INSIGHT GUIDES

JAPAN

PLAN & BOOK
YOUR TAILOR-MADE TRIP

BRAZIL **CHILE** **ECUADOR**

TAILOR-MADE TRIPS & UNIQUE EXPERIENCES CREATED BY LOCAL TRAVEL EXPERTS AT INSIGHTGUIDES.COM/HOLIDAYS

Insight Guides has been inspiring travellers with high-quality travel content for over 45 years. As well as our popular guidebooks, we now offer the opportunity to book tailor-made private trips completely personalised to your needs and interests. By connecting with one of our local experts, you will directly benefit from their expertise and local know-how, helping you create memories that will last a lifetime.

HOW INSIGHTGUIDES.COM/HOLIDAYS WORKS

STEP 1

Pick your dream destination and submit an enquiry, or modify an existing itinerary if you prefer.

STEP 2

Fill in a short form, sharing details of your travel plans and preferences with a local expert.

STEP 3

Your local expert will create your personalised itinerary, which you can amend until you are completely satisfied.

STEP 4

Book securely online. Pack your bags and enjoy your holiday! Your local expert will be available to answer questions during your trip.

BENEFITS OF PLANNING & BOOKING AT INSIGHTGUIDES.COM/HOLIDAYS

PLANNED BY LOCAL EXPERTS

The Insight Guides local experts are hand-picked, based on their experience in the travel industry and their impeccable standards of customer service.

SAVE TIME & MONEY

When a local expert plans your trip, you save time and money when you book, even during high season. You won't be charged for using a credit card either.

TAILOR-MADE TRIPS

Book with Insight Guides, and you will be in complete control of the planning process, from the initial selections to amending your final itinerary.

BOOK & TRAVEL STRESS-FREE

Enjoy stress-free travel when you use the Insight Guides secure online booking platform. All bookings come with a money-back guarantee.

WHAT OTHER TRAVELLERS THINK ABOUT TRIPS BOOKED AT INSIGHTGUIDES.COM/HOLIDAYS

DON'T MISS OUT BOOK NOW AT
INSIGHTGUIDES.COM/HOLIDAYS

CONTENTS

Travel tips

TRANSPORT

A – Z

LANGUAGE

FURTHER READING

Maps

LEGEND

○ Insight on
◙ Photo story

THE BEST OF JAPAN: TOP ATTRACTIONS

△ **Ginkaku-ji Temple and Gardens, Kyoto.** This temple is a wonderful place to see 15th-century Japanese architecture at its finest. See page 253.

▽ **Mount Fuji.** Japan's most iconic mountain dominates the skyline west of Tokyo, and is a Unesco World Heritage Site. Whether you climb it or gaze upon it from afar, it's easy to see why Fuji-san has captivated the Japanese for centuries. See page 184.

△ **Nikko.** Buried deep in forested mountains to the north of Tokyo, the outrageously lavish Tosho-gu Shrine complex in Nikko offers some of Japan's most spectacular architecture. If you just have time for one overnight trip from Tokyo, make it here. See page 186.

△ **Ryokan.** A night at a traditional inn (ryokan) is a quintessentially Japanese experience, combining refined luxury, elegance and the ultimate in relaxation. See page 369.

△ **Hiroshima's Peace Memorial Park.** Built in memory of the victims of the 1945 A-bomb attack that devastated Hiroshima, the Peace Park is a moving and poignant monument to the horrors of nuclear armament. See page 313.

△ **Roppongi at night.** Raucous nightclubs, cool bars and some of the chicest restaurants in Tokyo make a night out in Roppongi a must-do. It won't be cheap, but it will be very memorable. See page 160.

△ **Naoshima Island.** With cutting-edge galleries and a host of outdoor art installations, this tranquil island in the Seto Inland Sea is a bright star in Japan's contemporary art scene. See page 310.

▽ **Yaeyama Islands, Okinawa.** With pristine beaches, prime dive spots, a refreshingly laid-back pace of life and a distinctive local culture, it's sometimes hard to believe these islands are actually part of Japan. See page 359.

△ **Hiking the Northern Alps.** Breathtaking mountain scenery and hikes to suit all levels make the Northern Alps Japan's premier hiking ground. The pretty village of Kamikochi is the perfect base from which to explore the area. See page 201.

▽ **Japanese cuisine.** From refined Kyoto cuisine to steaming hot bowls of cheap ramen, and so much in between, Japan is a foodie's paradise. Don't go home without having your fill. See page 121.

THE BEST OF JAPAN: EDITOR'S CHOICE

Shinjuku Gyoen in spring, Tokyo.

BEST FOR FAMILIES

Kaiyukan Aquarium. Located in Osaka Bay, visitors can see aquatic species from various regions across the globe. Get up close in the feeling area and don't miss the chance to see giant whale sharks. See page 289.

DisneySea. An addition to Tokyo Disneyland but requiring a separate ticket. The themes here are all connected to water and a full day is recommended. See page 171.

Ghibli Museum. This museum-cum-amusement park in Tokyo's suburbs showcases the work of the renowned Studio Ghibli, including Miyazaki Hayao's famous anime. See page 173.

Universal Studios Japan. Hollywood special effects and fun rides, Osaka's theme park replicates its Los Angeles prototype. See page 289.

Miraikan. This museum in Odaiba has lots of hands-on activities for older kids to learn about cutting-edge robotics, space exploration and much more. See page 161.

ONLY IN JAPAN

Department terminals. A fascinating consumer concept – train platforms feeding passengers straight into department stores. Accessible station-store interfaces are found in Nihombashi, Ikebukuro and Shibuya in Tokyo.

High-tech toilets. At the other end of the spectrum to the squat toilet, many hotels, department stores and homes have *washlets*, toilets that will clean, dry and warm you, and on occasions make noises to cover any embarrassing sounds. See page 379.

Capsule hotels. Seal your door and fall into a contented sleep in these cosy, weightless cells – or sweat with claustrophobia. You either love or hate Japan's capsule hotels. See page 369.

Vending machines. It's the number and range that are unique to Japan: over 5 million on the last count, dispensing everything from disposable underwear to noodles. See page 126.

Japanese vending machines.

Universal Studios Japan.

BEST PARKS AND GARDENS

Koishikawa Botanical Garden. Although landscaped, the grounds of this fine Edo Period green haven have a natural and informal feel. The oldest garden in Tokyo. See page 155.
Shinjuku Gyoen. Enjoy the many species of plants, trees and flowers in a Tokyo park divided into different garden styles. There is a large botanical greenhouse for chilly days. See page 166.
Daitoku-ji. A complex of immeasurably beautiful Kyoto gardens. The most famous is Daisen-in, reminiscent of a Chinese painting. See page 254.
Ryoan-ji. Built in the 15th or 16th century, this famous Kyoto dry landscape temple garden was created as both a tool for meditation and as a work of art. A truly Zen experience. See page 255.
Ritsurin-koen. Completed in 1745, Ritsurin Park on Shikoku Island is one of the finest stroll gardens in Japan. See page 324.

Eko-in Temple and lodgings.

BEST MODERN ARCHITECTURE

Fuji TV Building. A Tange Kenzo masterpiece, this TV studio in Tokyo's man-made island Odaiba, with its suspended dome made of reinforced tungsten, seems to resemble the inside of a television set. See page 161.
Tokyo Big Sight. You'll probably do a double take when you see the inverted pyramids of this building in Tokyo's Odaiba district – it seems to defy gravity and common sense, but is still standing. See page 161.
Umeda Sky Building. A

Ritsurin-koen, Kagawa.

striking skyscraper in Osaka's Umeda district, this soaring building is pierced by a large hole at one point in its structure. See page 285.
ACROS Centre. Fukuoka is quite a laboratory for new architecture. ACROS, a culture centre, stands out for its ziggurat form and stepped terraces covered in hanging plants, creating the impression of a sci-fi jungle ruin. See page 336.
Tokyo Sky Tree. Some love it, some are distinctly underwhelmed, but this landmark can't be avoided – the world's second-tallest man-made structure towers 634 metres (2,080ft) above eastern Tokyo. See page 159.

BEST TRADITIONAL EXPERIENCES

Visit a castle. Himeji-jo is the best of Japan's original castles. Known as Shirasagi-jo, or the White Egret Castle, its graceful lines are said to resemble the bird as it is about to take flight. See page 293.
Watch the sumo. Centuries old and full of pomp and ceremony, an afternoon at one of the six annual 15-day grand tournaments is cracking good fun. See page 118.
Stay at a temple in Koya-san. Many temples have spartan accommodation available for travellers, but none are as atmospheric as this complex of temples and monasteries deep inside a mountainside forest. See page 279.
Fireworks. Summer means firework displays. The biggest and best is Tokyo's Sumida-gawa display in late July, but there are colourful events across the country in July and August. See page 375.
Festivals. *Matsuri* (festivals) big and small take place year-round all over the country, typified by traditional dancing, music and great street food. One of the best is the Gujo Odori dance festival in Gujo Hachiman, Honshu. See page 198.

Nada Fighting Festival, Himeji.

Neon lights in Tokyo.

BEST TEMPLES AND SHRINES

Asakusa Kannon Temple (Senso-ji). Tokyo's most visited temple hosts dozens of annual events and festivals. Nakamise, the approach street, is full of craft and dry-food goods. See page 158.

Kanda Myojin Shrine. One of Tokyo's liveliest shrine compounds, especially at weekends, when weddings, rituals and festivals are held. Bright and cheerful architecture. See page 153.

Meiji Shrine. A sublime setting at the centre of a forest in the middle of Tokyo. Gravel paths lead to the shrine, an example of pure Shinto design. See page 163.

Yamadera. Tohoku's most sacred temple complex, a veritable labyrinth of steps, pathways and stone stairways across a rocky hillside. Built to last in the 9th century. See page 219.

Golden Pavilion (Kinkaku-ji). It may be a 1950s rebuild, but the gilded Kinkaku-ji is understandably still Kyoto's most iconic sight. See page 254.

Itsukushima-jinja. Fabulously located on stilts and pillars rising 16 metres (52ft) above the waters of Miyajima, the walkways and platforms of this splendid, magical shrine seem to float in space. See page 315.

Yamadera Temple complex, Tohoku.

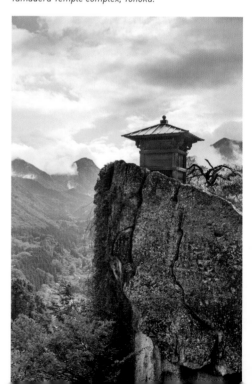

BEST OF MODERN JAPAN

Ride the *shinkansen*. You don't have to be a train-spotter to enjoy the super-slick *shinkansen*. It's extremely fast, unerringly efficient and aesthetically a joy to behold. See pages 168 and 367.

Shop for gadgets in Akihabara. Akihabara in Tokyo is known as "Electric Town" for good reason. The home electronics stores here carry the very latest gadgets and technology. See page 371.

Tokyo's urban complexes. Towering urban redevelopments like Tokyo Midtown, Ginza Six and Roppongi Hills have redefined central Tokyo. Fashionable and sleek, this is Japan at its most contemporary. See page 160.

Explore Shinjuku. Less fashionable than Roppongi, but buzzing with energy, Shinjuku has plenty of neon, bars and shops, not to mention Tokyo's main Koreatown, main gay district and biggest red-light area. See page 165.

BEST HOT SPRINGS

Dogo Onsen. These hot springs in Shikoku are the oldest in Japan. They are mentioned in the *Manyoshu*, the ancient collection of Japanese poetry (c.759). See page 329.

Beppu. A very busy spa town in Kyushu with eight different hot spring areas, each with different properties. The open-air "hell ponds" of boiling mud are a crowd-puller. See page 347.

Noboribetsu. There are 11 kinds of hot spring water at this spa resort in Hokkaido, including salt (for soothing pain), iron (for relieving rheumatism) and sodium bicarbonate (to attain smoother skin). See page 229.

Naruko. This once sacred site in Tohoku is over 1,000 years old. It is well known for its fine medicinal waters. See page 217.

Hakone. Only a couple of hours from central Tokyo, yet rich with bubbling volcanic valleys and mountain scenery, Hakone is a very popular weekend retreat for Tokyoites. See page 185.

Recreation of Frank Lloyd Wright's Imperial Hotel at the Meiji-Mura Museum.

Hot spring baths at Dogo Onsen, Shikoku.

BEST GALLERIES AND MUSEUMS

Edo Tokyo Museum. One of the finest museums in Japan, showcasing scale replicas of historic Tokyo from the 19th century to the present day. See page 155.

Tokyo National Museum. This museum on the edge of Ueno Park houses the largest collection of Japanese art and artefacts in the world. See page 158.

Meiji Mura Museum. This magnificent 100-hectare (250-acre) site near Nagoya houses 60 original Meiji-era buildings brought from around the country. See page 196.

Nagoya City Science Museum. Entertaining hands-on exhibits abound in this museum, which also boasts the world's largest planetarium, located in a giant silver globe. See page 195.

MONEY-SAVING TIPS

Cheap to sleep: Provided you eschew top-end hotels and restaurants, and the use of taxis, Japan can be a surprisingly affordable country to travel around. Accommodation in budget inns and business hotels ranges from as little as ¥3,000 to ¥6,000.

Travel: Buying a Japan Rail Pass before you arrive in Japan can save you a huge amount of money. Overnight buses, allowing you to save on sleeping accommodation, are cheaper than trains.

Shopping spree: Some department stores offer a 5 percent discount to foreign visitors and many local tourist offices issue regional discount cards to foreign visitors.

Set lunch: Look out for lunch set specials, which can be as cheap as ¥600. Fast-food joints have sets for as little as ¥350.

Cheers: Drinks at music clubs are sometimes included in the ticket price. Another good option are *tachinomiya* (standing bars), where you won't be expected to buy food and there is usually no table charge.

No tips: Tipping is almost non-existent in Japan, something that helps to offset daily costs.

THE BEST OF JAPAN: PLAN & BOOK YOUR TAILOR-MADE TRIP

Japan has two very contrasting sides. It's neon-lit cities are fast-paced and futuristic, but amongst the urban sprawl – and, indeed, when you venture into its diverse countryside – you'll find zen gardens, majestic castles and serene Shinto shrines. For this is a country proud of its centuries-old heritage and, thanks to its hyper-efficient infrastructure, much of it is doable in a week.

△ **Day 1, Tokyo.** The iconic elevated Yamanote railway line and the metro make this megalopolis easy to explore. Start your day with a tour around the Imperial Palace, the primary residence of the Emperor of Japan. Afterwards head north to Yasukuni-jinja, a Shinto shrine with a huge torii, before visiting the immersive Edo Tokyo Museum, which is full of local colour about the city. See page 145.

◁ **Day 2, Shinjuku.** If your first day was dedicated to Japan's imperial past, spend your second embracing the city's neon-lit, future-gen vibe. And where better than Shinjuku, Tokyo's sprawling, always-energetic entertainment centre which buzzes with shops, bars and restaurants. Refuel at one of the many *kaiten sushi-ya*, where delicious and affordable sushi is delivered on conveyor belts. See page 165.

△ **Day 3, Hakone.** Take a train from the behemoth red-brick Tokyo Station to Hakone, which takes about two hours. Set against the backdrop of the majestic, snow-capped Fuji-san, Hakone is known for its onsen, natural hot springs. If you can tear yourself away, visit the Hakone Open-Air Museum, with its superb outdoor sculpture and spend the night in a ryokan, a traditional Japanese inn. See page 185.

▽ **Day 4, Kyoto.** With its zen gardens, Buddhist temples, colourful shrines and elegant geisha (known as maiko and *geiko* in Kyoto), Kyoto defines traditional Japan. Be dazzled by the gilded Kinkaku-ji, a temple which is entirely covered in gold leaf; another iconic site is Fushimi Inari Taisha, a 9th-century shrine built in honour of the fox where over 10,000 torii lines its paths. See page 243.

△ **Day 5, Cherry blossom.** Stroll through Maruyama Park, which lies next to the Yasaka Shrine at the base of Kyoto's eastern mountains. In late-March and early April, the park is a popular spot for *hanami* (flower viewing), as its 680 cherry trees come into full bloom. The centrepiece has to be the decades-old *shidarezakura*, or weeping cherry tree, which is illuminated at night. See page 252.

▽ **Day 6, Osaka.** The *shinkansen* will whisk you from Kyoto to Osaka, Japan's second largest city, in under 15 minutes. Head for Umeda, a business area replete with skyscrapers including the futuristic Umeda Sky Building, where the 40th-floor observation deck affords an unparalleled cityscape. Minami – with its shopping, dining and nightlife – is where Osakans let their hair down. See page 283.

△▽ **Day 7, Kobe.** Just east of Osaka, perched on hills overlooking a harbour, Kobe is one of Japan's most attractive cities. It is also the origin of Kobe beef, a prized delicacy. Try it in Sannomiya, a bustling neighbourhood with a number of Kobe beef restaurants. Post-meal head to Wakamatsu Park, home of the quirky Tetsujin robot statue – all 50 tonnes of it. Surely a holiday snap worth having. See page 290.

We can plan and book tailor-made trips to over 70 destinations in the world. Whether you're after adventure or a family-friendly holiday, we have a trip for you, with all the activities you enjoy doing and the sights you want to see. All our trips are devised by local experts who get the most out of the destination. Visit **www.insightguides.com/holidays** to chat with one of our local travel experts.

A groundskeeper in Kenrokuen Garden.

A SINGULAR PLACE

From Buddhist effigies to virtual pop idols, imperial court dancers to robot pets, bamboo forests, ski slopes and coral reefs to mega-city fashion and architecture: an immense cultural and geographical diversity confronts the visitor to Japan.

Kappabashi kitchenware.

Japan is home to some of Asia's best sights, natural landscapes, cuisine and innovative culture, not to mention cutting-edge technologies and futuristic cities attracting the world's leading architects. The Japanese are prolific, curious travellers, but they also sense that their own country has everything the traveller could possibly desire.

The unifying metaphor of a country defined as one family, one language, one perspective, a land of order, rituals and rules, a xenophobic society of worker ants, conformists and whale slaughterers, a simulacrum of Western culture, crumbles under closer examination. If it's easy to belittle Japan's orthodoxies, it's equally easy to praise its originality and non-conformism, the pliability that allows it periodically to reinvent itself.

The dual stereotypes of Japan as the *Teahouse of the August Moon*, a place of mystique and graceful manners living in an exotic costume drama, or as a people characterised as early, super-advanced adopters of technology living in confined apartments, suffering the indignities of crowded subways and working conditions, have their origins in the popular imagination and the way the West, in particular, would like to think of Japan. Although there are elements of truth in these preconceptions, a more accurate cliché is Japan as the land of contrast, a notion few that have lived or visited the country would contest.

Elementary school students.

With roughly 6,800 islands, there is bound to be a lot of diversity. It is, quite literally, possible to experience Japan's superb powder snow on the ski slopes of Hokkaido one day, and to be testing the transparent blue seas of Okinawa's southernmost Yaeyama Islands the next, such is the geographical and climatic range.

Japan's vibrant cultural scene draws from the traditional arts and crafts as much as contemporary manga, anime artists, J-Pop icons and meta-pop fiction. The fussy aesthetics of the tea ceremony and flower arranging, the years of formal training required to perform *noh*, kabuki and bunraku, the rituals and ceremonies that punctuate its cultural calendar, contrast with its laid-back bars, live music houses and vibrant youth culture and street life.

Creating an itinerary can be challenging. Will you include castles, temples and millennia-old shrines, secluded heritage villages, pottery towns, old foreign settlements that are now cosmopolitan ports, exquisite crafts, traditional festivals, cutting-edge architecture, major art collections, hiking trails and rural hot-spring resorts, the cultural treasure houses of Kyoto and Nara, or focus on one of the world's largest concentrations of formal gardens?

Japan has rightly been called the storehouse of the world, a place where you can shop 'til you drop. Its reputation for world-class food and beverages precede it. In the spirit of trying to please every pocket, dishes can be sampled anywhere from stand-up soba eateries favoured by truck drivers and time-driven salaried workers, to the refinements of *kaiseki ryori*, Japan's haute cuisine.

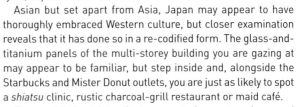

Asian but set apart from Asia, Japan may appear to have thoroughly embraced Western culture, but closer examination reveals that it has done so in a re-codified form. The glass-and-titanium panels of the multi-storey building you are gazing at may appear to be familiar, but step inside and, alongside the Starbucks and Mister Donut outlets, you are just as likely to spot a *shiatsu* clinic, rustic charcoal-grill restaurant or maid café.

The world's best intracity transportation system is served not only by the bullet train, but an increasingly competitive and

Yamadera Temple complex, Tohoku.

affordable airline network, inexpensive long-distance buses and a far-reaching ferry service, connecting visitors to Japan's intriguing small islands and their micro-cultures. Japan has never been cheap, but there has been considerable cost-cutting in recent years, reflected in more affordable deals on almost everything, from bargain basement restaurant lunches to accommodation.

It's an extraordinary place, offering the trip of a lifetime. If Japan has a *bête noire* at all, it is the friability of the earth's crust, manifest in earthquakes, tsunamis, volcanic eruptions and landslides. In 2018, 41 people died and 691 were injured during the Hokkaido Eastern Iburi earthquake. In 2014, 63 people died as Ontake-san in central Japan exploded without warning. But the most profound disaster of recent years took place on 11 March 2011, when a magnitude-9 earthquake and resultant tsunami

Utoro Port, Hokkaido.

caused three reactors in Fukushima nuclear power plant to go critical, that both the real and metaphorical cracks in Japan were exposed. The groundswell of activism prompted by the disaster, the mistrust of government and bureaucracy that grew in the wake of the catastrophe was an encouraging sign – a harbinger, perhaps, of another new Japan.

A NOTE ON STYLE

Wherever possible, we use Japanese terms for geographical names, appearing as suffixes to the proper name. For example, Mount Fuji is referred to as Fuji-san. Mountains may also appear with *-zan*, *-yama,* and for some active volcanoes, *-dake*. Islands are either *-shima* or *-jima,* lakes are *-ko*, and rivers are *-gawa* or *-kawa*. Shinto shrines end in *-jinja*, *-jingu* or *-gu*. Temples are Buddhist, with names ending in *-tera*, *-dera* or *-ji*. When referring to individuals, we follow the Japanese style: family name first, given name second.

Cooking traditional street food in Osaka.

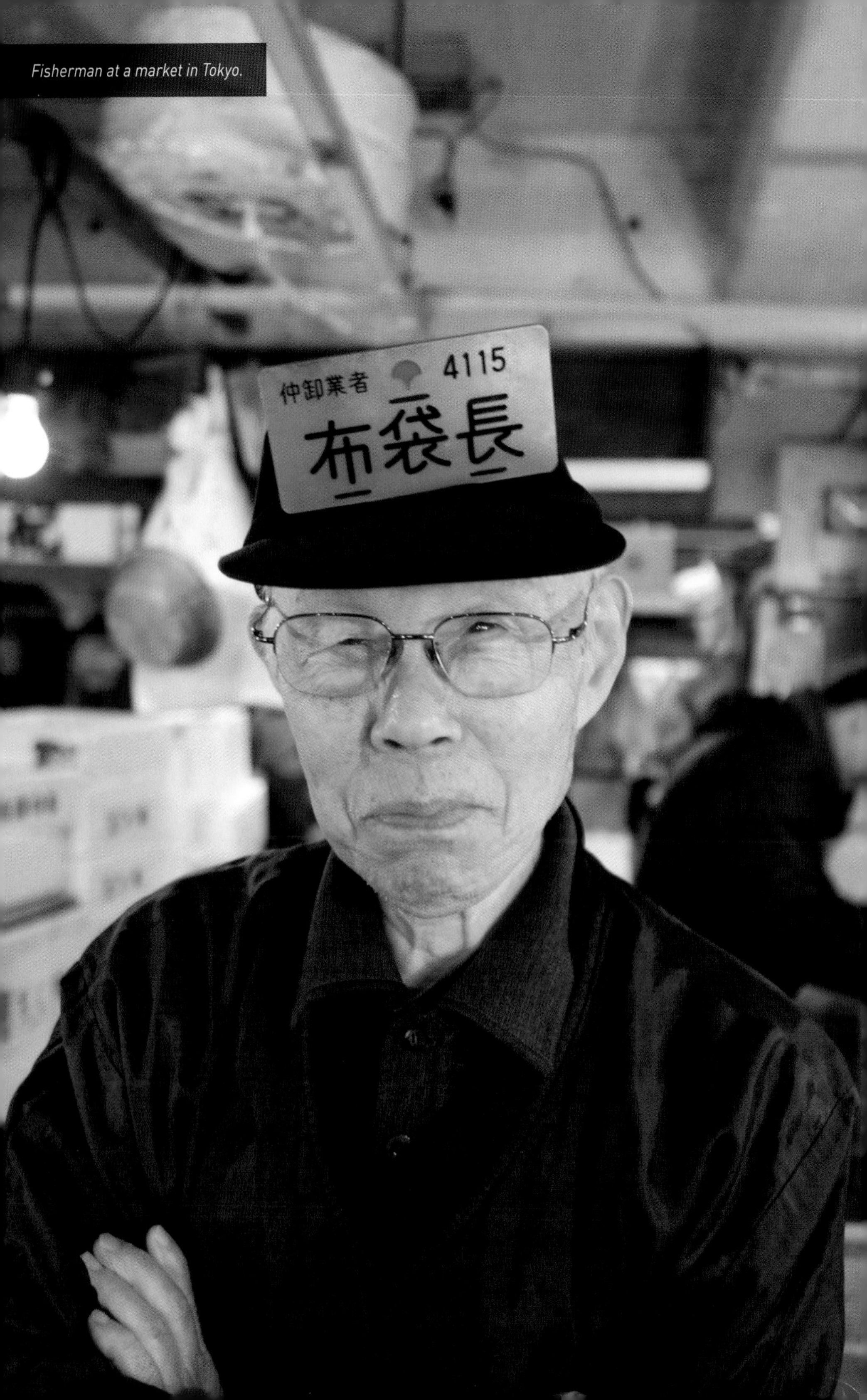

Fisherman at a market in Tokyo.

A NATION OF ISLANDS

An archipelago formed by the meeting of tectonic plates, Japan's thousands of islands are often rugged and violent, accented by soothing hot springs.

The Japanese like to think of themselves as a small people living in a snug but confined country. Scale, of course, is relative. If you come from Russia, then Japan is, indeed, a small country. If you hail from the UK, on the other hand, Japan, almost twice the size of the island of Great Britain, is expansive.

Japan is not the only archipelago in Asia. Like the Philippines and Indonesia, it boasts a huge number of islands – some 6,800, most of which are uninhabited. The impression of space and dimension comes from the country's length, from its northern tip on the Sea of Okhotsk – from where the Russian coast is visible on clear days – down to the subtropical islands of Okinawa, where, visibility permitting, the mountains of Taipei can be glimpsed. Buffeted by the winter ice drifts off Hokkaido and the freezing Sea of Japan on its west coast, the Pacific bathes its eastern seaboard and the East China Sea its southwestern shores.

While its inland prefectures may be relatively sheltered from the sea-born typhoons and constant threat of tsunamis that plague its coastline, geography has influenced the development of Japan in many ways. The most obvious is agriculture and fishing, with its rice fields and orchards set at a safe distance from the salt air, its coastline a series of harbours and fishing ports. It has also had an effect on architecture, evident in the pipe-stove chimneys used in private homes in Hokkaido with its bitter winters; the rurally sourced thatch traditionally used as roofing in regions like Tohoku and Hida; and in the coral, limestone and, more recently, cement used as building materials in Okinawa, whose islands stand squarely in the typhoon alley that begins its annual passage of destruction from the Philippines.

Jigoku-dani (Hell Gorge), Noboribetsu.

In Japanese mythology, the archipelago was formed from the tears of a goddess. Where each tear fell into the Pacific there arose an island to take its place. So goes the legend. But no less poetic – or dramatic – is the geological origin of this huge archipelago. The islands were born of massive crustal forces deep underground and shaped by volcanoes spitting out mountains of lava. The results seen today are impressive, with snow-capped mountain ranges and 30,000km (18,600 miles) of indented coastline.

The archipelago consists of five main islands – Kyushu, Shikoku, Honshu, Hokkaido and Okinawa – and about 6,800 smaller islands extending from southwest to northeast over a distance of some 3,800km (2,400 miles) off the east coast of mainland Asia. Honshu is by far the largest and most populous of all the islands. The main islands are noted for their rugged terrain, with 70 to 80 percent of the country being extremely mountainous. Most of the mountains were uplifted over millions of years as the oceanic crust of the Pacific collided with the continental plate of Asia. The oceanic crust submerged beneath the thicker continental crust, buckling the edge of it and forcing up the mountain chains that form the backbone of the Japanese archipelago and that of the Philippines to the south.

Sign for tsunami evacuation, Tohoku.

VOLCANOES

Other, singular peaks in Japan – including Fuji, the highest – are volcanic in origin. They were formed from molten lava that originated far below the earth's surface as the oceanic crust sank into the superheated depths of the upper mantle. The molten rock was forced up through fissures and faults, exploding onto the surface. Weather and glacial action did the rest.

One of the attractions of a visit to Japan is the possibility of seeing the milder geological forces in action. About 60 of Japan's 186 volcanoes are still active in geological terms, and occasionally they make their presence felt. Mihara on Oshima, one of the isles of Izu near Tokyo and part of Metropolitan Tokyo, exploded in 1986, forcing thousands

of residents to evacuate the island. A few years later, Unzen-dake on Kyushu violently erupted and devastated hundreds of kilometres of agricultural land. Sakura-jima, also on Kyushu, regularly spews ash. As recently as 2014, 63 people died as Ontake-san in central Japan exploded without warning, which was the most fatal eruption in Japan in over 100 years. Just eight months later, Shin-dake's massive eruption made all 137 residents of tiny Kuchinoerabu-jima flee the island.

Located above the Pacific Rim of Fire, Japan sits on top of four tectonic plates on the edge of a subduction zone, making it one of the most unstable regions on earth. The caldera of Mount Aso is periodically placed off-limits to tourists because of toxic emissions; Mount Asama in central Honshu has been erupting regularly for the last 1,500 years, most recently in 2019. Even iconic Mount Fuji is an active peak.

EARTHQUAKES AND TSUNAMIS

Earthquakes are far more frequent than volcanic eruptions, especially around the more seismologically active areas near Tokyo. On average Japan experiences about 7,500 quakes a year, though most are too small to be felt. It is an indicator, however, of how seismically active the islands are. The Japanese government currently spends billions of yen annually on earthquake detection – not that it works particularly well.

Complacency is a common problem anywhere and certainly was in Kobe, which had been declared to be outside any significant earthquake zone. Nevertheless, in 1995 a massive quake hit the city, killing more than 5,000 people and toppling high-rises. Mega-thrust earthquakes of the type that struck the coast of Miyagi Prefecture on 11 March 2011 tend to strike in pairs, with a relatively short interlude between. In 2015, tremors were felt across the country as a powerful 7.8-magnitude undersea earthquake struck south of Japan. Thankfully, no serious damage was reported.

The 3/11 tsunami revealed the dangers of locating concentrated communities along coastal areas. Local governments have been publishing hazard maps for low-lying residential coastal areas, the danger zones indicating that millions of people inhabit areas of alarming vulnerability. The ever-present threats have turned the Japanese into a stoic, resilient people, but also a rather fatalistic, even complacent one.

The events of 3/11 have changed both the physical and mental landscape of Japan.

Most Japanese tend not to dwell on the morbid aspects of the islands' geological activity, preferring to enjoy its pleasures instead. *Onsen*, or hot springs, are a tangible result of the massive quantities of heat released underground. For centuries hot springs have occupied a special place in Japanese culture, and today the pleasures of the *onsen* are a national pastime.

MOUNTAINS AND COASTAL PLAINS

Despite the dominance of mountains in these islands, the Japanese are not a mountain people, preferring instead to squeeze onto the coastal plains or into the valleys of the interior. Consequently separated from each other by mountains, which once took days to traverse, the populated areas tended to develop independently with distinct dialects and other social peculiarities; some local dialects, such as in Tohoku or Kyushu, are completely unintelligible to other Japanese. At the same time, isolation and efficient use of land meant that agriculture and communications evolved early in the country's history.

The highest non-volcanic peaks are in the so-called Japan Alps of central Honshu. Many of the landforms in these mountain ranges were sculpted by glaciers in an ice age over 27,000 years ago. Cirques, or depressions, left where glaciers formed, are still a common sight on some higher slopes. Debris brought down by melting ice can also be seen in lower regions.

WILDLIFE

To the Japanese, people are a part of nature and therefore anything people have constructed is considered part of the environment. The Japanese can look upon a garden – moulded, cut, sculptured and trimmed to perfect proportions – and still see it as a perfect expression of the natural order, not something artificial.

The result of this philosophy has generally been disastrous for the wildlife and ecosystems of Japan. The crested ibis, for example, common throughout the archipelago 100 years ago, was on the verge of extinction until recent conservation efforts turned things around. Efforts to save the red-crowned Japanese crane *(tancho)* have also been necessary, though its territory in eastern Hokkaido is now secure and numbers are on the rise.

Fish such as salmon and trout are no longer able to survive in Japan's polluted rivers and lakes. Brown bears have been hunted almost to extinction, and only recently have hunting laws been amended and the animal recognised as an endangered species.

Because of Japan's sheer length it is nevertheless able to host a veritable menagerie of fauna, including some, like the copper pheasant, wild boar, cormorants, kites, serow, Japanese giant salamander and horseshoe crab, that are indigenous to the archipelago. Of the other land

Japanese crane at Kushiro moor, Hokkaido.

⊘ TYPHOONS

Generally three or four typhoons hit Japan during the season, smaller ones in August building up to larger ones in September. The southern or Pacific side of Japan bears the brunt of these ferocious winds, which are quite capable of knocking down houses and wrecking ships. Fortunately for Japan, however, most typhoons have expended their energy in the Philippines or Taiwan before reaching the archipelago. While more frequent than Atlantic hurricanes or Indian Ocean cyclones, the Asian typhoons are also considerably smaller in size and strength. The Japanese don't use names for typhoons, just numbers.

mammals, the Japanese monkey, or macaque, is by far the most common in Japan. Originally a creature of the tropical rainforests, the macaque has adapted to the more temperate climates of these islands and can now be found throughout Kyushu, Shikoku and Honshu, although its numbers have been sharply reduced since the 1950s. During the winter months, macaques in Nagano and Hokkaido take to bathing in local hot springs.

Japan's sub-Arctic zone, centred on Hokkaido, is known for its hazel grouse, brown bears, Arctic hares, sticklebacks, foxes and

Cherry blossoms in Matsumoto.

humpback whales. Its temperate zone is home to mandarin ducks, sika deer, loggerhead turtles, porpoises, raccoon dogs, badgers and flying squirrels, its seas supporting fur seals and sea lions. The southern, subtropical regions support flying foxes, butterflies, crested serpent

> *The population of wild bears is again climbing, with the majority to be found in Hokkaido, which is estimated to have several thousand. Recent years have also seen a rise in human-bear encounters with bears leaving their natural habitat in search of food.*

eagles, lizards, sea serpents, manta rays, redfin fusiliers, parrot fish, anemone fish, lizards and the deadly habu snake.

There are several species that face near extinction, among them the Iriomote wildcat, a mostly nocturnal creature native to Iriomote Island; the black Amami rabbit; the Japanese otter; and the short-tailed albatross.

FLORA

In the far south of Japan, the islands of Okinawa have a distinctive fauna and flora. Here, the natural forests are subtropical, but many of the indigenous species of fauna have become rare or even extinct. Even so, a wealth of natural flora remains, with Japan's temperate species, like black pine, winter camellia, azaleas and plum contrasting with hibiscus, bougainvillea, giant tree ferns, luxuriant cycads, fukugi, ficus and banyan trees.

The most spectacular characteristic of these islands is the marine life. Most of the islands are surrounded by coral, home to a rich and colourful variety of warm-water fish. Yet once again the rapid growth of the tourist and leisure industry – especially that of scuba diving – and the bleaching effects of temperature rises caused by global warming, have taken a toll. Okinawa's coral reefs, however, continue to remain some of the finest in the world. The natural coral of Amami-jima, Yonaguni-jima, Miyako-jima, Iriomote-jima and the precious blue coral of Ishigaki-jima, the largest in the world, host an extraordinary rainbow of tropical fish and marine gardens.

In Hokkaido, the greater availability of space and natural moorland vegetation has led to the growth of the cattle and dairy industries. Meat is gradually becoming a more important part of the Japanese diet, just as rice is declining in popularity. In a sense, this is symptomatic of the way Japanese culture is changing. Younger generations are gradually turning away from the fish-and-rice diet to eat more meat and bread as Japan becomes more urbanised and Western in outlook.

CLIMATE

Extensive television and print coverage of the weather provides the Japanese with a major topic of conversation.

Japan's extremities, from its Siberian sub-Arctic zone in northern Hokkaido to the subtropical jungles of Okinawa, the Sea of Japan to the Pacific Ocean, straddle very different climatic regions.

Japan's seasons are similar to those of Europe and North America. The coldest months are December to February, with heavy snow on the Sea of Japan side of Hokkaido and Honshu, dry air on the Pacific Ocean side. Tokyo's urban growth has reduced evaporation levels, causing a drop in winter precipitation and concerns over water shortages.

CHERRY BLOSSOM TIME

Cherry trees *(sakura)* first blossom in Okinawa in late winter, reaching Hokkaido in mid-May. Celebrated with *hanami* parties, domestic tourism goes into overdrive. The media reports daily on the *sakura zensen* (cherry blossom front). The appeal of the blossom is its transience – it lasts at most a week.

Strong, southerly winds bring rain and the start of the *tsuyu*, rainy season. Temperatures rise and rains fall for about two months, easing around late June on the Pacific Ocean side, making way for the hot, humid summer, which lingers into September. As the warm air mass moves south, the rains return on the backs of devastating typhoons.

NATURAL RESOURCES

There are coalmines in Hokkaido and Kyushu, but coal production peaked in 1941 and many coalmining communities are now in serious decline. Nearly all of Japan's other raw materials, such as oil, minerals and metal ores, are imported. Timber is one resource Japan has in abundance, as most of the country's mountains are covered in natural or plantation forest. The natural cover varies from sub-Arctic conifers in Hokkaido to deciduous and evergreen temperate broad-leafed trees throughout the other three main islands and tropical plants in Okinawa. Yet despite a soaring demand for timber – used in the construction industry and for paper and disposable chopsticks – domestic production has actually fallen. The Japanese prefer to buy cheap, imported timber from the tropical rainforests of Southeast Asia, a practice that is causing considerable concern among many environmentalists as the rainforests of Borneo and Burma, and until recently Thailand, are being reduced to barren slopes.

Fishing is another rural occupation that has declined in activity, mainly because of a decline in fish stocks as a result of overexploitation. Japanese fleets now operate in international waters far away from home, and ports that once supported fishing fleets are turning towards other endeavours. One of the most lucrative of these is tourism. As the urban Japanese become more affluent and seek recreation outside the cities, ports and harbours are becoming leisure marinas, hotels and resorts are springing up all over the countryside, and mountains are being levelled in order to make way for golf courses. Yet, to Westerners, there is a paradox with this approach to ecology. It has been

The landing of tuna at a fishing port.

one of the proud boasts of the Japanese that they live close to and in harmony with nature – a strong theme in Japanese poetry and reflected in the Japanese preoccupation with the weather.

URBAN ZONES

By far the largest of Japan's few flat spaces is the Kanto plain, an area centred on Tokyo Bay and formed by a build-up of sediments resulting from Ice Age-induced changes in sea level. Other extensive areas of flat land occur in the Tohoku region, Hokkaido, and along the Nagoya–Osaka industrial belt.

Such is the concentration of resources in these plains that most of Japan's people, factories, farmland, housing and public facilities are all crowded onto approximately 20 percent of Japan's total land area. Thus, very little of what one might call countryside exists on the plains. Cities, towns and villages tend to merge into an indistinct urban blur that stretches endlessly across the flat land, with fields and farms dotted in between. In general, the plains are monochromatic, congested and less than aesthetic.

The main industrial regions are the Kanto and Kansai areas, which are centred on Tokyo and Osaka respectively. The Kanto area alone produces nearly a third of Japan's entire gross domestic product. If it were an independent nation, it would produce more goods and services than the United Kingdom.

Again, it is the Kanto region and Tokyo in particular that has benefited from Japan's prosperity since World War II. Metropolitan Tokyo had a nominal population of more than 13 million in 2017, but in fact the city spreads beyond its political boundaries north, south and west to form a massive urban complex that stretches across the entire Kanto plain. The actual population of this megalopolis is estimated at nearly 38 million people.

Metropolitan Tokyo and Yokohama are the first and second cities of Japan, respectively. Third in size is Osaka, with a population of 2.7 million, followed by Nagoya with 2.3 million. These cities have experienced phenomenal growth since World War II, as Japan's urban industrialisation and rural mechanisation drew people off the farms and into the cities.

Many rural communities are suffering from an increasingly aged population, as young people have fled the rural lifestyle.

The countryside lacks appeal and job opportunities, especially for the young. Farming on the typically tiny Japanese farms is inefficient. Unlike most other industrial nations, Japan has few natural resources and depends heavily upon manufacturing for wealth and employment. Recent years have seen the advent of the so-called U-Turn, by which young and retired people are relocating to rural areas looking for an alternative lifestyle to Japan's crowded urban zones. Many of them are setting up organic farms.

A farmer in the Tono Valley, Tohoku.

⊘ WORLD HERITAGE JAPAN

A long-overdue interest in ecotourism and the environment is now firmly embedded at both the government and local levels throughout Japan. At present there are 23 accredited Unesco sites in Japan. Natural heritage sites include Shirakami-Sanchi, a highland and woodland region crossing the borders of Aomori and Akita Prefectures, valued for its Siebold's beech forest and mountains; Shiretoko, a woodland and marine peninsula in the far north of Hokkaido; Yakushima Island south of Kagoshima Prefecture, home to millennia-old cypress trees and a warm, subtropical climate; the remote Ogasawara Islands, whose waters are a fine whale-watching venue; and the 2014 addition to the list, the sacred Fuji-san, the highest mountain in Japan.

All of Japan's five main islands have national and quasi-national parks. Among the oldest are Unzen and Kirishima in Kyushu, and Ise-Shima in Mie Prefecture. In all, there are 34 designated national parks in Japan, from the remote Rishiri-Rebun-Sarobetsu National Park in Hokkaido's far northwest, the marshlands of Oze National Park in the Kanto region, the peaks and watercourses of Chichibu Tama Kai National Park near Tokyo and the Sanin Kaigan area along the Sea of Japan, with its rugged coastline and desert-like Tottori Sand Dunes, to the jungles, waterfalls and priceless coral reefs of Okinawa's subtropical Iriomote-Ishigaki National Park.

ENVIRONMENTAL AWARENESS

Japan has one of the strangest landscapes on earth. Managed and contained, there are few areas spared the visible effects of a human hand.

Rivers flow through tiered cement embankments, environmentally questionable dams deface once pristine valleys, and mountains, lathered with concrete casing, exist to be tunnelled through, not lived on. Sea walls and breakers give the impression of a reinforced citadel. Even when there are great swathes of woodland, closer examination reveals serried ranks of trees, an industrial monoculture. Subordination, not coexistence, appears to be the mantra.

Japan's rapid, ill-considered post-war development has had catastrophic effects. Chemical pollution from industrial, domestic and agricultural sources and growing levels of seawater toxicity remain pressing issues. Japan has lobbied against a ban on the fishing of bluefin tuna, of which it consumes roughly 80 percent of the world's catch. Japanese whaling operates under a complex set of exemptions that allow it to hunt for scientific reasons. The only country undertaking long-distance whaling in the southern sanctuary of the Antarctic, Japan primarily catches minke whales, much of the catch ending up for sale as meat. Interestingly, the vast majority of Japanese are far more interested in whale-watching than devouring the unpopular meat.

Some 67 percent of the country is tree-covered, with single-species plantations of conifers dominating. Despite the abundance of timber, Japan imports roughly 80 percent of its lumber, employing a meagre 50,000 people in the forestry sector. Reviving its forestry industry would help to restore mountain streams by providing oxygen and nutrients, which would in turn help to cleanse its embattled coastlines.

The ancient cedar trees of Yakushima are lucky to have survived. By the 1970s, 80 percent of forest trees had been destroyed, most of the wood ending up as pulp. The island's listing as a Unesco World Heritage Site in 1993 quite literally saved Yakushima from extinction.

There is a growing awareness among citizens groups and at government levels that surviving natural beauty must be protected. The islands of Japan's Inland Sea offer hope. Petrochemical plants, oil refineries and the dumping of cyanogen and cadmium prompted one Japanese writer to comment that "the Seto Inland Sea had been turned into a sea of death". The fortunes of one island, Naoshima, home to an industrial waste-recycling plant, changed in 1992, when a small-scale art project was initiated with the idea of using art for community rejuvenation. On nearby Teshima, a former depository for toxic waste, a museum now sits among graduated rice fields, in which residents now

Cedar tree in the forest of Yakushima.

both produce and consume their own harvests. This project, and others that are planned to follow, provide an invaluable counter-model to reckless growth and industrial carnage.

Regarding vehicles, Japan is at the vanguard of development, with electric cars produced by Toyota and Nissan. Japan wants to set an example for green housing with the 2020 Olympic Village – a hydrogen-powered town located in Tokyo Bay. Japan's greenhouse-gas emissions hit a high in 2014, as the country had increased its dependence on fossil fuels following the closure of all its nuclear reactors in the aftermath of Fukushima. Amid protests, the government has been advocating a return to nuclear energy and on 11 August 2015, the first nuclear reactor started up again.

Kahō's "Fishing boats at dawn" woodblock print.

DECISIVE DATES

RISE OF CIVILISED JAPAN

10000 BC
Jomon culture produces Japan's earliest known examples of pottery.

3500–2000 BC
Population begins migrating inland.

300 BC
Migrants from Korea introduce rice cultivation.

AD 300
Kofun Period begins. Political and social institutions rapidly develop. Imperial line begins.

500–600
Buddhism arrives from Korea.

TIME OF THE WARLORDS

710
New capital established in Nara.

Toyotomi Hideyoshi.

794
Capital relocated to Kyoto. Rural areas neglected.

1180s
Estate holders develop military power. Warlord conflict ends Heian Period.

1185
Minamoto Yoritomo granted title of shogun, establishing base in Kamakura. The weakened imperial court stays in Kyoto.

1274
Mongols from China attempt unsuccessful invasion of Kyushu.

1333
Shogun Ashikaga Takauji returns capital to Kyoto, further eclipsing court influence.

1467
The Age of Warring States begins. Power of feudal lords increases.

1573
Warlord Oda Nobunaga conquers Kyoto and provinces, starting process of unification.

1582
Assassinated Nobunaga replaced by Toyotomi Hideyoshi.

1590
All of Japan is under Hideyoshi's control.

1597
Hideyoshi invades Korea but dies a year later.

1600
Edo Period begins. Tokugawa Ieyasu takes control after Battle of Sekigahara.

1603
Capital moves to Edo (present-day Tokyo). Edo becomes world's largest city.

1639
National seclusion policy begins.

1707
Mount Fuji erupts.

1720
Ban on importing foreign books lifted.

1853
Commodore Matthew Perry arrives with US naval ships, forcing Japan to accept trade and diplomatic contacts.

A 1796 print of a market at Nihonbashi.

RETURN OF IMPERIAL RULE

1868
Meiji Restoration returns emperor to power. Last shogun, Yoshinobu, retires. Name of capital changed to Tokyo (Eastern Capital).

1872
Samurai class abolished.

1877
Satsuma Rebellion crushed.

1889
New constitution promulgated.

1895
Japan wins Sino-Japanese War.

1904–6
Japan wins Russo-Japanese War.

1910
Japan annexes Korea.

1918
Economic chaos. Rice riots.

1923
Devastating Great Kanto Earthquake hits Tokyo area.

1926
Taisho emperor dies. Beginning of Showa Period.

1931
Manchuria occupied. Japan leaves League of Nations.

1936
Officers' insurgency – an attempt by a group of young

army officers to remove corrupt senior government figures – fails.

1937
Military advance on China.

1941
Japan attacks Pacific and Asian targets, occupying most of East Asia and western Pacific.

1945
American bombing raids destroy many major cities and industrial centres. Two atomic bombs dropped on Hiroshima and Nagasaki in August. Japanese surrender.

1946
New constitution places sovereignty with the people, not emperor.

1951
San Francisco Peace Treaty settles all war-related issues. Japan regains prewar industrial output.

1955
Socialist factions form Japan Socialist Party; Liberals and Democrats create the Liberal Democratic Party (LDP).

Atomic bombs devastated Hiroshima and Nagasaki.

A Japanese fan during the 2002 World Cup.

2002
Japan cohosts the football World Cup with South Korea.

2004
Unarmed peacekeeping mission sent to Iraq in support of US-led coalition.

2007
A 6.8-scale earthquake at the Kariwa plant in Niigata Prefecture causes fire and small amounts of radioactive leakage.

2009
LDP loses power to DPJ (Democratic Party of Japan) in landmark general election.

2010
China overtakes Japan as second-largest economy.

2011
A massive earthquake and tsunami, killing over 15,000 and leaving over 2,500 missing, shuts down reactors at the Fukushima power plant,

1964
The Summer Olympics are held in Tokyo.

1972
US returns Okinawa (having occupied it since the end of World War II).

1980s
Japan's economy climbs to second place.

1989
Emperor Hirohito dies, replaced by son Akihito.

END OF THE DREAM

1990
The "economic bubble" bursts.

1993
Coalition government replaced by another led by the Japan Socialist Party.

1995
Kobe earthquake kills over 5,000, leaving 300,000 homeless.

1998
Winter Olympics held in Nagano.

1999
Several die in nuclear accident at a uranium-reprocessing plant in Tokaimura.

The aftermath of the 2011 tsunami.

Japanese Prime Minister Shinzo Abe.

causing a nuclear meltdown and release of radioactive materials.

2012
LDP triumphs in general elections and Abe Shinzo becomes prime minister.

2014
The government approves a major change in military policy, paving the way for military operations overseas. A volcanic eruption on Mount Ontake claims 63 lives.

2015
Japan emerges from recession although growth is slack. The first nuclear reactor begins operating again, four years after Fukushima.

2016
A series of earthquakes strike Kumamoto Prefecture, killing over 50.

2018
Japan eases its immigration laws for foreign workers amid labour shortages due to the ageing population, allowing for hundreds of thousands of foreign immigrants.

2019
Akihito becomes the first Japanese emperor to abdicate since 1817 and is succeeded by his son, Naruhito. Japan hosts the first Rugby World Cup held in Asia.

2020
Tokyo becomes the first Asian city to host the Olympic Games twice.

Emperor Naruhito and Empress Masako during the enthronement ceremony.

Terracotta statues from Chiba and Gunma.

JAPAN'S EARLY CENTURIES

Migrations of people from the mainland across now submerged land bridges evolved into a feudal system of warlords and an aesthetic of profound elegance.

Shinto mythology holds that two celestial gods, descending to earth on a "floating bridge to heaven", dipped a spear into the earth, causing drops of brine to solidify into the archipelago's first group of islands. As one of the male gods was washing his face in the fertile sea, the Sun Goddess, Amaterasu, sprung from his left eye, bathing the world in light. Japanese mythology claims its first emperor, Jimmu, was a direct descendant of the Sun Goddess. Conferring on him the title Tenno, Lord of Heaven, all emperors up to the present day have been addressed in this way.

What we can say with certainty is that the lands that are now the Japanese archipelago have been inhabited by human beings for at least 30,000 years, and maybe for as long as 100,000 to 200,000 years. The shallow seas separating Japan from the Asian mainland were incomplete when these people first came and settled on the terrain. After people arrived, however, sea levels rose and eventually covered the land bridges.

Whether or not these settlers are the ancestors of the present Japanese remains a controversy. Extensive archaeological excavations of prehistoric sites in Japan only began during the 1960s.

It is generally agreed that Japan was settled by waves of people coming from South Asia and the northern regions of the Asian continent, and

Middle Jomon earthenware bowl.

that this migration very likely occurred over a long period.

JOMON PERIOD (C.10,000–300 BC)

The earliest millennia of Neolithic culture saw a warming in worldwide climate, reaching peak temperature levels between 8000 and 4000 BC. In Japan, this phenomenon led to rising sea levels, which cut any remaining land bridges to the Asian mainland. At the same time, the local waters produced more abundant species of fish and shellfish. New types of forest took root, sprang up and thrived. These natural developments in the environment set the stage for the Early Jomon Period. Japan's earliest pottery – belonging to the Jomon culture – has been

On 18 June 1877, zoologist Edward Sylvester Morse found the remains of a shell mound as he passed through the village of Omori. Morse's discovery of the pre-Bronze Age midden signalled the beginning of archaeology as a study in Japan.

dated at about 10,000 BC, possibly the oldest known in the world, say some experts.

The Early Jomon people were mostly coastal-living, food-gathering nomads. Dietary reliance on fish, shellfish and sea mammals gave rise to the community refuse heaps known as shell mounds, the archaeologist's primary source of information about these people. The Early Jomon people also hunted deer and wild pig. Artefacts include stone-blade tools and the earliest known cord-marked pottery (*jomon*, in fact, means cord-marked).

A Japanese dotaku (bronze bell).

Grinding stones, capped storage jars and other Middle Jomon artefacts indicate a much more intense involvement with plant cultivation.

The Late Jomon Period, dating from around 2000 BC, is marked by an increase of coastal fishing among villagers living along the Pacific shorelines of the main islands.

YAYOI PERIOD (C.300 BC–AD 300)

Named after an archaeological site near Tokyo University, the Yayoi Period was a time of significant cultural transition. It was ushered in around 300 BC by peoples who migrated from rice-growing areas of the Asian mainland into northern Kyushu via Korea and, most likely, Okinawa.

In a brief 600 years, Japan was transformed from a land of nomadic hunting-and-gathering communities into the more sedentary pattern of settled farming villages: tightly knit, autonomous rice-farming settlements sprang up and spread so rapidly in Kyushu and western Honshu that by AD 100 settlements were found in most parts of the country, except for the northern regions of Honshu and Hokkaido.

KOFUN PERIOD (C.300–710)

The break with Yayoi culture is represented by the construction of huge tombs of earth and stone in coastal areas of Kyushu and along the shores of the Inland Sea. *Haniwa*, hollow clay human and animal figures, and models of houses decorated the perimeters of these tombs. These were made, some experts have speculated, as substitutes for the living retainers and possessions of the departed noble or leader.

Political and social institutions developed rapidly. Each of the community clusters that defined itself as a "country" or "kingdom" had a hierarchical social structure, subjected to increasing influence by a burgeoning central power based in the Yamato plain, in what is now the area of Osaka and Nara. The imperial line, or the Yamato dynasty, was probably formed from a number of powerful *uji* (family-clan communities) that had developed in the Late Yayoi Period.

Buddhism came to Japan in the 6th century from Korea. Although it is said that writing accompanied the religion, it may be that Chinese writing techniques preceded it by as much as 100 to 150 years. In any case, it was literacy that made the imported religion accessible to the nobility, also exposing them to the Chinese classics and to the writings of sages such as Confucius. Social and political change naturally followed an increase in literacy.

The power of the Soga clan was enhanced by exclusive control of the imperial treasury and granaries and by the clan's monopolistic role as sponsor for new learning brought in from the Asian mainland. The reforms they introduced were aimed primarily at strengthening the central government and reducing the power of other clans at the imperial court. The reforms were far-reaching, including changes in social structure, economic and legal systems, provincial boundaries, bureaucracy and taxes.

The Nara-era Empress Komyo, believed to be a reincarnation of Kannon, the Goddess of Compassion, did much to alleviate the plight of the poor by creating orphanages and shelters for the sick after smallpox swept through Nara in 737.

NARA PERIOD (710–94)

An empress in the early 8th century again constructed a new capital, this one in the northwest of the Yamato plain and named Heijo-kyo, on the site of present-day Nara. The century that followed – the Nara Period – saw the full enforcement of the system of centralised imperial rule based on Chinese concepts (the *ritsuryo* system), as well as flourishing arts and culture.

With the enforcement of the *ritsuryo* system, the imperial government achieved tight control, with administration managed by a powerful grand council. All land used for rice cultivation was claimed to be under imperial ownership, which later led to heavy taxation of farmers.

HEIAN PERIOD (794–1185)

In the last decade of the 8th century, the capital was relocated yet again. As usual, the city was built on the Chinese model and was named Heian-kyo. It was the core around which the city of Kyoto developed. Its completion in 795 marked the beginning of the 400-year Heian Period.

The strength of the central government continued for several decades, but later in the 9th century the *ritsuryo* system gradually began to crumble under the bureaucratic system.

This was modified so that aristocrats and powerful temple guardians could own large estates *(shoen)*. Farmers, working imperial lands but faced with oppressive taxation, fled to these estates in large numbers. Thus the estate holders began to gain political – and military – power in the provinces.

Provincial areas were neglected by the imperial court. Banditry became widespread and local administrators were more interested in personal gain than in enforcing law and order. The result was that the lords of great estates continued to develop their own military power using skilled warriors called samurai.

Eventually they engaged in struggles amongst themselves, and the fighting ended the Heian Period dramatically and decisively.

KAMAKURA PERIOD (1185–1333)

The victor of the struggles, Minamoto Yoritomo, was granted the title of shogun (military commander) rather than emperor. He set up his base at Kamakura, far from Kyoto, and established an administrative structure and military headquarters, creating ministries to take care of samurai under his control.

Painting of Japanese warlord Minamoto-no Yoritomo, who established the first Samurai shogunate in Japan in the 12th century.

He convinced the emperor to sanction officials called *shugo* (military governors) and *jito* (stewards) in each province. The former were responsible for military control of the provinces and the latter for supervising the land, as well as collecting taxes. Both posts were answerable directly to the shogun himself, and thus government by the warrior class, located at a distance from the imperial capital, was created.

The origins of the samurai warriors can be traced to the 7th century when landowners began amassing power and wealth, creating a feudal system that needed defending. Some samurai, or *bushi*, were relatives or financial dependents of lords, others hired swords. The code of honour called bushido, "the way of the warrior," demanded absolute fidelity to one's lord, even above family loyalty. By 1100, the feudal lords and their samurai retainers held military and political power over much of the country.

This governing system was known as bakufu, or shogunate. The imperial court was, in effect, shoved into a corner and ignored. The court remained alive, however, though subsequent centuries saw its impoverishment. Still, it kept an important function in ritual and as a symbol.

A depiction of one of the battles of Kawanakajima.

Although the Kamakura Period was relatively brief, there were events and developments that profoundly affected the country. A revolutionary advance of agricultural techniques occurred that allowed greater production of food. Consequently, there was a significant increase in population and economic growth, with more intense settlement of the land, improved commerce and trade, the expansion of local markets, and the beginnings of a currency system. Contact with the Chinese mainland resumed on a private basis. Strong Buddhist leaders arose who preached doctrines that appealed to both the samurai and the common people.

The complexities of civil rule became top-heavy; the system of military governors and stewards started to crumble. More strain was added by the defence of the country against the two Mongol invasions in 1274 and 1281, both of which were unsuccessful due in great measure to the fortuitous occurrence of typhoons that destroyed the invading Mongol fleet.

MUROMACHI PERIOD (1333–1568)

A subsequent generalissimo, Ashikaga Takauji, returned the capital to Kyoto, enhancing the power of the shogunate over the imperial court.

The name of the period, Muromachi, comes from the area of Kyoto in which a later Ashikaga shogun, Yoshimitsu, built his residence. His life represents perhaps the high point of the Ashikaga shogunate. Yoshimitsu took an active role in court politics as well as excelling in his military duties as shogun.

⊙ CLAN WARS

Engrossed in a dream-like lifestyle, court intrigues and romantic dalliances, the Heian nobility failed to take note of the emergence of powerful and restive military clans. Most prominent were the Genji and Heike, also known as the Minamoto and Taira.

Wishing to rid himself of the dominant Fujiwara regents, the emperor enlisted the services of the Heike, who soon became embroiled in a power struggle with the Genji, one that led to the fierce Genpei Wars (1180–85). A struggle over imperial succession led to the Heike imprisoning the emperor and putting his grandson, whose mother happened to be a Heike, on the throne. The Genji counterattack, under the command of the cavalier young general Yoshitsune, annihilated the Heike in a decisive sea battle in 1185.

Battles took place at Mizushima, Shinohara, Yashima on Shikoku Island, and even in Uji, a town of great serenity. Shimonoseki's annual Kaikyo Festival reenacts the scene in which the red-and-white-bannered forces of the Genji and Heike fought their final battle at Dan-no-ura in the Shimonoseki straits between Honshu and Kyushu islands.

Even in remoter villages of places like Hida-Takayama in Gifu, visitors can find the descendants of communities formed from the fleeing remnants of the defeated Heike clan. The war between the two groups forms the main subject of the medieval *Tales of the Heike*.

Many scholars consider the Muromachi Period (1333–1568) the apex of Japanese garden design. With the development of Zen and the growing influence of its temples, small, exquisite stone gardens were constructed as aesthetic and contemplative spaces.

Overall, the Muromachi Period introduced the basic changes that would assure the economic growth and stability of the coming Edo Period. Agricultural techniques were improved, new crops were introduced, and irrigation and commercial farming expanded. Guilds of specialised craftsmen appeared, a money economy spread and trade increased markedly. Most importantly, towns and cities arose and grew; such development was accompanied by the appearance of merchant and service classes.

A later Ashikaga shogun was assassinated in 1441, which started the decline of the shogunate; the relationship between the shogun and the military governors of the provinces broke down. A decade of war and unrest marked the total erosion of centralised authority and a general dissolution of society. It ushered in the Age of Warring States, a century of battle that lasted from 1467 until 1568.

The almost total decentralisation of government that occurred in the Age of Warring States saw the development of what might be called a true type of feudal lord, the daimyo, backed up by vast armies.

MOMOYAMA PERIOD (1568–1600)

The short Momoyama Period is notable for the rise of Oda Nobunaga (1534–82), the first of three leaders to go about the business of unifying the country, who started by overrunning Kyoto. The other leaders were Toyotomi Hideyoshi (1536–98) and Tokugawa Ieyasu (1543–1616).

Nobunaga conquered the home provinces in a rigorous manner. He eliminated rivals and razed the temples of militant Buddhist sects around Kyoto that opposed him. Temple burning aside, he had a flair for culture.

Although he brought only about one-third of the country under his control, Nobunaga laid the foundation for the unification that would later follow. He was assassinated by a treacherous general in 1582.

Hideyoshi, Nobunaga's chief general, succeeded his master. With military brilliance, statesmanship and a certain amount of brass, he proceeded vigorously with the job of unifying Japan. By 1590, all territories of the country, directly or by proxy, were essentially under his control. But the government was still decentralised in a complex network of feudal relationships. Hideyoshi's hold on the country, based on oaths of fealty, was slippery at best. Still, he effected sweeping domestic reforms. The action that perhaps had the longest-lasting social

Screen depicting Jesuit priests and Portuguese merchants.

impact on Japanese history was his "sword hunt", in which all non-samurai were forced to give up their weapons. A class system was also introduced. In some areas, rich landlords had to make a difficult choice: declare themselves to be samurai and susceptible to the demands of the warrior's life, or else remain as commoners and thus subservient to the samurai class.

Hideyoshi made two attempts to conquer Korea, in 1592 and 1597, with the aim of taking over China. His death in 1598 brought this megalomaniacal effort to an end.

The cultural achievements of these three decades were astonishing. The country was in political ferment, yet at the same time glorious textiles, ceramics and paintings were produced.

THE EDO PERIOD

The rise of the great shogunates and their samurai warlords is instilled in the Japanese way of thinking and their behaviour, even today.

The political, economic, social, religious and intellectual facets of the Edo Period (1600–1868) are exceedingly complex. One often-cited general characteristic of this time is an increasingly prosperous merchant class emerging simultaneously with urban development. Edo (modern-day Tokyo) became one of the world's great cities and is thought to have had a population in excess of 1 million at the beginning of the 18th century – greater than London or Paris at the time.

THE TOKUGAWA SHOGUN

For many years, the shogun Hideyoshi had bemoaned his lack of a male heir. When in the twilight of his years an infant son, Hideyori, was born, Hideyoshi was ecstatic and became obsessed with founding a dynasty of warrior rulers. So he established a regency council of leading vassals and allies, foremost of whom was Tokugawa Ieyasu (1542–1616), who controlled the most territory in the realm after Hideyoshi. Members of the council swore loyalty to the infant; the boy was five at the time of Hideyoshi's death.

The death of Hideyoshi was naturally an opportunity for the ambitions of restless warlords to surface. Tokugawa Ieyasu had about half of the lords who were allied with Hideyoshi's son sign pledges to him within a year of Hideyoshi's death. In 1600, however, he was challenged by a military coalition of lords from western Japan. He won the encounter in the Battle of Sekigahara (near Kyoto) and became the islands' de facto ruler.

In 1603, Tokugawa Ieyasu was given the title of shogun by the still subservient but symbolically important emperor. He established his capital in Edo, handed his son the shogun title in 1605, and then retired to a life of intrigue and

Detail of a folding screen which depicts the siege of Osaka Castle in 1615.

scheming that was aimed at consolidating the position of his family (Ieyasu himself would die in 1616).

The primary problem facing Ieyasu was how to make a viable system out of the rather strange mix of a strong, central military power and a totally decentralised administrative structure. Eventually he devised a complex system that combined feudal authority and bureaucratic administration with the Tokugawa shoguns as supreme authority from whom the various lords, or daimyo, received their domains and to whom they allied themselves by oath.

While the military emphasis of the domain was curtailed, each daimyo had considerable

Tested on criminals' corpses, the Japanese sword, or katana, was the world's most beautiful instrument of death. After the abolition of the samurai class in the late 19th century, the sword-making town of Mino-Seki shrewdly became Japan's leading cutlery producer.

autonomy in the administration of his domain. The system sufficed to maintain peace and a growing prosperity for more than two centuries. Its flaws sprang from its inability to adapt well to social and political change, as would later be seen.

Ieyasu was Napoleonic in his passion for administration, and he thought of every device possible to assure that his descendants would retain power. Wanting to keep an eye on the daimyo, in 1635 he established the *sankin kotai* system, which required staggered attendance in Edo for the 300 independent feudal lords. The shogunate set up a rigid class hierarchy – warriors, farmers, artisans, merchants – and adopted a school of neo-Confucianism as the theoretical basis for social and political policy.

Whether in Edo or the countryside, every individual knew exactly what his or her position in society was and how to behave accordingly. For most of the Tokugawa decades, Japan's doors were closed to the outside. Long years of isolated peace slowly replaced the warrior's importance with that of the merchant. The standards of living for all classes increased, but at times the shogunate quelled conspicuous consumption among merchants.

GROWTH OF EDO

When Ieyasu first settled down in what would eventually become modern Tokyo, the area was little more than a collection of scattered farming and fishing villages. The little town of Edojuku, at the mouth of the Hirakawa River, contained only about 100 thatched huts in the shadow of a dilapidated castle, built in 1457 by the minor warlord Ota Dokan. A sophisticated poet and scholar, in 1485 he was betrayed and butchered at the behest of his own lord.

Ieyasu brought with him to Edo a ready-made population of considerable size. Huge numbers

of peasants, merchants and ronin (master-less samurai) poured into the new capital of the shogun to labour in the construction of the castle, mansions, warehouses and other infrastructure required to run the giant bureaucracy. The courses of rivers were changed, canals were dug and Hibiya Inlet, which brought Tokyo Bay lapping at the base of the castle hill, was filled in.

When the major daimyo and their entourage were in town, the samurai portion of the city's population probably topped 500,000, maybe even outnumbering the commoners. The samurai

Print of people walking in the Ryogoku Bridge area.

⊘ A SAMURAI'S WAY OF LIFE

The way of the samurai – *bushido* – was a serious path to follow, "a way of dying" to defend the honour of one's lord or one's own name. Often that meant *seppuku*, or ritual disembowelment. An unwritten code of behaviour and ethics, *bushido* came to the foreground during the Kamakura Period. In the Edo Period, *bushido* helped strengthen *bakufu*, or the shogunate government, by perfecting the feudal class system of samurai, farmer, artisan and merchant. The ruling samurai class was by far the most powerful. Only when the economy shifted from rice-based to monetary did the merchants take control of Edo, leaving the samurai increasingly in debt.

allotted themselves over 60 percent of the city's land. Another 20 percent went to hundreds of shrines and temples, which formed a spiritually protective ring around the outer edges of the city.

By the early 1700s, an estimated 1 to 1.4 million people lived in Edo, making it by far the largest city in the world at the time. During the same period, Kyoto had a population of 400,000 and Osaka 300,000. In 1801, when Britain's navy dominated the seas, Europe's largest city, London, had fewer than a million inhabitants. Japan's population hovered around 30 million

A depiction of some of the 47 ronin taking their revenge on Kira.

for most of the Edo era; less than 2 million belonged to the samurai families.

In general, the samurai gravitated to the hilly parts of the city, or *yamanote*, while the townspeople congregated – or were forced to do so – in the downtown lowlands, or *shitamachi*, especially along the Sumida River. More than half of Edo's residents were crammed into the 15 percent of the city comprising *shitamachi*, with a population density of about 70,000 people per square kilometre. Almost from the start, both *yamanote* and *shitamachi* began to encroach through landfill onto Tokyo Bay. (Even today in the modern city of Tokyo, these two districts retain distinctive characteristics.)

EDO CASTLE

The grounds of Ieyasu's huge castle, including the defensive moat system, were extensive. The complex was not actually completed until 1640 but was razed by fire seven years later.

The shogun's capital must have been a truly impressive city, backed by Fuji-san and laced with canals. It is often forgotten nowadays that most of Edo's supplies came by sea, especially from Osaka. In fact, one of the reasons Ieyasu had chosen the area for his capital was its easy access to the sea. But the swampy shore of Tokyo Bay itself was unsuitable for building docks and wharves; instead, canals and rivers threading inland from the bay served as ports.

This is not to suggest that the five great highways from the provinces, and especially from Kyoto, converging on the city were not also important. They were, especially the famous Tokaido, or East Sea Road, along which most of the feudal lords from Osaka and Kyoto travelled to Tokyo for their periodic and mandated stays in Edo. Tokaido also formed the central artery of the city itself between Shinagawa and Nihombashi.

The dichotomy between the refined – albeit somewhat inhibited – culture of upper-class *yamanote* and the robust, plebeian art and drama of lower-class *shitamachi* (which Edward Seidensticker aptly dubbed respectively as the "high city" and "low city") has been a consistent feature of life in Edo. The Edokko (Children of Edo) took delight in delight, and this appreciation of pleasure is grandly reflected in the popular culture of the time – the colour and splash of kabuki; the bunraku puppet drama; ukiyo-e woodblock prints depicting the world of actors, sumo stars, courtesans and geisha; the pleasure quarters, licensed and unlicensed; and the vigorous publishing world of both scholarship and trashy stories. All of these reflected the Edo pleasure in the material world and in a kind of high consumerism. The fact that men outnumbered women – two to one as late as 1721 – probably contributed to making the male population more than a bit rowdy and cantankerous. It would certainly explain the emphasis on catering to the sensual pleasures of men and in the rise of woodblock prints of a rather graphic, if not exaggerated, sexual nature.

The shogunate unsuccessfully tried banning both kabuki and prostitution. Eventually, the shogunate simply moved these debauched activities to locations that were less desirable.

RISE OF THE MERCHANTS

The establishment of the shogunate caused many economic changes. After the shogunate eliminated international trade, merchants and the increasingly powerful commercial conglomerates (zaibatsu) turned their attention to domestic distribution and marketing systems. The highways built by the Tokugawas, along with their standardisation of weights, measures and coinage, helped with the rise of the zaibatsu.

The samurai received their stipends in rice, but the economy was increasingly dependent upon money – not to the shogunate's liking, as the shogunate's economic foundation was based upon taxes paid in rice. The result was that the samurai borrowed from the merchants and increasingly went into debt.

Yet it was still controlled with rigid social and governmental systems. Internal pressures demanded change. Moreover, the world itself was not about to allow Japan to keep its doors closed. The industrial revolution was gaining momentum in Europe, and the Western powers were casting about for more countries into which to expand economic influence.

While others had tried rattling Japan's doors, it was the United States that yanked them open in 1853 with Commodore Matthew Perry and America's East India Squadron – the famous "Black Ships". He reappeared the following year with additional ships to back up his gunboat diplomacy and was successful: in 1858 a treaty of friendship and trade was signed with the United States, followed shortly by treaties with other Western powers.

The turmoil and tumult of the 15 years from 1853 to 1868 have been well documented in many books. The sense of Japan afloat in a sea of hostile powers who possessed more technology and had voracious ambitions may have acted to direct domestic energies away from internal wrangling. The shogun was in a tight squeeze with the arrival of Perry. His consensus with the daimyo regarding how to respond to the Black Ships – encouraging them to strengthen and improve defences in their own domains – eventually diluted his control over the daimyo. At the same time, an anti-Tokugawa movement amongst lower-level daimyo was stewing near Osaka and Kyoto.

Rebel daimyo captured the then powerless emperor and declared the restoration of imperial rule. Shogunate forces sought to reverse the situation in Kyoto but were defeated. The shogun yielded to the imperial court in 1868 – the Meiji Restoration. The emperor ascended again to head of state, and his reign would last until 1912.

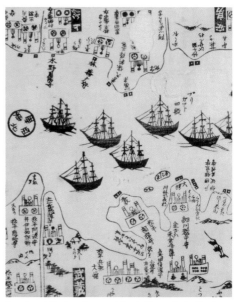

Drawing of Matthew Perry arriving in Uraga, Soshu Province.

⊘ THE 47 MASTERLESS SAMURAI

In 1701, the warlord Asano became angered at the taunting of a *hatamoto* (high-ranking samurai) named Kira, who had been assigned to teach him proper etiquette for receiving an imperial envoy. Asano drew his sword and wounded Kira, and so was ordered to commit ritual disembowelment, or *seppuku*. He did so. His lands were confiscated and his samurai left as *ronin*, or masterless warriors. A year later, the *ronin* took revenge by attacking Kira's mansion. Chopping off Kira's head, they took it to Asano's grave so that his spirit could finally rest. In turn, the 47 *ronin* were ordered by the shogun to commit *seppuku*, which they did together.

Mutsuhito, the Meiji emperor.

THE MODERN ERA

Once militarism was replaced by consumerism, Japan rapidly became one of the world's richest, safest and most advanced countries.

The Meiji Restoration of 1868, in which the ascension of the Meiji emperor as the nation's leader returned Japan to imperial rule, was a revolution of considerable proportions. Yet it was accomplished with surprisingly little bloodshed. The last shogun, Yoshinobu, retired in statesman-like fashion and gave up Edo Castle rather than precipitate a full-scale civil war. Power was officially returned to the emperor in the autumn of 1867.

But shogunate residue remained in Edo and not all the samurai gave up easily. At the Tokugawa family temple of Kan'ei-ji, most of which is now Tokyo's Ueno Park, 2,000 diehard Tokugawa loyalists – the Shogitai – chose to make a last, hopeless stand at the bloody Battle of Ueno.

MEIJI PERIOD (1868–1912)

In 1868, an imperial edict changed the name of Edo to Tokyo, or Eastern Capital, and Emperor Meiji moved his court from the imperial capital of Kyoto to Tokyo. Because at the end of the Edo Period the office of emperor had no longer been associated with a political system, the emperor's "restoration" could be used as a convenient symbol and vehicle for choosing from a wide range of governmental structures.

In a few decades, Japan effectively restructured itself as a political entity. In retrospect, this

A Japanese print from 1870 showing the various forms of transport employed by people.

seems astonishingly radical. Yet it did not happen overnight, but rather by a series of incremental modifications to the political system.

The leaders of the Meiji-era reforms were young, highly driven men, mostly in their 20s and 30s, like the egalitarian reformer Ryoma Sakamoto, political thinker Yukichi Fukuzawa, educator Shoin Yoshida and diplomat Arinori Mori.

This was the age of slogans. Only a few years ago, "Revere the emperor, expel the barbarians," had been the most resounding cry. Now the call was for *Bunmei Kaika*, "Civilisation and Enlightenment", "Western learning, Japanese spirit" and, significantly, *Fukoku Kyohei*, "Rich country, strong army". Compulsory education,

The new reforms included the abolition of practices like the tattooing of criminals, burning at the stake, crucifixion and torture. The mass murderess O-Den Takahashi – notorious for poisoning men – was the last person to be beheaded, in 1879.

the promotion of emperor-based Shinto and military service went hand in hand, laying the foundations for the nationalism and the state-sponsored indoctrination that would propel Japan towards the tragedy of World War II.

Meeting the Western powers as an equal was one of the guiding concerns of the Meiji years. This meant adopting anything Western, from railways to ballroom dancing. The pendulum first swung to extremes, from a total rejection of all native things (including an urge to abandon the Japanese language) to an emotional

Portrait of Meiji, Emperor of Japan, and the imperial family in 1900.

nationalism after the excesses of initial enthusiasm for foreign imports. But the employment of numerous foreign advisers (upwards of 3,000) ended as soon as the Japanese sensed that they could continue perfectly well on their own.

Japan took to Western industrialisation with enthusiasm. Interestingly, reformation had begun to take place even before the Meiji era in Kagoshima, Saga and Kamaishi, where the smelting of iron ore marked the beginnings of an industrial revolution. These regions belonged to fiefs controlled by the so-called *tozama* daimyo, or "outside territorial lords", who had never seen themselves as servants of the Tokugawa shoguns.

Many exhibitions were held during the Meiji era in Tokyo's Ueno Park, a showcase for new industries, technologies and gadgetry. The First National Industrial Exhibition, in 1877, attracted large crowds drawn to its displays of machinery, manufacturing, metallurgy and agriculture.

A new cabinet, consisting of 11 departments, was established to replace an unwieldy system of court management, and local governments were overhauled and reorganised along modern lines. New political groupings, with names like the Liberal Party and Reform Party, were formed. After a number of unsuccessful drafts over the years, a new constitution for the country was promulgated in 1889. This Meiji Constitution helped Japan become recognised as an advanced nation by the West.

Despite the creation of a parliament called the Diet, real power rested with the military, whose growing ranks were reinforced by Japan's victory in the Sino-Japanese War of 1894–5, an exercise in demonstrating the country's ability to wage modern warfare.

The clincher in making Japan a true world power, however, was winning the Russo-Japanese War of 1904–6, the first time that an Asian nation had defeated a European power. It didn't stop there. In 1910, Japan annexed Korea, ostensibly by treaty but actually under military threat, and occupied it until the end of World War II in 1945.

Emperor Meiji died in 1912. By then, Japan had consolidated its economy, defined a political system, changed its social structure and become an advanced nation.

TAISHO PERIOD (1912–26)

The short reign of Emperor Taisho saw the 20th century catch Japan in its grasp and carry it off on a strange and sometimes unpleasant odyssey.

World War I proved an enormous economic boom, and Japan seized the chance to enter Asian markets vacated by the European powers. With the defeat of Germany, some of its small Pacific territories came under Japanese control. But the inevitable deflation hit hard, and there were major rice riots in Tokyo in 1918.

The following year, politics became extremely polarised as the labour movement and leftists gained momentum. A new right, which believed in the politics of assassination rather than the ballot box, emerged from the political shadows. A series of political murders, including of prime ministers, followed over the next 15 years, helping to create the climate of violence that eventually let the military intervene in politics.

One of the founding members of the League of Nations in 1920, Japan failed to gain support from the US, Britain and Australia to have a dec-

of Japan as a world power contributed to the "Taisho Democracy", a time of healthy intellectual ferment that preceded the coming fascism.

SHOWA PERIOD (1926–89)

With the death of the Taisho emperor in 1926, Hirohito succeeded to the throne to begin the Showa Period and Japan's slide into war. Whatever the political, economic and social forces that produced the military government and the aggressive war effort, some observations can be made. The distribution of wealth was still

Photograph of a Tokyo street in the early 20th century.

laration of racial equality incorporated into its charter, a bitter snub to a country that had sat with the five big nations at the Paris Peace Conference after the war.

The most transforming event of the 1920s, however, was not political but the catastrophe of 1 September 1923, the Great Kanto Earthquake, which struck at just noon, when a good percentage of the city's charcoal and gas stoves were lit: fire, not the quake itself, caused the most damage. Ninety percent of Yokohama was destroyed.

During the Taisho Period, Japan began to bubble intellectually, becoming a beacon for independence-minded Asian thinkers. The growing prosperity (and accompanying problems), shrinking size of the world and relative youth

⊙ EMPERORS AND CALENDARS

Japan has a British-style constitutional monarchy and parliament. Since the 1868 Meiji Restoration, there have been four emperors, though since World War II they have been a figurehead (coronation dates in parentheses):

Meiji (Meiji Period) 1867 (1868)–1912
Taisho (Taisho Period) 1912 (1915)–1926
Hirohito (Showa Period) 1926 (1928)–1989
Akihito (Heisei Period) 1989 (1990)–present
Naruhito (Reiwa Period) 2019 (2019)–present

Japan uses two methods for indicating the year: the Western system (for example, 2016) and a system based on how long the current emperor has reigned (for example, Heisei 28).

uneven. The establishment factions included big business (the zaibatsu), the upper crust of government and military interests.

Political power within the country favoured establishment interests; suffrage was not universal. Non-establishment interests were weak because they had little recourse for expression, other than through imported political concepts – socialism and communism – that were distrusted and feared. A sense of territorial insecurity, coupled with domestic economic and demographic pressures, made military

European colonial powers had struck their Asian prey when they sensed a weakening or decay in the body politic of a sick state or failing kingdom. That this was done with impunity was made possible by the sense of entitlement that epitomised the West in its dealings with occupied territories.

There was little difference between the intentions of European nations and those of their Japanese colonial imitators when it came to entrapping and exploiting the peoples of Asia. The Burmese nationalist leader General Aung San couldn't have put it better when he said,

Inside the Peace Memorial Museum in Hiroshima.

hegemony seem a viable alternative, at least to the military.

MILITARISM'S RISE AND FALL

The pivotal point was the Manchurian Incident of 1931, in which Japanese military forces occupied Manchuria and set up the state of Manchuguo. Protest over this action by the League of Nations resulted in Japan leaving the League and following a policy of isolation.

Despite the Asia liberation rhetoric issuing from Tokyo, Japan's real aims were to secure self-sufficiency in strategic resources. Consolidating its empire in Asia would ensure this aim. The expansion of Japan's imperial hegemony was based on the European model. The

"If the British sucked our blood, the Japanese ground our bones!"

Within the military itself, extremist factionalism grew, and during the 1930s several plots of one kind or another sought to win power for different groups. The most famous is the 26 February Incident of 1936, a bloody military uprising that might have been a coup d'état had it not been based on vague, romantic ideas that did not include a practical plan of how to use power. This bolstered the civilian resistance to military involvement in politics. Yet in the summer of 1937 war erupted with China, and Japanese troops began a brutal campaign against the Chinese, which is infamous for the occupation of Nanjing and subsequent slaughter of between

150,000 and 300,000 civilians. Also known as the "Rape of Nanjing", this incident remains a controversial topic between Japan and China, South Korea and the Philippines.

Japan's colonial expansion into other parts of Asia and the Pacific was a replication of the Western powers' own search for resources, and was met with a series of economic sanctions imposed by the US, Britain and Holland. These included a crippling oil embargo, a factor which pushed Japan closer to confrontation with the Western powers. In 1940, Japan signed the

For a modern nation, the Shinto-orchestrated funeral of the Meiji emperor was a remarkable sight. A cortege drawn by white oxen, banner-bearers, bowmen and men bearing halberds passed through streets covered with sand to mute the sound of passing wheels.

Tripartite Act with Germany and Italy, thus formalising the Axis powers and promising mutual military support.

WORLD WAR II

Seeking to discourage Western intervention in Japan's Asian expansion and to break the trade embargo, the Japanese military launched pre-emptive attacks not only on the US's Pearl Harbor in December of 1941 (as well as targets in the US-held Philippines and Guam) but against European colonial holdings throughout Asia, including Malaya, Singapore and Hong Kong. The attack had the result of formally bringing the US into World War II, with their declaration of war on Japan alongside the other Allied nations. In less than a year, Japan had gained possession of most of East and Southeast Asia and the western Pacific. Their gains were profound, but the US and Allied troops had begun to press them back through 1944, and by early 1945 Japan was on the defensive. With the European battlefronts quietened, the US concentrated on the Pacific theatre of war.

Ignoring the Geneva Convention ban, the US continued its campaign of terror bombings on civilian areas of Japanese cities. The air raids were of an unprecedented ferocity. Many of the firebombs fell on the populations of Sumida-ku and other wards of eastern Tokyo during the 102 raids that were launched between January 1945 and Japan's surrender in August. Robert McNamara, whose name would later be linked with the Vietnam War, took part in planning the raids, recalling later that "in a single night we burned to death 100,000 civilians... men, women, and children."

Despite Germany's defeat in May of 1945, Japanese military leaders would not yield. Japan's intransigence, combined with mounting pressure from the US scientific lobby keen to test

⊘ SURRENDER PREVAILED

Evidence suggests that the Japanese military ignored civilian officials' pleas to end the war. Three days after the atomic bomb on Hiroshima, the imperial army's chief of staff assured the civilian government that a foreign invasion of Japan would be turned back. Informed of the second atomic bomb on Nagasaki, he repeated his claim. Despite this, on 14 August Hirohito prepared a surrender announcement. That night, 1,000 members of the army attempted a coup by surrounding the Imperial Palace, executing the emperor's guard commander and searching for the emperor's surrender edict. The coup was thwarted, and Japan surrendered on 15 August.

the effects of their labour, saw the dropping, in mid-August of the same year, of atomic bombs on the cities of Hiroshima and Nagasaki.

On 15 August 1945, Emperor Hirohito spoke on the radio – the first time commoners had heard his voice – and declared an unconditional surrender. Japan lost its empire, its right to independent foreign policy, the emperor's claim to divinity, and the army. More than 6 million soldiers and civilians returned home to Japan. War-crime trials convicted several thousand Japanese; 920 of them were executed.

Workers at the Nissan Motor Company factory in Tokyo.

⊙ WHAT KIND OF ARMY?

Article 9 of the post-war constitution, set up by the US, prohibits Japan from possessing or having the potential of an external military force. However, in 2014 the government voted to lift the ban on a Japanese army fighting overseas, in the most serious shift in the country's military stance since 1945. Currently, the *Jieitai*, or Self-Defence Force (SDF), which is technically an extension of the police force, exists in place of a military. In reality the SDF is a sophisticated military entity and one of the world's strongest armies, which already concerns Japan's neighbours. The SDF's responsibility extends 1,600km (1,000 miles) from Japan's shores.

Although the vast majority of Japanese today readily admit to their country's culpability in the war, the view still persists among some that Japan's ultimate defeat was the result more of a failure of strategy and rationality than of a descent into inhumanity. The American campaign to capture Okinawa reflected the quandary faced by many postwar Japanese, whose loathing for the savagery of American forces in the Pacific war zone and the atrocities of Hiroshima and Nagasaki was matched by a sense of betrayal and shame at the conduct of Japanese imperial forces.

A new 1946 constitution issued under the mandate of General Douglas MacArthur's occupation government guaranteed Western-style liberties, established a British-style parliamentary system, dismantled the pre-war industrial zaibatsu and renounced war as national policy. With the signing of the 1951 San Francisco Peace Treaty, American occupation of the country ended and Japan regained its sovereignty a year later. Okinawa, however, remained under US control until 1972.

ECONOMIC BOOM

Three significant characteristics help define post-war Japan in the 20th century: government-coordinated industrialisation and spectacular economic growth; the mocking of democracy by politicians; and Japan's ability to embrace transformation. With virtually every city in ruins after the US's zealous bombing campaign, young people felt a deep sense of betrayal and bitterness at having been indoctrinated into a militaristic mindset in schools and society, into an unshakable conviction in Japan's holy war. In response, they turned their backs on the past, throwing their energies into creating a culture and commerce that could be a creative and peaceful force in the world.

The decades following the war saw well-coordinated corporate and bureaucratic efforts to revive both business and the country. Protected by the American military umbrella, Japan was able to funnel maximum resources into its economy. With the urban population's explosive rise, farming's importance dropped to a fraction of the nation's gross national product, although the farmers' political power actually increased. Unusually for a developing or developed country, Japan's new national wealth was relatively evenly distributed amongst the people, leaving almost no one in an economic lower class. Unemployment remained low and industrial labour disputes and strikes were rare.

A significant boost to Japan's remarkable economic recovery was the Korean War (1950–53), during which the country benefited from a huge procurement trade, manufacturing goods for the American military. Japan's role in the war stimulated investment in equipment and industrial plants, and increased the country's confidence in competing on the international market. By the start of the 1960s, Japan's GNP had risen to fifth place in the world and Prime Minister Hayato Ikeda introduced a plan to double incomes by 1970. His goal was achieved in just seven years.

During post-war reconstruction, government regulation had served Japan's interests well. But as Japan joined the advanced industrial economies in the 1960s and 1970s, the one-way nature of Japan's markets strained relations with others, especially the US, its largest market, and Europe. Over-regulation and chummy

The funeral of Emperor Hirohito in 1989.

⊙ BUILDING, BUT FOR WHOM?

One of the major engines of growth in post-war Japan has been the construction industry. Following the war, most of Japan's infrastructure had to be rebuilt. Thirty years later, this development had become institutionalised to the point that it was a major political tool. Much of this money to fund lavish building projects comes from Japan's postal savings and pension funds. Public opinion has lately veered round to the belief that many of these projects are useless efforts solely for politicians' gain and glory.

Bullet-train lines have inexplicably been built to backwater towns. Two huge and quite expensive bridges between Shikoku and Honshu carry less than half the traffic that planners claimed, and tolls are more than US$50 one way. One of the world's longest (9.5km/6-mile) underwater tunnels, the Aqualine Expressway under Tokyo Bay, which opened in 1998, is rarely used, perhaps because of a US$40 toll and because it goes nowhere important. In the 1980s, Tokyo's former governor initiated an immense "sub-city" in Tokyo Bay at an estimated cost of US$100 billion. The city intended to sell or lease reclaimed land for huge profits, but then the economy's collapse instead put Tokyo deep in debt.

Successive recent prime ministers have come to power on the platform of structural reform. The battle over who really runs the country, though, continues.

business–government relationships saddled consumers with ridiculously high prices.

High rates of household savings created excess capital, used by business and the government for funding massive infrastructure projects. The economy accelerated with uncanny momentum, surpassing every other country except the United States. Japan became the new global paradigm for success and potency. The stock market was on a trajectory that, in the late 1980s, momentarily exceeded the New York Stock Exchange in volume and vigour. Real estate in Japan became

REIWA PERIOD (2019–PRESENT)

Citing old age and ill health, in 2019 Akihito became the first Japanese emperor since 1817 to abdicate the throne. His son, Naruhito, (b.1960) succeeded him, ushering the period of *Reiwa* ("beautiful harmony").

Atop the cauldron of hyper-inflated land values, Japan's "bubble economy" superheated in the late 1980s, only to begin collapsing in 1990. The stock market lost half its value in a short time, banks lost still unspeakable amounts on loans secured by now deflated land values, and

The Great Seto Bridge across the Inland Sea.

the planet's most valuable, and banks dished out money, securing the loans with highly overvalued land. Japan's rising sun seemed, for the moment, to outshine most of the world.

HEISEI PERIOD (1989–2019)

Emperor Hirohito died in 1989, the longest-reigning emperor (62 years) in Japan's recorded history. His son, Akihito, took the throne and adopted the period name of *Heisei,* which means "attainment of peace". He and his family made sustained efforts to humanise the imperial family and to deal tangentially with Japan's brutal past. But as a politically neutered figurehead, the emperor was not permitted to address politics, history or his father's place in history.

a blossoming Japanese self-righteousness as economic superpower took a cold shower. The country went into a recession followed by low growth in the new millennium.

In politics, life at the very top remained very good. For over six decades, one political party has dominated Japan – the dubiously named Liberal Democratic Party, or LDP. Institutionalised and immune to legal redress, *seiji fuhai,* or political corruption, festered unimpeded at the highest corporate and governmental levels. By the 1980s, *The Economist* opined that the ruling LDP government seemed to be "choking on its own corruption".

The LDP fell from grace in 1993 in an unusual backlash by voters, to be replaced by a coalition government. The LDP resuscitated itself by returning to control in 1996. By mid-1999 the party had formed a coalition with the Liberal Party and the new Komeito Party.

DISASTERS STRIKE

Two events within two months in the mid-1990s eroded Japanese self-confidence and world opinion yet further. In January of 1995, an earthquake hit Kobe, an important coastal port near Osaka. Kobe had been declared a low-risk area for earthquakes. The Great Hanshin Earthquake,

as it has been named, killed more than 5,000 people and left 300,000 homeless. Fires from igniting gas mains (said to be earthquake-proof) incinerated entire neighbourhoods of poorly constructed residences; elevated expressways and *shinkansen* rails toppled over like matchwood. Subway tunnels collapsed. Moreover, the local and national government response was nothing short of inept.

Two months after the Kobe earthquake, another event decimated Japanese confidence. In the heart of Tokyo, 12 people died and thousands were injured when the Tokyo subway system was flooded with sarin, a lethal nerve gas. It was in the middle of rush hour, and the prime target was Kasumigaseki Station, the subway stop for offices of the national government and parliament. The effect on the Japanese psyche was indescribable. The Japanese had long prided themselves on being perhaps the safest nation in the world, and believed that the Japanese could not engage in lethal terrorism against other Japanese, but the nerve-gas attack had been seemingly spontaneous and random.

The sarin gas attack – and other deadly deeds uncovered by investigators – were traced to a religious cult, Aum Shinrikyo, led by a nearly blind self-proclaimed prophet.

ECONOMIC DECLINE

The grimmest and most obvious fallout from Japan's economic stagnation, now well into its third decade, has been cynicism towards politicians, reflected in the humiliating losses at the polls by the LDP in the 2009 general election, resulting in the overwhelming victory of the Democratic Party of Japan (DPJ). With a succession of ineffectual leaders, however, the DPJ failed to staunch Japan's economic decline.

This was compounded by unprecedented levels of social destabilisation, an increase in crime, suicide and homelessness. Aware of Japan's vulnerability, American and European companies returned to Japan to buy up property and increase their market share of banking and other financial services. The success of an aggressive, highly motivated China, its enormous reserves of wealth and political clout, its ability to engage with governments in emerging

⊘ TOKYO'S NEXT EARTHQUAKE

Government studies in the 1990s estimated that there would be around 10,000 deaths in Tokyo if the 1923 earthquake were repeated today. Casualty estimates did not take into account subways. Over eight million people move in and out of Tokyo daily, mostly by train and subway, and should tunnels collapse, deaths in subways could reach tens of thousands alone. The Kobe quake was considerably more powerful than the 1923 earthquake that destroyed Tokyo. Should a Kobe-strength earthquake hit Tokyo, casualties could approach 100,000. Since the megaquake in Fukushima, seismologists, convinced that the foundations of the city have been seriously compromised, are preparing fresh predictions.

economies, to access the resources and raw materials it requires to sustain its growth, flabbergasted many people, as the Japanese economy slipped into third place in world ranking, behind the United States and China. The emergence of South Korean companies like Samsung and LG Electronics and Japan's inability to compete with the design cool of makers like Apple, badly hit the country's much-vaunted electronics sector. The sense of crisis felt by once titanic companies like Sony, Sharp and Panasonic, the engines of Japan's post-war growth, were com-

Reality of the tsunami disaster.

pounded by the prospect that these giants could fall into irreversible decline. These troubling developments were exacerbated by a series of corporate scandals and setbacks, including Toyota's recall of millions of cars suspected of design faults.

The magnitude-9 Great East Japan Earthquake of March 2011, and the tsunami and radioactive meltdown it triggered, was a major setback to the immediate prospect of recovery and rebirth. The fact that the government was keenly aware of the levels of risk posed by the nuclear accident, but chose to conceal the truth from the public, served to deepen the public's distrust of a risk-averse political system, one characterised by a diffuse leadership reluctant

> *Japan's government is called a parliamentary democracy. The prime minister, of the majority party, comes from the Diet. The emperor is head of state.*

to accept personal responsibility. As the world watched in appalled thrall the events of 11 March 2011, two things emerged: the duplicity of government, contrasted with the resilience, selflessness and stoicism of the Japanese, a people with the ability to come to terms with tragedy and the realities it dictates.

The DPJ was subsequently ejected from power as the LDP won a landslide victory in early parliamentary elections in 2012. On the appointment of his cabinet Prime Minister Abe Shinzo pledged to boost economic growth. Success came in 2013, when the weak yen resulted in export rises of over 10 percent. When the economy slipped back into recession in 2014, Abe called for snap elections to renew the mandate for his policies. Losing merely three out of 294 seats, the LDP retained its parliamentary majority.

Abe's economic policies, dubbed "Abenomics", aim to set the inflation rate at two percent, correcting excessive yen appreciation and stimulating private investment. As of 2019, there are signs of a continuing recovery from recession, although this is expected to be stymied by a looming global economic slowdown. Economic malaise and structural reforms aside, the government also faces such challenges as growing tensions with China and Russia over the disputed Senkaku and Kuril islands, restarting Japan's nuclear reactors following the arguably man-made Fukushima Daiichi meltdowns, and raising the birthrate and reversing population decline.

Two years after the triple calamity of earthquake, tsunami and meltdown, Tokyo won their bid to host the 2020 Summer Olympics, lifting hopes of a sustained recovery and giving a huge psychological boost to the entire nation. Despite the challenges they face, most Japanese enjoy a remarkably high quality of life on a spectacular archipelago that is inspiring ever-increasing numbers of tourists to visit its shores.

JAPAN'S ROYAL FAMILY

The Japanese monarchy is the oldest existing hereditary monarchy in the world; its head, the emperor, is the symbol of the state.

Royal mania hit a high on 9 June 1993, when tens of thousands of well-wishers turned out for a glimpse of the royal couple, Princess Masako and Crown Prince Naruhito, then heir to Japan's 2,600-year-old Chrysanthemum Throne.

A graduate of Tokyo, Oxford and Harvard universities and fluent in several languages, Owada Masako gave up a promising diplomatic career to marry Crown Prince Naruhito. Hopes, however, that she would become a "royal diplomat" who would give a human face to the Imperial Court were quickly dashed by the notoriously protocol-ridden Imperial Household Agency, and the princess was soon seen behaving in the self-effacing tradition of female royals.

In December 2001 Masako gave birth to a girl, Princess Aiko. As the practice of crowning a female as empress was terminated under the 1889 Meiji Constitution, which now limited the throne to male descendants, there was considerable pressure on Masako to produce a male heir, even as she grew older. After the birth of her daughter, she stayed largely out of the public eye, making only rare official appearances. The Agency has not been able to muzzle the reasons for Masako's long absence from public view. Hospitalised first in December 2003 with shingles, a stress-induced viral infection, she was said to have suffered from an "adjustment disorder" in 2004.

A HISTORY OF REPRESSION

Masako's problems were not the first of their kind in the modern history of the court. In 1963, after a miscarriage, Michiko, then Crown Princess, went into a three-month-long retreat. The first commoner to marry into the monarchy, she dealt with hostility for the miscarriage from the Agency and other royals.

In 2006, the succession crisis was resolved after Princess Kiko, the wife of Naruhito's younger brother Akishino, gave birth to a male heir, Prince Hisahito,

who is second in line to the throne after his father. The pressure on the royal family continues, but in recent years, Empress Masako (as she became in 2019) has made a few key public appearances, even undertaking some overseas engagements, fuelling hopes that her condition has improved.

Attempts were made by the Agency to halt the publication in 2006 of a controversial book by an Australian journalist, Ben Hills, called *Princess Masako: Prisoner of the Chrysanthemum Throne*.

The Masako story is interesting in what it reveals about the influence of the Imperial Household Agency and the way the media in Japan works, or fails to work, with regard to the royal family. Although it was an open

Emperor Naruhito with his wife Empress Masako and other members of the Japanese royal family.

secret among the press that Naruhito and Masako's wedding was scheduled for June 1993, a directive from the Agency extracted a vow of silence. It was not until early that year that the story was broken. The bamboo curtain has lifted a little since then, and stories have been covered by independent magazines in anonymously sourced articles, but for most Japanese publications such reporting remains off-limits.

In 2017, after Emperor Akihito, already in his 80s, had broadcast his desire to retire from his many duties in a rare video to the nation, the Diet enacted a special one-time law to allow him to step down. Akihito abdicated in April 2019 and was replaced as emperor by his son Naruhito, ushering in the Reiwa Period.

Socialising amongst the cherry blossoms in Matsumoto.

LIVING IN MODERN JAPAN

A place where social harmony is prized, Japan is beginning to embrace diversity and a more individual sense of identity.

There is an insistence on cultural stereotypes that often makes them too conveniently well entrenched to bother disputing. In the case of Japan they are myriad. The country, we are told, is a rice culture, despite the fact that before this crop was introduced from China, wheat cultivation and hunting were the order of the day. The Japanese, we are assured, are a monolithic ethnic family, although the Japanese, representing a melting pot that takes its ingredients from as far afield as Mongolia and Polynesia, are in fact a highly genetically diverse population.

Stereotypically, of whatever size or purpose, the group defines for the Japanese a person's individual purpose and function. And the group known as the Japanese – *nihon-jin*, or if especially nationalistic, *nippon-jin* – is the mother of all groups. Not exactly an irreverent comment, given that Amaterasu Omikami, or Sun Goddess, is the mythological foremother of the Japanese themselves. Television commentators and politicians repeatedly refer to *ware-ware Nippon-jin*, or "we Japanese" and the implicit definition of what "we Japanese" are or aren't, do or don't do, believe or don't believe. The compulsion to define identity even shows up in advertising.

JAPANESE ORIGINS

The Japanese sense of uniqueness extends down to a basic identity of a race and culture distinct from others. But the objective evidence strongly points to origins from the mainland.

From the 3rd century BC, waves of human migration from the Asian continent entered the Japanese archipelago, bringing along rice cultivation (including the use of tools), metallurgy and different social structures. These migrations are now considered to have brought

Strolling through the streets of Tokyo.

⊘ THE AINU

The population of the Ainu people today numbers around 25,000, yet they were early inhabitants of Hokkaido and also northern Honshu. Their origins are unclear; it was once thought that they were of Caucasian heritage, but blood and skeletal research strongly suggests connections with Siberia's Uralic population.

Nowadays there are few speakers of Ainu, which has much in common with other northern Asian languages and also with languages of Southeast Asia and some Pacific cultures. Traditional Ainu culture was one of hunting and gathering. Bears and salmon had an especially sacred place in Ainu traditions.

the ancestors of today's Japanese people, the Yamato, who displaced and pushed the resident – and decidedly different – Jomon population into the northern regions or other less desirable areas of the archipelago.

Theories regarding the racial origins of the Japanese cite both the north and the south – Manchuria and Siberia, and the South China or Indochina regions – as likely possibilities. Students of the subject differ as to which origin to favour. The southern physical type is the Malay; the northern type is the Mongolian. Today, both north and south Asia are considered equally valid as likely origins of the Japanese. Still, the precise configuration of the migrations and the cultural traits associated with areas of origin is subject to argument. (Toss in, too, other legitimate theories about migrations from Polynesia or Micronesia.)

There was substantial human immigration later – in addition to cultural and artistic influences – from the Korean Peninsula, a point vehemently denied by Japanese nationalists and racial purists despite the overwhelming archaeological and anthropological evidence. Whereas archaeology in many countries is considered the most neutral of disciplines, without political overtones of any kind, in Japan it can be rife with factions and rivalries. One group of "experts" in Japan has steadfastly refuted and rejected most modern, scientific dating methods, particularly when they are used to authenticate theories proposing a Japan–Korea connection. A breakthrough of sorts in the gridlock of denial came in 2001, when Emperor Akihito, in a speech on his 68th birthday, included a statement that the mother of Emperor Kanmu came from the former Paekche Kingdom of Korea, a clear acknowledgement of blood links between the two nations and royal lineage.

It may also be possible that the Korean and Japanese languages were mutually understandable, if not identical, some 2,000 years ago and that the people on the Korean Peninsula and the Japanese archipelago may have shared a common culture.

Shopping on Takeshita Street in Harajuku, Tokyo.

⊘ THE HINOMARU

When Okinawan Shoichi Chibana, the unassuming owner of a small supermarket, set fire to the *Hinomaru*, Japan's national flag, many people in the islands applauded the act, or at least empathised with it. Used as a shield to defend the emperor at the end of the war, and then occupied by the US until 1972, Okinawans have good reason to detest the flag as a symbol of oppression. For ordinary Japanese, feelings tend to be more ambivalent.

Visitors often note the lack of national flags displayed in public in Japan. The absence of visible nationalism, the cautious approach to patriotism, has its origin in the discomfort felt by many Japanese towards the period of indoctrination and thought-control they identify with Japan's wartime experience.

The displays of fringe extremism at Yasukuni Shrine in Tokyo, where the remains of convicted war criminals are interred, are an embarrassment to many Japanese, and reflect how deeply conflicted many people feel about the flag as a symbol of nationalism. Showings of the flag coincide with singing of the national anthem, the *Kimigayo*, another area of contention, especially among schoolteachers, some of whom have refused to sing or bow towards the flag. While nobody questions their love of country, many Japanese recoil from the idea of nationalism, yet are pressed by their government — in particular the Abe administration after 2012 — to be more patriotic.

UNIQUELY JAPANESE?

Perhaps the most substantial insulator of Japan from the outside is the modern language, which is spoken only in the islands. In fact, the grammar and syntax are considerably easier than those of most Germanic or Romance languages.

Some Japanese will retort, however, that it is undoubtedly one of the world's most difficult languages to learn. The language itself isn't, but the context of usage can be confusing and difficult for those not brought up within the Japanese culture. The increase in the number of non-Japanese speakers of the language has led to perceptions changing from astonishment at the foreigner speaking Japanese to an expectation that anyone who stays long enough should know the language.

The undercurrent in Japanese thinking and in Japanese traditions that all things Japanese, including the race, are "special", if not unique, is undergoing some re-examination. The former conviction that outsiders were incapable of fully appreciating – much less understanding – the distinctions and nuances of *being* Japanese and of Japanese ways has altered to a genuine appreciation of non-Japanese who do.

It was not always like this. It once seemed as if, to those who stayed long enough, and listened to the conversation and media, that only Japan had earthquakes, typhoons, tasty rice, misery, hot weather, bad memories of war, trees that change colour in autumn, snowfall, and fast trains. When French ski manufacturers first tried to export skis to Japan several decades ago, the Japanese government declared the skis unsuitable for the special and unique Japanese snow. Later, in the late 1980s when American beef producers were trying to increase exports to the Japanese market, the agriculture ministry argued that only Japanese beef was suitable for the special and unique digestive systems of the Japanese people. In the 1990s, respected university researchers even claimed that the Japanese were genetically unique in their ability to appreciate to the fullest the sounds of nature like crickets and waterfalls.

These days, with many Japanese enjoying extended periods abroad, contact with foreigners living in their midst, and an economy that is nothing if not global, many of these assumptions are being questioned and the sense of a uniquely different identity undermined.

JAPANESE MANNERS

In a country where physical crowding and complex interpersonal relationships have shaped the language and social manners over the centuries, even the slightest chance of offending, disappointing or inconveniencing another person is couched in a shower of soft words, bows and grave smiles. (Or worse, giggles, a sure signal of acute embarrassment or being uncomfortable.)

The extreme urban density in which the Japanese live has been somewhat relieved by extending city boundaries, the building of more

School children bow to their tour guide at Chuson Temple, Tohoku.

spacious apartment blocks and condominiums, and the preference for smaller families. They have been able to live in close quarters because of their instinctive good manners and mutual respect. Bowing remains a prominent part of the daily lives of the Japanese, a gesture that can mean apology, gratitude, greeting or farewell, and is a reminder of the courtly practices of a former age in many other countries.

There are few places where the virtues of selflessness are so vigorously applied. Part of this consideration for others devolves from the distaste for confrontation and the idea of avoiding any cause for *meiwaku* (bother, annoyance) to other people. Language itself, embodying an elaborate system of honorifics and inclining towards the deferential, plays an important part in maintaining an extraordinary level of civility throughout these congested islands.

To some foreigners, the Japanese language is excruciatingly indirect, requiring finesse in extracting the proper message. Raised in this social and cultural context, the Japanese easily read between the lines.

Sometimes the Japanese are able to use this to their advantage. Recent prime ministers have made efforts to acknowledge the past despite the vociferous views of right-wing politicians, nationalists and university scholars. Yet the linguistic nuances, when properly translated and understood, reveal not the expected apology as it first seems to be when translated from Japanese, but rather a promise of "reflection" or "remorse concerning unfortunate events", hardly an admission of wrong action or a sincere apology. Much of this, however, is the official position. Engage individuals in discussion on these topics and very different, more informed and measured opinions will often emerge.

Samurai houses in Nagamachi.

☉ LANGUAGE, SOCIETY, GENDER

The Japanese *keigo* (polite language) is a hold-over from the structured class system of feudal times, when politeness was reinforced with a sword. In modern times, *keigo* has been preserved as a key element in the deeply rooted Japanese tradition of deference to one's superiors.

Proper speech is a source of pride for most Japanese, and the use of *keigo* can be an art in itself. Moreover, simply shifting the politeness level up a notch – or down – can have the effect of sarcasm or insult. The younger generation tend to favour simpler language structures.

Perplexing to outsiders are the distinctions between the talk of males and females. Consider the first-person pronoun. Men have the option of several forms, the use of each dependent upon the situation and the people involved: *watakushi*, *watashi*, *boku* or *ore*, from most polite to exceedingly casual. Women have fewer options. Modulation and tone of voice also tend to vary between the sexes. Men try to affect a deep rumble, which can approach theatrical proportions. Women often tend to inflect a high, nasalised pitch; this so-called "nightingale voice" is said to be appealing to men.

Again, many of these distinctions are blurring, a fact reflected in the grumbles of an older generation bemused at the spectacle of young women adopting coarser, male speech modes and of young men affecting more effeminate mannerisms.

Marriage between Japanese and foreigners is hardly new, but the numbers have increased. In the past, marriage partners tended to be Westerners. Today many different nationalities form unions, impacting deeply on what is already a much more pluralistic society.

OBLIGATIONS

If apologies are linguistic puzzles, other expressions of social necessity, too, are interesting, if not curious. Strangely, the very word for "thank you" – *arigato* – literally means "You put me in a difficult position". *Oki no doku,* which is an expression of sympathy, means "poisonous feeling". And who would think of expressing regret or apology with *sumimasen,* which literally translates as "This situation or inconvenience will never end"?

Then there is that virtually untranslatable word, *giri.* To violate *giri* is simply unthinkable. *Giri* is often translated as a sense of duty and honour, but such a definition ignores the subtle communal and personal responsibilities behind *giri.* In Japan, there are unspoken responsibilities inherent to acceptance and participation within a group, whether in a friendship or with co-workers in an office, or in the sharing of communal village life. When the responsibility beckons, and the member of any group can easily recognise it without articulating it, the individual must meet and honour that responsibility while putting aside his or her work or personal desires.

FAMILY VALUES

No doubt there's a proverb somewhere saying that obligation, like charity, begins at home. It's true, for example, that in Japan the eldest child (once only the male but now the female as well) is expected to care for aged parents. Likewise, it is still true that the estate, if any, of a deceased parent automatically passes to the eldest child. In fact, these mutual obligations were once inviolable. Today, however, disputes over care for the aged and for inheritance of wealth are increasingly common and often decided in favour not of the parents or children, but of the national government because of prohibitively high inheritance taxes.

Often cited as the core of Japan's traditional social stability, extended families are nowadays as far removed from the original homestead as education, job opportunities and jet planes can take them. And although nostalgia for the hometown and simpler living have taken on a trendy air in recent years, especially as affluence spreads, the urban family is increasingly defining the contours of Japanese life. On the surface, the family appears both paternal (the man is nominally the household head) and maternal (as women still control the household budget and child rearing).

Family day out in Matsushima.

More opportunities for women in business, however, along with increased affluence and broader appetites for the good life, are slowly challenging this status quo.

A labour shortage combined with an equal opportunity employment law supposedly reinforced women's position in the workplace, but the law itself has no teeth as it does not carry penalties for companies failing to comply. The number of women in senior management positions remains deplorably low. What does continue to demand a great deal of respect in Japan is being a housewife and mother. The Global Gender Gap Index – which measures gender equality – ranked Japan 110th out of 149 countries in its 2018 survey, a deplorably low position for such a developed country.

In the Japan of pre-World War II, a young man often got married about the time his parents reminded him that he had reached the *tekireiki*, or appropriate marriageable age. His parents would take an active role in the selection of his bride, making sure she bore the markings of a good wife, wise mother and self-sacrificing daughter-in-law. They interviewed the woman's parents. Even birth records were checked (and often still are), ensuring that the woman's family tree had no bad apples or embarrassing branches. Love rarely entered the picture.

Batsu-ichi ("one X") is a nickname for those who are divorced. When a person gets divorced, an X is put through the spouse's name in the government's family registry.

and manages the daily household accounts. Occasionally, she takes part in activities of the neighbourhood association or of her children's school. She may also enjoy leisure activities such

A tour group at Kaiyukan Aquarium, Osaka.

Parents knew that the couple would eventually become fond of each other and maybe become good friends. The wife, having severed the ties to her own family through marriage, adhered to the customs and practices of her husband's family.

Despite the hardships, the wife generally chose to stay married. To divorce meant she would face penury and the censure – blame for the marital break-up was all hers – of her own family and that of the community.

The traditional wife follows a pattern that her grandmother followed in the pre-war years. Getting up earlier than her husband and children, she prepares the breakfasts and makes sure everyone gets off to work or school on time. During the day, she does the housework, goes shopping

as learning a foreign language. At night, she and the children will eat together, since her husband comes home much later in the evening. Upon his return, she will serve him (and his relatives, if present) his dinner and sit with him while he eats.

While the above is not as common or automatic as before, it is still a marital paradigm in both cities and rural areas. Yet some husbands, like their wives, have been exposed to Western lifestyles and trends and make an effort at being liberated men in the Western sense, cultural biases aside.

Accelerating this process of change is the dramatic increase in the number of divorce cases since the 1990s, a reflection of the growing desire of spouses, particularly wives, to fulfil personal aspirations over those of the family.

Some wives file for divorce when husbands retire from their jobs, demanding half of the husband's severance pay.

Some couples divorce before they even get started on a proper married life. It's called a Narita divorce in reference to the airport near Tokyo. Modern Japanese women have usually spent more time travelling overseas than their new husbands, who may never have been outside Japan because of the emphasis on career. Their first jaunt overseas, perhaps a honeymoon, is ripe with tension and ends in disaster because the woman is more self-reliant than the man. After returning home to Narita, Tokyo's international airport, they divorce.

Changing attitudes and the greater tolerance towards later or no marriage, childless couples, divorcees, single mothers, and the sense that such groups are no longer socially defective, have come less from a bolt of progressive enlightenment than the sheer numbers, the fact that so many people now fall into one or more of these categories.

ESSENTIAL EDUCATION

In the 6th century, Japan adopted major elements of Chinese culture, including Chinese ideographs, Buddhism and Confucianism, not to mention a heavily bureaucratic system of government that persists today. Education was based on the meritocratic selection of talented individuals, later to be bureaucrats, who would then be taught to read and write the *Analects* of Confucius and works related to Buddhism. This Chinese system of education and civil service was absorbed within Japanese society. With the rise of the Tokugawa clan to power in 1603, the pursuit of Western knowledge was strictly limited and controlled, and the study of Buddhist works declined in favour of Confucian ethics.

During the feudal period, education was available to common people in *terakoya*. (*Tera* means temple and *koya* refers to a small room.) These one-room temple schools offered the masses instruction in the written language and certain practical subjects, such as the use of the abacus and elementary arithmetic. Texts were similar to the Chinese classics used by the samurai. Many of the teachers were monks.

Defeat in 1945 brought to Japan a total reformation of the educational system. The new model was essentially American in structure: six years of elementary school, three years of junior high school and three years of high school. The first nine years were compulsory.

Visiting Dazaifu Temple, Fukuoka.

Entrance to higher education is determined by dreaded examinations, which are administered by the individual universities. For each school applied to, a complete set of entrance exams must be endured. There is no universal university admissions exam.

To help them reach the goal of passing the examinations, parents budget a considerable amount of their monthly income to send children to juku, or private cram schools, which are a multibillion-yen business. For the most disciplined of students, every night and weekend is spent at juku having their brains crammed with exam-passing information. It is all learned by rote and not deduction.

There is no doubt that the Japanese are united in a consensus that education is essential for

Hikikomori, or shut-ins, people who never leave their homes, are not peculiar to Japan, but their estimated numbers are: around a million, of whom 80 percent are male. Often their only connection with the outside world is via technology.

social cohesion, economic prosperity and prestige in the international arena. Unfortunately, both in the primary and university levels, form and rote usually take precedence over function and knowledge. Students are taught not analysis and discourse, but rather only the information needed to pass exams for entrance into the next level of their schooling.

Education is respected in Japan, and so are educators. In fact, the honorific for teacher – *sensei*, as in *Nakamura-sensei* – is the same as for physicians. Unfortunately, the responsibility

Shinjuku street pavement.

and professional pressure placed upon them is considerable, especially at the high-school level when students are preparing for their university exams. Holidays are rare for the teachers.

Even the Japanese themselves admit their educational system's shortcomings. The excessive emphasis on entrance examinations is a cause of much national concern and debate, as is the alienation of significant numbers of young people, violence in schools and bullying of pupils. The effectiveness and desirability of many of the orthodox teaching approaches are increasingly being questioned, and reforms are being considered. In the field of English, for example, several thousand native speakers, applying more innovative, interactive methods

> *The suicide rate in Japan remains one of the highest among developed nations, although it has dropped significantly in recent years. The country had the thirtieth highest rate in the world in 2016 according to the WHO, with around 14 suicides per 100,000 people.*

of learning, are employed at both state and privately run schools. Universities themselves are trying to attract more foreign students, a response in part to a troubling decline in the interest shown by young people in studying abroad that has led to much hand-wringing about the lack of ambition among youths.

GENERATION GAP

Few would contest that the majority of Japanese young people are positive, well-adjusted people with a sharper interest in and responsibility towards social issues and the need to be good global citizens than their elders. Older people, on the other hand, aided and abetted by the more established media, are apt to blame the growing insularity of Japanese youth for many of the country's troubles and its gloomy prospects.

To the young, the older generation seem soulless money-grabbers; while older people are quickly apt to label the younger generation as inward-looking, lethargic, passive and disengaged. The expression *shoshoku-danshi*, meaning herbivores or grass-eating men, is a derogative expression for flip-floppy youth, a generation that, without ambition or personal drive, are more interested in their pastimes and personal relationships than work. A more accurate picture is that, rather than aimless, they are victims of parents, cultural icons and leaders who have failed to offer them a road map for the future.

JAPAN'S IVY LEAGUE

Japanese social institutions in general, and schools in particular, are arranged hierarchically in terms of their ability to bestow economic and social status. The university heavyweights are mostly in Tokyo – Keio, Waseda, but above all Tokyo University, or Todai. Inspiring both awe and fierce competition for entrance, Todai regularly tops Japan's university league tables. The few who make it past its hallowed gates are virtually guaranteed a life of privilege. To prove the point, 80 percent of post-war prime ministers hail from Todai, while 90 percent of civil servants in the prestigious Finance and Home Affairs ministries call it their alma mater, and the same number in the all-important Trade and Industry Ministry.

Such orthodoxy belies Todai's radical past. In 1969, students organised a protest against the university system, barricading themselves in the lecture hall. The stand-off only ended when riot police fully armed with tear gas moved in and arrested 600 students.

WORKING LIFE

If the aim of education in Japan is essentially to obtain a well-paid job with a prestigious company, the chances of reaching that goal in Japan's current economic climate have faded for many Japanese. The term *kakusa shakai*, made from the words "gap" and "society," came into vogue in the early 1990s, reflecting a growing perception that a social contract that promised to deliver on the idea of an upwardly mobile middle class had defaulted. The consequent erosion of that class after decades of meagre growth and social-policy stagnation has created disparities between the affluent and a new underclass, inequality and a troubling bifurcation in the labour market.

The collapse of the kind of lifetime employment packages the larger companies were able to provide to a relatively small percentage of the workforce, together with the introduction of the

almost universal five-day week, has changed perceptions, encouraging a view that work and leisure are not incompatible, that job-hopping can improve your prospects, and that pursuing hobbies and interests, and making room for more family and private time, are important life goals.

Driven by the need for cost saving, there has been a near doubling in the number of non-regular workers over the past two decades. As welfare systems and safety nets are largely designed to protect regular workers, the one-third of the workforce now engaged

Uchiko Town, Shikoku.

⊘ CASTE AWAY

First there were the *eta* and *hinin*, the lowest orders of the Edo Period class system. All of that was supposed to have been abolished in 1871 with the issuing of the Emancipation Edict, but discrimination is not so easily uprooted, and for many Japanese, their descendants, known as *burakumin*, have remained "impure".

Outcasts were assigned the very worst jobs, working as gravediggers, tanners, executioners, butchers, and as performers in the lowest ranks of the entertainment world. No physical differences distinguish the *burakumin* today from ordinary Japanese, yet illegal lists of *burakumin*, of whom there are at least 3 million, are often purchased by corporations wishing to eliminate

them as job applicants.

Books, film and the media have often portrayed the modern day *burakumin* as members of Japan's criminal underworld. For many outcasts this has been the only way to make a living. The great Noh playwright Zeami, however, was a member of the sensui *kawaramono*, or "riverbank people". Others made their mark in the *bunraku* puppet theatre, as garden designers and *taiko* drummers. Eminent novelists Mishima Yukio and Yasunari Kawabata are said to have had *buraku* roots, as did the popular *enka* singer Hibari Misora. In more recent times, the influential LDP politician, Hiromu Nonaka, made a point in his early speeches of acknowledging his *buraku* origins.

in temporary work, often dead-end jobs that provide no health insurance coverage, social security benefits or pension programmes, are facing a bleak future as the "working poor", as the media has dubbed them.

Japan has been slow to expand its human resources, particularly in promoting the participation of women in the labour market and the hiring of more foreigners, although some firms like Uniqlo, Rakuten and Softbank have begun actively to recruit native English-speaking staff for their stores.

Exploring the Sankozo Museum, Chuson Temple, Tohoku.

Despite a declining population and workforce shortage, allowing immigrant labour into the market remains a contentious issue. From the Japanese perspective, the difficulties with multi-ethnicity in European countries like Britain, France and Germany has lent legitimacy to Japan's reluctance to open its doors to unskilled foreign workers and immigration, though immigration laws were loosened in 2018, paving the way for an influx of foreign workers.

SWEET UNIFORMITY

The idea that you are what you wear, that "these are my clothes, ergo this is my role", is nowhere more evident than in Japan. Conformism, still a powerful force in Japanese society, lends itself

naturally to uniformism. Individuality, as far as it exists – and it does – is generally of the kind that remains compatible with social rules. Even the radical urge is to be shared with others of a similar disposition.

Uniforms by their very nature unify, suggest strength in numbers – the perfect sartorial solution for a society that remains, despite all the surface experimentation, relatively rigid and tribal. Even Japanese youth, wearing clothes and accessories that highlight infinitesimal differences from the general pattern, have a way of suggesting that they are cut from the same cloth, part of a common weave.

Even the national costume, the kimono, categorises those who wear it into clearly defined groups conforming to certain unwritten rules and conventions of dress: young women are encouraged to wear bright, vibrant colours that offset their youth, older women to don more muted hues that bespeak their maturity.

Shibuya, Minato and Meguro wards remain the centres of Tokyo's theatre of dress. Harajuku, and its backstreet Urahara area in particular, is the fusion point where the assertion of Western individualism gets absorbed into oriental formalism. Here you will chance upon costumes reflecting almost every Anglo-Saxon popular culture fashion since the 1950s: from black-shirted Elvis clones, Minnie Mouse imitators, the checked shirts and chewed-up jeans of rockabilly hicks, the billowing, rainbow-coloured rags of hippie psychedelia, to post-punk and hip-hop. Harajuku is also where the pastiche "kawaii" fashions adopted by global popstars like Lady Gaga germinated.

While a few renegade brown and sand-coloured suits are occasionally glimpsed in commuter carriages, there isn't a great deal of colour on an average day, where black, grey and serge suits dominate among the male, white-collar class, forming an almost unbroken uniformity of taste. The only member of an institution daring enough to wear a purple suit in public is the gang or syndicate-affiliated thug, who is also, as a special concession to his outlaw status, allowed to sport ties printed with surfboards, cocktail sticks and naked women.

OLDEST SOCIETY IN HUMAN HISTORY

In 2017, the number of centenarians in Japan reached almost 68,000. Most were women. In

1965, there were only 150 Japanese centenarians; by 1993, there were 5,000. Okawa Misao, who died in 2015 at the age of 117, was the oldest Japanese person ever. The Japanese are living longer and having fewer children, and the skewed demographics are worrying government planners. The birth rate of roughly 1.4 children per woman is resulting in Japan becoming one of the world's oldest societies. The median age was estimated at 46.9 in 2016, topped in the world only by Monaco. Japan's 65-plus generation accounted for nearly 28 percent of the population in 2017, but it will reach 40 percent by 2060.

Japan as a whole has a negative population growth rate of -0.21 percent. It is expected that the number of people will shrink to under 100 million by 2050, compared to just over 126 million as of 2019. Many analysts believe that the ageing population, more than anything else, is the major factor behind Japan's demise as a world economic leader as the economy shifts to support a population of which at least a quarter is in retirement.

The reasons for this low growth rate are not hard to find. Japanese women enjoy the longest life expectancy in the world, in 2018 standing at 87, while for men it is 81, placing Japan second worldwide after Monaco. Furthermore, the overcrowded cities, where couples live in cramped apartments, occasionally with parents, are not conducive to large families, nor are the phenomenal costs of education and urban life.

Of concern is the cost of providing retirement pensions and old-age benefits. In order to maintain the Japanese pension system over the coming decades it will be necessary to raise the retirement age or allow more immigration. There has already been a hike in consumption tax to 10 percent. Another concern is nursing care, which will become an important problem. And as the population ages, the savings rate will drop, causing interest rates to rise and depleting the government's largest source of operating capital.

Japan may be the most over-analysed nation on earth, but the fact that issues like these are being openly debated hints also at the more vibrant civil society Japan has become.

Characters in the America-Mura district of Osaka.

◉ OKINAWAN LONGEVITY

Few people know how to age better than Okinawa's old folks. Sharp minds and physical vigour among those advanced in age may be a rarity in other parts of the world, but in these southern islands it's commonplace. Okinawa may have the highest proportion of centenarians in the world, with around 50 for every 100,000 people. That compares with about 10 to the same number of Americans. The authors of a best-selling book on longevity called *The Okinawa Program* (2001) discovered that elderly Okinawans have astonishingly clean arteries and low levels of cholesterol, and that heart disease and breast and prostate cancer are rare. The writers concluded that this enviable condition was attributable to the consumption of large amounts of tofu, seaweed and locally grown vegetables, regular exercise and a low-stress lifestyle.

In an effort to wean kids off burgers and cup noodles, so the young could live at least as long as their grandparents, the prefectural government launched its own health education programme. School meals now include such tried and tested local dishes like stir-fried papaya, *goya* (bitter melon) and egg, boiled pork, and rice with *wakame* (soft seaweed), in an attempt to return to their culinary roots. A case, perhaps, of the wisdom of the ages?

The Giant Lantern at Senso-ji, Asakusa.

RELIGION

To the outsider, the adaptability of worship and philosophy in Japan may seem contradictory and diffused. To the Japanese, beliefs are simply pragmatic and free from hypocrisy.

Polls asking Japanese in which religion they believe consistently yield results that total well over 100 percent – most say they are followers of both Shinto and Buddhism. The average Japanese thinks nothing of marrying at a Shinto shrine, burying loved ones in a Buddhist cemetery and boisterously celebrating Christmas. Although the devout Christian or Muslim – each with a monotheistic God demanding unswerving fidelity – might find this religious promiscuity hard to fathom, the typical Japanese sees no contradiction.

Traditionally, nearly every home was once equipped with a kami*dana*, a god-shelf with Shinto symbols, or else a butsudan, a Buddhist household altar containing memorials for the family's ancestors before which offerings of flowers, food, drink or incense are made daily. Most homes had both, and many still do.

The Japanese definitely seem to have a sense of religious piety and spiritual yearning, although it is very different from that in the West. The main difference seems to be that the line between the sacred and the profane is much less clearly drawn in Japan. In many ways, community life and religion are one and the same. Similarly, the distinction between good and bad, or sinful and righteous, is less clear in Japanese society. It is said that the West considers most things as black or white; in Japan, as elsewhere in Asia, there is a lot of grey.

SHINTO

A basic understanding of the Japanese religious sensibility must begin with Shinto, which influences virtually every aspect of Japanese culture and society. It is hard to give any simple definition of Shinto (literally, way of the gods, or kami), since it is not a systematised set of

Dazaifu Tenmangu shrine.

beliefs. There is no dogmatic set of rules nor even any holy script. The term shinto was not even invented until after the introduction of Buddhism, a date traditionally given as AD 552, and then only as a way of contrasting the native beliefs with that imported faith.

In general, it can be said that Shinto shares with many other animistic beliefs the concept that all natural objects and phenomena possess a spiritual side. It is this animism – mixed with ancestor worship, a shared trait with Buddhism – that characterises Shinto. A tree, for example, was revered by the ancient Japanese as a source of food, warmth, shelter and even clothing. For that reason, when a great tree was felled to provide wood for the Buddhist temple complexes at Nara or Kyoto, it was not used for several years in order to give the spirit within time to depart safely. Mountains, forests and even the oceans were also revered.

It should be recognised that the term kami, although often translated as "god", is quite different from the Western concept of divinity. The classic definition, as originally understood in Japan, was made by the 18th-century scholar Moto-ori Norinaga: "Anything whatsoever which was outside the ordinary, which possessed superior power, or which was awe-inspiring, was called kami."

In ancient Shinto there was also a belief in a kind of soul – *tamashii* – that lived on after death. An unrefined form of ancestor worship also existed, remnants of which can be seen in the observances of the spring and autumn equinoxes and in the Obon festivities in early autumn, which in Japan have both Shinto and Buddhist overtones.

Early Shinto had concepts of heaven and hell as well, although they were hazily conceived at best. There was no concept of sin, divine retribution or absolution for offenses committed.

Small shrine at the top of Kompira-san complex, Shikoku.

⊙ LIVING FAITH

Quizzed on the degree of their religious belief, most Japanese would say they are not pious, a way, in many cases, of deflecting the Westerner from viewing them as superstitious. Visitors will notice, however, how well attended its temples and shrines are. The rites and rituals aspire almost to the level of the performing arts. Sacred *kagura* dances, in fact, *are* performances, ones that take place on covered platforms set up in front of a shrine's main hall. In this way, religion may be seen as part of Japan's cultural life.

Detached from its metaphysical character, religion in Japan became a vehicle for a practical morality, but its non-rationality and absence of an overarching doctrinal system promoted an acceptance of things as they are and an openness to other faiths and beliefs that continues to permeate Japanese society, and to promote a polytheism that does not perceive the Buddhist temple and Shinto shrine as incompatible.

Aspects of faith are manifest. The market is carefully allocated: Shinto monopolises coming-of-age ceremonies, marriage and birth; Buddhism manages the more profitable market in death, the elaborate funerals, burial plots, posthumous names and memorial ceremonies.

Over half the population visit shrines over New Year to pray for the coming year, most often for success in examinations, luck in love and recovery from illness.

Prior to the arrival of Buddhism in the 6th century, Shinto lacked artistic or literary representation of beliefs and myths, and so it had no defined pantheon of deities.

It was commonly thought that the dead would eventually be reborn into this world, just as spring returns after winter.

There are 13 mainstream Shinto sects and numerous sub-sects in Japan today, but since World War II they have not been controlled by the government. In fact, it was only during the period from the Meiji Restoration of 1868 until the end of World War II that the state intervened in Shinto. During the Meiji Restoration, the government introduced *kokka* (national) Shinto as a political tool for controlling the people through the policy of *saisei it'chi* – the "unity of rites and politics".

Several shrines were established by the national government for various purposes as "national" shrines, including Yasukuni-jinja in Tokyo and the impressive Meiji-jingu, to the north of Shibuya in Tokyo, whose majestic architecture reminds the traveller that Emperor Meiji, enshrined within, was considered divine.

In fact, none of the national shrines – state inventions all – have much to do with traditional beliefs found within Shinto. Dismissing them as unimportant in the modern scheme of things, however, would be a sociological, if not religious, mistake.

Yasukuni-jinja is a case in point. A large and controversial Shinto shrine just north of the Imperial Palace in central Tokyo, it is an example (and a particularly notorious one) of the national shrines set up by the government authorities before World War II. It is here that the spirits of every soldier who has died in the name of the emperor since 1853 are enshrined (including war criminals executed by the Allies after World War II). Visits here – official or not – by the prime minister and members of government, less common these days, have usually been made to appease right-wing nationalists and are vociferously denounced by neighbouring countries such as China, South Korea and Taiwan.

SHINTO SHRINES

Shrines are of the Shinto religion, and their names often end in the suffixes *-gu*, *-jinja* or *-jingu*. Temples, on the other hand, are Buddhist and usually end with *-ji*, *-tera* or *-dera*. Quite often, temples and shrines are found side by side, or a temple or shrine will have a complementary adjunct on the same sacred grounds.

The thousands of Shinto shrines in Japan vary in size from tiny roadside boxes and intriguing cave-shrines, to large compounds such as the Grand Shrines at Ise and the Tosho-gu at Nikko,

Atsuta Shrine, Nagoya.

but nearly all share certain features.

First, there is at least one torii, shaped somewhat like the Greek letter *pi*. This gateway may have evolved from a bird's perch – a certain kind of bird having been a religious symbol in many animistic cults – and it may be made of wood, stone, metal or even concrete. Like the *shime-nawa* (sacred straw festoon), zigzag cuts of white paper, mounds of salt, and cleanly swept gravel, the torii serves to mark off areas considered sacred from those thought profane.

Often the largest building of the shrine is the inner sanctum, called the *honden*. This is the main dwelling of the deity. It is usually elevated above the other buildings and reached by a staircase. It is likely to be off-limits to visitors, but other than a mirror or, on rare occasions, an image, there is little to see inside. These objects, by the way, are the *mitama-shiro* or *go-shintai*, serving as spirit substitutes for the deity (*kami*) being worshipped. In front of the *honden* is the often quite spacious *haiden* or worship hall, used for ritual ceremonies. Usually this structure is merely a roof supported by pillars and open on all sides.

There are no elaborate rituals or prescribed procedures in worshipping at a shrine. On entering the grounds there is a stone water basin, often with ladles balanced across it, where one rinses mouth and hands in preparation for approaching the deity. It is customary to toss a small offering into the cashbox at the foot of the *haiden* before sounding the shaker to attract the attention of the god. Devout worshippers also clap their hands twice, making doubly sure the god is listening. Then, a deep bow is performed and held while the prayer is offered.

During matsuri, or festivals, the gods are taken out for rollicking rides through the streets in *mikoshi* (portable shrines) in order to bring

Ginkaku-ji Gardens, Kyoto.

☉ A WESTERN FAITH

Christianity came to Japan in the person of St Francis Xavier in 1549, and was received courteously by some of the feudal lords of Kyushu, where the famous missionary docked. The fact that Xavier had sailed from Goa in India caused some initial confusion, the Japanese mistaking the faith for a new form of Buddhism.

Rightly fearing that Christian missionary activities generally represented a prelude to occupation, the shogunate took a suspicious view of the faith. The military ruler Hideyoshi ordered the execution of 26 priests and converts in 1597, initiating a period of persecution that climaxed in the death of over 37,000 Christians after the end of the Shimabara Rebellion outside

Nagasaki in 1637. Henceforth, Christianity was banned and Japan's remaining Christians went underground.

Devout Catholics pay homage annually to the Nagasaki martyrs, but also to a number of Christians who were tortured and killed on the Otome Mountain Pass in the town of Tsuwano at the beginning of the Meiji Period, when there still existed much confusion over what should be done with Christians who had been secretly practising an outlawed faith for over 200 years.

With the introduction of religious suffrage, Western missionaries poured into Japan, building churches and opening schools. The religion has failed to make major inroads; today there are barely 2 million Christians in Japan.

the blessings of the kamisama to all the community. (This is one of the few times when Japanese collectively shed their social inhibitions and turn quite rowdy.)

BUDDHISM

The traditionally accepted date for Buddhism to have arrived in Japan is AD 552. While this may be true, it wasn't until centuries later that it ceased to be the exclusive province of aristocrats. This is somewhat ironic in view of the beliefs of the religion's founder, Sakyamuni –

being, sentient or non-sentient, shares a basic spiritual communion and that all are eventually destined for Buddhahood. Although all beings are separate in appearance, they are one and the same in reality. Every person's present situation is determined by past deeds, Buddhists believe. This is the principle of karma.

Since the main *Mahayana* sutras only appeared around 100 BC, it is not known to what extent they reflect the original thoughts of the Buddha. However, by the time it reached Japan's shores through China, Buddhism had changed tremen-

Raikyū-ji, a Buddhist temple in Takahashi.

born a prince in northeastern India (now part of Nepal) around 500 BC – who advocated a middle way between indulgence and asceticism.

The Buddha, as he came to be known, blamed all the world's pain and discontent on desire and claimed that through right living, desire could be negated and the "self" totally done away with through entry into the blissful state of nirvana, or Buddhahood. Buddha's followers came to believe that one who really knows the truth lives the life of truth and thus becomes truth itself. By overcoming all the conflicts of the ego, one can attain a universal, cosmic harmony with all.

Mahayana, meaning Greater Vehicle, was the form of Buddhism that became established throughout most of East Asia. It holds that every

dously from Sakyamuni's simple message, and was to undergo even more radical change when it encountered the beliefs that were held in the Japanese archipelago.

As early as the 6th century, for example, *Ryobu* Shinto began to emerge as a syncretic compromise with Buddhism. In this hybrid belief system, kamisama were regarded as temporary manifestations of the Buddhist deities. In time, Buddhist thought became influenced by the indigenous beliefs, deviating so far from the original that some scholars doubt whether the Japanese version really deserves to be called Buddhism.

For example, as the famed folklorist Yanagida Kunio once pointed out, if asked where people go after they die, the typical

Japanese will usually answer *Gokuraku*, which translates as Paradise. Contrast this with the more orthodox Buddhist tradition, which teaches that an individual will be repeatedly reborn until they attain the permanent state of nirvana, or extinction. In practice, however, Japanese usually return to their *furosato*, or ancestral home, for the two equinoxes as well as during the midsummer Obon, or Feast of the Dead, observances. The purpose of attending Obon is to be present when the family's ranking male ceremoniously offers food to the spirits of departed ancestors – spirits that return to earth for the occasion. From where do they return? Yanagida says most people will answer "the mountains", which hold a special place in Japanese religious lore. Certain peaks – Omine near Nara and, of course, Mount Fuji – are especially sacred.

Built of lava carried from the mother mountain, miniature Fuji replicas, known as *fujizuka*, were common in Edo, standing in as substitutes for people who, through infirmity or lack of funds, could not make the pilgrimage to the real mountain.

Combined with Buddhist notions of spirituality, the mountain became the locus of a heady mix of beliefs and doctrines during the Edo Period. The special significance of the peak to cults and quasi-religions like Shugendo, or mountain asceticism, was apparent in the length to which its followers would go to demonstrate their devotion. One celebrated mountain ascetic, Jikigyo Miroku, a man of unassailable moral rectitude by all accounts, went as far as to undertake a ritual suicide, a dedicatory fast to the death on the slopes of the mountain. Fuji's transcendent quality, the notion that it was the most proximate peak to heaven, was never questioned, even when its destructive forces were unleashed.

The keisaku is a wooden stick used to stop Zen Buddhists from losing focus during meditation.

AMIDA BUDDHISM

There are today an estimated 56 main divisions and 170 subdivisions in Japanese Buddhism. The single most popular sect is Jodo Shinshu,

Ⓞ NEW CULTS

The number of new religions and cults in Japan has proliferated since the 1970s. Many of these are quite legitimate, while others, though registered as religions, have raised concerns among the authorities.

The crackdown on cults began after Aum Shinrikyo's (Aum Supreme Truth) deadly sarin gas attack on a Tokyo subway in 1995. Headed by a nearly blind yoga instructor, Shoko Asahara, now in prison and facing execution, the group has since reinvented itself with a new image that renounces violence, calling itself Aleph. Membership is said to be growing.

There are dozens more small religious sects. Some have been publicly discredited. The scandal-ridden

neo-Buddhist Ho-no-Hana, run by a guru who claimed he could divine people's past and predict their future by examining the soles of their feet, was arrested after it emerged he had swindled followers out of millions of yen.

Other organisations, like Pana Wave, a group dedicated to fighting harmful electromagnetic waves by covering trees and other natural features in white cloth, and Fukudenkai, a cult founded by a guru who taught that the gaining of positive karma could be furthered by praying to a mound containing the nose rings of over 7 million cows, are generally considered harmless eccentricities.

founded in the 13th century by Shinran, who preached an "easy road to salvation" by means of the *nembutsu* prayer to the Amida, a bodhisattva who made a vow aeons ago to save all who placed faith in him or her and to guide them to the Blissful Land of Purity.

About half of Japanese Buddhists belong to either Jodo Shinshu or another form of Amidaism founded by Honen (1133–1212). Jodo Shinshu offers that it is not necessary to be "good" in order to be reborn into the Western Paradise and that the laity can become Buddhas as easily as priests. Amidaism is the Buddhist form closest to core Japanese beliefs due to its concern for moral judgement and its exaltation of inclinations beyond the mere good and evil.

ZEN EMPTINESS

The impact of that particularly eclectic form of Buddhism called Zen on Japanese culture is considerable, reaching far beyond the temple and entering into interior design, gardening, ink painting, calligraphy, the tea ceremony, cuisine and even military strategies.

Two Buddhist priests in the 12th and 13th centuries – Eisai, founder of the Rinzai Zen sect, and his disciple Dogen, who established the Soto Zen sect – brought the principle of "emptiness" into Japanese Buddhism.

Soto sect followers rely almost solely on *zazen*, or sitting meditation, and seek to emulate Sakyamuni, who reached the state of enlightenment while meditating without conscious thought in such a position. In contrast, the Rinzai sect also utilises *koan* riddles, such as the famous "What is the sound of one hand clapping?" *Koan* must be tackled with something beyond logic and non-logic; the riddles' function is to stimulate (or perhaps divert) the mind into a similar state.

Zen was influenced by both Daoism and the Wang Yangming school of neo-Confucianism, which stressed the "prime conscience" and the importance of action. They would describe the "Great Ultimate" as being akin to the hub of a well: empty but the point from which all action flows. For various reasons, Zen sects proved better able than the others to satisfy the spiritual needs of the samurai.

Whether through *zazen* or the use of *koan* posed by the Zen master, the goal is for the disciple to be provoked, excited or irritated to the point where he or she makes a non-intellectual leap into the void and experiences reality.

BUDDHIST TEMPLES

Under the Tokugawa shogunate, Japanese Buddhism lost much of its vigour, leading cynics to charge that priests were good for nothing else but burying people. An exaggeration, no doubt, but crematoriums still provide a good part of the income for most temples. The main building *(hondo)*, library *(bunko)*, bell tower *(shoro)*

Byodo-in Temple in Uji, Kyoto, dedicated to the Amida.

and other buildings of a temple complex can be exquisite architectural creations. But the one most easily admired is the pagoda, or *to*. The form in Japan is the result of evolution from the dome-shaped *stupa* (thought to represent an upside-down rice bowl), in which the bones of the Buddha and Buddhist saints were buried in India.

Images found in temples include Nyorai (Tathagata) Buddhas, such as Sakyamuni after Enlightenment and Maitreya (Miroku) or Future Buddhas, distinguished by a pose with one leg crossed over the other. Others include the *nio*, fierce-looking images flanking gates to many temples and derived from the Hindu gods Brahma and Indra.

📷 UNDERCURRENTS OF LIFE AND RITUAL

At the core of Japanese life are the ancient animist beliefs of Shinto, which inform daily life in basic ways, enriched by Buddhism introduced from China and Korea.

Buddhism and Shinto coexist, and on occasion appear to meld together. It is not uncommon to find Shinto shrines and Buddhist temples sharing the same sacred grounds, each tending to specific needs but complementing the other as a whole.

This cordial accommodation between the faiths only works in a civic society with high levels of tolerance. In the Meiji Period, with the promotion of emperor-centred Shintoism, an anti-Buddhist campaign was launched that was centred on nationalism and an antipathy towards a religion perceived as being of foreign provenance. This resulted in the destruction of many priceless Buddha images. During World War II, Zen Buddhists, in an effort to look patriotic, threw their support behind the militarists.

Shinto doesn't exist as doctrine, but rather as an integral undercurrent to one's daily life. Shinto is Japan's indigenous religion, but the term Shinto did not appear in any Japanese literature until the 6th century, and in fact the label came into existence only as a way to distinguish it from Buddhism, introduced from mainland Asia. Nor were there visual images of Shinto deities – kami – until the imagery of Buddhism established itself in the archipelago. Over the centuries, Daoism and Confucianism also influenced Shinto.

Ancient Shinto was polytheistic, maybe even pantheistic, and people believed kami existed not only in nature, but also in abstract ideas such as creation, growth and human judgement.

The Japanese may disclaim any strong religious beliefs, but stand in the grounds of a shrine at almost any time of the day, and you will see a steady trickle of worshippers.

Along with Mount Fuji and the bullet train, the massive torii gate that floats off the shores of Miyajima island has become one of the most easily recognised symbols of Japan.

Kimono are rarely worn in everyday life in Japan, but shrines that host weddings, children's coming-of-age rituals and other felicitous events are good places to glimpse them.

Shinto priests perform rituals that often appear arcane, not only to foreign visitors but even to the Japanese themselves.

A life of Shinto blessings

Traditions of Shinto (and of Buddhism, too) are the traditions of Japan itself. They pepper the daily lives of the Japanese, who perform them as routines of life when the urge or need arises.

Small votives *(ema)* are hung at shrines to seek good luck in exams or other secular rituals. Infants are brought to the shrine 30 to 100 days after birth to initiate the child as a new believer. Children dressed in kimono attend *shichi-go-san* (seven-five-three) on 15 November every year. Girls of three and seven years old and boys of five years old visit the shrine to thank the kami for their life so far and to pray for good health. In January, 20-year-olds return to the shrine to mark their attainment of adulthood. When they are married, it is usually a Shinto ceremony (although a separate Western-style ceremony is increasingly common). Death, however, is usually a time of Buddhist ritual and family remembrance.

The final cedar torii gate in a series of three leading to Meiji Shrine in Tokyo.

Kegs of sake, a sacred drink, are often donated to Shinto shrines and then displayed in the grounds.

An unusually decorated figure at Koya-san, a vast graveyard and mausoleum located in a dense cryptomeria forest.

ART, CRAFTS AND LITERATURE

With an aesthetic that goes back millennia, Japan's arts and crafts of today retain an intriguing depth and layers of history, culture and outlook.

Historically Japan has drawn many of its traditional art forms from continental Asia, but sci-fi novelist and Japan watcher William Gibson has written of the country now that "cultural change is essentially technologically driven". Referencing an extraordinary craft legacy in everything from painting and computer graphics to manga, rather than abandoning it, allows Japanese creators to yoke the authority of the traditional with the innovative and new. Ancient Japanese dramas, among the oldest still to be performed in the world, remain spectacles of unparalleled beauty and power, but so do the new works of its installation, pop and video artists, not to mention avant-garde flower arrangers. The international success of conceptual art figures like Kusama Yoyoi, the overseas exposure provided for art collective Chim Pom, and the success of individuals like 3D artist Miyanaga Aiko, hint at a restless exploration of ideas and forms that have their roots in centuries of creativity.

The earliest preserved distinctly Japanese artworks are those of the late Yayoi Period (300 BC–AD 300). These were small, tubular clay figurines called *haniwa*, some of which were set up like fences around imperial mausolea. Whatever their purpose may have been – substitutes for people buried alive in the tombs or magical instruments to ward off evil spirits or bandits – their immediate interest lies in their simplicity and charm. Although many of them are only cylinders, some of the *haniwa* (and there are hundreds) are figures of men and women, horses, monkeys and birds. Most are very simple, with only a few details of decoration – perhaps a sword or a necklace. They have large hollow spaces for the mouth and eyes, which prevented them from cracking when being fired and which add not only to their charm, but to their mystery.

Haniwa figurine (terracotta funerary art).

AESTHETIC IMPULSES

The *haniwa* figures are also important for another reason. We find in them – at the very beginning of the culture – many of the salient characteristics of almost all Japanese art. The *haniwa* are, so to speak, decorative. They are very much in this world, regardless of how much they may evoke the next. We want to create stories for them; as still in time as they are, we imagine a time before and after their mouths opened. And with their soft modelling and indolent lines they are recognisably human. These figures are not gods or angels: they smile, they shout, they gaze. In fact, there is little that is abstract about them. This is an "art of the real", which does not eliminate the fantastic or even the artificial.

The *haniwa* possess a beauty that seems almost uncannily to come from a natural aesthetic impulse. They occur during a lull in Japanese absorption of outside influences at a time when the culture was developing its own native hues.

RECOGNISING THE CONVENTIONS

The viewer needs only a few moments to get used to looking at Japanese art. He or she will soon recognise the conventions – the raised roofs to reveal scenes (no perspective here), the hooks for noses and slits for eyes, the seemingly

A sculpture of a future Buddha (maitreya), at Koryu-ji, Kyoto.

abstract patterns that resolve themselves into a few variations on plants and birds and insects.

Just look a little closer and the clothes and faces will soon take on individual qualities. There is no reason, either, to fear that cliché, "open space". There is and isn't any great metaphysical principle at work here – the idea is simple enough: like European Symbolist poetry of a millennium later, the Japanese knew that art evokes, it does not depict.

NARA AND KAMAKURA SCULPTURE

There are some superb examples of sculpture that date from before the Nara Period, such as the Miroku at Koryu-ji, in Kyoto. This is a delicately carved wooden statue of the Buddha of the Future.

In the Nara Period (646–794), with Japan's full-scale welcome of things Chinese, the native response to the real is fused with its spiritual aspirations without ever abandoning the former. Work is done in wood, clay, bronze, or by using the curious technique of hollow lacquer.

There are some fine early pieces to be seen in Yakushi-ji, in Nara, but visits must especially be made to Kofuku-ji and Todai-ji to see the numerous sculptures of the Buddha, of guardian deities and of monks.

It was also during this time that the 16-metre (52ft) high bronze Daibutsu (Great Buddha) in Nara was created. It was originally gilded bronze and incised with designs that can now only barely be discerned on some of the lotus petals upon which the figure sits.

The Nara Period ended with the move of the capital to Kyoto. With that – the beginning of the Heian Period (794–1185) – Japanese sculpture declined as other arts ascended and did not revive until the Kamakura Period several centuries later.

While Nara Period sculpture was both human and ideal, that of the Kamakura Period (1185–1333) was primarily human, passionate, personal and emotional. For example, the Kamakura Period produced more portraits of monks and demons than of aloof gods. Many of these can be seen in Todai-ji and Kofuku-ji in Nara. The Kamakura Period also produced its Daibutsu, which, though somewhat smaller than that in Nara, is equally affecting. Now sitting uncovered in the Kamakura hills, its impressiveness has been enhanced by time.

PAINTING

In the Heian Period, life itself became an art, and works of art became its decorative attendant. Kyoto's Byodo-in may have been meant as a model of the next world, but it only showed that life in this one was already exquisite. Japanese painting had long existed, particularly in the form of long, rolled and hand-held scrolls, but it had not flowered into great sophistication. These paintings, known as *Yamato-e*, might depict the changing seasons, famous beauty spots or illustrate well-known stories.

The best *Yamato-e* were of the latter type and depicted popular legends, warrior tales, or works of great literature such as the *Ise Monogatari* and *Genji Monogatari*, or *Tale of Genji*. The

> *The link between tattooing and woodblock printing during the Edo Period was strong. As woodblock printing acquired more colour and complexity, tattoo motifs and pigments grew more ambitious. Later, tattoos became associated with yakuza.*

popular legends might include a satirical look at pompous officials turned into battling frogs and rabbits, or a man who can't stop farting. Post-Heian warrior tales drew on the many heroic or sentimental tales collected in the *Heike Monogatari* and other stories. The scrolls are easy to follow and with their delicacy of line reveal the Japanese gift of design.

In the Kamakura Period, war and religion came together. This was the great period of Zen art, when *suiboku* (water-ink, or painting with black *sumi* ink) comes to the fore. One of the world's masterpieces of *suiboku-ga* can be seen in the National Museum in Tokyo: Sesshu's *Winter Landscape*. Owing to the sense of composition and the moods he evokes, Sesshu seems at times to be a contemporary artist. In fact, he died in 1506 at age 86.

In addition to calligraphy, *suiboku-ga* includes portraiture and landscape. An example of the principle "the line is the man himself" in portraiture is the stark portrait of the priest Ikkyu, in the National Museum in Tokyo (Tokyo Kokuritsu Hakubutsukan).

In *suiboku* landscape paintings, the emphasis is again on the real and on the visually pleasurable (Japanese landscape is rarely as profoundly mystical as that of China), and quite often also on the grotesque, the curious and the purely fantastic.

The Momoyama Period (late 16th century) is Japan's age of baroque. Filled with gold and silver, with very bright, flat colours (no shading or outlining), and embellished with lush scenes painted on screens and walls, it is one of the high points of Japan's decorative genius.

This is not to imply that monochrome was abandoned during the Momoyama Period. Far from it: there was a great deal of superb *sumi-e* (ink picture) screens and paintings done at this time. The overwhelming impression of Momoyama Period art, however, is of brilliance and gold, as one can see in the Jodan-no-ma and other ceremonial halls in Nijo Castle in Kyoto, with its painted walls

and gilded ceilings, or at nearby Nishi Hongan-ji, to the south of Nijo Castle, in the expansive *tai-mensho* (audience hall) and *Konoma* (stork room).

FLOATING WORLD

The Edo Period (1603–1868) is the great age of popular art, even though much great decorative art was also being made for the aristocracy or the military classes, especially by Koetsu, Sotatsu and Korin. The latter's gorgeous *Irises* – all violet and gold – is an excellent example of the art of the period and can be seen at the Nezu

Lacquerware from Nagano.

Institute of Fine Arts in Tokyo.

In the rigid society of the Edo Period, the artisan was the third of the four social classes, one step above the merchant, who was at the bottom (in theory, but increasingly at the top in practice). This was the age of the unknown craftsman, whose tools, hands and skills were part of a tradition and who learned techniques as an apprentice.

The art most associated with Edo Tokyo is ukiyo-e (literally, pictures of the floating world). Once again, the sublunary, fleshy human existence was a key element. Although woodblock printing had been used to reproduce sutras, for example, the technique first began to be used in a more popular vein in the early 18th century. At first, the prints were either monochromatic or hand-coloured with an orange-red. In time, two colours were used, then four, and so on.

Notable artists included Hiroshige Ando, Utamaro Kitagawa and Hokusai. Although the names of hundreds of ukiyo-e artists are known, it should be remembered that the production of these prints was a cooperative effort between many highly skilled people.

Early ukiyo-e, especially those by the first great master, Moronobu, are usually portraits of prostitutes from the Yoshiwara district of Old Edo or else illustrations for books. With polychrome

Designing textiles for kimonos in Kyoto.

printing in ukiyo-e, a number of "genres" became established. There were, for example, portraits of female beauties, often courtesans (*bijin ga*), kabuki actors in famous roles, the ever-present scenes of renowned places, and of plant and animal life. Suffice to say that ukiyo-e is one of the world's great graphic art forms, and in more ways than one. For example, the charmingly named *shunga* (literally, spring pictures) represent pornographic art of stupendous imagination, and comprised a large part of every ukiyo-e artist's oeuvre. Ironically, *shunga* is only occasionally exhibited in Japan (too pornographic, even though it is considerably tamer than what is found in some magazines).

The Japanese have never considered ukiyo-e to be "art". It was a publishing form and not art until

foreigners started collecting it. Only in the past few decades have Japanese collectors begun to realise the value of ukiyo-e. Yet the influence on Western artists has been considerable, especially amongst the Impressionists of the late 19th century. French engraver Félix Bracquemond fuelled the increasing interest in Japanese art – *Japonisme* – when he started distributing copies of Hokusai's sketches. Soon Manet, Zola, Whistler, Degas and Monet were all collecting ukiyo-e and adopting ukiyo-e motifs and themes in their own works.

LACQUERWARE

Japanese lacquer (*urushi*) is the sap of a certain tree (*Rhus verniciflua*) that has been refined and which may have pigment added. It has been used as a decorative coating on wood, leather and cloth for 1,500 years, but the earliest-known examples of lacquer in Japan – red-and-black-lacquered earthenware pots – date back 4,000 years. Lacquerware (*nurimono*) is a community craft – no one person can do all of the 50 steps involved in the plain coating on a wooden bowl. Decoration may involve another 30. The most common Japanese examples of lacquerware are food bowls and serving trays – tableware known as *shikki*.

CERAMICS

Japan is a treasure house of ceramic techniques, a craft that has long attracted many students from abroad. There are famous and numerous wares (*yaki*), the names of which have a certain amount of currency in antiques and crafts circles throughout the world. In general, pottery in Japan is stoneware or porcelain, that is, high-fired wares.

Earthenware and low-fired pottery are found in small quantities, usually in the form of humble utensils, in *Raku-yaki* – a rustic style produced by hand and without the use of a potter's

> *Okinawan bingata, a cotton and linen fabric, is soaked in natural pigments and vegetable dyes taken from wild plants. Covered in dazzling subtropical bird, flower, fan and shell motifs, quality bingata can take a craftsman between two and three weeks to complete.*

wheel – and in some of the enamelled wares of Kyoto and Satsuma, in southern Kyushu.

Located along the San-in coast, the great historical town of Hagi is a veritable time slip. The warren of old lanes that form a protective cobweb around the grounds of its ruined castle are full of craft shops and kilns busy with potter's wheels. Good pieces of the milky, translucent glazes of *Hagi-yaki* (Hagi ceramicware), ranked second only to *Raku-yaki* as utensils in the tea ceremony, are collectors' items. Quality *Hagi-yaki* improves with age, as the tea penetrates its porous surfaces, darkening them and adding a rich lustre.

Other major ceramic towns of note that lend their names to the pottery they produce can be found in Mashiko in Tochigi Prefecture and Imbe, near Okayama City, the home of Bizen-ware. There are several types of unglazed ware, of which the most famous is Bizen, which is made from hard clay and has a bronze-like texture after firing. Traditional glazes are mainly iron (ash glazes), though feldspathic glazes are sometimes used.

A fine concentration of pottery towns exists in Kyushu's Saga Prefecture, famed for Karatsu and Arita-ware as well as fine Imari porcelain. Porcelains are decorated with underglaze cobalt and overglaze enamels. The decorated porcelains produced by numerous kilns in the Arita area of northern Kyushu, shipped from the port of Imari from the 17th to the 19th century, are still avidly sought by antiques collectors, as is the Kutani porcelain of the Kanazawa area. The Kyushu Ceramic Museum in Arita (Kyushu Toji Bunkakan) is a good starting point for exploring the Saga region in more depth.

TEXTILES

This craft includes weaving and dyeing, as well as braiding *(kumihimo)* and quilting *(sashiko)*. Japan is a vast storehouse of textile techniques, one that Western craftspeople have yet to tap.

Of course, silks are the most famous and highly refined of Japanese textiles. The brocades used in *noh* drama costumes and in the apparel of the aristocracy and high clergy of bygone ages are among the highest achievements of textile art anywhere, as are the more humble but lyrical 16th-century *tsujigahana* "tie-dyed" silks.

Though little worn these days, the formal kimono, with its sumptuous silk and brocade designs, remains the national costume. In recent years, young people and modern designers have adapted the kimono so that it can be worn in a more casual way over Western clothes.

Japanese folk textiles are a world unto themselves. Cotton, hemp and ramie are the most common fibres, but the bark fibres of the *shina* tree, *kuzu* (kudzu), paper mulberry, plantain (in Okinawa) and other fibres were used in remote mountain areas.

Indigo is the predominant colour, and the *ikat* technique (known as *kasuri*) is the most popular for work clothes, quilt covers and the like.

Bizen-yaki: a type of Japanese pottery from Okayama.

⊘ MINGEI REVIVAL

Sensing a decline in Japanese folk crafts with the advent of the machine age, philosopher and art critic Yanagi Soetsu (1889–1961) set about reviving the production of simple, utilitarian but aesthetically beautiful objects, in a movement dubbed Mingei, or "ordinary people's art". Yanagi set up the Mingei-kan (Japan Folk Crafts Museum; www.mingeikan.or.jp) in Tokyo in 1936. It celebrates the legacy of such renowned craftsmen as the textile designer Keisuke Seizawa, the potters Kawai Kanjiro and Hamada Shoju, and the English ceramicist Bernard Leach. Thanks to Yanagi, and those who have followed, the movement today is alive and well.

MODERN LITERATURE

Japan has never been short of good writers. In over 1,000 years of literature, from *Genji Monogatari (The Tale of Genji)*, the world's first full-length novel, playwrights and novelists have recorded the Japanese experience and the mutations of the human condition.

The publication of Natsume Soseki's novel *Kokoro* (1914), concerned with the conflict between the old and a newly emerging Japan, arguably marks the beginning of modern Japanese literature. The immediate post-war period, with its more liberal values, saw an extraordinary efflorescence of literary works.

Jiro Osaragi's *The Journey* examines the upheavals of the American Occupation of Japan, while Nagai Kafu, that great chronicler of Tokyo life, consistently rejected the contemporary in works of plangent nostalgia such as *Geisha in Rivalry* and *A Strange Tale from East of the River*. The doubtful role of Western culture in Japanese life surfaces in the popular nihilism of Osamu Dazai's *The Setting Sun* and *No Longer Human*.

An astonishing number of Nobel-quality writers are associated with the period from the 1950s to early 1970s. The great Junichiro Tanizaki, author of modern classics like *The Makioka Sisters* and *Diary of a Mad Old Man*, never won a Nobel (although he was nominated), but two other contemporary writers, Yasunari Kawabata and Kenzaburo Oe, did. Yukio Mishima was nominated for works like *The Golden Pavilion* and *Forbidden Colours*, whose controversial topics, such as homosexuality, reflected the sensational life of the author himself.

For a blistering look at modern Japan, its drug addicts, dropouts and dispossessed, Murakami Ryu's *Almost Transparent Blue* is hard to beat. Haruki Murakami is the best-known author outside of Japan for his wondrously offbeat stories, such as *Kafka on the Shore* and *1Q84*.

Social issues are the stuff of a new wave of writers, many of them women. Miyuki Miyabe's *All She Was Worth* and *Shadow Family* are good examples of the Japanese social novel.

Finding a book in Tokyo.

⊘ HAIKU

In sharp contrast to the lavish indulgence in pleasure and the arts enjoyed by the townspeople of Edo during the Genroku Period (1688–1704) was a modest wattle hut, a hermitage on the east bank of the Sumida River. This was the one-time home of the great haiku poet Matsuo Basho.

Here he changed his name from Tosei to Basho, in tribute to a banana plantain palm *(basho)* that his disciples planted in the small garden beside his hut. According to his own account, he fondly identified himself with the ragged, easily torn but enduring fronds of the plant, comparing its leaves to "the injured tail of a phoenix". The tree, which the poet loved to sit beneath, appears in an early haiku from these days:

Storm-torn banana tree
All night I listen to rain
In a basin

Other great haiku writers include Masaoka Shiki (1867–1902), a major figure in the development of modern haiku, and Santoka Taneda (1882–1940), original poet of the "new haiku movement".

There were also *haijin* (women haiku poets), foremost among them the Buddhist nun Chiyo-ni (1703–75). The detail of her work is clear in this dramatic example:

How frightening
Her rouged fingers
Against white chrysanthemums

MANGA: THE DISPOSABLE ART

Hard-copy manga may be declining, but the image-powered entertainment, combining narrative, humour, stylised violence and sexuality, has made a natural transition to computer tablets and mobile phones.

The term 'manga' covers magazine and newspaper cartoons, comic strips, comic books and digitalised formats. Like all cultural forms it has its historical antecedents. Comic drawings and caricatures have been found in the 7th-century temple complex of Horyu-ji in Ikaruga; in Toshodai-ji, an 8th-century Buddhist temple in Nara; and in the ancient scroll drawing called *Choju Jinbutsu Giga*, in which birds and other creatures satirise the aristocracy and clergy of the time.

The master woodblock artist Hokusai is credited with coining the expression 'manga' to describe a form of adult storybook popular in the Edo Period (1600–1868).

The popularity of newspapers and magazines during the Taisho Period (1912–26) saw the dissemination of cartoons by popular illustrators such as Okamoto Ippei. A later artist, Osamu Tezuka, is credited as the "father of manga". Tezuka brought film techniques like panning, close-ups and jump cuts to manga, but is also credited with creating the unique look of Japanese manga, its characters singularly un-Japanese in appearance. From the early *Astro Boy*, Tezuka went on to explore more complex themes in *Black Jack*, about a brilliant, unlicensed surgeon, and *Adorufu ni Tsugu (Tell Adolf)*, which examined anti-Semitism.

More recent works, like *Dragon Ball* by Toriyama Akira, *Naruto* by Kishimoto Masashi or Oda Eiichiro's *One Piece*, all of whose total circulation runs into several hundred million copies, have been adapted into anime TV series and/or internationally marketable anime films.

It's almost impossible in Japan to avoid the manga-influenced cute and cartoonish, manifest in advertising, company and city mascots, stuffed animals and cosplay events, where young people dress up as their favourite characters.

Manga appeals to all age groups and sexes. The late Prime Minister, Hashimoto Ryutaro, is said to have enjoyed quiet evenings at home with his wife reading manga. Though the appeal is broad, categories exist. *Shonen* (young boys') magazines often feature noble crusades or quests to win the heart of a seemingly unobtainable girl, while *shojo* (young girls') comics, though lighter in impact, take a closer, more refreshing look at human relationships, often bending or blurring gender lines. The *Shonen-ai* (boy's love) genre is popular with women who enjoy explicit images of gay couples. The much commented-upon *hentai* (pervert) magazines, featuring violent sex and horror, in fact represent only a small part of the market.

Kyoto Manga Museum.

Today's manga includes a range of subjects from flower arranging to 'how-to' approaches to social relations, to abridged versions of classics like *The Tale of Genji*. A special genre known as *benkyo-manga*, or "study comics", is aimed at students. Needless to say, manga is a massive, multi-billion yen business, and successful illustrators have achieved celebrity status.

Because the manga style is so pervasive, it has influenced advertising, graphic and book design, and online publishing. Manga magazines, in fact, are decreasing in sales as the stories are effortlessly downloaded onto the more convenient handset of a mobile phone. As Donald Richie has said in his book *The Image Factory*, "Eyes that were once glued to the page are now pasted to the palm of the hand."

THE PERFORMING ARTS

Most of Japan's traditional performing arts look and sound otherworldly, if not sacred, to outsiders. Yet some were designed to entertain commoners.

For many of the traditional Japanese performing arts, the distinction between dance and drama is tenuous. Most traditional Japanese drama forms today developed out of some form of dance, and all, accordingly, employ musical accompaniment. Several of the forms also involve vocal disciplines to some extent, but not enough to qualify as opera.

There are five major traditional performing-art forms in Japan: *bugaku*, *noh*, kyogen, bunraku and kabuki. Only *bugaku*, *noh* and kyogen could be called classical – all are tightly contained and formal entertainments performed originally for the aristocracy. Both bunraku and kabuki are traditional stage arts but derived from the vigorous common-folk culture of the Edo Period. Another form, *kagura*, needs to be mentioned as well. Although it falls within what could be called folk drama, there is no single form of *kagura*. Rather, these offertory dance-drama-story-religious performances, held on festival days before the deity, all differ greatly throughout the country, involving anything from religious mystery to heroic epics, to bawdy buffoonery and symbolic sexual enactments – or a combination of all these elements.

BUGAKU

What the ancient indigenous dance and drama forms in Japan were is not known. There certainly must have been such expression before the cultural imports from the Asian mainland. During the 7th and 8th centuries, mainland culture from both Korea and China dominated the life of the archipelago's imperial court.

In AD 702, the court established a court music bureau to record, preserve and perform the continental music forms (gagaku) and dance (bugaku). Influences included not only dance from China

Bugaku, a traditional Japanese dance.

and Korea, but also from India and Southeast Asia. These dances are so highly stylised and abstract that there is little or no sense of story or dramatic event. The choreography is rigid and is usually symmetrical, since the dances are most often performed by two pairs of dancers.

The *bugaku* stage is a raised platform erected outdoors, independent of other structures and ascended by steps at the front and back. The performance area is carpeted with green silk, the stairs are lacquered black, the surrounding railings and posts are in cinnabar lacquer. Given that the *bugaku* repertoire has been preserved for almost 15 centuries, it is amazing to consider that about 60 different dances are known and performed today. These dances are categorised into "right" and "left", as was the custom in China. Left dances are slow, flowing and graceful, while right dances are relatively more humourous and spirited. *Bugaku* is classified into four categories: ceremonial, military, "running" (a more spirited genre) and children's dances.

Masks are often part of a *bugaku* dance. Those used for the dances still performed (and many of those preserved in temples and other repositories associated with dances no longer performed) closely resemble some of the masks employed in religious performances in Bhutan.

The Imperial Household Agency (keeper and administrator of the imperial family) maintains a *bugaku* section for the preservation and performance, at certain times of the year, of this ancient form. Additionally, some shrines and temples have kept up *bugaku* performances as part of festivals and other yearly observances.

NOH AND KYOGEN

What is called *noh* drama today dates from the early part of the 15th century. As an art form, its high degree of stylisation, monotonous-sounding vocal declamation (*utai*, a cross between chanting and dramatic narrative), and lack of overt action make it a distinctly acquired taste.

Such terms as classic dignity, grace and symbolism are used to describe the *noh* drama.

Noh was perfected by Kan'ami Kiyotsugu (1333–84) and his son, Zeami Motokiyo, who were playwrights, actors and aesthetic theorists of the highest level. Together they created about one-third of the 240 *noh* plays known today.

Buddhism had a profound influence on the content and dramatic structure of *noh*. The veil of "illusion" that we perceive as everyday "reality" is, in a sense, pierced momentarily by *noh* to expose something more basic, something that subsumes the senses.

Masks, highly stylised sets and props (when such things do appear), a tightly controlled style of movement, a voice style that projects and declaims but does not entice, and musical accompaniment – *hayashi* – of a few types of drum and a piercing fife mean that this form of play relies

A Japanese harp player in Kyoto.

☉ THOUSAND-YEAR-OLD MUSIC

There are solo or small-ensemble musical forms, particularly those featuring the harp-like *koto*, *shakuhachi* bamboo flute, *shamisen* and the numerous *taiko* (drum) and *minyon* (folk singing) troupes. But the most authentic (if not typical) form of Japanese music performed apart from drama or dance is *gagaku* (literally translated as "elegant music"). It is a kind of orchestral music developed in the 9th century and little changed since.

Quite unlike the popular entertainments described elsewhere, *gagaku* was strictly court music, almost never performed in public before World War II, and only occasionally now.

It employs esoteric instruments resembling – sometimes identical to – those used in India and China long before high-tech instruments such as the *koto* or the *sitar* were developed. These include drums, nose-flutes and bowed, single-stringed droners. Together with a slow, "courtly" tempo, *gagaku* is ideal for (and to most Japanese ears, synonymous with) funeral music. In fact, probably the first and only time the Japanese public has heard it in recent times was during the elaborate televised funeral of Emperor Showa (Hirohito) in 1989. Devotees to the form find tremendous excitement in *gagaku's* extended, soulful sounds and unrelieved tensions.

> There are some 240 plays in the kabuki repertoire of jidai-mono, or historical events and episodes, and sewa-mono, which deals with the lives of townspeople.

mostly on imagery and symbolism for its dramatic impact. In contrast to this sparse and uncluttered form of drama, the textiles used for *noh* costumes are the diametric opposite. The world's most opulent and gorgeous gold and silver and polychrome brocades are what the *noh* actor wears on stage. And *noh* masks are an art form in themselves.

As with Greek drama, the heavy and sober *noh* is performed in tandem with the light farces of kyogen (literally, crazy words), itself thought to reflect more directly the *sarugaku* antecedents it shares with *noh*. Although the dramatic methods have something in common with *noh*, kyogen does not use masks and is more direct and active. Traditionally it is performed during intermissions of a *noh* performance, but today it is often performed by itself. These farces are both part of and independent of *noh* – light-hearted, concerned with nonsense, and simple.

BUNRAKU

Japan's glorious puppet drama is a combination of three elements, which, about 400 years ago, fused into a composite: shamisen music, puppetry techniques and a form of narrative or epic-chanting called *joruri*. The result is bunraku, the puppet drama that is considered to be an equal with live-stage theatre performance. Although bunraku developed and matured in the two centuries after its creation, the origin of the puppetry techniques used is still shrouded in mystery. There are folk-puppet dramas scattered throughout Japan, but the centre of bunraku puppet drama is in Osaka.

The shamisen (a banjo-like instrument) entered Japan from the kingdom of the Ryukyus (now known as Okinawa) sometime in the 16th century and was adapted and spread throughout the country very quickly. Although the instrument only has three strings, music produced by the shamisen has great versatility and, in particular, lends itself well to dramatic emphasis.

Bunraku puppets *(ningyo)* are manipulated directly by hand and are quite large – it takes three men to handle one of the major puppets

in a play. The skills involved in manipulation of bunraku puppets are considerable. The narrative style derives from classic epics of heroism chanted to the accompaniment of a *biwa*, a form of lute that made its way to Japan from central Asia at an early date. Although there may be more than one shamisen to give musical density to the accompaniment, there is only one chanter. He uses different tones of voice to distinguish male from female characters, young from old, good from bad. Accent and intonation convey nuances of feeling and indicate shifts of scene.

Noh performance, Senso-ji Temple.

While bunraku and kabuki share many traits and have some plays in common, bunraku is the older of the two and it was kabuki that adopted elements of the puppet drama. The important point is that both bunraku and kabuki are popular theatre. Bunraku was for townspeople and intended as popular entertainment, much like Shakespeare's plays.

KABUKI

Plays for kabuki are still being written. Not many, granted, but the genre is alive, and like bunraku it is not "classical". Kabuki is the equivalent of cabaret spectacular, soap opera, morality play, religious pageant and tear-jerker. It is music and dance and story and colour and pathos and farce, everything any theatre-goer could want.

The highly stylised language of kabuki, the poses and posturing and eye-crossing for dramatic emphasis, the swashbuckling and acrobatics and flashy exits, instant costume changes and magic transformations – all are part of the fun.

Kabuki originated in the early years of the 17th century with a troupe of women who performed on the river bank at Kyoto what seems to have been a kind of dance (based on a dance performed at Buddhist festivals) and perhaps comic skits as well. Whether there was anything untoward in this performance probably will never be known, but

A puppet play (bunraku).

⊙ SHOCK DANCE

Performances may be announced at the last minute, venues moved from theatres to overgrown car parks, audiences exposed to sensory shocks. Welcome to *butoh*, Japan's most radical underground dance form. Stripped of the formalism of traditional Japanese dance, *butoh's* intensity, the exposed nerve points and primal emotions, the vision of semi-naked dancers smeared in white body paint, are definitely not for mainstream Japanese audiences. *Butoh's* appropriation of Western dance influences, but with an avowed aim to return to more elemental Japanese emotions, and its incorporation of taboo subjects have ensured that it remains radical.

the shogunal authorities seemed to think there was, and so in 1629 they banned women from appearing on stage. Male performers took their place, and to this day all kabuki performers are men; the discipline of the actor who takes female parts *(onnagata)* is particularly rigorous.

The female troupes were supplanted in short order by itinerant troupes of young men, who also got into trouble with the authorities. These groups were disbanded and the permanent theatre companies then developed in Kyoto, Osaka and Edo (now Tokyo) after the middle of the 17th century. Kabuki soon became the Edo Period's most popular entertainment.

The production of a kabuki play involves strict conventions governing gestures and other movements, colours, props, costumes, wigs and make-up. Even the types of textiles used for costumes are determined. (But there are places in a play left for spontaneous ad-libs.) The audience directs much attention to the performer or performers. The story is secondary and it will be well-known anyway. Kabuki devotees want to see favourite stars in familiar roles. Indeed, kabuki has been actor-centred since its beginning.

The training of a kabuki actor starts at about the age of three, when children are left by their actor parents backstage. The children internalise the atmosphere and the music's rhythms. With this kind of training, kabuki naturally becomes part of one's core early on in life. This facilitates the years of rigorous apprenticeship and training that every kabuki actor must undergo.

The kabuki stage has a number of unique features. The most striking is the walkway that extends from the stage to the doors at the rear of the theatre at stage level. Actors enter and exit through this stage extension (*hanamichi*, meaning flower path), and it is sometimes used as a venue of action. Another feature is the curtain, decorated in vertical stripes of black, green and orange, opened from stage right to left. The kabuki theatre also featured a revolving stage long before the concept arose in Europe.

THE NEW J-CULTURE

Modern Japanese drama dates from the emergence of *Shin-geki*, experimental, Western-style drama spearheaded by directors like Kaoru Osanai and Hogetsu Shimamura in the early 20th century. The first performance of Ibsen's contentious *A Doll's House* in 1910, with Matsui Sumako as Nora, electrified audiences.

The post-war period witnessed an extraordinary flowering in new theatre and performance. Young playwrights and directors, attuned to political polemic, placed their audiences in open areas, tents, and street venues, collapsing conventional ideas about space.

The performing arts in contemporary Japan are alive and well. The internationally acclaimed director Ninagawa Yukio was known for his innovative productions of classic Japanese theatre and Shakespeare, while theatre of the absurd figurehead Tanino Kurou is active on the international stage.

Music has always been a dynamic sector of the entertainment industry. Audiences for *Enka*, a soulful, vernacular form of song, with the emphasis on lament, have declined, but filling its place has been a surge in roots music. *Minyo* (folk music) from the Tohoku region, led by shamisen players the Yoshida Brothers, and drum troupes like Kodo from Sado Island, have toured abroad, but the biggest roots phenomena has been the resurgence of Okinawan music.

The haunting sound of the *sanshin*, a three-stringed instrument similar to the Japanese shamisen, defines, along with its unique vocal delivery, the sound of these remote islands.

While *shima-uta* (island song) remains the core of Okinawan music, the form has undergone exciting new developments. There have been several fruitful collaborations with overseas musicians. *Sanshin* player Yasukatsu Oshima has collaborated with US pianist

Geoffrey Keezer, while Kina Shoukichi and his band Champloose, key figures in the creation of contemporary Okinawan music, made an album with legendary blues guitarist Ry Cooder.

Japan's most successful and exportable musical entertainment form, however, has been J-Pop. With its origins in British sixties pop, the genre is big business. To many observers, J-Pop suggests transience, but there are several performers, like Hamasaki Ayumi and Amuro Namie, and bands like SMAP, all well into their late thirties and forties, who continue to be popular.

Kabuki performed in Oshika.

⊘ TAKARAZUKA

The Takarazuka Revue began their shows in 1914. Combining Japanese theatre, high drama, Broadway musicals and historic and literary heroes and heroines seen through the prism of a Harlequin novel, the company is composed entirely of women.

Women play both male and female parts, the best or most beautiful of the male impersonators, called *otokoyaku*, often achieving celebrity status from devoted fans. A measure of this devotion can be seen in the long queues and the gifts presented to the performers.

Competition to get into the Takarazuka's academy and its two-year course is fierce, and the training vigorous. For as long as they are members of the troupe,

they are not allowed to marry. Of the 2.5 million annual members of the audience, the vast majority are women. They also form the mainstay of the hundreds of fan clubs that exist throughout the country.

Like Bollywood films, audiences get a bit of everything, including lavish costumes and sumptuous sets. One of their most successful productions, *The Rose of Versailles*, was adapted from a manga series of the same name.

Explaining the appeal of the shows is more difficult. Some commentators have suggested that in a country where males are largely devoid of romantic tendencies, the performances fulfil the need for the fantasy of a sensitive male.

THE CINEMA OF JAPAN

Japanese cinema has always refused to embrace the values of Hollywood. In doing so, it has produced some of the world's most aesthetically beautiful and powerful films.

The Japanese cinema has been pronounced dead so many times over the past few years – perhaps most often by Japanese critics and filmmakers – that its stubborn survival, if not full resurrection, comes as a relief. Just when it seemed that Japanese audiences had turned away from domestic product dealing with their country's amazing history, along came the anime *Mononoke Hime (Princess Mononoke)* from Miyazaki Hayao, which smashed the previous all-time box-office record held by *E.T.* and then *Titanic*. What was so heartening about the success of the Miyazaki film was that Japanese people were indeed interested – in huge numbers – to see an epic historical fantasy about Japanese history, set in an ancient time filled with gods and demons, an era in which men and animals could still verbally communicate with each other. *Mononoke Hime* is a cartoon, or more accurately, anime (see page 101), which has always been taken more seriously in Japan than in the West.

Poster for the film 'Yojimbo' (1961).

JAPANESE STYLE

Dramatically, the classic three-act structure of Hollywood holds little place in Japanese cinema. Character and mood, rather than plot, are what propel many of its best films. Stories often trail off by the film's end without a "proper" ending, storylines (especially in *jidai-geki*, or historical dramas) can be unbelievably convoluted and confusing, even to the most ardent devotees, and most Japanese films move at a considerably slower pace.

In a typical Japanese movie, dynamic action stands in contrast to long, sustained scenes of inactive dialogue, or just silence. Directors not only take the time to smell the roses but to plant them, nurture them, and then watch them grow, quietly. Landscape and atmosphere also play key roles in Japanese cinema, perhaps tied into the other major religion of the country, the pantheistic Shinto. Floating mists, drops of water slowly falling into a stream, the soft, sad sound of cherry blossoms falling on an April day – all are familiar to Japanese audiences and alien to the rest of us.

Of course, it must also be said that such mass-market genres as *kaiju* (giant monster) and contemporary *yakuza* (gangster) movies are often just as breathlessly mounted as the latest Hollywood action flick.

There's also considerably more space in Japanese cinema for morally dubious protagonists since, in both the Shinto and Buddhist traditions, life is a balance between forces of good and evil, with both necessary to maintain life as we know it. Thus, a cold-blooded killer like the ronin (master-less samurai) Ogami Ito, who roams Japan with his tiny son Daigoro in a bamboo baby cart, dispatching others by decapitation and dis-embowelment in the popular *Sword of Vengeance* series of films, would baffle most Western audi-ences. Is he a good guy or a bad guy? Is he wearing a black hat or a white hat? The answer is both. And the dirty, amoral bodyguard portrayed by Mifune Toshiro in Kurosawa Akira's *Yojimbo* and *Sanjuro* would also fit this bill quite beautifully. He was the prototype for Clint Eastwood's Man with No Name in Sergio Leone's operatic spaghetti Westerns *A*

A scene from 'Tokyo Story' (1953).

⊘ OZU'S CAMERA EYE

Yasujiro Ozu (1903–63) was, arguably, Japan's great-est film director. The originality and technical skills of works like *Floating Weeds, But...* and *Record of a Tenement Gentleman* are still admired by film buffs and students. Ozu's work is a good example of Japanese cinema's ability to define a style and approach through limitation. In Ozu's case this took the form of the lingering single, long shot. An aes-thetic objectivity results from this restricted view. Ozu's best-known classic is *Tokyo Story (Tokyo Monogatari)*, a wonderful work of directorial under-statement routinely voted one of the best films of all time by bodies such as the British Film Institute.

Fistful of Dollars (a remake of *Yojimbo*), *For a Few Dollars More* and *The Good, the Bad and the Ugly*.

But what really makes Japanese film special isn't so much the bloodshed and ultraviolence, but rather the profound humanism and compassion ranging through its entire history. One would have to look deeply into other international cinemas to find efforts as profound as Kurosawa's *Ikiru* and *Ran*, Ozu's *Tokyo Story*, Kinoshita Keisuke's *Twenty-Four Eyes* or Mizoguchi's *The Life of Oharu*.

FILMMAKING STARS

The great, golden age of Japanese film, which lasted from the post-war 1950s until the late 1960s when the burgeoning availability of televi-sion laid it to waste, is certainly gone. The 'Big Four' major studios – Toho, Shochiku, Kadokawa and Toei – barely crank out enough domestic films in a year to fill a couple of the multiplexes that are suddenly springing up. But it's not over yet.

The death of Kurosawa Akira in 1998 was a particular blow. "Sensei", as he became known, almost single-handedly put Japanese film on the international map with *Rashômon*, which won top prize at the 1951 Venice Film Festival. His rising and falling fortunes over the next half-century were emblematic of the Japanese industry itself. Endlessly frustrated by unreceptive Japanese stu-dios and aborted projects, Kurosawa attempted suicide after a box-office failure in 1970. Yet he would go on to make five more films, at least two of which – *Kagemusha* and, particularly, *Ran* – would be counted among his greatest works. However, Kurosawa repeatedly had to look outside Japan to Francis Ford Coppola, George Lucas, Steven Spiel-berg and Serge Silberman for support.

Japanese film suffered a further shocking and unexpected blow by the still inexplicable 1997 suicide scandal of Itami Juzo. (A tabloid newspa-per was about to reveal a supposed relationship between the filmmaker and a younger woman.) Itami was responsible for some marvellously smart and funny dissections of contemporary life, all of them starring his wife, Miyamoto Nobuko: *The Funeral*, *Tampopo* and the societal exposés of the *Taxing Woman* films.

Another shock to the system was the 1996 death of actor Atsumi Kiyoshi, Japan's beloved Tora-san. Don't underestimate the impact of this character on the national consciousness (or Shochiku's box-office take). Over a span of nearly

30 years and 47 films, this itinerant amulet seller was to Japan what Chaplin's Little Tramp was to the world during the Silent Era, only more so. Within the restrictive, often suffocating bounds of Japanese society, Tora-san's gypsy-like existence had strong appeal to the millions of train-riding 9-to-5 businessmen, and his endlessly disappointing romances held women in thrall.

BRIGHT LIGHTS, NEW GENERATION

Although filmmaking styles have been altered for scaled-down financial resources and chang-

The 1997 film 'Hana-bi' (released as 'Fireworks' in the US) was written by and starred Takeshi Kitano.

ing audience tastes, there's much to recommend in Japan's current generation of filmmakers. Suo Masayuki's delightful *Shall We Dance?* (1996) was the highest-grossing foreign-language film ever to play in US movie theatres at the time and would undoubtedly have won the Oscar for foreign films had it not been disqualified by one of the Academy's innumerable arcane rules.

The anarchic, dark, violent and often funny ruminations by Takeshi "Beat" Kitano – a tremendously successful and popular comedian, actor, game-show host, raconteur and moviemaker – have won international acclaim, particularly the alternately tender and cataclysmic *Hana-Bi* (*Fireworks*), and *Zatoichi*, about the adventures of

Hung along Kyuome Kaido, the main street of Ome, a town west of Tokyo, are many old hand-painted movie signboards called kanban. From Nakahira Ko's 1956 Crazed Fruit to scenes from chanbara (samurai action films), the street is a boulevard of nostalgia.

a blind master swordsman, which won the Silver Lion award at Venice in 2003. Hirokazu Kore-eda's *Shoplifters* won the Palme d'Or at Cannes in 2018.

NATIONALISTIC DRAMAS

Japan's economic downturn of the 1990s produced greater box-office revenues. Much of this can be attributed to foreign films such as *Titanic*, which in Japan accounted for more than 70 percent of the revenues of foreign films.

Elsewhere there was scrutiny and criticism from the Japanese and international media with another film, *Unmei no Toki (Pride)*, a big-budget, nationalistic biopic from director Ito Shunya that sympathetically portrayed Japan's wartime Prime Minister, General Tojo Hideki. Asians were incensed that the man generally considered to be the prime instigator of Japanese Asian aggression – and the person responsible for what has become known as the Rape of Nanjing, in China – was depicted in the film to be battling for Asian interests against Western imperialism. *Pride* actually received a decent notice in *Daily Variety*, the primary American entertainment trade publication: "powerful, controversial, revisionist

☉ GODZILLA

To the Japanese people, Godzilla isn't some huge, lumbering, atomic-born giant lizard. He's their huge, lumbering, atomic-born giant lizard. With 35 movies since his debut in 1954's *Gojira* (a combination of the Japanese words for "gorilla" and "whale", anglicised to Godzilla for its US release two years later), this monster who towers above Tokyo smashing everything in his path is one of the most famous icons of post-war Japan. Naturally, despite (or more probably because of) its special effects and far-fetched plot, the first of the many Godzilla movies became a huge hit, not only in Japan but throughout Southeast Asia, the US and Europe.

courtroom drama... [the film's] different spin on famous events of the Pacific war is at times quite disturbing but is nonetheless fascinating and makes for most effective drama".

Japanese films about World War II have always veered wildly between the powerfully pacifistic (Ichikawa Kon's harsh *Fires on the Plain* and the stunningly emotional *The Burmese Harp*, also directed by Ichikawa) and jingoistic flag-waving. Often, war films try to have it both ways, especially in recent war movies in which popular teen idols, male and female, are cast in primary roles and then killed off tragically.

> *In Tokyo, the traveller often looks in vain for reminders of the past. Films with a Tokyo setting are therefore immensely important archival documents, ranging from Kenji Mizoguchi's 1929 Tokyo March to Isabel Coixet's Map of the Sounds of Tokyo (2009).*

'Mogari no Mori' ('The Mourning Forest') won the Grand Prix at the 2007 Cannes Film Festival.

HOLLYWOOD'S JAPAN

The claim that the Japanese enjoy nothing more than seeing themselves through the eyes of the outside world is corroborated by a glut of well-received Hollywood-made movies with Japanese locations and subjects. Hollywood had been fascinated with Japan as a setting for its dramas even before the 1958 John Wayne hit *The Barbarian and the Geisha*, or the 007 thriller *You Only Live Twice*, but the years round the turn of the millennium witnessed a Japan boom that seems unstoppable.

Memorable films include Ridley Scott's *Black Rain* (1989), filmed in Osaka, where a thriving criminal underworld provided theme and visual substance, and Paul Schrader's *Mishima* (1985), which looked at

the troubled but intriguing life of literary giant and right-wing imperialist Yukio Mishima.

Quentin Tarentino's 2003 *Kill Bill Volume 1* and its sequel *Kill Bill Volume 2* were homages to the Japanese *yakuza* film; Tom Cruise's portrayal of a transplanted American Civil War veteran in *The Last Samurai* was a smash hit in Japan; Sophia Coppola's Oscar-winning comedy *Lost in Translation*, which nevertheless received some criticism for its dated view of the Japanese, was filmed almost entirely in a Tokyo hotel and picked up an Oscar in 2003. The 2005 film version of Arthur Golden's novel *Memoirs of a Geisha* became a hit in Japan, where it was released under the title of its main character, *Sayuri*. Clint Eastwood's look at warfare from the American and Japanese perspective in *Flags of Our Fathers* and *Letters from Iwo Jima* (2006) are more sophisticated examples of how Japan has inspired Hollywood.

CONTEMPORARY FILM

The silver lining for Japan's silver screen after the erosion of the studio system has been more freedom for independent directors. Although many independent production companies have become mainstream now, their works are among the best being made today.

Early successes were Ichikawa Jun's *Tokyo Lullaby* and Iwai Shunji's 1996 *Swallowtail*, a story about an illegal Chinese alien from a foreigner-populated ghetto called Yentown who finds pop stardom only to be torn apart by tabloid journalists.

Addressing other shortcomings of contemporary existence are a number of thoughtful films by Kiyoshi Kurosawa, including *Journey to the Shore*, winning the Un Certain Regard Award for Best Director at the 2015 Cannes Film Festival.

Another take on society's shortcomings is Koreeda Hirokazu's *Nobody Knows*, based on the true story of a single mother who leaves her children. His film about children switched at birth, *Like Father, Like Son*, won a Jury Prize in Cannes.

ANIME

The Japanese have been in the anime business for a long time. Cartoonists like Kitayama Seitaro and Terauchi Junichi experimented with animated motion pictures as early as 1913.

Terauchi's first silhouette animation, *Kujira (The Whale)*, was made in 1927, a year before Walt Disney released his first Mickey Mouse cartoon. Highly influenced by manga (see page 89) – the thick comic books read by young and old in Japan – the link to anime is logical: the comic-book manga is a series of storyboards, a model used to great effect in anime. The similarities are natural as most animated films in Japan are adapted from bestselling comic books.

As for the more adult fare… well, here's where presentational differences are quite clear. Ultra-violence, raw sexuality and nudity, visionary and often apocalyptic views of the future, and extreme graphic style are the hallmarks of this genre, with most efforts falling into the science-fiction category. The better examples of these are truly stunning and original, such as Otomo Katsuhiro's 1989 classic *Akira* and, more recently, Oshii Mamoru's *The Ghost in the Shell*. Oshii went on to make the 2001 experimental anime *Avalon*, and to direct the 2008 feature *The Sky Crawlers*. One of the most commercially successful projects, tying in anime with the toy market and computer software, has been the 1998 *Pocket Monsters (Pokémon)* series, a huge hit overseas.

MIYAZAKI HAYAO AND STUDIO GHIBLI

But there's an alternative to the endless parade of animated juggernauts, cuddly toys and bare breasts – and his name is Miyazaki Hayao. Miyazaki heads the famed Studio Ghibli, which has been responsible for what many would consider to be the finest anime to emerge from Japan. Miyazaki got his start in TV anime, directing a popular multi-part version of Heidi before moving into features with *The Castle of Cagliostro*, based on a popular James Bondian character known as Lupin the Third. Since then, his films as director have included such fanciful, haunting and often humorous efforts as

Nausicaa of the Valley of the Wind, *Laputa – The Castle in the Sky*, *Porco Rosso*, *My Neighbour Totoro*, *Kiki's Delivery Service* and the gigantic box-office hit *Mononoke Hime*, or *Princess Mononoke*.

Shinto strongly informs *Princess Mononoke* – a complex story that is essentially about the inevitable clash between humans and the deities of nature – and the remarkable *Heise Tanuki Gassen Pompoko* (supervised by Miyazaki but directed by Ghibli's Takahata Isao), about raccoons fighting the destruction of their forest home in what would become the Tokyo suburb of Tama. Miyazaki's *Sen to Chihiro no Kamikakushi (Spirited Away)* received an Oscar for best animated feature in 2003. Miyazaki has since made *Ponyo*, a

'Spirited Away' is one of Studio Ghibli's best known anime films.

2009 feature about a girl who is half fish but wants to become human, and 2013's *The Wind Rises*, an award-winning drama about the designer of Mitsubishi fighter aircrafts. This was to be the director's final film before retiring, but a new offering, *How Do You Live?* is now slated for release in 2020.

There are other fine examples of ambitious anime directors who defy the supercharged sci-fi traditions, including Hosada Mamoru, director of *The Boy and the Beast* (2015). The anime scene's latest star is Makoto Shinkai, whose intimate *Your Name* (2016) became the world's second highest grossing anime (behind *Spirited Away*) with more than 360m dollars in worldwide revenue.

The traditional and historical Japanese village, Shirakawago.

ARCHITECTURE

With its post-and-beam construction, Japanese architecture allows flexible use of interior space and dissolves the rigid boundary between indoors and outdoors.

What kind of house would one build in Japan if one knew it might be blown apart in a natural disaster? Besides typhoons and earthquakes, Japan also has severe rains, which often cause flooding and landslides. How would one make a palace or temple or hall, a farmhouse or a gate to survive such destructive forces? These questions had to be faced by the designers of buildings in Japan's remote past and are still faced today.

The fact that Japan has the world's oldest wooden buildings (Horyu-ji, built about AD 607) and one of the world's largest wooden structures (at Todai-ji, some 50 metres/165ft high and said to have been rebuilt at only two-thirds its original size) suggests that the architectural system adopted by the Japanese was at least partially successful in creating structures that last. The devastation of the 1995 Kobe earthquake suggests otherwise. Indeed, rather than wind, earth or water, it is fire that is the greatest destroyer of buildings in Japan, although few buildings could have withstood the type of tsunami the world witnessed on 11 March 2011 along the devastated Tohoku coastline.

Nonetheless, Japanese architecture has influenced architectural design throughout the world. Its concepts of fluidity, modularity, making the most of limited space, and use of light and shadow have a great power and appeal, both aesthetically and as solutions to architectural problems in contemporary times.

Whatever factors determined how buildings were constructed in Japan – survival, tradition, aesthetics – some common characteristics can be found that define the tradition of Japanese architecture.

The oldest Japanese dwellings are the pit houses of the Neolithic Jomon culture, but the

The roof and gables of the Atsuta Shrine in Nagoya.

oldest structures to which the term "architecture" might be applied are the Grand Shrines of Ise (see page 281). First completed in the 5th century, the shrines have been ritually rebuilt 60 times – every 20 years. Each rebuilding takes years to accomplish, starting with the cutting of special cypress trees deep in the mountains, and involves special carpentry techniques as well as time-honoured rituals.

EARLY INFLUENCES

The introduction of Buddhism to Japan in AD 552 brought with it a whole raft of cultural and technical features, not least of which was the continental style of architecture. It is said that Korean builders came over to Japan and either built or supervised the building of the Horyu-ji (AD 607). The foundations of the vast temple that was the prototype of Horyu-ji can be seen in Kyongju, South Korea.

In the 8th century, at the capital in Nara, Chinese architectural influence became quite obvious, not only in the structures themselves, but in the adoption of the north–south grid plan of the streets, based on the layout of the Chinese capital. At this time, secular and sacred architecture were essentially the same, and palaces were often rededicated as temples. Both displayed red-lacquered columns and green roofs with pronounced upswinging curves in the eaves. Roofs were tiled.

FROM THE HEIAN PERIOD TO THE EDO PERIOD

The mutability of residence and temple held true in the subsequent Heian Period as well, as evidenced by the villa of the nobleman Fujiwara no Yorimichi (990–1074), which became the Phoenix Hall of Byodo-in, in Uji near Kyoto. The graceful *shinden-zukuri* style of this structure,

The Horyu-ji complex, Nara.

⊘ FORTIFIED ARCHITECTURE

Feudal-era castle towns were highly schematised. Revolving around the central fortress were merchant and shopkeepers' quarters. The temple district was positioned in the southeast, close to the elegant villas and attached gardens of the samurai. In small rural cities like Hikone and Matsue, this architectural paradigm remains largely intact.

A shift in castle design took place in 1579, when the warrior Oda Nobunaga chose a low hill with commanding views of the surrounding plains to build his towering, many-tiered *donjon*. Of the 12 original Japanese fortresses still in existence, and the countless replicas and reconstructions that have sprung up in the last century, most follow Nobunaga's template.

To make wooden structures more durable, castles were built on top of colossal, cut boulders. Each level was reinforced with plaster and clay to defend it against fire and artillery. Overhanging gables lend elegant curves to the design, colourful pendants were hung from the eaves, and symbolic dolphin statues were placed on the roof to act as talismans against fire.

Few Edo Period castles were destroyed in battle. Instead it took a more enlightened age to dismantle Japan's martial architecture. The new Meiji government, coming to power in 1868, demolished all but a handful of its citadels. Others were pulled down by local patriots, who saw them as symbols of feudalism.

utilised for the residences of Heian court nobles, is characterised by rectangular structures in symmetrical arrangement and linked by long corridors. The layout of Kyoto's Old Imperial Palace is similar, though it is a replica of this style.

When the imperial court at Kyoto lost the reins of power to the military government of the shogunate, located far to the east in Kamakura, the open and vulnerable *shinden* style was supplanted by a type of residential building more easily defended. This warrior style (*bukke-zukuri*) placed a number of rooms under one roof or a series of conjoined roofs and was surrounded by a defensive device, such as a fence, wall or moat, with guard towers and gates. Tiled roofs gave way to either shingled or thatched roofs. This period also saw the importation of Chinese Song-dynasty architectural styles for temples, particularly the so-called Zen style, which is characterised by shingled roofs, pillars set on carved stone plinths, and the "hidden roof" system developed in Japan, among other features.

In the subsequent Muromachi Period, which saw the purest expression of feudal government and its break-up into the Age of Warring States (15th century), Zen Buddhist influence transformed the warrior style into the *shoin* style. This at first was little more than the addition of a small reading or waiting room (*shoin*), with a deep sill that could be used as a desk, and decorative, built-in shelves to hold books or other objects. This room also displayed an alcove, the *toko-noma*, in which treasured objects could be effectively displayed. This *shoin* room eventually exerted its influence over the entire structure. Both the Golden Pavilion and the Silver Pavilion of Kyoto are examples of this style.

At the end of the Age of Warring States, firearms became common in warfare, and in response to this, massive castles were built. Few original structures remain today. Himeji Castle, with white walls and a soaring roof, is the finest example.

Political change brought the country into the Edo Period, and architecture saw a melding of the *shoin* style and teahouse concepts to produce the *sukiya* style, the grandest example of which is the Katsura Imperial Villa in Kyoto. This residential architecture displays an overall

lightness of members, a simplified roof and restrained, subtle ornamentation.

POST AND BEAM CONSTRUCTION

The favoured material of building construction is wood. Walls, foundations of castles, the podia of some structures, and a few novel experiments saw stone in limited use, usually without mortar. Yet, undoubtedly because it was plentiful, wood remained the material of preference, particularly the wood of conifers. This is reflected in the reforestation laws of the shogunate and various feudal

Himeji Castle, Okayama.

lords. The disappearance of certain types of large tree due to lumbering is reflected in certain historical changes in temple and shrine buildings.

This preference for wood is directly related to the fact that the basic structural system in Japanese architecture is post and beam. The structure is basically a box upon which a hat – the roof – rests. This system allows great freedom in the design of the roof, and the Japanese seemed to prefer large ones, sometimes exceeding half the total height of a structure. Roofs also became elaborate, with generous eaves, and often very heavy.

Straight lines dominate Japanese architecture, seemingly a natural result of using wood and the post-and-beam system. There are few curves and no arches. Post-and-beam boxes can also be combined and strung together in many ways to create fine aesthetic effects. The Katsura Imperial Villa in Kyoto represents the height of such architecture. Since posts or columns bear the weight of the roof, walls could be – and were – thin and non-supporting. This lightness was developed to the point that walls often ceased to be walls and became more like movable partitions instead.

This is the origin of fluidity or modularity, perhaps the single most noteworthy aspect of Japa-

Nishida-ke garden, Kanazawa, Ishikawa.

nese buildings. Interior spaces were partitioned so that rooms could become more versatile, to be combined or contracted. The former was accomplished through the use of sliding and removable door panels. A room could be divided by decorative standing screens, especially ones with gold backgrounds to act as a reflective surface and bring light into gloomy castle or palace interiors. Corridor width was the necessary width for two people with serving trays to pass one another.

LETTING THE OUTSIDE IN

The distinction between wall and door often disappears. This applies to outside walls – the "boundary" between interior and exterior – as

A Japanese ceramic bowl and a kimono look very different when seen in a traditional Japanese room rather than a room with plaster walls and glass windows.

well. External walls are often nothing more than a series of sliding wooden panels that can be easily removed, thus eliminating the solid border between inside and outside, a feature very much welcomed in Japan's humid summer. The veranda thus becomes a transitional space, connecting interior with exterior.

Since the floors of traditional Japanese buildings are generally raised, house floor and ground surface are not contiguous (except in the case of the packed-earth *doma*, the work and implement storage area of a farmhouse). In effect, this means that the indoor–outdoor fluidity is mainly visual and for circulation of air, not for movement of people.

In rural areas the veranda, when open, becomes a meeting place, to sit and talk with a neighbour.

TRADITIONAL MATERIALS

The materials used in traditional Japanese room interiors are few and limited, reflecting an ambivalence between interior and exterior, or perhaps a pleasure in harmonising rather than sharply demarking interior and exterior. Sliding door panels are either translucent shoji or the heavier, opaque fusuma paper screens, or of wood. Floors are of thick, resilient straw mats surfaced with woven reed (tatami mats), or of plain wood.

Supportive wooden posts remain exposed, and ceilings are generally of wood or of woven materials of various kinds. With the exception of lacquered surfaces, wood remains unpainted.

Because of the generous eaves of Japanese buildings, interiors tend to be dark and often may be gloomy. The use of translucent paper shoji screens to diffuse soft light helps, but the soft, natural colours of the room materials generally absorb rather than reflect light. The colours, lighting and textures of traditional Japanese rooms influenced the qualities of all objects to be used in them, including clothing.

DESIGN PRINCIPLES

The artistic unity or harmony of a building extends to its properties as well. Master carpenters, who were both the architects and the builders of traditional buildings, developed aesthetic proportions that applied to all elements of a single structure, as well as to individual buildings in a complex. There are special and sophisticated carpenter's measures that apply this system of aesthetic proportion to construction.

Teahouses show an awesome skill in building. Their lack of surface ornament, as seen in

Development is still taking its toll on Japan's architectural legacy, though an awakening preservation ethic is beginning to take root among citizen groups with an affection for older structures and a sense of the importance of visible history.

The Edo-Tokyo Open-Air Architectural Museum in Musashi-Koganei is a collection of buildings and structures that have been saved from the wrecking ball and collected inside a sympathetic setting in Koganei Park.

Exhibits include the former homes of the Mit-

A house in Uchiko, Shikoku.

the rustic simplicity of unpainted wood, is itself a design statement, the signature of the skilled artisan.

Historically, Japanese architecture shows a dialectic between imported and adapted continental styles (mainly from China, but some also from the Korean Peninsula) and native Japanese styles.

PRESERVATION ETHIC

In Japan, natural disasters, an erosive climate and a weak preservation ethic militate against architectural heritage. As Japan architecture scholar Mira Locher has written, "Buildings were understood to be part of the changing environment rather than permanent fixtures".

sui family, the important Meiji Period economist Korekiyo Takahashi, a Taisho-era bungalow from the garden suburb of Denenchofu, and a home designed in 1925 by the modernist architect Sutemi Horiguchi. Visitors can enter these homes and explore the rooms. Supplementing private residences are a photo studio, soy sauce and cosmetic shop, dry food store, and a number of intriguing urban features of the city, such as a fire observation tower, and even a Meiji-era police box that once stood at the entrance to Mansei Bridge.

The museum is a fitting introduction to the historical architecture of the capital and to the design aspirations of two very different ages.

INTO THE FUTURE

From the humble capsule hotel, a uniquely Japanese design that was not only based on space shuttle accommodation for astronauts but also the humble rental container, city architecture today is more ambitious. New structures like Tokyo Midtown, Design Sight 21_21, the Iceberg Tokyo Building, Keyaki Omotesando Building, Tokyo Sky Tree (the highest structure in the country, completed in 2012), Toranomon Hills, and Abeno Harukas in Osaka (the tallest skyscraper in Japan, opened in 2014), are the

To see authentic, steep thatch-roofed, A-framed farmhouses (gassho-zukuri), visit the villages of Shirakawa-go. The villages were made a Unesco World Heritage Site in 1995.

21_21 Design Sight, a design museum in Tokyo.

results of this experimentation. The modern anti-earthquake technology that provides shock absorbers and floating plates for cutting edge projects like these and for the more utilitarian new office blocks and upmarket condominiums is only available to the very affluent, however.

For the modernist, this is clearly a good time to be an architect in Japan. The country has the highest number of professional architects per capita in the world. After periods of hubris, showmanship and unlimited budgets, serious designers are in the ascendancy. Many of today's building projects are stand-out structures, designs of almost transcendental beauty and managed semantics in the midst of unconsidered construction sprawls. No ordinary structures, these are experiments by a distinguished group of designers to promote discourse on architecture.

A prime example is the De Beers Ginza Building, where the undulating facade appears to be experiencing a dramatic mutation, not unlike the self-regenerating surfaces of Shinjuku buildings in William Gibson's science fiction novel *Idoru*, or the folding structures in the film *Inception*.

⊘ AND THE WINNERS ARE...

They call it "architecture's Nobel": the annual Pritzker Prize was established in 1979. Since then, Japanese architects have been recipients no less than six times.

The first Japanese laureate, in 1987, was Tange Kenzo. Tange's famous aphorism, "Learning happens in corridors," marks his highly original, empirical approach to architecture. Fumihiko Maki won the prize in 1993. His designs include the National Museum of Art in Kyoto and the Tokyo Metropolitan Gymnasium. The 1995 winner Ando Tadao's body of work includes galleries, churches, museums and more. His preferred material is pre-cast concrete, his style spare and minimalist, mixing Japanese aesthetics and modernism.

The work of Sejima Kazuyo and Nishizawa Ryue is characterised by a sense of weightlessness and spatial ambiguity, seen in their designs for private homes, art venues and public buildings. The 2013 laureate was Ito Toyo, whose Sendai Mediatheque emerged almost unscathed from the 2011 earthquake. Ban Shigeru, who experiments with building materials, garnered the prize in 2014, and Arata Isozaki won the award in 2019.

Japan is experiencing a period of great creativity in architecture. Touted as Pritzker Prize potential is Kuma Kengo, whose sensitive, "low cost" design for a new National Stadium to host the Tokyo 2020 Olympics was chosen to replace the late Zaha Hadid's plan.

CITY SURFACES

Building materials are a response to environment, climate and design preference. The connection, even in the artefact of a Japanese city, is essentially one of nature to structure.

From the thin sliver of titanium that coats the soaring Global Tower in Beppu, through the Umeda Sky Building in Osaka, with its vaulting walls and great cavities of open, aerial space, to the honeycombed glass panels of the superb Prada building in Tokyo, Japan is a dreamscape for the experimental architect.

What characterises many of these new creations more than anything else is their surfacing. The "bubble" years of the 1980s were distinguished by a shift from industrial expansion to a post-industrial, information-oriented society with software elements dominating over hardware ones. In the shift towards an information-based economy, buildings have become sounding boards, global-age transmitters. One can almost see on the surfaces of these buildings the alternating currents of the economy.

This flexible system of choreographed space, layers of artificial skin and surface, is achieved with hi-tech materials which, at their most successful, create illusions of depth and space. This tendency is visible in the new surfaces and the floating contraptions surrounding the core of the building, in the use of lighter, non-durable, hi-tech industrial materials, such as liquid crystal glass, polycarbon, Teflon, perforated metal and stainless-steel sheets.

The merits of insubstantiality, of surface units that can be replaced at will, are highly visible in the works of architects Fumihiko Maki, Ando Tadao and Ito Toyo.

WRITING ON THE WALL

In acquiring the added function of advertising props, Japanese urban centres have been transformed into surfaces of running commercial text and scroll. In cities like Tokyo and Osaka, where pedestrians for the most part see one side of a building – the one overlooking the street – views are flattened into two-dimensional planes. Urban geographer Paul Waley has observed that "space

in the Japanese city is conceived only in the context of the immediate visual field. This gives it an episodic quality." If each panel is visualised as an episode, it is one in a narrative that is set on constant replay, or rewrite.

Where a former age delighted more in the texture and tone of walls and other urban exteriors, in contemporary, space-depleted urban Japan, utility dominates the use of walls and other surfaces. The result is panels hung with a forest of signage. Commercial advertising inscribes the city in a deliberate, expressive manner. The textual quality of Japanese cities, from their daylight advertising to night-time electrographics, permits urban spaces to be scanned and read: the city as streaming text. Like the city itself, this

Detail of the Prada Building in Tokyo.

commercial script can only be digested piecemeal, in lines of haiku length or even just a few syllables.

Signage in Japanese cities has developed to such an extent that, in some instances, entire buildings may be obscured by hanging objects and structures. Increasingly these are liquid constructions, facade-scale TV screens so carefully aligned and affixed that they appear as a seamless part of the building itself. These screens create, in what was hitherto an unassuming visual void, "a gate and a field within whose false depth a new, antithetical dimension of space and time opens up", as Vladimir Krstic has expressed it.

Are such liquid dreams the shape of things to come? For some, these seductive LCD screens may indeed be the writing on the wall.

📷 THE ART OF LANDSCAPING

Compact, organised and introspective: words stereotypically used to describe the Japanese might just as well be applied to their gardens.

In Japan, gardening as a conscious art form can be traced to its introduction from China and Korea in the 6th and 7th centuries. The balance between nature and man-made beauty, with water and mountain as prototypical images, are the principles that form the basis for the traditional Japanese garden. Artfully blended with ponds, banks of irises and moss-covered rocks, carefully contrived Japanese gardens are objects of quiet contemplation.

"In order to comprehend the beauty of a Japanese garden," the 19th-century writer Lafcadio Hearn wrote, "it is necessary to understand – or at least learn to understand – the beauty of stones." This is especially true of the *karesansui* (dry-landscape) garden. Zen Buddhism's quest for "inner truth", its rejection of superficiality and attachment embodied in the over-ornate styles of the day, gave birth to medieval temple gardens of a minimalist beauty.

The stroll garden, by contrast, was used to entertain and impress and creates an illusion of a long journey. As visitors strolled along carefully planned paths, around every twist and turn a new vista would appear. Famous scenes were recreated without the visitor having to undertake the arduous journey to the original sights. Among the views represented were miniaturised scenes from Kyoto such as the hillsides of Arashiyama. The idea of confined space, combined with the Zen idea of discovering limitless dimensions in the infinitely small, saw the creation of the *kansho-niwa*, or "contemplation garden": gardens created as both tools for meditation and works of art. Carefully framed to resemble a scroll, they are intended to be appreciated like a painting that changes with the seasons.

There is constant work to be done in the Japanese garden. When monks and gardeners are not raking sand and gravel, they are raking leaves.

Visitors pause on the small stone bridge over the pond that is part of the outer garden of the iconic Ryoan-ji stone garden.

The water lily is a common motif in Japanese gardens. Along with the sacred lotus, it is at its best in summer.

The creation of bamboo fences in Japan is an art in itself, with dozens of differing styles and wood types.

The riverbank people

Although routinely ascribed to the prominent designers of the day, or to professional rock-setting priests, many Kyoto gardens were likely to have been built by *sensui kawaramono*, the much despised riverbank underclass. The "*mono*" of the designation stands for "thing", clearly stigmatising this pariah class as non-humans. A combination of Buddhist and Shinto taboos against the killing of animals and other sordid forms of work – slaughtering and skinning of animals, execution of criminals, burial of the dead – placed these people well beyond the sphere of a rigidly hierarchical class system with the nobility and clergy at the apex, descending to farmers, artisans and merchants. The trade of stripping and tanning hides required large quantities of water, forcing the *kawaramono* to build their abodes along the banks of the waterways. The *kawaramono* services became indispensable as they acquired greater skills in planting trees and in the placing of rocks: they were able to surpass their masters in the art of gardening. Ironically, it may be that some of Kyoto's "purest" gardens were created by the hands of men regarded as impure to the point of being inhuman.

A solitary stone in Ryoan-ji, one of the most photographed gardens in the world. The ancient clay wall at the rear has been designated a national cultural treasure.

Raikyu-ji Temple garden in Bitchu-Takahashi is a wonderfully curvaceous work, with its lines created from azalea bushes and sand, replicating waves, water and currents.

Japanese gardens provide the opportunity to display Buddhist, and occasionally Shinto-style statuary.

SPORT AND LEISURE

The most popular sports are sumo, baseball and football –
one indigenous to the archipelago, the other two
introduced from abroad. All are passionately followed.

Although baseball has long been the athletic obsession of Japan, sumo (pronounced "s'mo") remains the "official" national sport. This is fitting, partly because of its 1500-plus year history, and also for its hoary, quasi-religious ritualism – but mostly because, in Japan, it's a more exciting sport.

While baseball and sumo are the two perennial spectator sports in Japan, professional football, introduced in the 1990s under the "J-League" banner, has proved its staying power in competing for the title of Japan's favourite sport.

Participant sports are few within Tokyo. It's just too expensive. Golf, the world knows, is fantastically popular in Japan, but only the well heeled can afford to play a proper round; the rest stand in cubicles at driving ranges and hit balls towards distant nets. Skiing is a fashionable sport and Japan has the mountains. The heyday of its popularity saw crowds and blaring loudspeakers everywhere, even on the slopes, making skiing here less than satisfying. The economic slowdown means more space for those who can still afford it. Taking up some of the slack have been large numbers of Australian visitors drawn to Hokkaido's fine powder snow. The Taiwanese, Chinese and Koreans have also been descending on Japan's slopes in recent years.

Now that the country is gearing up to host the 2020 Olympic and Paralympic Games – which will be held in Tokyo from 24 July to 9 August and from 25 August to 6 September respectively – it hopes to attract an ever-growing number of sports fans. Several of the 1964 Summer Olympics venues will be reused for the 2020 Games, 11 new ones are to be built, and the National Stadium, amid controversy, will receive a total revamp. The location of most sites is planned within 8km (5 miles) of the Olympic Village in Tokyo Bay.

High school baseball practice in Sapporo.

BASEBALL

Less popular than it used to be, baseball can still draw huge crowds, although only two clubs – Tokyo's Yomiuri Giants and Nishinomiya's Hanshin Tigers – turn much of a profit.

A national sport that sustains its year-round interest, baseball was introduced in the early 1870s by university professors from the United States. Its popularity quickly spread and it soon became the country's number one school sport. *Yakyu*, as baseball is technically called in Japanese, rivals sumo in both its popularity and declining audience numbers. The first professional baseball team was established in 1934, and today the two-league professional baseball system is a commercial business, drawing millions of spectators to stadiums.

Millions more watch on national television, and train commuters devour the pages of Japan's daily national sports newspapers, from April to October, for details of the previous night's baseball league action. The final of the All-Japan High School Baseball Championship is held at Koshien Stadium near Osaka in the summer, but even the play-offs attract keen audiences and are televised.

There are two major leagues in Japanese professional baseball. For top teams, the advertising and promotional value for the parent company (department stores, media giants and food processing companies) is considerable. The winners of each league pennant meet in Japan's version of the World Series, the best-of-seven Japan Series beginning in late October.

The Japanese rule allowing *gaijin* players in its professional leagues is one of the most interesting aspects of the system. Each Japanese team can list four foreign players on its 25-man game roster, who must be a mixture of position players and pitchers. There are critics, but most feel the situation is fine, since the colourful American players, with their occasional outbursts, make the Japanese game that much more interesting; the limit does, nonetheless, allow baseball in Japan to keep its identity as Japanese.

The rules of Japanese baseball are generally the same as for the US. There are, however, several peculiarities, such as the reversal of the ball-strike count in Japan making a full count 2-3, rather than 3-2.

Teams have their own supporters' sections, with trumpets, drums and tambourines, headed by cheerleaders paid by the team. The resulting din shatters the eardrums.

SUMO

Some people say sumo is the national sport, some say it's the national spirit. Sumo wrestlers,

If you ever wondered how sumo wrestlers bulk up, look no further than chankonabe, a staple stew consisting of meat, fish, udon noodles, vegetables, broth and tofu. The Ryogoku district of Tokyo has several chankonabe restaurants open to the public.

or rikishi, would probably say it's a long, hard grind to fleeting glory.

Sumo is a fascinating phenomenon because it involves so many different things: physical strength, centuries-old ritual, a complicated code of behaviour, religious overtones, a daunting hierarchy system and feudalistic training regimes.

The rikishi wrestle on a raised square of mud and sand, the dohyo. A circle within the square, the *tawara*, is made of rice-straw bales. The wrestler's goal is to force his opponent to touch the surface of the dohyo with some part of his

Sumo tournament in Nagoya pavilion.

body (other than the feet), or to set foot out of the ring. This happens very fast. The average sumo bout lasts no longer than six seconds.

Despite appearances to the contrary, rikishi are not slabs of flab. They are immensely strong, rigorously trained athletes, with solid muscle often loosely covered in fat. The biggest rikishi in history (a Hawaiian named Salevaa Atisanoe, retired and now a Japanese citizen, and whose sumo name was Konishiki) reached 253kg (557lbs) before slimming down a bit for his wedding. Most grand champions, however, have weighed between 110kg and 150kg (220–330lbs).

There are no weight divisions. During a tournament, the smallest will fight the largest. The waist is wrapped in sumo's only garment, a belt called the *mawashi*. The most dignified (and probably dullest) winning technique – called *yorikiri* – requires a two-handed grip on the *mawashi*, which allows the winner to lift and push his opponent out.

The sport was tainted by a series of scandals in 2011, connecting players and managers to gambling rings and even organised crime. Allegations of game-fixing were raised, the collective impact doing much to harm the sport's image and reduce audience attendance, although this image is now recovering.

hosts the event in July, and Fukuoka's annual sumo tournament takes place at the Fukuoka Kokusai Centre in November.

FOOTBALL

Like mountain climbing, football came to Japan via the enthusiasm of an Englishman, one Lieutenant Commander Douglas, a navy man who organised the first game here in 1873.

The turning point in Japanese football came much later though, with the establishment of the J-League in 1993, a costly undertaking that

Japanese football fans at the Asian Cup.

Six two-week tournaments are held each year. Three of these are in Tokyo's Kokugikan, in the Ryogoku area in the eastern part of the city, in January, May and September. There is a tournament in Osaka in March at the Osaka Furitsu Taiku Kaikan; the Aichi-ken Taiku-kan in Nagoya

Popular with retired Japanese of both genders, gateball is ubiquitous. Similar to croquet, played with a wooden mallet and three gates, the team game is ideal for land-pinched Japan. Grass being rare, the game is usually played on compacted earth.

provided its national team with the players, just a few years later, to compete in the 2002 World Cup. Japan cohosted the tourney with South Korea, reaching the last 16 for the first time in its football history. State-of-the-art stadiums, like those in Yokohama and Saitama, were built in readiness for the event.

Oddly, Tokyo was excluded from the J-League when it was first founded, an omission that has since been rectified with the addition of the FC Tokyo and Tokyo Verdy clubs. These teams play at the Ajinomoto Stadium in Chofu City, just to the west of Tokyo, which will also host games during the 2019 Rugby World Cup. The National Stadium was located right in the middle of the capital, but has since been demolished, to be replaced by the New National Stadium that will host the 2020 Summer Olympic Games (including athletics, rugby sevens and some football finals, as well as the opening and closing ceremonies).

The J-League currently has 18 teams. A crop of cups, contests and tournaments, including the J-League Cup, the Jomo Cup and the Emperor's Cup, have helped sustain the popularity of the game. Matches are played between February and October, with a summer break.

Standards are rising in the game, with several Japanese players now among the ranks of the

A pachinko parlour.

major European squads. The ruling that Japanese clubs can field up to five foreign players (unlimited for players from certain Asian countries) has helped both to kindle interest in the game and to raise the quality of play. The Nadeshiko Japan team won the Women's World Cup in 2011, sparking massive media interest in female football players.

Japanese football fans have created their own counter-entertainment to the matches, with colourful pennants, painted faces, team-inspired costumes, and a barrage of drums and other musical instruments that provide a continuous soundtrack to the games and the well-synchronised, good-natured frenzy of the supporters. Thankfully, hooliganism is still a foreign concept.

OTHER LEISURE ACTIVITIES

Leisure activities soared after companies adopted the five-day week in the 1980s. It's a serious business, and the Japanese manage to give the impression that leisure is hard work.

Originating in Nagoya, pachinko, a cross between pinball and the one-arm bandit, is a multimillion-yen business, and the parlours are everywhere. Pachinko has had to deal with a negative image. Notorious tax dodgers, many of the owners are second- or third-generation Koreans, whose donations to North Korea were a mainstay of that regime's economy. Recent years have seen the industry clean up, and the newer parlours offer coffee shops and smoke-free areas.

Melding technology and music, karaoke was always bound to be huge. Karaoke bars are still popular, but the karaoke box, rented by friends, is ever better as it provides privacy and a full menu of drinks and snacks.

Cycling clubs are popular in Japan, even in cities like Tokyo and Osaka. Country routes are the best options, though, for touring. Cycling terminals are located all over the country, catering to bicyclists with inexpensive accommodation.

Fishing remains largely the domain of men. The number of fishing publications and websites is staggering. With so many mountains, Japan is perfect for hiking, offering peaks up to 3,000 metres (10,000ft), or day hikes that start outside local railway stations. Mountains usually have huts providing very basic accommodation and

⊘ FOREIGN INVASIONS

It's no small irony that Japan's national sport, one replete with native Shinto-inspired rituals, should currently be dominated by foreigners. There has long been a sprinkling of Hawaiian and Fijian players, but recent years have seen the rise of Mongolian wrestlers into the very top ranks of sumo. Strong evidence suggests that the sport originated in Mongolia, and several world champions have been Mongolian. But what of Russian players, and even a European or two, making it to the semi-finals? Could it be that, like everything else Japanese, sumo is about to be embraced by the West not merely as a spectator sport, but a participant one?

meals for climbers. Others have cabins where hikers can spend the night; bring your own food. One twist on the theme of hiking includes ice climbing, the scaling of frozen waterfalls in winter.

Surrounded by sea and with so many rivers and lakes, Japan is a great destination for windsurfing, jet skiing and yachting, and renting equipment is easy. Decades ago, off-duty American servicemen took their surfboards down to Kamogawa on the Boso Peninsula in Chiba and, unwittingly, began the country's surf boom. White-water rafting, kayaking, canoeing and canyoning are common in the spring and summer months, with regions like Hakuba in Nagano Prefecture, Niseko in Hokkaido and Minakami in Gunma providing ideal stretches of river. In Okinawa, ocean and river kayaking among the mangrove forests is an option for ecotourists.

Interest in ecotourism has led to the growth of accommodation run by conservationists for people interested in flora and fauna. The number of birdwatchers in Japan is very high. The Wild Bird Society was founded in 1935, and today has more than 80 chapters nationwide. The opportunities for whale- and dolphin-watching have also increased. One of the best places to observe mammals in the spring months is the Ogasawara Islands. Ogata in Kochi Prefecture is a good option between April and October, while humpback whales appear off the shores of the Kerama Islands from the middle of January to the end of March.

Health has become synonymous with leisure, resort clinics and health centres now common features of most cities. Health and beauty treatments are often available at hot springs, where massage, mud baths, aromatherapy and facials are available.

With over 2,000 hot springs in Japan, the competition to attract visitors is intense. There is nothing quite like soaking in an outdoor bath in the winter, watching the steam rise and snowflakes fall into the steaming hot waters.

Diving in Okinawa.

☉ DIVING IN JAPAN

Many Japanese beaches and waters have been ruined by industrial pollution or commercial overuse. Beyond the main urban centres, however, the clear, emerald-green waters off the coast of Sado Island's west coast are well regarded by divers.

Most divers make for Okinawa. The translucent sea and dazzling coral lent the chain its original name, the Ryukyu Islands, which means "circle of jewels" in Chinese.

Mainland Okinawa is a fine place to start, but the further south you go, the clearer the waters and the better the coral. Miyako-jima is flat, a fact that has saved its crystalline waters from the chemical run-offs from farms located on hillier islands. Ranking high among the Okinawa's ecological wonders is the immensely important Shiraho Reef on Ishigaki Island, the world's largest expanse of blue coral.

Thankfully, the effects of global warming have yet to leach out the colours from Okinawa's milk-bush coral, home to large shoals of white-spotted parrot fish. Diving in this undersea world of honeycombed coral, caves, hollows and fish like rainbow runners, red fin fusilier and the strangely named Moorish idol, is like swimming through a dense, aquatic forest.

At the other extreme, Abashiri Lake in the far north of Hokkaido offers the chance of ice-diving during the winter, where you plunge beneath frozen water to see the coral.

THE MARTIAL ARTS

Martial arts masters are revered for their extreme physical fitness, rigorous mental training and discipline. Two categories exist: ones using weapons, and ones that are open-handed.

A general term for various types of fighting arts that originated in the Orient, most martial arts practised today came from China, Japan and Korea.

Two major martial arts evolved in Japan: the *bujutsu*, or ancient martial arts, and the *budo*, or new martial ways. Both are based on spiritual concepts embodied in Zen Buddhism. Most of the martial arts end in the suffix -*do*, usually translated as "way" or "path". Thus, kendo is the way of the sword. *Do* is also the root of *budo* and of *dojo* – the place where one studies and practises a martial art.

JAPANESE FORMS

The original form of judo, called jujutsu, was developed in the Edo Period (1603–1868). It was made up of different systems of fighting and defence, primarily without weapons, against either an armed or bare-handed opponent on the battlefield. The best-known judo hall in Japan is the Kodokan in Tokyo, where one can observe judoists practising in early evenings.

Karate, meaning "empty hand" in Japanese, is a form of unarmed combat in which a person kicks or strikes with the hands, elbows, knees or feet. In Japan, karate developed around the 1600s on the island of Okinawa. A Japanese clan had conquered the island and passed a strict law banning the ownership of weapons. As a result, the Okinawans – racially and culturally different from the Japanese – developed many of the unarmed techniques of modern karate.

Aikido is a system of pure self-defence derived from the traditional weaponless fighting techniques of jujutsu and its use of immobilising holds and twisting throws, whereby an attacker's own momentum and strength are made to work against him. Since aikido is primarily a self-defence system and does not require great physical strength, it has attracted many women and elderly practitioners.

Kendo is Japanese fencing based on the techniques of the samurai's two-handed sword. Kendo is a relatively recent term that implies spiritual discipline and fencing technique. (At the end of World War II, the US occupation authorities banned kendo as a militaristic practice, but it returned in 1957.)

Another martial art form that developed in Japan is ninjutsu ("the art of stealing in", or espionage). People who practise ninjutsu are called ninja. Mountain mystics developed ninjutsu in the late 1200s. At that time, ninja were masters in all forms of armed and unarmed combat, assassination and the skilful use of disguises, bombs and poisons. Although the rulers of Japan banned ninjutsu in the

Children learning judo.

1600s, the *ninja* practised it secretly and preserved its techniques. Today, ninjutsu is taught as a martial art with a non-violent philosophy.

One of the most sublime of martial arts is *kyudo*. Zen archery originated with the samurai class, but is now taught at Japanese schools and performed at special events like the famous women's annual archery performance and competition in Kyoto.

A famous women's *kyudo* competition takes place at the Sanjusangendo temple in Kyoto during the New Year holiday. *Yabusame*, or horseback archery, is another Zen discipline dating back to the Kamakura Period, in which an archer shoots an arrow at a wooden target. One of the best-known performances takes place at the Tsurugaoka Hachiman Shrine in Kamakura.

RIKISHI: LIFE ON THE BOTTOM AND ON TOP

Not only is the *rikishi*'s training one of harsh days and a long apprenticeship, but competition at the top is without weight classes or handicaps.

In sumo, life is best at the top. Only when a rikishi, or wrestler, makes it to the top ranks of ozeki or yokozuna (grand champion, the highest rank and rarely achieved) does life become easy. Those in the lower ranks become the ozeki's or yokozuna's servants and valets, doing nearly everything from running errands to scrubbing backs.

In most *beya* – the so-called stables in which wrestlers live a communal lifestyle with other rikishi – the day typically begins at 6am with practice, not breakfast. Harsh and tedious exercises work to develop the wrestlers' flexibility and strength, followed by repetitive practice matches amongst the *beya*'s wrestlers (the only time they wrestle one another, as wrestlers of the same *beya* don't compete during actual tournaments). Practice ends around noon, when the wrestlers bathe. Then the high-ranked wrestlers sit down to the day's first meal, served by the lower-ranked wrestlers. The food staple of the stable is *chankon-abe*, a high-calorie, nutritious stew of chicken, fish, miso or beef, to mention just a few of the possibilities. Side dishes of fried chicken, steak and bowls of rice – and even salads – fill out the meal.

Financially, rikishi can be divided into two groups: those who earn a salary and those who don't. Lower-ranked wrestlers receive no salary, although they earn a small tournament bonus (and food and lodging are provided). When a wrestler reaches the *juryo* level, he becomes a *sekitori*, or ranked wrestler, and so worthy of a salary of at least US$8,000 a month. An ozeki receives about $25,000 monthly, and a yokozuna $30,000. The winner of one of the six annual tournaments receives $100,000.

Ceremonial Sumo Tournament at the Yasukuni Shrine.

Colourful nobori (sumo banners), with wrestlers' names on show, add to the spectacle of the wrestling events.

Squatting in readiness for a practice session. Because of the weight and ritual poses, sumo wrestlers' knees have to be especially strong.

1972 champion Hasegawa Tatsutoshi is honoured with a portrait that hangs in the lobby at Ryugoku Station, where the Kokugikan National Stadium is located.

An ancient Shinto sport

Sumo has been around for at least 1,500 years. Japanese mythology relates an episode in which the destiny of the Japanese islands was once determined by the outcome of a sumo match between two gods. The victorious god started the Yamato imperial line.

While wrestling has always existed in nearly every culture, the origins of sumo as we know it were founded on Shinto rituals. Shrines were the venue for matches dedicated to the gods of good harvests. In the Nara and Heian periods sumo was a spectator sport for the imperial court, while during the militaristic Kamakura Period sumo was part of a warrior's training. Professional sumo arose during the 1700s and was quite similar to the sumo practised in today's matches.

Shinto rituals punctuate sumo. The stomping before a match *(shiko)* drives evil spirits from the ring (not to mention loosening the muscles) before a match. Salt is tossed into the ring for purification, as Shinto beliefs say that salt drives out evil spirits. Nearly 40kg (90lbs) of salt is thrown out in one tournament day.

Two wrestlers who appear to be slapping each other are actually following one of the many combat techniques that trainees have to acquire.

The sumo pit, which is a sacred site made of earth and encircled by Shinto ropes, is kept immaculately clean.

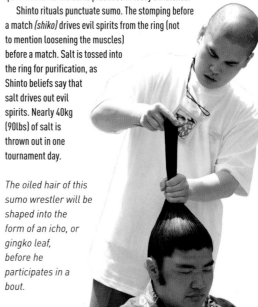

The oiled hair of this sumo wrestler will be shaped into the form of an icho, or gingko leaf, before he participates in a bout.

An example of kaiseki ryori.

FOOD AND DRINK

The Japanese islands are home to what is probably the world's most eclectic, diverse, detailed, potentially healthy and aesthetically appealing cuisine.

One of the myths about modern Japanese food is that it is necessarily healthy. In its original, purest form, when people ate brown rice, grilled fish, tofu and fresh mountain vegetables, it was everything a dietician would endorse. The food the Japanese typically eat today, on the other hand, contains an inordinate amount of salt, sugar and less healthy white rice, post-war additions to an otherwise healthy cuisine, which is now held responsible for the above-average incidence of stomach cancer in Japan and the alarming rise, especially among the young, of diabetes. Many people live on a diet of processed and ready-made food. Japan is among the world's biggest importers of beef. Vegetarians are not well provided for in Japan, with few restaurants catering to their needs. Fortunately, this doesn't mean that healthy food, corresponding to earlier Japanese tastes, is no longer popular or easily available.

Japan is a country of regional cuisines and, too, of seasonal cuisines. In fact, sampling local dishes is a fundamental purpose of travelling for many Japanese, whether it be a local *ekiben* box-lunch bought at the train station or an exquisite dinner at a remote ryokan. It would be foolish to even attempt a survey of the multitudinous regional and local cuisines. Even the Japanese don't try to know them all. To sample them all would be a worthy life's goal.

In the cities, there are almost too many places from which to choose. Two types of establishment that particularly deserve attention for their pure Japanese atmosphere are the *izaka-ya*, or pub, often with a string of red lanterns above its door, and the *taishu-sakaba*, a much larger tavern-like eatery that may also sport red lanterns. These red lanterns (*akachochin*) signify a traditional Japanese place for eating and drinking. Specialities

Restaurants in Dotonbori, Osaka.

include fried fish, shellfish, broiled dishes, tofu (bean curd) dishes, yakitori (skewered and broiled meat), fried rice balls and simple sashimi.

KAISEKI RYORI

At least one meal in Tokyo should be *kaiseki ryori*, a centuries-old form of Japanese cuisine served at restaurants or in ryokan over several elegant courses. (Be warned that authentic *kaiseki ryori* is very expensive.)

Fastidiously prepared, *kaiseki ryori* is so aesthetically pleasing that it's virtually an art form in Japan. The ingredients must be as fresh as the dawn.

The taste of *kaiseki ryori* relies on the inherent taste of the food itself, not on spices or similar additions. Rather than create distinctive flavours for their dishes, Japanese chefs seek above all to retain the natural flavours.

NOODLES

Japanese noodles are of three main types: soba, udon and *somen*. Made of buckwheat, soba noodles are thin and brownish, with a hearty consistency. Udon noodles, made of wheat, are usually off-white and thick to very thick. *Somen* noodles, also made of wheat, are as thin as vermicelli. Udon is usually eaten in hot dishes,

Tasty udon ramen.

⊘ EAT AND DRINK LIKE A LOCAL

At a traditional Japanese pub or *izaka-ya*, try the likes of *saba* (mackerel) or *nijimasu* (rainbow trout). Eat them *shioyaki*-style (salt broiled), accompanied by a good, cold Japanese beer or a very dry sake.

Izaka-ya, essentially drinking places, serve a wide variety of Japanese snack foods but not complete meals, whereas *koryori-ya*, being essentially eateries, serve light Japanese meals. Both types of establishment serve beer and sake, often *shochu* (a vodka-like spirit), and sometimes whisky. Both *izaka-ya* and *koryori-ya* often feature popular regional foods, invariably served with rice. Eating at one is a very Japanese experience.

while soba and *somen* may be eaten hot or cold, depending upon the season.

Another type of noodle called *hiyamugi* (iced noodles) is eaten only cold. *Hiyamugi* is made of the same ingredients as udon but is much thinner.

The most common type is soba, particularly delicious if not overburdened with non-buckwheat flour extender. Soba is usually served with wasabi (green horseradish), thinly sliced spring onions (scallions), a dip made of mirin (sweet sake), and *katsuobushi* (shaved flakes of dried bonito fish). Soba noodles in this form, when served chilled on a *zaru*, a type of bamboo tray, are called *zarusoba* and make a delicious summer meal. A rich source of vitamins B1 and C, soba is extremely nutritious.

Somen is another hot-weather favourite. Noted for its delicate flavour and adaptability to many garnishes, it can be served *gomoku-* (five-flavour) style with strips of omelette, chicken and vegetables; *gomadare*-style, with aubergine (eggplant), fish and *shiso* (beefsteak plant or Japanese basil); with fruit and hard-boiled swallow's eggs; or *hiyashi*-style: cold, with nothing but soy sauce containing sesame oil. As a light, refreshing treat on a hot summer day, *somen* is hard to beat.

One of Japan's great cold-weather favourites is udon served in a hot, soy-based broth with an egg, spring onions and other vegetables. Unlike soba and *somen*, udon is not placed in a dip before being eaten. A real body-warmer, this noodle is prized for its excellent texture.

Although essentially Chinese, so-called ramen noodles are eaten so obsessively in Japan that to omit mentioning them would be remiss. Ramen is served very hot in soy-flavoured broth with savoury ingredients, most typically strips of bamboo shoot and slices of spring onion and roast pork. Instant ramen is a mainstay of the home.

If short on time, try a *tachigui*soba-ya, "stand-and-eat soba". Train stations always have them, and a stand will sometimes be found on the platform. Prices are very reasonable, usually ranging from ¥200 or so for *kakesoba* (basic soba in broth) to somewhat higher for *tendama* (soba with raw egg and mixed ingredients fried together, tempura-style). Priced in between are tempura soba, *kitsune* (with fried tofu), *tanuki* (with tempura drippings), *tsukimi* (with raw egg), wakame (with kelp) and countless others.

SUSHI AND SASHIMI

Taste and visual pleasure converge in sushi and sashimi, both prepared with uncooked seafood. A good sushi shop, or *sushi-ya*, can be both expensive and confounding if one doesn't know what to ask for. Try, instead, a *kaiten sushi-ya*, where small dishes of sushi pass by on a conveyor belt along the counter. It lacks a certain elegance, but in a *kaiten sushi-ya* the uninitiated can study the sushi offerings at leisure and sample it for less cost. Then later, armed with new-found expertise, visit a proper *sushi-ya*.

Good sushi requires that the ingredients should be of high quality, that the rice be properly vinegared and steamed and that the topping should be as fresh as possible. (Thawed-out frozen fish just doesn't cut it.) Those who prefer raw fish and seafood without rice should order sashimi, served in a tray or on a plate with attention to the appearance. Often small bowls of sauce will be offered for dipping the sashimi.

The art of making noodles.

⊘ THE OKINAWA EFFECT

Japanese of all ages, with an eye to a more healthy diet, are turning their eyes south to the islands of Okinawa, or to one of the many Okinawan restaurants that have sprung up in recent years in cities throughout Japan.

Traditional cuisine can be summed up in the Okinawan concept of *nuchi gusui*, the healing power of food. The expression recalls the words of Dr Tokashiki Tsuka, a physician to the king of the Ryukyus, who wrote in his 1832 *Textbook of Herbal Medicine*, "If we nourish the spirit through proper food and drink, illness will cure itself."

Low in calorific density, rich in protein, fibre, flavanoids and other health-promoting properties, Okinawan cooking tends toward the stronger, spicier flavours found in Chinese cooking styles. Black sugar and *koregusu*, a condiment made from red peppers marinated in *awamori* (Okinawan firewater), are used in Okinawan cooking. A degree of self-discipline is required to follow the Okinawan way. The expression *hara hachi bu* is often invoked in Okinawa, meaning something like "eat until you are eight tenths full".

Many private houses in Okinawa have kitchen gardens, where the owners grow their own vegetables and cultivate dragon fruit, bananas, passion fruit, mango, papaya and custard apple. A visit to an Okinawan food market is a reminder that these islands sit in the sun-drenched subtropics.

NABEMONO

If hotpot dishes are your favourite, Japan is the place to be in autumn and winter. Every part of Japan, without exception, has its own distinctive *nabe-ryori* (pot dishes).

Nabemono are typically winter dishes and include *ishikari-nabe* (Hokkaido Prefecture), containing salmon, onions, Chinese cabbage, tofu, *konnyaku* (a jelly made of root starch) and *shungiku* (spring chrysanthemum); *hoto* (Yamanashi), with handmade udon, daikon (white radish), *ninjin* (carrot), *gobo* (burdock), squash,

A platter of sushi.

onions, Chinese cabbage and chicken; and *chiri-nabe* (Yamaguchi), containing fugu (blowfish) meat, Chinese cabbage, mushrooms, tofu and starch noodles.

BENTO

Like most modern countries, Japan is increasingly a land of fast food. The traditional Japanese box-lunch, bento, or, more respectfully, obento, has become a form of fast food in itself, with both convenience stores and *bento-ya* offering wide selections to take out. A bento box, flat and shallow, is used with small dividers to separate rice, pickles and whatever else might be inside. Bento is eaten at work, school, picnics and parties.

> *Fugu (blowfish, puffer or globefish), is the deadliest delicacy in Japan. It's prepared only by licensed chefs, as the liver and ovaries contain a poison with no known antidote. However, the taste of the finely cut sashimi slivers is superb.*

Just about anything can be used in bento, including Western imports such as spaghetti, sausage and hamburger. Schoolchildren take bento to school for lunch.

A special type of bento that has become an art in itself, not to mention a pursuit for the connoisseur, is the *ekiben* (from *eki*, for train station, and bento). Japan is a nation of obsessed train travellers.

Trains often make stops of just long enough duration to permit passengers to get off briefly and buy some of their favourite *meisanbutsu* (local specialities), especially the ubiquitous *ekiben*, to be eaten aboard the train.

TSUKEMONO

A Japanese meal always comes with *tsukemono*, or distinctive Japanese-style pickles. Pickles probably owe their origins to the practice of preserving foods in anticipation of famines. During the Edo Period pickles came into their own, and the *tsukemono-ya* (pickle shop) emerged as a new type of business. Ingredients used in Japanese pickles vary somewhat with the seasons. Common ingredients are Chinese cabbage, bamboo, turnips, *kyuri* (Japanese cucumber), hackberry, daikon, ginger root, *nasu* (Japanese aubergine), *udo* (a type of asparagus), *gobo* and many others.

Tsukemono add colour to a meal and offer a wide range of appealing textures, from crunch to squish, that might be missing from the main dishes. Pickles can serve to clear the palate for new tastes – such as in sushi, in which a bite of pickled ginger root rids the mouth of the aftertaste of an oily fish such as *aji* (mackerel) and prepares it for the delicate taste of *ebi* (prawn).

SEASONAL FOOD

Freshness equates with seasonality. Spring is the season for fresh fish and mountain vegetables and supplements like lotus root, butterbur, milk vetch and chrysanthemum leaves.

Typical garnishes would be a sprig of prickly ash leaves, or rice with chopped spring herbs. *Ayu* (sweetfish) is a great summer delicacy, along with horse mackerel and tuna. Chilled wheat noodles and cold tofu with grated ginger are served in this humid time. One-pot dishes like *yudofu*, tofu heated in hot water and served with soy sauce and citrus juice, are popular in the autumn. Saury pike are eaten and small snacks made of chestnuts and persimmon. This is also the crab and oyster season. Teriyaki dishes are popular in winter, especially chicken preparations grilled with sweet soy sauce. Yellowtail is a great favourite, along with carp and sardines.

ALFRESCO

The Japanese like to eat alfresco. Even in the cooler months, some restaurants will keep their chairs outside, hanging a transparent plastic curtain between terrace and pavement, or setting a stove among the tables. *Yatai* are outdoor eateries resembling tents. Cosy and intimate, customers usually sit and order from a counter. Some *oden* (fish cake stew) stalls provide miniature tables and chairs for customers.

Fukuoka in northern Kyushu is famous for its highly varied *yatai*. Besides local dishes like *tonkotsu ramen* (Chinese noodles in a white, garlic-laced soup made from a pork-bone stock), tempura and pieces of skewered chicken broiled over a charcoal fire, sophisticated Fukuoka *yatai* serve up salted bream, yellowtail and even steak dishes, Hakata's food stalls going out of their way to create an ambience not unlike that of an intimate restaurant.

SNACKING

The Japanese are inveterate snackers. Rice crackers called *sembei* are eaten with tea but also between meals. *Onigiri* rice balls are a mainstay as a snack for busy people. Yakitori (grilled chicken and vegetable skewers) goes well with cold beer; *oden*, fish cakes and vegetables simmered in a broth, are a light meal; while *okonomiyaki*, sometimes called "Japanese pizza", consists of bean sprouts, cabbage, carrot, boneless pieces of chicken breast, shrimp, shredded red ginger, dried bonito flakes, seaweed flakes and Japanese mountain yam and assorted garnishes added to a flour and baking-powder base.

FOREIGN INFLUENCES

Western food is routinely eaten, though it is often changed to satisfy the native palate. This means that spaghetti may have a topping of seaweed or *natto* (fermented soy bean), that steak is served with rice and that Western breakfasts are accompanied by a small salad.

Curry dishes have been a big favourite of the Japanese ever since curry powder was imported in the 19th-century by the British community living in Kobe. English-style curry, less fiery than its Indian counterpart and without

A street vendor offering snacks.

⊘ THE EELS OF SUMMER

Travellers will encounter many unusual dishes in Japan. Some fit in a category that Japanese commonly refer to as *stamina ryori*, or dishes intended to raise energy levels and "staying" power. Japan and especially Tokyo can be pretty enervating, so "stamina restaurants" (and drinks) are a common phenomenon. A popular summer dish is *unagi*, or broiled eel served on rice. It's said to help one withstand the hot and humid days of the Japanese summer – *doyo no iri*. Usually served with a sweetish *tare* sauce, *unagi* is rich in vitamins E and A, and it exceeds pork and beef in protein content yet contains fewer calories.

the food taboos that might exclude meats like beef, quickly established itself into the Japanese range of adapted tastes. To the despair of Indians living in Japan, the Japanese version is served with sticky rice and *fukujinzuke*, seven different thinly sliced vegetables pickled in sweetened soy sauce and salt. *Kare*-udon (curry-udon) is udon served in a thick, mildly spicy gravy.

Imported fruits such as loquat, fig, banana, papaya and mango have been enthusiastically absorbed onto the Japanese table. Some fruits

Wagashi – Japanese confectionery.

have been adapted in creative ways, like the ubiquitous strawberry, which was imported by the Dutch in the 17th century. Strawberry and cream sandwiches may not always be to the taste of foreigners, however.

JAPANESE CONFECTIONS

The Japanese had long enjoyed Chinese confections, but in the years between 1500 and 1640, the arrival of Europeans saw the advent of various types of sweet confectionery and cakes.

Desserts are usually limited to fresh fruit or *anmitsu*, a mixture of agar jelly cubes, *azuki* bean paste and boiled peas, served with tinned fruit like peach. Ice cream, *shiratama dango*

(sweet rice-flour balls) and a sweet black syrup called *mitsu* are often added.

Japanese confectionery, known as *wagashi*, is usually served with matcha, powdered green tea, or just after a meal. The main ingredient is *an*, a paste made from sugar and *azuki* beans, sweet potato and other ingredients. The two main types are *namagashi* (raw), a fresh sweet made from rice-flour doughs, and *higashi*, a hard, dry form made from sweetened powder. The more interesting and often decorative *namagashi* are seasonal in their ingredients and motifs. A puree made from boiled beans is combined with *kanten* (agar-agar) to make the popular *yokan*, a kind of jelly.

MINDING YOUR MANNERS

Although non-Japanese are not expected to know the rules, following them wherever possible creates a good impression. When you enter a Japanese restaurant the staff will greet you with a hearty *Irrashaimase!* (welcome). It is not necessary to respond, except with a smile. *Oshibori*, hot towels, are given out in many places. Use them to wash hands, but not the face.

Japanese food is eaten with chopsticks. You should never pass food from one set of utensils to another. With the exception of hot nabe dishes, when tucking into a communal dish, reverse the chopsticks so that the clean ends are used. Never place them sticking upwards in rice, which reminds people of the offering of rice made to the dead at funerals. Fingers can be used when eating sushi at a counter, but not at the table, where chopsticks are the norm. Slurping noodles is thought to improve their taste. Drinking the broth directly from the bowl is normal.

Unless you are required to buy a ticket for a dish at a vending machine, payment is usually made after the meal. There is no system of tipping. Generally, the Japanese frown upon eating in the street or in the subway, though you do see more people breaking this unwritten rule these days.

When drinking alcohol, never pour your own drink. The custom is to allow the host to pour first, then you reciprocate. You should raise the glass a little to receive the drink. After filling other people's glasses, it is acceptable, especially with beer, to pour for yourself.

SPIRITS IN BOTTLES

Whoever wrote the line, "If Venice is built on water, Tokyo is built on alcohol," was spot on. Drinking, in fact, is a national pastime.

Although Sapporo beer is probably Japan's largest liquid export these days, the quintessential Japanese drink remains sake.

A staple as much of Shinto ceremonies as of the rituals of the modern Japanese table, the quality of sake depends largely on the rice and water used in its fermentation. There are over 500 local sake breweries throughout Japan, and those in Niigata Prefecture are reckoned to be the best.

Sake is graded as *tokkyu* (special), *ikkyu* (first grade) and *nikyu* (second grade). Connoisseurs generally ignore these categories, established largely for tax purposes, in favour of the high-grade *junmaishu* (sake unmixed with added alcohol or sugar) and the very superior *ginjo-zukuri*, the purest sake on the market, a complex brew bulging with the kind of fragrance and fruity undertones associated with top French clarets. Serious drinkers tend to favour dry sake *(karakuchi)* over the sweet variety *(amakuchi)*.

Besides the classic clear sake, there is a variety, called *nigori-zake*, in which the rice solids have been left to sit in a thick sediment at the bottom of the bottle, resulting in a milky colour when shaken. A relative newcomer on the drinks scene, effervescent sake makes a lively end to a drinking session, or a light coda to a meal.

Unlike wine, sake does not age well and is best drunk within six months of bottling. Premium sake is at its best cold. Cheaper brands are often drunk hot during the winter.

A stronger tipple is *shochu*, a distilled spirit made from grain or potato. *Shochu* is often drunk with a soft drink or fruit juice, but straight, high-quality *shochu* has become de rigueur among young people. It can also be drunk *oyu-wari* (with a little hot water), which is a great way to warm up in cold weather.

OTHER SPIRITS

Okinawa has its own firewater, a spirit known as *awamori*. Made exclusively from Thai rather than Japanese rice, it is a reminder that these islands once enjoyed a thriving trade with Southeast Asia. Some *awamori* makers play music while the alcohol is fermenting in the belief it enhances the process. The Onna distillery in Okinawa places jars of *awamori* under the sea for a day, producing what they believe to be a more rounded, mellow Shinkai (Deep Sea) brand.

Ocha, Japanese tea, with variations, is a year-round drink. Japanese tea means green tea of various qualities. Tea is graded into the coarse and very cheap *bancha*, the better-quality leaves of *sencha* and, at the top,

Bottles of sake.

gyokuro, a fine brew made from the most tender bud leaves of the more mature bushes. *Mugicha* is a summer drink of chilled buckwheat tea. *Hoji-cha* is a roasted tea made from *bancha*. *Genmai-cha* is mixed with grains of roasted rice, giving it a rustic, nutty flavour.

Matcha, the thick, high-caffeine powdered green tea drunk in the tea ceremony, was originally intended to keep Zen monks from falling asleep during long hours of meditation. Bowls of *matcha au lait*, powdered green tea with hot or cold milk, have become a fixture with people who appreciate the tea ceremony or the abbreviated version of the powdered green tea that is often served in Japanese garden teahouses, but don't have the time or the requisite setting for the elaborate steps in the ritual.

JAPANESE FOOD

In his book *A Potter in Japan*, ceramicist Bernard Leach wrote, "There is a saying that the Chinese eat with their stomachs and the Japanese eat with their eyes".

A presentational, almost ritual cuisine, Japanese cooking demands that dishes should be contemplated, then consumed. According to this system of thinking, the satisfaction is as much aesthetic as gustatory.

Colours are important, a good example being *san-shoku*, a soba dish containing three types of buckwheat noodles: brown, white and green. Another popular three-colour combination consists of purple, green and white pickles. Asymmetrical arrangements of food on the plate are preferable, so that round fish or dumplings will be served on a long, narrow dish.

Great lengths are gone to in order to create aesthetic appeal. One popular rice cake, known as "the beautiful bay of Tango", is a pink-and-yellow confection resembling the form of a chestnut burr and named after a scenic spot that appears in the 8th-century poetry collection, the *Manyoshu*.

In spring, Japanese sweets, *wagashi*, may have a cherry blossom crest marked on them; in autumn a seasonally apposite chrysanthemum design. Tableware is also often visually matched with the season, especially in more expensive restaurants. Glass dishes and green bamboo vessels are associated with summer; stoneware and rough ceramic pots, along with wooden plates decorated with maple leaves, with autumn and winter. Fresh leaves may appear on dishes as a seasonal reminder. Visual appeal, of course, is not enough: the dishes must be beautiful, but good enough to eat.

Soba buckwheat noodles are a staple of Japanese restaurants, of both the sitting and standing variety.

The batter for tempura, a dish adapted from a Portuguese preparation, is used not only for fish, but a wide spectrum of vegetables and even leaves.

Osaka is known as one of the best cities in Japan to eat. Osakans, as this boldly advertised restaurant in the popular Dotonbori district shows, are not a shy or retiring people.

Mochi rice-based sweets, like this green tea flavoured offering, are popular gifts.

Empire of plastic

The practice of making life-like *sanpuru* (food samples) appears to have begun in the early years of the Meiji Restoration with the arrival of anatomical models made of hardened wax, which were used as teaching aids in the newly built schools of Western medicine. A businessman from Nara hit upon the idea of creating food models to promote restaurant menus. As visual aids models proved indispensable in demonstrating scale. The only problem was the models were apt to melt during Japan's humid summer months, so the material eventually changed to glazed plastic.

By the mid-70s the unsung creators of this highly original, uniquely Japanese genre had refined their products to such a degree that foreigners could discover in the finest examples a new pop art form. While they are certainly the most functional of sculptures, the best examples are mesmerising in their veracity. Viewed on an empty stomach they can seem like works of towering genius.

ike a lot of contemporary Japanese food, o-bento, or acked lunches, are heavy on salt, but wonderfully onvenient and often tasty.

n fish and meat-eating Japan, seijin-ryori, or temple ood, is the closest the country gets to an authentic raditional vegetarian cuisine.

Handmade noodles are considered the best, though restaurants serving them may charge a little extra.

Enjoying Japanese powder at Sapporoteine Ski Area, Mount Teine.

Two geishas walking through Fushimi Inari Shrine.

INTRODUCTION

A detailed guide to the entire country, with principal sights clearly cross-referenced by number to the maps.

Spread like cultured pearls in the western Pacific, the islands of the Japanese archipelago lie off the coast of China, Russia and Korea. Strung out for over 2,800km (1,700 miles) and covering 380,000 sq km (147,000 sq miles), the 6,800 or so islands are home to 127 million residents – twice the population of Italy, yet almost the same land area.

Nearly a third of Japan's population – over 42 million – lives in the Kanto region, on the main island of Honshu, where we begin with the nation's capital, Tokyo. Separate sections then cover areas around Tokyo, including Nikko and its lavish Tosho-gu Shrine complex to the north, Yokohama and the ancient capital of Kamakura to the south, and the iconic snow-capped Mount Fuji. Moving westwards, the Central Honshu section covers the commercial city of Nagoya, the breathtaking Northern Alps and areas along the northern coast of central Honshu.

Next is the largely rural Tohoku region in northern Honshu. Although its east coast was devastated by the 2011 earthquake and tsunami, Tohoku's inland attractions have remained untouched. The sedate Tono Valley and mountainside Yamadera Temple complex are a couple of the highlights. After Tohoku comes the northernmost island of Hokkaido, known for its harsh winters and stunning natural scenery, seen at its best in Daisetsuzan National Park.

We then move to the Kansai region, several hundred kilometres west of Tokyo, where many of Japan's most noteworthy sites are clustered. The focus here is on ancient *Umi Jigoku (Sea Hell).* Kyoto, the nation's capital city for over 1,000 years: a fabulous collection of temples, sanctuaries, geisha and Zen gardens. Nearby is the beauty of Nara – the country's cultural and artistic cradle. Also in Kansai is Osaka, Japan's second city, a lively business and nightlife centre.

Heading south, the next stops are Honshu's Chugoku region and the slow-paced islands of Shikoku and Kyushu. Chugoku's most famous sight is the city of Hiroshima, while Shikoku is home to the 88 temples of the centuries-old Shikoku pilgrimage route. Kyushu's warm climate, hot springs and active volcanoes give it a feel quite distinct from the rest of Japan.

Lastly, our attention turns to the Okinawa Islands. Stretching southwest from below Kyushu, they offer a unique culture and the best beaches and diving in Japan.

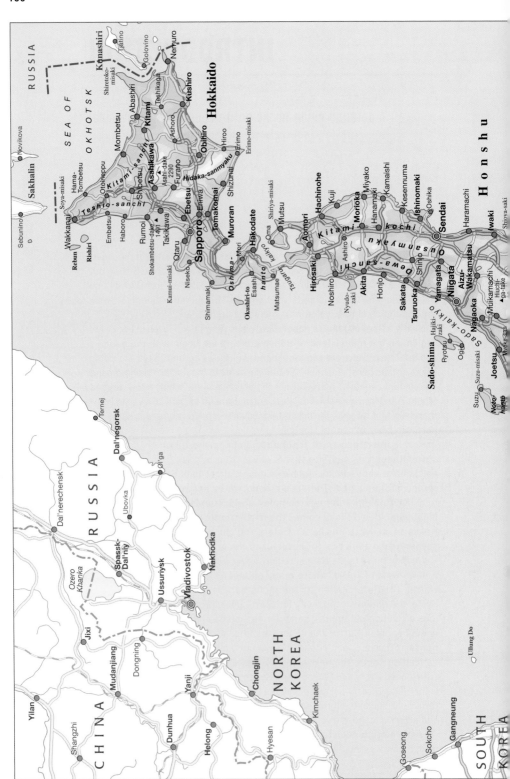

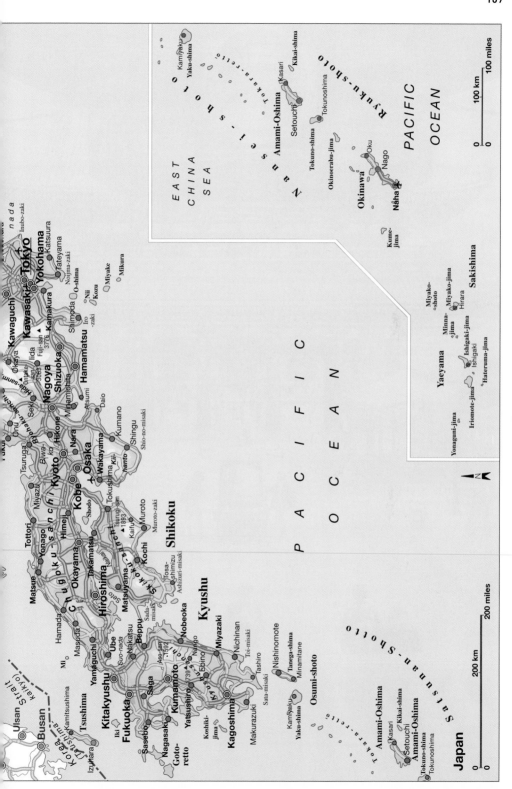

PACIFIC OCEAN

100 miles
100 km

Ryukyu-shoto

Kikai-shima
Kasari
Amami-Oshima
Setouchi
Tokuno-shima
Tokunoshima
Okinoerabu-jima
Oku
Nago
Okinawa
Nago
Naha

Kume-jima

EAST CHINA SEA

Nansei-shoto

Tokara-retto

Kami-Yaku
Yaku-shima

Sakishima

Miyako-shoto
Minna-jima
Miyako-jima
Hirara
Yaeyama
Ishigaki-jima
Ishigaki
Haterima-jima
Iriomote-jima
Yonaguni-jima

N

PACIFIC OCEAN

nada
Inubo-zaki
Katsuura
Tateyama
Kamakura
Kawaguchi
Kawasaki
TOKYO
YOKOHAMA
Nojima-zaki
O-shima
Shimoda
Nii
Kozu
Miyake
Mikura
Iro-zaki
Shizuoka
HAMAMATSU
Minamichita
Fuji-san 3776
Nagoya
Iida
Okaya
Seki
Kani
Ontake 3063
Hida-sanchi
Atsumi
Daio
Kumano
Shingu
Shio-no-misaki
Kumano
Kii-hanto
Wakayama
Nara
OSAKA
Kyoto
Hikone
Biwa-ko
Tsuruga
Miyazu
Yonago
Tottori
Matsue
Hamada
Mio
Masuda
Tsushima
Kamitsushima
Izuhara
Tsushima Strait
Ulsan
Busan
Korea Strait
Tsushima Kaikyo

Tokushima
Shodo
Tokushima-san
1893
Tsurugi-san
Kaifu
Muroto
Muroto-zaki
SHIKOKU
Kochi
Takamatsu
Matsuyama
Shiko-ku-sanchi
Seto
Saka
Sada-misaki
Tosa
Shimizu
Tosa-shimizu
Ashizuri-misaki

Chugoku-sanchi
HIROSHIMA
Okayama
Himeji
KOBE
Yonago

Matsue

Nada-nada
Suo-nada
Ube
Yamaguchi
Nakatsu
Beppu
KITAKYUSHU
FUKUOKA
Saga
Sasebo
Goto-retto
NAGASAKI
Kumamoto
Yatsushiro
Aso-san 1592
Kuma
Ebino
Hitoyoshi 739
Kagoshima
Makurazaki
Sata-misaki
Koshiki-jima
Kami-Yaku
Yaku-shima

KYUSHU
Nobeoka
Miyazaki
Nichinan
Toi-misaki
Tashiro
Nishinomote
Tanega-shima
Minamitane
Osumi-shoto

Satsunan-Shoto

Tokara-retto

Amami-Oshima
Kikai-shima
Kasari
Setouchi
Amami-Oshima
Tokuno-shima
Tokunoshima

200 miles
200 km

Japan

Senso-ji Temple.

KANTO PLAIN AND CHUBU

The central part of Honshu is Japan's heartland:
the vibrant metropolis of Tokyo spreads out on the
Kanto plain, while beyond the capital lie other
historic cities and the beauty of the Japan Alps.

*Tsurugaoka Hachiman-Gu
temple, Kamakura.*

Descriptions of the Kanto region can be misleading. It is Japan's largest alluvial plain, but it is certainly not an area of wide open spaces. None of the flat land extends far enough to offer a level, unbroken horizon. Most of Japan's longest rivers – the Tone, Naka, Ara, Tama and Sagami – pass through Kanto and empty into the Pacific, but few would call these concrete-lined conduits, managed and contained into near-obscurity, rivers at all.

Virtually nothing of interest about the region is recorded until Minamoto Yoritomo, the first Kamakura shogun, endowed Tokyo's Asakusa-jinja with 36 hectares (90 acres) of arable land around 1180. Later, in 1456, a village called Edo (Estuary Gate) was recorded when the first Edo castle was built by a small-time daimyo on the site of today's Imperial Palace. In 1600, a ship-wrecked Englishman became the first foreign guest at Edo, tutoring Tokugawa Ieyasu. Three years later, Ieyasu started the 250-year reign of the Tokugawa dynasty. Then, after centuries of growth, Edo got a name change – to Tokyo – when it became the country's capital with the Meiji Restoration of 1868.

Hakuba ski resort, Nagano.

Today, with more than 38 million people living in the Greater Tokyo area, Ieyasu's city is the heartbeat of Kanto. It offers visitors everything from the busy neon-drenched streets of Shinjuku and contemporary cool of Roppongi and Omotesando, to more traditional (though just as vibrant) neighbourhoods such as Asakusa.

The areas surrounding Tokyo have plenty of their own charms. To the west are Mount Fuji (or Fuji-san) and Hakone, offering beautiful scenery and relaxing hot springs, and to the north is Nikko and its magnificent Tosho-gu shrine complex. South is the Western-influenced city of Yokohama, which came to life with foreign trade after the Meiji Restoration, and the temple-laden ancient capital of Kamakura.

In the area known as Chubu, or Central Honshu, beyond Kanto, Japan is both highly industrial, as in Nagoya to the southwest, and rural, as in the delightful Noto Peninsula and elsewhere along the Sea of Japan (East Sea) coast. The area is also home to the historical city of Kanazawa, the mountainous resort city of Nagano, and the remoteness and drumming thunder of the island of Sado.

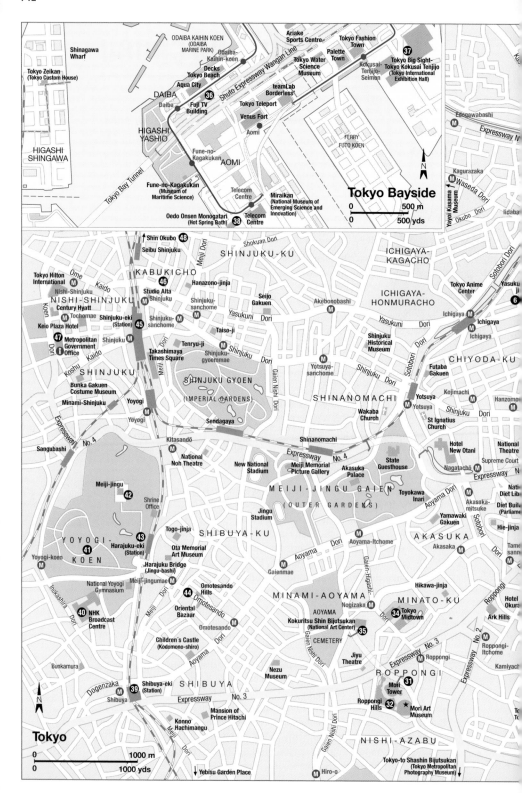

Shinagawa Wharf

Tokyo Zeikan (Tokyo Custom House)

HIGASHI SHINGAWA

ODAIBA KAIHIN KOEN (ODAIBA MARINE PARK)

Odaiba-Kaihin-koen

Decks Tokyo Beach

Aqua City

DAIBA

Daiba

Fuji TV Building

HIGASHI YASHIO

Fune-no-Kagakukan

AOMI

Fune-no-Kagakukan (Museum of Maritime Science)

Tokyo Bay Tunnel

Oedo Onsen Monogatari (Hot Spring Bath) 38

Shuto Expressway Wangan Line

Tokyo Water Science Museum

teamLab Borderless

Tokyo Teleport

Venus Fort

Aomi

Telecom Centre

Miraikan (National Museum of Emerging Science and Innovation)

Ariake Sports Centre

Tokyo Fashion Town

Palette Town

Kokusai-Tenjijo-Seimon

37

Tokyo Big Sight-Tokyo Kokusai Tenjijo (Tokyo International Exhibition Hall)

FERRY FUTO KOEN

Telecom Centre

36

Edogawabashi

Expressway N

Kagurazaka

Waseda Dori

Yayoi Kusama Museum

Okubo Dori

Iidaba

Tokyo Bayside

N

0   500 m

0   500 yds

Shin Okubo 48

Seibu Shinjuku

Shokuan Don

SHINJUKU-KU

ICHIGAYA-KAGACHO

Meiji Dori

Tokyo Hilton International

Ome Kaido

Nishi-Shinjuku

NISHI-SHINJUKU

Century Hyatt

Tochomae

Keio Plaza Hotel

Koen

47

Metropolitan Government Office

Koshu Kaido

SHINJUKU

Bunka Gakuen Costume Museum

Minami-Shinjuku

Shinjuku-eki (Station) 45

Shinjuku-sanchome

Shinjuku

Yoyogi

Yoyogi

KABUKICHO 46

Studio Alta Shinjuku

Shinjuku-sanchome

Taiso-ji

Tenryu-ji

Takashimaya Times Square

Shinjuku-gyoemmae

Hanazono-jinja

Seijo Gakuen

Yasukuni Dori

Shinjuku Dori

SHINJUKU GYOEN (IMPERIAL GARDENS)

Sendagaya

Kitasando

Akebonobashi

Yasukuni Dori

Yotsuya-sanchome

SHINANOMACHI

Wakaba Church

Shinjuku Dori

Shinjuku Historical Museum

Futaba Gakuen

Yotsuya

Yotsuya

St Ignatius Church

ICHIGAYA-HONMURACHO

Tokyo Anime Center

Ichigaya

Ichigaya

Ichigaya

Sotobori Dori

CHIYODA-KU

Kojimachi

Hanzomo

Yasuku ji

6

Galen Nishi Dori

National Noh Theatre

New National Stadium

Meiji Memorial Picture Gallery

Expressway No. 4

Akasuka Palace

State Guesthouse

Hotel New Otani

Nagatacho

National Theatre

Supreme Court

Expressway N

Sangubashi

Expressway No. 4

Meiji-jingu 42

Shrine Office

Togo-jinja

SHIBUYA-KU

MEIJI-JINGU GAIEN (OUTER GARDENS)

Jingu Stadium

Toyokawa Inari

Aoyama Dori

Akasaka-mitsuke

Yamawaki Gakuen

Nati Diet Lib

Diet Buil (Parliam

Hie-jinja

Tame sann

YOYOGI-KOEN

Yoyogi-koen

41

Harajuku-eki (Station) 43

Harajuku Bridge (Jingu-bashi)

Ota Memorial Art Museum

Aoyama

Aoyama-Itchome

Akasaka

AKASUKA

MINATO-KU

Roppongi-Itchome

Hotel Okura

Ark Hills

Inokashira Dori

National Yoyogi Gymnasium

40

NHK Broadcast Centre

Meiji-jingumae 44

Omotesando Hills

Oriental Bazaar

Omotesando

Children's Castle (Kodomono-shiro)

Bunkamura

Dogenzaka

Shibuya-eki (Station) 39

Shibuya

Aoyama

Omotesando

MINAMI-AOYAMA

AOYAMA

Kokuritsu Shin Bijutsukan (National Art Center)

35

Galen Nishi Dori

CEMETERY

Nezu Museum

Jiyu Theatre

Hikawa-jinja

Nogizaka

34 Tokyo Midtown

Expressway No. 3

Roppongi

Roppongi

Expressway No. 2

Kamiyach

To

Tokyo

N

Expressway No. 3

Konno Hachimangu

Mansion of Prince Hitachi

SHIBUYA

Meiji Dori

Galen-Higashi

ROPPONGI

Mori Tower

31

Roppongi Hills 32

★ Mori Art Museum

NISHI-AZABU

Tokyo-to Shashin Bijutsukan (Tokyo Metropolitan Photography Museum)

Hiro-o

Yebisu Garden Place

0   1000 m

0   1000 yds

The striking scenery of Tokyo.

TOKYO

The captivating Tokyo metropolitan area and its 38 million inhabitants sit snugly in the former capital of the shoguns, the whole existing rather dynamically in an active earthquake zone.

Japan has always been a country of villages. If Tokyo is Japan's biggest village – and it is by far, at over 620 sq km (240 sq miles) and over 12 million people in central Tokyo alone – then one can easily reduce Tokyo itself into a gathering of smaller villages anchored around major railway stations. Indeed, these stations are helpful for understanding Tokyo's layout, which doesn't have a central urban core.

Most of Tokyo's smaller "villages" lie on a circular rail line called Yamanote-sen, or Yamanote Line. There are 30 stations on the Yamanote and it takes about an hour to make the complete loop, actually an oval in shape. Whether on the Yamanote or one of the numerous other train and subway lines crisscrossing the city, most of Tokyo is accessible by one station or another, by one train or subway line, or many.

Roughly, Tokyoites consider the areas of Ginza, Hibiya, Marunouchi, Nihom-bashi and Yurakucho to encompass the very centre of the city – it's here that you will find some of the city's more expensive hotels, as well as Tokyo Station, the Imperial Palace and its vast grounds, and some of the most upmarket shopping and dining options in town. Moving northeast from here, but still in the larger central area, are the Akihabara and Kanda areas, and further on from them come Ueno and

Enjoying the sunshine in Ueno Park.

Asakusa, the point at which the centre becomes the "northeast" or "east end" (depending on who you ask) and Tokyo begins to reveal a more down-to-earth, traditionally working-class side – a part of town the Japanese call *shita-machi* (literally 'low city'). Following the Sumida River south from Asakusa comes Ryogoku, on the Sumida's east bank, a part of Tokyo's *shitamachi* known for its sumo connections. After Ryogoku the Sumida passes Nihom-bashi to its west and then begins to bend southwest, skirting the Tsukiji

Main attractions

Imperial Palace
Ginza
Akihabara
Korakuen
Ryogoku and Kiyosumi
Asakusa
Roppongi
Shibuya
Meiji-jingu
Shinjuku

Map on page 142

The Imperial Palace.

and Tsukishima districts before reaching the modern Odaiba and opening out into Tokyo Bay.

Heading west from the Imperial Palace grounds, Tokyo shows its modern sides – both brash and cultured. Here, Shinjuku is the epitome of a modern, thriving Asian city, mixing neon lights and skyscrapers with crowded, energetic streets. Shinjuku is home to the Tokyo Metropolitan Government, as well as the city's biggest red-light district, numerous department stores, Japan's best-known gay district, a Koreatown, and so much more. Just a few stations away on the Yamanote Line, Shibuya and Harajuku are colourful and youthful, while, also in the west, Omotesando and Roppongi represent cool, contemporary Tokyo like nowhere else – here it's all sleek design, great restaurants and cool cafés, hip boutiques and fashion houses.

It is something of a travel writing cliché to describe a city through its contrasts, or to mention how traditional elements of a city sit beside modern. But in Tokyo's case, that's what really does define the city. Walk 10 minutes from the Imperial Palace, for example, and you'll be surrounded by high-end European fashion houses and expensive department stores in Ginza. After a visit to Meiji-jingu and its sprawling park land, you are just a few minutes' walk from the teen fashion and cosplay stores (where fans can buy the outfits of their favourite manga characters) that cram the packed Takeshita street in Harajuku. Here glistening skyscrapers really do tower over centuries-old shrines, and as jumbled and chaotic as it can be for the senses, the city wouldn't feel right any other way. There really is nowhere else on earth quite like Tokyo. Today, the city is looking forward to the future and for ways to speed up progress as it gears up to host the 2020 Olympic Games.

CENTRAL TOKYO

IMPERIAL PALACE

In the centre of Tokyo is the **Imperial Palace**, or **Kokyo** ❶ (http://sankan.kunai-cho.go.jp), a functioning palace where

the Emperor and his family reside. Much of the grounds – including the palace itself – are closed to the public and secluded behind massive stone walls, old trees and Edo Period moats. Exceptions are the Emperor's birthday, 23 December (9.30–11.20am) and 2 January (9.30am–2.10pm), when the imperial family gives a public appearance and waves to the crowds from a balcony in the palace.

Most of the 110-hectare (270-acre) palace complex is forested or given over to private gardens and small ponds. The Showa Emperor (Hirohito), who reigned from 1926 until 1989, was a skilled biologist, and much of the inner garden area is a nature preserve. **Kokyo Gaien** ❷, the palace's outer garden to the southeast, is an expansive area of green and impeccably sculpted pine trees planted in 1889. A large, gravel-covered area leads to the famous postcard scene of **Niju-bashi** ❸, a distinctive bridge across an inner moat and one of the most widely recognised landmarks in Japan. Tourists come here by the busload for a group portrait in front of the bridge (bashi) and moat. Niju-bashi is both elegant and a functional entrance – the main gate – into the palace grounds. If you visit on 23 December or 2 January, this is where you enter. Behind is **Fushimi-yagura**, a lookout turret of the original Edo castle. Parts of the outer grounds were unpleasant places in 1945 immediately after the Emperor Hirohito announced Japan's surrender on the radio. Numerous loyal soldiers, refusing to admit defeat or surrender to the Allies, disembowelled themselves outside the palace.

Visitors are also permitted in the **Kokyo Higashi Gyoen** ❹ (tel: 03-5223-8071; http://sankan.kunaicho.go.jp; Mar–mid-Apr and Sept 9am–5pm, mid-Apr–Aug until 6pm, Oct until 4.30pm, Nov–Feb until 4pm), the East Imperial Garden of the palace, which can be entered through Ote-mon, Hirakawa-mon and Kitahanebashi-mon, three of the eight gates (mon) into the palace grounds. Inside are remains of the defences of Edo-jo, the shogunate's castle (jo), and the foundations of the

The Yasukuni shrine in Chiyoda is dedicated to those who died fighting on behalf of the Emperor of Japan.

◷ FROM EDO CASTLE TO IMPERIAL PALACE

The original Edo Castle, built by the Tokugawa shoguns, was an epic construction project of its time. It was built of granite and basaltic rocks quarried in the Izu Peninsula, 100km (60 miles) south. Several thousand boats made the two-week round trip. Offloaded near Kanda to the north, the stones were dragged on sleds by oxen and men provided by the shogun's warlords. In all, the castle took 40 years to build. That work, however, was soon lost: less than two decades after completion in 1636, much of the castle was reduced to ashes in a fire.

Of the original 21 defensive guard towers, or yagura, three still stand, including the Fushimi-yagura near Niju-bashi. Unfortunately, nothing substantial remains of the old Edo Castle itself, except for the three turrets and the donjon foundations, not to mention the moats and gates.

The Meiji emperor chose the shogunal castle site to be the new imperial residence in 1868 and moved there from Kyoto a year later, the city that until then had been the imperial capital for more than a millennium. The new Imperial Palace was completed in 1889 of exquisitely designed wood, but, like Edo Castle before it, it wasn't to last: in 1945 the Meiji palace was destroyed in Allied bombing raids. The current palace, still home to the imperial family, is a post-war construction.

castle's donjon, the primary lookout tower of the shogun's residence.

At the northern part of the old castle grounds in **Kitanomaru-koen** is the **Kokuritsu Kindai Bijutsukan** ❺ (National Museum of Modern Art; www.momat.go.jp; Tue–Thu, Sun 10am–5pm, Fri, Sat until 8pm). The modern building displays fine examples of Japan's contemporary artists, many of whom studied in Europe in the 20th century, in well-presented galleries. In the northern corner of Kitanomaru-koen is the octagonal martial-arts hall known as the **Nippon Budokan**. Built to host Olympic judo events in 1964, its gold topknot a gesture to the hairstyles of sumo wrestlers, the building is also used as a concert venue.

YASUKUNI SHRINE

West from Kitanomaru-koen, Yasukuni Avenue *(dori)* leads to **Yasukuni-jinja** ❻. What is said to be Japan's largest torii – eight storeys high, made of high-tension steel plates and weighing 100 tons – boldly announces the shrine. Its entrance nipping the

The Sumida River.

northern tip of the Imperial Palace grounds, this Shinto shrine is Japan's most controversial. Proponents say it honours those who died for Japan and the emperor; opponents say it glorifies Japanese aggression and honours convicted war criminals. Pinched between the two extremes are politicians, who must decide whether or not to attend annual ceremonies at the shrine. When a prime minister does visit, governments throughout Asia respond in loud disapproval. When a prime minister doesn't, Japan's vocal and politically influential rightists do likewise.

The souls of more than 2.5 million Japanese soldiers killed between 1868 (the shrine was founded in 1869) and World War II are enshrined at Yasukuni (literally peaceful country; www.yasukuni.or.jp; daily 6am–6pm, Nov–Feb until 5pm; free). In the shrine's archives, the names, dates and places of death for each soldier are recorded. The **Yushukan** (War Memorial Museum; daily 9am–4.30pm, until 9pm during Mitama Festival), part of Yasukuni-jinja, includes among its 100,000 pieces

⊘ BRIDGES WORTH CROSSING

How grateful I feel/As I step crisply over/The frost on the bridge – Matsuo Basho. When Shin Ohashi, or New Great Bridge, was completed in the capital of Edo in 1693, the great poet Matsuo Basho was sufficiently elated to compose the above haiku. Like many Edo Period writers and artists, Basho was a great admirer of the new bridges that were springing up across the capital.

Tokyo's Sumida River provides the setting for what is, perhaps, one of the most interesting concentrations of bridges in Japan. Each bridge has its own identity, and, if the woodblock prints and gazetteers of the time are to be believed, major bridges provided common, unlicensed space for all manner of activities, from full-moon viewing, freak shows and archery (read "prostitution") tents, to the shackling and public display of criminals.

The painted girders and bolts of the older bridges that have survived earthquakes, intense volumes of traffic and the hellfire of war, are reassuringly durable presences amidst the accelerated confusion of today's city. Sakurabashi, the last bridge of note, is an example of how such structures can have a benevolent effect on the environment. In 1985, river-facing Sumida and Taito wards constructed the bridge exclusively for the use of pedestrians.

samurai armour and a rocket-propelled kamikaze winged bomb.

On a more contemporary note, the **Tokyo Anime Center** (www.animecenter.jp; Tue–Sun 11am–7pm) in the DNP Plaza, across the bridge to the west, has exhibitions and displays on everything anime.

MARUNOUCHI AND TOKYO STATION'S SOUTHWEST SIDE

Directly east from the Imperial Palace and Kokyo Gaien is the **Marunouchi district** ⓐ, once an inlet of Tokyo Bay. Atop this landfill of Marunouchi – meaning "inside the wall" of the Edo castle fortifications – an exclusive residential area for Tokugawa samurai lords was created in the early 17th century. Known as Daimyo Koji, or the Little Lanes of the Great Lords, Marunouchi served not only as a buffer between the shogun's castle and the outside world of commoners but also permitted the shogun to keep an eye on his provincial warlords, whom he required to live in Edo on a rotating basis. Today it is filled with corporate headquarters and government offices.

A wide boulevard slices through these corporate buildings from the grounds of the Imperial Palace to **Tokyo-eki** ⓑ (Tokyo Station). While not Japan's busiest station – Shinjuku holds that honour – Tokyo Station is nonetheless sizeable, with 10 raised island platforms serving 20 tracks side by side, including the terminus for the *shinkansen* or bullet train. Beneath the main station are additional platforms for more trains and JR lines. The Marunouchi side of the station is fronted by the original station, built in 1914 of red brick in a European style. Air raids in 1945 damaged the station; an extensive renovation, completed in 2012, restored it to its former grandeur. Inside the concourse is the **Tokyo Station Gallery** (www.ejrcf.or.jp; Tue–Sun 10am–6pm, Fri until 8pm), which puts on exhibitions mostly comprised of 20th-century Japanese artists.

The red-brick facade of the station is surrounded by a grove of modern skyscrapers. The reconstructed and extended **Marunouchi Building** (Maru Biru, as it is commonly called), one of Tokyo's mini-city complexes, immediately catches the eye. Its gourmet food basement and four shopping levels attract large numbers of Japanese tourists from the countryside. The views of the palace grounds from the dozen or so restaurants on its 35th and 36th floors are especially good, as are the restaurants themselves. Maru Biru is the most visible example of the trendy makeover Marunouchi has recently been undergoing. Another is just south at the **Mitsubishi Ichigo-kan Museum** (http://mimt.jp; Tue–Sun 10am–6pm, Fri until 9pm), opened in 2010 in a Josiah Conder-designed red-brick building dating from the 1890s. The museum exhibits an eclectic mix of art, with past exhibitions having included French Impressionists and Japanese paper stencils.

Two blocks south of the Marunouchi Building, on the ground floor of the

Part of the Tokyo Station building.

Shin-Tokyo Building, is the **Tourist Information Centre** (daily 9am–5pm; tel: 03-3201-3331). If you are expecting to travel around Japan, visit this centre for extensive information on everything from walking tours through Tokyo to lodging in Okinawa. The staff speak English. Adjacent is the **Tokyo International Forum ⑨** (www.t-i-forum.co.jp), an echoing complex of concert and exhibition halls that is worth visiting just to check out Rafael Vinoly's sweeping steel and glass design, created to give the impression of a sailboat. On the first and third Sundays of each month the Forum is also the site of a great antiques market. South again are elevated train tracks extending from **Yurakucho-eki ⑩** (Yurakucho Station), constructed in 1910; the *shinkansen* and Yamanote-sen trains snake along the overhead tracks. Beside the station is a giant BIC Camera home electronics store selling everything from the latest camera gear to massage chairs. An elevated expressway over Harumi-dori defines the boundary between Ginza and Yurakucho.

Tokyo Station.

Towering on the opposite side of the expressway is the tall, curving exterior of the Hankyu department store, anchored at the ground by a musical clock and a hard-to-miss (or ignore) police box.

Even further southwards, along Hibiya-dori, is the towering **Imperial Hotel ⑪** (Teikoku Hoteru). The first Imperial Hotel opened in 1890. Its modest structure was later replaced by a wonderful Frank Lloyd Wright design; the day after it opened to the public in 1923, the Great Kanto Earthquake hit Tokyo. The hotel was one of the few buildings to escape destruction. The Wright building was replaced by the current structure in 1970. Across from the Imperial Hotel, **Hibiya-koen ⑫** (Hibiya Park) was Japan's first European-style plaza, opened in 1903. It quickly became a popular venue for rallies and demonstrations against rises in rice prices during the early 1900s. Nowadays, especially at weekends, it's a popular venue for all sorts of happier events – from annual fun runs to train festivals.

NIHOM-BASHI

Extending from the **Yaesu** central exit of Tokyo Station is Yaesu-dori, which intersects the major arteries of Chuo-dori and Showa-dori, running south to nearby Ginza and north to Ueno. On the corner of Yaesu and Chuo-dori, the **Artizon Museum** (www.artizon.museum), re-opened in January 2020, houses an important collection of European paintings. Highlighting the Impressionists and later artists like Picasso and Van Gogh, it also includes the work of Meiji-era Japanese painters. Moving north from here, Chuo-dori crosses Nihombashi-gawa over **Nihom-bashi ⑬** (Nihon Bridge). The ugly elevated Shuto Expressway directly above was erected for the 1964 Tokyo Olympics. Both the concrete-lined river and expressway serve to diminish the significance of the original 1603 arched wooden bridge, which was the centre of Edo Period Tokyo and the zero point for the five main roads leading out of Edo to the rest of Japan. The present stone bridge dates from 1911. With a new proposal to bury the expressway, its ornate dragons and pillars could soon be liberated from the eyesore above it. Just one block southwest of the bridge is the altogether more pleasant **Tako no Hakubutsukan** (Kite Museum; www. tako.gr.jp; Mon–Sat 11am–5pm). Over 2,000 kites cover the walls and ceiling of this cramped museum, many displaying Japanese motifs: manga characters, images from famous woodblock prints, armour-bearing warriors and depictions of Mount Fuji. Also in Nihom-bashi are the original branches of the Takashimaya (www.takashimaya.co.jp) and Mitsukoshi department stores, both stately affairs.

GINZA

Moving southwards on Chuo-dori from the Artizon Museum leads to Ginza, probably the most famous part of Tokyo. Ginza derives its name from *gin*, or silver. Japan once used three different coinage systems, each based upon silver, gold and copper. Tokugawa Ieyasu decided to simplify the system to only silver, and in 1612 he relocated the official mint from the countryside to Ginza. Two centuries later, the mint was once again shifted, to Nihom-bashi, but the name of Ginza stayed.

Ever since then, Ginza has always been associated in some way or another with money, or rather an excess of it. During the super-heated bubble economy of the late 1980s, for example, land in Ginza became the most expensive real estate in the world. Today, the boutiques and department stores that make Ginza Tokyo's most renowned shopping area are some of the priciest going, stocking the most recognisable high-end fashion brands. Likewise, the hostess clubs here, which boomed in the 1980s, are where seriously well-heeled businessmen can still drop hundreds of thousands of yen in a night on champagne and flirting.

Not that Ginza is always prohibitively expensive these days. Many of the

High-end designer stores in Ginza.

better restaurants in the area (and it has some of Tokyo's best) are no more expensive than in Omotesando or Roppongi, and you will find places to suit all budgets. Even the shopping has become cheaper in recent years – rubbing shoulders with the likes of Cartier and Louis Vuitton are affordable and extremely popular stores such as Gap, Uniqlo, Muji and H&M.

To get your bearings in Ginza head to the Mitsukoshi department store that anchors **Ginza 4-chome** ⓮, where Chuo-dori intersects Harumi-dori, the second main avenue. (Most Tokyo districts are subdivided into *chome*; Ginza has eight.) This intersection, **Ginza Crossing**, is the central point of Ginza. Head in any direction from here, on Chuo-dori, Harumi-dori or the many backstreets that shoot off the main avenues, and you will find the three things that define Ginza: places to eat, places to drink and even more places to shop.

ALONG HARUMI-DORI

Harumi-dori extends from Hibiya-koen back down through Ginza 4-chome and

Tsukiji and across the Sumida-gawa, Tokyo's barely accessible river (*gawa* or *kawa*). Down Harumi-dori, just past Showa-dori is the site of the **Kabuki-za** ⓯ (Kabuki Theatre; www.kabuki-bito. jp), founded in 1889. The theatre reopened in 2013 after extensive restoration, and now it boasts an English translation captioning system. Kabuki performances are staged twice daily (usually 11am and 4.30pm). Single act tickets are recommended for those who just want to get a general feel of kabuki. Although these are available only on the day of the performance and one person can buy just a single ticket, you will almost certainly have to queue as they remain very popular with tourists.

Closer towards the Sumida-gawa is **Tsukiji** ⓰, once home to a legendary wholesale fish market (*chuo oroshiuri ichiba*), now moved to a new home in Toyosu. *Tsukiji* means, simply, built land. As with Marunouchi, another landfill area near the Imperial Palace, the newly created land provided space for samurai estates, although of lower ranking than Marunouchi. In the mid-1800s, a part of

New Toyosu Fish Market.

G-19

大物冷凍

Tsukiji was set aside for foreigners and a hotel was constructed, which later burned to the ground.

The Tsukiji Fish Market was one of the most famous markets in the world and its early-morning tuna auction among Tokyo's prime attractions (for those willing to get up early enough). October 2018 saw the market relocate, in a long-speculated and controversial move, to Toyosu, but the Tuskiji Outer Market (www.tsukiji.or.jp; Mon–Sat 9am–2pm, many shops closed Wed) remains worthy of a visit. While the old wholesale auction provided visitors with a theatrical spectacle, it wasn't much of a shopping experience, whereas the new market is very much aimed at the everyday consumer – food stalls allow you to try the famous tuna in bite-size sushi or sashimi form, along with *nerimono* (fish balls), *tamagoyaki* (omelettes) and various other delicious morsels. Other shops sell beautiful knives and kitchenware, glazed bowls, clothing, and paper and wood products, while there are tea rooms, coffee shops and sit-down restaurants where you can take a breather. Some of the staff speak English, but this is not a place to haggle.

KANDA

If there is a book, however old and in whatever language, that seems unattainable, it can be found in **Kanda** ⓱, especially around Jimbocho Station. There are stores here specialising in art books, second-hand books, comic books – in English, French, German and Russian. The bookshops have been in Kanda since the 1880s, nearly as long as the nearby universities. Many of the early book printers established their shops in Kanda, followed later by several of the most famous publishers in Japan.

A short walk north past Ochanomizu Station and across the Kanda River are two important shrines. **Kanda Myojin**, a vividly coloured and decorated shrine dedicated to the rebel general Taira no Masakado, is a lively venue for Shinto-style weddings, rituals, cultural performances and one of the city's main festivals, the Kanda Matsuri. Continue

An electronics store in Akihabara.

up the slope to **Yushima Tenjin**, the city's foremost shrine of learning, a place much frequented by students supplicating the shrine's tutelary spirit for favourable exam results. The grounds of the shrine are a popular spot for plum-blossom viewing in mid-February.

AKIHABARA

The neighbourhood of **Akihabara** epitomises the old Edo tradition of merchants or craftsmen of a particular commodity congregating together. Akihabara is primarily devoted to the sales of all things electrical and electronic, with hundreds of shops vying for attention in a compact area around Chuo-dori. One of the biggest and most impressive stores is the giant branch of Yodobashi Camera (it sells all sort of home electronics, not just cameras; www.yodobashi.com) just east of Akihabara Station.

While Akihabara's "electric town" has its roots in post-war black-market trading, a more recent addition to Akihabara in the last decade or so has been the number of stores catering to Japan's legion of game, anime- and manga-obsessed otaku (geeks). Mixed in with the electrical and electronics stores are several big video arcades and lots of comic and DVD stores (and be warned, some sell sexual and violent material you wouldn't want kids to see), as well as places to buy cartoon-character costumes and cafés (called "maid cafés") where otaku are served fairly bland café fare by young women dressed in French maid outfits. To get a feel for that side of Akihabara, head to the large **Donkihote** store (www.donki.com; daily 9am–5am) on Sotokanda.

West of Akihabara, next to the Kanda-Jimbocho book quarter, the district of Ochanomizu is transected by the Kanda River. A minute to the north of the waterway is **Yushima Seido** (www.seido.or.jp; Mon–Fri 9.30am–5pm, Sat–Sun from 10am, winter until 4pm; free), an intriguing former academy and one of the few Confucian temples left in Japan. Ochanomizu's association with religion and learning, now obscured by a prevalence of ski shops

Girls posing as maids for a game launch in the Akihabara district of the city.

and stores selling musical instruments, can be sensed two blocks south of the temple, with the appearance of **Nikolai-do ⑲** (Nikolai Cathedral), a Russian Orthodox church, designed by British architect Josiah Conder in 1891. The building lost the top of its dome in the 1923 earthquake, but this has been replaced with a smaller one. Look out for the cathedral's beautiful stained-glass windows.

Meiji University has several academic buildings along Ochanomizu's main street, as well as the superb **Meiji Daigaku Kokogaku Hakubutsu-kan** (Archaeological Museum of Meiji University; www.meiji.ac.jp/museum; Mon–Sat 10am–5pm; free), housing a collection of objects found on digs around Japan sponsored by the university's archaeological faculty.

THEME PARKS AND GARDENS

Heading west along the river or taking the overground Sobu Line one station on, the Suidobashi district leads to a popular amusement area catering to all tastes. Most visible of these is the **Tokyo Dome City Amusement Park** and **La Qua hot spring spa complex**, sharing the same grounds. Among the highlights of the combined theme parks are a freefall parachute ride and a highly original roller coaster that passes over the rooftops and between the buildings here, offering at the same time a bird's-eye view of the city. Next to the park is the **Tokyo Domu ⑳** (Tokyo Dome, also called the Big Egg; www.tokyo-dome.co.jp), a venue used primarily for the Yomiuri Giants baseball matches, but also for major concerts, exhibitions and trade shows.

Easily approached by following directions in English and Japanese, the **Koishikawa Korakuen** (daily 9am–5pm), one of the city's finest Edo Period stroll gardens, stands in the shadow of the dome. The oldest garden in Tokyo, it was intended for amusement as much as aesthetic contemplation,

incorporating scenes from the Chinese classics as well as miniaturised Japanese landscapes.

Another generous expanse of green in this congested part of the city, the **Koishikawa Shokubutsu-en** (Koishikawa Botanical Garden; Tue–Sun 9am–4.30pm), lies to the north, easily accessed from Hakusan Station on the Mita Line and within the same Bunkyo Ward area. This research garden passed into the hands of the Tokyo University faculty in 1877 and over 100 species of herbs are grown here, amid trees and ponds.

EAST OF THE SUMIDA RIVER

East of Akihabara and on the other side of the Sumida-gawa, the area known as **Ryogoku** is the site of Tokyo's sumo arena, **Kokugikan ㉑**. A lot of very large men live in Ryogoku – it is the home of many of the sumo *beya*, or stables, as the training centres/dormitories for the rikishi (wrestlers) are called.

Behind the Kokugikan is the **Edo Tokyo Museum ㉒** (www.edo-tokyo-museum.or.jp; Tue–Sun 9.30am–5.30pm,

Central Tokyo in summer.

Sat until 7.30pm), a spectacular hall that encompasses a massive reconstruction of a part of *shitamachi* Edo from the 19th century. It is like walking onto the set of a samurai drama; there is even a lifelike dog relieving himself by the guard tower. Every 20 minutes, the lighting cycles through night and day. There are intricately constructed models of villages and a life-size reconstruction of Nihom-bashi, the Edo Period bridge. It has always been one of the finest museums in Japan, well planned and meticulously thought out. It still stays on top of museum trends – it has several new interactive exhibits and two floors cover the history of the 21st century.

Several other notable sights are located within this area, east of the Sumida River. Directly south along Kiyosumi Avenue, a few blocks in from the river, the intimate human scale of the exhibits and reconstructed buildings at the **Fukagawa Edo Museum** (www.kcf.or.jp/fukagawa; daily 9.30am–5pm, closed second and fourth Mon each month) is appealing after the massive Tokyo-Edo Museum. Opposite the museum, the **Kiyosumi Teien** (daily 9am–4.30pm) is a distinctive and very spacious Edo Period garden replete with a central pond set with miniature islands. The garden is especially worth a visit in November to take in the autumnal colours, and in June, when its small iris garden comes into bloom. South again from here, towards Kiba Station, is the **Museum of Contemporary Art** (www.mot-art-museum. jp; Tue–Sun 10am–6pm), a cavernous concrete building set beside pleasant parkland, which displays a mixture of works by contemporary Japanese and overseas artists.

NORTHERN AND EASTERN TOKYO

AROUND UENO

North of Tokyo Station and Akihabara, exactly eight minutes on the Yamanote train, is **Ueno-eki ㉓** (Ueno Station). It was once the commoners' part of town, in what was called *shitamachi* (literally the "low city"). Nowadays there's an aspect of urban life around Ueno not typically noticeable in Japan – the hundreds of homeless men and women who live in Ueno-koen.

Running parallel with elevated rail tracks leading south from Ueno Station is the bustling **Ameya Yokocho** (or Ameyoko; www.ameyoko.net; store times vary, but typically daily 10am–7pm) street market, which, like Akihabara's electrical stores, has its roots in postwar black-market trading. Although some people go a bit far in calling this one of Asia's great bazaars, the long, narrow street is undoubtedly one of the liveliest markets in Japan; the stalls and vocal traders here deal in everything from fresh fish and vegetables to Chinese medicines and cheap fashions.

West of the station, **Ueno-koen** (Ueno Park) is Tokyo's most distinctly park-like park: sprawling grounds with trees, flocks of scrounging pigeons,

Giants baseball team advertising posters inside the Tokyo Dome.

monuments and statues, homeless Japanese, a zoo, a big pond with lilies and waterfowl, and national museums. It's not quite as tidy and pristine as one might expect in Japan.

In the spring, Ueno-koen is cherished amongst Japanese for its blossoming cherry trees. The idea of blossom-viewing – *hanami*, a tradition extending back centuries – sounds peaceful, but in fact it is often a drunken and crowded party with few serene moments.

The **Tosho-gu** ㉔, a shrine adjacent to a five-storey pagoda, was established in 1627 (the present buildings date from a 1651 renovation) by a warlord on his own estate to honour the first Tokugawa shogun, Tokugawa Ieyasu. The path to Tosho-gu (literally, Illuminator of the East) is lined with dozens of large, symbolic stone or copper free-standing lanterns, all donated by warlords from throughout the land to cultivate a little merit with the shogun. Although not as embellished as it was in the Edo Period, the main shrine building is still a magnificent,

ornate building. The outer hall features murals painted by the famous Edo artist Kano Tanyu. Also interesting is the Chinese-style Kara-mon, a gate decorated with dragons that are meant to be ascending to and descending from heaven. It's said that the dragons slither over to the park's pond, Shinobazu-no-ike, under the cover of night to drink the water.

Shinobazu-no-ike (Shinobazu Pond) was once an inlet and is now a pond *(ike)* dense with lotus plants. A small peninsula juts into the pond with a Buddhist temple to Benten – goddess of mercy – perched on the end. A promenade follows the pond's 2km (1.2-mile) circumference. The **Shitamachi Fuzoku Shiryokan** ㉕ (Shitamachi Museum; www.taitocity.net/zaidan/shitamachi; Tue–Sun 9.30am–4.30pm), near the pond at the park's south entrance, is a hands-on exhibit of Edo commoners' daily life in the *shitamachi*, as this part of Edo Tokyo was known.

The **Kokuritsu Seiyo Bijutsukan** ㉖ (National Museum of Western Art; www.nmwa.go.jp; Tue–Thu 9.30am–5.30pm,

⊙ **Tip**

In late autumn and winter, the paths around Shinobazu Pond provide an earthy setting in which to sample *oden* (fishcakes, fried tofu and vegetables cooked in broth). Served from carts with seating around hot cauldrons, these warming snacks are best washed down with a glass of beer or sake.

Sumo practice tournament at the Kokugikan arena.

Fri–Sat until 8pm) has a collection of nearly 1,000 pieces, ranging from the Renaissance to the contemporary and including Gauguin, Rubens and Jackson Pollock, not to mention several sculptures by Rodin and a sizeable collection of 19th-century French art. The **Tokyo Kokuritsu Hakubutsu-kan** (Tokyo National Museum; www.tnm.jp; Tue–Sun at least 9.30am–5pm, but closing times vary, Fri–Sat often until 9pm) offers a superbly displayed collection of Asian art and archaeology, covering every period of Japanese history from the Jomon to the present. The main hall, holding the extensive Japanese collection, dates from 1937. Arching over the outside entrance to the museum grounds is an immense samurai-estate gate.

A 10-minute walk north of the museum following the walls of Kan'ei-ji, a temple established symbolically to protect the inauspicious northern entry point into Edo, takes you to **Yanaka**, a charming old quarter of winding lanes, temples, traditional shops, bathhouses, small art galleries,

Browsing the stalls on Ameyoko Street.

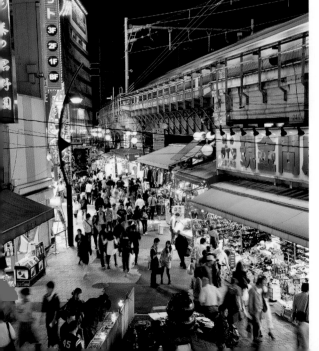

old wooden houses and a leafy, moss-covered cemetery full of time-eroded Buddhist statuary. West of Ueno is the most prestigious of Japanese universities, **Tokyo Daigaku** (Tokyo University), founded by imperial decree in the 1870s. The campus, more popularly known as Todai, was built on the estate of the powerful Maeda feudal lords after being transplanted from Kanda in the 1880s.

ASAKUSA

From the mid-1800s until World War II, **Asakusa** was a cultural nucleus of theatre and literature, and of cuisine and the sensual delights. The area's cultural and social flowering began with exile – first with the banishment to Asakusa of the Yoshiwara (the licensed prostitution district) in the 1600s, and then later with that of theatre, especially kabuki, in the 1800s.

The people of Asakusa were known as Edokko, or people of Edo. Asakusa dripped with *iki*, a sense of style and urbane polish, and with *inase*, or gallantry. It was the place to be seen in Edo Tokyo, reaching its heyday in the 1800s.

Anchoring Asakusa was **Senso-ji**, or **Asakusa Kannon** (www.senso-ji.jp; grounds 24hr, Main Hall 6am–5pm), perhaps the oldest Buddhist temple in the region and a draw for people from around Japan who brought with them spending money to make Asakusa prosper. Old places always start with a legend. Asakusa's legend has it that Senso-ji was founded in AD 628 when two fishermen netted a small statue of Kannon, the deity of mercy. A temple was built by the village leader to house it.

The south entrance to the temple, on Asakusa-dori, is a large gate called Kaminari-mon, or Thunder Gate. Here begins Nakamise-dori (literally, inside the shops), where two rows of red buildings funnel temple-goers northwards through a souvenir arcade before spilling out onto the temple grounds. Just east of here is the small

Hanayashiki (www.hanayashiki.net; daily, typically 10am–6pm, but times vary), Japan's oldest amusement park. A far cry from anything Disney has to offer (and some would say better for it), the park includes a sedate 1950s roller coaster and many other fun retro rides.

Other notable attractions include the interactive **Taiko-kan** (Drum Museum; Wed–Sun 10am–5pm), with dozens of different kinds of Japanese and other drums. It sits at the intersection of Kaminari-dori and Kokusai-dori, above a shop selling Buddhist and Shinto paraphernalia.

A few blocks east of the museum, the Nimi Building, topped with a giant chef's head and hat, comes into view. This announces the entrance to **Kappabashi Dogugai** ㉙ (Kappabashi Kitchenware Town), where restaurant and kitchen equipment is sold wholesale. Of main interest to foreign visitors are Kappabashi's plastic food samples of the type seen on display in restaurant windows, such as sushi platters, and plates of spaghetti with a fork suspended in the air.

In the other direction, east of Senso-ji, is the **Sumida-gawa** (Sumida River), which empties into Tokyo Bay. The exit for the Ginza Line, Tokyo's first subway line, which opened in 1927, surfaces near the Azuma-bashi (Azuma Bridge). Look across the river and you will see one of the most distinctive views of modern Tokyo. Towering 634 metres (2,080ft) high, the **Tokyo Sky Tree** ㉚ (observation deck open daily 8am–10pm; www.tokyo-skytree.jp) is a communications tower, completed in 2012, which also doubles as a tourist attraction – mainly because of the observation deck it has 450 metres (1,475ft) up, but also by virtue of being the world's second tallest structure. Completing the view is the head office of **Asahi Breweries**. Supposedly designed to look like a glass of golden beer complete with frothy head and a bead of foam running down the glass, locals have instead taken to calling it *unchi biru* (turd building) because the bead of foam looks like something a dog might produce.

The giant lantern at Senso-ji.

⊙ Fact

Roppongi Crossing is now one of the world's busiest junctions. However, during the Allied occupation, it was, as Robert Whiting says in his book *Tokyo Underworld*, occupied by "a police box, a small bookstore, and two vacant lots. At night, the surrounding side streets were so deserted that residents spoke of seeing ghosts".

The Tokyo Skytree.

SOUTHERN TOKYO

ROPPONGI AND MINATO

In the lower middle of the oval defined by the Yamanote-sen and just to the southwest of the Imperial Palace is an area favoured by Tokyo's expatriate community: **Minato-ku**, a Tokyo ward *(ku)* made up of Minamiaoyama, Akasaka, Roppongi, Nishiazabu and Hiroo. The area is peppered with embassies and high-priced expatriate (and company-subsidised) housing – US$10,000 a month rent is not unusual – and liberally spiced with trendy shops, cafés, bars and restaurants.

Up on a hill, **Roppongi** ㉛ is the heart of the area's social life and nightlife. Its main avenues are bright and loud, but don't confuse the activity here with the sex trade of Shinjuku's Kabukicho. A few of the bars and nightclubs aside, Roppongi is mainly a place for upscale food and drinks.

East of Roppongi along the road towards the Imperial Palace, the **Ark Hills** complex of offices, apartments and stores is the work of modernising construction mogul Mori Taikichiro. Riding the real-estate boom of the 1970s and 1980s, he owned more than 80 buildings in central Tokyo and was considered the world's richest private citizen at his death in 1993.

Pressing west along Roppongi-dori from the main crossing, the gigantic **Roppongi Hills** ㉜ is another Mori Corporation project, one of the most publicised in Japan. Towering and brash, the 16-hectare (40-acre) site, with its restaurants, nine-screen Toho cinema, public amphitheatre, apartments, Grand Hyatt hotel, and over 200 shops and interconnecting walkways, is undeniably impressive. A first-rate modern gallery, the **Mori Art Museum** (www.mori.art.museum; Wed–Mon 10am–10pm, Tue 10am–5pm), located on the 52nd and 53rd floors, holds temporary exhibitions. Superb views of the city can be had from the observation deck (Tokyo City View; http://tcv.roppongihills.com; daily 10am–11pm, Fri–Sat until 1am), adjacent to the gallery. There is also an open-air rooftop terrace on the 54th floor, which offers visitors views from 238 metres (780 ft) above the ground (Sky Deck; daily 11am–8pm).

Check the horizon to the south, towards the area known as Shiba: the red-and-white **Tokyo Tower** ㉝ (www.tokyotower.co.jp; daily 9am–11pm) juts skywards, looking industrial and out of place. Finished in 1958, its primary purpose was to broadcast television signals. Subsequent lyrical allusions to the Eiffel Tower or urban elegance were fabrications of creative writing. It's a less than graceful projection into the skyline – 333 metres (1,093ft) high – but views from the observation deck at 250 metres (820ft) are excellent.

Competing with Roppongi Hills, in fact right across the road from it, is the newer **Tokyo Midtown** (www.tokyo-midtown.com) ㉞ complex, built by the Mitsui Fudosan real-estate development company. Midtown's 248-metre (813ft) main tower is the most visible of its

five buildings, which between them are home to 73,000 sq metres (785,000 sq ft) of restaurants and shops. Of special note are Midtown's art venues: first, the **Suntory Museum of Art** (www.suntory.com/sma; Wed–Mon 10am–6pm, Fri–Sat until 8pm, closed for renovations until mid-May 2020) and its exhibitions of traditional Japanese artworks; second, Tadao Ando and Issey Miyake's **21_21 Design Sight** (www.2121designsight.jp; Wed–Mon 11am–8pm), a slick gallery and workshop focusing on modern art and design.

Adding to Roppongi's art credentials is the magnificent **National Art Center** ③⑤ (www.nact.jp; Wed–Mon 10am–6pm, Fri until 8pm). With 14,000 sq metres (150,000 sq ft) of exhibition space, but no permanent exhibits of its own, the centre has a constantly changing line-up of modern and traditional art on display.

TOKYO BAYSIDE

Tokyo-wan (Tokyo Bay) has shrunk over the centuries due to extensive landfill. The shoguns did it for the housing of their samurai, while politicians have done it in the past decades for glory and political favour. **Odaiba Island** is extremely popular with young people who flock to shopping and amusement treats like **Decks Tokyo Beach** (www.odaiba-decks.com); **Joyopolis** (http://tokyo-joypolis.com), a virtual-reality amusement park; and **Venus Fort** (www.venusfort.co.jp), a bizarre indoor shopping street with over 160 shops under an artificial sky that changes from sunny, to grey, to violet and stormy depending on the time of day and whims of its programmers. There's also **Palette Town** (www.palette-town.com), a leisure centre that includes a giant wheel and the stunning **teamLab Borderless** (http://borderless.team-lab.art; Mon–Fri 10am–7pm, Sat–Sun until 9pm), a spectacular art installation, opened in 2018, where mercurial, technicolour projections dance aross the gallery's surfaces.

The island has become an experimental zone for architects. One of the most outstanding designs is the highly visible **Fuji TV Building** ③⑥, a Kenzo Tange design, whose titanium-clad surfaces are connected by "sky corridors" and girders. The blue arch of the **Telecom Centre** is another chunk of postmodernism, but one that pales against the extraordinary **Tokyo Big Sight** ③⑦ (www.bigsight.jp), a convention centre and exhibition hall consisting of four inverted pyramids standing on a narrow base, which seems to defy gravity.

A curious addition to the island's futuristic structures is the **Oedo Onsen Monogatari** ③⑧ (http://daiba.ooedoonsen.jp; daily 11am–9am next day, last entry 7am), a traditional hot-spring bath designed along theme-park lines, where you could easily while away a whole day (or night) soaking in the baths, snacking, drinking and lounging about in a *yukata* (light kimono). Just a short walk from here is the fantastic **Miraikan** (Museum of Emerging Science and Innovation; www.miraikan.jst.go.jp;

Driving through Roppongi Hills.

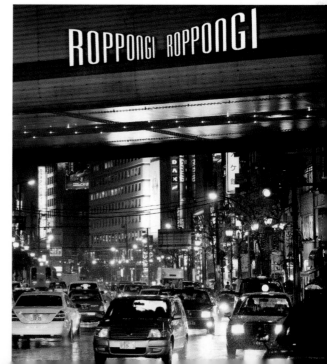

Wed–Mon 10am–5pm), with its robot-led tours of Japanese hi-tech designs. Geo-Cosmos, a high-resolution globe that shows real-time global weather patterns and ocean temperatures, is one of the museum's highlights.

In 2020, the waterfront around Harumi Pier will become home to the **Olympic and Paralympic Village**, a futuristic green town which is to present a showcase of sustainability to the world. A good view of the island and its futuristic constructions can be seen from a monorail that leaves Shimbashi Station for the artificial islands over the **Rainbow Bridge**. Odaiba can be reached on the driverless Yurikamome Line from Shimbashi Station.

WESTERN TOKYO

EBISU, SHIBUYA AND HARAJUKU

One stop south of Shibuya on the Yamanote Line, the expanded and redesigned south side of Ebisu Station is home to **Yebisu Garden Place** (http://gardenplace.jp), an enormous shopping, restaurant, hotel, office and entertainment complex. Located on the site of the old Yebisu Beer Brewery, the **Museum of Yebisu Beer** (www.sapporobeer.jp; Tue–Sun 11am–7pm; free) traces the history of the company, and has several daily tours of the facilities (Japanese only), followed by tastings. On the eastern side of the plaza is the important **Tokyo Photographic Art Museum** (http://topmuseum.jp), the city's foremost exhibition space for photography and video art.

Although many resident foreigners might nominate Roppongi to the east, **Shibuya** is one of the trendiest commercial neighbourhoods in the whole of Tokyo. Roppongi caters to foreigners and has done so with style for decades. Shibuya, on the other hand, caters to Japanese youth with money to spend and style to flaunt. Shibuya was a rural but bustling stop along one of the great highways built during the Tokugawa years and leading from Edo Tokyo. Later, mulberry (for an abortive attempt at silk production) and tea fields surrounded Shibuya's first railway station, which opened in 1885. Several private rail lines opened in the subsequent years, each with its own station. Finally, all the stations were consolidated at the current site of **Shibuya-eki** ③⑨ (Shibuya Station) in 1920. The most popular exit of Shibuya Station, opening to the northwest, is named after a dog who used to wait here for his owner every day at the same time, which he continued to do for nine years after his death. Outside that entrance you will find a statue erected in 1964 to the said dog, an Akita named Hachiko. This is a favourite spot to rendezvous. Shibuya is in the midst of a massive overhaul that will transform the district into a forest of soaring skyscrapers.

BEYOND SHIBUYA STATION

Beyond the Hachiko entrance is an immense intersection. Looking straight ahead, note the tall, cylindrical

A view of Tokyo Tower from the road.

Shibuya 109 building, a good reference for orientation. The crowded road to its right leads up a gentle hill to Tokyu department store, and adjacent to it, the **Bunkamura**, a performance hall built during the roaring 1980s (www.bunkamura.co.jp). Something is always going on inside – art, music, theatre – and the interior spaces are pleasantly cool on a hot day.

At the top of the hill to the left is the huge **NHK Broadcast Centre** ⑩, a 23-storey building with two dozen TV and radio studios. NHK is the government-run, viewer-subsidised television and radio broadcaster.

Nearby **Yoyogi-koen** ⑪ served as the Olympic Village during the 1964 summer games. Previously, the area was a barracks called Washington Heights for the US Army. Everything was eventually torn down, but rather than erecting something new, the site was turned into a park. It now includes a wild-bird park and playground. Yoyogi gained notoriety for some of the worst free music in town and for its punks and Elvis clones. Wannabe rock groups gave weekend "concerts" on a closed-off street, all playing at the same time and hoping to establish a following of adolescent girls that would cascade into Japan-wide popularity. The city government finally put an end to the well-planned spontaneity.

MEIJI SHRINE

Yoyogi-koen is an extension of one of Japan's most famous Shinto shrines, **Meiji-jingu** ⑫ (www.meijijingu.or.jp; daily sunrise–sunset). The shrine deifies Emperor Meiji and Empress Shoken. (Their remains, however, are in Kyoto.) The emperor was restored to rule in the 1868 Meiji Restoration, when the Tokugawa shogunate collapsed. The emperor died in 1912 and the empress two years later. The original shrine, built in 1920, was destroyed during World War II; the current shrine buildings were reconstructed in 1958. The shrine itself is constructed of Japanese cypress.

The grounds cover 70 hectares (175 acres) and were a favourite retreat of the emperor. The long walk to the shrine passes through a tunnel of trees and beneath three large torii gates, said to include one of the largest wooden gates in Japan: 12 metres (40ft) high with pillars more than a metre in diameter. Cypress wood over 1,700 years old from Taiwan was used for the gate.

The entrance to Meiji-jingu is near **Harajuku-eki** ⑬ (Harajuku Station), with an unusual wood-beamed, almost mock-Tudor architecture. Leading from the station are a number of hip and groovy avenues. For some reason, probably its proximity to once outrageous Yoyogi-koen, narrow Takeshitadori, a small side street between the station and Meiji-dori, has become a teeny-bopper avenue of shops. Harajuku Bridge (Jingu-bashi) is famous for its cosplayers, mostly young girls who hang out here every Sunday sporting stunning costumes that range from gothic Lolita to anime characters. The area lacks breathing room at weekends.

Inside Tokyo Midtown.

More room is found instead on the wide and upscale **Omotesando** , an avenue running from the southern end of Harajuku Station. Omotesando has a European feel about it from the expansiveness of the boulevard (at least for Japan) to the zelkovea trees that line it, not to mention the number of European fashion brands that have chic flagship stores here. The 12-storey (six above ground, six below) concrete-and-glass shopping and residential complex, **Omotesando Hills** (www.omotesandohills. com; Mon–Sat 11am–9pm, Sun until 10pm, individual shops and restaurants vary), was designed by Osaka-born Tadao Ando; it features high-profile stores and restaurants, and its six-level atrium, accented by a 700-metre (2,300ft) spiral ramp, is considered by many an architectural highlight of Tokyo. Across the road from Omotesando Hills is the garish faux-Chinese temple exterior of **Oriental Bazaar** (www.orientalbazaar.co.jp; Fri–Wed 10am–7pm), a very popular shop with travellers that sells everything from cheap and cheerful tourist T-shirts and plastic samurai swords to antique furniture and exquisite used kimono and yukata. The backstreets leading off Omotesando-dori are also home to many a hip café and boutique – well worth exploring if you have the time.

Beyond the far end of Omotesando-dori, several blocks on from the busy intersection straddled by Omotesando Station, the **Nezu Museum** (www.nezu-muse.or.jp; Tue–Sun 10am–5pm) is an oasis of tranquillity hidden behind a sandstone wall. It displays fine examples of Chinese bronzes, ceramic and lacquerware, calligraphy, textiles and Chinese and Japanese paintings. More alluring to some is the museum's delightful garden, a densely wooded landscape with a teahouse overlooking a small iris pond.

North of Omotesando is the site of the **New National Stadium**, which will host the opening and closing ceremonies at the 2020 Summer Olympic and Paralympic Games. The old stadium, which was completed in 1958 and used during the 1964 Olympics, was demolished in 2015 to be replaced with a sparkling design by

The Meiji-jingu shrine.

the late, great Zaha Hadid. When Hadid's architectural plan met criticism for its unusual and pricey design, it was controversially replaced with a scaled down design by local architect Kengo Kuma.

SHINJUKU

After building Edo Castle and settling down, Tokugawa Ieyasu had the **Shinjuku** area surveyed at the urging of some entrepreneurs. He then established a guard post – near today's Shinjuku 2-chome – along the Koshu Kaido, a road that led west into the mountains. Shinjuku (literally, new lodging) quickly became one of the largest urban towns in Edo, filled with shopkeepers, wholesale distributors, inns and teahouses. Shinjuku was also known for the male sensual delights, with "serving girls" working at 50 "inns". Unlike those in Asakusa, the women of Shinjuku worked without licences and were generally considered downscale.

Nowadays, it is said by the Japanese that **Shinjuku-eki** ⑮ (Shinjuku Station) is the world's busiest railway station. It is certainly a furiously busy place – approaching 3.7 million people use it daily – and congested, and if one is unfamiliar with the station, patience can melt within minutes.

Shinjuku Station is one of the most important stations in Japan, a major transfer point for both metropolitan and regional trains and for subways. As with most large urban stations in Japan, there are multitudinous shops and restaurants filling every unused space in the multilevel labyrinth above and below ground. In all, there are eight malls and department stores connected to the station, two of which have their own private rail tracks leading from Shinjuku: Keio, with a line that opened in 1915, and Odakyu, whose line began operation in 1927.

If you find the stores within the station uninspiring, leave by the station's east entrance onto Shinjuku-dori, where there are more department stores, including massive Isetan and Marui stores, thousands of other shops, and tens of thousands of people. This entrance of Shinjuku Station is a popular meeting spot. A small open plaza tempts the idle to linger, especially when there is something to watch on the immense outside television screen at Studio Alta.

This side of the station is a superb rambling area, which one can do for hours with little purpose. Many of those who do have a purpose enter **Kabukicho** ⑯, north of Yasukuni-dori. After World War II, residents of this area sought to establish a sophisticated entertainment area of cinemas and dance halls, and perhaps most importantly, a kabuki theatre, hence the name (*cho* means "ward" or "district"). But somewhat optimistically, the naming of the neighbourhood preceded actual construction of a kabuki theatre, which was never built. The cinemas were, however, and for many years Tokyo's best cinema-viewing was in Kabukicho; European films were very popular during the 1960s,

Tip

Groping, known as *chikan*, is a problem on Tokyo rush-hour trains, targeting mostly Japanese females. As a result, most trains and subways in Tokyo now designate a carriage, usually at the very front or back of a train, for women only on most rush-hour services.

Shopping on Takeshita Street in the Harajuku district is a colourful experience.

⊘ Eat

An old-fashioned and highly atmospheric row of tiny bars, *yakitori*, noodle and other cheap restaurants vie for space along Shomben Yokocho (more commonly known, rather unfortunately, as "piss alley"), just to the left of the underpass that connects East and West Shinjuku.

especially with intellectuals and political radicals. Eventually they moved elsewhere, leaving Kabukicho to the *yakuza*. Kabukicho is famous nowadays for its sexual entertainment, which tends towards voyeurism rather than participation. Also on the east side of Shinjuku but light years away in mood is **Shinjuku Gyoen** (Shinjuku Imperial Garden; mid-Mar–June, mid-Aug–Sept Tue–Sun 9am–6pm, Jul–mid-Aug until 7pm, Oct–mid-Mar until 4.30pm), a popular cherry-blossom-viewing venue in the spring that is divided into Japanese, French and English sections, and with vast lawns that are perfect for a picnic.

For more stately pursuits, follow Yasukuni-dori under the tracks to the west side of Shinjuku. (You could also exit the station directly to avoid the east side altogether.) Of most immediate interest are the numerous tall buildings on this side. Much of Tokyo is composed of either alluvial soil or landfill, both of which are geologically unstable foundations. Given the shakiness of Tokyo's land, not to mention

Tokyo's skyscraper district.

the experience of several devastating earthquakes, tall buildings in parts of Tokyo have been limited. But Shinjuku sits atop rather solid ground, giving architects the confidence to build what they claim are earthquake-proof buildings that utilise sophisticated techniques for stress dissipation and structure stabilisation.

TOKYO'S SKYLINE

The twin towers of the **Tokyo Metropolitan Government Office** 47 (http://metro.tokyo.jp) were conceived and started at the beginning of the so-called bubble economy in the 1980s. They were intended to make a statement that Tokyo was now one of the world's greatest and most powerful cities. Around 13,000 city employees fill the buildings each day.

At the top of both towers, on the 45th floors at 202 metres (660ft), expansive observation galleries with cafeterias offer Tokyo's finest views (north observatory daily, except second and fourth Mon, south observatory daily, except first and third Tue, 9.30am–11pm,

⊘ MEASURING EARTHQUAKES

Whenever there is an earthquake in Japan big enough to be felt (and Tokyo has plenty, especially with aftershocks from the 2011 earthquake), information on the quake's location, size and possibility of tsunami is immediately broadcast on TV – appearing as text at the top of the screen. The most important number you will see on screen is the intensity grade given to the earthquake, which ranges from 0 to 7 and is called *shindo*.

What do the numbers mean? Well, for most people indoors, a *shindo* 1 will register as a very gentle rocking, although some people might not notice it all. A *shindo* 4 can rattle doors and windows enough to make you take notice and perhaps consider getting under a table and bracing for something bigger. With *shindo* 5, which is divided into 5 Weak and 5 Strong (the latter being how most in Tokyo felt the 11 March 2011 earthquake), it can be difficult to walk, furniture can move, and unsecured bookshelves may topple. Move into the *shindo* 6 range, also divided into Weak and Strong, and the levels recorded in most of Fukushima, Iwate and Miyagi prefectures in March 2011, and it is impossible to stand, maybe even impossible to crawl, and less earthquake-resistant structures will begin to fall. *Shindo* 7, which was recorded in parts of Miyagi, cracks the earth, brings down even earthquake-resistant buildings and will throw people off their feet.

south observatory until 5.30pm, but until 11pm if north observatory closed; free). This section of Shinjuku, west of the railway tracks, supports a number of other impressive skyscrapers, the nearby NS and Sumitomo buildings and the Shinjuku Park Tower among them. The NTT InterCommunication Centre, an interactive, hi-tech site with an internet café and electronic library, is housed inside the impressive, 54-floor **Tokyo Opera City** (www.oper-acity.jp), another Kenzo Tange design. Opera City, as its name suggests, has a concert hall for classical music, as well as an art gallery (Tue–Thu 11am–7pm, Fri–Sat until 8pm) that puts on an interesting variety of exhibitions.

Shinjuku's most interesting shopping experience, the massive **Takashimaya Times Square** (www.takashimaya-global. com; shops Sun–Thu 10am–8pm, Fri–Sat until 8.30pm, restaurants daily 11am–11pm), is a short stroll from here near the station's south exit. Besides an upmarket Takashimaya department store, complete with restaurant floors, this shopping complex includes a branch of Tokyu Hands (the large home department store) and a Kinokuniya bookstore that has a big selection of English magazines and books.

"LITTLE ASIA"

If the streets of Kabukicho seem luridly exotic, **Shin Okubo** ⓰, a few minutes' walk directly north, brings you somewhere engagingly exotic. "Little Asia", as it is known, is home to Koreans, Thais, Filipinos, Chinese and even Russians, a lively mix of people, cultures and beliefs that is visible in the extraordinary range of restaurants, mini-markets, churches and shrines along Shin Okubo's main strip and back lanes. With its distinctly urban, working-class and cosmopolitan character, one wonders if Shin Okubo is a world apart from the capital, or the prototype for a new Tokyo.

The northeastern fringes of Shinjuku, near Kagarazuku Station, saw the opening in 2017 of the **Yayoi Kusama Museum** (http://yayoikusamamuseum.jp; Thu–Sun 11am–5.30pm), dedicated to the famous contemporary artist of the same name.

⊘ **Fact**

Kabukicho is notorious as a hangout for *yakuza* (Japanese mafia) and for its array of dubious sex clubs. Many of the "hostess" bars and other seedy establishments catering to Japanese men employ women from Thailand and the Philippines, often as indentured labour.

Lights in Shinjuku.

📷 JAPAN'S TRAINS

The *shinkansen*, which means "new trunk line", is a technological symbol of Japan to the world, but it's not the only train plying the islands.

Other countries have trains that are as fast as Japan's *shinkansen*. Others have trains with equally high levels of comfort, or that are arguably as aesthetically pleasing. But nobody puts all that into a single, unerringly efficient package quite like the Japanese. When it comes to fast trains, the Japanese simply do it better, and have been doing it longer – since 1959, when construction of the Tokaido *shinkansen*, or bullet train, began. Five years later, service on the Tokaido Line began between Tokyo and Osaka with 60 trains daily. Today, more than 150 million passengers a year use the Tokaido *shinkansen*. As for speed, several regularly scheduled trains operate at 300kmh (185mph), while currently in development is a Maglev train that registered top speeds of 603kmh (375mph) in testing in 2015, a world speed record for a manned train. By 2027, it should link Tokyo and Nagoya.

The Japanese live by the train and play by the train, literally and figuratively. The highest real-estate values are found near the railway or subway station.

For the Japanese, train travel is a life experience in itself in which the journey can be just as much fun as the destination. Take a train from Tokyo to a weekend getaway like Hakone, and the carriages can take on the atmosphere of a social club – everyone eating special bento and having a drink or two. It is even possible to charter a special train with tatami-mat carriages and go nowhere in particular, just party in locomotive style. Recent years have seen new luxury sleeper trains, like the Train Suite Shiki-Shima, plying Japan's scenic routes on multiday junkets costing several to tens of thousands of dollars.

Sleek, speedy and smooth, the shinkansen is the ultimate high-speed train. It takes years of experience before a driver can even think about joining the elite shinkansen ranks.

Not all trains are high-speed. Japan is very fond of its slow-moving historic lines too, like the 100-year-old Enoshima Electric Railway that serves the Kamakura area.

Japan Rail trains and private rail lines crisscross Japan's four main islands, affording access to all but the remotest of areas.

The Tokkaido shinkansen has an average delay of just 24 seconds, inclusive of natural disasters and other uncontrollable causes.

A primer of amazing facts

According to Japan Railways (JR), on any given day there are 8,600 people – drivers, train staff, controllers and maintenance engineers – involved in operating the Tokaido *shinkansen* line between Tokyo and Osaka. Each day the route's Series N700 trains, launched in 2007, or state-of-the art Series N700A, launched in 2013, make more than 400 regular runs along the 515km (320-mile) stretch of track between Japan's two biggest cities, each 16-car train carrying up to 1,323 passengers.

Each 16-car N700 weighs in at 715 tonnes, its motors generating 17 megawatts to move it through the 66 tunnels that the *shinkansen* uses between Tokyo and Osaka. The longest of these is 8km (5 miles), the shortest a mere 30 metres (100ft) long.

When the *shinkansen* is travelling at 270kph (170mph; not its top speed, but the limit imposed on the route), it will take almost 5km (3 miles) to come to a complete stop. Thanks to a system that allows the train to tilt up to one degree on bends, the N700 can maintain that 270kph (170 mph) even as it corners.

Inside the carriages, to cater to business travellers, the N700 comes with a power outlet for each pair of seats and free wireless LAN. It's a comfortable ride too, with spacious, reclinable seats, and a smoke-free environment (not always a given in Japan), as well as concession carts regularly going up and down the aisles.

Shinkansen and express trains have concession trolleys selling food and drinks, while the stations they stop at offer ekiben, a version of the bento box made with local ingredients and packaging.

Outside of rush hour, the painful grimaces of crushed commuters are replaced with vacant stares and heads buried in books or mobile phones.

White gloves are common on people working in public places. Conductors and drivers always wear them, as do the people who help squeeze passengers on to the worst rush-hour trains.

AROUND TOKYO

Trains make day trips from Tokyo easy. Head east to Disneyland; south to Yokohama, Kamakura and the Izu Peninsula; west to Mount Takao; and north to historic Kawagoe and Nikko.

Tokyo has enough attractions to keep visitors captivated for weeks, but anyone spending more than a few days in the capital should really make an effort to get out and explore beyond the city limits. To the south of Tokyo is the city of Yokohama, richly influenced by an influx of foreigners in the latter half of the 19th century, and beyond it are the ancient temples and shrines of the one-time capital Kamakura. West is the iconic Mount Fuji and in its shadow the restful hot springs of Hakone, while to the immediate east of Tokyo are the fun-filled Tokyo Disneyland and DisneySea. Arguably though, the most rewarding side trip is to the north, to the lavish Tosho-gu shrine complex built by the Tokugawa shoguns. And those are just for starters...

EAST OF TOKYO

DISNEYLAND AND CHIBA

Besides Narita Airport, what brings most visitors east to Chiba Prefecture today is **Tokyo Disneyland ❶** (www.tokyodisneyresort.jp; daily, usually from 8–9am until 10pm). Located on 874 hectares (2,160 acres) of reclaimed land in Urayasu, a city just across the Edo River from Tokyo, it is only a 15-minute train ride from Tokyo Station on the JR Keiyo Line to Maihama Station. All the attractions of the US and Hong Kong sister sites are here at Japan's own take on the Magic Kingdom.

Adjacent is a newer, contingent complex, the very popular **DisneySea** (www.tokyodisneyresort.jp; daily, usually from 8–9am until 10pm), which offers attractions designed along aquatic themes and legends. You may want to spend a whole day at each park, or you may want to avoid the crowds and cloying cuteness like the plague. Directly and indirectly, Tokyo Disneyland is responsible for somewhere in the region of 100,000 jobs – its total

Main attractions
Yokohama
Kamakura
Enoshima
Mount Takao
Izu Peninsula
Mount Fuji
Hakone
Kawagoe

Maps on pages
172, 177

Hakone hot springs.

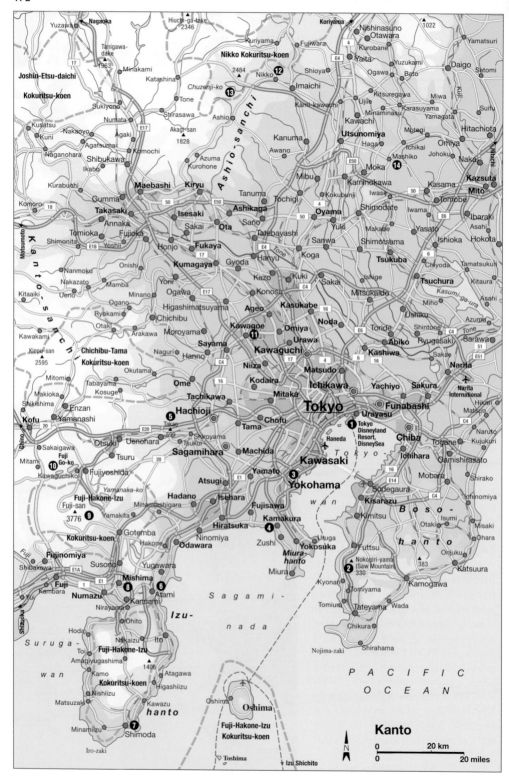

Kanto

economic impact on a par with Japan's camera industry.

Fans of anime have flocked to **Ghibli Museum** (www.ghibli-museum.jp; Wed–Mon 10am–6pm; online booking recommended) in Mitaka, in the west of Tokyo metropolis. This museum-cum-amusement park showcases the work of the renowned Studio Ghibli, who are behind the finest anime that has emerged from Japan in recent years, including Miyazaki Hayao's *Princess Mononoke* and *Spirited Away*.

AROUND NARITA

Most people are in a hurry to leave Narita Airport (officially known as the New Tokyo International Airport), which is a shame as the area has much to offer. First and foremost is Shinsho-ji, usually referred to simply as **Narita-san** (www.naritasan.or.jp; free guided walks daily 10am–3pm). A 15-minute walk from JR Narita or Keisei stations, this temple, said to date back to AD 940, is one of the most important in the entire Kanto region, drawing 12 million visitors a year, worshippers and sightseers alike, especially during the first three days of the New Year. It is the headquarters of the Shingon sect of esoteric Buddhism. The three-storey pagoda in front of the Great Main Hall is the original 18th-century building and is richly decorated with golden dragons' heads. A large garden with rivers and ornamental ponds is adjacent to the temple. Narita-san is also well known for its drive-in chapel at the side of the complex that welcomes drivers – and their vehicles – to be blessed by a priest and, for a fee (blessings everywhere always come with a charge), to be adorned with lucky amulets to protect against accidents.

For a digest of Japanese social history, the **Kokuritsu Rekishi Minzoku Hakubutsukan** (National Museum of Japanese History; www.rekihaku.ac.jp; Tue–Sun, Mar–Sept 9.30am–5pm, Oct–Feb 9.30am–4.30pm), in the former castle town of **Sakura**, is a short hop from the airport on the Keisei and JR Sobu lines. The comprehensive museum is set within the extensive landscaped grounds.

Nokogiri-yama ❷ (Saw Mountain) is located along the southwestern coastal region of Chiba's Boso Peninsula. It was known for its Boshu-seki stone from the 14th to the 18th centuries. The sites of the quarries left jagged edges resembling a saw, hence its name. The foot of Nokogiri-yama is a short walk from Hamakanaya Station on the JR Uchibo Line.

A cable car (www.mt-nokogiri.co.jp; daily 9am–5pm, mid-Nov–mid-Feb until 4pm, summer until 6pm) takes visitors halfway up the mountain, a number of steep flights of steps from there on providing enough physical effort to give the sensation of being a pilgrim, at least for the day. The top of the mountain affords a fine panorama of Tokyo Bay and Mount Fuji. On exceptionally clear days, faraway Suruga Bay in Shizuoka Prefecture can also be glimpsed. The holy mountain has quite an illustrious history, with enough sights to please everyone, including a 33-metre (110ft)

Disney character Mickey Mouse poses with a visitor at Tokyo Disneyland.

⊙ Tip

Yokohama and Kamakura
are easily accessible
from Tokyo Station on the
same train, the Yokosuka
Line. Other lines run
from Shinjuku and
Shibuya stations.
Yokohama is exactly 30
minutes from Tokyo,
Kamakura just one hour.

Kannon, Goddess of Mercy, carved into the rock face near the top of the mountain, and a cluster of 1,553 stone statues of *rakan* (disciples of the Buddha).

SOUTH OF TOKYO

YOKOHAMA

The very sound of **Yokohama** ❸ is somehow exotic. And although the city today is both an integral part of the Greater Tokyo area and a major urban centre in its own right, Yokohama has a distinctive personality and even a mystique, much of it stemming from its vital role as one of the greatest international seaports of the Far East.

When Commodore Matthew Perry and his armada of "black ships" arrived in 1853, Yokohama was just a poor fishing village next to a smelly swamp. Under the terms of a treaty negotiated in 1858 by the first US envoy to Japan, Townsend Harris, the port of Kanagawa, located on the Tokaido (the East Sea Road between Edo Tokyo and Kyoto), was to be opened to foreign settlement. But given its proximity to the important Tokaido, the shogunate reconsidered and instead built an artificial island on the mudflats of Yokohama for the foreigners.

That attempt to segregate the "red-haired barbarians" proved fortuitous for all concerned, since Yokohama's superb natural harbour helped international trade to flourish. The wild early days of the predominantly male community centred around such recreational facilities as Dirty Village, the incomparable Gankiro Teahouse and the local racetrack. Periodic attacks by sword-wielding, xenophobic samurai added to the lively atmosphere.

Eventually, foreign garrisons were brought in and the merchants could live in a more sedate environment. Honcho-dori became the centre of commercial activities, and the street is still lined with banks and office buildings. With a population of 3.7 million, Yokohama is second in size only to Tokyo.

Happily, however, many of those places worthy of exploring are concentrated in a relatively small area and can be covered for the most part by

*The Minato Mirai
21 development
in Yokohama.*

foot. Another aspect that makes Yokohama – only a 30-minute train ride from Tokyo – alluring is that its broad, relatively uncrowded streets (except on weekends) and laid-back atmosphere provide a perfect antidote to Tokyo's claustrophobia and frantic pace.

CENTRAL YOKOHAMA

Start a walking tour of central Yokohama at **Sakuragicho-eki** (Sakuragicho Station), which is the terminus for the Toyoko Line originating at Tokyo's Shibuya Station. Sakuragicho was also the last stop on Japan's first railway, which began service to Shimbashi in Tokyo in 1872. Central Yokohama is now dominated by the massive **Minato Mirai 21** (mm21) shopping and leisure complex, between Sakuragicho Station and the ocean. Trumpeted as the last great Japanese mega-complex to be constructed before the millennium (and after the economic meltdown in the 1990s), its 190 sq km (75 sq miles) are dominated by the 73-storey **Landmark Tower**, one of Japan's tallest buildings at 296 metres (970ft), with one of the highest observatory decks in Japan – Sky Garden on the 69th floor (www.yokohama-landmark.jp; daily 10am–9pm, Sat and summer until 10pm). Other buildings of note are the Yokohama Grand Inter-Continental Hotel, strikingly designed to resemble a sail, and the **Yokohama Port Museum** (www.nippon-maru.or.jp; Tue–Sun 10am–5pm). The *Nippon Maru*, a traditional sailing ship anchored nearby, is the museum's most impressive feature. The **Yokohama Museum of Art** (http://yokohama.art.museum; Fri–Wed 10am–6pm) has an excellent collection of 19th- and 20th-century paintings and modernist sculptures.

SOUTHEAST SIDE

On the southeast side of the Oka-gawa, a stream that separates Yokohama from Sakuragicho Station, is an area of old government buildings, banks and the like. Further on is a tree-lined street with red-brick pavements: Bashamichi-dori (Street of Horse Carriages). Here is the **Kanagawa Prefectural Museum of Cultural History** (http://ch.kanagawa-museum.jp;

⊙ Tip

Descend a long flight of steps from Nokogiri-yama and visit Japan's largest figure of the Buddha, the impressive Yakushi Nyorai. The distance from the base to the tip of the giant lotus bud that stands behind the statue's head measures an astonishing 31 metres (100ft).

Sketch of Matthew Perry and his staff arriving at an imperial tent during the 1854 negotiations.

⊙ PERRY'S ARRIVAL

More than two centuries of isolation evaporated in 1853 when Matthew Perry, a US naval officer, sailed four ships into Uraga, near Yokosuka. His sole mission was to force Japan into trade and diplomacy with the US, which then became an equal with Britain, France and Russia in East Asia.

He refused demands to leave and insisted that he be received. Mindful of China's recent defeat in the Opium Wars, the Japanese agreed to stall for time while improving their defences. In 1854 Perry reappeared in Tokyo Bay with nine ships to conclude a first treaty, which included a US consul in Japan and trade rights. Other countries then demanded treaties, which the shogun realised he could not refuse. This weakness helped hasten the collapse of the shogunate system.

The Yokohama Marine Tower.

A street in Yokohama's Chinatown.

Tue–Sun 9.30am–5pm). The building, dating from 1904, was formerly the head office of a bank. As one of the best surviving examples of the city's old commercial architecture, it has been designated a so-called Important Cultural Property by the national government. North of here, **Shinko Pier** is a man-made island jutting out into Yokohama Bay. For Japanese, the old "Akarenga" red-brick warehouses here, which now serve as a shopping mall, are a big attraction. Near them, the **Yokohama Cosmo World** amusement park (http://cosmoworld.jp; Fri–Wed 11am–at least 9pm, Sat–Sun and summer until 10pm) has plenty of fun attractions, including roller coasters, arcade games and a 112-metre (367ft) high Ferris wheel that affords great views of the city and bay.

In the same neighbourhood are the stately Yokohama Banker's Club and on the right, four blocks down, the lovely red-brick Yokohama Port Opening Memorial Hall, which miraculously survived the Great Kanto Earthquake of 1923 and the bombings of World War II. Also in the area are numerous offices for the prefectural government. This district is sometimes called the Bund and its oldest buildings have a distinctly European look, something shared with buildings along the Bund in Shanghai, built about the same time.

The **Yokohama Archives of History** (www.kaikou.city.yokohama.jp; Tue–Sun 9.30am–5pm), on the site of the former British consulate, houses a museum with various exhibits about Yokohama's fascinating history and a reading room with related audiovisual materials. Across the boulevard is the **Silk Centre**, with a delightful museum (www.silkcenter-kbkk.jp/museum/en; Tue–Sun 9.30am–5pm) on the history of that alluring fabric; at one time, Yokohama owed its prosperity primarily to silk, in which the local Indian community was intimately involved.

Yamashita-koen (Yamashita Park) is well worth a visit for the people-watching. On a clear summer night, a rock band is liable to be wailing away on a temporary stage several hundred metres offshore. The former passenger liner and hospital ship *Hikawa Maru* is permanently moored here and can be visited (Tue–Sun 10am–5pm). Further down the same road are the somewhat garish 106-metre (348ft) **Marine Tower** and the **Doll Museum** (www.doll-museum.jp; Tue–Sun 9.30am–5pm), with its collection of 3,500 dolls from Japan and overseas.

The aquarium at **Yokohama Hakkeijima Sea Paradise** (daily, but times vary, see www.seaparadise.co.jp) is very popular. Aquariums abound in Japan, and this is one of the finest in the country. Also at Sea Paradise is a 1.2km (0.75-mile) long roller coaster and the Blue Fall – a 107-metre (350ft), 125kph (80mph) chair-drop that claims to be one of the highest in the world.

CHINATOWN

No visit to Yokohama would be complete without a meal in **Chukagai**, Yokohama's Chinatown. This dozen or so

blocks is the largest Chinatown in Japan and is nearly as old as the port. The area within its five old gates accounts for 90 percent of the former foreign settlement. Chinatown also takes pride in the historical role it had in providing staunch support to Sun Yat-sen when he was here in exile trying to rally support for revolution on the Chinese mainland.

On days when a baseball game is on at nearby Yokohama Stadium, the area is visited by more than 200,000 people, the majority intent on dining at one of the approximately 150 local restaurants. Most also sneak in at least a peak at the exotic shops selling imported Chinese sweets and sundries from elsewhere in Asia. There are also many herbal medicine and teashops.

Back in the old days, the waterfront Bund often stood in contrast to the **Bluff**, or **Yamate Heights**, where the leading foreign merchants lived in palatial homes. Nanmon-dori in Chinatown was the central street that ran through the international settlement and connected the two. It became a local tradition – known as Zondag, from the Dutch word for Sunday – that on every Sunday the flags of the many nations represented there were flown and brass bands marched down the road. There is a foreign cemetery (gaijin bochi) where around 4,200 foreigners from 40 countries are buried. The adjacent **Yamate Museum** (Tue–Sun 11am–4pm), with quaint displays on the life of early foreign residents, sits near where one of Japan's earliest breweries was located.

Motomachi, a popular shopping street just below the Bluff and several hundred metres inland from Yamashita-koen, means "original town". This is something of a misnomer, because the area was developed long after Yokohama itself was established. Still, Motomachi, adjacent as it was to the foreign district (now Chinatown), has played an important role in the city's history by serving the needs of foreign vessels and their crews visiting the port. Motomachi's legacy of "foreignness" led to its revival in the 1960s and 1970s. However, the focus of fashion in Yokohama has shifted to Isezakicho, south of Kannai Station, and to the big

The Enoshima Electric Railway (Enoden).

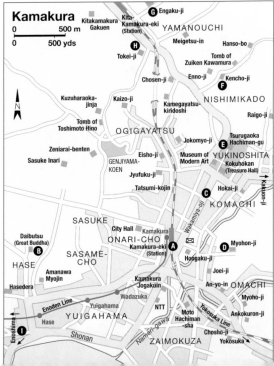

○ Fact

Zen and Nichiren forms of Buddhism reflect the removal of boundaries between Buddhism and Shinto, with Shinto the realm of daily life and Buddhism of the afterlife. Zen Buddhism's emphasis on austerity and simplicity harmonised well with the outlook of the Japanese samurai class.

department stores around Yokohama Station. A short bus ride south of the Yamate will bring you to the contiguous Negishi district and the **Sankeien Garden** (www.sankeien.or.jp; daily 9am–5pm). This classic Japanese garden was built by a prosperous silk merchant in 1906 and incorporates into its spacious grounds and lakeside area several tea-houses, a three-storey pagoda and the restored Rinshunkaku, a villa built by the shogun Tokugawa Yoshinobu.

KAMAKURA

Cradled in a spectacular natural amphi-theatre, **Kamakura** ❹ is bordered on three sides by wooded mountains and on the fourth by the blue Pacific. From 1192, when Minamoto Yoritomo made it the headquarters of the first shogu-nate, until 1333, when imperial forces breached its seven "impregnable" passes and annihilated the defenders, Kamakura was the de facto political and cultural capital of Japan. During those years, the military administra-tion based here built impressive tem-ples and commissioned notable works

of art, a great deal of them Zen-influ-enced. Despite the endemic violence of Japan's middle ages, most survived and can be viewed today.

It is a pity that the majority of visitors spend only a day or two in Kamakura, since it is best appreciated leisurely with visits to famous historical sites – there are 65 Buddhist temples and 19 Shinto shrines – interspersed with walks through the quiet surrounding hills. Kamakura is only an hour from Tokyo Station and 30 minutes from Yokohama on the JR Yokosuka Line. For that reason, much of it resembles an open-air madhouse at weekends, a time when it is highly recommended for the traveller to be elsewhere.

Visitors customarily begin their sightseeing from **Kamakura-eki** ❹ (Kamakura Station). In addition to the main rail line, there is a private electric-trolley line, the delightful Enoden (Enoshima Dentetsu; www.enoden.co.jp). The Enoden, which began operations in 1902, plies a meander-ing route with some wonderful views between Kamakura and Fujisawa, with 13 stops in between. For about half its 10km (6-mile) length, the carriages run along the ocean. When the trains are not crowded, the conductors allow surfers to bring their boards aboard. Unfortunately the charming old car-riages have been replaced with mod-ern ones, but if time permits, take the Enoden the entire length.

GREAT BUDDHA

Hop off the Enoden at Hase, the station closest to the **Daibutsu** ❸ (Great Bud-dha). A road leads to the statue. In the hills to the left and along the way are **Goryo-jinja** (next to the Enoden tracks), which holds a unique festival every 18 September with humorous characters sporting macabre masks; **Hase-dera** (www.hasedera.jp; daily, Mar–Sept 8am–5.30pm, Oct–Feb 8am–5pm), a temple with a 9-metre (30ft), 11-headed Hase Kannon statue, along with thousands

The Great Buddha in Kamakura.

of small *jiso* statues decked out in colourful bibs and bonnets and dedicated to lost babies (mostly due to abortion); and **Kosoku-ji** (daily sunrise–sunset), a temple known for its collection associated with the priest Nichiren. On a knoll to the right of the approach to the Buddha is the 1,200-year-old **Amanawa Shinmei shrine** (daily sunrise–sunset; free). Dedicated to the Sun Goddess, Amaterasu Omikami, the shrine offers majestic views.

Even first-time visitors to Japan have no doubt seen photos of Daibutsu, the Great Buddha. But if not, there's little chance of missing the colossus. At 11 metres (40ft) in height – not counting the pedestal – and weighing 93 tonnes, this representation of the compassionate Amida is unlikely to get lost in crowds posing for pictures below. The features of the statue were purposely designed out of proportion when it was cast in 1252 so that they look right when one is standing 4–5 metres (15ft) in front of it. For a fee, you can crawl around inside the statue. Astonishingly, the Great Buddha has survived the onslaughts of earthquakes, typhoons and tsunamis, like the one in 1495 that ripped away the wooden building that once enclosed it.

On the east side of Kamakura Station is **Wakamiya-oji** ⓒ, a broad boulevard that begins at the beach and heads inland under three massive torii archways to the Tsurugaoka Hachiman-gu. Parallel to Wakamiya-oji is **Kamachi-dori**, Kamakura's modest answer to Ginza and with little elbow room at weekends. The area abounds with all kinds of trendy shops and eating places, and many of the Japanese-style restaurants here and elsewhere in the city have incorporated Zen principles of cooking.

Along Kamachi-dori and especially on some of the side alleys, craft shops encourage serious browsing. Kamakura is most famous for *Kamakura-bori* (lacquerware), which originated in the area

in the 13th century for the production of utensils used in religious ceremonies. Unlike the traditional Chinese lacquerware from which it drew its inspiration, the first step in *Kamakura-bori* is to carve the design and then apply the lacquer. Like fine wine, *Kamakura-bori* improves with age, taking on richer and subtler hues and lustres.

NICHIREN TEMPLES

The area due east of Kamakura Station, on the other side of Wakamiya-oji, is largely the province of temples of the Nichiren sect. Although most foreigners have heard of Zen, few know much about Nichiren (1222–82) and his teachings, despite the fact that the iconoclast priest founded the only true Japanese Buddhist sect. Nichiren was an imposing personality who in his lifetime was nearly executed, exiled twice, and set upon by mobs on more than one occasion, and who continues to generate feelings of both respect and disdain centuries after his death. Nichiren's importance in political (as opposed to religious) history lies in his

⊙ **Tip**

The hills above Kamakura are laced with hiking trails good for an hour or a day of rambling. A good way to find them is just to follow any Japanese seemingly dressed, cow bells and all, for a hike in the Swiss Alps.

A souvenir shop in Kamakura.

prediction of the Mongol invasion as divine punishment for the failure of the authorities to accept his arguments. The irascible Nichiren seems to have been quite put out that the Mongols did not actually conquer the country.

The temples of **Myohon-ji**  (www. myohonji.or.jp), **Hongaku-ji**, **Chosho-ji** (all free and always open), **Myoho-ji** (daily 9.30am–4.30pm) and **Ankoku-ron-ji** (Tue–Sun 9.30am–5pm) are all Nichiren temples and are worth a visit. The Myohon-ji, for example, although only 10 minutes from the station, seems a world apart.

TSURUGAOKA HACHIMAN-GU

At the top end of Wakamiya-oji, the approach into **Tsurugaoka Hachi-man-gu** (www.hachimangu.or.jp; daily, Apr–Sept 5am–8.30pm, Oct–Mar 6am–8.30pm; free) crosses a steep, red, half-moon bridge that separates the Gempei Ponds. The name Gempei refers to the Minamoto (Genji) and Taira (Heike) clans, which fought to the end in the samurai power struggle known as the Gempei War. The three islands on the right – the Genji side – signify the Chinese character for birth, symbolising the victory of Yoritomo and his followers, while the four in the Heike Pond stand for the death of the rival Taira. Yoritomo's indomitable wife, Masako, who ironically was of Taira blood, apparently built the pond to rub in her husband's victory over the ill-fated heirs of Taira.

Behind the Heike Pond is the **Museum of Modern Art, Kamakura** (www.moma.pref.kanagawa.jp; Tue–Sun 9.30am–5pm), and a little past the Genji Pond is the modern and disaster-proof **Kokuhokan** (National Treasure Hall; Tue–Sun 9am–4.30pm). Each month the Kokuhokan teasingly changes the limited displays of the 2,000 treasures from the temples of Kamakura. Still, whatever is being shown at any given moment should be stimulating for those interested in Buddhist art.

Continuing up towards the main shrine, cross a 25-metre (80ft) dirt track, along which every 16 September mounted archers gallop and unloosen their arrows at targets in the ancient samurai ritual of *yabusame*. Next is an open area below the steps to the *hongu*, or shrine hall. Here is the red stage upon which Shizuka, Yoshit-sune's paramour, danced defiantly at the order of his vengeful half-brother Yoritomo, head of the Minamoto clan, using the occasion to sing the praises of her lover. The pregnant girl's courage sent Yoritomo into a furious and vengeful rage, and although he spared her life, he later executed her son.

Tsurugaoka Hachiman-gu's prominence on the top of Stork Mountain and the shrine's dedication to Hachiman, the god of war and tutelary deity of the Minamoto, made it the central point of reference for the numerous offices of the military government situated below. Actually, the shrine was founded way back in 1063 by one of Yoritomo's ancestors. Yoritomo's very unpretentious tomb is to be found off

Throngs of tourists visit the popular island of Enoshima during Golden Week.

to the right of the shrine near a hill. It is an austere grave befitting a samurai, unlike the monstrous mausoleums for the Tokugawa shoguns at Nikko, which look as if they were built for mafioso dons. Before exploring the hills north of the Tsurugaoka Hachiman-gu, **Hokuku-ji Temple** (daily 9am–4pm), a 10-minute walk, offers a closer retreat. Follow the road that runs east of the main entrance to the Hachiman-gu until you see signs on the right, pointing you across the river to the temple. Hokoku-ji's main draw is its tranquil bamboo forest, where visitors can repair to a tea pavilion for a bowl of thick, green matcha, the brew used in the tea ceremony.

TEMPLES AROUND KAMAKURA

Two isolated temples of great interest and few crowds are the **Kakuon-ji** (guided tours only, Mon–Fri between 10am–3pm, Sat–Sun until noon; call 0467-22-1195, in Japanese, to arrange), back in the hills behind Yoritomo's tomb, and the **Zuisen-ji** (www.kamakura-zuisenji.or.jp; daily 9am–5pm, Oct–Mar until 4.30pm), considerably to the east. The former was founded in 1296. Its Buddha Hall, dating to 1354, houses a beautiful Yakushi Nyorai flanked by guardians representing the sun and moon, as well as a shrine to the Black Jizo, whose indelible colour results from it constantly being scorched by the flames of hell in its efforts to save souls. Zuisen-ji has a Zen rock-and-water garden designed by its founder, the monk Muso Kokushi.

Another spot to visit that is not so far off the beaten track, but which is nevertheless largely missed by the tourist packs, is so-called **Harakiri Cave**, a 20-minute walk to the northeast of Kamakura Station past the shallow, meandering Nameri-gawa. In 1333, in what was then a temple called Tosho-ji, the last Kamakura regent, who had been scorned for his patronage of dog fights, died by his own hand while

surrounded by more than 800 of his cornered followers.

North of Tsurugaoka Hachiman-gu is **Kencho-ji**  (www.kenchoji.com; daily 8.30am–4.30pm), established in 1253 and perhaps Kamakura's most significant Zen temple. Before fires in the 1300s and 1400s razed the temple, Kencho-ji had 49 sub-temples. To the right of the main gate, San-mon, is the temple's bell (bonsho), cast in 1255 and inscribed by the temple's first abbot, a priest from China. The large juniper trees beyond the main gate are said to have been planted by the Chinese priest.

To the north is the station at **Kita Kamakura** (North Kamakura), the first stop beyond Kamakura. East of the station is **Engaku-ji** (www.engakuji.or.jp; daily, Apr–Oct 8am–5pm, Nov–Mar 8am–4pm), which dates from the late 13th century and was intended for the souls of those killed during the unsuccessful Mongol invasion the previous year. After the main gate and on the right are steps to a 2.5-metre (8ft) high bell cast in 1301, the largest temple bell in Kamakura. The bell's sound, it

Tsurugaoka Hachiman-gu.

is said, guides souls that have been
spared by the king of hell back to earth
and the living. Engaku-ji's Butsu-den
dates from 1964 and has been rebuilt
many times over the centuries after
fires and earthquakes.

Not far from Engaku-ji and on the
main road across the tracks between
Kita Kamakura and central Kamakura
is **Tokei-ji** (www.tokeiji.com; daily,
Mar–Oct 8.30am–4.30pm, Oct–Mar
8.30am–4pm), which can be seen
from Engaku-ji's bell tower. Begun
in the 1280s as a nunnery, Tokei-ji
became noted as a refuge for abused
wives. Women who found sanctuary
here worked as lay helpers for three
years, during which time they were
safe from husbands. At the end of the
three years, the women were released
from marriage.

ENOSHIMA

The wooded islet of **Enoshima** ❶ (Bay
Island) has many attractions in any
weather and is easily reached either
from Shinjuku in Tokyo on the private
Odayku Line (a pleasant 75-minute

*Mount Fuji viewed from
Lake Motosu.*

ride), or from Kamakura on the quaint
and rattling Enoden Electric Railway.
Avoid at the weekends and holidays.

The island, about 2km (1.2 miles) in
circumference, is a wooded hill surrounded by rocky beaches and cliffs.
But these days it hardly deserves the
name of island: the 600-metre (2,000ft)
long Benten Bridge, which connects
Enoshima to the bright lights of the
resort town of Katase, has gradually
turned into a major causeway. The
usually crowded beaches of Shichiriga-
hama and Miami stretch far to the east
and west. Still, access on foot or by car
is simple, and there is plenty of parking
space at the foot of the hill. Just beyond
where the causeway meets the island
is the yacht harbour, constructed for
the Summer Olympics in 1964.

The ascent of the hill begins at the
end of Benten Bridge along a narrow
street crammed with restaurants and
souvenir shops. This narrow street
leads up to the start of a series of
covered escalators, which make the
upward progress simple. First stop is
the charming **Enoshima-jinja** (http://
enoshimajinja.or.jp; daily 8.30am–5pm),
built in 1182 and dedicated to Benten,
the goddess of fortune. Her naked
statue used to reside in a cave on the
far side, but fears for her safety led to a
place in the shrine itself. On top, in the
Samuel Cocking Garden (daily 9am–
8pm) are tropical plants, greenhouses,
miniature trains, and restaurants and
patios providing views of the ocean.
An observation tower, the **Sea Candle**
(same times as the garden), 59 metres
(190ft) high and accessible by lift, gives
more exposed views.

The more spiritually minded might
like to visit the famous **Ryuko-ji**, a
temple near the station that features
a fine pagoda, albeit no older than the
20th century. The temple is dedicated
to Nichiren, founder of the only genuinely Japanese sect of Buddhism. It
was here that Nichiren was allegedly
saved from execution by a timely stroke

of lightning that hit the uplifted blade of the executioner's sword.

WEST OF TOKYO

MOUNT TAKAO

If you have a hankering to do some nature hiking within the boundaries of Greater Tokyo, the 599-metre (1,965ft) **Mount Takao ❺**, easily accessed on the Keio Line from Shinjuku Station, is the obvious choice. Seven trails wind up the mountain, three of them from just outside the Takao-san-guchi railway station. No. 1 trail is the most popular route up, though some visitors prefer to take the cable car or chairlift, which cuts almost 400 metres (1,300ft) off the climb, and then walk down via trail No. 6, a forest walk that includes a stream and freezing-cold waterfall popular with religious ascetics. The ascent takes you through the gloriously vivid colours of **Yakuo-in**, a temple founded in the 8th century. Mount Takao is something of a pilgrimage spot for botanists, its slopes and trails covered in nearly 500 types of wild as

well as cultivated plants and flowers. Serving the vast number of Tokyoites that head to Takao (almost 2.5 million annually), especially at weekends, are a plethora of food and souvenirs stalls dotted between the upper cable-car station and the summit.

IZU PENINSULA

Extending into the Pacific between Sagami and Sugura bays is **Izu-hanto** (Izu Peninsula), 60km (40 miles) long and 30km (20 miles) wide, and where countless bays, beaches and *onsen* (hot springs) meld with a very inviting climate to give Izu its reputation as a resort for all seasons. Seafood is excellent here, too. Trains run only along the eastern coast, however.

Eastern Izu begins at **Atami ❻**, a hot spring dating back more than 1,000 years. During the Edo Period, the shogun had its waters brought to the Edo palace so he could enjoy a relaxing bath. Today, Atami is still known for its ryokan and hot springs. Access from Tokyo is easy via the *shinkansen*, as well as on regular (and cheaper) trains. The **MOA**

> ◉ **Tip**
>
> It may have been humiliating for Japan at the time, but nowadays Perry's arrival is a tourist attraction. In the middle of May, Shimoda celebrates the Kurofune Matsuri (Black Ship Festival) in commemoration of Perry's landing with ceremonies, brass band parades, and, of course, spectacular fireworks.

Beautiful scenery at Hachijojima Island.

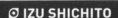

> ### ◉ IZU SHICHITO
>
> Time permitting, overnight or several day trips can be made from Tokyo to the ruggedly beautiful **Izu Shichito** (Izu Seven Islands; though there are actually nine), a group of mostly volcanic islands accessible only by boat or air. **Oshima** is the largest and closest. It is also the most touristy, albeit not yet overly so, with good deep-sea fishing, snorkelling, surfing, hot springs and an active volcano, Mount Mihara. Each of the seven main islands has something different to recommend it. **Niijima** is popular with young people during the summer, and has curious saltwater hot-spring pools at the edge of the sea. **Toshima** is the smallest, with a warm microclimate that supports camellia flowers; **Shikinejima** is a tranquil islet known for its hot springs; **Kozushima** is said to be the finest island for fishing; **Mikurajima** is the most unspoilt. Until 2013 visitors to **Miyakejima** had to wear gas masks to protect against the toxic gas produced by Mount Oyana, which erupted in 2000. The furthest-flung and most exotic of the islands is **Hachijojima**, 45 minutes by plane from Haneda. It is known for its semi-tropical flora and fruits, and locals produce an exquisite silk fabric known as *ki-hachijo*. For details, visit the Izu Islands Tourist Association website: www.tokyo-islands.com.

Museum of Art (www.moaart.or.jp; Fri–
Wed 9.30am–4.30pm), located above
the train station, has a fine collection
of ukiyo-e (woodblock prints), ceramics
and lacquer works, many of which have
been designated as National Treasures
and Important Cultural Properties by
the national government.

Those travellers who have read
James Clavell's *Shogun* may recognise **Ito**, south of Atami on the eastern
coast of Izu-hanto, as the temporary
abode of the shipwrecked Englishman
who ingratiated himself into Japanese
affairs. Today it is a popular hot-spring
resort, punctuated by the Kawana
resort complex in the south part of the
city. The **Ikeda Museum of 20th-Cen-
tury Art** (Thu–Tue 9am–5pm) offers
some 600 paintings and sculptures
by Matisse, Picasso, Chagall, Dalí and
other masters. South is another hot-
spring outpost, **Atagawa**, noted for
Atagawa Banana-Wanien (Atagawa
Tropical and Alligator Garden; daily
8.30am–5pm).

Shimoda ❼ is a somewhat sleepy
resort city at the southern terminus

of the railway line. A fine view of **Iro-
misaki** (Cape Iro) to the south can be
had from the top of **Nesugata-yama**,
three minutes by cable car from Shimoda Station. The view includes vol-
canically active Oshima, an island to
the east and part of Metropolitan Tokyo.

The first US consul general to Japan,
Townsend Harris, was based here,
arriving in 1856. This was the first permanent foreign consulate in Japan,
chosen by the shogun in part for its
remoteness and thus its distance
from centres of power. A monument in
Shimoda-koen (Shimoda Park) commemorates the occasion. The friendship treaty between Japan and the US
was signed at **Ryosen-ji** in 1854.

Central Izu is the cultural heart
of the peninsula. The **Taisha-jinja** in
Mishima ❽ (www.mishimataisha.or.jp;
daily 9am–4.30pm; free) is revered
as Izu's first shrine; its treasure hall
keeps documents of the first Kamakura shogun as well as swords and
other artefacts. The Egawa house in
Nirayama is the oldest private dwelling in Japan. **Shuzen-ji**, along the
Katsura-gawa, sprang up around a
temple founded by the monk Kobo Daishi; this quiet hot-spring town became
a favourite hideaway for Japan's great
literary talents such as Natsume
Soseki, Nobel Prize-winner Kawabata
Yasunari, and Kido Okamoto.

MOUNT FUJI AND HAKONE

The region around **Fuji-san** ❾ (Mount
Fuji but never Mount Fuji-san) has been
the inspiration for the works of many of
Japan's most celebrated writers, poets
and artists. Japan's most celebrated
woodblock print artist, Katsuhika
Hokusai (1760–1849), in particular,
dedicated much of his work to capturing the iconic peak. It would be hard to
find a mountain more highly praised for
its beauty than Fuji-san or a lake more
often photographed than Hakone's
Ashi-no-ko. The mountain also boasts
Unesco World Heritage status. Most

Hikers on Mount Takao.

of the region is designated a "national park", but due to Japan's rather weak laws protecting and restricting commercial exploitation of such assets, one can often consider a national park to be a "nature" amusement park.

Sweeping up from the Pacific to form a nearly perfect symmetrical cone 3,776 metres (12,388ft) above sea level, the elegantly shaped Fuji-san watches over Japan. Fuji's last eruption, in 1707, covered Edo Period Tokyo, some 100km (60 miles) away, with ash. Like many natural monuments held to be sacred and imbued with a living spirit, Fuji-san was off-limits to women for many centuries. It was not until 1867, when an Englishwoman boldly scaled the mountain, that there is any record of a woman climbing the peak. Today, half of the estimated 400,000 annual hikers are women.

Although climbers are known to set out to challenge the mountain throughout the year, the "official" climbing season for Fuji-san begins on 1 July and ends on 10 September. The mountain huts and services found along the trails to Fuji's peak are open only then. Expect thick crowds and a distinctly commercial atmosphere, not only around the facilities but along the entire trail to the top.

For those who wish to see the rising sun from Fuji's peak, start in the afternoon, stay overnight (forget sleeping – it's noisy) at one of the cabins near the top, and make the remaining climb while the sky is still dark. The other option is to climb through the night. The trails are well travelled and hard to miss. For detailed information, visit the official Fuji-san climbing website, www.fujisan-climb.jp.

Fuji Go-ko ⑩ (Fuji Five Lakes) skirts the northern base of Fuji-san as a year-round resort, probably more than most visitors seeking Japan's sacred mountain would expect or want. From east to west, the lakes are Yamanaka, Kawaguchi, Sai, Shoji and Motosu. (A

-ko added to the end of these names signifies "lake".)

Yamanaka-ko, which is the largest in the group, and the picturesque Kawaguchi-ko are the most frequented of the five, but some of the best spots are hidden near the smaller and more secluded Motosu-ko, Shoji-ko and Sai-ko. Some recommended visits include the Narusawa Ice Cave and Fugaku Wind Cave, both formed by the volcanic activities of one of Fuji's early eruptions.

Hakone is set against the backdrop of Fuji-san and has long been a popular place for rest and recreation. Hakone's 16 hot springs, including Tenzan (http://tenzan.jp), Hakone Kamon (www.hakone-kamon.jp), Hakone Yuryo (www.hakoney-uryo.jp), Yunosato Okada (www.yunosato-y.jp), Kappa Tengoku (www.kappa1059.co.jp) and Rakuyujurin Shizenkan are nestled in a shallow ravine where the Hayakawa and Sukumo rivers flow together. The inns here have natural mineral baths, but bathing is just part of Hakone's appeal, with the Hakone Open-Air Museum (www.hakone-oam.or.jp; daily 9am–5pm) offering a superb collection

Lake Ashi, Hakone, with a view to Mount Fuji.

☉ Fact

Amongst the world's major religions, Shinto is unique, with a supreme being, the Sun Goddess or Amaterasu Omikami, that is female. Her brother, Tsukuyomi, is the Moon God and ruler of night.

of sculpture, and the Pola Museum of Art (www.polamuseum.or.jp; daily 9am–5pm) a first-rate assemblage of Impressionist and Modernist paintings.

NORTH OF TOKYO

KAWAGOE

Kawagoe ⑪, a former castle town of dark wood, plaster and tile godowns (called *kura*), and ageing temples, prospered as a supplier of goods to Edo during the Tokugawa Period, hence its sobriquet "Little Edo".

It's a 15-minute walk north along Chuo-dori from Kawagoe Station to reach the historical core of the town. **Ichiban-gai** is Kawagoe's most famous street and the one with the largest concentration of *kura*.

The first main site reached on Chuo-dori is the **Yamazaki Art Museum** (www.mazak-art.com; Tue–Fri 10am–5.30pm, Sat–Sun 10am–5pm), which houses the Meiji-era paintings of Gaho Hashimoto and, unusually, includes a cup of green tea and traditional sweet in the admission fee.

Kawagoe's bell tower.

One block up from the Yamazaki Art Museum, down a lane to the right is the **Toki no Kane**, a wooden tower that has become the most photographed image of Kawagoe. The current structure was built after a fire broke out in 1893. Two blocks up across the street, the narrow lane on the left is **Kashi-ya Yoko-cho** (Confectioners' Row). Souvenirs and trinkets have been added to shops selling old-fashioned sweets and purple sweet potato ice cream. Several small atmospheric temples can be found just off of Kashi-ya Yokocho, and there is also the **Kurazukuri Shiryokan** (Tue–Sun 9am–5pm), a small museum housed in an 1850s tobacconist's that looks at *kura* and local history.

Heading several hundred metres east, little remains of Kawagoe Castle, but the exquisite **Honmaru-goten Palace** (Tue–Sun 9am–5pm), with its beautifully painted screens and archaeological artefacts, more than makes up for that. A 10-minute walk south takes you to **Kita-in**, an important Buddhist temple-museum with a traditional Japanese garden. Kita-in's main crowd-puller are the **Gohyaku Rakan** stones, 540 statues (although, oddly, *gohyaku* means 500) depicting disciples of the Buddha in different, highly realistic, sometimes humorous poses and expressions.

NIKKO

After learning that the main attraction at Nikko, a temple called Tosho-gu, comprises 42 structures and that 29 of these are embellished with some sort of carving – 5,147 in all, according to a six-year-long survey concluded in 1991 – more than a few travellers begin to realise that they've allotted too little time for Nikko.

The small city of **Nikko ⑫**, just under two hours north of Tokyo's Ueno Station on the Tobu Line, is of little interest in itself, serving merely as a commercial anchor to the splendours that decorate the nearby hillsides and

plateau across the river to the west from the main railway stations.

How this region – once a several-day trek from the shogunate's capital in Edo (present-day Tokyo) – was chosen as the site of Tokugawa Ieyasu's mausoleum is a story in itself. True, Nikko forms a sort of crown at the northern perimeter of the great Kanto Plain, of which Edo was the centre. However, Ieyasu was from Kansai, not Kanto, and he had established his capital in Kanto primarily to distance himself from the imperial forces in Kansai's Kyoto, forces he had vanquished to seize power in the first place.

Still, Ieyasu's grandson Iemitsu (1604–51) set in motion the process that turned this once out-of-the-way region into Tokugawa territory about 20 years after Ieyasu's death. In fact, Iemitsu himself and his successor Ietsuna – and the Tokugawa shoguns and princes for the next 250 years – made at least three annual pilgrimages to the site to pay tribute to the founder of the dynasty that kept Japan and its people isolated from the outside world.

THROUGH THE GATES

Ironically, however, given the Tokugawa aversion to things from outside Japan, many of the 5,000-odd carvings at **Tosho-gu** (www.toshogu.jp; daily, Apr–Oct 8am–5pm, Nov–Mar 8am–4pm) depict things foreign. The facade of the main shrine, for example, features carvings of three Chinese men, said to represent important figures of that country who, having turned down their chances to be kings or emperors, became folk heroes.

Most iconic of all is the famous, not to say fabulous, **Yomei-mon**, the gate beyond which only the highest-ranking samurai could pass into the inner sanctum of the shrine, and then only after laying aside their swords. This gate is a masterpiece. Technically, it is a 12-column, two-storey structure with hip-gable ends on right and left, and with cusped gables on four sides. This description, while accurate, is somewhat misleading, however. Even though its *keyaki*-wood columns are painted white to make it appear larger, the gate is quite small. Nearly every surface of the gate is adorned with delicate carvings of every sort – children at play, clouds, tree peonies, pines, bamboo, Japanese apricots, phoenixes, pheasants, cranes, wild ducks and other waterfowl, turtles, elephants, rabbits, a couple of furry tigers, Chinese lions and the traditional symbols of regal power, dragons.

A large, white dragon (one of 92 in and around the shrine) is the main feature of the central beam in front of the second storey of this fanciful structure, and two drawings of dragons appear on the ceiling of the porticoes. The drawing nearer the entrance is known as *noboriryu* or ascending dragon, while the other is *kudari-ryu* or descending dragon.

What lies beyond this gate? Another gate, of course: **Kara-mon** (Chinese Gate), also a National Treasure. It is smaller than the Yomei-mon (at about 3 by 2 metres, or 10 by 6.5ft, overall)

Yomei-mon, Nikko.

⊘ Tip

As a side trip from Nikko, one option is the quirky Edo Wonderland Nikko (www.edowonderland.net), a theme park where the extensive grounds look like a movie set of the old Edo days. You can catch a "real" ninja show, a mock trial in a magistrate's court, and see many other attractions. It is great entertainment and an enjoyable way to learn about the old days of pre-Meiji Japan.

and is also laden with carvings – dragons (ascending and descending, and lounging around), apricots, bamboo, tree peonies and more.

The ceiling has a carved figure of a fairy playing a harp, while on the ridge of the front gable is a bronze figure of a *tsutsuga*, which like quite a few other carvings and castings in the shrine precincts is not quite a real animal, but rather one created from hearsay and ancient myth and mixed with a healthy imagination.

To help get your bearings, the Kara-mon is the last barrier to pass through before reaching the entrance to the *haiden* (oratory) and the *honden* (main hall), which is the place most visitors remember as they are requested to remove shoes. An official guidebook describes *haiden* and *honden* as the "chief edifices of the shrine". Chief they are, but interesting they are not – at least not to the casual visitor who, not knowing what to look for, tends to shuffle along with the crowd and then returns to the shoe lockers without a pause.

Unfortunately, many of the key elements inside are partially or entirely hidden from the view achieved by this method. Confused (and no doubt somewhat bored) after their shuffle through the "chief edifices", most visitors exit, re-don their shoes and spend the next 10 minutes or so looking for the famous **Nemuri-neko**, or carving of the Sleeping Cat. Some never find it at all and make their way back down the hillside feeling somewhat cheated. To make sure this doesn't happen to you, do not follow the logical path back towards the Yomei-mon. Instead, turn left (right if facing the *haiden/honden* complex) until you are back on the terrace between Yomei-mon and Kara-mon. Next, advance straight ahead (paying the small fee charged at a makeshift entrance to the Oku no In, or Inner Precincts) and into the open-sided, red-lacquered corridor that skirts the foot of the steep hillside, atop which is the actual Tokugawa tomb. Nemuri-neko, a painted relief carving, is over the gateway.

This small grey cat, well-enough executed and rather cute but otherwise unremarkable, is said to symbolise tranquillity. The fact that it is asleep is taken to mean that all "harmful mice" have been sent packing and the shrine is therefore safe. The carved sparrows behind the dozing cat presumably aren't a threat.

SHOGUNATE TOMB

While here, climb the 200-odd stone steps to the top of the hill and the Tokugawa tomb, called **Hoto**, wherein it is said are the remains of Tokugawa Ieyasu. Some spectacular views of rooftops and the surrounding terrain are had from here. On the way past Tosho-gu, through the Yomei-mon to the main entrance and beyond, be sure to stop by the **Yakushido**, one of the few places in these sacred Shinto surroundings with a Buddhist atmosphere. It's off to the right. Here, too, remove shoes. The attraction of this building (it is not exactly a Buddhist temple) is the huge *naku-ryu*, or crying dragon, drawing on the ceiling.

Kara-mon.

It seems that when people stood under the original – drawn in India ink by Kano Yasunobu (1613–85) – and clapped their hands as in prayer, the dragon was heard to utter a long, agonised groan. What this was meant to signify is not recorded and perhaps we will never know, because in 1961 a fire destroyed the building – and the original drawing along with it. You can hear the current dragon cry today, if you pay for a brief tour of the temple that ends with one of the priests banging two wood blocks together under the dragon's head.

Among the other sights to take note of as one leaves the shrine are the sutra library, which boasts nearly 7,000 volumes of the Buddhist sutras in a large, revolving bookcase that was invented by the Chinese. Its other treasures include numerous stone, bronze and iron lanterns presented by the daimyo paying their respects to the shogunate and a pair of stone *tobikoe no shishi* (leaping lions) as the main pillars of the stone balustrade.

The bronze candelabrum, bronze lantern and large revolving lantern were presented by the government of the Netherlands to Japan in 1636. The revolving lantern in front of the drum tower is adorned with the three-leaf crests of the Tokugawa clan, but they are placed upside down, perhaps, as an official guidebook to the sutra library explains, "by mistake".

Here, also, are the sacred storehouses on the sides of the middle court. The upper one shows two elephants carved in relief, as well as the *mikoshi-gura* (sacred palanquin house), the repository for the sacred portable shrines used in the annual festival, and the *kagura-den* (sacred dance stage). The flower basket in the gilded panel at the right corner was probably inspired by a basket used by early Dutch traders; it is the only carving in the precincts that shows Western artistic influences.

Beyond the 40-metre (130ft) high, five-storey pagoda, its first storey decorated with the 12 signs of the Chinese zodiac, and just before reaching the 9-metre (30ft) tall **Omote-mon** (Front Gate), with its large images of the two deva kings, there is what may be the most famous carvings of all – not just in Nikko, but in all the world. Just under the eaves of the royal stables building, which is the only unlacquered structure in the shrine precincts, are the **Three Monkeys**: hear no evil, speak no evil, see no evil. Small carvings they are, despite their fame, but so are all 5,000-plus carvings at Tosho-gu.

Just a short stroll down the broad avenue leading from the Thousand Steps (there are only 10) entrance to Tosho-gu is the **Tosho-gu Homotsukan** (Tosho-gu Treasure House; daily, Apr–Oct 8am–5pm, Nov–Mar 8am–4pm), a small museum housing various ancient articles, including carvings, from Tosho-gu and other places around Nikko. During peak tourist seasons, a number of kiosks will set up in the small adjoining park, Koyoen, to sell beverages and food, lending a commercial flair to the area.

⊙ Fact

Hamada Shoji has been a great influence to potters all over the world. His glazing techniques are greatly copied and admired; *temmoku* iron glaze, rice-husk ash glaze and *kaki* persimmon glaze have become his trademarks.

A carving of the Three Monkeys in Nikko.

Continue west along the wide avenue for a few minutes to reach **Futarasan-jinja** (www.futarasan.jp; Apr–Oct 8am–5pm, Nov–Mar 8am–4pm), on the right side and away from Tosho-gu. Futar-asan-jinja enshrines the three primary Shinto deities: Okuninushi no Mikoto, his consort Tagorihime no Mikoto, and their son Ajisukitakahikone no Mikoto. All three are revered for having helped to create and then make prosperous the Japanese islands.

Within the grounds is a large bronze lantern called **Bake-doro** (Goblin Lantern), which is said to have once taken on the shape of a goblin so frightening that a samurai attacked it one night, leaving "sword scratches" that are still visible to this day.

BEYOND TOSHO-GU

Further afield but still within the general area of Tosho-gu are several other places of interest. One is the Futarasan-affiliated **Hon-gu**, established in 767 by the priest Shodo and one of the oldest shrines in Nikko. The present buildings date back only to the end of the 17th century, when the shrine was rebuilt after being destroyed by fire. Just behind it is **Shihonryu-ji**, also founded by Shodo. In fact, it is not a Shinto shrine but rather a Buddhist temple. It also was destroyed by fire and the present three-storey pagoda was erected in its place at the end of the 17th century. The pagoda and the image of the thousand-hand Kannon inside are the temple's main attractions.

Then there is **Rinno-ji** (www.rinnoji.or.jp; daily, Apr–Oct 8am–5pm, Nov–Mar 8am–4pm), a temple of the Tendai sect of Buddhism. Its significant claim is the fact that General Ulysses S. Grant, the 18th president of the United States and a hero of the American Civil War, stayed here during his eight-day trip to Japan and Nikko in 1879. It was one of Grant's few trips outside of North America. Actually, the temple has more than Grant-slept-here going for it. In its spirit hall are the tablets of its long line of abbots, all drawn from the imperial family. In another building, built in 1648 and still the largest in Nikko, are three quite amazing Buddhist statues, all measuring 8 metres (26ft) in height and worked in gilded wood.

NIKKO'S FORESTS

The lush forests of Nikko are filled with ancient trees. The majority are *sugi*, or Japanese cedar. When veiled in mist, one might think they have stood here since the beginning of time, or at the very least are part of a primeval virgin forest. They don't go back quite that far, but they are nevertheless very old, especially those trees in the Tosho-gu precincts proper and along the many kilometres of avenues and roads within and leading to Nikko. These cedars were planted as seedlings, one by one, from year to year, under the direction of a man named Matsudaira Masatsuna (1576–1648).

Matsudaira, so the story goes, was the daimyo of Kawagoe and one of the two persons honoured by edict of the shogun to supervise the construction

Chuzenji-ko.

of Tosho-gu. The extent of the man's personal wealth is not recorded nor how much of it was spent, in addition to the budget he was given by the Tokugawa shogun, in planting these trees.

However, it can be assumed that he wasn't very well off to begin with. When his turn to present a grand offering to the shrine came – all the daimyo were obliged to do this – Matsudaira was broke. What could he do as an offering, he wondered. Around 1631, several years before the shrine itself was finished, he began to transplant cedar seedlings – plentiful in the surrounding mountains (which he owned) – into strategic positions around the shrine grounds and along the seemingly endless roads. It took him 20 years and an estimated 25,000 seedlings. Today, these trees are what in part define Nikko and its surroundings for travellers. The beneficence continues. The trees and the banks along the avenues are protected as Natural Treasures and Places of Historical Importance under Japanese law.

Thanks to the numbers of visitors who flock to Nikko and the region's fine scenery, the area abounds with other diversions. Unfortunately, getting around without a vehicle is a problem. If money permits, rent a car (not cheap). If time permits, take a taxi or a bus (this will take longer) up the famed I-Ro-Ha switchback road to **Chuzenji-ko** , a large and quite picturesque lake due west of Nikko. From there, savour the altitude of 1,270 metres (4,170ft), clear air and lakeside scenery. A sightseeing boat leaves the pier, just across the road from the bus stop, for a one-hour tour of the lake. Its heavily wooded shores are lined with hotels, inns, campsites and other tourist wonders. Five minutes' walk in the opposite direction is the observatory of the 100-metre (320ft) high **Kegon Falls** (Kegon no Taki; http://kegon.jp); a lift descends right to the bottom of the gorge (daily, Mar–Apr, Nov 8am–5pm, May–Sept 7.30am–6pm, Oct

7.30am–5pm, Dec–Feb 9am–4.30pm), where a platform allows views of the thundering falls.

MASHIKO

Synonymous with a rustic, earthenware ceramic, the village of **Mashiko** ⓮, just 30km (20 miles) southeast of Nikko, is a living pottery village, with some 300 working kilns scattered among the surrounding paddy fields. Although Mashiko has been a craft village for over a millennium, its name was made in the 1930s when renowned potter Hamada Shoji built a kiln here, later to be joined by English ceramicist Bernard Leach. **Hamada's house and kiln**, located in the **Togei Messe** complex (www.mashiko-sankokan.net; Tue–Sun 9.30am–5pm), have been lovingly restored. Tourist information booths located in Utsunomiya Station (50 minutes from Tokyo Station by *shinkansen*), from where buses make the hour-long trip to Mashiko, provide leaflets and maps in English. A lively village with dozens of ceramic shops and stalls, Mashiko stages regular pottery fairs and festivals.

Owl figures.

View of the Japan Alps in the morning.

CENTRAL HONSHU

Central Honshu offers the modern city of Nagoya, a rugged coastline and historic castles, but it is the stupendous mountain scenery of the Japan Alps that is the real draw.

Central Honshu has an air of mystery about it. Yes, it has a big city in the shape of industrial Nagoya, but elsewhere it oozes history and tradition. In places, it still offers a glimpse of life before modernity crept in. All over the region, traditional crafts thrive – *kutani* ware in Kanazawa and Hida lacquerware in Takayama perhaps the two best known. Just outside Nagoya, in Gifu and Inuyama, they still practise a 1,300-year-old form of fishing, while in the charming town of Gujo Hachiman the main draw is a 400-year-old dance festival. In Shirakawa-go many villagers still live in traditional thatched houses that haven't changed for generations. And while tourism has no doubt played a part in keeping these traditions thriving, you get the feeling they would still be here even if the tour buses hadn't pulled up.

Central Honshu is blessed with rich nature too. The breathtaking peaks around Kamikochi are considered Japan's best hiking grounds for good reason, while Sado-jima off the northern coast of Niigata is beautifully rugged and wild. Visit the island in winter and you will soon understand why being exiled here – as so many were – was once considered a punishment. Better still, visit other parts of Niigata and Nagano in winter for fantastic skiing and snowboarding opportunities, or retreat to one of the region's hot spring resorts.

Crowds at Nagoya Station.

NAGOYA AND AROUND NAGOYA

Although known in Japan for its food – its flat, white *kishimen* noodles, its moriguchi-zuke pickles, its confection called *uiro*, its deep-fried *tebasaki* chicken wings, and all manner of dishes that use the local miso paste – **Nagoya ❶** is better recognised as a centre of industry, producing construction materials and automobiles, with just a few sights for the traveller. Nagoya is located almost precisely in the centre of Japan along the old Tokaido highway and is a major transport hub to and from other

Main attractions

Nagoya
Inuyama
Gujo Hachiman
Takayama
Shirakawa-go
Kamikochi
Kiso Valley
Kanazawa
Sado-jima

Map on page 194

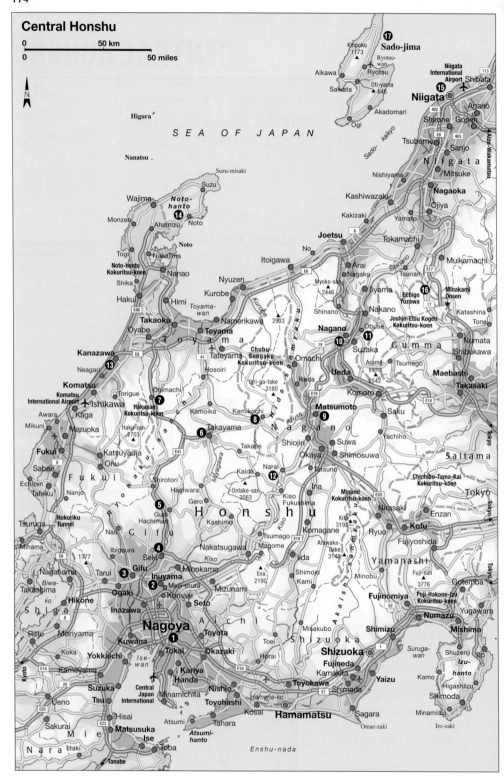

Central Honshu

0   50 km

0   50 miles

N

SEA OF JAPAN

Higura

Nanatsu

⑰ **Sado-jima**

Kinpoku 1173

Aikawa   Ryotsu-wan

Sawata   Ryotsu

Oti-yama 646

Ogi   Akadomari

Sado- kaikyo

Niigata International Airport   Shibata ⑮

Niigata   113

Agano

Shirone   Gosen

402

Tsubame   **Sanjo**

EB   403

N i i g a t a

Nishiyama   Mitsuke

Nagaoka

Kashiwazaki   Ojiya

Kakizaki   Yamato

8   Muikamachi

Joetsu   Tokamachi

No

Itoigawa   Shinano

Arai   Tsunan   E17

Nagako

EB   Myoko-san 2446

Tiyama

Shinano   Nakano   Echigo Yuzawa ⑯

Nagano ⑪   Obuse

Joshin-Etsu Kogen Kokuritsu-koen

⑩   Suzaka

19   Omachi   Asama-yama 2542

Ikeda   **Ueda**   Tsumago

E19   Komoro

Matsumoto   Saku

⑨

Shiojiri   Suwa   Yachiho

Okaya   Shimosuwa

Tatsuno   E20

Narai ⑫   Ina

Minami Kokuritsu-koen

Kiso Fukushima

Komagane

Nirasaki

Sado-hanto

Noto-hanto Kokuritsu-koen

Wajima   Noto-hanto ⑭

Monzen   Anamizu   Noto

Togi   Nakajima

Shika   Nanao

Hakui   Himi

E06   Toyama-wan

Takaoka   Namerikawa

Oyabe   **Toyama**

T o y a m a

Tateyama

Chubu Sangaku Kokuritsu-koen

41   Hosoiri

Yari-ga-take 3180

Kamikochi ⑧

Kanazawa

Neagari   ⑬

Komatsu

Komatsu International Airport   Ishikawa

Awara   Kaga

Mikuni

Maruoka

Fukui   Katsuyama

Sabae   Onu

Echizen

Tafeku   Nanjo

Hokuriku Tunnel

Tsuruga

Torigue   Ogimachi ⑦

Hakusan Kokuritsu-koen

Haku-san 2703

Kamoika   Takayama ⑥

Shirotori

Hagiwara

Gujo   ⑤

Hachiman

Gero

Kashimo

Ontake-san 3063

Ena 2190

Naka

G i f u

Nao   Ibigaura

④

Seki   **Gifu**

Inuyama ③

②

Meiji-mura

Komaki

Inazawa   **Seto**

F u k u i

2993

Shinano

Hakusan

H o n s h u

Kiso

Tsumago   Magome

Shimojo   Arawaka-dake 3149

Kami

Ida

Minobu

Kita 3192

Ryuo

Kofu

Fujiyoshida

Enzan

Tokyo

G u m m a

Numata

Shibukawa

Maebashi

Takasaki

E18

S a i t a m a

Chichibu-Tama-Kai Kokuritsu-koen

Tokyo

Y a m a n a s h i

Fuji-san 3776

Gotemba

Fuji-Hakone-Izu Kokuritsu-koen

52   Yugawara

Mihama

Nagahama   1377

Takashima   Tarui

Biwa-ko   ③ **Gifu**

Takashima   Ogaki

8   **Hikone**   **Inazawa**

S h i g a

Ritto   Moriyama

Koka   **Kuwana**

Yokkaichi

Kameyama

Kyoto   E1A

Suzuka

Ueno   **Tsu**

E25   Hisai

Sakurai   **Matsusaka**

M i e   **Ise**

N a r a   Iitaki   Toba

Tanabe

Nagoya ①

Toyota

Tokai   **Okazaki**

Kariya   Handa

Central Japan International

Minamichita

Nishio

Toyohashi

Kosai   **Hamamatsu**

Atsumi   Tahara

Atsumi-hanto

Misakubo

A i c h i

Toei

Horai

Toyokawa

Kamakita

Shimada

Hamana-ko

Fujineda

Yaizu

Sagara

Omae-zaki

S h i z u o k a

Shizuoka

Shimizu

Suruga-wan

Kamo   Higashizu

I z u-hanto

Shimoda

Minamiizu

Iro-zaki

Fujinomiya

Numazu

Mishima

Shuzenji-ko   Ito

Yugawara

Enshu-nada

Kiso

Nakatsugawa

Minokamo

Mizunami

Kaida

Takane

Kamoika

Takayama

Myogawa

Daisanmyaku

Akaishi

Kuzuryu

Kuzure-gawa

cities, including Tokyo and Osaka. It is Japan's fourth-largest city, with 2.2 million people.

Nagoya was originally planned by the shogun Tokugawa Ieyasu to be a castle town. He built **Nagoya-jo** (Nagoya Castle; www.nagoyajo.city.nagoya.jp; daily 9am–4.30pm) in 1612 for his ninth son, Yoshinao, but the town didn't really develop into a powerful presence. Much later, Nagoya had to be redesigned and reconstructed after suffering extensive air-raid damage in 1945. The castle, rebuilt in 1959 and now functioning as a cultural and historical museum, is considered Nagoya's primary attraction. The museum displays treasures of the Tokugawa family.

Nagoya's **Atsuta-jingu** (www.atsuta-jingu.or.jp; temple precincts always open and free; museum daily 9am–4.30pm, closed last Wed of the month and the following day) is second only to the Ise-jingu, in Mie Prefecture, in its importance to the emperor of Japan and Shintoism. One of the imperial family's three sacred treasures, the Kusanagi sword *(kusanagi no tsurugi)* is kept here. (The other two sacred treasures, the jewel and mirror, are kept at the Imperial Palace in Tokyo and at Ise, respectively.) All three treasures are said to have been given to the imperial family by the Sun Goddess Amaterasu Omikami. None are viewable by the public. Hundreds of ancient trees thrive amidst ancient artefacts, including the 600-year-old Nijugocho-bashi, a bridge made of 25 blocks of stone. The shrine's main festival is in June, though other events also take place throughout the year. More centrally located than Atsuta (which is south of the city centre) is the **Osu Kannon** temple. Originally located in Gifu, Tokugawa Ieyasu moved it to Nagoya in 1612, and although all the buildings are modern reconstructions, it's still an imposing sight – especially striking is the giant red paper lantern hanging before its main hall. Every 18th of the month, the grounds are used for a lively flea market.

There are museums all over Nagoya, ranging from the treasure-laden **Tokugawa Art Museum** (www.tokugawa-art-museum.jp; Tue–Sun 10am–5pm), displaying heirlooms of the Owari-Tokugawa family, and **Aichi Bijutsu-kan** (Arts Centre; www.aac.pref.aichi.jp; Tue–Sun 10am–6pm, Fri until 8pm), which features work from the 19th century to the present, to the state-of-the-art **Nagoya City Science Museum** (www.ncsm.city.nagoya.jp; daily 9.30am–5pm), which has plenty of entertaining hands-on exhibits for both children and adults to enjoy, and boasts one of the world's largest planetariums located in a giant silver globe. Another enjoyable and popular venue for a family visit is the **Port of Nagoya Public Aquarium** (www.nagoyaaqua.com; usually Tue–Sun 9.30am–5.30pm, summer until 8pm, winter until 5pm).

Celebrating part of Nagoya's more recent history is the **Toyota Commemorative Museum of Industry and Technology** (www.tcmit.org; Tue–Sun

Inuyama Castle.

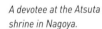

A devotee at the Atsuta shrine in Nagoya.

9.30am–5pm). Situated in cavernous red-brick buildings that once housed Toyota's looms (Toyota was a textile giant long before it branched out into cars), the museum gives insights into Japan's *monozukuri* (art of making things) culture and provides plenty of fun, hands-on activities aimed at kids. Alternatively, the **SCMAGLEV and Railway Park** (http://museum.jr-central.co.jp; Wed–Mon 10am–5.30pm), operated by Central Japan Railway Company, celebrates Japan's fast-train developments. Here, visitors can enter a life-size reproduction of a driver's cabin on the SeriesN700 *shinkansen*, learn how the superconducting Maglev works, or ride train-driving simulators.

OUTSIDE NAGOYA

Some 25km (15.5 miles) north of Nagoya is **Inuyama** ❷, site of Japan's oldest castle, built in the mid-1400s (http://inuyama-castle.jp; daily 9am–5pm). Standing in its original state above the Kiso-gawa, it has been owned by the same family since the 1600s. A little east of the castle is the exquisite

Meiji-mura, near Inuyama, contains the interior lobby of Frank Lloyd Wright's Imperial Hotel, transported from Tokyo.

Uraku-en (daily 9am–5pm, Dec–Feb until 4pm), a lush garden replete with several traditional teahouses, one of which, Joan, is considered to be one of the country's top three historic teahouses. Near Inuyama is **Meiji-mura** (Meiji Village; www.meijimura.com; Mar–July, Sep, Oct daily 9.30am–5pm, Aug daily 10am–5pm, Nov daily 9.30am–4pm, Dec–Feb Tue–Sun 10am–4pm), with 67 Meiji-era structures collected from around Japan and reassembled here. Of special note is the entrance hall and lobby of Frank Lloyd Wright's original Imperial Hotel, built in Tokyo and moved here when the latest hotel was built. Every March, one of Japan's strangest festivals (Hounen Matsuri) occurs not far from Inuyama, at a little shrine – **Tagata-jingu** – dedicated to phalluses (www.tagatajinja.com). A huge and anatomically correct phallus is carried through the streets, and crowds of men and especially women try to touch it, hoping to enhance their fertility. Equally traditional, but far less odd, are the *ukai* (cormorant fishing) displays that take place on Inuyama's Kiso River from June to mid-October.

Further north of Nagoya, **Gifu** ❸ has a modern clothing industry. But for Japanese tourists, Gifu is undoubtedly better known for its 1,300-year history of cormorant fishing *(ukai)* on the three rivers – the Kiso, Ibi and Nagara – that cut through the city. Today, *ukai* is distinctly a tourist attraction, with the collared birds doing their thing at night, illuminated by small fires suspended in iron baskets from the front of the boats (the displays take place most evenings from mid-May to mid-October; tickets can be bought at the tourist office in Gifu Station, www.gifucvb.or.jp). Gifu's highly respected craftsmen add another touch of tradition to the city, especially its lantern and umbrella makers.

Gifu's castle (**Gifu-jo**; times vary, but daily at least 9.30am–4.30pm) commands an impressive view from the top of Kinka-zan (Golden Flower

Mountain). It was built about seven centuries ago, has suffered numerous razings, and was last rebuilt in 1956. A three-minute gondola ride to the foot of the mountain arrives at Gifu-koen (Gifu Park) and the unspectacular **Museum of History** and the more interesting **Nawa Insect Museum** (www. nawakon.jp; Fri–Tue 10am–5pm, Feb also closed Tue). The latter, though small, contains various bugs, butterflies and spiders – some of which are uncomfortably large – from around the world. In all, its collection includes 300,000 specimens. Not far from here is **Shoho-ji temple** (www.gifu-daibutsu. com; daily 9am–5pm), an otherwise small and fairly run-down affair that has one spectacular saving grace – a giant gilded Buddha, 13.7 metres (45ft) high, that's well worth the admission fee to the main hall that it fills.

Finally, no summary of the Nagoya region would be complete without mention of **Seki ❹**, a sword-forging village a bit east of Gifu and the site of the Battle of Sekigahara, waged in the early 17th century between the forces of Tokugawa Ieyasu and Toyotomi Hideyori. The battle was a significant turning point in Japanese history and a catalyst for a complete shift in the archipelago's power structure. Although Tokugawa was outnumbered nearly two to one, his warriors slaughtered more than a third of the enemy troops to put Tokugawa on the shogun's throne, which he and his descendants held for the next 250-odd years. Today, only an unassuming stone marks the spot of Tokugawa's heroic triumph.

GUJO HACHIMAN

Writer and long-distance walker Alan Booth (who moved to Japan in 1970) was quick to sense something special when he wrote about **Gujo Hachiman ❺** in his classic travelogue *Looking for the Lost*: "What I was in fact approaching was a town of a kind I'd dreamed of finding when I'd first arrived in Japan almost 20 years before, a town so extraordinary that, when I went out to stroll around it that evening, I almost forgot to limp."

Cormorant fishing on Nagara River.

Gujo sits at the confluence of the very clean and beautiful Nagara and Yoshino rivers, their *ayu-* (sweetfish) rich waters popular with fishermen. The town sits in a mountain valley that long ago was a way station on an important trade route that led to the Sea of Japan (East Sea). An imposing fortress once stood here. Built as a symbol of the town's former importance, the current castle (**Gujo Hachiman-jo**; http://castle.gujohachiman. com; daily 9am–5pm, until 6pm during Gujo Odori season), dating from 1934, replaced the original. It's a stiff walk to the pinnacle, but the views from the top are commanding. This is the best place to appreciate the shape of the town, which, as all the local travel information will tell you, resembles a fish.

Hashimoto-cho, an old merchant area, remains the commercial heart of the town. Look behind the modern facades here and you will discover buildings which, in some cases, have stood here for centuries. The physical fabric of the town is as appealing as the setting, consisting of dark, stained-wood homes and shops, white plastered buildings, wooden bridges, steep walls constructed from boulders, and narrow stone-paved lanes. Museums, galleries and attractive shops selling local products like Tsumugi textiles can be found along these lanes.

Gujo Hachiman is known for its festivals, in particular the **Gujo Odori** dance festival that runs from mid-July to early September, climaxing in the middle with a frenetic four-day main festival in August. The 400-year-old event features thousands of dancers clad in colourful *yukata* (light kimonos), performing carefully choreographed movements accompanied by an almost hypnotic chant-like singing. During the festival, the local tourist office gives daily free **dance lessons** (at 11am, 1pm, 2pm and 3pm) to visitors, which are well worth trying. While you are at the tourist office, pick up one of their self-guided walking tour maps (also available online on www.gujohachiman. com/kanko/index_e.html) – following one of these for half a day is by far the best way to explore the town.

The Sanmachi Suji area, Takayama.

INTERIOR MOUNTAINS

TAKAYAMA TO THE COAST

High in the mountains is **Takayama** ❻, luring travellers with *onsen* (hot springs), hikes, tennis courts and other activities. Originally established in the 1500s as a castle town for the Kanamori family, Takayama retains an old charm nurtured by its ryokan (traditional inns), sake breweries and craft shops. One of its highlights, **Takayama-jinya** (Administrative House; daily 8.45am–5pm, Aug until 6pm, Nov–Feb until 4.30pm) dates from the early 1600s, although the current buildings are early 19th-century reconstructions. Among its displays is a torture chamber.

In the centre of Takayama, just east of the Miyagawa River, which runs through the town, is the **Sanmachi Suji** area, with three streets lined by museums, traditional shops, sake breweries and countless spots to eat. In the summer months it can be yet another tourist madhouse, but is well worth exploring nonetheless to soak up the old-Edo atmosphere given off by the area's old, wood buildings.

Museums abound in Takayama, but the not-to-miss museum is **Hida no Sato** (Hida Folk Village; www.hidanosato-tpo.jp; daily 8.30am–5pm), an open-air assembly of traditional houses that were collected from around the Takayama region and reassembled here. Artisans demonstrate regional folk crafts, and you can also try your hand here at making your own *sashiko* quilting and straw crafts. The **Kusakabe Mingeikan** (Folk Craft Museum; www.kusakabe-mingeikan.com; daily, Mar–Nov 9am–4.30pm, Dec–Feb until 4pm, Dec–Feb closed Tue) is another one worth checking out if you are interested in crafts. This former warehouse – designated as a National Treasure – displays wonderful examples of local Hida woodcarving *(ichii itobori)* and lacquerware work *(Hida-nuri)*.

Takayama is especially famous within Japan for two festivals: one in mid-April called *Sanno* matsuri (festival) with a procession of *yatai* (floats), and the Hachiman matsuri in October.

A thatched house in Shirakawa.

⊘ EAVES DROP

The name for Shirakawa-go's unique style of farmhouses, known as *gassho-zukuri*, or "praying hands," comes from the sharp "A" shape of their wooden frames, resembling the hands of monks pressed together in prayer. The thatched houses have been cleverly designed to withstand deep snowdrifts in the winter months.

Gently soaring structures, the roofs alone can reach an astonishing height of 9 metres (30ft). Constructed without nails, the wooden beams, tightly secured with rope, are a tribute to the traditional skills of Japanese carpenters. The smoke from *irori* open-hearth fires rises through the buildings, blackening rope and wood with soot, but also preserving them and killing off termites and thatch bugs in the process.

With the development of sericulture in the late 1800s, the large upper floors under the eaves were used to raise silkworms. Up to 30 people could inhabit one house, parents and their immediate family sleeping in a private room, servants and unmarried sons sharing an entire floor or two.

As privacy was virtually impossible in such circumstances, couples would retreat to the nearest wood or glade for snatched moments of intimacy, a practice that manifested itself nine months after the end of winter, with a noticeable rise in the birth rate.

If you aren't in Takayama for one of the festivals, you can get a good feel for them at the **Takayama Matsuri Yatai Kaikan** (www.hidahachimangu.jp; daily, Mar–Nov 9am–5pm, Dec–Feb 9am–4.30pm), which displays some of the festivals' floats.

SHIRAKAWA-GO AND GOKAYAMA

A safe haven for the defeated Taira clan, the regions of Shirakawa-go and Gokayama were once so secluded that during the later Edo Period Lord Maeda secretly produced gunpowder here. Until a road was constructed in 1925, villages here, set among thickly forested mountain valleys, were virtually inaccessible. Not so these days, especially after the area's designation in 1995 as a Unesco World Heritage Site, a mixed blessing guaranteeing the preservation of the region's unique architectural heritage, while inviting a blight of tourism on its fragile eco-structure. The beauty of the valleys and their distinctive A-frame thatched houses – *gassho-zukuri* – somehow manages to transcend the crowds.

The largest collection of steeply angled *gassho-zukuri* houses are concentrated in the village of **Ogimachi** ➐, easily accessed these days by buses from Takayama or Kanazawa. Hike up to an observation spot 10 minutes north of the main bus terminal for sweeping views of the valley and houses. **Wada-ke** (daily 9am–5pm), the first notable structure walking back in the direction of the main village, is one of several *gassho-zukuri* serving as museums. This one is a former family residence, once occupied by the Wada family, replete with household items and an impressive lacquerware collection.

A little south, **Myozen-ji Temple Museum** (daily, Apr–Nov 8.30am–5pm, Dec–Mar 9am–4pm) is a large building even by local standards. The great beams of its five storeys, once used by monks and priests as living quarters, are blackened from smoke from the first-floor open hearth used for cooking and to provide warmth. An adjacent thatched temple and bell tower add to the mood.

Although it has a rather contrived feel, the **Gassho-zukuri Folklore**

Hiking amongst spectacular scenery in Kamikochi.

Park (Shirakawa-go Minkaen; www. shirakawago-minkaen.jp; Mar–Nov daily 8.40am–5pm, Dec–Feb Fri–Wed 9am–4pm), a showcase collection of farmhouses relocated here after a dam on the nearby Sho-kawa threatened their existence, is well worth seeing. The open-air museum has 25 farmhouses and puts on demonstrations of weaving, carving and other handicrafts. Despite its World Heritage designation, Ogimachi, like all the villages here, is a working farming community. To get a sense of life here, an overnight stay in one of the *gassho-zukuri*, many now serving as guesthouses, is highly recommended.

Some 10km (6 miles) from Ogimachi, the hamlet of **Suganuma** consists of just 14 houses, 10 of which are *gassho-zukuri*. Despite its diminutive scale, it has two interesting museums, the **Gokayama Minzoku-kan**; and the **Ensho-no-Yakata** (both daily 9am–4pm), the first displaying household items from daily life, the second highlighting the clandestine production of gunpowder.

Another 8km (5 miles) north, **Ainokura** is another gem of rural architecture and life. Though requiring a 30-minute uphill hike from the village of Shimonashi, the village attracts a good number of visitors. The **Ainokura Minzoku-kan** (daily 8.30am–5pm) has interesting displays of local crafts, including handmade toys and washi paper, but it's the spectacular location of the village and endless meandering hiking trails leading from it across densely forested mountains that visitors come for.

KAMIKOCHI

In his novel *The House of Nire*, Kita Morio writes, "In the already fading light the linked peaks of the Alps were solid and harsh, all ranged there in the early dusk like a huge folding screen." One of the most ravishing panels of that folding screen, snow-dusted or gilded with sunlight according to the season, is Mount Hotaka and the high valley of **Kamikochi** ❽ at its feet.

The valley is a part of the **Chubu-Sangaku National Park** in the region of Nagano Prefecture known as Azumi. You know you have reached the area of Kamikochi when you begin to see

> ⊙ **Fact**
>
> Because of the 1998 Olympics, Nagano has a bullet train line direct from Tokyo Station, making crowds more dense. The journey from Tokyo takes one and three quarter hours.

Matsumoto Castle.

The waki-honjin at Tsumago used to be the main inn of the post town.

A quaint stop in Nagano.

cameo images of mountain peaks reflected in the ponds of the Azusa River Basin.

The unsettling paradox of visiting a rural area crowded out with nature-lovers can be avoided by visiting Kamikochi on a summer weekday, in early October, or in the spring shortly after the opening of the mountain road, which is unusable from 15 November to 22 April.

Most walkers set off from the bus terminal in the village, crossing the fast currents of the Azusa River by way of Kappa Bridge. The origin of this strange name (in Japanese folklore, *kappa* are malignant water sprites known in their worst tantrums of violence to tear a victim's bowels out through the anus) can only be guessed at.

After negotiating the bridge, trekkers usually pay brief homage at the Weston Memorial, which has a plaque dedicated to the Englishman who pioneered mountain climbing here at the turn of the 20th century. Trekkers then strike out on anything between a half-day excursion and a

full two-day-three-night circuit of a region many seasoned walkers regard as home to some of the finest hiking trails in Japan. For more information, the tourist offices in Takayama and Matsumoto can be a real help.

Matsumoto 9 is popular in summer with Japanese heading off into the mountains on bikes and on foot. In the 14th century it was the castle town of the Ogasawara clan. **Matsumoto-jo** (daily 8.30am–5pm) is an excellent example of a Japanese castle with its original donjon, dating from late 1590s. Three turrets and six floors are punctuated with fine historical displays and a nice view of the city and the Japan Alps from the top. South of the castle is the modern **Matsumoto City Museum of Art** (http://matsumoto-artmuse.jp; Tue–Sun 9am–5pm), home to many artworks by sculptor Kusama Yayoi, recognised the world over for her flamboyant polka dots.

Venue of the 1998 Winter Olympics, **Nagano** 10 is a moderately sized city of nearly 400,000 people and was established in the Kamakura Period as a temple town. That temple, Zenko-ji, dates from the 7th century and was the site for Ikko Sanzon, the first Buddha image in Japan. Northeast of Nagano, in **Obuse** 11, is the **Hokusai-kan** (Hokusai Museum; http://hokusai-kan.com; daily 9–5pm, July–Aug until 6pm; charge), with a decent collection of Hokusai's ukiyo-e, or woodblock prints.

KISO VALLEY

Taking the Chuo Line southwest of Matsumoto, you soon enter the Kiso Valley region between the Northern and Central Alps. The valley once formed part of the Nakasendo, one of the five key highways linking Edo with central Honshu. Despite vigorously promoted tourism, the region still manages to convey a sense of pre-industrial Japan.

The most affluent of the 11 post towns along the valley, **Narai** 12 and its 1km (0.6-mile) long main street boast

some of the best-preserved wooden buildings in the valley. Look out for the exquisite lattice-work called *renji-goshi*, as fine as filigree. **Nakamura-tei** (daily, Apr–Nov 9am–5pm, Dec–Mar until 4pm), a former comb merchant's shop, is now a museum where you can pick up a pamphlet on local architecture. Unlike the other post towns along the valley, this one permits traffic to pass along its main street. Depending on your point of view, this spoils the town or confirms that it is a living, working community rather than a historical showcase.

Time permitting, a half-day stopover in **Kiso Fukushima**, a sleepy, far less touristy post town south of Narai, provides a nice respite from the crowds. Inns line the Narai-gawa River. **Sumiyoshi-jinja**, an ancient shrine on a slope above the town, has an unusual sand and gravel garden designed by the modern landscape master Mirei Shigemori.

Following the Chuo Line south, **Tsumago** is a beautiful, well-appointed town whose carefully preserved buildings bespeak the efforts of the local community to restore and save their heritage. All high-tension wires and TV aerials have been banished from the scene, improving it no doubt, but giving the impression of a carefully managed open-air museum. It is still a beauty and well worth an overnight stay, if only to see the superb **Waki Honjin Okuya** (daily 9am–5pm), a folk museum located inside a spacious villa and former inn. The museum provides an excellent introduction to the town, with a large display of local products and daily items, as well as a fascinating photo display on the town before and after its restoration. Another, but smaller, local history museum sits next door. Ask at the **tourist information office** (www.tumago.jp; daily 8.30am–5pm) about a useful local service that arranges to have your luggage sent forward for you to your next accommodation in Magome, freeing you to

follow the lovely 8km (5-mile) hiking trail between the two towns.

Where Tsumago is tucked into the valley, **Magome** clings to the side of a hill offering terrific views of nearby Mount Ena. The town suffered a series of fires, the worst in 1895, so it is not as old as the other towns, but its stone paths, wood and plaster buildings, many now serving as shops and inns, have a weathered quality that makes them feel older. Shimazaki Toson, a Meiji Period author, is the town's pride and joy. The **Toson Kinenkan** (http://toson.jp; daily Apr–Oct 9am–5pm, Dec–Mar until 4pm, Dec–Mar closed Wed), a museum housed in a former inn, traces the writer's life through displays of original works and personal effects.

HOKURIKU AND THE SEA OF JAPAN (EAST SEA) COAST

SEA OF JAPAN (EAST SEA) COAST

On the coast of the Sea of Japan (East Sea), **Kanazawa** ⑬ came under the rule of the Maeda clan in the 16th

The teahouse in the grounds of Kenroku-en Garden, Kanazawa.

An installation at the 21st Century Museum of Contemporary Art.

Creating lacquerware in Wajima, Ishikawa.

century, a stewardship that lasted nearly three centuries and which supported a vigorous artistic effort. Lacking military or industrial targets, Kanazawa was spared bombing during World War II. Today, samurai houses in the Nagamachi area still line the twisting streets, and the Higashi-no-Kuruwa area still has geisha working its old tearooms. But that isn't the main reason Kanazawa is firmly planted on Japan's domestic tourist trail. The crowds come for **Kenroku-en** (Kenroku Garden; www. pref.ishikawa.jp/siro-niwa/kenrokuen; daily, Mar–mid-Oct 7am–6pm, mid-Oct–Feb 8am–5pm). Considered one of Japan's top gardens, it has its heritage in an ancient Chinese garden from the Song dynasty. Be warned, however, that being feverishly crowded, the garden is not for the contemplative.

A more peaceful, and much smaller, garden is **Gyokusen-en** (usually daily 9am–5pm). Designed by Korean Kim Yeocheol in the early 17th century, it combines a main pond in the shape of the Chinese character for water

(*mizu*), with two waterfalls, moss-covered rocks and several hundred varieties of plants to create a tranquil environment far removed from the nearby Kenroku-en. The garden's teahouse is an especially nice place for a break.

Gardens aside, Kanazawa is known for an overglaze-painted porcelain called *kutani-yaki*. You can see vibrant examples of that and other crafts at the **Ishikawa Prefectural Museum of Art** (www.ishibi.pref.ishikawa.jp; daily 9.30am–6pm), just to the west of Kenroku-en. An even better museum is the **21st Century Museum of Contemporary Art** (www.kanazawa21.jp/en; Tue–Sun 10am–6pm, Fri–Sat until 8pm), to the south of Kanazawa Park. The sleek circular building focuses only on art post-1980, both overseas and Japanese, and besides some very cool permanent installations it also puts on an ever-changing line-up of temporary exhibitions. Rounding out Kanazawa's main attractions is its castle, in **Kanazawa Castle Park** (www. pref.ishikawa.jp/siro-niwa/kanazawajou/

⊘ MINAKAMI

Minakami Onsen, in the north of Gunma Prefecture and bordering Niigata, calls itself a "four-season outdoor adventure resort" for good reason. In winter, the area is all about skiing, its nine ski fields (www.snowjapan.com) especially popular at weekends with Tokyoites. The rest of the year, Minakami is geared to hikers and adrenaline junkies, with rafting, bungee jumping, paragliding, canyoning and other activities available. For something a little more restful, year-round the area's 100 or so *onsen* (hot-spring baths) also make for the perfect place to unwind. If you are feeling really brave, head to the mixed-gender baths at Takaragawa Onsen (www.takaragawa.com; they also have gender-separated baths). Minakami is two hours from Tokyo, first by *shinkansen* to Jomo-Kogen, then by bus.

index.html; daily, Mar–mid-Oct 7am–6pm, mid-Oct–Feb 8am–5pm). It's mostly a reconstruction, but worth checking out anyway.

From Kanazawa consider an excursion out onto **Noto-hanto** ⑭ (Noto Peninsula), which jabs out into the Sea of Japan (East Sea) like a crooked finger. The sedate eastern coast, encircling a bay, is moderately developed for tourism. The western coast, sculpted by the vigorous winds and currents of the Sea of Japan (East Sea), is rocky and rustic. Noto's main town, **Wajima**, is noted for *Wajima-nuri*, a type of lacquerware, which you can learn more about at the **Wajima Shiki Kaikan** (Wajima Lacquerware Museum; www.wajimanuri.or.jp/frame-e.htm; daily 8.30am–5pm). Wajima is also known for its morning market (*asa-ichi*), which can take on a tourist-focused mood at times but is still interesting to visit.

NIIGATA AND AROUND

Moving north along the coast, there are few highlights until Niigata Prefecture. Although the city of **Niigata** ⑮ itself isn't the most exciting of places, it has enough affordable hotels and restaurants, not to mention transport links, to make for a good stepping stone before exploring the rest of the prefecture or before setting off north or east into Tohoku (see page 213). Being snow country, Niigata Prefecture is, not surprisingly, known for its skiing. It was here, inland in the Joetsu region of southern Niigata, that Austrian Major Theodore von Lerch first introduced skiing to Japan in 1911. The most popular ski area in Niigata today, **Echigo Yuzawa** ⑯, is also the most easily accessible from Tokyo – just 77 minutes on the *shinkansen* from Tokyo Station. The town has plenty of hotels and ryokan, most of which have their own hot springs, and is within a short bus ride from several good ski fields, including the modern and English-speaker-friendly

GALA Yuzawa (season mid-Dec–early May; http://gala.co.jp).

SADO-JIMA

Two hours from Niigata by ferry, **Sado-jima** ⑰ was first an island of exile in the 13th century and later, during the Edo Period, a prison colony. Japan's fifth-largest island at 1,900 sq km (850 sq miles), Sado is mountainous and probably most famous for the Kodo drummers, from a village near **Ogi**. In late August the muscular percussionists stage the Earth Celebration festival, three days of concerts alongside traditional music, arts and crafts workshops. The journey from Tokyo by bullet train and ferry is well worth the effort. If you are planning to go, transport and accommodation must be arranged well in advance. The island is associated in many Japanese minds with old, salt-encrusted temples, the clear bathing waters of its west coast, the old goldmine of **Sado Kinzan** (www.sado-kinzan.com; daily, Apr–Oct 8am–5.30pm, Nov–Mar 8.30am–5pm), and *okesa*, Sado's haunting music of exile.

Women relaxing at a hot spring in Yuzawa, Niigata.

Minakami Onsen.

Yamadera Temple.

Cape Kamui, Shakotan Peninsula, Hokkaido.

Birds flying over Lake Kussharo,
Akan National Park.

THE NORTH

Most Japanese regard the northern extents of Tohoku and Hokkaido as the ends of the earth, however close they are. Come here for nature at its most remote, beautiful and mysterious.

Chuson Temple.

"I might as well be going to the ends of the earth." That's how Basho, Japan's great 17th-century haiku poet, put it on the eve of his departure into the north in 1689. Back then, when Basho decided to prowl the backcountry, the roads were narrow and minimal, or non-existent. Today, Sendai, Tohoku's predominant city and north of Tokyo along the Pacific coast, is only two hours from Tokyo via *shinkansen*. From Sendai, you are then within striking distance of the Tono Valley – the epitome of rural Japan – the World Heritage shrines of Hiraizumi, the atmospheric mountainside temple complex of Yamadera, and many other intriguing sites.

Even the large island of Hokkaido, forcibly settled during the Meiji Restoration in the late 19th century, is but nine hours from Tokyo by train or two hours by plane. It's a relatively short trip to be transported to a remarkably different world – to ski the perfect powder snow of Niseko or explore the breathtaking natural surrounds of the Shiretoko Peninsula.

Native Ainu carvings on sale.

The north has always been perceived as remote and strange, existing outside the normal sphere of Japanese life, much like Alaska feels removed from the rest of the US. This is more down to psychology than distance – there is a seemingly limitless amount of open space and nature untouched by people.

The people of the north bear some responsibility, too. Tohoku was originally settled by itinerant warlords and soldiers who constructed castle fortresses to keep out potentially unfriendly neighbours, mostly from the south. These castle towns developed into insular communities with their own unique lifestyle, crafts, cottage industries and dialects.

Since the earthquake, tsunami and Fukushima nuclear disaster in March 2011 (see page 223), overseas perception of Tohoku is of a place that has been entirely devastated. Certainly, the level of destruction and loss along much of the east coast was beyond comprehension, and the rebuilding there will continue for decades. Yet much of Tohoku is as accessible, inviting and mysterious as it ever was.

TOHOKU

Its dialect is as thick as the winter snows that blow in over the Sea of Japan (East Sea) from Siberia. Tohoku's hold on northern Honshu makes it seem another world to Japan's urban majority.

Perhaps as a way of explaining and coping with the difficult realities of weather and topography, the northern portion of Honshu, known as Tohoku, remains filled with myths – clever foxes who turn into beautiful women and lure unsuspecting men to their doom, green-headed river creatures who snatch small children venturing too close to the water, and devils and ghosts in great abundance.

By Japanese standards, the Tohoku region is sparsely populated, with 9 million people in an area just under 67,000 sq km (26,000 sq miles). This northern part of Honshu comprises six prefectures: Aomori, Akita, Iwate, Miyagi, Yamagata and Fukushima – of these, it was Iwate, Fukushima and Miyagi on the east coast that bore the brunt of the damage from the March 2011 earthquake and tsunami (see page 223).

Its climate is comparable to New England in the United States, with the possible exception of the month of August, when certain parts of southern Tohoku slyly pretend they are on the equator. (In fact, the city of Yamagata held the record for the highest recorded temperature in Japan, 40.8°C or 104°F, from 1933 until it was topped, by 0.1°C, by Tajimi in Gifu Prefecture in 2007, and then by 0.3°C by Tokyo in 2018.)

Long known for its natural beauty, rugged mountains, sometimes

incomprehensible dialects, innumerable hot springs and harsh winters, especially on the Sea of Japan (East Sea) side, which gets the brunt of Siberian storms, Tohoku was once known as Michinoku (literally, interior or narrow road). The name was not as benign as it seems, for it implied a place rather uncivilised and lacking in culture. In the old days, a barrier wall was constructed at Shirakawa, in southern Fukushima, to separate the civilised world of the south from the barbarians in the north. Although the name was eventually

Main attractions

Sendai
Matsushima
Aizu-Wakamatsu
Yamadera Temple
   complex
Tono
Aomori
Towada-Hachimantai
   National Park

Map on page 214

Large lanterns at the Aomori Nebuta Festival.

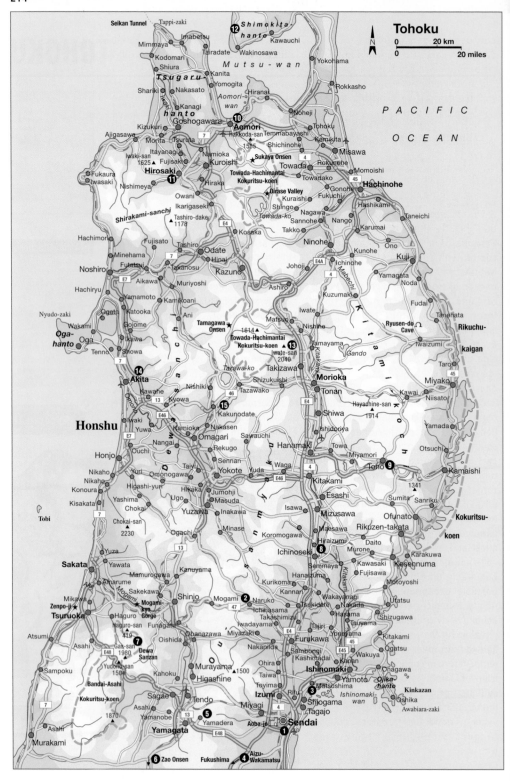

Tohoku

PACIFIC OCEAN

Honshu

changed to the innocent *tohoku* (literally, northeast), the region's image of cultural immaturity lingers for many urban Japanese to the south.

There is a certain irony in this, since it is generally agreed that Tohoku is perhaps the last bastion of traditional Japanese culture. To a large degree, the region has escaped the rapid modernisation that the rest of Japan has undergone since the end of World War II. In the north it is still possible to discover farms growing rice by methods used hundreds of years ago, tiny fishing villages nestled into cliffs overlooking unspoilt sea coasts, isolated hot-spring inns, and a people whose open friendliness is unstinting even as their dialect remains an exclusive mystery. No longer unknown, Tohoku is a place of spectacular beauty and a must-see for adventurous visitors.

SENDAI

The largest city in Tohoku and on the eastern coast, **Sendai ❶** was originally called Sentaijo after the Thousand Buddha Statue Temple that once graced the top of Aoba-yama, the wooded hilltop park. The name was changed to Sendai, or Thousand Generations, by the Date clan during their reign over the area, possibly in the mistaken belief that they would reign supreme for that long.

Sendai is today a cosmopolitan city of a little over 1 million people, the capital of Miyagi Prefecture, and the pre-eminent city of the entire Tohoku region. Sendai is the logical jumping-off point for exploring the rest of Tohoku. It is known as the Green City and the City of Trees, and visitors arriving on the *shinkansen* from treeless urban points south will understand why. From **Sendai-eki** (Sendai Station) the main boulevards running east and west are all tree-lined.

Those wide, European-style avenues are a pleasure to stroll along. The entire downtown area is small enough to cover in an hour or so of leisurely walking, if you feel so inclined. In one of Sendai's tallest buildings, the **SS-30 Building** with its 30 floors, one can relax in numerous top-floor restaurants that offer an excellent view of mountains to the north and west, the Pacific Ocean to the east and the city below. Close to the Sendai Station is **AER**, an even taller building with a free observation deck on the 31st floor (www.sendai-aer.jp; daily 10am–8pm; free). A 10-minute walk west up Aoba-dori from Sendai Station is **Ichiban-cho**, Sendai's main shopping arcade. Parts of it are covered in skylights and all of it is vehicle-free. Evenings suggest a walk a little further to Kokobuncho-dori, Sendai's main afterhours strip, where there are the usual (and seemingly endless) Japanese-style bars, nightclubs, discos, karaoke boxes and other entertainment.

Just beneath the surface, the traditional ways of Tohoku remain in Sendai. The visitor can still watch artisans and craftsmen making knives, tatami flooring and the famed *kayaki tansu*, or chests, in the traditional shops tucked into the shadows of much larger and more modern architecture.

The statue of Date Masamune.

Leafy Jyozenji Street in Sendai.

Sendai didn't come into its own until Date Masamune, the great one-eyed warlord of the north, moved to his newly constructed castle on Aoba-yama. Both **Aoba-jo** (Aoba Castle; also known as Sendai-jo; daily 9am–5pm, Nov–Mar until 4pm) and the Date family collapsed during the Meiji era, but the walls of Aoba-jo remain. In addition, a small museum, souvenir shop, shrine and statue of the great Masamune himself now occupy the grounds. Looking northwards and down from the castle grounds, one can see the Hirose-gawa river, unpolluted and thus unusual in Japan. Edible trout still swim downstream.

Zuihoden (www.zuihoden.com; daily, Feb–Nov 9am–4.30pm, Dec–Jan 9am–4pm), the burial site of Date Masamune, sits atop Kyogamine-yama. There are several cemeteries along the way up, as well as a beautiful Rinzai Zen temple, **Zuiho-ji**. Above the temple are steps leading to the mausoleum at the very top, and nearby are the tombs of samurai who committed ritual suicide when Masamune died. There is also an exhibition room displaying pictures taken when the mausoleum was opened during restoration, necessitated by bomb attacks near the end of World War II.

Osaki Hachiman-jinja (www.oosaki-hachiman.or.jp; daily sunrise–sunset) was originally built in 1100 and later moved to its present location by Date Masamune. Dedicated to the god of war or of archery, this shrine is one of Japan's national treasures. Walk up the 100 or so steps to the top – reportedly the count is never the same twice. Follow the stone-paved path lined with enormous cedar trees to the shrine, picturesquely set back in a small forest. It is done in Momoyama style with gold, black lacquer and bright colours.

There are several more modern attractions worth a look, especially in **Aobayama-koen** (Green Hill Park), including **Sendai-shi Hakubutsukan** (Sendai City Museum; www.city.sendai.jp/museum; Tue–Sun 9am–4.45pm) and a prefectural fine art museum. The municipal museum is interesting architecturally, with an extensive and permanent exhibition of the area's history. There is also a children's

Statue of Basho at the Yamadera Temple complex.

section where everything on display can be touched. The prefectural fine art museum has a sculpture wing with an outdoor sculpture garden. The **Sendai Mediatheque** (www.smt.jp; daily 9am–10pm, closed 4th Thursday of month), housed in an award-winning modern building, plays host to numerous cultural events and runs the "center for remembering 3.11", a project enabling all citizens to document restoration in the aftermath of the 2011 earthquake.

If you have the time and energy, consider the **Tohoku University Botanical Garden** (20 Mar–30 Nov Tue–Sun 9am–5pm, entry until 4pm), a place to cool off on a hot summer afternoon as well as to observe owls, bats and the region's flora and fauna. The observatory here is a relatively good place for star- and planet-viewing if you don't mind waiting in line. Finally, there's Kotsu-koen, a "traffic park" for children complete with roads, red lights, busy intersections and train tracks. Kids can cruise around in pedal-powered cars and get a taste for what real life is like on Japan's claustrophobic roads.

On the northern outskirts of Sendai, near Kitayama Station and a delightful place for a mountain stroll, are two Zen temples, **Rinno-ji** (www.rinno-ji.or.jp, daily 8am–5pm) and **Shifuku-ji**. Both date from the 15th century and were destroyed then rebuilt many times over the years. They offer beautiful Zen-inspired gardens, with azaleas and irises in the spring, brilliant foliage in autumn and dazzling winter scenes.

AROUND SENDAI

A short ride to the northwest of Sendai is **Naruko ❷**, Tohoku's most popular *onsen* (hot spring). Once a sacred site to honour the gods of the hot springs, Naruko is known for its medicinal waters (the treatment of nervous tension is a speciality here) and the production of wooden *kokeshi* dolls, with ball-shaped heads and limbless cylindrical bodies. Now produced in many regions, *kokeshi* originated in Tohoku as a winter industry.

Just north of Sendai is **Matsushima ❸**, considered by Japanese to be one of the three officially designated

Wooden kokeshi dolls.

Naruko onsen, Miyagi.

A five storey pagoda, Haguro-san, Yamagata.

most beautiful spots *(Nihon-sankei)* in Japan. (The others are on Miyazu Bay, north of Kyoto, and Miyajima, near Hiroshima.) Although the Miyagi coast was badly hit by the 2011 tsunami, the geography of the Matsushima Islands afforded some protection to their immediate surrounds, and tourism is back up and running again in the area. The bay is filled with beautiful pine-covered islets of all shapes and sizes, and a fleet of boats cruise the islands, sometimes in the form of ridiculous peacocks and other gimmicks. The poet Basho couldn't get enough of this place, declaring his arrival in Matsushima as the happiest moment of his life. While here, try the *sasa-kamaboko* (moulded fish paste) and the squid-on-a-stick.

AIZU-WAKAMATSU

Washing is a traditional process before praying in a temple.

Further south, in Tohoku's most southerly prefecture of Fukushima, the castle town of **Aizu-Wakamatsu ❹**, with its feudal history, pleasant parks and gardens, is also a centre for folk arts, ceramic and lacquerware making. Having opposed

the overthrow of the Tokugawa shogunate in 1868, and witnessed the deaths of 20 teenage samurais who committed suicide rather than surrender to the new imperial forces, Aizu's historical credentials are unassailable.

The bullet train from Tokyo Ueno Station to Koriyama eats up the miles, but the slower run from Tokyo's Asakusa Station on either the Tobu or Aizu lines is by far the more scenic route. If you are planning to stay overnight in Aizu, this route offers the option of stopping off at Nikko for the day.

Aizu's sights are spread out, so bus or bicycle are the best way around. A good place to orientate yourself is **Iimori-yama**, a hilltop affording excellent views in all directions. The peak can be reached via a steep staircase or care of an escalator. Japanese tourists come here mainly to pay homage to the **Byakkotai graves**. The Byakkotai (White Tigers) were the young warriors who committed ritual disembowelment after being severed from their main force and failing to get to the safety of Tsuruga Castle, which they mistakenly

thought was burning. Feelings are divided on whether this was the knee-jerk reaction of a culture of violence, or a noble gesture, but all agree on the tragic waste of life, the "heroes" aged 16 and 17. At the base of the hill are two small museums related to the Byakkotai, as well the architecturally quirky Sazaedo Pagoda (daily, Apr–Dec 8.15am–sunset, Jan–Mar 9am–4pm).

Some 2km (1.2 miles) south of the hill, **Buke-yashiki** (http://bukeyashiki.com; daily, Apr–Nov 8.30am–5pm, Dec–Mar 9am–4.30pm) is a skilful reproduction of samurai houses and, along with one or two original buildings, provides insights into the living conditions of the samurai class. Another 2km (1.2 miles) west, **Oyaku-en** (daily 8.30am–5pm) is a tranquil Japanese garden set in the grounds of a former villa owned by the local Matsudaira clan. A pond and stroll garden, it is also known as a medicinal garden – it still cultivates some 300 types of herbs, many of which are available at the garden shop. Teahouses always seem to have the best views of gardens. Repair to the small tatami-floored rooms here, where you will be served matcha, a traditional frothy green tea with a small Japanese confection.

TSURUGA CASTLE AND AROUND

A 15-minute walk from the garden, Aizu's warrior past is to the fore at **Tsuruga-jo** (www.tsurugajo.com; daily 8.30am–5pm), the town's reconstructed castle keep. The walls and moats of this great castle are original, the manicured park setting an afterthought. A good one, though, especially in spring when over 1,000 cherry trees burst into bloom, the white walls of the keep contrasting with the blue skies and pink blossom, an image reproduced on thousands of calendars. The dramatic castle exterior and views from the upper floors are more interesting than the lacklustre interiors and museum of local history.

If you are interested in Japan's best-known poison, sake, a popular warrior tipple, a 15-minute walk north takes you to the **Suheiro Sake Brewery** (daily 9am–5pm). Tours will take you through the sake brewing areas and to an informative museum, finishing up with tastings – be sure to try the sake-infused desserts in the café, too. The brewery has been in the same family since 1850 and is housed in a lovely old wooden building. Tours are in Japanese but English information is also available.

YAMADERA

The pride and joy of Yamagata Prefecture is the awesome temple complex of Risshaku-ji, better known as **Yamadera ❺** (www.rissyakuji.jp; daily 8am–5pm). It was founded in 860 by a Zen priest. Perched on the side of a mountain, its 40 or so temple buildings, connected by paths leading through ancient cedar forest, are a fantastic sight even for those who may by now feel templed-out. The main hall, **Kompon Chudo**, dates from the 14th century, other structures from the

Tsuruga Castle.

16th century. At the top of the 1,015 steps you'll need to ascend to reach it is **Okuno-in**, the holy of holies for the pilgrims who offer up prayers here. At the foot of the hillside, you'll come across a statue of the poet Basho, whose famous work *The Narrow Road to the Deep North* includes a haiku written while visiting Yamadera: *"How still it is! Stinging into the stones, The locust's trill."*

ZAO ONSEN

Some 20km (12 miles) southeast of Yamagata City, **Zao *Onsen*** ⑥ is one of the largest ski resorts in Tohoku (www.zao-spa.or.jp). The main focus of Zao Quasi National Park, it has dozens of runs to choose from – the longest of which is 10km (6 miles) – as well as night skiing during the months of December to late March. The Paradise and Juhyogen runs are the most interesting, passing groups of 'snow monsters'. Siberian winds whip up the snow into frozen droplets that coat fir trees along the slopes, turning them into weird and wonderful ice sculptures.

Zao *Onsen*, as the name suggests, is also an all-year hot-spring resort. There's nothing quite like tackling the hiking trails or ski slopes during the daytime, then having a pre-dinner soak in a mountain hot spring while contemplating the next step of your trip.

DEWA SANZAN

Standing 50km (30 miles) north of Yamagata City, the **Dewa Sanzan** ⑦ (Three Mountains of Dewa) are Yamagata's three holy mountains, where ascetic mountain priests called *yamabushi* still perform sacred rituals. Join the other pilgrims and walk the 2,446 steps to the summit of **Haguro-san**. Afterwards, travel down the Mogamigawa on a flat-bottomed boat while the boatman sings of the area's legends.

NORTHWARD FROM SENDAI

HIRAIZUMI AND AROUND

Exiting the station in **Hiraizumi** ⑧, in Iwate Prefecture, it's hard to believe that this ordinary-looking town once rivalled Kyoto in its cultural

Kyozo shrine.

splendours. But that was 850 years ago. Still, some remarkable remnants have survived from its glory days as the domain of the powerful Fujiwara clan.

The Fujiwaras ploughed their wealth into building projects of great splendour. Sadly, only two remain out of 40, but they are well worth the visit. **Chuson-ji** (www.chusonji.or.jp; daily, Mar–Oct 8.30am–5pm, Nov–Feb 8.30am–4.30pm) was founded by a Tendai priest in 850, then later rebuilt in the Heian Period style, one of a handful of buildings to have survived from that period. The temple's two great surviving treasures are the **Konjiki-do**, an astonishing structure covered almost entirely in gold leaf, the main altar inlaid with mother-of-pearl, lacquer and gilded copper; and the **Kyozo**, a sutra hall with an octagonal dais decorated with inlaid motifs, which was built in 1108. The more recently built **Sankozo** is a treasure hall housing valuable sutras in gold ink on indigo paper, a famous thousand-armed Kannon statue, and Fujiwara items, including lacquerware and swords.

Many people visit Hiraizumi to experience the wonderful **Motsu-ji** (www.motsuji.or.jp; daily, Apr–Oct 8.30am–5pm, Nov–Mar 8.30am–4.30pm), a temple home to a 12th-century garden, known as the Jodo-teien, and one of the few remaining Heian Period landscapes in Japan. The garden, with a central pond and scatterings of ancient foundation stones for a temple that once stood here, is alive with flowers in every season.

Heading northeast is the town of **Tono ⑨**, offering a perfectly preserved glimpse into feudal Japan. No modern trappings here. Farming is still done the old-fashioned way; note the *magariya* or traditional L-shaped farmhouses. The long side of the structure is for people, the short side for animals and ghosts. Do not go too near the rivers here – this is where the legendary *kappa* reside beneath the waters, waiting to pull people and horses under. (The traditional way to defeat a *kappa*, if encountered, is to bow in greeting, forcing the *kappa* to return the bow and thus drain the depression atop its

⊘ **Tip**

While in the vicinity of Dewa Sanzan, you might consider spending time in Bandai Kogen, a mountain area punctuated with beech trees, wetlands and almost 300 lakes. The jewel of these highlands is Bandai-san, a 1,819-metre (5,970ft) volcano next to Lake Inawashiro. It famously erupted in 1888, creating the distinctive topography you see today.

Having fun at Zao ski resort, Yamagata.

⊘ THE TOMB OF CHRIST

Tohoku is an area rich in mythology – the tale of the kappa in Tono being perhaps the most renowned. But there is one peculiar tale that is heard far less often than stories of the kappa, and it concerns the tomb of Jesus. The legend, which has its root in 1930s ultra-nationalism, goes that Jesus didn't actually die on the Cross. Instead, his brother apparently took his place, while Jesus fled to Japan, where he settled in what is now Aomori Prefecture, had a family and lived to the ripe old age of 105. His resting place, a mound topped by a crucifix, can be found in the village of Shingo, not far from the village's Legend of Christ Museum.

head of the *kappa's* life-giving fluid, water.) To the northwest is **Morioka**, Iwate's capital and famous – it claims – for its competitions for eating *wanko* soba. Other than that, it's rather unremarkable, but you will probably pass through the city if you opt to head to the far north of Tohoku.

AOMORI

Capital of Aomori Prefecture at the northern tip of Tohoku, the city of **Aomori ⑩** is a logical departure point for both Hokkaido and Towada-Hachimantai National Park to the south. **Hirosaki ⑪**, an hour's ride southwest from Aomori, is an old castle town with the most elegant (some say most difficult) regional dialect in Tohoku, as well as what Japanese chauvinists claim are Japan's most beautiful women. It is also noted for retaining a bit of the old samurai-era atmosphere. To the southeast are the Hakkoda Mountains, a volcanic massif boasting some of Japan's best backcountry skiing that runs down the middle of Aomori Prefecture to the river valley of Oirase.

The Tono Valley landscape.

Before entering this spectacular valley of steep cliffs, churning rapids and waterfalls, spend a night at **Sukayu Onsen**. The waters here are thought to be curative and the location is rustic and traditional.

North of Aomori lies the **Shimokita-hanto ⑫** (Shimokita Peninsula). The world's northernmost community of wild monkeys can be found here, as well as the ominous **Osore-zan mountain**, 870 metres (2,870ft) high. With its bubbling, multicoloured mud pits and clinging sulphur clouds, Osore's translation of "dread" or "terror" seems apt.

Southwest of Aomori, **Towada-Hachimantai Kokuritsu-koen** (Towada-Hachimantai National Park; www.env.go.jp/park/towada/index.html) covers a vast area, touching the borders of three prefectures – Aomori, Akita and Iwate. The onsen at **Tamagawa**, on the Akita side of Hachimantai Plateau, has hot, acidic and slightly radioactive water and is considered to be one of the best springs in the area. Excluding Hokkaido, this is Japan's last area of untamed wilderness, with several volcanoes, including **Iwate-san ⑬**, 2,040 metres (6,700ft) high and considered the Fuji-san of the north, with its bubbling mud pools, steam geysers and scenic splendour. South of stunning caldera lake **Towada-ko**, Iwate-san is one of eight active volcanoes in the Tohoku region.

West from Hachimantai is Akita Prefecture, home of **Tazawa-ko** (reportedly Japan's deepest lake) and the spectacular **Oga-hanto** (Oga Peninsula), home of the *namahage*, or the devils of the new year. These horrible creatures burst into local homes on 3 January each year and are not appeased until fed large quantities of sake and rice cakes. **Akita ⑭** is another little city with nothing to distinguish it, save perhaps its winters. **Kakunodate ⑮**, however, is noted for having preserved several samurai houses and streets, some lined with luscious cherry trees.

THE GREAT EAST JAPAN EARTHQUAKE

Few in Japan will forget where they were at 2.46pm on 11 March 2011, when a magnitude 9.0 earthquake, the fifth-largest recorded in world history, struck 72km (44 miles) east of Sendai in the northwestern Pacific Ocean.

The earthquake shook Tohoku for six minutes, in parts of Miyagi Prefecture registering the maximum earthquake intensity of 7 on Japan's intensity scale. The original shockwave was so large it was felt as far away as Kyushu.

Within 30 minutes, the original earthquake had been followed by magnitude 7.4 and 7.2 aftershocks. Over the next year, up to the first anniversary, more than 1,800 aftershocks measuring magnitude 4 or greater hit the region. But in many respects Japan was ready for that. The aftermath of the Kobe earthquake of 1995 saw earthquake-resistant building regulations come into effect and greater public awareness of how to react in a major quake.

The country, however, wasn't ready for what happened straight after the first quake in 2011. Within minutes, Japan's tsunami warning system kicked into effect, predicting a wave of up to 6 metres (20ft) to hit Miyagi within 30 minutes; lesser waves were predicted for elsewhere. What came was sadly far, far worse.

In Rikuzentakata in Iwate Prefecture, a 13-metre (43ft) wave breached the 6.5-metre (21ft) sea wall and engulfed the entire town. Eighty percent of the town's 8,000 houses were swept away and more than 2,000 were killed or remain unaccounted for. Similar horrors played out in many other towns and villages along Tohoku's east coast. By 2017, 19,575 deaths had been confirmed in Tohoku, 6,230 people had been injured, and 2,577 were still recorded as missing.

With waves funnelling up to 38 metres (125ft) in height in some areas the devastation was vast. Around 4.4 million households were left without electricity, over 45,000 buildings were destroyed and some 144,000 damaged.

Then, there was the Fukushima Daiichi nuclear accident. Studies following the accident found that the Japanese nuclear plants had not been adequately protected against tsunamis and that the accident was "man-made". All the country's reactors were closed down in the aftermath of the Fukushima meltdown. Before March 2011, nuclear energy had met 30 percent of the country's needs. Following the closure of all of its nuclear plants, Japan started to rely more heavily on fossil fuels thus increasing carbon dioxide emissions. Politicians and the business sector have pushed to reopen nuclear energy plants, although public anger against this has grown. Before any reactor is restarted, it has to meet stringent new safety requirements. Abe's government has pushed to reopen the country's nuclear reactors, but as of 2019, safety concerns meant their continued operation was uncertain.

In 2013, it was revealed that the Fukushima plant had continued to leak highly radioactive water into the Pacific Ocean, a fact that had been denied. Public pressure on and distrust of the government and TEPCO, the plant's operator, have led to a rise in NGOs and citizens' groups monitoring radiation levels in the environment and food supply nationwide. Their data, and that of the government and many independent overseas organisations, suggests that radiation levels in Tokyo and Kanto are normal. The safety of those living long-term on the edges of the exclusion zone in Fukushima is a different and hotly debated matter.

Rescuers work at the ruins in the city of Rikuzentakata.

A deer in Shiretoko National Park.

HOKKAIDO

The northern island of Hokkaido holds a special place in the Japanese imagination, conjuring up romantic images of misty mountains and wild lands where anything is possible.

Hokkaido has been part of the Japanese nation only since it was settled in the 19th century as an example of Meiji Restoration development. Nowadays, Hokkaido is to many Japanese as Alaska is to Americans: the northern extremity with a romantic sense of frontier, where summers are short and winters exceedingly cold, and where the people are just a little bit different for living there in the first place. Japan's northern island is where the temples and castles of the southern islands give way to mountains, forests and farms. You will find the residents here more direct and friendlier than their southern counterparts and, due to the Meiji-era Westernisation, quite sophisticated.

Hokkaido is also home to Japan's last indigenous people, the Ainu (see page 61), who research shows lack a genetic connection to today's Japanese. With a population of only 25,000, the Ainu are now a phantom culture with a nearly forgotten language, though efforts are being made to revive some aspects of their shamanic customs. Some Ainu can be seen in traditional costume, posing for tourist photos in Hokkaido, but most lead lives undistinguishable from any other Japanese.

Hokkaido has the feeling of remoteness, but this is mostly psychological. The Tokyo–Sapporo air corridor is one of the busiest in the world, and rail

lines running through the Seikan Tunnel also connect Honshu to southern Hokkaido – a journey that got faster in 2016 when trains on a new *shinkansen* route began service. Hokkaido offers the standard over-developed and tacky tourist traps and loudspeaker-enhanced "scenic" places so common throughout Japan. But Hokkaido can also be high adventure in the rustic north, with some of Japan's most undeveloped areas. Its climate parallels that of Quebec and Finland, and in winter icebergs scrape its shores.

Main attractions

Sapporo
Otaru
Niseko
Shikotsu-Toya National
 Park
Hakodate
Furano
Akan National Park
Shiretoko Peninsula
Abashiri

Maps on pages 227, 228

Dogsledge race, Wakkanai.

⊘ **Fact**

The Seikan Tunnel, opened in 1988, is the world's second longest after the Gotthard Base Tunnel in Switzerland, and deepest underwater tunnel at 53.9km (33.5 miles), although only about half of its total length is actually under the water. The tunnel links Honshu with Hokkaido, which are separated by the Tsugaru Strait.

In summer, hills and fields are riotous with wild flowers and filled with dairy cows.

SAPPORO

In southwest Hokkaido, **Sapporo** ❶ is the island's capital and its largest city, with 1.9 million people. It is an immensely liveable city, especially by Japanese standards. Streets are laid out in a grid, making navigation easy and useful addresses a reality, and they are also wider than most in Japan.

The city is anchored by **Odori-koen** Ⓐ (Odori Park), running east to west through the centre and perhaps one of Japan's liveliest, most charming boulevards. In the first week of February, this broad avenue is the venue for Sapporo's world-famous Snow Festival (www.snowfes.com). Snow statues and ice sculptures made by corporate, professional and amateur teams are decidedly complex and often quite large. In summer, beer gardens spring up on the grassy areas and people linger outdoors long into the night.

Snow Festival, Odori-koen, Sapporo.

Amongst the Japanese, a must-see is **Tokei-dai** Ⓑ (Clock Tower; daily 8.45am–5.10pm, closed fourth Mon of the month), an architecturally undistinguished wooden structure built in the late 1870s, which, despite possessing something of an exotic European allure for locals, is not really worth going out of one's way to see. Directly east of Odori-koen a couple of blocks is the **TV Tower** Ⓒ, with a decent viewing platform 90 metres (295ft) above the ground (www.tv-tower.co.jp; daily 9am–10pm). However to the north is the **Sapporo JR Tower**, whose observation deck on the 38th floor as well as restrooms with a sweeping view seem to be more popular with tourists these days (www.jr-tower.com/t38; daily 10am–11pm).

Just northwest of **Sapporo-eki** Ⓓ (Sapporo Station), itself a few blocks north of Odori-koen, is Hokkaido University. The university operates the nearby **Botanical Garden** Ⓔ (Tue–Sun, closing times vary, but at least 9am–3pm; only the greenhouse open Nov–Apr), which contains over 5,000 examples of Hokkaido's flora. Within its grounds is **Batchelor Kinenkan** (Batchelor Memorial Museum; daily, same times as the Botanical Garden), a museum with an excellent collection of Ainu artefacts and named after an Englishman who spent decades researching the Ainu of Japan. Rev. John Batchelor was a 19th-century minister who studied the indigenous people of both Hokkaido and Siberia. The collection of Ainu artefacts he left behind is probably the best in Japan.

To the east a couple of kilometres away is the **Sapporo Beer Museum** Ⓕ (www.sapporobeer.jp/english/brewery/s_museum; daily 11am–8pm) built on the site of the original brewery (Sapporo beer is now brewed in nearby Eniwa). Sapporo was Japan's first beer brewery, dating from the mid-1870s. Guided tours are only available in Japanese, but the informative museum exhibits

have English displays telling the story of the company and the history of Japanese beer. Tastings are also offered.

Two blocks south of Odori-koen is **Tanuki-koji**, a vibrant strip of restaurants and shops. The market of Nijo serves every dining and household need for locals and purveys souvenirs in abundance for eager first-time visitors. Finally, a couple more blocks south is **Susukino G**, Sapporo's nightlife and Red Light District.

West of Sapporo is **Otaru ❷**, once a fishing and trading centre and where many of the buildings are an eclectic blend of Western and 19th-century Japanese influences. Otaru is the gateway to the **Shakotan-hanto**, a peninsular microcosm of Hokkaido with its rugged coastlines, abundant campsites, ski areas, boating and fishing in the Sea of Japan (East Sea), and glorious sunsets from the capes (*misaki*) of Shakotan and Kamui. This area's proximity to Sapporo makes sightseeing hectic at times, especially during holidays and weekends. One of the island's most rewarding attractions

is the **Historical Village of Hokkaido** (www.kaitaku.or.jp/info/info.htm; Tue–Sun, May–Sept 9am–5pm, Oct–Feb 9am–4.30pm), an open-air museum set in parkland, displaying over 60 historical buildings from the 19th and early 20th centuries. The village is a fascinating re-creation of life in the early pioneering years of the island.

SOUTH OF SAPPORO

Japanese skiers (and more recently boarders) have been enjoying the perfect powder snow at **Niseko ❸**, 70km (45 miles) southwest of Otaru, for decades, but it has only been in recent years that Niseko has received international recognition. That has come in large part because of an influx of Australian developers who have invested heavily in holiday homes and ski resorts in the area, which now has five top-end resorts that, unlike other ski areas in Japan, are very much geared to overseas guests. The largest, the **Grand Hirafu** (www.grand-hirafu. jp), has 34 runs, but you will also find great backcountry snow, and plenty of

Old buildings on Otaru Canal.

Sapporo Beer Museum.

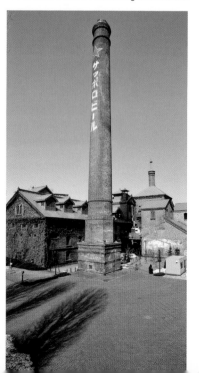

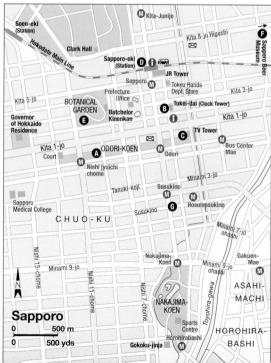

English-speaking guides able to take you to Niseko's incredible off-resort virgin slopes.

The ski season here lasts from December to early May, and the quality of the snow, some say, is the best in Asia. When the snow has receded, Niseko also offers good hiking, and year-round the area's natural hot springs make for great soaking.

The **Shikotsu-Toya Kokuritsu-koen** (Shikotsu-Toya National Park; www. env.go.jp/park/shikotsu/index.html) is Hokkaido's most accessible national park and thus highly commercial and often crowded. Closest to Sapporo is **Shikotsu-ko ❹**, a huge caldera lake. Shikotsu-Kohan, a fishing village, provides lodgings and tour boats of the lake, and

there are numerous youth hostels and campsites in the area.

Toya-ko ❺, south of Shikotsu, is a round caldera lake with a large island smack in the centre. Tour boats visit its islands, from where the view of 1,893-metre (6,200ft) high **Yotei-zan**, to the north, is best. Climbers can attack Yotei or three other peaks: Eniwa, Fuppushi and Tarumae. The last, on the south shore of Shikotsu-ko and rising to 1,040 metres (3,400ft), is a volcano that still steams and fumes; it is probably the best climb. The route to Tarumae from Shikotsu-ko passes through the eerie beauty of Koke no Domon (Moss Gorge). The resort areas around Toya-ko are boisterous in summer, with fireworks during the

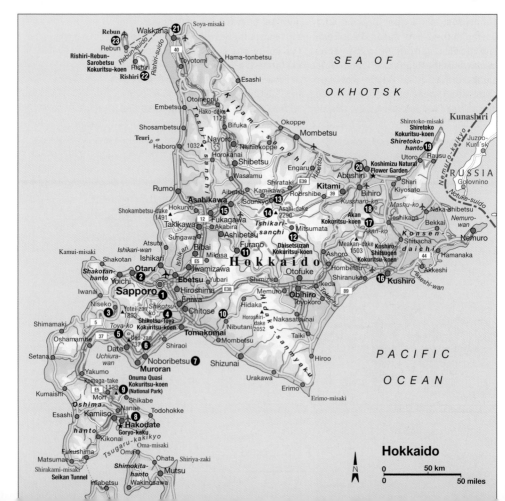

Hokkaido

0   50 km

0   50 miles

August festival season. There are many ryokan in the area, with hot-spring baths *(onsen)* having lake views. The must-see here is **Showa Shin-zan**, a small volcano just south that emerged unannounced from the earth in 1944. **Usu-zan** ❻, Showa Shin-zan's parent volcano, stands nearby. A cable car (www.wakasaresort.com; daily at least 9am–4pm, longer hours in summer) runs from near Showa Shin-zan up Usu-zan. At the top are the remains of trees destroyed when Usu-zan erupted in 1977, wreaking havoc on the resort. An even more devastating eruption occurred in 2000, destroying much of the area's tourist infrastructure. See it on film in the information centre in the Volcano Village on top, where you can also visit an eruption experience room.

The best route from Toya-ko east to the tourist hot spring of **Noboribetsu** ❼ is by bus through gorgeous Orofure Pass. Noboribetsu's notable sight and activity is at the Dai-Ichi Takimoto-kan Hotel (www.takimotokan.co.jp; daily, open 24 hours for guests, 9am–9pm for day visits), where 30 indoor, sex-segregated hot-spring baths, once of wood but now of marble, can hold 1,000 bathers simultaneously. There is nothing else like it.

There are two festivals in August at Noboribetsu, recommended only if you love crowds. For a gourmet treat in spring, ask for the *kegani koramushi*, or small freshwater crabs. While here, tour the volcanic Jigoku-dani (Hell Gorge) and go up to the summit of Shihorei.

HAKODATE

At the southern tip of Hokkaido and just across the Tsugaru Strait from Aomori and Honshu's northern tip is **Hakodate** ❽. Known for its rather wicked weather, Hakodate also offers one of the most romantic views from atop **Hakodate-yama**. In keeping with the national habit of ranking scenery and tourist spots, the Japanese consider this to be one of the top three night views in the world, together with those in Hong Kong and Naples. A cable car (www.334.co.jp; daily 10am–9pm, late Apr–mid-Oct until 10pm) climbs to its 334-metre (1,100ft) summit.

Horse riding by Toya-ko.

Hakodate is Hokkaido's historic city, with Japanese settlers arriving from the south as early as the 13th century. Russians followed in the mid-1700s. At the base of Hakodate-yama is **Motomachi**, a foreign enclave since the 1850s. In fact, Hakodate was one of three Japanese cities (along with Yokohama and Nagasaki) accessible to the West after Perry's opening of the country in the 1850s. Northeast of Motomachi is **Goryo-kaku**, a star-shaped fort (a typical Russian design) where loyalists of the collapsing Tokugawa shogunate lost the final battle against the Meiji imperial army in 1869. For an intriguing perspective on the ethnic and commercial routes into Hokkaido, see the city's premier museum, the **Hakodate City Museum of Northern Peoples** (daily, Apr–Oct 9am–7pm, Nov–Mar 9am–5pm). The museum has a fine collection of Ainu artefacts and Chinese and Siberian costumes.

Whereas Sapporo is a night city, Hakodate is at heart a morning city. Don't miss the fish market at dawn, when the squid fleet and the crab trappers return to port. Use the tram system, dating from 1913, to explore. For dinner, have Japan's freshest seafood. Crab and salmon are abundant and delicious; a unique salmon stew (*shake* nabe) called *sanpei-jiru* is truly remarkable. *Ika somen* – thinly sliced, noodle-like strips of raw squid – is the city's speciality.

ONUMA QUASI NATIONAL PARK

Some 20km (12 miles) north of Hakodate, **Onuma Quasi National Park**; (http://onumakouen.com) ❾ is easily reached in about 40 minutes by local train, making it the perfect day trip or overnight stay. Rated among the most stunning scenery in Japan, the park consists of three marshy lakes – Onuma, Junsai-numa and Konuma – and a 1,133-metre (3,700ft) peak, **Komaga-take**, a dormant volcano.

Onuma, the largest, is generally considered to be the most beautiful of the three lakes. The view across the lily-covered water to the soaring peak of the volcano in summer is certainly mightily impressive. The lake has over 100 islets, joined by walking bridges. Exploring the lakes on foot, or circuiting them by bicycle, is a good way to avoid the tour groups who are usually shepherded into boats for cruises. Hikers can enjoy stunning views of the lakes and surrounding countryside by taking one of the two 2.5-hour walking trails up the volcano.

NIBUTANI

Inland from Hokkaido's southern coast, some 50km (30 miles) east of Tomakomai port, **Nibutani** ❿ is an authentic Ainu village with a number of interesting, tastefully displayed exhibits and archival material.

There are two museums of special interest, the most outstanding being the **Kayano Shigeru Nibutani Ainu Museum** (daily 9am–4:30pm; Dec–Mar by appointment; tel: 01457-3215), where you'll find a first-rate

Night view of Hakodate from Hakodate-yama.

photo exhibition on Ainu fishing techniques, etchings showing Ainu hunting, everyday items, a giant stuffed salmon and a preserved emperor fish, and a number of Ainu huts with craftsmen inside engaged in making traditional artefacts.

A visit to the **Nibutani Ainu Culture Museum** (daily 9am–4.30pm; closed mid-Dec–mid-Jan, closed Mon mid-Nov–mid-Dec and mid-Jan–mid-Apr) will complete your education on the Ainu heritage. Original Ainu huts stand outside, in stark contrast to the modern concrete-and-glass museum building. Embroidered traditional costumes, exhibits on the religious life of the Ainu people, and videos of dances and rituals provide a highly visual introduction to Ainu life and culture.

FURANO

About 75km (45 miles) north of Nibutani, and an easy two-hour bus ride from Sapporo, **Furano** ⑪ is a very popular day trip from Sapporo for Japanese tourists. In summer they come for the undulating countryside and picturesque farmland (scenes that have a touch of Tolkien's Shire about them), which reaches the peak of its attractiveness in June and July, when Furano's vast lavender fields are in bloom.

In winter, the area attracts a different crowd – skiers and snowboarders. The **Furano Ski Resort** (www.snowfurano. com) on Mount Kitanomine is well developed and includes 24 courses as well as a major **Prince Hotel** just beside its slopes. If the idea of the very internationalised Niseko doesn't appeal, Furano, with its largely domestic crowd, might be the place for you.

DAISETSUZAN NATIONAL PARK

Wilder and colder than Akan and Shikotsu-Toya, **Daisetsuzan Kokuritsu-koen** ⑫ (Daisetsuzan National Park; www.env.go.jp/park/daisetsu/index.html) is the largest national park in Japan, covering 230,900 hectares (570,500 acres). Directly in the centre of Hokkaido, the climate is nearly always cool, even in summer. This is a landscape of volcanic peaks and steep

Exploring in Noboribetsu.

highlands, magnificent gorges, carpets of alpine wild flowers, and sightings of the park's rich wildlife, including deer, fox, bears and exotic birds. In the park there are also several good youth hostels and campsites.

Start at **Sounkyo** , a tourist village near the gorges of Sounkyo (Gorges Reaching to the Clouds), with chiselled walls of volcanic rock punctuated by feathery waterfalls and more than 100 metres (300ft) high. From Sounkyo, one of the park's two cable cars ends near the peak of Kuro, a jumping-off point for good hiking. The goal is Hokkaido's highest peak, **Asahi-dake** , 2,290 metres (7,500ft) high. Along the way, hikers come across vast tracts of creeping pine and virgin forests, barren timberline slopes, small lakes and side trails, volcanic vents, flower-covered hillsides, patches of year-round snow – and the inevitable pesky mosquitoes. Among the best festivals in Hokkaido are Sounkyo's Kyokoku Himatsuri, the Ainu Fire Festival in late June and Sounkyo's Ice Festival in winter.

Spring flora, Shiretoko National Park.

Lying 50km (30 miles) west of Sounkyo is **Asahikawa** , with a population of 350,000, it is one of Hokkaido's largest cities. It's known across Japan for its zoo, **Asahiyama Zoo**, and a local ramen variety (Asahikawa ramen), but is also worth visiting for the **Hokkaido Folk Arts and Crafts Museum village** (daily, times vary, but at least 9am–5pm), which houses three different craft museums. There is also the **Kawamura Kaneto Ainu Memorial Hall** (daily, July–Aug 9am–6pm, Sept–June 9am–5pm), which details Asahikawa's long association with the Ainu.

KUSHIRO AND AKAN NATIONAL PARK

To the east of Sapporo along the southern coast is the port city of **Kushiro** , where ultramodern architecture contrasts with one of Japan's most congenial dockside scenes, which includes a modern shopping and restaurant development called Fisherman's Wharf. Amongst the Japanese, Kushiro is noted mostly for the migrating red-crested cranes that put on elaborate and well-attended mating displays in the fields outside the city. Further east, Nemuro-hanto and the marshlands that stretch north from Kushiro along the eastern coastline are a recluse's paradise; Kushiroshitsugen Kokuritsu-koen (Kushiroshitsugen National Park; www.env.go.jp/park/kushiro/index.html) is the place to survey Japan's largest marsh and the river that meanders through it.

North of Kushiro in the centre of Hokkaido are the stunning virgin forests, volcanoes and caldera lakes that draw tens of thousands of visitors every year to 900-sq km (350-sq mile) **Akan Kokuritsu-koen** (Akan National Park; www.env.go.jp/park/akan/index.html), whose best staging point is Kushiro. Tour buses dominate this park, which makes a car or a bicycle a plus, and, as in many tourist areas, Ainu attractions are abundant. Within the park,

Akan-ko ⓱ is famous with the Japanese for *marimo* – odd, green algae balls also known as God's Fairies, which will either delight or bore you. **Akan Kohan**, the main town, has plenty of ryokan, youth hostels and campsites set in splendid natural surrounds. Two volcanic peaks, Oakan-dake and Meakan-dake, tempt climbers; Meakan is the preferred jaunt, partly because an *onsen* awaits the weary climber. North of Akan Kohan, Bokke has bubbling, hot mud.

The bus ride between Akan-ko and Mashu-ko to the northeast offers wonderful views at **Sogakudai** overlooking Meakan and Oakan. Mashu-ko is a landmark and is called Devil's Lake by the Ainu. Its 200-metre (650ft) high cliffs towering over misty waters have often served as leaps of death for lovers.

Less touristy is **Kussharo-ko** ⓲, at 80 sq km (30 sq miles) the largest inland lake in Hokkaido and home to "Kusshi", Japan's very own "Nessie", of whom there have been several alleged sightings. Three congenial *onsen* surround Kussharo: Kawayu, Wakoto and Sunayu, where hot sands provide a welcome novelty. **Io-san**, or Mount Sulphur, steams and reeks impressively and is worth a visit despite the commercialisation. **Bihoro**, a pass above Kussharo's west shore, has breathtaking vistas.

SHIRETOKO PENINSULA

Rich in land and marine ecosystems, a key region for salmon, sea mammals, migratory birds, woods of silver birch and resinous pine, home to deer and one of the world's largest concentrations of brown bear, it is not surprising that the outstanding biodiversity of the **Shiretoko** ⓳ region saw the area listed as a Unesco World Heritage Site.

Jutting out into the Sea of Okhotsk, this lonely, 70km (43-mile) long peninsula is one of the wildest and most remote regions in Japan, a fact that is reflected in its name, *Shiretoko*

translating from the Ainu language as "the end of the earth". Hardly any roads transect the half of the peninsula now designated as the **Shiretoko National Park** (www.env.go.jp/park/shiretoko/index.html), an expanse of virgin forest, volcanic peaks, waterfalls and hot springs. In midwinter the waters off the northern coast of the peninsula are frozen solid with pack ice. Most visits to the region are sensibly made in the months between June and September, although the frozen winter months have a crystalline beauty of their own.

Utoro, a spa town and fishing port, is the southeastern entrance and the area's main resort, with some useful amenities for an overnight stay and a helpful visitor centre. Though the town can be eschewed during the daytime, the lovely hot spring at **Iwaobetsu**, near Rausu-dake, the area's highest peak, is worth a half-day soak. Further up the coast, the **Shiretoko Shizen Centre** (http://center.shiretoko.or.jp; daily, 20 Apr–20 Oct 8am–5.30pm, 21 Oct–19 Apr 9am–4pm), has useful introduction material and film

Meakan-dake, Akan Kokuritsu-koen.

Fact

Japan and Russia, technically, are still at war, having never signed a peace accord after World War II. Part of the reason stems from a territorial dispute over what Russia calls the Kuril Islands, which include some of what Japan prefers to call the Northern Territories. Russia occupies all of these mineral-rich islands in the Sea of Okhotsk, but Japan believes the southernmost four of them, just 20km (12 miles) off Hokkaido, should be Japanese.

footage on the area, but the region's main attraction – the Shiretoko Go-Ko lakes – lies some 9km (6 miles) north of here. On the eastern side of the peninsula is **Rausu**, a pleasant fishing and *onsen* village.

FOREST PATHS AND LAKES

Shiretoko Go-ko, an area of forest paths and five exquisite lakes, is connected by wooden walkways. An observation point near the parking lot provides panoramic views across the lakes and forest towards the sea. Note that there are only four buses a day from Utoru to the lake. With a car or taxi, you can follow a dirt road up the peninsula to a stunningly located warm-water river and a series of waterfalls and hot springs collectively known as **Kamuiwakka-no-taki**. You can rent a pair of surprisingly comfortable straw sandals for the slippery hike up to the bathing pools.

From Shiretoko's high ground, visitors can gaze across the Nemuro Straits towards Kunashiri, an island

faithfully marked on all Japanese maps as part of their nation. Since World War II, however, this and other islands in the Northern Territories have been held by the Soviet Union, then Russia, the source of a long-running dispute that periodically sours relations between the two countries. Kunashiri, easily visible on a clear day, is a mere 25km (16 miles) away.

ALONG THE NORTHERN COAST

The best route away from the Shiretoko is west along the northern coast through the village of Shari and towards **Abashiri** ⑳ with its interesting but quirky prison museum, pleasant walks along Tofutsu-ko, and the wild-flower gardens. The **Abashiri Prison Museum** (www.kangoku.jp; daily, May–Sept 8:30am–6pm, Oct–Apr 9am–5pm) shows the preserved prison structures, including the minimalist cells that are barely adequate for this harsh climate. Japanese films about the *yakuza* (see page 291) often feature the notorious prison. Okhotsk

Icebreaking sightseeing boat, off Abashiri.

⊘ DRIFT ICE

In winter, the Sea of Okhotsk delivers one of Hokkaido's most distinctive attractions – drift ice watching. From January to April, the ice, (*ryuhyo*), moves across the northern coast, from where it is best seen from Abashiri or Shiretoko. Visitors can get up close on an ice-breaking sightseeing boat, gaze at the ice packs from shore, or even don a dry suit and go for a guided walk on it – followed, if they fancy, by a plunge into the waters.

A warmer option is to visit the Okhotsk Ryu-hyo Museum in Abashiri (www.ryuhyokan.com; daily, Apr–Oct 8.30am–6pm, Nov–Mar 9am–4.30pm), where you can watch ice floe videos or enter the museum's specially chilled "ice room" to touch blocks of ice. The tourist office in Abashiri Station can help arrange all the above.

Park, on the western fringes of Aba-shiri, is home to the fantastic **Hok-kaido Museum of Northern Peoples** (www.hoppohm.org; daily 9am–4.30pm, July–Sept until 5pm), housed in a striking pyramidal building, which compares the lives of the native people of Hokkaido with those of the Sami of Scandinavia and Inuit of North America. There is also the **Okhotsk Ryu-hyo Museum** (www.ryuhyokan.com; daily, Apr–Oct 8.30am–6pm, Nov–Mar 9am–4.30pm), dedicated to the winter drift ice that can be seen offshore. Best of all, however, Abashiri is at the beginning of Hokkaido's easiest long-distance bicycle route, a trip along the island's northern coast alongside the Sea of Okhotsk, which is popular with youths on summer holiday.

Wakkanai ㉑ lies at the northern-most tip of Hokkaido. In spring, the break-up of the ice pack to the north of Wakkanai is a mainstay of national television news. Wakkanai itself is undistinguished, although increasingly street and store signs in Russian suggest its popularity with Russians. In fact, the Russian island of Sakha-lin is often visible to the north. Wak-kanai is also a port for the export of older Japanese cars to Russia, where there is a thriving market for them, and it is the terminus for ferry ser-vices to some of the remote northern islands, including Rishiri and Rebun. Of course, in winter the ice pack can thwart travel by sea to these two small northwestern islands.

RISHIRI AND REBUN

The volcanic islands of **Rishiri** ㉒ and **Rebun** ㉓, part of the **Rishiri-Rebun-Sarobetsu Kokuritsu-koen** (Rishiri-Rebun-Sarobetsu National Park; www.env.go.jp/park/rishiri/index.html), are just west of Wakkanai, from where the ferry to the islands departs. Before boarding the ferry, visit the alpine wildflower reserve at **Sarobetsu**, a rainbow of colour as far as the eye

can see, especially in July. This is one of Hokkaido's real wonders. Rishiri and Rebun themselves offer various delights for the cyclist, hiker, camper and fisherman. It's possible to lodge at a minshuku (home-style inn) on either island and get up early in the morning with your host to go fishing in the Sea of Japan (East Sea).

Hiking is excellent. Rishiri offers the best hiking with a climb up Rishiri-san, poking upwards to 1,720 metres (5,620ft) above sea level, like Neptune's elbow. On Rebun, which is compara-tively flat, hike from Sukotan-misaki to Momiwa, or cycle from Kabuka to Funadomori to make the most of the rewarding coastline scenery. Joining a youth-hostel group is good insurance against getting lost.

Staying on these northern islands is an adventure. There is a hotel on Rishiri, the Kitaguni Grand, but stay-ing in a hostel (there are several on Rishiri and one on Rebun) or a min-shuku is a more down-to-earth choice and offers visitors a more authentic local experience.

Rishiri Island.

Abashiri Prison Museum.

THE GREAT OUTDOORS

A mountainous island archipelago that stretches from the frigid north to the subtropical south, Japan's great outdoors is vast. Hiking, skiing, soaking in hot springs – everything is possible here.

A week or two in Tokyo can leave the most city-hardened traveller in desperate need of fresh air and wide spaces, and Japan delivers both in abundance away from the capital.

The northern island of Hokkaido, in particular, is home to some the most rugged and wildest of Japan's national parks, among them Akan (see page 232) and its crystal-clear lakes, and Daisetsuzan (see page 231), which boasts 16 mountains over 2,000 metres (6,500ft) mixed with alpine meadows and a brown bear population that keeps hikers on their toes. At the other end of the archipelago, the southernmost of Japan's 29 national and 56 quasi-national parks, Iriomte-Ishigaki National Park in Okinawa, includes the Yaeyama Islands (see page 359) in the East China Sea. The dense forest and mangrove swamps on Iriomote Island here are the natural habitat for the critically endangered Iriomote wildcat. Other islands in Okinawa are home to underwater ecosystems that make for unforgettable dives.

More accessible, but equally striking, is Chubu-Sangaku National Park, straddling parts of Gifu, Nagano, Niigata and Toyama prefectures, and including arguably Japan's finest hiking grounds (see Kamikochi, page 201). Even Tokyo has a little bit of its own Great Outdoors. For an easy day trip into the mountains, head an hour west of Shinjuku to Mount Takao (see page 183) and chances are you will be rewarded with fine views west towards Mount Fuji (see page 184).

Warning for bears – "Don't go near nor feed them" – Shiretoko National Park.

On a clear day the easy hike up the 599-metre (1,965-ft) Mount Takao in western Tokyo affords magnificent views of Mount Fuji.

Be it Hokkaido backcountry or one of the resorts just an hour by shinkansen from central Tokyo, Japan offers plenty of great options for skiers and boarders.

Onsen come in many forms, from snowy rotemburo (outdoor onsen) to sake-infused waters and even mixed-gender baths. Some don't admit people with tattoos.

Soaking up the outdoors

Getting naked and sharing a bath with strangers might not sound appealing to everyone, but soaking in one of Japan's numerous natural hot-spring baths *(onsen)* really is one of the country's true pleasures. That's especially true if you find a *rotemburo*, or outdoor *onsen*, and soak surrounded by nature. Near Tokyo, Hakone and the Fuji area (see page 185) are known for ryokan with good baths, while Dogo *Onsen* in Shikoku, though without the stunning views, has the oldest known therapeutic waters in Japan and one of the county's most charming bathhouses (see page 329). Other great bathing areas are Beppu in Kyushu (see page 347), Noboribetsu in Hokkaido (see page 229) and Naruko in Tohoku (see page 217).

If you do try an *onsen*, there are a few points of etiquette to remember. First, throw any inhibitions out the window and strip off; you can't use the baths unless you are fully naked. Then, before getting into the bath, wash and rinse well at one of the stools in the separate wash area, making sure to be entirely soap-free before easing gently into the hot communal waters. Most *onsen* will give you a small towel or flannel to be used for washing and for a little modesty when walking about. When you get into the bath, leave this behind or rest it on your head – it shouldn't come into contact with the communal water. Those with tattoos should inquire as to the *onsen*'s policy: some forbid them, some ask patrons to cover them up, while others are accepting.

Nature and spirituality are frequently interwoven. In more extreme examples of this, frigid waterfalls can be used for practising shugyo (ascetic discipline).

With approximately 70 per cent of Japan's landmass mountainous, there's no shortage of stunning scenery and opportunities for outdoor activities.

The Japanese Alps provide some of the country's best hiking, with trails to suit all levels of hiker.

Gion, central Kyoto.

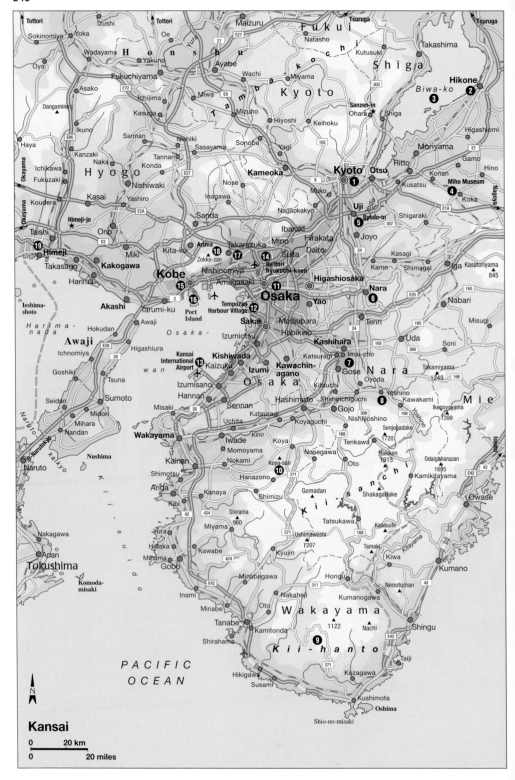

Kansai

0   20 km

0   20 miles

THE KANSAI REGION

In contrast with Kanto to the north, Kansai vibrates with entrepreneurial intensity. The region is also chock-full of cultural importance, and simply bursting with historical treasures.

Statue at Fushimi Inari Taisha, Kyoto.

The old Tokaido (Eastern Sea Road) that connected the ancient capital at Kyoto with the seat of the feudal shogunate at Kamakura (and later, with Edo Tokyo) has all but disappeared. But it was along that much-travelled highway, at a point where it passed through the Hakone hills, that the Kamakura bakufu (military government, or shogunate) set up a heavily armed outpost in the 13th century to stifle threats by the western warlords and imperial loyalists. It is from this post that the regions to the west got their name: Kansai, or Western Barrier.

In the Kamakura days, virtually all lands west and south of those barriers – including the Nagoya and Gifu regions (covered in the Central Honshu chapter) – were considered to be in Kansai. Since the Edo era, the definition has come to cover only the Kyoto, Nara, Osaka and Kobe areas.

Although much of Kansai is still rural, as we will see in the Southern Kansai chapter, declaring that one is from Kansai doesn't evoke a backwater image. Kyoto, Japan's capital for more than 1,000 years prior to Tokyo, is still the sophisticated heart of cultural Japan. Within day-trip distance of Kyoto's historic temples and shrines are the even more ancient temples of Japan's first capital, Nara, while the Kansai region also offers incredible natural beauty in places such as Lake Biwa and the hot springs of Arashiyama.

Todai-ji temple complex, Nara.

Osaka, only 40km (25 miles) from Kyoto, is quite different from Kyoto. An energetic, street-smart city, it is also the base for Japan's well-known electronics manufacturers, Panasonic Corporation (formerly called Matsushita Electric) and Sharp Corporation, and is a leader – together with Nagoya in Chubu – in the development of robotic production techniques. Tokyo may be Japan at its most modern, but the great commercial and industrial complexes of Osaka (and Kobe) are the centres of Japan's international commerce.

Put all its parts together and the Kansai region probably offers more diversity to the first-time visitor than does that megalopolis 500km (300 miles) to the north, Tokyo.

Kiyomizu-dera, a Buddhist temple in eastern Kyoto.

KYOTO

The former imperial capital was fortunately spared destruction during World War II and today retains pockets of Japan's elegant spiritual and architectural past.

Tokyo might have the national government and Osaka the entrepreneurial savvy, but **Kyoto** ❶ defines traditional Japan and possesses an ingrained aristocratic bloodline, punctuated by a history unrivalled by any other Japanese city. Home to no less than 17 Unesco World Heritage Sites, Kyoto is the country's artistic and cultural repository, ranking with Athens, Cairo and Beijing as a living museum. Still, don't expect a quiet, idyllic place. Kyoto is Japan's sixth-largest city, with a population reaching nearly 1.5 million. It is a large metropolis, crowded and noisy and, like most other Japanese cities, lacking aesthetic appeal in its modern contours. Even the temples can feel claustrophobic with busloads of tourists and students doing the rounds.

Rapid post-war modernisation saw tens of thousands of old traditional houses lining Kyoto's narrow back-streets razed to the ground in favour of modern, convenient living spaces. These old houses – splendid *kyo-machiya* – were of simplistic wooden facades and dancing rectilinear patterns; sliding paper doors; window slats in clay walls; lattices, trellises, benches, and hanging blinds of reeds and bamboo; and *inuyarai*, curved bamboo fences, that protruded out from the houses to protect against street traffic and dogs.

Kinkakuji Pavilion and Gardens.

Kyoto sits in a gradually sloping basin enclosed by a horseshoe of mountains on three sides, open southwards to the Nara plains, between the rivers Katsura-gawa to the west and Kamo-gawa to the east, and the Kitayama Mountains that stretch north to the Japan Sea.

Early April is when the cherry blossoms bloom, and by May, everything else has blossomed in ritual radiance. The rains of June offer a misty contrast to venerable temples and shrines, and also help to thin the crowds. The

Main attractions
Nishi and Higashi Hongan-ji
Kyoto Imperial Palace (Gosho)
Kyoto National Museum
Kiyomizu-dera
Gion
Ginkaku-ji (Silver Pavilion)
Kinkaku-ji (Golden Pavilion)
Ryoan-ji
Fushimi Inari Taisha

Maps on pages 240, 244

Kyoto

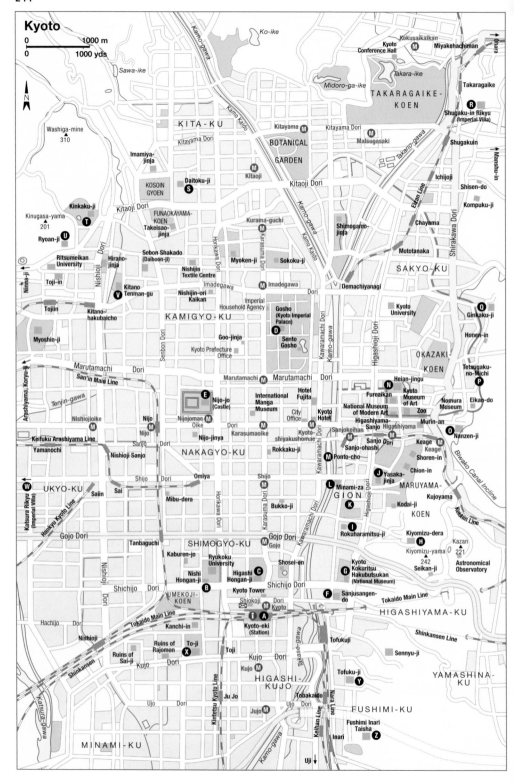

sticky heat *(mushi atsusa)* of summer is cooled by breezes from the surrounding mountains, making the long July and August evenings extremely pleasant. September and October deliver near-perfect temperatures for walking along Kyoto's temple paths. The autumn colours break out in earthy reds and oranges in November, making it one of the most popular times to visit.

The frigid, festive air of December and January is contagious all over town, while a light dusting of snow in February and March can cast Kyoto into a Zen-like state. Be aware that, at all the best times to visit Kyoto, most of Japan is doing likewise. Book well ahead for autumn and spring.

KYOTO'S BEGINNINGS

For nearly 1,100 years, from AD 794 until 1868, Kyoto was home to the emperor, and thus was capital of the nation. Japan's first permanent capital was established in Nara in 710, but by 784, the intrigues of power-hungry Buddhist priests forced Emperor Kammu to move the capital to Nagaoka, a nearby suburb of present-day Kyoto.

Ten years later, in 794, Kammu relocated the capital again to the village of Uda, renaming it Heian-kyo – the Capital of Peace. It wasn't until 988 that the use of *kyoto* (capital) began to appear in official records. A century later, Kyoto was the city's proper name.

The arrival of Buddhism in Japan in the 6th century brought great Chinese influence to the archipelago, reaching its peak of cultural flowering during the Heian Period (794–1185). Heian-kyo was built to a scale model of the Chinese Tang dynasty's (618–906) capital of Chang'an (now Xi'an), in China. Heian-kyo extended in a grid pattern still in evidence today for 5.2km (3.2 miles) from north to south and 4.4km (2.7 miles) east to west. Walls with 18 gates and a double moat surrounded the city. And because of earlier and persistent trouble with priests in Nara, Buddhist temples were forbidden inside the capital, explaining in part why many of Kyoto's most venerated temples are isolated in the hills surrounding the city.

Inside Kyoto Station.

Nijo Castle is surrounded by two concentric rings of fortifications.

Workers at the Nishijin Textile Centre.

Frequently levelled by earthquakes, floods, fires and wars over the centuries, the buildings of Kyoto have been moved, rebuilt and enlarged, and now represent a mosaic of historical periods. As a result, a scant few structures in Kyoto pre-date 1600, though many temples and shrines faithfully reproduce the earlier styles. It is commonly understood that a decision by the Americans not to bomb Kyoto during World War II – its historical heritage was considered too valuable – assured that these ancient structures stand today. Kyoto today offers some 1,600 Buddhist temples, 400 Shinto shrines, dozens of museums, two imperial villas, a palace, castle and thousands of arts and crafts shops.

AROUND KYOTO STATION

Most people first encounter Kyoto from inside the gargantuan **Kyoto-eki Ⓐ** (Kyoto Station), less than three hours from Tokyo by *shinkansen*. Construction of this futuristic 16-storey building, completed in 1997, created one of the hottest controversies in Kyoto's 1,200-year history. Preservationists, environmentalists, and much of the city's population were opposed to its construction, especially for the sheer size of the complex, its obstruction of the mountain skyline, and because its modern glass structure lacked any resemblance to traditional architecture.

The station area, and tragically much of central Kyoto, displays the characterless, cluttered sprawl of all Japanese cities. But fortunately, amid the thoughtless creations that increasingly plague the city are a vast treasure of sights behind fading imperial walls, down narrow lanes and amid the surrounding hills.

Directly north of Kyoto Station are two notable temples, Nishi (West) Hongan-ji and Higashi (East) Hongan-ji. As was the case with many of Kyoto's historical treasures, Japan's great unifier, Toyotomi Hideyoshi (1536–98), was responsible for establishing **Nishi Hongan-ji Ⓑ** (daily, Mar–Apr and Sept–Oct 5.30am–5.30pm, May–Aug 5.30am–6pm, Nov–Feb 5.30am–5pm; free). In 1591, Toyotomi brought the Jodo-shinshu Buddhist sect to the temple's current location. Its Chinese influences are many, and historians sometimes consider it the best example of Buddhist architecture still around. The *hondo*, or main hall, was rebuilt in 1760 after fire destroyed it. The founder's hall – *daishido* – contains a self-carved effigy of the sect's founder. Cremated after his death, his ashes were mixed with lacquer and then applied to the effigy. The study hall *(shoin)* contains a number of rooms named for their decorations: Wild Geese Chamber, Sparrow Chamber and Chrysanthemum Chamber.

To the east, **Higashi Hongan-ji Ⓒ** (www.higashihonganji.or.jp; daily, Mar–Oct 5.50am–5.30pm, Nov–Feb 6.20am–4.30pm; free) was established in 1603 when the first Tokugawa shogun, Ieyasu, wary of the Jodo-shinshu

monks' power at nearby Nishi Hongan-ji, attempted to thwart their influence by establishing an offshoot of the sect. Only the main hall and founder's hall are open to the public. The present buildings were erected in 1895 after fire destroyed the predecessors. When these current structures were being built, female devotees cut and donated their hair, which was woven into 50 ropes used during construction; some of the ropes are on display between the main temple buildings. Just two blocks east, the temple's tranquil **Shosei-en** (daily 9am–4pm) is a garden sanctuary of water, rocks and moss.

CENTRAL KYOTO

Due west on the other side of the Kamo-gawa, the **Gosho** ❶ (Kyoto Imperial Palace; free tours Mon–Fri; apply at Imperial Household Agency: tel: 075-211-1215; http://sankan.kunaicho.go.jp) remains the emperor's residence in Kyoto and is thus under the control of the Imperial Household Agency, which dictates every nuance and moment of the imperial family's life.

Originally built as a second palace for the emperor, the Kyoto Imperial Palace was used as a primary residence from 1331 until 1868, when Tokyo became the new residence with the fall of the shogunate and the Meiji restoration of the imperial system. The palace has gone through many restorations over the centuries; the current buildings were constructed in the mid-1800s. Shishinden (the Enthronement Hall), standing with its sweeping cedar roof before a silent stone courtyard, is an impressive emblem of imperial rule. It was constructed in the *shinden* style, where all buildings are connected by covered walkways or galleries. The court town that once surrounded the hall is now **Kyoto Gyoen**, the public Kyoto Imperial Park.

From the palace, a few blocks west is **Nishijin**, the weavers' quarter. The **Nishijin Textile Centre** (www.nishijin.or.jp; daily Mar–Oct 10am–6pm, until 5pm Nov–Feb; free) has excellent displays of working looms and woven goods as well as several kimono shows every day. After browsing the centre,

Imperial Palace, Kyoto.

Walking by the Kamo River.

walk through the narrow side streets – the ancient crafts of weaving and dyeing are still practised in the old wooden buildings.

South is **Nijo-jo** ❸ (daily 8.45am–5pm, entry until 4pm; Jan, July, Aug and Dec – closed Tuesdays), a castle begun in 1569 by the warlord Oda Nobunaga and finished by Tokugawa Ieyasu, ally to Oda Nobunaga, to demonstrate his military dominance over the city. In 1867, it served as the seat of government from where Emperor Meiji abolished the shogunate. Rectangular in shape, the castle's magnificent stone walls and gorgeous gold-leafed audience halls reflect the power of the Edo Period shoguns. The linking corridors of the castle's Ninomaru Palace feature "nightingale" (creaking) floors to warn of intruders, while the garden is a grand example of a lord's strolling garden.

Just south of the castle is **Nijo Jinya**, originally the home of a wealthy merchant and later used as an inn by visiting daimyo. The old manor house is full of trapdoors, secret passageways and hidden rooms. About 500 metres/yds east of Nijo-jo is the **Kyoto International Manga Museum** (www.kyotomm.jp; Thu–Tue 10am–6pm), which opened in 2006. Housed in an old elementary school, the museum has a vast collection of manga comics that covers every genre and which visitors can freely take off the shelves and read. It also holds regular manga art exhibitions and workshops.

EASTERN KYOTO

Just east of Kyoto Station and across the Kamo-gawa, **Sanjusangen-do** ❻ (Sanjusangen Hall, also called Rengeo-in; daily, Apr–Nov 15 8am–5pm, Nov 16–Mar 9am–4pm) was last rebuilt in 1266. The temple houses 33 (*sanju-san*) alcoves nestled between 33 pillars under a 120-metre (200ft) long roof. Inside is a 1,000-handed Kannon, the *bodhisattva* of mercy and compassion, and her 1,000 disciples. Each of their faces is different; Japanese look for the face that resembles their own – or that of a relative – to whom to make an offering. A famed

⊙ THE WATER CITY

Even in my sleep / I hear the sound of water / Flowing beneath my pillow" – Yoshi Osamu. Of all Japanese cities, Kyoto, with its rivers, commercial canals, irrigation channels, artesian wells and garden ponds is perhaps the most aquatic of Japan's inland urban centres, though in such a discreet way that you would hardly notice.

At one time there were literally thousands of wells in Kyoto. Wells were, and still are to some degree, an integral part of Kyoto life. They acquired a social function in the community, becoming focal points for informal gatherings. This practice among the townspeople of Kyoto gave birth to the expression "*Ido bata kaigi*" – literally, "to have a meeting around a well". Some private houses, if they are old enough, will still have them.

Glasses of water are often placed along with rice cakes and other delectables, in front of the stone figure of Jizo, a popular Buddhist saint found at roadsides or junctions. Fountains at the gates of Shinto shrines and strips of dyed cloth being fastened in the current of the Kamo River are constant reminders of the everyday importance of water.

Stroll anywhere in Kyoto and you are rarely beyond its presence. Water continues to be one of the main leitmotifs defining the character of the old imperial city.

archery festival, first started in 1606, takes place at the temple on the Sunday closest to 15 January.

On the opposite side of Shichijo-dori to the north is the **Kyoto Kokuritsu Hakubutsukan** ⑥ (Kyoto National Museum; www.kyohaku.go.jp; Tue–Sun 9.30am–5pm, Fri–Sat until 9pm, longer hours during special exhibitions), founded in 1897 and exhibiting artefacts of history, art and crafts. Several other temples are east of the museum. Up the Kiyomizu-zaka, a slope on the east side of Higashioji-dori, is **Kiyomizu-dera** ⑦ (www.kiyomizudera. or.jp; daily 6am–6pm, longer hours on weekends, holidays and special viewings in summer and autumn). The temple's main hall (hondo) sits perched out over the mountainside on massive wooden pilings. The veranda, or butai (dancing stage), juts out over the valley floor overlooking the city below. A popular Japanese proverb equates taking any big chance in life to jumping off the elevated stage at Kiyomizu. Founded in 788, Kiyomizu-dera predates Kyoto and is dedicated to the 11-faced Kannon. The two 3.6-metre (12ft) tall deva kings (nio) guarding the front gate speak the whole of Buddhist wisdom: the right one has lips pursed in the first letter of the Sanskrit alphabet, a, while the one on the left mouths om, the last letter. Behind the main hall with its dancing stage is Jishu, one of the most popular Shinto shrines in the country, and where the god of love and good marriage resides. (Most Buddhist temples in Japan also house some sort of Shinto shrine.) Don't trip over the "blind stones" (mekura-ishi) or the people walking between them with their eyes closed. The belief is that if you can negotiate the 20 metres (60ft) between the stones with eyes shut, silently repeating the name of your loved one, love and marriage are assured.

Steps lead down from Kiyomizu's main hall to **Otowa-no-taki**, a waterfall where visitors sip water from a spring said to bestow many health benefits, if not sheer divine power for the true believer. A short walk leads up the other side of the valley to a small pagoda with a view encompassing the entire hillside.

From Kiyomizu, return down the slope and follow a flight of stone steps down to Sannen-zaka, a street meaning "three-year slope". It is said that any pilgrim who trips or stumbles along this slope will have three years of bad luck. Today, the cobbled lane is less superstitiously known as Teapot Lane for all of the pottery shops lining its path. Continue to the charming Ninen-zaka, or "two-year slope". The restaurants near here are good for soba or udon noodles.

Back across Higashioji-dori sits **Rokuharamitsu-ji** ⑧ (www.rokuhara. or.jp; daily 8am–5pm), one of Kyoto's gems. At the rear of the main hall, built in 1363, is a museum with two fine Kamakura Period (1185–1333) sculptures: Taira-no Kiyomori, of the Heike clan, and Kuya, founder of the temple. The eyes of Kiyomori, presaging the

Statues of the thousand armed Kannon statues at Sanjusangen-do.

Admiring the exhibits at Kyoto International Manga Museum.

⊙ Fact

The many hostess-staffed "snack" bars in Gion are a pricey diversion in which an hour or two can easily cost US$500.

tragic destruction of his clan, sum up the anguish often seen in Kamakura Period art. Kuya, who popularised the chanting of the lotus sutra, is shown reciting magic syllables, each of which becomes Amida, the saviour.

North are the brilliant-orange buildings of **Yasaka-jinja** (www.yasaka-jinja.or.jp; always open; free), formerly called Gion-san, a name more commonly associated with the adjoining Gion pleasure quarter. One of the tallest granite torii in Japan, at 9 metres (30ft) in height, marks the portal to the shrine. From the shrine's back gate, one enters adjoining Maruyama-koen. The park is known for its beautiful garden and magnificent cherry blossoms in early April. Two interesting temples sit just beyond: **Chion-in** and **Shoren-in**.

GEISHA DISTRICT

East of the Kamo-gawa in central Kyoto, **Gion** ⓚ is Kyoto's famous pleasure quarter or geisha district, today an uncanny blend of traditional and modern architecture. In Kyoto, geisha are known as *maiko* and *geiko*, not geisha.

The word geisha in Old Kyoto referred to male entertainers dressed as women; in Tokyo and Osaka, however, it came to mean women. *Maiko* debut at about 16 years old and wear distinctive long trailing *obi*. At about 21, they may advance to the ranks of *geiko*, with their highly ornate kimono.

Along Gion's narrow streets one will rarely see *geiko*, but there's a good chance to catch sight of a *maiko* hurrying to entertain a guest – in recent years often harried by crowds of lens-wielding gawkers. The teahouses in the quarter are in the style of Kyoto's old *machiya* townhouses, but with added delicate touches such as the orange-pink plastered walls *(ichirikijaya)*. The best place to see the houses is along the alleyways that splinter off Hamani-koji, south of Shijo-dori. Just north of here is Gion Shimbashi, another well-preserved neighbourhood of old wooden buildings. At the intersection of Shijo-dori and the Kamo-gawa, **Minami-za** ⓛ, built in the early 1600s, is the oldest theatre in Japan and is still used for kabuki performances.

Exploring the Ponto-cho district.

ENTERTAINMENT AND NIGHTLIFE

For the height of imperial drama, try a *noh* play, which developed in Kyoto in the 14th century. Rooted in *sarugaku* (ballad operas), the lyrical and melodramatic form became known as *sarugaku no noh*, later shortened to *noh*. A classical presentation includes five plays with several humorous interludes *(kyogen)*. Most presentations today show only two plays and two interludes. *Noh* greatly departs from Western ideas of drama by abandoning realism in favour of symbolism.

Noh developed in Kyoto as one of Japan's original art forms, along with kabuki and bunraku (puppet theatre). Kabuki (ka-bu-ki, or singing-dancing-performing) was the last purely Japanese art form to flourish, developing during the Edo Period as a commoner's entertainment. Originally dancing shows performed by women, kabuki turned to men as performers when the shogun declared the form immoral and forbidden to women. It has more variety

and greater dynamic force than *noh* and appeals to a wider audience.

Other areas for traditional nightlife include traffic-free **Ponto-cho ⓜ** along the west bank of Kamo-gawa and just across from Gion. The narrow street is lined with interesting bars, restaurants and *tayu* (top-ranked courtesan) houses. Kawaramachi is another busy shopping, eating and entertainment neighbourhood, also located beyond the Kamo's west bank. An excellent spot to dine in summer are the restaurants along Kamo-gawa, between Shijo and Sanjo streets.

Cross over Sanjo-dori and continue north to **Okazaki-koen**. This park holds museums, halls, a library and zoo. The best of the lot is the highly informative, visually stimulating **Fureaikan** (https://kmtc.jp; daily 9am–5pm; free), a museum of traditional crafts housed in the basement of the Miyako Messe exhibition centre.

HEIAN-JINGU

An arching 24-metre (80ft) high torii leads from Okazaki-koen to the

A devotee at Yasaka Shrine.

Maiko performing a Kyoto-style dance.

⚙ GEISHA

Few things are as emblematic of Japan as geisha. Although misconstrued by many in the West to be high-class prostitutes (something that never fails to annoy the Japanese), the geisha are in fact trained to be companions and entertainers, traditionally providing refined conversation and performing song and dance for well-heeled male customers. Today, however, you don't have to be aristocratic or rich to partake in a little geisha company. Many travel agents sell reasonably priced tickets to geisha evenings, and some hotels and *ryokan* organize their own geisha events for guests.

Times have changed in other ways for the geisha. It is estimated before World War II there were nearly 80,000 of them across Japan, a number that has since dwindled to just several thousand with the modernisation of the country. The few that hope to become a modern-day geisha, however, still face a long and arduous journey.

Training customarily begins at age 15 (although it is common nowadays to begin at a later age) and it then takes five years before the apprentice can be called a *geiko*, a fully-fledged geisha. If you walk through Gion and catch a glimpse of a white-faced geisha in wooden *geta* sandals, shuffling awkwardly between teahouses, it will be one of these apprentices, or *maiko*. You can spot the *geiko* by the more elaborate design of their kimono.

vermilion-coloured gate of **Heian-jingu** (www.heianjingu.or.jp; daily, mid-Mar–Sept 6am–6pm, Oct–mid-Mar until 5.30pm; shrine – free), more of an architectural study than a Shinto centre. The shrine, dedicated to Kyoto's first and last emperors, is a replica of the original Imperial Palace built in 794 and last destroyed by fire in 1227. The shrine was erected in 1895 to commemorate Kyoto's 1,100th anniversary and displays architecture of the Heian Period, when Chinese influence was at its zenith. Shinto shrines took on Buddhist temple features during this period, when the plain wooden structures were first painted.

Passing through the shrine's massive gate, it's hard to imagine that the shrine is but a two-thirds-scale version of the original palace. The expansive, white-pebble courtyard leads the eye to the Daigoku-den, or main hall, where government business was conducted. The Blue Dragon and White Tiger pagodas dominate the view to the east and west. To the left of the main hall is the entrance to the garden, designed in the spirit of the Heian Period for the pleasures of walking and boating. Mirror ponds, dragon stepping stones and a Chinese-style bridge are some of the beguiling features.

TRANQUIL SHRINES

From Heian-jingu walk southeast to **Murin-an** (http://murin-an.jp, daily Apr–Sept 9am–6pm, Oct–Mar until 5pm), a 19th-century landscaped villa designed by the celebrated gardener Ogawa Jihei. The grass-covered grounds of this secluded garden, with its azalea-lined stream, incorporate an unspoilt view of Higashiyama. From the garden it is a short walk east to **Nanzen-ji** (www.nanzen.net; daily 8.40am–5pm, Dec–Feb until 4.30pm), which was originally the residence of 26-year-old Emperor Kameyama (1249–1305) after his abdication in 1274. Nanzen-ji sits nestled in a pine grove at the foot of Daimonji-yama and is part of the Rinzai school of Zen Buddhism, Zen's largest and best-known school. It's also one of Kyoto's most important Zen temples. The complex consists of

Hanami at night.

the main temple and 12 sub-temples, of which only four are regularly open to the public.

Nanzen-ji provides an example of the Zen's belief in the relationship between all things. The pine grove influences the architecture, art influences the garden, and taken together they all influence the observer. The temple reflects the Chinese style (kara-yo) that arrived in Japan along with Zen. This style, evolving through the Ashikaga Period (1338–1573), achieved a near-perfect balance between the lordly Chinese style and the lightness of the native Japanese style. Exploring the two buildings of the abbots' quarters – Daiho-jo and Shoho-jo – reveals how garden architecture and landscape painting interrelate. The quarters are full of famous paintings, like *Tiger in the Bamboo Grove*, and the surrounding gardens are renowned as some of the best in Japan. Here, the gardens are for sitting and contemplation, not strolling.

From Nanzen-ji, follow **Tetsugaku-no-Michi** ⓟ, or the Philosopher's Path, north past the Nomura Museum, Eikan-do temple and the intriguing hillside temple of Honen-in. The walk, named for the strolling path of Japanese philosopher Nishida Kitaro (1870–1945), snakes about 2km (1.2 miles) along the bank of a narrow canal to Ginkaku-ji. The quiet path – save for the crowds of tourists at times – is noted for its spring cherry blossoms and autumn foliage.

The walk ends at the Silver Pavilion, or **Ginkaku-ji** ⓠ (daily, Mar–Nov 8.30am–5pm, Dec–Feb 9am–4.30pm). The Ashikaga-era shogun who erected it in 1489 died before its completion and contrarily it remains without silver. However, its exquisite pavilion and Zen garden are not disappointing. The first floor of the pavilion was a residence and displays the Japanese *shinden* style. The second floor served as the altar room and shows a Chinese

Buddhist style. The mound of white stones (*Kogetsudai*) in the garden was designed to reflect moonlight onto the garden. The quaint tearoom in the northeastern section of the pavilion is touted as the oldest in Japan.

A 20-minute walk away directly north of the Silver Temple is **Kompuku-ji**, the first of three exquisite gardens. A dry landscape arrangement with a steep bank of azaleas, this temple is affiliated with the Rinzai school of Zen, but also has literary associations with Basho and Buson, two of Japan's greatest haiku masters. The narrow, bamboo entrance to **Shisen-do**, a rustic hermitage with an adjacent stone garden bordered by azaleas, maples and persimmon, is a short walk from here. Northeast on foot takes you to the tranquil precincts of **Manshu-in**, a hillside Tendai sect temple that dates from 1656.

TO THE NORTHEAST

In the northern foothills, the **Shugaku-in Rikyu** ⓡ (Shugaku-in Imperial Villa; free daily tours; apply at the Imperial

⊙ Shop

Antique-lovers should not miss Shinmonzen-dori, a few blocks north of Shijo-dori in the Gion. Dozens of shops sell screens, scrolls, *ukiyo-e* (woodblock) prints, Imari porcelain, lacquer, and bronzes from China, Korea and of course all over Japan.

The Shinto Heian shrine.

Household Agency before visiting; tel: 75-211-1215; http://sankan.kunaicho. go.jp) was built in 1659 as an emperor's retreat. This imperial villa seems pure fantasy compared to Katsura Imperial Villa. It consists of three large, separate gardens and villas. In Rakushiken (Middle Villa) stands a cedar door with carp painted on both sides. It is said that the carp would escape each night to swim in the villa's pond. Not until golden nets were painted over them, in the 18th century, did they stay put.

Hiei-zan, an 850-metre (2,800ft) mountain northeast of Shugaku-in Imperial Villa, has long held historic and religious importance to Kyoto. Here, **Enryaku-ji** (www.hieizan.or.jp) was founded to protect the new capital from evil northeast spirits. Apparently this exalted mission gave the temple's monks an inflated sense of importance. Over the decades, they became aggressive friars of the martial arts and swept into Kyoto on destructive raids. Their not-so-monastic rumbles were quenched by warlord Oda Nobunaga, who destroyed the temple in 1571.

Today, there are three pagodas and 100 sub-temples, some offering accommodation and making Hiei-zan one of the area's most accessible hiking areas.

TO THE NORTHWEST AND WEST

To the north and west of the city centre, skirting the foothills, are three renowned Zen temples that should not be missed. Established as a small monastery in 1315, the present buildings of **Daitoku-ji** ⑤ were built after 1468 when one of the several fires in its history burned down the temple. It is the holy of holies, where Zen married art. The great Zen calligrapher Ikkyu (d. 1481), painter Soga Dasoku (d. 1483), and founders of the tea ceremony Murata Juko (d. 1502) and Sen-no Rikyu (d. 1591) all came from Daitoku-ji. The great warlord Oda Nobunaga is buried here. Although a brutal warrior, Nobunaga was fundamental to the 16th-century unification of Japan and was a leading patron of the arts.

Some eight of Daitoku-ji's 22 subsidiary temples are open to the public. The three best-known are Daisen, Zuiho and Koto. In **Daisen-in** (daily, hours vary but at least 9am–4pm) is Kyoto's second most famous – maybe the best – Zen garden. Unlike the abstractions of other gardens, the Daisen garden more closely resembles the ink-wash paintings of Zen art.

The Daitoku complex has been criticised for its commercialism, but it is still worth the visit. This is also one of the best places to sample authentic Zen temple food, just like the monks eat.

Walk west along Kitaoji-dori past Funaokayama-koen to the best-known temple in Kyoto, if not all Japan: **Kinkaku-ji** ❶ (daily 9am–5pm), or the Golden Pavilion. It's a replica built in 1955 of a 15th-century structure and last re-covered in gold leaf in 1987. Each of the pavilion's three storeys reflects a different architectural style.

The Garden of Daisen-in at Daitoku-ji.

The first floor is of the palace style, the second floor of the samurai-house style, while the third floor reveals the Zen-temple style. The large pond in front of the pavilion and surrounding grounds give it a perfect setting.

The original temple was burned down in 1950 by a man who entered the Buddhist priesthood after being seduced by the pavilion's beauty. Thinking that his sense of aesthetics might approach perfection if he burned down the very object that had enchanted him in the first place, he did exactly that. The author and right-wing nationalist Mishima Yukio fictionalised the burning episode in his 1956 book, *Kinkakuji*.

Further west, visit **Ryoan-ji** (www. ryoanji.jp; daily, Mar–Nov 8am–5pm, Dec–Feb 8.30am–4.30pm), or Temple of the Peaceful Dragon, early in the day before the peace is shattered by the busloads of tourists and students. Here is the most famous Zen rock garden (*karesansui*, or dry landscape) in the world and one of Kyoto's main tourist attractions. The 16th-century garden is an abstract of an ink-wash painting executed in rock and stone. The sense of infinite space is said to lift the mind into a Zen state.

A little past Ryoan-ji to the west, **Ninna-ji**'s formidable gate with its fierce-looking *nio* guardians is one of the best in Japan. Returning east, **Myoshin-ji** (www.myoshinji.or.jp; daily tours 9.10am–4.40pm, Nov–Feb until 3.40pm) was founded in 1337 on the site of an imperial villa. Cast in 698, Japan's oldest bell hangs here. Tenth-century **Kitano Tenman-gu** (www. kitanotenmangu.or.jp; daily Apr–Sept 5am–6pm, Oct–Mar 5.30am–5.30pm) is one of Kyoto's most earthy shrines and hosts a popular antiques market on the 25th of each month. Its restrained wooden architecture enshrines Sugawara Michizane, a 9th-century scholar and statesman. Small wooden votives, or *ema* – with a picture of a horse on one side and a wish or prayer (most for success in school exams) written on the other side – hang in the courtyard. The shrine also celebrates the first calligraphy of the year, when

Catching a ride in Kyoto.

The Silver Pavilion at Ginkaku-ji.

schoolchildren offer their writings to the shrine. The present shrine structure was built in 1607. Tenman-gu is known for its splendid plum trees that bloom in the snows of February, and for the geisha who serve tea under the flowering trees.

UZAMASA DISTRICT

The Uzumasa district south of Ryoan-ji is home to two strikingly different sights: a temple of immense antiquity and cultural clout, and a cheesy but fun film studio.

Koryu-ji (daily 9am–5pm, Dec–Feb until 4.30pm) traces its roots to 622, when either Prince Shotoku or Hata no Kawakatsu, an important family of Korean lineage, founded the temple. It's a disputed point, but one that need not delay you in seeking out the treasures of this unique temple. The first building of note, the Kodo (Lecture Hall), is one of the oldest constructions in Kyoto, dating from 1165. The statues inside are even older, most dating from the 7th and 8th centuries. Impressive as they are,

these are overshadowed by the collection housed in the contemporary Reiho-kan (Treasure House; daily 9am–5pm, Dec–Feb until 4.30pm). The two most outstanding statues here are the image of Prince Shotoku at the age of 16, and Miroku Bosatsu, or Future Buddha.

For a more dramatic but decidedly lighter view of history, repair to the nearby Toei Uzumasa Eiga-mura (www.toei-eigamura.com; daily Mar–Nov 9am–5pm, Sat–Sun in Aug until 9pm, Dec–Feb 9.30am–4pm), a commercial studio renowned for churning out *chambara*-style, sword and Zen-flavoured samurai films and, now, TV dramas. Visitors can participate in acrobatic ninja shows and samurai sword fighting lessons.

One of Japan's most famous strolling gardens lies inside **Katsura Rikyu ⓦ** (Katsura Imperial Villa; applications for visits should be made to the Imperial Household Agency, which puts on several tours daily; tel: 75-211-1215; http://sankan.kunai-cho.go.jp), due west of Kyoto Station

The many torii at Fushimi Inari Taisha.

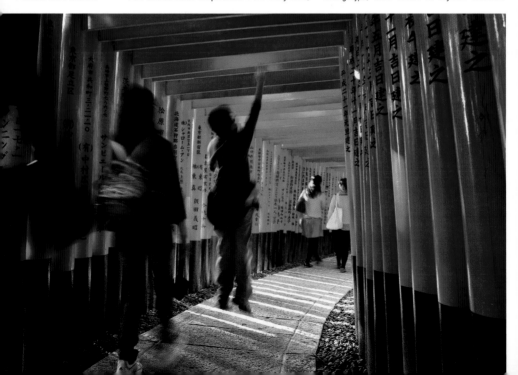

on the west side of Katsura-gawa. Its garden features a number of splendid teahouses overlooking a large central pond. Katsura, with its severe refinement, has exercised more influence on contemporary architecture than perhaps any other building in the whole of Japan.

SOUTH OF KYOTO STATION

Just south of Kyoto Station, **To-ji**  (www.toji.or.jp; daily mid-Apr–mid-Sept 8.30am–5pm, mid-Sept–mid-Mar until 4pm, mid-Mar–mid-Apr until 4.30pm) boasts one of the nation's enduring postcard images: the five-storey Goju-no-to pagoda. Rebuilt in 1644, and standing at 55 metres (180ft), it is Japan's tallest pagoda. The temple itself was established in 796 and today draws large crowds to its flea markets. Built next to the old city's south gate, To-ji became Japan's main Buddhist temple. Its main hall (kondo) reflects Buddhist traditions from India, China and Japan.

To the east up against the hills, **Tofuku-ji** (www.tofukuji.jp; daily 9am–4pm, Nov–early Dec 8.30am–4.30pm) contains Japan's oldest and most important Zen-style gate from the 15th century. Yet its 25 subsidiary temples are rarely visited and the grounds are usually quiet. Walk through the abbot's quarters (hojo) to the platform over the ravine looking down on Tsuten Bridge – it's one of the most delightful views in Kyoto. During the last week of November, don't miss the festival of old brushes and pens where writers and painters cast their old tools into a sacred fire.

A few blocks south of Tofuku-ji, tunnel-like paths of hundreds of bright-red torii tempt walkers. Actually, there are over 10,000 torii covering the paths of **Fushimi Inari Taisha** – the fox shrine founded in the 9th century in honour of the fox, which farmers believe is the messenger of the harvest god. Walk the full 4km (2.5-mile) course. Fushimi is renowned for its high-quality sake, and its famous brewery, Gakkien, is housed in an original Edo Period warehouse where visitors can sample products.

> **Tip**
>
> Both Japanese and foreign visitors need special permission to visit one of the imperial villas. Bring your passport to the Imperial Household Agency office at the Kyoto Imperial Palace early on the day you wish to visit – or apply online up to three months in advance (www.kunaicho.go.jp).

The Japanese rock garden at Ryoan-ji.

Tendai temple Sanzen-in in Ohara.

AROUND KYOTO

Just beyond Kyoto's hilly boundaries is the cradle of its ancient agricultural life. Some surprising cultural highlights nestle in the midst of this rustic scenery.

Who would expect to find ancient Buddhist statuary and a paradise garden in a mist-filled valley less than an hour from Kyoto Station, or to enter a futuristic art gallery, concealed in the side of a mountain? How about the villa of a silent-movie icon set among bamboo groves, or the largest lake in the country, just a short train or bus ride away? Equally impressive is Hikone Castle, one of only a handful of original fortresses to have survived.

The remnants of Kyoto's 1,000-year reign as Japan's capital can be seen all over Kyoto Prefecture and neighbouring Shiga Prefecture. In ancient times, retinues of powerful lords and shoguns would make way for Uji's yearly procession of wooden chests, carrying Japan's most valuable green-tea harvest. The brew still ranks as the very best, but the journey to Uji can now be made in just 45 minutes. Using Kyoto as a base, you could easily spend a week exploring beyond the city, starting with the highlights that follow.

OHARA

A pleasant 50-minute bus ride through the northeastern suburbs of Kyoto crosses a fertile valley plain into the village of **Ohara**. The area has a strong association with ancient Kyoto aristocracy: emperors, empresses, imperial kin and consorts who repaired here for

respite and refuge. Retired aristocracy, peasants, high priests and monks coexisted in a simple but rarefied atmosphere. Ohara has long been associated with the Buddhist faith. The legacy of beauty, calm and tradition clearly appeals to the handful of textile artists, potters and writers who have settled here.

Those with an interest in Japanese music will find **Jikko-in**, (daily 9am–4.30pm) on the eastern edge of Ohara, a worthy stop. Once the monks' quarters for the nearby Shorin-in temple, it was here that *shomyo* chanting was

◉ Main attractions
Enryaku-ji temple
The temples of Ohara
Hikone Castle
Lake Biwa
Miho Museum
Byodo-in
Arashiyama

Map on page 240

Lake Biwa from Hikone Castle.

⊙ Fact

The Shuheki-en Garden (Garden That Gathers Green) at Sanzen-in is to the south and east of the Kyaku-den, or reception hall. It is a pond-viewing garden created by the tea ceremony master Kanamori Sowa (1584–1656).

first brought to Japan from China by the monk Jakugen in the 11th century. This Tendai Buddhist music is thought to have had a significant influence on Japanese musical tradition. Today, bells and other instruments are exhibited in the tatami-matted guest hall.

SANZEN-IN

Ohara attracts a steady trickle of visitors, though most remain within the main temple district. A lane leading east from the main road winds up a hill beside a stream towards **Sanzen-in** (www.sanzenin. or.jp; daily, Mar–Dec 7th 8.30am–5pm, Dec 8th–Feb until 9am–4.30pm), Ohara's most important temple. Tubs of pickles, mountain vegetables, rice dumplings and a local speciality called *shiso-cha* (beefsteak-leaf tea) are sold along the way. The tea, which is slightly salty, supposedly contains flecks of gold.

Sanzen-in, like all the sacred sites here, is a sub-temple of Kyoto's grand **Enryaku-ji** (see page 254). Soft, flower-filled gardens, maples and massed hydrangea bushes replace the towering cedar forests that characterise the

Jakko-in, Ohara.

surroundings of the parent temple, blending in perfectly with the natural curvature of hill, forest line and mountain. Sanzen-in, standing in moss-covered grounds shaded by towering cryptomeria, is one of the great iconic images of cultural Japan.

The complex is an amalgam of buildings, some ancient, others more recently restored. Genshin, the retired abbot of Enryaku-ji temple in Kyoto, had the first Amida Hall built here in 985. The hall looks out over the garden, designed to evoke the unearthly beauty of the Pure Land sect. A statue of Amida, supposedly carved by Genshin himself with an intricate arabesque halo, is enshrined here.

OHARA'S OTHER TEMPLES

More earthly delights are laid out in the gardens above the temple where rhododendrons and bush clover make way for a newer hydrangea garden created by a former abbot of Sanzen-in. The earth is acidic on the hillside here, so the flowers are a watercolour-blue. The hydrangea, all 3,000 bushes, are best seen during the June rainy season. A

gravel path above Sanzen-in leads to **Raigo-in** (daily 9am–5pm), a temple located in a seldom-visited clearing in the forest. The main hall is still used for the study of *shomyo* chanting.

According to local legend, you are not supposed to hear Otonashi-no-Take (Soundless Falls), but if you continue up the same road a gentle splashing sound will soon be detected. The cascade is located amidst maple trees, cedar and clumps of wisteria. You cross a wooden bridge over a second river, the shallow, fast-flowing Ritsugawa, to reach the front lawn of **Shorin-in** (daily 9am–4.30pm), another temple often overlooked by visitors. An appealingly under-maintained garden and its main hall, a nicely weathered wooden building, date from the 1770s.

Nearby **Hosen-in** (daily 9am–5pm) is distinguished by a magnificent 700-year-old pine at its entrance. The unusual form looks vaguely familiar, turning out to be clipped into the resemblance of Fuji-san. The inner crane and turtle garden is framed like a painting or horizontal scroll by the pillars of

the tatami room visitors sit within to contemplate the scene while sipping green tea served with a delicate Japanese confection. **Jakko-in** (daily 9am–5pm, shorter hours in winter), built as a funerary temple for the Emperor Yumei in 594, lies across the fields along a lane lined with old houses and shops selling yet more varieties of pickles and local products. The original structure was destroyed in an arson attack in 2000 and was subsequently rebuilt. The temple is associated with the renowned *Tales of the Heike*, where it is described as a nunnery inhabited by the Empress Kenreimon-in. The compact garden here bears a remarkable resemblance to its description in the book.

If your thirst for solitude needs further quenching, a 40-minute walk north of Jakko-in leads to **Amida-ji** (daily 9am–4pm, Jan–Feb closed) temple in Kochitani (the Valley of Ancient Knowledge). A large Chinese-style gate marks the entrance to the route, a further 20-minute walk through an eerily still maple forest. There are no restaurants, shops or souvenir outlets

Genkyu-en garden in Hikone.

Enryaku-ji is a Tendai monastery overlooking Kyoto.

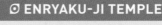

⊘ ENRYAKU-JI TEMPLE

Situated in western Shiga Prefecture, and overlooking Kyoto to its southwest, Enryaku-ji temple (www.hieizan.or.jp; daily Jan–Feb 9am–4.30pm, Mar–Nov 8.30am–4.30pm, Dec 9am–4pm) was once one of Japan's largest temple complexes – it encompassed 3,000 buildings and was famed for its warrior monks.

From its founding in the late 700s, the temple's power grew on the strength of imperial backing, but as has often been the way in Japanese history, support suddenly turned to rivalry: in 1471, the warlord Oda Nobunaga sent his troops to Enryaku-ji and levelled it.

The current complex, which was gradually rebuilt once the Tendai sect had returned to favour under Nobunaga's successor, Toyotomi Hideyoshi, is divided into three main compounds, of which visitors rightly tend to visit just two – the To-to, where most of the important buildings are located, and the Sai-to.

As for the monks, they are no longer warriors, but they do have a reputation for something else: marathon running. Running forms part of their extreme asceticism (though not all the monks do it), and since the Edo era the most devout have been attempting to reach enlightenment by running 40,000km in 1,000 days, divided into ten 100-day periods over seven years. Only 46 men have accomplished the feat since it started in 1585.

here, the faded colours, uneven floors and the musty air of wooden halls and corridors of the buildings adding to the ancient mystique of the valley.

HIKONE AND LAKE BIWA

A little over one hour from Kyoto on the JR Tokaido Line, **Hikone** ❷, the second-largest city in Shiga Prefecture, and one attractively situated on the shores of **Lake Biwa**, still manages to feel like the provincial castle town it once was. The tourist office (daily 5am–9pm) next to Hikone Station has helpful literature and the excellent English-language *Street Map & Guide to Hikone*.

Hikone Castle (daily 8.30am–5pm), the centrepiece of the town, dates from 1622, when local lords, the Ii family, had it constructed. One of Japan's few remaining original castles, it is also considered one of its finest. In keeping with the Japanese military's love of the cherry blossom, over 1,000 trees surround the castle. From the third storey there is a splendid view of the town and lake. Your castle admission ticket also allows you to enter nearby **Genkyu-en**

(daily 8.30am–5pm), once the Ii clan's private garden. The Chinese-influenced design, completed in 1677, is best appreciated from the raised teahouse, where for ¥500 you will be served powdered green tea (matcha) with a traditional sweet (tea is served between 9am–4pm).

For an even quieter setting, consult your map to find **Ryotan-ji** (daily 9am–5pm, mid-Nov–Feb until 4pm), a 17th-century temple to the south of the station that has two superb gardens – one the pond variety, the other a well-composed Zen garden – as well as a tea ceremony room once used by the Ii family. Look out for the pond garden's rock turtle island.

Lake Biwa ❸, or *Biwa-ko*, whose southern end cuts between Kyoto and Hikone (and which is easily accessed from either), is the largest freshwater lake in Japan, with a surface area of more than 670 sq km (260 sq miles). As a tourist attraction, it's known for its lakeside scenery, fishing and boating, but not all is well with these waters. Despite being "famous" for its fish and dishes that make use of the locally caught trout, previous over-use of agrochemicals in

Byodo-in temple and museum in Uji.

the area, poor wastewater treatment and other factors combined to make the lake quite polluted. Life-constricting red algae outbreaks are common.

MUSEUM IN THE MOUNTAIN

Art and architecture dovetail at the extraordinary **Miho Museum** ④ (mid-Mar–mid-June, mid-July–mid-Aug, Sept–Nov Tue–Sun 10am–5pm; for more precise details check www.miho.or.jp). The I.M. Pei-designed structure is located near the town of Shigaraki, inside a mountain in the lush green landscape of Shiga Prefecture. It is an unusual concept, a museum run by "new religion" leader Koyama Mihoko and her daughter Hiroko to promote their belief that spiritual completion comes through a fusing of art and nature. The result is stunning: as the electric shuttle bus emerges from a tunnel, transecting a giddy bridge over a deep valley, you disappear on the other side through a screen of tetrahedrons into the opposite mountain and the James Bond-like inner vault of the museum proper. The roof is an enormous glass-and-steel construction and the museum is divided into two wings. The north wing displays exquisite Japanese art objects, from Buddhist relics to ceramics and hanging scrolls, and the south wing contains art treasures from the great world civilisations, including Egypt, Assyria and ancient China.

BYODO-IN

About 10km (6 miles) south of Fushimi Inari Taisha, on the way to Nara and in the town of **Uji**, is one of Japan's most famous buildings, **Byodo-in** ⑤ (www.byodoin.or.jp; daily, garden: 8.30am–5.30pm).

Uji was a popular country retreat for aristocrats, and elegant retirement estates were built here. For members of the Heian Period imperial court in Kyoto, Uji, now reached in just 30 minutes by rail, must have felt a world away. From their well-situated villas, the nobility could enjoy watching the gentle range of green hills that stand as a backdrop to the majestic Uji River, the home even now of herons and sweetfish. One of these villas was owned by Fujiwara Michinaga, the emperor's chief

Hikone Castle.

Green tea flavoured ice cream on sale in Uji.

Togetsu-kyo Bridge, Arashiyama.

adviser. A closer glimpse of this era is found in Murasaki Shikibu's (a lady-in-waiting at the court) 11th-century narrative, *The Tale of Genji*, a tale of imperial court intrigue considered to be the world's first full-length novel. "He was obliged to move to Uji where fortunately he still possessed a small estate... after a time he began once more to take an interest in flowers and autumn woods, and would even spend hour after hour simply watching the river flow." Some years after Shikibu's work was completed, Yorimichi, the son of Fujiwara, converted the villa into a temple dedicated to Amida, the Buddha of the Western Paradise. The centrepiece of the project was the Amida Hall, commonly known as the Phoenix Hall, and the entire ensemble is known as Byodo-in. Amazingly, the building has survived centuries of weather, fire, earthquakes and years of neglect. In 1994 it was declared a Unesco World Heritage Site.

The best view of the perfectly balanced main building and its ornamental wings, seemingly floating on the surface of the water, can be had from across

the pond that surrounds the complex, an image that appears on the reverse side of the ¥10 coin. When the doors to the hall are open, a gilded statue of Amida, floating on a bed of lotuses, is visible within. Some of the more valuable or vulnerable objects in the hall, such as wall murals, wooden statues and the original temple bell, have been preserved and are housed in a modern **museum** (Byodo-in Museum Hoshokan; daily 9am–5pm) located in the complex.

UJI'S RIVERBANK

Besides Byodo-in, Uji has several other features of interest, not least of which is the river itself and its series of bridges, islands, shrines and teahouses lining its banks. The journey into Uji's past begins at the "Bridge of Floating Dreams", the modern version of the original 7th-century structure that spans the river. A narrow shopping street runs from here to Byodo-in. The first thing you will notice here is the smell of roasting tea. Fragrant *uji-cha* was first planted in the 13th century, and now Uji green tea is regarded as

the finest in Japan. On summer evenings, demonstrations of cormorant fishing take place along the river, adding to the magic of fireworks, poetry readings and other events.

ARASHIYAMA

Moving west from the centre of Kyoto, the **Arashiyama** district is where the dense urbanity begins to give way to a more pleasant semi-rural suburb, characterised by bamboo groves and the winding **Hozu-gawa River**. As with anywhere in and around Kyoto, Arashiyama has its fair share of temples, the most interesting visit being **Tenryu-ji** (www.tenryuji.com; daily 8.30am–5pm, late Mar–late Oct until 5.30pm). Built as a country home for the 13th-century emperor Kameyama, it ended up being converted into a temple in the 14th century. Most of the current buildings are modern reconstructions, but the temple's main garden – an exquisitely designed affair combining water and rock features set against a tree-covered hillside – supposedly dates back to Kameyama's day.

Near Tenryu-ji is the **Okochi Sanso** villa (daily 9am–5pm) that was once the home to a 1920s silent-movie star, Denjiro Okochi. As you wander through the villa's sprawling grounds, through moss and stone gardens and past tea ceremony pavilions, it soon becomes obvious that Denjiro must have been on a very tidy Hollywood-esque wage back in his day.

The other highlights of Arashiyama include the **Togetsu-kyo Bridge**, spanning the Hozu-gawa, the best place to see cherry blossoms in spring or the red leaves in autumn. The Hozu-gawa itself is a good place for taking a gentle boat tour, especially in spring or autumn when the trees along its banks are at their most colourful. South of the bridge, in the Arashiyama mountains, is the **Monkey Park Iwatayama** (www.kmpi.co.jp; daily 9am–4pm, mid-Mar–Oct until 4.30pm), where Japanese macaques roam freely on an observation deck, which also boasts good views down over the city. All of Arashiyama's sites can be taken in a single day trip from Kyoto.

You can sample the delights of green tea in shops in Uji.

NARA

Japan's capital in the 8th century, Nara later escaped the civil wars that shook the country. A repository of ancient treasures, it embodies Chinese, Korean and even Middle Eastern styles.

The ancient site of **Nara** belongs to an era before Zen gardens and tea ceremonies, before Japan became Japan. Buddhist thought from India and arts from as far as Greece and Turkey flowed east along the Silk Road and Nara was the last stop. Preserved here long after extinction in their home countries are the finest examples of Tang-dynasty architecture from China, early Korean religious sculpture and treasures from Iran.

Japan had its capital at Nara from AD 710 to 784, after which the government moved to Kyoto, 35km (22 miles) to the north, and the Nara area lost political importance. This was Nara's great blessing. As a result, it avoided the wars that destroyed other ancient capitals of China, Korea and Japan. It has also avoided the worst of the tourist crowds that are drawn to the more illustrious Kyoto. Many people that visit Nara do so as a day trip, opting to be nearer Kyoto's selection of hotels and restaurants.

Nara Buddhism represented an early exuberant form of Buddhist thought, rich in symbolism. Everywhere in Nara are mandala, the diagrams or arrangements symbolising cosmic truth. Represented at the centre is the essence of the main god. Expanding outward in circles or squares are other gods exerting their powers to help the centre. Mandala can be interpreted in everything

from the arrangement of statues on an altar to the layout of temple buildings. Every placement and gesture has meaning. For example, two guardian figures flank the gates to large temples. One has his mouth open, the other closed. These symbolise the sounds *a* and *om*, the first and last letters of the Sanskrit alphabet. Being first and last, they encompass all and hence have magical powers to protect against evil.

Hand gestures, clothing and implements are significant. Most ornate are the mandorla, or haloes, in which can

Main attractions
Nara Park
Kofuku-ji temple
Todai-ji temple
Kasuga Taisha
Shin Yakushi-ji temple
Horyu-ji temple
Asuka

Maps on pages
240, 268

Kofuku-ji.

be seen the intercultural impact of the Silk Road. The haloes originated in Indian Buddhism and travelled east to Japan and west to Europe, where they were adopted by Christianity. The flames in the halos signify divine light.

Statues with great power were hidden from the public and became the so-called secret Buddhas, shown only on rare occasions. For instance, the Kuze Kannon of Horyu-ji was hidden from the public for 1,000 years before seeing the light of day in the late 19th century. Many statues, Kuze Kannon included, are still only shown in the spring or autumn or on religious holidays.

OLD NARA

Old Nara, much larger than the city today, followed the traditional model of Chinese imperial cities: a sacred square with streets radiating from the central palace in a grid pattern. During the centuries of neglect after 784, the palaces of Nara disappeared, but the temples and shrines on the north-eastern edge of the city survived. This corner of the city is now a public park,

Nara-koen (Nara Park). Tame deer, sacred to the shrine of Kasuga Taisha, are its symbol.

A temple to the east of **Nara-eki ⓐ** (Nara Station) is **Kofuku-ji ⓑ** (www. kohfukuji.com; daily 9am–5pm), on the western side of Nara-koen. The patrons of Kofuku-ji were the Fujiwara clan, who gained power in the mid-7th century and succeeded in dominating the government for the next 500 years. Even after the capital moved to Kyoto, the Fujiwara continued to support Kofuku-ji as the family temple. Kofuku-ji is known for its two pagodas. The five-storey pagoda, built in 1426, is a copy of an original dating from 730 and is the second-tallest pagoda in Japan; the three-storey pagoda dates from 1114. The Central Golden Hall, which was destroyed for the seventh time in 1717, was restored to its original glory in 2018; 'golden' refers to the Buddha image inside, rather than the vermillion exterior.

The adjacent **Kokuhokan** (Treasure House; daily 9am–5pm) – a dreary, concrete building – offers the best

introduction to Japanese sculpture available. Most famous is the set of guardians (734) with sweet, child-like faces moulded out of dry lacquer. Of these, the six-armed Ashura is one of the best-loved statues in Japan. In addition, the museum displays a cast bronze head of Yakushi Nyorai, practically Egyptian in its abstract simplicity, and massive heads of temple guardians originally from statues that must have been 15–20 metres (50–65ft) high. Nara developed in an age before Japan became the land of the miniature. The buildings and statues aimed to exceed even the grandeur of Imperial China.

From Kofuku-ji, cross the street east to **Kokuritsu Hakubutsukan** Ⓒ (National Museum; www.narahaku.go.jp; Tue–Thu 9.30am–5pm, Fri–Sat until 8pm; longer hours during special exhibitions). The most interesting part of the museum is the East Gallery. At the end of October and the beginning of November, the normally hidden treasures of Todai-ji are displayed to the public. Regular displays include an array of Buddha images from past centuries and archaeological artefacts excavated from ancient tombs.

TODAI-JI AND AROUND

To the north across Nara-koen's central avenue is **Todai-ji** Ⓓ (www.todaiji.or.jp; daily, Apr–Oct 7.30am–5.30pm, Nov–Mar 8am–5pm), founded in 743 and the most important temple in Nara. Walk north towards the temple and you will be met by the **Nandai-mon**, a gate dating from 1199. With its 18 pillars and elaborate roof construction, it is one of the outstanding monuments of the Kamakura Period. Inside the gate stand great wooden statues, called *nio*, who guard the entrance to Todai-ji. They were carved around the 13th century. As an aside here, to the west of the Nandai-mon is the **Isuien Garden**. Constructed in the Meiji era, Isuien encompasses two beautifully sculpted stroll gardens, each centred on a large pond and offering a peaceful break from Nara's more visited temples.

Straight ahead from the Nandai-mon is Todai-ji, with the **Daibutsu-den** (Hall of the Great Buddha). Enshrining

⊙ **Tip**

The area south of Sarusawa Pond is an excellent place to find ryokan, traditional Japanese inns. Note that rates at these tend to go up at weekends and in the peak spring and autumn seasons.

Feeding the deer in Nara Park.

Nandai-mon pillars and beams at Todai-ji temple complex.

a monumental bronze image of Vairocana, the Cosmic Buddha, the hall was meant to proclaim the power of the imperial state. It was destroyed numerous times by fire; the present building dates from 1706. Although only two-thirds of its original size, Daibutsu-den is said to be the largest wooden structure in the world. The present building is not entirely a first-rate piece of architecture (note the pillars made of bound timbers, rather than single beams such as those of Nandai-mon). Still, the interior retains a sense of the medieval grandeur that was Nara.

The Buddha has been greatly altered in later restorations, but the petals of the lotus upon which the Buddha sits retain original engravings in fine lines showing Sakyamuni (the historical Buddha) as one of 110 billion avatars of Vairocana. The bronze statue is 16 metres (55ft) tall and weighs 500 tonnes. Like the statuary found in the nearby Sangatsu-do and Kaidan-in, it shows off Tempyo Period (729–764) art and craftsmanship.

Mochi (sticky rice snacks) on sale in Nara.

To the east of Daibutsu-den is a road lined with picturesque stone lanterns leading up the hill to two temples. **Sangatsu-do ❸** (March Hall), built in 746, contains a large central statue of Fukukenjaku Kannon (the Bodhisattva of compassion) radiating light beams and surrounded by a mandala arrangement of attendants and guardian beings. Next door is **Nigatsu-do** (February Hall), the perfect place for a final view of the park. Raised high over the city, this pyramidal building was frequently burned and rebuilt, most recently in 1669. Every 13 March since its founding in 752, the emperor sends an emissary at midnight with water symbolising the coming of spring. The arrival of the water is the occasion for a fire festival, with monks carrying burning pine running around the veranda and spinning sparks into the night. The building is closed to the public.

Kasuga Taisha ❻ (www.kasugataisha. or.jp; daily Apr–Sept 6am–6pm, Oct–Mar 6.30am–5pm, closed Mar 8–Mar 13, Dec 20–Jan 7) was originally built in AD 710, but its buildings have been

⊘ DIALECTICAL ROOTS

Japanese ranks ninth worldwide in number of native speakers, although no nation other than Japan has used Japanese as a language since World War II.

The origins of Japanese are not known with any certainty. A strong hypothesis connects Japanese to Korean, claiming that a language of southern Korea was imported into Kyushu over 2,000 years ago, along with the cultivation of rice.

Dialects abound in this archipelago punctuated by mountain peaks and deep valleys, not to mention the islands themselves. Some dialects – those of Kyushu and Tohoku come to mind – can be nearly unintelligible to many Japanese people when spoken by older generations. *Kyotsu-go*, or "common language", which is based on the Tokyo/Kanto dialect, linguistically unifies the islands.

reconstructed numerous times following the Shinto tradition that sacred structures be thoroughly rebuilt at intervals, often every 20 years, as is also the case with the shrines at Ise. Kasuga Taisha's treasure house is a modern structure housing the shrine's artefacts.

The city of Nara contains numerous other temples of historical importance. The most interesting temple outside Nara-koen is **Shin Yakushi-ji** Ⓖ (daily 9am–5pm) built in 747 to the southeast. This, along with Sangatsu-do, is one of the few original Nara buildings. The central figure of Yakushi Nyorai (Healer) grants aid to those suffering from ailments of the eyes and ears. Most unusual is the set of 12 clay guardian images still standing intact. Shin Yakushi-ji, tucked away among crowded streets in a forgotten part of town, is a favourite. Just a few steps west of the temple is the **Irie Taikichi Memorial Museum of Photography Nara City** (http://irietaikichi.jp; Tue–Sun 9.30am–4.30pm), with a splendid collection of images of Nara by the late Irie Taikichi and others.

NORTHWEST

Leaving Nara-koen behind, and heading a couple of kilometres northeastwards, is the old centre of the ancient city. The best place to begin here is **Hannya-ji** (www.hannyaji.com; daily 9am–5pm), the Temple of Wisdom. Surrounded by a garden of wild flowers, it has great charm. In the garden is a Kamakura-era gate with elegant upturned gables and a 13-storey Heian-era stone pagoda. The temple houses a Kamakura statue of Monju, the god of wisdom. Monju rides on his sacred lion, carrying in his hand the sword to cut through ignorance. A palace once stood near here, but today nothing survives but a large field with circular clipped hedges showing where the pillars used to stand. Just east of the palace field is **Hokke-ji** (www.hokkeji-nara.jp; daily 9am–5pm), a nunnery known for its 8th-century statue of Kannon.

North of Hokke-ji are imperial tomb mounds surrounded by moats, and beyond them to the northwest is **Akishino-dera** (daily 9.30am–4.30pm), patron temple of the arts. The original

A miko (female attendant) at Kasuga Taisha.

Nigatsudo temple at Todai-ji.

Shin Yakushi-ji was founded in 747.

Pagoda at the Horyu-ji temple complex.

temple was founded in 775, but the present hall dates from the Kamakura Period. Inside is Gigeiten, god of the arts and a favourite of Nara cognoscenti. The head is original Nara, with the delicacy of expression typical of dry lacquer. The body, a recreation from the Kamakura Period, has the S-curve of Chinese sculpture.

SOUTHWEST

Heading about 3km (1.8 miles) out of central Nara, the southwestern temples are a major destination for travellers. The first temple you reach heading from Nara-koen is **Toshodai-ji** (www.toshodaiji.jp; daily 8.30am–5pm), founded by the Chinese monk Ganjin in 751. The roof of the *kondo* (main hall) is the finest surviving example of Tang-dynasty architecture. Note the inward-curving fish tails on the roof, unique to Nara. **Yakushi-ji** (www.nara-yakushiji.com; daily 8.30am–5pm) is a 10-minute walk due south from Toshodai-ji. All of the original buildings have been destroyed by fires except the eastern pagoda, originally built in 698 and rebuilt in

718. This is constructed of a harmonious arrangement of three roofs, with smaller roofs underneath creating the illusion of six storeys. Unfortunately, the complex as a whole lacks the Nara charm due to modern reconstructions of the western pagoda (1981) and the main hall (1976). The main hall houses an original triad (considerably restored) of Yakushi flanked by Nikko, Light of the Sun, and Gakko, Light of the Moon.

HORYU-JI

To the southwest of Yakushi-ji, about 10km (6 miles) from Nara Station, is one of the region's standout sights: **Horyu-ji** (www.horyuji.or.jp; daily, late Feb–early Nov 8am–5pm, early Nov–late Feb 8am–4.30pm), home to the oldest wooden buildings in the world. Horyu-ji was founded in 607 by Prince Shotoku, the pivotal figure who established Chinese culture in Japan. The temple is something of a time capsule, preserving hundreds of art works from the 7th and 8th centuries. Horyu-ji is divided into two wings. Most visitors start from the western cloister. The main gate, dating

from 1438, leads to an avenue lined by earthen walls characteristic of Horyu-ji. Note the wood-grain patterns created by pressing the walls with boards, thought to make the walls earthquake resistant. At the end of the avenue is **Chumon** (Middle Gate). The pillars of the gate (dating from 607, rebuilt c.670) are famous for their entasis (outward curvature), a feature of Greek architecture that travelled to Japan via the Silk Road.

Inside the western cloister are the pagoda and *kondo* (main hall), built around 670. The *kondo* houses a rare group of bronzes dating from 620 in Wei style. They are distinguished by elongated faces, the "archaic smile" and the abstract, almost Art Deco lines of the falling drapery and the flames of the mandorla. In the centre is the Shaka Triad (Sakyamuni, the historical Buddha, with attendants). To the right is Yakushi and to the left is Amida, the Buddha of Paradise. Guardians, standing on demons, are Japan's oldest "Four Heavenly Kings".

One of the pleasures of Horyu-ji is the walk out through the cloister,

an old example of a Chinese form that influenced temples and palaces throughout eastern Asia. Outside the cloister, walk east to the two concrete buildings of the museum, **Daihozod-en** (Great Treasure House). These buildings are even uglier than the museum of Kofuku-ji, but the treasures inside are important. Among the displays in the museum are the Kudara Kannon from Korea, the portable shrine of Lady Tachibana and the Hyakuman pagodas, which contain strips of paper printed with short prayers. Published in 764 in an edition of 1 million, they are the world's oldest printed material.

From the museum there is a walk bordered by temples and earthen walls to the eastern cloister. In the centre is an octagonal building of Chinese inspiration, surmounted by a flaming jewel and known as the **Yumedono**, Hall of Dreams. Built around 740, it commemorates a dream of Prince Shotoku in which an angel appeared to him while he was copying the sutras. The Yumedono contains a secret Buddha, the Kuze Kannon, which is only

Yakushi-ji Temple.

on view in the spring and autumn. Behind the eastern cloister is **Chugu-ji**, a nunnery housing a wooden statue of Miroku, god of the future and the supreme statue of Nara. Possibly of Korean workmanship, it dates from the early 7th century. Although Miroku is enshrined in a drab concrete building, this is an ideal place to stop, rest and meditate for a while.

Slightly removed from the Horyu-ji complex are the two temples of **Hokki-ji** and **Horin-ji** (late Feb–early Nov 8.30am–5pm, early Nov–late Feb 8.30am–4.30pm), around 1km (0.6 miles) north of Chugu-ji. Hokki-ji contains a three-storey pagoda built in 706. Horin-ji was rebuilt only in 1975.

SOUTH YAMATO AND ASUKA

Travelling south of central Nara, into the south Yamato area, **Shakko-ji** and **Taima-dera** (www.taimadera.org; both daily 9am–5pm) are known for their thousands of varieties of peonies. Taima-dera contains two Nara Period pagodas and a "secret" mandala painting (an Edo Period copy is on view). On 14 May each year parishioners don masks of the Buddhas and parade through the grounds in a unique display of walking sculpture.

Asuka, the capital before Nara from 552 to 645, was the first city to have avenues on the Chinese grid pattern and large Buddhist temples. It was here that Prince Shotoku introduced Chinese law and philosophy. And it was here that the poems of the *Manyoshu*, Japan's first anthology of poetry, were written. Today, there is only a village of farmhouses and rice paddies, but the ruins conjure up an idea of the past. In Asuka, two burial mounds open to the public contain Japan's only known tomb murals. Excavated in 1972, they are displayed in a modern building often crowded with visitors. More evocative is the inner chamber of a 7th-century tumulus. The earthen covering has disappeared, leaving 75-tonne boulders exposed. **Tachibana-dera** stands at the site of Prince Shotoku's birthplace. Most of the temple's buildings date from the Edo Period, but the pleasant country surroundings exude something of old Asuka.

Hase-dera Temple.

Most important of the area's temples is **Asuka-dera** (daily, Apr–Sept 9am–5.30pm, Oct–Mar 9am–5pm), enshrining the Great Buddha of Asuka, a bronze image of Shaka (Sakyamuni) and Japan's oldest large-scale Buddhist statue.

EASTERN MOUNTAINS

Soon after leaving Sakurai, at the southeastern end of the Yamato Plain, the road begins to climb into verdant hills. The first stop is the temple of **Hase-dera** (www.hasedera.or.jp; daily, Apr–Sept 8.30am–5pm, Oct–Nov, Mar 9am–5pm, Dec–Feb 9am–4.30pm), known for its peony festival (Botan Matsuri) in the last week of April. A covered stairway of 399 steps hung with lanterns leads up to the main hall, which enshrines Japan's largest wooden statue, an 11-headed Kannon carved in 1538. A half-hour's drive to the east leads to the village of Ono. Turn south here on the winding road along the Muro-gawa. Across the river is the **Miroku Magaibutsu** cut into the cliff face. This is the largest hillside carving in Japan, dating from 1207.

NORTHERN HILLS

The northern and eastern hills are convenient for relaxing afternoon drives out of Nara, especially along the Nara Okuyama road, starting from behind Todai-ji. The jewel of the northern hills is **Joruri-ji** (daily, Mar–Nov 9am–5pm, Dec–Feb 10am–4pm), one of the few surviving Heian temples. The temple, established in 1179, is a miniature Buddhist Paradise. In the centre is a pond symbolising the lake of heaven. To the right is the Western Paradise and the temple of Nine Amida. During the year, the rays of the sun sweep across the temple lighting each Buddha image in turn. In a direct line across the pond is a pagoda with a statue of Yakushi, Lord of the Eastern Paradise. About a 1km (0.6-mile) walk into the hills are the **Tono-o Sekibutsu**, stone carvings dating from the Kamakura Period. Buddhas cut into the rock – in an abstract, even crude style, and covered with lichens – are called *magaibutsu* and have a magical aura about them. The hills of Nara contain hundreds of such carvings.

Ishibutai Kofun, Asuka.

The Koya-san Temple complex.

SOUTHERN KANSAI

The rugged mountains and ancient forests of the southern part of Kansai are a far cry from the region's urban centre. Like Kyoto and Nara to the north, however, the region is rich in history.

Fanning southwest and southeast from Nara, the largely rural southern Kansai region has some outstanding sights, both historic and modern. From a base in Nara or even Osaka or Kyoto, no visit to Kansai would be complete without a couple of days exploring the more remote south. At Koya-san, the mountain home of the Shingon sect of Buddhism, the more than 100 temples within ancient cryptomeria forest create an almost mystical aura befitting one of Japan's holiest sites, while the ancient Kumano Kodo pilgrimage trails to the east of the region wind through breathtaking mountain and forest scenery. Off the western coast, in the Seto Inland Sea, the traditional has given way to cutting-edge art on Naoshima – dubbed "Japan's art island" for good reason.

OUT OF NARA

It's an easy run directly south of Nara to **Imai-cho** ⑦, where the old quarter of the town is a 10-minute stroll from Yagi-nishiguchi Station. A thriving merchant town since the 17th century, Imai-cho has over 500 traditional wood-and-plaster houses, a half-dozen or so of which are open to the public. A real bonus is that most of the houses are occupied, making the town feel like a living entity rather

than a stagey museum set. A single ticket admits you to all the *machiya*, as these residences are known. The most interesting is the **Imanishi Jutaku** (Tue–Sun 9am–5pm), dating from 1650. Another notable building and Important Cultural Property is the Kawai Residence, which still functions as a private home and sake brewery.

The village of **Yoshino** ⑧, a quiet getaway at most times, is awash with visitors during the spring cherry blossom season when an astonishing

Map on page 240

Main attractions
Imai-cho
The Kii Peninsula
Kumano Kodo
Koya-san
The Grand Shrines of Ise

Pilgrims at Kumano Kodo, Wakayama.

Kumano Hongu Taisha is part of the Kumano Sanzan in the Wakayama Prefecture.

Yoshino-san in spring.

for the nicely appointed temples and shrines along and off the main street. **Kimpusen-ji** temple (www.kinpusen.or.jp; daily 8.30am–4.30pm), with its fierce guardian statues and a main hall, said to be the second-largest wooden building in Japan (after Todai-ji's Daibutsu-den in Nara), is a designated National Treasure.

Chikurin-in (www.chikurin.co.jp), a beautifully designed and finished temple, operates primarily as an upmarket Japanese inn, but has a fetching and quite famous stroll garden (daily 9am–8pm), said to have been partly designed by the tea master Sen no Rikyu. The garden uses Yoshino-san to great effect as borrowed scenery. To get to Yoshino take the Kintetsu Nara Line, changing onto the Kintetsu Yoshino Line at Kashihara-jingu-mae.

100,000 trees are in bloom. Grown at different elevations on the slopes of **Yoshino-san**, the earliest to bloom are at the bottom, the last at the top, an effect that stretches the viewing season to a full month.

It's an easy enough ascent from Yoshino Station to the village, which sits on the side of the mountain, but there is also a convenient cable car (Yoshino Ropeway; www.yokb315.co.jp). Before following the trails through the cherry trees, spare some time

THE KII PENINSULA

The **Kii-hanto** ❾ (peninsula) at the southern end of the Kansai region is Honshu's largest peninsula, an area known for the dense forests and

rugged mountains of its interior and a dramatic Pacific-facing coastline. The warm Kuroshio Current here has created a distinctive ecosystem and climate. On the one hand, the warm waters have helped produce the most poleward living coral reefs in the world; on the other the Kuroshio is blamed for making Kii the wettest place in the subtropics, with annual rainfall in the southern mountains nearly 5 metres (16.5ft). When typhoons batter Honshu in late summer and early autumn, Kii often takes the brunt of the damage. No wonder the people here have a reputation for being hardy folk.

A highlight of the Kii region is the **Kumano Kodo**, a network of four historic pilgrimage routes that have been granted Unesco World Heritage status. The routes would lead pilgrims between Kumano and religious sites such as the Grand Shrines of Ise (see page 281) and Koya-san, but today the pious have largely been replaced by tourists who come to gape at Kumano's sheer natural beauty – its remote mountains, tea fields and ancient woods – before soaking in the area's reportedly healing hot springs.

KOYA-SAN

Surrounded by 117 temples concealed within the green and mysterious canopies of cryptomeria trees and moss, spending a night at a *shukubo*, or temple lodging, on **Koya-san** ⑩ in the heart of the Kii-hanto is one of those quintessentially Japanese experiences not to be had with more conventional sights. Although easily accessed by train – take the Hashimoto and Nankai lines from Nara, about 40km (25 miles) to the east, to the terminus at Gokurakubashi Station and the cable car up to the mountain – Koya-san still manages to seem remote and isolated. The mountain became a major religious centre in 816, when the celebrated priest Kobo Daishi set up a temple here. Today it is a retreat, meditation centre and place of Buddhist study for trainee priests and monks, but it also offers simple

⊘ Tip

The graceful buildings of Kongobu-ji temple at Koya-san are worth seeing for their religious and secular treasures, including screen paintings by the respected Kano school of artists. There is also an impressive stone garden here called the Banryu-tei, which you can contemplate from the veranda.

View of the mountains from Kumano Kodo, Wakayama.

Daito at Koya-san.

Eko-in temple and lodgings at Koya-san.

resting place of everyone from commoners to members of the imperial family to Kobo Daishi himself. Followers of the priest believe that when he ascends to meet the Buddha, those buried near him will also rise to glory, hence the jam of tombs. Kobo Daishi's mausoleum at the far end of the cemetery, the most sacred spot on Koya-san, is located behind the **Lantern Hall** (daily 6am–5.30pm; free), where thousands of lights are kept burning. On the other side of the small town that serves all Koya-san's needs is the central religious compound known as the **Garan** (grounds always open; free), and also the symbol of the mountain, a two-storey vermilion pagoda called the **Daito** (daily 8.30am–5pm), or Great Stupa.

The Reiho-kan (www.reihokan.or.jp; Treasure Museum; daily 8.30am–5pm, May–Oct until 5.30pm) at Koya-san has a first-rate collection of priceless Buddhist art, including painted scrolls, silk paintings and mandalas. The exhibits are changed regularly through the year.

lodgings for travellers – mostly traditional Japanese rooms with tatami floors, sliding doors and shared toilets (for a list of temple accommodation, see www.shukubo.net).

Koya-san can be explored at random, but Ichinohashi, the entrance to **Okuno-in** cemetery, is a good starting point. In this veritable city of the dead, moss-covered tombstones mark the

THE SHRINES OF ISE

While not part of the Kansai district, Ise and its shrines, east from Nara and Kyoto, perhaps best exemplify the nature and purpose of the Japanese Shinto belief.

An excursion to Ise can be enlightening, but know beforehand that visitors are not allowed into the shrines' compounds under any circumstances.

No one can say exactly how long the two main shrines of what are collectively called the Grand Shrines of Ise have existed. Historical evidence suggests that **Naiku**, or the Inner Shrine, has been in place since around the 4th century, and **Geku**, or the Outer Shrine, since the late 5th century (www.isejingu. or.jp; both shrines: daily, Jan–Apr, and Sept 5am–6pm, May–Aug 5am–7pm, Oct–Dec 5am–5pm; free).

At Ise, the venerable cypress-wood (hinoki) shrine buildings stand today in perfect condition – almost new and mocking the ravages of time. The secret of the fine condition of these most sacred of Shinto shrines is sengu, or shrine removal, performed at Ise every 20 years over the past 13 centuries; the last and 62nd sengu took place in 2013. Sengu consists of the razing of the two main buildings of both shrines, along with 14 smaller auxiliary structures. In the sengu, before the existing structures are destroyed, new shrine buildings of identical scale and materials are erected on adjacent foundations set aside for that purpose. Then Japan's largest and most important Shinto festival, Jingu Shikinen Sengu, begins as the deities of the respective shrines are invited to pass from the old into the new structures. Later, the old structures are torn down and sections of the timbers sent to Shinto shrines throughout Japan. Visitors can learn more about the rebuilding of shrines in the recently opened Sengukan Museum (www.sengukan.jp; 9am–4.30pm; closed 4th Tue of month), adjacent to Geku.

Why this work? First, the 20-year period can be viewed as a transition point. In human life, it is a line of demarcation between generations. Thus, sengu perpetuates an appreciation and an awareness of the cultural and religious significance of the shrines from age to age. Two decades is also perhaps the most logical period in terms of passing on from generation to generation the technological expertise needed for the reconstruction.

Geku is dedicated to Toyouke no Omikami, the goddess of agriculture. The grounds of Geku cover about 90 hectares (220 acres). A thatched gateway stands at the outermost of the three formidable fences, which is as close as anyone except imperial personages, envoys and shrine officials get to Shoden, the main hall. The clean, simple lines of the building are the very essence of Japanese architecture, showing nary a trace of the often bolder Chinese and Korean influences that dominate shrines elsewhere in Japan.

Naiku is a few kilometres from Geku. Here, as in the Outer Shrine, the object of attention is enclosed in a series of fences and can be viewed only from the front of a thatched-roof gate in the outermost fence.

Naiku is said to contain the yata no kagami (sacred mirror), which, along with a sword and a jewel, constitute the Three Sacred Treasures of the Japanese imperial throne. Mythology says that the mirror was handed by Amaterasu Omikami to her grandson when he descended from heaven to reign on earth. She gave him the gift of rice agriculture and a blessing for Japan.

One of the various facilities of the Ise Shrine.

Neon lights on Dotonbori Canal, Osaka.

OSAKA AND KOBE

Tokyo may be where the bureaucrat and banker confer, but Osaka is where the entrepreneur and marketeer huddle, making it Japan's centre of commerce, with a gritty, refreshing straightforwardness.

Kyoto can lay fair claim to be Kansai's cultural heart, but it's Osaka – and to a lesser extent Kobe – that really epitomise the hustle and bustle for which Kansai is best known. Osaka has its fair share of historic attractions (where in Japan doesn't?) with the mighty Osaka Castle and temples such as Shitenno-ji, but it's areas like the buzzing, neon-drenched Dotonbori entertainment district, with its restaurants, bars and theatres, that best represent the city. The entertainment continues out in Osaka Bay, where the Universal Studios Japan amusement park is a huge draw for Japanese travellers. Like Osaka, Kobe offers visitors a mixture of fun and tradition. The European architecture in the Kitano-cho area, not to mention the colourful Nankinmachi Chinatown, can trace their roots to the early days of Kobe Port, while the Rokko Island development is all modern amusements. Away from these two cities, Himeji makes for one of the most rewarding day trips in Japan for anyone with an interest in feudal history – Himeji-jo is without a doubt the finest original castle still standing in Japan.

COMMERCIAL CONDUIT

Some Japanese look askance at **Osaka ⓫**, as if it belonged to another, somewhat unrelated, part of the hemisphere. Its humour is different and a

bit more rollicking than Tokyo. Even the language and intonation have a gritty, home-cooked flavour, raising eyebrows of disdain in sophisticated and bureaucratic Tokyo. Osaka is known for the character of its people: straightforward, business-savvy jay-walkers who know how to eat well. While sophisticated Kyotoites are said to spend their money on clothes, Osakans prefer to dispose of their hard-earned yen on culinary exploits.

Osaka goes by all sorts of nicknames – so many that they would put even an

Main attractions
Osaka Castle
Semba
Dotonbori
America-mura
Shitenno-ji temple
Osaka Bay
Kitano-cho
Port Island and Rokko
  Island
Takarazuka
Himeji

Maps on pages
240, 284

Kita-ku, Osaka.

enthusiastic civic promoter to sleep. Among them are the City of Water, for its numerous rivers and one-time canals, and City of a Thousand Bridges, for the nearly 1,000 *bashi* that span the waterways. But all the waterways and bridges have only served one purpose: moving goods and material in and out of Osaka, Japan's commercial trading centre to the world.

Osaka's business connection is documented as far back as the 4th century, when Emperor Nintoku made Naniwa (Osaka) his capital. His business acumen was considerable for a politician; for example, he astutely decided to rebate all taxes to local businesses for three years after he was informed of an impending recession. His ploy worked rather well and the Osaka business ethic was conceived, as was the unique language of its merchants, *akinai kotoba*.

The city's stellar port and river connection to the capital in Kyoto played a central role in its economic and cultural development. Merchants from around the country (and from China and Korea) flooded the city. Osaka grew in strength and economic power, culminating with the shogunate of legendary Toyotomi Hideyoshi (1536–98), who chose Osaka as his seat of government, built himself a fine castle, and then turned the city into Japan's foremost commercial and industrial centre.

For the next 270 years, Osaka was the "kitchen of Japan", with raw materials pouring in and high-quality finished products flowing out. Kyoto and fledgling Edo (present-day Tokyo) were consumers, Osaka the provider. When the capital and commercial centre moved to Tokyo, Osaka was – and remains – where the coin-of-the-realm is minted. And even though the aerial bombings of World War II nearly destroyed Osaka (unlike nearby Kyoto, spared the wrath of American air raids for its cultural, historic and religious landmarks), the city quickly returned to its commercial prominence and hustle.

CONTEMPORARY OSAKA

Osaka has an extensive, user-friendly subway and circular train line that makes exploring the city painless.

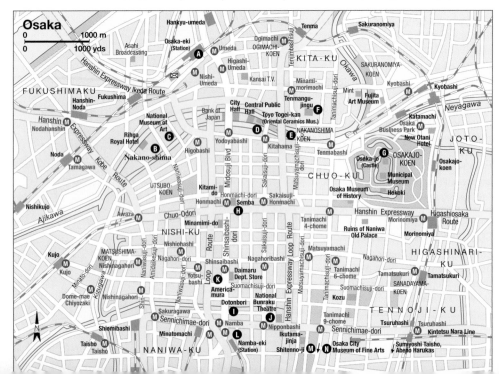

Flanking Chuo-ku (Central District) are two sides of the Osakan coin: one half centres on Umeda, in Kita-ku (North District), the northern area around Osaka Station, while the other side is Minami-ku (South District), the southern part of the city in and around Namba Station. While only 10 minutes apart by subway, they are worlds apart in mind and manner. Umeda is Osaka's newer face where most of the city's skyscrapers, offices, hotels and shopping centres are sprouting. Minami, the unpretentious side of the city, is claimed to be the real Osaka. Most Osakans will say that Umeda is where one works, but Minami is where the Osakan heart beats. It's also where the say-what-you-mean *Osaka-ben* (Osaka dialect) is spoken with pride.

Most trains (except the *shinkansen*, or bullet train) arrive at the **Osaka-eki Ⓐ** (Osaka Station) complex in Umeda, so it is from here that a tour of the city might start. At Osaka Station, *shinkansen* and other cross-country express trains meet with Osaka's three main north–south subway lines. Like most train stations in Japan, Osaka Station offers a large underground shopping mall. Meandering corridors connect station exits and entrances with department stores, hotels, hundreds of shops and boutiques, and uncountable places to eat. The main areas of the shopping mall cover over 3 hectares (7.5 acres). San-Ban-Gai, located directly under the Hankyu Umeda part of the station, has another collection of shops and restaurants.

From the Shin (New) Hankyu Hotel, cross under the railway tracks west to the twin towers of the futuristic Hiroshi Hara-designed **Umeda Sky Building**, where the 40th-floor Floating Garden observation deck (www.kuchu-teien. com; daily 9:30am–10.30pm) offers a 360-degree panoramic view of the city that are especially impressive when Osaka is lit up at night. In the basement is a 1960s retro-style restaurant food court.

Back up on the street from the station complex is Midosuji, Osaka's main north–south boulevard. South from Umeda is **Nakano-shima Ⓑ** (Nakano Island); this narrow island between the canals of Dojima-gawa and Tosabori-gawa is the centre of city government and home to many major Osaka companies. A footpath runs most of the way around Nakano-shima; sightseeing boats to tour the canals can be picked up nearby.

From Midosuji, follow the path on Nakano-shima west along the river, then turn left at the second bridge you come to and you will be at the **National Museum of Art, Osaka Ⓒ** (www.nmao.go.jp; Tue–Sun 10am–5pm, Fri and Sat until 8pm/9pm July–Sept; closed sometimes between exhibitions). Opened in 1977 as Japan's then fourth national museum, the NMAO's collection of 6,000 or so artworks leans mainly towards contemporary art and design, but also includes photography and ukiyo-e prints. It's certainly the best place in Osaka to get a taste for Japan's vibrant modern art scene.

Public transport in Osaka.

Heading back to Midosuji, follow the path east along the river, passing in front of Osaka City Hall, the library and the quaint, red-brick public hall. Across from the public hall is the superb **Toyo Togei-kan**  (Museum of Oriental Ceramics; www.moco.or.jp; Tue–Sun 9.30am–5pm), housing the famous Ataka collection of Chinese and Korean porcelain – one of the best collections in the world, with over 1,000 pieces. East of the museum is **Nakanoshima-koen** (Nakanoshima Park), with a rose garden and willow-draped paths.

The hard-to-miss Osaka Castle rising to the east is reached by following the footpath to the eastern end of Nakano-shima, then up the spiral ramp onto Tenjin-bashi. Walk north across the bridge, then right at the police box. A short jaunt ends at the entrance of **Sakuranomiya-koen** (Cherry Garden). A few blocks north of this point sits funky Osaka **Tenmangu** (www.tenjinsan.com) (daily 9am–5pm; free), dedicated to the god of learning. Kemasakuranomiya-koen (Kemasakuranomiya Park) has extensive

Umeda Sky Building, Osaka.

trails lined with cherry trees. If you're lucky enough to be here during the first or second week in April, you'll get a good look at Japan's national flower, the cherry blossom, in full bloom. In the evenings, uncountable numbers of Osakans will be at their merriest – and most uninhibited – while drinking and singing under the trees at lively *hanami* (flower-viewing) parties.

Follow the footpath about a kilometre along the river, then take the footbridge (Kawasaki-bashi) over the river to the castle straight ahead. Heading up and then down through an underpass and up onto an overpass eventually leads you to it. You can also take a taxi from Nakano-shima.

OSAKA CASTLE

Osaka-jo (Osaka Castle; www.osakacastle.net; daily 9am–5pm, hours may be longer in spring and summer) is the most visited site in the city. The magnificent castle on the hill is an ode to everything that was great in the past and even of future possibilities. Unfortunately for the romantic and the historian, it is not the original castle, but rather a replica. The main donjon, towering above the expansive gardens and stone walls, is a 1931 concrete re-creation of the original that was built by Toyotomi Hideyoshi in 1585. With the conscripted help of all the feudal lords of the nation and the labour of tens of thousands, the massive structure was completed in just three years. It was destroyed 30 years later by Tokugawa Ieyasa and then again rebuilt. Much of the original grounds, moats and walls still stand, however. Extensive restoration work to the castle building, which houses an impressive multistorey museum, was completed in 1997. The view from the top floor is impressive.

Immediately southwest of the castle grounds is the **Osaka Museum of History** (www.mus-his.city.osaka.jp; Wed–Mon 9.30am–5pm), which documents Osaka's history from its earliest days, through its feudal years, and on to its development as a modern, thriving city. With plenty of fun exhibits, the museum is especially accessible to kids.

South of Nakano-shima, head south on Midosuji under the ginkgo trees. Japan's thriving pharmaceutical industry started in Osaka with the import of Chinese herbal remedies, and most of Japan's drug companies still have their headquarters here along Doshomachi, just off Midosuji. Tucked away in a corner sits the pharmaceutical shrine of Sukuna-Hikona. It's a tiny little place that blossoms in importance entirely out of proportion to its size once a year on 22 and 23 November, when the Shinno Matsuri is held. The festival commemorates the discovery that ground tiger bones, among other things, combat malaria.

South on Midosuji is the district of Honmachi, where Midosuji and Honmachi boulevards cross. Just north of the crossing is **Semba ⒣**, the apparel wholesale area of Osaka. Most large wholesalers have outgrown their Semba origins, but some 1,000 small wholesalers still operate in the Semba Centre Building, a two-storey structure comprised of 10 adjoined buildings entirely under a 930-metre/yd long expanse of elevated highway. Many of Osaka's most venerated businesses got their start in Semba.

MINAMI

Follow Midosuji south until the next major crossing, Nagahori. The first landmark to look for is the Kisho Kurokawa-designed **Sony Tower**, at the mouth of Osaka's premier covered shopping street, the 560-metre/yd long Shinsaibashi-suji (www.shinsaibashi.or.jp), which extends south towards Namba Station. Here are more than 150 ancient little shops sitting in apparent ignorance of the outrageously fancy boutique plazas towering on either side.

South on Shinsaibashi is one of the most fascinating stretches in Osaka.

In the **Dotonbori ①** (www.dotonbori. or.jp) amusement quarter, neon lights illuminate giant moving crabs, prawns and octopuses that adorn the facades of neighbourhood seafood restaurants. At the Dotonbori Canal, Shinsaibashi ends and Ebisusuji begins. Venture about halfway across the **Ebisu-bashi**, a bridge across the canal, and squeeze in along the stone railing. Then sit tight for one of the best non-stop people-watching parades in the country.

There is more to Dotonbori than just the passing crowds, however. For hundreds of years, this was the theatrical heart of Japan with six kabuki theatres, five bunraku playhouses, and a myriad of other halls where the great storytellers and comics of Osaka performed. Today, most of the old theatres have been replaced by cinemas, among which the elegant old **Shochiku-za** is an architectural link to the golden age of black-and-white films. The venerable **Naka-za**, with its kabuki and geisha dances, and the vaudevillian Kado-za are still active, but they are the last of the legitimate theatres left

Osaka Castle.

The America-Mura district in Osaka.

Nightlife in Dotonbori.

in Dotonbori. Several years ago, the Bunraku Puppet Theatre moved from its old Asahi-za home to the **National Bunraku Theatre** ⓙ (www.ntj.jac.go.jp), a few blocks to the east, where besides bunraku you can catch kabuki and other performances of traditional theatre, music and dance.

Just south of Naka-za, the alley named Hozenji Yokocho is lined with scores of traditional Osaka eating and drinking establishments – some can be quite expensive, so confirm prices before ordering. Continue down the alley to **Hozen-ji**, one of the most visited and venerated temples in Osaka. Local businessmen come to pray for good business, young couples to ask for happy futures and older people to pray for good health – all in all, a very serviceable temple.

For a glimpse of a more modern Japan, stroll through **America-mura** ⓚ (America Village) tucked into the narrow streets on the west side of Midosuji. This potpourri of Americana done Japanese-style is where stylish youth are out en masse to see and be seen. The area is filled with used-clothing boutiques and makeshift flea markets, where vintage Levis can fetch thousands of dollars.

South is the wide boulevard of Sen-nichimae-dori, and the Sennichimae shopping arcade, a typical blue-collar area of pachinko parlours, cinemas and cheap restaurants. The arcade leads to one of Osaka's most famous wholesale areas, Doguyasuji, an entire market devoted to kitchen and restaurant supplies, similar to Kappabashi-dori in Tokyo.

From Doguyasuji, it's just two blocks to **Namba-eki** ⓛ (Namba Station), where there is nothing too remarkable save the vast underground and overground shopping arcades of Namba City and Namba Walk, good places to find a café or somewhere affordable for lunch or dinner. Three main subway lines connect at Namba Station, also the terminus for both the Kintetsu and Nankai railways serving Nara, Wakayama and points south.

SOUTH OF OSAKA CENTRE

Founded in 593 by Prince Shotoku, **Shitenno-ji temple** ⓜ (www.shitennoji. or.jp daily 8.30am–4pm, Apr–Sept until 4.30pm) is the oldest Buddhist temple in Japan, though none of its original structures has survived. The current complex, a heartless concrete reconstruction 2km (1.2 miles) southeast of Namba, has at least kept to the original layout, and there is a touch of genuine antiquity in the torii gate at the main entrance, which dates from the 13th century.

It's a lively, well-patronised site, however, and on festival days swells with the faithful. Its **Treasure House** (daily 8.30am–4pm, Apr–Sept until 4.30pm), encased in a modern white building, has a small collection of Buddhist art, a wonderful display of sumptuous costumes and mandalas used in court dance.

It's a short walk south, via **Isshin-ji**, a smaller but well-supported temple

with a mischievous display of half-naked dancing girls on the entrance gate, to the **Osaka City Museum of Fine Arts** (www. osaka-art-museum.jp; Tue–Sun 9.30am–5pm). The museum houses a fine collection of ancient Japanese Jomon pottery and Edo Period and Chinese art.

Contiguous with the museum is **Tennoji-koen** (daily 7am–10pm; free), with a modern conservatory stuffed with hothouse plants and trees. Integral to the park is **Keitakuen**, a moderately interesting Japanese garden bequeathed by Baron Sumitomo, a member of the giant trading company of the same name. A block west from the southwest corner of the park is **Spa World** (www.spaworld.co.jp; 10am–8.45am next day), home to water slides, pools, saunas and, more importantly, 15 hot-spring baths representing different hot-spring styles from around Asia and Europe. A block south of the southeast corner of the park is **Abeno Harukas**, the tallest skyscraper in Japan, which has a popular observation deck as well as a few restaurants and cafés boasting good views down over the city (www.abenoharukas-300.jp; daily 9am–10pm).

Some 5km (3 miles) south on the Hankai Tram Line, **Sumiyoshi Taisha** (www.sumiyoshitaisha.net; daily, Apr–Sept 6am–5pm, Oct–Mar 6.30am–5pm; free), with a pedigree dating to 211, is Osaka's most prestigious shrine. Of special interest is the style of architecture, known as *sumiyoshi zukuri*, a Shinto design with its exposed logs and finials and a thatched roof. The brilliant-red building is immediately recognisable after you cross the drum-shaped Sori-hashi Bridge.

OSAKA BAY

In the far west of Osaka along **Osaka-wan** (Osaka Bay), **Tempozan Harbour Village** ⑫ makes an excellent place to explore for a half-day. The highlight of this waterfront development is the excellent and enormous **Kai-yukan Aquarium** (www.kaiyukan.com;

daily usually 10am–8pm, hours vary by season), where visitors can get a close-up glimpse of giant whale sharks and immense spider crabs. Other attractions nearby include **Tempozan Market Place**, a mall full of shops, restaurants and amusements for kids. At 112 metres (368ft) high and difficult to miss, what was once the world's largest Ferris wheel also looms nearby. Osaka's newest and brashest addition to its western waterfront is the **Universal Studios Japan** theme park (http://usj.co.jp; daily 8.30–9.30am until 7–10pm). Water taxis and a shuttle train whisk visitors to the park, where simulated rides include the special effects found on the recreated sets of *Harry Potter* or *Jurassic Park* and, for a more sobering experience, the city's extraordinary **Liberty Osaka** (www.liberty.or.jp; Wed–Fri 10am–4pm, Sat 1–5pm, closed Sun–Tue and 4th Fri and Sat of month), 2km (1.2 miles) west of the studios. It is a human rights museum that takes a frank and disturbing look at some of the skeletons in Japan's own cupboard.

Performance of a puppet play (bunraku).

Seemingly afloat in Osaka Bay, **Kansai International Airport** ❸ opened in the late 1990s as an alternative to Tokyo's overextended Narita. On an artificial island and away from developed areas, the airport allows flights 24 hours daily, whereas Narita is closed late at night.

For those without time to explore the age-old traditional architecture in the Japanese countryside, consider a trip to **Hattori Ryokuchi-koen** ❹, north of central Osaka and near the old international airport. Here is an open-air museum (www.occh.or.jp/minka; Tue–Sun 9.30am–5pm) of old Japanese-style farmhouses displaying nine different styles of *minka* farmhouse with thatched roofs.

KOBE

The Chinese *kanji* characters for Kobe translate as "god's door". But **Kobe** ❺, 30km (20 miles) west of Osaka, is more like a doorsill – a long and narrow ledge squeezed between the coastal mountains and Osaka Bay. Although lacking in fantastic attractions for

Universal Studios, Osaka.

travellers – and so usually overlooked – Kobe is one of the most liveable and attractive cities in Japan, perched on hills overlooking a harbour.

In 1995, Kobe was jolted by the horrific Great Hanshin Earthquake, which killed more than 6,000 people in the Kobe area. Entire neighbourhoods, especially in the western sections of the city, were flattened when Japanese-style homes – wooden post-and-beam frames with heavy tiled roofs – collapsed and burned in the resulting fires. Buildings and elevated roads, mostly of contemporary concrete construction, collapsed spectacularly. Transport routes were severely damaged, including Kobe's container-port facilities, which are on landfill.

The earthquake wreaked havoc beyond anyone's belief and the government's inept emergency response was equally astounding. Dire predictions that Kobe would take several years to rebuild proved true; it was not until the summer of 1998 that the last of the tens of thousands of displaced residents were finally able to resettle into homes after four years in temporary housing. Today Kobe has returned to normal.

Those arriving in Kobe by *shinkansen* will disembark at **Shin Kobe-eki** (Shin Kobe Station; regular trains from Osaka and Kyoto stop at Sannomiya-eki). A few blocks to the east and still on high ground, **Kitano-cho** is where rich foreign traders once staked out impressive residences at the turn of the 20th century, their growing influence freeing them from the foreign ghetto originally allocated near the wharves. Presenting a fanciful potpourri of European and American architectural styles, several of these *ijinkan* – foreign residences – now sharing the hill with trendy boutiques and restaurants are open to the public. Westerners tend to find the interiors unexceptional, but one standout is the impeccably restored **Kazamidori-no-Yakata** (www.kobe-kazamidori. com; daily 9am–6pm), recognisable by the weathercock atop it, which offers an intimate glimpse into the lifestyle of long-time foreign residents.

While exploring the neighbourhood, try to locate the Muslim mosque, Jewish synagogue, the Catholic, Baptist and Russian Orthodox churches, and the Jain temple, all within a few blocks of one another in a unique assemblage for an Asian city this size.

The cardinal point on the Kobe compass is **Sannomiya**, where **Sannomiya-eki** (Sannomiya Station) is embraced by this popular shopping and entertainment district. Extending west from Sannomiya, parallel shopping arcades extend to Motomachi-eki (Motomachi Station) and beyond. The arcade directly beneath the overhead tracks is the remnant of a black market that surfaced amid the post-World War II rubble and today is a bonus for bargain-hunters seeking second-hand or imitation goods.

South of Motomachi Station and just west of the elegant Daimaru department store, look for the dragon gate announcing **Nankinmachi**, which is Kobe's two-block-long Chinatown. Although not of the standard and calibre of Chinatowns elsewhere in the world, this small but vibrant enclave surpasses anything that can be seen in the historic ports of Yokohama and Nagasaki.

From Chinatown, it's a short walk south to **Meriken Hatoba** and the waterfront. The surrounding redeveloped wharf frontage is the site of an informative and strikingly designed **Kobe Maritime Museum** (www.kobe-maritime-museum.com; Tue–Sun 10am–5pm). A visit here could also include a ride to the top of adjacent **Port Tower** and a harbour cruise.

PORT ISLAND

Offshore is the hard-to-ignore **Port Island** ⓰, also its Japanese name. In a feat of near science fiction and biblical dimensions, Kobe has "recycled" its surplus mountains to build up from the sea floor two of the world's largest artificial islands. This massive undertaking was to confirm Kobe as a prime trading port.

The *Portliner* monorail from Sannomiya Station provides a convenient

Yakuzas with tattoos during a summer festival.

⊙ YAKUZA

Yakuza (organised crime) originated in the 1600s, when the unemployed samurai terrorised people for leisure. Later, men called *bakuto* were hired by the shogun to gamble with labourers paid by the government to reclaim some of the substantial wages. The *bakuto* introduced the custom of *yubitsume* (severing the top joint of the little finger), as an act of apology to the boss, and tattooing.

The most notorious group is the Yamaguchi-gumi, which originated in Kobe in the 1910s. It is by far Japan's biggest *yakuza* group, accounting for nearly half of the country's estimated 80,000 *yakuza*.

The *yakuza* have established alliances with Chinese Triads, Italian and US Mafia. Legitimate businesses mask their criminal activities, but the members themselves are generally open about being *yakuza*.

Kobe's Chinatown (Nankinmachi) is one of the three designated Chinatowns in Japan.

elevated loop ride around Port Island. Here – and on neighbouring **Rokko Island** (hard-hit by the earthquake) and also reachable by a monorail from JR Sumiyoshi Station – visitors can get a first-hand look at the future of container vessels. Rokko island's high-tech **Fashion Museum** (www.fashionmuseum.or.jp; Tue–Sun 10am–6pm) is housed in a futuristic building as arresting as the exhibitions themselves. The centre of the island has swanky hotels, sports and convention facilities, plus an amusement park and a couple more small museums. Port Island is also where the jet-boat shuttle from **Kobe City Air Terminal** (KCAT) departs for the 30-minute ride to the Kansai International Airport.

Port Island is a good point from which to gaze back at Kobe, especially at night, when it becomes a flickering tiara augmented by two insignia on the mountainside. One symbol is an anchor and the other a pair of interlocking fans representing the unification of Hyogo Prefecture and Kobe. It was due to the fan-shaped perfection

Strolling through Kobe's Chinatown.

of the harbours that the trading port flourished back in AD 700.

For an intriguing look at the cultural side of foreign trade, drop in at the nearby **Kobe City Museum** (Tue–Sun 10am–5pm), housed in a former bank. This small, admirable museum focuses on Japan's early encounters with the West and features a rare collection of *namban* ("southern barbarian") art, works inspired by contacts with the first Portuguese and Spanish traders who arrived here during the 16th and 17th centuries.

Finally, down the coast from Sannomiya at the southern end of Kobe is one of the largest beaches in western Japan, **Suma**, where there is the Aqualife Park (http://sumasui.jp; daily 9am–5pm, Dec–Feb closed Wed), with a large aquarium and a dolphin show. From the vantage point of Suma's beach, the Akashi Kaikyo Ohashi, claimed to be the world's longest suspension bridge, can be seen connecting Japan's main island of Honshu to Shikoku via the large island of Awaji.

About 10km (6 miles) southwest of Sannomiya, and accessed by Shin Nagata Station, is possibly Kobe's most distinctive attraction. Built at a cost of nearly $1.5 million, weighing in at 50 tonnes, and standing 18 metres (59ft) tall, the statue of the **Tetsujin** robot from Mitsuteru Yokoyama's *Tetsujin 28* manga comic series (later an anime series too) stands in the otherwise nondescript Wakamatsu Park. There's nothing else to see here – just a chance to stand, stare and wonder at Tetsujin.

BEYOND OSAKA AND KOBE

Theatre-lovers and the culturally adventurous might want to make the trek (about 30 minutes from Osaka's Umeda Station or Kobe's Sannomiya Station) out to **Takarazuka** , where high-stepping women have been staging flashy musical extravaganzas for nearly 90 years. Back in 1910, Takarazuka was a small town at the end of the then newly opened Hankyu rail line. In order to attract passengers, the train company built a resort and put together an all-female performing company. There are 400 performers divided into four casts, two performing simultaneously here and in Tokyo, while the other two troupes rehearse. For details of shows and performance times at the **Takarazuka Grand Theatre** in Takarazuka, as well as at the **Tokyo Takarazuka Theatre**, see www.kageki.hankyu.co.jp.

To the west, scalding hot springs *(onsen)* await weary hikers north of scenic, 930-metre (3,000ft) high **Rokko-zan** in the town of **Arima** ⑱. Reached by bus and cable car from Rokko Station, this ancient spa boasts all the usual hot-springs amenities and is also the home of nationally recognised basket-makers.

One bargain in town is the public **Arima Onsen Kinnoyu** (http://arimaspa-kingin.jp; daily 8am–10pm, closed second and fourth Tue of every month), where for ¥650 one can bathe in the same curative waters offered at the much costlier inns. Arima's waters are said to soothe all human ailments except love.

HIMEJI

At the upper end of Chugoku, the industrial city of **Himeji** ⑲ makes for a great side trip from either Kobe or Osaka. The city is dominated by a marvellous snow-white castle that seems to hover above the town. Variously called the White Egret or Heron Castle, **Himeji-jo** (Himeji Castle; www.city.himeji.lg.jp/guide/castle; daily, late Apr–Aug 9am–6pm, Sept–late Apr until 5pm) is a 15-minute stroll from the *shinkansen* station along a road lined with modern sculptures. Resting resplendent on the banks of the Senba-gawa, this is the largest and most elegant of the dozen existing medieval castles in Japan. Although the city was extensively bombed during World War II, the castle emerged unscathed and has

been maintained in pristine condition. It reopened in 2015 after a comprehensive renovation.

The site occupied by the castle has been fortified since 1333, and an actual castle was built here in 1580 by Toyotomi Hideyoshi. In 1681, Ikeda Terumasa, Tokugawa Ieyasu's son-in-law, rebuilt and expanded the castle to its present form. Castles in this period served both as military strongholds and as administrative centres. Terumasa's design, with financial help from the shogunate, elegantly merged martial necessity and artistic form on a scale previously unknown in Japan.

The castle's construction was a Herculean task requiring 400 tonnes of wood, 75,000 tiles weighing a total of 3,000 tonnes, and a huge number of large stones. These stones weren't easy to come by and tales of their procurement live on in the ramparts. Ancient stone coffins mined from nearby tombs can be seen in one part of the precinct. The contribution of a millstone, from a woman living in the town below the castle, is still remembered today.

The Fashion Museum in Kobe.

Arima at night, Hyogo.

The castle was never tested in battle, but walking up past the succession of defensive lines – three concentric moats surrounding high, curved ramparts punctuated by gates and watchtowers with arrow slits and gun ports – it seems an impregnable bastion. Roads within the castle grounds twist and turn, the better to confuse hostile forces if the outer defences were breached, and the uppermost floors of the castle contain hidden places where troops could continue to shoot at the enemy until the bitter end.

Himeji-jo is a hillock (as distinct from a mountain or flatland) castle atop a 45-metre (150ft) hill. There are spectacular views from the main donjon, which rises 30 metres (100ft) from the castle grounds. *Shachihoko*, huge ornamental fish that were strategically placed on the roof as charms to ward off fire, can be seen close up from the top floor; some now support lightning rods.

An attractive angle on Himeji-jo in any season is from the grounds of the surprisingly quiet **Himeji Koko-en**

Blossoms at Himeji-jo.

(www.himeji-machishin.jp/ryokka/kokoen; daily, late Apr–Aug 9am–6pm, Sept–late Apr 9am–5pm), located next to the castle moat on the site of old samurai residences. Built in 1992, to celebrate the 100th anniversary of the Himeji receiving city status, Koko-en is a beautiful composite of nine separate Edo-style gardens with a teahouse and pools with carp. You can buy a combined ticket to the castle and gardens.

The **Hyogo-kenritsu Rekishi Hakubutsukan** (Hyogo Prefectural Museum of History; www.hyogo-c.ed.jp/~rekihaku-bo/; Tue–Sun 10am–5pm) nearby to the north contains informative displays about Japanese castles, including the most magnificent of them all, Himeji. It is the best of Himeji's several museums. For information on others, as well as on several worthwhile shrines, visit the **tourist office** (daily 9am–7pm) on the first floor of JR Himeji Station; the English-speaking staff here can help you plan a full day's worth of activities and also have free rental bicycles, which make for a great way to get around the city.

EARTHQUAKES

From time to time over the centuries, major quakes have wreaked havoc on Japan, most recently the devastating earthquake in Tohoku on 11 March 2011.

Japan is highly prone to earthquakes. There are minor shakes recorded on seismological instruments almost every day, and bigger ones that startle people from their sleep, rattle dishes and knock objects off shelves occur several times a year.

The reason for the earthquakes is that the Japanese archipelago is at a place where three moving segments of the earth's crust – the Pacific Plate, the Philippine Plate and the Eurasian Plate – come into violent contact. This also explains Japan's volcanic activity and its many hot springs.

The Philippine Plate is the prime culprit, sliding in under central Honshu in a northeastern direction at about 3cm (1.25in) a year. The movement, in turn, puts stress on the primary fault that affects Tokyo and other earthquake-prone regions. Add to this a nest of faults spread widely under the islands, sometimes as deep as 100km (60 miles).

In Tokyo, the danger from earthquakes is made worse because much of the city is on unconsolidated alluvial soil and on landfill. This is a very poor foundation, which makes buildings tremble and oscillate more than they would on solid ground. Much of the waterfront damage during the 1995 Kobe earthquake was also because of landfill liquefaction, and a great deal of the remaining damage was due to fire from burst gas mains.

A COUNTRY AT RISK

A major tremor whiplashes the Tokyo area every 60 or 70 years on average, and the last one, the Great Kanto Earthquake – a 7.9-magnitude jolt on the Richter scale – took place in 1923. At that time, most of the central part of the city was levelled and totally destroyed by fire, and more than 100,000 people were killed. Close to Ryogoku Station, 40,000 people were incinerated when a fire tornado swept across an open area where they had sought safety.

More recently, in Kobe, earthquake-proof structures collapsed like jelly during a 7.2-magnitude earthquake in 1995. Rescue and relief plans proved unworkable, and government response, both on the local and national levels, was inept and embarrassingly inadequate. Nearly 6,000 people died.

Experts say that Tokyo is now much safer than it was in 1923, and far safer than Kobe in 1995. Buildings, bridges and elevated highways are reinforced and built according to the latest techniques, something in which Japan has invested heavily in recent decades. In addition, much of the city has been made fireproof. There are also shelters and elaborate plans to provide help should the worst happen.

But there are still concerns about whether or not Japan – and the world's largest metropolitan area, Tokyo – can ever be fully prepared.

Tokyo is the world's most populated city, with extensive underground networks of subways and gas lines, and above ground, glass-covered buildings and many flimsily constructed residences. In a reassessment of Tokyo's preparedness after the catastrophic earthquake of 3/11, experts believe a 7.3-magnitude earthquake (with a *shindo* intensity level of 7) directly under northern Tokyo Bay could destroy some 390,000 buildings and kill 9,600 people in the Greater Tokyo area.

Nishinomiya after the Kobe earthquake in 1995.

📷 KIMONOS FOR ALL SEASONS AND STYLES

Adopted from ancient Chinese court attire, the Japanese kimono today is mostly a ceremonial dress of exquisite textures and appeal.

Western dress is the norm amongst today's Japanese, and few wear traditional attire except on special occasions such as weddings or festivals. But when a busy street of suited businessmen and trendy schoolgirls is punctuated by the colours and elegance of a kimono, Japan momentarily reverts to another time and place.

Contrary to popular belief, the kimono did not originate in Japan. Like many things "distinctly" Japanese, the kimono has its roots in China – the Chinese court. During the Nara Period (710–84), the Japanese imperial court adopted the Chinese-style p'ao, a long, kimono-like gown brilliant with colours and embellishment; kimono styles used by Japanese women during this time were similar to the p'ao garments of women in Tang-dynasty China. Indeed, the Heian-era court dress worn by Japan's emperor and empress today during special occasions displays Chinese characteristics unchanged since the 12th century.

As did most things adopted by the Japanese over the centuries, the kimono underwent changes that eventually made it distinctly Japanese. During the Muromachi Period (1338–1573), for example, women introduced the obi (sash), and adapted the kimono sleeves to fit Japanese climate and styles.

Visit a shrine in November and you might see kids – girls aged 3 or 7 and boys aged 5 – in kimono as part of the Shichi-go-san rituals.

Kyoto is a great place to discover kimono. You could wander about Gion hoping for a glimpse of a geisha, or better yet take a trip to the Nishijin Textile Centre for the daily kimono fashion show.

Geisha and maiko are the most obvious examples of kimono being worn for work, but the traditional attire is also worn by staff at ryokan and in some traditional restaurants.

The obi (sash) – often ornate and made of embroidered silk – today is about 25 cm (10 in) wide and 3.7 m (12 ft) long.

The obi: simple and exquisite

Once a simple and narrow sash introduced by Muromachi Period women, the *obi* has evolved into one of the most beautiful – and complicated – aspects of the kimono today.

The *obi*'s need came about when the Japanese made changes to the adopted Chinese-court *p'ao*. A short-sleeved form of kimono *(kosode)* began to be worn as an outer garment, constrained by the *obi*. Later, the *obi* took on increased importance when women of the feudal estates wore an elaborate and exquisite outer kimono called *uchikake*. As centuries passed, only married women wore the *kosode*, while unmarried women wore the long-sleeved *furisode*.

The wider and more embellished silk sash seen today developed in the early 1700s during the Edo Period. This *obi* can be tied in a number of ways and may be embellished with *netsuke*, beautifully carved images used to cinch cords and fasten the details of the woman's *obi*.

Most young Japanese rarely, if ever, wear traditional kimono like these – more commonly they might wear a light cotton yukata to a summer festival or at an onsen.

While the basic kimono design is consistent and often features seasonal motifs, regional and ceremonial differences abound. There are even subtle differences between kimono for single and married women.

It's not just the kimono itself that has to be immaculate. A lot of time and effort also has to go into the accompanying hair and make-up.

Taketomi Island, Okinawa.

Cycling through the old streets of Uchiko, Shikoku.

THE SOUTH

Southern Japan includes western Honshu and two main islands, Kyushu and Shikoku, along with Okinawa. All are sea facing but that's where the similarities end.

Itsukushima-jinja, Hiroshima.

The "south" is called "western" Japan by the Japanese, although this part of the archipelago does extend southwards. Chugoku (Western Honshu), Shikoku and Kyushu are all very different, yet have one element in common: Seto Naikai, or the Inland Sea. All three regions also face the open ocean, and as a result, each area has widely varying climates and local qualities.

The Honshu coast along the Inland Sea, where you will find Hiroshima, is markedly different from the Sea of Japan (East Sea) side. Likewise, Shikoku, the smallest of Japan's four main islands, could as well be in a different hemisphere from the one occupied by the islands of Okinawa. As for Kyushu, there are those who believe this large island, particularly the southern part, is a nation unto itself and who cite the long tradition of fierce independence stemming from the Satsuma clans, not to mention Kyushu's thick dialect, as proof.

Even in the most populous and industrial cities of Kyushu and Shikoku, and even Chugoku, the pace is mellow compared with Tokyo and Osaka. Not all is idyllic down this way, however. The southern parts lie in the path of seasonal typhoons and thus are regularly given good soakings by torrential rains. Moreover, there are more active volcanoes on Kyushu than on any other Japanese island.

Ibusuki public hot spring, Kyushu.

These volcanoes have given the archipelago an unlimited variety of ceramic-quality clays, along with natural chemicals for glazes. Kyushu and parts of Chugoku are noted for their hearty pottery, an art form with a considerable amount of Korean influence.

Shikoku, Chugoku and Kyushu are large enough to keep travellers occupied for quite some time. Smaller gems await even further south, however. Like pearls upon the ocean, islands drip away from Kyushu's southern tip and stretch down to within 200km (125 miles) of Taiwan. This string of islands, Nansai-shoto, is over 1,200km (750 miles) in length. Best known by foreigners is Okinawa for its historical importance in World War II and also for its cultural uniqueness.

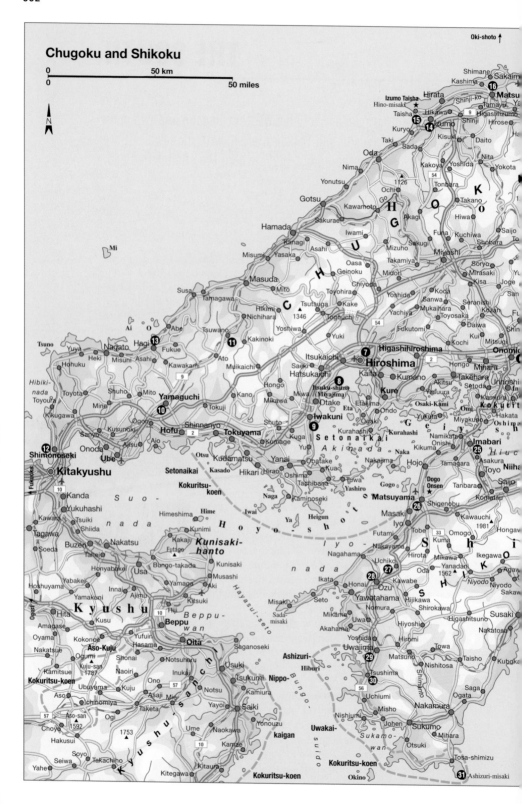

Chugoku and Shikoku

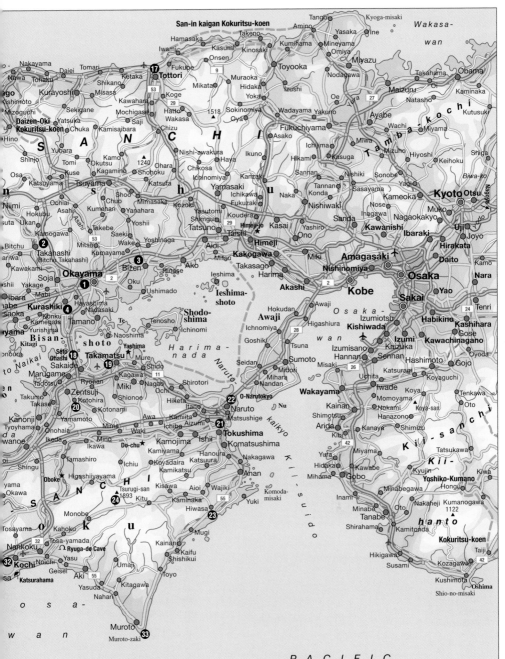

San-in kaigan Kokuritsu-koen

Wakasa-wan

PACIFIC

OCEAN

View of the Inland Sea at Naruto,
Shikoku.

CHUGOKU

Chugoku means "centre country". This varied region was once Japan's heartland, with the historic towns and shrines to prove it – as well as evocative Hiroshima and its altogether more recent associations.

Most travellers would look at a map of Japan's main island of Honshu and consider Chugoku to be the southern part. The Japanese, however, consider it to be the western part. In fact, of course, it is southwest. Compass directions aside, the Chugoku region spreads over the bottom third of Honshu, bounded by Seto Naikai (Inland Sea) to the south and the Sea of Japan (East Sea) to the north. Not many foreign travellers get to Chugoku other than to its main cities of Okayama and Hiroshima. The region includes the prefectures of Okayama, Hiroshima, Yamaguchi, Shimane and Tottori, and it offers some splendid views of rustic Japan, especially along the Sea of Japan (East Sea) coast.

Seto Naikai, or the Seto Inland Sea, is a 9,500-sq km (3,700-sq mile) body of water surrounded by Kyushu, Shikoku and the western extent of Honshu, dotted with more than 1,000 small islands. Osaka, Kobe and Hiroshima are all on the sea's coast. Although largely industrialised these days, the sea coast still retains some exquisite vistas, enough for the area to have been designated Japan's first national park in 1934 (for more about the different islands in the Inland Sea, see page 310).

The Chugoku region's most visited sites are Hiroshima, with its Gembaku Dome and Peace Memorial Park

a testament to the horrors of nuclear conflict, and the nearby floating shrine at Miyajima. But the region offers more than its most common postcard images. On the Seto Naikai coast, the town of Kurashiki reveals a sophisticated tradition of crafts and art, while towns like Tsuwano are rich with remnants of medieval Japan. Take time to explore the whole region and you will be treated to the intriguing mix of rural traditions, Edo-era history, ancient myth and Western influences that make Chugoku so diverse.

Okayama
Takahashi
Kurashiki
Tomonoura
Hiroshima
Miyajima
Yamaguchi
Tsuwano
Hagi
Matsue

Maps on pages 302, 312

Genbaku Dome and Cenotaph, Hiroshima.

OKAYAMA

The rapidly growing city of **Okayama ❶** has asserted itself as the region's most dynamic metropolis. For this reason it often finds itself playing host to visiting foreigners, mostly on business and not for sightseeing, although it does have a handful of worthwhile attractions. The most notable of these, the **Koraku-en** (Koraku Garden; www.okayama-korakuen. jp; daily, 20 Mar–Sept 7.30am–6pm, Oct–19 Mar 8am–5pm) was originally laid out in 1686 for the warlord Ikeda. Located on an island in the Asahi-gawa across from **Okayama-jo** (Okayama or Crow Castle because of its black exterior; www.okayama-kanko.net/ujo/index. html; daily 9am–5.30pm), Koraku-en is unusual for its large grassy areas and the cultivation of such crops as rice and wheat. Tea is also grown and harvested here and teahouses are scattered throughout the fine strolling garden, which Japan ranks among its top three.

Other sights in Okayama include the **Orient Museum** (www.orientmuseum. jp), with exhibits tracing the impact of Near Eastern civilisation on Japan; the

Okayama Prefectural Museum of Art (http://okayama-kenbi.info); and the compact **Yumeji Art Museum** (https://yumeji-art-museum.com), with works by Yumeji Takehisa (all Tue–Sun 9am–5pm).

TAKAHASHI

Takahashi ❷ is one of those towns that is easy to overlook. Lying 30km (20 miles) northwest of Okayama, it takes just under one hour to get here by rail on the JR Hakubi Line, a pleasant journey along the attractive, well-contoured Takahashi-gawa. The shallow, winding river is well stocked with *ayu* (sweetfish), a local speciality found on the menus of most of the town's traditional restaurants or, sprinkled with salt and smoked over a charcoal brazier, served from roadside stalls.

Takahashi enjoys a modest celebrity among travellers and cognoscenti of curious and obscure places. A provincial town with mountain and valley settings, its cultural credentials are unimpeachable, and most of its sights are conveniently located within walking distance of the station.

Raikyu-ji Zen Garden, Takahashi.

Pausing to pick up a local map at the information office (Mon–Fri 8am–6pm, Sat 8.30am–5pm) at the bus terminus beside the station, make your way to **Raikyu-ji** (http://raikyuji.com; daily 9am–5pm), a Rinzai school of Zen temple; the temple's date of origin is disputed, but most historians concur that a rebuilding took place under the orders of the shogun Ankoku in 1339. However illustrious the temple and its collection of hanging scrolls and sutras may be, it is its magnificent garden that sets the site apart.

Created by Kobori Enshu, a member of the local nobility who would go on to become one of the foremost designers of gardens in Japanese landscape history, the small but dynamic balanced asymmetry of the garden is classified as a *karesansui* (dry landscape) type. Enshu finished the garden, also known as "Tsurukame Garden" on account of its crane- and turtle-shaped islands (signifying longevity), in 1609. Mount Atago can be glimpsed in the distance beyond the garden proper, forming the classic "borrowed view" frequently incorporated into such designs.

If Raikyu-ji represents Takahashi's spiritual and artistic heritage, **Takahashi-jo** (also known as Bitchu-Matsuyama-jo; daily, Apr–Sept 9am–5.30pm, Oct–Mar 9am–4.30pm), the town's castle, stands for its martial traditions. This well-appointed fortress, constructed on the peak of Gagyuzan-san, is at 430 metres (1,400ft) Japan's highest castle, something of a tourist draw for the town. Adding to elevation as a formidable defence, the lower and middle levels of the mountain were further fortified with samurai villas and farmhouses designed to act as a second line of defence in the event (tested on several occasions) of attack. Interestingly enough, many of the homes here in the district of **Ishibiya-cho**, grand constructions sitting on raised ground above stone walls and foundations, are still occupied by the descendants of Takahashi's old samurai families.

Meiji- and Taisho-era wooden buildings and private estates face the Kouya-gawa as it runs through the centre of Takahashi, their Japanese features mixing effortlessly with the occidental experimentation in architecture associated with the time. The Takahashi church and the wooden Takahashi Elementary School, now serving, along with the **Haibara Samurai House** (daily 9am–5pm) in Ishibiya-cho as local history museums, are good examples of this blending. Like the Haibara Samurai House, the **Takahashi History Museum** (Wed–Mon 9am–5pm) houses items closely associated with this period of contact with the West, expressing Japan's fascination with Western science, design and the new technology that would lead to the transformation of Japan from a feudal backwater to an advanced nation. Exhibits include an old Morse code set, a symbol and harbinger of modernity, period clocks and a microscope. There are also local exhibits

Koraku-en, Okayama.

Making Bizen pottery.

predating this period, and a fine collection of black-and-white photos of the town.

Bizen ❸, about 45 minutes by train east along the coast from Okayama, is famous for its unglazed, coarse pottery that is frequently enhanced by kiln "accidents", such as a stray leaf or a bit of straw sticking to the side of a pot that leaves an interesting pattern after firing. There are more than 100 kilns in Imbe, the 700-year-old pottery-making section of Bizen, along with several museums, including the **Bizen Togei Bijutsukan** (Ceramics Museum; Tue–Sun 9.30am–5pm) and Fujiwara Kei Kinenkan gallery.

KURASHIKI

Punting at Bikan District, Kurashiki, Okayama.

West of Okayama, **Kurashiki ❹** is a textile-producing city containing the pearl of Japanese tourist attractions: an arts district that brings world-class Japanese and international art and traditional crafts together in an exquisite setting. Some 13.5 hectares (33 acres) of 300-year-old rice warehouses, Meiji-era factories, and the homes of

samurai and wealthy merchant families have been elegantly preserved and converted into museums, craft shops and art galleries. Kurashiki is for walkers, with most of the attractions within a block or two of the central canal. The streets and alleys bordering on this canal look much as they did during the town's cultural and economic zenith in the 18th century. Automobiles are not allowed to disturb the atmosphere of its preserved quarter.

During the Edo Period, Kurashiki was a central collection and storage site for the shogun's taxes and tribute – paid in rice – from communities throughout western Honshu, Seto Naikai and Shikoku. Numerous stone rice warehouses (*kura*) are clustered around willow-lined canals, thus giving the town its name. Their striking designs employ black tiles deeply set in bright-white mortar, capped by roofs of black tile. Stone bridges, arched so that barges piled high with sacks of rice from the hinterland could pass below them, span the waterways. Kurashiki's preservation was largely the work of Ohara Magosaburo,

the wealthy scion of Kurashiki's leading family. The Ohara family's textile mills were the primary source of employment in Kurashiki during the Meiji Period, by which time rice levies had been replaced by cash taxes, thus making the city's huge rice warehouses redundant.

Ohara Magosaburo built the nation's first museum of Western art in 1930, the **Ohara Museum of Art** (www.ohara. or.jp; Tue–Sun 9am–5pm), and stocked it with works by El Greco, Monet, Matisse, Renoir, Gauguin and Picasso. The neoclassical building remains the city's centrepiece, although new galleries have proliferated around it over the years. The restored *kura* next to the main gallery are likely to be of more interest to visitors already familiar with European art as they contain Japanese folk art and a fine collection of ancient Chinese art. Other rooms are devoted to the works of the great *mingei* (Japanese folk art) potters such as Hamada Shoji, Kawai Kanjiro and Tomimoto Kenkichi.

Many of Kurashiki's warehouses-turned-art-houses are devoted to preserving and revitalising *mingei*. Among the most interesting is the **Japanese Rural Toy Museum** (www.gangukan.jp; daily 10am–5pm, Mar–Nov 9.30am–5pm). The first floor is packed with traditional Japanese toys, dolls and kites, while a collection of toys from around the world can be seen on the second floor. In all there are over 5,000 toys on display. The adjacent toy store is as interesting as the museum. Next door, the **Kurashiki Mingei-kan** (Museum of Folk Craft; http://kurashiki-mingeikan.com; Tue–Sun, Mar–Nov 9am–5pm, Dec–Feb 9am–4.15pm) displays around 4,000 simple, handmade objects that are or were used in everyday life. The building that houses this museum was remodelled from four two-storey wooden rice granaries.

Visitors can learn about the daily life of one of Kurashiki's leading families at the **Ohashi House** (http://ohashi-ke.com; Tue–Sun 9am–5pm, Apr–Sept Sat

until 6pm), constructed in 1796 for a merchant family. Of samurai status, the house is much larger than typical merchant houses of that time. Note the unusual roof tiles. Ivy Square, an arts complex created out of the red-brick textile factories that brought about the Ohara family fortune, houses the Kurabo Memorial Hall, with displays on the textile industry as well as scores of shops and restaurants.

TOMONOURA

Some 14km (9 miles) south of the JR *shinkansen* stop at Fukuyama, a 30-minute bus ride from outside the station takes you to the delightful fishing port of **Tomonoura** ❺. In this well-preserved but working town at the very extremity of the Numakuma Peninsula, southern enough for garden cacti, one may savour the smell of the sea, squawking gulls and the sight of kites wheeling over temple roofs. It also offers fleeting images of history– the warrior Masashige passed through here on his way to Kyushu, as did the Empress Jingu.

Takahashi Castle.

The port town of Tomonoura.

People in front of Yayoi Kusama's art installation on Naoshima Island.

Succoured, as it always has been by the sea, Tomonoura has not entirely escaped Japan's post-war uglification programme, as some of its cement installations testify. The town seems to have had its last flirt with concrete in the 1980s, however, and then mercifully left it at that.

The waters here are abundant in sea bream, a local speciality. You'll also see octopus, caught on lines rather than in pots or nets, being hauled from the water just below the sea walls, gleaming and full of life. The raised bund along the port also provides space for women to set up stalls under temporary plastic roofing, where the local catch is displayed and tasty fare sold. Shrimps are sold directly from their drying frames, from street stalls or from the doorways and entrance halls of private homes, conveying the largely accurate impression that most of the inhabitants of this village are engaged in one way or another with the sea.

The sea bream netting methods can be glimpsed in simulated form in the models and photographs at the

Tomonoura Museum of History (Tue–Sun 9am–5pm). From the museum grounds, a commanding view of grey, undulating ceramic roofs, their eaves interlocking, suggests a community that is also tightly knit. Donald Richie (see page 387), a profoundly attentive traveller, described the town at the end of the 1960s as having "the casual look of most towns where progress has been late in arriving. It is a crosswork of little streets like those in Italian mountain villages."

Tagashima-jo, the ruins of an old castle that once stood on the headland above the harbour, and its adjacent temple, Empuku-ji, offer another angle on the town. Here you can glimpse the harbour to the west, and **Benten-jima**, a tiny island, to the east. Of Indian provenance, the goddess Benten is a sensuous figure, now firmly inducted into the Shinto pantheon and serving as the patroness of music, the arts and beauty.

Half the enjoyment of this little town, where it is still possible to lose your bearings, is to explore its labyrinth of lanes and stone alleys, noting the old

⊘ ISLANDS OF THE SETO NAIKAI

The islands that bejewel the Seto Inland Sea have a diversity of riches. The most prominent of the islands, **Naoshima** (see page 325), has risen to international attention for the contemporary art galleries that have transformed it from a collection of sleepy fishing communities to an undoubted high point on Japan's art scene. Often overlooked, however, are smaller islands nearby, such as **Teshima** and its picturesque rice terraces and the quiet **Inu-jima** – both have had less dramatic, but nonetheless impressive, art renaissances.

Naoshima's larger neighbour, **Shodoshima** (see page 326), is an altogether different affair. Head here not for art, but to soak up the slow-paced, traditional way of life. Many of the islanders are still involved in Shodoshima's traditional industries of fishing, soy sauce production and making sesame oil.

Away to the west, off the coast off Onomichi, **Ikuchi-jima** reveals another side of the Seto Naikai. Palm-lined beaches and citrus groves make it a beautiful setting for one of Japan's most distinctive temples, Kosan-ji – known as the "Nikko of the west" because of its flamboyant design. Rounding out the variety is **Omishima** next door, which has one of the oldest shrines in the country, the Kamakura-era Oyamazumi-jinja. You could easily amuse yourself for weeks hopping from island to island.

wooden houses, ship's chandlers, and the bijoux gardens that can be glimpsed behind timeworn fences. One area of streets near the harbour contains the **Shichikyo-ochi Ruins**, a misleading name for what is in fact a graceful ensemble of wood-and-plaster sake breweries and warehouses dating from the mid-18th to the 19th century.

Despite its diminutive scale, there are several temples of note in Tomonoura. **Io-ji** was supposedly founded by Kobo Daishi, a priest who, if only half the temples that claim a connection are true, must have been one of Buddhism's most itinerant pilgrims. **Fukuzen-ji** (daily 8am–5pm), a reception hall located near the ferry terminus and once used to receive Korean missions, inspired flights of calligraphy from envoys, such as the man of letters I-pan-o, who were overcome with the beauty of the view. Only slightly disfigured by small concrete installations and power lines, it remains largely intact.

Moving west along the coast, **Onomichi** ❻ was an important commercial port 800 years ago. Wealthy merchants flocked to the city during the Edo Period, building 81 temples on the steep slopes overlooking the sea to celebrate their prosperity. With the coming of the railway in the late 19th century, however, commerce literally passed the city by. Because of its relative lack of importance, American bombers also passed by Onomichi, and when the *shinkansen* route was mapped, Onomichi was passed over again. As a result of its slide into relative obscurity, the city has retained much of its pre-Meiji heritage. Some 25 of the old temples remain, the most interesting being the 1,100-year-old **Senko-ji**, which is best reached via the tram. From here, walk down the hill towards town, taking in as many temples as you can stand.

HIROSHIMA

One moment – 8.15am, 6 August 1945 – irrevocably changed world history. An atomic flash signalled the instant destruction of **Hiroshima** ❼, the eventual loss of over 200,000 lives, and forever linked the city's name with

Tomonoura fishing village.

⊘ Tip

The best way to see Hiroshima is from a tram. As other Japanese cities tore up their tram lines after World War II, their cars were sent to Hiroshima; as a result, the city acquired an eclectic collection of tram cars, many dating back to the 1940s.

nuclear holocaust and mass killings. The immediate and lasting impact on Hiroshima gives concrete reality to the horrors of atomic and nuclear war. Unlike Nagasaki, the second city to receive such an attack but which doesn't dwell much on past history, there seem to be reminders of Hiroshima's atomic bombing around virtually every corner in the city.

Amazingly, Hiroshima's people quickly rebuilt a vibrant city from the ashes, making it larger and more prosperous than the old one and leaving a few carefully chosen scars to memorialise its abiding atomic legacy. Hiroshima was chosen for the first atomic-bomb attack because of its military importance. The city was one of Japan's most vital military depots and industrial areas (a fact that goes unmentioned in the atomic bomb museum). However, Hiroshima's military significance predates World War II by several hundred years: troops were staged here in preparation for the invasion of Korea in 1582. A castle incorporating the latest construction and

defensive techniques was built here seven years later by the Mori clan. It rested on pilings driven into reclaimed swampland, and the outer moats were built above the level of the surrounding land so that their walls could be breached, flooding the plain where siege troops would likely mass. The castle was an important bastion of the Tokugawa shogun's forces, a western outpost facing the often hostile Choshu and Satsuma clans.

In the 19th century, **Hiroshima-jo** Ⓐ (Hiroshima Castle; daily, Mar–Nov 9am–6pm, Dec–Feb 9am–5pm) was occupied by the emperor during the occupation of Manchuria. The castle also served as an important Japanese Army headquarters during World War II and was completely destroyed by the atomic bomb. Reconstructed in 1958, the castle contains an excellent museum.

A few blocks east of the castle, **Shukkei-en** Ⓑ (Shukkei Garden; http://shukkeien.jp; daily, Apr–Sept 9am–6pm, Oct–Mar 9am–5pm) was built on the banks of the Kyobashi-gawa in 1620 in emulation of a famous Chinese lake.

Peace Memorial Museum in Hiroshima.

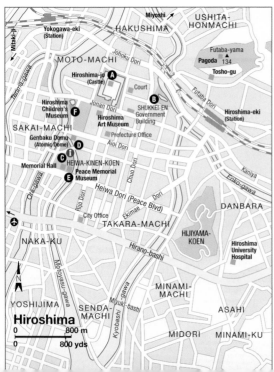

Early spring brings cherry blossoms to the garden, while azaleas bloom a little later, and multicoloured carp inhabit the garden's central pond throughout the year.

The **Heiwa Kinen-koen** ⊙ (Peace Memorial Park), southwest of the castle and wedged between the Motoyasu and Ota rivers, is adjacent to the **Genbaku Domu** ⊙ (Atomic Dome), a World Heritage site that marks ground zero of Hiroshima's atomic explosion. At its maximum intensity, the temperature approached that on the sun's surface and almost everything within sight was vapourised instantly. The famous building with the carefully maintained skeletal dome once housed the Industrial Promotion Hall and was one of the few surviving vertical structures. Today the park has a serene air; men perhaps old enough to remember the explosion sit meditatively on benches, the sonorous tones of the Peace Bell echo through the trees, and the solemnity is disturbed only by the exuberance of children who dash about with clipboards in hand for their school projects

and then stand silent in prayer before the many shrines.

Tange Kenzo designed the heart of the park complex, which comprises the **Peace Memorial Museum** ⊙ (www. pcf.city.hiroshima.jp; daily, Mar–Nov 8.30am–6pm, Aug 8.30am–7pm, Dec–Feb 8.30am–5pm), Peace Memorial Hall, the Cenotaph and Peace Flame. The museum contains graphic portrayals of the bombing. Although the museum is filled with powerful images of terrible suffering, it certainly is not the hall of horrors one might expect. A visit is nonetheless an emotional experience, even though the museum has been accused of failing to place the bombing in historical perspective, mainly as a result of right-wing nationalist opposition – it seems to suggest that the bomb fell on Hiroshima, figuratively as well as literally, out of the blue. There is little mention of Japan's brutal war record, and the suffering meted out on other peoples. The museum's Main Building reopened in 2019 after two years of renovation. It contains artefacts documenting the

Hiroshima Castle.

Photograph of the injured on the day of the atomic bomb in Hiroshima.

⊙ BLACK RAIN

"It was like a white magnesium flash... We first thought to escape to the parade grounds, but we couldn't because there was a huge sheet of fire in front of us... Hiroshima was completely enveloped in flames. We felt terribly hot and could not breathe well at all. After a while, a whirlpool of fire approached us from the south. It was like a big tornado of fire spreading over the full width of the street. Whenever the fire touched, wherever the fire touched, it burned... After a while, it began to rain. The fire and the smoke made us so thirsty... As it began to rain, people opened their mouths and turned their faces towards the sky and tried to drink the rain... It was a black rain with big drops."

Takakura Akiko
300 metres (1,000ft) from ground zero

horrors of 8 August 1945, including victims' clothing and personal effects. The East Building includes video testimonies from survivors, some of whom are still alive.

The **Cenotaph**'s inverted U-shape reflects the design of the thatched-roof houses of Japanese antiquity. It contains a stone chest with the names of the victims of the atomic bombing and bears an inscription, "Sleep in peace: the error will not be repeated". The **Peace Flame** and Atomic Dome can be seen through it. The statue of the children killed by the bombing is dedicated to Sasaki Sadako, who died of leukaemia caused by radiation when she was just 12 years old. She believed that if she could fold 1,000 paper cranes – a symbol of happiness and longevity for Japanese – she would be cured. Despite her illness, she managed to complete folding 1,000 cranes. As she did not get better, she started on a second thousand. She had reached some 1,500 when she finally died in 1955, 10 years after the atomic bomb exploded. Her spirited actions inspired

Torii at Miyajima.

an outpouring of national feeling and her classmates completed the second thousand paper cranes. Today, schoolchildren from all over the country bring paper cranes by the tens of thousands to lay around Sadako's memorial, a tribute that is simultaneously heart-rending, beautiful, and a terrible condemnation of militarism.

Many visitors ring the Peace Bell before crossing the Motoyasu-gawa to the dome. Colourful rowing boats can be rented by the hour near the **Heiwa Ohashi** (Peace Bridge), offering a more cheerful perspective on Hiroshima. Sightseeing cruises depart from the nearby pier. By the river, and just east of the Peace Memorial Museum, is the **Hiroshima Children's Museum ❻** (www. pyonta.city.hiroshima.jp; Tue–Sun 9am–5pm; free except for planetarium). It offers a refreshing break from the sombre park, with a planetarium and plenty of fun, hands-on science exhibits.

Half an hour away and northwest of central Hiroshima, **Mitaki-ji** is set in a lush forest with three waterfalls. Buddhas adorn the hillsides, and a fierce,

life-size baby-killing devil statue of wood hangs out on the temple's porch. A friendly dog often welcomes visitors to the teahouse, which is decorated with a colourful collection of masks and kites. The walk from the central train station to the temple grounds passes a group of graves belonging to many unknown atomic-bomb victims.

MIYAJIMA

Though it is formally called **Itsuku-shima** (Strict Island), this major Hiro-shima-area tourist attraction, which boasts World Heritage status, is better known as **Miyajima ❽**, the Island of Shrines. To find the spirit and splen-dour of Miyajima, one of the country's holiest sites, visitors must make their way through herds of tame deer and the litter left by thousands of tourists. Most of the island is covered with unin-habited virgin forest. A good way to see it is from the 1.6km (1-mile) long cable car (http://miyajima-ropeway.info; daily, Mar–Oct 9am–5pm, Nov 8am–5pm, Dec–Feb 9am–4.30pm) that runs over Momijidani-koen to the top of Misen.

The large crimson torii (shrine gate), rising out of the sea in front of the **Itsukushima-jinja** (daily sunrise–sun-set), is probably the most familiar Jap-anese cultural icon and representative of Shintoism. But this torii, which is plastered on nearly every travel poster and guidebook that has anything to do with Japan, hasn't suffered from the overexposure. For those who stay overnight on the island, it is especially breathtaking in the evening, when the crowds have returned to the mainland.

The current gate was built in 1874, but a similar torii has lured visitors for seven centuries. The island's spiritual roots are much older, however. The first shrine, honouring Amaterasu's three daughters – goddesses of the sea – was built in the 6th century. To maintain the island's "purity", births and deaths have been prohibited on Miyajima from the earliest times.

The entire island was dedicated as a sanctuary by Taira no Kiyomori, who ordered the Itsukushima-jinga to be completely rebuilt in 1168.

Itsukushima-jinga itself rests on stilts and seems to float like a giant ship when the tide comes in. Costumes and masks used in the *bugaku* dance festival (first week of January) and the *noh* plays, performed in mid-April, are on display in the Asazaya (morn-ing prayer room), which is reached via a bridge. Next to Itsuku-shima, one of the oldest *noh* theatres in Japan, built in 1568, also seems to float a few inches above the sea. A nearby build-ing contains hundreds of government-designated National Treasures and Important Cultural Objects, including illuminated sutras made by the Taira clan in the 1160s.

A five-storey pagoda, built in 1407, and the hall of **Senjokaku** (A Thousand Mats) are at the top of a hill behind Itsukushima-jinga. Senjokaku, built in 1587, is the great warlord Toyotomi Hideyoshi's contribution to Miyajima. The island has a number of noteworthy

The Yamaguchi-go steam train in Yamaguchi.

Peace Memorial Park and Cenotaph, Hiroshima.

matsuri, like its February **Oyster Festival** and a pine torch parade in December. The best of these utilise the island and shrine's stunning setting. Look out for the 17 June Kangensai with its traditional music and boat parade, and on 14 August, the **Hanabi Matsuri**, a huge firework display in front of the shrine.

TO THE WEST

Iwakuni ❾, 44km (27 miles) west of Hiroshima, is on both the *shinkansen* and JR San-yo Line. The stations are located to the west and east of the central area, where most of the sights are. Each has a useful tourist information office with handouts in English.

Iwakuni's premier sight is, without question, **Kintai-kyo** (http://kintai-kyo.iwakuni-city.net), the Brocade Sash Bridge, a graceful span that undulates between five steep arches, a popular image with tourist promoters and directors of TV samurai dramas looking for instant image bites. The original bridge, built in 1673, was destroyed in a flood in 1950. Rebuilt a few years later, the present construction is almost indistinguishable from the original. There's a small toll charge to cross the bridge.

On the far side of the bridge, **Kikko-koen**, a pleasant parkland area, includes the surviving residences of an old samurai district and a ruined moat that once served a castle, **Iwakuni-jo** (daily 9am–4.45pm; closed final two weeks of Dec). The castle was relocated into a more commanding and picturesque spot when it was rebuilt in 1960. There's a cable car to take you to the top of the hill, but the walk is hardly strenuous.

If you happen to be in Iwakuni during the summer months from June to August, you can, for a fee, board a night boat to observe *ukai*, a visually exciting, traditional method of fishing using cormorants and baskets of burning flames that light up the river surfaces.

YAMAGUCHI

Though the bullet train numbers nearby Shin–Yagamuchi among its stops, the provincial city of **Yamaguchi** ❿ is better known for another form

Kintai-kyo, Iwakuni, Yamaguchi.

of transport: a 1937 locomotive, one of the few in Japan to remain in regular service. Operating during weekends and holidays from late March to November, the gleaming steam engine, called the **SL Yamaguchi-go**, runs between the castle town of Tsuwano and Shin-Yamaguchi. Tickets sell fast and need booking well in advance.

During the Sengoku era (1467–1573), Japan's century of anarchy, much of the cultural and political life of the country shifted to the relative security of Yamaguchi. Many literati, noblemen and their retinues sought refuge here, bringing with them the sensibilities and tastes of the imperial capital, Kyoto. Several of Yamaguchi's easily sought-out temples and shrines date from this period.

Japan's first Christian missionary, the Basque priest Francis Xavier, stayed in Yamaguchi for two months trying, without much success, to convert the locals. Xavier and his mission are still remembered with affection in Yamaguchi, though, where there is a gleaming **Yamaguchi Xavier Memorial Church** (www.xavier.jp). A strikingly modern structure, a pyramid of silver and eggshell white, it is crowned with metallic towers, sculptures and a brace of suspended bells. Its stained-glass windows and coloured jars of burning candles create the effect of a slightly dimmed café-gallery.

Were the Yamaguchi Post Office to be looking for an image to place on a commemorative stamp of their prefectural capital, they would no doubt choose the city's magisterial five-storey pagoda, built in the grounds of the **Ruriko-ji** temple (grounds always open; free; pagoda museum: daily 9am–5pm). Made from Japanese cypress, each roof a fraction steeper than the one below it, the pagoda, typical of the Muromachi-era Zen Kyoto style, is strikingly situated beside an ornamental pond graced by bushes and topiary, the effect only slightly marred by a tape recording giving an account of the history of the building.

SESSHU-TEI GARDEN

A kilometre (0.6 miles) or so northeast of the pagoda, the **Sesshu-tei** (daily 8am–4.30pm, Apr–Nov until 5pm), named after its designer, the master painter and priest Sesshu, is a Zen-inspired garden, a combination of dry landscape and moss, an arrangement of stones, rocks, lawn and lily pad pond. It's best viewed in its intended entirety from the broad wooden veranda at the rear of the temple, from where the garden resembles a horizontal scroll.

Transected by the only moderately busy Route 9, it is possible to preserve some of the serenity of Sesshu's garden by following a path along the **Ichinosaka-gawa** as it makes a sinuous course back to the town centre. Crossed by pedestrian bridges, the banks of the stream, a place of water reeds and azaleas, is a popular walk in springtime when its cherry trees are in full blossom, while in the summer there are swarms of fireflies.

Koi pond in Tsuwano.

Castle town of Hagi, Yamaguchi.

TSUWANO

Easily accessed from either Yamaguchi City or Hagi, **Tsuwano** ⑪ is one of the best-preserved medieval towns in Japan, and another of its "Little Kyotos" – but, unlike many other self-titled "Little Kyotos", Tsuwano really does live up to the billing. Its exquisite samurai and merchant houses, temples and museums are located in a narrow, photogenic ravine. An extraordinary 80,000 colourful carp live in shallow streams and culverts that run between the main road, Tonomachi-dori and the walls of the samurai residences. The fish were stocked as a food resource in case of a siege, and the streams would provide ready water in the event of fire.

The tourist information centre (daily 9am–5pm) near the station has a very decent English guidebook to the town.

A one-minute walk into the woods directly west of the station leads to the **Otome Toge Maria Chapel** (always open), an attractive structure built in 1951 to honour the memory of Christians persecuted during the Meiji Period in the late 19th century. Thousands were relocated to areas across Japan, including Tsuwano, and were either forced to convert, tortured, or killed. With its pavilion roofs and modest spire, this rustic chapel exhibits a blend of Japanese and Western architectural styles.

Following Tonomachi-dori southeast of the station, the spire of Tsuwano's 1931 **Catholic Church** is the town's other Christian site of interest. It's a modest sight, but worth a few minutes to view the stained-glass windows. A moderately interesting folk museum (Tsuwano Minzoku Museum; Apr–Nov Sat–Sun 8.30am–4.30pm) stands nearby on the banks of the Tsuwano-gawa. The building, known as the **Yorokan**, once served as a school for young samurai.

On the other side of the rail tracks from here are two shrines of interest – **Yasaka-jinja**, known for its July Heron Dance festival, and, further on, **Taikodani Inari-jinja**, an Inari fox shrine with a tunnel of bright-red torii gates wending its way uphill

to the main shrine and its colourful Shinto paraphernalia.

Climb or take the cable car from here up to the site of **Tsuwano-jo**, remains of another hilltop castle with the best views of the town. The original castle was built in 1295 as a bulwark against a possible Mongol attack, a very real threat at that time. Ironically, it was the Meiji era's passion for reckless modernisation, and dismantling feudal castles, that reduced Tsuwano-jo to a ruin.

SHIMONOSEKI

At the western limit of Honshu, **Shimonoseki** ⓬ is the gateway to Kyushu and to Korea as well, with *shinkansen* (bullet train) service to Hakata Station in Fukuoka and daily overnight ferries to Busan, South Korea. There isn't much reason to linger here, but one of the largest aquariums in Asia, the **Shimonoseki Kaikyokan** (www.kaikyokan.com; daily 9.30am–5.30pm), and the Akama shrine may be of interest to those waiting for a boat to Korea.

Shimonoseki has been an important port over many centuries, although today it is less so. The area was also the site of some of Japan's most important sea battles. History and literature students will recall that the final scenes of *Tale of the Heike* were set here. It is where the exiled empress dowager hurled herself and the infant emperor into the swirling tides. Several spots in the area claim to be the actual location, but, in fact, any would do, as the cliffs are high and the waters do swirl frighteningly as the Sea of Japan (East Sea) meets the Seto Naikai.

HAGI

From Shimonoseki, the coastal road loops back east along the northern coast of Honshu and the Sea of Japan (East Sea). Samurai footsteps echo through the narrow streets in the heart of **Hagi** ⓭, and indeed the whole town resounds to the beat of historical events that have shaped Japan as it is today. If there is one reason to journey to this part of the coast, it is here in Hagi – a place that is as picturesque as it is fascinating.

Many of the statesmen who played significant parts in the Meiji Restoration came from here, Korean potters brought their art and flourished in Hagi, and it is the site of some of the earliest steps taken in glass-making.

Start where Hagi itself started, at the castle site at the foot of **Shizuki-yama**. Built on the orders of Terumoto Mori in 1604, who then presided over the area that is now Yamaguchi Prefecture, the castle stood until 1874, when it was pulled down to express allegiance to the new Meiji government, which had returned the emperor to power. Parts of the walls and the former dungeon remain today (castle ruins: daily, Mar 8.30am–6pm, Apr–Oct 8am–6.30am, Nov–Feb 8.30am–4.30pm), and there's a Japanese teahouse in the adjacent gardens.

⊙ Tip

The port of Shimonoseki provides a nightly ferry connection to Busan in Korea. With prices from just ¥9,000, the eight-hour crossing is an extremely cheap option if you are travelling around Asia. There are also low-cost ferry connections to parts of China. Check www.shimonoseki-port.com for details.

Hagi pottery.

The Tottori dunes.

Izumo Taisha, Shimane.

From here, head to the Asa Mori clan residence, the largest of the surviving samurai houses that arose in Hagi beyond the castle walls, or, just a few steps away beyond a natural, grassy sea wall, **Kikugahama beach**, a sandy curve with clean water for a pleasant swim. The streets of the castle town, or Jokamachi, were divided into three sections: one for lower-ranking samurai, a second for rich politicians and the third for merchants. As you wander its lanes – particularly Edoya, Iseya and Kikuya – every turn reveals another pocket of days gone by. Doctor's son Kido Takayoshi, one of the Meiji Restoration's dynamos, grew up in a house on Edoya. Another prominent Restoration figure, Takasugi Shinsaku, lived on Kikuya and was cured of smallpox by Dr Aoki Shusuke, another inhabitant of Edoya. All their residences are on view to the public. After the Meiji Restoration, a number of *natsu mikan* (orange or tangerine) trees were planted in Hagi, mainly to provide some relief to the unemployed samurai. Many trees dot the Horiuchi (inner moat) district,

and in May and June the scent of the blossoms is almost intoxicating.

Hagi's other great influence on Japan is its pottery, ranked the second-most beautiful in the country after that of Kyoto. At first glance it can appear deceptively simple and rustic, but closer examination reveals subdued colours and classical features, especially in the glazing that is exceptionally clear and vivid.

Lesser known is Hagi's glass, introduced around 1860 as the Edo Period drew to a close and using European techniques. After a century-long hiatus, the old techniques are now being used again to make Hagi glass.

ALONG THE SEA OF JAPAN (EAST SEA)

Further on along the coast, **Shimane** and its modest peninsula consist of three ancient districts: Izumo, Iwami and the islands of Oki-shoto. It is one of the longest-inhabited areas of Japan and offers special insights into the cultural heritage of the nation. **Izumo** ⑭ covers the eastern part of

the prefecture and is known as the mythical province where the history of Japan began. Several shrines, temples and ancient buildings can be seen around the prefecture, including the **Izumo Taisha** ⑮ (shrine: always open, free; Treasure Hall: daily 8.30am–4.30pm), the oldest Shinto shrine in the country. Dedicated to the spirit god of marriage, it is paid particular heed by couples.

Shinji-ko sits at the eastern end of the prefecture. The lake's 45km (30-mile) coastline offers beautiful sights throughout the year, and sunset over the lake is one of the finest evening scenes in Japan. At the eastern end of the lake sits **Matsue-jo** (daily, Apr–Sept 8.30am–6.30pm, Oct–Mar 8.30am–5pm). Often called Plover Castle because of its shape, the castle was built in 1611 by Yoshiharu Horio, a samurai general. It is the only remaining castle in the Izumo area and very little has been done to modernise it, so the feeling inside is truly authentic. Across the castle moat to the north lies Shiominawate, an area where ranking samurai once lived.

Matsue ⑯ was also the home of a renowned writer and observer of Japan, Lafcadio Hearn (1850–1904). Greek-born Hearn was raised in the US and went to Japan in 1891 as a *Harper's* magazine reporter. In his many years in Japan, he wrote numerous works, including *Kwaidan: Stories and Studies of Strange Things*; *Shadowings*, *Japan: An Attempt at Interpretation*; *Bushido: The Soul of Japan*; and *A Daughter of the Samurai*. Although written over a century ago, his observations carry well over time. Along with Matsue's other cultural credentials, such as its samurai dwellings, history museum and the interesting Karakoro Art Studio with its exhibits of local crafts, is the **Lafcadio Hearn Memorial Museum** (www.hearn-museum-matsue.jp; daily, Apr–Sept 8.30am–6.30pm, Oct–Mar 8.30am–5pm). Also in Matsue is the

ancient shrine of **Kamosu**. Its unique architectural style, *taisha-zukuri*, is the oldest architectural style in Japan.

About 16km (10 miles) southeast of Matsue, the **Adachi Museum of Art** (www.adachi-museum.or.jp; daily, Apr–Sept 9am–5.30pm, Oct–Mar 9am–5pm) is well worth a detour. The collection covers Japanese art from the Meiji era through to the present, and while that is impressive enough in its own right, it's almost secondary to the pristine gardens, complete with teahouses, that make up the museum's 43,000 sq metres (465,000 sq ft) of grounds.

Continuing east along the coast brings one to **Tottori** Prefecture, with a rural reputation not too dissimilar to Tohoku's. Though its tourist attractions are few and far between, Tottori does lure visitors with one thing very un-Japanese – large **sand dunes** *(sakyu)* (www.tottori-tour.jp/en/sightseeing/456) on the coast by **Tottori City** ⑰ that attract nearly 2 million tourists to enjoy diversions like camel-riding and sandboarding annually.

Quote

"That trees, at least Japanese trees, have souls, cannot seem an unnatural fancy to one who has seen the blossoming of the *umenoki* and the *sakuranoki*. This is a popular belief in Izumo and elsewhere."

In a Japanese Garden by Lafcadio Hearn

A statue of Adachi Zenko.

A pilgrim on the route of 88 temples.

SHIKOKU

Japan's fourth-largest island is an area of rugged terrain with open exposure to Pacific typhoons. Difficult to access until relatively recently, here its people are fiercely independent.

The least developed and rarely visited of Japan's four biggest islands, Shikoku's attractions (and drawbacks) are attendant on its relative isolation. The island can provide a more "Japanese" experience than either Honshu or Kyushu. Its people are not as familiar with foreigners and its atmosphere has been less influenced by the homogenising aspects of modern culture. It is also more diffused. Places likely to be of interest to travellers here are relatively far apart and more difficult to get to than on the more widely travelled pathways.

Shikoku's separate identity is not as isolated as before. The smallest of Japan's four main islands, it was the last to be linked by bridge with Honshu, the largest and most populated of Japan's islands. In 1988 the completion of the **Seto Ohashi**  bridge, which took 10 years and nearly US$1 billion to build, gave Shikoku a ground transport link to the rest of Japan. At 12.3km (7.5 miles) in length, it is one of the longer double-deck bridges in the world, carrying four lanes of traffic above dual rail tracks. Since its completion another two bridges have been added to improve further Shikoku's connections with the main island.

The most numerous and distinctive visitors crossing into Shikoku today are *ohenrosan* – devout Buddhist pilgrims making the rounds of the 88 holy temples and shrines established by the priest Kobo Daishi 1,200 years ago. In the feudal period, it was common for white-robed pilgrims to complete the circuit on foot, a feat requiring more than two months. Today's pilgrims usually make the rounds in two weeks or less via bus, though recent years have seen a surge in both young Japanese and foreigners attempting all or part of the route.

Shikoku is split into northern and southern sections by steep, rugged mountains. The relatively dry northern

Main attractions

Takamatsu
Kotohira
Tokushima
Naruto
Matsuyama
Dogo Onsen Honkan
Uchiko and Ozu
Ashizuri-misaki
Kochi

Map on page 302

The Great Seto Bridge.

The Konpira-san Temple complex has a nautical theme, as sailors, in particular, believe this temple brings good fortune.

Ritsurin Garden, Takamatsu.

part, facing the **Seto Naikai** (Inland Sea), is more industrialised, and in cities like the fairly cosmopolitan Takamatsu feels really no different from Honshu. The south is wilder, warmer and wetter, offering opportunities to experience Japan at its most rugged and rural, especially in the small fishing and farming communities towards the southern capes. The weather here is most favourable in early spring and at the beginning of autumn.

TAKAMATSU

The capital of Kagawa Prefecture, **Takamatsu** ⑲ is the main railway terminal and ferry port in eastern Shikoku. **Ritsurin-koen** (Ritsurin Park; www.my-kagawa.jp/ritsuringarden; daily from 5.30–7am until 5–7pm, depending on the season) contains one of the finest traditional gardens in Japan, with 54 hectares (133 acres) of ponds, hills, pine forests and a botanical garden. One of the garden's best rewards is a cup of tea at the beautiful Kikugetsutei teahouse. The **Kagawa Museum** (Tue–Sun 9am–5pm), near the entrance

to the park, displays comprehensive collections of crafts from Shikoku and throughout Japan. However, the region's most popular craft are the distinctive *sanuki*-udon noodles, served daily at thousands of udon restaurants throughout the area.

A few kilometres east by train from the centre of Takamatsu is **Yashima**. It was one of the seemingly countless battlefields of the Gempei War (1180–85) between the Minamoto and Taira clans. The architectural embodiments of Shikoku's past – an open-air kabuki theatre, a vine suspension bridge, thatch-roofed farmhouses and a variety of other traditional buildings – have been collected and preserved in **Shikoku-mura** (Shikoku Village; www.shikokumura.or.jp; daily, Apr–Oct 8.30am–6pm, Nov–Mar 8.30am–5.30pm). This tiny part of Shikoku Island was itself once an island; now a narrow strip connects it to the mainland. It juts out into the Seto Naikai and provides extensive views, particularly from Yashima's lofty temple on the hill. In addition to the temple's

beautiful garden you can visit its Treasure House, stuffed with interesting relics and local art and craft objects.

Southwest of Takamatsu, **Kotohira** ⑳ is home to one of the most famous and popular shrines in Japan, **Kotohira-gu** (also called Konpira-san; the main precinct is free, but some buildings require an entrance fee). Dedicated to Okuninushi no Mikoto, the guardian of seafarers, the shrine has lured sailors and fishermen seeking propitious sailing since the shrine's inception in the 11th century. In recent years, their numbers have been swelled by the 4 million tourists arriving each year. The main shrine is at the end of a long, steep path lined with stone lanterns. A trip to the top of the 785 stairs and back takes at least an hour.

The **Kanamaru-za** (www.konpirakabuki. jp), restored to its original early 19th-century condition, is the oldest existing kabuki theatre in Japan. Its stage, resonating with the fading echoes of thousands of performances, is exciting to visit even when empty. In the third week of April, the nation's best kabuki actors bring it alive. The revolving section is turned by strong men pushing the 150-year-old mechanism under the stage, and the audience is seated on cushions on tatami.

Off the coast of Takamatsu, in the Seto Naikai, are two islands worth a day trip or overnight visit. **Naoshima Island**, a 20-minute ferry ride from Takamatsu's port (also accessible by ferry from Okayama), is nationally renowned for its collection of contemporary art galleries. Until the 1990s, the small fishing island had seen several decades of decline, its population shrinking as the island's youth shunned traditional island life or work at its largest employer – a Mitsubishi metals processing plant. Then along came the publishing group Benesse, who chose Naoshima's idyllic setting for its Art Site Naoshima contemporary art initiative.

Naoshima's three major and very sleek contemporary art galleries – **Benesse House Museum** (http:// benesse-artsite.jp/art/benessehouse-museum.html; daily 8am–9pm), **Lee Ufan Museum** (http://benesse-artsite.jp/

Bar sign in Naruto.

Naoshima Island.

◎ Tip

Tokushima Prefecture's southern end is surfing country. The place to head to is Kaifu, about 25km (15.5 miles) south of Hiwasa on the JR line – there are plenty of surf shops here for renting gear before heading out to ride the breakers at Kaifu Point or moving to the equally good Shishikui beach a few kilometres further south.

art/lee-ufan.html; Tue–Sun 10am–5pm, Mar–Sept until 6pm) and **Chichu Art Museum** (http://benesse-artsite.jp/art/chichu.html; Tue–Sun 10am–5pm, Mar–Sept until 6pm) – feature work by local artists and international stars such as Pollock, Warhol, Walter de Maria, Lee Ufan and James Turrell. Naoshima's **Art House Project** (most installations: Tue–Sun 10am–4.30pm) has also seen several traditional houses and other structures in Honmura Village transformed into art installations, while art can also be found in other unexpected places. Some 20 installations dot the beaches and cliff tops near Benesse House and the even the local public bath (**I Love Yu**; Tue–Sun 1am–9pm) has been bombed inside and out with pop art and erotica. The **Ando Museum** (http://benesse-artsite.jp/art/ando-museum.html; Tue–Sun 10am–4.30pm), opened in 2013 and dedicated to the world-renowned architect Tadao Ando's work, is the most recent addition.

An hour by ferry is **Shodoshima**, which among its attractions has several soy-sauce plants that can be toured and great views of the Inland Sea from its mountainous interior.

EASTERN SHIKOKU

Tokushima Prefecture faces Osaka Bay and the Pacific Ocean along the western end of Shikoku. In ancient times, Tokushima was known as Awa no Kuni – Millet Country. Today, most of the prefecture's traditional arts still use the Chinese characters for Awa no Kuni. The Awa Odori – the summer "crazy dance" festival – is held in mid-August and is perhaps the most humorous of Japanese festivals, with residents and tourists joining in processional dances and contests for the "biggest fool of all". Another home-grown entertainment are puppet shows featuring giant puppets accompanied by shamisen and performed by farmers between growing seasons.

The garden of the old castle of **Tokushima ㉑** is set against the backdrop of forest-covered Shiro-yama. The garden consists of a traditional landscaped area with a fountain. Over a quarter of the 88 Kobo Daishi temples are in the immediate vicinity of

The Awa Odori dance festival in Tokushima.

◎ DANCING JAPAN

"You're a fool if you dance and a fool if you don't, so dance, fool!" goes the rallying cry of the centuries-old Awa Odori dance festival in Tokushima. Over four days every 12–15 August, more than 1 million people descend on the city to watch some 80,000 dancers prance through the streets like lunatics on the run. Dressed in colourful *yukata* and driven by a pounding two-beat drum rhythm accompanied by *shamisen* and flute, the dancers produce an intoxicating display that invariably goes on long into the night and has spectators starting their own impromptu dance parties across the city.

You can get a taste of the Awa Odori year-round at the Awa Odori Museum (www.awaodori-kaikan.jp; daily 9am–5pm), where local dance troupes also put on several displays daily.

Tokushima. Along the once prosperous and busy main highway through the centre of town are several old, fire-resistant *kura* (warehouses) used by merchants to store their goods in earlier times.

About 20km (12 miles) to the north, **Naruto** ㉒ faces the **Naruto-kaikyo** (Naruto Straits), where the **O-Naru-tokyo** (Great Naruto Bridge) connects Tokushima with Awaji-shima and is one of the longer suspension bridges in Asia. The attraction to travellers is not the bridge, however, but rather the countless whirlpools, some as large as 20 metres (60ft) in diameter, that swirl in the Naruto Straits flowing beneath the bridge. The whirlpools are largest in the spring and autumn, when tides reach a speed of 20kmh (12mph). Sightseeing boats chug right up to the whirlpools during peak tourism season.

The 100km (60-mile) coastline of Tokushima Prefecture holds some of the best beaches in Japan. Along the centre of the coast, **Komoda-misaki** (Cape Komoda) stretches out into the Pacific. The peninsula is noted for its luxuriant subtropical flora. The offshore reefs, washed by the warm Japan Current, are the site of some of the best surf-fishing in Japan. The area is also noted as an egg-laying location for giant loggerhead turtles. In **Hiwasa** ㉓ to the south is a sea turtle museum. Also in Hiwasa is **Yakuo-ji**, the 23rd temple on the great Shikoku pilgrimage and famous for its series of paintings of the miseries of the Buddhist hell. The temple is thought to ward off evil. Men and women in their *yakudoshi* (unlucky years) visit here to ask for divine help by placing a one-yen coin on each step as they climb up to the temple. The grounds of Yakuo-ji afford fine views of Hiwasa harbour.

INLAND SHIKOKU

Tsurugi-san ㉔ (1,893 metres/6,200ft) dominates the interior of eastern Shikoku and is one of the main peaks of Shikoku. In contrast to its name – meaning "broadsword" – the crest of the mountain slopes gently. A lift brings visitors up to near the summit, followed by a 40-minute hike to the peak. A lodging

Oku-Iya double vine bridges (kazura-bashi).

Oboke Gorge.

Train in Matsuyama.

Matsuyama's Dogo Onsen.

house, skiing area and old shrines make Tsurugi a major recreation area.

South of Tsurugi-san, the gorge of **Konose** lies deep in the mountains at the source of the Naka-gawa. It is a site of magnificent natural beauty, and in autumn, red and yellow foliage covers the surrounding mountains.

To the west of Tsurugi-san is the gorge at **Oboke**, formed by the upper reaches of the Yoshino-gawa. The site is noted for towering cliffs and giant rocks polished like marble from the cascading waters. Spring and autumn are the best times to see the gorge, which is also visited by busloads of tourists, however. The **Iya Valley**, with its hot springs, river rafting, and the much-photographed pair of unique vine bridges, are a little east of Oboke.

The **Yoshino-gawa Valley**, north of Tsurugi-san and running due west from Tokushima, holds most of the area's main attractions. The valley is full of ancient temples, shrines, museums and cultural sites. The area is also peppered with *ai yashiki* (indigo-dyeing plants); *Awa*-style indigo dyeing

has flourished as the main industry of Tokushima for centuries.

About 30km (20 miles) up the Yoshino-gawa from Tokushima is **Do-chu** (Earthen Pillars). The strangely shaped pillars were formed over millions of years as the result of soil erosion. Nearby are the historic streets of Udatsu and the Awagami traditional paper factory. The entire valley is served by the JR Yoshinogawa rail line from Tokushima.

WESTERN SHIKOKU

Facing the Seto Naikai along Shikoku's northwestern shore, Ehime Prefecture was described as early as AD 712 in the *Kojiki*, Japan's first chronicle of historical events and legends. Ehime has many historical places, hot springs and festivals.

Several castles dot the Ehime landscape, **Imabari-jo** in **Imabari** ㉕ being one of them. It is a rare coastal castle built in 1604 by Takatora Todo. The massive walls and moats, filled by water from the sea, let its masters fight attacks by land or sea. Shikoku's best-known castle is **Matsuyama-jo**

(www.matsuyamajo.jp; daily 9am–5pm, Aug until 5.30pm, Dec–Jan until 4.30pm), which stands in the middle of the city of **Matsuyama** ㉖, with a slightly incongruous baseball park and athletic stadium at its base. It was completed in 1603, burned down but was rebuilt on a slightly smaller scale in 1642, struck by lightning and razed to the ground in 1784, and then not fully rebuilt until 1854. The present-day edifice is a result of restoration work completed in 1986, so it's not exactly an original, but the cable-car ride up to it is fun, and this is a good place to get your bearings.

Away to the west near **Dogo-koen** stands the **Dogo Onsen Honkan** (www.dogo.or.jp). People in Matsuyama have been coming to Dogo for more than a century, taking off their shoes at the entrance to the rambling three-storey castle affair topped with a white heron and leaving their clothes and cares behind as they wallow in the glory of the alkaline hot spas. It is thought that they've been doing so for as long as 3,000 years – Dogo Onsen is reckoned to

be the oldest hot spring in use in Japan. It was first mentioned in the early 8th-century *Kojiki* ('record of ancient matters') and also in the mid-8th-century *Manyoshu* book of poetry.

One can get a basic soak in **Kami-no-yu** (Water of the Gods; daily 6am–11pm) for a few hundred yen, but that would be like going to a Michelin-starred restaurant and merely nibbling on the breadsticks. Pay the full price and head up Dogo's precipitous stairways to **Tama-no-yu** (Water of the Spirits; daily 6am–10pm). Language is not a problem as smiling ladies point the way to a private tatami room where you can leave clothes in a locker, don a *yukata* and head for the bath itself.

Males and females go their separate ways at this point, and then, as in all onsen, you soap and thoroughly rinse off, sitting on a little wooden stool and dousing your body from a wooden bucket. Then it's time to lower yourself inch by inch into the waters (hot but not scalding) and let the body gradually adjust. It's a tingling cleanliness that washes over you, relaxing the body

⊙ **Fact**

Japan's countless hot springs – there are more here than in any other country – are indicative of the islands' continuing volcanism. They are found in all parts of Japan in every landscape, from mountain tops to city centres, but they vary widely in chemical composition.

Kabuki theatre, Uchiko.

⊙ Tip

Note that in Japanese onsen no clothes are worn (though a small hand towel offers a little modesty while walking around), and you should thoroughly wash and rinse before entering the water, as the pools are communal and used only for soaking. Those with tattoos may be asked to cover up or refrain.

and bringing a drowsy contentment to the mind. After 10 or 20 minutes, heave yourself out, dry off, dress and climb back up to the tatami room. The maid will pull out your sitting pillows and serve tea and marzipan balls. The balcony looks out over tiled roofs and trees, and laughter and the contented buzz of conversation drifts over from adjoining rooms.

Also in Dogo, **Ishite-ji**, the 51st temple on Shikoku's 88-temple pilgrimage, was built by the decree of Emperor Shomu in 728. It was restored by the great priest Kobo in the early 9th century. Its treasure hall (daily 8am–5pm) holds some 300 important historical articles.

One of Ehime's more interesting historical sites is the kabuki theatre in **Uchiko** ㉗. This full-scale kabuki theatre was built in 1916 in the Irimoya zukuri style, its tiled roof typical of the housing style of the 1800s. Its restoration in 1985 preserved the old-style drum tower on the top floor, a rotating stage, an elevated passageway and box seats. Ten kilometres (6 miles) southwest of Uchiko, the small town of

Cape Ashizuri-Misaki.

Ozu ㉘ calls itself "mini Kyoto". Among the traditional attractions that have helped give it that tag are summer **cormorant fishing** (ukai) displays along Ozu's Hiji-kawa River and several old sukiya-style villas about town. Ozu also has Japan's newest castle, an impressive 2004 reconstruction of the original 16th-century, four-storey **Ozu-jo**.

Continuing south, **Uwajima-jo** was built in 1595 by Takatora Todo. The castle's three-storeyed tower stands atop an 80-metre (260ft) hill overlooking the city of **Uwajima** ㉙, noted throughout Japan for bullfights. The curious visitor drawn to Uwajima by tales of **Taga-jinja** and its sex museum (daily 8am–5pm) should be aware that many of the more tantalising exhibits within this shrine are locked away in glass cases and there is little interpretation in English, although, of course, most of the items on display – from lurid photos to well-proportioned fertility sculptures – are self-explanatory.

To the south in **Tsushima** ㉚ is a strolling garden, **Nanrakuen-koen**, covering more than 15 hectares (37 acres) and the largest on Shikoku. Developed in 1985, the garden has four theme areas: mountains, villages, towns and the sea. Some 30,000 irises, which bloom in early May, cover most of the gardens. Near Nanrakuen-koen is a gorge, **Nametoko**, carved out by the Shimanto-gawa, which is reported to be the last clear river in Japan. The gorge runs through Ashizuri-Uwakai National Park (www.env.go.jp/park/ashizuri/index.html).

Ehime Prefecture is also noted for its many and varied festivals: the Ikazaki Kite Festival in May displays Ehime's 300-year history of kite-making; the Saijo Festival in October features 80 moveable shrines; the Niihama Drum Festival in October includes a competition between 33 massive drums, or taiko. Other festivals include bullfights, samba competitions and the Matsuyama Spring Festival in April.

SOUTHERN SHIKOKU

Two large capes frame Kochi Prefecture. On the far western side of Kochi lies **Ashizuri-misaki ③**. This cape is noted for towering marble cliffs and Japan's first underwater park. In early spring, camellias cover the cape in a dazzling red carpet of blossoms.

The prefecture of Kochi broadly encircles the wide **Tosa-wan** (Tosa Bay), with its capital of **Kochi ②** facing the south on a flat plain. Kochi is best known for the role its leading families played in forging the alliance between the Satsuma and Choshu clans and the ensuing imperial Meiji Restoration of 1868. Its most renowned citizen from this period is Sakamoto Ryoma. Sakamoto – from a half-merchant, half-samurai family – left the class system and set up a trading company in Nagasaki.

While there, he helped establish a network of anti-Tokugawa samurai but was assassinated in Kyoto in 1867 – just a year before the overthrow of the shogun and restoration of the emperor to legitimate rule. He is remembered in the museum at **Kochi-jo** (Kochi Castle; daily 9am–5pm), an elegant castle built in the 17th century and rebuilt in the 18th. A market is held every Sunday on the road leading to the castle's Ote gate. The market is popular with local residents, with as many as 700 small stalls selling vegetables, antiques, plants and just about everything else imaginable; it runs for about 1km (0.6 miles) along both sides of the road. A statue of Sakamoto Ryoma graces the beach at **Katsurahama**, more famous as one of the few locations in Japan where dogfighting is legal. This beautiful beach is also a popular spot for admiring the moon. Katsurahama-koen is nearby, and there are many places of interest, such as an aquarium (http://katurahama-aq.jp; daily 9am–5pm).

Ryuga-do (daily, Mar–Nov 8.30am–5pm, Dec–Feb 8.30am–4.30pm), a limestone cave 25km (15 miles) east of Kochi and gradually moulded over a period of 50 million years, boasts a mysterious natural beauty that enthrals everyone who visits. The scenic Skyline Drive to the top of the mountain where the cave is buried offers a wonderful vista of the Pacific Ocean.

A few kilometres west of Kochi, in **Ino**, is a fabulous paper museum. Ino has a long history of papermaking, and Kochi paper is famous throughout Japan. (For a place to be viable in Japan's domestic tourism industry, it must be "famous" for something, no matter how insignificant.) In the museum, visitors can try their hand at papermaking in addition to observing the papermaking process.

On the far eastern side of Kochi from Ashizuri-misaki, **Muroto-zaki ③** points out southwards into the Pacific Ocean. The cape is warm year-round, and at its tip the towering waves of the Pacific have eroded the rocks and reefs into strange shapes. The area is also noted for its connection with the venerable Kobo Daishi, founder of the Shingon sect of Buddhism.

Statue of Kobo Daishi in Shikoku.

KYUSHU

The fascinating history of Nagasaki and the dramatic setting of Kagoshima, facing Japan's most active volcano, draw visitors to Kyushu, birthplace of some of Japan's most independently minded leaders.

Kyushu is far to the south and, it seems at times, almost forgotten by the rest of Japan. Yet the region has always been in the vanguard of development and change. Kyushu is where the Yamato tribe – and thus the Japanese people – first took root in what was to become their homeland. It was Kyushu that withstood the onslaught of the Mongols from the mainland. It is also from where the Japanese first struck out on foreign conquest – the invasion of Korea in 1594 – and where ancient Chinese and Korean culture entered the archipelago as foundations for Japanese art and philosophy. In later years, it was one of the few places where Westerners had a foothold in the xenophobic islands. Kyushu's main cities aren't as cosmopolitan as Tokyo or Osaka, but there is a more welcoming warmth here for visitors, possibly related to the island's long history of openness to outsiders.

Any traveller coming from the north usually enters Kyushu at **Kitakyushu ❶**, considered by some as a city in search of a soul – it is an amalgamation of five cities (Moji, Kokura, Yawata, Tobata and Wakamatsu) with a combined population of almost 1 million. The civic marriage was arranged by Tokyo bureaucrats in 1963, but it has yet to be consummated by a blending of culture or politics. It is a lacklustre

city with little of interest for travellers. Kitakyushu is linked to Shimonoseki on Honshu by a bridge across the Kanmon Strait. Immense steel mills (now an endangered species) and factories were built here to take advantage of the region's rich coal deposits.

Don't, however, let Kitakyushu put you off – Kyushu has so much else to offer, from the hot springs of Beppu and subtropical islands like Yakushima, to charming cities such as Nagasaki, and the fine ceramics of Arita. And that's just scratching the surface.

⊙ Main attractions
Fukuoka
Dazaifu
Yanagawa
Nagasaki
Shimabara Peninsula
Beppu hot springs
Kagoshima and Sakura-jima
Yaku-shima Island

Maps on pages 334, 341

Businessmen in Fukuoka.

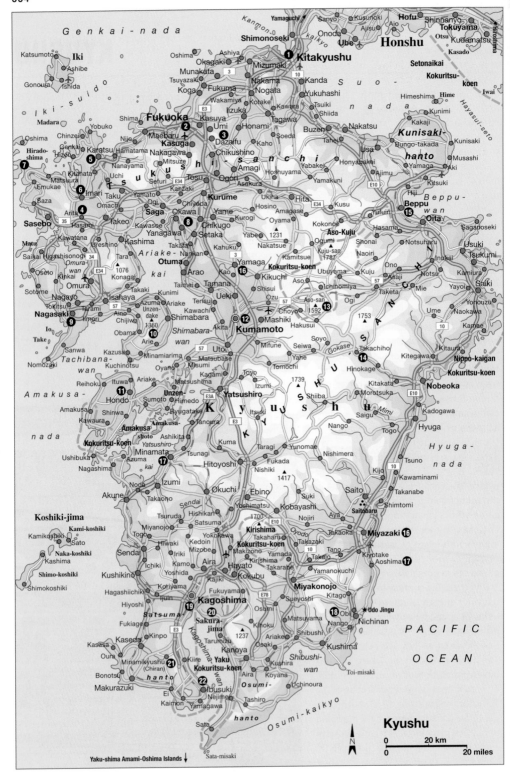

Kyushu

N

| 0 | | 20 km |
| 0 | | 20 miles |

FUKUOKA

Northern Kyushu has a long history of overseas influence. In the 13th century it was targeted by foreign invaders, but other "imports" have been of a more peaceful nature. **Fukuoka** ❷ is reportedly where both tea and Buddhism were introduced to Japan, and Korean captives brought back here were responsible for starting up a sizeable pottery industry. Today, with a population of over 1.5 million, Fukuoka has the beating of Kitakyushu as the largest city on Kyushu. It certainly has more soul.

The city remains an important hub in regional trade and commerce, but while shopping and hotel complexes such as the glistening Canal City dominate the skyline, Fukuoka still retains a lot of charm at ground level. Canals crisscross the central urban area and in the evenings and at weekends small stalls selling snacks and alcohol are set up on the paths beside the water, each an oasis of relaxation and merriment for the hordes of harried *sararimen* ("salarymen") wending their way home from work.

Fukuoka's history has not always been benign. During the Nara and Heian periods, the area was the principal Japanese port for trade with China and Korea, but in 1274 a reconnaissance force of some 30,000 Mongols landed near Fukuoka after annihilating garrisons on the islands of Tsushima and Iki, just to the north of Kyushu in the Korea Strait. The invaders enjoyed similar success on Kyushu, but the death of their commander, along with serious storms that threatened their ships, forced them to retreat. Seven years later, in 1281, Kublai Khan dispatched another Mongol expeditionary force of 150,000 troops, the largest amphibious assault recorded in history prior to World War II. Backed by a ferocious armoury of catapults and cannons, the Mongols gradually wore down the tenacious Japanese resistance, but when they were on the brink of victory after 53 days of fighting, a terrific typhoon – kamikaze (literally, divine wind) – sent most of the invading fleet to the bottom of the sea. Remnants of the defensive wall

⊙ Tip

Fukuoka City International Association (www.fcif.or.jp) daily Mon–Fri 8.45am–6pm), located on the eighth floor of the IMS Building in Tenjin, is an excellent information centre with noticeboards, events calendars, brochures and newspapers in English. http://fukuoka-now.com is another good source of local info and event listings.

Stall selling ramen, Fukuoka.

⊙ FUKUOKA'S YATAI

Yatai – food street stalls – aren't by any means unique to Fukuoka. In fact, most cities have them somewhere. It is doubtful, however, that any have as many of these little mobile kitchens, or indeed as vibrant a *yatai* scene, as Fukuoka, where they have become one of the best known city symbols. Usually open from nightfall to early morning, and covered by cheap plastic tenting that creates something akin to a mini, ramshackle izakaya just big enough for a small handful of customers, there are *yatai* specialising in all manner of cuisine – from staples such as ramen, oden and yakitori to more unusual *yatai* fare like French cuisine. The best places to go *yatai* hunting are Tenjin and Nakasu. Some stalls also sell alcoholic beverages.

⊙ Fact

Hakata Gion Yamagasa takes place in the first half of July. Seven enormous floats are displayed around Fukuoka for a fortnight. On the 15th, groups of brawny men race the floats, which each weigh a tonne, through the streets in a hilarious tumult of noise, excitement and general frenzy.

built to repel the Mongols can still be seen on the outskirts of Fukuoka, although nowadays they are rather unimpressive.

Modern Fukuoka traces its roots to 1601, when a castle was built on the west side of the **Naka-gawa** in what is today Ohori Park, and the town that grew up around the castle took the same name of Fukuoka. Only the castle's walls survive nowadays, but they provide an excellent view over the city. Hakata, a town for merchants who enjoyed a less important status than the ruling samurai, was built on the other side of the river. Hakata-ku has been a ward within Fukuoka since 1889, but the name remains – **Hakata-eki** (Hakata Station), the southern terminus of the *shinkansen* line; Hakata clay dolls; and the popular Hakata Yamagasa festival are all named after the merchant city. In its role as the crossroads between Japan and China, Fukuoka was the place where Zen Buddhism first touched the archipelago's shores. Located northwest of Hakata Station near Mikasa-gawa, **Shofuku-ji**

(always open; free) is the oldest Zen temple in Japan, founded in 1195 by Eisai after years of study in China. Sadly, much of the temple suffered bomb damage during World War II and the current complex is only a fraction of its former self. Eisai is also credited with bringing the first tea seeds into the country.

The **Sumiyoshi-jinja**, the oldest extant Shinto shrine on Kyushu, was built in 1623. South of Shofuku-ji and due west of the train station, it sits atop a hill that provides an excellent city view. A museum, **Hakata Machiya Furusato-kan** (www.hakatamachiya.com; daily 10am–6pm, Jul–Aug 9am–6pm), chronicling the history of the city, is located on a street running almost opposite **Kushida-jinja** (daily 4am–10pm; free, but charge for the shrine's small museum) in the central district of Nakasu, the city's most important shrine.

All in all, Fukuoka today is still very much open to outside influence and sees itself as the cultural crossroads of this part of Asia. The downtown **ACROS Centre** (www.acros.or.jp),

Canal City Mall.

⊙ CANAL DREAMS

Fukuoka's modernity and willingness to experiment is exemplified by the Canal City shopping and entertainment complex (http://canalcity.co.jp). Canal City was created by California architect Jon Jerde, who also designed Universal Studios' cartoon-like City Walk, and the giant Mall of America. Opened in 1996, it was the first mall of its kind in Kyushu to mix shopping and leisure activities in one unified space. Curvaceous walls, like opera or window balconies, with overhanging plants, overlook an artificial canal, with outdoor retail booths and a performance space. Sleek cafés, restaurants and a number of import clothing stores are represented here, along with a 13-theatre IMAX cinema. Canal City's fountains use rain and waste water, which is treated within the complex.

easily recognisable for its imaginative stepped-garden exterior, stages international opera, ballet, symphony orchestras and popular musical extravaganzas, as well as more traditional Japanese performances.

Two other significant structures overlook life in the city. A mammoth seaside stadium, **Fukuoka Yahuoku! Dome**, is home to the SoftBank Hawks baseball team, while the adjacent shopping mall **Markis Fukuoka Momochi** (daily 10am–10pm), opened in 2018, houses cafés, restaurants, shops and a cinema. And a little further along the coast above Momochi-koen stands the 234-metre (768ft) **Fukuoka Tower** (www.fukuokatower.co.jp; daily 9.30am–10pm), with two observation towers that provide stunning views over the surrounding area.

Other points of interest in Fukuoka include **Fukuoka-shi Bijutsukan** (Fukuoka Art Museum; www.fukuoka-art-museum.jp; Tue–Sun 9.30am–5.30pm, July–Oct until 8pm Fri and Sat), a museum housing a collection of Japanese art, and **Ohori-koen** (Ohori Park), a pleasant park harbouring the remains of **Fukuoka-jo** (Fukuoka Castle) and reconstructions of its turret and gates.

DAZAIFU AND AROUND

Forty minutes from Fukuoka and inland to the southeast, **Dazaifu** ❸ is home to **Tenman-gu** (www.dazaifutenmangu.or.jp; main hall: daily, hours vary seasonally but at least 6.30am–6.30pm, until 8.30pm Fri and Sat; free), a shrine built in 1591 to commemorate the poet-scholar Sugawara Michizane, who died in AD 903 after being unjustly exiled from the court in Kyoto. Successive mishaps befell Kyoto supposedly because of Sugawara's banishment. As a result, he gradually came to be acknowledged as *Tenman*, a deity of culture and scholars.

Nowadays, students of all ages tramp over the bright-orange shrine's arched bridge to beseech his help in passing school examinations, which can make or break careers and lives in Japan. Sections of defensive walls built after the first Mongol invasion can still be seen on the road to Dazaifu.

Dazaifu offers a lot more than just a simple pilgrimage to Tenman-gu and its commercial offerings. Rather than bearing left at the end of the approach road to the shrine, turn right and, tucked into a small lane, you will come across a stark Zen garden fronting the grounds of **Komyozen-ji** temple (daily 8am–5pm). Remove your shoes to enter its dimly lit wooden corridors, where Buddhist art and other treasures lurk in the unlit rooms that the temple's trickle of visitors file past. Look closer and you might spot a small camphor statue, Korean bowl or earth-coloured teacup, objects that have been sitting in the shadows for centuries. The rear walkways provide a slightly elevated view of another rock, gravel and moss garden below. Also near Tenmangu is the **Kyushu National Museum** (www.kyuhaku.jp/en; Tue–Sun 9.30am–5pm, Fri–Sat until

Fukuoka Yahuoku! Dome is home of the SoftBank Hawks baseball team.

Dazaifu temple Rock Garden.

Dazaifu shrine.

8pm), which houses a fine collection of artefacts from around Asia and details the influences other Asian cultures have had on Japanese art and crafts.

The **Kanzeon-ji** temple (grounds: always open, free; Treasure Hall: daily 9am–5pm), with its rare ordination stage and great bell, is a 15-minute walk from here. Its Treasure House contains a number of highly prized statues, some of the figures masked, including an unusual horse-headed Kannon. A short walk further on, near a small museum to the site, are the remains of the Tofuro, or City Tower, a lookout post used during the Yamato Period when rebellious tribes, like the Kumaso in southern Kyushu, threatened the realm. There are several axially arranged foundation stones here of former administrative buildings.

Dazaifu's heady blend of religion, historical relics and academia dissolve in the curative waters of **Futsu-kaichi Onsen**, just 3km (2 miles) south. Although this is the closest spa town to Fukuoka, Kyushu's largest city, it rarely gets crowded even at weekends. There

Ceramics made in Arita.

are three hot springs here, conveniently lumped together – the perfect place to nurse out the day's aches and pains.

CERAMIC CITIES

When Ri Simpei, an ordinary Korean potter, first chanced upon *kaolin* clay – the essential ingredient for producing fine porcelain – in **Arita ❹**, 50km (30 miles) west of Fukuoka around the turn of the 17th century, he probably had little notion of the ramifications of his discovery.

Nearly 400 years later, Arita and its neighbours **Karatsu ❺** and **Imari ❻** are the hub of a thriving pottery industry. The delicate craftsmanship and brightly coloured glazes that are the hallmarks of pottery from this region are prized all over Japan, and further afield, too. Simpei and the other potters who were brought over from Korea as prisoners of the Nabeshima daimyo were kept under close guard so their trade secrets did not slip out.

To understand something about those times, the **Nabeshima Hanyo-koen** at Okawachiyama (a short bus ride from Imari) portrays the sort of techniques Simpei and his fellow workers used and the conditions in which they lived. There are plenty of working potteries in the area as well, but **Kyushu Toji Bunkakan** (Kyushu Ceramic Museum; http://saga-museum. jp/ceramic; Tue–Sun 9am–5pm) in Arita is the best place to view the full range of Kyushu pottery. Imaizumi Imaemon and Sakaida Kakiemon are celebrated workshops with galleries and shops open to the public.

Karatsu is also highly regarded for its stoneware. Several galleries and workshops, including the Nakazato Taro-emon and the Ryuta kilns, are open to visitors. The Hikiyama Tenijo museum exhibits 19th-century Karatsu *kunchi* festival floats, which are paraded through the town every 2–4 November. **Saga**, a pottery town in its own right, is an excellent base from which to explore

the three principal ceramic centres of Arita, Imari and Karatsu.

For a breath of ocean air, take a stroll or hire a bike to explore the pine groves of **Niji-no-Matsubara**, which stretch along the beach found at Matsuragate.

HIRADO

Some 40km (25 miles) west of Imari, the focus shifts to Japan's early Christians. The first foreign settlement in Japan was established by Dutch traders on **Hirado-shima ❼** (Hirado Island) in 1550, although the one-time island is now connected to the mainland by a bridge. The Francis Xavier Memorial Chapel consecrates the Spanish saint's visit to Hirado after he was expelled from Kagoshima in southern Kyushu. European activity here ended when the Dutch were forced to move to Dejima, in Nagasaki harbour, in 1641. But secretive Christians maintained a version of the faith here for centuries afterwards, often under the threat of imprisonment and death. This bit of historical lore has provided the basis for a thriving domestic tourist industry here, with "real" icons for sale.

YANAGAWA

Like Kyoto, **Yanagawa ❽**, under an hour on the Nishitetsu Omuta Line from Fukuoka Station, is a water city. The angularity of Yanagawa's grid of canals contrasts intriguingly with the winding lanes of the Old Town that transects it. An aerial view would no doubt reveal something like an octopus on a chequerboard.

Yanagawa was founded by the Kamachi clan in the 16th century. Its water sources, however, are far older, dating back to the Yayoi Period, when an area of damp lowland existed near the mouth of several rivers that funnelled into the nearby Ariake Sea. Canals were dug to drain the land and improve its agricultural prospects. The canals remain more or less intact, covering a total length of 470km (290

miles). In fact, 12 percent of the town's surface area is water.

It's a comfortable place to stroll through, though many visitors elect to view the town, its willow-lined canals flowing by old samurai villas, luxuriating back gardens and old brick storehouses, from the comfort of a canal barge. The vessels are propelled by boatmen who, like Oxbridge punters, use poles to propel the barges along the currentless waterways. During winter months the boats install quilts with heaters placed underneath.

If you opt to walk, one building in particular worth checking out is the **Former Residence of the Toshima Family** (Wed–Mon 9am–5pm), which is built in sukiya style, complete with thatched roof and pretty ornamental garden. Pick up a free copy of the "strolling map" from Yanagawa's tourist office (or download it from www.yanagawa-net.com), and it will lead you to many more intriguing buildings.

Eating baked and steamed *unagi no seiromushi*, rice and eel steamed with a sauce made from sugar and soy, with

Fugu/blowfish sashimi.

Hirado with Xavier Memorial Chapel in the background.

⊙ Fact

Fugu, or blowfish, is the local speciality and is reputed to be especially good if prepared incorrectly, deadly toxins can poison the diner. For this reason you have to go to a specialist fish restaurant to sample it. Be warned – the extra training the chef needs to prepare the blowfish, and the inherent risk in serving it, are reflected in the price.

a finely sliced omelette on top, is part of the Yanagawa experience. The fish is said to increase a person's stamina and virility, especially during the dog days of summer. At lunchtime the whole town seems to smell of baked eel, as charcoal-coloured smoke billows out into the street from vents at the side of restaurants. In winter, visitors can sample duck. *Yanagawa* nabe, small fish cooked with local vegetables and egg in an earthenware pot, is another local speciality.

NAGASAKI

Like Hiroshima, **Nagasaki** ➒ is a name automatically associated with the atomic bomb that brought World War II to its terrible and tumultuous climax. It is particularly ironic that this devastating manifestation of Western technology should have been detonated in a city that was one of the first to open up to the outside world and where foreign inventions and ways were once eagerly adopted.

The path was not always smooth, of course, and many early Christian converts were brutally executed and foreign

Pleasure boats exploring Yanagawa's canals.

residents were expelled from time to time. But Nagasaki was one of the first Japanese cities to take a serious interest in Western medicine. It was here, too, that the first railway and modern shipyard in Japan were established.

Now home to nearly half a million people, Nagasaki clings to steep hills wrapped around a very active deepwater harbour, competing with Kobe for designation as Japan's San Francisco. Like San Francisco, it has a lively Chinatown and a continuing spirit of receptiveness to novel ideas. As it is one of the most interesting cities in Japan, even travellers on a restricted time budget should allow for two days or more to explore Nagasaki and its surroundings.

Nagasaki's harbour has played a prominent role in Japan's relations with the outside world. Dutch traders initiated the first sustained European presence here, on an island in the harbour that also acted as a conduit for most of the early Christian missionaries. The port at Nagasaki was established in 1571 to serve Portuguese traders. A decade later, Omura Sumitada, a local daimyo who had grown rich on trade with the foreigners, turned over partial administration of the port to the Jesuit missionaries who followed in the merchants' wake.

A generation later, fearing that the Christians and their converts would subvert his authority, the shogun Toyotomi Hideyoshi banned Christianity. He ordered six Spanish priests and 20 Japanese Christians, including two teenage boys, to be rounded up in Kyoto and Osaka. They were brought to Nagasaki and crucified in 1597 as a warning to Japan's largest Christian community. A memorial constructed in 1962 and related Memorial Hall (www.peacenagasaki.go.jp; daily May–Aug 8.30am–6.30pm, Sept–Apr 8.30am–5.30pm) stands in **Nishizaka-koen** (Nishizaka Park) on the spot of the crucifixions, near **Nagasaki-eki** ➊ (Nagasaki Station) at the north end of downtown.

Christianity was utterly and viciously suppressed following the Christian-led Shimbara Rebellion of 40,000 peasants south of Nagasaki in 1637. As a result, Japan's sole officially sanctioned contact with Europeans for the next two centuries was through a settlement on **Dejima** Ⓑ (http://nagasakidejima.jp), in Nagasaki harbour and south of the present-day Nagasaki Station. The artificial island – now part of the mainland – was built for Portuguese traders but it was occupied by the Dutch after the Portuguese were banished in 1638. Its occupants were confined to a small, walled area and contact with Japanese was limited to a small circle of officials, traders, prostitutes and, in the later years, scholars.

As no other Europeans were permitted in Japan until 1854, whatever news of European technology and culture filtered into Japan came through this settlement. The **Shiryokan** (Dejima Museum; daily 8am–9pm) near the site preserves relics of the settlement.

Like the Dutch, Nagasaki's Chinese, mostly from Fujian along China's southern coast, were officially confined to a walled ghetto, but restrictions on their movements were not as strictly enforced. The Chinese in Nagasaki left the only pure Chinese architecture to be found in Japan, along with one of the country's three remaining Chinatowns (the others are in Yokohama and Kobe). The narrow and winding streets of **Shinchimachi** are filled with Chinese restaurants catering to tourists, as there are very few Chinese remaining in Nagasaki.

Two popular "Chinese" dishes in Japan, saraudon (meat, seafood and vegetables served on a bed of crispy noodles) and champpon (similar, except served in broth instead of with crispy noodles), were invented in Shinchimachi. Like most of the foreign food served in Japan, they bear only a passing resemblance to the original but they are still quite palatable. On the subject of food, the other "foreign" delicacy that survives in Nagasaki is the kasutera, or sponge cake, that is supposedly baked to an old Portuguese recipe and sold (in exquisitely wrapped packages) in bakeries around town.

Peace Statue in Peace Park, Nagasaki.

Nagasaki City Temple.

The Chinese community was granted permission to build its own temples. Teramachi (Temple Town) contains two of the oldest Chinese temples in Japan, as well as numerous Japanese Buddhist temples and graveyards. **Kofuku-ji** (www.kohfukuji.com; daily 9am–5pm), founded in 1620, was built on the edge of the original Chinatown in the northeast part of town. The Chinese quarters burned down in 1698; the current Shinchi-machi occupies land designated for Chinese merchants following the fire. Centrally located, **Sofuku-ji** Ⓓ (daily 8am–5pm) is a bright, elaborate Ming-style temple and is in better condition than most Ming-era temples in China. The Masodo (Hall of the Bodhisattva) contains an image of the goddess of the seas, flanked by fierce guardians reputed to have thousand-mile vision. Nagasaki's premier shrine, **Suwa-jinja**, is a 10-minute walk north. Points of interest include a graceful main hall, a curious collection of guardian lions and an imposing horse statue, and the shrine's dynamic festival, the Kunchi

Sofoku-ji Temple.

Matsuri, held annually on 7–9 October. A few blocks west of Suwa is the **Nagasaki Museum of History and Culture** (www.nmhc.jp; daily 8.30am–7pm; closed third Mon of each month), which gives insights into Nagasaki's role as a meeting point between Japan and other cultures.

Within walking distance of the temples, the **Nakashima-gawa** (Nakashima River) is spanned by a picturesque range of bridges. The best known and most photographed is **Megane-bashi** Ⓔ, whose English translation of Spectacles Bridge makes immediate sense when there is enough water in the river to ensure a good reflection. The original bridge was the oldest stone arch bridge in Japan, built in 1634 by a priest from Kofuku-ji. However, a flood in 1962 destroyed it and the present structure is a carbon-copy restoration.

True to its traditional receptiveness to new ideas, Nagasaki embarked on an aggressive modernisation campaign in the latter part of the 19th century. Thomas Glover, a Scotsman, was one of the first and most significant of the European traders who arrived soon after Commodore Matthew Perry's Black Ships reopened the country. Glover helped Nagasaki achieve many Japanese firsts: the first railway, the first mint and the first printing press with movable type were all built in Nagasaki as a result of his efforts. He was also very active in supporting the rebels who defeated the shogun's forces – mainly through a profitable line in gun-running – and re-established the emperor's rule in 1868 in the Meiji Restoration. There is considerable controversy over whether Glover's marriage to a geisha did, as many guidebooks assert, inspire Puccini's opera *Madame Butterfly*. Glover also built the first Western-style mansion in Japan.

At the southern end of the city, **Glover-en** Ⓕ (Glover Gardens; www.

glover-garden.jp; daily, late Apr–early-Oct 8am–9.30pm, early Oct–late Apr 8am–6pm, some periods until 8pm) contains this mansion, built in 1863, and several other early Meiji-era, Western-style houses – elegant mixtures of Japanese and European architecture plus the inevitable statues of Puccini and his tragic Japanese heroine. It is amusing to wander around the grounds today, which now have vending machines, covered escalators and recorded announcements, and speculate that these are technological innovations of which Glover himself would have approved.

If your trip does not coincide with the annual Kunchi Festival in early October, when Chinese-style dragon dances and parades are held in the vicinity of Suwa-jinja, a trip to the **Kunchi Shiryokan** (Performing Arts Museum; daily 8am–6pm) near Glover Garden will at least give a visitor some idea of the floats and costumes involved.

Nearby in the same neighbourhood is **Oura Tenshu-do** (Oura Catholic Church; daily 8am–6pm), said to be the oldest Gothic-style structure in Japan. Completed in 1865, it is dedicated to the 26 Christian martyrs who were crucified in the 16th century and has some fine examples of stained glass. Signposts point along a paved footpath east of the church to an interesting enclave of foreign influence, the **Dutch Slopes**.

The highly conspicuous **Koshi-byo**, a red and orange lacquered Confucian temple (http://nagasaki-koushibyou.com, daily 8.30am–5.30pm), lies close by the slopes. It's one of just a handful of Confucian temples in Japan, and the treasures within its sanctuary are sumptuous.

A CITY REMEMBERS

A simple stone obelisk stands at the epicentre ("hypocentre" in Japan) of the atomic blast that devastated much of Nagasaki on the morning of 9 August 1945. The plutonium bomb, which was nearly twice as powerful as the uranium bomb dropped earlier over Hiroshima, landed about 3km (2 miles) off course over **Urakami**, a Christian village just to the north of downtown. (The Mitsubishi Heavy Industry shipyard, on

Spectacles Bridge, Nagasaki.

the west side of the port and the first modern shipbuilding facility in Japan, was the intended target; the pilot's vision was hampered by poor visibility.)

Urakami Roman Catholic Church, the largest Christian church in Japan, stood a few hundred metres from the epicentre; it was rebuilt in 1958. Headless statues of saints scorched in the blast remain as mute witnesses to the tragedy. A similarly poignant memorial is the small hut used by Dr Takashi Nagai, who struggled to treat bomb victims as best he could until he himself succumbed to radiation sickness in 1951.

The **Atomic Bomb Museum** Ⓖ (http://nagasakipeace.jp; daily, May–Aug 8.30am–6.30pm, Sept–Apr 8.30am–5.30pm) at the International Culture Hall contains photos, relics and poignant details of the blast and its 150,000 victims. Simple objects – a melted bottle, the charred remains of a kimono – as well as photos of victims provide stark evidence of the bomb's destructive powers.

As important as its displays are, the museum fails to provide historical context or background to the bombing. Arguments for and against this revolve around whether it is appropriate to include Japan's appalling war record, and thereby attribute partial blame for the bombing to the Japanese, or whether this undoubted atrocity against humanity should be allowed to stand for itself.

Heiwa-koen Ⓗ (Peace Park) is dominated by the Peace Statue – a man with right hand pointing to the sky (signalling the threat from the atomic bomb) and left hand extended (symbolising world peace). The Peace Fountain, on the south side of the park, was built in remembrance of the bomb victims who died crying for water. Heiwa-koen was built on the site of a former jail, whose occupants and warders were all killed in the blast. On the other side of the harbour, the cable car (Nagasaki Ropeway; www.nagasaki-ropeway.jp; daily 9am–10pm) climbing the 332-metre (1,089ft) peak of **Inasa-yama** Ⓘ provides fantastic vistas of the harbour and surrounding hills, especially at night. Further south is the Mitsubishi shipyard, the intended target for the atomic bomb.

An hour out of Nagasaki stands **Huis Ten Bosch** (www.huistenbosch.co.jp; daily, closing times varying often, but at least 9am–7pm last admission), one of the most graceful theme parks in Japan with many replicas of Dutch buildings and windmills, canals and clogs galore. Theme park is perhaps an inaccurate description, as Huis Ten Bosch has been carefully constructed on environmentally friendly lines and stands as a modern-day testimony to the area's close links with the Dutch. There is something particularly Japanese about the place in the way that the replicas are built to look precisely like the originals, even to the point of making the Amsterdam canal houses lean out at an angle over the water. Once through the pricey gate most attractions are free, and watching the Japanese tourists

Huis Ten Bosch.

dressing up in traditional Dutch clothing for photos is as much fun as examining the architecture.

SHIMABARA PENINSULA

Leaving Nagasaki a scenic route takes travellers through **Shimabara Peninsula** and the Amakusa Islands to Kumamoto on a combination of buses and ferries. Down the peninsula, roughly midway between Nagasaki and Kumamoto, is **Unzen-dake** ⑩, whose *jigoku* (hell) pits of boiling mud and coloured mineral waters are less dramatic but less commercialised than those in Beppu, on the east coast of Kyushu. In the 17th century, Christians who refused to renounce their faith were thrown into these *jigoku*. The town is named after the 1,360-metre (4,460ft) volcano Unzen-dake, on the peninsula and in **Unzen-Amakusa Kokuritsu-koen** (Unzen-Amakusa National Park; www.env.go.jp/park/unzen/index. html). Unzen erupted in 1991, causing widespread death and damage. **Shimabara-jo** (Shimabara Castle; daily 9am–5.30pm), destroyed in a 1637 Christian rebellion, was reconstructed in 1964. The castle houses a museum displaying the *fumi-e* Christian images, which suspected believers were forced to walk upon. **Amakusa-shoto** (Amakusa Islands), about 70 islands in all, lie between Unzen and Kumamoto. The Kirishitankan in **Hondo** ⑪ is a museum with relics of the Amakusa Christians.

KUMAMOTO

Although it isn't a popular tourist destination, **Kumamoto** ⑫ is an interesting and dynamic provincial capital. This city of over 0.7 million people is best known for its 17th-century castle, 350-year-old **Suizenji-jojuen** (Suizenji Park), and its horse-meat sashimi. Kumamoto also has the most successful technical research park (adjacent to the airport) in Japan. Kumamoto Prefecture has a sister-state relationship with the American state of Montana, due more to the power and influence of the former American ambassador to Japan, Mike Mansfield, a Montanan, than to any similarity between the two places.

Atomic Bomb Museum.

⊘ MINAMATA

The bay near **Minamata**, in the southern part of Kumamoto Prefecture, is a monument to the excesses of industry. A severely debilitating and often fatal ailment known as Minamata disease was traced to shellfish and other products taken from its waters, into which industries had been discharging mercury and other wastes for decades. Legislation hurriedly passed by the Diet soon after the disease's discovery in the 1970s now constitutes the basis of Japan's still weak pollution controls. Nevertheless, litigation regarding the responsibility for the mercury dumping was dragged out until the mid-1990s, with no entity admitting responsibility. Minamata Bay itself has been reclaimed and turned into an ecological park with numerous green spaces, restaurants and gift shop.

Kumamoto-jo (Kumamoto Castle; http://kumamoto-guide.jp/kumamoto-castle) was built in 1607 by Kato Kiyomasa. Unfortunately, the castle's 49 towers were made of wood and most were incinerated in an 1877 siege and damaged again in an earthquake in April, 2016. The castle's grandeur can still be observed from Ninomaru Square and Kato Shrine, but it's advisable to check the website for areas open to tourists as restoration proceeds.

Honmyo-ji (daily 6am–5pm), a Nichiren temple housing Kato's tomb, can be seen from the castle's towers. The basement of the **Kumamoto Prefectural Traditional Crafts Centre** (http://kumamoto-kougeikan.jp; Tue–Sun 9am–5pm), across the street from the castle, is a good place to enjoy a cup of tea, while the first floor has a colourful collection of toys, tools, jewellery and ceramics produced by Kumamoto craftsmen. The museum is part of the prefecture's efforts to sustain traditional crafts, largely abandoned after World War II. **Suizenji-Jojuen** (daily, Mar–Oct 7.30am–6pm, Nov–Feb

Kumamoto-jo.

8.30am–5pm), designed in 1632 and south of the modern city, contains in its lush, sprawling grounds landscaped models of Mount Fuji and a 400-year-old teahouse that serves matcha and sweets.

The Kyushu Kokusai Kanko Bus has regular departures for **Aso-Kuju Kokuritsu-koen** (Aso-Kuju National Park; www.env.go.jp/park/aso/index.html), but the JR Hohi Line switchback train from Kumamoto to Aso affords great views.

Signposts along the roads welcome visitors to *Hi-no-Kuni*, the "Land of Fire". **Mount Aso** ⑬ is actually a series of five volcanic cones, its massive caldera stretching to a circumference of 128km (80 miles). Of the five peaks, Daikanbo, at 936 metres (3,070ft), is the highest. **Nakadake**, the massive, highly active crater, which is the highlight of an Aso trip for many, emits sulphurous fumes and high-temperature gases that occasionally bring hiking above the basin to an abrupt halt. It last erupted in 2019, and the area within 1km of the crater was still off-limits at the time of writing (check the latest information on www.aso.ne.jp/~volcano/eng/index.html). The ideal way to explore the area beyond the main road connecting the caldera with the town would normally be by bicycle – a steep ride up, a blissful one down – or time permitting, on foot. You could also get to Mount Aso's crater edge by cable car (however, due to increased volcanic activity, the service was suspended at the time of writing).

Once in the caldera, a striking shape materialises on the right-hand side of the road. This is the grass-covered hill known as **Komezuka**, the name meaning "inverted rice-bowl". Equally suggestive of the ziggurat or burial mound of some ancient nature cult, it is a configuration of great beauty.

Buses en route for Nakadake stop a little further on at Kusasenri-ga-Hama, a circular plain that was originally a minor crater. A large pond at its centre serves as a watering hole for cattle and horses. The **Aso Volcano Museum** (www.asomuse.jp; daily 9am–5pm), with its 170-degree multiscreens relaying images of the crater and its catchment area, is also here. All this subterranean activity means superb hot springs, most found in the caldera itself, though there are *onsen* retreats tucked away in the highlands nearby as well.

East of Kumamoto and on the other side of Aso, the shrine at **Takachiho** ⑭ is where the *iwato kagura*, a sacred dance, is performed for tourists every night (daily 8pm). **Takachiho-kyo** (Takachiho Gorge), with its 80-metre (260ft) cliffs, is another one of the many spots where the Sun Goddess Amaterasu is said to have emerged from her cave to create the islands and people of the archipelago. A cave near the shrine at Iwato is touted as the very one.

HOT SPRINGS

If seeking to go to hell and back, head for **Beppu** ⑮ on the northeastern coast of Kyushu. The resort town is famous – and thus highly commercialised – for its *jigoku*, or variously coloured ponds of water and mud that steam and boil, as well as its hot springs. A popular destination for Japanese tourists, Beppu is gaudy and rather tacky and a far cry from the serene elegance of Japanese travel posters. Besides the hype, there are other hells, more than can be experienced in a lifetime, including: Blood Pond Hell, a vermillion-coloured boiling pond; Sea Hell, a boiling mud pond 120 metres (400ft) deep; and Mountain Hell, a mud pond in the hills, complete with statues of gorillas. All these are far too hot for bathing, but in the many *onsen* inns, comfortable hot-sand and hot-mud baths are available.

A more serene and sophisticated hot-spring resort, **Yufuin**, less than an hour inland from Beppu, is known for its galleries, elegant country inns, fashionable guesthouses, and the beautiful morning mists that rise from the warm, thermal waters of **Lake Kinrin**. Bicycles can be rented for a circuit of the lake, and hiking trails taken up nearby Mount Yufu or through the woods.

About 40km (25 miles) south along the coast from Beppu, the **Usuki Sekibutsu** (http://sekibutsu.com; daily 6am–6pm, Apr–Sept until 7pm), a collection of more than 60 stone Buddhas, is all that remains of the **Mangetsu-ji**, once an important temple. The stone images are some of the most exquisite and mysterious Buddhist images in Japan. It takes less than an hour to take in the statues, but it's still worth the jaunt here and back from Beppu.

Descending Kyushu's rugged east coast to its southern end, the pleasant provincial city of **Miyazaki** ⑯, with its locally grown mangoes, palm-lined streets and golf, pool and spa resort Phoenix Seagaia Resort (www.seagaia.co.jp) is a convenient stopover on the

Fact

Obi was once a thriving merchant centre. The main road through the castle town has several fine examples of whitewashed merchant houses dating from the Edo to early Showa periods, some now serving as stores and museums.

Shimabara-jo.

way to the Nichinan coast that stretches south of the city. The delightfully rural Nichinan Line train follows the shore, taking a slightly inland route.

Aoshima , a seaside resort with plenty of action and animation of the modern kind at its beaches, cafés, hotels and amusement arcades, is the most popular stop on the line. Patronised by sun-worshippers and weekend surfers, Aoshima's main draw is its tiny subtropical island of the same name, surrounded by great platforms of "devil's washboard" – eroded rock formations with row upon row of shallow pools and indented octopusshaped rings sunk into long furrows of basalt – which disappear at high tide.

OBI AND ITS CASTLE

The crowds rarely make it as far as the old samurai town of **Obi**, a few stops slightly inland on the Nichinan Line and another town that has taken to calling itself "Little Kyoto". A quiet trickle of discerning Japanese visitors (and virtually no foreigners as yet) file in and out of its gardens and samurai

villas, though you will often find yourself left alone.

At the core of the old quarter, 15 minutes on foot from Obi Station, Otemon-dori, a ramrod-straight avenue lined with old houses, plaster storerooms and stone and clay walls topped with ceramic tiles, leads to the superbly restored Ote-mon, or main gate, the entrance to the **Obi Castle** grounds (daily 9.30am–4.30pm).

Destroyed in 1870, only its walls, carefully reconstructed in the original style using joinery rather than nails, and a whitewashed history museum, remain. Up a further flight of steps in the castle precincts, the Edo Period **Matsuo-no-Maru** (daily 9am–5pm), the residence of Lord Ito's most senior wife (yes, he had a few!), is a faithful replica of the original, complete with women's quarters, reception rooms and the *chashitsu*, a beautifully stark tea-ceremony room.

The wooden gate to the **Yoshokan** (daily 9am–5pm), former residence of the Ito clan, is just to the left of the Ote-mon. Obi's most graceful samurai

Beppu Hot Springs.

residence, this airy construction was built for the family's chief retainer and then requisitioned for their own use after feudal holdings were abolished in the Meiji era. All the rooms in the Yoshokan face south in conformity with tradition and the rules of geomancy. Each chamber overlooks a fine dry landscape garden with the ultimate *shakkei*, or "borrowed view", in the form of Mount Atago.

Proceeding south, **Ishinami beach** is one of the finest stretches of unspoilt white sand along the Nichinan coast. **Kojima**, at the southern end of the cove, is inhabited by wild monkeys. A cluster of rustic farmhouses, doubling in the summer months as minshuku (lodgings), lie within a short stroll of the beach. **Toi Misaki**, a scenic but overdeveloped cape marred by tacky hotels and other resort facilities, marks the southern tip of this extraordinary, timeworn coast.

KAGOSHIMA

This prefecture in the far south of Kyushu consists of two peninsulas, Satsuma and Osumi, that encircle **Kagoshima-wan** (Kagoshima Bay), and also a chain of islands stretching south towards Okinawa. **Kagoshima ⑲**, on the interior side of Satsuma-hanto and the southernmost metropolis in Kyushu, is situated on large Kagoshima Bay. It is famous for being Japan's most polluted city. The pollution comes from **Sakura-jima ⑳** (Cherry Blossom Island), the very active volcano east across the bay that rises 1,120 metres (3,670ft) directly above the water. The mountain has erupted more than 5,000 times since 1955, sending clouds of ash and often large boulders raining down on Kagoshima. (Umbrellas are used as much against ash as against rain.) More than half a million people live within 10km (6 miles) of Sakura-jima's crater. No other major city is as precariously positioned; Naples,

Kagoshima's sister city, is twice as far from Vesuvius.

Sakura-jima itself can be reached via a short ferry ride from Kagoshima or by road around the periphery of the bay. As the name indicates, it was once an island, but an eruption in 1914 spilled some 3 billion tonnes of lava down its southeast flank, joining it to the peninsula. There are dramatic views from the **Yogan Tenbodai** on the southeast side of Sakura-jima. Extra-large daikon (Japanese radishes) grow in the rich volcanic soil, along with kumquats, summer oranges and other fruits.

SATSUMA CLANS

Aside from the ash and sometimes polluted air of Kagoshima, the city itself is delightful and retains the spirit of the once-powerful Satsuma clans, from whom the area takes its name. The Satsumas were ruled by the Shimazu daimyo, among the most dynamic of the Japanese hereditary rulers, for seven centuries. The Shimazu's distance from Edo Tokyo bred a fierce

⊘ **Fact**

Minamikyushu is best known for its miniature Edo Period gardens, six of which are open to the public. Background scenery, such as mountains, forest and hills, are used as part of the garden as "borrowed views". The top of the hedges are clipped into angles to match the outline of the hills.

Minamata disease memorial, with a box containing the names of those that died.

independence here in southern Kyushu. The Shimazu were open to new ideas from abroad. They welcomed Francis Xavier to Kagoshima, the first Japanese city he visited, in 1549. Returning from Japan's ill-fated invasion of the Korean peninsula in the early 17th century, the Shimazu brought captive Korean potters to Kagoshima, where they developed Satsuma-ware.

Despite their receptiveness to outsiders, the Satsuma clans opposed the Edo shogunate's capitulation to European demands that Japan open its ports to trade. Demonstrating resistance to the shogun's edicts, Shimazu retainers killed an Englishman near Edo in 1862. The British retaliated the following year by sending a squadron of ships to bombard Kagoshima. To the British sailors' surprise, the lords of Satsuma admired this demonstration of modern naval power. They welcomed Her Majesty's officers to the still smoking city and purchased some of their ships. In 1866, the Satsuma clans joined with the rival Choshu clan in a successful military coup against the shogun, which restored imperial rule with the Meiji Restoration in 1868. (Close relations between the Japanese and British navies lasted until the 1920s, and Satsuma clansmen dominated Japan's navy until World War II.)

Satsuma-ware and the more rustic Kuro-Satsuma pottery can be purchased in **Naeshirogawa**, a village that was settled by Korean potters in the 1600s. In addition to pottery, Kagoshima is known for *kiriko* cut glass.

Iso-koen, containing a garden laid out in 1661, provides excellent views of Sakura-jima. Just outside the park, the **Shoko Shuseikan** (History Museum; www.shuseikan.jp; daily 8.30am–5.30pm) houses one of the first Western-style factories in Japan. It contains exhibits on the factory and the Shimazu family, whose mansion has also been preserved.

The cemetery of Nanshu holds the remains of Saigo Takamori (1827–77), who led the forces that defeated the shogun. Saigo later perished after leading the 1877 rebellion against the Meiji regime he had created. Saigo made his last stand at the hill called Shiroyama. With defeat inevitable, he had a loyal follower decapitate him.

Twelve buses leave Kagoshima every day for the near-1.5-hour ride south to **Minamikyushu** (formerly Chiran) ㉑, a charming samurai town set in a pastoral landscape of striking warmth, a concentration of green volcanic peaks, tea plantations and white stucco-faced houses.

The *tokko-tai*, better known in the West as kamikaze pilots, flew from what was then called Chiran and other bases in southern Kyushu, on the first leg of their one-way missions. Visitors should view the **Tokko Heiwa Kaikan** (Peace Museum for Kamikaze Pilots; www.chiran-tokkou. jp; 9am–5pm), a 3–4km (2–3-mile)

A Yaku-shima cedar.

taxi or bus ride into the hills north of town. A rather splendid plane, superior to the hastily refurbished trainers most flew, greets visitors to the open space beside the museum. The museum's centrepiece, its **Peace Hall**, was completed in 1975. Its collection, though chilling, is more sentimental than gruesome, with drawers full of uniforms, flying gear and adolescent mascots, its walls and cabinets bristling with letters and photos. In one image, a pilot tightens the rising-sun *hachimaki* bandanna of a comrade, a symbol of samurai valour and pre-battle composure, around the head of a doomed but smiling youth.

Ibusuki ㉒ is a spa town southeast of Minamikyushu with hot-sand baths near **Kaimon-dake**, a 900-metre (3,000ft) volcano looking much like Fuji.

YAKU-SHIMA

A circular island 1,000km (600 miles) southwest of Tokyo and 135km (80 miles) from Kagoshima, **Yaku-shima** is a naturalist's fantasy, declared a UN World Heritage Site in 1993 for its flora. There is the rare Yakushima rhododendron, and the *Yaku-sugi* cedar trees that are over 1,000 years old. (Youthful cedar trees less than 1,000 years old are *ko-sugi*.) Existing at 700 to 1,500 metres (2,300–5,000ft) on the slopes of some of Yaku-shima's 40 peaks that are higher than 1,000 metres (600ft), the cedar trees are like elderly sages amidst the dense foliage. The largest cedar is said to be the world's biggest, with a circumference of 43 metres (141ft) at its roots, a trunk circumference of 16.4 metres (54ft) and a height of 25 metres (80ft). The Japanese also claim that it is the oldest in the world at 7,200 years, but there is some dispute about this.

Waterfalls and lush hiking trails lace this ancient volcanic island, which is nearly 30km (20 miles) in diameter. Once you are done exploring them, head to the island's coast, where you will find several good dive spots and places worth snorkelling. The two small towns of **Anbo** and **Miyanoura** are home to most of the island's 13,000 people and have accommodation and places to rent dive gear.

AMAMI ISLANDS

Just before Kyushu gives way to Okinawa, and some 300km (200 miles) south of Yaku-shima, are the **Amami Islands**. The largest of these eight islands, **Amami Oshima**, reached by air or ferry from Kyushu, has some great diving spots that take divers to vivid coral in a rich ocean ecosystem. On land, which is 95 percent covered by forest and thick mangrove, the island's wildlife is on a par with Yakushima – it's home to a rare species of hare and the beautiful Lidth's jay bird. Less travelled than many of the Okinawan Islands, with which it shares a Ryukyuan cultural heritage, a trip here is something you will share with few other foreign travellers.

Sakurajima volcano.

Snorkeling in Okinawa.

OKINAWA

Once an independent kingdom called Ryukyu, Okinawa is a world of its own. Bloodied by World War II, sultry Okinawa is today Japan's domestic resort escape.

Extending for 1,200km (746 miles) southwest from Kyushu, the 70-plus islands of the Ryukyus, or **Nansei-shoto**, stretch across the ocean to within 200km (125 miles) of Taiwan. For centuries, the Okinawans minded their own business and accommodated themselves to outsiders. But during the age of imperialism in the late 19th century, their independence fell prey to the ambitions of powerful neighbours.

Ryukyu is the Japanese pronunciation of the Chinese name Liugiu, which is what the Ming-dynasty Chinese called the islands. Taken over by Japan, which then long ignored the islands like a faraway province, Okinawa was the final beachhead for a planned Allied invasion of the Japanese archipelago in World War II. The battle for Okinawa was bloody for both sides and for the Okinawan civilians. Placed under American control by the UN following the end of World War II, the islands reverted to Japanese sovereignty in 1972. Now, all islands north of the main island of Okinawa are part of Kyushu, and the main island and islands to the south are in Okinawa Prefecture.

Okinawa sits in a subtropical belt, blessed with average temperatures of around 23°C (73°F). A short rainy season blankets the area in heavy rains during May and June. Spring and autumn are enjoyable, typhoons in September and October notwithstanding.

There are the exquisite white-sand beaches and azure waters of the Yaeyama and Kerama Islands, not to mention some unusual flora and fauna – no wonder Okinawa is, along with Guam, Japan's backyard resort escape. Not that Okinawa is only about beaches – Unesco recognised the local Ryukyu culture in 2000, when they designated a group of historic Ryukyuan sites, including Shuri Castle, as Japan's 11th World Heritage Site.

Main attractions
Naha
Himeyuri-no-To
Okinawa World
Nakagusuku
Motobu Peninsula
Zamami Island
Miyako Island
Ishigaki Island

Maps on pages
354, 359

Shisa figurine, Taketomi Island.

Awamori cup and jar.

Okinawans are proud of their heritage and will often remind travellers that they are not Japanese. A fine and relaxing manner in which to gauge the differences between Okinawa and the rest of Japan is a visit to a local pub to listen to the frequently plaintive sounds of the *sanshin*, the three-stringed, snakeskin-covered Okinawan banjo known elsewhere as the shamisen. Traditional Okinawan dance and theatre differ considerably from their Japanese counterparts.

Okinawans are also quite proud of their exquisite textiles, which are typically hand-woven from linen and silk and feature beautiful designs created with painted-on dyes. The designs traditionally differed by area, and the *bingata* stencil-dyed fabric, originally made exclusively for aristocrats, is the most highly prized of the fabrics.

And no visit to Okinawa would be complete without sampling Okinawa's distinctive food and drink, ranging from "delicacies" such as pig ears and trotters to the fiery Okinawan version of shochu, *awamori*, which packs a vodka-like punch.

Making sanshin, an Okinawan musical instrument.

NAHA

The centre of Okinawa's tourism is the city of **Naha ❶**, and Naha's centre of tourist activity is Kokusai-dori (International Road), which is a jangle of typical Japanese urban architecture – cluttered and without aesthetic appeal – and crowds of walkers and swarms of vehicles. Yet only a short distance away are typically Okinawan neighbourhoods. **Naminou-gu**, a small Confucian shrine, and the **Gokoku-ji**, a temple that was once considered a national religious centre, are along the waterfront not far from the central post office and just north of an old pleasure quarter that retains its fair share of bars, cabarets and steakhouses.

Okinawan crafts are a delight. Active since 1617, the **Tsuboya** pottery district, off Himeyuri-dori and southeast of Kokusai-dori, houses two dozen kilns that make everything from the *kara-kara* flasks once carried by country gentlemen to the fearsome *shisa* figures that guard dwellings. Tsuboya's pottery history began in the early 1600s when a Korean potter was forced to

settle here after being taken prisoner. Pottery made in Tsuboya bears 17th-century Korean characteristics, as is also the case in Kyushu. The **Tsuboya Ceramic Museum** (Tue–Sun 10am–6pm), built in the late 1990s, with pottery displays and models of reconstructed local buildings, is an excellent introduction to the history of the area.

Naha is the perfect spot for first experiments with Okinawan cuisine. Now familiar with the sashimi, *unagi*, *yaki*soba and other delicacies of central Japan, travellers might brave *mimiga* (sliced pig ears with vinegar), *ashite-bichi* (stewed pig legs), *rafutei* (pork simmered in miso, sugar, rice wine and soy sauce), *goya champuru* (stir-fried meat and melon), or one of the many kinds of local *somen* noodles. *Awamori*, the local distilled rice brew served with ice and water, packs a wallop that puts all else to shame.

SHURI

The first castle on **Shuri**, west of downtown on a hill overlooking Naha and the oceans beyond, was established in 1237. Under the second Sho dynasty, established in 1469 by King Sho En, Shuri became a mighty palace and temple complex. Shuri remained the political and cultural centre of the Ryukyus until 1879, when the last Okinawan king, Sho Tai, was forced to abdicate by the Meiji government in Tokyo. During the 82-day battle of Okinawa in 1945, when the Japanese Army chose Okinawa as the last stand against the Allies before an anticipated invasion of the main Japanese islands, **Shuri-jo** (Shuri Castle; http://oki-park.jp; daily Apr–June and Oct–Nov 8am–7.30pm, July–Sept until 8.30pm, Dec–Mar until 6.30pm) was the headquarters of the Japanese forces. It was destroyed in the fighting. Pre-war accounts describe a marvel on a par in architectural and artistic interest with Kyoto, Nara and Nikko. Much of the castle's stonework has now been rebuilt.

Nearby, **Ryutan-koen** is an expansive park barely able to absorb the hordes of tour buses or the clusters of tour groups posing for photographs with classically attired Okinawan women in front of **Shuri no Mon**, the traditional gate to the castle grounds. The **Tama-udon**, minutes from the gate, contains the bodies of Sho En and other members of his family. The nearby **Okinawa Prefectural Museum** (Tue–Sun 9am–6pm, Fri–Sat until 8pm) is a very slick facility that presents a good digest of Okinawa's rich history and culture.

SOUTH OF NAHA

Southern Okinawa is noted for caves. The most famous caves are the tunnel labyrinths at **Tomigusuku**, near the Naha airport and the last headquarters of the Imperial Navy. The military commanders refused to surrender as the Allies pounded the island's south with naval bombardments; over 4,000 Japanese men committed suicide. Reminders and memorials of the bloodiest battle of the Pacific war that cost the lives of 13,000 Americans,

Shaping terracotta in Tsuboya.

110,000 Japanese and 140,000 Okinawan civilians (one-eighth of the population) are numerous throughout the south of the island.

The coastal highway south past the international airport leads to **Itoman**, claimed to be the home of some of the most fearless sailors in the world. Itoman's mid-August tug-of-war with intertwined "male" and "female" ropes draws crowds from afar. Several heavily promoted and developed caverns pepper the southern coastline, including **Hakugin-do**, a cavern with a shrine dedicated to the guardian deity of Itoman.

The story of **Himeyuri-no-To ②** (Lily of the Valley Tower) is famous: it involves a deep pit where a group of high-school girls and their teachers committed suicide – rather than endure the possibility of capture by Americans – after singing their school song. **Mabuniga-oka**, on a promontory overlooking the ocean, is the site of the last resistance of the Japanese Army. Just east of here is the **Okinawa Prefecture Peace Memorial Museum**

US Marine Corps' Futemma Air Station in Ginowan.

(http://www.peace-museum.pref.okinawa. jp; daily 9am–5pm), which documents the Battle of Okinawa and the suffering of the people of the islands during World War II.

Gyokusen-do is said to be East Asia's largest cave. Only about one-fifth of it is open to the public; unfortunately, in this part visitors have broken off most of the stalactites and stalagmites, and the cave's floor has been pockmarked by footprints. Not to worry, though, as the caves are part of the larger **Okinawa World ❸** (www.gyokusendo.co.jp/okinawaworld; daily 9am–6pm), a "village" with extensive attractions related to local culture, arts and crafts. One of the quirkier places here is **Habu-koen** (Snake Park; www. habu-park.com; daily 9am–6pm), where there are swimming races between mongooses and *habu* snakes, whose venom is strong enough to fell a horse.

A 5km (3-mile) ferry ride from **Chinen ❹** on Okinawa's southeast coast brings visitors to small and flat **Kudaka-jima**, the so-called island of the gods. This is where the great

⊙ US BASES

It's impossible to talk about Okinawa without the long-running debate over US military bases on the islands cropping up. For locals, it's certainly an emotive subject – while the bases contribute greatly to the local economy, the majority of islanders want no US military presence at all on the islands. The noise and disturbances caused by major bases such as Kadena and Futenma, both north of Naha, is one reason. Cases of US military personnel making a nuisance of themselves, or worse, is another; although with the subject of the bases being so sensitive (and political), it isn't unheard of for incidents to get quickly blown out of proportion.

One common complaint from Okinawans is this: why, when they represent only 1 percent of the country's landmass, do they get almost 75 percent of US bases? Part of the answer is that nowhere else in Japan wants them to be relocated to their front step.

Shinzo Abe's promise that Futenma airbase would cease operations by 2019 passed with no resolution to the problem in sight. Plans have been drafted for 9,000 marines to be moved to Guam, Hawaii or Australia, while 10,000 will stay on the island in a new base in Henoko, also in Okinawa. However, many Okinawan people are against the construction of a new facility and would like to see all American bases simply moved off the island.

ancestress of the Ryukyuan people, Amamikiyo, is said to have descended from heaven and bestowed on them the five grains. The people of these isolated, storm-swept islands came to believe that their fate rested in the hands of the gods, and an arcane priestess cult still survives, albeit only just. Covered with sugar cane and *fukugi* trees, Kudaka-jima, which has a resident population of about 200 people, is a somnolent place. Until the 1990s, it transformed in mid-November every 12th year for the five-day Izaiho Festival, in which local women served collectively as *noro*, or priestesses, to perform rites and communicate with the gods. The *noro* are still on the island, but because of a dwindling female population, the festival has been in hiatus since 1990. Kudaka still has its charms though. Like other *utaki*, or sacred places throughout Okinawa, visitors often remark that the sounds of the sea, wind and the singing birds seem strangely louder here.

CENTRAL AND NORTHERN OKINAWA

About 15km (9 miles) north of Shuri are the ruins of the castle at **Nakagusuku ⑤**, built in the 15th century, and the largest in Okinawa. These ruins are part of the same World Heritage package as Shuri, but they aren't the only worthwhile attraction here. The Nakamura home in Nakagusuku offers an insight into how an 18th-century gentry family lived.

Back on the west coast, the main road north of Naha, towards Moon Bay, passes **Ryukyu-mura** (www.ryukyumura. co.jp; daily 9am–6pm), a cultural heritage village that has preserved some genuine traditional farmhouses and other tangible features of Okinawan culture. Despite the souvenir-dominated entrance and exit areas, the "village" is an intriguing digest that includes displays of Okinawan crafts like textile weaving and dyeing, Eisa

dancing and performances on the *sanshin*. Okinawan dishes and sweets made from the local brown sugar are readily available. You could easily spend half a day here, soaking up the Ryukyu culture.

Jutting out from the west coast about two-thirds of the way to the northern tip of Okinawa, **Motobu-hanto ⑥** (Motobu Peninsula) was the site of an ocean exposition in the 1970s. Most of the tourist-focused offerings are on the exposition's former site, Exposition Memorial Park, including several exhibitions about Okinawan culture and the ocean. The restored ruins of **Nakijin-jo** (Nakijin Castle; daily 8am–6pm, May–Aug until 7pm), on the peninsula's northern tip, are a fine place to watch a sunset. Offshore, tiny **Ie-jima** is where a famous US war correspondent, Ernie Pyle, was killed in World War II. Also on the Motobu-hanto is the **Ocean Expo Park** (http://churaumi.okinawa; daily, Mar–Sept 8.30am–8pm, Oct–Feb 8.30am–6.30pm). Among the attractions that make this a good family trip are a fine aquarium, a planetarium, a museum

Shuri Castle.

◎ Tip

Okinawa has plenty of excellent diving opportunities. The best three places to check out are Zamami-jima in the Kerama Islands, Irabu off Miyako-jima, and Shiraho-no-umi on Ishigaki, home to the world's longest blue coral reef.

View from Nakijin Castle.

documenting the lives of fishing communities in Southeast Asia, several small beaches, local crafts and arts, and a small kids' adventure area.

A visit to the far north of Okinawa, or *yanbaru*, will reward the adventurous with rugged hills, beaches and secluded fishing villages, along with some of the friendliest people anywhere. In the village of **Kijoka ❼**, you can watch the various steps required to produce the plantain-fibre textile *bashofu*. The view at **Hedo-misaki ❽**, the cape at the northern tip of the island, is stunning. But don't go wandering off in the bush in *yanbaru*, as this is home to the *habu* – the deadly poisonous snake found in Okinawa.

One of the Ryukyu's sacred islands is **Iheya-jima ❾**, to the northeast of Okinawa. According to Okinawan legend, King Jimmu Tenno began his conquest of Japan from here. Moreover, a huge cave on the island, referred to as the "Hiding Place", is said to be the very cave where the Sun Goddess Amaterasu hid herself until the other deities could coax her out, thereby restoring light to the world.

OUTER ISLANDS

The best way to experience the Ryukyuan way of life is to visit the outer islands, or *saki-shima*, reached by ferry or air from Naha. The 20 **Kerama Islands ❿** are only 35km (20 miles) west of Naha, and the coral reefs in the surrounding waters provide excellent scuba diving. A favourite diving and beach spot, **Zamami-jima** is a largely unspoilt island with its own dialect and customs. The **tourist information office** (www.vill.zamami. okinawa.jp; daily 9am–5pm) in the harbour has a good map in English of the island. Zamami is a major centre for whale-watching. It may surprise foreigners to learn that a good many Japanese are just as concerned as they are about preserving whales – Japan's pro-whaling lobby is a minority, but one with powerful connections. The tourist office includes the Zamami Whale-Watching Association, which runs two-and-a-half-hour boat trips daily at 10.30am and 1pm, from January through to early April.

Further afield is the Miyako group of eight islands. **Miyako-jima ⓫**, the main island, is an hour by air or 10 hours by boat from Naha. The beaches here are some of the finest in Japan, most notably **Yonaha Maihama beach** on Miyako-jima (known as Maibama by locals). This 7km (4.5-mile) strip of mostly undeveloped (save for a large Tokyu Resort) white sand is sandwiched by azure waters and subtropical trees, and is a good place to look for marine sports or just relax in relative peace and quiet. Nearby **Irabu**, an island that can be reached by boat from Miyako-jima, offers attractive scenery and fine diving.

At Miyako-jima's port of **Hirara** are the *o-honoyama* (tax stones). After the samurai of Satsuma (now Kagoshima) on Kyushu invaded the Ryukyu kingdom in 1609, it became in everything but name a tributary to that fief's lord, even though the country also continued to pay tribute to the Ming dynasty in China. At the time, all children on Miyako-jima were paraded once a year before the *ninto-zeiseki*. Those taller than the stone had to pay the tax or else were shipped off to work as forced labour. This system was only abolished in 1918. Miyako-jima earned a place in Japanese school books when five local fishermen spotted the Czarist fleet steaming towards Japan during the Russo-Japanese War (1904–5). The timely warning allowed the Imperial Navy, under Admiral Togo Shigenori, to surprise and annihilate the Russians in the Battle of Tsushima Straits.

YAEYAMA ISLANDS

The narrator of Kushi Fusako's short story *Memoirs of a Declining Ryukyuan Woman* observes, "We always seem to be at the tail end of history, dragged along roads already ruined by others." Efforts to stamp out traditional Okinawan customs by the mainland Japanese government were only partially successful in the **Yaeyama Islands**, where the indigenous beliefs of these parts, the animism and shamanistic practices that predated the Japanese acquisition of the islands, survive and serve as the prime reason for paying a visit – nowhere is Ryukyu culture better felt than here. Further from Tokyo than from Taipei, the Yaeyamas assimilated both Chinese and Japanese influences. These remote islanders have also been influenced by Southeast Asians, allowing for other, more exotic influences to creep in. Being out of the mainstream has benefited the islands in a number of other ways. The Yaeyamas were fortunate enough to be left comparatively unaffected by Japanese colonial policies of the last century and to have emerged unscathed from both the pitched battles of World War II and the effects of the subsequent American Occupation of Okinawa, which only ended in 1972.

ISHIGAKI

Ishigaki-jima ⑫ is the main island of the Yaeyama chain and its administrative centre. Its name signifies "stone walls", a derivation from the local dialect *"Ishiagira"*, meaning "a place of many stones". Its airport and harbour serve the other outlying islands in the group. Ishigaki offers visitors more creature comforts than are normally found on the other islands, and a larger number of conventional sights, but also makes an excellent base from which to explore islands whose names and locations are unfamiliar even to many Japanese people.

Ishigaki's island feel is intensified by the roadside presence of colourful dugout canoes, more suggestive of Polynesia than Japan. Samples of the region's unique culture can be seen

Yaeyama Islands

⊙ Fact

Iriomote is noted for its rare flora and fauna. The Iriomote wildcat, a nocturnal feline, was discovered in 1965 and is endemic to the island. Other rare species include the atlas moth, the yellow-margined box turtle and the crested serpent eagle.

at the **Yaeyama Museum** (Tue–Sun 9am–5pm), where good examples of ancient Panori ceramics, old Yaeyama-*jofu* textiles and more canoes can be found. Also of interest in the town itself is the beautifully preserved **Miyara Donchi** (Wed–Mon 9am–5pm), the ancestral home of the Matsushige family. Modelled on aristocratic buildings at the royal capital of Shuri in Naha, it is the only such house left in Okinawa. Built in 1819, its stone garden, made from pitted coral in the Chinese manner, and sprouting with myriad tropical plants, sets it far apart from mainland Japanese dry landscape arrangements.

The white beaches, clear blue waters, coral and tropical fish are ideal for snorkelling and diving. A bus ride from the port, protected **Shiraho-no-umi** on the southeast coast boasts the world's largest blue coral reef. Heading north along the western shore, the **Ishigaki Yaima Village** (www.yaimamura.com; daily 9am–5.30pm), a cultural heritage village in a lovely setting on a hill above

Nagura Bay, has well-preserved Okinawan buildings, gardens and an exhibition on the history of the islands' weaving styles. Ishigaki is of considerable ecological importance. **Kabira Bay** on the north shore is unquestionably the island's most spectacular marine landscape. Here, green islets rise like loaves of bread from crystal-clear, steeply shelving emerald waters. But be warned that Japan's best views often come with an excess of tourist stalls – Kabira is no exception, but is still well worth a visit. Just 5km (3 miles) east of Kabira Bay, **Yonehara beach** is a wonderful place to snorkel the teeming coral.

Although **Taketomi-jima** can be reached by ferry in just 12 minutes from Ishigaki's port, it remains a time capsule among these southern seas, the hospitality of its 400 or so inhabitants a measure of how well it has retained its identity. The name Taketomi signifies "prosperous bamboo", stands of which can be seen at the roadsides or in the centre of this island, whose circumference stretches to little more than 9km (5.5 miles). These days the island is noted for its sumptuous flowers and plant life. Bougainvillea and hibiscus, traditionally used in this part of Okinawa to decorate graves and Buddhist altars, spill over walls made from volcanic rock, built as a defence against the furious typhoons that strike the islands from late September to early October.

Kondoi Misaki, the island's finest beach, located along the southwestern shore, is known for its star-shaped sand grains, actually the remains of tiny, fossilised sea creatures. Taketomi is also famous as the source of *minsa*, an indigo fabric often used as a belt for a women's kimono. *Minsa* is only produced on Taketomi. Strips of the material can be seen drying on the stone walls of the village, or at the **Mingei-kan**, a weaving

Humpback whale watching.

centre where you can observe women at work on the fabrics.

A ferry also goes to the large island of **Iriomote** ⓭, which is no doubt the most unusual island in the Japanese archipelago – a touch of New Guinea in Japan. Except for the towns of Ohara in the southeast and Funaura in the north, the island is mostly tropical rainforest. Thankfully, development on the island has so far not run amok, and the majority of accommodation are hostels, minshuku (lodgings) or small developments. River trips along the broad, Amazonian-like **Urauchi-gawa** on Iriomote Island include trekking through the jungle to a series of natural waterfalls. The island is home to the nocturnal Iriomote lynx, one of the world's rarest species of cat.

Yonaguni-jima ⓮, a forested island with some of the chain's most spectacular diving and snorkelling offerings, is now accessible by plane. Yonaguni is Okinawa's most westerly island, a mere 125km (78 miles) from Taiwan.

SOUTHERNMOST POINT

It is worth making the sometimes choppy, 50-minute crossing from Ishigaki port to **Hateruma-jima** ⓯, a rustic island out on a limb among the southern Yaeyamas, a place where empty roads lead not to hotels and shops, but to an infinity of sea and sky. The name "Hateruma" means "the end of the coral", an indication that this is Japan's southernmost island, its last landmass. Local maps to the island's **Southernmost Point Monument**, a cement and rock affair stuck on top of a bluff above the cliffs, read "Beyond here, the Philippines." Renting a bicycle for the day nicely matches the rhythm and pace of this small, 6km (4-mile) long island.

Ghostly banyan trees, *fukugi* and Indian almond trees dot the island. Among the island flowers are bamboo orchids, hibiscus and plumeria. Taking root also in the sand of Hateruma's superb **Nishi-no-Hama**, or West Beach, are pineapple-like *pandanus* trees. For divers, underwater Hateruma is a glorious filigree of coral, stone holes, rock arches and deep-blue silhouettes.

Iriomote Island.

Kabira Bay, Ishigaki-jima.

A surfer carrying his board to Enoshima Beach.

JAPAN

TRAVEL TIPS

TRANSPORT

By air

Tokyo, the main gateway to Japan, is served by two main airports: **New Tokyo International Airport** (Narita), 66km (41 miles) east of the city, and **Tokyo International Airport** (Haneda), 20km (12 miles) to the south of the city centre. The airports are usually simply referred to as Narita and Haneda. Narita is the main international airport serving the Kanto region. While Haneda has been increasing its international routes in recent years, its main function is still as Tokyo's domestic hub.

Narita Airport

Although it is a little inconveniently located, Narita Airport's services have vastly improved since its renewal and extension, completed in 2009. It has three terminals and two runways. The terminals have currency-exchange counters, ATMs, restaurants and cafés, internet facilities, post offices and health clinics, and a range of shops including duty-free. Terminal 2 has a children's playroom, day rooms for taking a nap, and showers.
General and flight info: 0476-34-8000; www.narita-airport.jp
Tourist info: 0476-30-3383 (Terminal 1); 0476-34-5877 (Terminal 2)

Haneda Airport

Haneda is Tokyo's hub for domestic flights. Both domestic airlines – Japan Air Lines (JAL) and All Nippon Airways (ANA) – operate flights throughout Japan from Haneda. Since the opening of its new international terminal in 2010 and the launch of long-haul daytime services in 2014, Haneda has also offered flights to many major

cities overseas, including London, New York, Paris, Bangkok and Beijing.

Haneda's two domestic terminals are well designed, with Japanese, Western and Chinese restaurants, cafés, shops, a post office, information desks and a bookstore. The sleek international terminal has a similarly good selection of facilities, in addition to one floor designed to look like an Edo-era town.
Airport info: 03-5757-8111; http://www.haneda-airport.jp/inter/en/ (international); www.tokyo-airport-bldg.co.jp (domestic)

Osaka-Kansai Airport

Kansai International Airport (www.kansai-airport.or.jp/en) in Osaka serves the entire Kansai region, especially Osaka, Kyoto and Kobe. Airport facilities are good, city transport rapid and efficient.

Central Japan International Airport, Nagoya

This international airport (www.centrair.jp), commonly known as Centrair, is handily located between Tokyo and Osaka. Flight routes include those to and from the USA, Continental Europe and numerous

Asian destinations, including Singapore, Thailand and Hong Kong.

Fukuoka Airport

Western Japan's main arrival and departure point from overseas, this international airport (www.fuk-ab.co.jp) provides flights to Asian destinations, as well as domestic routes.

Naha Airport

The main gateway to Okinawa, Naha International Airport's (http://www.naha-airport.co.jp) main overseas destinations are Hong Kong, Shanghai, Taipei and Seoul.

Niigata Airport

The main international airport in northern Japan (www.niigata-airport.gr.jp), Niigata provides useful links to Harbin, Shanghai, Xian, Guam, Vladivostok and other Asian airports, in addition to domestic routes.

New Chitose Airport, Sapporo

The main gateway to Hokkaido, New Chitose (http://www.new-chitose-airport.jp), just outside Sapporo, provides numerous domestic connections, as well as handy links to Seoul, Taipei, Beijing, Shanghai, Hong Kong and Bangkok.

⊘ Key airlines

All Nippon Airways (ANA)
1-5-2, Shiodome-City Center, Higashi-Shimbashi, Tokyo
Tel: 03-6741-1120
www.ana.co.jp
American Airlines
2-4-11, Higashi-Shinagawa, Shinagawa-ku, Tokyo
Tel: 03-4333-7675
www.aa.com
British Airways
Tel: 03-3298-5238
www.britishairways.com
Qantas Airways

Tel: 03-6833-0700 (in Tokyo), 0120-207-020 (toll free, outside of Tokyo)
www.qantas.com.au
Singapore Airlines
1-10-1-1021 Yurakucho, Chiyoda-ku, Tokyo
Tel: 03-3213-3431
www.singaporeair.com
United Airlines
Tel: 03-6732-5011
www.united.com
Virgin Atlantic Airways
www.virgin-atlantic.com

Women-only carriage on a Japanese train.

More gateways

A number of smaller airports, including those in Nagasaki, Kumamoto and Kagoshima, may be worth checking out for their connections to and from Asian destinations in South Korea, Hong Kong, China and other East Asian destinations.

Flying from the UK and the US

The three big-name airlines serving Tokyo direct from the UK are British Airways, JAL, and ANA. Flying time direct from London is 11–13 hours.

Coming from the US or Canada, you are spoilt for choice. Besides JAL and ANA, among the better-known airlines are Delta, United Airlines and American Airlines. Direct flights from North America's west coast take about 9–11 hours, and from the east coast roughly 12–14 hours.

Tokyo is an increasingly important transport hub for direct flights from major Asian destinations like Beijing, Shanghai, Hong Kong, Bangkok and further afield from Singapore, Bali and Sydney.

While fares vary between airlines, April, August and December tend to be the most expensive times to fly to Japan from the UK or US as they coincide with the country's Golden Week, O-Bon and Year End–New Year holidays. Flying a few days either side of these peak periods can result in huge savings.

Other departure points

JAL and Qantas have daily flights to Japan from Australia. JAL, ANA, Air Canada and American Airlines offer flights between Japan and North America. Air New Zealand and JAL have daily flights to Japan from New Zealand. There are innumerable flights from the main cities of Continental Europe, such as Paris, Frankfurt, Rome and Amsterdam. Cathay Pacific, JAL, ANA and Air China are the main airlines serving Hong Kong and China, but there are cheaper carriers also. Singapore Airlines, Thai Airways International, JAL and ANA are among many companies serving Southeast Asian destinations such as Bangkok, Singapore, Ho Chi Minh City and Jakarta.

By sea

Although few people arrive in Tokyo by sea, the slow approach to this speed-defined city would certainly be a novelty. Japan's ferry services are quite extensive, at least in their connections with South Korea and China.

There is a regular boat service between South Korea's port of Busan and Shimonoseki in Japan (www.kampuferry.co.jp). The latter also has connections to the ports of Taicang (www.ssferry.co.jp) in China. A hydrofoil (www.jrbeetle.co.jp) as well as a ferry (www.camellia-line.co.jp) travel between Busan and Hakata in Japan.

Ferries from Shanghai (www.shanghai-ferry.co.jp) arrive in Osaka, from where passengers travel either by rail or air to Tokyo. In summer, a ferry operates between Wakkanai (www.hs-line.com) in northern Hokkaido and Korsakov in Russia.

GETTING AROUND

On arrival

From Narita Airport

A taxi to downtown Tokyo from Narita costs between ¥20,000 and ¥30,000, depending on destination and traffic.

Fixed fare taxis cost between ¥16,000 and ¥26,500. Most people prefer either the bus or train as they are much cheaper. By bus or taxi, it's 90 minutes to 2.5 hours by road.

Bus: a regular limousine bus service (www.limousinebus.co.jp) runs between Narita and TCAT (Tokyo City Air Terminal) in central Tokyo, to Tokyo and Shinjuku stations, and to most major hotels in Tokyo. Tickets (around ¥3,200) are bought at the airport after clearing immigration and customs. There are several routes depending on destination. Buses are boarded outside the terminal at the kerb, and will accept any amount of luggage at no extra charge. The buses leave every 10 to 20 minutes, depending on the route, taking 90 minutes to 2.5 hours to arrive at central hotels. There are also buses to Yokohama and Haneda Airport.

Trains: there are two train alternatives into Tokyo: Japan Railways (JR) Narita Express (www.jreast.co.jp/e/nex) and the Keisei Skyliner (www.keisei.co.jp). Both are almost twice as fast as taxi or bus, but not as convenient, as once you arrive at a station, you'll have to make arrangements for transport around the city. Be aware also that, while the city's train system is all-encompassing, carrying luggage through train and subway is a feat of considerable effort, involving long hikes and Fuji-like climbs. If you have more than one piece of luggage, don't even think about getting around or reaching your hotel by either overhead train or subway, especially during the hot and humid summer months. Instead, consider the limousine bus or the baggage delivery service available at the airport.

In terms of connections, the Narita Express is more convenient, stopping at JR stations in Chiba, Tokyo (Station), Shinjuku, Ikebukuro, Yokohama and Ofuna. The Skyliner stops just at Ueno Station and nearby Nippori. Both have services approximately every 30 minutes and take about the same time to reach Tokyo – 41 minutes to Ueno on the Skyliner and 53 minutes to Tokyo Station on the Narita Express – and neither has restrictions on luggage. Both also offer a comfortable ride, with smart modern carriages and far more legroom than you would have had if you flew economy to Narita.

The Narita Express costs between ¥3,020 and ¥4,620 for standard class and tickets can be bought up to a month in advance at travel agents, Floor B1 of the airport or at the station before boarding. The Keisei Skyliner costs ¥2,790 and tickets can also be bought in advance or at the station. If you are travelling during a peak holiday period, it is advisable to book train tickets when heading to Narita. From Narita into Tokyo, you will have no problems getting tickets upon arrival.

Domestic air connections: Narita operates domestic flights to a number of cities, including Sapporo, Osaka, Nagoya and Naha. If making a domestic air connection to elsewhere, you must take the taxi, bus or train into Tokyo and make the connection at Haneda Airport. The limousine bus will take you directly from Narita to Haneda, as will a very expensive taxi ride.

Baggage delivery: many residents of Japan take advantage of Japan's fast and reliable delivery network. After clearing immigration and customs, take your luggage to one of the several JAL ABC, GPA or KTC counters. Often a queue indicates the counters. For about ¥2,000–4,000 per bag, they can deliver the luggage by the following day wherever you are.

From Haneda Airport

If you are coming into Haneda Airport, a taxi to the city centre will cost ¥7,000 to ¥8,000 and takes about 30–40 minutes. Provided your luggage is light, you can take either the Monorail to Hamamatsucho Station on the JR Yamanote Line or take the Keikyu Line to Shinagawa Station. Both trips take 13 minutes.

Subway entrance in Fukuoka.

From Kansai Airport

The Kansai International Airport (KIX) has replaced Osaka Airport (Itami) as the international air terminus for the Kansai region. It was also intended to relieve the overcrowding at Narita Airport, which has restricted operating hours. Today, lots of domestic flights fly from Itami.

The second-largest and the first 24-hour-operation airport in Japan, Kansai International Airport opened in 1994. It is located southeast of Osaka Bay, 5km (8 miles) off the coast and about 60km (37 miles) from JR Shin-Osaka Station for *shinkansen* (bullet train) connections. The airport, constructed on an artificial island in Osaka Bay and one of the world's most expensive airports – ¥2,730 departure tax – is architecturally impressive and extremely functional. All international and domestic connections at KIX are made at the same terminal in a matter of minutes. Make sure to confirm that domestic flight connections are from KIX and not Itami-Osaka Airport. Despite being on an island, getting to and from KIX is relatively easy: two railways, two expressways and some 10 limousine bus lines connect the island to every point in Kansai. A high-speed ferry service also connects to Kobe Airport.

For travel information, the **Kansai Tourist Information Centre** is located in the arrival lobby (1st Floor) and is open daily 7am–10pm. There is another information centre in Terminal 2 (daily 11.30am–7.30pm). For handling currency exchange, there are 17 currency exchange bureaus with one or more open 6am–11pm. Cash machines are also plentiful. The only bank that conducts normal business operations at the airport is the Mitsubishi UFJ (MUFG) on the second floor (Mon–Fri 9am–3pm). Japan Rail Passes can be validated either at the JR West Information Counter in the International Arrivals Lobby (1st Floor, daily 10.30am–6.30pm), at the TIS-Travel Service Centre (daily 10am–6pm) or at the green-coloured Midori-no-madoguchi Reservations Ticket Office (daily 5.30am–11pm) at JR Kansai Airport Station.

To/from Osaka

Train: JR (Japan Railways) Haruka Express, with reserved seating, runs between KIX and Osaka's Tennoji

Station (30 min) and Shin Osaka Station (50 min), where you catch the *shinkansen*, or bullet train. This connects KIX with Osaka's Tennoji Station (30 min), while the Nankai Railways Airport Express connects with Namba Station's Osaka City Air Terminal (O-CAT), which offers express baggage check-in (45 min). **JR West train information**: tel: 0570-00-2486 (daily 6am–11pm), www.westjr.co.jp.

Nankai train information tel: 0724-56-6203.

Bus: there are a number of deluxe buses between KIX and various Osaka hotels and rail stations, including the 24-hour limousine bus service to Osaka Station. For bus information call Kansai International Airport Information Service (24-hours), tel: 0724-55-2500, or inquire at one of the eight information counters at the airport.

To/from Kyoto

Train: JR Haruka Express, reserved seats, connects Kyoto Station with KIX (75 min). For JR train information tel: 0570-00-2486.

Bus: a bus leaves Kyoto Station for KIX and takes about 85 minutes. For bus information call Kansai International Airport Information Service (24-hours): tel: 0724-55-2500.

To/from Nara

Bus: a bus runs from KIX to Nara JR Station (90 min). For bus information call Kansai International Airport Information Service (24-hours): tel: 0724-55-2500.

To/from Kobe

Bus: connect by bus from KIX to Kobe's Sannomiya Station (90 min). For bus information, Kansai International Airport Information Service (24-hours): tel: 0724-55-2500.

Ferry: the Kobe Bay Shuttle is the best and fastest way to get to or from Kobe. The Bay Shuttle runs between KIX and the Kobe Airport on Port Island (30 min), where the Port Liner automated train service is provided to Kobe's Sannomiya Station. For Bay Shuttle information tel: 078-304-0033.

From Sendai

25 minutes from town and linked by regular bus services. Domestic flights connect to most cities (Tokyo 45 minutes and Osaka 1 hour 30

min). International flights have decreased since the March 2011 earthquake, and now connect mostly to China, Korea and Taiwan.

From Sapporo

35 minutes from town and linked by regular bus services. Domestic flights connect to most cities (Tokyo 2 hours and Osaka 3 hours). International flights connect to China, Hawaii, Hong Kong, Korea, the Philippines, Russia, Singapore, and Taiwan.

From Hiroshima

50 minutes from town and linked by regular bus services. Domestic flights connect to most cities (Tokyo 1 hour 20 min and Osaka 45 min). International flights connect to China, Hong Kong, Korea and Taiwan.

From Fukuoka

Domestic flights connect to most cities (Tokyo 1 hour 40 min and Osaka-Itami 1 hour 5 min). International flights connect to China, Guam, Korea, Philippines, Singapore, Taiwan and Thailand.

From Nagasaki

One hour or more from town and linked by regular bus services. Domestic flights connect to most cities (Tokyo 2 hours to 2 hours 30 min and Osaka 1 hour). International flights connect to China, Hong Kong and Korea.

From Okinawa

15 minutes from Naha and linked by regular bus services. Domestic flights

The bullet train in Kyoto.

connect to most cities (Tokyo 3 hours and Osaka 2 hours). International flights connect to China, Hong Kong, Korea, Singapore and Taiwan.

Public transport

Rail

Japan has one of the most efficient and extensive rail networks in the world. Rail service is provided by **Japan Railways (JR)** and several regional private lines. The trains on important routes run every few minutes. High-speed trains – such as JR's **shinkansen**, sometimes called the bullet train, which travels at speeds of up to 300kph (185mph) – offer a good alternative to air and long-distance bus travel. Between Tokyo and Kyoto, travel times and prices are similar for both air and *shinkansen*. The train, however, is from city centre to city centre; plane, from airport to airport.

Subway systems in Japan are clean, safe, and convenient. They are faster than congested road transport. However, they are notorious for being crowded, especially during morning and evening rush hours.

All subway stations post timetables. Regular service is Monday to Friday. The Saturday, Sunday and holiday timetable has slightly fewer trains. Trains run until just after midnight, so be sure to check the time of the last train if you're out late. All stations have a route map with fares for each stop near the ticket machines, but not always in English. Your present location is shown with a red mark.

The fares are regulated on a station-to-station basis, so if you cannot determine the fare required, just purchase the cheapest ticket available. You can pay the difference, if needed, at the exit gate upon arrival at your destination.

A child's ticket is half fare. Ticket machines accept ¥1,000 notes in addition to coins. At most stations there will also be machines that accept ¥5,000 and ¥10,000 bills.

Savings can be made by buying a *teiki* (train pass). Major subway and overland train stations issue passes. Another way to save on train fares is to buy a *kaisuken*, a series of 11 tickets between two destinations for the price of 10.

Station arrivals are announced in Japanese inside the trains, but these are often difficult to understand. There is usually a map of the stops on the line and connecting lines above the train doors, often written in both Japanese and English.

Timetables and subway system maps in Japanese can be obtained at most stations, and in English at major train and subway stations.

⊘ Japan Rail Pass

Japan's rail services are unsurpassed in the world. Extremely efficient, they go nearly everywhere, even to the remotest neck of the woods.

Foreign travellers intending to travel in Japan should consider the Japan Rail Pass (www. japanrailpass.net). The pass allows for virtually unlimited travel on the national JR network, including the *shinkansen*, or bullet trains. Passes must be purchased outside Japan, and you must be travelling in Japan under the visa entry status of "temporary visitor".

Once in Japan, the pass must initially be validated at a JR Travel Centre (which are everywhere in Japan). Once it is validated, reservations can be made at any so-called Green Window (*midori no madoguchi*) at major stations.

While trains are not especially cheap in Japan (long-distance fares equal air fares), the pass is a great deal. A 7-day pass costs around ¥30,000 – less than the round-trip fare from Narita Airport to Kyoto via Tokyo.

Standard/First-class
7-day/¥29,110/¥38,880
14-day/¥46,390/¥62,950
21-day/¥59,350/¥81,870
Children aged 6 to 11 travel at half of the above prices. Children under 6 travel free.

Discount tickets

In the major cities, there are special tickets that allow unlimited travel for one day and are good value. They can be purchased at ticket windows and sometimes at special ticket machines, often marked in English.

Tokyo

Nine of Tokyo's 13 subway lines are now collectively known as the Tokyo Metro. The remaining four are run by the Tokyo Metropolitan Bureau of Transportation, and are referred to as Toei lines.

Tokyo Furii Kippu (Tokyo 1-Day Ticket): one-day pass for JR trains and Toei trains and buses. All may be used as often as you want (except JR express trains). ¥1,600.

Tokunai Pass: unlimited-use, one-day pass in Tokyo for use only on JR trains (except JR express trains) running within the 23 wards of Tokyo. ¥760.

Toei One-Day Pass (Toei Marugoto Kippu): unlimited-use, one-day pass for Toei trains, buses and subway trains within Tokyo on any day within a 6-month period. Approx. ¥700.

Kyoto

Unlimited-use, one-day bus and subway train ticket that can be used on all city buses and subway trains in the Kyoto area. One day, ¥900; 2 days, ¥1,700. www2.city.kyoto.lg.jp/kotsu/webguide.

Osaka Amazing Pass

Unlimited-use pass for buses, new trams and subway trains, and which also includes free admission to 35 tourist sites and gives discounts

Taxi in Tokyo.

to some other attractions. One day ¥2,700; 2 days ¥3,600. www.osp.osaka-info.jp/en

Train discounts

If you have not purchased a Japan Rail Pass or don't qualify, JR and the private railways offer a number of special fare discounts. Amongst them:

JR Discount round-trip: a 10 percent discount to destinations more than 600km (370 miles) one-way.

Excursion tickets: a saving of around 20 percent for direct travel between a starting point and a designated area in which unlimited travel can be made. One good example is the 2-day (¥5,700) or 3-day (¥6,100) Hakone Free Pass available at Shinjuku Station, which covers travel to and from Hakone on the Odakyu Line, as well travel on seven types of transport within the Hakone area. It also gives discounted admission to some tourist sites.

Package tours: discount lodging as well as discounted rail and bus travel. Packages may be purchased at JR travel centres, at a Green Window (midori no madoguchi) or leading travel agents.

JR Seishun 18 Kippu: a coupon available during parts of spring, summer and winter for five days' travel, each section used for one day's unlimited train travel. Good for ordinary JR trains, rapid JR trains, and the JR ferry-boat between Miyajimaguchi and Miyajima Island. Passengers may get on and off as many times as wanted at any JR station and at the JR ferry terminal within the same date. Price is ¥11,850 both for adults and children. It may be shared by several people, provided they travel together and do not split the coupon (so for example, five people can use it on one day).

Regional rail passes

Another option for cutting travel costs is to look out for special regional travel passes. The JNTO keeps an up-to-date list of such passes on its website (www.jnto.go.jp). Among these are:

Hokkaido Rail Pass: a coupon that allows 3 days' (¥16,500), Flexible 4 days' (¥22,000), 5 days' (¥22,000) or 7 days' (¥24,000) travel on all JR Hokkaido train and bus services.

JR West Sanyo Area Pass: a coupon for 7 days' (¥20,000) unlimited travel on JR shinkansen, limited-express and regular trains in the Osaka-Sanyo area.

JR East Pass: a coupon valid for two weeks allowing 5 days' (¥19,250–20,360) unlimited use of JR shinkansen and limited-express services within the entire JR East area (essentially the northern half of Honshu, including Tokyo).

JR All Kyushu Area Pass: a coupon giving 5 days' (¥18,000) or 3 days' (¥15,000) unlimited use on JR trains within the Kyushu region. There is also a much cheaper pass for Northern Kysushu Area only.

Private transport

Driving in Japan is a headache. Roads are narrow and crowded, signs confusing, rental cars and petrol expensive. Motorway and bridge tolls are very costly. If at all possible, consider flying or, better, taking the train.

☉ Taxis

Taxis are the most comfortable way of getting around, but also the most expensive. The basic fare in Tokyo is ¥430 for the flag drop. A short trip can easily run from ¥3,000 to ¥5,000. No tipping is expected or required. Taxis are readily available at almost every city-centre street corner, major hotel and railway station. A red light in the front window is illuminated if the taxi is available.

Don't touch the door when getting in or out of a taxi. The doors on taxis are operated by the driver with a remote lever. Get out, walk away and forget the door.

Most taxi drivers speak only Japanese, so it can be helpful to have your destination written in Japanese. As many taxi drivers rely on their in-car navigation systems rather than an in-depth knowledge of the streets, having the address for them to input will also prevent them getting lost.

Don't be surprised if an available taxi ignores you late at night; the driver is looking for a sarariman – and a nice, tidy fare – on his way back to the suburbs.

A

Accommodation

There are hotels everywhere, but unfortunately not all of them are up to international standards. Those that are reflect it in their price. However, convenience is a very dear commodity here, so often you are paying for the location more than the service or luxury.

Be aware that many hotels offer only twin beds, which are the most popular arrangement in Japan. Smoking rooms (and even entire floors in budget accommodation) may have a thick stench of stale smoke. Hotel rooms are also quite compact. Even a ¥20,000 room in a deluxe hotel can be snug. So-called business hotels (favoured by many Japanese business travellers), generally found in the moderate and budget categories, have rooms that are not just snug, but cramped. As a rule, smaller hotels have fewer amenities, including no room service. If you are not intending to luxuriate all day in your room, though, these can be good bases for exploring destinations. Most business hotels and Western-style hotels provide free in-room Wi-fi or broadband internet, but not all traditional accommodation such as ryokan (Japanese-style inns). In most hotels and all ryokan, you are provided with a yukata (light kimono) robe, toothbrush, razor, shower cap, etc.

Western-style hotels offer rooms whose rates may vary from ¥8,000 to ¥40,000. There are hotels that also provide Japanese-style guest rooms and landscaped gardens. Others have restaurants serving Continental food as well as local cuisines.

Capsule hotels, conveniently located near key stations, provide Apollo spacecraft-style compactness as a last resort for the drunk, stranded or merely inquisitive. Capsule cells come complete with TV, air conditioning, a radio and alarm. Complexes have showers, bath, sauna and sometimes restaurants. Rates are around ¥4,000. The majority are for men only, but a few have women-only floors.

Ryokan exude an atmosphere of traditional Japanese living and a stay will be a rewarding experience. The average charges per person range from ¥10,000 to ¥25,000, depending on the type of bath facilities and dining offered, but the rates at a truly elegant ryokan can rise far higher.

There are about 80,000 ryokan in Japan, of which 1,200 are members of the Japan Ryokan Association (JRA; www.ryokan.or.jp), which ensures that a high standard of service is maintained. Guests sleep in rooms covered with tatami (straw) mats, on futon. Ryokan usually have large gender-separated communal baths (often using hot spring water) as well as small in-room baths and showers. In some ryokan there are also private hot spring baths available for rent. At higher-end ryokan both morning and evening meals are served in the guest's room, but more typically breakfast is served in a large dining hall.

Minshuku are small, family-run bed-and-breakfast lodgings operated within private homes, without the frills (toiletries and yukata gowns, etc). Guests are expected to fold up their futon bedding and tidy it away for the day. A stay in a minshuku will give you a more intimate experience of Japanese home life. Rates are from ¥5,000 up.

Japanese Inn Group (c/o Turtle Inn Nikko, 2-16 Takumi-cho, Nikko-shi, Tochigi 321-1433; tel: 0288-53-3168; info@japaneseinngroup.com; www.japaneseinngroup.com) offers the foreign traveller recommendations and bookings for traditional Japanese inns, usually with traditional tatami floors, futon bedding, yukata and Japanese-style baths. The Japanese Inn Group consists of about 90 reasonable ryokan, hotels, minshuku and pensions located throughout Japan. Most member facilities are small, family-run Japanese-style accommodation with a hometown atmosphere and affordable rates (per person between ¥4,000–¥8,000), with meals extra.

There are plenty of websites in Japan for booking accommodation, but most are in Japanese only. The best local sites in English and which offer reasonable discounts are Japanican (www.japanican.com) with more than 4,000 hotels and ryokan, and plenty of tours and package options, and Rakuten (http://travel.rakuten.com), a very popular multilingual site for all sorts of online shopping, and with a travel section that includes more than 5,000 hotels, ryokan and other types of accommodation in Japan.

The National Art Center, Tokyo.

Addresses

Finding an address in Japan can be tricky, even for taxi drivers. Especially in a city like Tokyo or Osaka, where addresses are written in a descending order – *ku* (ward), then *cho* or *matchi* (district), followed by the *chome* (an area of a few blocks) designations. The English rendition of addresses, and the one used in this guide, would result in a location appearing like this: Regency Hotel, 5F, 4-9-11 Shibuya, Minato-ku. In Japan the ground floor equals the first. Floor numbers are often shown on the outside of the building.

If you are stuck, ask at the nearest police box, where they have detailed area maps, and are usually helpful.

Admission charges

Admission fees in Japan are generally high. At cinemas, you can expect to pay around ¥1,900, although prices are usually discounted to ¥1,100 the first day of the month. Most cinemas also offer ¥1,100 tickets to women every Wednesday. Major museums and galleries usually cost between ¥1,000 and ¥1,500, while admission to a club or disco will typically be ¥1,500 to ¥3,000, including one or two drinks.

One way of saving on museum and gallery charges in Tokyo is with a Grutto Pass (www.rekibun.or.jp/grutto). The pass costs ¥2,200 but gives admission or discounted admission to 80 museums and galleries. You can buy one at most major museums or from tourist information centres, and the pass is valid for two months.

Many local tourism boards have similar passes available. The staff at the centres will be able to tell you about any multi-attraction tickets available in the area, which are quite common and offer substantial savings on museum, temple and shrine admission charges.

Arts

Japan's arts scene runs the gamut from traditional theatre such as kabuki and *noh* to cutting-edge contemporary art, with much of it made accessible to English-speakers in Tokyo. Most of the arts action is concentrated in the big cities, but Japan also has arty surprises waiting in

A sculptor carving a Buddha face on a tree.

some out-of-the-way places, most notably on the islands of the Seto Naikai (see page 305) and even on the rugged Sado Island (see page 205) off Niigata. For up-to-date listings of art shows and performances, check out the listings websites and magazines on page 378.

Bathhouses

Whether at a hot spring, a local *sento* (bathhouse) or at a traditional inn, the procedure for this quintessentially Japanese experience is the same. Disrobe, enter the bathroom (hide your modesty with a small washcloth), and wash and rinse thoroughly before easing into the typically large communal hot bath – which is for soaking, not washing. Note that people with tattoos may be refused or asked to cover up.

Budgeting for your trip

Japan has a reputation for being expensive, a legacy of the 1980s bubble-economy years when the country was flush with cash. Compared to other Asian destinations Japan remains expensive but, despite recent signs of a turnaround in its economy, 20 years of stagnation have left a dent in the cost-of-living index. Compared to European capitals, cities like Tokyo, Osaka and Kyoto begin to look quite affordable.

Accommodation can run from as little as ¥3,500 for a room in a modest inn or guesthouse to over ¥50,000 in a top hotel. Food is exceptionally good value, and the choices are remarkable. A decent set lunch

can cost as little as ¥650, less if you opt for a meal at a Japanese fast-food chain like Yoshinoya, the beef-bowl restaurants found in every Japanese city. American fast-food chains like McDonald's have dropped their prices in recent years, and their ¥100-menu has been a big hit with consumers. Family restaurant chains are very good value, and provide free coffee refills. Convenience stores are good places for affordable snacks, lunchtime fillers like *onigiri*, instant ramen and soba. Supermarkets will often have lunch boxes (bento) for as little as ¥300.

Taxis are a major expense if you use them regularly, with base tariffs starting at ¥430, rising quickly if you get stuck in a traffic jam. Subway and commuter train tickets are much more reasonable, with base fares starting at ¥170 for two or three stops. Rates are slightly different for each line.

There is no tipping system in Japan, and prices quoted usually include a service charge and consumption tax, all of which makes a significant difference.

Business hours

Officially, business is done on a 9am–5pm basis, but this is in theory only. The Japanese will often do overtime until 8 or 9pm. In general, **government** offices are open from 8.30 or 9am to 4 or 5pm Monday to Friday, and from 9am to noon on Saturdays. **Main post offices** are open 9am to 7pm Monday to Friday, 9am to 5pm on Saturday and 9am to noon on Sunday and holidays. **Branch post offices** are open 9am to 5pm Monday to Friday. **Department stores** and larger shops open daily from 10am to 7.30 or 8pm, although some close once or twice a month, which varies with each store. **Restaurants** are generally open for lunch from 11.30am to 2pm and for dinner from 5 to 9 or 10pm, although in major cities they often stay open much later. **Major companies** and **offices** are open from 9am to 5pm Monday to Friday. Some are also open on Saturday mornings. Most **small shops** open between 9 and 11am and close between 6 and 8pm. Convenience stores are open 24 hours.

Business travellers

When you meet a Japanese person, wait to see if she or he shakes your hand or bows, and then follow suit. Younger people are more comfortable with the handshake in general. Dressing smartly is part of doing business in Japan, something you should emulate.

The Japanese love of consensus, of trying to avoid confrontation wherever possible, is legendary, and can make doing business in Japan a frustrating experience. Don't expect rapid decisions, or a meeting to yield quick results. Long-term relationships are important to the Japanese business community, and these may take time to develop.

At meetings expect stiff formality to prevail, although a certain amount of small talk and civilities can break the ice. It may seem an elliptical approach, but circling around a topic before getting down to business is the norm. The pecking order for sitting is important: wait for others to decide this. The same applies to social situations like dinner.

The exchange of business cards is a vital ritual at first meetings. Make sure you have a good supply as they can go fast. If possible, have your cards printed on one side in *katakana* script, so that non-English-speakers can pronounce it easily and do not jot down names or make notes on these cards. Don't be surprised or offended if you are asked questions regarding age, education, family background and company service. Identity and "proper" affiliation are very important in Japan. One other thing to remember is that, no matter how daunting business etiquette may seem, as a foreigner you are given plenty of leeway – making an effort is more important than getting everything right.

C

Children

With a little advance planning Japan is a perfectly feasible place to bring children. There are many choices of activities, from amusement parks, children-oriented museums, zoos, aquariums and toy shops. When exploring Japanese cities with kids, try to avoid train rush hours, especially when using pushchairs.

Where public-toilet facilities are often inadequate in Japan, department stores usually have family rooms and play areas. Stores and malls are good places to eat, with plenty of set meals for children. Many of the bigger hotels offer babysitting services.

Children's activities

Bringing children to Japan is a relatively easy task, given that the Japanese love kids and that the country is both safe and hygienic, with plenty of health and food products targeting toddlers to teens. There is plenty to keep children interested, though too many temples may tire even the most tolerant child. Overhead and subway trains and buses are free for kids under six; those aged 6–11 pay half-price. Trains, subway trains and buses have seating designated for small children and pregnant women (along with the elderly), although if they are full don't expect many people who shouldn't be sitting in them to give up their seats. Children under three go free on domestic flights, but have to share a seat with a parent; fares for kids aged 3–11 are half-price. If you are looking for some free fun for kids, you will find small (though not always pristine) children's playgrounds with slides, swings and so on in most city neighbourhoods. In many major home electronics stores, especially in Akihabara, kids (and adults!) can also often test out the latest video games for free.

Climate

When untravelled Japanese talk about living in a country that has four seasons – as if this is unique to Japan – technically they are talking about an area which at the very most extends from parts of northern to certain areas of western Honshu Island. These are the only regions that can truly be said to have four distinct seasons. This limited but culturally dominant belt, embracing both Tokyo and the former imperial capital of Kyoto, has influenced not only perceptions about the four seasons but almost every statement on Japanese culture.

Spring begins in the south, with the cherry blossoms coming out in Okinawa in February. Hokkaido, where the winter snow can linger well into April, will enjoy the blossoms in May. In general, May is a warm and pleasant month, while June sees the onset of the humid rainy season, known poetically as *tsuyu* (dew). This drizzly spell lasts about a month. Hokkaido, as its tourist brochures never fail to mention, is exempt from this. Midsummer is hot and sticky, with the mercury rising into the mid- and upper thirties ⁰C. Typhoons occur mostly between August and October.

Many Japanese will say that October and November are the finest months to visit their country – the crisp, well-defined days of autumn, when the skies are often blue. Winter can be harsh in Hokkaido and the Japan Sea side of the country, with heavy snowdrifts. Clear skies and low humidity are the rewards of January and February, the coldest months. March is generally chilly, overcast and changeable. But again, bear in mind that, while one set of travellers will be enjoying the ski slopes of Hokkaido in that month, others may be taking their first tentative dip in the blue, coral waters of Okinawa.

Clothing

Although Japanese people place a great deal of importance on clothing

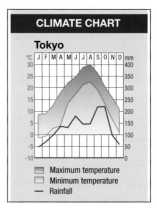

CLIMATE CHART

Tokyo

- Maximum temperature
- Minimum temperature
- Rainfall

and appearance in general, provided that clothes are clean, casual wear is perfectly in order for most occasions. In business situations, suits are definitely de rigueur, although in summer many companies now let staff work without a jacket and tie to reduce the need for air conditioning and thus conserve energy.

The weather is relatively predictable, so dress for the season, bringing a thick jacket for winter, light cotton or linen clothes for the late spring and summer. A light jacket will usually suffice for spring and autumn. Check world weather reports for last-minute adjustments, though, before starting out on your trip.

Crime and security

While the number of offences committed throughout Japan remains about one-eighth the number in the United States, crime has risen over the past two decades, particularly among Japanese youth. Personal security is far higher than in Western countries, and visitors routinely comment on the fact that they never feel threatened walking in Japanese streets.

Theft of luggage and money is rare, although some pickpockets do work the Tokyo and Osaka subway and trains. The media is always full of reports of crimes committed by foreigners, especially Asian immigrants, though when closely examined, many of these turn out to be visa violations or activities connected to Japan's sex industry.

Organised crime, while often violent, is unlikely to affect the traveller or ordinary citizen as these are usually the result of turf disputes. The police generally turn a blind eye to prostitution, gambling, ticket touting, illegal immigration and the protection rackets operated by the *yakuza* gangs, only conducting crackdowns when intergang rivalry threatens the public domain.

If an incident occurs, report it to the nearest *koban* (police box). These are located in every neighbourhood, especially in busy areas and outside major railway stations. If possible go with an eyewitness or a native speaker. For police contact details, see page 373.

Women travellers

Japan is not a dangerous place for women travellers on their own, although a certain amount of harassment, from which foreign women are not entirely excluded, does occasionally occur on crowded trains. There are anti-groping posters on most trains and at stations. The meaning of the term *seku-hara* (sexual harassment) is finally sinking in at the workplace, although Japan still lags behind Western countries in this regard, evident in degrading TV shows (not all late at night), tabloid papers and the thinly veiled ads for prostitution services and manga books glorifying sexual violence towards women.

That said, it is safer to walk, travel, eat and drink anywhere in Japan than in most Western countries. Although red-light areas of large cities are inadvisable for women to walk alone in, two women together are unlikely to suffer anything worse than leering.

Customs regulations

Japan strictly prohibits the import and use of narcotic drugs, firearms and ammunition. If caught in possession of any of these, the offender can expect no leniency. You can bring any currency into Japan, but amounts of cash over ¥1 million need to be declared to customs. You are also allowed to bring with you into Japan, free of tax, three 760ml (25fl oz) bottles of spirits, 400 cigarettes and 100 cigars or 500g of tobacco, and 56ml (2fl oz) of perfume. There is no duty-free allowance for valuables whose value exceeds ¥200,000. For more information visit www.customs.go.jp.

Foreign tourists can make purchases of electronics worth over ¥10,000 and of consumable goods over ¥5,000 exempt from the consumption tax of 10 percent. A passport is required for all tax-free purchases, and they can only be made in licensed shops (mostly major department stores).

E

Eating out

Japan is an eater's paradise, and the diversity of possibilities would fill a separate guide (for a broad-brush survey of Japanese cuisine, see page 121). Alleys are lined with restaurants, whole buildings sometimes

⊘ Electricity

The power supply is 100 volts AC. Eastern cities in Japan, including Tokyo, run on 50 cycles, while those in the west such as Kyoto, Osaka and Nagoya use 60 cycles. Sockets are two-pin and most hotels will have adaptors.

occupied with nothing else; entire blocks have been taken over in some cities. You certainly won't need to look hard to find somewhere good to eat. In the app, you will find plenty of suggestions for good eats in most of the main areas covered in the guide, and in particular you will find restaurants that offer opportunities to try classic Japanese dishes and the country's fine and diverse range of regional fare. If you want a McDonald's, a bento lunch box or a simple coffee shop, just walk down any street; if you want something memorable, remember that restaurants rated ¥¥¥ or ¥¥¥¥ will need a reservation in advance.

Economical eating and drinking

Japan has faced a mixed economy ever since the economic bubble burst in the late 1980s, but every cloud has its silver lining. One positive outcome of the economic malaise, at least from the point of view of travellers and the fully employed Japanese, has been the cut-throat competitiveness of the food sector throughout Japan, particularly with set lunch offerings. Bargain deals in all kinds of restaurants, even in traditionally more expensive areas like Tokyo's Ginza, are the norm.

It's quite common for Japanese to buy meals (especially for lunch while at work) at convenience stores like 7-Eleven, Lawson and Family Mart. The competition between convenience stores is stiff, so the food is made fresh daily and though it wouldn't win any culinary awards, it represents really good value for money, with many dishes under ¥450. Many restaurants also offer filling "lunch set specials" which can be as cheap as ¥600. Fast-food joints have sets for as little as ¥350.

Family restaurants like Denny's, Coco's and Volks often have a free coffee refill service after the first cup, though you will find far better deals on food elsewhere. Tipping is almost non-existent in Japan, which helps offset costs.

Away from the budget end, don't expect to escape from most decent restaurants for less than ¥3,000 per person, excluding drinks. On average, a night on the upscale side of town can run in the region of ¥10,000. If you're on a budget, stick to medium-range restaurants, *izaka-ya*, street stands and convenience stores.

Be aware that some restaurants, typically at the more expensive end of the spectrum, will add a 10 or 15 percent service charge to your bill. Some *izaka-ya* and mid-range establishments will add a flat fee of a few hundred yen as a table charge.

If you just want to grab a quick drink without having to order food (as most *izaka-ya* insist upon), the best and cheapest option is to find a standing bar, or *tachinomiya*, where it is not uncommon to get a medium-size draught beer or glass of sake for ¥300. Another option is to find a Western-style pub, which is easily done in the major cities, although expect to pay upward of ¥800 a pint after the common 5–7pm happy-hour period.

Where and what to eat

Japan has myriad different places to eat and drink. At the budget end, besides those mentioned above, are local fast-food joints such as Yoshinoya, where the speciality is *gyu-don*, a bowl of rice covered in simmered beef and onions, and rivals like Matsuya, where alongside the *gyu-don* they also serve cheap curry rice.

Moving up a notch on the culinary totem pole are the many *teishoku* (set meal) restaurants that do a roaring trade at lunch with home-style cooking – the classic trio of rice, pickles and miso soup served with a main dish such as a piece of fish or a breaded pork cutlet. With so much competition in the big cities (Tokyo alone has some 150,000 licensed restaurants), you can always get a good feed for under ¥1,000 (very often under ¥800). Other similarly priced restaurants, specialising in ramen, soba noodles or a host of other cuisines abound. The traveller need only walk down any main street in any town or city to find numerous possibilities. Plastic food in display cases or photographic menus make decisions both

easier and more difficult – too many choices. Look, sniff, and enter.

At dinner, *izaka-ya* (pubs) make for a great place to try a variety of dishes and have a drink without spending too much. As you will see in the listings that follow, every part of Japan has its local specialities, and there are numerous restaurants that specialise in a single dish or individual style of cuisine. Most of these tend to have a more refined atmosphere than a typical *izaka-ya* and traditional decor, and, depending on the type of cuisine, the price can vary from budget to bank-breaking. If you can afford it, at least once push the boat out for a *kaiseki* dinner – it represents Japanese cuisine at its most subtle and exquisite.

Eating etiquette

Good table manners, Japanese-style, go a long way. Here are a few tips:

The wet towel (*o-shibori*) you receive to freshen up at the beginning of the meal should be neatly rolled up when you've finished, and don't use it on anything except your hands, no matter how often you see middle-aged men washing their faces with them before eating!

It is bad manners to wave your chopsticks around, to use them to point at someone, to stick them upright in your rice (an allusion to death) or to pull dishes forward with them. If you have a communally shared bowl of food, then it is considered good form (though not everyone does it) to turn your chopsticks around and use the reverse points to pick up the food.

Japanese-style soups (*suimono*) and noodles in broth (except ramen) are sipped straight from the bowl. Whereas it is altogether acceptable form in Japan to slurp noodle dishes, there is no need to slurp soups. Sip them directly from the bowl without a spoon, as this is the best way to savour their delicate flavour.

For dishes that are dipped in sauce, such as tempura and sashimi, hold the sauce dish with one hand and dip the food into it with the chopsticks. Soy sauce should not be splashed onto a dish. Rather, pour it into the small soy-sauce dish, only a little at a time and use it sparingly.

You will rarely see Japanese eating and walking at the same time. They buy the food or snack, then find a place to sit properly and finish it

completely. The same restraint goes for eating or drinking on the subway or commuter trains – wait until you are off the train.

If you are eating with Japanese acquaintances, it is polite to say *itadakimasu* (the equivalent of saying "bon appétit", even if you garble the pronunciation) before eating, and then *gochisosama deshita* (literally "you prepared a feast") once you've finished. It's also good form to say *gochisosama deshita* to staff when you are leaving a restaurant. To toast the first drink of the night, raise your glass and say *kampai*.

Embassies and consulates

Australia, 2-1-14 Mita, Minato-ku. Tel: 03-5232-4111 (www.japan.embassy. gov.au/tkyo/home.html).

Canada, 7-3-38 Akasaka, Minato-ku. Tel: 03-5412-6200 (www.japan.gc.ca).

India, 2-2-11 Kudan-minami, Chiyoda-ku. Tel: 03-3262-2391 (www. indembassy-tokyo.gov.in/home.html).

Ireland, 2-10-7 Kojimachi, Chiyoda-ku. Tel: 03-3263-0695 (www. dfa.ie/irish-embassy/japan).

New Zealand, 20-40 Kamiyamacho, Shibuya-ku. Tel: 03-3467-2271 (www. mfat.govt.nz/en/countries-and-regions/ north-asia/japan/new-zealand-embassy).

Singapore, 5-12-3 Roppongi, Minato-ku. Tel: 03-3586-9111 (www. mfa.gov.sg/content/mfa/overseasmission/ tokyo.html).

United Kingdom, 1 Ichibancho, Chiyoda-ku. Tel: 03-5211-1100 (www. gov.uk/world/japan).

United States, 1-10-5 Akasaka, Minato-ku. Tel: 03-3224-5000 (http:// jp.usembassy.gov/).

US Consulate General in Osaka, 2-11-5 Nishi-temma, Kita-ku, Osaka. Tel: 06-6315-5900 (http:// jp.usembassy.gov/embassy-consulates/ osaka/).

Emergencies

Police: 110

Fire and ambulance: 119

Police info in English: 03-3501-0110 (Mon–Fri 8.30am–5.15pm)

Emergency calls can be made from any phone without using coins or prepaid telephone cards.

Japan Helpline, 24-hour information and help about everything, in English. Tel: 0570-000-911, www. jhelp.com.

For **medical information**, call 03-5285-8181 in Tokyo (English spoken; daily Mon–Fri 5am–10pm, Sat–Sun 9am–10pm).

Etiquette

At work and in most formal situations, the Japanese may seem a very reticent and reserved people, lacking in spontaneity or personality. There are books and theories explaining this behaviour, but it only provides one side of the picture. Japanese (especially men) can become extremely raucous when drinking and often let out their real opinions and feelings after a few drinks. The next morning in the office, all is forgotten. Intentionally.

On the crowded trains you will find yourself being pushed and bumped around. You do not need to be very polite here; just push along with everyone else. It is often said that the Japanese are only polite with their shoes off, which means that they are polite and courteous with people they know well and would be indoors with (where shoes are almost always removed).

For the Japanese, the distinction between inside and outside the home is important. Inside the entrance to all homes (and some restaurants) is an area for removing shoes. You then step up into the living area, wearing slippers or in your stockinged feet. (Slippers are never worn on tatami mats, however, only socks or bare feet.) Taking shoes off keeps the house clean, besides being more relaxing, and it also increases the amount of usable space, since you can sit on the floor without worrying about getting dirty. The toilet, however, is one area of the house that is considered dirty, so separate slippers are provided for use there.

The custom of bowing has, in many cases, become somewhat a conditioned reflex. Foreigners, in general, are not expected to bow, and this is especially evident if a Japanese person first reaches out to shake hands.

As for punctuality and keeping appointments, outside of business the Japanese have a reputation for not being very punctual. At several of the famous meeting places (in Tokyo, in front of Ginza's Sony Building or at the Hachiko entrance to Shibuya Station, as examples) you can observe people waiting for someone, often for an hour or more.

After several apologies and explanations, everything is usually forgotten and forgiven.

The way the Japanese usually speak and express themselves gives a very good picture of their culture. Except when talking to close friends and family, direct statements of fact are most often avoided as this implies that the speaker has a superior knowledge, and this is considered impolite. Therefore, much beating about the bush is done, which often leads to misunderstandings and seems like a waste of time to foreigners, but this must be taken into consideration when dealing with the Japanese.

In their own language, the Japanese are adept at reading between the lines and interpreting deft nuances of words and tone.

In any case, whatever happens, foreigners, who are blissfully unaware of these points, are usually forgiven for any breach of etiquette, so there's no need to spend time worrying about what is right and wrong. The cardinal rule is to try to be courteous at all times. Japanese behaviour in general is situational, and the Japanese themselves often do not know the right thing to do in any given situation. "It all depends on the situation," remarks the smart alec, but it's often fun for everyone involved when one of "us" makes a slip. Sometimes it actually helps to break the ice and put everyone in a more relaxed mood.

F

Festivals

Festivals, or *matsuri*, seem to be happening at any given time somewhere in Japan, and indeed have been an important part of Japanese life for hundreds of years. Many of the festivals have their roots in the long history of Japan's agricultural society. In today's ever-modernising Japan, they are one of the few occasions when the Japanese can dress up and relive the past. Below is a list of the most important festivals (for public holidays, see page 379). For information on forthcoming events going on during any particular week or month, please consult the Tourist Information Centre (see page 381) or www.jnto.go.jp.

January

The first **sumo** tournament of the year, **Hatsu-basho**, is held for 15 days at Tokyo's Kokugikan in mid-January. Shujin-no-hi (Adults' Day) falls on the second Monday of January, when 20-year-olds visit shrines in their finest kimonos.

February

On the 3rd is **Setsubun**, the traditional bean-throwing ceremony that is meant to purify the home of evil. Roasted beans are scattered from the inside of the house to the outside while people shout, *"Oni wa soto"* (Devils, go out!), and from the outside of the home to the inside while *"Fuku wa uchi"* (Good luck, come in) is shouted. The same ceremony is also held at temples and shrines. Plum Viewing festivals begin in early to late February. The most famous viewing spot in Tokyo, Yushima Tenjin shrine, holds *ikebana* and tea-ceremony displays at this time. Sapporo's famous *Yuki Matsuri* (Snow Festival) in early February features giant statues sculpted from snow and ice.

March

On the 3rd is *Hina Matsuri* (Girls' Day), a festival for little girls. Small *Hina* dolls, representing imperial court figures, are decorated and displayed at home and in several public places. *Yamabushi* mountain monks perform the Fire-Walking Ceremony in mid-March at the foot of Mount Takao outside Tokyo. Spectators can test their mettle by walking barefoot across the smouldering coals of the fires. Many shrines throughout Japan have their Daruma Fairs on 3–4 March, selling red, white and black dolls of the famous Zen monk. One of the two empty eyes should be painted in upon undertaking a new, difficult task, the other filled in upon its successful completion.

April

From early to mid-April across much of Japan is *O-hanami* (cherry-blossom-viewing), one of the important spring rites. People love to turn out and picnic, drink sake and sing songs under the pink blossoms. Kyoto has a multitude of blossom-viewing parties, the most famous being at Daigo-ji. In Tokyo, Ueno Park attracts big o-hanami crowds and is a very lively place for a picnic, while Chidorigafuchi moat at

Tokyo's Imperial Palace is especially photogenic. On 8 April is **Hana Matsuri** (Birthday of Buddha), when commemorative services are held at various temples such as Gokoku-ji, Senso-ji, Zojo-ji and Hommon-ji. A colourful display of horseback archery is put on by men dressed in medieval costumes during the Yabusame Festival in Sumida Park in mid-April. Acrobatic marionettes balance on towering festival floats as they are carried across the bridges of the town in the **Takayama Festival** on 14–15 April.

May

In mid-May, the **Natsu-basho** (summer **sumo** tournament) is held for 15 days at the Kokugikan in Tokyo. On the 3rd Saturday and Sunday, the **Sanja Matsuri** is held. This is one of the big Edo festivals honouring the three fishermen who found the image of Kannon in the river. Tokyo's Asakusa-jinja Senso-ji Temple is a great place to go at this time to see the dancing, music and many portable shrines. In mid-May the huge **Kanda Festival**, one of Tokyo's most important *matsuri*, is held every other year. Processions and floats and portable shrines parade through this downtown area. A fine historical costume parade takes place in Kyoto during the 15 May **Aoi Matsuri** (Hollyhock Festival). There's a similar event on 17 May, with horseback archery, at the Tosho-gu shrine in Nikko.

June

The summer rains blanket Kyoto from mid-June to mid-July. Kifune-jinja, dedicated to the god of water, celebrates the season in a vibrant water festival. Torchlight performances of *noh* plays are held 1–2 June at the Heian Shrine. On the second Sunday is **Torigoe Jinja Taisai**, a night-time festival, when the biggest and heaviest portable shrine in Tokyo is carried through the streets by lantern light. It all happens at the Torigoe Shrine. From the 10th to the 16th on even-numbered years is **Sanno Sai**, another big Edo festival featuring a *gyoretsu* (people parading in traditional costumes) on Saturday at the Hie Shrine. June is the season for iris-viewing, the best locations being the Iris Garden in the grounds of the Meiji shrine in Tokyo and the Iris Garden in Tokyo's Kiyosumi Teien.

July

From the 6th to the 8th is the **Asagao Ichi** (Morning Glory Fair) in Tokyo, when over 100 merchants set up stalls selling the flower at Iriya Kishibojin. On 7 July is the **Tanabata Matsuri**, a festival celebrating the only day of the year when, according to the legend, the Weaver Princess (Vega) and her lover the Cowherder (Altair) can cross the Milky Way to meet. People write their wishes on coloured paper, hang them on bamboo branches, and then float them down a river the next day. Also in Tokyo, 9–10 July is the **Hozuki Ichi** (Ground Cherry Fair) at Senso-ji from early morning to midnight. A visit to this temple on the 10th is meant to be equal to 46,000 visits at other times. On the last Saturday of July, the **Sumida-gawa Hanabi Taikai** (Sumida River Fireworks) is held. This is the biggest fireworks display in Tokyo, and the best places to watch the display are between the Kototoi and Shirahige bridges, or at the Komagata Bridge. Fukuoka's pride and joy, its Hakata Yamagasa, takes place 1–15 July, an event that sees colourful portable shrines carried through the streets. Kyoto's grandest event, the 17 July Gion Matsuri, features massive floats hung with fine silks and paper lanterns.

August

Late July/early August hosts a more contemporary event that is fast becoming a tradition: international and local acts gather for the huge, three-day Fuji Rock Festival in Naeba. Between the 13th and the 15th is the **O-Bon** festival, when people return to their hometowns to clean up graves and offer prayers to the souls of departed ancestors. The traditional **Bon Odori** folk dances are held all over around this time. The best known, running for almost two months, is in Gujo Hachiman. The largest single turnout of dancers is in Tokushima during its more renowned Awa Odori. Both Aomori and Hirosaki hold Nebuta and Neputa Matsuri on 1–7 August. Giant paper figures are lit up from inside like lanterns.

September

Mid-September is the time for moon-viewing, with many events across Kyoto. Osawa Pond has been known since Heian times as one of Japan's three great moon-viewing sites. This is also a good time of year for dinner, with moon-viewing, on one of the *yakatabune* barges that sail around Tokyo Bay. On 16 September at the Tsurugaoka Hachimangu Shrine in Kamakura is an annual display of *yabusame* (horseback archery) performed by riders in samurai armour.

October

From mid- to late October is chrysanthemum-viewing time, and there are flower displays dotted around the cities. Nagasaki's Okunchi Matsuri, on 7–9 October, is an interesting blend of Chinese, European and Shinto, with dragon dances and floats representing Dutch galleons. Kyoto's Jidai Matsuri, on 22 October, is a splendid, quietly dignified costume parade.

November

The 15th is **Shichi-Go-San** (Seven-Five-Three), a ceremony for 5-year-old boys and 3- and 7-year-old girls. The children usually dress up in kimonos and *hakama* (loose trousers) and are taken to visit a shrine.

December

Kaomise (face-showing) is Kyoto's gala kabuki performance at Minami-za, when the actors reveal their real faces. On 7–8 December, Senbon Shaka-do celebrates the day of Buddha's enlightenment with a radish-boiling ceremony to help ward off evil. The 14th is **Gishi Sai**, a memorial service for the famous 47 Ronin who, on this day in 1702, avenged the death of their master and later committed ritual suicide. They are buried at the Sengaku-ji in Tokyo, where the service is held. On 31 December at the stroke of midnight, every temple bell in the country begins to toll. The bells toll 108 times, for the 108 evil human passions. This is called **Joya no Kane**, and the general public are allowed to strike the bells at various temples.

G

Guides and travel agencies

Guides and escorts

Japan Guide Association, 603, International Building, 1-6-1 Kanda

Izumicho, Chiyoda-ku, Tokyo. Tel: 03-3863-2895, www.jga21c.or.jp.
Japan Federation of Certified Guides, Hatoya Building, 2-29-7 Nakano, Nakano-ku, Tokyo. Tel: 03-3380-6611, http://jfg-e.jp.

Goodwill guides

Goodwill Guides are volunteers who assist overseas visitors. All volunteers are registered with the JNTO. With over 40,000 members, the guides are affiliated with more than 80 groups throughout Japan, and guides are available in over two dozen regions to offer local information or guide you on walking tours. For a list of volunteer guides throughout Japan visit www.jnto.go.jp.

Travel agencies

The following agencies offer travel services for foreign travellers:
Kyoto Tourist Information Center, 2nd floor of Kyoto Station. Tel: 075-343-0548.
Nippon Travel Agency, Nihonbashi Dia Bldg. 11F, 1-19-1, Nihonbashi, Chuo-ku, Tokyo 103. Tel: 03-6895-8344, www.ntainbound.com.
Japan Dream Tours, 1-13-10-2A Hatchobori, Chuo-ku, Tokyo. Tel: 03-6280-4646, http://japandreamtours.com.
Osaka Visitors Information Center, Nankai Terminal Bldg 1F, 5-1-60 Namba, Cnuo-ku, Osaka. Tel: 06-6131-4550, http://osaka-info.jp.
Okinawa Tourist Service, 1-2-3 Matsuo, Naha, Okinawa 900. Tel: 098-862-1111, www.otsinfo.co.jp.

Health and medical care

In general, levels of hygiene are very high, and it is very unlikely that you will become ill as a result of eating or drinking something. The tap water, though heavily chlorinated, is drinkable. Most food is of a high standard. However, because the Japanese place so much emphasis on presentation and how food looks, there is wide use of chemical fertilisers in Japan, and therefore it is not recommended to eat the skins of fruits and some vegetables.

Medical services

Try to remember that you are in Japan and must be prepared to adapt to the Japanese system.

Although some doctors may speak English, the receptionist and nursing staff will not, so it is advisable to bring along a Japanese-speaking friend or someone who can speak both languages. If you show up at a hospital or clinic without an appointment, you have to be prepared to wait your turn. Here is a list of hospitals and clinics in Tokyo where you would have no problem in being understood or treated. They all have different administrative systems and hours for outpatient treatment.

Hospitals in Tokyo

International Catholic Hospital (Seibo Byoin), 2-5-1 Nakaochiai, Shinjuku-ku. Tel: 03-3951-1111, www.seibokai.or.jp. Open Mon–Sat 8–11am and 2–8pm. Closed 3rd Sat of the month.
Red Cross Medical Centre (Nisseki), 4-1-22 Hiroo, Shibuya-ku. Tel: 03-3400-1311, www.med.jrc.or.jp. Open Mon–Fri 8.30am–3pm.
St Luke's International Hospital (Seiroka Byoin), 9-1 Akashicho, Chuo-ku. Tel: 03-5550-7120, http://hospital.luke.ac.jp. Open Mon–Sat 8.30am–5pm.
Tokyo Adventist Hospital (Tokyo Eisei Byoin), 3-17-3 Amanuma, Suginami-ku. Tel: 03-3392-6151, www.tokyoeisei.com. Open Mon–Fri 9am–12.30pm, Mon–Thu 2–5.30pm.
Toho Fujin Women's Clinic, 5-3-10 Kiba, Koto-ku. Tel: 03-3630-0303, www.toho-clinic.or.jp. Open Mon–Fri 9–11.30am, 1.30–5.30pm, Sat 9–11.30am, 1.30–4pm.
Japan Helpline, 24-hour information on everything, including finding hospitals and emergency medical care (English). Tel: 0570-000-911, www.jhelp.com.
For **hospital information**, call 03-5285-8181 in Tokyo (English spoken; daily 9am–8pm).

Pharmacies

Most Western-brand, over-the-counter medicines are hard to find in Japan, and when they are available, prices are high. High-street drugstores such as Matsumoto Kiyoshi (www.matsukiyo.co.jp) and Tomods (www.tomods.jp) can help you with Japanese or Chinese remedies. It's best to bring your own preferred cold and allergy medicines with you, but note that many popular brands, like Sudafed, contain small amounts of amphetamine-like drugs and are illegal in Japan.

Be aware that while drugstores stock useful regular medication and may be able to advise you on coping with minor problems, they do not dispense prescription drugs. Prescriptions can only be obtained through a hospital or clinic after a consultation. The medicine will be issued to you on the same premises or you will be directed to a nearby pharmacist.
American Pharmacy, Marunouchi Building (basement), Chiyoda-ku. Open Mon–Fri 9am–9pm, Sat 10am–9pm, Sun 10am–8pm.
Pharmacy at Tokyo Medical and Surgical Clinic, 32 Shiba Koen Building, 3-4-30 Shiba-Koen, Minato-ku. Tel: 03-3434-5817, www.tmsc.jp. Mon–Fri 9am–5.30pm, Sat 9am–1pm.
Yakuju Pharmacy Roppongi Izumi Garden, 1-6-1 Roppongi, Minato-ku. Tel: 03-3568-3370, www.yakuju.co.jp. Open Mon–Fri 9am–7pm, Sat 9.30am–2pm and 3–5pm.

Dentists

Royal Dental Office, 4-10-11 Roppongi, Minato-ku. Tel: 03-3404-0819, www.royal-dental-roppongi.com.
Tokyo Clinic Dental Office, 2F, 32 Shiba Koen Bldg, 3-4-30, Shiba-Koen, Minato-ku. Tel: 03-3431-4225, www.tcdo.jp.

Optical care

Fuji Optical Service International, 1F, Otemachi Bldg, 1-6-1 Otemachi, Chiyoda-ku. Tel: 03-3214-4751, www.fujimegane.co.jp.
MinamiAoyama Eye Clinic, Renai Aoyama Building 4F 3-3-11 Kitaaoyama, Minato-ku, Tokyo. Tel: 03-5772-1451, http://minamiaoyama.or.jp.

Internet

Free internet hotspots are widespread in Japan; you will find them at airports, train and subway stations, department and convenience stores, restaurants and bars, as well as along major shopping streets. Most of these services require registration. Japan Connected-free Wi-Fi and Travel Japan Wi-Fi are two handy smartphone apps that offer you access to thousands of hotspots without having to sign up for each one individually. Western-style and business hotels also provide in-room broadband or Wi-Fi, usually free; however, some high-end establishments may charge a daily fee. You can find a list of hotspots on www.freespot.com/users/map_e.html. Paid mobile internet providers that offer services to visitors include docomo (http://visitor.docomowifi.com/en) and Wi2 (http://wi2.co.jp) – a week can cost less than ¥1000. Another solution is buying a data SIM card for your device (virtually all smartphones and tablets should be compatible with the Japanese mobile-phone system) or renting a pocket Wi-Fi from a phone rental company (see Mobile Phones).

Internet cafés

While 24-hour manga cafés are very competitive, there are also prefectural and city culture/exchange centres that typically have machines available free for a limited time. Most airports also have internet-connected computers available, typically at ¥100/10 minutes. Tourist offices will always have a list of cafés and access points handy and in some cases will have their own free or paid internet-connected computers along a Wi-Fi hotspot.

L

Left luggage

Carry as little luggage as possible when travelling in Japan. Trains and stations, especially, are not designed for travellers with more than a small overnight bag. If you're thinking of making all your Tokyo train connections while hauling several large bags – forget it. The train/subway map looks neat and tidy, but station connections are serious hikes with no trolleys or porters available, and seemingly endless stairs. Hotels, of course, will usually store luggage for guests heading off on adventures.

Several companies, including JAL ABC (www.jalabc.com), GPA (www.gpanet.co.jp), Yamoto Transport (www.kuronekoyamato.co.jp) and Sagawa Express (www.sagawa-exp.co.jp) offer convenient baggage delivery services, which are very popular with the Japanese. Depending on the destination, it will cost you ¥2000–4000 to have each luggage item

delivered from the airport to your hotel. In most cases you should be able to arrange with your hotel for the baggage to be sent to your next accommodation, which will make multi-destination travelling more enjoyable.

International airports. For security reasons, bombs in particular, the international airports have no coin lockers. There are cloakrooms, however, at international airports. While staff may not speak English, forms are bilingual and the staff will know why you're standing there. At Narita:

JAL ABC: Terminal 1 and 2: 6 locations both in arrivals and departure halls. ¥300–800 per day per bag, with no time limit for storage. Open daily 7am–9pm.

GPA (Green Port Agency): Terminal 1 and 2: 6 locations both in arrivals and departure halls, 1F. ¥300–800 per day per bag, 30-day limit. Open daily 7am–last fight.

Train and subway stations. Most train and subway stations have coin lockers of varying sizes for ¥300 to ¥800 per day, depending on station and size of the locker. Time limits vary, so check, but are typically 3 days. After that, contents are removed. You'll have no problem finding lockers; Japanese use them as a habit and convenience.

Cloakrooms for large bags (around ¥600 per item) are located at several main JR stations, however they often require that luggage is reclaimed on the same day.

Tokyo Station, outside Yaesu south exit, 7.30am–8.30pm.

Ueno Station, in front of central exit, 8am–8pm.

Shin Osaka Station, outside the central exit, 9am–8pm.

Kyoto Station, Karasuma central exit and Hachijo central exit, 8am–8pm.

LGBTQ travellers

Unlike other developed countries, homosexuality in Japan is still kept very much under wraps. This is not to say that it is invisible. Gay and transvestite celebrities often appear on TV, and it isn't hard to find comic books and films with gay themes. Tokyo's Shinjuku ni-chome district is the undisputed centre of the gay scene in Japan. There are over 300 gay bars and clubs located around its central street, Naka-dori. Outside Tokyo and Osaka, however, the gay scene is very difficult to gain access

to. Badi (www.badi.jp) is Japan's premier publication for gay men, but there are classified ads and occasional coverage of the scene in the free magazine Metropolis (http://metropolisjapan.com) as well as on websites such as Time Out Tokyo (www.timeout.com/tokyo).

Gay websites

www.utopia-asia.com/tipsjapn.htm General coverage of gay life in Japan, with club and venue listings.
www.tokyowrestling.com Webzine for women, with loads of info on Tokyo's lesbian scene.

Gay venues

AiiRO Café
7F, Tenka Bldg, 1F, 2-18-1, Shinjuku, Shinjuku-ku
Tel: 03-6273-0740, www.aliving.net/aiirocafe.
Formerly known as Advocates Café, this is a popular meeting place for both Japanese and foreigners.
Kinsmen
2F, 2-18-5, Shinjuku, Shinjuku-ku
Tel: 03-3354-4949, http://kinsmen2.sakura.ne.jp.
The male-only counterpart to Kinswomyn.

Lost property

The Japanese are quite honest about handing in found items. If you've lost a wallet packed with cash, a camera or an overnight bag, chances are it will be safe. In fact, you often hear stories of lost wedding rings, computers and other valuables finding their way home.

JR trains: Items left on trains will usually be kept for a couple of days at the nearest station. After that, they are taken to one of the major stations to be stored for five more days. The best thing to do is call the JR East Infoline 050-2016-1603, daily 10am–6pm.

Subways: On the Toei trains, or on Tokyo city-operated buses, enquire about lost property at terminals the same day, or call the lost-and-found centre, on 03-3812-2011 (Japanese only), Mon–Fri 9am–7pm.

Taxis: All taxi companies in Tokyo report unclaimed items to a single centre, the Tokyo Taxi Kindaika Centre. Tel: 03-3648-0300 (Japanese only).

Police: As a last resort, contact the police. The Tokyo Metropolitan Police Department maintains an absolutely immense lost-and-found centre, with everything from forgotten umbrellas (zillions of them) to bags full of cash. Tel: 03-3814-4151, Mon–Fri 8.30am–5.15pm. English spoken sometimes, Japanese mostly.

M

Maps

The JNTO in Tokyo and elsewhere provide lots of adequate maps, including walking and hiking tours. Kodansha's **Tokyo City Atlas: A Bilingual Guide** is highly detailed and very useful. There is a similar atlas on Osaka and Kyoto. *Insight Flexi Map Tokyo* is laminated and immensely durable.

Media

Television

There are several terrestrial TV channels. One is from the quasi-national Japan Broadcasting Corporation (NHK) and the other five are private-sector commercial networks. NHK also broadcasts on two satellite channels, plus a high-definition TV channel. A small percentage of the programmes – including news bulletins – is bilingual, offering English on the sub-channel. Ask your hotel reception which button to press to see if the programme has this service. NHK's 7pm and 9pm news broadcast are always available with an English sub-channel.

Overseas networks CNN and BBC are available on satellite and cable TV at most large hotels.

Radio

The main foreign-language radio station is Inter FM (89.7 Mhz in Tokyo, 76.5 Mhz in Yokohama; www.interfm.co.jp), which broadcasts news and music mainly in English. J-Wave (81.3 Mhz; www.j-wave.co.jp) also has some shows in English. The American Forces Network Eagle (810 AM), broadcast by the US Armed Forces, airs music, news, US sports and some National Public Radio shows.

Newspapers

There are two daily newspapers in English. The *Japan Times* (www.japan-times.co.jp) is the premier English-language paper and the oldest, followed by *The Daily Yomiuri* (www.yomiuri.co.jp), which is comprised largely of wire stories and translations from the Japanese-language *Yomiuri Shimbun*. The *Nikkei* (www.nikkei.com) is a financial digest.

Magazines

Many English-language magazines are published in Japan, though the quality is not always the best. They tend to fall into three categories: events magazines, those focusing on Japanese culture, and custom publications for members' clubs, chambers of commerce and the like. Of the first group, look out for *Time Out Tokyo* (www.timeout.com/tokyo) and a free monthly *Metropolis* (https://metropolisjapan.com). J@pan.Inc (www.japaninc.com) is an internet- and business-related monthly magazine. The best event coverage is online, and there are now several online magazines up and running. Most of the custom publications are also available, at least in part, online.

Money

The unit of currency is the yen (¥), and the coins are ¥1, ¥5, ¥10, ¥50, ¥100 and ¥500. Bills are ¥1,000, ¥2,000, ¥5,000 and ¥10,000. Exchange rates are around US$1 = ¥80–125; £1 = ¥120–195; €1 = ¥100–145. Japanese stores, services and merchants are legally forbidden to accept foreign currencies. You can buy yen at foreign exchange banks and other authorised money changers on presentation of your passport. At the international airports at Narita and Osaka the banks are open 24 hours. Traveller's cheques can only be cashed at banks and major hotels, and are not accepted elsewhere.

Credit cards

Major credit cards, such as American Express, Diners Club, MasterCard and Visa, are accepted at establishments in and around Tokyo and Osaka/Kyoto, and there is no surcharge for their use. Unfortunately, acceptance is sporadic. Even at establishments displaying acceptance of Visa or MasterCard, for example, some will refuse to accept cards issued by banks overseas. If they refuse your card, don't get testy. Carry lots of cash instead, just in case.

American Express. Tel: 03-3220-6100; card member services (including lost/stolen cards): 0120-020-120 (toll-free).
Diners Club. Tel: 0120-074-024 (toll-free).
MasterCard. Tel: 03-5728-5200.
Visa. Tel: 006633-800-553 (toll-free).

Banks

Despite the wide use of computers and online systems, Japanese banks are often slow and inefficient in many fields. Especially when transferring money in or out of the country, you can expect the process to take a long time and to be costly. Also, small neighbourhood branches are often not able to process any international transactions. In order to send money out of the country, or cash foreign cheques, you will find it much easier to go to a major branch, where someone *may* be able to speak English and usually understand what you want to do. (An exception is Citibank, which is experienced in dealing with non-Japanese customers. If you are a Citibank customer elsewhere, your chances in Japan are much, much better.)

Banks open Mon–Fri 9am–3pm for normal banking. Cash dispensers (ATMs) are everywhere in Japan, even in convenience stores. The problem is that many of them can't be used for cash advances on cards issued abroad. Machines in Seven-Eleven convenience stores and at post offices usually accept most overseas cash cards, and will be among the few that can be operated in English. Just in case you can't find one of these, carry plenty of cash with you.

Tipping

No tipping remains the rule in Japan, except for unusual or exceptional services. Porters at large stations and airports charge a flat rate of around ¥300 per piece of luggage. Taxi drivers don't expect any tips, nor do hotel staff. The only exception are country inns, where older generations still hand a ¥1,000 note discreetly to the maid who takes them to their room and serves a welcome tea and sweets. You don't need to worry about doing this yourself.

N

Nightlife

Below is a brief round-up of the main nightlife areas in the regions covered in this guide. For up-to-date event listings for these areas, contact the local tourist information centres or check out the magazines and websites listed in the A–Z chapter (see page 378).

Kanto and Chubu

In **Tokyo** you will find plenty of places to burn money at night. If trendy bars and restaurants with sleekly designed interiors are your thing, head to Omotesando, Aoyama or Roppongi; the last is also home to a few raucous nightclubs. For a more bohemian feel, the bars in narrow alleys of Golden Gai, neighbouring Kabukicho in Shinjuku, are well worth exploring. Likewise Kabukicho itself, despite its sleazy reputation, has some great bars and small live music venues. More youthful are the bars, music venues and clubs in Shibuya and Harajuku, while hipsters will find something in the Koenji, Naka-Meguro or Shimokitazawa areas. If it's a more down-to-earth night out at an *izaka-ya* you want, you will find something wherever you are in Tokyo. The gay scene is centred around Shinjuku's Ni-chome area.

Heading west, to **Nagoya**, the place to explore is Sakae, the city's main entertainment district, and home to many a good bar, restaurant, *izaka-ya* and club.

The north

The north doesn't have much of a reputation for rip-roaring nightlife – not beyond the normal realms of *izaka-ya* that is – but the Susukino area of **Sapporo** is a definite exception. Head here for bars, clubs, restaurants and a fair sprinkling of sleazier establishments.

Kansai

Kansai is at its most raucous and liveliest in **Osaka**'s Dotonbori district, while the America-mura area has good watering holes. The narrow alleys of Osaka's Hozenji Yokocho are best for traditional restaurants and atmospheric *izaka-ya*. **Kyoto**, like Tokyo and Osaka, has a great nightlife, ranging from cool clubs and bars to lively *izaka-ya* and live music venues. Much of this activity is concentrated in the Kiya-machi area, around Sanjo and Shijo stations, as well as in Gion and Pontocho, alongside the Kamogawa River.

The south

Shikoku and Kyushu might have a fairly sedate vibe compared to Tokyo or Osaka, but the locals know how to have a rollicking night out. On **Shikoku**, Tokushima's Akita-machi, Kochi's Obiya-machi, and Matsuyama's Niban-cho and Sanban-cho areas are the liveliest entertainment districts, while on **Kyushu** head to Fukuoka's Nakasu area or Nagasaki's Shianbashi area. On **Okinawa**, the best nightlife is concentrated in central Naha.

P

Photography

Although there are no limitations on what you can photograph, beyond the obvious taboos of military installations, you should use your discretion in religious sites, particularly when there are rites and rituals taking place. As many Japanese are avid amateur photographers, camera shops are plentiful.

Postal services

There are nearly 30,000 post offices in Japan, which means they are ubiquitous. In addition to postal services, post offices offer savings services; in fact, the post office is Japan's largest holder of personal savings. Postal services are efficient and fast, but expensive for both international and domestic post.

For daytime opening hours, see Business Hours. For night owls, there's a 24-hour window at the **Tokyo Central Post Office**, located on the ground floor of the JP Tower near the Marunouchi side of Tokyo Station. Tel: 03-3217-5231. For 24-hour, 365-day international mail services, try also the main Shibuya post office (1-12-13 Shibuya, tel: 03-5469-9907).

International express mail: Larger post offices offer EMS services; for some reason, the isolated post offices outside the major cities of Tokyo and Osaka may require that an account be opened, though it's just a formality. If language is proving to be a problem in getting a package sent via EMS, this could be the reason.

International parcel post: foreign parcel post cannot exceed 30kg

(66lbs) per package to any international destination. For heavier packages or those that exceed certain size or content restrictions (which vary by country), a commercial courier service must be used.

Postal information (English-language). Tel: 0570-046-111, www.post.japanpost.jp.

Courier services

DHL. Tel: 0120-392-580, www.dhl.co.jp.
Federal Express. Tel: 0120-003-200 (toll-free), www.fedex.com/en-jp.

Public holidays

1 January: Ganjitsu (New Year's Day)
Second Monday in January: Seijin no Hi (Coming-of-Age Day)
11 February: Kenkoku Kinen no Hi (National Foundation Day)
23 February: Emperor's Birthday
Around 21 March: Shumbun no Hi (Vernal Equinox Day)
29 April: Showa no Hi (Showa Day)
3 May: Kempo Kinembi (Constitution Memorial Day)
4 May: Midori no Hi (Green Day)
5 May: Kodomo no Hi (Children's Day)
Third Monday in July: Umi no Hi (National Maritime Day)
11 August: Yama no Hi (Mountain Day), celebrated from 2016
Third Monday in September: Keiro no Hi (Respect-for-the-Aged Day)
Around 23 September: Shubun no Hi (Autumnal Equinox Day)
Second Monday in October: Taiiku no Hi (Sports Day)
3 November: Bunka no Hi (Culture Day)
23 November: Kinro Kansha no Hi (Labour Thanksgiving Day)
If a holiday falls on a Sunday, the following Monday will be a "substitute holiday".

Holidays to avoid

There are three periods of the year when the Japanese travel and holiday en masse. You would be wise not to make any travel plans during this time:
New Year: from around 27 December to 4 January. Most museum and galleries are closed then.
Golden Week: from 29 April to 5 May.
Obon: a week around 15 August.

Public toilets

The Asian squatting type toilet, which takes some getting used to, is supposed to be the most hygienic (no part of your body actually touches them) and physiologically best. Thankfully for Western visitors, in Tokyo and other major cities, they have mostly been replaced with Western-style toilets. By law, every coffee shop and restaurant, etc, must have its own toilet, or access to one in the same building. Toilets in train stations and other large places are often dirty and smelly.

If you can't find a public toilet your best bet is to find a large department store, which will have all the necessary facilities.

Hi-tech toilets with push-button control panels are common – approximately 70 percent of homes in Tokyo have them, as do most department stores and Western-style hotels and business hotels. There are special enhancements such as heated seats, hot-air dryers, and a device that plays the sound of flushing water to conceal any embarrassing noises.

R

Religious services

Protestant
United Church of Christ in Japan, Ginza Church, 4-2-1 Ginza, Chuo-ku. Tel: 03-3561-0236, www.ginza-church.com.

Baptist
Tokyo Baptist Church, 9-2 Hachiyama-cho, Shibuya-ku. Tel: 03-3461-8425, www.tokyobaptist.org.

Lutheran
St Paul International Lutheran Church, 1-2-32 Fujimi-cho, Chiyoda-ku. Tel: 03-3261-3740, www.spilchurchtokyo.org.

Catholic
Azabu Church, 3-21-6 Nishi-Azabu, Minato-ku. Tel: 03-3408-1500, http://azabu-catholic.jp.
Franciscan Chapel Center, 4-2-37 Roppongi, Minato-ku. Tel: 03-3401-2141, http://franciscanchapelcentertokyo.org.

Anglican Episcopal
St Alban's Church, 3-6-25 Shiba-Koen, Minato-ku. Tel: 03-3431-8534, www.saintalbans.jp.

Muslim
Hiroo Mosque, 3-4-18 Moto-Azabu, Minato-ku. Tel: 03-3404-6622, www.aii-t.org.
Islamic Centre Japan, 1-16-11 Ohara, Setagaya-ku. Tel: 03-3460-6169, http://islamcenter.or.jp.

Jewish
Jewish Community of Japan, 3-8-8 Hiroo, Shibuya-ku. Tel: 03-3400-2559, www.jccjapan.or.jp.

T

Telephones

Japan's country code: 81
Domestic area codes:
Fukuoka: 092
Hiroshima: 082
Kagoshima: 099
Kobe: 078
Kyoto: 075
Nagasaki: 095
Nagoya: 052
Naha: 098
Osaka: 06
Sapporo: 011
Sendai: 022
Tokyo: 03
Yokohama: 045

Although the number of payphones has decreased in recent years, they are still plentiful. To use the public telephones just insert a ¥10- or a ¥100-coin and dial the number desired – ¥10 pays for one minute (a few older phones accept ¥10-coins only).

Most common are green and grey phones, all taking prepaid telephone cards and some taking only prepaid cards, no coins. No change is returned for unused portions of coins. Telephone cards can be obtained at any Nippon Telegraph and Telephone (NTT) office, many shops, kiosks and convenience stores, or through special vending machines near telephones.

Domestic calls, expensive over 60km (37 miles), are cheaper at night and on weekends and holidays by as much as 40 percent.

Toll-free numbers
Domestic telephone numbers that begin with "0120" or "0088" are toll-free, or "freephone", calls.

International calls
Making international calls from Japan is fairly painless. Using public telephones, international calls can be made from specially marked – in English and Japanese – telephones, which will be green, grey or multicoloured; look for an IDD sticker on the phone or booth. The grey phones use prepaid cards and have small screens displaying operating instructions in both Japanese and English.

Western-style hotels can usually provide international call services too.

To make a **person-to-person**, **reverse charge** (collect) or **credit-card** call from anywhere in Japan through KDDI, the dominant international telecom company, simply dial 001.

KDDI Information, international telephone information, in English: 0057 (toll-free).

Mobile phones
Mobile phones are ubiquitous in Japan; as is the case across the developed world, on crowded commuter trains it often seems like everyone is whiling away the boredom playing with their phones.

Japan uses mobile-network systems such as UMTS 2100MHz, CDMA2000 800MHz and LTE. If you come from a country that uses the more common GSM system found in Asia, UK, Europe, Australia and New Zealand, your phone may not work here, but this is rather a thing of the past now, and only older handsets may pose a problem. Virtually all smartphones operate also on UMTS 2100MHz and some on CDMA2000 and will work in Japan. Check your phone specifications if unsure, as you will have to rent a handset that hooks up with the local network. Japan's international airports all have mobile phone counters, where you can rent handsets and/or local SIM cards to avoid international roaming charges. The largest of the several operators are NTT Docomo (tel: 0120-005-250 English spoken, www.nttdocomo.co.jp), KDDI with its brand au by KDDI (tel: 0120-959-472 English spoken, www.au.com/english) and SoftBank (tel: 0800-919-0157 English spoken, www.softbank.jp/en). If you subscribe to SoftBank's US subsidiary Sprint then you can use your current SIM card for just a small weekly roaming fee. Mobile phone rental companies include JAL ABC (www.

jalabc.com), Pupuru (www.pupuru. com), Rentafone Japan (www.renta-fonejapan.com) and Softbank (www. softbank-rental.jp).

Most mobile phone numbers begin with 090 or 080.

Tourist information

Tourist offices

The Japan National Tourism Organisation (JNTO) is an excellent source of information on visas, culture, accommodation, tours, etc. You can log on at www.jnto.go.jp.

JNTO Overseas Offices
Australia: Level 4, 56 Clarence Street, Sydney NSW 2000. Tel: 02-9279-2177, www.jnto.org.au.
Canada: 481 University Ave, Suite 306, Toronto, Ont. M5G 2E9. Tel: 416-366-7140, www.ilovejapan.ca.
Hong Kong: Unit 807–809, 8F, Prosperity Millennia Plaza, 663 King's Road, North Point. Tel: 2968-5688, www.welcome2japan.hk.
United Kingdom: 3rd Floor, 32 Queensway, London W2 3RX. Tel: 020-7398-5670, www.seejapan.co.uk.
United States:
Los Angeles: 707 Wilshire Blvd Suite 4325, Los Angeles, CA 90017. Tel: 213-623-1952, www.us.jnto.go.jp.
New York: One Grand Central Place, 60 East 42nd Street, Suite 448, New York, NY 10165. Tel: 212-757-5640, www.us.jnto.go.jp.

Tourist information centres

Tokyo, 1F, Tokyo Metropolitan Government Building, 2-8-1 Nishi-Shinjuku, Tokyo 100-0005. Tel: 03-5321-3077. Open daily 9.30am–6.30pm.
Shinjuku Expressway Bus Terminal, 3F, 5-24-55 Sendagaya, Shibuya-ku, Tokyo. Tel: 03-6274-8192.
Kyoto Office (TIC): JR Kyoto Station 2F, Shimogyo-ku, Kyoto 600-8216. Tel: 075-343-0548. Open daily 8.30am–7pm.

⏱ Time zone

Japan is GMT +9 hours; EST (New York) +14 hours; and PST (Los Angeles) +17. Japan does not have summer daylight saving time. The idea is periodically mooted, and then dismissed in deference to the nation's farmers, a powerful electoral lobby.

Tourist information

Tokyo: Tel: 03-3201-3331
Yokohama: Tel: 045-441-7300
Nagoya: Tel: 052-541-4301
Sendai: Tel: 022-222-4069
Sapporo: Tel: 011-213-5088
Kyoto: Tel: 075-343-0548

Local tourist websites

There are a number of useful local websites to help you plan your visit. The links below are full of advice on what to see and suggestions of where to stay, plus the latest news on local events and festivals in each area.

Kyoto City Tourist and Cultural Information System: www.pref.kyoto. jp/en/index.html.
Osaka Tourist Guide: www.city.osaka. lg.jp.
Hokkaido Tourist Association: www. visit-hokkaido.jp.
Koyasan Tourist Association: http:// eng.shukubo.net.
Kyushu Tourism Promotion Organization: www.welcomekyushu. com.
Okinawa Conventions and Visitors Bureau: www.visitokinawa.jp.

Translators and interpreters

Most languages are covered for translation or interpretation by big translation companies, for example ILC (tel: 03-3940-2821, www.ilcsug-amo.com), or check with a hotel business centre. Be aware that rates are not cheap.

Travellers with disabilities

In general, Japan is not user-friendly for the disabled and still lags behind most Western cities. Although there has been a gradual increase in disabled facilities in recent years, such as ramps and multiuse toilets in hotels and public areas, in most cases doors, lifts, toilets and just about everything else have not been designed for wheelchairs. It is a struggle for the disabled to get around Japan, but it can be done. Traditionally, people with disabilities kept a low profile, as they were sometimes considered an embarrassment for the family. More recently, however, disabled people have become a more visible and accepted part of society.

Forget about using a wheelchair in train or subway stations, much less trains during rush hour, 7–9am and 5–7pm. The crowds are just too thick.

To request assistance when travelling on JR East lines, call the JR English InfoLine at 050-2016-1603 (daily 10am–6pm). They can give information on disabled facilities and give you the contact numbers for different stations, so you can call in advance to arrange assistance. Even without advance notice, in many stations staff will help with escalators, lifts and getting on and off the train, although a wait of up to an hour may be involved if you haven't called ahead.

It is possible to reserve a special seat for wheelchairs on the shinkansen, or bullet train. Reservations can be made from one month to two days before departure. You must also call ahead to use the elevators for the shinkansen platforms.

Narita Airport's website (www. narita-airport.jp) has information for disabled travellers. The very comprehensive online English-language guide, Accessible Tokyo, is another useful resource: http://accessible. jp.org. For help in emergencies or personal distress, telephone Tokyo English Life Line 03-5774-0992 (http://telljp.com; daily 9am–11pm), or the 24-hour Japan Helpline 0570-000-911 (www.jhelp.com).

U

Useful addresses

Organisations

American Chamber of Commerce, Masonic 39 MT Bldg 10F, 2-4-5 Azabudai, Minato-ku. Tel: 03-3433-5381, www.accj.or.jp.
British Council, 1-2 Kagurazaka, Shinjuku-ku. Tel: 03-3235-8031, www.britishcouncil.jp.
Foreign Correspondents' Club, Yurakucho Denki Bldg, 20F, 1-7-1 Yurakucho, Chiyoda-ku. Tel: 03-3211-3161, www.fccj.or.jp.
Institut Franco-Japonais, 15 Ichigaya Funagawaracho, Shinjuku-ku. Tel: 03-5206-2500, www.institutfrancais.jp.
The Japan Foundation Library, 4-4-1 Yotsuya, Shinjuku-ku. Tel: 03-5369-6086, www.jpf.go.jp.
JETRO (Japan External Trade Organisation), Ark Mori Building 6F, 12-32-1, Akasaka, Minato-ku. Tel: 03-3582-5511, www.jetro.go.jp.

Kyoto City International Foundation, 2-1 Torii-cho, Awataguchi, Sakyo-ku, Kyoto. Tel: 075-752-3010, www.kcif. or.jp.

Visas and passports

A proper visa is necessary for foreigners living in Japan and engaged in business or study. Passengers with confirmed departure reservations can obtain a stopover pass for up to 72 hours.

Japan has an agreement with 68 countries, whose nationals do not require visas for tourism purposes as of July, 2017. They include: Australia, Canada, New Zealand, United States and most European countries (for stays of up to 90 days).

Visitors from Ireland, the UK and several other European nations may reside in Japan for up to 6 months providing they are not earning an income.

For further details and requirements for other nationalities, contact your nearest Japanese diplomatic mission or log on to www. mofa.go.jp.

Extension of stay

Foreigners wishing to extend their stay in Japan must report, in person, to the Immigration Bureau within two weeks before their visa expiration. Present your passport, completed application forms and documents certifying the reasons for extension. The fee is ¥4,000.

Foreigners living in Japan must obtain a re-entry permit from the Immigration Bureau if they leave Japan and plan to return. Present, in person, your passport and certificate of alien registration (held by foreign residents in Japan) along with the appropriate re-entry form to the Immigration Office. Fees are charged for both single and multiple re-entry permits.

Those wishing to transfer visas to new passports must report to the Immigration Bureau in Tokyo. Present both old and new passports and certificate of alien registration. No charge is required.

Ministry of Foreign Affairs, www. mofa.go.jp. Information on the current rules and regulations regarding visas.

Immigration Bureau of Japan, www. immi-moj.go.jp. Information on regulations on entry and stay for foreign nationals.

Tokyo Regional Immigration Bureau, 5-5-30, Konan, Minato-ku, Tokyo. Tel: 03-5796-7111.

Yokohama District Immigration Office, 10-7 Torihama-cho, Kanazawa-ku. Tel: 045-769-1720.

Osaka Regional Immigration Bureau, 1-29-53 Nankou Kita, Suminoe-ku. Tel: 06-4703-2100.

Foreign residents' registration

In 2012, the alien registration system was discontinued and replaced with a national foreign-residents-registration system. Foreigners who have been granted permission to stay for over 90 days are required to register at the regional immigration office. For details, contact a regional immigration bureau or the Immigration Information Centre (tel: 0570-013904 Mon–Fri 8.30am–5.15pm, www.immi-moj.go.jp).

Websites

ACCJ Journal: the American Chamber of Commerce magazine provides insightful stories related to doing business in Japan. http://journal.accj.or.jp.

The Asahi Shimbun Asia & Japan Watch: the English online edition of centre-left national daily. www.asahi.com/ajw.

Endless Discovery: a multimedia site on Japanese attractions run by the Japan Tourism Agency. www.jnto.org.au.

Eurobiz Japan: if you are interested in business in Japan, the online version of the European Business Council's magazine is a good source of stories. http://eurobiz.jp.

Gurunavi: country-wide restaurant, bar and culture listings. http://gurunavi.com.

Japan-guide.com: extensive and up-to-date travel data. www.japan-guide.com.

IFLYER: Japan's largest club and concert listings portal. http://iflyer.tv.

Japan Monthly Web Magazine: an absorbing site run by the Japan National Tourist Organisation. http://japan-magazine.jnto.go.jp.

Japan National Tourist Organisation: excellent links and travel info. www.jnto.go.jp.

The Japan Times: a good online site for Japan's oldest English-language newspaper, which has nearly everything covered. www.japantimes.co.jp.

Japan Today: a good source for short, translated news stories, from national and business news to more quirky fare. www.japantoday.com.

The Mainichi: English online edition of centrist national daily *The Mainichi Shimbun*. http://mainichi.jp/english/

Metropolis: the website of the English magazine *Metropolis* is packed with insightful information on Japanese culture and lifestyle. http://metropolisjapan.com.

Outdoor Japan: regularly updated site on the great outdoors including live weather forecasts, activity guides and some good features. http://outdoorjapan.com.

Savvy Tokyo: helpful data and insights for foreign women in Japan. http://savvytokyo.com.

Skiing Hokkaido: all the skiing information and resort details from Hokkaido. www.skiing-hokkaido.com.

Stanford University: scholarly links for the more highbrow surfer. http://library.stanford.edu/guides/japanese-e-resources.

Time Out Tokyo: bilingual site with lots of event listings, activity ideas, reviews, and plenty of interesting articles on travel and culture. www.timeout.com/tokyo.

Tokyo Food Page: updates on food, sake and beer. Tips on the best places to eat in Tokyo, Yokohama, Kyoto, Osaka and Nagoya, plus some great recipes. www.bento.com.

Tokyo Art Beat: Tokyo's most extensive arts and exhibitions portal. www.tokyoartbeat.com.

Tokyo Metro: a site for keeping up with Tokyo's ever-growing subway system. www.tokyometro.jp/en.

☉ Weights and measures

Japan follows the metric system, except in cases governed by strong tradition. For example, rice and sake are measured in units of 1.8 litres and rooms are measured by a standard tatami mat size. Ancient measures are also used for carpentry in Shinto temples and for making kimonos.

LANGUAGE

The visitor will have few language problems within the confines of airports and the major hotels, but outside these the going can get tough. Despite being unable to communicate verbally, however, the visitor, while illiterate, now has a number of tools like Google Translate's scanning function to assist them.

Written Japanese is made up of three different sets of characters: two simple home-grown syllabaries, hiragana and katakana, consisting of 46 characters each; and the much more formidable Chinese ideograms, kanji. Knowledge of just under two thousand of these is necessary to read a daily newspaper.

While the enormous effort required to memorise this number of kanji (it takes the Japanese most of their school career to do so) is clearly unjustifiable for those with only a passing interest in the language, a few hours spent learning the two syllabaries would not be time wasted for those who can afford it.

Hiragana can be useful for identifying which station your train has

Japanese road sign.

stopped at; the platforms are plastered with hiragana versions of the station name so that children who have not yet learned kanji can see where they are. Station names are usually (but not always) posted in roman script *(romanji)* as well, but not always as obviously. Katakana is used to transliterate foreign words. Western-style restaurants often simply list the foreign names for the dishes on their menus in katakana.

PRONUNCIATION

With its small number of simple and unvarying vowel sounds, the pronunciation of Japanese should be easy for those who speak Western languages, which are rich in vowel sounds, and Japanese has nothing like the tonal system of Chinese.

Vowels have only one sound. Don't be sloppy with their pronunciations.

a – between fat and the u in but
e – like the e in egg
i – like the i in ink
o – like the o in orange
u – like the u in butcher

When they occur in the middle of words between voiceless consonants (ch, f, h, k, p, s, sh, t and ts), i and u are often almost silent. For example, *Takeshita* is really pronounced *Takesh'ta* while *sukiyaki* sounds more like *s'kiyaki*.

In spite of the seemingly simple pronunciation of Japanese, a lot of foreigners manage to mangle the language into a form which is almost impossible for the native speaker to understand. It is mainly intonation that is responsible for this. It would be untrue to claim that the Japanese language has no rise and fall in pitch but it is certainly "flatter" in character than Western languages.

It is important to avoid stressing syllables within words; whereas an English-speaker would naturally stress either the second or third syllable of Hiroshima, for example, in Japanese the four syllables should be stressed equally.

Another problem lies in long (actually double) vowel sounds. These are often indicated by a line above the vowel, or simply by a double vowel. To pronounce these long vowels properly, it is simply necessary to give the vowel sound double length.

WORDS AND PHRASES

Essential phrases

Do you speak English? *eego ga dekimasu ka?*
Please write it down *kaite kudasai*
Pardon? *sumimasen*
I understand *wakarimashita*
I don't understand/I don't know *wakarimasen*
Yes/No *hai/iie*
OK *ookee*
please *onegai shimasu*
Thank you (very much) *(doomo) arigatoo*

Greetings

Good morning *ohayoo gozaimasu*
Hello (afternoon) *kon-nichi-wa*
Good evening *konban-wa*
Goodnight *oyasumi nasai*
Goodbye *sayoonara* (*shitsure shimasu* for formal occasions)
How are you? *ogenki desu ka?*
My name is... *... to moshimasu*
I'm Mr/Ms Smith *watashi wa Smith desu*
Are you Mr/Ms Honda? *Honda-san desu ka?*
I'm American *Amerika-jin desu*
I'm British *Igirisu-jin desu*
I'm Australian *Oosutoraria-jin desu*
I'm Canadian *Kanada-jin desu*

Asking for directions

Excuse me, where is the toilet?
sumimasen, toire wa doko desu ka?
**Excuse me, is there a post office
near here?** *sumimasen, kono chikaku
ni, yubin-kyoku wa arimasu ka?*
on the left/right *hidari/migi ni*
bakery *pan-ya*
stationer's *bunboogu-ya*
pharmacy *yakkyoku*
bookshop *hon-ya*
supermarket *suupaa*
department store *depaato*
restaurant *resutoran*
hotel *hoteru*
station *eki*
taxi rank *takushii noriba*
bank *ginkoo*
hospital *byooin*
police station *kooban*

Out shopping

This one *kore*
That one (near the other person)
sore
That one (near neither of you) *are*
Do you have...? *...(wa) arimasu ka?*
How much is it? *ikura desu ka?*
I'll take this *kore o kudasai*

Boarding the train

ticket (office) *kippu (uriba)*
reserved seat *shitei seki*
unreserved seat *jiyu seki*
first-class car *guriin sha*
**Which platform does the train for
Nagoya leave from?** *Nagoya yuki wa
namban sen desu ka?*
Thank you (very much) *(doomo) arigato gozaimasu* (informally, *doomo* is
enough)
Don't mention it *doitashimashite*
Thanks for the meal *gochisosama
deshita*

Ramen noodles.

Here you are *doozo*
After you *doozo*
Of course, go ahead *doozo* (in
answer to "May I...?")

Days/time

(On) Sunday *nichi-yoobi (ni)*
(Next) Monday *(raishu no)
getsu-yoobi*
(Last) Tuesday *(senshu no) ka-yoobi*
(Every) Wednesday *(maishu)
sui-yoobi*
(This) Thursday *(konshu no)
moku-yoobi*
Friday *kin-yoobi*
Saturday *do-yoobi*
yesterday *kino*
today *kyo*
This morning *kesa*
This evening *konya*
tomorrow *ashita*
What time is it? *nan-ji desu ka?*

Months/seasons

January *ichi-gatsu*
February *ni-gatsu*
March *san-gatsu*
April *shi-gatsu*

May *go-gatsu*
June *roku-gatsu*
July *shichi-gatsu*
August *hachi-gatsu*
September *ku-gatsu*
October *juu-gatsu*
November *juu-ichi-gatsu*
December *juu-ni-gatsu*

At the hotel

Western-style hotel *hoteru*
business hotel *bijinesu hoteru*
love hotel *rabu hoteru*
Japanese-style inn *ryokan*
guesthouse *minshuku*
temple accommodation *shukuboo*
youth hostel *yuusu hosuteru*
I have a reservation *yoyaku shite
arimasu*
Do you have a room? *heya wa arimasu ka?*
I'd like a single/double room *shin-
guru/daburu ruumu o onegai shimasu*
I'd like a room with ... *... tsuki no heya
o onegai shimasu*
twin beds *tsuin beddo*
double bed *daburu beddo*
bath/shower *o furo/shawa*
air conditioning *eakon*

Ueno Station ticket hall, Tokyo.

Yasaka Shrine, Kyoto.

TV/telephone *terebi/denwa*
How much is it? *ikura desu ka?*
Can I see the room please? *heya o misete kudasai*
That's fine, I'll take it *kekkoo desu, tomarimasu*
No, I won't take it *sumimasen, yamete okimasu*

At the restaurant

A table for two, please *futari onegai shimasu*
The bill, please *o-kanjoo onegai shimasu*
tsukemono **pickled vegetables**
sashimi **raw fish served with soy sauce and horseradish** *(wasabi)*
sushi **rice balls topped with fish/seafood**
tempura **battered vegetables, fish or seafood**
okonomiyaki **pizza/savoury pancake**
chankonabe **chicken and vegetable stew often served to sumo wrestlers**
gyoza **meat or vegetable dumplings**
soba **buckwheat noodles**
udon **thick wheat-flour noodles**
tonkotsu ramen **pork broth-based dish with Chinese noodles**
tonkatsu **breaded deep-fried pork**
yakitori **grilled chicken on skewers**
sukiyaki **thin slices of beef and vegetables in aromatic sauce**

shabu-shabu **thin slices of beef or pork cooked in broth**
karee raisu **Japanese curry on rice**
teppanyaki **griddled meat/fish**
kamameshi **rice casserole**
biiru **beer**
ocha **green tea**
o-sake/nihonshu **sake**
hiya/hitohada/atsukan **cold/lukewarm/hot** (used for sake temperatures)
mizu **water**
mineraru wootaa **mineral water**

Sightseeing

Where is the ...? *... wa doko desu ka*
art gallery *bijutsu-kan*

botanical garden *shokubutsu-en*
Buddhist temple *o-tera*
castle *o-shiro*
museum *hakubutsu kan*
Imperial palace *kookyo*
Shinto shrine *jinja*
Can you show me on the map? *kono chizu de oshiete kudasai*

Numbers

Counting is very complicated in Japanese. Counting up to 10 on their fingers, the Japanese will use general numbers, which are: *ichi, ni, san, shi* (or *yon*), *go, roku, shichi* (or *nana*), *hachi, ku* (or *kyuu*), *juu*. If they are counting bottles, they will say: *ip-pon, ni-hon, sam-bon, yon-hon, go-hon...* The suffix will change according to what is being counted, and there are more than 100 suffix groups. Commonly used categories of counter include flat objects (stamps, paper, etc), long thin objects (pens, bottles, umbrellas) and people. You will be fairly safe with the following "all purpose" numbers below, which don't need suffixes:

one *hitotsu*
two *futatsu*
three *mittsu*
four *yottsu*
five *itsutsu*
six *muttsu*
seven *nanatsu*
eight *yattsu*
nine *kokonotsu*
ten *too*

If you want five of something, point at it and say, *itsutsu kudasai*. Or hold up the appropriate number of fingers or write the number down. Thankfully the counter system only applies to numbers 1–10; after 10 the general numbers are used for all things.

⊘ A question of grammar

Japanese **questions** are formed by adding the grammar marker *ka* (a verbal question mark) to the verb at the end of a sentence. In Japanese the verb always comes last, with the basic rule for word order within a sentence being subject – object – verb.

Japanese **nouns** have no articles (a, an, the) and very few plural forms. Whether a noun is singular or plural is judged from the context.

Personal pronouns are rarely used in Japanese. For "you", either use the person's family name + -*san*, or omit the pronoun completely if it's clear who you are addressing. **I** *watashi*; **we** *watashi tachi*.

Japanese do not usually use **first names**, but the family name, most commonly followed by -*san* (more formally by -*sama*), which can stand for Mr, Mrs, Miss or Ms. With close acquaintances or children, -*san* is often replaced by the casual -*chan* or -*kun*.

FURTHER READING

HISTORY

Bells of Nagasaki by Dr Takashi Nagai. No longer in print but nonetheless worth scouring Tokyo's used bookstores for, Nagai gives a very personal and heart-wrenching account of the atomic bombing of Nagasaki and its horrific aftermath.

Dogs & Demons: Tales From the Dark Side of Japan by Alex Kerr. A brutal appraisal of Japan's post-war economic, social and environmental policies by a former long-term Japan resident.

Embracing Defeat: Japan in the Aftermath of World War II by John Dower. A Pulitzer Prize-winning look at how Japan rose from the ashes of World War II and transformed itself into a peaceful democracy.

Japan Story: In Search of a Nation by Christopher Harding. An in-depth account of Japan's recent history, from Japan's Meiji-era emergence from international isolation to the modern day. Published in 2018.

FICTION

Green Tea to Go: Stories from Tokyo by Leza Lowitz. A collection of short stories set in modern Japan.

Hokkaido scenery.

Tokyo Stories: A Literary Stroll by Lawrence Rogers. An anthology of translated short stories by Japanese writers that covers Japan's capital through the 20th century.

SOCIETY AND CULTURE

Bending Adversity: Japan and the Art of Survival by David Pilling. Authored by the *Financial Times Asia* editor and published in 2015, this enjoyable book offers vivid reportage and an observant examination of Japan's survivalist mentality through recent disasters and historical catastrophes.

The Chrysanthemum and the Sword: Patterns of Japanese Culture by Ruth Benedict. A seminal study of Japanese social, political and economic life that is still insightful some 75 years after it was first published.

The Enigma of Japanese Power by Karel van Wolferen. Wolferen's weighty tome on the interwoven worlds of Japanese business, bureaucracy and politics is heavy reading, but is regarded as a classic work.

Learning to Bow: Inside the Heart of Japan by Bruce S. Feiler. Many people have written about teaching

Takeshita Street, Tokyo.

English in Japan, but few of the results are as readable or culturally insightful as Feiler's account of teaching at a rural high school.

The Life And Death of Yukio Mishima by Henry Scott-Stokes. Veteran journalist Scott-Stokes, a former Tokyo bureau chief for The Times and New York Times, provides a fascinating insight into the life and times of his close friend Mishima, one of Japan's most influential and controversial modern-day authors.

Pink Samurai by Nicholas Bornoff. A worthwhile though not comprehensive guide to the role of sexuality in past and present Japanese society.

Reimaging Japan: The Quest for a Future That Works. A collection of 80 thought-provoking essays from Japanese and overseas thinkers and business leaders on how Japan can rebuild and prosper after the 11 March 2011 earthquake, tsunami and nuclear tragedies. Contributors include Masayoshi Son, Howard Schultz and Carlos Ghosn; edited by McKinsey and Company.

Speed Tribes by Karl Taro Greenfeld. This foray into the violent worlds of Japan's subcultures offers a striking contrast to the image of Japan as an orderly, regimented society.

You Gotta Have Wa by Robert Whiting. In his third book Whiting gives us an often comical look at the trials and tribulations of American baseball players plying their trade in Japan.

Zen & Japanese Culture by Daisetz Suzuki. An in-depth yet accessible study of the multi-faceted role of Zen in Japanese society.

Sake casks at Atsuta Shrine, Nagoya.

TRAVEL GUIDES AND TRAVELOGUE

The Gardens of Japan by Teiji Itoh. Beautifully illustrated guide that covers all the main gardening styles and introduces some of Japan's most famous gardens in the process.
The Inland Sea by Donald Richie. It may be 40 years old, but Richie's travelogue of the Inland Sea is still a captivating and relevant read.
Japan: A Bilingual Atlas. Detailed and accurate maps of the entire country along with useful close-ups and transportation maps for Japan's major cities.
Kyoto: 29 Walks in Japan's Ancient Capital by John H. Martin and Phyllis G. Martin. A collection of guided walks covering Kyoto's main sights as well as many of its overlooked nooks and crannies, in the process taking the reader deep into the history of the city.
Looking for the Lost by Alan Booth. Along with Booth's first book, *The Roads to Sata*, this classic trilogy of walking tales offers some of the most insightful, touching and funniest travel writing on Japan.
Sado: Japan's Island in Exile by Angus Waycott. A fascinating account of the author's eight-day walk around Sado Island, off the coast of Niigata, that details not just the history and traditions of the rugged island but also delves into the workings of Japanese society.
Tokyo by Donald Richie. An in-depth and colourful guide to the various districts of Tokyo by one of the most respected foreign experts on Japan.
Tokyo: 30 Walks in the World's Most Exciting City by John H. Martin and Phyllis G. Martin. A collection of guided walks around Tokyo, as well as areas nearby such as Hakone,

⊘ Send us your thoughts

We do our best to ensure the information in our books is as accurate and up-to-date as possible. The books are updated on a regular basis using local contacts, who painstakingly add, amend and correct as required. However, some details (such as telephone numbers and opening times) are liable to change, and we are ultimately reliant on our readers to put us in the picture.

We welcome your feedback, especially your experience of using the book "on the road". Maybe you came across a great bar or new attraction we missed.

We will acknowledge all contributions, and we'll offer an Insight Guide to the best letters received.

Please write to us at:
Insight Guides
PO Box 7910
London SE1 1WE

Or email us at:
hello@insightguides.com

that delves deep into Edo's roots and subsequent development.
Hokkaido Highway Blues by Will Ferguson. In his debut novel Ferguson spins a humorous and at turns moving tale of his quest to hitch-hike from the southern to northern tip of the country.
Tokyo: A Bilingual Atlas. A handy and detailed collection of maps covering Tokyo's streets, trains and subways.

YAKUZA

Confessions of a Yakuza by Junichi Saga. This largely biographical novel of a dying gangster boss, as told to his doctor, charts gangster Eiji Ijichi's rise through the *yakuza* ranks and his experiences of war, prison and the traditional *yakuza* way of life.
Tokyo Underworld by Robert Whiting. A great *yakuza* book centred on the rise and fall of Italian-American Tokyo mafia boss Nick Zapapetti.
Tokyo Vice: An American Reporter on the Police Beat in Japan by Jake Adelstein. Told like a classic PI novel, Adelstein's biographical account of his time on the crime beat at Japan's biggest newspaper and the subsequent *yakuza* scoop that nearly cost him his life is a gripping read, rife with gallows humour and clinical reporting.
Yakuza Moon by Shoko Tendo. Born into a *yakuza* family, Tendo offers a rare woman's perspective on *yakuza* life. Her story is a survivor's tale of drug addiction, rape and family strife, but ultimately reconciliation and redemption.

OTHER INSIGHT GUIDES

Other Insight Guides to this part of the world include: Tokyo, Beijing, China, Hong Kong, South Korea, Taipei and Taiwan.

Route-based Insight Explore Guides highlight the best city walks and tours, with itineraries for all tastes. Destinations in this series include Tokyo, Hong Kong, Singapore and Shanghai.

Insight Fleximaps are full-colour, laminated and easy-to-fold maps with clear cartography, and photography describing a place's top sights. Titles in this series to destinations in this region include: Beijing, Hong Kong, Seoul, Shanghai, Singapore, Taipei and Tokyo.

CREDITS

PHOTO CREDITS

COVER CREDITS

INSIGHT GUIDE CREDITS

Distribution
UK, Ireland and Europe
Apa Publications (UK) Ltd;
sales@insightguides.com
United States and Canada
Ingram Publisher Services;
ips@ingramcontent.com
Australia and New Zealand
Woodslane; info@woodslane.com.au
Southeast Asia
Apa Publications (SN) Pte;
singaporeoffice@insightguides.com
Worldwide
Apa Publications (UK) Ltd;
sales@insightguides.com
Special Sales, Content Licensing and CoPublishing
Insight Guides can be purchased in bulk quantities at discounted prices. We can create special editions, personalised jackets and corporate imprints tailored to your needs. sales@insightguides.com
www.insightguides.biz

Printed in Poland by Pozkal

All Rights Reserved
© 2020 Apa Digital (CH) AG and
Apa Publications (UK) Ltd

First Edition 1992
Seventh Edition 2020

www.insightguides.com

Editor: Zara Sekhavati
Author: Rob Goss and Stephen Mansfield
Updater: Daniel Stables
Head of DTP and Pre-Press: Rebeka Davies
Managing Editor: Carine Tracanelli
Picture Editor: Tom Smyth
Picture research: Aude Vauconsant
Cartography: original cartography Berndtson & Berndtson, updated by Carte

CONTRIBUTORS

This new edition of *Insight Guide Japan* was updated by travel writer, **Daniel Stables**. Daniel is a travel writer and journalist based in Manchester. He writes about Asia, Europe, the Americas and the Middle East, and has worked on several Insight Guides titles and for various websites and magazines. His work can be found at

his website, danielstables.co.uk.
  He has built on the comprehensive work of **Rob Goss** and **Stephen Mansfield**, who wrote the last edition of the book, drawing on their detailed knowledge of all things Japan.
  The book was edited by **Zara Sekhavati** and the index compiled by **Penny Phenix**.

ABOUT INSIGHT GUIDES

Insight Guides have more than 45 years' experience of publishing high-quality, visual travel guides. We produce 400 full-colour titles, in both print and digital form, covering more than 200 destinations across the globe, in a variety of formats to meet your different needs.
  Insight Guides are written by local authors, whose expertise is evident in the extensive historical and cultural

background features. Each destination is carefully researched by regional experts to ensure our guides provide the very latest information. All the reviews in **Insight Guides** are independent; we strive to maintain an impartial view. Our reviews are carefully selected to guide you to the best places to eat, go out and shop, so you can be confident that when we say a place is special, we really mean it.

Legend

City maps

Freeway/Highway/Motorway
Divided Highway
Main Roads
Minor Roads
Pedestrian Roads
Steps
Footpath
Railway
Funicular Railway
Cable Car
Tunnel
City Wall
Important Building
Built Up Area
Other Land
Transport Hub
Park
Pedestrian Area
Bus Station
Tourist Information
Main Post Office
Cathedral/Church
Mosque
Synagogue
Statue/Monument
Beach
Airport

Regional maps

Freeway/Highway/Motorway (with junction)
Freeway/Highway/Motorway (under construction)
Divided Highway
Main Road
Secondary Road
Minor Road
Track
Footpath
International Boundary
State/Province Boundary
National Park/Reserve
Marine Park
Ferry Route
Marshland/Swamp
Glacier   Salt Lake
Airport/Airfield
Ancient Site
Border Control
Cable Car
Castle/Castle Ruins
Cave
Chateau/Stately Home
Church/Church Ruins
Crater
Lighthouse
Mountain Peak
Place of Interest
Viewpoint

INDEX

MAIN REFERENCES ARE IN BOLD TYPE

INSIGHT ⊙ GUIDES

OFF THE SHELF

Since 1970, INSIGHT GUIDES has provided a unique perspective on the world's best travel destinations by using specially commissioned photography and illuminating text written by local authors.

Whether you're planning a city break, a walking tour or the journey of a lifetime, our superb range of guidebooks and phrasebooks will inspire you to discover more about your chosen destination.

INSIGHT GUIDES

offer a unique combination of stunning photos, absorbing narrative and detailed maps, providing all the inspiration and information you need.

PHRASEBOOKS & DICTIONARIES

help users to feel at home, when away. Pocket-sized with a free app to download, they go where you do.

CITY GUIDES

pack hundreds of great photos into a smaller format with detailed practical information, so you can navigate the world's top cities with confidence.

EXPLORE GUIDES

feature easy-to-follow walks and itineraries in the world's most exciting destinations, with our choice of the best places to eat and drink along the way.

POCKET GUIDES

combine concise information on where to go and what to do in a handy compact format, ideal on the ground. Includes a full-colour, fold-out map.

EXPERIENCE GUIDES

feature offbeat perspectives and secret gems for experienced travellers, with a collection of over 100 ideas for a memorable stay in a city.

www.insightguides.com

Tokyo Subway

SOURCES
of the
WESTERN
TRADITION

SOURCES
of the
WESTERN
TRADITION

EIGHTH EDITION

VOLUME I: FROM ANCIENT TIMES
TO THE ENLIGHTENMENT

Marvin Perry

Baruch College, City University of New York

George W. Bock, Editorial Associate

WADSWORTH
CENGAGE Learning

Australia • Brazil • Japan • Korea • Mexico • Singapore • Spain • United Kingdom • United States

WADSWORTH
CENGAGE Learning™

Sources of the Western Tradition:
Volume I: From Ancient Times
to the Enlightenment, Eighth Edition
Marvin Perry

Senior Publisher: Suzanne Jeans

Senior Sponsoring Editor: Nancy Blaine

Assistant Editor: Lauren Floyd

Editorial Assistant: Emma Goehring

Executive Marketing Manager:
Diane Wenckebach

Marketing Coordinator: Lorreen Pelletier

Senior Marketing Communications Manager:
Heather Baxley

Associate Content Project Manager:
Anne Finley

Senior Art Director: Cate Rickard Barr

Senior Print Buyer: Judy Inouye

Senior Rights Acquisition Specialist, Text:
Katie Huha

Senior Image Rights Acquisition Specialist:
Jennifer Meyer Dare

Production Service: PreMediaGlobal

Cover Designer: Roy R. Neuhaus

Cover Image: Detail from *Virgil Writing*
before Artemis: The Georgics. Virgil: Works,
with commentary by Servius. Ms. 493, fol.
29r. Medieval manuscript, French, 1469.
Bibliotheque Municipale, Dijon, France/
Giraudon/Art Resource, NY

Compositor: PreMediaGlobal

For product information and technology assistance, contact us at
Cengage Learning Customer & Sales Support, 1-800-354-9706

For permission to use material from this text or product,
submit all requests online at **www.cengage.com/permissions.**
Further permissions questions can be emailed to
permissionrequest@cengage.com.

Library of Congress Control Number: 2010928285

ISBN-13: 978-0-495-91320-7

ISBN-10: 0-495-91320-0

Wadsworth
20 Channel Center Street
Boston, MA 02210
USA

Cengage Learning is a leading provider of customized learning solutions with
office locations around the globe, including Singapore, the United Kingdom,
Australia, Mexico, Brazil, and Japan. Locate your local office at:
international.cengage.com/region

Cengage Learning products are represented in Canada by
Nelson Education, Ltd.

For your course and learning solutions, visit **www.cengage.com.**

Purchase any of our products at your local college store or at our preferred
online store **www.cengagebrain.com.**

Printed in the United States of America
1 2 3 4 5 6 7 14 13 12 11 10

Contents

CHAPTER 6 *Early Christianity* 166

PART TWO: THE MIDDLE AGES 201

CHAPTER 7 *The Early Middle Ages* 201

CHAPTER 8 *The High and Late Middle Ages   232*

Preface

Teachers of the Western Civilization survey have long recognized the pedagogical value of primary sources, which are the raw materials of history. The eighth edition of *Sources of the Western Tradition* contains a wide assortment of documents—some 217 in Volume I and 213 in Volume II and principally primary sources—that have been carefully selected and edited to fit the needs of the survey and to supplement standard texts.

I have based my choice of documents for the two volumes on several criteria. To introduce students to those ideas and values that characterize the Western tradition, *Sources of the Western Tradition* emphasizes primarily the works of the great thinkers. While focusing on the great ideas that have shaped the Western heritage, however, the reader also provides a balanced treatment of political, economic, and social history. I have tried to select documents that capture the characteristic outlook of an age and provide a sense of the movement and development of Western history. The readings are of sufficient length to convey their essential meaning, and I have carefully extracted those passages that focus on the documents' main ideas.

An important feature of the reader is the grouping of several documents that illuminate a single theme; such a constellation of related readings reinforces understanding of important themes and invites comparison, analysis, and interpretation. For example, in Volume I, Chapter 9, *The Renaissance*, Section 1, "The Humanists' Fascination with Antiquity" contains three interrelated readings: the first by Petrarch, shows his commitment to classical culture; in the second, Leonardo Bruni discusses the value of studying Greek literature and proposes a humanist educational program; and in the third, Petrus Paulus Vergerius also discusses the importance of liberal studies. In Volume II, Chapter 13, *World War II*, Section 11, "Resistance" contains four readings: in the first, Albert Camus explains

why he joined the French Resistance; the second reproduces the leaflets distributed during the war by Hans and Sophie Scholl denouncing the Nazis; the third selection is by Marek Edelman, one of the surviving commanders of the memorable Warsaw Ghetto uprising; and the final selection by Tadeusz Bor-Komorowski, Commander of the Polish Home Army, recounts the Poles' valiant effort to drive the Germans from Warsaw.

An overriding concern of mine in preparing this compilation was to make the documents accessible—to enable students to comprehend and to interpret historical documents on their own. I have provided several pedagogical features to facilitate this aim. Introductions of three types explain the historical setting, the authors' intent, and the meaning and significance of the readings. First, introductions to each chapter—thirteen in Volume I and fifteen in Volume II—provide comprehensive overviews of periods. Second, introductions to each numbered section or grouping treat the historical background for the reading(s) that follow(s). Third, each reading has a brief headnote that provides specific details about that reading.

Within some readings, interlinear notes, clearly set off from the text of the document, serve as transitions and suggest the main themes of the passages that follow. Used primarily in longer extracts of the great thinkers, these interlinear notes help to guide students through the readings.

To aid students' comprehension, brief, bracketed editorial definitions or notes that explain unfamiliar or foreign terms are inserted into the running text. When terms or concepts in the documents require fuller explanations, these appear at the bottom of pages as editors' footnotes. Where helpful, I have retained the notes of authors, translators, or editors from whose works the documents were acquired. (The latter have asterisks, daggers, et cetera, to distinguish them from my numbered explanatory notes.) The review questions that appear at the ends of sections enable students to check their understanding of the documents; sometimes the questions ask for comparisons with other readings, linking or contrasting key concepts.

For ancient sources, I have generally selected recent translations that are both faithful to the text and readable. For some seventeenth- and eighteenth-century English documents, the archaic spelling has been retained, when this does not preclude comprehension, in order to show students how the English language has evolved over time.

For the eighth edition I have reworked most chapters, dropping some documents and adding new ones. All new documents have been carefully edited: extraneous passages deleted, notes inserted to explain historical events, names identified, and technical terms defined. Throughout the book, I have extended the constellation format that groups related documents into one section.

The eighth edition of Volume I contains 23 new documents. In Chapter 2, I have added passages from *Exodus* to the constellation "Humaneness of Hebrew Law" and have significantly enriched the introduction. In Chapter 3, I have inserted a new section, "Early Greek Philosophy: The Emancipation of Thought from Myth," which includes excerpts from Aristotle on Thales of Miletus, as well as excerpts from Anaximander and Pythagoras. The section "Greek Drama" now features *Antigone* by Sophocles. In the section "The Status of Women in Classical Greek Society," *Medea* has joined *Lysistrata*. Added to the section "The Decline of the Republic" in Chapter 4 is Velleius Paterculus' account of Octavian's triumph over Mark Antony. Chapter 6 includes three new selections: the first covers The Dead Sea Scrolls; the second is on Rabbinic Judaism: Ethical Concerns; and the third features Pope Gelasius I's elucidation of the proper relationship between church and state. A section on jihad has been added to Chapter 7. It includes sayings attributed to the Prophet and Ibn Taymiyyah's understanding of

the religious and moral duty to participate in jihad. In that same chapter, added to the constellation "Converting the Germanic Peoples to Christianity," is an account by Bishop Martin of Braga of the persistence of paganism in the countryside.

In Chapter 8, I have added an account of German towns forming an alliance to protect merchants to the section "The Revival of Trade and the Growth of Towns." Also in Chapter 8, Thomas Aquinas' argument for the death sentence for unrepentant heretics has been inserted in the section "Religious Dissent," and a selection from Adelard of Bath, an early exponent of investigating the natural world, has been incorporated into the section, "Medieval Learning: Synthesis of Reason and Christian Faith." The section "The Jews in the Middle Ages" also has a new selection—an account of Philip II's expulsion of the Jews from France; the section "The Fourteenth Century: An Age of Adversity" has a new selection on the extermination of the Albigensians (or Cathars). In Chapter 9, I have enriched the constellation "The Humanists' Fascination with Antiquity" with a passage from Petrus Paulus Vergerius' educational treatise in which he stresses the importance of liberal studies. In Chapter 10, in the section "The German Peasants Revolt," I have inserted passages from a pamphlet by an unknown author that clearly states the peasants' grievances. The section "Spanish Oppression of Amerindians" in Chapter 11 has been enhanced with a statement by Spain's chief crown jurist justifying on theological grounds Spanish domination of the Amerindians. Chapter 12 now begins with Nicholas Copernicus' discussion of his breakthrough in astronomy that precipitated the Scientific Revolution.

Volume II contains 33 new selections. The new selection for Chapter 2, *The Scientific Revolution*, which is reproduced from Volume I, is described above. Added to Chapter 4 is Gracchus Babeuf's call for the elimination of private property during the French Revolution. Chapter 5 now includes Friedrich Engels' famous description of slums in Britain's rapidly growing urban centers. In Chapter 6, an excerpt from Goethe's *Faust* has been incorporated into the "Romanticism" constellation. Also inserted into that chapter is a new section, "Repression," which contains the Karlsbad Decrees that were designed to stifle liberalism and nationalism in the German states. Introducing the section "Realism in Literature" in Chapter 7 is now an early definition of realism by Vissarion Belinsky, a Russian intellectual. Broadening the section "Anti-Semitism: Regression to the Irrational" in Chapter 8 is a description of the murderous Kishinev Pogrom in Russia. In Chapter 9, an excerpt from *The Black Man's Burden* by Edmund Morel, who was distressed by the mistreatment of Africans in the Congo, has been added to the section "European Rule in Africa." Also inserted into Chapter 9 is a new section, "Chinese Resentment of Western Imperialism," that contains selections focusing on the anti-Western and anti-Christian outlook of the Boxers. An account of the militarist spirit of French students prior to World War I has been added to the section "Militarism" in Chapter 11. Also inserted into the chapter is a new constellation, "Women at War," that depicts the employment of women in British factories and the opposition to female employment in Germany.

Chapter 12 contains a new section, "The Great Depression," that depicts the suffering of working people in Britain and Germany. Another new section, "Resistance," has been incorporated into Chapter 13 (for a description of the four selections in that section, see page above). A survivor's account of the fire-bombing of Dresden has been added to the section "The End of the Third Reich," also in Chapter 13. In Chapter 14, *Europe: A New Era,* the first section, "The Aftermath: Devastation and Demoralization" has been completely revised. It now includes a description of a ruined Germany by distinguished journalist Theodore H. White, accounts of the ordeal of Jewish survivors dwelling in camps for displaced persons, and the expulsion of Germans from Czechoslovakia. In the same chapter, added to the section "Communist Repression" is Roy

Medvedev's discussion of Stalin's last years. Another selection by Theodore H. White, this time on Germany's economic resurgence, has been incorporated into "The New Germany: Economic Miracle and Confronting the Past." The chapter ends with a new section, "The Soviet Union: Restructuring and Openness," that features excerpts from Mikhail S. Gorbachev's *Perestroika*.

Chapter 15 has been completely revised to reflect issues of current importance. The new section "Russia: Creeping Autocracy and Burgeoning Nationalism" contains the article Vladimir Putin: A New Tsar in the Kremlin? In another new section, "Child Soldiers," Ishmael Beah describes his terrifying ordeal as a boy soldier in Sierra Leone. Augmenting the section "Radical Islamic Terrorists" is a report by the European Union on this growing problem and an appeal by Abdurrahman Wahid, the former president of Indonesia, for Muslims to unite and defeat the radicals who are distorting Islam's true meaning. In the section "Islam in Europe: Failure of Assimilation," Walter Laqueur, a prominent American historian with strong ties to Europe, discusses the threat to Europe's future posed by a burgeoning Muslim population. In 2008, the United States State Department prepared a comprehensive study of global anti-Semitism, excerpts of which are reproduced in the new section, "Resurgence of Anti-Semitism." The closing section, "In Defense of European Values," contains excerpts from *The Betrayal of the West*, French sociologist Jacques Ellul's defense of Western civilization from its detractors.

I wish to thank the following instructors for their critical reading of the manuscript: Richard Brabander, Bridgewater State College; Elena Osokina, University of South Carolina; and Janusz Duzinkiewicz, Purdue University. I would be remiss if I did not also thank Sylvia Gray, Portland Community College, who took the initiative to suggest to the publisher a significant improvement in the Hebrew Law selection.

I am grateful to the staff of Wadsworth/ Cengage Learning who lent their talents to the project. As in previous editions, Nancy Blaine, senior sponsoring editor, provided useful guidelines. A special thanks to Lauren Floyd, assistant editor, who efficiently prepared the revision for production. I also thank Anne Finley, associate content project manager, who, with the very capable assistance of freelancer Karunakaran Gunasekaran, skillfully guided the book through production. Also deserving of my gratitude are Greg Teague, copy editor, who read the manuscript with a trained eye; Katie Huha, senior rights specialist, who managed the difficult task of obtaining text permissions smoothly; Jennifer Meyer Dare, senior photo editor, who oversaw the selection and research of the chapter-opening photos; and Cate Rickard Barr, senior art director, who managed the design of the cover.

I am pleased that my friend George Bock continues to evaluate with a trained eye proposed new selections and introductions and to proofread so diligently. I thank my wife Phyllis Perry for her encouragement and computer expertise, which saved me time and aggravation. Unfortunately, Angela Von Laue, who had assisted me since the death of her husband Theo in 2000, has taken a too early retirement from the book. I miss her research and proofreading skills.

M.P.

Prologue
Examining Primary Sources

When historians try to reconstruct and apprehend past events, they rely on primary or original sources—official documents prepared by institutions and eyewitness reports. Similarly, when they attempt to describe the essential outlook or world-view of a given era, people, or movement, historians examine other types of primary sources—the literature, art, philosophy, and religious expressions of the time. These original sources differ from secondary or derivative sources—accounts of events and times written at a later date by people who may or may not have had access to primary sources. *Sources of the Western Tradition* consists principally of primary sources, which are the raw materials of history; they provide historians with the basic facts, details, and thinking needed for an accurate reconstruction of the past.

Historians have to examine a document with a critical spirit. The first question asked is: Is the document authentic and reliable? An early illustration of critical historical awareness was demonstrated by the Renaissance thinker Lorenzo Valla (c. 1407–1457) in *Declamation Concerning the False Decretals of Constantine*. The so-called Donation of Constantine, which was used by popes to support their claim to temporal authority, stated that the fourth-century Roman emperor Constantine had given the papacy dominion over the western Empire. By showing that some of the words in the document were unknown in Constantine's time and therefore could not have been used by the emperor, Valla proved that the document was forged by church officials several hundred years after Constantine's death. A more recent example of the need for caution is shown by the discovery of the "Hitler Diaries" in the mid–1980s. Several prominent historians "authenticated" the manuscript before it was exposed as a forgery—the paper dated from the 1950s and

Hitler died in 1945. Nor can all eyewitness accounts be trusted, something Thucydides, the great Greek historian, noted 2,400 years ago.

[E]ither I was present myself at the events which I have described or else I heard of them from eye-witnesses whose reports I have checked with as much thoroughness as possible. Not that even so the truth was easy to discover: different eye-witnesses give different accounts of the same events, speaking out of partiality for one side or the other or else from imperfect memories.

An eyewitness's personal bias can render a document worthless. For example, in *The Auschwitz Lie* (1973), Thies Christophersen, a former SS guard at Auschwitz-Birkenau, denied the existence of gas chambers and mass killings in the notorious Nazi death camp, which he described as a sort of resort where prisoners, after work, could swim, listen to music in their rooms, or visit a brothel. Years later he was captured on videotape—he mistakenly thought the interviewers were fellow neo-Nazis—confessing that he had lied about the gas chambers because of loyalty to the SS and his desire to protect Germany's honor.

After examining the relevant primary sources and deciding on their usefulness, historians have to construct a consistent narrative and provide a plausible interpretation. Ideally, this requires that they examine documentary evidence in a wholly neutral, detached, and objective way. But is it possible to write history without being influenced by one's own particular viewpoint and personal biases?

No doubt several historians examining the same material might draw differing conclusions, and each could argue his or her position persuasively. This is not surprising, for history is not an exact science and historians, like all individuals, are influenced by their upbringing and education, by their thoughts and feelings. Conflicting interpretations of historical events and periods are expected and acceptable features of historiography. But what is not acceptable is the deliberate distortion and suppression of evidence in order to substantiate one's own prejudices.

A flagrant example of writers of history misusing sources and distorting evidence in order to fortify their own prejudices is the recent case of British historian David Irving, author of numerous books on World War II, several of them well reviewed. Increasingly Irving revealed an undisguised admiration for Hitler and an antipathy toward Jews, which led him to minimize and disguise atrocities committed by the Third Reich. Addressing neo-Nazi audiences in several lands, he asserted that the Holocaust is "a major fraud. . . . There were no gas chambers. They were fakes and frauds." In *Lying About Hitler: History, Holocaust and the David Irving Trial* (2001), Richard J. Evans, a specialist in modern German history with a broad background in archival research, exposed instance after instance of how Irving, in his attempt to whitewash Hitler, misquoted sources, "misrepresented data, . . . skewed documents [and] ignored or deliberately suppressed material when it ran counter to his arguments. . . . [W]hen I followed Irving's claims and statements back to the original documents on which they purported to rest . . . Irving's work in this respect was revealed as a house of cards, a vast apparatus of deception and deceit."

The sources in this anthology can be read on several levels. First, they enhance understanding of the historical period in which they were written, shedding light on how people lived and thought and the chief concerns of the time. Several of the sources, written by some of humanity's greatest minds, have broader implications. They are founts of wisdom, providing insights of enduring value into human nature and the human condition. The documents also reveal the evolution of those core ideas and values—reason, freedom, and respect for human dignity—that constitute the Western heritage. Equally important, several documents reveal the precariousness of these values and the threats to them. It is the hope of the editors that an understanding of the evolution of the Western tradition will foster a renewed commitment to its essential ideals.

The documents in these volumes often represent human beings struggling with the vital questions of their day. As such they invite the reader to react actively and imaginatively to the times in which they were produced and to the individuals who produced them. The documents should also be approached with a critical eye. The reader has always to raise several pointed questions regarding the author's motivation, objectivity, logic, and accuracy. In addition, depending on the content of a particular document, the reader should consider the following questions: What does the document reveal about the times in which it was written? About the author? About the nature, evolution, and meaning of the Western tradition? About human nature and human relations? About good and evil? About progress? About war and peace? About gender relations? About life and death? Doubtless other questions will come to mind. In many instances, no doubt, the documents will impel readers to reflect on current issues and their own lives.

CHAPTER 1

The Near East

STROLL IN THE GARDEN, Eighteenth Dynasty, c. 1350 B.C. This relief portrays Tutankhamun and his wife Ankhesenamun. *(Bildarchiv Preussischer Kulturbesitz/Art Resource, NY)*

The world's first civilizations arose some five thousand years ago in the river valleys of Mesopotamia (later Iraq) and Egypt. In these Near Eastern lands people built cities, organized states with definite boundaries, invented writing, engaged in large-scale trade, practiced specialization of labor, and erected huge monuments: all activities that historians associate with civilization. Scholars emphasize the fact that civilizations emerged in the river valleys—the Tigris and Euphrates in Mesopotamia and the Nile in Egypt. When they overflowed their banks, these rivers deposited fertile soil, which could provide a food surplus required to sustain life in cities. The early inhabitants of these valleys drained swamps and built irrigation works, enabling them to harness the rivers for human advantage. In the process they also strengthened the bonds of cooperation, a necessary ingredient of civilization.

Religion and myth were the central forces in these early civilizations. They pervaded all phases of life, providing people with satisfying explanations for the operations of nature and the mystery of death and justifying traditional rules of morality. Natural objects—the sun, the river, the mountain—were seen as either gods or as the abodes of gods. The political life of the Near East was theocratic; that is, people regarded their rulers either as divine or as representatives of the gods and believed that law originated with the gods. Near Eastern art and literature were dominated by religious themes.

The Sumerians, founders of urban life in Mesopotamia, developed twelve city-states in the region of the lower Euphrates near the Persian Gulf. Each city-state included a city and the farmland around it; each had its own government and was independent of the other city-states. In time the Sumerians were conquered, and their cities were incorporated into kingdoms and empires. However, as Akkadians, Elamites, Babylonians, and other peoples of the region adopted and built upon Sumerian religion, art, and literary forms, the Sumerian achievement became the basis of a coherent Mesopotamian civilization that lasted some three thousand years.

Early in its history Egypt became a centralized state under the rule of a pharaoh, who was viewed as both a man and a god. The pharaoh's authority was all-embracing, and all Egyptians were subservient to him. Early in their history, the Egyptians developed cultural patterns that were to endure for three thousand years; the ancient Egyptians looked to the past, seeking to maintain the ways of their ancestors.

Although the cultural patterns of both civilizations were similar—in both, religion and theocratic kingship played a dominant role—there were significant differences between the two. Whereas in Egypt the pharaoh was considered divine, rulers in Mesopotamia were regarded as exceptional human beings whom the gods had selected to act as their agents. Second, the natural environment of the Egyptians fostered a sense of security and an optimistic outlook toward life.

Natural barriers—deserts, the Mediterranean Sea, and cataracts in the Nile—protected Egypt from invasion, and the overflowing of the Nile was regular and predictable, ensuring a good harvest. In contrast, Mesopotamia, without natural barriers, suffered from frequent invasions, and the Tigris and Euphrates rivers were unpredictable. Sometimes there was insufficient overflow, and the land was afflicted with drought; at other times, rampaging floods devastated the fields. These conditions promoted a pessimistic outlook, which pervaded Mesopotamian civilization.

After 1500 B.C., the Near East entered a period of empire building. In the late sixth century B.C., the Persians, the greatest of the empire builders, conquered all the lands from the Nile River to the Indus River in India. Persia united Egypt, Mesopotamia, and other Near Eastern lands into a world-state and brought together the region's various cultural traditions. In the first half of the fifth century B.C., the Persians tried to add the city-states of Greece to their empire; the ensuing conflict was of critical importance for the history of Western civilization.

Egyptians, Mesopotamians, and other Near Eastern peoples developed a rich urban culture and made important contributions to later civilizations. They established bureaucracies, demonstrated creativity in art and literature, fashioned effective systems of mathematics, and advanced the knowledge of architecture, metallurgy, and engineering. The wheel, the plow, the phonetic alphabet, and the calendar derive from the Near East. Both the Hebrews and the Greeks, the principal sources of Western civilization, had contact with these older civilizations and adopted many of their cultural forms. But, as we shall see, even more important for the shaping of Western civilization was how the Hebrews and the Greeks broke with the essential style of Near Eastern society and conceived new outlooks, new points of departure for the human mind.

1 Mesopotamian Protest Against Death

The *Epic of Gilgamesh*, the greatest work of Mesopotamian literature, was written about 2000 B.C. It utilized legends about Gilgamesh, probably a historical figure who ruled the city of Uruk about 2600 B.C. The story deals with a profound theme—the human protest against death. In the end, Gilgamesh learns to accept reality: there is no escape from death. While the *Epic of Gilgamesh* is an expression of the pessimism that pervaded Mesopotamian life, it also reveals the Mesopotamians' struggle to come to terms with reality.

EPIC OF GILGAMESH[1]

The *Epic of Gilgamesh* involves the gods in human activities. Because King Gilgamesh, son of a human father and the goddess Ninsun, drives his subjects too hard, they appeal to the gods for help. The gods decide that a man of Gilgamesh's immense vigor and strength requires a rival with similar attributes with whom he can contend. The creation goddess, Aruru, is instructed to create a man worthy of Gilgamesh. From clay she fashions Enkidu in the image of Anu, the god of the heavens and father of all the gods. Enkidu is a powerful man who roams with the animals and destroys traps set by hunters, one of whom appeals to King Gilgamesh. The two of them, accompanied by a harlot, find Enkidu at a watering place frequented by animals. The harlot removes her clothes and seduces Enkidu, who spends a week with her, oblivious to everything else. After this encounter, the bond between Enkidu and the animals is broken. He now enters civilization and is befriended by Gilgamesh, with whom he slays the terrible monster Humbaba.

Returning to Uruk after the encounter with Humbaba, Gilgamesh washes away the grime of battle and dons his royal clothes; thus arrayed he attracts the goddess of love, Ishtar, patroness of Uruk, who proposes marriage, but because of Ishtar's previous marriages and infidelities, Gilgamesh refuses. Ishtar falls into a bitter rage and appeals to her father, the god Anu, to unleash the fearful Bull of Heaven on Gilgamesh. However, Gilgamesh and Enkidu together slay the beast. To avenge the deaths of Humbaba and the Bull of Heaven, the gods decide that Enkidu shall die. In the following passage, Enkidu dreams of his impending death and the House of Darkness, from which no one returns.

When the daylight came Enkidu got up and cried to Gilgamesh, "O my brother, such a dream I had last night. Anu, Enlil, Ea and heavenly Shamash took counsel together, and Anu said to Enlil, 'Because they have killed the Bull of Heaven, and because they have killed Humbaba who guarded the Cedar Mountain one of the two must die.'. . ."

So Enkidu lay stretched out before Gilgamesh: his tears ran down in streams and he said to Gilgamesh, "O my brother, so dear as you are to me, brother, yet they will take me from you." Again he said, "I must sit down on the threshold of the dead and never again will I see my dear brother with my eyes."

. . . In bitterness of spirit he poured out his heart to his friend. "It was I who cut down the cedar, I who levelled the forest, I who slew Humbaba and now see what has become of me. Listen, my friend, this is the dream I dreamed last night. The heavens roared, and earth rumbled back an answer; between them stood I before an awful being, the sombre-faced man-bird; he had directed on me his purpose. His was a vampire face, his foot was a lion's foot, his hand was an eagle's talon. He fell on me and his claws were in my hair, he held me fast and I smothered; then he transformed me so that my arms became wings covered with feathers. He turned his stare towards me, and he led me away to the palace of Irkalla, the Queen of Darkness, to the house from which none who enters ever returns, down the road from which there is no coming back.

"There is the house whose people sit in darkness; dust is their food and clay their meat. They are clothed like birds with wings for covering, they see no light, they sit in darkness.

---

[1]Throughout the text, titles original to the source appear in italics. Titles added by the editors are not italicized.

I entered the house of dust and I saw the kings of the earth, their crowns put away for ever; rulers and princes, all those who once wore kingly crowns and ruled the world in the days of old. They who had stood in the place of the gods like Anu and Enlil, stood now like servants to fetch baked meats in the house of dust, to carry cooked meat and cold water from the waterskin. In the house of dust which I entered were high priests and acolytes, priests of the incantation and of ecstasy; there were servers of the temple, and there was Etana, that king of Kish whom the eagle carried to heaven in the days of old. I saw also Samuqan, god of cattle, and there was Ereshkigal the Queen of the Underworld; and Belit-Sheri squatted in front of her, she who is recorder of the gods and keeps the book of death. She held a tablet from which she read. She raised her head, she saw me and spoke: 'Who has brought this one here?' Then I awoke like a man drained of blood who wanders alone in a waste of rushes; like one whom the bailiff has seized and his heart pounds with terror."

Gilgamesh had peeled off his clothes, he listened to his words and wept quick tears, Gilgamesh listened and his tears flowed. . . .

This day on which Enkidu dreamed came to an end and he lay stricken with sickness. One whole day he lay on his bed and his suffering increased. He said to Gilgamesh, the friend on whose account he had left the wilderness, "Once I ran for you, for the water of life, and I now have nothing." A second day he lay on his bed and Gilgamesh watched over him but the sickness increased. A third day he lay on his bed, he called out to Gilgamesh, rousing him up. Now he was weak and his eyes were blind with weeping. Ten days he lay and his suffering increased, eleven and twelve days he lay on his bed of pain. Then he called to Gilgamesh, "My friend, the great goddess cursed me and I must die in shame. I shall not die like a man fallen in battle; I feared to fall, but happy is the man who falls in the battle, for I must die in shame." And Gilgamesh wept over Enkidu. With the first light of dawn he raised his voice and said to the counsellors of Uruk:

"Hear me, great ones of Uruk,
I weep for Enkidu, my friend,
Bitterly moaning like a woman mourning
I weep for my brother.
O Enkidu, my brother,
You were the axe at my side,
My hand's strength, the sword in my belt,
The shield before me,
A glorious robe, my fairest ornament;
An evil Fate has robbed me.

. . .

All the people of Eridu
Weep for you Enkidu.

. . .

What is this sleep which holds you now?
You are lost in the dark and cannot hear me."

He touched his heart but it did not beat, nor did he lift his eyes again. When Gilgamesh touched his heart it did not beat. So Gilgamesh laid a veil, as one veils the bride, over his friend. He began to rage like a lion, like a lioness robbed of her whelps. This way and that he paced round the bed, he tore out his hair and strewed it around. He dragged off his splendid robes and flung them down as though they were abominations.

In the first light of dawn Gilgamesh cried out, "I made you rest on a royal bed, you reclined on a couch at my left hand, the princes of the earth kissed your feet. I will cause all the people of Uruk to weep over you and raise the dirge of the dead. The joyful people will stoop with sorrow; and when you have gone to the earth I will let my hair grow long for your sake, I will wander through the wilderness in the skin of a lion." The next day also, in the first light, Gilgamesh lamented; seven days and seven nights he wept for Enkidu, until the worm fastened on him. Only then he gave him up to the earth, for the Anunnaki, the judges [of the dead],[2] had seized him. . . .

---

[2] Throughout the text, words in brackets have been added as glosses by the editors. Brackets around glosses from the original sources have been changed to parentheses to distinguish them.

In his despair, Gilgamesh is confronted with the reality of his own death. Yearning for eternal life, he seeks Utnapishtim, legendary king of the city of Shurrupak, a man to whom the gods had granted everlasting life.

Bitterly Gilgamesh wept for his friend Enkidu; he wandered over the wilderness as a hunter, he roamed over the plains; in his bitterness he cried, "How can I rest, how can I be at peace? Despair is in my heart. What my brother is now, that shall I be when I am dead. Because I am afraid of death I will go as best I can to find Utnapishtim whom they call the Faraway, for he has entered the assembly of the gods." So Gilgamesh travelled over the wilderness, he wandered over the grasslands, a long journey, in search of Utnapishtim, whom the gods took after the deluge; and they set him to live in the land of Dilmun, in the garden of the sun; and to him alone of men they gave everlasting life. . . .

In the garden of the gods, Gilgamesh speaks with Siduri, the divine winemaker, who tells him that his search for eternal life is hopeless.

". . . My friend who was very dear to me and who endured dangers beside me, Enkidu my brother, whom I loved, the end of mortality has overtaken him. I wept for him seven days and nights till the worm fastened on him. Because of my brother I am afraid of death, because of my brother I stray through the wilderness and cannot rest. But now, young woman, maker of wine, since I have seen your face do not let me see the face of death which I dread so much."

She answered, "Gilgamesh, where are you hurrying to? You will never find that life for which you are looking. When the gods created man they allotted to him death, but life they retained in their own keeping. As for you, Gilgamesh, fill your belly with good things; day and night, night and day, dance and be merry, feast and rejoice. Let your clothes be fresh, bathe yourself in water, cherish the little child that holds your hand, and make your wife happy in your embrace; for this too is the lot of man."

But Gilgamesh said to Siduri, the young woman, "How can I be silent, how can I rest, when Enkidu whom I love is dust, and I too shall die and be laid in the earth. You live by the sea-shore and look into the heart of it; young woman, tell me now, which is the way to Utnapishtim, the son of Ubara-Tutu? What directions are there for the passage; give me, oh, give me directions, I will cross the Ocean if it is possible; if it is not I will wander still farther in the wilderness.". . .

Siduri instructs Gilgamesh how to reach Utnapishtim. Ferried across the "waters of death" by a boatman, Gilgamesh meets Utnapishtim. But he, too, cannot give Gilgamesh the eternal life for which he yearns.

. . . "Oh father Utnapishtim, you who have entered the assembly of the gods, I wish to question you concerning the living and the dead, how shall I find the life for which I am searching?"

Utnapishtim said, "There is no permanence. Do we build a house to stand for ever, do we seal a contract to hold for all time? Do brothers divide an inheritance to keep for ever, does the flood-time of rivers endure? It is only the nymph of the dragon-fly who sheds her larva and sees the sun in his glory. From the days of old there is no permanence. The sleeping and the dead, how alike they are, they are like a painted death. What is there between the master and the servant when both have fulfilled their doom? When the Anunnaki, the judges, come together, and Mammetun the mother of destinies, together they decree the fates of men. Life and death they allot but the day of death they do not disclose."

The tale concludes with one of several Near Eastern flood stories that preceded the account of Noah in Genesis.

1. Describe the condition of the dead as envisioned in Enkidu's dream.
2. Describe the stages of Gilgamesh's reaction to Enkidu's death. Do these seem plausible psychologically? Explain.
3. What philosophic consolation did the goddess Siduri and Utnapishtim offer Gilgamesh?
4. Historians often comment on the pessimism or sense of the tragic that is reflected in Mesopotamian literature. To what extent is this true in the story of Gilgamesh?

2   Mesopotamian Concepts of Justice

A significant source of information about the life of the ancient peoples of Mesopotamia is a code of laws issued about 1750 B.C. by the Babylonian king Hammurabi (1792–1750 B.C.). Discovered by archaeologists in 1901, the code was inscribed on a stone that shows the king accepting the laws from the sun god, Shamash, who was also the Babylonian god of justice.

These laws offer striking insights into the moral values, class structure, gender relationships, and roles of kingship and religion in Babylonian society. The 282 laws cover a range of public and private matters: marriage and family relations, negligence, fraud, commercial contracts, duties of public officials, property and inheritance, crimes and punishments, and techniques of legal procedure. The prologue to the code reveals the Mesopotamian concept of the priest-king— a ruler chosen by a god to administer his will on earth. In it, Hammurabi asserted that he had a divine duty to uphold justice in the land, to punish the wicked, and to further the welfare of the people.

CODE OF HAMMURABI

Two distinct approaches to choice of punishment for crime are found in Hammurabi's code with its numerous laws. In some instances, the guilty party is required to pay a monetary compensation to the victim, a tradition traceable to the earliest known Sumerian laws. Another approach, also found in the later Hebrew codes of law, is the principle of exact retaliation: "an eye for an eye, a tooth for a tooth."

Another feature of Hammurabi's code is that the penalties vary according to the social status of the victim. Three classes are represented: free men and women (called *patricians* in the reading here); commoners (or *plebeians*), not wholly free, but dependents of the state or perhaps serfs on landed estates; and slaves. The patricians are protected by the law of retaliation. People of the lower classes receive only monetary compensation if they are victims of a crime.

196. If a man has knocked out the eye of a patrician, his eye shall be knocked out.

197. If he has broken the limb of a patrician, his limb shall be broken.

198. If he has knocked out the eye of a plebeian or has broken the limb of a plebeian, he shall pay one mina[1] of silver.

199. If he has knocked out the eye of a patrician's servant, or broken the limb of a patrician's servant, he shall pay half his value.

200. If a patrician has knocked out the tooth of a man that is his equal, his tooth shall be knocked out.

201. If he has knocked out the tooth of a plebeian, he shall pay one-third of a mina of silver. . . .

209. If a man has struck a free woman with child, and has caused her to miscarry, he shall pay ten shekels[2] for her miscarriage.

210. If that woman die, his daughter shall be killed.

211. If it be the daughter of a plebeian, that has miscarried through his blows, he shall pay five shekels of silver.

212. If that woman die, he shall pay half a mina of silver.

213. If he has struck a man's maid and caused her to miscarry, he shall pay two shekels of silver.

214. If that woman die, he shall pay one-third of a mina of silver.

Many laws relating to business transactions show the importance of trade in Mesopotamian society and the willingness of the government to intervene in order to regulate the practices of the marketplace.

---

218. If a surgeon has operated with the bronze lancet on a patrician for a serious injury, and has caused his death, or has removed a cataract for a patrician, with the bronze lancet, and has made him lose his eye, his hands shall be cut off.

219. If the surgeon has treated a serious injury of a plebeian's slave, with the bronze lancet, and has caused his death, he shall render slave for slave.

220. If he has removed a cataract with the bronze lancet, and made the slave lose his eye, he shall pay half his value.

221. If a surgeon has cured the limb of a patrician, or has doctored a diseased bowel, the patient shall pay five shekels of silver to the surgeon.

222. If he be a plebeian, he shall pay three shekels of silver.

223. If he be a man's slave, the owner of the slave shall give two shekels of silver to the doctor. . . .

228. If a builder has built a house for a man, and finished it, he shall pay him a fee of two shekels of silver, for each *SAR*[3] built on.

229. If a builder has built a house for a man, and has not made his work sound, and the house he built has fallen, and caused the death of its owner, that builder shall be put to death.

230. If it is the owner's son that is killed, the builder's son shall be put to death.

231. If it is the slave of the owner that is killed, the builder shall give slave for slave to the owner of the house.

232. If he has caused the loss of goods, he shall render back whatever he has destroyed. Moreover, because he did not make sound the house he built, and it fell, at his own cost he shall rebuild the house that fell. . . .

271. If a man has hired oxen, a wagon, and its driver, he shall pay one hundred and sixty *KA*[4] of corn daily. . . .

275. If a man has hired a boat, its hire is three *ŠE*[5] of silver daily.

---

[1]The mina was a weight of silver used to express monetary value. (Throughout the text, the editors' notes carry numbers, whereas notes from the original sources are indicated by asterisks, daggers, et cetera. An exception is made for editorial notes pertaining to Scriptures, which have symbols rather than numbers.)

[2]The shekel, also a weight of monetary value, was worth far less than the mina.

[3]*SAR* was a measure of land.

[4]*KA* stood for a bulk measure.

[5]*ŠE* was another monetary weight of silver.

The outcome of some procedures depended on the will of the gods: for example, an accused woman could place her fate in the hands of a god by plunging into a river, canal, or reservoir; if she did not drown, she was declared innocent. In other cases, legal culpability could be removed by invoking a god to bear witness to the truth of one's testimony. The law was particularly harsh on perjurers and those who made grave charges that they could not prove in court.

The buyer shall recoup himself from the seller's estate.

The laws concerned with family relationships placed great power in the hands of husbands and fathers, yet the code tried to protect women and children from neglect and mistreatment. Divorce initiated by either husband or wife was permitted under specific circumstances.

1. If a man has accused another of laying a *nêrtu* (death spell?) upon him, but has not proved it, he shall be put to death.

2. If a man has accused another of laying a *kišpu* (spell) upon him, but has not proved it, the accused shall go to the sacred river, he shall plunge into the sacred river, and if the sacred river shall conquer him, he that accused him shall take possession of his house. If the sacred river shall show his innocence and he is saved, his accuser shall be put to death. He that plunged into the sacred river shall appropriate the house of him that accused him.

3. If a man has borne false witness in a trial, or has not established the statement that he has made, if that case be a capital trial, that man shall be put to death.

4. If he has borne false witness in a civil law case, he shall pay the damages in that suit. . . .

9. If a man has lost property and some of it be detected in the possession of another, and the holder has said, "A man sold it to me, I bought it in the presence of witnesses"; and if the claimant has said, "I can bring witnesses who know it to be property lost by me"; then the alleged buyer on his part shall produce the man who sold it to him and the witnesses before whom he bought it; the claimant shall on his part produce the witnesses who know it to be his lost property. The judge shall examine their pleas. The witnesses to the sale and the witnesses who identify the lost property shall state on oath what they know. Such a seller is the thief and shall be put to death. The owner of the lost property shall recover his lost property.

141. If a man's wife, living in her husband's house, has persisted in going out, has acted the fool, has wasted her house, has belittled her husband, he shall prosecute her. If her husband has said, "I divorce her," she shall go her way; he shall give her nothing as her price of divorce. If her husband has said, "I will not divorce her," he may take another woman to wife; the wife shall live as a slave in her husband's house.

142. If a woman has hated her husband and has said, "You shall not possess me," her past shall be inquired into, as to what she lacks. If she has been discreet, and has no vice, and her husband has gone out, and has greatly belittled her, that woman has no blame, she shall take her marriage-portion and go off to her father's house.

143. If she has not been discreet, has gone out, ruined her house, belittled her husband, she shall be drowned. . . .

148. If a man has married a wife and a disease has seized her, if he is determined to marry a second wife, he shall marry her. He shall not divorce the wife whom the disease has seized. In the home they made together she shall dwell, and he shall maintain her as long as she lives. . . .

168. If a man has determined to disinherit his son and has declared before the judge, "I cut off my son," the judge shall inquire into the son's past, and, if the son has not committed a grave misdemeanor such as should cut him off from sonship, the father shall (not) disinherit his son.

169. If he has committed a grave crime against his father, which cuts him off from sonship, for

the first offence he shall pardon him. If he has committed a grave crime a second time, the father shall cut off his son from sonship. . . .

195. If a son has struck his father, his hands shall be cut off.

One of the most unusual features of the law dealt with the failure of the government officials of a city or a district to prevent banditry. The code held the governor responsible for the breach of the peace and required him to compensate the bandit's victim. Government officials found guilty of extortion, bribery, or use of public employees for private purposes were severely punished.

---

23. If the highwayman has not been caught, the man that has been robbed shall state on oath what he has lost and the city or district governor in whose territory or district the robbery took place shall restore to him what he has lost.

24. If a life (has been lost), the city or district governor shall pay one mina of silver to the deceased's relatives. . . .

34. If either a governor, or a prefect, has appropriated the property of a levymaster,[6] has hired him out, has robbed him by high-handedness at a trial, has taken the salary which the king gave to him, that governor, or prefect, shall be put to death. . . .

---

[6]A levymaster was a military official.

REVIEW QUESTIONS

1. What does Hammurabi's code reveal about the social structure of Babylonian society?
2. Explain the role of religion in the administration of law in Babylonia.
3. How did Hammurabi seek to regulate business practices among the Babylonian people?
4. What do the laws indicate about the status of women in Babylonian society?
5. How did Hammurabi try to control corrupt practices among the government officials of Babylonia?

---

3 Divine Kingship in Egypt

Theocratic monarchy, in which the ruler was considered either a god or a representative of the gods, was the basic political institution of ancient Near Eastern civilization. Kings were believed to rule in accordance with divine commands, and law was viewed as god-given. Theocracy as a form of government that subordinates the individual to the gods and their earthly representatives is compatible with mythical thought that sees nature and human destiny controlled by divine beings.

The theocratic mind of the Near East did not conceive the idea of political freedom. Mesopotamians and Egyptians were not free citizens but subjects who obeyed unquestioningly the edicts of their god-kings or priest-kings. Nor did Near Easterners arrive at a rational way of analyzing the nature and purpose of government and the merits or demerits of political institutions. To them the power of their gods and rulers was absolute and not an issue for discussion or reflection.

Divine kingship was the basic political institution of ancient Egyptian civilization. The Egyptians believed their king or pharaoh to be both a god and a man, the earthly embodiment of the god Horus. He was regarded as a benevolent protector who controlled the flood waters of the Nile, kept the irrigation system in working order, maintained justice in the land, and expressed the will of the gods by his words. It was expected that when the pharaoh died and joined his fellow gods, he would still help his living subjects. The Egyptians rejoiced in the rule of their all-powerful god-king.

HYMNS TO THE PHARAOHS

The first reading is a hymn to the new god-king Ramesses IV (c. 1166 B.C.). The second reading is a hymn to a deceased pharaoh, perhaps Unnos (c. 2600 B.C.).

TO RAMESSES IV

What a happy day! Heaven and earth rejoice, (for) thou art the great lord of Egypt.

They that had fled have come again to their towns, and they that were hidden have again come forth.

They that hungered are satisfied and happy, and they that thirsted are drunken.

They that were naked are clad in fine linen, and they that were dirty have white garments.

They that were in prison are set free, and he that was in bonds is full of joy.

They that were at strife in this land are reconciled. High Niles [beneficial floods] have come from their sources, that they may refresh the hearts of others.

Widows, their houses stand open, and they suffer travellers to enter.

Maidens rejoice and repeat their songs of gladness (?). They are arrayed in ornaments and say (?): "——— he createth generation on generation. Thou ruler, thou wilt endure for ever."

The ships rejoice on the deep ———.
They come to land with wind or oars,
They are satisfied . . . when it is said:
"King Hekmaatrē-Beloved-of-Amūn[1] again weareth the crown.
The son of [the sun-god] Rē, Ramesses, hath received the office of his father."

———
[1] Hekmaatrē was another name of this pharaoh.

All lands say unto him:
"Beautiful is Horus on the throne of Amūn who sendeth him forth,
(Amūn) the protector of the Prince, who bringeth every land."

TO A DECEASED PHARAOH

The King has not died the death: he has become one who rises (like the morning sun) from the horizon. He rests from life (like the setting sun) in the West, but he dawns anew in the East. O King, you have not departed dead: you have departed living! Have you said that he would die?—nay, he dies not: this king lives for ever. He has escaped his day of death. O lofty one among the imperishable stars!—you shall not ever perish. Loose the embalming bandages!—they are not bandages (at all): they are the tresses of the goddess Nephthys (as she leans down over you). Men fall, and their name ceases to be: therefore God takes hold of this king by his arm, and leads him to the sky, that he may not die upon earth amongst men. This king flies away from you, you mortals. He is not of the earth, he is of the sky. He flies as a cloud to the sky, he who was like a bird at the masthead. He goes up to heaven like the hawks, and his feathers are like those of the wild geese; he rushes at heaven like a crane, he kisses heaven like the falcon, he leaps to heaven like the locust.

He ascends to the sky! He ascends to the sky on the wind, on the wind! The stairs of the sky are let down for him that he may ascend thereon to heaven. O gods, put your arms under the king: raise him, lift him to the sky. To the sky! To the sky! To the great throne amongst the gods!

GUIDELINES FOR THE RULER

Generally, pharaohs were mindful of their responsibilities. To prepare his son to rule, a pharaoh or his vizier (a high executive officer) might compile a list of instructions, like the ones that follow. These instructions were most likely composed by a vizier of King Issi (c. 2400 B.C.).

If thou art a leader and givest command to the multitude, strive after every excellence, until there be no fault in thy nature. Truth is good and its worth is lasting, and it hath not been disturbed since the day of its creator,* whereas he that transgresseth its ordinances is punished. It lieth as a (right) path in front of him that knoweth nothing. Wrong-doing (?) hath never yet brought its venture to port. Evil indeed winneth wealth, but the strength of truth is that it endureth, and the (upright) man saith: "It is the property of my father.". . .†

The following excerpts come from the instructions of Amenemhet I (1991–1962 B.C.), who prepared them for his son.

I gave to the poor and nourished the orphan, I caused him that was nothing to reach the goal, even as him that was of account. . . .

None hungered in my years, none thirsted in them. Men dwelt in (peace) through that which I wrought; . . . all that I commanded was as it should be. . . .

These instructions were prepared for King Merikare (c. 2050 B.C.) by his father.

Be not evil, it is good to be kindly. Cause thy monument‡ to endure through the love of thee. . . . Then men thank God on thine account, men praise thy goodness and pray for thine health. . . . But keep thine eyes open, one that is trusting will become one that is afflicted. . . .

Do right so long as thou abidest on the earth. Calm the weeper, oppress no widow, expel no man from the possessions of his father. . . . Take heed lest thou punish wrongfully.

Exalt not the son of one of high degree more than him that is of lowly birth, but take to thyself a man because of his actions.

---

*Rē [the sun god], who brought truth into the world.
†That my father brought me up in the ways of truth is the best thing that he has bequeathed me.

‡The remembrance of thee.

REVIEW QUESTIONS

1. What were the duties expected of an Egyptian king?
2. Discuss the role of religion in sustaining the authority of rulers over their subjects.

4 Religious Inspiration of Akhenaten

Pharaoh Amenhotep IV (1369–1353 B.C.) was a religious mystic who conceived of divinity in a manner approaching monotheism. He suppressed the worship of the many gods of Egypt and insisted that only Aton—the sun god—and himself, the king and son of Aton, be worshiped by the Egyptians. Aton was viewed as the creator of the world, a god of love, peace, and justice. To promote the exclusive worship of Aton and himself, Amenhotep changed his name to Akhenaten ("It is well with Aton"), and near modern Tell El-Amarna he built a new capital city, Akhetaten, which became the center of the new religious cult. The new religion perished quickly after Akhenaten's death. There is no evidence that this step toward a monotheistic conception of the divine had any later influence on the Hebrews.

The masses of Egypt were not influenced by Akhenaten's religious inspiration, and he was resisted by the priests, who clung to traditional beliefs. His immediate successors abandoned the new capital and had the monuments to Aton destroyed.

HYMN TO ATON

Akhenaten's religious outlook inspired remarkable works of art and literature. In the following hymn, Akhenaten glorifies Aton in words that are reminiscent of Psalm 104.

Thou appearest beautifully on the horizon of
    heaven,
Thou living Aton, the beginning of life!
When thou art risen on the eastern horizon,
Thou hast filled every land with thy beauty.
Thou art gracious, great, glistening, and high
    over every land;
Thy rays encompass the lands to the limit of all
    that thou hast made. . . .
At daybreak, when thou arisest on the horizon,
When thou shinest as the Aton by day,
Thou drivest away the darkness and givest thy rays.
The Two Lands[1] are in festivity *every day*,
Awake and standing upon (their) feet,
For thou hast raised them up.
Washing their bodies, taking (their) clothing,

Their arms are (raised) in praise at thy appearance.
All the world, they do their work.

All beasts are content with their pasturage;
Trees and plants are flourishing.
The birds which fly from their nests,
Their wings are (stretched out) in praise to thy *ka*.[2]
All beasts spring upon (their) feet.
Whatever flies and alights,
They live when thou hast risen (for) them.
The ships are sailing north and south as well,
For every way is open at thy appearance.
The fish in the river dart before thy face;
Thy rays are in the midst of the great green sea.

Creator of seed in women,
Thou who makest fluid into man,

---

[1]The Two Lands were the two political divisions of Egypt—Upper and Lower Egypt. They were usually governed by the same king.

[2]The *ka* was a protective and guiding spirit, which each person was thought to have.

Who maintainest the son in the womb of his
  mother,
Who soothest him with that which stills his
  weeping,
Thou nurse (even) in the womb,
Who givest breath to sustain all that he had made!
When he descends from the womb to *breathe*
On the day when he is born,
Thou openest his mouth completely,
Thou suppliest his necessities.
When the chick in the egg speaks within the shell,
Thou givest him breath within it to maintain him.
When thou hast made him his fulfillment
  within the egg, to break it,
He comes forth from the egg to speak at his
  completed (time);
He walks upon his legs when he comes forth
  from it.

How manifold it is, what thou hast made!
They are hidden from the face (of man).
O sole god, like whom there is no other!
Thou didst create the world according to thy
  desire,
Whilst thou wert alone:
All men, cattle, and wild beasts,
Whatever is on earth, going upon (its) feet,

And what is on high, flying with its wings.
The countries of Syria and Nubia,[3] the *land* of
  Egypt,
Thou settest every man in his place,
Thou suppliest their necessities:
Everyone has his food, and his time of life is
  reckoned.
Their tongues are separate in speech,
And their natures as well;
Their skins are distinguished,
As thou distinguishest the foreign peoples.
Thou makest a Nile in the underworld,[4]
Thou bringest it forth as thou desirest
To maintain the people (of Egypt)
According as thou madest them for thyself,
The lord of all of them, wearying (himself)
  with them,
The lord of every land, rising for them,
The Aton of the day, great of majesty.

———

[3]Syria was an ancient country, larger than modern Syria, north of modern Israel and Jordan; Nubia was a kingdom located south of the first cataract of the Nile. It is now in Sudan.
[4]The Egyptians believed that the source of their Nile was in a huge body of water, which they called Nun, under the earth.

REVIEW QUESTIONS

1. Why was the sun a likely choice for a god conceived as one and universal?
2. What were some of the gifts of Aton to humanity?
3. What does the poem reveal about Akhenaten's view of the world and its peoples?

---

5 Love, Passion, and Misogyny in Ancient Egypt

As in most ancient societies, Egyptian women were concerned principally with marriage, children, and household. But in comparison to other societies, Egyptian women suffered fewer disabilities. They had legal rights, could enter the priesthood, a truly prestigious position, and, like men, were thought to have access to the other world after death.

Both men and women came under love's power, and the Egyptians wrote numerous poems that expressed both the joy and pain of love.

LOVE POETRY

In the first selection, a young man admires his loved one's beauty. In this instance, the word *sister*[1] is probably not to be taken literally; it is intended as an expression of endearment.

The *One*, the sister without peer,
The handsomest of all!
She looks like the rising morning star
At the start of a happy year.
Shining bright, fair of skin,
Lovely the look of her eyes,
Sweet the speech of her lips,
She has not a word too much.
Upright neck, shining breast,
Hair true lapis lazuli;
Arms surpassing gold,
Fingers like lotus buds.
Heavy thighs, narrow waist,
Her legs parade her beauty;
With graceful step she treads the ground,
Captures my heart by her movements.
She causes all men's necks
To turn about to see her;
Joy has he whom she embraces,
He is like the first of men!

Without his love the young man suffers.

Seven days since I saw my sister,
And sickness invaded me;
I am heavy in all my limbs,
My body has forsaken me.
When the physicians come to me,
My heart rejects their remedies;

The magicians are quite helpless,
My sickness is not discerned.
To tell me "She is here" would revive me!
Her name would make me rise;
Her messenger's coming and going,
That would revive my heart!
My sister is better than all prescriptions,
She does more for me than all medicines;
Her coming to me is my amulet,
The sight of her makes me well!
When she opens her eyes my body is young,
Her speaking makes me strong;
Embracing her expels my malady—
Seven days since she went from me!

Egyptian women also experience love and vent their feelings.

My heart *flutters* hastily,
When I think of my love of you;
It lets me not act sensibly,
It leaps (from) its place.
It lets me not put on a dress,
Nor wrap my scarf around me;
I put no paint upon my eyes,
I'm even not anointed.

"Don't wait, go there," says it to me,
As often as I think of him;
My heart, don't act so stupidly,
Why do you play the fool?
Sit still, the brother comes to you,
And many eyes as well!
Let not the people say of me:
"A woman fallen through love!"
Be steady when you think of him,
My heart, do not *flutter*!

---

[1]Since Egyptians were interested in maintaining pure bloodlines, incestuous relationships, including brother and sister, were not uncommon. Therefore, the word *sister*, when used by a lover, may be taken figuratively or literally, depending on the circumstances.

THE INSTRUCTION OF ANKHSHESHONQ

Some Egyptian men held unflattering views of women. In his advice to his son, the priest Ankhsheshonq, who lived sometime between 300 B.C. and 50 B.C., expresses such misogynistic views.

Do not take to yourself a woman whose husband is alive, lest he become your enemy. . . .

Let your wife see your wealth; do not trust her with it. . . .

Do not open your heart to your wife or to your servant.

Open it to your mother; she is a woman of discretion. . . .

Instructing a woman is like having a sack of sand whose side is split open.

Her savings are stolen goods.

What she does with her husband today she does with another man tomorrow. . . .

Do not rejoice in your wife's beauty; her heart is set on her lover. . . .

A woman lets herself be loved according to the character of her husband. . . .

He who violates a married woman on the bed will have his wife violated on the ground. . . .

He who makes love to a woman of the street will have his purse cut open on its side. . . .

He who makes love to a married woman is killed on her doorstep. . . .

Do not marry an impious woman, lest she give your children an impious upbringing.

If a woman is at peace with her husband they will never fare badly.

If a woman whispers about her husband [they will never] fare well.

If a woman does not desire the property of her husband she has another man [in her] heart. . . .

If a wife is of nobler birth than her husband he should give way to her.

REVIEW QUESTIONS

1. On the basis of these poems, what similarities do you discern between our standards of beauty and an ancient Egyptian's?
2. Which piece of the priest's advice would a misogynist today consider the wisest?

6 Empire Builders

After 1500 B.C. Near Eastern history was marked by empire building, which led to the intermingling of peoples and cultural traditions and to the extension of civilization well beyond the river valleys. Two of the leading empire builders were the Assyrians and the Persians.

THE ASSYRIAN EMPIRE
INSCRIPTION OF TIGLATHPILESER I

The Assyrians, a Semitic people from the region of what is now northern Iraq, went through several stages of empire building. At its height in the seventh century B.C., the Assyrian Empire stretched from Egypt to Persia (modern Iran). The king, representative of the god Ashur, governed absolutely, and nobles, appointed by the crown, kept order in the provinces. Traveling inspectors checked on the performance of these officials. A network of roads and an effective messenger service enabled Assyrian rulers to keep informed about potential unrest and to crush rebellions. Conquered peoples were permitted a substantial amount of independence so long as they paid tribute to their Assyrian overlords, but uprisings were ruthlessly suppressed.

In the following reading, Tiglathpileser I (1115–1077 B.C.) describes his conquests and the subjugation of rebellious subjects.

Tiglath-pileser, the powerful king, king of hosts, who has no rival, king of the four quarters (of the world), king of all rulers, lord of lords, king of kings; the lofty prince . . . who rules over the nations, . . . the legitimate shepherd whose name is exalted above all rulers; the lofty judge, whose weapons Ashur[1] has sharpened, and whose name, as ruler over the four quarters (of the world), he has proclaimed forever; the conqueror of distant lands, which form the boundaries on north and south; the brilliant day, whose splendour overthrows the world's regions; the terrible, destroying flame, which like the rush of the storm sweeps over the enemy's country; who . . . has no adversary, and overthrows the foes of Ashur.

Ashur and the great gods who have enlarged my kingdom, who have given me strength and power as my portion, commanded me to extend the territory of their (the gods') country, putting into my hand their powerful weapons, the cyclone of battle. I subjugated lands and mountains, cities and their rulers, enemies of Ashur, and conquered their territories. With sixty kings I fought, spreading terror (among them), and achieved a glorious victory over them. A rival in combat, or an adversary in battle, I did not have. To Assyria I added more land, to its people I added more people, enlarging the boundaries of my land and conquering all (neighbouring?) territories.

In the beginning of my government, five kings . . . with an army of twenty thousand men . . .—and whose power no king had ever broken and overcome in battle—trusting to their strength rushed down and conquered the land of Qummuh (Commagene).[2] With the help of Ashur, my lord, I gathered my war chariots and assembled my warriors; I made no delay, but traversed Kashiari,[3] an almost impassable region. I waged battle in Qummuh with these five kings and their twenty thousand soldiers and accomplished their defeat. Like the Thunderer (the storm god Adad) I crushed the corpses of their warriors in the battle that caused their overthrow. I made their blood to flow over all the ravines and high places of mountains. I cut off their heads and piled them up at the walls of their cities like heaps of grain. I carried off their booty, their goods, and their property beyond reckoning. Six thousand, the rest of their troops,

---

[1]Ashur was the patron god of the Assyrians. He is identified with the earlier Babylonian god Marduk.

[2]Commagene was a region along the upper Euphrates River in northern Syria.
[3]Kashiari was a mountainous area in Mesopotamia.

who had fled before my weapons and had thrown themselves at my feet, I took away as prisoners and added to the people of my country.

At that time I marched also against the people of Qummuh, who had become unsubmissive, withholding the tax and tribute due to Ashur, my lord. I conquered Qummuh to its whole extent, and carried off their booty, their goods, and their property; I burned their cities with fire, destroyed, and devastated.

THE PERSIAN EMPIRE
INSCRIPTIONS OF CYRUS AND DARIUS I

Under Cyrus the Great and his son and successor, Cambyses, the Persians conquered all lands between the Nile in Egypt and the Indus River in India. This conquest took twenty-five years, from 550 to 525 B.C. The Near Eastern conception of absolute monarchy justified by religion reached its culminating expression in the person of the Persian king who, it was believed, ruled this vast empire with divine approval. The Persian kings developed an effective system of administration—based in part on an Assyrian model—which gave stability and a degree of unity to their extensive territories.

In the following inscription, Cyrus the Great describes his accomplishments.

I am Cyrus, king of the world, great king, legitimate king, king of Babylon, king of Sumer and Akkad, king of the four rims (of the earth), son of Cambyses, great king, king of Anshan, grandson of Cyrus, great king, king of Anshan, descendant of Teispes, great king, king of Anshan, of a family (which) always (exercised) kingship; whose rule Bel and Nebo love, whom they want as king to please their hearts.

When I entered Babylon as a friend and (when) I established the seat of the government in the palace of the ruler under jubilation and rejoicing, Marduk, the great lord, (induced) the magnanimous inhabitants of Babylon (to love me), and I was daily endeavouring to worship him. My numerous troops walked around in Babylon in peace, I did not allow anybody to terrorize (any place) of the (country of Sumer) and Akkad. I strove for peace in Babylon and in all his (other) sacred cities. As to the inhabitants of Babylon, (I abolished) the corvée[1] (lit.: yoke) which was against their (social) standing. I brought relief to their dilapidated housing, putting (thus) an end to their (main) complaints. Marduk, the great lord, was well pleased with my deeds and sent friendly blessings to myself, Cyrus, the king who worships him, to Cambyses, my son, the offspring of (my) loins, as well as to all my troops, and we all (praised) his great (godhead) joyously, standing before him in peace.

All the kings of the entire world from the Upper to the Lower Sea, those who are seated in throne rooms, (those who) live in other (types of buildings as well as) all the kings of the West land living in tents,* brought their heavy tributes and kissed my feet in Babylon. (As to the region) from . . . as far as Ashur and Susa, Agade, Eshnunna, the towns Zamban, Me-Turnu, Der as well as the region of the Gutians, I returned to (these) sacred cities on the other side of the Tigris, the sanctuaries of which

---

[1]The corvée was labor that local authorities required of ordinary citizens, often on public works such as the maintenance of roads.

*This phrase refers either to the way of life of a nomadic or a primitive society in contradistinction to that of an urban.

have been ruins for a long time, the images which (used) to live therein and established for them permanent sanctuaries. I (also) gathered all their (former) inhabitants and returned (to them) their habitations. Furthermore, I resettled upon the command of Marduk, the great lord, all the gods of Sumer and Akkad whom Nabonidus has brought into Babylon to the anger of the lord of the gods, unharmed, in their (former) chapels, the places which make them happy.

May all the gods whom I have resettled in their sacred cities ask daily Bel and Nebo for a long life for me and may they recommend me (to him); to Marduk, my lord, they may say this: "Cyrus, the king who worships you, and Cambyses, his son, . . ." . . . all of them I settled in a peaceful place . . . ducks and doves, . . . I endeavoured to fortify/repair their dwelling places. . . . (six lines destroyed)

Besides providing impressive political and administrative unity, the Persian Empire fused and perpetuated the various cultural traditions of the Near East. This cultural fusion is reflected in the following inscription, which describes the construction of the palace at Susa by King Darius I (522–486 B.C.).

A great god is Ahuramazda, who created this earth,
who created yonder firmament, who created man,
who created welfare for man, who
made Darius king, one king of many,
one lord of many.—I am Darius,
great king, king of kings, king of countries, king
of this earth, son of Hystaspes, the
Achaemenian.—Says Darius the king:
  Ahuramazda
the greatest of gods, he created me; he
made me king; he to me this kingdom
granted, the great (kingdom), with good
  horses, with
good men. By the grace of Ahuramazda my
  father
Hystaspes and Arsames my grandfather
then both were living when Ahuramazda

made me king of this earth. Ahuramazda
created for me the horse on the whole earth, and
man; he made me king. Ahuramazda
granted me aid, Ahuramazda I reverenced,
Ahuramazda the greatest of gods—what he
  told me
to do, all that by my hand was done,
all that Ahuramazda did.—By the grace of
  Ahuramazda this palace I made which at Susa
was made. From afar to here its ornamentation
  was brought.
The earth was dug until I came to rock-bottom.
When the excavation was made, then rubble
  was filled in, one
part 40 feet in depth, the other 20 feet in depth.
On this rubble the palace was constructed.—
And that the earth was dug down, and that rubble
was filled in and that brick was moulded, the
  Babylonian
folk, it did (that). The timber cedar,
this—a mountain named Lebanon—from
  there was
brought; the Assyrian folk, it brought it to
Babylon; from Babylon the Karkians and
  Ionians
brought it to Susa. The oak from Gandara
was brought and from Carmania. The gold
  from Sardis and from Bactria was brought,
  which was wrought here. The stone—lapis
  lazuli and serpentine—
which was wrought here, this from Sogdiana
was brought. The stone hematite, this from
  Chorasmia
was brought, which was wrought here. The
  silver and
the copper from Egypt were brought. The
  ornamentation
with which the wall was adorned, that from
  Ionia
was brought. The ivory, which was brought
  here, from
Ethiopia and from India and from Arachosia
was brought. The stone pillars which here
were wrought—a place named Abirāduš in
Uja—from there were brought; the stone-masons
who there worked, those were Ionians and
Sardians.—The artisans who the structure
wrought, those were Medes and Egyptians;

those who worked on the fine stones, those were Sardians and Egyptians. The men who worked on the brick (work), those were Babylonians and Ionians; those who (worked) at the wall, those were Medes and Egyptians.—Says Darius the king: by the grace

of Ahuramazda (this) fine well-laid well-walled (palace)
I made. Me may Ahuramazda protect, and what by me was done, and what my father (has done), and my country.

REVIEW QUESTIONS

1. What role do the inscriptions suggest the gods played in establishing and extending the rule of the Assyrian and Persian kings?
2. What appear to have been the character and purposes of warfare in the Assyrian and Persian empires?
3. In what ways did the great royal palace at Susa symbolize both the culture and extent of the Persian Empire?

7 The Myth-Making Outlook of the Ancient Near East

The civilizations of the ancient Near East were based on a way of thinking that is fundamentally different from the modern scientific outlook. The peoples of Mesopotamia and Egypt interpreted nature and human experience through myths, which narrated the deeds of gods who in some distant past had brought forth the world and human beings. These myths made the universe and life intelligible for Near Eastern people.

The difference between scientific thinking and mythical thinking is profound. The scientific mind views physical nature as an *it*—inanimate, impersonal, and governed by universal law. The myth-making (mythopoeic) mind sees nature as personified—alive, with individual wills, gods, and demons who manipulate things according to their desires. The scientific mind holds that natural objects obey universal rules; hence the location of planets, the speed of objects, and the onset of a hurricane can be predicted. The myth-making mind has no awareness of repetitive laws inherent in nature; rather it attributes all occurrences to the actions of gods, whose behavior is often unpredictable. The scientific mind appeals to reason—it analyzes nature logically and systematically and searches for general principles that govern the phenomena. The myth-making mind explains nature and human experience by narrating stories about the gods and their deeds. Myth is an expression of the poetic imagination; it proclaims a truth that is emotionally satisfying, not one produced by intellectual analysis and synthesis. It gives order to human experiences and justifies traditional rules of morality. Mythical explanations of nature and human experience, appealing essentially to the imagination, enrich perception and feeling; they make life seem less overwhelming and death less frightening.

PERSONIFICATION OF NATURAL OBJECTS

The mythopoeic mind accounts for causation by personifying inanimate substances. To explain through personification is to seek the *who* behind events, to attribute these events to the will of a god (or to an object suffused with divine presence). Thus if a river did not rise, it was because it refused to do so; either the river or the gods were angry at the people.

The following excerpts from Mesopotamian literature are examples of personification. While we regard table salt as an ordinary mineral, to the Mesopotamians it was alive, a fellow being. In one passage, a person appeals to salt to end his bewitchment. In another, an afflicted person who believes himself bewitched calls on fire to destroy his enemies.

O SALT

O Salt, created in a clean place,
For food of gods did *Enlil* [father of the
    Sumerian gods] destine thee.
Without thee no meal is set out in *Ekur*,
Without thee god, king, lord, and prince do
    not smell incense.
I am so-and-so, the son of so-and-so,
Held captive by enchantment,
Held in fever by bewitchment.
O Salt, break my enchantment! Loose my spell!
Take from me the bewitchment!—And as My
    Creator
I shall extol thee.

SCORCHING FIRE

Scorching Fire, warlike son of Heaven,
Thou, the fiercest of thy brethren,
Who like Moon and Sun decidest lawsuits—
Judge thou my case, hand down the verdict.
Burn the man and woman who bewitched me;
Burn, O Fire, the man and woman who
    bewitched me;
Scorch, O Fire, the man and woman who
    bewitched me;
Burn them, O Fire;
Scorch them, O Fire;
Take hold of them, O Fire;
Consume them, O Fire;
Destroy them, O Fire.

LAMENT FOR UR THE GODS AND HUMAN DESTINY

Mesopotamians and Egyptians believed that their destinies were determined by the gods. Drought, hurricanes, sickness, law, and foreign invasion were all attributed to divine intervention. In the "Lament for Ur," the assembly of the gods decides to punish the Sumerian city-state of Ur.

Enlil called the storm.
  The people mourn.
Winds of abundance he took from the land.
  The people mourn.

Good winds he took away from Sumer.
  The people mourn.
Deputed evil winds.
  The people mourn.

Entrusted them to Kingaluda, tender of storms.
He called the storm that annihilates the land.
    The people mourn.
He called disastrous winds.
    The people mourn.
Enlil—choosing Gibil as his helper—
called the (great) hurricane of heaven.
    The people mourn.
The (blinding) hurricane howling across the
        skies—
    the people mourn—
the storm that annihilates the land roaring over
        the earth—
    the people mourn—
the tempest unsubduable like breaks
        through levees,
beats down upon, devours the city's ships,
(all these) he gathered at the base of heaven.
    The people mourn.

(Great) fires he lit that heralded the storm.
    The people mourn.
And lit on either flank of furious winds the
    searing heat of desert.
Like flaming heat of noon this fire
        scorched.

It is this storm that destroys the city:

The storm ordered by Enlil in hate,
    the storm which wears away the country,

covered Ur like a cloth,
    veiled it like a linen sheet.

When it clears away all is over:

On that day did the storm leave the city;
    that city was a ruin.
O father Nanna, that town was left a ruin.
    The people mourn.
On that day did the storm leave the country.
    The people mourn.
Its people ('s corpses), not potsherds,
    littered the approaches.
The walls were gaping;
the high gates, the roads,
    were piled with dead.
In the wide streets,
    where feasting crowds (once) gathered,
jumbled they lay.

In all the streets and roadways
    bodies lay.
In open fields that used to fill with dancers,
    the people lay in heaps.

The country's blood now filled its holes,
    like metal in a mold;
bodies dissolved—like butter
    left in the sun.

The assembly of the gods has decided,
    and the decision has been carried out.

REVIEW QUESTIONS

1. What is myth? How does mythical thinking differ from scientific thinking?
2. It has been said that humans are mythmaking animals and that all human societies
   sustain themselves by creating myths. Discuss.
3. On what occasions might the ancient Mesopotamians have turned to the gods for help?
4. How did the ancient Mesopotamians explain natural disasters?

CHAPTER 2
The Hebrews

A SCULPTURED RELIEF from the triumphal Arch of Titus showing Jewish captives bearing the menorah and vessels from the holy temple burned by the Romans at the end of the Jewish revolt, first century A.D. *(Alinari/Art Resource, NY)*

Two ancient peoples, the Hebrews (Jews) and the Greeks, are the principal founders of Western civilization. From the Hebrews derives the concept of *ethical monotheism*—the belief in one God who demands righteous behavior from his human creations—which is an essential element of the Western tradition.

According to biblical tradition, the Hebrews originated in Mesopotamia and migrated to Canaan (Palestine). Some Hebrews who journeyed to Egypt to become farmers and herdsmen were forced to labor for the Egyptian state. In the thirteenth century B.C., Moses, who believed that he was doing God's bidding, led the Hebrews from Egypt—the biblical Exodus. While wandering in the Sinai Desert, the Hebrews were uplifted and united by a belief in Yahweh, the One God. In the eleventh century B.C., some two hundred years after they had begun the conquest of Canaan, the Hebrews were unified under the leadership of Saul, their first king. Under Solomon (d. 922 B.C.) the kingdom of Israel reached the height of its power and splendor.

The Hebrews borrowed elements from the older civilizations of the Near East. Thus there are parallels between Babylonian literature and biblical accounts of the Creation, the Flood, and the Tower of Babel. Nevertheless, Israelite religion marks a profound break with the outlook of the surrounding civilizations of the Near East.

There are two fundamental characteristics of ancient Near Eastern religion. First, the Near Eastern mind saw gods everywhere in nature: the moon and stars, rivers and mountains, thunder and wind storms were either gods or the dwelling places of gods. The Near Eastern mind invented myths—stories about the gods' birth, deeds, death, and resurrection. Second, Near Eastern gods were not fully sovereign. They were not eternal but were born or created; their very existence and power depended on some prior realm. They grew old, became ill, required food, and even died—all limitations on their power. The gods were subject to magic and destiny—forces that preceded them in time and surpassed them in power—and if the gods did wrong, destiny, or fate, punished them.

Hebrew religious thought evolved through the history and experience of the Jewish people. Over the centuries the Hebrew view of God came to differ markedly from Near Eastern ideas about the gods and the world. For the Hebrews, God was not only one, he was also *transcendent*—above nature. This means that natural objects were not divine, holy, or alive, but were merely God's creations. In contrast to the Near Eastern gods, Yahweh was fully *sovereign*, absolutely free; there were no limitations whatsoever on his power. He was eternal and the source of all in the universe; he did not answer to fate but himself determined the consequences of wrongdoing; he was not subject to any primordial power or to anything outside or above him.

The Hebrew conception of God led to a revolutionary view of the human being. The Hebrews believed that God had given the individual moral autonomy—the capacity to choose between good and evil. There-fore, men and women had to measure their actions by God's laws and were responsible for their own behavior. Such an outlook led people to become aware of themselves—their moral potential and personal worth. From the Hebrews came a fundamental value of the Western tradition—the inviolable worth and dignity of the individual.

1 Hebrew Cosmogony and Anthropology

The Hebrew Scriptures, which form the Old Testament of the Christian Bible, are a collection of thirty-nine books written over several centuries by several authors. It is a record of more than a thousand years of ancient Jewish history and religious development. Among the topics treated in Genesis, the first book of the Bible, are God's creation of the universe and human beings, the original human condition in the Garden of Eden, and the origin of evil with Adam and Eve's disobedience of God and their resultant expulsion from Eden.

GENESIS

The first two chapters from the book of Genesis follow. The first chapter presents the *cosmogony* and *anthropology* of the Jews. Hebrew cosmogony—that is, their view of the generation of the universe and all that is in it—exemplifies God's majesty and power. Although Genesis is similar to other Near Eastern creation myths, it also sharply breaks with the essential outlook of the time. In Genesis, nature is no longer inhabited by mythical gods, and inanimate objects are not suffused with life. The Hebrews did not worship the moon and stars and moun-tains and rivers, but they regarded nature as the orderly creation of one supreme and eternal being.

How the Hebrews conceived of the creation of men and women and their position in the universe—the anthropology of the Jews—is dealt with in verses 26–31. The Hebrews' conception of the individual created in God's image and subordinate to nothing except God is as revolutionary as their idea of God, for this conception confers great value and dignity upon human beings.

1 In the beginning God created the heavens and the earth. [2]The earth was without form and void, and darkness was upon the face of the deep; and the Spirit of God was moving over the face of the waters.

3 And God said, "Let there be light"; and there was light. [4]And God saw that the light was good; and God separated the light from the darkness. [5]God called the light Day, and the darkness he called Night. And there was evening and there was morning, one day.

6 And God said, "Let there be a firmament in the midst of the waters, and let it separate the waters from the waters." [7]And God made

the firmament and separated the waters which were under the firmament from the waters which were above the firmament. And it was so. [8]And God called the firmament Heaven. And there was evening and there was morning, a second day.

9 And God said, "Let the waters under the heavens be gathered together into one place, and let the dry land appear." And it was so. [10]God called the dry land Earth, and the waters that were gathered together he called Seas. And God saw that it was good. [11]And God said, "Let the earth put forth vegetation, plants yielding seed, and fruit trees bearing fruit in which is their seed, each according to its kind, upon the earth." And it was so. [12]The earth brought forth vegetation, plants yielding seed according to their own kinds, and trees bearing fruit in which is their seed, each according to its kind. And God saw that it was good. [13]And there was evening and there was morning, a third day.

14 And God said, "Let there be lights in the firmament of the heavens to separate the day from the night; and let them be for signs and for seasons and for days and years, [15]and let them be lights in the firmament of the heavens to give light upon the earth." And it was so. [16]And God made the two great lights, the greater light to rule the day, and the lesser light to rule the night; he made the stars also. [17]And God set them in the firmament of the heavens to give light upon the earth, [18]to rule over the day and over the night, and to separate the light from the darkness. And God saw that it was good. [19]And there was evening and there was morning, a fourth day.

20 And God said, "Let the waters bring forth swarms of living creatures, and let birds fly above the earth across the firmament of the heavens." [21]So God created the great sea monsters and every living creature that moves, with which the waters swarm, according to their kinds, and every winged bird according to its kind. And God saw that it was good. [22]And God blessed them, saying, "Be fruitful and multiply and fill the waters in the seas, and let birds multiply on the earth." [23]And there was evening and there was morning, a fifth day.

24 And God said, "Let the earth bring forth living creatures according to their kinds: cattle and creeping things and beasts of the earth according to their kinds." And it was so. [25]And God made the beasts of the earth according to their kinds and the cattle according to their kinds, and everything that creeps upon the ground according to its kind. And God saw that it was good.

26 Then God said, "Let us make man in our image, after our likeness; and let them have dominion over the fish of the sea, and over the birds of the air, and over the cattle, and over all the earth, and over every creeping thing that creeps upon the earth." [27]So God created man in his own image, in the image of God he created him; male and female he created them. [28]And God blessed them, and God said to them, "Be fruitful and multiply, and fill the earth and subdue it; and have dominion over the fish of the sea and over the birds of the air and over every living thing that moves upon the earth." [29]And God said, "Behold, I have given you every plant yielding seed which is upon the face of all the earth, and every tree with seed in its fruit; you shall have them for food. [30]And to every beast of the earth, and to every bird of the air, and to everything that creeps on the earth, everything that has the breath of life, I have given every green plant for food." And it was so. [31]And God saw everything that he had made, and behold, it was very good. And there was evening and there was morning, a sixth day. (Genesis 1)

The second chapter of Genesis contains a more detailed description of God's creation of woman.

---

18 Then the LORD God said, "It is not good that the man should be alone; I will make him a helper fit for him." [19]So out of the ground the LORD God formed every beast of the field

and every bird of the air, and brought them to the man to see what he would call them; and whatever the man called every living creature, that was its name. ²⁰The man gave names to all cattle, and to the birds of the air, and to every beast of the field; but for the man there was not found a helper fit for him. ²¹So the LORD God caused a deep sleep to fall upon the man, and while he slept took one of his ribs and closed up its place with flesh; ²²and the rib which the LORD God had taken from the man he made into a woman and brought her to the man.

23 Then the man said,
"This at last is bone of my bones
      and flesh of my flesh;
she shall be called Woman,
      because she was taken out of Man."

24 Therefore a man leaves his father and his mother and cleaves to his wife, and they become one flesh. ²⁵And the man and his wife were both naked, and were not ashamed. (Genesis 2)

REVIEW QUESTIONS

1. What conception of God emerges from these two chapters in Genesis?
2. What does the book of Genesis reveal about Hebrew conceptions of male and female relationships?
3. What relationship does the book of Genesis suggest between humans and other creations of God such as the earth, plants, and animals?

---

2 Human Sinfulness

The Hebrews defined sin as a violation of God's laws and a breach of his Covenant. This offense against God corrupts his created order, which was intended to be beneficial to human beings, and brings suffering into the world. Biblical writers regarded sin as a universal phenomenon, an ever-present menace to both individual and group life, deserving of God's punishment. Yet even when God inflicts terrible pain on the Hebrews for violating his law, he still remains compassionate and merciful, an inducement to sinners to renew their commitment to God's teachings.

GENESIS
THE ORIGINS OF SIN

The third chapter of Genesis deals with the origin of evil. When Adam and Eve disobeyed God by eating from the tree of knowledge, they were driven from the Garden of Eden. For the Hebrews the expulsion from paradise marks the beginning of human history, suffering, and death. This passage provides one of the fundamental explanations of evil in the Western tradition, the Judaic conception, later to be refashioned by Saint Paul into the Christian notion of original sin. The language of the biblical narrative is seemingly naive and framed in mythic imagery, but the ideas that it presents are profound and timeless.

1 Now the serpent was more subtle than any other wild creature that the Lord God had made. He said to the woman, "Did God say, 'You shall not eat of any tree of the garden'?" ²And the woman said to the serpent, "We may eat of the fruit of the trees of the garden; ³but God said, 'You shall not eat of the fruit of the tree which is in the midst of the garden, neither shall you touch it, lest you die.'" ⁴But the serpent said to the woman, "You will not die. ⁵For God knows that when you eat of it your eyes will be opened, and you will be like God, knowing good and evil." ⁶So when the woman saw that the tree was good for food, and that it was a delight to the eyes, and that the tree was to be desired to make one wise, she took of its fruit and ate; and she also gave some to her husband, and he ate. ⁷Then the eyes of both were opened, and they knew that they were naked; and they sewed fig leaves together and made themselves aprons.

8 And they heard the sound of the Lord God walking in the garden in the cool of the day, and the man and his wife hid themselves from the presence of the Lord God among the trees of the garden. ⁹But the Lord God called to the man, and said to him, "Where are you?" ¹⁰And he said, "I heard the sound of thee in the garden, and I was afraid, because I was naked; and I hid myself." ¹¹He said, "Who told you that you were naked? Have you eaten of the tree of which I commanded you not to eat?" ¹²The man said, "The woman whom thou gavest to be with me, she gave me fruit of the tree, and I ate." ¹³Then the Lord God said to the woman, "What is this that you have done?" The woman said, "The serpent beguiled me, and I ate."

14 The Lord God said to the serpent,
"Because you have done this,
     cursed are you above all cattle,
     and above all wild animals;
upon your belly you shall go,
     and dust you shall eat
     all the days of your life.

¹⁵I will put enmity between you and the
     woman,
     and between your seed and her seed;
he shall bruise your head,
     and you shall bruise his heel."
¹⁶To the woman he said,
"I will greatly multiply your pain in
     childbearing;
     in pain you shall bring forth children,
yet your desire shall be for your husband,
     and he shall rule over you."
17 And to Adam he said,
"Because you have listened to the voice of
     your wife,
     and have eaten of the tree
of which I commanded you,
     'You shall not eat of it,'
cursed is the ground because of you;
     in toil you shall eat of it all the days of
     your life;
¹⁸thorns and thistles it shall bring forth to you;
     and you shall eat the plants of the field.
¹⁹In the sweat of your face
     you shall eat bread
till you return to the ground,
     for out of it you were taken;
you are dust,
     and to dust you shall return."

20 The man called his wife's name Eve, because she was the mother of all living. ²¹And the Lord God made for Adam and for his wife garments of skins, and clothed them.

22 Then the Lord God said, "Behold, the man has become like one of us, knowing good and evil; and now, lest he put forth his hand and take also of the tree of life, and eat, and live for ever"—²³therefore the Lord God sent him forth from the garden of Eden, to till the ground from which he was taken. ²⁴He drove out the man; and at the east of the garden of Eden he placed the cherubim [winged angels], and a flaming sword which turned every way, to guard the way to the tree of life. (Genesis 3)

REVIEW QUESTION

1. What does the story of Adam and Eve reveal about Hebrew conceptions of good and evil?

3   The Covenant and the Ten Commandments

Central to Hebrew religious thought was the Covenant that the Hebrews believed had been made between God and themselves. The Hebrews believed that God had chosen them to be the first recipients of his law. They did not hold that this honor was bestowed on them because they were better than other nations or that they had done something special to earn it. Rather they viewed the Covenant as an awesome responsibility; God had chosen them to set an example of righteous behavior to the other nations.

EXODUS
THE COVENANT

As described in Exodus, the Israelite leader Moses received the Covenant on Mount Sinai at the time of the Hebrews' flight from Egypt and wanderings in the wilderness of the Sinai Desert.

3 And Moses went up to God, and the LORD called to him out of the mountain, saying, "Thus you shall say to the house of Jacob, and tell the people of Israel: ⁴You have seen what I did to the Egyptians, and how I bore you on eagles' wings and brought you to myself. ⁵Now therefore, if you will obey my voice and keep my covenant, you shall be my own possession among all peoples; for all the earth is mine, ⁶and you shall be to me a kingdom of priests and a holy nation. These are the words which you shall speak to the children of Israel."

7 So Moses came and called the elders of the people, and set before them all these words which the LORD had commanded him. ⁸And all the people answered together and said, "All that the LORD has spoken we will do." And Moses reported the words of the people to the LORD. ⁹And the LORD said to Moses, "Lo, I am coming to you in a thick cloud, that the people may hear when I speak with you, and may also believe you for ever." (Exodus 19)

EXODUS
THE TEN COMMANDMENTS

Together with the Covenant, Moses received the Ten Commandments, which specified God's moral laws. Exodus 20 sets forth the Ten Commandments.

17 Then Moses brought the people out of the camp to meet God; and they took their stand at the foot of the mountain. ¹⁸And Mount

Sinai was wrapped in smoke, because the LORD descended upon it in fire; and the smoke of it went up like the smoke of a kiln, and the whole mountain quaked greatly. [19]And as the sound of the trumpet grew louder and louder, Moses spoke, and God answered him in thunder. [20]And the LORD came down upon Mount Sinai, to the top of the mountain; and the LORD called Moses to the top of the mountain, and Moses went up. (Exodus 19)

1 And God spoke all these words, saying,

2 "I am the LORD your God, who brought you out of the land of Egypt, out of the house of bondage.

3 "You shall have no other gods before me.

4 "You shall not make yourself a graven image, or any likeness of anything that is in heaven above, or that is in the earth beneath, or that is in the water under the earth; [5]you shall not bow down to them or serve them; for I the LORD your God am a jealous God, visiting the iniquity of the fathers upon the children to the third and the fourth generation of those who hate me, [6]but showing steadfast love to thousands of those who love me and keep my commandments.

7 "You shall not take the name of the LORD your God in vain; for the LORD will not hold him guiltless who takes his name in vain.

8 "Remember the sabbath day, to keep it holy. [9]Six days you shall labor, and do all your work; [10]but the seventh day is a sabbath to the LORD your God; in it you shall not do any work, you, or your son, or your daughter, your manservant, or your maidservant, or your cattle, or the sojourner who is within your gates; [11]for in six days the LORD made heaven and earth, the sea, and all that is in them, and rested the seventh day; therefore the LORD blessed the sabbath day and hallowed it.

12 "Honor your father and your mother, that your days may be long in the land which the LORD your God gives you.

13 "You shall not kill.

14 "You shall not commit adultery.

15 "You shall not steal.

16 "You shall not bear false witness against your neighbor.

17 "You shall not covet your neighbor's house; you shall not covet your neighbor's wife, or his manservant, or his maidservant, or his ox, or his ass, or anything that is your neighbor's."

18 Now when all the people perceived the thunderings and the lightnings and the sound of the trumpet and the mountain smoking, the people were afraid and trembled; and they stood afar off, [19]and said to Moses, "You speak to us, and we will hear; but let not God speak to us, lest we die." [20]And Moses said to the people, "Do not fear; for God has come to prove you, and that the fear of him may be before your eyes, that you may not sin."

21 And the people stood afar off, while Moses drew near to the thick cloud where God was. (Exodus 20)

REVIEW QUESTIONS

1. What were the terms of the Covenant between God and the Hebrews?
2. The belief that some laws were divine in origin was shared by many Near Eastern peoples, including the Hebrews. How has this belief shaped subsequent Western civilization?

4 Humaneness of Hebrew Law

The new awareness of the individual that was produced by the Hebrew concept of God found expression in Hebrew law, which was recorded in the Torah, the first five books of the Scriptures. For the Hebrews, the source of law was, of course, God, and because God is good, his law must be concerned with human welfare. Thus Hebrew law showed a respect for life: it protected the stranger, widows, orphans, and the destitute and slaves from cruel masters. Elders and judges who implemented the law were expected to be guided by God's command to pursue righteousness as the prophet Micah enjoined: "And what does the Lord require of you but to do justice and to love kindness and to walk humbly with your God?"

Israelite law incorporated elements of the customary law and legal codes of the older civilizations of the Near East. For example, in Deuteronomy the law prescribes the treatment of a murder committed in areas where there are no witnesses and no indication of who committed the crime. The elders in the nearest village are required to declare that the inhabitants of their village did not commit the murder and to assume responsibility for bringing the unknown assailant to justice. These requirements bear striking similarity to several Near Eastern texts. Another example involves the theft of a herd or flock animal. The penalties in both Exodus and Babylonian documents are similar: the guilty party has to return more animals than were stolen. And both Babylonian and Hebrew law endorse the principle of "an eye for an eye." However, it seems that for the Hebrews, this law of retaliation was eventually replaced by the formula of proportionate compensation for the damage inflicted. The person responsible for the loss of another's eye or tooth could compensate the injured party in other ways.

There are also fundamental differences between biblical law and the other law codes of the Near East. Hebrew laws were more concerned with people than with property. For example, whereas Babylonian law prescribed death for house invasion and theft, the Bible does not permit taking a life for a crime against property. Hebrew law rejected the idea, so clearly demonstrated in the Code of Hammurabi, of one law for nobles and another for commoners. Nor did Hebrew law permit substitutionary punishment common to Near Eastern law codes. For example, if due to faulty construction a house collapsed killing the homeowner's son, Babylonian law required that the builder's son be put to death. No such provision is found in biblical law. Hebrew law was more considerate of the slave than the law codes of other Near Eastern peoples: "When you buy a Hebrew slave, he shall serve six years, and in the seventh he shall go out free, for nothing." Also in contrast to Near Eastern law, a Hebrew father had no legal sanction to kill his daughter for having premarital sex.

While biblical law valued human life and was concerned with human welfare, it also contained provisions that shock us as cruel, for example: ordering the slaughter of the enemies in war, the stoning to death of one's family members who chose to serve other gods, and the execution of homosexuals. Over the centuries, however, there arose an oral and interpretive tradition that made the written law less rigid and led the Hebrews to adapt to changing cultural conditions.

EXODUS
CRIME AND PUNISHMENT

For the Hebrews the most serious crimes were grave sins against God, including idolatry, blasphemy, apostasy, profaning the sabbath, and adultery,* which were all punishable by death. They viewed such rebellion as a threat to the entire community, for it might cause God to annul the Covenant, the special relationship he had with the Hebrews that was the foundation of their existence as a nation. Believing that God would blame them if they failed to take action, the entire community felt a responsibility to punish by death these dangerous offenders in their midst.

Hebrew law dealt with a multiplicity of crimes, including assaults and murder. Because each human being was a bearer of God's image, murder was viewed as an attack on God. In Near Eastern legal codes, if a noble killed a commoner, his punishment might be financial compensation to the family. Such class differences did not enter into Israelite law, which required the murderer to pay with his own life; there was no death penalty in cases of involuntary homicide, and the law provided places of refuge where the person who killed by accident would be protected from people seeking vengeance. Hebrew law also prescribed the death penalty for children who physically or verbally abused their parents. However, because the parents' approval was necessary for the court to implement the law, it is highly likely that only rarely was it put into effect. Kidnapping with the object of selling the victim to caravan traders for transportation to foreign slave markets was another capital crime.

The following passages from Exodus illustrate Hebrew views of crime and punishment.

12 "Whoever strikes a man so that he dies shall be put to death. [13]But if he did not lie in wait for him, but God let him fall into his hand, then I will appoint for you a place to which he may flee. [14]But if a man wilfully attacks another to kill him treacherously, you shall take him from my altar, that he may die.

15 "Whoever strikes his father or his mother shall be put to death.

16 "Whoever steals a man, whether he sells him or is found in possession of him, shall be put to death.

17 "Whoever curses his father or his mother shall be put to death.

18 "When men quarrel and one strikes the other with a stone or with his fist and the man does not die but keeps his bed, [19]then if the man rises again and walks abroad with his staff, he that struck him shall be clear; only he shall pay for the loss of his time, and shall have him thoroughly healed.

20 "When a man strikes his slave, male or female, with a rod and the slave dies under his hand, he shall be punished. [21]But if the slave survives a day or two, he is not to be punished; for the slave is his money.

22 "When men strive together, and hurt a woman with child, so that there is a miscarriage, and yet no harm follows, the one who hurt her

---

*Although the Scriptures exhort husbands to be faithful, the death penalty only applied if his infidelity were conducted with another man's wife. No exception was made for an adulteress wife.

shall be fined, according as the woman's husband shall lay upon him; and he shall pay as the judges determine. [23]If any harm follows, then you shall give life for life, [24]eye for eye, tooth for tooth, hand for hand, foot for foot, [25]burn for burn, wound for wound, stripe for stripe.

26 "When a man strikes the eye of his slave, male or female, and destroys it, he shall let the slave go free for the eye's sake. [27]If he knocks out the tooth of his slave, male or female, he shall let the slave go free for the tooth's sake.

22 "If a man steals an ox or a sheep, and kills it or sells it, he shall pay five oxen for an ox, and four sheep for a sheep. He shall make restitution; if he has nothing, then he shall be sold for his theft. [4]If the stolen beast is found alive in his possession, whether it is an ox or an ass or a sheep, he shall pay double.

16 "If a man seduces a virgin who is not betrothed, and lies with her, he shall give the marriage present for her, and make her his wife. [17]If her father utterly refuses to give her to him, he shall pay money equivalent to the marriage present for virgins.

18 "You shall not permit a sorceress to live.

19 "Whoever lies with a beast shall be put to death.

20 "Whoever sacrifices to any god, save to the LORD only, shall be utterly destroyed.

21 "You shall not wrong a stranger or oppress him, for you were strangers in the land of Egypt. [22]You shall not afflict any widow or orphan. [23]If you do afflict them, and they cry out to me, I will surely hear their cry; [24]and my wrath will burn, and I will kill you with the sword, and your wives shall become widows and your children fatherless.

25 "If you lend money to any of my people with you who is poor, you shall not be to him as a creditor, and you shall not exact interest from him. [26]If ever you take your neighbor's garment in pledge, you shall restore it to him before the sun goes down; [27]for that is his only covering, it is his mantle for his body; in what else shall he sleep? And if he cries to me, I will hear, for I am compassionate.

28 "You shall not revile God, nor curse a ruler of your people.

LEVITICUS
NEIGHBOR AND COMMUNITY

To the Hebrews, laws governing economic, social, and political relationships gave practical expression to God's universal standards of morality. Leviticus, the third book in the Scriptures, contains laws governing actions dealing with neighbors and the community.

9 "When you reap the harvest of your land, you shall not reap your field to its very border, neither shall you gather the gleanings after your harvest. [10]And you shall not strip your vineyard bare, neither shall you gather the fallen grapes of your vineyard; you shall leave them for the poor and for the sojourner: I am the LORD your God.

11 "You shall not steal, nor deal falsely, nor lie to one another. [12]And you shall not swear by my name falsely, and so profane the name of your God: I am the LORD.

13 "You shall not oppress your neighbor or rob him. The wages of a hired servant shall not remain with you all night until the morning. [14]You shall not curse the deaf or put a stumbling

block before the blind, but you shall fear your God: I am the LORD.

15 "You shall do no injustice in judgment; you shall not be partial to the poor or defer to the great, but in righteousness shall you judge your neighbor. [16]You shall not go up and down as a slanderer among your people, and you shall not stand forth against the life of your neighbor: I am the LORD.

17 "You shall not hate your brother in your heart, but you shall reason with your neighbor, lest you bear sin because of him. [18]You shall not take vengeance or bear any grudge against the sons of your own people, but you shall love your neighbor as yourself: I am the LORD. . . .

33 "When a stranger sojourns with you in your land, you shall not do him wrong. [34]The stranger who sojourns with you shall be to you as the native among you, and you shall love him as yourself. . . ." (Leviticus 19)

DEUTERONOMY
JUDGES, WITNESSES, AND JUSTICE

The book of Deuteronomy was composed in the seventh century B.C., some six centuries after the exodus from Egypt. Written as though it were a last speech of Moses advising the people how to govern themselves as they entered the land of Canaan, Deuteronomy reflects the new problems faced by the Hebrews who had already established a kingdom and lived in a settled urban society. In presenting their reform program, the authors of Deuteronomy linked their message to the authority of Moses. The central theme of these verses is the attainment of justice.

18 "You shall appoint judges and officers in all your towns which the LORD your God gives you, according to your tribes; and they shall judge the people with righteous judgment. [19]You shall not pervert justice; you shall not show partiality; and you shall not take a bribe, for a bribe blinds the eyes of the wise and subverts the cause of the righteous. [20]Justice, and only justice, you shall follow, that you may live and inherit the land which the LORD your God gives you." (Deuteronomy 16)

———

15 "A single witness shall not prevail against a man for any crime or for any wrong in connection with any offence that he has committed; only on the evidence of two witnesses, or of three witnesses, shall a charge be sustained. [16]If a malicious witness rises against any man to accuse him of wrongdoing, [17]then both parties to the dispute shall appear before the LORD, before the priests and the judges who are in office in those days; [18]the judges shall inquire diligently, and if the witness is a false witness and has accused his brother falsely, [19]then you shall do to him as he had meant to do to his brother; so you shall purge the evil from the midst of you." (Deuteronomy 19)

———

15 "You shall not give up to his master a slave who has escaped from his master to you; [16]he shall dwell with you, in your midst, in the place which he shall choose within one of your towns, where it pleases him best; you shall not oppress him." (Deuteronomy 23)

———

14 "You shall not oppress a hired servant who is poor and needy, whether he is one of your brethren or one of the sojourners who are in your land within your towns; ¹⁵you shall give him his hire on the day he earns it, before the sun goes down (for he is poor, and sets his heart upon it); lest he cry against you to the LORD, and it be sin in you.

16 "The fathers shall not be put to death for the children, nor shall the children be put to death for the fathers; every man shall be put to death for his own sin.

17 "You shall not pervert the justice due to the sojourner or to the fatherless, or take a widow's garment in pledge; ¹⁸but you shall remember that you were a slave in Egypt and the LORD your God redeemed you from there; therefore I command you to do this.

19 "When you reap your harvest in your field, and have forgotten a sheaf in the field, you shall not go back to get it; it shall be for the sojourner, the fatherless, and the widow; that the LORD your God may bless you in all the work of your hands. ²⁰When you beat your olive trees, you shall not go over the boughs again; it shall be for the sojourner, the fatherless, and the widow. ²¹When you gather the grapes of your vineyard, you shall not glean it afterward; it shall be for the sojourner, the fatherless, and the widow. ²²You shall remember that you were a slave in the land of Egypt; therefore I command you to do this." (Deuteronomy 24)

REVIEW QUESTIONS

1. Show how an awareness of social justice pervaded Hebrew law.
2. How did the legal procedures of Hebrew law try to ensure fair treatment of all ranks of society?
3. What facets of Hebrew law do you consider especially humane? Excessively severe?

5 God's Greatness and Human Dignity

The Hebrew view of God produced a remarkable new concept of human dignity. In God's plan for the universe, the Hebrews believed, human beings are the highest creation, subordinate only to God. Of all God's creatures, only they have been given the freedom to choose between good and evil. To human beings God granted dominion over the earth and the seas.

The Psalms in the Hebrew Scriptures contain 150 hymns extolling Yahweh, some of them written by King David, who ruled c. 1000–961 B.C. In addition to his great success as a warrior and administrator, David was renowned as a harpist and composer.

PSALM 8

In the following song, the psalmist rejoices in the greatness of God. He marvels in the Lord's love for human beings, expressed in their having been given dominion over the earth and its creatures.

O LORD, our Lord,
how majestic is thy name in all the earth!

Thou whose glory above the heavens is
       chanted
   ²by the mouth of babes and infants,
thou hast founded a bulwark because of thy
       foes,
   to still the enemy and the avenger.

³When I look at thy heavens, the work of thy
       fingers,
   the moon and the stars which thou hast
       established;
⁴what is man that thou art mindful of him,

and the son of man that thou dost care for
       him?
⁵Yet thou hast made him little less than God,
   and dost crown him with glory and honor.
⁶Thou hast given him dominion over the works
       of thy hands;
   thou hast put all things under his feet,
⁷all sheep and oxen,
   and also the beasts of the field,
⁸the birds of the air, and the fish of the sea,
   whatever passes along the paths of the sea.

⁹O LORD, our Lord,
   how majestic is thy name in all the earth!

PSALM 104

**Psalm 104 praises God's majesty and lauds him for the wonders of his creation—
the earth and all its creatures.**

Bless, the LORD, O my soul!
O LORD my God, thou art very great!
Thou art clothed with honor and majesty,
²who coverest thyself with light as with a
       garment,
who hast stretched out the heavens like a tent,
³who hast laid the beams of thy chambers
       on the waters,
who makest the clouds thy chariot,
   who ridest on the wings of the wind,
⁴who makest the winds thy messengers,
   fire and flame thy ministers.
⁵Thou didst set the earth on its foundations, so
       that it should never be shaken.
⁶Thou didst cover it with the deep as with a
       garment;
   the waters stood above the mountains.
⁷At thy rebuke they fled;
   at the sound of thy thunder they took to
       flight.
⁸The mountains rose, the valleys sank down
   to the place which thou didst appoint for
       them.

⁹Thou didst set a bound which they should not
       pass,
   so that they might not again cover the earth.
¹⁰Thou makest springs gush forth in the valleys;
   they flow between the hills,
¹¹they give drink to every beast of the field;
   the wild asses quench their thirst.
¹²By them the birds of the air have their
       habitation;
   they sing among the branches.
¹³From thy lofty abode thou waterest the
       mountains;
   the earth is satisfied with the fruit of thy work.

¹⁴Thou dost cause the grass to grow for the
       cattle,
   and plants for man to cultivate,
that he may bring forth food from the earth,
¹⁵and wine to gladden the heart of man,
oil to make his face shine,
   and bread to strengthen man's heart.
¹⁶The trees of the LORD are watered abundantly,
   the cedars of Lebanon which he planted.

¹⁷In them the birds build their nests;
  the stork has her home in the fir trees.
¹⁸The high mountains are for the wild goats;
  the rocks are a refuge for the badgers.
¹⁹Thou hast made the moon to mark the
    seasons;
  the sun knows its time for setting.
²⁰Thou makest darkness, and it is night,
  when all the beasts of the forest creep forth,
²¹The young lions roar for their prey,
  seeking their food from God.
²²When the sun rises, they get them away and
    lie down in their dens.
²³Man goes forth to his work
  and to his labor until the evening.
²⁴O LORD, how manifold are thy works!
  In wisdom hast thou made them all;
  the earth is full of thy creatures.
²⁵Yonder is the sea, great and wide,
  which teems with things innumerable,
  living things both small and great.
²⁶There go the ships,
  and Leviathan [a sea monster]
    which thou didst form to sport in it.

²⁷These all look to thee,
  to give them their food in due season.

²⁸When thou givest to them, they gather it up;
  when thou openest thy hand, they are
    filled with good things.
²⁹When thou hidest thy face, they are
    dismayed;
  when thou takest away their breath, they
    die
  and return to their dust.
³⁰When thou sendest forth thy Spirit, they are
    created;
  and thou renewest the face of the ground.

³¹May the glory of the LORD endure for ever,
  may the LORD rejoice in his works,
³²who looks on the earth and it trembles,
  who touches the mountains and they
    smoke!
³³I will sing to the LORD as long as I live;
  I will sing praise to my God while I have
    being.
³⁴May my meditation be pleasing to him,
  for I rejoice in the LORD.
³⁵Let sinners be consumed from the earth,
  and let the wicked be no more!
Bless the LORD, O my soul!
Praise the LORD!

REVIEW QUESTIONS

1. What do the Psalms reveal about the Hebrew view of God? Of human beings? Of nature?
2. Compare Psalm 104 with Akhenaten's Hymn to Aton (pages 13–14).

---

6 The Problem of Undeserved Suffering

Why do the righteous often suffer and the wicked prosper? And why does God permit such injustice? These profound questions continue to intrigue religious thinkers. The Book of Job does not provide conclusive answers to these questions, but it does impel us to ponder them and to think about our relationship to God.

JOB
"[GOD] DESTROYS BOTH
THE BLAMELESS AND THE WICKED"

Written sometime between the seventh and the fourth centuries B.C., the Book of Job is one of the best examples of Hebrew wisdom literature. In the prologue, the first two chapters of the book, God tells Satan[1] that there is none like his servant Job, "a whole-hearted and an upright man that feareth God and shunneth evil." Satan replies that Job is loyal only because God has protected him from misfortune. Put an end to his good fortune, says Satan, and Job "will blaspheme Thee to Thy face." Accepting the challenge, God permits Satan to destroy Job's children, take away his possessions, and afflict him with painful boils all over his body. Still Job does not curse God.

So far Job has accepted his fate uncomplainingly. But then in the company of three friends, Eliphaz, Bildad, and Zophar, he laments his misfortune and protests that God has treated him unjustly. Why is this happening, he asks, since he has not knowingly sinned? And why does a merciful God continue to make him suffer?

1 After this Job opened his mouth and cursed the day of his birth.

[2]And Job said:

[3]"Let the day perish wherein I was born, and the night which said, 'A man-child is conceived.'

[4]Let that day be darkness! . . .

[11]"Why did I not die at birth, come forth from the womb and expire? . . .

(Job 3)

————

[11]"Therefore I will not restrain my mouth; I will speak in the anguish of my spirit; I will complain in the bitterness of my soul.

[12]Am I the sea, or a sea monster, that thou settest a guard over me?

[13]When I say, 'My bed will comfort me, my couch will ease my complaint,'

[14]then thou dost scare me with dreams and terrify me with visions,

[15]so that I would choose strangling and death rather than my bones.

[16]I loathe my life; I would not live for ever. Let me alone, for my days are a breath.

[17]What is man, that thou dost make so much of him, and that thou dost set thy mind upon him,

[18]dost visit him every morning, and test him every moment?

[19]How long wilt thou not look away from me, nor let me alone till I swallow my spittle?

[20]If I sin, what do I do to thee, thou watcher of men? Why hast thou made me thy mark [target]? Why have I become a burden to thee?

[21]Why dost thou not pardon my transgression and take away my iniquity? For now I shall lie in the earth; thou wilt seek me, but I shall not be." . . .

(Job 7)

————

[1]At this stage in Jewish thought, Satan is simply a member of God's court; he is not the enemy of God and the leader of the forces of evil as he is later depicted, particularly at the time of Jesus and in early Christian writings.

Job's friends take the orthodox position that "God will not cast away an innocent man, /Neither will he uphold the evil-doers. . . ." But Job replies that God is destroying an innocent man.

²²It is all one; therefore I say,
   he destroys both the blameless and the wicked.
²³When disaster brings sudden death,
   he mocks at the calamity of the innocent.
²⁴The earth is given into the hand of the wicked;
   he covers the faces of its judges—
   if it is not he, who then is it? . . . (Job 9)

—

¹¹God gives me up to the ungodly,
   and casts me into the hands of the wicked.
¹²I was at ease, and he broke me asunder;
   he seized me by the neck and dashed me to pieces;
he set me up as his target,
¹³his archers surround me.
He slashes open my kidneys, and does not spare;
   he pours out my gall on the ground.
¹⁴He breaks me with breach upon breach;
   he runs upon me like a warrior. . . .
¹⁶My face is red with weeping,
   and on my eyelids is deep darkness;
¹⁷although there is no violence in my hands,
   and my prayer is pure. . . . (Job 16)

—

⁶[K]now then that God has put me in the wrong,
   and closed his net about me.
⁷Behold, I cry out, 'Violence!' but I am not answered;
   I call aloud, but there is no justice.
⁸He has walled up my way, so that I cannot pass,
   and he has set darkness upon my paths.
⁹He has stripped from me my glory,
   and taken the crown from my head.

¹⁰He breaks me down on every side, and I am gone,
   and my hope has he pulled up like a tree.
¹¹He has kindled his wrath against me,
   and counts me as his adversary. (Job 19)

Job protests that the wicked often go unpunished, while he who aspired to righteousness is made to suffer.

⁷Why do the wicked live,
   reach old age, and grow mighty in power?
⁸Their children are established in their presence,
   and their offspring before their eyes.
⁹Their houses are safe from fear,
   and no rod of God is upon them.
¹⁰Their bull breeds without fail;
   their cow calves, and does not cast her calf.
¹¹They send forth their little ones like a flock,
   and their children dance.
¹²They sing to the tambourine and the lyre,
   and rejoice to the sound of the pipe.
¹³They spend their days in prosperity,
   and in peace they go down to Sheol.
¹⁴They say to God, 'Depart from us!
   We do not desire the knowledge of thy ways.
¹⁵What is the Almighty, that we should serve him?
   And what profit do we get if we pray to him?' (Job 21)

—

¹² . . . I delivered the poor who cried,
   and the fatherless who had none to help him.
¹³The blessing of him who was about to perish came upon me,
   and I caused the widow's heart to sing for joy.
¹⁴I put on righteousness, and it clothed me;
   my justice was like a robe and a turban.
¹⁵I was eyes to the blind,
   and feet to the lame.

¹⁶I was a father to the poor,
and I searched out the cause of him whom I
did not know.
¹⁷I broke the fangs of the unrighteous,
and made him drop his prey from his teeth.
(Job 29)

––––––

¹⁶"And now my soul is poured out within me;
days of affliction have taken hold of me.
¹⁷The night racks my bones,
and the pain that gnaws me takes no rest.
¹⁸With violence it seizes my garment;
it binds me about like the collar of my tunic.
¹⁹God has cast me into the mire,
and I have become like dust and ashes.
²⁰I cry to thee and thou dost not answer me;
I stand, and thou dost not heed me.
²¹Thou hast turned cruel to me;
with the might of thy hand thou dost
persecute me.
²²Thou liftest me up on the wind, thou makest
me ride on it,
and thou tossest me about in the roar of the
storm.
²³Yea, I know that thou wilt bring me to death,
and to the house appointed for all living.
(Job 30)

––––––

Elihu, a young man, joins the sympo-
sium. He is angry with Job for his self-
righteousness, for trying to justify himself
rather than God, and with Job's friends,
for having found no answer to Job's
dilemma. But in proclaiming God's justice, Elihu essentially repeats the friends'
arguments.

¹⁰"Therefore, hear me, you men of under-
standing,
far be it from God that he should do
wickedness,
and from the Almighty that he should do
wrong.

¹¹For according to the work of a man he will
requite him,
and according to his ways he will make it
befall him.
¹²Of a truth, God will not do wickedly,
and the Almighty will not pervert justice.
¹³Who gave him charge over the earth
and who laid on him the whole world?
¹⁴If he should take back his spirit to himself,
and gather to himself his breath,
¹⁵all flesh would perish together,
and man would return to dust.
¹⁶"If you have understanding, hear this;
listen to what I say. . . .
³¹"For has any one said to God,
'I have borne chastisement; I will not offend
any more;
³²teach me what I do not see:
if I have done iniquity, I will do it no more'?
³³Will he then make requital to suit you,
because you reject it?
For you must choose, and not I; therefore
declare what you know.
³⁴Men of understanding will say to me,
and the wise man who hears me will say:
³⁵'Job speaks without knowledge,
his words are without insight.'
³⁶Would that Job were tried to the end,
because he answers like wicked men.
³⁷For he adds rebellion to his sin;
he claps his hands among us,
and multiplies his words against God."
(Job 34)

––––––

⁵"Behold, God is mighty, and does not despise
any;
he is mighty in strength of understanding.
⁶He does not keep the wicked alive,
but gives the afflicted their right.
⁷He does not withdraw his eyes from the
righteous,
but with kings upon the throne
he sets them for ever, and they are exalted.
⁸And if they are bound in fetters
and caught in the cords of affliction,

⁹then he declares to them their work
   and their transgressions, that they are
      behaving arrogantly.
¹⁰He opens their ears to instruction,
   and commands that they return from
      iniquity.
¹¹If they hearken and serve him,
   they complete their days in prosperity,
   and their years in pleasantness.
¹²But if they do not hearken, they perish by
      the sword,
   and die without knowledge. (Job 36)

Then God, "out of the whirlwind," replies to Job. But in God's response, we do not find a clear answer to the problem of undeserved suffering. Instead, God, in a series of rhetorical questions, reminds Job that he alone is the creator and sustainer of the universe and that it is the obligation of Job, a mere mortal, to honor his creator and not find fault with him. Awed by God's majesty and power, a humbled Job declares, "I abhor my words and repent." In an epilogue, God responds by restoring Job's good fortune.

REVIEW QUESTIONS

1. Do you see ways in which Job could have strengthened his case?
2. Do you have an answer to Job's dilemma? Explain.

7 The Age of Classical Prophecy

Ancient Jewish history was marked by the rise of prophets—spiritually inspired persons who believed that God had chosen them to remind the Jews of their duties to God and his law. These prophets carried God's message to the leaders and the people and warned of divine punishments for disobedience to God's commandments.

The prophetic movement—the age of classical prophecy—which emerged in the eighth century B.C., creatively expanded Hebrew religious thought. Prophets denounced exploitation of the poor, the greed of the wealthy, and the oppressive behavior of the powerful as a betrayal of Yahweh, a violation of his moral laws. They insisted that the core of Hebrew faith was not ritual but morality. Their concern for the poor and their attack on injustice received reemphasis in the Christian faith and thus became incorporated into the Western ideal of social justice.

AMOS AND *ISAIAH* SOCIAL JUSTICE

By the eighth century a significant disparity existed between the wealthy and the poor. Small farmers in debt to moneylenders faced the loss of their land or even bondage. Amos, a mid-eighth-century prophet, felt a tremendous compulsion to speak out in the name of God against these injustices.

²¹"I hate, I despise your feasts,
  and I take no delight in your solemn
    assemblies.
²²Even though you offer me your burnt
    offerings and cereal offerings,
  I will not accept them,
and the peace offerings of your fatted beasts
  I will not look upon.
²³Take away from me the noise of your songs;
  to the melody of your harps I will not listen.
²⁴But let justice roll down like waters,
  and righteousness like an everflowing stream.
    (Amos 5)

The prophets' insistence that rituals were not
the essence of the law and their passion for
righteousness are voiced in the Scriptures by
Isaiah of Jerusalem, who lived in the mid-
eighth century B.C. Scholars agree that Isaiah
of Jerusalem did not write all sixty-six chapters that make up the Book of Isaiah. Some
material appears to have been written by his
disciples and interpreters, and Chapters 40
to 55, composed two centuries later, are attributed to a person given the name Second
Isaiah. The following verses come from Isaiah of Jerusalem.

---

¹¹"What to me is the multitude of your
    sacrifices?
  says the LORD;
I have had enough of burnt offerings of rams
  and the fat of fed beasts;
I do not delight in the blood of bulls, or of
  lambs, or of he-goats. . . .
¹³Bring no more vain offerings;
  incense is an abomination to me.
  New moon and sabbath and the calling of
    assemblies—

I cannot endure iniquity and solemn
    assembly.
¹⁴Your new moons and your appointed feasts
  my soul hates;
they have become a burden to me,
  I am weary of bearing them.
¹⁵When you spread forth your hands,
  I will hide my eyes from you;
even though you make many prayers,
  I will not listen;
  your hands are full of blood.
¹⁶Wash yourselves; make yourselves clean;
  remove the evil of your doings
  from before my eyes;
cease to do evil,
¹⁷ learn to do good;
seek justice,
  correct oppression;
defend the fatherless,
  plead for the widow.
    (Isaiah 1)

Isaiah denounces the rich and the powerful
for exploiting the poor.

---

¹³The LORD has taken his place to contend,
  he stands to judge his people.
¹⁴The LORD enters into judgment
  with the elders and princes of his people:
"It is you who have devoured the vineyard,
  the spoil of the poor is in your houses.
¹⁵What do you mean by crushing my people,
  by grinding the face of the poor?"
    says the Lord GOD of hosts.
    (Isaiah 3)

ISAIAH
PEACE AND HUMANITY

Isaiah of Jerusalem envisioned the unity of all people under God. This universalism drew out the full implications of Hebrew monotheism. In Isaiah's vision all peoples would live together in peace and harmony. Some of these lines are inscribed on the building that houses the United Nations in New York City.

²It shall come to pass in the latter days
  that the mountain of the house of the LORD
shall be established as the highest of the
    mountains,
  and shall be raised above the hills;
and all the nations shall flow to it,
³ and many peoples shall come, and say:
"Come, let us go up to the mountain of the
    LORD,
  to the house of the God of Jacob;
that he may teach us his ways
  and that we may walk in his paths."

For out of Zion shall go forth the law,
  and the word of the LORD from Jerusalem.
⁴He shall judge between the nations,
  and shall decide for many peoples;
and they shall beat their swords into
    plowshares,
  and their spears into pruning hooks;
nation shall not lift up sword against nation,
  neither shall they learn war any more.
    (Isaiah 2)

REVIEW QUESTIONS

1. What were some of the ritual acts and ceremonies practiced by the Hebrews?
2. What was the prophets' attitude toward rituals?
3. What social reforms did the prophets seek?
4. What does the concept *humanity* mean? The Hebrew prophets are one source of the idea of humanity. Discuss this statement.

CHAPTER 3

The Greeks

THE ACROPOLIS OF ATHENS. Many of Athens' most important temples, including the Parthenon, were located on the Acropolis. *(Robert Harding World Imagery)*

Hebrew ethical monotheism, which gave value to the individual, is one source of Western civilization. Another source derives from the ancient Greeks, who originated scientific and philosophic thought, created democracy, and developed a humanistic outlook. From about 750 B.C. to 338 B.C. the Greek world consisted of small, independent, and self-governing city-states. Within this political-social context, the Greeks made their outstanding contributions to civilization.

In contrast to the Egyptians and Mesopotamians, the Greeks developed rational-scientific, rather than mythical, interpretations of nature and the human community. In trying to understand nature, Greek philosophers proposed physical explanations; that is, they gradually omitted the gods from their accounts of how nature came to be the way it is. Greek intellectuals also analyzed government, law, and ethics in logical and systematic ways. It was the great achievement of Greek thinkers to rise above magic, miracles, mystery, and custom and to assert that reason was the avenue to knowledge. The emergence of rational attitudes did not, of course, end traditional religion, particularly for the peasants, who remained devoted to their ancient cults, gods, and shrines. But what distinguishes the Greeks is that alongside an older religious-mythical tradition arose a philosophic-scientific view of the natural world and human culture.

The Greeks, who defined human beings by their capacity to use reason, also defined the principle of political liberty. Egyptians and Mesopotamians were subject to the authority of god-kings and priest-kings; the common people did not participate in political life, and there was no awareness of individual liberty. In contrast, many Greek city-states, particularly Athens, developed democratic institutions and attitudes. In the middle of the fifth century B.C., when Athenian democracy was at its height, adult male citizens were eligible to hold public office and were equal before the law; in the Assembly, which met some forty times a year, they debated and voted on the key issues of state. Whereas Mesopotamians and Egyptians believed that law had been given to them by the gods, the Greeks came to understand that law was a human creation, a product of human reason. The Athenians abhorred rule by absolute rulers and held that people can govern themselves. While expressing admiration for the Greek political achievement, modern critics also point out several limitations of Greek democracy, notably slavery and the inability of women to participate in political life.

The Greeks originated the Western humanist tradition. They valued the human personality and sought the full cultivation of human talent. In the Greek view, a man of worth pursued excellence; that is, he sought to mold himself in accordance with the highest standards and ideals. Greek art, for example, made the human form the focal point of attention and exalted the nobility, dignity, self-assurance, and beauty of the human being.

Greek culture has a distinctive style that enables us to see it as an organic whole. To the English classicist H. D. F. Kitto, the common thread that runs through Greek philosophy, literature, and art is "a sense of the wholeness of things"—the conviction that the universe contains an inherent order, that law governs both nature and human affairs, and that this orderliness can be comprehended by human reason.

Although the Greek city-states shared a common culture, they frequently warred with each other. Particularly ruinous was the Peloponnesian War (431–404 B.C.) between Athens and Sparta and their allies. The drawn-out conflict, marked by massacres and civil wars within city-states, shattered the Greek world spiritually. Increasingly, a narrow individualism and worsening factional disputes weakened the bonds of community within the various city-states. Moreover, learning little from the Peloponnesian War, the Greeks continued their internecine conflicts. Finally, by 338 B.C. the weakened city-states were conquered by Philip II of Macedonia, a kingdom to the north of Greece. Although the Greek cities continued to exist, they had lost their political independence; Greek civilization was entering a new phase.

Philip's famous son, Alexander the Great, a romantic adventurer and brilliant commander, inherited the Macedonian kingdom and conquered the vast Persian Empire. After Alexander died in 323 B.C. at the age of thirty-two, his generals could not hold together the empire, which extended from Egypt to the frontiers of India. By 275 B.C. it was broken into three parts, each named for a dynasty: the Ptolemies in Egypt, the Seleucids in Asia, and the Antigonids in Macedonia and Greece. The rulers of these kingdoms were Macedonians, and their generals and high officials were Greek; the style of government, not in the democratic tradition of the Greek city-states, was modeled after the absolute rule by priest-kings and god-kings typical of the Near East.

Alexander's conquest of the Near East marks a second stage in the evolution of Greek civilization (Hellenism). The first stage, the *Hellenic Age*, began about 800 B.C. with the earliest city-states and lasted until Alexander's death; at that time Greek civilization entered the *Hellenistic Age*, which lasted until 30 B.C., when Egypt, the last Hellenistic kingdom, lost its independence to Rome.

The Hellenistic Age inherited many cultural achievements of the earlier Hellenic Age, but crucial differences exist between the two eras. The self-sufficient and independent *polis* (city-state), the center of life in the Hellenic Age, was diminished in power and importance by larger political units, kingdoms headed by absolute monarchs. Although Greek cities continued to exercise considerable control over domestic affairs, they had lost to powerful monarchs their freedom of action in foreign affairs.

A second characteristic of the Hellenistic Age was cosmopolitanism, an intermingling of peoples and cultural traditions. In the Hellenic Age, the Greeks had drawn a sharp distinction between Greek and non-Greek. In the wake of Alexander's conquests, however, thousands of Greek soldiers, merchants, and administrators settled in Near Eastern lands, bringing with them Greek language, customs, and culture. Many upper-class citizens of Near Eastern cities, regardless of their ethnic backgrounds, came under the influence of Greek civilization. At the same time, Mesopotamian, Egyptian, and Persian ways, particularly religious practices and beliefs, spread westward into regions under the sway of Greek civilization.

1 Homer: The Educator of Greece

The poet Homer, who probably lived during the eighth century B.C., helped shape the Greek outlook. His great epics, *The Iliad* and *The Odyssey*, contain the embryo of the Greek humanist tradition: the concern with man and his achievements. "To strive always for excellence and to surpass all others"—in these words lies the essence of the Homeric hero's outlook. In the warrior-aristocratic world of Homer, excellence is primarily interpreted as bravery and skill in battle. The Homeric hero is driven to demonstrate his prowess, to assert himself, to win honor, and to earn a reputation.

The Iliad deals in poetic form with the Trojan War, which probably was waged in the thirteenth century B.C., between the Mycenaean Greeks and the Trojans of Asia Minor. At the outset Homer states his theme: the wrath of Achilles that brought so much suffering to the Greeks. Agamemnon, their king, has deprived the great warrior Achilles of his rightful prize, the captive girl Briseis. Achilles will not submit to this grave insult to his honor and refuses to join the Greeks in combat against the Trojans. In this way he intends to make Agamemnon pay for his arrogance, for without the Greeks' greatest warrior, Agamemnon will have no easy victories. With Achilles on the sidelines, the Greeks suffer severe losses.

Destiny is at work: the "wicked arrogance" of Agamemnon and the "ruinous wrath" of Achilles have caused suffering and death among the Greek forces. For Homer, human existence has a pattern—a universal plan governs human affairs. People, even the gods, operate within a certain unalterable framework; their deeds are subject to the demands of destiny or necessity. Later Greek thinkers would express this idea of a universal order in philosophic and scientific terms.

Homer
THE ILIAD

The following passages from *The Iliad* illustrate the Homeric ideal of excellence. In the first, Hector of Troy, son of King Priam, prepares for battle. Hector's wife Andromache pleads with him to stay within the city walls, but Hector, in the tradition of the Homeric hero, feels compelled to engage in combat to show his worth and gain honor.

Hector looked at his son and smiled, but said nothing. Andromache, bursting into tears, went up to him and put her hand in his. "Hector," she said, "you are possessed. This bravery of yours will be your end. You do not think of your little boy or your unhappy wife, whom you will make a widow soon. Some day the Achaeans [Greeks] are bound to kill you in a massed attack. And when I lose you I might as well be dead. There will be no comfort left, when you have met your doom—nothing but grief. I have no father, no mother, now. My father fell to the great Achilles when he sacked our lovely town, Cilician Thebe[1] of the High Gates. . . . I had seven brothers too at home. In one day all of them went down to Hades' House.[2] The great Achilles of the swift feet killed them all. . . .

"So you, Hector, are father and mother and brother to me, as well as my beloved husband. Have pity on me now; stay here on the tower; and do not make your boy an orphan and your wife a widow. . . ."

"All that, my dear," said the great Hector of the glittering helmet, "is surely my concern. But if I hid myself like a coward and refused to fight, I could never face the Trojans and the Trojan ladies in their trailing gowns. Besides, it would go against the grain, for I have trained myself always, like a good soldier, to take my place in the front line and win glory for my father and myself. . . ."

As he finished, glorious Hector held out his arms to take his boy. But the child shrank back with a cry to the bosom of his girdled nurse, alarmed by his father's appearance. He was frightened by the bronze of the helmet and the horsehair plume that he saw nodding grimly down at him. His father and his lady mother had to laugh. But noble Hector quickly took his helmet off and put the dazzling thing on the ground. Then he kissed his son, dandled him in his arms, and prayed to Zeus [the chief god] and the other gods: "Zeus, and you other gods, grant that this boy of mine may be, like me, pre-eminent in Troy; as strong and brave as I; a mighty king of Ilium [Troy]. May people say, when he comes back from battle, 'Here is a better man than his father.' Let him bring home the bloodstained armour of the enemy he has killed, and make his mother happy."

Hector handed the boy to his wife, who took him to her fragrant breast. She was smiling through her tears, and when her husband saw this he was moved. He stroked her with his hand and said: "My dear, I beg you not to be too much distressed. No one is going to send me down to Hades before my proper time. But Fate is a thing that no man born of woman, coward or hero, can escape. Go home now, and attend to your own work, the loom and the spindle, and see that the maidservants get on with theirs. War is men's business; and this war is the business of every man in Ilium, myself above all."

---

[1] In *The Iliad* the Cilices lived in southern Asia Minor.
[2] Hades refers both to the god of the underworld and to the underworld itself.

Many brave Greek warriors die in battle, including Achilles' best friend Patroclus, slain by the Trojan Hector. Achilles now sets aside his quarrel with Agamemnon (who has appealed to Achilles) and joins the battle. King Priam urges his son not to fight the mighty Achilles, but Hector, despite his fears, faces Achilles and meets his death. In this passage, the grief-stricken Priam goes to Achilles and requests Hector's body. Achilles responds with compassion. This scene shows that although Homer sees the essence of life as the pursuit of glory, he is also sensitive to life's brevity and to the suffering that pervades human existence.

. . . Big though Priam was, he came in unobserved, went up to Achilles, grasped his knees and kissed his hands, the terrible, man-killing hands that had slaughtered many of his sons. Achilles was astounded when he saw King Priam, and so were all his men. . . .

But Priam was already praying to Achilles. "Most worshipful Achilles," he said, "think of your own father, who is the same age as I, and so has nothing but miserable old age ahead of him. No doubt his neighbours are oppressing him and there is nobody to save him from their depredations. Yet he at least has one consolation. While he knows that you are still alive, he can look forward day by day to seeing his beloved son come back from Troy; whereas my fortunes are completely broken. I had the best sons in the whole of this broad realm, and now not one, not one I say, is left. There were fifty when the Achaean expedition came. Nineteen of them were borne by one mother and the rest by other ladies in my palace. Most of them have fallen in action,

and Hector, the only one I still could count on, the bulwark of Troy and the Trojans, has now been killed by you, fighting for his native land. It is to get him back from you that I have come to the Achaean ships, bringing this princely ransom with me. Achilles, fear the gods, and be merciful to me, remembering your own father, though I am even more entitled to compassion, since I have brought myself to do a thing that no one else on earth has done—I have raised to my lips the hand of the man who killed my son."

Priam had set Achilles thinking of his own father and brought him to the verge of tears. Taking the old man's hand, he gently put him from him; and overcome by their memories they both broke down. Priam, crouching at Achilles' feet, wept bitterly for man-slaying Hector, and Achilles wept for his father, and then again for Patroclus. The house was filled with the sounds of their lamentation. But presently, when he had had enough of tears and recovered his composure, the excellent Achilles leapt from his chair, and in compassion for the old man's grey head and grey beard, took him by the arm and raised him. Then he spoke to him from his heart: "You are indeed a man of sorrows and have suffered much. How could you dare to come by yourself to the Achaean ships into the presence of a man who has killed so many of your gallant sons? You have a heart of iron. But pray be seated now, here on this chair, and let us leave our sorrows, bitter though they are, locked up in our own hearts, for weeping is cold comfort and does little good. We men are wretched things, and the gods, who have no cares themselves, have woven sorrow into the very pattern of our lives."

REVIEW QUESTIONS

1. What glimpses do we get from Homer's *Iliad* of the respective roles of men and women in Greek society?
2. Homer's epic poems were studied and even memorized by Greek schoolchildren. What values would the poems have taught these youngsters to emulate?
3. What lessons about the human condition did Achilles draw from the tragic events of the Trojan War?

2 Lyric Poetry

During the seventh century B.C., lyric poetry began to supplant epic poetry. Greek lyric poetry was intended to be sung to the musical accompaniment of a lyre, a stringed instrument. In fact the word *lyric* means "accompanied by the lyre." Lyric poetry was much more concerned with a poet's own opinions and inner emotions than with the great deeds of heroes as recounted in epic poetry.

Sappho
LOVE, PASSION, AND FRIENDSHIP

The greatest female lyric poet in antiquity was Sappho, who lived around 600 B.C. on the island of Lesbos. She was a member of the aristocracy and married a man named Cercylas, with whom she had one daughter, Cleïs. Unfortunately, just one complete poem, of twenty-eight lines, still remains; the rest of her poems exist only in fragments. Nonetheless, Sappho is credited with creating the metric stanza that bears her name—*Sapphic*. She established a "finishing" school to teach music and singing to well-to-do girls and to prepare them for marriage. With great tenderness, she wrote poems of friendship and love. Although some of her poems are about love between women and men, a number of verses are addressed to women, suggesting a homoerotic interest. The sensual and erotic nature of these poems indicates that Sappho was bisexual. Such sexual behavior was, however, tolerated in ancient Greece, for it did not deprive a woman of her status as a virgin, since it was nonprocreative.

In this first fragment, Sappho likens her absent friend, Anactoria, to a defiant Helen of Troy, who (in spite of Homer's claims to the contrary) willingly left Sparta to sail away to Troy with her lover Paris, son of the Trojan King Priam.

Some an army on horseback, some an army on
　　foot
and some say a fleet of ships is the loveliest sight
on this dark earth; but I say it is whatever you
　　desire:

and it is perfectly possible to make this clear
to all; for Helen, the woman who by far
　　surpassed
all others in her beauty, left her husband—
the best of all men—

behind and sailed far away to Troy; she did not
　　spare
a single thought for her child nor for her dear
　　parents

but [the goddess of love] led her astray
[to desire. . . .]

　　　　　　[. . . which]
reminds me now of Anactoria
although far away,

whose long-desired footstep, whose radiant,
　　sparkling face
I would rather see before me than the chariots
of Lydia[1] or the armour of men
who fight wars on foot. . . .

_____

[1]Lydia was an ancient kingdom in the western part of Asia Minor.

The following poetic fragments also deal with the power of love. In the first one, Sappho frankly addresses passion between women.

. . . frankly I wish that I were dead:
she was weeping as she took her leave from me

and many times she told me this:
"Oh what sadness we have suffered,
Sappho, for I'm leaving you against my will."
So I gave this answer to her:
"Go, be happy but remember
me there, for you know how we have cherished you,

if not, then I would remind you
[of the joy we have known,] of all
the loveliness that we have shared together;

for many wreaths of violets,
of roses and of crocuses
. . . you wove around yourself by my side

. . . and many twisted garlands
which you had woven from the blooms
of flowers, you placed around your slender neck

. . . and you were anointed with
a perfume, scented with blossom,
. . . although it was fit for a queen

and on a bed, soft and tender
. . . you satisfied your desire. . . ."

In this fragment, Sappho admits that Aphrodite, the goddess of love, has left her powerless to resist desire.

Mother dear, I simply cannot weave my cloth;
                                    I'm overpowered
by desire for a slender youth—and it's all
                                    Aphrodite's fault

Sappho loved her daughter dearly and speaks of her love for Cleïs in the following fragment.

I have a child; so fair
As golden flowers is she,
My Cleïs, all my care.
I'd not give her away
For Lydia's wide sway
Nor lands men long to see.

A lost love is the subject of this fragment, as Aphrodite responds to Sappho's plea for assistance.

Immortal Aphrodite, on your patterned throne,
daughter of Zeus, guile-weaver,
I beg you, goddess, don't subjugate my heart
with anguish, with grief

but come here to me now, if ever in the past
you have heard my distant pleas
and listened; leaving your father's golden house
you came to me then

with your chariot yoked; beautiful swift sparrows
brought you around the dark earth
with a whirl of wings, beating fast, from heaven
down through the mid-air

to reach me quickly; then you, my sacred
    goddess,
your immortal face smiling,
asked me what had gone wrong this time and
    this time
why was I begging

and what in my demented heart, I wanted
    most:
"Who shall I persuade this time
to take you back, yet once again, to her love;
who wrongs you, Sappho?

For if she runs away, soon she shall run after,
if she shuns gifts, she shall give,
if she does not love you, soon she shall even
against her own will."

So come to me now, free me from this aching
    pain,
fulfil everything that

my heart desires to be fulfilled: you, yes
   you,
will be my ally.

Greek society mandated that women should
marry and bear children, thus surrendering
their symbol of female honor—virginity. In
this poem, Sappho recounts the trauma a
woman may experience when she loses her
virginity.

FIRST VOICE
Virginity O my virginity!
Where will you go when I lose you?

SECOND VOICE
I'm off to a place I shall never come back from
Dear Bride!
I shall never come back to you
Never!

REVIEW QUESTION

1. Which lines in Sappho's poems have the most appeal for you? Why?

---

3 Early Greek Philosophy: The Emancipation of Thought from Myth

In the sixth century B.C., Greeks living in the city of Miletus in Ionia, the coast
of Asia Minor, conceived a nonmythical way of viewing nature, a feat that marks
the origins of philosophic and scientific thought. Traditionally, natural occurrences like earthquakes and lighting had been attributed to the gods. But early
Greek thinkers, called cosmologists because they were interested in the nature
and structure of the universe, were the first to see nature as a system governed
by laws that the intellect could ascertain. The cosmologists sought physical
rather than supernatural explanations for natural events. This new approach
made possible a self-conscious and systematic investigation of nature and a critical appraisal of proposed theories; in contrast, the mythical view that the gods
regulate nature did not invite discussion and questioning.

Aristotle
THALES OF MILETUS

Thales of Miletus (c. 624–c. 548 B.C.) is considered the founder of Ionian philosophy. He wanted to know how nature came to be the way it is, and he did not turn
to traditional legends for an answer. Thales said that water was the basic element
of nature and that through a natural process—similar to the formation of ice or
steam—water gave rise to everything else in the universe. Thales revolutionized
thought because in searching for a first cause in nature he omitted the gods. What
we know about Thales' view of nature comes essentially from Aristotle. A brief
reference to Thales from Aristotle's *Metaphysics* follows.

Most of the philosophers thought that principles in the form of matter were the only principles of all things: for the original source of all existing things, that from which a thing first comes-into-being and into which it is finally destroyed, the substance persisting but changing in its qualities, this they declare is the element and first principle of existing things... for there must be some natural substance, either one or more than one, from which the other things come-into-being, while it is preserved. Over the number, however, and the form of this kind of principle they do not all agree; but Thales, the founder of this type of philosophy, says that it is water (and therefore declared that the earth is on water), perhaps taking this supposition from seeing the nurture of all things to be moist, and the warm itself coming-to-be from this and living by this (that from which they come-to-be being the principle of all things)—taking the supposition both from this and from the seeds of all things having a moist nature, water being the natural principle of moist things.

ANAXIMANDER

Anaximander (c. 611–547 B.C.), another Ionian, also held that a single element was the wellspring of nature, but he rejected any specific substance such as water, holding instead that something indefinite, which he called the Boundless or the Infinite, was the source of all things. Anaximander attempted to explain how natural objects and living things had derived from this primary mass. What is remarkable about Anaximander's cosmogony was the omission of the gods or any supernatural agency in the origin of life and the formation of the world. All that we know about Anaximander comes from brief passages in the writings of several ancient scholars.

Of those who say that it is one, moving, and infinite, Anaximander, son of Praxiades, a Milesian, the successor and pupil of Thales, said that the principle and element of existing things was the *apeiron* (indefinite, *or* infinite), being the first to introduce this name of the material principle. He says that it is neither water nor any other of the so-called elements, but some other *apeiron* nature, from which come into being all the heavens and the worlds in them. . . .

———

He says that that which is productive from the eternal of hot and cold was separated off at the coming-to-be of this world, and that a kind of sphere of flame from this was formed round the air surrounding the earth, like bark round a tree. When this was broken off and shut off in certain circles, the sun and the moon and the stars were formed. . . .

The heavenly bodies come into being as a circle of fire separated off from the fire in the world, and enclosed by air. There are breathing holes, certain pipe-like passages, at which the heavenly bodies show themselves; accordingly eclipses occur when the breathing-holes are blocked up. The moon is seen now waxing, now waning according to the blocking or opening of the channels. The circle of the sun is 27 times the size of (the earth, that of) the moon (18 times); the sun is highest, and the circles of the fixed stars are lowest. . . .

———

Winds occur when the finest vapours of the air are separated off and when they are set in motion by congregation; rain occurs from the exhalation that issues upwards from the things beneath the sun, and lightning whenever wind breaks out and cleaves the clouds. . . .

———

(On thunder, lightning, thunderbolts, whirl-winds and typhoons.) Anaximander says that all these things occur as a result of wind: for whenever it is shut up in a thick cloud and then bursts out forcibly, through its fineness and lightness, then the bursting makes the noise, while the rift against the blackness of the cloud makes the flash. . . .

———

Anaximander said that the first living creatures were born in moisture, enclosed in thorny barks; and that as their age increased they came forth on to the drier part and, when the bark had broken off, they lived a different kind of life for a short time.

———

Further he says that in the beginning man was born from creatures of a different kind; because other creatures are soon self-supporting, but man alone needs prolonged nursing. For this reason he would not have survived if this had been his original form.

———

Anaximander of Miletus conceived that there arose from heated water and earth either fish or creatures very like fish; in these man grew, in the form of embryos retained within until puberty; then at last the fish-like creatures burst and men and women who were already able to nourish themselves stepped forth.

Living creatures came into being from moisture evaporated by the sun. Man was originally similar to another creature—that is, to a fish.

———

{H}e declares . . . that originally men came into being inside fishes, and that having been nurtured there—like sharks—and having become adequate to look after themselves, they then came forth and took to the land.

Aristotle
PYTHAGORAS

Pythagoras (c. 580–507 B.C.) was born on the island of Samos, a major Greek cultural and commercial center in the eastern Aegean Sea; as a young man, he migrated to southern Italy, where the Greeks had established colonies. A deep religiosity pervaded the thought of Pythagoras and his followers, who sought to purify the soul and to achieve salvation. Believing that the soul undergoes a reincarnation in animals, Pythagoreans would not eat meat. The Pythagoreans' great contribution to scientific thought was their conviction that nature contains an inherent mathematical order. Thus, continuity exists between the Pythagoreans and Isaac Newton and Albert Einstein, who expressed the laws underlying the cosmos in mathematical terms more than two thousand years later. Aristotle's description of the Pythagoreans follows.

. . . the Pythagoreans, as they are called, devoted themselves to mathematics; they were the first to advance this study, and having been brought up in it they thought its principles were the principles of all things. Since of these principles numbers are by nature the first, and in numbers they seemed to see many resemblances to the things that exist and come into being—more than in fire and earth and water (such and such a modi-fication of numbers being justice, another being soul and reason, another being opportunity—and similarly almost all other things being numerically expressible); since, again, they saw that the attributes and the ratios of the musical scales were expressible in numbers; since, then, all other things seemed in their whole nature to be modelled after numbers, and numbers seemed to be the first things in the whole of nature, they supposed the elements of numbers to be the elements of all things, and the whole heaven to be a musical scale and a number. And all the properties of numbers and scales which they could show to agree with the attributes and parts and the whole arrangement of the heavens, they collected and fitted into their scheme.

REVIEW QUESTIONS

1. Why is Thales considered the first philosopher in the Western world?
2. Compare the Babylonian and Hebrew accounts of the origin of the world and human beings with that of Anaximander. How do they differ in purpose and literary genre?
3. What is the significance of Pythagoras' view that nature contains an inherent mathematical order?
4. Early Greek philosophy marks a break with mythical thinking and the emergence of rational scientific thinking. Discuss this statement.

4 The Expansion of Reason

The method of inquiry initiated by the Ionian natural philosophers found expression in other areas of Greek culture. Thus, in the Greek medical school headed by Hippocrates (c. 460–377 B.C.) on the island of Cos, doctors consciously attacked magical practices and beliefs, seeing them as hindrances to understanding causes and cures of disease. The historian Thucydides (c. 460–400 B.C.) sought logical explanations for human events, and the Sophists applied reason to traditional religion, law, and morality.

Hippocrates
THE SACRED DISEASE
THE SEPARATION OF MEDICINE FROM MYTH

In the following excerpt from *The Sacred Disease*, a Hippocratic doctor rejects the belief that epilepsy is a sacred disease. Instead he maintains that epilepsy, like all other diseases, has a natural explanation and denounces as "charlatans and quacks" those who claim that gods cause the disease.

I. I am about to discuss the disease called "sacred." It is not, in my opinion, any more divine or more sacred than other diseases, but has a natural cause, and its supposed divine origin is due to men's inexperience, and to their wonder at its peculiar character. Now while men continue to believe in its divine origin because they are at a loss to understand it, they really disprove its divinity by the facile method of healing which they adopt, consisting as it does of purifications and incantations. But if it is to be considered divine just because it is wonderful, there will be not one sacred disease but many, for I will show that other diseases are no less wonderful and portentous, and yet nobody considers them sacred. For instance, quotidian fevers, tertians and quartans seem to me to be no less sacred and god-sent than this disease,* but nobody wonders at them. . . .

II. My own view is that those who first attributed a sacred character to this malady were like the magicians, purifiers, charlatans and quacks of our own day, men who claim great piety and superior knowledge. Being at a loss, and having no treatment which would help, they concealed and sheltered themselves behind superstition, and called this illness sacred, in order that their utter ignorance might not be manifest. They added a plausible story, and established a method of treatment that secured their own position. They used purifications and incantations; they forbade the use of baths, and of many foods that are unsuitable for sick folk. . . .

*Because of the regularity of the attacks of fever, which occur every day (quotidians), every other day (tertians), or with intermission of two whole days (quartans).

But if to eat or apply these things engenders and increases the disease, while to refrain works a cure, then neither is godhead to blame nor are the purifications beneficial; it is the foods that cure or hurt, and the power of godhead disappears.

III. Accordingly I hold that those who attempt in this manner to cure these diseases cannot consider them either sacred or divine; for when they are removed by such purifications and by such treatment as this, there is nothing to prevent the production of attacks in men by devices that are similar. If so, something human is to blame, and not godhead. He who by purifications and magic can take away such an affliction can also by similar means bring it on, so that by this argument the action of godhead is disproved. By these sayings and devices they claim superior knowledge, and deceive men by prescribing for them purifications and cleansings, most of their talk turning on the intervention of gods and spirits.

Thucydides
METHOD OF HISTORICAL INQUIRY

Thucydides' history was another expression of the movement from myth to reason that pervaded every aspect of Greek culture. Mesopotamians and Egyptians kept annals purporting to narrate the deeds of gods and their human agents. The Greeks carefully investigated events—the first people to examine the past with a critical eye. Thucydides examined men's actions and their motives, explicitly rejected divine explanations for human occurrences, searched for natural causes, and based his conclusions on evidence. In this approach, he was influenced by the empiricism of the Hippocratic physicians. For Thucydides, a work of history, as distinguished from poetry, was a creation of the rational mind and not an expression of the poetic imagination. Thus, in Thucydides' *History of the Peloponnesian War* there was no place for legend, for myth, for the fabulous—all hindrances to historical truth. In the following passage, Thucydides describes his method of inquiry.

I began my history at the very outbreak of the war, in the belief that it was going to be a great war and more worth writing about than any of those which had taken place in the past. My belief was based on the fact that the two sides were at the very height of their power and preparedness, and I saw, too, that the rest of the Hellenic [Greek] world was committed to one side or the other; even those who were not immediately engaged were deliberating on the courses which they were to take later. This was the greatest disturbance in the history of the Hellenes, affecting also a large part of the non-Hellenic world, and indeed, I might almost say, the whole of mankind. For though I have found it impossible, because of its remoteness in time, to acquire a really precise knowledge of the distant past or even of the history preceding our own period, yet, after looking back into it as far as I can, all the evidence leads me to conclude that these periods were not great periods either in warfare or in anything else. . . .

In investigating past history, and in forming the conclusions which I have formed, it must be admitted that one cannot rely on every detail which has come down to us by way of tradition. People are inclined to accept all stories of ancient times in an uncritical way—even when these stories concern their own native countries. . . .

. . . Most people, in fact, will not take trouble in finding out the truth, but are much more inclined to accept the first story they hear.

However, I do not think that one will be far wrong in accepting the conclusions I have reached from the evidence which I have put forward. It is better evidence than that of the poets, who exaggerate the importance of their themes, or of the prose chroniclers, who are less interested in telling the truth than in catching the attention of their public, whose authorities cannot be checked, and whose subject-matter, owing to the passage of time, is mostly lost in the unreliable streams of mythology. We may claim instead to have used only the plainest evidence and to have reached conclusions which are reasonably accurate, considering that we have been dealing with ancient history. As for this present war, even though people are apt to think that the war in which they are fighting is the greatest of all wars and, when it is over, to relapse again into their admiration of the past, nevertheless, if one looks at the facts themselves, one will see that this was the greatest war of all.

In this history I have made use of set speeches some of which were delivered just before and others during the war. I have found it difficult to remember the precise words used in the speeches which I listened to myself and my various informants have experienced the same difficulty; so my method has been, while keeping as closely as possible to the general sense of the words that were actually used, to make the speakers say what, in my opinion, was called for by each situation.

And with regard to my factual reporting of the events of the war I have made it a principle not to write down the first story that came my way, and not even to be guided by my own general impressions; either I was present myself at the events which I have described or else I heard of them from eyewitnesses whose reports I have checked with as much thoroughness as possible. Not that even so the truth was easy to discover: different eyewitnesses give different accounts of the same events, speaking out of partiality for one side or the other or else from imperfect memories. And it may well be that my history will seem less easy to read because of the absence in it of a romantic element. It will be enough for me, however, if these words of mine are judged useful by those who want to understand clearly the events which happened in the past and which (human nature being what it is) will, at some time or other and in much the same ways, be repeated in the future. My work is not a piece of writing designed to meet the taste of an immediate public, but was done to last for ever.

Critias
RELIGION AS A HUMAN INVENTION

After the Greek philosophers of Asia Minor began to employ natural, rather than supernatural, explanations for nature, Greek thinkers on the mainland applied reason to human affairs. Exemplifying this trend were the Sophists, who wandered from city to city teaching rhetoric, grammar, poetry, mathematics, music, and gymnastics. The Sophists sought to develop their students' minds, and they created a secular curriculum—for these reasons they enriched the humanist tradition of the West.

The Sophist Critias (c. 480–403 B.C.) was a poet, philosopher, orator, and historian; also he was originally an eager follower of Socrates. Later, Critias became the most bloodthirsty of the so-called Thirty Tyrants, oligarchs who seized control of Athens in 404 B.C. and massacred their democratic opponents. The following passage, a surviving fragment of a play by Critias, demonstrates the Sophists' use of critical thought.

There was a time when the life of men was unordered, bestial and the slave of force, when there was no reward for the virtuous and no punishment for the wicked. Then, I think, men devised retributory laws, in order that Justice might be dictator and have arrogance as its slave, and if anyone sinned, he was punished. Then, when the laws forbade them to commit open crimes of violence, and they began to do them in secret, a wise and clever man invented fear (of the gods) for mortals, that there might be some means of frightening the wicked, even if they do anything or say or think it in secret. Hence he introduced the Divine (religion), saying that there is a God flourishing with immortal life, hearing and seeing with his mind, and thinking of everything and caring about these things, and having divine nature, who will hear everything said among mortals, and will be able to see all that is done. And even if you plan anything evil in secret, you will not escape the gods in this; for they have surpassing intelligence. In saying these words, he introduced the pleasantest of teachings, covering up the truth with a false theory; and he said that the gods dwelt there where he could most frighten men by saying it, whence he knew that fears exist for mortals and rewards for the hard life: in the upper periphery, where they saw lightnings and heard the dread rumblings of thunder, and the starry-faced body of heaven, the beautiful embroidery of Time the skilled craftsman, whence come forth the bright mass of the sun, and the wet shower upon the earth. With such fears did he surround mankind, through which he well established the deity with his argument, and in a fitting place, and quenched lawlessness among men. . . . Thus, I think, for the first time did someone persuade mortals to believe in a race of deities.

REVIEW QUESTIONS

1. Hippocrates distinguishes between magic and medicine. Discuss this statement.
2. What were some of the methods that Thucydides promised to use to make his history more accurate and credible?
3. What was revolutionary about Critias' approach to religion?

5 Humanism

The Greeks conceived the humanist outlook, one of the pillars of Western civilization. They urged human beings to develop their physical, intellectual, and moral capacities to the fullest, to shape themselves according to the highest standards, and to make their lives as harmonious as a flawless work of art. Such an aspiration required intelligence and self-mastery.

Pindar
THE PURSUIT OF EXCELLENCE

The poet Pindar (c. 518–438 B.C.) expressed the Greek view of excellence in his praise for a victorious athlete. Life is essentially tragic—triumphs are short-lived, misfortunes are many, and ultimately death overtakes everyone; still, human beings must demonstrate their worth by striving for excellence.

He who wins of a sudden, some noble prize
In the rich years of youth
Is raised high with hope; his manhood takes
  wings;
He has in his heart what is better than
  wealth
But brief is the season of man's delight.

Soon it falls to the ground;
Some dire decision uproots it.
—Thing of a day! such is man: a shadow in a
  dream.
Yet when god-given splendour visits him
A bright radiance plays over him, and how
  sweet is life!

Sophocles
LAUDING HUMAN TALENTS

In a famous passage from his play *Antigone*, Sophocles (c. 496–406 B.C.) lauded human talents.

Wonders are many, and none is more wonderful than man; the power that crosses the white sea, driven by the stormy south-wind, making a path under surges that threaten to engulf him; and Earth, the eldest of the gods, the immortal, the unwearied, doth he wear, turning the soil, with the offspring of horses, as the ploughs go to and fro year to year.

And the light-hearted race of birds, and the tribes of savage beasts, and the sea-brood of the deep, he snares in the meshes of his woven toils, he leads captive, man excellent in wit. And he masters by his arts the beast whose lair is in the wilds, who roams the hills; he tames the horse of shaggy mane, he puts the yoke upon its neck, he tames the tireless mountain bull.

And speech, and wind-swift thought, and all the moods that mould a state, hath he taught himself; and how to flee the arrows of the frost, when 'tis hard lodging under the clear sky, and the arrows of the rushing rain; yea, he hath resource for all; without resources he meets nothing that must come: only against Death shall he call for aid in vain; but from baffling maladies he hath devised escapes.

Cunning beyond fancy's dream is the fertile skill which brings him, now to evil, now to good. When he honors the laws of the land, and that justice which he hath sworn by the gods to uphold, proudly stands his city: no city hath he who, for his rashness, dwells with sin. Never may he share my hearth, never think my thoughts, who doth these things!

REVIEW QUESTIONS

1. In what sense does Pindar consider life to be tragic?
2. What human virtues did the Greek poets extoll?

---

6 The Persian Wars

In 499 B.C., the Ionian Greeks in Asia Minor revolted against their Persian rulers; Athens sent twenty ships to aid the Ionians. To punish the Athenians, Darius I, king of Persia, sent a force to the peninsula of Attica, where Athens is located. In 490 B.C., on the plains of Marathon, an Athenian army of about ten thousand men defeated the Persians. Ten years later, Xerxes, Darius' son and heir, organized a huge invasion force aimed at making Greece a Persian province. Realizing that their independence and freedom were at stake, many Greek cities put aside their quarrels and united against the common enemy. In 480 B.C., on the Bay of Salamis near Athens, the Athenian navy defeated the Persian armada, and the next year the Spartan army crushed the Persians at Plataea.

Herodotus
THE HISTORIES

Herodotus (c. 484–c. 424 B.C.), often called "the father of history," wrote about the most important events of his lifetime, the Persian Wars. He took note of the strategy that lay behind the Greek victory in the battle of Salamis. He tells us that the Athenian general Themistocles (c. 527–460 B.C.) sent a slave to the Persian commander with the story that some of Athens' allies, fearing entrapment, were planning to sail out of the Bay of Salamis. As Themistocles hoped, the Persians, eager for a decisive victory, sailed into the narrow waters of the bay. Unable to deploy its more numerous ships in this cramped space, the Persian fleet was destroyed by the Greek ships.

Although the gods were present in Herodotus' narrative, they played a far less important role than they had in Greek mythology or in Near Eastern annals. Herodotus visited Persian lands and found much to praise there. Nevertheless, he was struck by the contrast between Greek freedom and Persian absolutism, between the free Greek citizen and the Persian subject who knew only obedience to the king's commands.

A second theme prevalent in *The Histories* is punishment for *hubris*, or arrogance. Xerxes, in seeking to rule both Asia and Greece, was seen as exhibiting such arrogance. In the following excerpt, Herodotus discusses Xerxes' ambition.

In this book, the result of my inquiries into history, I hope to do two things: to preserve the memory of the past by putting on record the astonishing achievements both of our own and of the Asiatic peoples; secondly, and more particularly, to show how the two races came into conflict. . . .

———

Xerxes began his reign by building up an army for a campaign in Egypt. The invasion of Greece was at first by no means an object of his thoughts; but Mardonius—the son of Bogryas and Darius' sister and thus cousin to the king—who was present in court and had more influence with Xerxes than anyone else in the country, used constantly to talk to him on the subject. "Master," he would say, "the Athenians have done us great injury, and it is only right that they should be punished for their crimes. By all means finish the task you already have in hand; but when you have tamed the arrogance of Egypt, then lead an army against Athens. Do that, and your name will be held in honour all over the world, and people will think twice in future before they invade your country." And to the argument for revenge he would add that Europe was a very beautiful place; it produced every kind of garden tree; the land there was everything that land should be—it was, in short, too good for anyone in the world except the Persian king. Mardonius' motive for urging the campaign was love of mischief and adventure and the hope of becoming governor of Greece himself; and after much persistence he persuaded Xerxes to make the attempt. . . .

After the conquest of Egypt, when he was on the point of taking in hand the expedition against Athens, Xerxes called a conference of the leading men in the country, to find out their attitude towards the war and explain to them his own wishes. When they met, he addressed them as follows: "Do not suppose, gentlemen, that I am departing from precedent in the course of action I intend to undertake. We Persians have a way of living, which I have inherited from my predecessors and propose to follow. . . . Of our past history you need no reminder; for you know well enough the famous deeds of Cyrus,[1] Cambyses,[2] and my father Darius, and their additions to our empire. Now I myself, ever since my accession, have been thinking how not to fall short of the kings who have sat upon this throne before me, and how to add as much power as they did to the Persian empire. And now at last I have found a way to win for Persia not glory only but a country as large and as rich as our own—indeed richer than our own—and at the same time to get satisfaction and revenge. That, then, is the object of this meeting—that I may disclose to you what it is that I intend to do. I will bridge the Hellespont[3] and march an army through Europe into Greece, and punish the Athenians

———

[1] Cyrus, the founder of the Persian Empire, ruled from 559 to 529 B.C.

[2] Cambyses was king of Persia from 529 to 521 B.C. When he conquered Egypt, it temporarily became a Persian province.

[3] The Hellespont is the narrow strait connecting the Aegean Sea with the Sea of Marmora. At one point it is less than a mile wide.

for the outrage they committed upon my father and upon us. As you saw, Darius himself was making his preparations for war against these men; but death prevented him from carrying out his purpose. I therefore on his behalf, and for the benefit of all my subjects, will not rest until I have taken Athens and burnt it to the ground, in revenge for the injury which the Athenians without provocation once did to me and my father. These men, you remember, came to Sardis with Aristagoras[4] the Milesian— a mere slave of ours—and burnt the temples, and the trees that grew about them; and you know all too well how they served our troops under Datis and Artaphernes.[5] when they landed upon Greek soil. For these reasons I have now prepared to make war upon them, and, when I consider the matter, I find several advantages in the venture: if we crush the Athenians and their neighbours in the Peloponnese,[6] we shall so extend the empire of Persia that its boundaries will be God's own sky. With your help I shall pass through Europe from end to end and make it all one country, so that the sun will not look down upon any land beyond the boundaries of what is ours. For if what I am told is true, there is not a city or nation in the world which will be able to withstand us, once Athens and Sparta are out of the way. Thus the guilty and the innocent alike shall bear the yoke of servitude. . . ."

The first to speak after the king was Mardonius. "Of all Persians who have ever lived," he began, "and of all who are yet to be born, you, my lord, are the greatest. Every word you have spoken is true and excellent, and you will not allow the wretched Ionians in Europe to make fools of us. It would indeed be an odd thing if we who have defeated and enslaved the Sacae, Indians, Ethiopians, Assyrians,[7] and many other great nations for no fault of their own, but merely to extend the boundaries of our empire, should fail now to punish the Greeks who have been guilty of injuring us without provocation. . . . Well then, my lord, who is likely to resist you when you march against them with the millions of Asia at your back, and the whole Persian fleet? Believe me, it is not in the Greek character to take so desperate a risk. But should I be wrong—should the courage born of ignorance and folly drive them to do battle with us, then they will learn that we are the best soldiers in the world. Nevertheless, let us take this business seriously and spare no pains; success is never automatic in this world—nothing is achieved without trying."

Xerxes' proposals were made to sound plausible enough by these words of Mardonius, and when he stopped speaking there was a silence. For a while nobody dared to put forward the opposite view, until Artabanus, taking courage from the fact of his relationship to the king— he was a son of Hystaspes and therefore Xerxes' uncle—rose to speak. . . . "It is my duty to tell you what you have to fear from them: you have said you mean to bridge the Hellespont and march through Europe to Greece. Now suppose—and it is not impossible—that you were to suffer a reverse by sea or land, or even both. These Greeks are said to be great fighters—and indeed one might well guess as much from the fact that the Athenians alone destroyed the great army we sent to attack them under Datis and Artaphernes. Or, if you will, suppose they were to succeed upon one element only—suppose they fell upon our fleet and defeated it, and then sailed to the Hellespont and

---

[4]Aristagoras, the ruler of Miletus, encouraged the other cities of Ionia to revolt against the Persians.
[5]Datis and Artaphernes were the commanders of the Persian forces defeated by the Athenians at Marathon.
[6]The Peloponnese (Peloponnesus) is the largst peninsula of southern Greece.

[7]The Sacae lived in Bactria, above the Iranian Plateau; the Indians just west of the Indus River. Ethiopia of that time means a land along the west side of the Red Sea. The Assyrians were a people inhabiting land between the Tigris and Euphrates rivers.

destroyed the bridge: then, my lord, you would indeed be in peril. . . .

"I urge you, therefore, to abandon this plan; take my advice and do not run any such terrible risk when there is no necessity to do so. . . .

"You know, my lord, that amongst living creatures it is the great ones that God smites with his thunder, out of envy of their pride. The little ones do not vex him. It is always the great buildings and the tall trees which are struck by lightning. It is God's way to bring the lofty low. Often a great army is destroyed by a little one, when God in his envy puts fear into the men's hearts, or sends a thunderstorm, and they are cut to pieces in a way they do not deserve. For God tolerates pride in none but Himself."

REVIEW QUESTIONS

1. What were the motives of the Persians in planning Xerxes' invasion of Greece? What do these motives suggest about the nature of the Persian imperial system?
2. What factors did the Persians consider in choosing a strategy for the war?
3. Herodotus was not a witness to the debate between Mardonius and Artabanus. Which lines do you think represent his own view rather than that of the Persians?
4. What dangers did Artabanus foresee in the proposed invasion of Greece?

7 Greek Drama

Western drama is an art form that originated in Greece. It had its beginnings in the religious ceremonies of the Greeks and initially served a ritual function linking the Greeks with their gods. In the hands of the great Greek dramatists, drama gradually became less concerned with the activities of the gods, emphasizing instead human personality and universal human themes.

Sophocles
ANTIGONE

In *Antigone*, the dramatist Sophocles expresses the Greeks' high esteem for humanity and its potential. He also deals with a theme that recurs in Western thought over the centuries: the conflict between individual morality and the requirements of the state, between personal conscience and the state's laws. Creon, king of Thebes, forbids the burial of Polyneikes, Antigone's brother, because he rebelled against the state. The body, decrees Creon, shall remain unburied, food for dogs and vultures, despite the fact that Antigone is his niece and betrothed to his son. Antigone believes that a higher law compels her to bury her brother, even though this means certain death for her and for her sister Ismene, if the later helps Antigone.

SCENE II

CREON (*to* ANTIGONE)
You there. You, looking at the ground. Tell me.
Do you admit this or deny it? Which?

ANTIGONE
Yes, I admit it. I do not deny it.

CREON (*to* GUARD)
Go. You are free. The charge is dropped.
Exit GUARD
Now you,
Answer this question. Make your answer brief.
You knew there was a law forbidding this?

ANTIGONE
Of course I knew it. Why not? It was public,

CREON
And you have dared to disobey the law?

ANTIGONE
Yes, For this law was not proclaimed by Zeus,
Or by the gods who rule the world below.
I do not think your edicts have such power
That they can override the laws of heaven,
Unwritten and unfailing, laws whose life
Belongs not to today or yesterday
But to time everlasting; and no man
Knows the first moment that they had
    their being.
If I transgressed these laws because I feared
The arrogance of man, how to the gods
Could I make satisfaction? Well I know,
Being a mortal, that I have to die,
Even without your proclamations. Yet
If I must die before my time is come,
That is a blessing. Because to one who lives,
As I live, in the midst of sorrows, death
Is of necessity desirable.
For me, to face death is a trifling pain
That does not trouble me. But to have left
The body of my brother, my own brother,
Lying unburied would be bitter grief.
And if these acts of mine seem foolish
    to you,
Perhaps a fool accuses me of folly.

CHORUS
The violent daughter of a violent father,
She cannot bend before a storm of evils.

CREON (*to* ANTIGONE)
Stubborn? Self-willed? People like that, I tell
    you,
Are the first to come to grief. The hardest
    iron,
Baked in the fire, most quickly flies to
    pieces.
An unruly horse is taught obedience
By a touch of the curb. How can you be so
    proud?
You, a mere slave? (*to* CHORUS) She was well
    schooled already
In insolence, when she defied the law.
And now look at her! Boasting, insolent,
Exulting in what she did. And if she
    triumphs
and goes unpunished, I am no man—she is.
If she were more than niece, if she were
    closer
Than anyone who worships at my altar,
She would not even then escape her doom,
A dreadful death. Nor would her sister. Yes,
Her sister had a share in burying him.
(*to* ATTENDANT) Go bring her here. I have just
    seen her, raving,
Beside herself. Even before they act,
Traitors who plot their treason in the dark
Betray themselves like that. Detestable!
(*to* ANTIGONE) But hateful also is an
    evil-doer
Who, caught red-handed, glorifies the
    crime.

ANTIGONE
Now you have caught me, will you do more
    than kill me?

CREON
No, only that. With that I am satisfied.

ANTIGONE
Then why do you delay? You have said
    nothing

I do not hate. I pray you never will.
And you hate what I say. Yet how could I
Have won more splendid honor than by giving
Due burial to my brother? All men here
Would grant me their approval, if their lips
Were not sealed up in fear. But you, a king,
Blessed by good fortune in much else besides,
Can speak and act with perfect liberty.

CREON
All of these Thebans disagree with you.

ANTIGONE
No. They agree, but they control their tongues.

CREON
You feel no shame in acting without their
   help?

ANTIGONE
I feel no shame in honoring a brother.

CREON
Another brother died who fought against him.

ANTIGONE
Two brothers. The two sons of the same
   parents.

CREON
Honor to one is outrage to the other.

ANTIGONE
Eteocles will not feel himself dishonored.

CREON
What! When his rites are offered to a traitor?

ANTIGONE
It was his brother, not his slave, who died.

CREON
One who attacked the land that he defended.

ANTIGONE
The gods still wish those rites to be performed.

CREON
Are they just pleased with the unjust as their
   equals?

ANTIGONE
That may be virtuous in the world below.

CREON
No. Even there a foe is never a friend.

ANTIGONE
I am not made for hatred but for love.

CREON
Then go down to the dead. If you must love,
Love them. While I yet live, no woman
   rules me.

CHORUS
Look there. Ismene, weeping as sisters weep,
The shadow of a cloud of grief lies deep.
On her face, darkly flushed; and in her pain
Her tears are falling like a flood of rain.
           Enter ISMENE *and* ATTENDANTS

CREON
You viper! Lying hidden in my house,
Sucking my blood in secret, while I reared,
Unknowingly, two subverters of my throne.
Do you confess that you have taken part
In this man's burial, or deny it? Speak.

ISMENE
If she will recognize my right to say so,
I shared the action and I share the blame.

ANTIGONE
No. That would not be just. I never let you
Take any part in what you disapproved of.

ISMENE
In your calamity, I am not ashamed
To stand beside you, beaten by this tempest.

ANTIGONE
The dead are witnesses of what I did,
To love in words alone is not enough.

ISMENE
Do not reject me, Sister! Let me die
Beside you, and do honor to the dead.

ANTIGONE
No. You will neither share my death nor claim
What I have done. My death will be sufficient.

ISMENE
What happiness can I have when you are gone?

ANTIGONE

Ask Creon that. He is the one you value.

ISMENE

Do you gain anything by taunting me?

ANTIGONE

Ah, no! by taunting you, I hurt myself.

ISMENE

How can I help you? Tell me what I can do.

ANTIGONE

Protect yourself. I do not grudge your safety.

ISMENE

Antigone! Shall I not share your fate?

ANTIGONE

We both have made our choices life, and death.

ISMENE

At least I tried to stop you. I protested.

ANTIGONE

Some have approved your way; and others,
    mine.

ISMENE

Yet now I share your guilt. I too am ruined.

ANTIGONE

Take courage. Live your life. But I long since
Gave myself up to death to help the dead. . . .

Haemon, grief-stricken at the condemnation of his fiancée Antigone, approaches his
father Creon, and tries to resolve the crisis.
Creon is suspicious about Haemon's loyalty.

CREON

We soon shall know better than seers could tell
    us.
My son, Antigone is condemned to death.
Nothing can change my sentence. Have you
    learned
Her fate and come here in a storm of anger,
Or do you love me and support my acts?

HAEMON

Father, I am your son. Your greater knowledge

Will trace the path way that I mean to follow.
My marriage cannot be of more importance
Than to be guided always by your wisdom.

CREON

Yes, Haemon, this should be the law you
    live by!
In all things to obey your father's will.
Men pray for children round them in their
    homes
Only to see them dutiful and quick
With hatred to require their father's foe,
With honor to repay their father's friend.
But what is there to say of one whose children
Prove to be valueless? That he has fathered
Grief for himself and laughter for his foes.
Then, Haemon, do not, at the rule of pleasure,
Unseat your reason for a woman's sake.
This comfort soon grows cold in your embrace:
A wicked wife to share your bed and home.
Is there a deeper wound than to find worthless
The one you love? Turn from this girl with
    loathing,
As from an enemy, and let her go
To get a husband in the world below.
For I have found her openly rebellious,
Her only out of all the city. Therefore,
I will not break the oath that I have sworn.
I will have her killed. Vainly she will invoke
The bond of kindred blood the gods make
    sacred.
If I permit disloyalty to breed
In my own house, I nurture it in strangers.
He who is righteous with his kin is righteous
In the state also. Therefore, I cannot pardon
One who does violence to the laws or thinks
To dictate to his rulers; for whoever
May be the man appointed by the city,
That man must be obeyed in everything,
Little or great, just or unjust. And surely
He who was thus obedient would be found
As good a ruler as he was a subject;
And in a storm of spears he would stand fast
With loyal courage at his comrade's side.
But disobedience is the worst of evils.
For it is this that ruins cities; this
Makes our homes desolate; armies of allies

Through this break up in rout. But most men find
Their happiness and safety in obedience.
Therefore we must support the law, and never
Be beaten by a woman. It is better
To fall by a man's hand, if we must fall,
Than to be known as weaker than a girl.

CHORUS
We may in our old age have lost our judgment,
And yet to us you seem to have spoken wisely.

HAEMON
The gods have given men the gift of reason,
Greatest of all things that we call our own.
I have no skill, nor do I wish to have it,
To show where you have spoken wrongly. Yet
Some other's thought, beside your own, might prove
To be of value. Therefore it is my duty,
My natural duty as your son, to notice,
On your behalf, all that men say, or do,
Or find to blame. For your frown frightens them,
So that the citizen dares not say a word
That would offend you. I can hear, however,
Murmurs in darkness and laments for her.
They say: "No woman ever less deserved
Her doom, no woman ever was to die
So shamefully for deeds so glorious.
For when her brother fell in bloody battle,
She would not let his body lie unburied
To be devoured by carrion dogs or birds.
Does such a woman not deserve reward,
Rewards of golden honor?" This I hear,
A rumor spread in secrecy and darkness.
Father, I prize nothing in life so highly
As your well-being. How can children have
A nobler honor than their father's fame
Or father than his son's? Then do not think
Your mood must never alter; do not feel
Your word, and yours alone, must be correct.
For if a man believes that he is right
And only he, that no one equals him
In what he says or thinks, he will be found
Empty when searched and rested. Because
  a man

Even if he wise, feels no disgrace
In learning many things, in taking care
Not to be over-rigid. You have seen
Trees on the margin of a stream in winter:
Those yielding to the flood save every twig,
And those resisting perish root and branch.
So, too, the mariner who never slackens
His taut sheet overturns his craft and spends
Keel uppermost the last part of his voyage.
Let your resentment die. Let yourself change.
For I believe—if I, a younger man,
May have a sound opinion—it is best
That men by nature should be wise in all
  things.
But most men find they cannot reach that goal;
And when this happens, it is also good
To learn to listen to wise counselors.

CHORUS
Sir, when his words are timely, you should heed them.
And Haemon, you should profit by his words.
Each one of you has spoken reasonably.

CREON
Are men as old as I am to be taught
How to behave by men as young as he?

HAEMON
Not to do wrong. If I am young, ignore
My youth. Consider only what I do.

CREON
Have you done well in honoring the rebellious?

HAEMON
Those who do wrong should not command respect.

CREON
Then that disease has not infected her?

HAEMON
All of our city with one voice denies it.

CREON
Does Thebes give orders for the way I rule?

HAEMON
How young your are! How young in saying that!

CREON
Am I to govern by another's judgment?

HAEMON
A city that is one man's is no city.

CREON
A city is the king's. That much is sure.

HAEMON
You would rule well in a deserted country.

REVIEW QUESTIONS

1. What was Antigone's justification for disobeying the command of the king? Provide examples of historical figures who have employed a similar justification for their actions.
2. Why did Creon react so violently to Antigone's action?
3. Which lines best reveal Antigone's position? Creon's position?

---

8 Athenian Greatness

The Persian Wars were decisive in the history of the West. Had the Greeks been defeated, it is very likely that their cultural and political vitality would have been aborted. The confidence and pride that came with victory, however, propelled Athens into a golden age.

Thucydides
THE FUNERAL ORATION OF PERICLES

The central figure in Athenian political life for much of the period after the Persian Wars was Pericles (c. 495–429 B.C.), a gifted statesman and military commander. In the opening stage of the Peloponnesian War between Athens and Sparta (431–404 B.C.), Pericles delivered an oration in honor of the Athenian war dead. In this speech, as reconstructed by the historian Thucydides, Pericles brilliantly described Athenian greatness.

Pericles contrasted Sparta's narrow conception of excellence with the Athenian ideal of the self-sufficiency of the human spirit. The Spartans subordinated all personal goals and interests to the demands of the Spartan state. As such, Sparta—a totally militarized society—was as close as the ancient Greeks came to a modern totalitarian society. The Athenians, said Pericles, did not require grinding military discipline in order to fight bravely for their city. Their cultivation of the mind and love of beauty did not make them less courageous.

To be sure, Pericles' "Funeral Oration," intended to bolster the morale of a people locked in a brutal war, idealized Athenian society. Athenians did not always behave in accordance with Pericles' high principles. Nevertheless, as both Pericles and Thucydides knew, Athenian democracy was an extraordinary achievement.

"Let me say that our system of government does not copy the institutions of our neighbours. It is more the case of our being a model to others, than of our imitating anyone else. Our constitution is called a democracy because power is in the hands not of a minority but of the whole people. When it is a question of settling private disputes, everyone is equal before the law; when it is a question of putting one person before another in positions of public responsibility, what counts is not membership of a particular class, but the actual ability which the man possesses. No one, so long as he has it in him to be of service to the state, is kept in political obscurity because of poverty. And, just as our political life is free and open, so is our day-to-day life in our relations with each other. We do not get into a state with our next-door neighbour if he enjoys himself in his own way, nor do we give him the kind of black looks which, though they do no real harm, still do hurt people's feelings. We are free and tolerant in our private lives; but in public affairs we keep to the law. This is because it commands our deep respect.

"We give our obedience to those whom we put in positions of authority, and we obey the laws themselves, especially those which are for the protection of the oppressed, and those unwritten laws which it is an acknowledged shame to break.

"And here is another point. When our work is over, we are in a position to enjoy all kinds of recreation for our spirits. There are various kinds of contests [in poetry, drama, music, and athletics] and sacrifices regularly throughout the year; in our own homes we find a beauty and a good taste which delight us every day and which drive away our cares. Then the greatness of our city brings it about that all the good things from all over the world flow in to us, so that to us it seems just as natural to enjoy foreign goods as our own local products.

"Then there is a great difference between us and our opponents, in our attitude towards military security. Here are some examples:

Our city is open to the world, and we have no periodical deportations in order to prevent people observing or finding out secrets which might be of military advantage to the enemy. This is because we rely, not on secret weapons, but on our own real courage and loyalty. There is a difference, too, in our educational systems. The Spartans, from their earliest boyhood, are submitted to the most laborious training in courage; we pass our lives without all these restrictions, and yet are just as ready to face the same dangers as they are. Here is a proof of this: When the Spartans invade our land, they do not come by themselves, but bring all their allies with them; whereas we, when we launch an attack abroad, do the job by ourselves, and, though fighting on foreign soil, do not often fail to defeat opponents who are fighting for their own hearths and homes. As a matter of fact none of our enemies has ever yet been confronted with our total strength, because we have to divide our attention between our navy and the many missions on which our troops are sent on land. Yet, if our enemies engage a detachment of our forces and defeat it, they give themselves credit for having thrown back our entire army; or, if they lose, they claim that they were beaten by us in full strength. There are certain advantages, I think, in our way of meeting danger voluntarily, with an easy mind, instead of with a laborious training, with natural rather than with state-induced courage. We do not have to spend our time practising to meet sufferings which are still in the future; and when they are actually upon us we show ourselves just as brave as these others who are always in strict training. This is one point in which, I think, our city deserves to be admired. There are also others:

"Our love of what is beautiful does not lead to extravagance; our love of the things of the mind does not make us soft. We regard wealth as something to be properly used, rather than as something to boast about. As for poverty, no one need be ashamed to admit it: the real shame is in not taking practical measures to escape from it. Here each individual is interested not only in his own affairs but in the affairs of the state as well: even those who are mostly occupied with their own business are extremely well-informed on general politics—this is a peculiarity of ours: we do not say that a man who takes no interest in politics is a man who minds his own business; we say that he has no business here at all. We Athenians, in our own persons, take our decisions on policy or submit them to proper discussions: for we do not think that there is an incompatibility between words and deeds; the worst thing is to rush into action before the consequences have been properly debated. And this is another point where we differ from other people. We are capable at the same time of taking risks and of estimating them beforehand. Others are brave out of ignorance; and, when they stop to think, they begin to fear. But the man who can most truly be accounted brave is he who best knows the meaning of what is sweet in life and of what is terrible, and then goes out undeterred to meet what is to come.

"Again, in questions of general good feeling there is a great contrast between us and most other people. We make friends by doing good to others, not by receiving good from them. This makes our friendship all the more reliable, since we want to keep alive the gratitude of those who are in our debt by showing continued goodwill to them: whereas the feelings of one who owes us something lack the same enthusiasm, since he knows that, when he repays our kindness, it will be more like paying back a debt than giving something spontaneously. We are unique in this. When we do kindnesses to others, we do not do them out of any calculations of profit or loss: we do them without afterthought, relying on our free liberality. Taking everything together then, I declare that our city is an education to Greece, and I declare that in my opinion each single one of our citizens, in all the manifold aspects of life, is able to show himself the rightful lord and owner of his own person, and do this, moreover, with exceptional grace and exceptional versatility. And to show that this is no empty boasting for the present occasion, but real tangible fact, you have only to consider the power which our city possesses and which has been won by those very qualities which I have mentioned. Athens, alone of the states we know, comes to her testing time in a greatness that surpasses what was imagined of her. In her case, and in her case alone, no invading enemy is ashamed at being defeated, and no subject can complain of being governed by people unfit for their responsibilities. Mighty indeed are the marks and monuments of our empire which we have left. Future ages will wonder at us, as the present age wonders at us now."

REVIEW QUESTIONS

1. According to Pericles, what are the chief characteristics of a democratic society?
2. What were the attitudes of the Athenians to such things as wealth, learning, and public affairs?
3. How did the Athenians differ from the Spartans in their views on education and military training?

9   The Status of Women in Classical Greek Society

Women occupied a subordinate position in Greek society. A woman's chief functions were to bear male heirs for her husband and to manage his household. In Athens, respectable women were secluded in their homes; they did not go into the marketplace or eat at the same table as their husbands and guests. Nor did women have political rights; they could not vote or hold office. In order to exercise her property rights, a woman was represented by a male guardian—usually a father, husband, brother, or son.

Parents usually arranged the marriage of their daughters. A father who discovered that his daughter had been unchaste could sell her into slavery. Adultery was a crime. A husband was compelled by law to divorce his adulterous wife and could have her lover executed.

Euripides
MEDEA

The Greek dramatist Euripides (c. 485–406 B.C.) applied a keen critical spirit to the great question of individual life versus the demands of society. His play *Medea* focuses on a strong-willed woman whose despair at being cast off by her husband leads her to exact a terrible revenge. But in the following passage, Medea might speak for the deepest feelings of any Greek woman.

It was everything to me to think well of one
man,
And he, my own husband, has turned out
wholly vile.
Of all things which are living and can form a
judgement
We women are the most unfortunate creatures.
Firstly, with an excess of wealth it is required
For us to buy a husband and take for our bodies
A master; for not to take one is even worse.
And now the question is serious whether we
take
A good or bad one; for there is no easy escape
For a woman, nor can she say no to her marriage.
She arrives among new modes of behaviour
and manners,
And needs prophetic power, unless she has
learnt at home,
How best to manage him who shares the bed
with her.

And if we work out all this well and carefully,
And the husband lives with us and lightly
bears his yoke,
Then life is enviable. If not, I'd rather die.
A man, when he's tired of the company in his
home,
Goes out of the house and puts an end to his
boredom
And turns to a friend or companion of his own
age.
But we are forced to keep our eyes on one
alone.
What they say of us is that we have a peaceful
time
Living at home, while they do the fighting in
war.
How wrong they are! I would very much
rather stand
Three times in the front of battle than bear one
child.

Aristophanes
LYSISTRATA

Aristophanes (c. 448–c. 380 B.C.), greatest Athenian comic playwright, wrote *Lysistrata* in 412 B.C. to convey his revulsion for the Peloponnesian War that was destroying Greece. In the play, the women of Athens, led by Lysistrata, resolve to refrain from sexual relations with their husbands until the men make peace. When the women seize the Acropolis—the rocky hill in the center of Athens— the men resort to force but are doused with water. At this point a commissioner, accompanied by four constables, enters and complains about the disturbance; Koryphaios, one of the doused men, vents his anger. The ensuing dialogue between the commissioner and Lysistrata reflects some attitudes of Greek men and women toward each other.

COMMISSIONER . . . That's what women are good for: a complete disaster.

MAN I Save your breath for actual crimes, Commissioner. Look what's happened to us. Insolence, insults, insufferable effrontery, and apart from that, they've soaked us. It looks as though we pissed in our tunics.

COMMISSIONER By Poseidon, that liquid deity, you got what you deserved. It's all our own fault. We taught them all they know. We are the forgers of fornication. We sowed in them sexual license and now we reap rebellion . . . *(shrugs)* What do you expect? This is what happens. . . . *(indicates doors of Acropolis)* Take my own case.

I'm the Commissioner for Public Safety. I've got men to pay. I need the money and look what happens. The women have shut me out of the public treasury. *(taking command)* All right, men. On your feet. Take up that log over there. Form a line. Get a move on. You can get drunk later. I'll give you a hand. *(They ram the gates without success. After three tries, as they are stepping back, Lysistrata opens the door. Calonike and Myrrhine accompany her.)*

LYSISTRATA Put that thing down! I'm coming out of my own free will. What we want here is not bolts and bars and locks, but common sense.

COMMISSIONER Sense? Common sense? You . . . you . . . you . . . Where's a policeman? Arrest her! Tie her hands behind her back.

LYSISTRATA *(who is carrying wool on a spindle or a knitting needle)* By Artemis, goddess of the hunt, if he touches me, you'll be dropping one man from your payroll. *(Lysistrata jabs him)*

COMMISSIONER What's this? Retreat? Get back in there. Grab her, the two of you.

MYRRHINE *(holding a large chamber pot)* By Artemis, goddess of the dew, if you lay a hand on her, I'll kick the shit out of you.

COMMISSIONER Shit? Disgusting. Arrest her for using obscene language.

CALONIKE *(carrying a lamp)* By Artemis, goddess of light, if you lay a finger on her, you'll need a doctor.

COMMISSIONER Apprehend that woman. Get her, NOW!

BOEOTIAN *(from the roof, with a broom)* By Artemis, goddess of witchcraft, if you go near her, I'll break your head open.

COMMISSIONER Good God, what a mess. Athens' finest disgraced! Defeated by a gaggle of girls. Close ranks, men! On your marks, get set, CHARGE!

LYSISTRATA (*holds her hands up and they stop*) Hold it! We've got four battalions of fully equipped infantry women back there.

COMMISSIONER Go inside and disarm them.

LYSISTRATA (*gives a loud whistle and women crowd the bottlenecks and the doorway with brooms, pots and pans, etc.*) Attack! Destroy them, you sifters of flour and beaters of eggs, you pressers of garlic, you dough girls, you bar maids, you market militia. Scratch them and tear them, bite and kick. Fall back, don't strip the enemy—the day is ours. (*the policemen are overpowered*)

COMMISSIONER (*in tears*) Another glorious military victory for Athens!

LYSISTRATA What did you think we were? There's not an ounce of servility in us. A woman scorned is something to be reckoned with. You underestimated the capacity of freeborn women.

COMMISSIONER Capacity? I sure as hell did. You'd cause a drought in the saloons if they let you in.

MAN I Your honor, there's no use talking to animals. I know you're a civil servant, but don't overdo it.

MAN II Didn't we tell you? They gave us a public bath, fully dressed, without any soap.

WOMAN I What did you expect, sonny? You made the first move—we made the second. Try it again and you'll get another black eye. (*flute*) We are really sweet little stay-at-homes by nature, all sweetness and light, good little virgins, perfect dolls (*they all rock to and fro coyly*). But if you stick your finger in a hornet's nest, you're going to get stung.

MEN ALL (*and drums—they beat their feet rhythmically on the ground*)
Oh Zeus, Oh Zeus.
Of all the beasts that thou has wrought,
What monster's worse than woman?
Who shall encompass with his thought
Their endless crimes? Let me tell you . . . no man!

They've seized the heights, the rock, the shrine.
But to what end I know not.
There must be *reasons* for the crime (*to audience*)
Do you know why? (*pause*) I thought not.

MAN I Scrutinize those women. Assess their rebuttals.

MAN II 'Twould be culpable negligence not to probe this affair to the bottom.

COMMISSIONER (*as if before a jury*) My first question is this, gentlemen of the . . . What possible motive could you have had in seizing the Treasury?

LYSISTRATA We wanted to keep the money. *No money, no war.*

COMMISSIONER You think that money is the cause of the war?

LYSISTRATA Money is the cause of all our problems. . . . They'll not get another penny.

COMMISSIONER Then what do you propose to do?

LYSISTRATA Control the Treasury.

COMMISSIONER Control the Treasury?

LYSISTRATA Control the Treasury. National economics and home economics—they're one and the same.

COMMISSIONER No, they're not.

LYSISTRATA Why do you say so?

COMMISSIONER The national economy is for the war effort.

LYSISTRATA Who needs the war effort?

COMMISSIONER How can we protect the city?

LYSISTRATA Leave that to us.

ALL MEN You?

ALL WOMEN Us.

COMMISSIONER God save us.

LYSISTRATA Leave that to us.

COMMISSIONER Subversive nonsense!

LYSISTRATA Why get so upset? There's no stopping us now.

COMMISSIONER It's a downright crime.

LYSISTRATA We *must* save you.

COMMISSIONER (*pouting*) What if I don't want to be saved?

LYSISTRATA All the more reason to.

COMMISSIONER Might I ask where you got these ideas of war and peace?

LYSISTRATA If you'll allow me, I'll tell you.

COMMISSIONER Out with it then, or I'll . . .

LYSISTRATA Relax and put your hands down.

COMMISSIONER I can't help myself. You make me so damned angry.

CALONIKE Watch it.

COMMISSIONER Watch it yourself, you old wind bag.

LYSISTRATA Because of our natural self-restraint, we women have tolerated you men ever since this war began. We tolerated you and kept our thoughts to ourselves. (You never let us utter a peep, anyway.) But that does not mean that we were happy with you. We knew you all too well. Very often, in the evening, at suppertime, we would listen to you talk of some enormously important decision you had made. Deep down inside all we felt was pain, but we would force a smile and ask, "How was the assembly today, dear? Did you get to talk about peace?" And my husband would answer, "None of your business. Shut up!" And I would shut up.

CALONIKE I wouldn't have.

COMMISSIONER I'd have shut your mouth for you.

LYSISTRATA But then we would find out that you had passed a more disgusting resolution, and I would ask you, "Darling, how did you manage to do something so absolutely stupid?" And my husband would glare at me and threaten to slap my face if I did not attend to the distaff side of things. And then he'd always quote Homer: "The men must see to the fighting."

COMMISSIONER Well done. Well done.

LYSISTRATA What do you mean? Not to let us advise against your idiocy was bad enough, but then again we'd actually hear you out in public saying things like, "Who can we draft? There's not a man left in the country." Someone else would say, "Quite right, not a man left. Pity." And so we women got together and decided to save Greece. There was no time to lose. Therefore, you keep quiet for a change and listen to us. For we have valuable advice to give this country. If you'll listen, we'll put you back on your feet again.

COMMISSIONER You'll do what? I'm not going to put up with this. I'm not going . . .

LYSISTRATA SILENCE!

COMMISSIONER I categorically decline to be silent for a woman. Women wear hats.

LYSISTRATA If that's what is bothering you, try one on and shut up! (puts one on him)

CALONIKE Here's a spindle.

MYRRHINE And a basket of wool.

CALONIKE Go on home. There's a sweetheart. Put on your girdle, wind your wool, and mind the beans don't boil over.

LYSISTRATA "THE WOMEN MUST SEE TO THE FIGHTING."

COMMISSIONER Beside the point, beside the point. Things are in a tangle. How can you set them straight?

LYSISTRATA Simple.

COMMISSIONER Explain.

LYSISTRATA Do you know anything about weaving? Say the wool gets tangled. We lift it up, like this, and work out the knots by winding it this way and that, up and down, on the spindles. That's how we'll unravel the war. We'll send our envoys this way and that, up and down, all over Greece.

COMMISSIONER Wool? Spindles? Are you out of your mind? War is a serious business.

LYSISTRATA If you had any sense, you'd learn a lesson from women's work.

COMMISSIONER Prove it.

LYSISTRATA The first thing we have to do is give the wool a good wash, get the dirt out of the fleece. We beat out the musk and pick out the hickies. Do the same for the city. Lambast the loafers and discard the dodgers. Then our spoiled wool—that's like your job-hunting sycophants—sack the spongers, decapitate the dabblers. But toss together into the wool basket the good [resident] aliens, the allies, the strangers, and begin spinning them into a ball. The colonies are loose threads; pick up the ends and gather them in. Wind them all into one, make a great bobbin of yarn, and weave, without bias

or seam, a garment of government fit for the people.

COMMISSIONER It's all very well this weaving and bobbing—when you have absolutely no earthly idea what a war means.

LYSISTRATA You disgusting excuse for a man! The pain of giving birth was only our first pain. You took our boys and sent *them to their deaths in Sicily.*

COMMISSIONER Quiet! I beg you, let that memory lie still.

LYSISTRATA And now, when youth and beauty are still with us and our blood is hot, you take our husbands away, and we sleep alone. That's bad enough for us married women. But I pity the virgins growing old, alone in their beds.

COMMISSIONER Well, men grow old too, you know.

LYSISTRATA But it's not the same. A soldier's discharged, bald as a coot he may be, and ... zap! he marries a nymphette. But a woman only has one summer, and when that has slipped by, she can spend her days and her years consulting oracles and fortune tellers, but they'll never send her a husband.

———

MEN ALL There's something rotten in the state of Athens.
An ominous aroma of constitutional rot.
My nose can smell a radical dissenter,
An anarchist, tyrannous, feminist plot.

The Spartans are behind it.
They must have masterminded
This anarchist, tyrannous, feminist plot.

REVIEW QUESTIONS

1. List several reasons Medea gives to support her claim that "we women are the most unfortunate creatures."

were the grievances of Greek women as listed by Aristophanes?
attitudes of ancient Greek males toward females are reflected in the
contemporary world?

---

10 The Peloponnesian War

After the defeat of the Persian invaders in 479 B.C., the Athenians organized a mutual defense pact, called the Delian League, among the smaller Greek states. With the largest population and greatest wealth and naval forces, Athens became the dominant power within the league. In the course of time, Athens converted the alliance from an organization of equal sovereign states to an empire under Athenian control. This outcome aroused suspicion among the other Greek states in the Peloponnese, particularly Sparta, that an imperialistic Athens was a threat to their own independence and freedom. That fear precipitated the Peloponnesian War (431–404 B.C.), which devastated the Greek world during the late fifth century B.C.

Elected general during the war, Thucydides was banished from Athens for failing to rescue Amphipolis, a town under attack by Sparta. During his twenty-year exile, Thucydides gathered information about the war, which he correctly viewed as an event of world-historical importance. He was also right to regard his account as a unique documentary achievement that would serve as a model for future historians.

Above all, Thucydides studied politics, the lifeblood of Athenian society. For him, history was essentially the study of political behavior. Consistent with the Greek character, Thucydides sought underlying patterns and general truths pertaining to statesmanship and political power. His chronicle contains rich insights into human nature, the techniques of demagogues, the ruinous consequences of mob behavior, and the spiritual deterioration of men under the stress of war.

Thucydides
THE MELIAN DIALOGUE AND THE REVOLUTION AT CORCYRA

The Athenians, who saw no conflict between imperialism and democracy, considered it natural for strong states to dominate weaker ones. This view coincided with the position of those Sophists who argued that might makes right. The classic expression of this view is found in Thucydides' history.

During the war, Athens decided to invade the island of Melos, which resisted this unprovoked act of aggression. Thucydides reconstructed a dialogue based on a meeting between Athenian envoys and Melian officials, who tried unsuccessfully to persuade the Athenians not to launch an unjust war. Subsequently, Athens attacked. After capturing the town, the Athenians slaughtered the men, enslaved the women and children, and colonized the territory. The first selection is the famous Melian Dialogue. In the second selection, Thucydides describes the revolution in Corcyra, one of several conflicts that broke out within the city-states during the Peloponnesian War.

MELIANS No one can object to each of us putting forward our own views in a calm atmosphere. That is perfectly reasonable. What is scarcely consistent with such a proposal is the present threat, indeed the certainty, of your making war on us. We see that you have come prepared to judge the argument yourselves, and that the likely end of it all will be either war, if we prove that we are in the right, and so refuse to surrender, or else slavery.

ATHENIANS If you are going to spend the time in enumerating your suspicions about the future, or if you have met here for any other reason except to look the facts in the face and on the basis of these facts to consider how you can save your city from destruction, there is no point in our going on with this discussion. If, however, you will do as we suggest, then we will speak on.

MELIANS It is natural and understandable that people who are placed as we are should have recourse to all kinds of arguments and different points of view. However, you are right in saying that we are met together here to discuss the safety of our country and, if you will have it so, the discussion shall proceed on the lines that you have laid down.

ATHENIANS Then we on our side will use no fine phrases saying, for example, that we have a right to our empire because we defeated the Persians, or that we have come against you now because of the injuries you have done us—a great mass of words that nobody would believe. And we ask you on your side not to imagine that you will influence us by saying that you, though a colony of Sparta, have not joined Sparta in the war, or that you have never done us any harm. Instead we recommend that you should try to get what it is possible for you to get, taking into consideration what we both really do think; since you know as well as we do that when these matters are discussed by practical people, the standard of justice depends on the equality of power to compel and that in fact the strong do what they have the power to do and the weak accept what they have to accept.

MELIANS Then in our view (since you force us to leave justice out of account and to confine ourselves to self-interest)—in our view it is at any rate useful that you should not destroy a principle that is to the general good of all men—namely, that in the case of all who fall into danger there should be such a thing as fair play and just dealing, and that such people should be allowed to use and to profit by arguments that fall short of a mathematical accuracy. And this is a principle which affects you as much as anybody, since your own fall would be visited by the most terrible vengeance and would be an example to the world.

ATHENIANS . . . What we shall do now is to show you that it is for the good of our own empire that we are here and that it is for the preservation of your city that we shall say what we are going to say. We do not want any trouble in bringing you into our empire, and we want you to be spared for the good both of yourselves and of ourselves.

MELIANS And how could it be just as good for us to be the slaves as for you to be the masters?

ATHENIANS You, by giving in, would save yourselves from disaster; we, by not destroying you, would be able to profit from you.

MELIANS So you would not agree to our being neutral, friends instead of enemies, but allies of neither side?

ATHENIANS No, because it is not so much your hostility that injures us; it is rather the case that, if we were on friendly terms with you, our subjects would regard that as a sign of weakness in us, whereas your hatred is evidence of our power. . . . [Our subjects think] that those who still preserve their independence do so because they are strong, and that if we fail to attack them it is because we are afraid. So that by conquering you we shall increase not only the size but the security of our empire. We rule the sea and you are islanders, and weaker islanders too than the others; it is therefore particularly important that you should not escape. . . .

MELIANS Then surely, if such hazards are taken by you to keep your empire . . . we who are still free would show ourselves great cowards and weaklings if we failed to face everything that comes rather than submit to slavery.

ATHENIANS No, not if you are sensible. This is no fair fight, with honour on one side and shame on the other. It is rather a question of saving your lives and not resisting those who are far too strong for you.

MELIANS Yet we know that in war fortune sometimes makes the odds more level than could be expected from the difference in numbers of the two sides. And if we surrender, then all our hope is lost at once, whereas, so long as we remain in action, there is still a hope that we may yet stand upright.

ATHENIANS Hope, that comforter in danger! If one already has solid advantages to fall back upon, one can indulge in hope. . . . [D]o not be like those people who, as so commonly happens, miss the chance of saving themselves in a human and practical way, and, when every clear and distinct hope has left them in their adversity, turn to what is blind and vague, to prophecies and oracles and such things which by encouraging hope lead men to ruin.

MELIANS It is difficult, and you may be sure that we know it, for us to oppose your power. . . . Nevertheless we trust that the gods will give us fortune as good as yours, because we are standing for what is right against what is wrong; and as for what we lack in power, we trust that it will be made up for by our alliance with the Spartans, who are bound, if for no other reason, then for honour's sake, and because we are their kinsmen, to come to our help. Our confidence, therefore, is not so entirely irrational as you think.

ATHENIANS . . . Our opinion of the gods and our knowledge of men lead us to conclude that it is a general and necessary law of nature to rule wherever one can. . . . [W]ith regard to your views about Sparta and your confidence that she, out of a sense of honour, will come to your aid, we must say that we congratulate you on your simplicity but do not envy you your folly. . . .

. . . You, if you take the right view . . . will see that there is nothing disgraceful in giving way to the greatest city in Hellas when she is offering you such reasonable terms—alliance on a tribute-paying basis and liberty to enjoy your own property. And, when you are allowed to choose between war and safety, you will not be so insensitively arrogant as to make the wrong choice. This is the safe rule—to stand up to one's equals, to behave with deference towards one's superiors, and to treat one's inferiors with moderation. Think it over again, then, when we have withdrawn from the meeting, and let this be a point that constantly recurs to your minds—that you are discussing the fate of your country, that you have only one country, and that its future for good or ill depends on this one single decision which you are going to make.

The Athenians then withdrew from the discussion. The Melians, left to themselves, reached a conclusion which was much the same as they had indicated in their previous replies. Their answer was as follows:

MELIANS Our decision, Athenians, is just the same as it was at first. We are not prepared to give up in a short moment the liberty which our city has enjoyed from its foundation for 700 years. We put our trust in the fortune that the gods will send and which has saved us up to now, and in the help of men—that is, of the Spartans; and so we shall try to save ourselves. But we invite you to allow us to be friends of yours and enemies to neither side, to make a treaty which shall be agreeable to both you and us, and so to leave our country.

During the war, revolutions broke out in several city-states as democrats, those who believed in decision making by citizen participation, and oligarchs, those who wanted the rule of a select few, competed for power. In these conflicts, traditional standards of morality were set aside and dangerous passions were unleashed. Thucydides' account of the revolution at Corcyra shows how the stresses of war precipitated a moral collapse and a deterioration in the quality of political life.

. . . The Corcyraeans continued to massacre those of their own citizens whom they considered to be their enemies. Their victims were accused of conspiring to overthrow the democracy, but in fact men were often killed on grounds of personal hatred or else by their debtors because of the money that they owed. There was death in every shape and form. And, as usually happens in such situations, people went to every extreme and beyond it. There were fathers who killed their sons; men were dragged from the temples or butchered on the very altars; some were actually walled up in the temple of Dionysus [a god of drunken revelry] and died there.

So savage was the progress of this revolution, and it seemed all the more so because it was one of the first which had broken out. Later, of course, practically the whole of the Hellenic world was convulsed, with rival parties in every state—democratic leaders trying to bring in

the Athenians, and oligarchs trying to bring in the Spartans. In peacetime there would have been no excuse and no desire for calling them in, but in time of war, when each party could always count upon an alliance which would do harm to its opponents and at the same time strengthen its own position, it became a natural thing for anyone who wanted a change of government to call in help from outside. In the various cities these revolutions were the cause of many calamities—as happens and always will happen while human nature is what it is, though there may be different degrees of savagery, and, as different circumstances arise, the general rules will admit of some variety. In times of peace and prosperity cities and individuals alike follow higher standards, because they are not forced into a situation where they have to do what they do not want to do. But war is a stern teacher; in depriving them of the power of easily satisfying their daily wants, it brings most people's minds down to the level of their actual circumstances.

So revolutions broke out in city after city, and in places where the revolutions occurred late the knowledge of what had happened previously in other places caused still new extravagances of revolutionary zeal, expressed by an elaboration in the methods of seizing power and by unheard-of atrocities in revenge. To fit in with the change of events, words, too, had to change their usual meanings. What used to be described as a thoughtless act of aggression was now regarded as the courage one would expect to find in a party member; to think of the future and wait was merely another way of saying one was a coward; any idea of moderation was just an attempt to disguise one's unmanly character; ability to understand a question from all sides meant that one was totally unfitted for action. Fanatical enthusiasm was the mark of a real man, and to plot against an enemy behind his back was perfectly legitimate self-defence. Anyone who held violent opinions could always be trusted, and anyone who objected to them became a suspect. To plot successfully was a sign of intelligence, but it was still cleverer to see that a plot was hatching. If one attempted to provide against having to do either, one was disrupting the unity of the party and acting out of fear of the opposition. In short, it was equally praiseworthy to get one's blow in first against someone who was going to do wrong, and to denounce someone who had no intention of doing any wrong at all. Family relations were a weaker tie than party membership, since party members were more ready to go to any extreme for any reason whatever. These parties were not formed to enjoy the benefits of the established laws, but to acquire power by overthrowing the existing regime and the members of these parties felt confidence in each other not because of any fellowship in a religious communion, but because they were partners in crime. If an opponent made a reasonable speech, the party in power, so far from giving it a generous reception, took every precaution to see that it had no practical effect. . . .

Love of power, operating through greed and through personal ambition, was the cause of all these evils. To this must be added the violent fanaticism which came into play once the struggle had broken out. Leaders of parties in the cities had programmes which appeared admirable—on one side political equality for the masses, on the other the safe and sound government of the aristocracy—but in professing to serve the public interest they were seeking to win the prizes for themselves. In their struggles for ascendancy nothing was barred; terrible indeed were the actions to which they committed themselves, and in taking revenge they went farther still. Here they were deterred neither by the claims of justice nor by the interests of the state; their one standard was the pleasure of their own party at that particular moment, and so, either by means of condemning their enemies on an illegal vote or by violently usurping power over them, they were always ready to satisfy the hatreds of the hour. Thus neither side had any use for conscientious motives; more interest was shown in those who could produce attractive

arguments to justify some disgraceful action. As for the citizens who held moderate views, they were destroyed by both the extreme parties, either for not taking part in the struggle or in envy at the possibility that they might survive.

As the result of these revolutions, there was a general deterioration of character throughout the Greek world. The simple way of looking at things, which is so much the mark of a noble nature, was regarded as a ridiculous quality and soon ceased to exist. Society had become divided into two ideologically hostile camps, and each side viewed the other with suspicion. As for ending this state of affairs, no guarantee could be given that would be trusted, no oath sworn that people would fear to break; everyone had come to the conclusion that it was hopeless to expect a permanent settlement and so, instead of being able to feel confident in others, they devoted their energies to providing against being injured themselves. As a rule those who were least remarkable for intelligence showed the greater powers of survival. Such people recognized their own deficiencies and the superior intelligence of their opponents; fearing that they might lose a debate or find themselves outmanoeuvred in intrigue by their quick-witted enemies, they boldly launched straight into action; while their opponents, over-confident in the belief that they would see what was happening in advance, and not thinking it necessary to seize by force what they could secure by policy, were the more easily destroyed because they were off their guard.

Certainly it was in Corcyra that there occurred the first examples of the breakdown of law and order. There was the revenge taken in their hour of triumph by those who had in the past been arrogantly oppressed instead of wisely governed; there were the wicked resolutions taken by those who, particularly under the pressure of misfortune, wished to escape from their usual poverty and coveted the property of their neighbours; there were the savage and pitiless actions into which men were carried not so much for the sake of gain as because they were swept away into an internecine struggle by their ungovernable passions. Then, with the ordinary conventions of civilized life thrown into confusion, human nature, always ready to offend even where laws exist, showed itself proudly in its true colours, as something incapable of controlling passion, insubordinate to the idea of justice, the enemy to anything superior to itself; for, if it had not been for the pernicious power of envy, men would not so have exalted vengeance above innocence and profit above justice. Indeed, it is true that in these acts of revenge on others men take it upon themselves to begin the process of repealing those general laws of humanity which are there to give a hope of salvation to all who are in distress, instead of leaving those laws in existence, remembering that there may come a time when they, too, will be in danger and will need their protection.

REVIEW QUESTIONS

1. In what way did the debate between the Athenians and Melians reflect the new rationalist spirit in Greek society?
2. Evaluate the performance of the Melian negotiators.
3. What types of political behavior did Thucydides hold in contempt?

11 Socrates: The Rational Individual

Socrates (469–399 B.C.) marked a decisive turning point in Greek philosophy and in the history of Western thought. The Socratic conception of the rational individual became an essential component of the tradition of classical humanism. Socrates agreed with the Sophists that the study of physical nature was less important than the study of man. But whereas the Sophists concentrated on teaching specific skills—how to excel in debates, for example—Socrates was concerned with comprehending and improving human character. Although ethical concerns lay at the center of Socrates' thought, he never provided a list of ethical commands; in Socratic philosophy, there is nothing comparable to the Ten Commandments. What he did provide was a method—the dialectic or dialogue—of arriving at knowledge, including moral values.

For Socrates, the dialogue (the asking and answering of questions between two or more individuals) was the sole avenue to moral insights and self-knowledge. The interchange implied that a human mind was not a passive vessel into which a teacher poured knowledge. Participants in a dialogue were obliged to play an active role and to think critically about human values. The use of the dialogue implied further that relations between people should involve rational discussion through which people learn from each other and improve themselves.

When Socrates was seventy, he was accused by his enemies of corrupting the youth of Athens and of not believing in the city's gods but in other, new divinities, and he went on trial for his life.

Plato
THE APOLOGY

Knowledge of Socrates' trial comes principally from *The Apology* written by Plato, Socrates' most illustrious student. (The original meaning of *apology* was a defense or explanation.) In the first passage from *The Apology*, presented below, Socrates tells the court that the Delphic Oracle, the prophetess of Apollo at Delphi, had said that there was no one wiser than Socrates. Not considering himself wise, Socrates resolved to discover what the oracle meant, by conversing with people reputed to be wise.

I went to a man who seemed wise: thinking that there, if anywhere, I should prove the answer wrong, and be able to say to the oracle, "You said that I am the wisest of men; but this man is wiser than I am." So I examined him—I need not tell you his name, he was a public man, but this was the result, Athenians. When I conversed with him, I came to see that, though many persons, and chiefly he himself, thought that he was wise, yet he was not wise. And then I tried to show him that he was not wise, though he fancied that he was; and by that I gained his hatred, and the hatred of many of the bystanders. So when I went away, I thought to myself, "I am wiser than this man: neither of us probably knows anything that is really good, but he thinks that he has knowledge, when he has it not, while I, seeing that I have no knowledge, do not think that I have." In this point, at least, I seem to be a little wiser than he is; I do not think that I know what I do not know. Next I went to another man, who seemed to be still wiser, with just the same result. And there again I gained his hatred. . . . After the public men I went to the poets, tragic, dithyrambic [frenzied], and others, thinking there to find myself manifestly more ignorant than they. So I took up the poems on which I thought that they had spent most pains, and asked them what they meant wishing also for instruction. I am ashamed to tell you the truth, my friends, but I must say it. In short, almost any of the bystanders would have spoken better about the works of these poets than the poets themselves.

So I soon found that it is not by wisdom that the poets create their works, but by a certain natural power, and by inspiration, like soothsayers and prophets: for though such persons say many fine things, they know nothing of what they say. And the poets seemed to me to be in a like case. And at the same time I perceived that, because of their poetry, they thought that they were the wisest of men in other matters too, which they were not. So I went away again, thinking that I had the same advantage over them as over the public men.

Finally I went to the artisans: for I was conscious, in a word, that I had no knowledge at all, and I was sure that I should find that they knew many fine things. And in that I was not mistaken. They knew what I did not know, and so far they were wiser than I. But, Athenians, it seemed to me that the skilled craftsmen made the same mistake as the poets. Each of them claimed to have great wisdom in the highest matters because he was skilful in his own art; and this fault of theirs threw their real wisdom into the shade. So I asked myself on behalf of the oracle whether I would choose to remain as I was, neither wise in their wisdom nor ignorant in their ignorance, or to have both, as they had them. And I made answer to myself and to the oracle that it were better for me to remain as I was.

This search, Athenians, has gained me much hatred of a very fierce and bitter kind, which has caused many false accusations against me; and I am called by the name of wise. For the bystanders always think that I am wise myself in any matter wherein I convict another man of ignorance. But in truth, my friends, perhaps it is God who is wise: and by this oracle he may have meant that man's wisdom is worth little or nothing. He did not mean, I think, that Socrates is wise: he only took me as an example, and made use of my name, as though he would say to men: "He among you is wisest, who, like Socrates, is convinced that for wisdom he is verily worthless." And therefore I still go about searching and testing every man whom I think wise, whether he be a citizen or a stranger, according to the word of the God [Apollo]; and whenever I find that he is not wise, I point that out to him in the service of the God. And I am so busy in this pursuit that I have never had leisure to take any part worth mentioning in public matters, or to look after my private affairs. I am in very great poverty by my service to the God.

And besides this, the young men who follow me about, who are the sons of wealthy persons and with much leisure, by nature delight in hearing men cross-questioned: and they often imitate me among themselves: then they try their hand at cross-questioning other people. And, I imagine, they find a great abundance of men who think that they know a great deal, when in truth they know little or nothing. And then the persons who are cross-questioned are angry with me instead of with themselves: and say that Socrates is an abominable fellow who corrupts the young. And when they are asked, Why, what does he do? what does he teach? they have nothing to say; but, not to seem at a loss, they repeat the stock charges against all philosophers, and say that he investigates things in the air and under the earth, and that he teaches people to disbelieve in the gods, and "to make the worst appear the better reason." For I fancy they would not like to confess the truth, that they are shown up as mere ignorant pretenders to knowledge. And so they have filled your ears with their fierce slanders for a long time, for they are zealous and fierce, and numerous: they are well-disciplined too, and plausible in speech. . . .

Had Socrates been willing to compromise and to stop teaching his philosophy, it is likely that he would not have received the death penalty. However, for Socrates the pursuit of truth was the highest human activity; it involved the person's whole being. It transformed the individual, enabling him to live in accordance with moral values that had been arrived at through thought and that could be defended rationally.

. . . But I know well that it is evil and base to do wrong and to disobey my better, whether he be man or god. And I will never choose what I know to be evil, and fear and fly from what may possibly be a good. And so, even if you acquit me now, and do not listen to Anytus' [his prosecutor's] argument that I ought never to have been brought to trial, if I was to be acquitted; and that as it is, you are bound to put me to death, because if I were to escape, all your children would forthwith be utterly corrupted by practising what Socrates teaches: if you were therefore to say to me, "Socrates, this time we will not listen to Anytus: we will let you go: but on this condition, that you cease from carrying on this search, and from philosophy: if you are found doing that again, you shall die:" I say, if you offered to let me go on these terms, I should reply:—"Athenians, I hold you in the highest regard and love; but I will obey the God rather than you: and as long as I have breath and power I will not cease from philosophy, and from exhorting you and setting forth the truth to any of you whom I meet, saying as I am wont, 'My excellent friend, you are a citizen of Athens, a city very great and very famous for wisdom and power of mind: are you not ashamed of caring so much for the making of money, and for reputation and honour? Will you not spend thought or care on wisdom and truth and the perfecting of your soul?' " And if he dispute my words, and say that he does care for these things, I shall not forthwith release him and go away: I shall question him and cross-examine him: and if I think that he has not virtue, though he says that he has, I shall reproach him for setting the least value on the most important things; and the greater value on the more worthless. This shall I do to every one whom I meet, old or young, citizen or stranger; but especially to the citizens, for they are more nearly akin to me. For know well, the God commands me so to do. And I think that nothing better has ever happened to you in your city than my service to the God. For I spend my whole life in going about persuading you all, both young and old, to give your first and chiefest care to the perfection of your souls: and not till you have done that to care for your bodies or your wealth. I tell you, that virtue does not come from wealth, but that wealth and every other good, whether public or private, which men have, come from virtue. If then I corrupt the youth by this teaching, the mischief is great; but if any man says that I teach anything else, he speaks falsely. And therefore, Athenians, I say, either listen to Anytus, or do not listen to him: either acquit me, or do not acquit me: but be sure that I shall not alter my life; no, not if I have to die for it many times.

Do not interrupt me, Athenians. Remember the request which I made to you, and listen to my words. I think that it will do you good to hear them. I have something more to say to you, at which perhaps you will cry out: but do not do that. Be sure that if you kill me, a man such as I say I am, you will harm yourselves more than you will harm me. Meletus [another prosecutor] and Anytus can do me no harm; that is impossible, for I do not think that God will allow a good man to be harmed by a bad one. They may indeed kill me, or drive me into exile, or deprive me of my civil rights; and perhaps Meletus and others think these things great evils. But I do not think so: I think that to do as he is doing, and to try to kill a man unjustly, is a much greater evil. And now, Athenians, I am not going to argue for my own sake at all, as you might think, but for yours, that you may not sin against the God and reject his gift to you, by condemning me. If you put me to death, you will hardly find another man to fill my place. The God has sent me to

attack the city, if I may use a ludicrous simile, just as if it were a great and noble horse, which was rather sluggish from its size and needed a gadfly to rouse it: and I think that I am the gadfly that the God has set upon the city: for I never cease settling on you as it were at every point, and rousing, and exhorting, and reproaching each man of you all day long. You will hardly find any one else, my friends, to fill my place: and, if you take my advice, you will spare my life. You are indignant, as drowsy persons are when they are awakened, and, of course, if you are persuaded by Anytus, you could easily kill me with a single blow, and then sleep on undisturbed for the rest of your lives. . . .

Perhaps someone will say, "Why cannot you withdraw from Athens, Socrates, and hold your peace?" It is the most difficult thing in the world to make you understand why I cannot do that. If I say that I cannot hold my peace because that would be to disobey the God, you will think that I am not in earnest and will not believe me. And if I tell you that no greater good can happen to a man than to discuss human excellence every day and the other matters about which you have heard me arguing and examining myself and others, and that an unexamined life is not worth living, then you will believe me still less. But that is so, my friends, though it is not easy to persuade you. . . .

Socrates is convicted and sentenced to death.

. . . Perhaps, my friends, you think that I have been convicted because I was wanting in the arguments by which I could have persuaded you to acquit me, if I had thought it right to do or to say anything to escape punishment. It is not so. I have been convicted because I was wanting, not in arguments, but in impudence and shamelessness—because I would not plead before you as you would have liked to hear me plead, or appeal to you with weeping and wailing, or say and do many other things which I maintain are unworthy of me, but which you have been accustomed to from other men. But when I was defending myself, I thought that I ought not to do anything unworthy of a free man because of the danger which I ran, and I have not changed my mind now. I would very much rather defend myself as I did, and die, than as you would have had me do, and live. . . .

And now I wish to prophesy to you, Athenians, who have condemned me. For I am going to die, and that is the time when men have most prophetic power. And I prophesy to you who have sentenced me to death that a far more severe punishment than you have inflicted on me will surely overtake you as soon as I am dead.

You have done this thing, thinking that you will be relieved from having to give an account of your lives. But I say that the result will be very different. There will be more men who will call you to account, whom I have held back, though you did not recognize it. And they will be harsher toward you than I have been, for they will be younger, and you will be more indignant with them. For if you think that you will restrain men from reproaching you for not living as you should, by putting them to death, you are very much mistaken. That way of escape is neither possible nor honorable. It is much more honorable and much easier not to suppress others, but to make yourselves as good as you can. This is my parting prophecy to you who have condemned me.

REVIEW QUESTIONS

1. What is the nature of Socrates' wisdom?
2. Was Socrates a subversive force in Athenian society? Explain your answer.
3. According to Socrates, what is the true vocation of a philosopher? What price may the philosopher pay for his effort?
4. Compare and contrast the vocation of Socrates as a philosopher to that of the Hebrew prophets.
5. Why did some Athenians believe that Socrates corrupted the young?
6. What did Socrates say would be his reaction if he were offered an acquittal on the condition that he give up teaching his philosophy? What were his reasons?

12 Plato: The Philosopher-King

Plato (c. 429–347 B.C.), an Athenian aristocrat and disciple of Socrates, based his philosophy on Socrates' teachings. Plato was greatly affected by the deterioration of Athenian politics during and immediately after the Peloponnesian War. The rise of demagogues, the violent conflicts between oligarchs and democrats, and the execution of Socrates convinced Plato that Athenian democracy was a failure. His hostility toward democracy also stemmed from his upper-class background and temperament.

Socratic philosophy held promise of reforming the individual through the critical use of reason. Plato felt that the individual could not undergo a moral transformation while living in a wicked and corrupt society. For the individual to be able to achieve virtue, the state must be reformed.

Plato
THE REPUBLIC

In *The Republic*, Plato proposed organizing government in harmony with the needs of human nature. Those people who are driven by a desire for food, possessions, and sexual gratification, Plato said, should be farmers, tradesmen, or artisans. Those who are naturally courageous and assertive should be soldiers. And the few who have the capacity for wisdom—the philosophers—should be entrusted with political power.

 In the ideal state, Plato asserted, the many would be ruled by the few who have a natural endowment for leadership. These philosopher-kings, the finest product of the state's carefully designed educational program, would wield absolute power: the people would lose their right to participate in political affairs, and the state would manufacture propaganda and strictly control education in order to keep the masses obedient. In exchange, the citizens would gain leaders distinguished by their rationality, wisdom, and virtue. In the form of a dialogue between Socrates and a man called Glaucon, Plato in the following reading presents his views on the character of the philosopher.

[SOCRATES] Unless either philosophers become kings in their countries or those who are now called kings and rulers come to be sufficiently inspired with a genuine desire for wisdom; unless that is to say, political power and philosophy meet together . . . there can be no rest from troubles, my dear Glaucon, for states, nor yet, as I believe, for all mankind. . . . There is no other way of happiness either for the state or for the individual. . . .

Now . . . we must, I think, define . . . whom we mean by these lovers of wisdom who, we have dared to assert, ought to be our rulers. Once we have a clear view of their character, we shall be able to defend our position by pointing to some who are naturally fitted to combine philosophic study with political leadership, while the rest of the world should accept their guidance and let philosophy alone.

[GLAUCON] Yes, this is the moment for a definition. . . .

[S] . . . One trait of the philosophic nature we may take as already granted: a constant passion for any knowledge that will reveal to them something of that reality which endures for ever and is not always passing into and out of existence. And, we may add, their desire is to know the whole of that reality; they will not willingly renounce any part of it as relatively small and insignificant, as we said before when we compared them to the lover and to the man who covets honour.

[G] True.

[S] Is there not another trait which the nature we are seeking cannot fail to possess—truthfulness, a love of truth and a hatred for falsehood that will not tolerate untruth in any form?

[G] Yes, it is natural to expect that.

[S] It is not merely natural, but entirely necessary that an instinctive passion for any object should extend to all that is closely akin to it; and there is nothing more closely akin to wisdom than truth. So the same nature cannot love wisdom and falsehood; the genuine lover of knowledge cannot fail, from his youth up, to strive after the whole of truth.

[G] I perfectly agree.

[S] Now we surely know that when a man's desires set strongly in one direction, in every other channel they flow more feebly, like a stream diverted into another bed. So when the current has set towards knowledge and all that goes with it, desire will abandon those pleasures of which the body is the instrument and be concerned only with the pleasure which the soul enjoys independently—if, that is to say, the love of wisdom is more than a mere pretence. Accordingly, such a one will be temperate and no lover of money; for he will be the last person to care about the things for the sake of which money is eagerly sought and lavishly spent.

[G] That is true.

[S] Again, in seeking to distinguish the philosophic nature, you must not overlook the least touch of meanness. Nothing could be more contrary than pettiness to a mind constantly bent on grasping the whole of things, both divine and human.

[G] Quite true.

[S] And do you suppose that one who is so high-minded and whose thought can contemplate all time and all existence will count this life of man a matter of much concern?

[G] No, he could not.

[S] So for such a man death will have no terrors.

[G] None.

[S] A mean and cowardly nature, then, can have no part in the genuine pursuit of wisdom.

[G] I think not.

[S] And if a man is temperate and free from the love of money, meanness, pretentiousness, and cowardice, he will not be hard to deal with or dishonest. So, as another indication of the philosophic temper, you will observe whether, from youth up, he is fair-minded, gentle, and sociable.

[G] Certainly.

[S] Also you will not fail to notice whether he is quick or slow to learn. No one can be expected to take a reasonable delight in a task in which much painful effort makes little headway. And if he cannot retain what he learns, his forgetfulness will leave no room in his head for knowledge; and so, having all his toil for nothing, he can only end by hating himself as well

as his fruitless occupation. We must not, then, count a forgetful mind as competent to pursue wisdom; we must require a good memory.

[G] By all means.

[S] Further, there is in some natures a crudity and awkwardness that can only tend to a lack of measure and proportion; and there is a close affinity between proportion and truth. Hence, besides our other requirements, we shall look for a mind endowed with measure and grace, which will be instinctively drawn to see every reality in its true light.

[G] Yes.

[S] Well then, now that we have enumerated the qualities of a mind destined to take its full part in the apprehension of reality, have you any doubt about their being indispensable and all necessarily going together?

[G] None whatever.

[S] Then have you any fault to find with a pursuit which none can worthily follow who is not by nature quick to learn and to remember, magnanimous and gracious, the friend and kinsman of truth, justice, courage, temperance?

Plato said that genuine philosophers are "those whose passion it is to see the truth." For Plato, unlike the Sophists, standards of beauty, justice, and goodness exist that are universally valid—that apply to all peoples at all times. Plato held that these standards are in a higher world, the realm of Forms or Ideas. This world of Forms is known only through the mind, not the senses. For example, a sculptor observes many bodies but they all possess flaws; in his mind's eye he perceives the world of Ideas and tries to reproduce with his art the perfect human form. Plato says that the ordinary person, basing opinion on everyday experience, has an imperfect understanding of beauty, goodness, and justice, whereas the philosopher, through reason, reaches beyond sense perception to the realm of Forms and discovers truth. Such people are the natural rulers of the state; only they are capable of a correct understanding of justice; only they have the wisdom to reform the state in the best interests of all its citizens.

The distinction between a higher world of truth and a lower world of imperfection, deception, and illusion is illustrated in Plato's famous Allegory of the Cave. Plato, through the dialogue of Socrates and Glaucon, compares those persons without a knowledge of the Forms to prisoners in a dark cave.

[S] Next, said I, here is a parable to illustrate the degrees in which our nature may be enlightened or unenlightened. Imagine the condition of men living in a sort of cavernous chamber underground, with an entrance open to the light and a long passage all down the cave. Here they have been from childhood, chained by the leg and also by the neck, so that they cannot move and can see only what is in front of them, because the chains will not let them turn their heads. At some distance higher up is the light of a fire burning behind them; and between the prisoners and the fire is a track with a parapet built along it, like the screen at a puppet-show, which hides the performers while they show their puppets over the top.

[G] I see, said he.

[S] Now behind this parapet imagine persons carrying along various artificial objects, including figures of men and animals in wood or stone or other materials, which project above the parapet. Naturally, some of these persons will be talking, others silent.

[G] It is a strange picture, he said, and a strange sort of prisoners.

[S] Like ourselves, I replied; for in the first place prisoners so confined would have seen nothing of themselves or of one another, except the shadows thrown by the fire-light on the wall of the Cave facing them, would they?

[G] Not if all their lives they had been prevented from moving their heads.

[S] And they would have seen as little of the objects carried past.

[G] Of course.

[S] Now, if they could talk to one another, would they not suppose that their words referred only to those passing shadows which they saw?

[G] Necessarily.

[S] And suppose their prison had an echo from the wall facing them? When one of the people crossing behind them spoke, they could only suppose that the sound came from the shadow passing before their eyes.

[G] No doubt.

[S] In every way, then, such prisoners would recognize as reality nothing but the shadows of those artificial objects.

[G] Inevitably. . . .

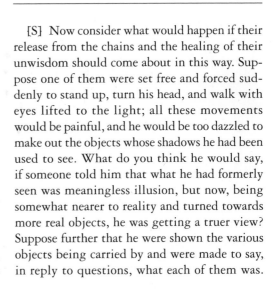

To the prisoners chained in the cave, the shadows of the artificial objects constitute reality. When a freed prisoner ascends from the cave to the sunlight, he sees a totally different world. Returning to the cave, he tries to tell the prisoners that the shadows are only poor imitations of reality, but they laugh at him, for their opinions have been shaped by the only world they know. The meaning of the parable is clear: the philosophers who ascend to the higher world of Forms possess true knowledge; everyone else possesses mere opinions, deceptive beliefs, and illusions. The philosophers have a duty to guide the ignorant.

[S] Now consider what would happen if their release from the chains and the healing of their unwisdom should come about in this way. Suppose one of them were set free and forced suddenly to stand up, turn his head, and walk with eyes lifted to the light; all these movements would be painful, and he would be too dazzled to make out the objects whose shadows he had been used to see. What do you think he would say, if someone told him that what he had formerly seen was meaningless illusion, but now, being somewhat nearer to reality and turned towards more real objects, he was getting a truer view? Suppose further that he were shown the various objects being carried by and were made to say, in reply to questions, what each of them was.

Would he not be perplexed and believe the objects now shown him to be not so real as what he formerly saw?

[G] Yes, not nearly so real.

[S] And if he were forced to look at the fire-light itself, would not his eyes ache, so that he would try to escape and turn back to the things which he could see distinctly, convinced that they really were clearer than these other objects now being shown to him?

[G] Yes.

[S] And suppose someone were to drag him away forcibly up the steep and rugged ascent and not let him go until he had hauled him out into the sunlight, would he not suffer pain and vexation at such treatment, and, when he had come out into the light, find his eyes so full of its radiance that he could not see a single one of the things that he was now told were real?

[G] Certainly he would not see them all at once.

[S] He would need, then, to grow accustomed before he could see things in that upper world. At first it would be easiest to make out shadows, and then the images of men and things reflected in water, and later on the things themselves. After that, it would be easier to watch the heavenly bodies and the sky itself by night, looking at the light of the moon and stars rather than the Sun and the Sun's light in the day-time.

[G] Yes, surely.

[S] Last of all, he would be able to look at the Sun and contemplate its nature, not as it appears when reflected in water or any alien medium, but as it is in itself in its own domain.

[G] No doubt.

[S] And now he would begin to draw the conclusion that it is the Sun that produces the seasons and the course of the year and controls everything in the visible world, and moreover is in a way the cause of all that he and his companions used to see.

[G] Clearly he would come at last to that conclusion.

[S] Then if he called to mind his fellow prisoners and what passed for wisdom in his former dwelling place, he would surely think himself happy in the change and be sorry for them. They may have had a practice of honouring and commending one another, with prizes for the man who had the keenest eye for the passing shadows and the best memory for the order in which they followed or accompanied one another, so that he could make a good guess as to which was going to come next. Would our released prisoner be likely to covet those prizes or to envy the men exalted to honour and power in the Cave? Would he not feel like Homer's Achilles, that he would far sooner "be on earth as a hired servant in the house of a landless man" or endure anything rather than go back to his old beliefs and live in the old way?

[G] Yes, he would prefer any fate to such a life.

[S] Now imagine what would happen if he went down again to take his former seat in the Cave. Coming suddenly out of the sunlight, his eyes would be filled with darkness. He might be required once more to deliver his opinion on those shadows, in competition with the prisoners who had never been released, while his eyesight was still dim and unsteady; and it might take some time to become used to the darkness. They would laugh at him and say that he had gone up only to come back with his sight ruined; it was worth no one's while even to attempt the ascent. If they could lay hands on the man who was trying to set them free and lead them up, they would kill him.

[G] Yes, they would.

[S] Every feature in this parable, my dear Glaucon, is meant to fit our earlier analysis. The prison dwelling corresponds to the region revealed to us through the sense of sight, and the firelight within it to the power of the Sun. The ascent to see the things in the upper world you may take as standing for the upward journey of the soul into the region of the intelligible; then you will be in possession of what I surmise, since that is what you wish to be told.

Heaven knows whether it is true; but this, at any rate, is how it appears to me. In the world of knowledge, the last thing to be perceived and only with great difficulty is the essential Form of Goodness. Once it is perceived, the conclusion must follow that, for all things, this is the cause of whatever is right and good; in the visible world it gives birth to light and to the lord of light, while it is itself sovereign in the intelligible world and the parent of intelligence and truth. Without having had a vision of this Form no one can act with wisdom, either in his own life or in matters of state. . . .

For Plato, the perfect state, like the well-formed soul, is one governed by reason. By contrast, in the imperfect state, as in the imperfect soul, greed, selfishness, desire, and disorder predominate. Democracy is flawed, said Plato, because most people lack the ability to deal intelligently with matters of state. In the end, said Plato, the democratic state degenerates into anarchy, and the way is prepared for a tyrant. Plato viewed the tyrant as the most despicable of persons. A slave to his own passions, said Plato, the tyrant is like a lunatic who "dreams that he can lord it over all mankind and heaven besides." The character of the philosopher is the very opposite of the sick soul of the tyrant. In the following passage, Plato discusses what he regards as democracy's weaknesses.

[S] And when the poor win, the result is a democracy. They kill some of the opposite party, banish others, and grant the rest an equal share in civil rights and government, officials being usually appointed by lot.

[G] Yes, that is how a democracy comes to be established, whether by force of arms or because the other party is terrorized into giving way.

[S] Now what is the character of this new régime? Obviously the way they govern themselves will throw light on the democratic type of man.

[G] No doubt.

[S] First of all, they are free. Liberty and free speech are rife everywhere; anyone is allowed to do what he likes.

[G] Yes, so we are told.

[S] That being so, every man will arrange his own manner of life to suit his pleasure. The result will be a greater variety of individuals than under any other constitution. So it may be the finest of all, with its variegated pattern of all sorts of characters. Many people may think it the best, just as women and children might admire a mixture of colours of every shade in the pattern of a dress. At any rate if we are in search of a constitution, here is a good place to look for one. A democracy is so free that it contains a sample of every kind; and perhaps anyone who intends to found a state, as we have been doing, ought first to visit this emporium of constitutions and choose the model he likes best.

[G] He will find plenty to choose from.

[S] Here, too, you are not obliged to be in authority, however competent you may be, or to submit to authority, if you do not like it; you need not fight when your fellow citizens are at war, nor remain at peace when they do, unless you want peace; and though you may have no legal right to hold office or sit on juries, you will do so all the same if the fancy takes you. . . .

. . . When he [the democrat] is told that some pleasures should be sought and valued as arising from desires of a higher order, others chastised and enslaved because the desires are base, he will shut the gates of the citadel against the messengers of truth, shaking his head and declaring that one appetite is as good as another and all must have their equal rights. So he spends his days indulging the pleasure of the moment, now intoxicated with wine and music, and then taking to a spare diet and drinking nothing but water; one day in hard training, the next doing nothing at all, the third apparently immersed in study. Every now and then he takes a part in politics, leaping to his feet to say or do whatever comes into his head. . . . His life is subject to no order or restraint, and he has no wish to change an existence which he calls pleasant, free, and happy.

That well describes the life of one whose motto is liberty and equality. . . .

In a democratic country you will be told that liberty is its noblest possession, which makes it the only fit place for a free spirit to live in.

[G] True; that is often said.

[S] Well then, as I was saying, perhaps the insatiable desire for this good to the neglect of everything else may transform a democracy and lead to a demand for despotism. A democratic state may fall under the influence of unprincipled leaders, ready to minister to its thirst for liberty with too deep draughts of this heady wine; and then, if its rulers are not complaisant enough to give it unstinted freedom, they will be arraigned as accursed oligarchs and punished. Law-abiding citizens will be insulted as nonentities who hug their chains; and all praise and honour will be bestowed, both publicly and in private, on rulers who behave like subjects and subjects who behave like rulers. In such a state the spirit of liberty is bound to go to all lengths. . . .

. . . The parent falls into the habit of behaving like the child, and the child like the parent: the father is afraid of his sons, and they show no fear or respect for their parents, in order to assert their freedom. . . . To descend to smaller matters, the schoolmaster timidly flatters his pupils, and the pupils make light of their masters as well as of their attendants. Generally speaking, the young copy their elders, argue with them, and will not do as they are told; while the old, anxious not to be thought disagreeable tyrants, imitate the young and condescend to enter into their jokes and amusements. . . .

Putting all these items together, you can see the result: the citizens become so sensitive that they resent the slightest application of control as intolerable tyranny, and in their resolve to have no master they end by disregarding even the law, written or unwritten.

[G] Yes, I know that only too well.

[S] Such then, I should say, is the seed, so full of fair promise, from which springs despotism.

REVIEW QUESTIONS

1. According to Plato, what were the character traits a philosopher should possess? What traits should he avoid?
2. In terms of the Allegory of the Cave, what is real and what is illusion?
3. Why did Plato believe that philosophers would make the best rulers?
4. In Plato's view, what were the principal arguments against democracy? What is your assessment of his critique?

13 Aristotle: Science, Politics, and Ethics

Aristotle (384–322 B.C.) was born at Stagira, a Greek city-state on the Macedonian coast. About 367 B.C., he came to Athens to study with Plato, and he remained a member of Plato's Academy for twenty years. In 342 B.C., Philip II, king of Macedonia, invited Aristotle to tutor his son Alexander, who was then fourteen-years old. When Alexander succeeded Philip and set out to conquer the Persian Empire, Aristotle left Macedonia for Athens, where he opened a school of philosophy called the Lyceum, named for a nearby temple to Apollo Lyceus. Aristotle synthesized the thought of earlier philosophers, including his teacher Plato, and was the leading authority of his day in virtually every field of knowledge.

Aristotle
HISTORY OF ANIMALS, POLITICS,
AND NICOMACHEAN ETHICS

Scientific thinking encompasses both rationalism and empiricism. Rationalism—pursuit of truth through thought alone, independent of experience with the natural world—was advocated by Plato. This approach points in the direction of theoretical mathematics. Like Plato, Aristotle valued reason, but unlike his teacher he also had great respect for the concrete details of nature obtained through sense experience. In *History of Animals*, Aristotle demonstrated his empirical approach: observing nature and collecting, classifying, and analyzing data. Aristotle's empiricism is the foundation of such sciences as geology, botany, and biology. The first excerpt, a careful observation of the development of a chick embryo, illustrates Aristotle's empiricism.

When he turned to the study of politics, Aristotle also followed an empirical methodology. He undertook a series of historical studies of the constitutions of 158 Greek states. The most significant and complete study that has survived describes the constitution of Athens. On the basis of these extensive surveys, Aristotle proceeded to write *Politics*, his masterwork of political philosophy, excerpted in the second reading.

Like Socrates and Plato, Aristotle based his ethics on reason. People could achieve moral well-being, said Aristotle, when they avoided extremes of behavior and rationally chose the way of moderation. In his *Nicomachean Ethics*, dedicated to his son Nicomachus, Aristotle described the "proud man." This passage, excerpted in the third reading, sketches characteristics that make up the Greek ideal of excellence.

HISTORY OF ANIMALS

. . . With the common hen after three days and three nights there is the first indication of the embryo; with larger birds the interval being longer, with smaller birds shorter. Meanwhile the yolk comes into being, rising towards the sharp end, where the primal element of the egg is situated, and where the egg gets hatched; and the heart appears, like a speck of blood, in the white of the egg. This point beats and moves as though endowed with life, . . . and a membrane carrying bloody fibres now envelops the yolk. . . . A little afterwards the body is differentiated, at first very small and white. The head is clearly distinguished, and in it the eyes, swollen out to a great extent. This condition of the eyes lasts on for a good while, as it is only by degrees that they diminish in size and collapse. At the outset the under portion of the body appears insignificant in comparison with the upper portion. . . . The life-element of the chick is in the white of the egg, and the nutriment comes through the navel-string out of the yolk.

When the egg is now ten days old the chick and all its parts are distinctly visible. The head is still larger than the rest of its body, and the eyes larger than the head, but still devoid of vision. The eyes, if removed about this time, are found to be larger than beans, and black; if the cuticle be peeled off them there is a white and cold liquid inside, quite glittering in the sunlight, but there is no hard substance whatsoever. Such is the condition of the head and eyes. At this time also the larger internal organs are visible. . . .

About the twentieth day, if you open the egg and touch the chick, it moves inside and chirps; and it is already coming to be covered with down, when, after the twentieth day is past, the chick begins to break the shell. The head is situated over the right leg close to the flank, and the wing is placed over the head. . . .

In the following selection from Politics, Aristotle begins by defining the nature of a state and its purpose.

POLITICS

It is clear therefore that the state cannot be defined merely as a community dwelling in the same place and preventing its members from wrong-doing and promoting the exchange of goods and services. Certainly all these must be present if there is to be a state, but even the presence of every one of them does not *ipso facto* [by that fact] make a state. The state is intended to enable all, in their households and their kinships, to live *well*, meaning by that a full and satisfying life. . . .

He then addresses the problem of where the sovereign power of the state ought to reside.

. . . "Where ought the sovereign power of the state to reside?" With the people? With the propertied classes? With the good? With one man, the best of all the good? With one man, the tyrant? There are objections to all these. Thus suppose we say the people is the supreme authority, then if they use their numerical superiority to make a distribution of the property of the rich, is not that unjust? It has been done by a valid decision of the sovereign power, yet what can we call it save the very height of injustice? Again, if the majority, having laid their hands on everything, distribute the possessions of the few, they are obviously destroying the state. But

that cannot be goodness which destroys its possessor and justice cannot be destructive of the state. So it is clear that this process, though it may be the law, cannot be just. Or, if that is just, the actions taken by a tyrant must be just; his superior power enables him to use force, just as the masses force their will on the rich. Thirdly, if it is just for the few and wealthy to rule, and if they too rob and plunder and help themselves to the goods of the many, is that just? If it is, then it is just in the former case also. The answer clearly is that all these three are bad and unjust. The fourth alternative, that the good should rule and have the supreme authority, is also not free from objection; it means that all the rest must be without official standing, debarred from holding office under the constitution. The fifth alternative, that one man, the best, should rule, is no better; by making the number of rulers fewer we leave still larger numbers without official standing. It might be objected too that it is a bad thing for any human being, subject to all possible disorders and affections of the human mind, to be the sovereign authority, which ought to be reserved for the law itself. . . .

. . . [A]t the moment it would seem that the most defensible, perhaps even the truest, answer to the question would be to say that the majority ought to be sovereign. . . . For where there are many people, each has some share of goodness and intelligence, and when these are brought together, they become as it were one multiple man with many pairs of feet and hands and many minds. So too in regard to character and powers of perception. That is why the general public is a better judge of works of music and poetry; some judge some parts, some others, but their joint pronouncement is a verdict upon the whole. . . .

Aristotle seeks to determine what is the best constitution. His conclusion reflects the premise developed in his Ethics that moderation, or the middle way, is the path to virtue in all things. So, Aristotle says that in forming a constitution for the state, power should reside in the hands of the middle class rather than the aristocracy or the poor.

If we were right when in our *Ethics* we stated that Virtue is a Mean and that the happy life is life free and unhindered and according to virtue, then the best life must be the middle way, [or the mean] . . . between two extremes which it is open to those at either end to attain. And the same principle must be applicable to the goodness or badness of cities and states. For the constitution of a city is really the way it lives.

In all states there are three sections of the community—the very well-off, the very badly off, and those in between. Seeing therefore that it is agreed that moderation and a middle position are best, it is clear that in the matter of possessions to own a middling amount is best of all. This condition is most obedient to reason, and following reason is just what is difficult both for the exceedingly rich, handsome, strong, and well-born, and for the opposite, the extremely poor, the weak, and the downtrodden. The former commit deeds of violence on a large scale, the latter are delinquent and wicked in petty ways. The misdeeds of the one class are due to *hubris* [overweening pride, arrogance], the misdeeds of the other to rascality. . . . There are other drawbacks about the two extremes. Those who have a super-abundance of all that makes for success, strength, riches, friends, and so forth, neither wish to hold office nor understand the work; and this is ingrained in them from childhood on; even at school they are so full of their superiority that they have never learned to do what they are told. Those on the other hand who are greatly deficient in these qualities are too subservient. So they cannot command and can only obey in a servile régime, while the others cannot obey in any régime and can command only in a master-slave relationship. The result is a state not of free men but of slaves and masters, the one full of envy, the other of contempt. Nothing could be farther

removed from friendship or from the whole idea of a shared partnership in a state. . . . The state aims to consist as far as possible of those who are like and equal, a condition found chiefly among the middle section. . . . The middle class is also the steadiest element, the least eager for change. They neither covet, like the poor, the possessions of others, nor do others covet theirs, as the poor covet those of the rich. . . .

It is clear then both that the political partnership which operates through the middle class is best, and also that those cities have every chance of being well-governed in which the middle class is large, stronger if possible than the other two together, or at any rate stronger than one of them. . . . For this reason it is a happy state of affairs when those who take part in the life of the state have a moderate but adequate amount of property. . . . Tyranny often emerges from an over-enthusiastic democracy or from an oligarchy, but much more rarely from middle-class constitutions or from those very near to them.

The superiority of the middle type of constitution is clear also from the fact that it alone is free from fighting among factions. Where the middle element is large, there least of all arise faction and counter-faction among citizens. . . .

The following selection from Ethics shows how Aristotle's ethical theory rests on the principles of moderation and balance. Aristotle notes that some people become "angry at the wrong things, more than is right, and longer, and cannot be appeased until they inflict vengeance or punishment." On the other extreme, foolish and slavish people endure every insult without defending themselves. Between these extremes is the proud man, "who is angry at the right thing and with the right people, and, further, as he ought, when he ought, and as long as he ought." Even-tempered and moderate in all things, such a man "tends to be unperturbed and not to be led by passion."

ETHICS

. . . In the first place, then, as has been said, the proud man is concerned with honours; yet he will also bear himself with moderation towards wealth and power and all good or evil fortune, whatever may befall him, and will be neither over-joyed by good fortune nor over-pained by evil. For not even towards honour does he bear himself as if it were a very great thing. . . .

He does not run into trifling dangers, nor is he fond of danger, because he honours few things; but he will face great dangers, and when he is in danger he is unsparing of his life, knowing that there are conditions on which life is not worth having. And he is the sort of man to confer benefits, but he is ashamed of receiving them; for the one is the mark of a superior, the other of an inferior. And he is apt to confer greater benefits in return; for thus the original benefactor besides being paid will incur a debt to him, and will be the gainer by the transaction. They seem also to remember any service they have done, but not those they have received (for he who receives a service is inferior to him who has done it, but the proud man wishes to be superior), and to hear of the former with pleasure, of the latter with displeasure. . . . It is a mark of the proud man also to ask for nothing or scarcely anything, but to give help readily, and to be dignified towards people who enjoy high position and good fortune, but unassuming towards those of the middle class; for it is a difficult and lofty thing to be superior to the former, but easy to be so to the latter, and a lofty bearing over the former is no mark of ill-breeding, but among humble people it is as vulgar as a display of strength against the weak. Again, it is characteristic of the proud man not to aim at the things commonly held in honour, or the things in which others excel; to be sluggish and to hold back except where great honour or a great work is at stake, and to be a man of few deeds, but of great and notable ones. He must also be open in his hate and in his love (for to conceal one's feelings, i.e., to care less for truth than for what people will think, is a coward's part), and must speak and act openly; for he is free of speech because he is contemptuous, and he is given to telling the truth, except when he speaks in irony to the vulgar. He must be unable to make his life revolve round another, unless it be a friend; for this is slavish, and for this reason all flatterers are servile and people lacking in self-respect are flatterers. Nor is he given to admiration; for nothing to him is great. Nor is he mindful of wrongs; for it is not the part of a proud man to have a long memory, especially for wrongs, but rather to overlook them. Nor is he a gossip; for he will speak neither about himself nor about another, since he cares not to be praised nor for others to be blamed; nor again is he given to praise; and for the same reason he is not an evil-speaker, even about his enemies, except from haughtiness. With regard to necessary or small matters he is least of all men given to lamentation or the asking of favours; for it is the part of one who takes such matters seriously to behave so with respect to them. He is one who will possess beautiful and profitless things rather than profitable and useful ones; for this is more proper to a character that suffices to itself.

Further, a slow step is thought proper to the proud man, a deep voice, and a level utterance; for the man who takes few things seriously is not likely to be hurried, nor the man who thinks nothing great to be excited, while a shrill voice and a rapid gait are the results of hurry and excitement.

Such, then, is the proud man; the man who falls short of him is unduly humble, and the man who goes beyond him is vain.

REVIEW QUESTIONS

1. What evidence in Aristotle's description of chick embryo development illustrates his use of empirical methods of scientific inquiry?

2. Why did Aristotle believe that state power was best left in the hands of the middle classes? Why did he fear government by the poor, the tyrant, the few, the good, or the rich?
3. According to Aristotle, how did the "proud man," a man of excellence, relate to others? To worldly success and riches?
4. What kind of moral values did the proud man cultivate?
5. Aristotle urged both self-sufficiency and moderation as guiding principles in human life. In what specific ways would the proud man demonstrate these virtues?

14 Hellenistic Culture: Universalism and Individualism

During the Hellenistic Age, Greek civilization spread to the Near East in the wake of Alexander's conquests, and Mesopotamian, Egyptian, Persian, and Jewish traditions—particularly religious beliefs—moved westward. Thousands of Greeks settled in newly established cities throughout the ancient Near East, carrying with them Greek urban institutions and culture—laws, cults, educational methods, artistic and architectural styles, customs, and dress. The new Hellenistic cities were dominated by a Greek upper class, which recruited native non-Greeks to its ranks to the degree that they became *Hellenized*—that is, they adopted the Greek language and lifestyle. Through intermarriage, education in Greek schools, and the prospect of political and economic advantage, non-Greeks came to participate in and contribute to a common Greek civilization that spread from the western Mediterranean to the Indus River.

Cultural exchange permeated all phases of cultural life. Sculpture showed the influence of many lands. Historians wrote world histories, not just local ones. Greek astronomers worked with data collected over the centuries by the Babylonians. Greeks increasingly demonstrated a fascination with Near Eastern religious cults. Philosophers helped to break down the barriers between peoples by asserting that all inhabit a single fatherland. As the philosopher Crates said, "My fatherland has no single tower, no single roof. The whole earth is my citadel, a home ready for us all to live in."

Plutarch
CULTURAL FUSION

The Greek biographer Plutarch (c. A.D. 46–120) provides a glowing account of Alexander the Great in the following passage. Plutarch saw Alexander as a philosopher in action and an apostle of universalism and human brotherhood. Many modern historians reject this assessment of Alexander's intentions, but the scope of his conquests and their significance in reducing the distinctions between Near Easterners and Greeks remain impressive.

[W]hen Alexander was civilizing Asia, Homer was commonly read, and the children of the Persians, of the Susianians, and of the Gedrosians[1] learned to chant the tragedies of Sophocles and Euripides. . . . yet through Alexander Bactria[2] and the Caucasus learned to revere the gods of the Greeks. Plato wrote a book on the One Ideal Constitution, but because of its forbidding character he could not persuade anyone to adopt it; but Alexander established more than seventy cities among savage tribes, and sowed all Asia[3] with Grecian magistracies, and thus overcame its uncivilized and brutish manner of living. Although few of us read Plato's *Laws*, yet hundreds of thousands have made use of Alexander's laws, and continue to use them. Those who were vanquished by Alexander are happier than those who escaped his hand; for these had no one to put an end to the wretchedness of their existence, while the victor compelled those others to lead a happy life. . . . Thus Alexander's new subjects would not have been civilized, had they not been vanquished; Egypt would not have its Alexandria, nor Mesopotamia its Seleuceia, nor Sogdiana its Prophthasia, nor India its Bucephalia,[4] nor the Caucasus a Greek city hard by; for by the founding of cities in these places savagery was extinguished and the worse element, gaining familiarity with the better, changed under its influence. If, then, philosophers take the greatest pride in civilizing and rendering adaptable the intractable and untutored elements in human character, and if Alexander has been shown to have changed the savage natures of countless tribes, it is with good reason that he should be regarded as a very great philosopher.

Moreover, the much-admired *Republic* of Zeno, the founder of the Stoic sect, may be summed up in this one main principle: that all the inhabitants of this world of ours should not live differentiated by their respective rules of justice into separate cities and communities, but that we should consider men to be of one community and one polity, and that we should have a common life and an order common to us all, even as a herd that feeds together and shares the pasturage of a common field. This Zeno wrote, giving shape to a dream or, as it were, shadowy picture of a well-ordered and philosophic commonwealth; but it was Alexander who gave effect to the idea. For Alexander did not follow Aristotle's advice to treat the Greeks as if he were their leader, and other peoples as if he were their master; to have regard for the Greeks as for friends and kindred, but to conduct himself toward other peoples as though they were plants or animals; for to do so would have been to cumber his leadership with numerous battles and banishments and festering seditions. But, as he believed that he came as a heaven-sent governor to all, and as a mediator for the whole world, those whom he could not persuade to unite with him, he conquered by force of arms, and he brought together into one body all men everywhere, uniting and mixing in one great loving-cup, as it were, men's lives, their characters, their marriages, their very habits of life. He bade them all consider as their fatherland the whole inhabited earth, as their stronghold and protection his camp, as akin to them all good men, and as foreigners only the wicked; they should not distinguish between Grecian and foreigner by Grecian cloak and targe [shield], or scimitar [curved sword] and jacket; but the distinguishing mark of the Grecian should be seen in virtue, and that of the foreigner in iniquity; clothing and food, marriage and manner of life they should regard as common to all, being blended into one by ties of blood and children. . . .

---

[1] The Susianians lived in and near the city of Susa, the capital of the Persian Empire; the Gedrosians lived just north of the Arabian Sea, in what is now southeastern Iran and western Pakistan.

[2] Bactria, a northeastern province of the ancient Persian Empire, was located in the area of modern Afghanistan and Central Asia.

[3] "All Asia" referred to western Asia Minor at first, then, as Alexander's conquests spread further, the term was broadened to include the other territory to the east, extending to what is now India and Central Asia.

[4] Seleuceia (named for one of Alexander's generals) was near modern Baghdad. Prophthasia, a city founded by Alexander, was in Sogdiana, north of modern Afghanistan. Bucephalia, on a northern branch of the Indus River, was named for Alexander's horse Bucephalus.

. . . For he did not overrun Asia like a robber nor was he minded to tear and rend it, as if it were booty and plunder bestowed by unexpected good fortune, after the manner in which Hannibal later descended upon Italy. . . . But Alexander desired to render all upon earth subject to one law of reason and one form of government and to reveal all men as one people, and to this purpose he made himself conform. But if the deity that sent down Alexander's soul into this world of ours had not recalled him quickly, one law would govern all mankind, and they all would look toward one rule of justice as though toward a common source of light. But as it is, that part of the world which has not looked upon Alexander has remained without sunlight.

Epicurus
SELF-SUFFICIENCY

Hellenistic philosophy marks a second stage in the evolution of Greek thought. In the Hellenic Age, philosophers dealt primarily with the individual's relationship to the city-state. In the Hellenistic Age, philosophers were concerned with defining the individual's relationship to a wider, often competitive and hostile community that consisted of a variety of peoples and cultures. In particular, the later philosophers sought to help people become ethically self-sufficient so that they could attain peace of mind in such an environment. Among the most significant schools of philosophy that emerged during the Hellenistic Age were Stoicism and Epicureanism.

Epicureanism was named for its founder, Epicurus (341–270 B.C.), who established a school at Athens in 307 or 306 B.C. To achieve peace of mind, taught Epicurus, one should refrain from worrying about death or pleasing the gods, avoid intense involvements in public affairs, cultivate friendships, and pursue pleasure prudently. The following excerpts from Epicurus' works reveal his prescription for achieving emotional well-being. The passages have been grouped according to particular subjects.

THE GODS

. . . We must grasp this point, that the principal disturbance in the minds of men arises because they think that these celestial bodies are blessed and immortal, and yet have wills and actions and motives inconsistent with these attributes; and because they are always expecting or imagining some everlasting misery [inflicted on them by the gods], such as is depicted in legends, or even fear the loss of feeling in death . . . and, again, because they are brought to this pass not by reasoned opinion, but rather by some irrational presentiment . . . and, by learning the true causes of celestial phenomena and all other occurrences that come to pass from time to time, we shall free ourselves from all which produces the utmost fear in other men.

It is vain to ask of the gods what a man is capable of supplying for himself.

DEATH

. . . So death, the most terrifying of ills, is nothing to us, since so long as we exist, death is not with us; but when death comes, then we do not exist. It does not then concern either the living or the dead, since for the former it is not, and the latter are no more.

But the many at one moment shun death as the greatest of evils, at another yearn for it as a respite from the evils in life. But the wise man neither seeks to escape life nor fears the cessation of life, for neither does life offend him nor does the absence of life seem to be any evil. And just as with food he does not seek simply the larger share and nothing else, but rather the most pleasant, so he seeks to enjoy not the longest period of time, but the most pleasant.

REASON AND PHILOSOPHY

Let no one when young delay to study philosophy, nor when he is old grow weary of his study. For no one can come too early or too late to secure the health of his soul. And the man who says that the age for philosophy has either not yet come or has gone by is like the man who says that the age for happiness is not yet come to him, or has passed away. Wherefore both when young and old a man must study philosophy, that as he grows old he may be young in blessings through the grateful recollection of what has been and that in youth he may be old as well, since he will know no fear of what is to come. We must then meditate on the things that make our happiness, seeing that when that is with us we have all, but when it is absent we do all to win it.

———

A man cannot dispel his fear about the most important matters if he does not know what is the nature of the universe but suspects the truth of some mythical story. So that without natural science it is not possible to attain our pleasures unalloyed.

———

We must not pretend to study philosophy, but study it in reality: for it is not the appearance of health that we need, but real health.

LIVING WELL

When, therefore, we maintain that pleasure is the end, we do not mean the pleasures of profligates and those that consist in sensuality, as is supposed by some who are either ignorant or disagree with us or do not understand, but freedom from pain in the body and from trouble in the mind. For it is not continuous drinkings and revellings, nor the satisfaction of lusts, nor the enjoyment of fish and other luxuries of the wealthy table, which produce a pleasant life, but sober reasoning, searching out the motives for all choice and avoidance, and banishing mere opinions, to which are due the greatest disturbance of the spirit.

Of all this the beginning and the greatest good is prudence. Wherefore prudence is a more precious thing even than philosophy; for from prudence are sprung all the other virtues, and it teaches us that it is not possible to live pleasantly without living prudently and honourably and justly. . . .

———

Of all the things which wisdom acquires to produce the blessedness of the complete life, far the greatest is the possession of friendship.

———

We must release ourselves from the prison of affairs and politics.

———

A free life cannot acquire many possessions, because this is not easy to do without servility to mobs or monarchs. . . .

———

The noble soul occupies itself with wisdom and friendship. . . .

———

The first measure of security is to watch over one's youth and to guard against what makes havoc of all by means of pestering desires.

REVIEW QUESTIONS

1. According to Plutarch, what benefits did Alexander confer on the peoples he conquered?
2. In Plutarch's view, how did Alexander's policies reflect Stoic philosophic ideals?
3. What did Epicurus believe were the chief causes of emotional distress among human beings?
4. What advice did he offer for achieving inner peace and happiness?
5. How did Epicurean teachings both continue and break with traditional Greek values?

---

15 Greek Culture and the Jews in the Hellenistic Age

Like other Near Eastern people, the Jews—both in Judea and the Diaspora (Jews who lived outside Palestine)—came under the influence of Hellenism. As Greek settlements sprang up in Judea, Jews had increasing contact with Greek soldiers, artisans, and merchants. Some Jewish scholars came to admire the rich Greek philosophical tradition. The Hebrew Scriptures were translated into Greek for use by Greek-speaking Jews, Greek words entered the Hebrew language, and newly constructed synagogues employed Hellenistic architectural styles. Radical Hellenizers, mainly prosperous aristocrats, adopted Greek games, dress, entertainment, and eating habits; these efforts to assimilate pagan ways were resisted by simple folk and the devout who clung tenaciously to Mosaic law. Thus Greek influences both enriched Hebrew culture and threatened its integrity.

FIRST BOOK OF MACCABEES JEWISH RESISTANCE TO FORCED HELLENIZATION

The clash of Greek and Hebrew cultures came to a head when the Seleucid king Antiochus IV (174–163 B.C.) decided to impose Hellenization upon the Jews of Judea. (His predecessor, Antiochus III, had seized Palestine from Ptolemaic Egypt.) In 167 B.C. he desecrated the Temple in Jerusalem by erecting an altar to Zeus in the Temple court and offering pigs, unclean animals in Jewish law, as a sacrifice. He forbade ritual circumcision, the sign of the covenant between Jews and their god, Yahweh. In the following selection from the *First Book of the Maccabees*, an anonymous Jewish historian writing shortly after 134 B.C. describes the causes of the great rebellion against forced Hellenization. The text reveals that some Jews were already so Hellenized that they supported the policies of the Seleucid king.

The outrage of loyalist Jews against forced Hellenization was epitomized by Mattathias, whose battle cry was "Let everybody who is zealous for the Law and stands by the covenant come out after me." Led by one of Mattathias' sons, Judah the Maccabeus (the "hammerer"), the Jews successfully fought the Syrians, venting their anger also against the Hellenized Jews who sided with Antiochus. In 140 B.C., the Jews, under Judah's brother Simon, regained their independence.

THE PERSECUTION

41 Then the king wrote to his whole kingdom that all should be one people, [42]and that each should give up his customs. [43]All the Gentiles accepted the command of the king. Many even from Israel gladly adopted his religion; they sacrificed to idols and profaned the sabbath. [44]And the king sent letters by messengers to Jerusalem and the cities of Judah; he directed them to follow customs strange to the land, [45]to forbid burnt offerings and sacrifices and drink offerings in the sanctuary, to profane sabbaths and feasts, [46]to defile the sanctuary and the priests, [47]to build altars and sacred precincts and shrines for idols, to sacrifice swine and unclean animals, [48]and to leave their sons uncircumcised. They were to make themselves abominable by everything unclean and profane, [49]so that they should forget the [Mosaic] law and change all the ordinances. [50]"And whoever does not obey the command of the king shall die."

51 In such words he wrote to his whole kingdom. And he appointed inspectors over all the people and commanded the cities of Judah to offer sacrifice, city by city. [52]Many of the people, every one who forsook the law, joined them, and they did evil in the land; [53]they drove Israel into hiding in every place of refuge they had.

54 Now on the fifteenth day of Chislev [in 167 B.C.] they erected a desolating sacrilege upon the altar of burnt offering. They also built altars in the surrounding cities of Judah, [55]and burned incense at the doors of the houses and in the streets. [56]The books of the law which they found they tore to pieces and burned with fire. [57]Where the book of the covenant was found in the possession of any one, or if any one adhered to the law, the decree of the king condemned him to death. [58]They kept using violence against Israel, against those found month after month in the cities. [59]And on the twenty-fifth day of the month they offered sacrifice on the altar which was upon the altar of burnt offering. [60]According to the decree, they put to death the women who had their children circumcised, [61]and their families and those who circumcised them; and they hung the infants from their mothers' necks.

62 But many in Israel stood firm and were resolved in their hearts not to eat unclean food. [63]They chose to die rather than to be defiled by food or to profane the holy covenant; and they did die. [64]And very great wrath came upon Israel.

Philo of Alexandria
APPRECIATION OF GREEK CULTURE AND SYNTHESIS OF REASON AND REVELATION

Living in the cosmopolitan world of Alexandria dominated by Greek thought and culture, Alexandrian Jews felt compelled to demonstrate that their faith was not incompatible with reason, that there was no insurmountable gulf separating

Mosaic religion from Greek philosophy. The leading figure in this effort to explain and justify the Hebrew Scriptures in terms of Greek philosophy—to prove that Mosaic law, revealed by God, was compatible with truth discovered by natural reason—was Philo of Alexandria (c. 20 B.C.–A.D. 50). Scion of a wealthy, aristocratic Jewish family, Philo was intimately familiar with the Greek cultural tradition and greatly admired Plato. He believed that Plato's view of God, as presented in the *Timaeus*, was compatible with Hebrew Scripture. In that work Plato had posited an eternal God who had existed prior to his creation of the world and continued to exist as an incorporeal and transcendent being.

On several points Philo disagreed with Greek philosophy. For example, holding that only God was eternal, he could not accept the Platonic view of the eternity of Ideas or Forms. Nor could he accept the position of Greek philosophy that the laws of nature were inexorable, for this precluded divine miracles. In these and other instances, Philo skillfully used the tools of Greek logic to harmonize differing viewpoints. His blending of Platonism with Scripture would be continued by Christian thinkers who admired Philo's achievement.

In the following selections, Philo expresses his admiration for Greek culture.

There was a time when I had leisure for philosophy and for the contemplation of the universe and its contents, when I made its spirit my own in all its beauty and loveliness and true blessedness, when my constant companions were divine themes and verities, wherein I rejoiced with a joy that never cloyed or sated. I had no base or abject thoughts nor grovelled in search of reputation or of wealth or bodily comforts, but seemed always to be borne aloft into the heights with a soul possessed by some God-sent inspiration, a fellow-traveller with the sun and moon and the whole heaven and universe. Ah then I gazed down from the upper air, and straining the mind's eye beheld, as from some commanding peak, the multitudinous world-wide spectacles of earthly things, and blessed my lot in that I had escaped by main force from the plagues of mortal life. But, as it proved, my steps were dogged by the deadliest of mischiefs, the hater of the good, envy, which suddenly set upon me and ceased not to pull me down with violence till it had plunged me in the ocean of civil cares, in which I am swept away, unable even to raise my head above the water. Yet amid my groans I hold my own, for, planted in my soul from my earliest days I keep the yearning for culture which

ever has pity and compassion for me, lifts me up and relieves my pain. To this I owe it that sometimes I raise my head and with the soul's eyes—dimly indeed because the mist of extraneous affairs has clouded their clear vision—I yet make shift to look around me in my desire to inhale a breath of life pure and unmixed with evil. And if unexpectedly I obtain a spell of fine weather and a calm from civil turmoils, I get me wings and ride the waves and almost tread the lower air, wafted by the breezes of knowledge which often urges me to come to spend my days with her, a truant as it were from merciless masters in the shape not only of men but of affairs, which pour in upon me like a torrent from different sides. Yet it is well for me to give thanks to God even for this, that though submerged I am not sucked down into the depths, but can also open the soul's eyes, which in my despair of comforting hope I thought had now lost their sight, and am irradiated by the light of wisdom, and am not given over to lifelong darkness. So behold me daring, not only to read the sacred messages of Moses, but also in my love of knowledge to peer into each of them and unfold and reveal what is not known to the multitude.

———

. . . For instance when first I was incited by the goads of philosophy to desire her I consorted in early youth with one of her handmaids, Grammar, and all that I begat by her, writing, reading and study of the writings of the poets, I dedicated to her mistress. And again I kept company with another, namely Geometry, and was charmed with her beauty, for she shewed symmetry and proportion in every part. Yet I took none of her children for my private use, but brought them as a gift to the lawful wife. Again my ardour moved me to keep company with a third; rich in rhythm, harmony and melody was she, and her name was Music, and from her I begat diatonics, chromatics and enharmonics, conjunct and disjunct melodies, conforming with the consonance of the fourth, fifth or octave intervals. And again of none of these did I make a secret hoard, wishing to see the lawful wife a lady of wealth with a host of servants ministering to her.

Philo sought to demonstrate the truth of Judaism to a non-Jewish culture. In the selections below, he employs the categories of Greek philosophy to provide proof for God's existence and his creation of the universe.

Doubtless hard to unriddle and hard to apprehend is the Father and Ruler of all, but that is no reason why we should shrink from searching for Him. But in such searching two principal questions arise which demand the consideration of the genuine philosopher. One is whether the Deity exists, a question necessitated by those who practise atheism, the worst form of wickedness, the other is what the Deity is in essence. Now to answer the first question does not need much labour, but the second is not only difficult but perhaps impossible to solve. Still, both must be examined. We see then that any piece of work always involves the knowledge of a workman. Who can look upon statues or painting without thinking at once of a sculptor or painter? Who can see clothes or ships or houses without getting the idea of a weaver and a shipwright and a housebuilder? And when one enters a well-ordered city in which the arrangements for civil life are very admirably managed, what else will he suppose but that this city is directed by good rulers? So then he who comes to the truly Great City, this world, and beholds hills and plains teeming with animals and plants, the rivers, springfed or winter torrents, streaming along, the seas with their expanses, the air with its happily tempered phases, the yearly seasons passing into each other, and then the sun and moon ruling the day and night, and the other heavenly bodies fixed or planetary and the whole firmament revolving in rhythmic order, must he not naturally or rather necessarily gain the conception of the Maker and Father and Ruler also? For none of the works of human art is self-made, and the highest art and knowledge is shewn in this universe, so that surely it has been wrought by one of excellent knowledge and absolute perfection. In this way we have gained the conception of the existence of God.

REVIEW QUESTIONS

1. Why were some Jews attracted to Greek culture? Why were others repelled?
2. How did the directives of Antiochus IV violate Jewish beliefs?
3. What Hellenistic elements can be seen in the writings of Philo of Alexandria?

CHAPTER 4

The Roman Republic

FORUM IN ROME. The forum, a large rectangular space that served as a marketplace, was the center of a Roman city. In Rome itself, the forum evolved into a political center surrounded by large public buildings. *(Atlantide Phototravel/Corbis)*

The city-state was the foundation of Greek society in the Hellenic Age; in the Hellenistic Age, Greek cities became subordinate to kingdoms, larger political units ruled by autocratic monarchs. Hellenistic philosophers conceived of a still broader political arrangement: A world-state in which people of different nationalities were bound together by the ties of common citizenship and law that applied to all. It was Rome's great achievement to construct such a world-state.

Roman history falls into two broad periods—the Republic and the Empire. The Roman Republic began in 509 B.C. with the overthrow of the Etruscan monarchy and lasted until 27 B.C., when Octavian (Augustus) became in effect the first Roman emperor, ending almost five hundred years of republican self-government. For the next five hundred years, Rome would be governed by emperors.

In 264 B.C., when the Roman Republic had established dominion over the Italian peninsula, there were four other great powers in the Mediterranean world. Carthage controlled North Africa, Corsica, Sardinia, and parts of Spain and Sicily. The other powers—Macedonia, Egypt, and Syria—were the three Hellenistic kingdoms carved out of the empire of Alexander the Great. By 146 B.C., Rome had emerged victorious over the other powers, and by 30 B.C. they were all Roman provinces.

The Roman Republic, which had conquered a vast empire, was destroyed not by foreign armies but by internal weaknesses. In the century after 133 B.C., the senate, which had governed Rome well during its march to empire, degenerated into a self-seeking oligarchy; it failed to resolve critical domestic problems and fought to preserve its own power and prestige. When Rome had been threatened by foreign enemies, all classes united in a spirit of patriotism. This social harmony broke down when the threat from outside diminished, and the Republic was torn by internal dissension and civil war.

1 Rome's March to World Empire

By 146 B.C., Rome had become the dominant state in the Mediterranean world. Roman expansion had occurred in three main stages: the uniting of the Italian peninsula, which gave Rome the manpower that transformed it from a city-state into a great power; the collision with Carthage, from which Rome emerged as ruler of the western Mediterranean; and the subjugation of the Hellenistic states, which brought Romans in close contact with Greek civilization. As Rome expanded territorially, its leaders enlarged their vision. Instead of restricting citizenship to people having ethnic kinship, Rome assimilated other peoples into its political community. Just as law had grown to cope with the earlier grievances of the plebeians, so it adjusted to the new situations resulting from the creation of a multinational empire. The city of Rome was evolving into the city of humanity—the cosmopolis envisioned by the Stoics.

Polybius
THE ROMAN ARMY

The discipline and dedication of the citizen-soldiers help explain Rome's success in conquering a world empire. In the following account, Polybius (c. 200–c. 118 B.C.) tells how the commanders enforced obedience and fostered heroism.

A court-martial composed of the tribunes immediately sits to try him [a soldier], and if he is found guilty, he is punished by beating (*fustuarium*). This is carried out as follows. The tribune takes a cudgel and lightly touches the condemned man with it, whereupon all the soldiers fall upon him with clubs and stones, and usually kill him in the camp itself. But even those who contrive to escape are no better off. How indeed could they be? They are not allowed to return to their homes, and none of their family would dare to receive such a man into the house. Those who have once fallen into this misfortune are completely and finally ruined. The *optio* [lieutenant] and the *decurio* [sergeant] of the squadron are liable to the same punishment if they fail to pass on the proper orders at the proper moment to the patrols and the *decurio* of the next squadron. The consequence of the extreme severity of this penalty and of the absolute impossibility of avoiding it is that the night watches of the Roman army are faultlessly kept.

The ordinary soldiers are answerable to the tribunes [elected military administrators] and the tribunes to the consuls [commanders]. A tribune, and in the case of the allies a prefect [commander of a large unit], has power to inflict fines, distrain on [confiscate] goods, and to order a flogging. The punishment of beating to death is also inflicted upon those who steal from the camp, those who give false evidence, those who in full manhood commit homosexual offences, and finally upon anyone who has been punished three times for the same

offence. The above are the offences which are punished as crimes. The following actions are regarded as unmanly and dishonourable in a soldier: to make a false report to the tribune of your courage in the field in order to earn distinction; to leave the post to which you have been assigned in a covering force because of fear; and similarly to throw away out of fear any of your weapons on the field of battle. For this reason the men who have been posted to a covering force are often doomed to certain death. This is because they will remain at their posts even when they are overwhelmingly outnumbered on account of their dread of the punishment that awaits them. Again, those who have lost a shield or a sword or any other weapon on the battlefield often hurl themselves upon the enemy hoping that they will either recover the weapon they have lost, or else escape by death from the inevitable disgrace and the humiliations they would suffer at home.

If it ever happens that a large body of men break and run in this way and whole maniples [units of 120 to 300 men] desert their posts under extreme pressure, the officers reject the idea of beating to death or executing all who are guilty, but the solution they adopt is as effective as it is terrifying. The tribune calls the legion [large military unit] on parade and brings to the front those who are guilty of having left the ranks. He then reprimands them sharply, and finally chooses by lot some five or eight or twenty of the offenders, the number being calculated so that it represents about a tenth[1] of those who have shown themselves guilty of cowardice. Those on whom the lot has fallen are mercilessly clubbed to death in the manner I have already described. The rest are put on rations of barley instead of wheat, and are ordered to quarter themselves outside the camp in a place which has no defences. The danger and the fear of drawing the fatal lot threatens every man equally, and since there is no certainty on whom it may fall, and the public disgrace of receiving rations of barley is shared by all alike, the Romans have adopted the best possible practice both to inspire terror and to repair the harm done by any weakening of their warlike spirit.

The Romans also have an excellent method of encouraging young soldiers to face danger. Whenever any have especially distinguished themselves in a battle, the general assembles the troops and calls forward those he considers to have shown exceptional courage. He praises them first for their gallantry in action and for anything in their previous conduct which is particularly worthy of mention, and then he distributes gifts such as the following: to a man who has wounded one of the enemy, a spear; to one who has killed and stripped an enemy, a cup if he is in the infantry, or horse-trappings if in the cavalry—originally the gift was simply a lance. These presentations are not made to men who have wounded or stripped an enemy in the course of a pitched battle, or at the storming of a city, but to those who during a skirmish or some

---

[1]This custom is the origin of the word *decimate*, from the Latin *decem*, ten.

similar situation in which there is no necessity to engage in single combat, have voluntarily and deliberately exposed themselves to danger.

At the storming of a city the first man to scale the wall is awarded a crown of gold. In the same way those who have shielded and saved one of their fellow-citizens or of the allies are honoured with gifts from the consul, and the men whose lives they have preserved present them of their own free will with a crown; if not, they are compelled to do so by the tribunes who judge the case. Moreover, a man who has been saved in this way reveres his rescuer as a father for the rest of his life and must treat him as if he were a parent. And so by means of such incentives even those who stay at home feel the impulse to emulate such achievements in the field no less than those who are present and see and hear what takes place. For the men who receive these trophies not only enjoy great prestige in the army and soon afterwards in their homes, but they are also singled out for precedence in religious processions when they return. On these occasions nobody is allowed to wear decorations save those who have been honoured for their bravery by the consuls, and it is the custom to hang up the trophies they have won in the most conspicuous places in their houses, and to regard them as proofs and visible symbols of their valour. So when we consider this people's almost obsessive concern with military rewards and punishments, and the immense importance which they attach to both, it is not surprising that they emerge with brilliant success from every war in which they engage.

REVIEW QUESTIONS

1. How did the Romans ensure good discipline among their soldiers?
2. What factors mentioned by Polybius help explain Rome's emergence as a great power?

2   The Punic Wars

In 264 B.C., Rome, which had just completed its conquest of Italy, went to war with Carthage, the dominant power in the western Mediterranean. A threat to the north Sicilian city of Messana (now Messina) was the immediate cause of the war. Rome feared that Carthage might use Messana as a springboard from which to attack the cities of southern Italy, which were allied to Rome, or to interfere with their trade. The First Punic War (264–241 B.C.) was a grueling conflict; drawing manpower from its loyal allies, Rome finally prevailed. Carthage surrendered Sicily to Rome, and three years later Rome seized the large islands of Corsica and Sardinia, west of Italy, from a weakened Carthage.

Livy
THE SECOND PUNIC WAR: THE THREAT FROM HANNIBAL

Carthaginian expansion in Spain led to the Second Punic War (218–201 B.C.). The Carthaginian army was led by Hannibal (247–183 B.C.), whose military genius impressed and frightened Rome. Hannibal brought the battle to Rome by leading his seasoned army, including war elephants, across the Alps into Italy.

Hannibal demonstrated his superb generalship at the battle of Cannae in 216 B.C., where the Carthaginians destroyed a Roman army of sixty thousand. Hannibal removed some of his soldiers in the center and commanded the thin line to retreat as the Romans charged. Believing that the enemy was on the run, the Romans continued their headlong thrust into the Carthaginian center. Then, according to plan, Carthaginian troops stationed on the wings attacked the Roman flanks and the cavalry closed in on the Roman rear, completely encircling the Roman troops. News of the disaster, one of the worst in the Republic's history, brought anguish to Romans, who feared that Hannibal would march on the capital itself. Adding to Rome's distress was the desertion of some of its Italian allies to Hannibal. In the following passage, the Roman historian Livy (59 B.C.–A.D. 17) describes the mood in Rome after Cannae.

. . . Never, without an enemy actually within the gates, had there been such terror and confusion in the city [Rome]. To write of it is beyond my strength, so I shall not attempt to describe what any words of mine would only make less than the truth. In the previous year a consul and his army had been lost at Trasimene [location of an overwhelming defeat for Rome], and now there was news not merely of another similar blow, but of a multiple calamity—two consular armies annihilated, both consuls[1] dead, Rome left without a force in the field, without a commander, without a single soldier, Apulia and Samnium [two provinces in southern Italy] in Hannibal's hands, and now nearly the whole of Italy overrun. No other nation in the world

---

[1]The consuls served dual offices as elected magistrates of Rome in peacetime and commanders-in-chief of the Roman army.

could have suffered so tremendous a series of disasters, and not been overwhelmed. It was unparalleled in history: the naval defeat off the Aegates islands,* a defeat which forced the Carthaginians to abandon Sicily and Sardinia and suffer themselves to pay taxes and tribute to Rome; the final defeat in Africa to which Hannibal himself afterwards succumbed—neither the one nor the other was in any way comparable to what Rome had now to face, except in the fact that they were not borne with so high a courage.

The praetors[2] Philus and Pomponius summoned the Senate[3] to meet . . . to consider the defence of the City, as nobody doubted that Hannibal, now that the armies were destroyed, would attack Rome—the final operation to crown his victory. It was not easy to work out a plan: their troubles, already great enough, were made worse by the lack of firm news; the streets were loud with the wailing and weeping of women, and nothing yet being clearly known, living and dead alike were being mourned in nearly every house in the city. In these circumstances, Quintus Fabius Maximus[4] put forward some proposals: riders, he suggested, lightly equipped, should be sent out along the Appian and Latin Ways[5] to question any survivors they might meet roaming the countryside, and report any tidings they could get from them of what had happened to the consuls and the armies. If the gods, in pity for the empire, had suffered any of the Roman name to survive, they should inquire where they were, where Hannibal went after the battle, what his plans were, what he was doing, and what he was likely to do next. The task of collecting this information should be entrusted to vigorous and active men. There was also a task, Fabius suggested, for the Senate itself to perform, as there was a lack of public officers: this was, to get rid of the general confusion in the city and restore some sort of order. Women must be forbidden to appear out of doors, and compelled to stay in their homes; family mourning should be checked, and silence imposed everywhere; anyone with news to report should be taken to the praetors, and all individuals should await in their homes the news which personally concerned them. Furthermore, guards should be posted at the gates to prevent anyone from leaving the city, and every man and woman should be made to believe that there was no hope of safety except within the walls of Rome. Once, he ended, the present noise and disorder were under control, then would be the proper time to recall the Senate and debate measures for defence.

The proposals of Fabius won unanimous support. The city magistrates cleared the crowds out of the forum and the senators went off to restore some sort of order in the streets. . . .

How much more serious was the defeat at Cannae than those which had preceded it can be seen by the behaviour of Rome's allies: before that fatal day their loyalty had remained unshaken; now it began to waver, for the simple reason that they despaired of the survival of Roman power. The following peoples went over to the Carthaginian cause: the Atellani, Calatini, Hirpini, some of the Apulians, all the Samnites except the Pentri, the Bruttii, the Lucanians, the Uzentini, and nearly all the Greek settlements on the coast, namely Tarentum, Metapontum, Croton, and Locri, and all the Gauls on the Italian side of the Alps.

But neither the defeats they had suffered nor the subsequent defection of all these allied peoples moved the Romans ever to breathe a word about peace.

---

*The end of the First Punic war in 241 B.C.

[2]Praetors were magistrates who governed the city of Rome when the consuls were absent.

[3]The senate, originally drawn from the patrician caste, was the true ruler of Rome. It advised the magistrates on all matters of public policy.

[4]Fabius (Quintus Fabius Maximus Verrucosus, nicknamed "the Delayer," d. 203 B.C.) was elected consul several times, but his tactics in trying to avoid pitched battles displeased the Romans. However, Fabius' successors were totally defeated at Cannae, and Fabius, elected consul for the fifth time, recaptured Tarentum in 209.

[5]The Appian Way, parts of which exist today, was the main highway from Rome southward to Campania. The Latin Way (Via Latina), a parallel route, passed through hill towns before rejoining the Appian Way.

Appian of Alexandria
THE THIRD PUNIC WAR:
THE DESTRUCTION OF CARTHAGE

Despite his brilliant victory at Cannae, Hannibal lacked the manpower to deal Rome a knockout blow, and the Romans, respecting Hannibal's generalship, refused to engage his army in another major encounter. Finally, when Rome invaded North Africa and threatened Carthage, Hannibal quit Italy to defend his homeland and was defeated at the battle of Zama in 202 B.C.

Although Carthage, now a second-rate power, no longer posed a threat, Rome started the Third Punic War in 149 B.C. Driven by old hatreds and the traumatic memory of Hannibal's near conquest of Italy, Rome resolved to destroy Carthage. After Carthage fell in 146 B.C., Rome sold the survivors into slavery, obliterated the city, and turned the land into a province, which was named Africa. The savage and irrational behavior of Rome toward a helpless Carthage showed an early deterioration in senatorial leadership. In the following passage, Appian of Alexandria (A.D. 95–c. 165) describes the destruction of Carthage by the Romans under Scipio Aemilianus (185–129 B.C.).

Now Scipio hastened to the attack of Byrsa, the strongest part of the city [of Carthage], where the greater part of the inhabitants had taken refuge. There were three streets ascending from the forum to this fortress, along which, on either side, were houses built closely together and six stories high, from which the Romans were assailed with missiles. They were compelled, therefore, to possess themselves of the first ones and use those as a means of expelling the occupants of the next. When they had mastered the first, they threw timbers from one to another over the narrow passageways, and crossed as on bridges. While war was raging in this way on the roofs, another fight was going on among those who met each other in the streets below. All places were filled with groans, shrieks, shouts, and every kind of agony. Some were stabbed, others were hurled alive from the roofs to the pavement, some of them alighting on the heads of spears or other pointed weapons, or swords. No one dared to set fire to the houses on account of those who were still on the roofs, until Scipio reached Byrsa. Then he set fire to the three streets all together, and gave orders to keep the passageways clear of burning material so that the army might move back and forth freely.

Then came new scenes of horror. As the fire spread and carried everything down, the soldiers did not wait to destroy the buildings little by little, but all in a heap. So the crashing grew louder, and many corpses fell with the stones into the midst. Others were seen still living, especially old men, women, and young children who had hidden in the inmost nooks of the houses, some of them wounded, some more or less burned, and uttering piteous cries. Still others, thrust out and falling from such a height with the stones, timbers, and fire, were torn asunder in all shapes of horror, crushed and mangled. Nor was this the end of their miseries, for the street cleaners, who were removing the rubbish with axes, mattocks, and forks, and making the roads passable, tossed with these instruments the dead and the living together into holes in the ground, dragging them along like sticks and stones and turning them over with their iron tools. Trenches were filled with men. Some who were thrown in head foremost, with their legs sticking out of the ground, writhed a long time. Others fell with their feet downward and their heads above ground. Horses ran over them, crushing their faces and skulls, not purposely on the part of the riders, but in their headlong haste. Nor did the street cleaners do these things on purpose; but the tug of war, the glory of approaching victory, the rush of the soldiery, the orders of the officers, the blast of the trumpets, tribunes and centurions[1] marching their cohorts hither and thither—all together made everybody frantic and heedless of the spectacles under their eyes.

Six days and nights were consumed in this kind of fighting, the soldiers being changed so that they might not be worn out with toil, slaughter, want of sleep, and those horrid sights. . . .

Scipio, beholding this city, which had flourished 700 years from its foundation and had ruled over so many lands, islands, and seas, rich with arms and fleets, elephants and money, equal to the mightiest monarchies but far surpassing them in bravery and high spirit (since without ships or arms, and in the face of famine, it had sustained continuous war for three years), now come to its end in total destruction—Scipio, beholding this spectacle, is said to have shed tears and publicly lamented the fortune of the enemy. After meditating by himself a long time and reflecting on the rise and fall of cities, nations, and empires, as well as of individuals, upon the fate of Troy, that once proud city, upon that of the Assyrians, the Medes, and the Persians, greatest of all, and later the splendid Macedonian empire, either voluntarily or otherwise the words of the poet escaped his lips:—

"The day shall come in which our
    sacred Troy
And Priam,[2] and the people over
    whom
Spear-bearing Priam rules, shall
    perish all."
(*The Iliad*, vi, 448, 449; Bryant's translation.)

Being asked by Polybius in familiar conversation (for Polybius had been his tutor) what he meant by using these words, he said that he did not hesitate frankly to name his own country, for whose fate he feared when he considered the mutability of human affairs. And Polybius wrote this down just as he heard it.

---

[1]Centurions were noncommissioned officers, each commanding a hundred men; attached to each legion were six military tribunes, who had been voted in by the citizens of Rome in the general elections.

[2]Priam, in Homer's epic poem *The Iliad*, was the king of Troy at the time of the Trojan War.

REVIEW QUESTIONS

1. Describe the mood in Rome after the battle of Cannae.
2. After the Roman disaster at Cannae, what actions did Quintus Fabius Maximus propose?
3. What do you think prompted Scipio Aemilianus to quote the lines from Homer's *Iliad*?

3 The Spread of Greek Philosophy to Rome

One of the chief consequences of Roman expansion was growing contact with Greek culture. During the third century B.C., Greek civilization started to exercise an increasing and fruitful influence on the Roman mind. Greek teachers, both slave and free, came to Rome and introduced Romans to Hellenic cultural achievements.

As they conquered the eastern Mediterranean, Roman generals began to ship libraries and works of art from Greek cities to Rome. Roman sculpture and painting imitated Greek prototypes. In time, Romans acquired from Greece knowledge of scientific thought, medicine, and geography. Roman writers and orators used Greek history, poetry, and oratory as models. Roman philosophers borrowed the ideas of Greek philosophical schools and adapted them to Roman culture.

Lucretius
DENUNCIATION OF RELIGION

The writings of the Greek philosopher Epicurus soon won admirers in Rome. Lucretius (c. 96–c. 55 B.C.), the leading Roman Epicurean philosopher, lived in a time of civil war, which was fostered by two generals, Marius and Sulla. Distraught by the seemingly endless strife, Lucretius yearned for philosophical tranquillity. Like Epicurus, he believed that religion prompted people to perform evil deeds and caused them to experience terrible anxiety about death and eternal punishment. Like his mentor, Lucretius advanced a materialistic conception of nature, one that left no room for the activity of gods—mechanical laws, not the gods, governed all physical happenings. To dispel the fear of punishment after death, Lucretius marshaled arguments to prove that the soul perishes with the body. He proposed that the simple life, devoid of political involvement and excessive passion, was the highest good. Epicurus' disparagement of politics and public service and rejection of the goals of power and glory ran counter to the accepted Roman ideal of virtue. On the other hand, his praise of the quiet life amid a community of friends and his advice on how to deal with life's misfortunes with serenity had great appeal to first-century Romans who were disgusted with civil strife.

In the following selection from *On the Nature of Things*, Lucretius expresses his hostility to religion and his admiration for Epicurus, "the first to stand firm in defiance" of the fables about the gods.

When before our eyes man's life lay groveling,
  prostrate,
Crushed to the dust under the burden of
  Religion
(Which thrust its head from heaven, its
  horrible face
Glowering over mankind born to die),
One man, a Greek [Epicurus], was the first
  mortal who dared
Oppose his eyes, the first to stand firm in
  defiance.
Not the fables of gods, nor lightning, nor the
  menacing
Rumble of heaven could daunt him, but all
  the more

They whetted his keen mind with longing
  to be
First to smash open the tight-barred gates of
  Nature.
His vigor of mind prevailed. . . .
Religion now lies trampled beneath our feet,
And we are made gods by the victory.

Lucretius attempts to explain why people came to believe in powerful gods.

How the idea of gods spread to all nations,
Stocking their cities with altars and making
  men tremble

To undertake the solemn rites, which flourish
With all our luxury and magnificence
(Even now sowing in us the seeds of horror,
Urging us on to rear across the world
New shrines to the gods to crowd on festival
   days),
Is not hard to explain in a few words.
In those days mortal men saw while awake
The excellent countenances of the gods,
Or rather in dreams they gasped at their vast
   size.
Men lent sensation to these giant forms
For they moved their limbs, it seemed, and
   spoke proud words
As arrogant as their beauty and great strength.
Eternal life they gave them, for their faces
And their physiques persisted ever-present,
And they thought that beings endowed with
   such great power
Could never be put to rout by any force.
They thought the gods preeminently blest,
For the fear of death could hardly trouble them;
Also because in dreams they saw them do
Miraculous things, and many, without an effort.
Then too they saw the systems of the sky
Turn in sure order, and the changing seasons,
But could not understand why this occurred.
Their refuge, then: assign to the gods all things,
Have them steer all things with a single nod.
In the heavens they placed the holy haunts of
   the gods. . . .

Unhappy human race—to grant such feats
To gods, and then to add vindictiveness!
What wailing did they bring forth for
   themselves,
What wounds for us, what tears for our
   descendants!
It's no piety to be seen at every altar,
To cover your head and turn to the stone idol,
Or to flatten yourself on the ground and lift
   your palms
To the shrines, or to spray altars with the blood
Of cattle—so much!—or to string vow on vow.
To observe all things with a mind at peace
Is piety. For when we look up to the heavenly

Shrines of this great world, the stars that
   glitter, the sky
Studded, when we think of the journeying sun
   and moon,
Then in hearts heavy-laden with other cares
Trouble is roused to boot, and rears its
   head—
That the limitless power of gods, the power
   that wheels
The stars and planets, may be aimed at us.
Then ignorance assails the mind in doubt
About the universe's origin,
About the end, how long the walls of the world
Can suffer the straining of such stir and motion,
Or whether, granted everlasting health
By the gods, they can in endless course disdain
The turning age and the vast strength of time.
And worse, whose soul does not contract in fear
Of the gods, whose limbs don't crawl with
   terror when
The scorched earth under the terrible
   lightning bolt
Quakes, and a grumbling rolls through the
   great sky?
Don't people and nations tremble, and
   arrogant kings
Cringe, stricken into shock by fear of the gods,
Lest for some foul deed done or proud word said
The heavy time has come to pay the price?
When a high hard gale across the plains of the sea
Rakes a commander and his fleet along
With all his mighty elephants and legions,
Won't he beseech the "Peace of the Gods" in
   terror
And pray for peaceful breezes and fair winds?
In vain, for the whirlpool's got him anyway
And borne him down unto the shoals of
   Death.
So thoroughly is human grandeur crushed
By a hidden force; the glorious rods and axes,
Those splendid mockeries, are trampled under.
Well, when the whole earth staggers underfoot
And cities are battered and fall, or threaten to fall,
What wonder if self-loathing seizes men
And they grant wondrous power over all affairs
To gods, to steer and rule the universe?

Cicero
ADVOCATE OF STOICISM

Marcus Tullius Cicero, a leading Roman statesman, was also a distinguished orator, an unsurpassed Latin stylist, and a student of Greek philosophy. His letters, more than eight hundred of which have survived, provide modern historians with valuable insights into late republican politics. His orations before the Senate and law courts have been models of eloquence and rhetorical technique for students of Latin and later European languages.

Like many other Romans, Cicero was influenced by the Greek philosophy of Stoicism. Cicero adopted the Stoic belief that natural law governs the universe and applies to all and that all belong to a common humanity. The gift of reason, which is common to all people, enables us to comprehend this natural law and to order our lives in accordance with its principles, which are unchangeable and eternal. Natural law as understood by right reason commands people to do what is right and deters them from doing what is wrong. Thus there is a unity of knowledge and virtue. For Cicero, the laws of the state should accord with the natural law underlying the universe. Adherence to such rationally formulated laws creates a moral bond among citizens and the peoples of all nations and states. In the following passage from his philosophic treatise *The Laws*, Cicero explored the implications of the Stoic concept of natural law.

. . . Now let us investigate the origins of Justice.

Well then, the most learned men have determined to begin with Law, and it would seem that they are right, if, according to their definition, Law is the highest reason, implanted in Nature, which commands what ought to be done and forbids the opposite. This reason, when firmly fixed and fully developed in the human mind, is Law. And so they believe that Law is intelligence whose natural function it is to command right conduct and forbid wrongdoing. They think that this quality has derived its name in Greek from the idea of granting to every man his own, and in our language I believe it has been named from the idea of choosing. For as they have attributed the idea of fairness to the word law, so we have given it that of selection, though both ideas properly belong to Law. Now if this is correct, as I think it to be in general, then the origin of Justice is to be found in Law, for Law is a natural force; it is the mind and reason of the intelligent man, the standard by which Justice and Injustice are measured. But since our whole discussion has to do with the reasoning of the populace, it will sometimes be necessary to speak in the popular manner, and give the name of law to that which in written form decrees whatever it wishes, either by command or prohibition. For such is the crowd's definition of law. But in determining what Justice is, let us begin with that supreme Law which had its origin ages before any written law existed or any State had been established.

. . . I shall seek the root of Justice in Nature, under whose guidance our whole discussion must be conducted.

. . . [T]hat animal which we call man, endowed with foresight and quick intelligence, complex, keen, possessing memory, full of reason and prudence, has been given a certain distinguished status by the supreme God who created him; for he is the only one among so many different kinds and varieties of living beings who has a share in reason and thought, while all the rest are deprived of it. But what is more divine, I will not say in man only, but in all heaven and earth, than reason? And reason, when it is full grown and perfected, is rightly called wisdom. Therefore, since there is nothing better than reason, and since it exists both in man and God, the first common possession of man and God is reason. But those who have reason in common must also have right reason in common. And since right reason is Law, we must believe that men have Law also in common with the gods. Further, those who share Law must also share Justice; and those who share these are to be regarded as members of the same commonwealth. If indeed they obey the same authorities and powers, this is true in a far greater degree; but as a matter of fact they do obey this celestial system, the divine mind, and the God of transcendent power. Hence we must now conceive of this whole universe as one commonwealth of which both gods and men are members.

Moreover, virtue exists in man and God alike, but in no other creature besides; virtue, however, is nothing else than Nature perfected and developed to its highest point; therefore there is a likeness between man and God. As this is true, what relationship could be closer or clearer than this one? For this reason, Nature has lavishly yielded such a wealth of things adapted to man's convenience and use that what she produces seems intended as a gift to us, and not brought forth by chance; and this is true, not only of what the fertile earth bountifully bestows in the form of grain and fruit, but also of the animals; for it is clear that some of them have been created to be man's slaves, some to supply him with their products, and others

to serve as his food. Moreover innumerable arts have been discovered through the teachings of Nature; for it is by a skilful imitation of her that reason has acquired the necessities of life. . . .

. . . [O]ut of all the material of the philosophers' discussions, surely there comes nothing more valuable than the full realization that we are born for Justice, and that right is based, not upon men's opinions, but upon Nature. This fact will immediately be plain if you once get a clear conception of man's fellowship and union with his fellow-men. For no single thing is so like another, so exactly its counterpart, as all of us are to one another. Nay, if bad habits and false beliefs did not twist the weaker minds and turn them in whatever direction they are inclined, no one would be so like his own self as all men would be like all others. And so, however we may define man, a single definition will apply to all. This is a sufficient proof that there is no difference in kind between man and man; for if there were, one definition could not be applicable to all men; and indeed reason, which alone raises us above the level of the beasts and enables us to draw inferences, to prove and disprove, to discuss and solve problems, and to come to conclusions, is certainly common to us all, and, though varying in what it learns, at least in the capacity to learn it is invariable. For the same things are invariably perceived by the senses, and those things which stimulate the senses, stimulate them in the same way in all men; and those rudimentary beginnings of intelligence to which I have referred, which are imprinted on our minds, are imprinted on all minds alike; and speech, the mind's interpreter, though differing in the choice of words, agrees in the sentiments expressed. In fact, there is no human being of any race who, if he finds a guide, cannot attain to virtue.

Cato the Elder
HOSTILITY TO GREEK PHILOSOPHY

Some conservative Romans were hostile to the Greek influence, which they felt threatened traditional Roman values. Cato the Elder (also the Censor; 234–149 B.C.) denounced Socrates for undermining respect for Athenian law and warned that Greek philosophy might lure Roman youth into similar subversive behavior. The following passage from Plutarch's *Lives* shows Cato's hostility to Greek philosophy.

He was now grown old, when Carneades the Academic, and Diogenes the Stoic, came as deputies from Athens to Rome, praying for release from a penalty of five hundred talents laid on the Athenians, in a suit, to which they did not appear, in which the Oropians were plaintiffs and Sicyonians[1] judges. All the most studious youth immediately waited on these philosophers, and frequently, with admiration, heard them speak. But the gracefulness of Carneades's oratory, whose ability was really greatest, and his reputation equal to it, gathered large and favourable audiences, and ere long filled, like a wind, all the city with the sound of it. So that it soon began to be told that a Greek, famous even to admiration, winning and carrying all before him, had impressed so strange a love upon the young men, that quitting all their pleasures and pastimes, they ran mad, as it were, after philosophy; which indeed much pleased the Romans in general; nor could they but with much pleasure see the youth receive so welcomely the Greek literature, and frequent the company of learned men. But Cato, on the other side, seeing the passion for words flowing into the city, from the beginning took it ill, fearing lest the youth should be diverted that way, and so should prefer the glory of speaking well before that of arms and

doing well. And when the fame of the philosophers increased in the city, and Caius Acilius, a person of distinction, at his own request, became their interpreter to the senate at their first audience, Cato resolved, under some specious pretence, to have all philosophers cleared out of the city; and, coming into the senate, blamed the magistrates for letting these deputies stay so long a time without being despatched, though they were persons that could easily persuade the people to what they pleased; that therefore in all haste something should be determined about their petition, that so they might go home again to their own schools, and declaim to the Greek children, and leave the Roman youth to be obedient, as hitherto, to their own laws and governors.

Yet he did this not out of any anger, as some think, to Carneades; but because he wholly despised philosophy, and out of a kind of pride scoffed at the Greek studies and literature; as, for example, he would say, that Socrates was a prating, seditious fellow, who did his best to tyrannise over his country, to undermine the ancient customs, and to entice and withdraw the citizens to opinions contrary to the laws. Ridiculing the school of Isocrates,[2] he would add, that his scholars grew old men before they had done learning with him, as if they were to use their art and plead causes in the

---

[1]The Oropians came from the town of Oropus in east central Greece. Sicyonians came from the city of Sicyon in southern Greece.

[2]Isocrates (436–338 B.C.) was an Athenian orator whose students distinguished themselves as orators, historians, and statesmen.

court of Minos in the next world. And to frighten his son from anything that was Greek, in a more vehement tone than became one of his age, he pronounced, as it were, with the voice of an oracle, that the Romans would certainly be destroyed when they began once to be infected with Greek literature; though time indeed has shown the vanity of this his prophecy; as, in truth, the city of Rome has risen to its highest fortune while entertaining Grecian learning. Nor had he an aversion only against the Greek philosophers, but the physicians also; for having, it seems, heard how Hippocrates, when the king of Persia sent for him, with offers of a fee of several talents, said, that he would never assist barbarians who were enemies of the Greeks; he affirmed, that this was now become a common oath taken by all physicians, and enjoined his son to have a care and avoid them.

REVIEW QUESTIONS

1. Why was Lucretius critical of religion?
2. According to Lucretius, why did people first begin to believe in gods? Compare his view to that of Critias.
3. What is Cicero's view on the nature of law and what conclusions does he derive from it?
4. Why does Cicero conclude that the sense of justice is common to all humans? What implication does he draw from this conclusion?
5. Why did Cato fear Carneades in particular and Greek thought in general?

---

4 Roman Slavery

Slavery was practiced in ancient times, in many lands, and among most peoples. Although conditions might vary in detail from place to place, essentially a slave was considered legally to be a piece of property, not a person with normal citizen's rights. Age, sex, skills, ethnic origin, demeanor, appearance, and personal character determined a slave's value in the marketplace. The status of slave was usually hereditary, but a person might be enslaved for debt or as a penalty for crime. Pirates would kidnap and sell their captives as slaves. But the most common source of slaves was defeated people captured during wars. They were assigned to all kinds of work, and their labors were vital in sustaining the luxury and leisure of the Roman upper classes. Even families of modest fortunes could usually afford a slave to do domestic chores, to help farm, or to assist in the family's business or craft.

Diodorus Siculus
SLAVES: TORMENT AND REVOLT

The Roman war machine created hundreds of thousands of slaves during the last centuries of the Republic and the early centuries of the imperial age. Under the Republic, the Romans were notably harsh toward slaves; until the full influence of Greek Stoic philosophy penetrated the governing class, little was done to protect them from the absolute power of their Roman masters. Diodorus

Siculus, a Greek historian, describes the condition of Roman slaves toiling in silver and gold mines in Iberia (present-day Spain) and then tells of an uprising of slaves that lasted from 135 to 132 B.C.

THE ORDEAL OF SLAVES IN THE MINES

. . . After the Romans had made themselves masters of Iberia, a multitude of Italians have swarmed to the mines and taken great wealth away with them, such was their greed. For they purchase a multitude of slaves whom they turn over to the overseers of the working of the mines; and these men, opening shafts in a number of places and digging deep into the ground, seek out the seams of earth which are rich in silver and gold; and not only do they go into the ground a great distance, but they also push their diggings many stades [measure equalling about 607 feet] in depth and run galleries off at every angle, turning this way and that, in this manner bringing up from the depths the ore which gives them the profit they are seeking. . . .

But to continue with the mines, the slaves who are engaged in the working of them produce for their masters revenues in sums defying belief, but they themselves wear out their bodies both by day and by night in the diggings under the earth, dying in large numbers because of the exceptional hardships they endure. For no respite or pause is granted them in their labours, but compelled beneath blows of the overseers to endure the severity of their plight, they throw away their lives in this wretched manner, although certain of them who can endure it, by virtue of their bodily strength and their persevering souls, suffer such hardships over a long period; indeed death in their eyes is more to be desired than life, because of the magnitude of the hardships they must bear.

A SLAVE REVOLT IN SICILY

There was never a sedition of slaves so great as that which occurred in Sicily, whereby many cities met with grave calamities, innumerable men and women, together with their children, experienced the greatest misfortunes, and all the island was in danger of falling into the power of fugitive slaves. . . .

. . . The Servile [slave] War broke out for the following reason. The Sicilians, having shot up in prosperity and acquired great wealth, began to purchase a vast number of slaves, to whose bodies, as they were brought in droves from the slave markets, they at once applied marks and brands. The young men they used as cowherds, the others in such ways as they happened to be useful. But they treated them with a heavy hand in their service, and granted them the most meagre care, the bare minimum for food and clothing. . . .

The slaves, distressed by their hardships, and frequently outraged and beaten beyond all reason, could not endure their treatment. Getting together as opportunity offered, they discussed the possibility of revolt, until at last they put their plans into action. . . . The beginning of the whole revolt took place as follows.

There was a certain Damophilus of Enna [a city in central Sicily], a man of great wealth but insolent of manner; he had abused his slaves to excess, and his wife Megallis vied even with her husband in punishing the slaves and in her general inhumanity towards them. The slaves, reduced by this degrading treatment to the level of brutes, conspired to revolt and to murder their masters. Going to Eunus [a Syrian slave believed to be a seer and magician] they asked him whether their resolve had the favour of the gods. He, resorting to his usual mummery, promised them the favour of the gods, and soon persuaded them to act at once. Immediately, therefore, they brought together four hundred of their fellow slaves and, having armed themselves in such ways as opportunity permitted, they fell upon the city of Enna, with Eunus at their head and working his miracle of the flames of fire for their benefit. When they found their way into the houses they shed much blood, sparing not even suckling babes. Rather they tore them from the breast and dashed them to the ground, while as for the women—and under their husbands' very eyes—but words cannot tell the extent of their outrages and acts of lewdness! By now a great multitude of slaves from the city had joined them, who, after first demonstrating against their own masters their utter ruthlessness, then turned to the slaughter of others. When Eunus and his men learned that Damophilus and his wife were in the garden that lay near the city, they sent some of their band and dragged them off, both the man and his wife, fettered and with hands bound behind their backs, subjecting them to many outrages along the way. Only in the case of the couple's daughter were the slaves seen to show consideration throughout, and this was because of her kindly nature, in that to the extent of her power she was always compassionate and ready to succour the slaves. Thereby it was demonstrated that the others were treated as they were, not because of some "natural savagery of slaves," but rather in revenge for wrongs previously received. The men appointed to the task, having dragged Damophilus and Megallis into the city, as we said, brought them to the theatre, where the crowd of rebels had assembled. But when Damophilus attempted to devise a plea to get them off safe and was winning over many of the crowd with his words, Hermeias and Zeuxis, men bitterly disposed towards him, denounced him as a cheat, and without waiting for a formal trial by the assembly the one ran him through the chest with a sword, the other chopped off his head with an axe. Thereupon Eunus was chosen king, not for his manly courage or his ability as a military leader, but solely for his marvels and his setting of the revolt in motion. . . .

Established as the rebels' supreme commander, he called an assembly and put to death all the citizenry of Enna except for those who were skilled in the manufacture of arms: these he put in chains and assigned them to this task. He gave Megallis to the maidservants to deal with as they might wish; they subjected her to torture and threw her over a precipice. He himself murdered his own masters, Antigenes and Pytho. Having set a diadem upon his head, and arrayed himself in full royal style, he proclaimed his wife queen (she

was a fellow Syrian and of the same city), and appointed to the royal council such men as seemed to be gifted with superior intelligence. . . .

. . . In three days Eunus had armed, as best he could, more than six thousand men, besides others in his train who had only axes and hatchets, or slings, or sickles, or fire-hardened stakes, or even kitchen spits; and he went about ravaging the countryside. Then, since he kept recruiting untold numbers of slaves, he ventured even to do battle with Roman generals, and on joining combat repeatedly overcame them with his superior numbers, for he now had more than ten thousand soldiers.

Soon after, engaging in battle with a general arrived from Rome, Lucius Hypsaeus [the Roman governor], who had eight thousand Sicilian troops, the rebels were victorious, since they now numbered twenty thousand. Before long their band reached a total of two hundred thousand,[1] and in numerous battles with the Romans they acquitted themselves well, and failed but seldom. As word of this was bruited about, a revolt of one hundred and fifty slaves, banded together, flared up in Rome, of more than a thousand in Attica, and of yet others in Delos [an island off the southeastern Greek coast] and many other places. But thanks to the speed with which forces were brought up and to the severity of their punitive measures, the magistrates of these communities at once disposed of the rebels and brought to their senses any who were wavering on the verge of revolt. In Sicily, however, the trouble grew. Cities were captured with all their inhabitants, and many armies were cut to pieces by the rebels, until Rupilius, the Roman commander, recovered Tauromenium [Taormina] for the Romans by placing it under strict siege and confining the rebels under conditions of unspeakable duress and famine: conditions such that, beginning by eating the children, they progressed to

---

[1] The ancients often exaggerated numbers; the slaves probably raised an army of some 70,000.

the women, and did not altogether abstain even from eating one another. . . .

Finally, after Sarapion, a Syrian, had betrayed the citadel, the general laid hands on all the runaway slaves in the city, whom, after torture, he threw over a cliff. From there he advanced to Enna, which he put under siege in much the same manner, bringing the rebels into extreme straits and frustrating their hopes. . . . Rupilius captured this city also by betrayal, since its strength was impregnable to force of arms. Eunus, taking with him his bodyguards, a thousand strong, fled in unmanly fashion. . . .

. . . He met such an end as befitted his knavery, and died at Morgantina [in central Sicily]. Thereupon Rupilius, traversing the whole of Sicily with a few picked troops, sooner than had been expected rid it of every nest of robbers.

Appian of Alexandria
THE REVOLT OF SPARTACUS

In 73 B.C., gladiators led by Spartacus broke out of their barracks and were joined by tens of thousands of runaways. Spartacus aimed to escape from Italy to Gaul and Thrace, the homelands—Spartacus was a Thracian—of many slaves. The slave army, which grew to some 150,000, defeated Roman armies and devastated southern Italy before the superior might of Rome prevailed. Some six thousand of the defeated slaves were tortured and crucified on the road from Capua to Rome. The following account of the rebellion was written by Appian of Alexandria in the second century A.D.

In Italy, at this same time, Spartacus, a Thracian who had once fought against the Romans and after being taken prisoner and sold had become a gladiator in a troop which was kept to provide entertainments at Capua, persuaded about seventy of his fellows to risk their lives for freedom rather than for exhibition as a spectacle. With them, he overpowered their guards and escaped. Then he equipped himself and his companions with staves and daggers seized from travellers and took refuge on Mount Vesuvius, where he allowed many runaway domestic slaves and some free farm hands to join him. With the gladiators Oenomaus and Crixus as his subordinates he plundered the nearby areas, and because he divided the spoils in equal shares his numbers quickly swelled. The first commander sent against him was Varinius Glaber, and the second Publius Valerius; instead of legionary forces they had anyone they could quickly conscript on the way, because the Romans did not yet class the affair as a war, but as a kind of raid akin to piracy, and they were defeated when they attacked him. Spartacus himself actually captured Varinius' horse from under him; so nearly was a Roman general taken prisoner by a gladiator. After this, people flocked in still greater numbers to join Spartacus: his army now numbered 70,000 and he began to manufacture weapons and gather stores.

The government in Rome now despatched the consuls with two legions. Crixus, at the head of 3,000 men, was defeated and killed by one of them at Mount Garganus, with the loss of two-thirds of his force. Spartacus, who was eager to go through the Apennines to the Alpine regions, and then to Celtic lands from the Alps, was intercepted and prevented from escaping by the other consul, while his colleague conducted the pursuit. But Spartacus turned on each of them and defeated them separately. In the aftermath they retreated in confusion, while

Spartacus, first sacrificing 300 Roman prisoners to Crixus, made for Rome with 120,000 foot soldiers after burning the useless equipment and putting all the prisoners to death and slaughtering the draught animals to free himself of all encumbrances; and although a large number of deserters approached him he refused to accept any of them. When the consuls made another stand in Picenum, there was a further great struggle and on that occasion also a great Roman defeat. Spartacus, however, changed his mind about marching on Rome because he was not yet a match for the defenders and his troops did not all have soldier's arms and equipment (no town had joined their cause, and they were all slaves, deserters and human flotsam). He seized the mountains around Thurii, together with the town itself, and then prevented traders bringing in gold and silver, barred his own men from acquiring any, and bought exclusively iron and bronze at good prices without harming those who brought them. As a result they had plenty of raw material and were well equipped and made frequent raiding expeditions. They again confronted the Romans in battle, defeated them, and on that occasion too returned to camp laden with booty.

The war had now lasted three years and was causing the Romans great concern, although at the beginning it had been laughed at and regarded as trivial because it was against gladiators. When the appointment of other generals was proposed there was universal reluctance to stand, and no one put himself forward until Licinius Crassus, distinguished both for his family and his wealth, undertook to assume the post, and led six legions against Spartacus; to these he added the two consular legions when he reached the front. He immediately punished the latter for their repeated defeats, making them draw lots for every tenth man to be put to death. According to some, this was not what happened; instead, when he himself had suffered defeat after engaging the enemy with his whole force he had them all draw lots for the tenth place and put to death up to 4,000 men without being in the least deterred by their numbers. Whatever

the truth, he established himself in the eyes of his men as more to be feared than a defeat at the hands of the enemy, and forthwith won a victory over 10,000 of Spartacus' men who were encamped separately somewhere. He killed two-thirds of them and marched confidently against Spartacus himself. After winning a brilliant victory, he pursued Spartacus as he fled towards the sea with the intention of sailing across to Sicily, overtook him, and walled him in with ditches, earthworks, and palisades. Spartacus then tried to force his way out and reach the Samnite country, but Crassus killed almost 6,000 of his opponents at the beginning of the day and nearly as many more at evening, at the cost of three dead and seven wounded from the Roman army; so effective had their punishment been in altering their will to win. Spartacus, who was waiting for some cavalry that were on their way to him, no longer went into battle with his full force, but conducted many separate harassing operations against his besiegers; he made sudden and repeated sorties against them, set fire to bundles of wood which he had thrown into the ditches, and made their work difficult. He crucified a Roman prisoner in no-man's land to demonstrate to his own troops the fate awaiting them if they were defeated. When the government at Rome heard of the siege and contemplated the dishonour they would incur from a protracted war with gladiators, they appointed Pompeius, who had recently arrived from Spain, to an additional command in the field, in the belief that the task of dealing with Spartacus was now substantial and difficult. As a result of this appointment Crassus pressed on urgently with every means of attacking Spartacus, to stop Pompeius stealing his glory, while Spartacus, thinking to forestall Pompeius, invited Crassus to negotiate. When Crassus spurned the offer, Spartacus decided to make a desperate attempt, and with the cavalry which had by now arrived forced a way through the encircling fortifications with his whole army and retired towards Brundisium, with Crassus in pursuit. But when he discovered that Lucullus, who was on his way back from his victory over Mithridates, was there, he despaired of everything and, at the head of a still large force, joined battle with Crassus.

The fight was long, and bitterly contested, since so many tens of thousands of men had no other hope. Spartacus himself was wounded by a spear-thrust in the thigh, but went down on one knee, held his shield in front of him, and fought off his attackers until he and a great number of his followers were encircled and fell. The rest of his army was already in disorder and was cut down in huge numbers; consequently their losses were not easy to estimate (though the Romans lost about 1,000 men), and Spartacus' body was never found. Since there was still a very large number of fugitives from the battle in the mountains, Crassus proceeded against them. They formed themselves into four groups and kept up their resistance until there were only 6,000 survivors, who were taken prisoner and crucified all the way along the road from Rome to Capua.

REVIEW QUESTIONS

1. What was the character of slavery under the early Romans?
2. According to Diodorus Siculus, what was the impact of slavery on the moral character of both masters and slaves? Compare with that of Seneca (see page 141).
3. Judging from Appian's account, how would you describe Spartacus' character?

5 Women in Republican Society

The status of women in late republican Roman society was considerably better than that of Greek women during the classical age. Like Greek law, Roman law had originally placed each female under the jurisdiction of a male, the *pater-familias* (literally, "family father"), but Roman women obtained some freedom from male control during the times of the late Republic and the early Empire. Although women never achieved full civil equality and they could not formally participate in the political institutions of Rome, they did eventually exercise much practical control over their own property and indirectly exercised political influence through their husbands, sons, and fathers.

Quintus Lucretius Vespillo
A FUNERAL EULOGY FOR A ROMAN WIFE

Documenting intimate relationships between Roman men and women is difficult because ordinary people were unlikely to write about such things. Although personal records are scant or now lost, glimpses have survived in the writings of historians and poets or as inscriptions on tombstones.

In the late Republic, it became more common for distinguished men to pronounce funeral eulogies for distinguished female as well as male members of their families. One such eulogy was composed by the ex-Consul Quintus Lucretius Vespillo for his wife Turia, who died about 8 B.C. Though marriages among persons of the higher social ranks were usually undertaken for political and economic considerations, clearly this couple had gone beyond such a formal alliance to achieve a most touching love.

Before the day fixed for our marriage, you were suddenly left an orphan, by the murder of your parents in the solitude of the country. . . .

Through your efforts chiefly, their death did not remain unavenged. . . .

In our day, marriages of such long duration, not dissolved by divorce, but terminated by death alone, are indeed rare. For our union was prolonged in unclouded happiness for forty-one years. Would that it had been my lot to put an end to this our good fortune and that I as the older—which was more just—had yielded to fate.

Why recall your inestimable qualities, your modesty, deference, affability, your amiable disposition, your faithful attendance to the household duties, your enlightened religion, your unassuming elegance, the modest simplicity and refinement of your manners? Need I speak of your attachment to your kindred, your affection for your family—when you respected my mother as you did your own parents and cared for her tomb as you did for that of your own mother and father,—you who share countless other virtues with Roman ladies most jealous of their fair name? These qualities which I claim for you are your own, equalled or excelled by but few; for the experience of men teaches us how rare they are.

With common prudence we have preserved all the patrimony which you received from your parents. Intrusting it all to me, you were not troubled with the care of increasing it; thus did we share the task of administering it, that I undertook to protect your fortune, and you to guard mine. . . .

You gave proof of your generosity not only towards several of your kin, but especially in your filial devotion. . . . You brought up in your own home, in the enjoyment of mutual benefits, some young girls of your kinship. And that these might attain to a station in life worthy of our family, you provided them with dowries. . . .

I owe you no less a debt than Cæsar Augustus [27 B.C.–A.D. 14, emperor of Rome] himself, for this my return from exile to my native land. For unless you had prepared the way for my safety, even Cæsar's promises of assistance had been of no avail. So I owe no less a debt to your loyal devotion than to the clemency of Cæsar.

Why shall I now conjure up the memory of our domestic counsels and plans stored away in the hidden recesses of the heart?—That, aroused by the sudden arrival of messages from you to a realization of the present and imminent perils, I was saved by your counsel? That you suffered me not to be recklessly carried away by a foolish rashness, or that, when bent on more temperate plans, you provided for me a safe retreat, having as sharers in your plans for my safety, when an exile,—fraught with danger as they were for you all,—your sister and her husband. . . .

Vespillo then relates what happened to his wife when she begged his enemy M. Lepidus to honor her husband's writ of pardon from Octavian Caesar.

. . . Then prostrating yourself at his feet, he not only did not raise you up,—but, dragged along and abused as though a common slave, your body all covered with bruises, yet with unflinching steadfastness of purpose, you recalled to him Cæsar's edict (of pardon) and the letter of felicitation on my return, that accompanied it. Braving his taunts and suffering the most brutal treatment, you denounced these cruelties publicly so that he (Lepidus) was branded as the author of all my perils and misfortunes. And his punishment was not long delayed.

Could such courage remain without effect? Your unexampled patience furnished the occasion for Cæsar's clemency, and, by guarding my life, he branded the infamous and savage cruelty (of the tyrant Lepidus). . . .

When all the world was again at peace and the Republic reestablished, peaceful and happy days followed. We longed for children, which an envious fate denied us. Had Fortune smiled on us in this, what had been lacking to complete our happiness? But an adverse destiny put an end to our hopes. . . . Disconsolate to see me without children . . . you wished to put an end to my chagrin by proposing to me a divorce, offering to yield the place to another spouse more fertile, with the only intention of searching for and providing for me a spouse worthy of our mutual affection, whose children you assured me you would have treated as your own. . . .

I will admit that I was so irritated and shocked by such a proposition that I had difficulty in restraining my anger and remaining master of myself. You spoke of divorce before the decree of fate [death] had forced us to separate, and I could not comprehend how you could conceive of any reason why you, still living, should not be my wife, you who during my exile had always remained most faithful and loyal. . . .

Would that our time of life had permitted our union to have endured until I, the older, had passed away—which was more just—and that you might perform for me the last sad rites and that I might have departed, leaving you behind, with a daughter to replace me at your side.

By fate's decree your course was run before mine. You left me the grief, the heart-ache, the longing for you, the sad fate to live alone. . . .

The conclusion of this discourse will be that you have deserved all, and that I remain with the chagrin of not being able to give you all. Your wishes have always been my supreme law; and whatever it will be permitted me to accord them still, in this I shall not fail.

May the gods, the Manes [spirits of dead ancestors, considered godlike], assure and protect your repose!

REVIEW QUESTIONS

1. What does Vespillo's eulogy reveal about the virtues a Roman husband might expect in his wife? What duties were expected of a wife?
2. In your opinion, what was Turia's most commendable quality?

6   The Decline of the Republic

In 133 B.C. the Romans effectively controlled all the lands that touched the Mediterranean Sea. The old enemies of Rome, Carthage, and Macedonia had become Roman provinces; the Hellenistic kingdoms of Syria and Egypt were clients of Rome without effective power to challenge Roman hegemony. The Mediterranean Sea had become a "Roman lake."

Yet, at the very moment of its imperial supremacy, the internal order and institutions of the Roman Republic began to break down. The senatorial leaders, who had served Rome responsibly in its march to empire, no longer governed effectively. The ruling class engaged in shameless corruption in administering the provinces, resorted to bribery and force to maintain control over public offices, and failed to solve the deeply rooted problems that afflicted the state.

Triggering the Republic's downhill slide was an agricultural crisis that destroyed the small independent peasant.

Plutarch
TIBERIUS GRACCHUS

The wars of expansion had a disastrous effect on Roman agriculture. Hannibal's ravaging of Italian farmlands and the obligatory military service that kept peasants away from their fields for long periods left many small farms in near ruins. The importation of thousands of prisoners of war to toil as slaves on large plantations also kept small farmers from this work. Sinking ever deeper into debt and poverty, many lost their lands and went to Rome, where lack of jobs condemned them to permanent poverty. The once sturdy and independent Roman farmer, who had done all that his country had asked of him, became part of a vast urban underclass—poor, embittered, and alienated.

Tiberius Gracchus (163–133 B.C.), a scion of one of Rome's most honored families, was distressed by this injustice. Moreover, he realized that small landowners were the backbone of the Roman army. Elected tribune (an office created in 493 B.C. to protect plebeian rights), Tiberius Gracchus in 133 B.C. proposed land reforms that the senatorial nobility regarded as a potential menace to their property. They also viewed Tiberius Gracchus as a threat to their political authority. The Roman nobility feared that this popular reformer was building a following among the commoners in order to undermine senatorial rule and that his real ambition was to subvert republican institutions and to become a tyrant, a one-man ruler. This fear was strengthened when Tiberius, in violation of constitutional custom, announced that he would seek reelection as tribune. Senatorial extremists killed Tiberius Gracchus and some three hundred of his followers. The Republic had entered an age of political violence that would eventually destroy it. (Tiberius' younger brother, Gaius, became tribune in 123 B.C. and suffered a fate similar to his brother's.) The following account of Tiberius Gracchus is by Plutarch, the second-century Greek biographer.

Of the territory which the Romans won in war from their neighbours, a part they sold, and a part they made common land, and assigned it for occupation to the poor and indigent among the citizens, on payment of a small rent into the public treasury. And when the rich began to offer larger rents and drove out the poor, a law was enacted forbidding the holding by one person of more than five hundred acres of land. For a short time this enactment gave a check to the rapacity of the rich, and was of assistance to the poor, who remained in their places on the land which they had rented and occupied the allotment which each had held from the outset. But later on the neighbouring rich men, by means of fictitious personages, transferred these rentals to themselves, and finally held most of the land openly in their own names. Then the poor, who had been ejected from their land, no longer showed themselves eager for military service, and neglected the bringing up of children, so that soon all Italy was conscious of a dearth of freemen, and was filled with gangs of foreign slaves, by whose aid the rich cultivated their estates, from which they had driven away the free citizens. An attempt was therefore made to rectify this evil, and by Caius Laelius[1] the comrade

---

[1] Caius Laelius Sapiens, a leading military hero in the Third Punic War and a close friend of Scipio Aemilianus, the conqueror of Carthage, attempted unsuccessfully to resettle the poor on public land.

of Scipio; but the men of influence opposed his measures, and he, fearing the disturbance which might ensue, desisted, and received the surname of *Wise* or *Prudent* [for the Latin word "sapiens" would seem to have either meaning]. Tiberius, however, on being elected tribune of the people, took the matter directly in hand. . . .

He did not, however, draw up his law by himself, but took counsel with the citizens who were foremost in virtue and reputation. . . .

. . . And it is thought that a law dealing with injustice and rapacity so great was never drawn up in milder and gentler terms. For men who ought to have been punished for their disobedience and to have surrendered with payment of a fine the land which they were illegally enjoying, these men it merely ordered to abandon their injust acquisitions upon being paid their value, and to admit into ownership of them such citizens as needed assistance. But although the rectification of the wrong was so considerate, the people were satisfied to let bygones be bygones if they could be secure from such wrong in the future; the men of wealth and substance, however, were led by their greed to hate the law, and by their wrath and contentiousness to hate the law-giver, and tried to dissuade the people by alleging that Tiberius was introducing a re-distribution of land for the confusion of the body politic, and was stirring up a general revolution.

But they accomplished nothing; for Tiberius, striving to support a measure which was honourable and just with an eloquence that would have adorned even a meaner cause, was formidable and invincible, whenever, with the people crowding around the rostra [speaker's platforms], he took his stand there and pleaded for the poor. "The wild beasts that roam over Italy," he would say, "have every one of them a cave or lair to lurk in; but the men who fight and die for Italy enjoy the common air and light, indeed, but nothing else; houseless and homeless they wander about with their wives and children. And it is with lying lips that their imperators[2] exhort the soldiers in their battles to defend sepulchres and shrines from the enemy; for not a man of them has an hereditary altar, not one of all these many Romans an ancestral tomb, but they fight and die to support others in wealth and luxury, and though they are styled masters of the world, they have not a single clod of earth that is their own."

Such words as these, the product of a lofty spirit and genuine feeling, and falling upon the ears of a people profoundly moved and fully aroused to the speaker's support, no adversary of Tiberius could successfully withstand.

---

[2]First, a commander, general, or captain in the army, later *imperator* meant "emperor."

Cicero
JUSTIFYING CAESAR'S ASSASSINATION

In the century following the assassination of Tiberius Gracchus in 133 B.C., the Republic was torn by conspiracies to seize the state, civil wars, assassinations, mob violence, and confiscations of property by political opponents.

In 49 B.C., Julius Caesar (100–44 B.C.), a talented and ambitious commander, marched on Rome. After defeating the Senate's forces, he was appointed dictator for ten years. A creative statesman, Caesar introduced reforms to resolve the grievances of Romans and provincials. Some senators feared that Caesar aimed to establish a typical Hellenistic monarchy over Rome with himself as absolute king. The very word *king* was abhorrent to patriotic Romans, who gloried in their status as free citizens of a five-centuries-old republic. Finally, on the Ides (the fifteenth) of March, 44 B.C., Julius Caesar was slain by some sixty senators, who acted, they said, to restore the liberty of the Roman people. Their leaders were Marcus Junius Brutus (82–42 B.C.) and Gaius Cassius (d. 42 B.C.), both of whom Caesar had previously pardoned.

In the following reading from *On Duties*, Cicero, who was not one of the assassins, justifies the killing of Caesar.

Our tyrant deserved his death for having made an exception of the one thing that was the blackest crime of all. Why do we gather instances of petty crime—legacies criminally obtained and fraudulent buying and selling? Behold, here you have a man who was ambitious to be king of the Roman People and master of the whole world; and he achieved it! The man who maintains that such an ambition is morally right is a madman; for he justifies the destruction of law and liberty and thinks their hideous and detestable suppression glorious. But if anyone agrees that it is not morally right to be king in a state that once was free and that ought to be free now, and yet imagines that it is advantageous for him who can reach that position, with what remonstrance or rather with what appeal should I try to tear him away from so strange a delusion? For, oh ye immortal gods! can the most horrible and hideous of all murders—that of fatherland—bring advantage to anybody, even though he who has committed such a crime receives from his enslaved fellow-citizens the title of "Father of his Country"?

Velleius Paterculus
THE TRIUMPH OF OCTAVIAN

The assassination of Julius Caesar plunged Rome into renewed civil war in which thousands more perished. Two of Caesar's trusted lieutenants, Mark Antony and Lepidus, joined with Octavian, Caesar's adopted son, and defeated the armies of Brutus and Cassius, two principal conspirators in the plot against Caesar. After Lepidus was forced into political obscurity, Antony and Octavian fought each other, with Rome as the prize. In 31 B.C., at the naval battle of Actium in western Greece, Octavian crushed the forces of Antony and his wife, Egypt's Queen Cleopatra. Both Antony and Cleopatra had fled to Egypt prior to the battle. The following year Octavian pursued the couple to Egypt where both committed suicide. Following is Velleius Paterculus' (c. 19 B.C.–c. A.D. 31) account of Octavian's triumph.

Then, in the consulate of Cæsar and Corvinus Messala, the decisive contest was waged at Actium, where, long before the engagement, it was easy to foresee, that victory would attend the Julian party. On [Octavian's] side, both the soldiers and the commander were full of vigour; on [Anthony's], everything was feeble: on this, the seamen were in full strength; on the other, they were greatly reduced by want: on this, the ships were moderate in size and active; on the opposite, they were more formidable only in appearance. From this side not a man deserted to Anthony; from the other, deserters came daily to Cæsar....

At length arrived the day of the grand dispute, when Cæsar and Anthony, with their fleets in line of battle, came to a general engagement; one fighting for the preservation, the other for the destruction of the world....

When the engagement began, every thing on one side was complete, the commander, the seamen, the soldiers; on the other, nothing but the soldiers. Cleopatra first began the flight, and Anthony chose to accompany her, rather than remain with his men in battle. Thus a general, whose duty it had been to punish deserters, became a deserter of his own army. His men, though deprived of their chief, maintained the fight a long time with most determined resolution; and many, even when they despaired of victory, continued it to death. Cæsar, although he could have conquered them with the sword, wished rather to subdue them by words; and calling aloud, and pointing, shewed them that Anthony had fled; asking them for whom, and against whom, they fought. At last, after a long struggle in favour of their absent leader, they were with difficulty prevailed on to lay down their arms, and yield the victory; and Cæsar granted them life and pardon more readily than they were persuaded to ask them of him. It was universally allowed, that the soldiers acted the part of an excellent commander, and the commander that of a most dastardly soldier. So that you can easily judge, whether, in case of

success, he would have regulated his conduct by his own judgment, or by Cleopatra's, since by hers he was determined to fly. The army on land submitted in like manner, after [its commander] had precipitately fled to Anthony.

What blessings that day procured to the world, what an improvement it produced in the state of the public welfare, no man can attempt to recount in such a hasty narrative as this abridgment. The victory was attended with the greatest clemency: very few were put to death....

In the next year, Cæsar followed the Queen and Anthony to Alexandria, and brought the war to a final conclusion. Anthony killed himself courageously enough, so as to compensate by his death for many crimes of effeminacy. Cleopatra, eluding the vigilance of her guards, had an asp brought to her, and by its bite put an end to her life, without betraying any womanish fear. It reflected honour on Cæsar's success and his merciful disposition, that not one of who bore arms against him was put to death by him. Decimus Brutus perished by the cruelty of Anthony; and the same Anthony, when Sextus Pompey was conquered by him, although he had pledged his honour to secure even his dignity, yet he bereft him of that and life together. Brutus and Cassius died voluntary deaths, without making trial of the disposition of the conquerors. The end of Anthony and Cleopatra we have now related. Canidius died in a more cowardly manner than was consonant to his frequent professions. Of the murderers of Cæsar, Cassius Parmensis was the last victim of vengeance, as Trebonius had been the first.

Sallust
MORAL DETERIORATION

In the dark days of the Republic after the assassination of Julius Caesar in 44 B.C., the Roman politician and historian Sallust (Gaius Sallustius Crispus, 86–35 B.C.) reflected on the causes of the Republic's collapse. In his account of a failed coup d'état that occurred in 63 B.C., Sallust contrasted the virtues of the early Republic with the moral decline that set in after the destruction of Carthage. Having failed to be elected consul in 63 B.C., Catiline, a Roman noble, organized a conspiracy to seize the state. The coup d'état was thwarted by the vigorous action of the consul Cicero, who arrested the known conspirators and had them executed. Catiline, who led an army against the forces loyal to the government, was defeated and killed.

In peace and war [in the early Republic], as I have said, virtue was held in high esteem. The closest unity prevailed, and avarice was a thing almost unknown. Justice and righteousness were upheld not so much by law as by natural instinct. They quarrelled and fought with their country's foes; between themselves the citizens contended only for honour. In making offerings to the gods they spared no expense; at home they lived frugally and never betrayed a friend. By combining boldness in war with fair dealing when peace was restored, they protected themselves and the state. There are convincing proofs of this. In time of war, soldiers were often punished for attacking against orders or for being slow to obey a signal of recall from battle, whereas few ever ventured to desert their standards or to give ground when hard pressed. In peace, they governed by conferring benefits on their subjects, not by intimidation; and when wronged they would rather pardon than seek vengeance.

Thus by hard work and just dealing the power of the state increased. Mighty kings were vanquished, savage tribes and huge nations were brought to their knees; and when Carthage, Rome's rival in her quest for empire, had been annihilated [in 146 B.C.], every land and sea lay open to her. It was then that fortune turned unkind and confounded all her enterprises. To the men who had so easily endured toil and peril, anxiety and adversity, the leisure and riches which are generally regarded as so desirable proved a burden and a curse. Growing love of money, and the lust for power which followed it, engendered every kind of evil. Avarice destroyed honour, integrity, and every other virtue, and instead taught men to be proud and cruel, to neglect religion, and to hold nothing too sacred to sell. Ambition tempted many to be false, to have one thought hidden in their hearts, another ready on their tongues, to become a man's friend or enemy not because they judged him worthy or unworthy but because they thought it would pay them, and to put on the semblance of virtues that they had not. At first these vices grew slowly and sometimes met with punishment; later on, when the disease had spread like a plague, Rome changed: her government, once so just and admirable, became harsh and unendurable.

Reflecting on the last stages of the Republic's decline, Sallust believed that men had learned a most dangerous lesson: that they could gain power and wealth through violence and corruption rather than through virtue and self-restraint.

Never in its history—it seems to me—had the empire of Rome been in such a miserable plight. From east to west all the world had been vanquished by her armies and obeyed her will; at home there was profound peace and abundance of wealth, which mortal men esteem the chiefest of blessings. Yet there were Roman citizens obstinately determined to destroy both themselves and their country. In spite of two senatorial decrees, not one man among all the conspirators was induced by the promise of reward to betray their plans, and not one deserted from Catiline's camp. A deadly moral contagion had infected all their minds. And this madness was not confined to those actually implicated in the plot. The whole of the lower orders, impatient for a new régime, looked with favour on Catiline's enterprise.* In this they only did what might have been expected of them. In every country paupers envy respectable citizens and make heroes of unprincipled characters, hating the established order of things and hankering after innovation; discontented with their own lot, they

---

*This surely cannot have been true. Sallust must be exaggerating the popular support for the conspiracy.

are bent on general upheaval. Turmoil and rebellion bring them carefree profit, since poverty has nothing to lose.

The city populace were especially eager to fling themselves into a revolutionary adventure. There were several reasons for this. To begin with, those who had made themselves conspicuous anywhere by vice and shameless audacity, those who had wasted their substance by disgraceful excesses, and those whom scandalous or criminal conduct had exiled from their homes—all these had poured into Rome till it was like a sewer. Many, remembering Sulla's victory,[1] and seeing men who had served under him as common soldiers now risen to be senators, or so rich that they lived as luxuriously as kings, began to hope that they too, if they took up arms, might find victory a source of profit. Young men from the country, whose labour on the farms had barely kept them from starvation, had been attracted by the private and public doles available at Rome, and preferred an idle city life to such thankless toil. These, like all the rest, stood to gain by public calamities. It is no wonder, therefore, that these paupers, devoid of moral scruple and incited by ambitious hopes, should have held their country as cheap as they held themselves. Those also to whom Sulla's victory had brought disaster by the proscription of their parents, the confiscation of

their property, and the curtailment of their civil rights, looked forward with no less sanguine expectations to what might result from the coming struggle. Moreover, all the factions opposed to the Senate would rather see the state embroiled than accept their own exclusion from political power.

Such was the evil condition by which, after an interval of some years, Rome was once more afflicted. After the restoration of the power of the tribunes in the consulship of Pompey and Crassus,[*2] this very important office was obtained by certain men whose youth intensified their natural aggressiveness. These tribunes began to rouse the mob by inveighing against the Senate, and then inflamed popular passion still further by handing out bribes and promises, whereby they won renown and influence for themselves. They were strenuously opposed by most of the nobility, who posed as defenders of the Senate but were really concerned to maintain their own privileged position. The whole truth—to put it in a word—is that although all disturbers of the peace in this period put forward specious pretexts, claiming either to be protecting the rights of the people or to be strengthening the authority of the Senate, this was mere pretence: in reality, every one of them was fighting for his personal aggrandizement. Lacking all self-restraint, they [stopped] at nothing to gain their ends, and both sides made ruthless use of any successes they won.

---

[1]Lucius Cornelius Sulla (c. 138–78 B.C.) was a successful politician and general, whose rivalry with another politician and general, Gaius Marius (c. 155–86 B.C.), led to civil war. After seizing Rome and massacring his opponents, Sulla made himself dictator and increased the power of the aristocratic senate, suppressing the office of tribune of the people. The latter had been used by Tiberius and Gaius Gracchus, among others, to better the condition of the poorer classes.

---

*In 70 B.C.

[2]Pompey (Gnaeus Pompeius, 106–48 B.C.) and Crassus (Marcus Licinius Crassus, c. 115–53 B.C.) held the office of consul in 55 B.C. In 59 B.C., together with Julius Caesar, they had formed a political alliance called a triumvirate (meaning "group of three men"), which dominated Roman government for the next decade.

REVIEW QUESTIONS

1. What factors created a socioeconomic class struggle in the late Roman Republic?
2. According to Plutarch, what was the reaction of the senatorial order to the reforms proposed by Tiberius Gracchus?
3. Why did Cicero consider Caesar guilty of "the blackest crime of all"?
4. How did Octavian's triumph over Anthony and Cleopatra foreshadow the way he might govern the Roman Empire?
5. To what virtues did Sallust attribute the greatness of Rome?
6. What vices did Sallust believe could ruin a great state? Does his analysis have any contemporary significance?

CHAPTER 5

The Roman Empire

THE ROMAN COLOSSEUM. Rome's largest amphitheater, the Colosseum could seat some forty-five to fifty thousand spectators. *(Scala/Ministero per i Beni e le Attività culturali/Art Resource, NY)*

In the chaotic years following Julius Caesar's assassination in 44 B.C., Octavian (Augustus) emerged victorious over his rivals, becoming the unchallenged ruler of Rome. Although eager for personal power, Augustus was by no means a self-seeking tyrant; he was a creative statesman who prevented the renewal of civil war that had plagued the Republic and introduced needed reforms in Italy and the provinces. His long reign, from 27 B.C. to A.D. 14, marks the beginning of the *Pax Romana*, the Roman Peace, which endured until A.D. 180.

The period of the Pax Romana was one of the finest in the ancient world. Revolts against Roman rule were few, and Roman legions ably defended the Empire's borders. The Mediterranean world had never enjoyed so many years of peace, effective government, and economic well-being. Stretching from Britain to the Arabian Desert and from the Danube River to the sands of the Sahara, the Roman Empire united some sixty million people. In many ways the Roman Empire was the fulfillment of the universalism and cosmopolitanism of the Hellenistic Age. The same law bound together Italians, Spaniards, North Africans, Greeks, Syrians, and other peoples. Although dissatisfaction was sometimes violently expressed and separatist tendencies persisted, notably in Judea and Gaul, people from diverse backgrounds viewed themselves as Romans even though they had never set foot in the capital city.

In the seventy years following Augustus' reign, political life was sometimes marred by conspiracies and assassinations, particularly after an emperor's death left the throne vacant. Marcus Cocceius Nerva, who reigned from A.D. 96 to 98, introduced a practice that led to orderly succession and gave Rome four exceptionally competent emperors. He adopted as his son and designated as his heir Trajan (Marcus Ulpius Traianus), a man of proven ability. From the accession of Nerva to the death of Marcus Aurelius Antoninus in A.D. 180, the Roman Empire was ruled by the "Five Good Emperors." Marcus Aurelius abandoned the use of adoption and allowed his son Commodus (Lucius Aelius Aurelius, A.D. 180–192) to succeed to the throne. An extravagant despot, Commodus was murdered in A.D. 192.

During the third century the Roman Empire suffered hard times, and the ordered civilization of the Pax Romana was shattered. The Empire was plunged into anarchy as generals vied for the throne. Taking advantage of the weakened border defenses, the barbarians (Germanic tribesmen) crossed the Danube frontier and pillaged Roman cities. Both civil war and barbarian attacks greatly disrupted the Roman economy, which even during good times suffered from basic weaknesses.

Two later emperors—Diocletian (G. Aurelius Valerius Diocletianus, A.D. 285–305) and Constantine (Flavius Valerius Constantinus,

A.D. 306–337)—tried to keep the Empire from dissolution by tightening control over the citizenry. Although heavy taxes, requisitioning of goods, and forced labor provided some stability, these measures also turned many citizens against the oppressive state. At the end of the fourth and the opening of the fifth century, several barbarian tribes poured into the weakened Empire in great numbers. In succeeding decades Germanic tribes overran Roman provinces and set up kingdoms on lands that had been Roman. The Roman Empire in the west fell; the eastern provinces, however, survived as the Byzantine Empire.

The history of the Roman Empire influenced Western civilization in many ways. From Latin, the language of Rome, came the Romance languages: French, Italian, Spanish, Portuguese, and Romanian. Roman law became the basis of the legal codes of most modern European states. Rome preserved Greek culture, the foundation of Western learning and aesthetics, and spread it to other lands. And Christianity, the religion of the West, was born in the Roman Empire.

1 The Imperial Office

The greatest achievement of Caesar Augustus (Octavian), grandnephew and adopted son of Julius Caesar, was undoubtedly the step-by-step building of a new constitutional structure for the Roman Empire. This political system, called by modern historians the Principate, has been described as a monarchy disguised as an oligarchical republic. The Roman antimonarchial tradition, nurtured for five centuries under the Republican regime, had contributed directly to Julius Caesar's assassination. Augustus was wise enough, as he created a stable central executive office for the Empire, to camouflage the monarchial reality of his regime by maintaining the outer forms of the old Republic's constitution.

Augustus' chief innovation was creating the office of *Princeps* (First Citizen), which combined a number of Republican offices and powers and placed them at the disposal of one man. Desiring to maintain the appearance of traditional Republican government, he refused to be called king. The Senate gave him the semireligious and revered name Augustus (venerable). In effect, however, he was the first Roman emperor. He cultivated the support of the traditional constituents of the Roman state—the senatorial nobility, knights (those who bid for the right to collect public revenues), public contractors, residents of the capital, soldiers and veterans, and the wealthy and politically useful provincial subjects of Rome. At the time of his death in A.D. 14, Augustus successfully passed on his imperial office to his chosen heir, his adopted son Tiberius.

Augustus
THE ACHIEVEMENTS OF THE
DIVINE AUGUSTUS

In *Res gestae divi Augusti* (The Achievements of the Divine Augustus), a document composed shortly before his death and left to be published with his will, Augustus gave an account of those achievements for which he wanted to be remembered. A careful reading reveals the image Augustus chose to promote to justify his emperorship. It also describes the many responsibilities of holders of that office.

I drove into exile the murderers of my father [Julius Caesar], avenging their crime through tribunals established by law; and afterwards, when they made war on the republic, I twice defeated them in battle.

I undertook many civil and foreign wars by land and sea throughout the world, and as victor I spared the lives of all citizens who asked for mercy. When foreign peoples could safely be pardoned I preferred to preserve rather than to exterminate them. The Roman citizens who took the soldier's oath of obedience to me numbered about 500,000. I settled rather more than 300,000 of these in colonies or sent them back to their home towns after their period of service; to all these I assigned lands or gave money as rewards for their military service. . . .

The dictatorship was offered to me by both senate and people in my absence and when I was at Rome in the consulship of Marcus Marcellus and Lucius Arruntius, but I refused it. I did not decline in the great dearth of corn to undertake the charge of the corn-supply, which I so administered that within a few days I delivered the whole city from apprehension and immediate danger at my own cost and by my own efforts. . . . The senate and people of Rome agreed that I should be appointed supervisor of laws and morals without a colleague and with supreme power, but I would not accept any office inconsistent with the custom of our ancestors. The measures that the senate then desired me to take I carried out in virtue of my tribunician power. . . .

To each member of the Roman plebs [common populace] I paid under my father's will 300 sesterces,[1] and in my own name I gave them 400 each from the booty of war in my fifth consulship, and once again in my tenth consulship I paid out 400 sesterces as a largesse to each man from my own patrimony, and in my eleventh consulship I bought grain with my own money and distributed twelve rations apiece, and in the twelfth year of my tribunician power I gave every man 400 sesterces for the third time. These largesses of mine never reached fewer than 250,000 persons. . . .

. . . I paid monetary rewards to soldiers whom I settled in their home towns after completion of their service, and on this account I expended about 400,000,000 sesterces.

Four times I assisted the treasury with my own money, so that I transferred to the administrators of the treasury 150,000,000 sesterces. . . .

I restored the Capitol[2] and the theatre of Pompey, both works at great expense without

---

[1]Sesterces, during the reign of Augustus, were small coins of bronze, each worth one hundredth of a gold *aureus*, or a quarter of a silver denarius, the basic coin of the Roman monetary system. Brunt (editor of source) notes that a Roman legionary soldier of this period earned 900 sesterces a year, out of which the cost of uniform, food, and arms was deducted. A Roman whose assessed wealth came to at least 400,000 sesterces qualified to enter the order of knights; to be a senator required one million sesterces.
[2]Here "Capitol" refers to the temple of Jupiter, patron of Rome, on the Capitoline Hill.

inscribing my own name on either. I restored the channels of the aqueducts, which in several places were falling into disrepair through age, and I brought water from a new spring into the aqueduct called Marcia, doubling the supply. I completed the Forum Julium[3] and the basilica between the temples of Castor and Saturn,[4] works begun and almost finished by my father. . . .

I gave three gladiatorial games in my own name and five in that of my sons or grandsons; at these games some 10,000 men took part in combat. Twice in my own name and a third time in that of my grandson I presented to the people displays by athletes summoned from all parts. I produced shows in my own name four times and in place of other magistrates twenty-three times. . . . I gave beast-hunts of African beasts in my own name or in that of my sons and grandsons in the circus or forum or amphitheatre on twenty-six occasions, on which about 3,500 beasts were destroyed.

I made the sea peaceful and freed it of pirates. In that war I captured about 30,000 slaves who had escaped from their masters and taken up arms against the republic, and I handed them over to their masters for punishment.

I extended the territory of all those provinces of the Roman people on whose borders lay peoples not subject to our government. I brought peace to the Gallic and Spanish provinces as well as to Germany, throughout the area bordering on the [Atlantic] Ocean from Cadiz [in Spain] to the mouth of the Elbe [in northwestern Germany]. I secured the pacification of the Alps. . . . The Pannonian peoples [in western Hungary] . . . were conquered through the agency of Tiberius Nero[5] who was then my stepson and legate; I brought them into the empire of the Roman people, and extended the frontier of Illyricum[6] to the banks of the Danube. . . .

In my sixth and seventh consulships, after I had extinguished civil wars, and at a time when with universal consent I was in complete control of affairs, I transferred the republic from my power to the dominion of the senate and people of Rome. For this service of mine I was named Augustus by decree of the senate, and the doorposts of my house were publicly wreathed with bay leaves and a civic crown was fixed over my door and a golden shield was set in the Curia Julia,[7] which, as attested by the inscription thereon, was given me by the senate and people of Rome on account of my courage, clemency, justice and piety. After this time I excelled all in influence, although I possessed no more official power than others who were my colleagues in the several magistracies.

In my thirteenth consulship the senate, the equestrian order and the whole people of Rome gave me the title of Father of my Country. . . .

---

[3]The Forum (Square) Julium was surrounded by a covered portico. Begun by Julius Caesar, it was finished by Augustus.
[4]Saturn was a Roman agricultural god associated with the Greek god Cronus. Castor, brother of Pollux and Helen of Troy, was the son of Jupiter by a mortal. The twins Castor and Pollux were deified in Rome for having helped the Romans in a battle.

[5]Tiberius Nero, Augustus' adopted son and designated heir, reigned as emperor from A.D. 14 to 37.
[6]Illyricum was a Roman province on the eastern coast of the Adriatic Sea.
[7]The Curia Julia, also begun by Julius Caesar and completed by Augustus, was a courthouse.

Tacitus
THE IMPOSITION OF ONE-MAN RULE

Not all Romans accepted Augustus' own evaluation of his achievements. In this reading, the Roman historian Cornelius Tacitus (c. A.D. 55–c. 117) described how Augustus seduced the Roman people into accepting monarchial rule.

[Augustus] seduced the army with bonuses, and his cheap food policy was successful bait for civilians. Indeed, he attracted everybody's goodwill by the enjoyable gift of peace. Then he gradually pushed ahead and absorbed the functions of the senate, the officials, and even the law. Opposition did not exist. War or judicial murder had disposed of all men of spirit. Upperclass survivors found that slavish obedience was the way to succeed, both politically and financially. They had profited from the revolution, and so now they liked the security of the existing arrangement better than the dangerous uncertainties of the old régime. Besides, the new order was popular in the provinces. There, government by Senate and People was looked upon sceptically as a matter of sparring dignitaries and extortionate officials. The legal system had provided no remedy against these, since it was wholly incapacitated by violence, favouritism, and—most of all—bribery.

To safeguard his domination Augustus made his sister's son Marcellus a priest and an aedile[1]—in spite of his extreme youth—and singled out Marcus Agrippa,[2] a commoner but a first-rate soldier who had helped to win his victories, by the award of two consecutive consulships; after the death of Marcellus, Agrippa was chosen by Augustus as his son-in-law. Next the emperor had his stepsons Tiberius and Nero Drusus[3] hailed publicly as victorious generals. . . .

At this time there was no longer any fighting—except a war against the Germans. . . . In the capital the situation was calm. The titles of officials remained the same. Actium[4] had been won before the younger men were born. Even most of the older generation had come into a world of civil wars. Practically no one had ever seen truly Republican government. The country had been transformed, and there was nothing left of the fine old Roman character. Political equality was a thing of the past; all eyes watched for imperial commands.

---

[1]An aedile was a minor municipal magistrate, responsible for petty criminal cases, and for the supervision of markets and public games—gladiator combats and chariot races.

[2]Marcus Agrippa (c. 63–12 B.C.), Augustus' son-in-law, was his closest associate and virtually co-emperor; he predeceased Augustus.
[3]Nero Drusus (38–9 B.C.), one of Augustus' stepsons, was the father of Emperor Claudius (ruled A.D. 41–54).
[4]The Battle of Actium, fought in the sea off west-central Greece, pitted forces of Antony and Cleopatra against those of Octavian (Augustus). Octavian's victory gave him sole control of the Roman Empire.

REVIEW QUESTIONS

1. Describe the functions of a Roman emperor as suggested by the career of Caesar Augustus.
2. What constituencies did Caesar Augustus have to serve?
3. How did Augustus disguise the monarchial character of his regime?

---

2 Imperial Culture

The reign of Augustus marks the golden age of Latin literature. This outpouring of literary works stemmed in part from the patronage of authors by Augustus and other prominent Romans. Roman poets and dramatists used Greek models, just as Roman philosophers, mathematicians, scientists, doctors, and geographers did. Not surprisingly, writers of the Augustan Age often expressed strong patriotic sentiments and were extravagant in their praise of Augustus.

Virgil
THE AENEID

The poet Virgil (Publius Vergilius Maro, 70–19 B.C.) admired Augustus, who was his patron, for ending the civil wars and bringing order to the Roman world. Augustus urged Virgil to compose a grand opus that would glorify Rome's imperial achievement—the emperor knew that he would find an honored place in such a work. It took Virgil ten years to produce the *Aeneid*, which was not fully completed when he died. Augustus disobeyed Virgil's deathbed request that the manuscript be destroyed, and the patriotic poem became Rome's national epic.

The *Aeneid* was greatly influenced by Homer's *Iliad* and *Odyssey*. In *The Iliad*, Homer dealt with the conflict between the early Greeks and the Trojans. Roman legend held that a Trojan remnant led by Prince Aeneas, son of Venus (the goddess of love) and a mortal father, Anchises, escaped the sacking of Troy. (Caesar Augustus claimed descent from the goddess Venus through Aeneas.) In book six, Aeneas, escorted by the Sybil, prophetess and priestess of Apollo, descends to the underworld in order to reach his father. There his father's soul describes the illustrious future that will be Rome's.

. . . Turn your two eyes
This way and see this people, your own Romans.
Here is Caesar, and all the line of Iulus
   [founder of the Julian family],
All who shall one day pass under the dome
Of the great sky: this is the man, this one,
Of whom so often you have heard the promise,
Caesar Augustus, son of the deified [Julius
   Caesar],
Who shall bring once again an Age of Gold
To Latium,[1] to the land where Saturn [Roman
   god] reigned
In early times. He will extend his power

Beyond the Garamants[2] and Indians,
Over far territories north and south

   . . .

Others will cast more tenderly in bronze
Their breathing figures, I can well believe,
And bring more lifelike portraits out of marble;
Argue more eloquently, use the pointer
To trace the paths of heaven accurately
And accurately foretell the rising stars.
Roman, remember by your strength to rule
Earth's peoples—for your arts are to be these:
To pacify, to impose the rule of law,
To spare the conquered, battle down the proud.

---

[1]Latium was the ancient country in which stood the towns of Lavinium and Alba Longa; Rome was established in that region and became its most significant city.

[2]The Garamants (Garamantes) were a warlike nomadic people living in the northwestern Sahara.

Ovid
THE ART OF LOVE

The greatest of the Latin elegists during the golden age was Publius Ovidius Naso or Ovid (43 B.C.–A.D. 17). Unlike Virgil, Ovid did not experience the civil wars during his adult years. Consequently, he was less inclined to praise the

Augustan peace. He was married three times and supposedly had a mistress, Corinna, to whom he wrote *Amores* (love letters). As a result of his marriages and affairs, Ovid's poetry reveals a preference for romance and humor and a fondness for love and sensual themes.

Ovid is best remembered for his advice to lovers contained in his most famous work—*Ars Amatoria* (Art of Love). Written when Ovid was fifty years old, the poem concerns itself with the art of seduction and is written in a worldly wise yet witty manner. It is divided into three books; the first and second tell how to attract and retain a woman who is the object of a man's desire.

Women can always be caught; that's the first
    rule of the game.
Sooner would birds in the spring be silent, or
    locusts in August,
Sooner would hounds run away when the fierce
    rabbits pursue,
Than would a woman, well-wooed, refuse to
    succumb to a lover;
She'll make you think she means No! while she
    is planning her Yes!
Love on the sly [stolen love] delights men; it is
    equally pleasing to women.
Men are poor at pretense; women can hide their
    desire.
It's a convention, no more [than that], that
    men play the part of pursuer.
Women don't run after us; mousetraps don't
    run after mice.

Play the role of the lover, give the impression
    of heartache;
No matter what your device, that you must
    make her believe,
Nor is it very hard—they all of them think
    that they're lovely,
Even the ugliest hag dotes on her beauty's
    appeal.
More than once, you will find, the pretense
    ends in conviction,
More than once the romance proves, after all, to
    be true.
So, girls, don't be too harsh on the men you
    suspect of pretending:
Some day the butterfly, Truth, breaks from the
    lying cocoon.
Flattery works on the mind as the waves on the
    bank of a river:

Praise her face and her hair; praise her fingers
    and toes.
Tears are a good thing, too; they move the most
    adamant natures.
Let her, if possible, see tears on your cheeks, in
    your eyes.
This is not easy: sometimes the eyes will not
    stream at your bidding.
What can be done about this?—get your hands
    wet, and apply.

What about sending her poems? A very diffi-
    cult question.
Poems, I am sorry to say, aren't worth so much
    in this town.
Oh, they are praised, to be sure; but the girls
    want something more costly.
Even illiterates please, if they have money to burn.
Ours is a Golden Age, and gold can purchase
    you honors,
All the "Golden Mean" means is, gold is the end.
Homer himself, if he came attended by all of
    the Muses,
With no scrip in his purse, would be kicked
    out of the house.
There are a few, very few, bright girls with a
    real education,
Some (perhaps) here and there, willing to give
    it a try.
So, go ahead, praise both: the worth of the song
    matters little
Just so you make it sound lovely while reading
    aloud.
Whether or not she can tell one kind of verse
    from another,
If there's a line in her praise she will assume,
    "It's a gift!"

Juvenal
THE SATIRES

Juvenal (Decimus Junius Juvenalis, c. A.D. 60–c. 131), Rome's greatest satirical poet, found much fault with the Rome of his day. The streets were crowded, noisy, and unsafe; bullies itched to fight; criminals stole and murdered; the poor suffered even more than other Romans. The following excerpt from *The Satires* is Juvenal's account of the underside of life in Rome.

. . . A man's word
Is believed just to the extent of the
   wealth in his coffers stored.
Though he swear on all the altars from
   here to Samothrace,[1]
A poor man isn't believed. . . .

Anyway, a poor man's the butt of jokes if
   his cloak has a rip
Or is dirty, if his toga is slightly soiled, if
   a strip
Of leather is split in his shoes and gapes,
   if coarse thread shows
New stitches patching not one but many
   holes. Of the woes
Of unhappy poverty, none is more
   difficult to bear
Than that it heaps men with ridicule.
   Says an usher, "How dare
You sit there? Get out of the rows
   reserved for knights to share. . . ."

. . . What poor man ever inherits
A fortune or gets appointed as clerk to a
   magistrate?
Long ago the penniless Romans ought to
   have staged a great
Mass walkout. It's no easy job for a man
   to advance
When his talents are balked by his
   impoverished circumstance,

But in Rome it's harder than
   elsewhere. . . .
Here most of the sick die off because
   they get no sleep
(But the sickness is brought on by the
   undigested heap
Of sour food in their burning stomachs),
   for what rented flat
Allows you to sleep? Only rich men in
   this city have that.
There lies the root of the illness—carts
   rumbling in narrow streets
And cursing drivers stalled in a traffic
   jam—it defeats
All hope of rest. . . .

. . . Though we hurry, we merely crawl;
We're blocked by a surging mass ahead,
   a pushing wall
Of people behind. A man jabs me,
   elbowing through, one socks
A chair pole against me, one cracks my
   skull with a beam, one knocks
A wine cask against my ear. My legs are
   caked with splashing
Mud, from all sides the weight of
   enormous feet comes smashing
On mine, and a soldier stamps his
   hobnails through to my sole. . . .

. . . a piece of a pot
Falls down on my head, how often a
   broken vessel is shot
From the upper windows, with what a
   force it strikes and dints
The cobblestones! . . .

---

[1]Samothrace, an island in the northern Aegean Sea, is best known today as the place where the famous statue of the Winged Victory (Nike) was found.

The besotted bully, denied his chance in
  the shabby bars
Of killing somebody, suffers torments,
  itching to fight.
Like Achilles[2] bemoaning his friend, he
  tosses about all night,
Now flat on his face, now on his back—
  there's no way at all
He can rest, for some men can't sleep till
  after a bloody brawl.
But however rash and hot with youth
  and flushed with wine,
He avoids the noble whose crimson cloak
  and long double line
Of guards with brass lamps and torches
  show they're too much to handle.
But for me, whom the moon escorts, or
  the feeble light of a candle
Whose wick I husband and trim—he
  has no respect for me.
Now hear how the pitiful fight begins—
  if a fight it be,

When he delivers the punches and I am
  beaten to pulp.
He blocks my way and tells me to stop.
  I stop, with a gulp—
What else can you do when a madman
  stronger than you attacks? . . .

This is the poor man's freedom: having
  been soundly mauled
And cut to pieces by fists, he begs and
  prays, half dead,
To be allowed to go home with a few
  teeth still in his head.

But these aren't your only terrors. For
  you can never restrain
The criminal element. Lock up your
  house, put bolt and chain
On your shop, but when all's quiet,
  someone will rob you or he'll
Be a cutthroat perhaps and do you in
  quickly with cold steel. . . .

---

[2]Achilles, the Greeks' most formidable warrior in Homer's
Iliad, was torn by grief when his best friend Patroclus was
killed by the Trojans.

REVIEW QUESTIONS

1. Why are some poems a valuable source for historians?
2. According to Virgil, what was Rome's destiny and the basis of its greatness?
3. Which of Ovid's suggestions do you consider very clever? very foolish?
4. According to Juvenal, what were some of the hazards of urban life in ancient Rome?

3 Roman Stoicism

Stoicism, the leading school of thought in the Hellenistic world, appealed to
Roman thinkers. Founded by Zeno of Citium (335–267 B.C.), who established an
academy in Athens, Stoicism taught that universal principles, or natural law, un-
derlay the universe. Natural laws applied to all people and were grasped through
reason, which was common to all human beings. Stoicism gave expression to the
universalism of the Hellenistic Age; it held that all people—Greek and barbarian,
free and slave, rich and poor—were essentially equal, for they all had the capacity

to reason and were all governed by the same universal laws. Living according to the law of reason that pervades the cosmos provides the individual with the inner fortitude to deal with life's misfortunes, said the Stoics; it is the path to virtue. In the tradition of Socrates, the Stoics regarded people as morally self-sufficient, capable of regulating their own lives. The Romans valued the Stoic emphasis on self-discipline and the molding of character according to worthy standards. The Stoic doctrine of natural law that applied to all peoples harmonized with the requirements of Rome's multinational Empire.

Seneca
THE MORAL EPISTLES

Lucius Annaeus Seneca (4 B.C.–A.D. 65) was born at Cordoba (Cordova), Spain, into a highly educated family: his father, for example, was a distinguished rhetorician, politician, and historian. Sent to school in Rome, Seneca studied rhetoric and philosophy, particularly Stoicism. From A.D. 54 to 62, he was a key advisor to the emperor Nero (A.D. 54–68). Later the notoriously unstable emperor accused Seneca of participating in a conspiracy against him and compelled him to commit suicide.

In traditional Stoic fashion, Seneca held that individuals belong to two commonwealths, the city where they are born and the kingdom of humanity, which is worldwide. In serving this superior commonwealth, individuals become aware of their moral potential. The virtuous tone of Seneca's writings (they had a great appeal to Christians) contrasted with the realities of his life, for Seneca used his political influence for self-enrichment and condoned murder to enhance his political power. Despite this discrepancy between Seneca's words and deeds, he was one of the few Romans to denounce the gladiatorial events as barbaric, and he urged humane treatment of slaves.

The sentiments expressed in these two moral essays, written in the form of epistles (letters) to his friend Lucilius, a prominent Roman civil servant, reveal Seneca's Stoic humanitarianism.

ON GLADIATORS

But nothing is more harmful to a good disposition than to while the time away at some public show. I return from such entertainments more greedy, more dissipated, nay, even more cruel and inhuman. By chance I fell in with a public show at midday, expecting some sport, buffoonery [clownish amusement], or other relaxation, now that the spectators had seen their fill of human gore. All the bloody deeds of the morning were mere mercy: for now, all trifling apart, they commit downright murder. The combatants have nothing with which to shield the body; they are exposed to every stroke of their antagonist; and every stroke is a wound. And this some prefer to their fighting well armored! There is no helmet or shield to repel the blow; no defense, no art—for these are but so many balks and delays of death. In the morning men are exposed to lions and bears; at noon gladiators who fight to the death are ordered out against one another, and the conqueror is detained for another slaughter. Death alone puts an end to this business. "Kill, burn, scourge," is all they cry. "Why is he so afraid of the sword's point? Why is he so timorous to kill? Why does he not die more manfully?" They are urged on with floggings if they refuse to fight and are obliged to give and take wounds with an open breast. They are called upon to cut one another's throats.

ON SLAVERY

It by no means displeases me, Lucilius, to hear from those who confer with you, that you live on friendly terms with your slaves. This attests to your good sense and education. Are they slaves? No, they are men; they are comrades; they are humble friends. Nay, rather fellow-servants, if you reflect on the equal power of Fortune over both you and them. I therefore laugh at those who think it scandalous for a gentleman to permit, at times, his servant to sit down with him at supper. Why should he not? It is only proud custom that has ordained that a master dine surrounded by at least a dozen slaves and stuff himself, while the poor servants are not allowed to open their lips, even to speak. The slightest murmur is restrained by a rod; nor are mere accidents excused, such as a cough, a sneeze, or a hiccup. Silence interrupted by a word is sure to be punished severely. Thus the slaves must stand, perhaps the whole night, without taking a bit of food or drink or speaking a word. Whence it often happens that such as are not allowed to speak before their masters will speak disrespectfully of them behind their backs. In contrast, those slaves who have been allowed not only to speak before their masters, but sometimes with them, whose mouths were not sewed up, have been ready to incur the most imminent danger, even to the sacrificing of their lives, for their master's safety. Slaves are not naturally our enemies, but we make them such.

I pass by the more cruel and inhuman actions, wherein we treat slaves not as men but as beasts of burden. . . .

Were you to consider, that he whom you call your slave, is sprung from the same origin, enjoys the same climate, breathes the same air, and is subject to the same condition of life and death as yourself, you will think it possible to see him as a free-born person, as he is free to see you as a slave. After the fall of Marius,[1] how many people born of the most splendid parentage and not unjustly expecting a senatorial office for their exploits in war, did fortune cut down? She made one a shepherd, another a caretaker of a country cottage. Can you now despise the man whose fortune is such, into which, while you despise it, you may fall?

I will not discuss at length the treatment of slaves towards whom we behave cruelly and arrogantly. But this is the essence of what I would prescribe: treat your inferiors as you would have a superior treat you. As often as you think of the power that you have over a slave, reflect on the power that your master has over you. But you say, "I have no master." Be it so. The world goes well with you at present; it may not do so always. You may one day be a slave yourself. Do you know at what time Hecuba[2] became a slave, or Croesus,[3] or the mother of Darius,[4] or Plato, or Diogenes?[5] Live therefore courteously with your slave; talk with him, dine with him.

---

[1]Gaius Marius (c. 155–86 B.C.) was a famous Roman general.
[2]In *The Iliad*, Hecuba, the wife of Priam, king of Troy, was enslaved by the Greeks after their conquest of Troy.
[3]Croesus, king of Lydia in Asia Minor from 560 to 546 B.C., was famous for his wealth, but died in slavery after losing his kingdom in battle.
[4]Darius III of Persia (336–330 B.C.) was defeated by Alexander the Great, who also captured Darius' mother, wives, and children.
[5]Diogenes (c. 412–323 B.C.), a famous Greek philosopher of the Cynic school, was captured by pirates and put up for sale in Crete. He is reported to have said, "Sell me to that man; he needs a master." He was bought by a wealthy Greek, who restored his freedom.

Marcus Aurelius
MEDITATIONS

Emperor Marcus Aurelius Antoninus (A.D. 161–180) was the last of the great Roman Stoics and the last of the so-called Five Good Emperors. His death brought an end to the Pax Romana. A gentle and peace-loving man, Marcus Aurelius was not spared violence and personal misfortune during his reign. Troops returning from Syria brought back a plague, which spread throughout the Empire. Marcus hurried to the East to quell an uprising by the commander of the forces in Asia, who declared himself emperor. Although the mutiny quickly died out, Marcus Aurelius' wife perished on the journey. Four of his five sons died young, and his fifth son, Commodus, who succeeded to the throne, was a cruel tyrant.

For the last fourteen years of his life, Marcus Aurelius had to deal with tribesmen from north of the Danube who broke through the defenses and plundered what is now the Balkan peninsula. Marcus took personal command of the hard-pressed legions on the frontier. During this period he wrote the *Meditations*, twelve books containing his reflections on duty, human dignity, the self-sufficiency of reason, and other themes traditionally discussed by Stoic thinkers. Written in Greek, this deeply personal expression of Stoic philosophy has been called "the highest ethical product of the ancient mind." Excerpts from the *Meditations* follow.

BOOK TWO

Begin each day by telling yourself: Today I shall be meeting with interference, ingratitude, insolence, disloyalty, ill-will, and selfishness—all of them due to the offenders' ignorance of what is good or evil. But for my part I have long perceived the nature of good and its nobility, the nature of evil and its meanness, and also the nature of the [evildoer] himself, who is my brother (not in the physical sense, but as a fellow-creature similarly endowed with reason and a share of the divine); therefore none of those things can injure me, for nobody can implicate me in what is degrading. Neither can I be angry with my brother or fall foul of him; for he and I were born to work together, like a man's two hands, feet, or eyelids, or like the upper and lower rows of his teeth. To obstruct each other is against Nature's law—and what is irritation or aversion but a form of obstruction?

A little flesh, a little breath, and a Reason to rule all—that is myself. . . . As one already on the threshold of death, think nothing of the first—of its viscid [thick] blood, its bones, its web of nerves and veins and arteries. The breath, too; what is that? A whiff of wind; and not even the same wind, but every moment puffed out and drawn in anew. But the third, the Reason, the master—on this you must concentrate. Now that your hairs are grey, let it play the part of a slave no more, twitching puppetwise at every pull of self-interest; and cease to fume at destiny by ever grumbling at today or lamenting over tomorrow. . . .

Hour by hour resolve firmly, like a Roman and a man, to do what comes to hand with correct and natural dignity, and with humanity, independence, and justice. Allow your mind freedom from all other considerations. This you can do, if you will approach each action as though it were your last, dismissing the wayward thought, the emotional recoil from the commands of reason, the desire to create an impression, the admiration of self, the discontent with your lot. See how little a man needs to master, for his days to flow on in quietness and piety: he has but to observe these few counsels, and the gods will ask nothing more.

BOOK THREE

If mortal life can offer you anything better than justice and truth, self-control and courage—that is, peace of mind in the evident conformity of your actions to the laws of reason, and peace of mind under the visitations of a destiny you cannot control—if, I say, you can discern any higher ideal, why, turn to it with your whole soul, and rejoice in the prize you have found. . . .

Never value the advantages derived from anything involving breach of faith, loss of self-respect, hatred, suspicion, or execration of others, insincerity, or the desire for something which has to be veiled and curtained. One whose chief regard is for his own mind, and for the divinity within him and the service of its goodness, will strike no poses, utter no complaints, and crave neither for solitude nor yet for a crowd. . . . No other care has he in life but to keep his mind from straying into paths incompatible with those of an intelligent and social being. . . .

BOOK FOUR

Men seek for seclusion in the wilderness, by the seashore, or in the mountains—a dream you have cherished only too fondly yourself. But such fancies are wholly unworthy of a philosopher, since at any moment you choose you can retire within yourself. Nowhere can man find a quieter or more untroubled retreat than in his own soul; above all, he who possesses resources in himself, which he need only contemplate to secure immediate ease of mind—the ease that is but another word for a well-ordered spirit. Avail yourself often, then, of this retirement, and so continually renew yourself. Make your rules of life brief, yet so as to embrace the fundamentals;

recurrence to them will then suffice to remove all vexation, and send you back without fretting to the duties to which you must return. . . .

If the power of thought is universal among mankind, so likewise is the possession of reason, making us rational creatures. It follows, therefore, that this reason speaks no less universally to us all with its "thou shalt" or "thou shalt not." So then there is a world-law; which in turn means that we are all fellow-citizens and share a common citizenship, and that the world is a single city. Is there any other common citizenship that can be claimed by all humanity? And it is from this world-polity that mind, reason, and law themselves derive. If not, whence else? As the earthy portion of me has its origin from earth, the watery from a different element, my breath from one source and my hot and fiery parts from another of their own elsewhere (for nothing comes from nothing, or can return to nothing), so too there must be an origin for the mind. . . .

BOOK FIVE

At day's first light have in readiness, against disinclination to leave your bed, the thought that "I am rising for the work of man." Must I grumble at setting out to do what I was born for, and for the sake of which I have been brought into the world? Is this the purpose of my creation, to lie here under the blankets and keep myself warm? "Ah, but it is a great deal more pleasant!" Was it for pleasure, then, that you were born, and not for work, not for effort? Look at the plants, the sparrows, ants, spiders, bees, all busy at their own tasks, each doing his part towards a coherent world-order; and will you refuse man's share of the work, instead of being prompt to carry out Nature's bidding? "Yes, but one must have some repose as well." Granted; but repose has its limits set by nature, in the same way as food and drink have; and you overstep these limits, you go beyond the point of sufficiency; while on the other hand, when action is in question, you stop short of what you could well achieve.

REVIEW QUESTIONS

1. What virtues did Stoics believe should guide human actions?
2. What Stoic philosophic principle influenced Seneca's view of the proper relationship between slaves and masters?
3. According to Marcus Aurelius, what was the purpose of human life?
4. How did a Stoic seek to achieve tranquillity of mind and spirit?

4 Roman Law

One of the most significant legacies of Rome to Western civilization is the system of law developed by the Romans over many centuries. Roman law evolved into three distinct types: the civil law (*ius civile*), which was peculiar to the Roman state and applicable only to its citizens; the law of nature (*ius naturale*), an unchanging, everlasting, universal law that was binding on all persons by reason of their common humanity; the law of nations (*ius gentium*), an international law governing the relationship between Romans and other peoples. The law of nations was fashioned by Roman jurists as Rome came into contact with and conquered other cultures; it incorporated elements from Roman civil law and the legal traditions of the other peoples, particularly the Greeks. Roman jurists held that the law of nations accorded with natural law: that is, it rested upon principles of reason that were common to all humans.

Justinian
CORPUS IURIS CIVILIS

The principles of Roman law are drawn from many sources, from the statutes of emperors, edicts of magistrates, and commentaries of learned jurists, such as Ulpian (Domitius Ulpianus, d. A.D. 228), Gaius (c. A.D. 130–180), and Julius Paulus (second–third century A.D.). These past laws and judicial commentaries were culled and selectively incorporated in the *Corpus Iuris Civilis*, the imperial code drawn up by order of Emperor Justinian (A.D. 527–565) and promulgated in A.D. 534. It has been said that next to the Bible, no book has had a deeper impact on Western civilization than Justinian's code. It became the official body of laws of the eastern Roman (or Byzantine) Empire through the Middle Ages and was gradually reintroduced into Western Europe in the twelfth century. Roman law continued in the postmedieval world and formed the basis of common law in all Western lands except England and its dependencies, where its influence was less marked. Some principles of Roman law are readily recognizable in today's legal systems, as the following excerpts indicate.

- The Divine Trajan stated in a Rescript addressed to Julius Frontonus that anyone who is absent should not be convicted of crime. Likewise, no one should be convicted on suspicion; for the Divine Trajan stated in a Rescript to Assiduus Severus: "It is better to permit the crime of a guilty person to go unpunished than to condemn one who is innocent."

- No one suffers a penalty for merely thinking.

- Proof is incumbent upon the party who affirms a fact, not upon him who denies it.

- In inflicting penalties, the age and inexperience of the guilty party must always be taken into account.

- Nothing is so opposed to consent, which is the basis of *bona fide* contracts, as force and fear; and to approve anything of this kind is contrary to good morals.

- The crime or the punishment of a father can place no stigma upon his son; for each one is subjected to fate in accordance with his conduct, and no one is appointed the successor of the crime of another.

- Women are excluded from all civil or public employments; therefore they cannot be judges, or perform the duties of magistrates, or bring suits in court, or become sureties for others, or act as attorneys.

- A minor, also, must abstain from all civil employments.

- Every person should support his own offspring, and anyone who thinks that he can abandon his child shall be subjected to the penalty prescribed by law. We do not give any right to masters or to patrons to recover children who have been abandoned, when children exposed by them, as it were, to death, have been rescued through motives of pity, for no one can say that a child whom he has left to perish belongs to him.

- The authority and observance of long-established custom should not be treated with contempt, but it should not prevail to the extent of overcoming either reason or law.

Not all principles of Roman law have been incorporated into the legal codes of modern societies. One example is the use of torture to test the testimony of witnesses, particularly those of low social status. In those lands where Roman law remained in effect, torture was legal until the eighteenth century, when it was purged from European judicial systems.

- Torture is employed in the detection of crime, but a beginning should not be made with its application; and, therefore, in the first place, evidence should be resorted to, and if the party is liable to suspicion, he shall be compelled by torture to reveal his accomplices and crimes.

- Where several culprits are implicated in the same offence, they should be examined in such a way as to begin with the one who appears to be more timid than the others, and of tender age.

- Torture is not applied in [financial] matters, unless when an investigation is made with reference to property belonging to an estate; other things, however, are established by oath, or by the evidence of witnesses.

- Torture should not be inflicted upon a minor under fourteen years of age, as the Divine Pius stated in a Rescript addressed to Caecilius Jubentinus.

- All persons, however, without exception, shall be tortured in a case of high treason which has reference to princes, if their testimony is necessary, and circumstances demand it.

- Torture should not be applied to the extent that the accuser demands, but as reason and moderation may dictate.

- In questions where freedom is involved it is not necessary to seek for the truth by the torture of those whose status is in dispute.

- It was declared by the Imperial Constitutions that while confidence should not always be reposed in torture, it ought not to be rejected as absolutely unworthy of it, as the evidence obtained is weak and dangerous, and inimical to the truth; for most persons, either through their power of endurance, or through the severity of the torment, so despise suffering that the truth can in no way be extorted from them.

Others are so little able to suffer that they prefer to lie rather than to endure the question, and hence it happens that they make confessions of different kinds, and they not only implicate themselves, but others as well.

- The Edict of the Divine Augustus, which he published during the Consulate of Vivius Avitus and Lucius Apronianus, is as follows: "I do not think that torture should be inflicted in every instance, and upon every person; but when capital and atrocious crimes cannot be detected and proved except by means of the torture of slaves, I hold that it is most effective for ascertaining the truth, and should be employed."

REVIEW QUESTIONS

1. What is the *ius naturale* and what are its implications when applied to particular legal cases?
2. What is the *ius gentium* and what were its origins?
3. What provisions of Justinian's code are reflected in present-day legal systems in Europe and America?
4. Why are both torture and slavery in the modern world seen as incompatible with the basic premises of natural law?

5 Provincial Administration

During the Pax Romana, Roman officials governed territories that extended from Britain, Spain, and present-day Morocco in the west to Mesopotamia and Armenia in the east; from the Rhine and Danube rivers in Western and Central Europe to the Sahara in northern Africa. The Empire reached its greatest geographic extent under Emperor Trajan (A.D. 98–117), who conquered Dacia (heartland of modern Romania). The basic unit of political administration, the city, met most of the daily political and social needs of the population. Above the level of the city governments were the Roman provincial authorities, led by governors usually appointed by and responsible directly to the emperor. The senate's role in governing the provinces gradually declined, and the burdens of ruling the vast territory fell largely on the emperor. This enormous task proved daunting for all but the most energetic and conscientious emperors.

CORRESPONDENCE BETWEEN PLINY THE YOUNGER AND EMPEROR TRAJAN

A series of letters exchanged between Emperor Trajan and Gaius Plinius Caecilius (Pliny the Younger, c. A.D. 61–c. 112), governor of the Roman province of Bithynia, located in the northwestern corner of Asia Minor, reveal the many problems Roman provincial officials faced. Given the highly personal character of the imperial office, provincial officials like Pliny, even when urged not to do so, tended to refer most problems directly to the emperor for policy guidance.

XXXIII

Pliny to the Emperor Trajan

While I was visiting another part of the province, a widespread fire broke out in Nicomedia[1] which destroyed many private houses and also two public buildings (the Elder Citizens' Club and the Temple of Isis)[2] although a road runs between them. It was fanned by the strong breeze in the early stages, but it would not have spread so far but for the apathy of the populace; for it is generally agreed that people stood watching the disaster without bestirring themselves to do anything to stop it. Apart from this, there is not a single fire engine anywhere in the town, not a bucket nor any apparatus for fighting a fire. These will now be provided on my instructions.

Will you, Sir, consider whether you think a company of firemen might be formed, limited to 150 members? I will see that no one shall be admitted who is not genuinely a fireman, and that the privileges granted shall not be abused: it will not be difficult to keep such small numbers under observation.

XXXIV

Trajan to Pliny

You may very well have had the idea that it should be possible to form a company of firemen at Nicomedia on the model of those existing elsewhere, but we must remember that it is societies like these which have been responsible for the political disturbances in your province, particularly in its towns. If people assemble for a common purpose, whatever name we give them and for whatever reason, they soon turn into a political club. It is a better policy then to provide the equipment necessary for dealing with fires, and to instruct property owners to make use of it, calling on the help of the crowds which collect if they find it necessary.

XXXIX

Pliny to the Emperor Trajan

The theatre at Nicaea,[3] Sir, is more than half built but is still unfinished, and has already cost more than ten million sesterces,[4] or so I am told—I have not yet examined the relevant accounts. I am afraid it may be money wasted. The building is sinking and showing immense cracks, either because the soil is damp and soft or the stone used was poor and friable [crumbly]. We shall certainly have to consider whether it is to be finished or abandoned, or even demolished,

---

[1]Nicomedia was the capital city of the province of Bithynia (northern Turkey today).
[2]Isis, the chief Egyptian goddess and consort of Osiris, was widely worshiped throughout the Roman Empire.

[3]Nicaea was another city in Bithynia. The Roman theater was an open-air structure, consisting of the flat stage used by the performers, the orchestra (close to the stage, a place where senators and nobles sat), and the auditorium, a sloped stand or rows of stone benches on which the rest of the audience sat. Dramas and declamations of poetry were given in the theaters.
[4]One sestertius (plural, sesterces) equals one quarter of a silver denarius.

as the foundations and substructure intended to hold up the building may have cost a lot but look none too solid to me. There are many additions to the theatre promised by private individuals, such as a colonnade on either side and a gallery above the auditorium,[5] but all these are now held up by the stoppage of work on the main building which must be finished first.

The citizens of Nicaea have also begun to rebuild their gymnasium[6] (which was destroyed by fire before my arrival) on a much larger and more extensive scale than before. They have already spent a large sum, which may be to little purpose, for the buildings are badly planned and too scattered. Moreover, an architect— admittedly a rival of the one who drew up the designs—has given the opinion that the walls cannot support the superstructure in spite of being twenty-two feet thick, as the rubble core has no facing of brick.

The people of Claudiopolis[7] are also building, or rather excavating, an enormous public bath in a hollow at the foot of a mountain. The money for this is coming either from the admission fees already paid by the new members of the town council elected by your gracious favour, or from what they will pay at my demand. So I am afraid there is misapplication of public funds at Nicaea....

...I am therefore compelled to ask you to send out an architect to inspect both theatre and bath and decide whether it will be more practicable, in view of what has already been spent, to keep to the original plans and finish both buildings as best we can, or to make any necessary alterations and changes of site so that we do not throw away more money in an attempt to make some use of the original outlay.

---

[5] The word *auditorium* was also used in the modern sense, a lecture room or courtroom; the word means "listening place."

[6] As now, a gymnasium was a place where Greek and Roman wrestlers competed, and other small-scale athletic feats were performed. It was also a hall where citizens heard lectures or debates and socialized.

[7] Claudiopolis was another city in the Roman province of Bithynia.

XL

Trajan to Pliny

The future of the unfinished theatre at Nicaea can best be settled by you on the spot. It will be sufficient for me if you let me know your decision. But, once the main building is finished, you will have to see that private individuals carry out their promises of adding to the theatre.

These poor Greeks all love a gymnasium; so it may be that they were too ambitious in their plans at Nicaea. They will have to be content with one which suits their real needs.

As for the bath at Claudiopolis, which you say has been started in an unsuitable site, you must decide yourself what advice to give. You cannot lack architects: every province has skilled men trained for this work. It is a mistake to think they can be sent out more quickly from Rome when they usually come to us from Greece.

XXXI

Pliny to the Emperor Trajan

You may stoop when necessary, Sir, to give ear to my problems, without prejudice to your eminent position, seeing that I have your authority to refer to you when in doubt.

In several cities, notably Nicomedia and Nicaea, there are people who were sentenced to service in the mines or the arena, or to other similar punishments, but are now performing the duties of public slaves and receiving an annual salary for their work. Since this was told me I have long been debating what to do. I felt it was too hard on the men to send them back to work out their sentences after a lapse of many years, when most of them are old by now, and by all accounts are quietly leading honest lives, but I did not think it quite right to retain criminals in public service; and though I realized there was nothing to be gained by supporting these men at public expense if they did no work, they might be a potential danger if they were left to starve. I was therefore obliged to leave the whole question in suspense until I could consult you.

You may perhaps want to know how they came to be released from the sentences passed on them. I asked this question myself, but received no satisfactory answer to give you, and although the records of their sentences were produced, there were no documents to prove their release. But people have stated on their behalf that they had been released by order of the previous governors or their deputies, and this is confirmed by the unlikelihood that any unauthorized person would take this responsibility.

XXXII

Trajan to Pliny

Let us not forget that the chief reason for sending you to your province was the evident need for many reforms. Nothing in fact stands more in need of correction than the situation described in your letter, where criminals under sentence have not only been released without authority but are actually restored to the status of honest officials. Those among them who were sentenced within the last ten years and were released by no proper authority must therefore be sent back to work out their sentences. But if the men are elderly and have sentences dating back farther than ten years, they can be employed in work not far removed from penal labour, cleaning public baths and sewers, or repairing streets and highways, the usual employment for men of this type.

XXVI

Pliny to the Emperor Trajan

As a result of your generosity to me, Sir, Rosianus Germinus became one of my closest friends; for when I was consul he was my quaestor [financial officer]. I always found him devoted to my interests, and ever since then he has treated me with the greatest deference and increased the warmth of our public relations by many personal services. I therefore pray you to give your personal attention to my request

for his advancement; if you place any confidence in my advice you will bestow on him your favour. He will not fail to earn further promotion in whatever post you place him. I am sparing in my praises because I trust that his sincerity, integrity and application are well known to you already from the high offices he has held in Rome beneath your own eyes, as well as from his service in the army under your command.

I still feel that I have not given adequate expression to the warmth of my affection, and so once more I pray you, Sir, most urgently, to permit me to rejoice as soon as possible in the due promotion of my quaestor—that is to say, in my own advancement in his person.

LXV

Pliny to the Emperor Trajan

A very considerable question, Sir, in which the whole province is interested, has been lately started, concerning the state and maintenance of what are called *foundlings* [abandoned infants]. I have examined the rulings of former Princes upon this head, but not finding any thing in them either particular or general relating to the Bithynians, I thought it necessary to apply to you for your directions. For in a point which requires the special interposition of your authority, I could not content myself with following precedents.

An edict of the Emperor Augustus (as pretended) was read to me, concerning Asia*; also a letter from Vespasian to the Lacedaemonians, and another from Titus to the same, with one likewise from him to the Achaeans. Also a letter from Domitian to the Proconsuls Avidius Nigrinus and Armenius Brocchus, and another to the Lacedaemonians: but I have not transmitted them to you, as well because they were ill-copied (and some of them, too, of doubtful authority) as because I imagine the true copies are preserved in your Record Office.

---

*I.e., the Roman province so called.

LXVI
Trajan to Pliny

The question concerning free-born persons who have been exposed [abandoned] as infants and reared in slavery by those who took them up, has been frequently discussed; but I do not find in the archives of the Princes my predecessors, any general regulation upon this head, extending to all the provinces. There are, indeed, letters of Domitian to Avidius Nigrinus and Armenius Brocchus, which perhaps ought to be observed; but Bithynia is not comprehended in the provinces therein mentioned. I am of opinion therefore, that those who desire emancipation upon this ground should not be debarred from publicly asserting their freedom, nor be obliged to purchase it by repaying the cost of their maintenance.

REVIEW QUESTION

1. What kinds of political and administrative problems in the Roman Empire are suggested by the letters of Trajan and Pliny?

---

6 The Roman Peace

The two-hundred-year period from Augustus' assumption of sole power in 27 B.C. to the death of Emperor Marcus Aurelius in A.D. 180 marks the Pax Romana, the Roman Peace. Roman poets and officials extolled the Roman achievement—the creation of a well-run world-state that brought order and stability to the different nations of the Mediterranean world.

Aelius Aristides
THE ROMAN ORATION
THE BLESSINGS OF THE PAX ROMANA

In the following reading, Aelius Aristides (A.D. 117–187), a Greek intellectual, glowingly praises the Pax Romana in an oration that was probably delivered in Rome. In the tradition of Roman orators, Aristides used hyperbole and exaggeration. Nevertheless, the oration does capture the universalism and cosmopolitanism that characterized the Roman Empire.

"If one considers the vast extent of your empire he must be amazed that so small a fraction of it rules the world, but when he beholds the city and its spaciousness it is not astonishing that all the habitable world is ruled by such a capital. . . . Your possessions equal the sun's course. . . . You do not rule within fixed boundaries, nor can anyone dictate the limits of your sway. . . . Whatever any people produces can be found here, at all times and in abundance. . . . Egypt, Sicily, and the civilized part of Africa are your farms; ships are continually coming and going. . . .

"Vast as it is, your empire is more remarkable for its thoroughness than its scope: there are no dissident or rebellious enclaves. . . . The whole world prays in unison that your empire may endure forever.

"Governors sent out to cities and peoples each rule their charges, but in their relations to each other they are equally subjects. The principal difference between governors and their charges is this—they demonstrate the proper way to be a subject. So great is their reverence for the great Ruler [the emperor], who administers all things. Him they believe to know their business better than they themselves do, and hence they respect and heed him more than one would a master overseeing a task and giving orders. No one is so self-assured that he can remain unmoved upon hearing the emperor's name; he rises in prayer and adoration and utters a twofold prayer—to the gods for the Ruler, and to the Ruler for himself. And if the governors are in the least doubt concerning the justice of claims or suits of the governed, public or private, they send to the Ruler for instructions at once and await his reply, as a chorus awaits its trainer's directions. Hence the Ruler need not exhaust himself by traveling to various parts to settle matters in person. It is easy for him to abide in his place and manage the world through letters; these arrive almost as soon as written, as if borne on wings.

"But the most marvelous and admirable achievement of all, and the one deserving our fullest gratitude, is this. . . . You alone of the imperial powers of history rule over men who are free. You have not assigned this or that region to this nabob or that mogul. . . . But just as citizens in an individual city might designate magistrates, so you, whose city is the whole world, appoint governors to protect and provide for the governed, as if they were elective, not to lord it over their charges. As a result, so far from [treating] the office as if it were their own, governors make way for their successors readily when their term is up, and may not even await their coming. Appeals to a higher jurisdiction are as easy as appeals from parish to county. . . .

"But the most notable and praiseworthy feature of all, a thing unparalleled, is your magnanimous conception of citizenship. All of your subjects (and this implies the whole world) you have divided into two parts: the better endowed and more virile, wherever they may be, you have granted citizenship and even kinship; the rest you govern as obedient subjects. Neither the seas nor expanse of land bars citizenship; Asia and Europe are not differentiated. Careers are open to talent. . . . Rich and poor find contentment and profit in your system; there is no other way of life. Your polity is a single and all-embracing harmony. . . .

"You have not put walls around your city, as if you were hiding it or avoiding your subjects; to do so you considered ignoble and inconsistent with your principles, as if a master should show fear of his slaves. You did not overlook walls, however, but placed them round the empire, not the city. The splendid and distant walls you erected are worthy of you; to men within their circuit they are visible, but it requires a journey of months and years from the city to see them. Beyond the outermost ring of the civilized world you drew a second circle, larger in radius and easier to defend, like the outer fortifications of a city. Here you built walls and established cities in diverse parts. The cities you filled with colonists; you introduced arts and crafts and established an orderly culture. . . . Your military organization makes all others childish. Your soldiers and officers you train to prevail not only over the enemy but over themselves. The soldier lives under discipline daily, and none ever deserts the post assigned him.

"You alone are, so to speak, natural rulers. Your predecessors were masters and slaves in turn; as rulers they were counterfeits, and reversed their positions like players in a ball game. . . . You have measured out the world, bridged rivers, cut roads through mountains, filled the wastes with posting stations, introduced orderly and refined modes of life. . . .

"Be all gods and their offspring invoked to grant that this empire and this city flourish forever and never cease until stones float upon the sea and trees forbear to sprout in the springtide. May the great Ruler and his sons be preserved to administer all things well."

Tacitus
THE OTHER SIDE OF THE PAX ROMANA

Not all peoples in the Roman Empire welcomed Roman rule. Some nations, particularly Jews, Gauls, Britons, and Egyptians, saw themselves as victims of brutal domination and rose in revolt against their Roman governors. Our knowledge of their motives and grievances is usually secondhand, being found in the records of their enemies—the Romans and their collaborators.

Cornelius Tacitus, Roman historian and orator, wrote a biography of his father-in-law, Agricola (A.D. 40–93), a general who completed the conquest of northern Britain. In this work, Tacitus describes the character and motives of Roman imperialism from a Briton's viewpoint. The speech that follows is uttered by Calgacus, a leader of the northern, or Caledonian, tribes during the Roman campaign in the years A.D. 77–83. The ideas expressed, however, are those that Tacitus, a well-informed Roman of high social rank, believed the victims of Roman military conquest held about their situation.

"Whenever I consider why we are fighting and how we have reached this crisis, I have a strong sense that this day of your splendid rally may mean the dawn of liberty for the whole of Britain. You have mustered to a man, and to a man you are free. There are no lands behind us, and even the sea is menaced by the Roman fleet. The clash of battle—the hero's glory—has become the safest refuge for the coward. Battles against Rome have been lost and won before—but never without hope; we were always there in reserve. We, the choice flower of Britain, were treasured in her most secret places. Out of sight of subject shores, we kept even our eyes free from the defilement of tyranny. We, the last men on earth, the last of the free, have been shielded till today by the very remoteness and the seclusion for which we are famed. We have enjoyed the impressiveness of the unknown. But today the boundary of Britain is exposed; beyond us lies no nation, nothing but waves and rocks and the Romans, more deadly still than they, for you find in them an arrogance which no reasonable submission can elude. Brigands of the world, they have exhausted the land by their indiscriminate plunder, and now they ransack the sea. The wealth of an enemy excites their [greed], his poverty their lust of power. East and West have failed to glut their maw [stomach]. They are unique in being as violently tempted to attack the poor as the wealthy. Robbery, butchery, rapine, the liars call Empire; they create a desolation and call it peace.

"We instinctively love our children and our kinsmen above all else. These are torn from us by conscription to slave in other lands. Our wives and sisters, even if they are not raped by Roman enemies, are seduced by them in the guise of guests and friends. Our goods and fortunes are ground down to pay tribute, our land and its harvest to supply corn, our bodies and hands to build roads through woods and swamps—all under blows and insults. Slaves, born into slavery, once sold, get their keep from their masters. But as for Britain, never a day passes but she pays and feeds her enslavers. In a private household it is the latest arrival who is always the butt of his fellow-slaves; so, in this establishment, where all the world have long been slaves, it is we, the cheap new acquisitions, who are picked out for extirpation. You see, we have no fertile lands, no mines, no harbours, which we might be spared to work. Courage and martial spirit we have, but the master does not relish them in the subject. Even our remoteness and seclusion, while they protect, expose us to suspicion. Abandon, then, all hope of mercy and at last take courage, whether it is life or honour that you hold most dear. . . . Let us, then, uncorrupted, unconquered as we are, ready to fight for freedom but never to repent failure, prove at the first clash of arms what heroes Caledonia[1] has been holding in reserve. . . . Or can you seriously think

that those Gauls or Germans[2]—and, to our bitter shame, many Britons too!— are bound to Rome by genuine loyalty or love? They may be lending their life-blood to foreign tyrants, but they were enemies of Rome much longer than they have been her slaves. Apprehension and terror are weak bonds of affection; once break them, and, where fear ends, hatred will begin. All that can goad men to victory is on our side. . . . In the ranks of our very enemies we shall find hands to help us. . . . They [the Romans] have nothing in reserve that need alarm us—only forts without garrisons, colonies of grey-beards, towns sick and distracted between rebel subjects and tyrant masters. Here before us is their general, here his army; behind are the tribute, the mines and all the other whips to scourge slaves. Whether you are to endure these for ever or take summary vengeance, this field must decide. On, then, into action and, as you go, think of those that went before you and of those that shall come after."

---

[2]The Gauls consisted of several groups of tribes in modern Belgium, the Netherlands, France, and Switzerland. The Germans (Germani) who had been conquered by Rome lived north of the Gauls, just south of the Rhine; the rest of the Germani occupied a large territory north and east of the Rhine.

---

[1]Caledonia was the name given by the Romans to the section of Scotland north of what is now the Firth of Forth.

REVIEW QUESTIONS

1. According to Aelius Aristides, how did Roman rule benefit the peoples of the Roman Empire?
2. What views about Rome do you think Tacitus wishes to express through the speech he attributes to Calgacus the Briton?

---

7 Third-Century Crisis

An extravagant tyrant, Marcus Aurelius' son Commodus (Lucius Aelius Aurelius, A.D. 180–192) was an unworthy successor, and his reign marks the close of the Pax Romana. For the next hundred years the Empire was burdened by economic, political, and military crises. For much of the third century, barbarian tribesmen broke through the northern frontier defenses and plundered the Balkans, Greece,

Asia Minor, northern Italy, Gaul, and Spain; the Persians invaded the Empire from the east. The legions, consisting predominantly of the least Romanized provincials, used their weapons to place their own commanders on the throne. During the ensuing civil wars, the soldiers looted the towns as if they were an invading army. Rome was drifting into anarchy.

The devastations by barbarians and the soldiers wrecked the economy, which was further damaged by crushing taxes and requisitions of goods and by inflation caused by debased coinage. Everywhere, people were fleeing from plundering barbarians or soldiers, from warring armies, and from government officials who extorted taxes and goods and services from an already overburdened population.

Dio Cassius
CARACALLA'S EXTORTIONS

The reign (A.D. 211–217) of Caracalla provides an early example of the crushing demands imposed by the state on its citizenry. The following account comes from the *Roman History* of Dio Cassius.

[Caracalla] was fond of spending money upon the soldiers, great numbers of whom he kept in attendance upon him, alleging one excuse after another and one war after another; but he made it his business to strip, despoil, and grind down all the rest of mankind, and the senators by no means least. In the first place, there were the gold crowns that he was repeatedly demanding, on the constant pretext that he had conquered some enemy or other; and I am not referring, either, to the actual manufacture of the crowns— for what does that amount to?—but to the vast amount of money constantly being given under that name by the cities for the customary "crowning," as it is called, of the emperors. Then there were the provisions that we were required to furnish in great quantities on all occasions, and this without receiving any remuneration and sometimes actually at additional cost to ourselves—all of which supplies he either bestowed upon the soldiers or else peddled out; and there were the gifts which he demanded from the wealthy citizens and from the various communities; and the taxes, both the new ones which he promulgated and the ten per cent tax that he instituted in place of the five per cent tax applying to the emancipation of slaves, to bequests, and to all legacies. . . . But apart from all these burdens, we were also compelled to build at our own expense all sorts of houses for him whenever he set out from Rome, and costly lodgings in the middle of even the very shortest journeys; yet he not only never lived in them, but in some cases was not destined even to see them. Moreover, we constructed amphitheatres and race-courses wherever he spent the winter or expected to spend it, all without receiving any contribution from him; and they were all promptly demolished, the sole reason for their being built in the first place being, apparently, that we might become impoverished.

The emperor himself kept spending the money upon the soldiers, as we have said, and upon wild beasts and horses; for he was for ever killing vast numbers of animals, both wild and domesticated, forcing us to furnish most of them, though he did buy a few. One day he slew a hundred boars at one time with his own hands. . . . In everything he was very hot-headed and very fickle, and he furthermore possessed the craftiness of his mother and the Syrians, to which race she belonged. He would appoint some freedman or other wealthy person to be director of the games in order that the man might spend money in this way also; and he would salute the spectators with his whip from the arena below and beg for gold pieces like a performer of the lowest class. . . . To such an extent was the entire world, so far as it owned his sway, devastated throughout his whole reign, that on one occasion the Romans at a horse-race shouted in unison this, among other things: "We shall do the living to death,* that we may bury the dead." Indeed, he often used to say: "Nobody in the world should have money but me; and I want it to bestow upon the soldiers." Once when Julia [Domna, his mother] chided him for spending vast sums upon them and said, "There is no longer any source of revenue, either just or unjust, left to us," he replied, exhibiting his sword, "Be of good cheer, mother: for as long as we have this, we shall not run short of money."

Moreover to those who flattered him he distributed both money and goods.

———

*Or . . . "We are stripping the living."

PETITION TO EMPEROR PHILIP

A petition presented about A.D. 245 to Emperor Philip (M. Julius Philippus, A.D. 244–249) reveals the desperation of the peasants.

We who flee as suppliants to the refuge of your divinity are the entire population of your most sacred estate. We are suffering extortion and illegal exactions beyond all reason at the hands of those who ought to preserve the public welfare. . . . Military commanders, soldiers, and powerful and influential men in the city and your officials . . . swoop down upon us, take us away from our work, requisition our plow oxen, and illegally exact what is not due them. As a result we are suffering extraordinary injustice by this extortion. We wrote about all this to your majesty, Augustus,[1] when you held the prefecture of the Praetorian Guard[2] . . . and how your divinity was moved the rescript [emperor's official answer] quoted herewith makes clear: "We have transmitted the content of your petition to the governor, who will see to it that there is no further cause for complaint." But inasmuch as this rescript has brought us no aid, it has resulted that we are still suffering throughout the countryside illegal exactions of what is not owing, as certain parties assault us and trample upon us unjustly, and we are still suffering extraordinary extortion at the hands of the officials, and our resources have been exhausted and the estates deserted.

———

[1]The title Augustus was originally given by the senate to Octavian, the first emperor. It later became the title of all his successors.

[2]The Praetorian Guard, commanded by a prefect (*praefectus*), was the official troop of imperial bodyguards.

Herodian
EXTORTIONS OF MAXIMINUS

Raised to imperial office by his own rebellious troops, Maximinus (A.D. 235–238) was desperate for money to pay the soldiers and to run the state. He therefore robbed the urban middle class. This account of Maximinus comes from Herodian of Antioch (c. A.D. 165–c. 255), a Syrian Greek who served in the imperial bureaucracy. He wrote a history of the Roman Empire that covered the time from the death of Marcus Aurelius (A.D. 180) to the accession of Gordian III (A.D. 238).

. . . Other battles took place in which Maximinus won praise for his personal participation, for fighting with his own hands, and for being in every conflict the best man on the field. . . . He threatened (and was determined) to defeat and subjugate the German nations as far as the ocean.

This is the kind of military man the emperor was, and his actions would have added to his reputation if he had not been much too ruthless and severe toward his associates and subjects. What profit was there in killing barbarians when greater slaughter occurred in Rome and the provinces? Or in carrying off booty captured from the enemy when he robbed his fellow countrymen of all their property? . . . Anyone who was merely summoned into court by an informer was immediately judged guilty, and left with all his property confiscated. It was thus possible every day to see men who yesterday had been rich, today reduced to paupers, so great was the avarice of the tyrant, who pretended to be insuring a continuous supply of money for the soldiers. The emperor's ears were always open to slanderous charges, and he spared neither age nor position. He arrested on slight and trivial charges many men who had governed provinces and commanded armies, who had won the honor of a consulship, or had gained fame by military victories. . . . After insulting and torturing these prisoners, he condemned them to exile or death.

As long as his actions affected only individuals and the calamities suffered were wholly private, the people of the cities and provinces were not particularly concerned with what the emperor was doing. Unpleasant things which happen to those who seem to be fortunate or wealthy are not only a matter of indifference to the mob, but they often bring pleasure to mean and malicious men, who envy the powerful and the prosperous. After Maximinus had impoverished most of the distinguished men and confiscated their estates, which he considered small and insignificant and not sufficient for his purposes, he turned to the public treasuries; all the funds which had been collected for the citizens' welfare or for gifts, all the funds being held in reserve for shows or festivals, he transferred to his own personal fortune. The offerings which belonged to the temples, the statues of the gods, the tokens of honor of the heroes, the decorations on public buildings, the adornments of the city, in short, any material suitable for making coins, he handed over to the mints. But what especially irked the people and aroused public indignation was the fact that, although no fighting was going on and no enemy was under arms anywhere, Rome appeared to be a city under siege. Some citizens, with angry shaking of fists, set guards around the temples, preferring to die before the altars than to stand by and see their country ravaged. From that time on, particularly in the cities and the provinces, the hearts of the people were filled with rage. The soldiers too were disgusted with his activities, for their relatives and fellow citizens complained that Maximinus was acting solely for the benefit of the military.

For these reasons, and justifiably, the people were aroused to hatred and thoughts of revolt.

REVIEW QUESTIONS

1. How did the Roman emperors abuse their power?
2. What evidence do these documents provide of the citizens' growing hate for the Roman state?

8 The Demise of Rome

The conquest of the western provinces of the Roman Empire by various Germanic tribes in the fifth century A.D. was made easier by the apathy and frequent collaboration of Roman citizens themselves. Many Romans had grown to hate the bureaucratic oppressors who crushed them with constant demands for excessive and unfair taxes, forced labor on government projects, extortion, and all the evils of a police state. In some areas of Gaul and Spain, peasants had revolted and successfully defended their homes and farms against the Roman authorities. When such barbarians as the Visigoths, Vandals, and Ostrogoths entered the region, many Romans welcomed them as liberators and cooperated with them in establishing their new kingdoms.

Ammianus Marcellinus
THE BATTLE OF ADRIANOPLE

The problem of guarding the frontier became increasingly urgent in the last part of the fourth century. The Huns, a nomadic people from central Asia, swept across the plains of Russia with their armed cavalry. They subdued the Ostrogoths, a Germanic tribe in Ukraine, and put pressure on the Germanic Visigoths, who had migrated along the Danube into what is now Romania.

Encamped on the Danube, the Visigoths, desperate to escape from the Huns, petitioned the eastern emperor Valens to let them take refuge within the Roman Empire. Not eager to resort to force to keep the Goths out and hoping that they would prove useful allies against other enemies, Valens permitted them to cross the Danube. But after imperial officials plundered their possessions and carried off some into slavery, the Goths took up arms against the Empire.

In A.D. 378, the Goths and the Romans fought each other in a historic battle at Adrianople. The Visigoths routed the Roman forces, killing or capturing perhaps as much as two-thirds of the Roman army. Emperor Valens perished in what was Rome's worst defeat since Cannae in the war with Hannibal. The Visigoths were on Roman territory to stay. The battle of Adrianople signified that Rome could no longer defend its borders. The Roman historian Ammianus Marcellinus (A.D. 330–c. 400) describes this historic battle in the following reading.

. . . In the meantime a report spread extensively through the nations of the Goths, that a race of men, hitherto unknown, had suddenly descended like a whirlwind from the lofty mountains, as if they had risen from some secret recess of the earth, and were ravaging and destroying everything which came in their way. And then the greater part of the population . . . resolved to flee and to seek a home remote from all knowledge of the [Huns]; and after a long deliberation where to fix their abode, they resolved that a retreat into Thrace [within the Roman Empire] was the most suitable for these two reasons: first of all, because it is a district most fertile in grass; and also because by the great breadth of the Danube, it is wholly separated from the [Huns]. . . .

[Valens] sent forth several officers to bring this ferocious people and their wagons into our territory. And such great pains were taken to gratify this nation which was destined to overthrow the empire of Rome, that not one was left behind, not even of those who were stricken with mortal disease. Moreover, having obtained permission of the emperor to cross the Danube and to cultivate some districts in Thrace, they crossed the stream day and night, without ceasing, embarking in troops on board ships and rafts, and canoes made of the hollow trunks of trees, in which enterprise, as the Danube is the most difficult of all rivers to navigate, and was at that time swollen with continual rains, a great many were drowned, who, because they were too numerous for the vessels, tried to swim across, and in spite of all their exertions were swept away by the stream.

In this way, through the turbulent zeal of violent people, the ruin of the Roman empire was brought on. This, at all events, is neither obscure nor uncertain, that the unhappy officers who were intrusted with the charge of conducting the multitude of the barbarians across

the river, though they repeatedly endeavoured to calculate their numbers, at last abandoned the attempt as hopeless; and the man who would wish to ascertain the number might as well (as the most illustrious of poets [Virgil] says) attempt to count the waves in the African sea, or the grains of sand tossed about by the zephyr. . . .

But after the innumerable multitudes of different nations, diffused over all our provinces, and spreading themselves over the vast expanse of our plains, filled all the champaign country and all the mountain ranges . . . the emperor assigned them a temporary provision for their immediate support, and ordered lands to be assigned them to cultivate.

At that time the defences of our provinces were much exposed and the armies of barbarians spread over them like the lava of Mount Etna. . . .

The barbarians, like beasts who had broken loose from their cages poured unrestrainedly over the vast extent of country. . . .

When the Goths proved to be enemies of Rome, the eastern emperor Valens led his army to Adrianople and pitched camp. As he waited impatiently for the arrival of Gratian, the western emperor, he took counsel with his officers.

Some, following the advice of Sebastian [Valens's nephew] recommended with urgency that he should at once go forth to battle; while Victor, master-general of the cavalry, a Sarmatian by birth, but a man of slow and cautious temper, recommended him to wait for his imperial colleague, and this advice was supported by several officers, who suggested that the reinforcement of [Gratian, the western emperor's] army would be likely to awe the fiery arrogance of the barbarians.

However, the fatal obstinacy of the emperor prevailed, fortified by the flattery of some of the princes, who advised him to hasten with all speed so that Gratian might have no share in a victory which, as they fancied, was already almost gained. . . .

The Roman army draws near the Goths, and the battle begins.

Then, having traversed the broken ground, which divided the two armies, as the burning day was progressing towards noon, at last, after marching eight miles, our men came in sight of the wagons of the enemy all arranged in a circle. According to their custom, the barbarian host raised a fierce and hideous yell, while the Roman generals marshalled their line of battle. The right wing of the cavalry was placed in front; the chief portion of the infantry was kept in reserve.

But the left wing of the cavalry, of which a considerable number were still straggling on the road, were advancing with speed, though with great difficulty. . . .

[I]n the meantime the cavalry of the Goths had returned . . . ; these descending from the mountains like a thunderbolt, spread confusion and slaughter among all whom in their rapid charge they came across.

And while arms and missiles of all kinds were meeting in fierce conflict, and Bellona [the goddess of war], blowing her mournful trumpet, was raging more fiercely than usual to inflict disaster on the Romans, our men began to retreat; but roused by the reproaches of their officers, they made a fresh stand, and the battle increased like a conflagration, terrifying our soldiers, numbers of whom were pierced by strokes from the javelins hurled at them, and from arrows.

Then the two lines of battle dashed against each other, like the rams of warships, and thrusting with all their might, were tossed to and fro, like the waves of the sea. Our left wing had advanced actually up to the wagons, with the intent to push on still further if they were properly supported; but they were deserted by the rest of the cavalry, and so pressed upon by the superior numbers of the enemy, that they were overwhelmed and beaten down, like the ruin of a vast rampart. Presently our infantry also was left unsupported, while the different companies became so huddled together that a soldier could hardly draw his sword, or withdraw his hand after he had once stretched it out. And by this time such clouds of dust arose that it was scarcely possible to see the sky, which resounded with horrible cries; and in consequence, the darts, which were bearing death on every side, reached their mark, and fell with deadly effect because no one could see them beforehand so as to guard against them.

But when the barbarians, rushing on with their enormous host, beat down our horses and men, and left no spot to which our ranks could fall back to deploy, they were so closely packed that it was impossible to escape by forcing a way through them. Our men at last began to despise death, and again took to their swords, and slew all they encountered, while with mutual blows of battleaxes, helmets, and breastplates were dashed in pieces.

Then you might see the barbarian towering in his fierceness, hissing or shouting, fall with his legs pierced through, or his right hand cut off, sword and all, or his side transfixed, and still, in the last gasp of life, casting round him defiant glances. The plain was covered with carcasses, strewing the mutual ruin of the combatants, while the groans of the dying, or of men fearfully wounded, were intense and caused great dismay all around.

Amidst all this great tumult and confusion our infantry were exhausted by toil and danger, till at last they had neither strength left to fight, nor spirits to plan anything; their spears were broken by the frequent collisions, so that they were forced to content themselves with their drawn swords, which they thrust into the dense battalions of the enemy, disregarding their own safety, and seeing that every possibility of escape was cut off from them.

The ground, covered with streams of blood, made their feet slip, so that all that they endeavoured to do was to sell their lives as dearly as possible; and with such vehemence did they resist their enemies who pressed on them, that some were even killed by their own weapons. At last one black pool of blood disfigured everything, and wherever the eye turned, it could see nothing but piled-up heaps of dead, and lifeless corpses trampled on without mercy.

The sun being now high in the heavens, having traversed the sign of Leo, and reached the abode of the heavenly Virgo, scorched the Romans, who were emaciated by hunger, worn out with toil, and scarcely able to support even the weight of their armour. At last our columns were entirely beaten back by the overpowering weight of the barbarians, and so they took to disorderly flight, which is the only resource in extremity, each man trying to save himself as well as he could.

While they were all flying and scattering themselves over roads with which they were unacquainted, the emperor, bewildered with terrible fear, made his way over heaps of dead, and fled to the battalions of the Lancearii and the Mattiarii, who, till the superior numbers of the enemy became wholly irresistible, stood firm and immovable. As soon as he saw him, Trajan [the Roman commander] exclaimed that all hope was lost, unless the emperor, thus deserted by his guards, could be protected by the aid of his foreign allies.

When this exclamation was heard, a count named Victor hastened to bring up with all speed the Batavians, who were placed in the reserve and who ought to have been near at hand, but as none of them could be found, he too retreated, and in a similar manner Richomeres and Saturninus [other Roman officers] saved themselves from danger.

So now, with rage flashing in their eyes, the barbarians pursued our men, who were in a state of torpor, the warmth of their veins having deserted them. Many were slain without knowing who smote them; some were overwhelmed by the mere weight of the crowd which pressed upon them; and some were slain by wounds—inflicted by their own comrades. The barbarians spared neither those who yielded nor those who resisted.

Besides these, many half-slain lay blocking up the roads, unable to endure the torture of their wounds; and heaps of dead horses were piled up and filled the plain with their carcasses. At last a dark moonless night put an end to the irremediable disaster which cost the Roman state so dear.

Just when it first became dark, the emperor being among a crowd of common soldiers, as it was believed—for no one said either that he had seen him, or been near him—was mortally wounded with an arrow, and, very shortly after, died, though his body was never found. For as some of the enemy loitered for a long time about the field in order to plunder the dead, none of the defeated army or of the inhabitants ventured to go to them. . . .

. . . Many illustrious men fell in this disastrous defeat. . . . Scarcely one-third of the whole army escaped. Nor, except the battle of Cannae, is so destructive a slaughter recorded in our annals.

After this disastrous battle, when night had veiled the earth in darkness, those who survived fled, some to the right, some to the left, or wherever fear guided them, each man seeking refuge among his relations, as no one could think of anything but himself, while all fancied the lances of the enemy sticking in their backs. And far off were heard the miserable wailings of those who were left behind—the sobs of the dying, and the agonizing groans of the wounded.

But when daylight returned, the conquerors, like wild beasts rendered still more savage by the blood they had tasted and allured by the temptations of groundless hope, marched in a dense column upon Adrianople.

Salvian
POLITICAL AND SOCIAL INJUSTICE

The growing hatred of citizens for the Roman state is well delineated in a book called *The Governance of God*, by Salvian (Salvianus) of Marseilles (c. A.D. 400–470). A Christian priest, Salvian, was an eyewitness to the end of Roman rule in Gaul. He describes the political and moral causes of the collapse of the Roman state in the West in the following reading.

What towns, as well as what municipalities and villages are there in which there are not as many tyrants as *curiales*.[1] Perhaps they glory in this name of tyrant because it seems to be considered powerful and honored. For, almost all robbers rejoice and boast, if they are said to be more fierce than they really are. What place is there, as I have said, where the bowels of widows and orphans are not devoured by the leading men of the cities, and with them those of almost all holy men? . . . Not one of them [widows and orphans], therefore, is safe. In a manner, except for the very powerful, neither is anyone safe from the devastation of general brigandage, unless they are like the robbers themselves. To this state of affairs, indeed, to this crime has the world come that, unless one is bad, he cannot be safe. . . .

All the while, the poor are despoiled, the widows groan, the orphans are tread underfoot, so much so that many of them, and they are not of obscure birth and have received a liberal education, flee to the enemy lest they die from the pain of public persecution. They seek among the barbarians the dignity of the Roman because they cannot bear barbarous indignity among the Romans. Although these Romans differ in religion and language from the barbarians to whom they flee, and differ from them in respect to filthiness of body and clothing, nevertheless, as I have said, they prefer to bear among the barbarians a worship unlike their own rather than rampant injustice among the Romans.

Salvian tells how Roman citizens are deserting Rome to live under the rule of the Goths and other barbarian invaders. Moreover, in many parts of Spain and Gaul (France), peasants called *Bagaudae* have rebelled and established zones free from Roman authority.

Thus, far and wide, they migrate either to the Goths[2] or to the Bagaudae, or to other barbarians

---

[1] The *curiales* were members of the municipal councils. In the late years of the Roman Empire, they were forced to act as tax collectors for the central government and to pay from their own pockets whatever sums they could not collect from the overtaxed inhabitants.

[2] The Goths were Germanic tribes that invaded Rome. The Visigoths invaded Italy in the early fifth century and seized Rome for a few days. This was the first time in eight centuries that a foreign enemy had entered the capital. Later the Visigoths occupied large areas of Spain and Gaul. In the late fifth century, the Ostrogoths invaded and conquered Italy, establishing a kingdom there.

everywhere in power; yet they do not repent having migrated. They prefer to live as freemen under an outward form of captivity than as captives under an appearance of liberty. Therefore, the name of Roman citizens, at one time not only greatly valued but dearly bought, is now repudiated and fled from, and it is almost considered not only base but even deserving of abhorrence.

And what can be a greater testimony of Roman wickedness than that many men, upright and noble and to whom the position of being a Roman citizen should be considered as of the highest splendor and dignity, have been driven by the cruelty of Roman wickedness to such a state of mind that they do not wish to be Romans? . . .

I am now about to speak of the Bagaudae who were despoiled, oppressed and murdered by evil and cruel judges. After they had lost the right of Roman citizenship, they also lost the honor of bearing the Roman name. We blame their misfortunes on themselves. We ascribe to them a name which signifies their downfall. We give to them a name of which we ourselves are the cause. We call them rebels. We call those outlaws whom we compelled to be criminal.

For, by what other ways did they become Bagaudae, except by our wickedness, except by the wicked ways of judges, except by the proscription and pillage of those who have turned the assessments of public taxes into the benefit of their own gain and have made the tax levies their own booty? Like wild beasts, they did not rule but devoured their subjects, and feasted not only on the spoils of men, as most robbers are wont to do, but even on their torn flesh and, as I may say, on their blood.

Thus it happened that men, strangled and killed by the robberies of judges, began to live as barbarians because they were not permitted

to be Romans. They became satisfied to be what they were not, because they were not permitted to be what they were. They were compelled to defend their lives at least, because they saw that they had already completely lost their liberty. . . .

But what else can these wretched people wish for, they who suffer the incessant and even continuous destruction of public tax levies. To them there is always imminent a heavy and relentless proscription. They desert their homes, lest they be tortured in their very homes. They seek exile, lest they suffer torture. The enemy is more lenient to them than the tax collectors. This is proved by this very fact, that they flee to the enemy in order to avoid the full force of the heavy tax levy. This very tax levying, although hard and inhuman, would nevertheless be less heavy and harsh if all would bear it equally and in common. Taxation is made more shameful and burdensome because all do not bear the burden of all. They extort tribute from the poor man for the taxes of the rich, and the weaker carry the load for the stronger. There is no other reason that they cannot bear all the taxation except that the burden imposed on the wretched is greater than their resources. . . .

Therefore, in the districts taken over by the barbarians, there is one desire among all the Romans, that they should never again find it necessary to pass under Roman jurisdiction. In those regions, it is the one and general prayer of the Roman people that they be allowed to carry on the life they lead with the barbarians. And we wonder why the Goths are not conquered by our portion of the population, when the Romans prefer to live among them rather than with us. Our brothers, therefore, are not only altogether unwilling to flee to us from them, but they even cast us aside in order to flee to them.

Saint Jerome
THE FATE OF ROME

Saint Jerome (Hieronymus, c. A.D. 340–420) was one of the major theologians and scriptural scholars of the late Roman period. He left Rome itself to join a monastery in Bethlehem in Judea, where he studied Hebrew and began work on a monumental new translation of the Hebrew and Christian Scriptures into Latin. This new edition, called the Vulgate (written in the Latin of the common people), became the standard text of the Bible in the Western church for more than a thousand years. In the following letter to Agenuchia, a highborn lady of Gaul, Saint Jerome bemoans the fate of Rome, once so proud and powerful. The letter, dated A.D. 409, was written at a critical moment: the Visigoths had accepted a huge ransom to end their siege of Rome.

Nations innumerable and most savage have invaded all Gaul. The whole region between the Alps and the Pyrenees, the ocean and the Rhine, has been devastated by the Quadi, the Vandals, the Sarmati, the Alani, the Gepidae, the hostile Heruli, the Saxons, the Burgundians, the Alemanni, and the Pannonians [barbarian tribes]. O wretched Empire! Mayence [Mainz], formerly so noble a city, has been taken and ruined, and in the church many thousands of men have been massacred. Worms has been destroyed after a long siege. Rheims, that powerful city, Amiens, Arras, Speyer, Strasburg,*—all have seen their citizens led away captive into Germany. Aquitaine and the provinces of Lyons and Narbonne, all save a few towns, have been depopulated; and these the sword threatens without, while hunger ravages within. I cannot speak without tears of Toulouse, which the merits of the holy Bishop Exuperius have prevailed so far to save from destruction. Spain, even, is in daily terror lest it perish, remembering the invasion of the Cimbri;[1] and whatsoever the other provinces have suffered once, they continue to suffer in their fear.

I will keep silence concerning the rest, lest I seem to despair of the mercy of God. For a long time, from the Black Sea to the Julian Alps,[2] those things which are ours have not been ours; and for thirty years, since the Danube boundary was broken, war has been waged in the very midst of the Roman Empire. Our tears are dried by old age. Except a few old men, all were born in captivity and siege, and do not desire the liberty they never knew. . . .

> When the Visigoths led by Alaric sacked Rome in 410, Jerome lamented in another passage.

Who could believe that Rome, built upon the conquest of the whole world, would fall to the ground? that the mother herself would become the tomb of her peoples?

---

*The names of modern cities here used are not in all cases exact equivalents for the names of the regions mentioned by Jerome.

[1]The Cimbri, originally from what is now Denmark, spread southward to invade Spain, Gaul, and Italy in the late part of the second century B.C. They were defeated by the Roman general Marius (c. 157–86 B.C.).
[2]The mountains called the Julian Alps are in northwest Slovenia.

Pope Gregory I
THE END OF ROMAN GLORY

In the late sixth century, the Lombards, the last Germanic tribe to invade those lands that had once been Roman, swept down the Tiber valley and in 593 were at the gates of Rome. At that time, Pope Gregory I, the Great (590–604), descendant of a prominent and wealthy Roman senatorial family, reflected on Rome, once the mistress of the world.

We see on all sides sorrows; we hear on all sides groans. Cities are destroyed, fortifications razed to the ground, fields devastated, the land reduced to solitude. No husbandman is left in the field, few inhabitants remain in the cities, and yet these scanty remnants of the human race are still each day smitten without ceasing. . . . Some men are led away captive, others are mutilated, others slain before our eyes. What is there, then, my brethren to please us in this world?

What Rome herself, once deemed the Mistress of the World, has now become, we see—wasted away with afflictions, grievous and many, with the loss of citizens, the assaults of enemies, the frequent fall of ruined buildings. . . . For where is the Senate? Where is the People [the State]? The bones are dissolved, the flesh is consumed, all the pomp of the dignities of this world is gone. . . .

Yet even we who remain few as we are, still are daily smitten with the sword, still are daily crushed by innumerable afflictions. . . . For the Senate is no more, and the People has perished, yet sorrow and sighing are multiplied daily among the few that are left. Rome is, as it were, already empty and burning. . . . But where are they who once rejoiced in her glory? Where is their pomp? Where their pride? Where their constant and immediate joy? . . .

. . . The Sons of men of the world, when they wished for worldly advancement came together from all parts of the earth to this city. But now behold! she is desolate. Behold! she is wasted away. No one hastens to her for worldly advancement.

REVIEW QUESTIONS

1. How does Ammianus account for Rome's defeat at Adrianople?
2. What conditions in late Roman society undermined the social and political bonds between the rulers and the ruled?
3. What were the consequences of the Germanic invasions as depicted by Saint Jerome and Pope Gregory I?

CHAPTER 6
Early Christianity

FOURTEENTH-CENTURY FRENCH PSALTER depicting monks singing. *(Bridgeman-Giraudon/Art Resource, NY)*

Christianity, the core religion of Western civilization, emerged during the first century of the Roman Empire. The first Christians were followers of Jesus Christ, a Jew, who, in the tradition of the Hebrew prophets, called for a moral reformation of the individual. Jesus' life, teachings, crucifixion, and the belief that he had risen from the dead convinced his followers that Jesus was divine and had shown humanity the way to salvation. Dedicated disciples spread this message throughout the Mediterranean world.

Surviving persecution and gaining in numbers, Christianity appealed to all classes from slave to aristocrat and had become the state religion of Rome by the end of the fourth century. The reasons for the spread and triumph of Christianity are diverse. The poor and oppressed of the Roman world were drawn to Jesus' message of love and compassion, his concern for humanity; the promise of eternal life had an immense attraction to people who were burdened with misfortune and fearful of death. Jesus' call for a moral transformation of the individual addressed itself to the inner conscience of men and women of all social classes.

The Judeo-Christian and Greco-Roman (classical humanist) traditions constitute the foundations of Western civilization. Nevertheless, they represent two contrasting views of the world. For classical humanists, the ultimate aim of life was the achievement of excellence in this world, the maximum cultivation of human talent; Christians subordinated this world to a higher reality. For Christians, the principal purpose of life was the attainment of salvation—entrance into a heavenly kingdom after death.

In the Greco-Roman tradition, reason was autonomous; that is, the intellect depended on its own powers and neither required nor accepted guidance from a supernatural authority. For example, Socrates held that ethical standards were arrived at through rational thought alone; they were not divine commandments revealed to human beings by a heavenly lawmaker. Conservative Christian churchmen, believing that Greek intellectualism posed a threat to Christian teachings, wanted nothing to do with Greek philosophy. But other Christians, recognizing the value of Greek philosophy, sought to integrate Greek learning into the Christian framework. Greek philosophy, they said, could help Christians clarify, organize, and explain their teachings. Those who advocated studying and utilizing Greek philosophy prevailed; thus Christianity preserved rational thought, the priceless achievement of the Greek mind. In the process, however, philosophy lost its autonomy, for early Christian thinkers insisted that to reason properly one must first believe in God and his revelation, with the Bible as the ultimate authority. Without these prior conditions, the Christians argued, reason would lead to error. Thus, for early Christian thinkers, unlike their Greek predecessors, reason was not autonomous: it was subject to divine authority as interpreted by the church.

In the late Roman Empire, when Roman institutions were breaking down and classical values were being discarded, Christianity was a dynamic movement. Surviving the barbarian invasions, the Christian church gave form and direction to the European culture that emerged in the Middle Ages.

---

1 The Teachings of Jesus

During the reign (A.D. 14–37) of the Emperor Tiberius, the Roman governor in Judea, Pontius Pilate, executed on charges of sedition an obscure Jewish religious teacher, Jesus of Nazareth. While performing healings and exorcisms, Jesus expounded a message of hope and salvation for sinners who repented. To the Jews who were attracted to Jesus' person and teachings, Jesus appeared to be a new prophet or even the long-awaited Messiah, the divinely promised leader who would restore Israel to freedom and usher in a new age.

Jesus made enemies among those powerful Jewish leaders who believed that the popular preacher was undermining their authority and weakening respect for their teachings on the requirements of Jewish law. The Romans viewed Jesus as a political agitator who might lead the Jews in a revolt against Roman rule. Some Jewish leaders denounced Jesus to the Roman authorities, who executed him.

After the death of Jesus, his loyal followers, who believed in his resurrection, continued to preach his teachings, forming small congregations of those faithful to his mission and words. They soon spread out as missionaries to Jewish and Gentile communities throughout the Roman Empire. These followers of Jesus, the Messiah, or in Greek, *Christos* (the Anointed One), were the founders of the Christian church.

Like Socrates, Jesus himself never wrote a book; all we know of his life and teachings are the recollections of his disciples, passed down orally until put in written form some thirty to seventy years after his death. These primary sources include the gospels ("good news") attributed to the Saints Mark, Matthew, Luke, and John; the letters of Saint Paul and others; the Acts of the Apostles, a historical account of their missionary work; and the book of Revelation, a prophetic portrayal of the coming messianic kingdom of Jesus and God's destruction of the powers of evil. These works, written several decades after Jesus' death and collected together definitively in the fourth century, comprise the New Testament, the Christian sacred scriptures. They reflect the ways in which the early Christians remembered Jesus' teachings and the meaning of his life and ministry.

THE GOSPEL ACCORDING TO SAINT MARK

In this reading from Saint Mark's gospel, Jesus stated in a few words the core of his ethical teaching.

28 And one of the scribes[*] came up and heard them disputing with one another, and seeing that he answered them well, asked him, "Which commandment is the first of all?" [29] Jesus answered, "The first is, 'Hear, O Israel: The Lord our God, the Lord is one;[†][30] and you shall love the Lord your God with all your heart, and with all your soul, and with all your mind, and with all your strength.' [31] The second is this, 'You shall love your neighbor as yourself.' There is no other commandment greater than these." [32] And the scribe said to him, "You are right, Teacher; you have truly said that he is one, and there is no other but he; [33] and to love him with all the heart, and with all the understanding, and with all the strength, and to love one's neighbor as oneself, is much more than all whole burnt offerings and sacrifices." [34] And when Jesus saw that he answered wisely, he said to him, "You are not far from the kingdom of God." And after that no one dared to ask him any question. (Mark 12)

---

[*]Scribes were not only copyists of the scrolls that contained Jewish law, but they were also students of that law.
Editors' footnotes for Bible readings in this chapter are not numbered, to eliminate confusion with verse numbers.—Eds.
[†]"Hear, O Israel" occurs in the Book of Deuteronomy in the Hebrew Scriptures as the "first law," that of monotheism (one God). Here, as a Jew, Jesus was reminding his followers of this fact.—Eds.

THE GOSPEL ACCORDING TO SAINT MATTHEW

In the gospel of Saint Matthew, Jesus outlined to his disciples the attitudes pleasing to God; this is the famous Sermon on the Mount.

1 Seeing the crowds, he went up on the mountain, and when he sat down his disciples came to him. [2] And he opened his mouth and taught them, saying:

3 "Blessed are the poor in spirit, for theirs is the kingdom of heaven.

4 "Blessed are those who mourn, for they shall be comforted.

5 "Blessed are the meek, for they shall inherit the earth.

6 "Blessed are those who hunger and thirst for righteousness, for they shall be satisfied.

7 "Blessed are the merciful, for they shall obtain mercy.

8 "Blessed are the pure in heart, for they shall see God.

9 "Blessed are the peacemakers, for they shall be called sons of God.

10 "Blessed are those who are persecuted for righteousness' sake, for theirs is the kingdom of heaven.

11 "Blessed are you when men revile you and persecute you and utter all kinds of evil against you falsely on my account. [12] Rejoice and be glad, for your reward is great in heaven, for so men persecuted the prophets who were before you. . . ."

A characteristic feature of Jesus' teaching—one that angered the Jewish leaders—was a demand that his followers go beyond the letter of the Jewish law. In the tradition of the Hebrew prophets, Jesus stressed the ethical demands that underlie this law and urged a moral transformation of human character, based on a love of God and neighbor. In the next reading from Saint Matthew, Jesus reinterpreted the Hebrew commandments on killing, adultery, divorce, vengeance, the definition of a neighbor, and almsgiving.

---

17 "Think not that I have come to abolish the law and the prophets; I have come not to abolish them but to fulfil them. . . .

21 "You have heard that it was said to the men of old, 'You shall not kill; and whoever kills shall be liable to judgment.' [22]But I say to you that every one who is angry with his brother shall be liable to judgment; whoever insults his brother shall be liable to the council, and whoever says, 'You fool!' shall be liable to the hell of fire. [23]So if you are offering your gift at the altar, and there remember that your brother has something against you, [24]leave your gift there before the altar and go; first be reconciled to your brother, and then come and offer your gift. [25]Make friends quickly with your accuser. . . .

27 "You have heard that it was said, 'You shall not commit adultery.' [28]But I say to you that every one who looks at a woman lustfully has already committed adultery with her in his heart. [29]If your right eye causes you to sin, pluck it out and throw it away; it is better that you lose one of your members than that your whole body be thrown into hell. [30]And if your right hand causes you to sin, cut it off and throw it away; it is better that you lose one of your members than that your whole body go into hell.

31 "It was also said, 'Whoever divorces his wife, let him give her a certificate of divorce.' [32]But I say to you that every one who divorces his wife, except on the ground of unchastity, makes her an adulteress; and whoever marries a divorced woman commits adultery. . . .

38 "You have heard that it was said, 'An eye for an eye and a tooth for a tooth.' [39]But I say to you, Do not resist one who is evil. But if any one strikes you on the right cheek, turn to him the other also; [40]and if any one would sue you and take your coat, let him have your cloak as well; [41]and if any one forces you to go one mile, go with him two miles. [42]Give to him who begs from you, and do not refuse him who would borrow from you.

43 "You have heard that it was said, 'You shall love your neighbor and hate your enemy.' [44]But I say to you, Love your enemies and pray for those who persecute you, [45]so that you may be sons of your Father who is in heaven. . . . (Matthew 5)

1 "Beware of practicing your piety before men in order to be seen by them; for then you will have no reward from your Father who is in heaven.

2 "Thus, when you give alms, sound no trumpet before you, as the hypocrites do in the synagogues[‡] and in the streets, that they may be praised by men. Truly, I say to you, they have their reward. [3]But when you give alms, do not let your left hand know what your right hand is doing, [4]so that your alms may be in secret; and your Father who sees in secret will reward you. . . ." (Matthew 6)

---

‡Synagogues, originally a name given to substitutes outside Judea for the Temple in Jerusalem, coexisted with the Temple; they were places for public prayer and study of the Hebrew Scriptures.—Eds.

REVIEW QUESTIONS

1. What did Jesus believe to be the basic tenets of his teachings?
2. Why might his message appeal to many people?

---

2 The Dead Sea Scrolls

Between 1947 and 1956 some 800 documents, written primarily in Hebrew but also in Aramaic and Greek, were discovered in eleven caves on the shore of the Dead Sea, thirteen miles east of Jerusalem. Relying on advanced radiocarbon dating tests and textual analysis, scholars conclude that the documents were written in stages between 200 B.C. and 70 A.D. The oldest copies of Old Testament writings ever found, these scrolls, many of them fragments but some intact manuscripts, are of considerable historical and religious importance. For example, the Isaiah Scroll, is a thousand years older than the earliest known surviving text. The scrolls also contain some previously unknown psalms and unknown stories about Joseph, Moses, and other biblical figures; commentaries on the Hebrew Scriptures; wisdom writings; and rules for the Essenes, the Jewish sect that wrote the scrolls.

The Essenes were a devout Jewish sect that established a semimonastic community in the barren Judean Desert at Qumran to live more holy lives. Rejecting the Temple priests as corrupt—the "Sons of Darkness"—they were led by a priest called the "Teacher of Righteousness." Although the scrolls make no reference to Jesus or his followers, scholars do find parallels between the Qumran community and the Jesus movement. Like Jesus, for example, the community spoke of the end of days that they believed was imminent. Both the Qumran community and Jesus' early followers considered themselves the true Israel, referred to themselves as the "sons of light," and anticipated a coming messianic age.

The Qumran Community
THE COMMUNITY RULE

The following selection from the sect's Community Rule shows the members commitment to the Law of Moses that commands righteous behavior.

V *And this is the Rule for the men of the Community who have freely pledged themselves to be converted from all evil and to cling to all His commandments according to His will.*

They shall separate from the congregation of the men of injustice and shall unite, with respect to the Law and possessions, under the authority of the sons of Zadok, the Priests who keep the Covenant, and of the multitude of the men of the Community who hold fast to the Covenant. Every decision concerning doctrine, property, and justice shall be determined by them.

They shall practise truth and humility in common, and justice and uprightness and charity and modesty in all their ways. No man shall walk in the stubbornness of his heart so that he strays after his heart and eyes and evil inclination, but he shall circumcise in the Community the foreskin of evil inclination and of stiffness of neck that they may lay a foundation of truth for Israel, for the Community of the everlasting Covenant. They shall atone for all those in Aaron who have freely pledged themselves to holiness,

and for those in Israel who have freely pledged themselves to the House of Truth, and for those who join them to live in community and to take part in the trial and judgement and condemnation of all those who transgress the precepts.

On joining the Community, this shall be their code of behaviour with respect to all these precepts.

Whoever approaches the Council of the Community shall enter the Covenant of God in the presence of all who have freely pledged themselves. He shall undertake by a binding oath to return with all his heart and soul to every commandment of the Law of Moses in accordance with all that has been revealed of it to the sons of Zadok, the Priests, Keepers of the Covenant and Seekers of His will, and to the multitude of the men of their Covenant who together have freely pledged themselves to His truth and to walking in the way of His delight. And he shall undertake by the Covenant to separate from all the men of injustice who walk in the way of wickedness.

For they are not reckoned in His Covenant. They have neither inquired nor sought after Him concerning His laws that they might know the hidden things in which they have sinfully erred; and matters revealed they have treated with insolence. Therefore Wrath shall rise up to condemn, and Vengeance shall be executed by the curses of the Covenant, and great chastisements of eternal destruction shall be visited on them, leaving no remnant. They shall not enter the water to partake of the pure Meal of the men of holiness, for they shall not be cleansed unless they turn from their wickedness: for all who transgress His word are unclean. Likewise, no man shall consort with him in regard to his work or property lest he be burdened with the guilt of his sin. He shall indeed keep away from him in all things: as it is written, *Keep away from all that is false* (Exod. xxiii, 7). No member of the Community shall follow them in matters of doctrine and justice, or eat or drink anything of theirs, or take anything from them except for a price; as it is written, *Keep away from the man in whose nostrils is breath, for wherein is he counted?* (Isa. ii, 22). For all those not reckoned in His Covenant are to be set apart, together with all that is theirs. None of the men of holiness shall lean upon works of vanity: for they are all vanity who know not His Covenant, and He will blot from the world all them that despise His word. All their deeds are defilement before Him, and all their property unclean.

But when a man enters the Covenant to walk according to all these precepts that he may be joined to the holy Congregation, they shall examine his spirit in community with respect to his understanding and practice of the Law, under the authority of the sons of Aaron who have freely pledged themselves in the Community to restore His Covenant and to heed all the precepts commanded by Him, and of the multitude of Israel who have freely pledged themselves in the Community to return to His Covenant. They shall inscribe them in order, one after another, according to their understanding and their deeds, that every one may obey his companion, the man of lesser rank obeying his superior. And they shall examine their spirit and deeds yearly, so that each man may be advanced in accordance with his understanding and perfection of way, or moved down in accordance with his distortions. They shall rebuke one another in truth, humility, and charity. Let no man address his companion with anger, or ill-temper, or obduracy, or with envy prompted by the spirit of wickedness. Let him not hate him [because of his uncircumcised] heart, but let him rebuke him on the very same day lest he incur guilt because of him. And furthermore, let no man accuse his companion before the Congregation without having admonished him in the presence of witnesses.

These are the ways in which all of them shall walk, each man with his companion, wherever they dwell. The man of lesser rank shall obey the greater in matters of work and money. They shall eat in common and bless in common and deliberate in common.

REVIEW QUESTION

1. Compare the ideas expressed in the Dead Sea Scrolls with those in the gospels of St. Mark and St. Matthew.

---

3 Christianity and Greco-Roman Learning

Should the cultural inheritance of the Greco-Roman world be retained or discarded? This was a formidable problem for early Christian thinkers. Those who urged abandoning Greco-Roman learning argued that such knowledge would corrupt the morality of the young and would lead Christians to doubt

Scripture. On the other hand, several Christian intellectuals, particularly those educated in the Greco-Roman classics, defended the study of pagan works. Their view ultimately prevailed.

Christians preserved the intellectual tradition of Greece. However, philosophy underwent a crucial change: philosophic thought among Christians had to be directed in accordance with the requirements of their faith. The intellect was not fully autonomous; it could not question or challenge Christian teachings but had to accept the church's dictums regarding God's existence, the creation of the universe, the mission of Jesus, and the purpose of life and death.

Tertullian
WHAT HAS JERUSALEM TO DO WITH ATHENS?

A native of Carthage, Tertullian (Quintus Septimus Florens Tertullianus, c.A.D. 160–c. 240) became a Christian about A.D. 190 and thereafter was a defender of Christian morals against both pagans and less rigorous Christians. He emphasized the sacredness of life and the Christian abhorrence of violence. His *Prescriptions Against Heretics* reveals hostility toward Greco-Roman learning, an attitude shared by some other early Christian thinkers.

. . . Worldly wisdom culminates in philosophy with its rash interpretation of God's nature and purpose. It is philosophy that supplies the heresies[1] with their equipment. . . . The idea of a mortal soul was picked up from the Epicureans, and the denial of the restitution of the flesh was taken from the common tradition of the philosophical schools. . . . Heretics and philosophers [ponder] the same themes and are caught up in the same discussions. What is the origin of evil and why? The origin of man, and how? . . . A plague on Aristotle, who taught them dialectic [logical argumentation], the art which destroys as much as it builds, which changes its opinions like a coat, forces its conjectures, is stubborn in argument, works hard at being contentious and is a burden even to itself. For it reconsiders every point to make sure it never finishes a discussion.

From philosophy come those fables and . . . fruitless questionings, those "words that creep

like as doth a canker." To hold us back from such things, the Apostle [Paul] testifies expressly in his letter to the Colossians [Colossians 2:8] that we should beware of philosophy. "Take heed lest any man [beguile] you through philosophy or vain deceit, after the tradition of men," against the providence of the Holy Ghost. He had been at Athens where he had come to grips with the human wisdom which attacks and perverts truth, being itself divided up into its own swarm of heresies by the variety of its mutually antagonistic sects. What has Jerusalem to do with Athens, the Church with [Plato's] Academy, the Christian with the heretic? Our principles come from the Porch of Solomon,[2] who had himself taught that the Lord is to be sought in simplicity of heart. I have no use for a Stoic or a Platonic or a

---

[1] A heresy is any belief that differs from official or standard doctrine.

[2] The Stoic philosophers took their name from the Greek word *stoa*, porch, the place where Zeno, their founder, used to teach. *Porch of Solomon* is used to designate the teachings of King Solomon, who built the great Temple in Jerusalem. Tertullian makes it clear he follows Solomon's wisdom.

dialectic Christianity. After Jesus Christ we have no need of speculation, after the Gospel no need of research. When we come to believe, we have no desire to believe anything else; for we begin by believing that there is nothing else which we have to believe.

Clement of Alexandria
IN DEFENSE OF
GREEK LEARNING

In the following passage, Clement of Alexandria (c. A.D. 150–c. 220) expresses his admiration for Greek learning. A Greek Christian theologian, Clement combined Christianity with Platonism.

The Greeks should not be condemned by those who have merely glanced at their writings, for comprehension of these works requires careful investigation. Philosophy is not the originator of false practices and base deeds as some have calumniated it; nor does it beguile us and lead us away from faith.

Rather philosophy is a clear image of truth, a divine gift to the Greeks. Before the advent of the Lord, philosophy helped the Greeks to attain righteousness, and it is now conducive to piety; it supplies a preparatory teaching for those who will later embrace the faith. God is the cause of all good things: some given primarily in the form of the Old and the New Testament; others are the consequence of philosophy. Perchance too philosophy was given to the Greeks primarily till the Lord should call the Greeks to serve him. Thus philosophy acted as a schoolmaster to the Greeks, preparing them for Christ, as the laws of the Jews prepared them for Christ.

The way of truth is one. But into it, as into a perennial river, streams flow from all sides. We assert that philosophy, which is characterized by investigation into the form and nature of things, is the truth of which the Lord Himself said, "I am the truth." Thus Greek preparatory culture, including philosophy itself, is shown to have come down from God to men.

Some do not wish to touch either philosophy or logic or to learn natural science. They demand bare faith alone, as if they wished, without bestowing any care on the vine, straightway to gather clusters from the first. I call him truly learned who brings everything to bear on the truth; so that from geometry, music, grammar, and philosophy itself, he culls what is useful and guards the faith against assault. And he who brings everything to bear on a right life, learning from Greeks and non-Greeks, this man is an experienced searcher after truth. And how necessary it is for him who desires to be partaker of the power of God to treat of intellectual subjects by philosophising.

According to some, Greek philosophy apprehended the truth accidentally, dimly, partially. Others will have it that Greek philosophy was instituted by the devil. Several hold that certain powers descending from heaven inspired the whole of philosophy. But if Greek philosophy does not comprehend the whole of truth and does not encompass God's commandments, yet it prepares the way for God's teachings; training in some way or other, molding character, and fitting him who believes in Providence for the reception of truth.

Saint Augustine
APPROPRIATING PAGAN LEARNING AND INSTITUTIONS FOR CHRISTIAN ENDS

Saint Augustine (see page 196) also argued that pagan learning and institutions could be put to good use by Christians.

Any statements by those who are called philosophers, especially the Platonists, which happen to be true and consistent with our faith should not cause alarm, but be claimed for our own use, as it were from owners who have no right to them. Like the treasures of the ancient Egyptians, who possessed not only idols and heavy burdens, which the people of Israel hated and shunned, but also vessels and ornaments of silver and gold, and clothes, which on leaving Egypt the people of Israel, in order to make better use of them, surreptitiously claimed for themselves (they did this not on their own authority but at God's command) . . . similarly all the branches of pagan learning contain not only false and superstitious fantasies and burdensome studies that involve unnecessary effort, which each one of us must loathe and avoid as under Christ's guidance we abandon the company of pagans, but also studies for liberated minds which are more appropriate to the service of the truth, and some very useful moral instruction, as well as the various truths about monotheism to be found in their writers. These treasures . . . which were used wickedly and harmfully in the service of demons must be removed by Christians, as they separate themselves in spirit from the wretched company of pagans, and applied to their true function, that of preaching the gospel. As for their clothing—which corresponds to human institutions, but those appropriate to human society, which in this life we cannot do without—this may be accepted and kept for conversion to Christian purposes. This is exactly what many good and faithful Christians have done.

REVIEW QUESTIONS

1. Why did Tertullian oppose the study of pagan literature on the part of Christians?
2. Why did Clement of Alexandria favor the study of pagan learning? Why did Saint Augustine?
3. What might have been the consequences if the Christian church had followed the advice of Tertullian rather than that of Clement?

4 The Persecutions

Under Roman law, all cults had to be approved by the authorities, and religious associations were licensed by the state. At first, the Christians were assumed to be members of a Jewish sect, and as Judaism was a legal religion, the authorities did not intervene in the work of the Christian missionaries except as they were involved in disputes within the Jewish community. By the reign of Emperor Nero (A.D. 54–68), Roman officials had become aware that the new Christian churches were composed of many Gentiles as well as Jews, and could no longer reasonably be considered a legitimate part of the privileged Jewish religious community. The first major persecution broke out in the city of Rome when Nero, to put down a rumor that he had set afire a large section of the city, decided to focus blame for the disaster on the small Christian community. When the unpopular Christians were arrested, they pleaded guilty not to arson, but to the crime of being Christians: that is, to belonging to an illegal sect or association. The penalty for such unlicensed association was death. Those who denied they were Christians and agreed to offer sacrifice to the gods of Rome were released.

PERSECUTIONS AT LYONS AND VIENNE

During the second century, Christians in the Roman Empire were at times victims of mob actions, usually stimulated by some disaster like an outbreak of disease, an earthquake, a drought, or other communal catastrophes attributed to the anger of the gods. Christians' pacifism and their refusal to participate in the worship of the state deities, in processions and festivals, and in theatrical performances and gladiatorial games, made them increasingly unpopular.

The next reading is a letter sent in A.D. 177 by the Christians of the cities of Lyons and Vienne in Gaul (France) to fellow Christians in Asia and Phrygia (both in modern Turkey). The letter describes a group of Christians arrested and reviled by enraged mobs.

First, indeed, they [the Christians] endured nobly the sufferings heaped upon them by the general populace, clamors, blows, being dragged along, robberies, stonings, imprisonments, and all that an enraged mob loves to inflict on opponents and enemies. Then they were taken to the forum by . . . the ordained authorities of the city and were examined in the presence of the whole multitude. Having confessed, they were imprisoned until the arrival of the governor. When they were afterwards brought before him . . . he treated us with all manner of cruelty. . . .

. . . [Some refused to renounce their faith in Christ, but others] appeared unprepared and untrained and still weak, unable to endure the strain of a great contest. Of these about ten became apostates [renounced their religion], who caused us great pain and excessive sorrow, and weakened the zeal of the others who had not

yet been seized, and who, although suffering all kinds of evil, were constantly with the martyrs and did not abandon them. . . . And some of our servants who were heathens were seized because the governor had ordered that we should all be examined in public.

These by the wiles of Satan, fearing the tortures which they saw the saints suffering and urged by the soldiers to do this, accused us falsely of Thyestean banquets[1] and Oedipodean incests[2] and of deeds which it is not lawful for us to speak of, or think of, and which we do not believe men ever committed. When these accusations were reported all raged like wild beasts against us. . . . Then finally the holy martyrs

---

[1]Thyestes, in Greek myth, was forced to eat his own sons at a banquet; the reference is to cannibalism.
[2]Oedipus, the protagonist of several Greek dramas, unwittingly committed incest with his mother.

endured sufferings beyond all description and Satan strove earnestly that some blasphemies might be uttered by them also.

But the whole rage of the people, governor and soldiers was aroused exceedingly against Sanctus, deacon from Vienne, and against Maturus, a recent convert but a noble combatant, and against Attalus, a native of Pergamum [a city in Asia Minor], who had always been a pillar and a foundation in that place, and against Blandina [a slave] through whom Christ showed that what appears mean, deformed and contemptible to men is of great glory with God through love for Him, shown in power and not boasting in appearance. For while we all, together with her mistress on earth, who was herself also one of the combatants among the martyrs, feared lest in the strife she should be unable to make her confession on account of her bodily weakness, Blandina was filled with such power that she was delivered and raised above those who took turns in torturing her in every manner from dawn till evening; and they confessed that they were defeated and had nothing more which they could do to her. They marvelled at her endurance, for her whole body was mangled and broken; and they testified that one form of torture was sufficient to destroy life, to say nothing of so many and so great tortures. But the blessed one, like a noble athlete, renewed her strength . . . , and her comfort, refreshment and relief from suffering was in saying, "I am a Christian" and "Nothing vile is done by us."

. . . Maturus, Sanctus, Blandina and Attalus were therefore led to the wild beasts in the amphitheatre, and in order to give to the heathen public a spectacle of cruelty, a day was especially appointed for our people to fight with the wild beasts. Accordingly Maturus and Sanctus again passed through the whole torture in the amphitheatre, not as if they had suffered nothing at all before, but rather as if having overcome the adversary already in many kinds of contests they were now striving for the crown itself. They endured again the running the gauntlet customary in that place and the attacks from the wild beasts and everything that the raging multitude, who cried out from one place or another, desired, and at last the iron chair in which their bodies were roasted and tormented them with the fumes. Not even with this did the tortures cease, but they raged still more, desiring to overcome their patience, and they did not hear a word from Sanctus except the confession [that he was a Christian] which he had made from the beginning. These accordingly, after their life had continued for a very long time through the great conflict, died at last, after having furnished a spectacle to the world throughout that day instead of all the varieties of gladiatorial combats.

But Blandina suspended on a stake was exposed as food for the wild beasts which should fall upon her. Because she seemed to be suspended in the manner of a cross and because of her earnest prayers, she encouraged the contestants greatly. They looking upon her in her conflict, beheld with their eyes, through their sister, Him who had suffered for them in order to persuade those who trust in Him that everyone who suffers for the glory of Christ has eternal fellowship with the living God. And as none of the beasts touched her at that time, she was taken down from the stake and led away again to the prison, to be preserved for another contest. . . .

The Roman authorities frequently set free anyone who denied his Christian faith and was willing to worship a Roman god, usually the divine emperor.

. . . For Caesar had written that these [Christians] should be put to death, but if any should deny they should be dismissed. At the beginning of the festival held there, which is attended by throngs of people from all nations, the governor had the blessed ones brought to the judgment-seat to be a show and spectacle for the multitude. Therefore he examined them again, and as many as seemed to be Roman citizens he had beheaded, the others he sent to the wild beasts.

Christ was glorified greatly in those who had previously denied him, for contrary to the expectation of the heathen, they confessed. For these were examined separately as about to be set free, and when they confessed, they were added to the number of the martyrs. But those who never had a particle of faith . . . or any thought of the fear of God . . . blasphemed [slandered Christianity] the way through their apostasy. . . .

. . . The bodies of the martyrs after having been exposed and exhibited in every manner for six days, were afterwards burned and reduced to ashes by the lawless men and thrown in the river Rhone which flows close by, so that no remnants of them might still be seen on the earth. And they did this as if they were able to overcome God and prevent their coming to life again, in order, as some said, "that they may have no hope of a resurrection, trusting in which they bring to us a certain foreign and strange religion, and despise awful punishments and are ready with joy to suffer death. Now let us see whether they will rise again, and if their God is able to aid them and rescue them from our hands."

REVIEW QUESTIONS

1. What do the stories of the martyrs tell us about the character of Roman society?
2. Tertullian claimed that "the blood of the martyrs was the seed of the faith." How did the persecutions strengthen Christianity?

5 Monastic Life

In the late third century A.D., inspired by Jesus' example of self-denial and seeking to escape from the distractions of worldly concerns, some zealous Christians withdrew to the deserts of Roman Egypt in search of peace and isolation. They turned their minds wholly to prayer, contemplation, and ascetic practices. These hermits were the earliest Christian monks. In time, some hermits banded together to form monastic communities, living under written rules that established a form of monastic government and way of life.

The hermit or monk "took up the Cross"—that is, emulated the way of Christ through a life of prayer, introspective self-examination, hard work, and ascetic practices like fasting, sexual abstinence, physical deprivation, and poverty. The hermitage and the monastery were schools for sanctity; thus the hermits and monks have been the spiritual models for many male and female Christians from late Roman times down to the present age.

The many early Christians who were drawn to the austerity of the African desert sought to escape the distractions of the world, to find religious insight and come closer to God. These hermits and mystics produced a vast body of literature describing their lives and experiences. Written first in Greek by the participants themselves, these accounts were translated into Latin in the fourth, fifth, and sixth centuries, and finally collected into a comprehensive work, *Vitae Patrum* (Lives of the Fathers), in the seventeenth century.

Saint Jerome
THE AGONY OF SOLITUDE IN THE DESERT

The Christian's vision of the world was honed in the isolation of the desert. The price of such insight was the agony that came with self-denial and solitude. Saint Jerome (A.D. 374–419), who lived in the desert during the fourth century, vividly described this suffering in a letter written to his female pupil Eustochium. He recounts the effects of the desert's austerity, which debilitated his body and disoriented his mind with delirious memories of earlier years and "enchantments" in Rome.

"Oh, how many times did I, set in the desert, in that vast solitude parched with the fires of the sun that offers a dread abiding to the monk, how often did I think myself back in the old Roman enchantments. There I sat solitary, full of bitterness; my disfigured limbs shuddered away from the sackcloth, my dirty skin was taking on the hue of the Ethiopian's flesh: every day tears, every day sighing: and if in spite of my struggles sleep would tower over and sink upon me, my battered body ached on the naked earth. Of food and drink I say nothing, since even a sick monk uses only cold water, and to take anything cooked is wanton luxury. Yet that same I, who for fear of hell condemned myself to such a prison, I, the comrade of scorpions and wild beasts, was there, watching the maidens in their dances: my face haggard with fasting, my mind burnt with desire in my frigid body, and the fires of lust alone leaped before a man prematurely dead. So, destitute of all aid, I used to lie at the feet of Christ, watering them with my tears, wiping them with my hair, struggling to subdue my rebellious flesh with seven days' fasting. I do not blush to confess the misery of my hapless days: rather could I weep that I am not what I was once. I remember crying out till day became one with night, nor ceasing to beat my breast until my Lord would chide and tranquillity return. I grew to dread even my cell, with its knowledge of my imaginings; and grim and angry with myself, would set out solitary to explore the desert: and wherever I would spy the depth of a valley or a mountainside or a precipitous rock, there was my place of prayer, there the torture-house of my unhappy flesh: and, the Lord Himself is witness, after many tears, and eyes that clung to heaven, I would sometimes seem to myself to be one with the angelic hosts."

Cassian of Marseilles
ON THE DANGERS AND FRUITS OF SOLITUDE

Cassian of Marseilles (c. 360–c. 435), who lived as an ascetic in the Egyptian desert and later founded monasteries in France, believed that the Christian hermit's most fearsome enemy was an emotional state that he called *accidie*. One of the dangers of solitude, *accidie* was a tedium or perturbation of the heart, an awesome apathy, boredom, and mental distraction, with which the desert fathers had forever to contend.

It is akin to dejection and especially felt by wandering monks and solitaries, a persistent and obnoxious enemy to such as dwell in the desert, disturbing the monk especially about midday, like a fever mounting at a regular time, and bringing its highest tide of inflammation at definite accustomed hours to the sick soul. And so some of the Fathers declare it to be the demon of noontide which is spoken of in the xcth Psalm.[1]

When this besieges the unhappy mind, it begets aversion from the place, boredom with one's cell, and scorn and contempt for one's brethren, whether they be dwelling with one or some way off, as careless and unspiritually minded persons. Also, towards any work that may be done within the enclosure of our own lair, we become listless and inert. It will not suffer us to stay in our cell, or to attend to our reading: we lament that in all this while, living in the same spot, we have made no progress, we sigh and complain that bereft of sympathetic fellowship we have no spiritual fruit; and bewail ourselves as empty of all spiritual profit, abiding vacant and useless in this place; and we that could guide others and be of value to multitudes have edified no man, enriched no man

with our precept and example. We praise other and far distant monasteries, describing them as more helpful to one's progress, more congenial to one's soul's health. We paint the fellowship of the brethren there, its suavity, its richness in spiritual conversation, contrasting it with the harshness of all that is at hand, where not only is there no edification to be had from any of the brethren who dwell here, but where one cannot even procure one's victuals without enormous toil. Finally we conclude that there is no health for us so long as we stay in this place, short of abandoning that cell wherein to tarry further will be only to perish with it, and betaking ourselves elsewhere as quickly as possible.

And so the wise Fathers in Egypt would in no way suffer the monks, especially the younger, to be idle, measuring the state of their heart and their progress in patience and humility by their steadiness at work; and not only might they accept nothing from anyone towards their support, but out of their own toil they supplied such brethren as came by, or were from foreign parts, and did send huge stores of victuals and provisions throughout Libya, a barren and hungry land, and to those that pined in the squalor of the prisons in the towns. . . . There was a saying approved by the ancient Fathers in Egypt; that a busy monk is besieged by a single devil: but an idle one destroyed by spirits innumerable.

---

[1]Ps. 90 in the Douai Bible; Ps. 91 in most modern editions.

Saint Benedict of Nursia
THE BENEDICTINE RULE

The monastic way of life soon spread from Egypt to Palestine and Syria and eventually throughout the Christian Roman Empire. In Italy, Benedict of Nursia (c. 480–547), scion of a wealthy Roman family, founded twelve monasteries, the best known being at Monte Cassino in the mountains of southern Italy. Benedict wrote a set of rules for the governance of his monks; the Benedictine Rule became the model for many monasteries throughout Latin Christendom. In the following extract, Benedict summarizes the purpose and principles of monastic life.

. . . Therefore we are constrained to found a school for the service of the Lord. In its organization we hope we shall ordain nothing severe, nothing burdensome; but if there should result anything a little irksome by the demands of justice for the correction of vices and the persevering of charity, do not therefore, through fear, avoid the way of salvation, which cannot be entered upon save through a narrow entrance, but in which, as life progresses and the heart becomes filled with faith, one walks in the unspeakable sweetness of love; but never departing from His control, and persevering in His doctrine in the monastery until death, let us with patience share in the sufferings of Christ, that we may be worthy to be partakers in His kingdom. . . .

WHAT THE ABBOT SHOULD BE LIKE

The abbot who is worthy to rule a monastery ought to remember by what name they are called, and to justify by their deeds the name of a superior. For he is believed to take the place of Christ in the monastery, since he is called by his name, as the apostle says: "Ye have received the spirit of adoption of sons, whereby we call, Abba, Father."

And so the abbot ought not (God forbid) to teach or decree or order anything apart from the precept of the Lord; but his rules and his teaching ought always to be leavened with the leaven of divine justice in the minds of his disciples; and let the abbot be always mindful that in the great judgment of God, both his teaching and the obedience of his disciples will be weighed in the balance. And let the abbot know that whatever the master finds lacking in the sheep will be charged to the fault of the shepherd. Only in case the pastor has shown the greatest diligence in his management of an unruly and disobedient flock, and has given his whole care to the correction of their evil doings, will that pastor be cleared at the judgment of God and be able to say with the prophet, "I have not hid thy righteousness within

my heart, I have declared thy faithfulness and thy salvation, but they despising have scorned me"; then let the punishment of eternal death itself fall upon the disobedient sheep of his care.

Therefore when anyone takes on himself the name of abbot, he should govern his disciples by a twofold teaching, that is, let him show forth all the good and holy things by his deeds rather than by his words; to ready disciples he ought to set forth the commands of God in words, but to the hard of heart, and to the simple-minded he ought to illustrate the divine precepts in his deeds. And all things which he has taught his disciples to be wrong, let him demonstrate in his action that they should not be done, lest sometime God should say to him, a sinner: "Why dost thou declare my statutes or take my testimony in thy mouth? Thou hast hated instruction and cast My word behind thee"; and again: "Thou who hast seen the mote in thy brother's eyes, hast not seen the beam in thine own eye."

Let him not be a respecter of persons in the monastery. Let not one be loved more than another, unless he shall have found someone to be better than another in good deeds and in obedience; let not a freeman be preferred to one coming from servitude, unless there be some good and reasonable cause; but if according to the dictates of justice it shall have seemed best to the abbot, let him do this with anyone of any rank whatsoever; otherwise let each keep his own place, since, whether bound or free, we are all one in Christ, and under one God we bear the same burden of service, for there is no respect of persons with God; only in this regard are we distinguished with him if we are found better and more humble than others in our good deeds. Therefore let his love for all be the same, and let one discipline be put upon all according to merit. . . .

ABOUT CALLING THE BROTHERS TO COUNCIL

Whenever anything especial is to be done in the monastery, the abbot shall convoke the whole body and himself set forth the matter at issue. And after listening to the advice of the brothers, he shall consider it by himself, and shall do what he shall have judged most useful. Now we say all should be called to the council, because the Lord often reveals to the younger brother what is best to be done.

But let the brothers give advice with all subjection of humility and not presume to defend boldly what seemed good to them, but rather rely on the judgment of the abbot, and all obey him in what he has judged to be for their welfare. But just as it is fitting that the disciples obey the master, so is it incumbent on him to dispose everything wisely and justly.

Therefore, let all follow the rule of the master in all things, and let no one depart from it rashly; let no one in the monastery follow the desire of his own heart. And let no one strive with his abbot shamelessly either within or without the monastery; and if he shall have presumed to do so, let him be subjected to the regular discipline. And let the abbot himself do all things in the fear of God and in the observance of the rule, knowing that he must without doubt render account unto God, the most just judge, for all his judgments.

If there are any matters of minor importance to be done for the welfare of the monastery, let the abbot take the advice only of the elders, as it is written: "Do all things with counsel, and after it is done thou wilt not repent."

CONCERNING THOSE WHO, BEING OFTEN REBUKED, DO NOT AMEND

If any brother, having frequently been rebuked for any fault, do not amend even after he has been excommunicated, a more severe rebuke shall fall upon him;—that is, the punishment of the lash shall be inflicted upon him. But if he do not even then amend; or, if perchance—which God forbid,—swelled with pride he try even to defend his works: then the abbot shall act as a wise physician. If he have applied . . . the ointments of exhortation, the medicaments [medicines] of the Divine Scriptures; if he have proceeded to the last blasting of excommunication, or to blows with rods, and if he sees that his efforts avail nothing:

let him also—what is greater—call in the prayer of himself and all the brothers for him: that God who can do all things may work a cure upon an infirm brother. But if he be not healed even in this way, then at last the abbot may use the pruning knife, as the apostle says: "Remove evil from you," etc.: lest one diseased sheep contaminate the whole flock.

WHETHER BROTHERS WHO LEAVE THE MONASTERY OUGHT AGAIN TO BE RECEIVED

A brother who goes out, or is cast out, of the monastery for his own fault, if he wish to return, shall first promise every amends for the fault on account of which he departed; and thus he shall be received into the lowest degree—so that thereby his humility may be proved. But if he again depart, up to the third time he shall be received. Knowing that after this every opportunity of return is denied to him.

CONCERNING BOYS UNDER AGE, HOW THEY SHALL BE CORRECTED

Every age or intelligence ought to have its proper bounds. Therefore as often as boys or youths, or those who are less able to understand how great is the punishment of excommunication: as often as such persons offend, they shall either be afflicted with excessive fasts, or coerced with severe blows, that they may be healed.

CONCERNING THE RECEPTION OF GUESTS

All guests who come shall be received as though they were Christ; for He Himself said: "I was a stranger and ye took Me in." And to all, fitting honour shall be shown; but, most of all, to servants of the faith and to pilgrims. When, therefore, a guest is announced, the prior or the brothers shall run to meet him, with every office of love. And first they shall pray together; and thus they shall be joined together in peace. Which kiss of peace shall not first be offered, unless a prayer have preceded; on account of the wiles of the devil. In the salutation itself, moreover, all humility shall be exhibited. In the case of all guests arriving or departing: with inclined head, or with prostrating of the whole body upon the ground, Christ, who is also received in them, shall be adored.

The monks gathered together for prayer seven times in the course of the day. Prayers were chanted from set texts.

CONCERNING THE ART OF SINGING

Whereas we believe that there is a divine presence, and that the eyes of the Lord look down everywhere upon the good and the evil: chiefly then, without any doubt, we may believe that this is the case when we are assisting at divine service. Therefore let us always be mindful of what the prophets say: "Serve the Lord in all fear"; and before the face of the Divinity and His angels; and let us so stand and again, "Sing wisely"; and "in the sight of the angels I will sing unto thee." Therefore let us consider how we ought to conduct ourselves and sing that our voice may accord with our intention.

CONCERNING REVERENCE FOR PRAYER

If when to powerful men we wish to suggest anything, we do not presume to do it unless with reverence and humility: how much more should we supplicate with all humility, and devotion of purity, God who is the Lord of all. And let us know that we are heard, not for much speaking, but for purity of heart and compunction of tears. And, therefore, prayer ought to be brief and pure; unless perchance it be prolonged by the influence of the inspiration of the divine grace. When assembled together, then, let the prayer be altogether brief; and, the sign being given by the prior, let us rise together.

CONCERNING THE DAILY MANUAL LABOUR

Idleness is the enemy of the soul. And therefore, at fixed times, the brothers ought to be occupied in manual labour; and again, at fixed times, in sacred reading.

CONCERNING HUMILITY

. . . If we wish to attain to the height of the greatest humility, and to that divine exaltation which is attained by the humility of this present life, we must mount by our own acts that ladder which appeared in a dream to Jacob,[1] upon which angels appeared unto him ascending and descending. For that ascent and descent can only be understood by us to be this: to ascend by humility, to descend through pride. . . .

Now the first grade of humility is this: keeping the fear of God before his eyes, let him avoid forgetfulness and ever remember all the precepts of the Lord; and continually consider in his heart that eternal life which is prepared for those who fear God, just as the mockers of God fall into hell. . . .

The fifth grade of humility is this, if one reveals to the abbot in humble confession all the vain imaginings that come into his heart, and all the evil he has done in secret. . . .

This is the eighth grade of humility; if a monk do nothing except what the common rule of the monastery or the examples of his superior urges him to do.

The ninth grade of humility is this: if a monk keep his tongue from speaking and keeping silence speaks only in answer to questions, since the Scripture says that "sin is not escaped by much speaking," and "a talkative man is not established in the earth."

The tenth grade of humility is this, that he be not easily moved nor prompt to laughter, since it is written: "The fool raiseth his voice in laughter."

---

[1]Jacob, a patriarch of ancient Israel, had a dream about angels ascending and descending a ladder between heaven and earth; the dream is recounted in the Old Testament.

The eleventh grade of humility is this: if, when the monk speaks, he says few words and those to the point, slowly and without laughter, humbly and gravely; and be not loud of voice, as it is written: "A wise man is known by his few words."

The twelfth grade of humility is this: that a monk conduct himself with humility not only in his heart but also in his bearing, in the sight of all; that is, in the service of God, in the oratory [chapel], in the monastery, in the garden, on the road, in the field; and everywhere, sitting or walking or standing, let him always have his head bowed, and his eyes fixed on the ground. Always mindful of his sins, let him think of himself as being already tried in the great judgment, saying in his heart what that publican, spoken of in the gospel, said with his eyes fixed on the earth: "Lord, I a sinner am not worthy to lift mine eyes to the heavens;" and again with the prophet: "I am bowed down and humbled wheresoever I go." . . .

REVIEW QUESTIONS

1. Why did the desert fathers feel that solitude and self-mortification were the best ways to serve Christ?
2. What would you recommend for a Christian today as the best way to serve God?
3. Describe the government of a Benedictine monastery.
4. How did monasticism help to shape Western cultural values?

6 Christianity and Society

Although the principal concern of Jesus' followers was the attainment of salvation, Christians still had to deal with the world and its ways. In the process of doing so, they developed attitudes and customs that have had an enduring influence on Western culture.

Lactantius
ACQUISITIVENESS AS THE SOURCE OF EVIL

Early Christian theologians were concerned primarily with preparation for the afterlife, but they also aspired to shape a just social order on earth. For them devotion to God and neighbor, as Jesus had commanded, was the basis for achieving a just society. This meant having compassion for the poor and needy, distributing earthly goods more fairly, and eschewing greed.

A particularly insightful early Christian view of social justice is found in *Divine Institutes*, written by the fourth-century Christian apologist L. Caecilius Firmianus Lactantius. Relying on classical themes rather than Genesis, Lactantius describes an early Golden Age in which people lived in peace and "without insatiable and obsessive greed laying claim to everything." It was a time in which no one went "short of what nature produced for all. . . . [The] haves bestowed their goods so plentifully upon the have-nots that all were equally well off." But when an evil king seized the throne, justice was extirpated, hatred and deceit flourished, and the worship of God disappeared. As concern for the common good dissipated, "So began conflict and treachery and pride in the shedding of human blood." In the following passages from *Divine Institutes*, Lactantius shows that greed is the source of evil and is the principal cause for the degeneration of society.

Acquisitiveness was the source of all these evils, acquisitiveness which sprang out of the contempt of true majesty. It was not simply that those who had plenty of something would not share it with others, but they actually got hold of others' goods and turned them all to their private profit; so that, whereas previously property had been a matter of one person contributing his labor for the use of all, now it was the concentration of goods in a few wealthy households. First they began to accumulate and monopolize the necessaries of life and keep them inaccessible, to bring others under their power as slaves. The gifts of heaven they made out to be their own—not for humanity's sake, for they had none of that, but to sweep up every means that could serve their acquisitive greed. They had laws passed which represented as "justice" the grossest inequities and injustices, to protect their rapacious practice and purpose against mass resistance. So they laid claim to authority to sanction what force, resources, and sheer unscrupulousness had achieved for them. And since there was actually no trace of justice in them—which would have been expressed in humanity, equality, and compassion—they began to find satisfaction in arrogant and inegalitarian self-promotion, which put them on a higher rank than others, with retinues of staff, armed guards, and distinguishing dress. This is the origin of honors, marks of nobility, official status: relying on the terror of the axe and sword, they were to rule a cowed and craven people with the "right of masters." Such was the condition of human life introduced by the king who, after driving his father out by war, established not a kingdom but an unprincipled tyranny by force of arms, destroying that "golden age" of justice and

forcing men to be harsh and conscienceless—all by the singular means of diverting worship from God to himself, a demand enforced by terror of his pitiless power. . . .

. . . For God who gives being and life to men wished us all to be equal, that is, alike. He laid down the same terms of life for us all, making us capable of wisdom and promising us immortality, excluding nobody from the benefits of heaven. And so, as he gives us all a place in the daylight, waters the earth for us all, provides nourishment and precious, relaxing sleep, no less does he endow us all with moral equality. With him there is no slave or master. Since we all have the same father, so we are all alike his freeborn children. No one is poor in his eyes, except for want of justice; no one is rich except in moral qualities. No one is prominent, except in being incorruptible; no one is famous, except for works of mercy performed on a grand scale; no one has the title "Excellency" without accomplishing all the stages of moral growth. And that is why neither the Romans nor the Greeks could sustain justice, since they had so many levels of disparity in their societies, separating poorest from richest, powerless from powerful, the obscure from the most elevated dignities of royal state. Where all are not alike, there is no equality; and inequality is enough to rule out justice, the very point of which is to afford like treatment to those who have entered this life on like terms. . . .

But someone will say, "Don't you have poor and rich, slaves and masters, in your community [of Christians]? Aren't there distinctions between one member and another?" Not at all! That is precisely the reason that we address one another as "Brother," since we believe we are one another's equals. Since human worth is measured in spiritual not in physical terms, we ignore our various physical situations; slaves are not slaves to us, but we treat them and address them as brothers in the spirit, fellow slaves in devotion to God. Wealth, too, is no ground of distinction, except insofar as it provides the opportunity for preeminence in good works. To be rich is not a matter of *having*, but of *using* riches for the tasks of justice; and those whom one would suppose poor are actually no less rich, in that they are short of nothing and hanker after nothing. Yet although our attitude of humility makes us one another's equals, free and slave, rich and poor, there are, in fact, distinctions which God makes, distinctions in virtue, that is: the juster, the higher. For if justice means behaving as the equal of inferiors, then, although it is *equality* that one excels in, yet by conducting oneself not merely as the equal of one's inferiors but as their subordinate, one will attain a far *higher* rank of dignity in God's sight. It is true, the brevity and fragility of everything in this transitory life makes men compete with one another for

status—a most repellent, most self-assertive style of behavior, and entirely irrelevant to mature rationality, since this whole realm of earthly preoccupation runs counter to the values of heaven. For as "the wisdom of men is utter folly with God" (1 Cor. 3:19) . . . so it follows that one who achieves earthly prominence is insignificant and contemptible to God. Leaving aside all the highly regarded goods of this world that militate against virtue and weaken our mental resources, what security is there in rank, wealth, or power, when God can bring even kings lower than the low? And so among the commands which God took care to give us, he included this in particular: "Whoever exalts himself will be humbled, and whoever humbles himself will be exalted" (Matt. 23:12). We learn from this wholesome prescription that whoever adopts a modest, unassuming style in the sight of men, stands out with distinction in the sight of God. There is truth in the quotation from Euripides, which goes: What are taken here for evils may be known in heaven for goods.

Saint Benedict of Nursia
THE CHRISTIAN WAY OF LIFE

In the following selection from his monastic book of rules, Saint Benedict of Nursia advises his monks on the attitudes and conduct necessary to live a virtuous Christian life.

WHAT ARE THE INSTRUMENTS OF GOOD WORKS?

In the first place, to love the Lord God with the whole heart, whole soul, whole strength, then his neighbor as himself.

Then not to kill, not to commit adultery, not to steal, not to covet, not to bear false witness, to honor all men, and what anyone would not have done to him, let him not do to another.

To deny himself, that he may follow Christ, to chasten the body, to renounce luxuries, to love fasting. To relieve the poor, to clothe the naked, to visit the sick, to bury the dead, to help in tribulation, to console the afflicted.

To make himself a stranger to the affairs of the world, to prefer nothing before the love of Christ, not to give way to anger, not to bear any grudge, not to harbour deceit in the heart, not to forsake charity. Not to swear, lest haply he perjure himself, to utter truth from his heart and his mouth. Not to return evil for evil, not to do injuries, but rather to bear them patiently, to love his enemies, not to curse again those who curse him, but rather to bless them, to endure persecution for righteousness' sake. Not to be proud, not given to wine, not gluttonous, not addicted to sleep, not slothful, not given to murmur, not a slanderer. To commit his hope to God; when he sees anything good in himself to attribute it to God, and not to himself, but let him always know that which is evil is his own doing, and impute it to himself. To fear the day of judgment, to dread hell, to desire eternal life with all spiritual longing, to have the expectation of death every day before his eyes. To watch over his actions at all times, to know certainly that in all places the eye of God is upon him; those evil thoughts which come into his heart to dash to pieces on Christ, and to make them known to his spiritual senior. To keep his lips from evil and wicked discourse, not to be fond of much talking, not to speak vain words or such as provoke laughter, not to love much or violent laughter. To give willing attention to the sacred readings, to pray frequently every day, to confess his past sins to God, in prayer, with tears and groanings; from thence forward to reform as to those sins.

Not to fulfill the desires of the flesh, to hate his own will, in all things to obey the commands of the abbot, even though he himself (which God forbid) should do otherwise, remembering our Lord's commands: "What they say, do; but what they do, do ye not." Not to desire to be called a saint before he is one, but first to be one that he may be truly called one; every day to fulfill the commands of God in his deeds, to love chastity, to hate no one, not to have jealousy or envy, not to love contention, to avoid self-conceit; to reverence seniors, to love juniors, to pray for enemies in the love of Christ, to be reconciled with his adversary, before the going down of the sun, and never to despair of the mercy of God. . . .

The Apostle Paul
THE SUBMISSIVE ROLE OF WOMEN

After the execution of Jesus by the Roman authorities in Judea around A.D. 30, his disciples, believing that he had risen from the dead, sought a clearer understanding of his life and teachings. They became convinced that Jesus' mission, calling people to repent their sins and receive God's forgiveness and to conduct their lives according to a high code of ethics, must be carried on. They proceeded to spread the "good news" to their fellow Jews and eventually to other peoples throughout the Roman world.

The disciples of Jesus were soon joined in this great mission by a man known to us as Saint Paul, the first great theologian of the new Christian church. Saint Paul started his life as a pious Jew named Saul. Born around A.D. 5 in Tarsus, a Greek city in Asia Minor, Paul enjoyed Roman citizenship. He studied the Hebrew Scriptures in Judea and joined in the early persecution of Jesus' followers. Yet through a visionary experience, Paul was converted to the belief that Jesus was the Messiah. He traveled widely throughout Syria, Asia Minor, and Greece, converting both Jews and non-Jews. He kept in touch with the new Christian communities by visits and letters. Several of the latter are included in the New Testament. He died around A.D. 65.

Passages in the New Testament concerning the role of women in Christian society have greatly affected the Western view of the relationship between the sexes. Paul's letter to the Ephesians and his first letter to Timothy contain passages emphasizing the traditional, submissive role of women in the Christian church. Although conservative theologians accept the Pauline authorship of these letters, liberal scholars date Ephesians about A.D. 95, thirty years after Paul's death, and 1 Timothy about A.D. 130. If the later dates are correct, the following passages reflect the attitude of the developing Christian church rather than Paul's own opinion. Nonetheless, these passages, and others like them, have had an enormous influence on Christian attitudes toward women.

EPHESIANS 6
The morals of the home

Be subject to one another out of reverence for Christ. Wives should be subject to their husbands as to the Lord, since, as Christ is head of the Church and saves the whole body, so is a husband the head of his wife; and as the Church is subject to Christ, so should wives be to their husbands, in everything. Husbands should love their wives, just as Christ loved the Church and sacrificed himself for her to make her holy by washing her in cleansing water with a form of words, so that when he took the Church to himself she would be glorious, with no speck or wrinkle or anything like that, but holy and faultless. In the same way, husbands must love their wives as they love their own bodies; for a man to love his wife is for him to love himself. A man never hates his own body, but he feeds it and looks after it; and that is the way Christ treats the Church, because we are parts of his body. *This is why a man leaves his father and mother and becomes attached to his wife, and the two become one flesh.* This mystery has great significance, but I am applying it to Christ and the Church. To sum up: you also, each one of you, must love his wife as he loves himself; and let every wife respect her husband.

TIMOTHY 2
Women in the assembly

Similarly, women are to wear suitable clothes and to be dressed quietly and modestly, without braided hair or gold and jewellery or expensive clothes; their adornment is to do the good works that are proper for women who claim to be religious. During instruction, a woman should be quiet and respectful. I give no permission for a woman to teach or to have authority over a man. A woman ought to be quiet, because Adam was formed first and Eve afterwards, and it was not Adam who was led astray but the woman who was led astray and fell into sin. Nevertheless, she will be saved by child-bearing, provided she lives a sensible life and is constant in faith and love and holiness.

REVIEW QUESTIONS

1. Lactantius assails human greed and social inequality as evil. What does he conceive as the natural condition of human beings, and how does he justify his assertion?
2. Why would Benedict's message appeal to many people?
3. In your opinion, which of Paul's views have merit today? Which do you reject?

7 Jews in the Era of Early Christianity

Numerous links connect early Christianity and Judaism. Jesus himself and his earliest followers, including the Twelve Apostles, were Jews who were faithful to Jewish law. Jesus' message was first spread in synagogues throughout the Roman Empire. Early Christianity's affirmation of the preciousness of the human being, created in God's image, its belief that God rules history, its awareness of human sinfulness, its call for repentance, and its appeal to God for forgiveness are rooted in Judaism. The Christian reference to God as a "merciful Father" derives from Jewish prayer. Also rooted in Judaism are the moral norms proclaimed by Jesus in the Sermon on the Mount and on other occasions. For example, "Thou shalt love thy neighbor as thyself" was the motto of the Jewish sage Hillel, a contemporary of Jesus, who founded a school. The great value that the Torah gives to charity was inherited by Christianity. Jesus' use of parables to convey his teachings, the concept of the Messiah, respect for the Sabbath, and congregational worship also stem from Judaism. And, of course, Christians viewed the Hebrew Scriptures as God's word.

Over the years, however, Christians forgot or devalued this relationship to Judaism, and some thinkers began to show hostility toward Judaism and Jews that had tragic consequences in later centuries. Several factors fueled this anti-Judaism: resentment against Jews for their refusal to embrace Jesus; the polemics of the Jewish establishment against the followers of Jesus; the role in Jesus' death ascribed to Jews by the New Testament; resentment against those Christians who Judaized—that is, continued to observe Jewish festivals and the Jewish Sabbath, regard the synagogue as holy, and practice circumcision; and anger that Judaism remained a vital religion, for this undermined the conviction that Christianity was the fulfillment of Judaism and the one true faith.

What made Christian anti-Judaism particularly ominous was the effort of some theologians to demonize the Jewish people. The myth emerged that the Jews, murderers of the incarnate God who embodied all that was good, were a cursed people, children of the Devil, whose suffering was intended by God.

The diabolization of the Jew, which bore no relationship to the actual behavior of Jews or to their highly ethical religion, and the "theology of victimization," which held that the Jews were collectively and eternally cursed for denying Christ, became powerful myths, which, over the centuries, poisoned Christians' hearts and minds against Jews, spurring innumerable humiliations, persecutions, and massacres.

Saint John Chrysostom
CHRISTIAN DEMONIZATION OF JEWS

A particularly fierce attack on Jews was made by John Chrysostom (347–407), a prominent church father. John sought to discourage Christians from participating in Jewish festivals, which still maintained their attraction for converts. In a series of sermons, he repeatedly castigated the Jews as demons and deicides. Since Jews are hated by God, he told the congregation, it is also a Christian's duty to hate these pitiable and miserable people.

What is this disease? The festivals of the pitiful and miserable Jews are soon to march upon us one after the other and in quick succession: the feast of Trumpets,* the feast of Tabernacles,† the fasts.‡ There are many in our ranks who say they think as we do. Yet some of these are going to watch the festivals and others will join the Jews in keeping their feasts and observing their fasts. I wish to drive this perverse custom from the Church right now. . . . But now that the Jewish festivals are close by and at the very door, if I should fail to cure those who are sick with the Judaizing disease, I am afraid that, because of their ill-suited association and deep ignorance, some Christians may partake in the Jews' transgressions; once they have done so, I fear my discourses on these transgressions will be in vain. For if they hear no word from me today, they will then join the Jews in their fasts; once they have committed this sin, it will be useless for me to apply the remedy.

And so it is that I hasten to anticipate this danger and prevent it. . . .

But do not be surprised that I called the Jews pitiable. They really are pitiable and miserable. When so many blessings from heaven came into their hands, they thrust them aside and were at great pains to reject them. . . . From their childhood they read the prophets, but they crucified him whom the prophets had foretold. We did not hear the divine prophecies but we did worship him of whom they prophesied. And so they are pitiful because they rejected the blessings which were sent to them, while others seized hold of these blessings and drew them to themselves. . . .

Many, I know, respect the Jews and think that their present way of life is a venerable one.

This is why I hasten to uproot and tear out this deadly opinion. . . . [T]he synagogue is not only a brothel and a theater; it also is a den of robbers and a lodging for wild beasts. . . . [W]hen God forsakes a people, what hope of salvation is left? When God forsakes a place, that place becomes the dwelling of demons.

But at any rate the Jews say that they, too, adore God. God forbid that I say that. No Jew adores God! Who says so? The Son of God says so. For he said: "If you were to know my Father, you would also know me. But you neither know me nor do you know my Father."§ Could I produce a witness more trustworthy than the Son of God?

If, then, the Jews fail to know the Father, if they crucified the Son, if they thrust off the help of the Spirit, who should not make bold to declare plainly that the synagogue is a dwelling of demons? God is not worshipped there. Heaven forbid! From now on it remains a place of idolatry. But still some people pay it honor as a holy place. . . .

. . . In our churches we hear countless discourses on eternal punishments, on rivers of fire, on the venomous worm, on bonds that cannot be burst, on exterior darkness. But the Jews neither know nor dream of these things. They live for their bellies, they gape for the things of this world, their condition is no better than that of pigs or goats because of their wanton ways and excessive gluttony. They know but one thing: to fill their bellies and be drunk, to get all cut and bruised, to be hurt and wounded while fighting for their favorite charioteers. . . .

. . . Indeed the synagogue is less deserving of honor than any inn. It is not merely a lodging place for robbers and cheats but also for demons. This is true not only of the synagogues but also of the souls of the Jews, as I shall try to prove at the end of my discourse. . . .

But I must get back again to those who are sick. Consider, then, with whom they are sharing

---

*This is the New Year or Rosh Ha-Shanah, which falls on the first of Tishri (Sept.–Oct.).
†This falls on the fifteenth of Tishri and lasts a week, during which the Jews danced and "made merry before the Lord" (cf. Lv 23.33–43).
‡The fasts here referred to would seem to be the Ten Days of Penitence between Rosh Ha-Shanah and Yom Kippur (the Day of Atonement).

---

§John 8:19.

their fasts. It is with those who shouted: "Crucify him, Crucify him,"‖ with those who said: "His blood be upon us and upon our children."# . . . Is it not strange that those who worship the Crucified keep common festival with those who crucified him? Is it not a sign of folly and the worst madness?

Since there are some who think of the synagogue as a holy place, I must say a few words to them. Why do you reverence that place? Must you not despise it, hold it in abomination, run away from it? They answer that the Law and the books of the prophets are kept there. What is this? Will any place where these books are be a holy place? By no means! This is the reason above all others why I hate the synagogue and abhor it. They have the prophets but do not believe them; they read the sacred writings but reject their witness—and this is a mark of men guilty of the greatest outrage.

Tell me this. If you were to see a venerable man, illustrious and renowned, dragged off into a tavern or den of robbers: if you were to see him outraged, beaten, and subjected there to the worst violence, would you have held that tavern or den in high esteem because that great and esteemed man had been inside it while undergoing that violent treatment? I think not. Rather, for this very reason you would have hated and abhorred the place.

Let that be your judgment about the synagogue, too. For they brought the books of Moses and the prophets along with them into the synagogue, not to honor them but to outrage them with dishonor. When they say that Moses and

the prophets knew not Christ and said nothing about his coming, what greater outrage could they do to those holy men than to accuse them of failing to recognize their Master, than to say that those saintly prophets are partners of their impiety? And so it is that we must hate both them and their synagogue all the more because of their offensive treatment of those holy men. . . .

Therefore, flee the gatherings and holy places of the Jews. Let no man venerate the synagogue because of the holy books; let him hate and avoid it because the Jews outrage and maltreat the holy ones, because they refuse to believe their words, because they accuse them of the ultimate impiety. . . .

Certainly it is the time for me to show that demons dwell in the synagogue, not only in the place itself but also in the souls of the Jews. . . . Do you see that demons dwell in their souls and that these demons are more dangerous than the ones of old? And this is very reasonable. In the old days the Jews acted impiously toward the prophets; now they outrage the Master of the prophets. Tell me this. Do you not shudder to come into the same place with men possessed, who have so many unclean spirits, who have been reared amid slaughter and bloodshed? Must you share a greeting with them and exchange a bare word? Must you not turn away from them since they are the common disgrace and infection of the whole world? Have they not come to every form of wickedness? Have not all the prophets spent themselves making many and long speeches of accusation against them?**. . .

Tell me this. If a man were to have slain your son, would you endure to look upon him, or to accept his greeting? Would you not shun him as a wicked demon, as the devil himself? They slew the Son of your Lord; do you have the boldness to enter with them under the same roof? After he was slain he heaped such honor upon you that he made you his brother and coheir. But you dishonor him so much that you pay honor to those who slew him on the cross, that

---

‖Lk 23.21.
#Mt 27.25. Chrysostom obviously holds the position, which was common for centuries, that all Jews are responsible for Christ's passion and death. Vatican II's "Declaration on the Relationship of the Church to Non-Christian Religions" states that these "cannot be blamed on all the Jews then living, without distinction, nor upon the Jews of today. Although the Church is the new people of God, the Jews should not be presented as repudiated or cursed by God, as if such views followed from the holy Scriptures." A footnote at this point says that Cardinal Bea and others explained Mt 27.25 as the cry of a Jerusalem crowd that had no right to speak for the whole Jewish people.

**Chrysostom argues from the guilt of their forebears to the guilt of contemporary Jews.

you observe with them the fellowship of the festivals, that you go to their profane places, enter their unclean doors, and share in the tables of demons. For I am persuaded to call the fasting of the Jews a table of demons because they slew God. If the Jews are acting against God, must they not be serving the demons? . . .

Meanwhile, I ask you to rescue your brothers, to set them free from their error, and to bring them back to the truth. . . . I want them to learn these facts from you and to free themselves from their wicked association with the Jews. I want them then to show themselves sincere and genuine Christians. I want them to shun the evil gatherings of the Jews and their synagogues, both in the city and in the suburbs, because these are robbers' dens and dwellings of demons.

Rabbinic Judaism
ETHICAL CONCERNS

Contrary to the hopes of Early Christian theologians, Jews generally did not convert to the new religion but preserved their ancient faith, which took the form called Rabbinic Judaism. Evolving in the centuries following the destruction of the Temple in Jerusalem, the center of Jewish religious life, by the Romans in A.D. 70, Rabbinic Judaism parallels the period of Early Christianity. The rabbis who shaped this development in Jewish thought maintained that to understand properly the written law—the Torah revealed at Sinai—it was necessary to study the oral tradition—the wisdom transmitted over the centuries by word of mouth. Rabbinical writings interpreted the oral tradition to elucidate the behavior the Torah demanded of Jews. The Talmud, which is a compilation of the discussions and decisions of the rabbis during this period, provided Jews with an authoritative set of rules that governed every phase of Jewish life for centuries.

The rabbinical literature shows the rabbis great concern with ethical considerations as the following excerpts from the Talmud illustrate.

He who does charity and justice is as if he had filled the whole world with kindness.

Sukkah, 49

———

Charity knows neither race nor creed.

Gittin, 61a

———

He who gives charity serves the Holy One daily, and sanctifies His Name.

———

The Good Impulse seeks the joy of the Torah; the Evil Impulse, the joy of women, wine and arrogance.

Zohar, i, 202a

———

He is called a man who subdues his impulses.

Zohar, ii, 128a

———

God created the Evil Impulse, but also the Torah as its antidote.

Kiddushin, 30a

———

Upon the heart of man lies the stone of the Evil Inclination.

Bereshit Rabbah, 70, 8

———

Rabbi Simeon ben Lakish said: "Man should always rouse his good impulse against the Evil, and he may thus succeed in overcoming it. But if not, more potent means are at his command, such as immersing himself in the study of the Torah."

Berakot, 5a

———

When the wrong-doer makes amends (confesses and begs forgiveness), it is the duty of the injured party to forgive him: "When thou hast mercy upon thy, fellow, thou hast One to have mercy on thee; but if thou hast not mercy upon thy fellow, thou hast none to have mercy on thee."

Tanhuma, Buber, Wayyera, par. 30

———

R. Zeira said: "I was privileged to know a man with perfect trust in God. He set aside hours for the study of the Torah, and no matter how much he stood to lose, he would never desist from his period of study. He would say: 'If God desires to send me profit, He can do so after my time of study.' "

Y. Sotah, 9

———

Judaism is not only ethical, but ethics constitutes its essence, its nature—"its beginning, its middle and its end."

Midrash Tanhuma, Wayishlah

———

When man appears before the Throne of Judgment, the first question he is asked is not— "Have you believed in God," or, "Have you prayed or performed ritual acts," but "Have you dealt honorably, faithfully in all your dealings with your fellow-man?"

Shabbat, 31a

———

The Rabbis have taught: "For the sake of peaceful intercourse or for the sake of the Torah whose ways are ways of peace, the non-Jewish poor may gather unharvested produce left over in Jewish fields, in the same fashion as the Jewish poor. The non-Jewish poor shall receive food and garments from Jewish charity funds the same as Jews. If the non-Jewish sick have no friends, they should be visited the same as the Jewish sick. If no one claims the body of the non-Jewish dead, they should be buried by Jews, the same as the Jewish dead. When a Jew sees a non-Jew at work in the field, he should greet him with words of blessing, even in the forbidden seventh year when a Jewish worker should be shunned."

Gittin, 61

———

It is forbidden to rob the idolator.

Y. Baba Metzia, 2, 5

———

Even an idolator can be a Zaddik [righteous person].

Bemidbar Rabbah, 8, 2

———

Even a non-Jew who speaks words of wisdom is called a wise man.

Megillah, 16

———

The just among the Gentiles are priests of God.

Eliyahu Zuta, 20

———

The righteous among the Gentiles will have a share in the World-to-Come.

Yalkut Shimeoni, Prophets, Section 296

———

To rob or defraud a Gentile is worse than to rob an Israelite "on account of the profanation of the Name"—the Israelite lays the wrong to the individual; the Gentile blames the religion.

Tosefta Baba Kamma, 10, 15

———

That man's life is indeed enriched who is wedded to a virtuous woman.

Shabbat, 25b

———

A man without a wife lives without good, without help, without joy, without blessing and without forgiveness.

Kohelet Rabbah, 9, 7

A man should be careful not to irritate his wife and cause her to weep.

Baba Metzia, 59

———

REVIEW QUESTIONS

1. In what ways did John Chrysostom demonize the Jews?
2. What is the historical significance of this form of anti-Judaism?
3. Among the ethical considerations expressed in the Talmud, enumerate those that seem compatible with Early Christianity. Are any incompatible?

---

8 Church and State

Emperor Constantine's conversion to Christianity in the early fourth century dramatically changed the Christian church's relationship to the Roman state. After nearly three centuries of periodic persecution, the church now enjoyed imperial patronage, and Christianity was an accepted religion. Though still not a majority of the population, the Christian community grew rapidly through the fourth century and gained new power.

Finally, about 392, Emperor Theodosius I (A.D. 379–395) outlawed the traditional pagan cults and established Christianity as the official religion of the Roman state. Though welcome, this new status created problems for the church, which was treated more and more as if it were a department of the imperial government. Interference in matters of doctrine and discipline by imperial rulers was resisted by a clergy used to internal freedom of action, who recognized no spiritual authority but Christ and the Scriptures.

Pope Gelasius I
LETTER TO EMPEROR ANASTASIUS

In the late fifth century, Pope Gelasius I (492–496), the bishop of Rome, tried to establish clear boundaries between the legitimate sphere of authority of the state and that of the church. In the following letter to the Emperor Anastasius (491–518), written in 494, Pope Gelasius I established the church's theoretical ground rules for church–state relations over the next thousand years.

. . . Two there are, august emperor, by which this world is chiefly ruled, the sacred authority (*ductoritas*) of the priesthood and the royal power (*potestas*). Of these the responsibility of the priests is more weighty in so far as they will answer for the kings of men themselves at the divine judgement. You know, most clement son, that, although you take precedence over all mankind in dignity, nevertheless you piously bow the neck to those who have charge of divine affairs and seek from them the means of your salvation, and hence you realize that, in the order of religion, in matters concerning the reception and right administration of the heavenly sacraments, you ought to submit yourself rather than rule, and that in these matters you should depend on their judgement rather than seek to bend them to your will. For if the bishops themselves, recognizing that the imperial office was conferred on you by divine disposition, obey your laws so far as the sphere of public order is concerned lest they seem to obstruct your decrees in mundane matters, with what zeal, I ask you, ought you to obey those who have been charged with administering the sacred mysteries? Moreover, just as no light risk attends pontiffs[1] who keep silent in matters concerning the service of God, so too no little danger threatens those who' show scorn—which God forbid—when they ought to obey. And if the hearts of the faithful should be submitted to all priests in general who rightly administer divine things, how much more should assent be given to the bishop of that see[2] which the Most High [God] wished to be pre-eminent over all priests, and which the devotion of the whole church has honored ever since. As Your Piety is certainly well aware, no one can ever raise himself by purely human means to the privilege and place of him whom the voice of Christ has set before all, whom the church has always venerated and held in devotion as its primate.[3] The things which are established by divine judgement can be assailed by human presumption; they cannot be overthrown by anyone's power.

---

[1]Originally designating a Roman magistrate, the Latin word *pontifex* became applied to any priest. Here it refers to bishops.
[2]A see is a bishop's center of authority or community, over which he has power of decision in religious matters.
[3]The primate (originally from a Latin word for first) is the "first" bishop; that is, the bishop of Rome, who, as the successor of Saint Peter, was recognized as the presiding bishop over the entire Christian church.

REVIEW QUESTIONS

1. Why did Gelasius think that priests have greater responsibilities than secular rulers?
2. What argument did the pope make to persuade the emperor that divine affairs were not the business of an emperor?
3. What principle did Gelasius propose for church–state relations?

---

9 The Christian World-View

Building on the life and teachings of Jesus as reported in the Gospels and apostolic letters collected in the New Testament, the early Christian thinkers formulated a comprehensive world-view. The Christian view stressed the sinful nature of human beings—their almost unlimited capacity for evildoing. The church taught that only through the gift of God's grace could individuals overcome the consequences of sin and obtain salvation. Christian leaders drew a sharp distinction between a spiritual realm (called the City of God by Saint Augustine) and the secular world (the City of Man), where Christians had to live out their earthly, material existence. Christians were urged to live in the world, but not to live by its values. Rather, they were to imitate the ways of Jesus in thought, word, and deed, as interpreted by the authorities of the church.

The task of living a Christian life in a secular world was not easy. Not the least of the problems was how Christians could relate to the political power structure of earthly societies. The task of finding a Christian basis for relations between church and state has been a continuous process since early Christian times. It has had wide repercussions in creating a distinctive Christian view of the legitimate powers of the state.

Saint Augustine
THE CITY OF GOD

Augustine (Aurelius Augustinus, A.D. 354–430), bishop of Hippo (now Souk-Ahras in modern Algeria), was one of the great theologians of the early Christian church. He formulated a view of life and of the individual that became definitive for Western Christians until it was partially superseded by the writings of Thomas Aquinas in the thirteenth century. Although Augustine admired the achievements of Socrates and Plato, he could not accept their central premise: that in the search for truth the individual relied on reason alone.

The sacking of Rome by the Visigoths in A.D. 410 shocked the entire Roman world. Pagans blamed the catastrophe on the Christians; by abandoning the old gods, said pagans, Christians had brought down the wrath of heaven on Rome. In reply to these charges, Saint Augustine wrote the *City of God*, setting forth the Christian view of the world and humanity.

The theme of the first group of passages from Augustine's *City of God* is a crucial element in the Christian outlook: that when human beings turn away from God to follow their own desires as Adam and Eve did—the original sin—they fall into evil and become afflicted with many miseries, which can be relieved only through God's grace.

I have already said, in previous Books, that God had two purposes in deriving all men from one man. His first purpose was to give unity to the human race by the likeness of nature. His second purpose was to bind mankind by the bond of peace, through blood relationship, into one harmonious whole. I have said further that no member of this race would ever have died had not the first two [Adam and Eve]—one created from nothing and the second from the first—merited this death by disobedience. The sin which they committed was so great that it impaired all human nature—in this sense, that the nature has been transmitted to posterity with a propensity to sin and a necessity to die. . . .

When a man lives "according to man" and not "according to God" he is like the Devil. . . .

When man lives according to himself, that is to say, according to human ways and not according to God's will, then surely he lives according to falsehood. Man himself, of course, is not a lie, since God who is his Author and Creator could not be the Author and Creator of a lie. Rather, man has been so constituted in truth that he was meant to live not according to himself but to Him who made him—that is, he was meant to do the will of God rather than his own. It is a lie not to live as a man was created to live.

Man indeed desires happiness even when he does so live as to make happiness impossible. . . . The happiness of man can come not from himself but only from God, and that to live according to oneself is to sin, and to sin is to lose God. . . .

Moreover, our first parents [Adam and Eve] only fell openly into the sin of disobedience because, secretly, they had begun to be guilty. Actually, their bad deed could not have been done had not bad will preceded it; what is more, the root of their bad will was nothing else than pride. For, "pride is the beginning of all sin." And what is pride but an appetite for inordinate exaltation? Now, exaltation is inordinate when the soul cuts itself off from the very Source [God] to which it should keep close and somehow makes itself and becomes an end to itself. This takes place when the soul becomes inordinately pleased with itself, and such self-pleasing occurs when the soul falls away from the unchangeable Good which ought to please the soul far more than the soul can please itself. Now, this falling away is the soul's own doing, for, if the will had merely remained firm in the love of that higher immutable Good which lighted its mind into knowledge and warmed its will into love, it would not have turned away in search of satisfaction in itself and, by so doing, have lost that light and warmth. And thus Eve would not have believed that the serpent's lie was true, nor would Adam have preferred the will of his wife to the will of God. . . .

This life of ours—if a life so full of such great ills can properly be called a life—bears witness to the fact that, from its very start, the race of mortal men has been a race condemned. Think, first, of that dreadful abyss of ignorance from which all error flows and so engulfs the sons of Adam in a darksome pool that no one can escape without the toll of toils and tears and fears. Then, take our very love for all those things that prove so vain and poisonous and breed so many heartaches, troubles, griefs, and fears; such insane joys in discord, strife, and war; such wrath and plots of enemies, deceivers, sycophants; such fraud and theft and robbery; such perfidy and pride, envy and ambition, homicide and murder, cruelty and savagery, lawlessness and lust; all the shameless passions of the impure—fornication and adultery, incest and unnatural sins, rape and countless other uncleannesses too nasty to be mentioned; the sins against religion—sacrilege and heresy, blasphemy and perjury; the iniquities against our neighbors—calumnies and cheating, lies and false witness, violence to persons and property; the injustices of the courts and the innumerable other miseries and maladies that fill the world, yet escape attention.

It is true that it is wicked men who do such things, but the source of all such sins is that radical canker [sinfulness] in the mind and will that is innate in every son of Adam. . . .

Yet, for all this blight of ignorance and folly, fallen man has not been left without some ministries of Providence, nor has God, in His anger, shut up His mercies. There are still within the reach of man himself, if only he will pay the price of toil and trouble, the twin resources of law and education. With the one, he can make war on human passion; with the other, he can keep the light of learning lit even in the darkness of our native ignorance. . . .

From this all but hell of unhappiness here on earth, nothing can save us but the grace of Jesus Christ, who is our Saviour, Lord and God. In fact, the very meaning of the name, Jesus, is Saviour, and when we say "save" we mean, especially, that He saves us from passing from the misery of this mortal life to a still more miserable condition, which is not so much a life as death. . . .

Augustine saw a conflict between the earthly city, visible, temporal, and corrupt, and the City of God, invisible, eternal, and perfect. Those Christians favored with God's grace lived in this earthly city as strangers and pilgrims passing through on their journey to their true homeland, the heavenly kingdom. The fate of the earthly city was of no ultimate concern to these Christians. For Augustine, this earthly world represented the forces of evil that would finally be destroyed at the end of time, when Christ would come again.

What we see, then, is that two societies have issued from two kinds of love. Worldly society has flowered from a selfish love which dared to despise even God, whereas the communion of saints is rooted in a love of God that is ready to trample on self. In a word, this latter relies on the Lord, whereas the other boasts that it can get along by itself. The city of man seeks the praise of men, whereas the height of glory for the other is to hear God in the witness of conscience. The one lifts up its head in its own boasting; the other says to God: "Thou art my glory, thou liftest up my head."

In the city of the world both the rulers themselves and the people they dominate are dominated by the lust for domination; whereas in the City of God all citizens serve one another in charity, whether they serve by the responsibilities of office or by the duties of obedience. The one city loves its leaders as symbols of its own strength; the other says to its God: "I love thee, O Lord, my strength." Hence, even the wise men in the city of man live according to man, and their only goal has been the goods of their bodies or of the mind or of both; though some of them have reached a knowledge of God, "they did not glorify him as God or give thanks but became vain in their reasonings, and their senseless minds have been darkened. For while professing to be wise" (that is to say, while glorying in their own wisdom, under the domination of pride), "they have become fools, and they have changed the glory of the

incorruptible God for an image made like to corruptible man and to birds and four-footed beasts and creeping things" (meaning that they either led their people, or imitated them, in adoring idols shaped like these things), "and they worshiped and served the creature rather than the Creator who is blessed forever." In the City of God, on the contrary, there is no merely human wisdom, but there is a piety which worships the true God as He should be worshiped and has as its goal that reward of all holiness whether in the society of saints on earth or in that of angels of heaven, which is "that God may be all in all." . . .

Augustine says that history reveals the intermingling of the City of God and the City of Man in time and space, and the incessant combat between the partisans of these two cities. This struggle will continue until time itself is annulled by God when Christ returns and the saints are separated from sinners at the Last Judgment. Then the saints will join Jesus and be with him for eternity, and the sinners will be separated from God and confined to hell, also for eternity.

. . . In the eternal City of God, each and all of the citizens are personally immortal with an immortality which the holy angels never lost and which even human beings can come to share. This is to be achieved by the supreme omnipotence of the Creator, the Founder of the City. . . .

Who can measure the happiness of heaven, where no evil at all can touch us, no good will be out of reach; where life is to be one long laud extolling God, who will be all in all; where there will be no weariness to call for rest, no need to call for toil, no place for any energy but praise. . . .

. . . There will be such poise, such grace, such beauty as become a place where nothing unbecoming can be found. Wherever the spirit wills, there, in a flash, will the body be. Nor will the spirit ever will anything unbecoming either to itself or to the body.

In heaven, all glory will be true glory, since no one could ever err in praising too little or too much. True honor will never be denied where due, never be given where undeserved, and, since none but the worthy are permitted there, no one will unworthily [pursue] glory. Perfect peace will reign, since nothing in ourselves or in any others could disturb this peace.

REVIEW QUESTIONS

1. According to Augustine, what was the origin of the unity of the human race? What was the origin of human sinfulness?
2. Describe Augustine's conception of the two cities—the City of God and the City of Man—and the radical implications of this teaching in shaping Christian culture.

CHAPTER 7

The Early Middle Ages

CORONATION OF CHARLEMAGNE. The crowning of Charlemagne by the pope implied that the emperor had a spiritual responsibility to spread and defend the faith. *(Scala/Art Resource, NY)*

The establishment of Germanic kingdoms in the fifth and sixth centuries on Roman lands marked the end of the ancient world and the start of the Middle Ages, a period that spanned a thousand years. During the Middle Ages the center of Western civilization shifted northward from the lands bordering the Mediterranean Sea to parts of Europe that Greco-Roman civilization had barely penetrated.

The Early Middle Ages (500–1050) marked an age of transition. The humanist culture that characterized the Greco-Roman past had disintegrated, and a new civilization was emerging in Latin Christendom, which covered Western and Central Europe. Medieval civilization consisted of a blending of the remnants of Greco-Roman culture with Germanic customs and Christian principles. The central element was Christianity; the Christian view of a transcendent God and the quest for salvation pervaded the medieval outlook, and the church was the dominant institution.

During the Early Middle Ages, Latin Christendom was a pioneer society struggling to overcome invasions, a breakdown of central authority, a decline in trade and town life, and a deterioration of highly refined culture. The Latin Christian church, centered in Rome and headed by the pope, progressively gave form and unity to the new civilization. Christian clergy preserved some of the learning of the ancient world, which they incorporated into the Christian outlook. Dedicated missionaries converted various Germanic, Celtic, and Slavic peoples to Latin Christianity. From Italy to the North Sea and from Ireland to Poland, an emerging Christian tradition was providing unity to people with differing customs and beliefs.

The center of emerging medieval civilization was the kingdom of the Franks, located in Gaul (France) and western Germany. Migrating westward from their homeland in the valley of the Rhine River, the Germanic Franks conquered Roman Gaul in the fifth and sixth centuries. Charlemagne (768–814), the greatest of the Frankish rulers, added large areas of Germany and Italy to his kingdom. On Christmas Day in the year 800, Pope Leo III crowned Charlemagne emperor of the Romans, a sign that the memory of Imperial Rome still persisted. Without Roman law, a professional civil service, and great cities serving as centers of trade, however, Charlemagne's empire was only a pale shadow of the Roman Empire. Rather, the crowning of a German king as emperor of the Romans by the pope signified something new: the intermingling of Germanic, Christian, and Roman elements that came to characterize medieval Latin Christendom.

Charlemagne's empire rested more on the strength of the emperor's personality than it did on viable institutions. Charlemagne's heirs were unable to hold the empire together; power passed gradually into the hands of large landholders, who exercised governmental authority in their own regions. Also contributing to this decline in centralized authority were devastating raids by Muslims from Spain, North Africa, and Mediterranean islands; Northmen from Scandinavia; and Magyars from western Asia. Europe had entered an age of feudalism, in which public authority was dispersed among lords and held as if it were private inheritable property.

Feudalism rested on an economic base known as manorialism. Although family farms owned by free peasants still existed, the essential agricultural arrangement in medieval society was the village community (manor), headed by a lord or his steward and farmed by serfs, who were bound to the land. A lord controlled at least one manorial village; great lords might possess scores. Much land was held by various clerical institutions; the church's manors were similar to those run by nonclerics.

Feudalism was an improvised response to the challenge posed by ineffectual central authority, and it provided some order and law during a period of breakdown. Medieval feudal practices were not uniform but differed from region to region. In later centuries, when kings reasserted their authority and fashioned strong central governments, the power of lords declined.

Latin Christendom (Western and Central Europe) was only one of three new civilizations based on religion that emerged after the decline of the Roman Empire; Byzantium and Islam were the other two. During the Early Middle Ages both of these eastern civilizations were far more advanced than Latin Christendom. And yet it was Latin Christendom, not Byzantine or Islamic civilizations, that eventually produced the modern world.

---

1 The Byzantine Cultural Achievement

During the Early Middle Ages, when learning was in retreat in Latin Christendom, Byzantine civilization preserved the intellectual tradition of ancient Greece. Although the Roman Empire in the West fell to the German tribes, the eastern provinces of the Empire survived. They did so because they were richer, more urbanized, and more populous and because the main thrust of the Germanic and Hunnish invaders had been directed at the western regions. In the eastern parts, Byzantine civilization took shape. Its religion was Christianity, its culture Greek, and its machinery of administration Roman. Contacts with Byzantine learning during the High Middle Ages stimulated learning in the Latin West.

Theophylact Simocattes
THE VALUE OF REASON AND HISTORY

In the following selection Theophylact Simocattes, a seventh-century Byzantine historian, shows respect for the tradition of reason that was inherited from the classical world and familiarity with Homer, the wellspring of Greek literature. Like Thucydides, he values history, considering it a far better avenue to knowledge than the myths and fables created or embellished by poets.

Man is adorned not only by the endowments of nature but also by the fruits of his own efforts. For reason, which he possesses, is an admirable and divine trait by which he renders to God his adoration and homage. Through reason he enters into knowledge of himself and does not remain ignorant of the ordering of his creation. Accordingly, through reason men come together with each other and, turning away from external considerations, they direct their thoughts toward the mystery of their own nature.

Reason has given many good things to men and is an excellent helpmate of nature. The things which nature has withheld from man, reason provides in the most effective manner, embellishing those things which are seen, adding spice to those that are tasted, roughening or softening things to the touch, composing poetry and music for the ear, soothing the soul by lessening discord, and bringing sounds into concord. Is not reason also the most persuasive master of the crafts?—reason which has made a well-woven tunic from wool, which from wood has constructed carts for farmers, oars for sailors, and small wicker shields for soldiers as protection against the dangers of the battlefield.

Most important of all, reason provides the hearer with that pleasure which reflects the greatest amount of experience, the study of history, which is the instructor of the spirit. Nothing can be more seductive than history for the minds of those who desire to learn. It is sufficient to cite an example from Homer to demonstrate this: Soon after he had been thrown on the beach by violent waves of the sea, the son of Laertes, Odysseus, almost naked and

with his body emaciated from the mishap of the shipwreck, was graciously received at the court of Alcinous. There he was clothed in a bright robe and given a place at the table of the king. Although only just arrived, he was granted permission to speak and an opportunity to relate his adventures. His recital pleased the Phocaeans so much that the banquet seemed to have changed into a theater. Indeed, they lent him an attention altogether remarkable, nor did they feel during his long narration any tedium, although he described the many misfortunes he had suffered. For listening brings an overwhelming desire (to hear more) and thus easily accepts a strange tale.

It is for this reason that in learning the poets are considered most estimable, for they realize that the spirits of men are fond of stories, always yearning to acquire knowledge and thirsty for strange narrations. Thus the poets create myths for men and clothe their phrases with adornments, fleshing out the fables with method, and embellishing their nonsense with meter as if with enchanted spells. This artifice has succeeded so well that poets are considered to be theologians, intimately associated with the gods. It is believed that through the poets' mouths the gods reveal their own personal affairs and also whether a felicitous or a calamitous event will happen to men in their lifetime.

This being so, one may term history the common teacher of all men: it shows which course to follow and which to avoid as profitless. The most competent generals are those who have been instructed by history, for history reveals how to draw up troops and by what means to outmaneuver the enemy through ambush. History renders these generals more prudent because they know about the misfortunes of others, and it directs them through observation of the mistakes of others. Similarly, it has shown that men become happier through good conduct, pushing men to higher peaks of virtue through gradual advances. For the old man history is his support and staff, while for the young, it is the fairest and wisest instructor, applying (the fruit of) great experience to new situations and thus anticipating somewhat the lessons of time. I now dedicate my own zeal and efforts to history, although I know that I am undertaking a greater task than I am able to fulfill effectively, since I lack elegance of expression, profundity of thought, purity of syntax, and skill in composition. If any parts of my work should prove pleasing in any way, let this be ascribed rather to the result of chance than to my own skill.

REVIEW QUESTION

1. Why did Theophylact value reason? History? What is his debt to ancient Greece?

2 Islam

The vital new religion of Islam emerged in the seventh century among the Arabs of Arabia. Its founder was Muhammad (c. 570–632), a prosperous merchant in Mecca, a trading city near the Red Sea. When Muhammad was about forty, he believed that he was visited by the angel Gabriel, who ordered him to "recite in the name of the Lord!" Transformed by this vision, Muhammad was convinced that he had been chosen to serve as a prophet.

Although most desert Arabs worshiped tribal gods, in the towns and trading centers many Arabs were familiar with Judaism and Christianity, and some had accepted the idea of one God. Rejecting the many deities of the tribal religions, Muhammad offered the Arabs a new monotheistic faith, Islam, which means "surrender to Allah" (God).

THE KORAN

Islamic standards of morality and rules governing daily life are set by the Koran, the book that Muslims believe contains the words of Allah as revealed to Muhammad. Muslims see their religion as the completion and perfection of Judaism and Christianity. They regard the ancient Hebrew prophets as sent from God and value their messages about compassion and the oneness of humanity. Muslims also regard Jesus as a great prophet but do not consider him divine. They see Muhammad as the last and greatest of the prophets and believe that he was entirely human, not divine. Muslims worship only Allah, the creator and ruler of heaven and earth, a single, all-powerful God who is merciful, compassionate, and just. Following are excerpts from the Koran.

GOD

God: there is no god but Him, the Living, the Eternal One. Neither slumber nor sleep overtakes Him. His is what the heavens and the earth contain. Who can intercede with Him except by His permission? He knows what is before and behind men. They can grasp only that part of His knowledge which He wills. His throne is as vast as the heavens and the earth, and the preservation of both does not weary Him. He is the Exalted, the Immense One. (2:255–257)

———

In the Name of God, the Compassionate, the Merciful

It is the Merciful who has taught the Koran.

He created man and taught him articulate speech. The sun and the moon pursue their ordered course. The plants and the trees bow down in adoration.

He raised the heaven on high and set the balance of all things, that you might not transgress that balance. Give just weight and full measure.

He laid the earth for His creatures, with all its fruits and blossom-bearing palm, chaff-covered grain and scented herbs. Which of your Lord's blessings would you deny?

He created man from potter's clay, and the jinn [spirits] from smokeless fire. Which of your Lord's blessings would you deny? (55:1–18)

———

All that is in the heavens and the earth gives glory to God. He is the Mighty, the Wise One.

It is He that has sovereignty over the heavens and the earth. He ordains life and death, and has power over all things.

He is the First and the Last, the Visible and the Unseen. He has knowledge of all things.

It was He who created the heavens and the earth in six days, and then mounted the throne. He knows all that goes into the earth and all that emerges from it, all that comes down from heaven and all that ascends to it. He is with you wherever you are. God is cognizant of all your actions.

He has sovereignty over the heavens and the earth. To God shall all things return. He causes the night to pass into the day, and causes the day to pass into the night. He has knowledge of the inmost thoughts of men. (57:1–7)

RIGHTEOUSNESS AND MERCY

Righteousness does not consist in whether you face towards the East or the West. The righteous man is he who believes in God and the Last Day, in the angels and the Book and the prophets; who, though he loves it dearly, gives away his wealth to kinsfolk, to orphans, to the destitute, to the traveller in need and to beggars, and for the redemption of captives; who attends to his prayers and renders the alms levy; who is true to his promises and steadfast in trial and adversity and in times of war. Such are the true believers; such are the God-fearing. (2:176–178)

———

Serve God and associate none with Him. Show kindness to parents and kindred, to orphans and to the destitute, to near and distant neighbours, to those that keep company with you, to the traveller in need, and to the slaves you own. God does not love arrogant and boastful men, who are themselves niggardly and enjoin others to be niggardly; who conceal the riches which God of His bounty has bestowed upon them (We have prepared a shameful punishment for the unbelievers); and who spend their wealth for the sake of ostentation, believing neither in God nor in the Last Day. He that chooses Satan for his friend, an evil friend has he. (4:36–39)

CHRISTIANITY

And remember the angels' words to Mary. They said:* "God has chosen you. He has made you pure and exalted you above womankind.

———

*Cf. Luke i, 26–38.

Mary, be obedient to your Lord; bow down and worship with the worshippers."

This is an account of a divine secret. We reveal it to you.[†] You were not present when they cast lots to see which of them should have charge of Mary; nor were you present when they argued about her.

The angels said to Mary: "God bids you rejoice in a word from Him. His name is the Messiah, Jesus the son of Mary. He shall be noble in this world and in the hereafter, and shall be one of those who are favoured. He shall preach to men in his cradle and in the prime of manhood, and shall lead a righteous life."

"Lord," she said, "how can I bear a child when no man has touched me?"

He replied: "Even thus. God creates whom He will. When He decrees a thing He need only say: 'Be,' and it is. He will instruct him in the Scriptures and in wisdom, in the Torah and in the Gospel, and send him forth as an apostle to the Israelites. He will say: 'I bring you a sign from your Lord. From clay I will make for you the likeness of a bird. I shall breathe into it and, by God's leave, it shall become a living bird. By God's leave I shall heal the blind man and the leper, and raise the dead to life. I shall tell you what to eat and what to store up in your houses. Surely that will be a sign for you, if you are true believers. I come to confirm the Torah which preceded me and to make lawful to you some of the things you are forbidden. I bring you a sign from your Lord: therefore fear God and obey me. God is my Lord and your Lord: therefore serve Him. That is a straight path.'" (3:42–51)

———

People of the Book,[‡] do not transgress the bounds of your religion. Speak nothing but the truth about God. The Messiah, Jesus the son of Mary, was no more than God's apostle and His Word which He cast to Mary: a spirit from Him. So believe in God and His apostles and do not say: "Three" [a reference to the Trinity] Forbear, and it shall be better for you. God is but one God. God forbid that He should have a son! His is all that the heavens and the earth contain. God is the all-sufficient protector. The Messiah does not disdain to be a servant of God, nor do the angels who are nearest to Him. Those who through arrogance disdain His service shall all be brought before Him. (4:171–172)

HEAVEN AND HELL

THAT WHICH IS COMING

In the Name of God, the Compassionate, the Merciful

When that which is coming comes—and no soul shall then deny its coming—some shall be abased and others exalted.

When the earth shakes and quivers, and the mountains crumble away and scatter abroad into fine dust, you shall be divided into three multitudes: those on the right (blessed shall be those on the right); those on the left (damned shall be those on the left); and those to the fore (foremost shall be those). Such are they that shall be brought near to their Lord in the gardens of delight: a whole multitude from the men of old, but only a few from the latter generations.

They shall recline on jewelled couches face to face, and there shall wait on them immortal youths with bowls and ewers and a cup of purest wine (that will neither pain their heads nor take away their reason); with fruits of their own choice and flesh of fowls that they relish. And theirs shall be the dark-eyed houris [beautiful virgins], chaste as hidden pearls: a guerdon [reward] for their deeds.

There they shall hear no idle talk, no sinful speech, but only the greeting, "Peace! Peace!" Those on the right hand – happy shall be those on the right hand! They shall recline on couches raised on high in the shade of thornless [cedars] and clusters of talh;[§] amidst gushing waters and abundant fruits, unforbidden, neverending.

We created the houris and made them virgins, loving companions for those on the right

———

[†]Muhammad.
[‡]Christians.

———

[§]Probably the banana fruit.

hand: a multitude from the men of old, and a multitude from the later generations.

As for those on the left hand (wretched shall be those on the left hand!) they shall dwell amidst scorching winds and seething water: in the shade of pitch-black smoke, neither cool nor refreshing. For they have lived in comfort and persisted in the heinous sin,‖ saying: "When we are once dead and turned to dust and bones, shall we be raised to life? And our forefathers, too?"

Say: "Those of old, and those of the present age, shall be brought together on an appointed day. As for you sinners who deny the truth, you shall eat the fruit of the Zaqqūm tree and fill your bellies with it. You shall drink scalding water: yet you shall drink it as the thirsty camel drinks."

‖Idolatry.

Such shall be their fare on the Day of Reckoning. (56:1–56)

WOMEN

Men have authority over women because God has made the one superior to the other, and because they spend their wealth to maintain them. Good women are obedient. They guard their unseen parts because God has guarded them. As for those from whom you fear disobedience, admonish them and send them to beds apart and beat them. Then if they obey you, take no further action against them. Surely God is high, supreme.

If you fear a breach between a man and his wife, appoint an arbiter from his people and another from hers. If they wish to be reconciled God will bring them together again. Surely God is all-knowing and wise. (4:34–35)

REVIEW QUESTIONS

1. Compare and contrast the views of God and morality described in the Koran with those found in the Hebrew Scriptures and the New Testament.
2. What advice does the Koran give to Christians?

---

3   Muslim Relations with Christians and Jews

The Koran regards Jesus as a righteous prophet who performed miracles but rejects his divinity and denounces as blasphemers those who believe in it. Muslims accept the Hebrew Scriptures as God's revelation but are often critical of Jews, probably because of their opposition to Muhammad in Medina. In Islamic lands both Christians and Jews were called the people of the Book and were granted the status of *dhimmis*—minorities who lived under the protection of Islamic authority. They were not required to convert and were free to practice their faith in private and to govern their own communities. For these privileges, they had to accept a subordinate status, which included payment of a poll tax and humiliating restrictions on their activities (described in the following documents). Despite these prohibitions, Christians and Jews generally enjoyed toleration and some rose to positions of prominence. Jews in particular lived in greater security than they did in Christian lands where, in the High and Late Middle Ages, they were subject to frequent persecution, including expulsion and massacre. Although some passages in the Koran disparage Jews, medieval Muslims, unlike in the Latin West, did not teach that Jews were agents of Satan.

LEGAL TEXTS AND DECREES: RESTRICTIONS ON *DHIMMIS*

The first document describing restrictions on Jews and Christians is from a legal text drawn up in the eighth and ninth centuries. The second is a decree issued by a caliph in 1354. The Arabic terms in brackets were inserted by Bernard Lewis, the translator.

"You will be subject to the authority of Islam and to no contrary authority. You will not refuse to carry out any obligation which we think fit to impose upon you by virtue of this authority.

If any one of you speaks improperly of Muhammad, may God bless and save him, the Book of God, or of His religion, he forfeits the protection [*dhimma*] of God, of the Commander of the Faithful, and of all the Muslims; he has contravened the conditions upon which he was given his safe-conduct; his property and his life are at the disposal of the Commander of the Faithful.

If one of them commits fornication with a Muslim woman or goes through a form of marriage with her or robs a Muslim on the highway or subverts a Muslim from his religion or gives aid to those who made war against the Muslims by fighting with them or by showing them the weak points of the Muslims, or by harboring their spies, he has contravened his pact [*'ahd*], and his life and his property are at the disposal of the Muslims.

If he commits some lesser offense against the property or the honor of a Muslim or against an infidel under Muslim protection, with a pact or safe-conduct, he shall be punished.

We shall supervise all your dealings with Muslims. If there is anything in which you are engaged which is not lawful for a Muslim, we shall reject it and punish you for it. If you sell a Muslim something we hold forbidden, such as wine, pig, blood, or carrion, and the like, we shall annul the sale, confiscate the price if it has been paid, and not return the thing to you if it still exists, but pour it out if it is wine or blood and burn it if it is carrion; if the purchaser has already consumed it, we shall not oblige him to pay for it, but we shall punish you for it.

You shall not give a Muslim anything to eat or drink which is forbidden, nor marry him in the presence of witnesses chosen from among you nor by wedding rites we hold to be invalid. . . .

If any of you steals and the victim takes him before a judge, his hand shall be cut off if his crime is punishable by this penalty, and he shall make restitution. . . .

You may not display crosses in Muslim cities, nor proclaim polytheism, nor build churches or meeting places for your prayers, nor strike clappers, nor proclaim your polytheistic beliefs on the subject of Jesus, son of [Mary], or any other to a Muslim.

You shall wear the girdle [*zunnār*] over all your garments, your cloaks and the rest, so that the girdles are not hidden. You shall differentiate yourselves by your saddles and your mounts, and you shall distinguish your and their headgear [*qalansuwa*] by a mark which you shall place on your headgear. You shall not occupy the middle of the road or the seats in the market, obstructing Muslims.

Every free adult male of sound mind among you shall have to pay a poll tax [*jizya*] of one dinar, in good coin, at the beginning of each year. He shall not be able to leave his city until he pays his poll tax or appoints someone to pay it on his behalf, with no further liability until the beginning of the year. The poor among you is liable for the poll tax, which should be paid for him. Poverty does not free you from any obligation, nor does it abrogate your pact [*dhimma*]. . . . You are subject to no taxes on your money other than the poll tax as long as you stay in your country or travel around in the lands of the Muslims otherwise than as a merchant. You may in no circumstances enter Mecca. If you travel for trade, you shall pay to the Muslims a tenth part of all your merchandise. You may go wherever you wish in the lands of the Muslims, except [holy] Mecca, and reside wherever you wish in the lands of the Muslims, except the Hijāz, where you may only stay for three days in any city, after which you must leave. . . .

We owe you protection, for yourselves and for property which it is lawful for you to hold according to our laws, against anybody, Muslim or other, who seeks to wrong you, as we would protect our own persons and property, and we administer justice to you in matters under our jurisdiction as we do with our own property. But no one among you can ask us to protect any forbidden thing which you own, such as blood, carrion, wine, or pigs, as we would protect lawful property. We shall not prevent you from having them, but we shall not allow you to display them in the cities of the Muslims. If a Muslim or any other buys such merchandise, we shall not compel him to pay the price, because these are forbidden things and therefore have no price which could be legally enforced. But we shall restrain him from troubling you in this, and if he persists he shall be punished, though not by enforcing payment for what he took from you.

You must observe all the conditions which we have imposed.

———

A noble decree, to the effect that all the communities of Jews, Christians, and Samaritans in the Egyptian lands and the God-guarded realms of Islam and their dependencies must conform to the covenant accorded by the Commander of the Faithful ʿUmar ibn al-Khaṭṭāb, may God be pleased with him, to the members of these communities in bygone times, as follows: That they shall not build any new convent or church or hermitage in the lands of Islam, nor rebuild any such building which is destroyed; that they shall not harbor spies nor any who are suspect to the Muslims, nor shall they deceitfully plot against the Muslims; that they shall not teach their children the Qurʾān; that they shall not make public display of polytheism; that they shall not obstruct any of their relatives who wish to accept Islam; that they shall not dress like the Muslims, but shall wear blue and yellow distinguishing dress; that their women shall be prevented from dressing like Muslim women; that they shall not ride with stirrups nor gird a sword, nor ride on a horse or mule but only on donkeys, side-seat on litters; that they shall not sell intoxicating drinks; that they shall keep to their special dress wherever they are; that they shall wear girdles not made of silk around their waists; that the Christian woman who appears in public shall wear a cotton veil, dyed blue, and the Jewess a yellow veil; that none of them shall enter the bath except wearing a sign around his neck which distinguishes him from the Muslims, such as a ring made of iron or lead or some other material; that they shall not build themselves houses higher than the houses of the Muslims, nor equal to them, but only lower; that they shall knock lightly with their clappers and not raise their voices in their churches; that they shall not work in the service of our exalted state, may God strengthen its foundations, nor in the service of any of the amirs, may Almighty God strengthen them, nor shall any of them hold a position which would give him authority over any of the Muslims; that jurisdiction over the estates of the dead among them shall be according to the noble Muhammadan Holy Law and that the rules of administrative confiscation will be applied to them equally as to the Muslim dead; that the women of the protected communities shall not enter public bathhouses together with the Muslim women, but that separate bathhouses shall be made for them, into which they shall enter. All this is in accordance with the rulings of the doctors of the Holy Law, as has been explained.

1. What was the purpose of the restrictions imposed on Christians and Jews?

---

4 Jihad

Muhammad had conveyed to his followers their religious obligation to perform jihad, a complex term whose two essential meanings are an internal striving by an individual for moral self-improvement (Greater Jihad) and a collective military struggle to defend Islam against its enemies and to extend Muslim power over other lands so that all people will be subject to Allah (Lesser Jihad). Historically the doctrine of jihad held that the Islamic community (umma), the recipient of Allah's revelation is commanded to make Allah's directives supreme over the whole world. Either by conversion or conquest, infidels are destined to submit to Islamic jurisdiction.

Westerners, who are repulsed by the Islamic concept of jihad and feel threatened by jihadist terrorists, generally interpret jihad as a Muslim's fanatical duty to engage in holy war against the perceived enemies of Islam. Seeking to defend their faith against critics who attack contemporary Islam as an incubator of terrorism, some Muslim intellectuals and religious authorities often respond by stressing Islam's peaceful, tolerant, and humanitarian characteristics, its command to win converts by preaching and persuasion. Central to their argument is the traditional distinction in Islam between the Lesser Jihad and the Greater Jihad. Over the centuries, however, most classical Islamic theologians and jurists interpreted jihad as a military obligation to advance Islamic power. And that is how Islamic terrorists interpret it today.

SAYINGS ATTRIBUTED TO THE PROPHET

Muhammad glorified jihad and criticized those who did not participate in it, calling them "hypocrites" and "sick in heart." The Koran states: "Those who are killed in the path of God, He does not let their good deeds go for nothing. The *hadith*, which consists of an assemblage of sayings and actions attributed to Muhammad and is a major source of Islamic law, contains numerous passages prescribing and lauding jihad as the following excerpts indicate.

I asked Allah's Apostle, "O Allah's Apostle! What is the best deed?" He replied, "To offer the prayers at their early stated fixed times." I asked, "What is next in goodness?" He replied, "To be good and dutiful to your parents." I further asked, what is next in goodness?" He replied, "To participate in Jihad in Allah's Cause."

A man came to Allah's Apostle and said, "Instruct me as to such a deed as equals Jihad (in reward)." He replied, "I do not find such a deed."

———

The Prophet said, "Last night two men came to me (in a dream) and made me ascend a tree and then admitted me into a better and superior house, better of which I have never seen. One of them said, 'This house is the house of martyrs'."

———

The Prophet said, "A single endeavor (of fighting) in Allah's Cause in the forenoon or in the afternoon is better than the world and whatever is in it."

———

The Prophet said, "Nobody who dies and finds good from Allah (in the Hereafter) would wish to come back to this world even if he were given the whole world and whatever is in it, except the martyr who, on seeing the superiority of martyrdom, would like to come back to the world and get killed again (in Allah's Cause)."

Narrated Anas: The Prophet said, "A single endeavor (of fighting) in Allah's Cause in the afternoon or in the forenoon is better than all the world and whatever is in it. A place in Paradise as small as the bow or lash of one of you is better than all the world and whatever is in it."

———

A man whose face was covered with an iron mask (i.e., clad in armor) came to the Prophet and said, "O Allah's Apostle! Shall I fight or embrace Islam first?" The Prophet said, 'Embrace Islam first and then fight.' So he embraced Islam, and was martyred. Allah's Apostle said, "A little work, but a great reward." (He did very little (after embracing Islam), but he will be rewarded in abundance).

———

A man came to the Prophet and asked, "A man fights for war booty; another fights for fame and a third fights for showing off; which of them fights in Allah's Cause?" The Prophet said, "He who fights that Allah's Word (i.e., Islam) should be superior, fights in Allah's Cause."

———

Allah's Apostle said, "Anyone whose both feet get covered with dust in Allah's Cause will not be touched by the (Hell) fire."

Ibn Taymiyyah
THE RELIGIOUS AND MORAL DOCTRINE OF JIHAD

Present-day Islamists who advocate jihad against the enemies of Islam often quote extensively Shaykh ul-Islaam Taqi al-Din Ahmad ibn Taymiyyah (1263–1328), a Syrian theologian who regarded jihad as a Muslim's religious and moral duty as the following excerpt from his writings reveals.

The benefit of jihad is general, extending not only to the person who participates in it but also to others. . . . More than any other act it implies love and devotion for God, Who is exalted, trust in Him, the surrender of one's life and property to Him. . . . Any individuals or community that participates in it, finds itself between two blissful outcomes: either victory and triumph or martyrdom and Paradise. . . . Now, it is in jihad that one can live and die in ultimate happiness, both in this world and in the hereafter. Abandoning it means losing entirely or partially both kinds of happiness. There are people who want to perform religious and temporal deeds full of hardship in spite of their lack of benefit, whereas actually jihad is religiously and temporally more beneficial than any other deed full of hardship. . . . The death of a martyr. . . . is the best of all manners of dying.

REVIEW QUESTIONS

1. What is the meaning of jihad defined in the Hadith? What reasons led Muslims to perform jihad?
2. How, according to Ibn Taymiyyah, does jihad provide ultimate happiness?

5 Islam and Greek Learning

In the eighth and ninth centuries, Muslim civilization, which creatively integrated Arabic, Byzantine, Persian, and Indian cultural traditions, entered its golden age. Muslim science, philosophy, and mathematics, based largely on the achievements of the ancient Greeks, made brilliant contributions to the sum of knowledge at a time when Latin Christendom had lost much of Greco-Roman thought and culture. The Muslims had acquired Greek learning from the older Persian and Byzantine civilizations, which had kept alive the Greek inheritance. By translating Greek works into Arabic and commenting on them, Muslim scholars performed the great historical task of preserving the philosophical and scientific heritage of ancient Greece. Along with this heritage, the original contributions of Muslim scholars and scientists were also passed on to Christian Europe.

Avicenna
LOVE OF LEARNING

The most eminent Muslim thinker, Ibn-Sina, known to the West as Avicenna (980–1037), was a poet, doctor, scientist, and philosopher who wrote on every field of knowledge. His philosophical works, which relied heavily on Aristotle, had an important influence on medieval Christian thinkers. In his autobiography, excerpted below, Avicenna describes his love for learning and his debt to ancient Greece.

[In] Bukhara [in present-day Uzbekistan] I was put under teachers of the Koran and of letters. By the time I was ten I had mastered the Koran and a great deal of literature, so that I was marvelled at for my aptitude. . . . Then there came to Bukhara a man called Abū ʿAbd Allāh al-Nātilī who claimed to be a philosopher; my father invited him to stay in our house, hoping that I would learn from him also. Before his advent I had already occupied myself with

Muslim jurisprudence, attending Ismāʿīl the Ascetic; so I was an excellent enquirer, having become familiar with the methods of postulation and the techniques of rebuttal according to the usages of the canon lawyers. I now commenced reading the *Isagoge* (of Porphyry)[1] with al-Nātilī: when he mentioned to me the definition of *genus* as a term applied to a number of things of different species in answer to the question "What is it?" I set about verifying this definition in a manner such as he had never heard. He marvelled at me exceedingly, and warned my father that I should not engage in any other occupation but learning; whatever problem he stated to me, I showed a better mental conception of it than he. So I continued until I had read all the straightforward parts of Logic with him; as for the subtler points, he had no acquaintance with them.

From then onward I took to reading texts by myself; I studied the commentaries, until I had completely mastered the science of Logic. Similarly with Euclid[2] I read the first five or six figures with him, and thereafter undertook on my own account to solve the entire remainder of the book. Next I moved on to the *Almagest* (of Ptolemy)[3]; when I had finished the prolegomena [introductory essay] and reached the geometrical figures, al-Nātilī told me to go on reading and to solve the problems by myself; I should merely revise what I read with him, so that he might indicate to me what was right and what was wrong. The truth is that he did not really teach this book; I began to solve the work, and many were the complicated figures of which he had no knowledge until I presented

them to him, and made him understand them. Then al-Nātilī took leave of me, setting out for Gurganj.

I now occupied myself with mastering the various texts and commentaries on natural science and metaphysics, until all the gates of knowledge were open to me. Next I desired to study medicine, and proceeded to read all the books that have been written on this subject. Medicine is not a difficult science, and naturally I excelled in it in a very short time, so that qualified physicians began to read medicine with me. I also undertook to treat the sick, and methods of treatment derived from practical experience revealed themselves to me such as baffle description. At the same time I continued between whiles to study and dispute on law, being now sixteen years of age.

The next eighteen months I devoted entirely to reading; I studied Logic once again, and all the parts of philosophy. During all this time I did not sleep one night through, nor devoted my attention to any other matter by day. I prepared a set of files; with each proof I examined, I set down the syllogistic premises and put them in order in the files, then I examined what deductions might be drawn from them. I observed methodically the conditions of the premises, and proceeded until the truth of each particular problem was confirmed for me. Whenever I found myself perplexed by a problem, or could not find the middle term in any syllogism, I would repair to the mosque and pray, adoring the All-Creator, until my puzzle was resolved and my difficulty made easy. At night I would return home, set the lamp before me, and busy myself with reading and writing; whenever sleep overcame me or I was conscious of some weakness, I turned aside to drink a glass of wine until my strength returned to me; then I went back to my reading. If ever the least slumber overtook me, I would dream of the precise problem which I was considering as I fell asleep; in that way many problems revealed themselves to me while sleeping. So I continued until I had made myself master of all the sciences; I now comprehended them to the limits of

---

[1]Porphyry (A.D. 233–c. 305) wrote a history of philosophy and edited the lectures of Plotinus, the Neoplatonist. The *Isagoge* was Porphyry's introduction to the categories of Aristotle.

[2]Euclid, an Alexandrian mathematician who lived around 300 B.C. He creatively synthesized earlier developments in geometry.

[3]Ptolemy, a mathematician, geographer, and astronomer who worked at Alexandria in the second century A.D. His *Almagest*, a Greek-Arabic term meaning "the greatest," summed up antiquity's knowledge of astronomy and became the authoritative text during the Middle Ages.

human possibility. All that I learned during that time is exactly as I know it now; I have added nothing more to my knowledge to this day.

I was now a master of Logic, natural sciences and mathematics. I therefore returned to metaphysics; I read the *Metaphysica* (of Aristotle), but did not understand its contents and was baffled by the author's intention; I read it over forty times, until I had the text by heart. Even then I did not understand it or what the author meant, and I despaired within myself, saying, "This is a book which there is no way of understanding." But one day at noon I chanced to be in the booksellers' quarter, and a broker was there with a volume in his hand which he was calling for sale. He offered it to me, but I returned it to him impatiently, believing that there was no use in this particular science. However he said to me, "Buy this book from me: it is cheap, and I will sell it to you for four dirhams. The owner is in need of the money." So I bought it, and found that it was a book by Abū Naṣr al-Fārābī *On the Objects of the Metaphysica*. I returned home and hastened to read it; and at once the objects of that book became clear to me, for I had it all by heart. I rejoiced at this, and upon the next day distributed much in alms to the poor in gratitude to Almighty God.

Now the Sultan of Bukhara at that time was Nūḥ ibn Manṣūr, and it happened that he fell sick of a malady which baffled all the physicians. My name was famous among them because of the breadth of my reading; they therefore mentioned me in his presence, and begged him to summon me. I attended the sick-room, and collaborated with them in treating the royal patient. So I came to be enrolled in his service. One day I asked his leave to enter their library, to examine the contents and read the books on medicine; he granted my request, and I entered a mansion with many chambers, each chamber having chests of books piled one upon another. In one apartment were books on language and poetry, in another law, and so on; each apartment was set aside for books on a single science. I glanced through the catalogue of the works of the ancient Greeks, and asked for those which I required; and I saw books whose very names are as yet unknown to many—works which I had never seen before and have not seen since. I read these books, taking notes of their contents; I came to realize the place each man occupied in his particular science.

So by the time I reached my eighteenth year I had exhausted all these sciences. My memory for learning was at that period of my life better than it is now, but to-day I am more mature; apart from this my knowledge is exactly the same, nothing further having been added to my store since then.

REVIEW QUESTIONS

1. Provide examples of Avicenna's familiarity with Greek learning.
2. Show how Avicenna combined Greek learning with Islamic teachings.

---

6 Converting the Germanic Peoples to Christianity

From its beginnings, Christianity sought to carry to all peoples its offer of salvation through faith in Jesus. After Christianity had become the religion of the Roman state, pagan cults were suppressed. When the western Roman provinces fell under the power of invading Germanic tribes, Christian Romans faced the task of converting their new rulers to their religion.

The ability of the Christian religion to penetrate and absorb alien cultures while preserving its own core beliefs was continually to be tested in the Early Middle Ages. Roman Britain had been invaded in the fifth century by various tribes from northwestern Germany, Denmark, and the Netherlands. Among these tribes were the Angles (from which the word *English* is derived), the Saxons, and the Jutes. The Romano-Britons, who were Christians, were forced to retreat westward to occupy what became the Celtic-speaking Christian principalities of Cornwall, Wales, and Cumberland. Pagan Germans ruled the rest of England.

Bede
HISTORY OF THE ENGLISH CHURCH AND PEOPLE

The English monk called the Venerable Bede (673–735), in his *History of the English Church and People*, cites a letter from Pope Gregory I (the Great) written in 601. In the letter, the pope forwarded instructions for Augustine of Canterbury, whom he had appointed leader of a mission to convert the English to Christianity. He wrote his emissary to tell Augustine to win the favor of the pagan English by accommodating the requirements of Christian beliefs to the existing non-Christian cultural practices, as the excerpt shows.

When these [missionaries] had left, the holy father Gregory sent after them letters worthy of our notice, which show most clearly his unwearying interest in the salvation of our nation. The letter runs as follows:

"To our well loved son Abbot[1] Mellitus: Gregory, servant of the servants of God.

"Since the departure of yourself and your companions, we have been somewhat anxious, because we have received no news of the success of your journey. Therefore, when by God's help you reach our most reverend brother, Bishop Augustine,[2] we wish you to inform him that we have been giving careful thought to the affairs of the English, and have come to the conclusion that the temples of the idols in that country should on no account be destroyed. He is to destroy the idols, but the temples themselves are to be aspersed [sprinkled] with holy water, altars set up, and relics enclosed in them. For if these temples are well built, they are to be purified from devil-worship,[3] and dedicated to the service of the true God. In this way, we hope that the people, seeing that its temples are not destroyed, may abandon idolatry and resort to these places as before, and may come to know and adore the true God. And since they have a custom of sacrificing many oxen to devils, let some other solemnity be substituted in its place, such as a day of Dedication[4] or the Festivals of the holy martyrs [saints' days] whose relics are

---

[1]The elected head of a monastic community, the abbot was supposed to rule justly and paternally following the constitution (rule) of the community.
[2]Augustine (not to be confused with Augustine of Hippo) was an Italian monk who was sent in 597 to convert the English to Christianity. He established his see (bishopric) at Canterbury and founded others at Rochester and London, successfully directing missionary activity in the southern part of what is now England.

[3]As Christianity was monotheistic, it denied the validity of any other gods. Therefore, Christians customarily designated the pagan deities as "devils," or evil spirits.
[4]The anniversary of the dedication or consecration of a church was celebrated as a holiday.

enshrined there. On such occasions they might well construct shelters of boughs for themselves around the churches that were once temples, and celebrate the solemnity with devout feasting. They are no longer to sacrifice beasts to the Devil, but they may kill them for food to the praise of God, and give thanks to the Giver of all gifts for His bounty. If the people are allowed some worldly pleasures in this way, they will more readily come to desire the joys of the spirit. For it is certainly impossible to eradicate all errors from obstinate minds at one stroke, and whoever wishes to climb to a mountain top climbs gradually step by step, and not in one leap. It was in this way that God revealed Himself to the Israelite people in Egypt, permitting the sacrifices formerly offered to the Devil to be offered thenceforward to Himself instead. So He bade them sacrifice beasts to Him, so that, once they became enlightened, they might abandon a wrong conception of sacrifice, and adopt the right. For, while they were to continue to offer beasts as before, they were to offer them to God instead of to idols, thus transforming the idea of sacrifice. Of your kindness, you are to inform our brother Augustine of this policy, so that he may consider how he may best implement it on the spot. God keep you safe, my very dear son." . . .

Einhard
FORCIBLE CONVERSION UNDER CHARLEMAGNE

Although most conversions were based on peaceful persuasion or a voluntary act of consent, occasionally Christianity was imposed by force. Thus, after his long wars against the pagan Saxons, Charlemagne required the Saxons to adopt Christianity and be assimilated into the Frankish kingdom. In his biography of Charlemagne, the Frankish historian Einhard (770–840) described this event.

No war ever undertaken by the Frank nation was carried on with such persistence and bitterness, or cost so much labor, because the Saxons,[1] like almost all the tribes of Germany, were a fierce people, given to the worship of devils, and hostile to our religion, and did not consider it dishonorable to transgress and violate all law, human and divine. Then there were peculiar circumstances that tended to cause a breach of peace every day. Except in a few places, where large forests or mountain ridges intervened and made the bounds certain, the line between ourselves and the Saxons passed almost in its whole extent through an open country, so that there was no end to the murders, thefts, and arsons on both sides. In this way the Franks became so embittered that they at last resolved to make reprisals no longer, but to come to open war with the Saxons [in 772]. Accordingly war was begun against them, and was waged for thirty-three successive years with great fury; more, however, to the disadvantage of the Saxons than of the Franks. It could doubtless have been brought to an end sooner, had it not been for the faithlessness of the Saxons. It is hard to say how often they were conquered, and humbly submitting to the King, promised to do what was enjoined upon them, gave without

---

[1] The Saxons were members of a Germanic tribe living between the Rhine and Elbe rivers.

hesitation the required hostages, and received the officers sent them from the King. They were sometimes so much weakened and reduced that they promised to renounce the worship of devils, and to adopt Christianity, but they were no less ready to violate these terms than prompt to accept them, so that it is impossible to tell which came easier to them to do; scarcely a year passed from the beginning of the war without such changes on their part. But the King did not suffer his high purpose and steadfastness—firm alike in good and evil fortune—to be wearied by any fickleness on their part, or to be turned from the task that he had undertaken; on the contrary, he never allowed their faithless behavior to go unpunished, but either took the field against them in person, or sent his counts[2] with

an army to wreak vengeance and exact righteous satisfaction. At last, after conquering and subduing all who had offered resistance, he took ten thousand of those that lived on the banks of the Elbe,[3] and settled them, with their wives and children, in many different bodies here and there in Gaul and Germany. The war that had lasted so many years was at length ended by their acceding to the terms offered by the King; which were renunciation of their national religious customs and the worship of devils, acceptance of the sacraments of the Christian faith and religion, and union with the Franks to form one people.

_____

[3]The Elbe River, in central Germany, flows northwestward into the North Sea.

_____

[2]Counts were royal officials exercising the king's authority in districts called counties.

Martin of Braga
THE PERSISTENCE OF PAGANISM IN THE COUNTRYSIDE

The persistence of paganism in the countryside remained an ongoing and serious problem for the clergy. Bishop Martin of Braga (c. 520–580), in *On the Castigation of Rustics,* a letter to another bishop in Spain that he expected to be delivered as a sermon to peasants, denounced Christian converts for retaining traditional religious beliefs, practices, and cults despite the pact they had made with God in baptism. In particular, he railed against the peasants' worship of sacred trees and stones and their attempt to divine the future through magic. Following is an excerpt from *On the Castigation of Rustics.*

You promised to renounce the Devil and his angels and all his evil works. And you confessed you believed in Father, Son, and Holy Spirit, and hoped, at the end of the age, for the resurrection of the flesh and eternal life.

See what a bond and confession God holds from you! And how can any of you, who has

renounced the Devil and his angels and his evil works, now return again to the worship of the Devil? For to burn candles at stones and trees and springs, and where three roads meet, what is it but the worship of the Devil? To observe divinations and auguries and the days of idols, what is it but worship of the Devil?

To observe the "days" of Vulcan [August 23] and the first days of each month, to adorn tables and hang up laurels, to watch the foot, and to pour out fruit and wine over a log in the hearth, and to put bread in a spring, what is it but the worship of the Devil? For women to invoke Minerva in their weaving, to keep weddings for the "day" of Venus [Friday], and to consider which day one should set out on a journey, what is it but the worship of the Devil? To mutter spells over herbs and invoke the names of demons in incantations, what is it but the worship of the Devil? And many other things which it takes too long to say. And you do all these things *after* renouncing the Devil, after Baptism, and, returning to the worship of demons and to their evil works, you have betrayed your Faith and broken the pact you made with God. You have abandoned the Sign of the Cross you received in Baptism, and you give heed to signs of the Devil by little birds and sneezing and many other things. Why does no augury harm me or any other upright Christian? Because, where the Sign of the Cross has gone before, the sign of the Devil is nothing. Why does it harm you? Because you despise the Sign of Cross and fear the sign you made for yourselves. Likewise you have abandoned the Holy Incantation, that is the Creed you received in Baptism, and the Lord's Prayer, and you cling to diabolical incantations and chants. Whoever, therefore, having despised the Sign of the Cross of Christ, turns to other signs, has lost the Sign of the Cross which he received in Baptism. So, too, he who has other incantations invented by magicians and enchanters, has lost the Creed and the Lord's Prayer, which he received in the Faith of Christ, and has trampled underfoot the Faith of Christ, for one cannot worship God and the Devil at once.

If, therefore, beloved sons, you acknowledge that all the things we have said are true, if a man knows he has done these things after Baptism, and has broken the Faith of Christ, let him not despair of himself, nor say in his heart, "Since I have done such great evil after Baptism, perhaps God will not forgive me my sins." Do not doubt the mercy of God. Only make such a pact in your heart with God that, from now onward, you will no longer worship demons, nor adore anything except the God of Heaven, nor commit murder, nor adultery nor fornication, nor steal nor perjure yourself. And when you have promised this to God of your whole heart, and, further, have ceased to commit these sins, trust in God's pardon, for thus says the Lord by the prophet: "In whatever day the unjust shall forget his iniquities and do justice, I also will forget all his iniquities" (Ezekiel 18:21). God, therefore, waits for repentance. But that repentance is true when a man no longer does the evil he did but both asks for pardon for his past [sins] and bewares lest he return again to them in the future, and, on the other hand; practices good, both providing alms for the hungry poor, refreshing the tired guest, and, whatever he does not wish another should do to him, not doing to another, for in this word the commandments of God are fulfilled.

REVIEW QUESTIONS

1. Give examples of the methods Pope Gregory I suggested for introducing Christianity in pagan England.
2. Compare the methods Charlemagne used to convert the Saxons with the instruction given by Pope Gregory I to Augustine of Canterbury.
3. What is Bishop Martin of Braga's concept of devil worship? How did he believe Christianity could overcome it?

7 The Transmission of Learning

Learning, which had been in retreat in the Late Roman Empire, continued its decline in the unsettled conditions following Rome's demise. The old Roman schools closed, and many scientific and literary works of the ancient world were either lost or neglected. Knowledge of the Greek language in Western Europe virtually disappeared, and except for clerics, few people could read or write Latin. The few learned people generally did not engage in original thought but preserved and transmitted surviving elements of the Greco-Roman past.

One such scholar was Cassiodorus (c. 490–575), who served three Ostrogothic kings in Italy. Cassiodorus wrote theological treatises and the twelve-volume *History of the Goths*, but his principal achievement was collecting Greek and Latin manuscripts. Like other Christian scholars before and after him, Cassiodorus maintained that the study of secular literature was an aid to understanding sacred writings. He retired to a monastery where he fostered the monastic practice of copying Christian and pagan manuscripts. Without this effort of monks, many important secular and Christian writings might have perished.

Cassiodorus
THE MONK AS SCRIBE

In the following reading from his Introduction to *Divine and Human Readings*, Cassiodorus gave his views on the importance of the monastic scribe's vocation. Cassiodorus believed that through his pen the scribe preaches the word of God and is inspired by his text to know God more fully.

ON SCRIBES AND THE REMEMBERING OF CORRECT SPELLING

1. I admit that among those of your tasks which require physical effort that of the scribe,[1] if he writes correctly, appeals most to me; and it appeals, perhaps not without reason, for by reading the Divine Scriptures he wholesomely instructs his own mind and by copying the precepts of the Lord he spreads them far and wide. Happy his design, praiseworthy his zeal, to preach to men with the hand alone, to unleash

tongues with the fingers, to give salvation silently to mortals, and to fight against the illicit temptations of the devil with pen and ink. Every word of the Lord written by the scribe is a wound inflicted on Satan. And so, though seated in one spot, with the dissemination of his work he travels through different provinces. The product of his toil is read in holy places; people hear the means by which they may turn themselves away from base desire and serve the Lord with heart undefiled. Though absent, he labors at his task. I cannot deny that he may receive a renovation of life from these many blessings, if only he accomplishes things of this sort, not with a vain show of ambition, but with upright zeal. Man multiplies the heavenly

---

[1]Scribes were persons trained to copy by hand the texts of books, or to take dictation.

words, and in a certain metaphorical sense, if one may so express himself, that which the virtue of the Holy Trinity utters is written by a trinity of fingers. O sight glorious to those who contemplate it carefully! With gliding pen the heavenly words are copied so that the devil's craft, by means of which he caused the head of the Lord to be struck during His passion, may be destroyed. They deserve praise too for seeming in some way to imitate the action of the Lord, who, though it was expressed figuratively, wrote His law with the use of His all-powerful finger. Much indeed is there to be said about such a distinguished art, but it is enough to mention the fact that those men are called scribes *(librarii)* who serve zealously the just scales *(libra)* of the Lord.

2. But lest in performing this great service copyists introduce faulty words with letters changed or lest an untutored corrector fail to know how to correct mistakes, let them read the works of ancient authors on orthography [spelling]. . . .

. . . I have collected as many of these works as possible with eager curiosity. . . . [If you] read [them] with unremitting zeal, they will completely free you from the fog of ignorance, so that what was previously unknown may become for the most part very well known.

3. In addition to these things we have provided workers skilled in bookbinding, in order that a handsome external form may clothe the beauty of sacred letters; in some measure, perhaps, we imitate the example in the parable of the Lord,* who amid the glory of the heavenly banquet has clothed in wedding garments those whom He judges worthy of being invited to the table. And for the binders, in fitting manner, unless I err, we have represented various styles of binding in a single codex,[2] that he who so desires may choose for himself the type of cover he prefers.

4. We have also prepared cleverly constructed lamps which preserve their illuminating flames and feed their own fire and without human attendance abundantly maintain a very full clearness of most copious light; and the fat oil in them does not fail, although it is burned continually with a bright flame.

5. Nor have we by any means allowed you to be unacquainted with the hour meters which have been discovered to be very useful to the human race. I have provided a sundial for you for bright days and a water clock which points out the hour continually both day and night, since on some days the bright sun is frequently absent, and rain water passes in marvellous fashion into the ground, because the fiery force of the sun, regulated from above, fails. And so the art of man has brought into harmony elements which are naturally separated; the hour meters are so reliable that you consider an act of either as having been arranged by messengers. These instruments, then, have been provided in order that the soldiers of Christ,[3] warned by most definite signs, may be summoned to the carrying out of their divine task as if by sounding trumpets.

---

*Matthew 22:11.

[2]A codex consists of the rectangular sheets on which scribes have written, bound together on one side like a modern book. Invented in the late first century A.D., the codex gradually replaced scrolls as the predominant way to store written texts.
[3]"Soldiers of Christ" is a metaphor to describe the monks in their vocation.

REVIEW QUESTIONS

1. What was the function of a scribe?
2. What contributions did the monasteries make in the development of medieval culture?

8   The Carolingian Renaissance

The Early Middle Ages witnessed a marked decline in learning and the arts. Patronage of both the liberal and the visual arts by the old Roman aristocracy was not widely copied by the Germanic ruling class that replaced the Romans. Support for learning and the arts shifted from secular to ecclesiastical patrons. Monasteries became the new centers for intellectual and artistic activities, and Christian themes and values almost entirely displaced the worldly values of Greco-Roman culture.

Under the patronage of Charlemagne (742–814), the great Frankish emperor, a conscious revival of classical Greek and Roman learning and the visual arts occurred. Charlemagne realized that his great empire could not be effectively governed without a cadre of literate clergy and administrators. To educate the leaders of the Frankish empire, Charlemagne sponsored a number of reforms designed to improve the educational institutions and the quality of literacy and learning in his realm. At court, he completely reformed the school conducted for the children of his family and his courtiers and recruited the best scholars in Western Europe to staff it. Among these scholars was the English deacon Alcuin of York (735–804), who became his chief advisor on educational and religious affairs. They aimed at restoring classical learning to serve the needs of the new Christian culture.

Einhard
CHARLEMAGNE'S APPRECIATION OF LEARNING

The revival of classical learning and the visual arts under Charlemagne is called the Carolingian Renaissance, a cultural awakening that helped shape medieval civilization. One of Charlemagne's most significant decisions was ordering the making of copies of old manuscripts dating back to Roman times. Much of today's knowledge of Roman learning and literature comes from surviving Carolingian copies of older Latin texts that no longer exist. In the first reading, Charlemagne's biographer Einhard describes Western Europe's greatest royal patron of the liberal arts since the fall of the Western Roman Empire.

Charles [Charlemagne] had the gift of ready and fluent speech, and could express whatever he had to say with the utmost clearness. He was not satisfied with command of his native language merely, but gave attention to the study of foreign ones, and in particular was such a master of Latin that he could speak it as well as his native tongue; but he could understand Greek better than he could speak it. He was so eloquent, indeed, that he might have passed for a teacher of eloquence. He most zealously cultivated the liberal arts, held those who taught them in great esteem, and conferred great honors upon them. He took lessons in grammar of the deacon Peter of Pisa,[1] at that time an aged man. Another deacon, Albin of Britain, surnamed Alcuin, a man of Saxon extraction, who was the greatest scholar of the day, was his teacher in other branches of learning. The King spent much time and labor with him studying rhetoric, dialectics, and especially astronomy; he learned to reckon, and used to investigate the motions of the heavenly bodies most curiously, with an intelligent scrutiny. He also tried to write, and used to keep tablets and blanks in bed under his pillow, that at leisure hours he might accustom his hand to form the letters; however, as he did not begin his efforts in due season, but late in life, they met with ill success.

He cherished with the greatest fervor and devotion the principles of the Christian religion, which had been instilled into him from infancy. Hence it was that he built the beautiful basilica[2] at Aix-la-Chapelle,[3] which he adorned with gold and silver and lamps, and with rails and doors of solid brass. He had the columns and marbles for this structure brought from Rome and Ravenna,[4] for he could not find such as were suitable elsewhere. He was a constant worshipper at this church as long as his health permitted, going morning and evening, even after nightfall, besides attending mass; and he took care that all the services there conducted should be administered with the utmost possible propriety, very often warning the sextons not to let any improper or unclean thing be brought into the building or remain in it. He provided it with a great number of sacred vessels of gold and silver and with such a quantity of clerical robes that not even the doorkeepers who fill the humblest office in the church were obliged to wear their everyday clothes when in the exercise of their duties. He was at great pains to improve the church reading and psalmody [singing], for he was well skilled in both, although he neither read in public nor sang, except in a low tone and with others.

He was very forward in succoring the poor, and in that gratuitous generosity which the Greeks call alms, so much so that he not only made a point of giving in his own country and his own kingdom, but when he discovered that there were Christians living in poverty in Syria, Egypt, and Africa, at Jerusalem, Alexandria, and Carthage, he had compassion on their wants, and used to send money over the seas to them. . . .

---

[1]Peter of Pisa, a famous grammarian (in Latin, the international language of the Middle Ages), was brought from Italy to teach at the school in Charlemagne's palace. He encouraged interest in pre-Christian classical writing, which influenced the court poets of that era.

[2]A basilica is usually a rectangular-shaped church, whose main chamber is divided by columns into a central nave and side aisles. There was usually a semicircular apse at the narrow end facing the east, which was the visual focal point and the location of the main altar.

[3]Aix-la-Chapelle, now Aachen, was Charlemagne's capital. It was located in what is now western Germany, near the Netherlands–Belgium frontier.

---

[4]Ravenna, in northeastern Italy, was the final capital of the Western Roman Empire, in the fifth century; in the sixth and seventh centuries it was the capital of the Byzantine governors of Italy. Ravenna is famous for its magnificent sixth-century churches and mosaic art.

Charlemagne
AN INJUNCTION TO MONASTERIES TO CULTIVATE LETTERS

In a letter to the Abbot Baugulf of Fulda (in Germany), Charlemagne announced his decision to use monasteries as schools for training future clergymen in grammar, writing, and rhetoric.

Charles, by the grace of God, King of the Franks and Lombards and Patrician of the Romans, to Abbot Baugulf and to all the congregation, also to the faithful committed to you, we have directed a loving greeting by our ambassadors in the name of omnipotent God.

Be it known, therefore, to your devotion pleasing to God, that we, together with our faithful, have considered it to be useful that the bishoprics and monasteries entrusted by the favor of Christ to our control, in addition to the [rule] of monastic life and the intercourse of holy religion, . . . also ought to be zealous in [the cultivation of letters], teaching those who by the gift of God are able to learn, according to the capacity of each individual, so that just as the observance of the rule imparts order and grace to honesty of morals, so also zeal in teaching and learning may do the same for sentences, so that those who desire to please God by living rightly should not neglect to please him also by speaking correctly. For it is written: "Either from thy words thou shalt be justified or from thy words thou shalt be condemned."*

For although correct conduct may be better than knowledge, nevertheless knowledge precedes conduct. Therefore, each one ought to study what he desires to accomplish, so that . . . the mind may know more fully what ought to be done, as the tongue hastens in the praises of omnipotent God without the hindrances of errors. For since errors should be shunned by all men, . . . the more they ought to be avoided

as far as possible by those who are chosen for this very purpose alone, so that they ought to be the especial servants of truth. For when in the years . . . [past], letters were often written to us from several monasteries in which it was stated that the brethren who dwelt there offered up in our behalf sacred and pious prayers, we have recognized in most of these letters both correct thoughts and uncouth expressions; because what pious devotion dictated faithfully to the mind, the tongue, uneducated on account of the neglect of study, was not able to express in the letter without error. . . . We began to fear lest perchance, as the skill in writing was less, so also the wisdom for understanding the Holy Scriptures might be much less than it rightly ought to be. And we all know well that, although errors of speech are dangerous, far more dangerous are errors of the understanding. Therefore, we exhort you not only not to neglect the study of letters, but also with most humble mind, pleasing to God, to study earnestly in order that you may be able more easily and more correctly to penetrate the mysteries of the divine Scriptures. Since, moreover, images . . . and similar figures are found in the sacred pages, no one doubts that each one in reading these will understand the spiritual sense more quickly if previously he shall have been fully instructed in the mastery of letters. Such men truly are to be chosen for this work as have both the will and the ability to learn and a desire to instruct others. And may this be done with a zeal as great as the earnestness with which we command it.

---

*Matthew, xii. 37.

REVIEW QUESTION

1. Why was Charlemagne so anxious to raise the educational standards of both the clergy and laity of his empire? How did he go about doing it?

9 The Feudal Lord: Vassal and Warrior

In societies in which the state's role in regulating human relationships is minimal, law and order are maintained through custom and contract. This condition prevailed in the Early Middle Ages, particularly among the Germanic peoples. Laws were based on the community's assumptions about what was right and wrong, enforced by public opinion and community-approved use of force. To enforce law and to protect oneself and one's family, a person formed contractual ties with others and sought security and justice in mutual aid. A principal form of such a contract was called vassalage. By its terms, two free men of different means bound themselves to assistance and loyal support. The socially and economically superior man was called the lord; the man of inferior social status was called the vassal. The vassal pledged to be loyal and fight on behalf of his lord when called upon, in return for the lord's loyalty and protection when they were needed. The contract was lifelong and had deep emotional meaning in addition to the obvious self-interest of both parties.

Vassalage was a dynamic relationship, ever changing in content and meaning according to time, place, and circumstances. In the Carolingian Empire, vassalage was practiced by all members of the free class wealthy enough to afford weapons. Charlemagne and his successors tried to use vassalage as a means of controlling their warlike subjects and organizing them to serve more effectively for the defense of the royal family's realms. Eventually, the kings' vassals used their military skills, their own landed wealth, and their political power to diminish royal power. The royal vassals then became the true center of authority within medieval society.

An important part of the lord–vassal relationship was the lord's grant of a fief to his vassal. The fief might be any object of value that reflected the vassal's social status and the lord's respect for his services. A fief could be a warhorse, sword, and suit of armor; a public office; a right to collect a tax or toll; or authority to hold a court of justice in a specified district. The most sought-after fief was a land grant—one or more manors from which to draw income. Fiefs were held for the duration of the bond of vassalage. If the bond was broken by death or disloyalty, the fief was forfeited to its grantor. By the late ninth century, however, fiefs had become hereditary, as had the right to be a vassal to a specific lord.

Galbert of Bruges
COMMENDATION AND
THE OATH OF FEALTY

This reading contains an eyewitness account of the ceremony of commendation or investiture in which vassals swore an oath of fealty (loyalty) to their new lord, William Clito, the count of Flanders, in 1127, and were then invested with their fiefs. The account comes from an early twelfth-century chronicle written by a Flemish notary, Galbert of Bruges (a major medieval commercial city in Flanders, now part of Belgium).

Through the whole remaining part of the day those who had been previously enfeoffed [given fiefs] by the most pious count Charles,[1] did homage to the count, taking up now again their fiefs and offices and whatever they had before rightfully and legitimately obtained. On Thursday the seventh of April, homages were again made to the count being completed in the following order of faith and security.

First they did their homage thus: The count asked if he was willing to become completely his

man, and the other replied, "I am willing"; and with clasped hands, surrounded by the hands of the count, they were bound together by a kiss. Secondly, he who had done homage gave his fealty to the representative of the count in these words, "I promise on my faith that I will in future be faithful to count William, and will observe my homage to him completely against all persons in good faith and without deceit," and thirdly, he took his oath to this upon the relics of the saints. Afterward, with a little rod which the count held in his hand, he gave investitures to all who by this agreement had given their security and homage and accompanying oath.

---

[1]Charles, count of Flanders, was murdered on March 2, 1127.

Bishop Fulbert of Chartres
OBLIGATIONS OF LORDS AND VASSALS

In a letter written in 1020 to William, Duke of Aquitaine, Bishop Fulbert (c. 962–1028) of Chartres summarizes the obligations of the lord and the vassal.

To William most glorious duke of the Aquitanians,[1] bishop Fulbert [asks] the favor of his prayers.

Asked to write something concerning the form of fealty, I have noted briefly for you on the authority of the books the things which follow. He who swears fealty to his lord ought always to have these six things in memory; what is harmless, safe, honorable, useful, easy, practicable. Harmless, that is to say that he should not be injurious to his lord in his body; safe, that he should not be injurious to him in his secrets or in the defences through which he is able to be secure; honorable, that he should not be injurious to him in his justice or in other matters that pertain to his honor; useful, that he should not be injurious to him in his

possessions; easy or practicable, that that good which his lord is able to do easily, he make not difficult, nor that which is practicable he make impossible to him.

However, that the faithful vassal should avoid these injuries is proper, but not for this does he deserve his holding; for it is not sufficient to abstain from evil, unless what is good is done also. It remains, therefore, that in the same six things mentioned above he should faithfully counsel and aid his lord, if he wishes to be looked upon as worthy of his benefice and to be safe concerning the fealty which he has sworn.

The lord also ought to act toward his faithful vassal reciprocally in all these things. And if he does not do this he will be justly considered guilty of bad faith, just as the former, if he should be detected in the avoidance of or the doing of or the consenting to them, would be perfidious and perjured.

---

[1]The Aquitanians inhabited the kingdom of Aquitaine in southwestern France—later a province of France.

Bertran de Born
IN PRAISE OF COMBAT

Feudal lords did not engage in productive labor as did serfs, merchants, and craftsmen. Manual labor and commerce were considered degrading for men of their rank and skills. Lords were professional warriors; combat was what they relished, trained for, and eagerly sought. They used their wealth to obtain armor and weapons; and even their sports, hunting and tournaments, prepared them for battle.

The spirit of the feudal warrior is expressed in the following poem by Bertran de Born (c. 1140–c. 1215), a French nobleman from the bishopric of Perigord in southern France. He is acknowledged to have been a superior poet of his day, a good warrior, and a clever intriguer who stirred up troubles between the kings of France and England. His poetry captures the excitement and pageantry of medieval warfare.

I love the springtide of the year
When leaves and blossoms do abound,
And well it pleases me to hear
The birds that make the woods resound
With their exulting voices.
And very well it pleases me
Tents and pavilions pitched to see,
And oh, my heart rejoices

To see armed knights in panoply [full armor]
Of war on meadow and on lea [pasture].

I like to see men put to flight
By scouts throughout the countryside,
I like to see, armed for the fight,
A host of men together ride;
And my delight's unbounded

When castles strong I see assailed,
And outworks smashed, whose strength has
    failed,
And near the walls, surrounded
By moats, and by strong stakes enrailed,
The host that has the ramparts scaled.

And well I like a noble lord
When boldly the attack he leads,
For he, whene'er he wields his sword,
Inspires his men by his brave deeds,
Their hearts with courage filling.
When tide of battle's at the flood,

Each soldier then, in fighting mood,
To follow should be willing,
For no man is accounted good
Till blows he's given and withstood.

Axes and swords and spears and darts,
Shields battered in with many a blow,
We'll see when first the battle starts,
And clash of arms as foe meets foe;
The steeds of dead and dying
Wildly will rush throughout the field,
And all who wish to be revealed
As brave will e'er be trying
How best their axes they may wield,
For they would rather die than yield.

Not so much joy in sleep have I,
Eating and drinking please me less
Than hearing on all sides the cry
"At them!" and horses riderless
Among the woodlands neighing.
And well I like to hear the call
Of "Help!" and see the wounded fall,
Loudly for mercy praying,
And see the dead, both great and small,
Pierced by sharp spearheads one and all.

Barons, without delaying,
Pawn every city, castle, hall,
And never cease to fight and brawl.

REVIEW QUESTIONS

1. In the Middle Ages, contracts were symbolized and publicly noted by the use of various ritual acts or gestures. Explain how the contract of vassalage was signified by specific rituals or actions.
2. What were some of the ethical and emotive dimensions of vassalage? Describe the mutual obligations of lords and vassals.
3. What personal qualities were expected from a medieval leader in combat? What challenge did the Germanic warrior spirit present to the leaders of the Christian church?

---

10 The Burdens of Serfdom

The feudal lord's way of life was made possible by the toil of the serfs who worked on the manors. Serfs, who were not free persons, had some rights but also many burdensome obligations. Unlike slaves, they could not be sold off the land or dispossessed from their landholdings. Their tenure on their farms was hereditary, but they owed heavy rent to the landlord in the form of labor and a share of their crops and livestock. There were many restrictions on their personal freedom: they needed the landlord's permission to leave the estate, to marry, or to pass on personal property to their heirs. In return, they received security; they were defended by the landlords against outside aggressors or fellow serfs.

The labor services usually took up half the work week of the serf. He was required to plant, plow, and harvest the lord's fields, repair roads, fix fences, clear ditches, and cart goods to barns and markets. Although specific obligations varied from time to time and manor to manor, they were sufficiently onerous to encourage the serfs to seek freedom; in later centuries, when the opportunity presented itself, a serf might flee to a nearby town or to newly developed lands, or might purchase certain freedoms from the manorial lord. The serfs' struggle to rid themselves of the burdens of serfdom took centuries. It was largely successful in Western Europe by the fifteenth century. But in Eastern Europe, serfdom was imposed on the formerly free peasantry in the sixteenth and seventeenth centuries. Remnants of serfdom in Western Europe survived until the French Revolution. Serfdom was abolished in Central and Eastern Europe in the mid-nineteenth century.

Bishop Adalbero of Laon
THE TRIPARTITE SOCIETY

Medieval thinkers came to see their society divided into three different but complementary groups: clergy, lords, and serfs. Each group had its own responsibilities—priests guided the souls of the faithful; lords protected society from its enemies; and the serfs' toil provided sustenance for everyone. Written in about 1020, the following statement by Bishop Adalbero of Laon, France, illustrates the tripartite nature of medieval society.

The community of the faithful is a single body, but the condition of society is threefold in order. For human law distinguishes two classes. Nobles and serfs, indeed, are not governed by the same ordinance. . . . The former are the warriors and the protectors of the churches. They are the defenders of the people, of both great and small, in short, of everyone, and at the same time they ensure their own safety. The other class is that of the serfs. This luckless breed possesses nothing except at the cost of its own labour. Who could, reckoning with an abacus, add up the sum of the cares with which the peasants are occupied, of their journeys on foot, of their hard labours? The serfs provide money, clothes, and food, for the rest; no free man could exist without serfs.

Is there a task to be done? Does anyone want to put himself out? We see kings and prelates make themselves the serfs of their serfs; [but in truth] the master, who claims to feed his serf, is fed by him. And the serf never sees an end to his tears and his sighs. God's house, which we think of as one, is thus divided into three; some pray, others fight, and yet others work. The three groups, which coexist, cannot bear to be separated; the services rendered by one are a precondition for the labours of the two others; each in his turn takes it upon himself to relieve the whole. Thus the threefold assembly is none the less united, and it is thus that law has been able to triumph, and that the world has been able to enjoy peace.

Ralph Glaber, Monk of Cluny
FAMINE

Among the hardships burdening medieval peasants was famine, which particularly afflicted the poor. The following passage by Ralph Glaber, monk of Cluny in France, describes the terrible famine of 1032–1034.

The famine started to spread its ravages and one could have feared the disappearance of almost the entire human race. The atmospheric conditions became so unfavourable that no suitable time could be found to sow seed, and that, especially because of the floods, there was no means of reaping the harvest. . . . Continual rains had soaked into all the soil to the point where during three years no one could dig furrows capable of taking the seed. At harvest-time, weeds and ill-omened tares had covered the whole surface of the fields. A [half bushel] of grain sown, where it gave the best yields, . . . produced barely a fistful. If by chance one found some food for sale, the seller could charge an outrageous price just as he pleased. However, when they had eaten the wild beasts and birds, the people started, under the sway of a devouring hunger, to collect all sorts of

carrion [decaying flesh] and other things which are horrible to mention to eat. Some in order to escape death had recourse to forest roots and water-weed. Finally, horror takes hold of us listening to the perversions which then reigned among the human race. Alas! O woe! Something rarely heard of throughout the ages: rabid hunger made men devour human flesh. Travellers were kidnapped by people stronger than they were, their limbs were cut off, cooked on the fire and eaten. Many people who moved from one place to another to flee the famine, and who had found hospitality on the way, were murdered in the night, and served as food for those who had welcomed them. Many showed a fruit or an egg to children, enticed them into out-of-the-way spots, killed them, and devoured them. Bodies of the dead were in many places torn out of the ground and equally served to appease hunger. . . . Then people tried an experiment in the region of Mâcon which had never before, to our knowledge, been tried anywhere. Many people took out of the ground a white soil which looked like clay, mixed it with what flour or bran they had, and made out of this mixture loaves with which, they reckoned, they would not die of hunger; this practice however brought only an illusory hope of rescue and an illusory relief. One only saw pale and emaciated faces; many people had a skin distended with swellings; the human voice itself became thin, like the little cries of dying birds. The corpses of the dead, who were so numerous that they had to lie scattered without burial, served as food for the wolves, who thereafter continued for a long time to seek their pittance among men. And since it was not possible, as we said, to bury each person individually because of the great number of the dead, in certain places men who feared God dug what were commonly called charnel pits, into which the bodies of the dead were thrown by the 500 or more, as many as there was space for, pellmell, half naked or without any covering; crossroads and the edges of fields served as cemeteries. Although some heard say that they would find it better to take themselves off to other regions, many were those who perished along the way of starvation.

William of Jumièges and Wace
FAILED REBELLION

Occasionally, peasant anger at their treatment at the hands of lords led to open rebellion as illustrated in the following account by a Norman monk of an uprising of Norman peasants in 977.

He had scarcely reigned or been duke for any length of time when there arose in that land a war which was to cause great misery. The peasants and villeins [partly freed serfs], those from the woodlands and those from the plains (I do not know through whose instigation it happened or who started it in the first place), held a number of councils in groups of twenty, thirty and a hundred. They were devising a plan such that, if they could succeed in it and bring it to fruition, harm would be done to the highest noblemen. They discussed this in private and many of them swore between themselves that never again would they willingly have a lord or a governor. Lords did them nothing but harm and they could get nothing out of them, from either their produce or their labours; each day they were experiencing great suffering. They were enduring pain and hardship. Things used to be bad, but now they were worse; every day their beasts were being taken to pay for aids and service. There were so many complaints and legal actions and so many old and new customs that they could not have an hour's peace. Every day they were subject to [unjust treatment by their lords]. . . .

There were so many provosts and beadles [lesser officials], so many bailiffs, old and new, that they had no peace for a single hour; all day long they descended on them. They could not defend themselves in court; each one of them wanted his due. These men had their beasts taken by force and they did not dare take a stand or defend themselves. They could not go on living like this; they would have to abandon their lands. They could get no protection against either their lord or his men, who did not keep any agreement with them.

"Son of a whore!" said some, "why do we put up with all the harm which is being done to us?

Let us free ourselves from their control! We are men as they are; we have the same limbs as they do, we are their equal physically and are able to endure as much as they can. The only thing we lack is courage. Let us unite on oath, defend our goods and ourselves and stick together. If they wish to wage war on us, against one knight we have thirty or forty peasants, skilful and valiant. Thirty men in the flower of their youth will be cowardly and shameful if they cannot defend themselves against one man, providing they are willing to join forces. With clubs and large stakes, arrows and staffs, axes, bows and pikes, and stones for those who have no arms, let us defend ourselves against knights with the large number of men we have. In this way we can go into woods, cut down trees and take what we will, catch fish in the rivers and venison in the forests. We will do as we wish with everything, with the woods, the ponds and the meadows."

Lords generally crushed these rebellions with great ferocity.

With such talk and such words, and other even more foolish remarks, they all agreed on this plan and all swore they would join forces and defend themselves together. They chose I do not know which or how many of the most intelligent amongst them and the best speakers who would go round the country receiving oaths. But a plan transmitted to so many people could not be concealed for long. Whether it was from vassals or men-at-arms, women or children, through drunkenness or anger, Richard very soon heard that the peasants were forming a commune and would

take away what was rightfully his, from him and the other lords who had peasants and [tenants]. He sent for his uncle Ralph and related the whole affair to him; Ralph was the very valiant count of Évreux and very skilled in many things.

"My lord," he said, "do not worry; leave the peasants to me, for you would only regret taking action yourself. But send me your household troops, send me your knights."

"Willingly," Richard replied to him. Then Ralph sent his spies and his couriers to many places. He did so much spying and had his spies make so many enquiries, with both the sick and the healthy, that he caught and captured the peasants who were arranging the meetings and receiving the oaths. Ralph was very angry and did not want to bring them to trial; he gave them all cause to feel sad and sorrowful. He had the teeth of many of them pulled out and others' feet cut off, their eyes put out and their hands cut off; yet others he had branded on the hamstrings. He did not care who died as a result. The others he had roasted alive and others plunged into molten lead. He had them all so well dealt with that they were hideous to behold. Henceforth, they were not seen anywhere without being easily recognised. Then the commune came to an end and the peasants made no more moves; they all withdrew and abandoned what they had undertaken, as a result of the fear caused by seeing their friends injured and maimed. The rich peasants paid for all this, but they settled their debt from their own purses; they were left with nothing which could be taken from them while they could still be put to ransom. They reached the best agreements they could with their lords.

REVIEW QUESTIONS

1. What hardships did medieval peasants face?
2. On the basis of these documents, how do you think lords viewed serfs?

CHAPTER 8

The High and Late Middle Ages

CHRISTINE DE PISAN, who wrote in praise of the virtues, abilities, and accomplishments of women, presenting her manuscript to Isabel of Bavaria. *(Historical Picture Archive/Corbis)*

The High Middle Ages (1050–1300) were an era of growth and vitality in Latin Christendom. Improvements in technology and cultivation of new lands led to an increase in agricultural production; the growing food supply, in turn, reduced the number of deaths from starvation and malnutrition, and better cultivation methods freed more people to engage in nonagricultural pursuits, particularly commerce.

During the Early Middle Ages, Italian towns had maintained a weak link with the Byzantine lands in the eastern Mediterranean. In the eleventh century, the Italians gained ascendancy over Muslim fleets in the Mediterranean and rapidly expanded their trade with the Byzantine Empire and North Africa. The growing population provided a market for silk, sugar, spices, dyes, and other Eastern goods. Other mercantile avenues opened up between Scandinavia and the Atlantic coast; between northern France, Flanders, and England; and along the rivers between the Baltic Sea in the north and the Black Sea and Constantinople in the southeast.

The revival of trade and the improved production of food led to the rebirth of towns in the eleventh century. During the Early Middle Ages, urban life had largely disappeared in Latin Christendom except in Italy, and even Italian towns had declined since Roman times both in population and as centers of trade and culture. During the twelfth century, towns throughout Latin Christendom became active centers of commerce and intellectual life. The rebirth of town life made possible the rise of a new social class: the middle class, consisting of merchants and artisans. These townspeople differed significantly from the clergy, the nobles, and the serfs—the other social strata in medieval society. The world of the townspeople was the marketplace rather than the church, the castle, or the manorial village. These merchants and artisans resisted efforts by lords to impose obligations upon them, as their livelihood required freedom from such constraints. The middle class became a dynamic force for change.

The High Middle Ages were also characterized by political and religious vitality. Strong kings extended their authority over more and more territory, often at the expense of feudal lords; in the process, they laid the foundation of the modern European state system. By the eleventh century the autonomy of the church—its freedom to select its own leaders and to fulfill its moral responsibilities—was threatened by kings and lords who appointed bishops and abbots to ecclesiastical offices. In effect, the churches and monasteries were at the mercy of temporal rulers, who distributed church positions as patronage, awarding them to their families, vassals, and loyal servants. These political appointees often lacked the spiritual character to maintain high standards of discipline among the priests or monks they supervised. Many clergy resented the subordination of the church to the economic and political interests of kings and lords. They held that for the church to fulfill its spiritual mission, it must be free from lay control.

The crisis within the church was dramatically addressed by a small band of clergy, mostly monks, who managed to elect to the papacy a series of committed reformers. These popes condemned clerical marriages, deeming them uncanonical, because they risked subordinating the church's interests to those of the clergymen's wives and children. Priests were required to be celibate like bishops and monks. The reformers also pressed for the systematic exclusion of the laity from participation in the governing of the church. In calling for the abolition of lay investiture (that is, the formal installation of clergy to their office by temporal lords), the papacy encountered bitter opposition. As head of the church, charged with the mission of saving souls, the papacy refused to accept a subordinate position to temporal rulers.

Economic, political, and religious vitality was complemented by a cultural and intellectual awakening. The twelfth and thirteenth centuries marked the high point of medieval civilization. The Christian outlook, with its otherworldly emphasis, shaped and inspired this awakening. Christian scholars rediscovered the writings of ancient Greek thinkers, which they tried to harmonize with Christian teachings. In the process, they constructed an impressive philosophical system that integrated Greek rationalism into the Christian world-view. The study of Roman law was revived, and some of its elements were incorporated into church law. A varied literature expressed both secular and religious themes, and a distinctive form of architecture, the Gothic, conveyed the overriding Christian concern with things spiritual.

During the Late Middle Ages, roughly the fourteenth and early fifteenth centuries, medieval civilization declined. In contrast to the vigor of the twelfth and thirteenth centuries, the fourteenth century was burdened by crop failures, famine, plagues, and reduced population. The church also came under attack from reformers who challenged clerical authority and questioned church teachings; from powerful kings who resisted papal interference in the political life of their kingdoms; and from political theorists who asserted that the pope had no authority to intervene in matters of state. In the city-states of Italy, a growing secularism signified a break with medieval other-worldliness and heralded the emergence of the modern outlook. Known as the Renaissance, this development is discussed in Chapter 9.

1 The Revival of Trade and the Growth of Towns

Several factors contributed to economic vitality in the High Middle Ages: the end of the Viking raids in northwestern Europe, greater political stability provided by kings and powerful lords, and increased agricultural productivity, which freed some people to work at other pursuits and facilitated a population increase. The prime movers in trade were the merchant adventurers, a new class of entrepreneurs. Neither bound to the soil nor obligated to lifelong military service, merchants traveled the sea lanes and land roads to distant places in search of goods that could profitably be traded in other markets.

HOW TO SUCCEED IN BUSINESS

In the following reading from *The King's Mirror,* an anonymous thirteenth-century Norseman outlined the characteristics and skills a merchant needed and described the hazards of the job. In typical medieval fashion, he emphasized the moral dimensions of commercial transactions.

The man who is to be a trader will have to brave many perils, sometimes at sea and sometimes in heathen lands, but nearly always among alien peoples; and it must be his constant purpose to act discreetly wherever he happens to be. On the sea he must be alert and fearless.

When you are in a market town, or wherever you are, be polite and agreeable; then you will secure the friendship of all good men. Make it a habit to rise early in the morning, and go first and immediately to church. . . .

. . . When the services are over, go out to look after your business affairs. If you are unacquainted with the traffic of the town, observe carefully how those who are reputed the best and most prominent merchants conduct their business. You must also be careful to examine the wares that you buy before the purchase is finally made to make sure that they are sound and flawless. And whenever you make a purchase, call in a few trusty men to serve as witnesses as to how the bargain was made.

You should keep occupied with your business till breakfast or, if necessity demands it, till midday; after that you should eat your meal.

Keep your table well provided and set with a white cloth, clean victuals, and good drinks. Serve enjoyable meals, if you can afford it. After the meal you may either take a nap or stroll about a little while for pastime and to see what other good merchants are employed with, or whether any new wares have come to the borough which you ought to buy. On returning to your lodgings examine your wares, lest they suffer damage after coming into your hands. If they are found to be injured and you are about to dispose of them, do not conceal the flaws from the purchaser: show him what the defects are and make such a bargain as you can; then you cannot be called a deceiver. Also put a good price on your wares, though not too high, and yet very near what you see can be obtained; then you cannot be called a foister [trickster].

Finally, remember this, that whenever you have an hour to spare you should give thought to your studies, especially to the law books; for it is clear that those who gain knowledge from books have keener wits than others, since those who are the most learned have the best proofs for their knowledge. Make a study of all the laws. . . . If you are acquainted with the law, you will not be annoyed by quibbles when you have suits to bring against men of your own class, but will be able to plead according to law in every case.

But although I have most to say about laws, I regard no man perfect in knowledge unless he has thoroughly learned and mastered the customs of the place where he is sojourning. And if you wish to become perfect in knowledge, you must learn all the languages, first of all Latin and French, for these idioms are most widely used; and yet, do not neglect your native tongue or speech.

. . . Train yourself to be as active as possible, though not so as to injure your health. Strive never to be downcast, for a downcast mind is always morbid; try rather to be friendly and genial at all times, of an even temper and never moody. Be upright and teach the right to every man who wishes to learn from you; and always associate with the best men. Guard your tongue carefully; this is good counsel, for your tongue may honor you, but it may also condemn you. Though you be angry speak few words and never in passion; for unless one is careful, he may utter words in wrath that he would later give gold to have unspoken. On the whole, I know of no revenge, though many employ it, that profits a man less than to bandy heated words with another, even though he has a quarrel to settle with him. You shall know of a truth that no virtue is higher or stronger than the power to keep one's tongue from foul or profane speech, tattling, or slanderous talk in any form. If children be given to you, let them not grow up without learning a trade; for we may expect a man to keep closer to knowledge and business when he comes of age, if he is trained in youth while under control.

And further, there are certain things which you must beware of and shun like the devil himself: these are drinking, chess, harlots, quarreling, and throwing dice for stakes. For upon such foundations the greatest calamities are built; and unless they strive to avoid these things, few only are able to live long without blame or sin.

Observe carefully how the sky is lighted, the course of the heavenly bodies, the grouping of the hours, and the points of the horizon. Learn also how to mark the movements of the ocean and to discern how its turmoil ebbs and swells; for that is knowledge which all must possess who wish to trade abroad. Learn arithmetic thoroughly, for merchants have great need of that.

If you come to a place where the king or some other chief who is in authority has his officials, seek to win their friendship; and if they demand any necessary fees on the ruler's behalf, be prompt to render all such payments, lest by holding too tightly to little things you lose the greater. . . . If you can dispose of your wares at suitable prices, do not hold them long; for it is the wont of merchants to buy constantly and to sell rapidly. . . .

. . . If you attend carefully to all these things, with God's mercy you may hope for success. This, too, you must keep constantly in mind, if you wish to be counted a wise man, that you ought never to let a day pass without learning something that will profit you. Be not like those who think it beneath their dignity to hear or learn from others such things even as might avail them much if they knew them. For a man must regard it as great an honor to learn as to teach, if he wishes to be considered thoroughly informed. . . .

. . . Always buy good clothes and eat good fare if your means permit; and never keep unruly or quarrelsome men as attendants or messmates. Keep your temper calm though not to the point of suffering abuse or bringing upon yourself the reproach of cowardice. Though necessity may force you into strife, be not in a hurry to take revenge; first make sure that your effort will succeed and strike where it ought. Never display a heated temper when you see that you are likely to fail, but be sure to maintain your honor at some later time, unless your opponent should offer a satisfactory atonement.

If your wealth takes on rapid growth, divide it and invest it in a partnership trade in fields where you do not yourself travel; but be cautious in selecting partners. Always let Almighty God, the holy Virgin Mary, and the saint whom you have most frequently called upon to intercede for you be counted among your partners. Watch with care over the property which the saints are to share with you and always bring it faithfully to the place to which it was originally promised.

ORDINANCES OF THE GUILD MERCHANTS OF SOUTHAMPTON

Along with revived trade and burgeoning towns in the High Middle Ages came the formation of businessmen's associations, called guilds. Merchant guilds encompassed all townspeople engaged in commerce. Carpenters, bakers, shoemakers, and other skilled craftsmen formed guilds that specialized in each occupation. Though women were employed in many trades, working under male guild masters, they were rarely admitted to full membership. Guilds composed exclusively of women existed in only a few places like Paris and Cologne. Guilds tried to eliminate competition by barring outsiders from doing business in the town, by limiting membership, by fixing the price of their goods, and by setting quality standards. Guilds provided for the social needs of their members, too, as the following selection of guild regulations for the seaport of Southampton, England, show. The document itself belongs to the fourteenth century, but several of the regulations had been framed earlier.

6. . . . And if a guildsman be ill and in town, one shall send to him two loaves and a gallon of wine, and one dish of cooked food; and two of the approved men of the guild shall go to visit him and look to his condition.

7. And when a guildsman dies, all those who are of the guild and in the town shall be at the service of the dead, and guildsmen shall carry the body, and bring it to the place of sepulture [burial]. And he who will not do this shall pay, on his oath, twopence to be given to the poor. And those of the ward where the dead man shall be, shall find a man to watch with the body the night that the dead person shall lie in his house. . . .

9. And when a guildsman dies, his eldest-born son or his next heir shall have the seat of his father, or of his uncle, if his father was not a guildsman, but of no one else. Nor can any husband, by reason of his wife, either have a seat in the guild or demand it by any right of his wife's ancestors. . . .

10. And no one ought nor can lawfully sell or give his seat in the guild to any man. And the son of a guildsman, other than his eldest, shall be admitted to the guild on payment of ten shillings [120 pence], and shall take the oath.

11. And if any guildsman be imprisoned in England in time of peace, the alderman, with the seneschal[1] . . . shall go at the cost of the

---

[1]An alderman was the chief of the guild, and a seneschal acted as its treasurer and vice-president.

guild to procure the release of him that is in prison.

12. And if any guildsman strike another with his fist, and be thereof attainted [found guilty], he shall lose his guildship until he has purchased it again for ten shillings, and shall take the oath like a new member. And if a guildsman strike another with a stick or a knife, or any other weapon, whatever it may be, he shall lose his guildship and his franchise,[2] and shall be held a stranger, until he be reconciled to good people of the guild, and have made satisfaction to the person whom he has injured, and be fined to the guild twenty shillings, which shall not be [forgiven or refunded]. . . .

19. And no one shall buy anything in the town of Southampton to sell it again in the same town, unless he be of the guild merchant or of the franchise. And if any one do so and be attainted (thereof), all that he has so bought shall be forfeited to the king. And no one shall be quit of custom unless he has done so as to be of the guild or of the franchise, and this from year to year.

20. And no one shall buy honey, seim [lard], salt herring, or any kind of oil, or millstones, or fresh hides, or any kind of fresh skins, except a guildsman; nor keep a tavern for wine, or sell cloth by retail, except on a market day or fair day; nor keep above five quarters of corn in his granary to sell by retail, if he is not a guildsman; and whoever shall do this, and be attainted (thereof), shall forfeit all to the king.

21. No one of the guild shall be partner or joint dealer in any of the foresaid merchandises with any person who is (not?) of the guild, by any manner of coverture [concealment], art, contrivance, collusion, or any other manner. And whosoever shall do this, and be attainted (thereof), the goods so bought shall be forefeited to the king, and the guildsman shall lose his guildship.

22. And if any guildsman fall into poverty and have not wherewith to live, and cannot work, he shall be provided for: when the guild shall be held he shall have one mark from the guild to relieve his condition. No one of the guild or franchise shall avow another's goods for his own, by which the custom of the town may be defrauded. And if any one so do, and be attainted (thereof), he shall lose the guildship and the franchise, and the merchandise so avowed shall be forfeited to the king. . . .

41. No butcher or cook shall sell to any man other than wholesome and clean provisions, and well cooked; and if any do, and he be thereof attainted, he shall be put in the pillory an hour of the day, or give two shillings to the town for the offence.

42. And that no butcher or cook throw into the street any filth or other matter whereby the town or the street become more dirty, filthy, or corrupt; and if any one do this, and be attainted, he shall pay a fine of twelve pence, as often as he shall offend in the manner aforesaid.

43. No man shall have any pigs going about in the street, or have before his door, or in the street, muck or dung beyond two nights; and if any one has, let whoever will take it away; and he who shall have acted contrary to this statute shall be grievously fined.

---

[2]A person's franchise was the privilege of citizenship in the town.

ALLIANCE OF GERMAN TOWNS TO PROTECT MERCHANTS, 1253

The following document relates how several German cities entered into an alliance to protect merchants who were exposed to frequent dangers to life and property. Federations like the one described below grew into the famed Hanseatic League, which in the fourteenth century had a membership of about one hundred towns, mainly German. The league actively combated pirates and brigands and built lighthouses to promote safe navigation.

In the name of the holy and indivisible Trinity, Amen. The magistrates, consuls, and the whole community of burghers and citizens in Münster, Dortmund, Soest, and Lippstadt, to all who may read this document, greeting:

We hereby make known to all men, now and in the future, that because of the manifold dangers to which we are constantly exposed, of capture, robbery, and many other injuries, we have, by common counsel and consent, decided to unite in a perpetual confederation under the following terms, and we have mutually given and received word and oath:

First, that if any man shall take captive one of our citizens or seize his goods without just cause, we will altogether deny to him opportunity to trade in all our cities aforesaid. And if the castellan of any lord shall be the author of an injury that has been done, the afore-mentioned privileges shall be altogether withheld from the lord of that castellan, and from all his soldiers and servants, and all others dwelling with him in his castle. . . .

If any robber has taken goods from one of our citizens . . . and the injured man shall go to any one of our [federated] cities seeking counsel and aid, in order that justice may be done upon the malefactor, the citizens of that city shall act as they would be obliged to act if executing justice for a similar crime committed against one of their own fellow-citizens.

And if any of our burgesses shall chance to go to any of our cities and fear to go forth because of peril to life and property, the burgesses of that city shall conduct him to a place whence his fellow-citizens can receive him in safety.

If a knight shall be denounced to us on reasonable grounds as a violator of faith and honor, we will denounce him in all our cities, and will by mutual consent withhold from him all privileges in our cities until he shall pay the whole debt for which he broke his word.

If any one of us shall buy goods taken from any of our confederates by theft or robbery, . . . he shall not offer the goods at retail anywhere and shall be held guilty with the thief and robber.

REVIEW QUESTIONS

1. What attitudes were merchants encouraged to cultivate when dealing with customers and fellow merchants? How did their outlook differ from that of medieval clergy and nobility?
2. What business practices were recommended to merchants?
3. What was a guild and how did it benefit its members?
4. What method does the document presenting the rules for the Hanseatic League employ for subduing pirates, brigands, kidnappers, and dishonored knights?

2 Papal Supremacy

As the sole interpreters of God's revelation and the sole ministers of his sacraments, the clergy imposed and supervised the moral standards of Christendom. Papal theory maintained that human society was part of a divinely ordered universe, governed by God's universal law, and as the supreme spiritual leader of Christendom, the pope was charged with the mission of establishing a Christian society on earth. Popes maintained that all kings came under their power. Disobeying the pope, God's viceroy on earth, constituted disobedience to God himself. Responsible for implementing God's law, the pope could never take a subordinate position to kings, an attitude that led to a conflict between church and state in the High and Late Middle Ages as the power of monarchs grew.

Pope Gregory VII
THE *DICTATUS PAPAE*

Like no other pope before him, Gregory VII (1073–1085) asserted the preeminence of the papacy over secular rulers. He declared that princes should "not seek to subdue or subject holy Church to themselves as a handmaiden; but indeed let them fittingly strive to honor her eyes, namely the priests of the Lord, by acknowledging them as masters and fathers." His exaltation of the spiritual authority of the church encouraged future popes to challenge the state whenever it threatened the supremacy of Christian moral teachings or the church's freedom to carry out its mission. The exalted conception of the papacy as the central authority in the Christian church was expressed in its most extreme and detailed form in a series of propositions called the *Dictatus papae* (Rules of the Pope), which appear as numbered paragraphs in the excerpt below. Drawn up by the papal government during the pontificate of Gregory VII, the *Dictatus papae* represents claims and ambitions that would inspire many popes and theologians throughout the Middle Ages.

1. That the Roman church was established by God alone.
2. That the Roman pontiff [bishop] alone is rightly called universal.
3. That he alone has the power to depose and reinstate bishops.
4. That his legate [emissary], even if he be of lower ecclesiastical rank, presides over bishops in council, and has the power to give sentence of deposition against them.
5. That the pope has the power to depose those who are absent (*i.e.*, without giving them a hearing).
6. That, among other things, we ought not to remain in the same house with those whom he has excommunicated.
7. That he alone has the right, according to the necessity of the occasion, to make new laws, to create new bishoprics, to make a monastery of a chapter of canons,[1] and *vice versa*, and either to divide a rich bishopric or to unite several poor ones.

---

[1] A chapter of canons is a corporate ecclesiastical body composed of priests who administer cathedrals or monastic communities.

8. That he alone may use the imperial insignia.

9. That all princes shall kiss the foot of the pope alone.

10. That his name alone is to be recited in the churches.

11. That the name applied to him belongs to him alone.

12. That he has the power to depose emperors.

13. That he has the right to transfer bishops from one see to another when it becomes necessary.

14. That he has the right to ordain as a cleric anyone from any part of the church whatsoever.

15. That anyone ordained by him may rule (as bishop) over another church, but cannot serve (as priest) in it, and that such a cleric may not receive a higher rank from any other bishop.

16. That no general synod may be called without his order.

17. That no action of a synod and no book shall be regarded as canonical [official] without his authority.

18. That his decree can be annulled by no one, and that he can annul the decrees of anyone.

19. That he can be judged by no one.

20. That no one shall dare to condemn a person who has appealed to the apostolic seat.

21. That the important cases of any church whatsoever shall be referred to the Roman church (that is, to the pope).

22. That the Roman church has never erred and will never err to all eternity, according to the testimony of the holy scriptures.

23. That the Roman pontiff who has been canonically ordained is made holy by the merits of St. Peter, according to the testimony of St. Ennodius, bishop of Pavia, which is confirmed by many of the holy fathers, as is shown by the decrees of the blessed pope Symmachus.

24. That by his command or permission subjects may accuse their rulers.

25. That he can depose and reinstate bishops without the calling of a synod.

26. That no one can be regarded as catholic who does not agree with the Roman church.

27. That he has the power to absolve subjects from their oath of fidelity to wicked rulers.

Pope Innocent III
"ROYAL POWER DERIVES ITS DIGNITY FROM THE PONTIFICAL AUTHORITY"

In the tradition of Gregory VII, Innocent III (1198–1216), the most powerful of medieval popes, asserts the claim for papal supremacy.

The Creator of the universe set up two great luminaries in the firmament of heaven; the greater light to rule the day, the lesser light to rule the night. In the same way for the firmament of the universal Church, which is spoken of as heaven, he appointed two great dignities; the greater to bear rule over souls (these being, as it were, days), the lesser to bear rule over bodies (those being, as it were nights). These dignities are the pontifical authority and the royal power. Furthermore, the moon derives her light from the sun, and is in truth inferior to the sun in both size and quality, in position as well as effect. In the same way the royal power derives its dignity from the pontifical authority: and the more closely it cleaves to the sphere of that authority the less is the light with which it is adorned; the further it is removed, the more it increases in splendour.

REVIEW QUESTION

1. Why were papal claims likely to stir a conflict with secular rulers?

3   The Crusades

In the eleventh century the Seljuk Turks, recent converts to Islam, conquered vast regions of the Near East including most of Asia Minor, the heartland of the Byzantine Empire. When the Seljuk empire crumbled, Byzantine emperor Alexius I Comnenus (1081–1118), seeing an opportunity to regain lost lands, appealed to Latin princes and the pope for assistance, an appeal answered by Urban II (1088–1099).

In 1095 at the Council of Clermont, Pope Urban II in a dramatic speech urged Frankish lords to take up the sword against the Muslims, an event that marked the beginning of the Crusades—the struggle to regain the Holy Land from Islam. A Christian army mobilized by the papacy to defend the Christian faith accorded with the papal concept of a just war. Moreover, Urban hoped that such a venture might bring the Byzantine church under papal authority. Nobles viewed Urban's appeal as a great adventure that held the promise of glory, wealth, and new lands; they were also motivated by religious reasons: recovery of Christian holy places and a church-approved way of doing penance for their sins.

The Crusades demonstrated the growing strength and confidence of Latin Christendom, which previously had been on the defensive against Islam; it was also part of a wider movement of expansion on the part of Latin Christians. In the eleventh century, Italians had already driven the Muslims from Sardinia; Normans had taken Sicily from the Muslims and southern Italy from Byzantium; and Christian knights, supported by the papacy, were engaged in a long struggle to expel the Muslim Moors from Spain.

The First Crusade demonstrated Christian fanaticism as well as idealism and growing power, as contingents of crusaders robbed and massacred thousands of Jews in the Rhineland. The First Crusade was climaxed by the storming of Jerusalem in June 1099 and the slaughter of the city's inhabitants.

Robert the Monk
APPEAL OF URBAN II TO THE FRANKS

Pope Urban's speech, as reported by Robert the Monk, shows how skillfully the pope appealed to the Frankish lords.

"O race of the Franks, O people who live beyond the mountains, O people loved and chosen of God, as is clear from your many deeds, distinguished over all other nations by the situation of your land, your catholic faith, and your regard for the holy church, we have a special message and exhortation for you. For we wish you to know what a grave matter has brought us to your country. The sad news has come from Jerusalem and Constantinople that the people of Persia, an accursed and foreign race [the Turks], enemies of God, 'a generation that set not their heart aright, and whose spirit was not steadfast with God' (Ps. 78:8), have invaded the lands of those Christians and devastated them with the sword, rapine, and fire. Some of the Christians they have carried away as slaves, others they have put to death. The churches they have either destroyed or turned into mosques. They desecrate and overthrow the altars. . . . They have taken from the Greek empire a tract of land so large that it takes more than two months to walk through it. Whose duty is it to avenge this and recover that land, if not yours? For to you more than to other nations the Lord has given the military spirit, courage, agile bodies, and the bravery to strike down those who resist you. Let your minds be stirred to bravery by the deeds of your forefathers, and by the efficiency and greatness of . . . [Charlemagne], and of . . . his son [Louis the Pious], and of the other kings who have destroyed [Muslim] kingdoms, and established Christianity in their lands. You should be moved especially by the holy grave of our Lord and Saviour which is now held by unclean peoples, and by the holy places which are treated with dishonor and irreverently befouled with their uncleanness.

"O bravest of knights, descendants of unconquered ancestors, do not be weaker than they, but remember their courage. . . . Let no possessions keep you back, no solicitude for your property. Your land [France] is shut in on all sides by the sea and mountains, and is too thickly populated. There is not much wealth here, and the soil scarcely yields enough to support you. On this account you kill and devour each other, and carry on war and mutually destroy each other. Let your hatred and quarrels cease, your civil wars come to an end,

and all your dissensions stop. Set out on the road to the holy sepulchre [site of Jesus' burial], take the land from that wicked people, and make it your own. That land which, as the Scripture says, is flowing with milk and honey, God gave to the children of Israel. Jerusalem is the best of all lands, more fruitful than all others, as it were a second Paradise of delights. This land our Saviour [Jesus] made illustrious by his birth, beautiful with his life, and sacred with his suffering; he redeemed it with his death and glorified it with his tomb. This royal city is now held captive by her enemies, and made pagan by those who know not God. She asks and longs to be liberated and does not cease to beg you to come to her aid. She asks aid especially from you because, as I have said, God has given more of the military spirit to you than to other nations. Set out on this journey and you will obtain the remission of your sins and be sure of the incorruptible glory of the kingdom of heaven."

When Pope Urban had said this and much more of the same sort, all who were present were moved to cry out with one accord, "It is the will of God, it is the will of God." When the pope heard this he raised his eyes to heaven and gave thanks to God, and, commanding silence with a gesture of his hand, he said: "My dear brethren. . . . [L]et these words be your battle cry, because God caused you to speak them. Whenever you meet the enemy in battle, you shall all cry out, 'It is the will of God, it is the will of God.' . . . Whoever therefore shall determine to make this journey and shall make a vow to God and shall offer himself as a living sacrifice, holy, acceptable to God (Rom. 12:1), shall wear a cross on his brow or on his breast. And when he returns after having fulfilled his vow he shall wear the cross on his back. In this way he will obey the command of the Lord, 'Whosoever doth not bear his cross and come after me is not worthy of me'" (Luke 14:27).

William of Tyre
THE CAPTURE OF JERUSALEM

Over the centuries, some have praised the Crusades for inspiring idealism and heroism. Others, however, have castigated the movement for corrupting the Christian spirit and unleashing intolerance and fanaticism, which resulted in the slaughter of Jews in the Rhineland and of Muslims and Jews in Jerusalem—all in the name of Christ.

The Crusaders captured Jerusalem in 1099 after a difficult siege, overcoming its defenses and breaking into the city. The following account of the massacre in the Holy City was written by William of Tyre (c. 1130–c. 1184), archbishop of the Crusader kingdom established in Tyre.

It was a Friday at the ninth hour. Verily, it seemed divinely ordained that the faithful who were fighting for the glory of the Saviour should have obtained the consummation of their desires at the same hour and on the very day on which the Lord had suffered in that city for the salvation of the world. It was on that day, as we read, that the first man was created and the second was delivered over to death for the salvation of the first. It was fitting, therefore, that, at that very hour, those who were members of His body and imitators of Him should triumph in His name over His enemies. . . .

. . . Regardless of age and condition, they laid low, without distinction, every enemy encountered. Everywhere was frightful carnage, everywhere lay heaps of severed heads, so that soon it was impossible to pass or to go from one place to another except over the bodies of the slain. Already the leaders had forced their way by various routes almost to the center of the city and wrought unspeakable slaughter as they advanced. A host of people followed in their train, athirst for the blood of the enemy and wholly intent upon destruction. . . . So frightful was the massacre throughout the city, so terrible the shedding of blood, that even the victors experienced sensations of horror and loathing. . . .

. . . A crowd of knights and foot soldiers . . . massacred all those who had taken refuge [in the court of the Temple]. No mercy was shown to anyone, and the whole place was flooded with the blood of the victims.

It was indeed the righteous judgment of God which ordained that those who had profaned the sanctuary of the Lord by their superstitious rites and had caused it to be an alien place to His faithful people should expiate their sin by death and, by pouring out their own blood, purify the sacred precincts.

It was impossible to look upon the vast numbers of the slain without horror; everywhere lay fragments of human bodies, and the very ground was covered with the blood of the slain. It was not alone the spectacle of headless bodies and mutilated limbs strewn in all directions that roused horror in all who looked upon them. Still more dreadful was it to gaze upon the victors themselves, dripping with blood from head to foot, an ominous sight which brought terror to all who met them. It is reported that within the Temple enclosure alone about ten thousand infidels perished, in addition to those who lay slain everywhere throughout the city in the streets and squares, the number of whom was estimated as no less.

The rest of the soldiers roved through the city in search of wretched survivors who might be hiding in the narrow portals and byways to escape death. These were dragged out into public view and slain like sheep. Some formed into bands and broke into houses where they laid violent hands on heads of families, on their wives, children, and their entire households. These victims were either put to the sword or dashed headlong to the ground from some elevated place so that they perished miserably. Each marauder claimed as his own in perpetuity the particular house which he had entered, together with all it contained. For before the capture of the city the pilgrims had agreed that, after it had been taken by force, whatever each man might win for himself should be his forever by right of possession, without molestation. Consequently the pilgrims searched the city most carefully and boldly killed the citizens. They penetrated into the most retired and out-of-the-way places and broke open the most private apartments of the foe. At the entrance of each house, as it was taken, the victor hung up his shield and his arms, as a sign to all who approached not to pause there but to pass by that place as already in possession of another. . . .

When at last the city had been set in order in this way, arms were laid aside. Then, clad in fresh garments, with clean hands and bare feet, in humility and contrition, they began to make the rounds of the venerable places which the Saviour had deigned to sanctify and make glorious with His bodily presence. With tearful sighs and heartfelt emotion they pressed kisses upon these revered spots. With especial veneration they approached the church of the Passion and Resurrection of the Lord. Here the leaders were met by the clergy and the faithful citizens of Jerusalem. These Christians who for so many years had borne the heavy yoke of undeserved bondage were eager to show their gratitude to the Redeemer for their restoration to liberty. Bearing in their hands crosses and relics of the saints, they led the way into the church to the accompaniment of hymns and sacred songs.

It was a pleasant sight and a source of spiritual joy to witness the pious devotion and deep fervor with which the pilgrims drew near to the holy places, the exultation of heart and happiness of spirit with which they kissed the memorials of the Lord's sojourn upon earth. On all sides were tears, everywhere sighs, not such as grief and anxiety are wont to cause, but such as fervent devotion and the satisfaction of spiritual joy produce as an offering to the Lord. Not alone in the church but throughout all Jerusalem arose the voice of a people giving thanks unto the Lord until it seemed as if the sound must be borne to the very heavens. Verily, of them might it well be said, "The voice of rejoicing and salvation is in the tabernacles of the righteous [Ps. 118:15]."

James of Vitry
"THE REMISSION OF SINS AND THE REWARD OF ETERNAL LIFE"

Many nobles set off for the Holy Land seeking adventure and economic gain. But it is likely that a religious impulse was the principal motive for joining a crusader army. The following sermon by James of Vitry (1160/1170–1240), a French bishop who was a propagandist for the Fifth Crusade and accompanied the crusading army, appeals to the nobles' hope for remission of sins and entrance into heaven.

[T]hose crusaders who prepare themselves for the service of God, truly confessed and contrite, are considered true martyrs while they are in the service of Christ, freed from venial and also mortal sins,[1] from all the penitence enjoined upon them, absolved from the punishment for their sins in this world and the punishment of purgatory[2] in the next, safe from the tortures of hell, in the glory and honour of being crowned in eternal beatitude.

The spouses and children are included in these benefits in as much as they contribute to expenses. But [crusaders] can also greatly help their deceased parents who have left their goods to them, if [the crusaders] take the cross with the intention of helping [their parents]. If it is possible to come to the aid of the dead by giving alms and doing other good works, what greater alms are there but to offer oneself and one's belongings to God and pledge one's soul to Christ, to leave behind one's spouse, children, relatives and birthplace for the service of Christ alone, to expose oneself to dangers on land, dangers on sea, the dangers of thieves, the dangers of predators, the dangers of battles for the love of the Crucified? Therefore, have no doubt at all that this pilgrimage affords not only you the remission of sins and the reward of eternal life, but that whatever good you do on this journey on behalf of your spouses, children and parents, whether living or dead, will profit them greatly.

This is the full and plenary indulgence[3] that the pope concedes to you according to the keys that were given to him by God. This is like *the fountain open to the house of David for washing away* all sins and acquiring heavenly rewards.

---

[1]Venial sin: a minor transgression against God's laws that does not deprive the soul of divine grace or salvation; mortal sin: a deliberate and serious transgression of God's laws, such as murder, that deprives the soul of salvation and leads to eternal damnation.
[2]Purgatory: a place where the soul spends time paying for the person's sins before it can be admitted into heaven.

[3]Plenary indulgence: the complete remission of venial sins incurred by the sinner; the remission of mortal sins is dependent further on God's grace.

REVIEW QUESTIONS

1. Modern political propaganda frequently uses popular fears, prejudices, moral idealism, and patriotic fervor to shape public opinion. Discuss the techniques used by Pope Urban II to create public support for the Crusade.
2. What types of people did Pope Urban II address and what were his motives?
3. Why did William of Tyre believe that the massacre in Jerusalem was an act of religious purification?
4. Why do you think James of Vitry's sermon appealed to his listeners?

---

4 Religious Dissent
—⁂—

Like many groups held together by common ideology, the medieval church wanted to protect its doctrines from novel, dissident, or erroneous interpretations. To ensure orthodoxy and competency, therefore, all preachers were licensed by the bishop; unlicensed preaching, especially by unschooled laymen, was forbidden. In the western church, heresy had not been a serious problem in the post-Roman period. But in the twelfth century, heretical movements attracted significant numbers of supporters among both the clergy and laity and cut across frontiers and social classes.

Thomas Aquinas
DEATH FOR UNREPENTANT HERETICS

In the first selection, Thomas Aquinas (see page 251), the leading theologian of the Middle Ages, argues that unrepentant heretics should be executed.

With regard to heretics two points must be observed: one, on their own side, the other, on the side of the Church. On their own side there is the sin, whereby they deserve not only to be separated from the Church by excommunication, but also to be severed from the world by death. For it is a much graver matter to corrupt the faith which quickens the soul, than to forge money, which supports temporal life. Wherefore if forgers of money and other evildoers are forthwith condemned to death by the secular authority, much more reason is there for heretics, as soon as they are convicted of heresy, to be not only excommunicated but even put to death.

On the part of the Church, however, there is mercy which looks to the conversion of the wanderer, wherefore she condemns not at once, but *after the first and second admonition,* as the Apostle directs: after that, if he is yet stubborn, the Church no longer hoping for his conversion, looks to the salvation of others, by excommunicating him and separating him from the Church, and furthermore delivers him to the secular tribunal to be exterminated thereby from the world by death.

Bernard Gui
THE WALDENSIAN HERESY

One major heretical movement was that of the Waldensians, or Poor Men of Lyons, founded about 1173 by Peter Waldo (d. 1217), a rich merchant of Lyons, France, who gave away his wealth to the poor and began to preach in villages in southeastern France. Neither a priest nor a theologian, Waldo had the Bible translated from Latin into the common language of the people and preached the gospel message without the consent of church authorities. Small groups of Waldo's converts soon were found in towns and villages throughout southeastern France, northern Italy, and Switzerland. Within less than a decade, the Waldensians had aroused the clergy's hostility and were condemned as heretics by Pope Lucius III at a council in Verona in 1184. Gradually, influenced by other heretical groups, the Waldensians adopted a more radical stance toward the medieval church. In the following reading from *Manual of an Inquisitor*, a fourteenth-century Dominican friar, Bernard Gui, describes the origin and the teachings of the Waldensians. The Waldensian criticisms of the church would be echoed in the writings of the leading Protestant reformers of the sixteenth century.

The sect and heresy of the Waldenses or Poor of Lyons began about the year of our Lord 1170. Its moving spirit and founder was a certain citizen of Lyons named Waldes, or Waldens, from whom his followers received their name. He was a rich man who, having given up all his property, resolved to devote himself to poverty and to evangelical perfection, just as the apostles had done. He had procured for himself translations of the Gospels and some other books of the Bible in vernacular French, also some texts from St. Augustine, St. Jerome, St. Ambrose, and St. Gregory, arranged topically, which he and his adherents called "sentences." On frequently reading these over among themselves, although very seldom understanding them aright, they were carried away by their emotions and, although they had but little learning, they usurped the function of the apostles by daring to preach "in the streets and the broad ways."

This man Waldes, or Waldens, won over to a like presumption many people of both sexes, made men and women his accomplices, and sent them out to preach as his disciples. They, men and women alike, although they were stupid and uneducated, wandered through villages, entered homes, preached in the squares and even in churches, the men especially, and spread many errors everywhere. Moreover, when they were summoned by the archbishop of Lyons, John of the Fair Hands, and by him forbidden such audacity, they were not at all willing to obey, alleging as excuse for their madness that "we ought to obey God rather than men," Who had commanded His apostles to "preach the gospel to every creature." By virtue of a false profession of poverty and a feigned appearance of sanctity, they arrogated to themselves what had been said to the apostles. Boldly declaring that they were imitators and successors of these apostles, they cast aspersions upon prelates and clergy for abundant wealth and lives of luxury.

Thus, through presumptuously usurping the office of preaching, they became teachers of error. After they had been warned to desist, they rendered themselves disobedient and contumacious, for which they were excommunicated and driven from that city and their native land. Finally, indeed, because they remained obdurate, they were pronounced schismatics [rebels] at a certain council which was held at Rome . . . and were then condemned as heretics. And so, as they had grown in number on the earth, they scattered throughout that province and neighboring areas and into the region of Lombardy [northern Italy]. Separated and cut off from the Church, when they mingled with other heretics and imbibed their errors, they combined with their own fantasies the errors and heresies of heretics of earlier days. . . .

. . . Now, the principal heresy of the aforesaid Waldenses was and still continues to be contempt of ecclesiastical authority. Then, having been excommunicated for this and given over to Satan, they were plunged by him into countless errors, and they combined with their own fantasies the errors of heretics of an earlier day.

The foolish followers and impious teachers of this sect hold and teach that they are not subject to our lord pope, the Roman pontiff, or to other prelates of the Roman Church, for they declare that the Roman Church persecutes and censures them unjustly and unduly. Also, they declare positively that they cannot be excommunicated by the said Roman pontiff and prelates, to none of whom ought obedience be given should he enjoin or command the members and teachers of this sect to desert and abjure it—this despite the fact that it has been condemned as heretical by the Roman Church.

Also, they hold and teach that every oath, in or out of court, without exception or qualification, has been forbidden by God as unlawful and sinful. . . .

Also, out of the same font of error, the aforesaid sect and heresy declares that any judicial process is forbidden by God and is, consequently, a sin and that it is contrary to God's command for any judge, in any case or for any reason, to sentence a man to corporal punishment involving bloodshed, or to death. They seize on the words of the Holy Gospels—"Judge not that ye be not judged"; "Thou shalt not kill"; and other similar passages—without the proper explanation essential to their interpretation. This they do without understanding the sense or accepting the signification or explanation which the Holy Roman Church wisely perceives and transmits to the faithful in accordance with the teaching of the Fathers [early Christian theologians], the doctors, and the canonical decrees.

Also, as it strays from the way and the right path, this sect does not accept or consider valid, but despises, rejects, and damns the canonical decrees, the decretals [judgments] of the supreme pontiffs, the rules concerning observance of fasts and holy days, and the precepts of the Fathers.

Also, in a more pernicious error in respect of the sacrament of penance and the keys [papal powers to legislate] of the Church, these [Waldensians] hold, and teach that, just as the apostles had it from Christ, they have from God alone and from no other the power to hear confessions from men and women who wish to confess to them, to give absolution, and to impose penance. And they do hear the confessions of such persons, they do give absolution [forgiveness] and impose penance, although they are not priests or clerics ordained by any bishop of the Roman Church but are laymen and nothing more. They do not claim to have any such power from the Roman Church, but rather disclaim it. . . .

Also, this sect and heresy ridicules the indulgences [remissions of punishments due to sin] which are published and granted by prelates of the Church, asserting that they are of no value whatever.

In regard to the sacrament of the Eucharist [communion, celebration of the Last Supper] they err, saying, not publicly but in private among themselves, that if the priest who celebrates or consecrates the Mass is a sinner, the bread and wine do not change into the body and blood of Christ in the sacrament of the altar; and in their view anyone is a sinner who is not a member of their sect. Also, they say that any righteous person, even though he be a layman and not a cleric ordained by a Catholic bishop, can perform the consecration of the body and blood of Christ, provided only that he be a member of their sect. This they apply even to women, with the same proviso that they belong to their sect. Thus they teach that every holy person is a priest.

REVIEW QUESTIONS

1. On what grounds does Aquinas argue that the crime of the heretic deserves excommunication and death? What kind of leniency could the heretic expect from the Church?
2. What was the Waldensian attitude toward the wealth and the temporal powers exercised by the medieval church?
3. How did the Waldensians differ from the orthodox church on the role of the clergy and the administration of the sacraments?

---

5 Medieval Learning: Synthesis of Reason and Christian Faith

The twelfth century witnessed a revived interest in classical learning and the founding of universities. Traditional theology was broadened by the application of a new system of critical analysis, called scholasticism. Scholastic thinkers assumed that some teachings of Christianity, which they accepted as true by faith, could also be demonstrated to be true by reason. They sought to explain and clarify theological doctrines by subjecting them to logical analysis.

Adelard of Bath
A QUESTIONING SPIRIT

In the High and Late Middle Ages, ancient scientific texts, particularly the works of Aristotle, were translated from Greek and Arabic into Latin. Influenced by Aristotle's naturalistic and empirical approach, several medieval scholars devoted greater attention to investigating the natural world. An early exponent of this emerging scientific outlook was Adelard of Bath (c. 1080–c. 1145). Born in England, Adelard studied in France and traveled in Muslim lands, becoming an advocate of Arabic science.

Adelard's *Natural Questions* was written before the major Greek works were translated into Latin and made available to Western European scholars. But it does show a growing curiosity and a questioning spirit, attitudes that are crucial to scientific thinking. *Natural Questions* is a dialogue between Adelard and his nephew; reproduced below are some of Adelard's responses to his nephew's queries.

ADELARD I take nothing away from God, for whatever exists is from Him and because of Him. But the natural order does not exist confusedly and without rational arrangement, and human reason should be listened to concerning those things it treats of. But when it completely fails, then the matter should be referred to God. Therefore, since we have not yet completely lost the use of our minds, let us return to reason. . . .

. . . It is difficult for me to talk with you about animals, for I have learned one thing, under the guidance of reason, from Arabic teachers; but you, captivated by a show of authority, are led around by a halter. For what should we call authority but a halter? Indeed, just as brute animals are led about by a halter wherever you please, and are not told where or why, but see the rope by which they are held and follow it alone, thus the authority of writers leads many of you, caught and bound by animal-like credulity, into danger. Whence some men, usurping the name of authority for themselves, have employed great license in writing, to such an extent that they do not hesitate to present the false as true to such animal-like men. For why not fill up sheets of paper, and why not write on the back too, when you usually have such readers today who require no rational explanation and put their trust only in the ancient name of a title? For they do not understand that reason has been given to each person so that he might discern the true from the false, using reason as the chief judge. For if reason were not the universal judge, it would have been given to each of us in vain. It would be sufficient that it were given to one (or a few at most), and the rest would be content with their authority and decisions. Further, those very people who are called authorities only secured the trust of their successors because they followed reason; and whoever is ignorant of reason or ignores it is deservedly considered to be blind. I will cut short this discussion of the fact that in my judgment authority should be avoided. But I do assert this, that first we ought to seek the reason for anything, and then if we find an authority it may be added. Authority alone cannot make a philosopher believe anything, nor should it be adduced for this purpose. . . .

NEPHEW One should listen to what you say but not believe it. But I shall gird myself for higher things, so that, as far as my little knowledge permits, light might come forth from the smoke. For although I am ignorant of the Greeks' boasts, and I have not seen Vulcan's cave (i.e., Mt. Aetna), nevertheless I have learned both to know what is true and to disprove what is false, and I have considerable skill in this. So continue! I want to find out what you think about human nature. For although you may consider what you have already said to be very important, nevertheless, if you do not know yourself, I think that your remarks have little value. For men ought most properly to investigate man. . . .

ADELARD I believe that man is dearer to the Creator than all the other animals. Nevertheless it does not happen that he is born with natural weapons or is suited for swift flight. But he has something which is much better and more worthy, reason I mean, by which he so far excels the brutes that by means of it he can tame them, put bits in their mouths, and train them to perform various tasks. You see, therefore, by how much the gift of reason excels bodily defenses. . . .

NEPHEW Since we have been discussing things having to do with the brain, explain, if you can, how the philosophers determined the physical location of imagination, reason and memory. For both Aristotle in the *physics* (an erroneous reference) and other philosophers in other works, have been able to determine that the operations of imagination are carried on in the front part of the brain, reason in the middle,

and memory in the back, and so they have given these three areas the names imaginative, rational and memorial. But by what skill were they able to determine the site of each operation of the mind and to assign to each small area of the brain its proper function, since these operations cannot be perceived by any sense?

ADELARD To one who does not understand, everything seems impossible: but when things are understood, everything becomes clear. I would guess that whoever first undertook this task learned something about it from sense experience. Probably, someone who had formerly had a very active imagination suffered an injury to the front of his head and afterwards no longer possessed the imaginative faculty, although his reason and memory remained unaffected. And when this happened it was noticed by the philosopher. And similarly injuries to other parts of the head impeded other functions of the mind so that it could be established with certainty which areas of the brain controlled which mental functions, especially since in some men these areas are marked by very fine lines. Therefore, from evidence of this sort, which could be perceived by the senses, an insensible and intellectual operation of the mind has been made clear.

Thomas Aquinas
SUMMA THEOLOGICA

For most of the Middle Ages, religious thought was dominated by the influence of Saint Augustine (d. 430), the greatest of the Latin church fathers. Augustine placed little value on the study of nature; for him, the City of Man (the world) was a sinful place from which people tried to escape in order to enter the City of God (heaven). Regarding God as the source of knowing, he held that reason by itself was an inadequate guide to knowledge: without faith in revealed truth, there could be no understanding. An alternative approach to that of Augustine was provided by Thomas Aquinas (1225–1274), a friar of the Order of Preachers (Dominicans), who taught theology at Paris and later in Italy. Both Augustine and Aquinas believed that God was the source of all truth, that human nature was corrupted by the imprint of the original sin of Adam and Eve, and that God revealed himself through the Bible and in the person of Jesus Christ. But, in contrast to Augustine, Aquinas expressed great confidence in the power of reason and favored applying it to investigate the natural world.

Aquinas held that as both faith and reason came from God, they were not in opposition to each other; properly understood, they supported each other. Because reason was no enemy of faith, it should not be feared. In addition to showing renewed respect for reason, Aquinas—influenced by Aristotelian empiricism (the acquisition of knowledge of nature through experience)—valued knowledge of the natural world. He saw the natural and supernatural worlds not as irreconcilable and hostile to each other, but as a continuous ascending hierarchy of divinely created orders of being moving progressively toward the Supreme Being. In constructing a synthesis of Christianity and Aristotelianism, Aquinas gave renewed importance to the natural world, human reason, and the creative human spirit. Nevertheless, by holding that reason was subordinate to faith, he remained a typically medieval thinker.

In the opening reading from his most ambitious work, the *Summa Theologica* [Highest Theology], Thomas Aquinas asserts that reason by itself is insufficient to lead human beings to salvation.

WHETHER, BESIDES THE PHILOSOPHICAL SCIENCES, ANY FURTHER DOCTRINE IS REQUIRED?

It was necessary for man's salvation that there should be a knowledge revealed by God, besides the philosophical sciences investigated by human reason. First, because man is directed to God as to an end that surpasses the grasp of his reason. . . . But the end must first be known by men who are to direct their thoughts and actions to the end. Hence it was necessary for the salvation of man that certain truths which exceed human reason should be made known to him by divine revelation. Even as regards those truths about God which human reason can investigate, it was necessary that man be taught by a divine revelation. For the truth about God, such as reason can know it, would only be known by a few, and that after a long time, and with the admixture of many errors; whereas man's whole salvation, which is in God, depends upon the knowledge of this truth. Therefore, in order that the salvation of men might be brought about more fitly and more surely, it was necessary that they be taught divine truths

by divine revelation. It was therefore necessary that, besides the philosophical sciences investigated by reason, there should be a sacred science by way of revelation.

In the next selection, Aquinas uses the categories of Aristotelian philosophy to demonstrate through natural reason God's existence.

WHETHER GOD EXISTS?

The existence of God can be proved in five ways.

The first and more manifest way is the argument from motion. It is certain, and evident to our senses, that in the world some things are in motion. Now whatever is moved is moved by another, for nothing can be moved except it is in potentiality to that towards which it is moved; whereas a thing moves inasmuch as it is in act. For motion is nothing else than the reduction of something from potentiality to actuality. But nothing can be reduced from potentiality to actuality, except by something in a state of actuality. Thus that which is actually hot, as fire, makes wood, which is potentially hot, to be actually hot, and thereby moves and changes it. Now it is not possible that the same thing should be at once in actuality and potentiality in the same respect, but only in different respects. For what is actually hot cannot simultaneously be potentially hot; but it is simultaneously potentially cold. It is therefore impossible that in the same respect and in the same way a thing should be both mover and moved, *i.e.,* that it should move itself. Therefore, whatever is moved must be moved by another. If that by which it is moved be itself moved, then this also must needs be moved by another, and that by another again. But this cannot go on to infinity, because then there would be no first mover, and, consequently, no other mover, seeing that subsequent movers move only inasmuch as they are moved by the first mover; as the staff moves only because it is moved by the hand. Therefore it is necessary to arrive at a first mover, moved by no other; and this everyone understands to be God.

The second way is from the nature of efficient cause. In the world of sensible things we find there is an order of efficient causes. There is no case known (neither is it, indeed, possible) in which a thing is found to be the efficient cause of itself; for so it would be prior to itself, which is impossible. Now in efficient causes it is not possible to go on to infinity, because in all efficient causes following in order, the first is the cause of the intermediate cause, and the intermediate is the cause of the ultimate cause, whether the intermediate cause be several, or one only. Now to take away the cause is to take away the effect. Therefore, if there be no first cause among efficient causes, there will be no ultimate, nor any intermediate, cause. But if in efficient causes it is possible to go on to infinity, there will be no first efficient cause, neither will there be an ultimate effect, nor any intermediate efficient causes; all of which is plainly false. Therefore it is necessary to admit a first efficient cause, to which everyone gives the name of God.

The third way is taken from possibility and necessity, and runs thus. We find in nature things that are possible to be and not to be, since they are found to be generated, and to be corrupted, and consequently, it is possible for them to be and not to be. But it is impossible for these always to exist, for that which can not-be at some time is not. Therefore, if everything can not-be, then at one time there was nothing in existence. Now if this were true, even now there would be nothing in existence, because that which does not exist begins to exist only through something already existing. Therefore, if at one time nothing was in existence, it would have been impossible for anything to have begun to exist; and thus even now nothing would be in existence—which is absurd. Therefore, not all beings are merely possible, but there must exist something the existence of which is necessary. But every necessary thing either has its necessity caused by another, or not. Now it is impossible to go on to infinity in necessary things which have their necessity caused by another, as has been already proved in regard to efficient causes. Therefore we cannot but admit the existence of some being having of itself its own necessity, and not receiving it from another, but rather causing in others their necessity. This all men speak of as God.

The fourth way is taken from the graduation to be found in things. Among beings there are some more and some less good, true, noble, and the like. But *more* and *less* are predicated of different things according as they resemble in their different ways something which is the maximum, as a thing is said to be hotter according as it more nearly resembles that which is hottest; so that there is something which is truest, something best, something noblest, and, consequently, something which is most being, for those things that are greatest in truth are greatest in being. . . . Now the maximum in any genus is the cause of all in that genus, as fire, which is the maximum of heat, is the cause of all hot things. . . . Therefore there must also be something which is to all beings the cause of their being, goodness, and every other perfection; and this we call God.

The fifth way is taken from the governance of the world. We see that things which lack knowledge, such as natural bodies, act for an end, and this is evident from their acting always, or nearly always, in the same way, so as to obtain the best result. Hence it is plain that they achieve their end, not fortuitously, but designedly. Now whatever lacks knowledge cannot move towards an end, unless it be directed by some being endowed with knowledge and intelligence; as the arrow is directed by the archer. Therefore some intelligent being exists by whom all natural things are directed to their end; and this being we call God.

REVIEW QUESTIONS

1. What ideas of Adelard of Bath encouraged further scientific study of the natural world in the Middle Ages?
2. According to Thomas Aquinas, when does a person require more than reason to arrive at truth?
3. Show how Aquinas used both logic and an empirical method to prove the existence of God.

6 Medieval Universities

The twelfth century witnessed a revival of classical learning and cultural creativity. Gothic cathedrals, an enduring testament to the creativeness of the religious spirit, were erected throughout Europe. Roman authors were again read and their style imitated. Latin translations of Greek philosophical and scientific texts stimulated scholars; the reintroduction of the study of Roman law began to influence political theory and institutions. These were some of the major changes that would leave a permanent mark on subsequent Western culture.

A significant achievement of this age was the emergence of universities. Arising spontaneously among teachers of the liberal arts and students of the higher studies of law, theology, and medicine, the universities gave more formal and lasting institutional structure to the more advanced levels of schooling. The medieval universities were largely dedicated to educating young men for careers as lawyers, judges, teachers, diplomats, and administrators of both church and state. The educational foundation for such professional careers was the study of grammar, rhetoric, logic, mathematics, and theology.

Geoffrey Chaucer
AN OXFORD CLERIC

In his masterpiece, *The Canterbury Tales*, English poet and diplomat Geoffrey Chaucer (c. 1340–1400) describes a typical student on pilgrimage to the shrine of Saint Thomas à Becket in Canterbury.

An *Oxford Cleric*, still a student though,
One who had taken logic long ago,
Was there; his horse was thinner than a rake,
And he was not too fat, I undertake,
But had a hollow look, a sober stare.
The thread upon his overcoat was bare;
He had found no preferment [employment] in
    the church
And he was too unworldly to make search
For secular employment. By his bed
He preferred having twenty books, in red
And black, of Aristotle's philosophy,
To having fine clothes, fiddle, or psaltery
    [a book of Psalms used for daily prayer].
Though a philosopher, as I have told,

He had not found the stone for making gold.[1]
Whatever money from his friends he took
He spent on learning or another book
And prayed for them most earnestly, returning
Thanks to them thus for paying for his learning.
His only care was study, and indeed
He never spoke a word more than was need,
Formal at that, respectful in the extreme,
Short, to the point, and lofty in this theme.
The thought of moral virtue filled his speech
And he would gladly learn, and gladly teach.

———

[1]The *philosopher's stone* was the name given to the mythical substance, searched for by alchemists, that would turn base metals into gold.

STUDENT LETTERS

The relationship between fathers and their sons enrolled at universities has not changed all that much since the Middle Ages, as the letters that follow demonstrate.

FATHERS TO SONS

I

I have recently discovered that you live dissolutely and slothfully, preferring license to restraint and play to work and strumming a guitar while the others are at their studies, whence it happens that you have read but one volume of law while your more industrious companions have read several. Wherefore I have decided to exhort you herewith to repent utterly of your dissolute and careless ways, that you may no longer be called a waster and your shame may be turned to good repute.

II

I have learned—not from your master, although he ought not to hide such things from me, but from a certain trustworthy source—that you do not study in your room or act in the schools as a good student should, but play and wander about, disobedient to your master and indulging in sport and in certain other dishonorable practices which I do not now care to explain by letter.

SONS TO FATHERS

I

"Well-beloved father, I have not a penny, nor can I get any save through you, for all things at the University are so dear: nor can I study in my Code or my Digest, for they are all tattered. Moreover, I owe ten crowns in dues to the Provost, and can find no man to lend them to me; I send you word of greetings and of money.

The Student hath need of many things if he will profit here; his father and his kin must needs supply him freely, that he be not compelled to pawn his books, but have ready money in his purse, with gowns and furs and decent clothing, or he will be damned for a beggar; wherefore, that men may not take me for a beast, I send you word of greetings and of money.

Wines are dear, and hostels, and other good things; I owe in every street, and am hard bested to free myself from such snares. Dear father, deign to help me! I fear to be excommunicated; already have I been cited, and there is not even a dry bone in my larder. If I find not the money before this feast of Easter, the church door will be shut in my face: wherefore grant my supplication, for I send you word of greetings and of money.

L'ENVOY

Well-beloved father, to ease my debts contracted at the tavern, at the baker's, with the doctor and the bedells [a minor college official], and to pay my subscriptions to the laundress and the barber, I send you word of greetings and of money."

II

Sing unto the Lord a new song, praise him with stringed instruments and organs, rejoice upon the high-sounding cymbals, for your son has held a glorious disputation, which was attended by a great number of teachers and scholars. He answered all questions without a mistake, and no one could get the better of him or prevail against his arguments. Moreover he celebrated a famous banquet, at which both rich and poor were honoured as never before, and he has duly begun to give lectures which are already so popular that others' classrooms are deserted and his own are filled.

A Wandering Scholar
"IN THE TAVERN LET ME DIE"

During the Middle Ages, errant students and idle clerks roamed the highways as free spirits, searching for adventure or at least for diversion. Some had given up their studies for lack of funds; others were restless or unable to secure the position they desired. These vagabonds sometimes amused themselves by composing poetry that ridiculed clerics and sang the praises of wine, gambling, and women. The following poem was written in Latin by a poet known as the "Archpoeta," who lived in the twelfth century.

Down the highway broad I walk,
Like a youth in mind,
Implicate myself in vice,
Virtue stays behind,

Avid for the world's delight
More than for salvation,
Dead in soul, I care but for
Body's exultation.

Prelate, you most circumspect,
Grace I would entreat,
It's a good death that I die,
Such a death is sweet,
O, my heart is wounded sore
When a lass comes near it,
If there's one I cannot touch,
Her I rape in spirit.

It is most difficult indeed
Overcoming Nature,
Keeping pure our mind and thought
Near a girlish creature.
Young like me, one can't observe
Rules that are unfeeling,
Can't ignore such shapes and curves
Tempting and appealing.

Who when into fire is pushed
Is by fire not scorched?
Whoso in Pavia[1] stayed
Has not been debauched,
Where Dame Venus with a sign
Gives young men a shake-up,
Snares them with her luring eyes,
With her tempting makeup?

Secondly I've been accused
That I yield to gambling,
Yet when gambling strips me bare,
Then I can't go rambling,
For outside I quake with cold
While my heart glows white,
In this state far better song,
Finer verse I write.

Thirdly to the tavern I
Must refer in turn,
This I've spurned not in the past
Nor will ever spurn,
Till the holy angels come
With a chant supernal,
Singing masses for the dead—
Requiem eternal.

In the tavern let me die,
That's my resolution,

Bring me wine for lips so dry
At life's dissolution.
Joyfully the angel's choir
Then will sing my glory:
"Sit deus propicius
Huic potatori."*

Through the cup new light bursts up
In my spirit's flare,
Nectar stimulates my heart
Etherward to fare.
Wine that in the tavern flows
Has a richer flavor
Than the watered stuff our lord's
Steward likes to savor.

———

Special gifts on every man
Mother Nature lavished;
I can never write a verse
When by hunger ravished,
If I'm famished, one small boy
Bests me in a trice,
Thirst and hunger I detest
Like my own demise.

Special gifts for every man
Nature will produce,
I, when I compose my verse,
Vintage wine must use,
All the best the cellar's casks
Hold of these libations.
Such a wine calls forth from me
Copious conversations.

My verse has the quality
Of the wine I sip,
I can not do much until
Food has passed my lip,
What I write when starved and parched
Is of lowest class,
When I'm tight, with verse I make
Ovid I surpass.[2]

———

---

[1]Pavia, a city in northern Italy, drew many students in the Middle Ages.

*May God be well-disposed to this toper [drunkard].
[2]Roman poet (43 B.C.–A.D. 17), author of the *Metamorphoses*, who was considered a master of metrical form.

As a poet ne'er can I
Be appreciated
Till my stomach has been well
Filled with food and sated,
When god Bacchus[3] gains my brain's
Lofty citadel,
Phoebus[4] rushes in to voice
Many a miracle.

See, my own depravity
I have now confessed,
Disapproval of my sins
Have my friends expressed.
Not a single one of these
His own sins confesses,
Though he also likes the dice,
Likes the world's excesses.

---

[3]Bacchus is an alternative name for Dionysus, the Greek
god of wine and ecstasy.
[4]Phoebus is another name for the Greek god Apollo, who
represented male beauty and moral excellence.

REVIEW QUESTIONS

1. How do medieval students resemble their modern counterparts? How do they
   differ?
2. What virtues did Archpoeta find in his vices?

---

7 The Jews in the Middle Ages

Toward the end of the eleventh century, small communities of Jews were living in
many of the larger towns of Christian Europe. Most of these Jews were descended
from Jewish inhabitants of the Roman Empire. Under the protection of the Roman
law or of individual Germanic kings, they had managed to survive amid a sometimes hostile Christian population. But religious fanaticism unleashed by the call
for the First Crusade undermined Christian–Jewish relations gravely. Bands of
Crusaders began systematically to attack and massacre the Jewish inhabitants of
Rhineland towns. Thousands were killed—many because they refused to convert
to Christianity—and their houses were looted and burned. Efforts by the bishops
and civil authorities to protect their Jewish subjects were largely ineffective. After
the First Crusade, anti-Semitism became endemic in Latin Christendom.

Albert of Aix-la-Chapelle
MASSACRE OF THE JEWS OF MAINZ

In this reading, Albert, a twelfth-century priest of the city of Aix-la-Chapelle,
describes the massacre of Jews (1096) at the beginning of the First Crusade.

At the beginning of summer in the same year in which Peter [the Hermit] and Gottschalk,[1] after collecting an army, had set out, there assembled in like fashion a large and innumerable host of Christians from diverse kingdoms and lands; namely, from the realms of France, England, Flanders, and Lorraine. . . . I know not whether by a judgment of the Lord, or by some error of mind, they rose in a spirit of cruelty against the Jewish people scattered throughout these cities and slaughtered them without mercy, especially in the Kingdom of Lorraine,[2] asserting it to be the beginning of their expedition and their duty against the enemies of the Christian faith. This slaughter of Jews was done first by citizens of Cologne.[3] These suddenly fell upon a small band of Jews and severely wounded and killed many; they destroyed the houses and synagogues of the Jews and divided among themselves a very large amount of money. When the Jews saw this cruelty, about two hundred in the silence of the night began flight by boat to Neuss. The pilgrims and crusaders discovered them, and after taking away all their possessions, inflicted on them similar slaughter, leaving not even one alive.

Not long after this, they started upon their journey, as they had vowed, and arrived in a great multitude at the city of Mainz. There Count Emico, a nobleman, a very mighty man in this region, was awaiting, with a large band of Teutons [German soldiers], the arrival of the pilgrims who were coming thither from diverse lands by the King's highway.

The Jews of this city, knowing of the slaughter of their brethren, and that they themselves could not escape the hands of so many, fled in hope of safety to Bishop Rothard. They put an infinite treasure in his guard and trust, having much faith in his protection, because he was Bishop of the city. Then that excellent Bishop of the city cautiously set aside the incredible amount of money received from them. He placed the Jews in the very spacious hall of his own house, away from the sight of Count Emico and his followers, that they might remain safe and sound in a very secure and strong place.

But Emico and the rest of his band held a council and, after sunrise, attacked the Jews in the hall with arrows and lances. Breaking the bolts and doors, they killed the Jews, about seven hundred in number, who in vain resisted the force and attack of so many thousands. They killed the women, also, and with their swords pierced tender children of whatever age and sex. The Jews, seeing that their Christian enemies were attacking them and their children, and that they were sparing no age, likewise fell upon one another, brother, children, wives, and sisters, and thus they perished at each other's hands. Horrible to say, mothers cut the throats of nursing children with knives and stabbed others, preferring them to perish thus by their own hands rather than to be killed by the weapons of the uncircumcised.

From this cruel slaughter of the Jews a few escaped; and a few because of fear, rather than because of love of the Christian faith, were baptized. With very great spoils taken from these people, Count Emico, Clarebold, Thomas, and all that intolerable company of men and women then continued on their way to Jerusalem.

---

[1]A brilliant propagandist, Peter the Hermit raised a large army of poor and sparsely armed Frenchmen, who marched to Cologne to begin a Crusade to the Holy Land. Most of them were killed by Turkish forces after crossing into Asia Minor. Gottschalk was a German priest who gathered a band of undisciplined soldiers to join the First Crusade. His forces were killed by Hungarians defending their families and property from these Crusaders.

[2]Lorraine, a duchy in the western part of the Holy Roman Empire, is now part of France.

[3]Cologne (Köln), founded by the Romans in the first century A.D., was the largest city in the Rhine Valley, a center of commerce, industry, and learning. Its politically powerful archbishop was a prince of the Holy Roman Empire.

A DECREE BY POPE INNOCENT III

Regarding the Jews as wicked because they refused to accept Christ, the church wanted them to live in humiliation. However, the church did at times seek to protect them from violence.

The Fourth Lateran Council, which was organized by Innocent III (1198–1216), the most powerful of medieval popes, barred Jews from public office and required them to wear a distinguishing badge on their clothing, a sign of their degradation. Yet Innocent, as the following passage indicates, also cautioned against harming Jews. The passage, however, reveals some of the torments faced by Jews.

. . . We decree that no Christian shall use violence to compel the Jews to accept baptism. But if a Jew, of his own accord, because of a change in his faith, shall have taken refuge with Christians, after his wish has been made known, he may be made a Christian without any opposition. For anyone who has not of his own will sought Christian baptism cannot have the true Christian faith. No Christian shall do the Jews any personal injury, except in executing the judgments of a judge, or deprive them of their possessions, or change the rights and privileges which they have been accustomed to have. During the celebration of their festivals, no one shall disturb them by beating them with clubs or by throwing stones at them. No one shall compel them to render any services except those which they have been accustomed to render. And to prevent the baseness and avarice of wicked men we forbid anyone to deface or damage their cemeteries or to extort money from them by threatening to exhume the bodies of their dead. . . .

THE LIBEL OF RITUAL MURDER

Despite efforts by some popes to protect Jews, outbreaks of violence toward them persisted and bizarre myths about them emerged, often fomented by the clergy. Jews were seen as agents of Satan conspiring to destroy Christendom and as sorcerers employing black magic against Christians. Perhaps the most absurd (and dangerous) charge against the Jewish people was the accusation of ritual murder—that the Jews, requiring Christian blood for the Passover service, sacrificed a Christian child. Despite the vehement denials of Jews and the protests of some enlightened Christian leaders, hundreds of such libelous accusations were made, resulting in the torture, trials, murder, and expulsion of many Jews. Allegations of ritual murder and accompanying trials persisted into the twentieth century, to the consternation and anger of enlightened people who regarded the charge as so much nonsense, a lingering medieval fabrication and superstition.

In the next passage, an English chronicler reports on the death of one young Harold of Gloucester purported to be murdered by Jews in 1168.

. . . [The eight-year-old] boy Harold, who is buried in the Church of St. Peter the Apostle, at Gloucester . . ., is said to have been carried away secretly by Jews, in the opinion of many,* on Feb. 21, and by them hidden till March 16. On that night, on the sixth of the preceding feast, the Jews of all England coming together as if to circumcise a certain boy, pretend deceitfully that they are about to celebrate the feast [Passover] appointed by law in such case, and deceiving the citizens of Gloucester with that fraud, they tortured the lad placed before them with immense tortures. It is true no Christian was present, or saw or heard the deed, nor have we found that anything was betrayed by any Jew. But a little while after when the whole convent of monks of Gloucester and almost all the citizens of that city, and innumerable persons coming to the spectacle, saw the wounds of the dead body, scars of fire, the thorns fixed on his head, and liquid wax poured into the eyes and face, and touched it with the diligent examination of their hands, those tortures were believed or guessed to have been inflicted on him in that manner. It was clear that they had made him a glorious martyr to Christ, being slain without sin, and having bound his feet with his own girdle, threw him into the river Severn. (The body is taken to St. Peter's Church, and there performs miracles.)

---

*Even the chronicler puts it doubly doubtfully.

Philip II Augustus
EXPULSION OF THE JEWS FROM FRANCE

At various times in the Middle Ages and Early Modern times, monarchs and town authorities expelled Jews from their lands after first confiscating their property. So numerous were these expulsions that by 1541, virtually all of Western Europe and most of Central Europe were largely devoid of Jews.

In 1181, Philip II Augustus had Jews arrested in their synagogues on the Sabbath, extracted an enormous sum from them, and canceled all debts payable to Jews but made one-fifth payable to his treasury. A year later, he banished the Jews from his royal domain. The king filled his coffers by seizing and selling Jewish land, homes, barns, and other properties. Synagogues were converted into churches. Running out of money, Philip permitted the Jews to return a few years later but imposed heavy taxes on their economic activities, principally money-lending.

In succeeding years Jews would face additional expulsions from French lands. In 1306, Philip IV the Fair, seeking to replenish his treasury, condemned Jews to exile. All their property, except for a few coins and the clothes they were wearing, was forfeited to the king, and all loan records were transferred to the exchequer so that Philip could collect every penny of principal and interest. Other recalls and expulsions ensued in the fourteenth century, but a final expulsion in 1394 brought an end to France's thousand-year-old Jewish community.

Following is a contemporary account of Philip Augustus' banishment of the Jews from France in 1182. The author begins with the widely believed myth that Jews engaged in ritual murder.

[Philip Augustus had often heard] that the Jews who dwelt in Paris were wont every year on Easter day, or during the sacred week of our Lord's Passion, to go down secretly into underground vaults and kill a Christian as a sort of sacrifice in contempt of the Christian religion. For a long time they had persisted in this wickedness, inspired by the devil, and in Philip's father's time many of them had been seized and burned with fire. St. Richard, whose body rests in the church of the Holy Innocents-in-the-Fields in Paris, was thus put to death and crucified by the Jews, and through martyrdom went in blessedness to God. Wherefore many miracles have been wrought by the hand of God through the prayers and intercessions of St. Richard, to the glory of God, as we have heard.

And because the most Christian King Philip inquired diligently, and came to know full well these and many other iniquities of the Jews in his forefathers' days, therefore he burned with zeal, and in the same year in which he was invested at Rheims with the holy governance of the kingdom of the French, upon a Sabbath, the first of March, by his command, the Jews throughout all France were seized in their synagogues and then bespoiled of their gold and silver and garments, as the Jews themselves had spoiled the Egyptians at their exodus from Egypt. This was a harbinger of their expulsion, which by God's will soon followed. . . .

At this time a great multitude of Jews had been dwelling in France for a long time past, for they had flocked thither from divers parts of the world, because peace abode among the French, and liberality; for the Jews had heard how the kings of the French were prompt to act against their enemies, and were very merciful toward their subjects. And therefore their elders and men wise in the law of Moses, who were called by the Jews *didascali,* made resolve to come to Paris.

When they had made a long sojourn there, they grew so rich that they claimed as their own almost half of the whole city, and had Christians in their houses as menservants and maidservants, who were open backsliders from the faith of Jesus Christ, and *judaized* with the Jews. And this was contrary to the decree of God and the law of the Church. And whereas the Lord had said by the mouth of Moses in Deuteronomy (xxiii, 19, 20), "Thou shalt not lend upon usury to thy brother," but "to a stranger," the Jews in their wickedness understood by "stranger" every Christian, and they took from the Christians their money at usury. And so heavily burdened in this wise were citizens and soldiers and peasants in the suburbs, and in the various towns and villages, that many of them were constrained to part with their possessions. Others were bound under oath in houses of the Jews in Paris, held as if captives in prison.

The most Christian King Philip heard of these things, and compassion was stirred within him. He took counsel with a certain hermit, Bernard by name, a holy and religious man, who at that time dwelt in the forest of Vincennes, and asked him what he should do. By his advice the king released all Christians of his kingdom from their debts to the Jews, and kept a fifth part of the whole amount for himself.

Finally came the culmination of their wickedness. Certain ecclesiastical vessels consecrated to God—the chalices and crosses of gold and silver bearing the image of our Lord Jesus Christ crucified—had been pledged to the Jews by way of security when the need of the churches was pressing. These they used so vilely, in their impiety and scorn of the Christian religion, that from the cups in which the body and blood of our Lord Jesus Christ was consecrated they gave their children cakes soaked in wine. . . .

In the year of our Lord's Incarnation 1182, in the month of April, which is called by the Jews Nisan, an edict went forth from the most serene king, Philip Augustus, that all the Jews of his kingdom should be prepared to go forth by the coming feast of St. John the Baptist. And then the king gave them leave to sell each his movable goods before the time fixed, that is, the feast of St. John the Baptist. But their real estate, that is, houses, fields, vineyards, barns, winepresses, and such like, he reserved for himself and his successors, the kings of the French.

When the faithless Jews heard this edict some of them were born again of water and the Holy Spirit and converted to the Lord, remaining steadfast in the faith of our Lord Jesus Christ. To them the king, out of regard for the Christian religion, restored all their possessions in their entirety, and gave them perpetual liberty.

Others were blinded by their ancient error and persisted in their perfidy; and they sought to win with gifts and golden promises the great of the land,—counts, barons, archbishops, bishops,—that through their influence and advice, and through the promise of infinite wealth, they might turn the king's mind from his firm intention. But the merciful and compassionate God, who does not forsake those who put their hope in him and who doth humble those who glory in their strength, . . . so fortified the illustrious king that he could not be moved by prayers nor promises of temporal things. . . .

The infidel Jews, perceiving that the great of the land, through whom they had been accustomed easily to bend the king's predecessors to their will, had suffered repulse, and astonished and stupefied by the strength of mind of Philip the king and his constancy in the Lord, exclaimed, "Scema Israhel!" and prepared to sell all their household goods. The time was now at hand when the king had ordered them to leave France altogether, and it could not be in any way prolonged. Then did the Jews sell all their movable possessions in great haste, while their landed property reverted to the crown. Thus the Jews, having sold their goods and taken the price for the expenses of their journey, departed with their wives and children and all their households in the aforesaid year of the Lord 1182.

Maimonides
JEWISH LEARNING

Medieval Jews, despite frequent persecution, carried on a rich cultural and intellectual life based on their ancestral religion. The foremost Jewish scholar of the Middle Ages was Moses ben Maimon, also called by the Greek name Maimonides (1135–1204), who was born in Córdoba, Spain, then under Muslim rule. After his family emigrated from Spain, Maimonides went to Egypt, where he became physician to the sultan. During his lifetime, Maimonides achieved fame as a philosopher, theologian, mathematician, and physician; he was recognized as the leading Jewish sage of his day, and his writings were respected by Christian and Muslim thinkers as well. Like Christian scholastics and Muslim philosophers, Maimonides tried to harmonize faith with reason, to reconcile the Hebrew Scriptures and the Talmud (Jewish biblical commentary) with Greek philosophy. In his writings on ethical themes, Maimonides demonstrated piety, wisdom, and humanity. In the following passages, he discusses education and charity.

EDUCATION

Every man in Israel [every Jew] is obliged to study the Torah,[1] whether he be poor or rich, whether he be physically healthy or ailing, whether he be in full vigor of youth or of great age and weakened vitality; even if he be dependent upon alms for his livelihood, or going around from door to door begging his daily bread, yea, even he who has a wife and children to support is obliged to have an appointed time for the study of the Torah, both during the day and at night, for it is said: "But thou shalt meditate therein day and night" (Joshua, I.8).

Some of the great scholars in Israel were hewers of wood, some of them drawers of water, and some of them blind: nevertheless they engaged themselves in the study of the Torah by day and by night. Moreover, they are included among those who translated the tradition as it was transmitted from mouth of man to mouth of man, even from the mouth of Moses our Master [the biblical Moses].

Until what age in life is one obliged to study the Torah? Even until the day of one's demise; for it is said: "And lest they depart from thy heart all the days of thy life" (Deut. 4.9). Forsooth, as long as one will not occupy himself with study he forgets what he did study.

One is obligated to divide his time of study by three; one third for the study of Holy Writ, one third for the study of the Oral Torah [the interpretations of the Torah], and one third for thinking and reflecting so that he may understand the end of a thing from its beginning, and deduct one matter from another, and compare one matter to another. . . .

When a master gave a lesson which the disciples did not understand, he should not get angry at them and be moody, but go over it again and repeat it even many times, until they will understand the depth of the treatise. Likewise, a disciple shall not say, I understood, and he did not understand; but he should repeat and ask even many times. If the master angers at him and becomes moody, he may say to him: "Master, it is Torah, and I need instruction, but my mind is short of understanding!"

A disciple shall not feel ashamed before his fellows who mastered the subject the first or the second time, whereas he did not grasp it until after hearing it many times, for if he will be ashamed of such a thing, he will find himself coming in and going out of the . . . [school] without any instructions at all. The sages, therefore, said: "he who is bashful cannot be instructed and he who is in an angry mood cannot instruct." . . .

Even as a man is under command to honor his father and fear him, so is he obliged to honor his master, but fear him yet more than his father; his father brought him to life upon this world but his master who taught him wisdom, brings him to life in the world to come. . . .

Care for the poor is ingrained in the Jewish tradition. Rabbis gave the highest value to assistance, given in secret, that helps a poor person to become self-supporting. Maimonides drew upon this rabbinical tradition in his discussion of charity.

CHARITY

The law of the Torah commanded us to practise *tsedakah*,[2] support the needy and help them financially. The command in connection with this duty occurs in various expressions; e.g., "Thou shalt surely open thy hand unto him" (Deut. xv. 8), "Thou shalt uphold him; as a stranger and a settler shall he live with thee" (Lev. xxv. 35). The intention in these passages is identical, viz., that we should console the

---

[1]The Torah refers to the first five books of the Hebrew Scriptures, which the Jews believed were written by Moses. In time, *Torah* also acquired a broader meaning that encompassed the entire Hebrew Scriptures and the various commentaries.

[2]The term *tsedakah* is derived from *tsédek* (righteousness); it denotes showing kindness to others.

poor man and support him to the extent of sufficiency. . . .

There are eight degrees in alms-giving, one higher than the other: Supreme above all is to give assistance to a co-religionist who has fallen on evil times by presenting him with a gift or loan, or entering into a partnership with him, or procuring him work, thereby helping him to become self-supporting.

Inferior to this is giving charity to the poor in such a way that the giver and recipient are unknown to each other. This is, indeed, the performance of a commandment from disinterested motives; and it is exemplified by the Institution of the Chamber of the Silent which existed in the Temple,[3] where the righteous secretly deposited their alms and the respectable poor were secretly assisted.[*]

Next in order is the donation of money to the charitable fund of the Community, to which

no contribution should be made without the donors feeling confident that the administration is honest, prudent and capable of proper management.

Below this degree is the instance where the donor is aware to whom he is giving the alms but the recipient is unaware from whom he received them; as, e.g., the great Sages who used to go about secretly throwing money through the doors of the poor. This is quite a proper course to adopt and a great virtue where the administrators of a charitable fund are not acting fairly.

Inferior to this degree is the case where the recipient knows the identity of the donor, but not *vice versa*; as, e.g., the great Sages who used to tie sums of money in linen bundles and throw them behind their backs for poor men to pick up, so that they should not feel shame.

The next four degrees in their order are: the man who gives money to the poor before he is asked; the man who gives money to the poor after he is asked; the man who gives less than he should, but does it with good grace; and lastly, he who gives grudgingly.

---

[3]The Temple to which Maimonides refers was the Temple in Jerusalem, destroyed by the Romans in A.D. 70.
[*]This system of charity was adopted by Jews in several Palestinian and Babylonian cities.

REVIEW QUESTIONS

1. What were the apparent motives of those who attacked the Jews at Cologne and elsewhere at the time of the First Crusade?
2. What harassments and abuses were Jews likely to suffer in late medieval society?
3. What was the attitude of the papacy toward Jews?
4. Why were Christians prone to believe the absurd myth that Jews committed ritual murder?
5. Analyze the motives of Philip II Augustus for expelling the Jews from France. How might Jewish spokesmen respond to his accusations?
6. Discuss the roles of scholarship, education, and charity in medieval Jewish culture.

8 Troubadour Love Songs

In the late twelfth century, new kinds of poetry with a distinctive set of themes began to be created at the castles and courts in France, Italy, Spain, and Germany. The poets were themselves knights or noblewomen who composed their poems to be sung or read aloud for the entertainment of fellow feudal nobles. The subject was always that of the love between man and woman.

The original inspiration for the new troubadour poetry was probably the Arab poetry of Spain and Sicily, where the theme of courtly love was developed earlier. What was revolutionary in later European poetry was its treatment of the relationship between men and women. The troubadours reversed the traditional view of men as superior and women as inferior and dependent in their relationships. They introduced what is called "courtly love," a love relationship in which the woman is the superior and dominant figure, the man inferior and dependent. The male courts the lady, paying homage to her beauty and virtue. He suffers humiliation and frustration at her will and expresses the erotic tensions that consume him.

LOVE AS JOYOUS, PAINFUL, AND HUMOROUS

The following poems were all composed by southern French troubadours. In the first selection a poet sings the praises of his beloved.

I wandered through a garden, 'twas
    filled with flowers the rarest,
And of all these brilliant blossoms
    I culled the very fairest;
So fine its shape, so sweet its scent, its
    hues so richly blent,
That heaven, I'm sure, created it itself
    to represent.
My lady is so charming, my lady is so
    meek,
Such tenderness is in her smile, such
    beauty in her cheek;
Such kisses blossom on her lip, such
    love illumines her eye—
Oh, never was there neath the stars a
    man so blest as I!
I gaze, I thrill with joy, I weep, in song
    my feelings flow—
A song of hope, delight, desire, with
    passion all aglow—

A fervent song, a pleading song, a song
    in every line—
Of thanks and praise to her who lists no
    other songs but mine.
Oh, hear me sweet! Oh, kiss me sweet!
    Oh, clasp me tenderly!
Thy beauties many, many touch, but
    none that love like me.

The following two poems tell of a lover's failure to win the affections of his beloved.

Now that the air is fresher
and the world turned green,
I shall sing once more
of the one I love and desire,
but we are so far apart
that I cannot go and witness
how my words might please her.

And nothing can console me
but death, for evil tongues
(may God curse them)
have made us part.
And alas, I so desired her
that now I moan and cry
half mad with grief.

I sing of her, yet her beauty
is greater than I can tell,
with her fresh color, lovely eyes,
and white skin, untanned
and untainted by rouge.
She is so pure and noble
that no one can speak ill of her.

But above all, one must praise,
it seems to me, her truthfulness,
her manners and her gracious speech,
for she never would betray a friend;
and I was mad to believe
what I heard tell of her
and thus cause her to be angry.

I never intended to complain;
and even now, if she so desires,
she could bring me happiness
by granting what I seek.
I cannot go on like this much longer,
for since she's been so far away
I've scarcely slept or eaten.

Love is sweet to look upon
but bitter upon parting;
one day it makes you weep
and another skip and dance,
for now I know that the more
one enters love's service,
the more fickle it becomes.

Messenger, go with Godspeed
and bring this to my lady,
for I cannot stay here much longer
and live, or be cured elsewhere,
unless I have her next to me,
naked, to kiss and embrace
within a curtained room.

———

I said my heart was like to break,
 And that my soul was cast,
By passion's tide, just like a wreck
 Disabled by the blast.

I swore an oath that what I felt
 Was like to turn my head;
I sighed—such sighs!—and then I knelt,
 But not a word she said!

I preached of Grace in moving strain;
 I told her she was fair;
I whispered what renown she'd gain,
 By listening to my prayer.

I spoke of needle and of pole,
 And other things I'd read;
But unto all my rigmarole—
 Why not a word she said!

I prayed her then my love to test,
 To send me near or far—
I'd squelch the dragon in his den,
 I'd yoke him to my car.

I'd risk for her, as faithful knight,
 My eyes, or limbs, or head,
Being quite prepared to fool or fight—
 But not a word she said!

I argued that, if poor in cash,
 Yet I was rich in mind;
Of rivals vowed to make a hash,
 When such I chanced to find.

I knit my brows, I clenched my hand,
 I tried to wake her dread;
In quiet wise, you'll understand—
 But not a word she said!

———

Troubadours could also be playful. Sometimes they mocked women who labored too hard to preserve a youthful beauty.

———

That creature so splendid is but an old jade;
Of ointment and padding her beauty is made;
Unpainted if you had the hap to behold her,
You'd find her all wrinkles from forehead to
 shoulder.

What a shame for a woman who has lost all her
  grace
To waste thus her time in bedaubing
  her face!
To neglect her poor soul I am sure is not right
  of her,
For a body that's going to corruption
  in spite of her.

Sometimes they even mocked this obsession
with romance.

You say the moon is all aglow,
  The nightingale a-singing—
I'd rather watch the red wine flow,
  And hear the goblets ringing.

You say 'tis sweet to hear the gale
  Creep sighing through the willows—
I'd rather hear a merry tale,
  'Mid a group of jolly fellows!

You say 'tis sweet the stars to view
  Upon the waters gleaming—
I'd rather see, 'twixt me and you
  And the post, my supper steaming.

REVIEW QUESTION

1. What do these troubadours' love songs reveal about the tradition of courtly love?

9 The Status of Women in Medieval Society

The precise status of a woman in medieval society differed immensely depending
on the time, the place, and her class. The majority of women managed families
and households, often taking part in farm work or crafts connected with the family livelihood. However, their legal rights, social standing, and power were inferior to those of adult males in their own families. During the High Middle Ages,
the Christian church increasingly supported a patriarchal structure of authority
in church and civil society that left women effectively under the domination of
males, clerical and lay. Although clerical teachings tended to demean women,
several church doctrines also recognized the inherent dignity of a woman. The
church regarded marriage as a sacrament, considered adultery a sin, and subjected men and women to the same moral standards. Neither sex had any special
advantage in attaining salvation.

Despite legal, social, and economic handicaps imposed upon them by males,
some women successfully assumed positions of power and achievement. A few
ruled kingdoms and principalities or headed convents and religious orders.
Others organized guilds; founded nunneries; practiced various crafts; served as
teachers, physicians, and midwives; and operated small businesses. Some showed
talent as poets, dramatists, and artists.

Jacopone da Todi
PRAISE OF THE VIRGIN MARY
"O THOU MOTHER, FOUNT OF LOVE"

The ambivalence that medieval men, particularly intellectuals, expressed toward women arose from several sources. First, medieval authors, who highly esteemed the writings of the ancient Greeks and Romans, were influenced by the hostility of classical authors toward women who did not accept their position as subordinate and inferior to men. Classical writers maintained that women were less intelligent, more carnal, and more devious than men. Second, prejudice against women was fostered by the clerical insistence that celibacy was superior to marriage (because the former made it possible to escape the distractions of the flesh and family life and concentrate on spiritual matters). Third, the Christian view of men and women as equals in the sight of God was obscured by certain scriptural texts, such as Saint Paul's "Let your women keep silence in the churches: for it is not permitted unto them to speak" (1 Cor. 14:34); and "Wives, submit yourselves unto your own husbands, as unto the Lord" (Eph. 5:22). This negative view of women was symbolized by the Old Testament portrait of Eve as the archetypal temptress who led Adam to sin. One medieval writer expressed it this way: "Between Adam and God in paradise there was but one woman and she had no rest until she had succeeded in banishing her husband from the garden of delights and in condemning Christ to the torments of the cross."

Countering this negative image was the New Testament picture of Mary, whose acceptance of her role as the mother of Jesus made salvation possible for all people. The highest expression of devotion to the Virgin Mary was reached in the twelfth and thirteenth centuries with the growing notion that Mary was preserved from original sin and remained free of sin throughout her life. Moreover, medieval Christians believed that Mary, by devoting her entire life to her son in his work of redemption, cooperated with him in his ministry. Therefore, as the mother of God she was able to intercede with her son on behalf of individual Christians. The numerous artistic depictions of Mary as the Mother of God and the Queen of Heaven, as well as the multitude of churches named after the Virgin, are evidence of the popular piety that the cult of Mary generated throughout the Middle Ages.

The following poem by Italian religious poet Jacopone da Todi (c. 1230–1306) is a tribute to the Virgin Mary.

At the Cross her station keeping
Stood the mournful mother weeping,
    Close to Jesus to the last;
    Through her heart, His sorrow sharing,
All His bitter anguish bearing,
    Now at length the sword had passed.

O how sad and sore distressed
Was that mother highly blest
    Of the sole-begotten One!
Christ above in torment hangs:
She beneath Him holds the pangs
Of her dying glorious Son.

Is there one who would not weep
Whelmed in miseries so deep
    Christ's dear mother to behold?
Can the human heart refrain
From partaking in her pain,
    In that mother's pain untold?

Bruised, derided, cursed, defiled,
She held her tender Child
    All with bloody scourges rent;
For the sins of His own nation,
Saw Him hang in desolation,
    Till His spirit forth he sent.

O thou mother, fount of love,
Touch my spirit from above,
    Make my heart with thine accord!
Make me feel as thou hast felt;
Make my soul to glow and melt
    With the love of Christ my Lord.

Holy mother, pierce me through!
In my heart each wound renew
    Of my Saviour crucified;
Let me share with thee His pain,
Who for all my sins was slain,
    Who for me in torments died.

Let me mingle tears with thee,
Mourning Him who mourned for me,
    All the days that I may live;
By the Cross with thee to stay,
There with thee to weep and pray,
    Is all I ask of thee to give.

Virgin of all virgins blest!
Listen to my fond request:
    Let me share thy grief divine;
Let me, to my latest breath,
In my body bear the death
    Of that dying Son of thine.

Wounded with His every wound,
Steep my soul till it hath swooned
    In His very blood away;
Be to me, O virgin, nigh,
Lest in flames I burn and die
    In His awful judgment day:

Christ, when Thou shalt call me hence,
Be Thy mother my defence,
    Be Thy cross my victory
While my body here decays,
May my soul Thy goodness praise,
    Safe in paradise with Thee.

Christine de Pisan
THE CITY OF LADIES

In the Late Middle Ages (or early Renaissance), a remarkable woman took up the task of defending women from their many male detractors. Christine de Pisan (1364–c. 1429) was born in Venice but moved with her parents to Paris, where her father was court physician and astrologer. She married a court notary when she was fifteen, had three children, and was left a widow and penniless ten years later. She decided to use her unusually good education to become a professional writer, an unheard-of occupation for a woman at that time. She won the patronage and friendship of noble ladies at the French royal court and produced many poems and books, including a biography of King Charles V and several polemical attacks upon the poets who slandered womankind. The most famous of these is *The City of Ladies*, written in 1405. In it Christine de Pisan questioned three allegorical figures—Reason, Rectitude, and Justice—about the lies and slanders of males concerning the virtues and achievements of women. The book is really a history of famous women and their accomplishments in many fields of endeavour. In the following passages, she challenged the traditional medieval attitude toward women. In questioning Lady Reason about the alleged inferiority of women to men, de Pisan cleverly changed the subject to that of virtue, proclaiming the equality of the sexes in attaining it.

"My lady [Lady Reason], according to what I understand from you, woman is a most noble creature. But even so, Cicero [Roman statesman] says that a man should never serve any woman and that he who does so debases himself, for no man should ever serve anyone lower than him."

She replied, "The man or the woman in whom resides greater virtue is the higher; neither the loftiness nor the lowliness of a person lies in the body according to the sex, but in the perfection of conduct and virtues. And surely he is happy who serves the Virgin [Mary, the mother of Jesus], who is above all the angels."

"My lady, one of the Catos[1]—who was such a great orator—said, nevertheless, that if this world were without women, we would converse with the gods."

She replied, "You can now see the foolishness of the man who is considered wise, because, thanks to a woman, man reigns with God. And if anyone would say that man was banished because of Lady Eve, I tell you that he gained more through [the Virgin] Mary than he lost through Eve when humanity was conjoined to the Godhead,[2] which would never have taken place if Eve's misdeed [eating the forbidden fruit] had not occurred. Thus man and woman should be glad for this sin, through which such an honor

has come about. For as low as human nature fell through this creature woman, was human nature lifted higher by this same creature. And as for conversing with the gods, as this Cato has said, if there had been no woman, he spoke truer than he knew, for he was a pagan, and among those of this belief, gods were thought to reside in Hell as well as in Heaven, that is, the devils whom they called the gods of Hell—so that it is no lie that these gods would have conversed with men, if Mary had not lived."

In this next passage, de Pisan discusses the slander that women are not as intelligent as men.

". . . But please enlighten me again, whether it has ever pleased this God, who has bestowed so many favors on women, to honor the feminine sex with the privilege of the virtue of high understanding and great learning, and whether women ever have a clever enough mind for this. I wish very much to know this because men maintain that the mind of women can learn only a little."

She [Lady Reason] answered, "My daughter, since I told you before, you know quite well that the opposite of their opinion is true, and to show you this even more clearly, I will give you proof through examples. I tell you again—and don't doubt the contrary—if it were customary to send daughters to school like sons, and if they were then taught the natural sciences,

---

[1]Several Roman statesmen bore the name Cato. Cato the Censor (234–149 B.C.) was a vigorous critic of women.
[2]This clause refers to the Christian belief that God became a human being in the person of Jesus Christ.

they would learn as thoroughly and understand the subtleties of all the arts and sciences as well as sons. And by chance there happen to be such women, for, as I touched on before, just as women have more delicate bodies than men, weaker and less able to perform many tasks, so do they have minds that are freer and sharper whenever they apply themselves."

"My lady, what are you saying? With all due respect, could you dwell longer on this point, please. Certainly men would never admit this answer is true, unless it is explained more plainly, for they believe that one normally sees that men know more than women do."

She answered, "Do you know why women know less?"

"Not unless you tell me, my lady."

"Without the slightest doubt, it is because they are not involved in many different things, but stay at home, where it is enough for them to run the household, and there is nothing which so instructs a reasonable creature as the exercise and experience of many different things."

"My lady, since they have minds skilled in conceptualizing and learning, just like men, why don't women learn more?"

She replied, "Because, my daughter, the public does not require them to get involved in the affairs which men are commissioned to execute, just as I told you before. It is enough for women to perform the usual duties to which they are ordained. As for judging from experience, since one sees that women usually know less than men, that therefore their capacity for understanding is less, look at men who farm the flatlands or who live in the mountains. You will find that in many countries they seem completely savage because they are so simpleminded. All the same, there is no doubt that Nature provided them with the qualities of body and mind found in the wisest and most learned men. . . ."

Next, Christine de Pisan argues in favor of giving young women the same opportunities for learning as men.

Following these remarks, I, Christine, spoke, "My lady, I realize that women have accomplished many good things and that even if evil women have done evil, it seems to me, nevertheless, that the benefits accrued and still accruing because of good women—particularly the wise and literary ones and those educated in the natural sciences whom I mentioned above—outweigh the evil. Therefore, I am amazed by the opinion of some men who claim that they do not want their daughters, wives, or kinswomen to be educated because their mores would be ruined as a result."

She responded, "Here you can clearly see that not all opinions of men are based on reason and that these men are wrong. For it must not be presumed that mores necessarily grow worse from knowing the moral sciences, which teach the virtues, indeed, there is not the slightest doubt that moral education amends and ennobles them. How could anyone think or believe that whoever follows good teaching or doctrine is the worse for it? Such an opinion cannot be expressed or maintained. I do not mean that it would be good for a man or a woman to study the art of divination or those fields of learning which are forbidden—for the holy Church did not remove them from common use without good reason—but it should not be believed that women are the worse for knowing what is good. . . .

". . . To speak of more recent times, without searching for examples in ancient history, Giovanni Andrea, a solemn law professor in Bologna [Italy] not quite sixty years ago, was not of the opinion that it was bad for women to be educated. He had a fair and good daughter, named Novella, who was educated in the law to such an advanced degree that when he was occupied by some task and not at leisure to present his lectures to his students, he would send Novella, his daughter, in his place to lecture to the students from his chair. And to prevent her beauty from distracting the concentration of his audience, she had a little curtain drawn in front of her. In this manner she could on occasion supplement and lighten her father's occupation. . . ."

A Merchant of Paris
ON LOVE AND MARRIAGE

It is difficult to generalize about so intimate a relationship as marriage. It is too intensely individual, and marital love is seldom captured by words that are not either trite or highly poetic in character. But in the late fourteenth century (c. 1393), a merchant of Paris, a man of mature years and experience, tried to put in words for his fifteen-year-old child bride some practical advice as to what a good wife should be and should do for her loving husband. The young lady was of higher social status than her husband, and he clearly expected that she would marry again after his death. His instructions were for her eyes only, but the manuscript survived in at least three copies. Discovered and published in French in 1846, it offers a rare look at the marital values and expectations of a wealthy, pious, and practical businessman living in one of the largest and most cosmopolitan cities of late medieval Europe.

WHEN TWO GOOD AND HONEST PEOPLE ARE MARRIED

I believe that when two good and honest people are married, all other affections, except their love for each other, are withdrawn, annulled, and forgotten. It seems to me that when they are together they look at each other more than they look at others, they come together and embrace each other, and they would rather talk and communicate with each other than with anyone else. When they are separated, they think of each other and say in their hearts: "This is what I will do, this is what I will say, this is what I will ask him when I see him again." All their special pleasures, greatest desires, and perfect joys are in pleasing and obeying each other. But if they don't love one another, they have no more than a routine sense of duty and respect for each other, which is not enough between many couples.

BE VERY LOVING AND INTIMATE WITH YOUR HUSBAND

You ought to be very loving and intimate with your husband, more than with all other living creatures; moderately loving and intimate with your good and nearest kinsfolk and your husband's kinsfolk; very distant with all other men; and entirely aloof from conceited and idle young men who have more expenses than income, and who, without property or good lineage, go dancing; and also distant from courtiers of very great lords. Moreover, have nothing to do with men and women who are said to lead corrupt, amorous, or dissolute lives.

Concerning what I have said about being very loving to your husband, it is certainly true that every man ought to love and cherish his wife, and every woman should love and cherish her husband: for he is her beginning. I can prove this, for it is found in the second chapter of the first book of the Bible, called Genesis. . . .

Do not think that someone else will hide for you that which you yourself have not been able to conceal. Be secretive and discreet with everyone except your husband. For you should conceal nothing from him, but tell him everything, and he should also tell you everything. . . . You two, man and woman, ought to be as one, and at all times and in all places the one should act on the other's advice. This is how good and wise people act and ought to act. . . .

HOW GOOD WIVES ACT TOWARD THEIR HUSBANDS, AND GOOD HUSBANDS TOWARD THEIR WIVES, WHEN THEY GO ASTRAY

Husbands ought to hide and conceal the follies of their wives and lovingly protect them from future mistakes, as did an honorable man of Venice.

In that city there was a married couple with three children. As the wife lay on her deathbed, she confessed, among other things, that one of the children was not her husband's. The confessor at length told her that he would seek advice about how to counsel her and return. This confessor went to the doctor who was looking after her and asked the nature of her illness. The doctor said that she would not be able to recover from it. Then the confessor went to her and told her that he didn't see how God would give her salvation unless she begged her husband for forgiveness for the wrong she had done him. She summoned her husband; had everyone removed from the room except her mother and her confessor, who placed her, and held her, on her knees on the bed: and before her husband, with folded hands, humbly begged pardon for having sinned in the law of his marriage and having had one of her children with another man. She would have said more, but her husband cried out: "Stop! Stop! Stop! Don't say anything else." Then he kissed her and pardoned her, saying: "Say no more. Don't tell me or anyone else which of your children it is; for I want to love each as much as the other—so equally that you will not be blamed during your lifetime or after your death. For through your blame, I will be dishonored, and because of it, your children, and others through them—that is, our relations—will receive vile and everlasting reproach. Therefore, don't say anything. I don't want to know any more. So that no one can ever say that I do wrong by the other

two, whichever it is, I will give him in my lifetime what would come to him under our laws of succession."

So, dear sister, you see that the wise man bent his heart to save his wife's reputation, which would affect his children. This shows you what wise men and women ought to do for each other to save their honor.

CHERISH YOUR HUSBAND'S PERSON CAREFULLY

Dear sister, if you have another husband after me, be aware that you must take very good care of his person. For generally when a woman has lost her first husband and marriage, it is hard for her, depending on her social status, to find a second who is to her liking, and she remains forsaken and helpless for a long time, and even more so when she loses the second. Therefore, cherish your husband's person carefully.

I entreat you to keep his linen clean, for this is up to you. Because the care of outside affairs is men's work, a husband must look after these things, and go and come, run here and there in rain, wind, snow, and hail—sometimes wet, sometimes dry, sometimes sweating, other times shivering, badly fed, badly housed, badly shod, badly bedded—and nothing harms him because he is cheered by the anticipation of the care his wife will take of him on his return—of the pleasures, joys, and comforts she will provide, or have provided for him in her presence: to have his shoes off before a good fire, to have his feet washed, to have clean shoes and hose, to be well fed, provided with good drink, well served, well honored, well bedded in white sheets and white nightcaps, well covered with good furs, and comforted with other joys and amusements, intimacies, affections, and secrets about which I am silent. And on the next day fresh linen and garments.

Indeed, dear sister, these favors cause a man to love and desire the return home and the sight of his good wife, and to be reserved with others. And so I advise you to comfort your second husband on all his homecomings, and persevere in this.

Also keep peace with him. Remember the country proverb that says there are three things that drive a good man from his home: a house with a bad roof, a smoking chimney, and a quarrelsome woman. Dear sister, I beg you, in order to preserve your husband's love and good will, be loving, amiable, and sweet with him. . . . By my soul! I believe doing good is the only enchantment, and one can no better bewitch a man than by giving him what pleases him.

Therefore, dear sister, I pray you to bewitch and bewitch again the husband whom you will have, preserve him from a badly covered house and a smoky chimney, and be not quarrelsome with him, but be sweet, amiable, and peaceful. Mind that in winter he has a good fire without smoke, and that he is well couched and covered between your breasts, and there bewitch him.

REVIEW QUESTIONS

1. How does Jacopone da Todi's poem present a positive image of women through its depiction of Mary?
2. Evaluate the arguments used by Christine de Pisan in her defense of women.
3. What is the merchant's attitude toward women in general and marriage in particular?
4. Which of the merchant's instructions to his wife do you consider most valuable in a good marriage?

---

10 Sexual Nonconformity: Satan's Lures

The clergy sought to impose uniform sexual standards throughout Christendom. They regarded sexual practices that were not intended for procreation, including homosexuality and masturbation, as violations of natural law and God's will and as Satan's temptations that lead to eternal damnation.

Robert of Flamborough
PROHIBITION OF SEXUAL SINS[1]

The Fourth Lateran Council (1215) decreed that it was necessary for a Christian to go to confession at least once a year. Not doing so could be interpreted as a sign of heresy, which the church might investigate. This requirement gave the clergy tremendous control over the moral outlook of Christians throughout Europe. The following "interview" was a creation of Robert of Flamborough, an English schoolman or scholar who heard confessions of clerics studying at the University of Paris in the early thirteenth century; it was designed as a model to be used by confessors. Although not an actual interview, it does reveal the sexual standards the clergy aspired to uphold and the sexual behavior they sought to suppress.

---

[1]The brackets and the notes within the document were inserted by Michael Goodrich, the editor of the volume from which this selection was taken.

Have you been lustful? The following things pertain to lust: extravagance, shamelessness, licentiousness, impudence, hesitation, flattery, allurements, voluptuousness, dissoluteness, feebleness, scurrility, and coitus. Extravagance is clear; likewise shamelessness. Hesitation is when a man acts without confidence. Flattery is when a man flatters others and accepts flattery from others. Allurements are clear. Voluptuousnes is when a man follows his longings, his desires. Dissoluteness may be found in gestures, words, deeds and attire. Feebleness is clear. Scurrility is when a man acts like a clown. Concerning all these things, do you ask pardon, etc.?

Priest: Those things which you otherwise do, do with confidence . . . and patiently . . . and firmly . . . and with perseverance . . . and with a relaxed mind. . . .

There remains coitus [intercourse], which is lust in the strict sense of the word. Have you ever been polluted with lust?

PENITENT: Many times.
PRIEST: Ever against nature?
PENITENT: Many times.
PRIEST: Ever with a man?
PENITENT: Many times.
PRIEST: With clerics or laymen?
PENITENT: With both clerics and laymen.
PRIEST: Married or single laymen?
PENITENT: Both.
PRIEST: With how many married persons?
PENITENT: I don't know.
PRIEST: You therefore don't know how often?
PENITENT: Correct.
PRIEST: Let's try to find out what we can. How long were you with those persons?
PENITENT: For seven years.
PRIEST: In what [priestly] order?
PENITENT: In the priesthood for two years, in the diaconate for two years, in the sub-diaconate for two years, and as an acolyte for a year. I sinned with single persons, but I don't know how many or how often.
PRIEST: Did you sin with clerics?
PENITENT: I sinned with both secular clergy and religious [monastic clergy].

PRIEST: Tell me with how many secular and how many religious clergy, in which order you and they were in when you sinned together, and whether they possessed the office of archdeacon, dean, abbot, or bishop. Did you ever introduce some innocent person to that sin? Tell me how many and what order you were then in.

He may afterward be asked whether he ever sinned any more against nature, if he had anyone "in an extraordinary way." If he should ask in what "extraordinary way," I won't answer him; he'll see for himself. I never mention anything to him from which he might derive some reason to sin, but only speak in a general way about things which everyone knows are sins. I painfully wrench a confession of masturbation out of him and likewise from a woman, but the method of getting this out should not be written down. Just as I asked a man whether he has done anything against nature, so I ask a woman, and in fact about every kind of fornication. Second, I inquire about adultery, then about every kind of fornication; afterward I ask about incest in this way:

Did you approach your female cousins? Say how often and how they were related to you. Afterward I inquire as above. Did you approach two females related to you by blood? Say how many times and how they are related, and afterward as above. You had how many [such female relatives] after your male relatives [had them]? Say how they [the males] are related to you, and afterward as above.

Did you approach a nun or another *conversa?*[1] Say to which order they belonged, and afterward as above.

Did you ever deflower a virgin? Did you approach your godmother (*commater*)? Your aunt? Your daughter? Your father's daughter? Your godfather's daughter? A woman during menstruation? An infidel, Jew, Gentile, heretic? Say how many times and how much. A woman in childbirth? A woman who has not been purified?[2] You should inquire about all of this as above.

---

[1] A woman who has taken a vow.
[2] Forty days after childbirth.

Did you approach a pregnant woman? I ask this because many little children are weakened in this way, crippled and oppressed. If someone is oppressed by your having sexual relations you should in my opinion never serve as a minister in any order or be promoted without papal dispensation. During menstruation or childbirth many lepers, epileptics, and children with evil characteristics are conceived.

Have you committed fornication in a holy place or on a holy day? Ask where and how often this has happened, in what order, with whom and what kind of fornication it was. If you have fornicated in a holy place like a church which has been consecrated or a cemetery, the place itself is reconciled by a simple priest in a private capacity, or solemnly by a bishop. It is reconciled by a simple priest in a private capacity if the crime is hidden, and solemnly by a bishop if the crime becomes known. For this purpose a special office and special masses are held. The simple priest

ought to walk around the place and sprinkle water which has been blessed in a dedicated church, singing seven Psalms and a litany. It is reconciled as for homicide, for whatever kind of fornication, if blood was shed there during a quarrel, [but] as if for theft according to some.

Did you approach prostitutes? You should be afraid lest she be your cousin or related by marriage, or vowed to enter religion, or because one of your relatives had had her, or for some other reason.

Did you procure her not for yourself? Say how often. . . . From the aforesaid inquiries you should know well enough what is to be investigated. Have you ever solicited another person through someone else? Inquire as above.

Were you ever "infamous" due to fornication? Something was said above concerning infamy. Did you ever fail to confess and approach the altar without contrition after fornication or in hatred or with a desire to sin? . . .

Peter Damian
CONDEMNATION OF HOMOSEXUALITY

In the following selection, Peter Damian (1007–1072), a prominent cleric, denounces homosexuality and holds that clergy who engage in this behavior are unable to carry out their spiritual duties and should be dismissed from their positions.

XVI

A Deserving Condemnation of Abominable Shamefulness

Truly, this vice is never to be compared with any other vice because it surpasses the enormity of all vices. Indeed, this vice is the death of bodies, the destruction of souls. It pollutes the flesh, it extinguishes the light of the mind. It evicts the Holy Spirit from the temple of the human heart; it introduces the devil who incites to lust. It casts into error; it completely removes the truth from the mind that has been deceived. It prepares snares for

those entering; it shuts up those who fall into the pit so they cannot get out. It opens hell; it closes the door of heaven. It makes a citizen of the heavenly Jerusalem into an heir of infernal Babylon. It makes of the star of heaven the stubble of eternal fire; it cuts off a member of the Church and casts it into the consuming fire of boiling Gehenna [Hell]. This vice tries to overturn the walls of the heavenly homeland and is busy repairing the renewed bulwarks of Sodom. For it is this which violates sobriety, kills modesty, strangles chastity, and butchers irreparable virginity with the dagger of unclean contagion. It defiles everything, stains everything, pollutes everything. And as for itself, it permits nothing pure, nothing clean, nothing other than filth...."

This vice casts men from the choir of the ecclesiastical community and compels them to pray with the possessed and with those who work for the devil. It separates the soul from God to join it with devils. This most pestilential queen of the sodomists makes the followers of her tyrannical laws filthy to men and hateful to God. She commands to join in evil wars against God.... She humiliates in church, condemns in law, defiles in secret, shames in public, gnaws the conscience as though with worms, sears the flesh as though with fire.... A person who himself participates in a sinful act ought not to be a judge of the crime in confession as long as he hesitates in any way to confess that he has sinned himself by joining in the sin of another.... The miserable flesh burns with the heat of lust.... In fact, after this most poisonous serpent once sinks its fangs into the unhappy soul, sense is snatched away, memory is borne off, the sharpness of the mind is obscured. It becomes unmindful of God and even forgetful of itself. This plague undermines the foundation of faith, weakens the strength of hope, destroys the bond of charity; it takes away justice, subverts fortitude, banishes temperance, blunts the keenness of prudence.

And what more should I say since it expels the whole host of the virtues from the chamber of the human heart and introduces every barbarous vice as if the bolts of the doors were pulled out....

Indeed, whomever this most atrocious beast once seizes upon with bloodthirsty jaws, it restrains with its bonds from every form of good work and immediately unleashes him down the steep descent of the most evil depravity. In fact, when one has fallen into this abyss of extreme ruin he becomes an exile from the heavenly homeland, separated from the body of Christ, confounded by the authority of the whole Church, condemned by the judgment of all the holy fathers. He is despised among men on earth and rejected from the community of heavenly citizens.... Burdened with the weight of the crime, he cannot arise nor conceal his evil for long in the hiding-place of ignorance. He cannot rejoice here while he lives nor can he hope there when he dies, since he is compelled to bear the disgrace of human derision now and afterwards the torment of eternal damnation.

XIX
The Service of an Unworthy Priest Is the Ruin of the People

O guilty, carnal men, why do you desire the height of ecclesiastical dignity with so much burning ambition? Why is it that you try with such desire to ensnare the people of God in the bonds of your own ruin? Is it not enough for you to throw yourselves down the steep cliffs of outrageous crime without having to involve others in the peril of your own ruin? ...

Or how can anyone who does not know whether he himself is pleasing to God ask God for forgiveness for others? ...

Therefore, the person who is still bound by earthly desires should beware lest, by more gravely igniting the anger of the strict Judge, he become the author of the ruin of his subordinates while he takes pleasure in his exalted position. So, if culpable vice still rules over him, a person should prudently take stock of himself before he dares to assume the position of the sacerdotal office, lest one who is perverted by his own crime should desire to become the intercessor for the faults of others. Be careful, be careful, and be afraid of igniting inextinguishably God's fury towards you; fear lest you provoke more sharply by your very prayers the one you offend openly by acting evilly. Intent on your own ruin, beware of becoming responsible for the ruin of another.

REVIEW QUESTION

1. What do these documents tell you about medieval sexual standards and practices?

11 Medieval Contributions to the Tradition of Liberty

In several ways the Middle Ages contributed to the development of liberty in the Western world. Townsmen organized themselves into revolutionary associations called communes to demand freedom from the domination of feudal lords. They successfully won personal liberties, the end of feudal labor services and arbitrary tax levies, and a system of municipal self-government. Another development crucial to the tradition of liberty was the resistance of lords to kings who attempted to interfere with the lords' customary rights. These actions helped to establish the tradition that kings were not above the law and could not rule arbitrarily or absolutely. There is a direct link between modern parliaments and medieval representative institutions, particularly in the case of the English Parliament.

By justifying resistance to tyrannical authority, medieval theologians made a significant contribution to the growth of liberty. They held that a monarch's powers were limited by God's laws and by what was for the common good of Christian people. Some argued that a monarch who ignored or violated the laws and liberties of the people or the church became a tyrant and forfeited his right to be ruler. Such rulers could be, and some in fact were, deposed.

John of Salisbury
POLICRATICUS
A DEFENSE OF TYRANNICIDE

One prelate who opposed the rule of tyrants was an Englishman, John of Salisbury (c. 1115–1180), who became bishop of Chartres, France, in 1176. He composed a statesman's handbook, *Policraticus*, explicitly defending the assassination of tyrants. Paraphrasing the Roman statesman Cicero, John held that it was right, lawful, and just to slay a tyrant.

. . . A tyrant, then, as the philosophers have described him, is one who oppresses the people by the rulership based upon force, while he who rules in accordance with the laws is a prince. Law is the gift of God, the model of equity, a standard of justice, a likeness of the divine will, the guardian of well-being, a bond of union and solidarity between peoples, a rule defining duties, a barrier against the vices and the destroyer thereof, a punishment of violence and all wrong-doing. The law is assailed by force or by fraud, and, as it were, either wrecked by the fury of the lion or undermined by the wiles of the serpent. In whatever way this comes to pass, it is plain that it is the grace of God which is being assailed and that it is God himself who in a sense is challenged to battle. The prince fights for the laws and the liberty of the people; the tyrant thinks nothing done unless he brings the laws to nought and reduces the people to slavery. Hence the prince is a kind of likeness of divinity; and the tyrant, on the contrary, a likeness of the boldness of the Adversary [the devil], even of the wickedness of Lucifer. . . .

The prince, as the likeness of the Deity, is to be loved, worshipped and cherished; the tyrant, the likeness of wickedness, is generally to be even killed. The origin of tyranny is iniquity, and springing from a poisonous root, it is a tree which grows and sprouts into a baleful pestilent growth, and to which the axe must by all means be laid.

MAGNA CARTA

Feudal nobles sought to limit the arbitrary powers of kings by compelling them to issue written charters of liberties. These earliest constitutions spelled out the rights of subjects and the obligations of rulers. In 1215 King John of England (1199–1216) was compelled to recognize the liberties of his vassals, the clergy, and the towns in the Great Charter (*Magna Carta*). The king and his agents were forbidden to act arbitrarily, and the king swore to govern by due process of law. Similar written constitutions checking the powers of kings and princes were achieved in other parts of Europe.

The Magna Carta asserted the feudal rights of the subjects of a monarch who allegedly tried to rule by personal will rather than by law. Though many of its detailed clauses subsequently lost their significance, three notions embedded in the Magna Carta became rooted in English constitutional tradition: that the king cannot levy a tax without the consent of his feudal council (later Parliament); that no one may be imprisoned or otherwise damaged except through due process of law and trial by jury of his (or her) peers; and that the king himself is subject to the law, and if he violates the rights of his subjects, he may be legally disobeyed and deposed. Significant portions of the document follow.

1. In the first place [I, John] have granted to God and by this our present Charter have confirmed, for us and our heirs in perpetuity, that the English church shall be free, and shall have its rights undiminished and its liberties unimpaired. . . . We have also granted to all the free men of our realm for ourselves and our heirs for ever, all the liberties written below, to have and hold, them and their heirs from us and our heirs. . . .

12. No scutage[1] or aid[2] is to be levied in our realm except by the common counsel of our realm, unless it is for the ransom of our person, the knighting of our eldest son or the first marriage of our eldest daughter; and for these only a reasonable aid is to be levied. Aids from the city of London are to be treated likewise.

13. And the city of London is to have all its ancient liberties and free customs both by land and water. Furthermore, we will and grant that all other cities, boroughs, towns and ports shall have all their liberties and free customs.

14. And to obtain the common counsel of the realm for the assessment of an aid (except in the three cases aforesaid) or a scutage, we will have archbishops, bishops, abbots, earls and greater barons[3] summoned individually by our letters;

---

[1]Scutage was a tax paid by knights to the king of England, their feudal overlord, in place of performing actual military service. In the absence of danger of war, the levying of scutage was considered an abuse of the king's authority.

[2]Aid, in this sense, was any obligation, usually financial, due from a vassal to his lord. The word was later used to indicate a tax on income or property paid by his subjects to the English king.

[3]Barons were vassals holding fiefs directly from the king; earls ("counts" in other lands) were nobles who managed counties or shires.

and we shall also have summoned generally through our sheriffs and bailiffs[4] all those who hold of us in chief [hold a fief from the king], with at least forty days' notice, and at a fixed place; and in all letters of summons we will state the reason for the summons. And when the summons has thus been made, the business shall go forward on the day arranged according to the counsel of those present, even if not all those summoned have come. . . .

20. A free man shall not be amerced [fined] for a trivial offence, except in accordance with the degree of the offence; and for a serious offence he shall be amerced according to its gravity, saving his livelihood; and a merchant likewise, saving his merchandise; in the same way a villein [serf] shall be amerced saving his wainage;[5] if they fall into our mercy. And none of the aforesaid amercements shall be imposed except by the testimony of reputable men of the neighbourhood.

21. Earls and barons shall not be amerced except by their peers and only in accordance with the nature of the offence. . . .

38. Henceforth no bailiff shall put anyone on trial by his own unsupported allegation, without bringing credible witnesses to the charge.

_____

[4]The sheriff was a royal official responsible for the carrying out of laws in a shire or county; bailiffs were his assistants.
[5]*Wainage* (or *gainage*) is a collective term meaning farming tools and implements, including such things as wagons (wains).

39. No free man shall be taken or imprisoned or disseised [dispossessed] or outlawed or exiled or in any way ruined, nor will we go or send against him, except by the lawful judgement of his peers or by the law of the land.

40. To no one will we sell, to no one will we deny or delay right or justice.

41. All merchants are to be safe and secure in leaving and entering England, and in staying and travelling in England, both by land and by water, to buy and sell free from all maletotes [unjust taxes] by the ancient and rightful customs, except, in time of war, such as come from an enemy country. And if such are found in our land at the outbreak of war they shall be detained without damage to their persons or goods, until we or our chief justiciar [legal official] know how the merchants of our land are treated in the enemy country; and if ours are safe there, the others shall be safe in our land.

42. Henceforth anyone, saving his allegiance due to us, may leave our realm and return safe and secure by land and water, save for a short period in time of war on account of the general interest of the realm and excepting those imprisoned and outlawed according to the law of the land, and natives of an enemy country, and merchants, who shall be treated as aforesaid. . . .

REVIEW QUESTIONS

1. How does John of Salisbury distinguish a legitimate king from a tyrant?
2. Compare John of Salisbury's view of tyranny with Thomas Jefferson's use of the term.
3. In the selected passages of the Magna Carta, what specific liberties were guaranteed by the king to his subjects?
4. Why is this document considered a landmark in English history?

12 The Fourteenth Century: An Age of Adversity

During the Late Middle Ages, roughly the fourteenth and early fifteenth centuries, medieval civilization was in decline. The fourteenth century, an age of adversity, was marked by crop failures, famine, population decline, plagues, stagnating production, unemployment, inflation, devastating warfare, and abandoned villages. Violent rebellions by the poor of the towns and countryside were ruthlessly suppressed by the upper classes. The century witnessed flights into mysticism, outbreaks of mass hysteria, and massacres of Jews; it was an age of pessimism and general insecurity. The papacy declined in power, heresy proliferated, and the synthesis of faith and reason, erected by Christian thinkers during the High Middle Ages, began to disintegrate. These developments were signs that the stable and coherent civilization of the thirteenth century was drawing to a close.

Jean de Venette
THE BLACK DEATH

Until the fourteenth century, the population of Europe had increased steadily from its low point in the centuries immediately following the fall of the Roman Empire in the West. Particularly from the eleventh century on, landlords tried to raise their income by bringing new land into cultivation. By improving farming technology, building dikes, draining marshland, and clearing forests, European peasants produced much more food, which permitted more people to survive and multiply. That advance in population tapered off by the early fourteenth century due to many crop failures and wars, which wasted the countryside and led to economic stagnation. But the greatest catastrophe began in the fall of 1347, when sailors returning to Sicily from eastern Mediterranean ports brought with them a new disease, bubonic plague. Within the next three years, from one-quarter to one-third of the population of Europe died from what became known, because of some of its symptoms, as the Black Death. Most who caught the plague died, though some survived. No one knew its cause or cure. We now know that the bacteria were transmitted by fleas from infected rats. The unsanitary living conditions of medieval towns and low standards of personal cleanliness helped to spread the disease. The people were so terrified by the incomprehensible pattern of the disease's progress that superstition, hysteria, and breakdown of civility were common.

The progress of the plague as it made its way through Europe and speculation on its causes, the terrible toll of victims, and various moral responses to the crisis are described in the following reading from the chronicle of Jean de Venette (c. 1308–c. 1368), a French friar who lived through the events described.

In A.D. 1348, the people of France and of almost the whole world were struck by a blow other than war. For in addition to the famine which I described in the beginning and to the wars which I described in the course of this narrative, pestilence and its attendant tribulations appeared again in various parts of the world. . . . All this year and the next, the mortality of men and women, of the young even more than of the old, in Paris and in the kingdom of France, and also, it is said, in other parts of the world, was so great that it was almost impossible to bury the dead. People lay ill little more than two or three days and died suddenly, as it were in full health. He who was well one day was dead the next and being carried to his grave. Swellings appeared suddenly in the armpit or in the groin—in many cases both—and they were infallible signs of death. This sickness or pestilence was called an epidemic by the doctors. Nothing like the great numbers who died in the years 1348 and 1349 has been heard of or seen or read of in times past. This plague and disease came from *ymaginatione* or association and contagion, for if a well man visited the sick he only rarely evaded the risk of death. Wherefore in many towns timid priests withdrew, leaving the exercise of their ministry to such of the religious as were more daring. In many places not two out of twenty remained alive. So high was the mortality at the Hôtel-Dieu [an early hospital] in Paris that for a long time, more than five hundred dead were carried daily with great devotion in carts to the cemetery of the Holy Innocents in Paris for burial. A very great number of the saintly sisters of the Hôtel-Dieu who, not fearing to die, nursed the sick in all sweetness and humility, with no thought of honor, a number too often renewed by death, rest in peace with Christ, as we may piously believe.

This plague, it is said, began among the unbelievers [Muslims], came to Italy, and then crossing the Alps reached Avignon [site of the papacy in that period], where it attacked several cardinals and took from them their whole household. Then it spread, unforeseen, to France, through Gascony [now part of the south of France] and

Spain, little by little, from town to town, from village to village, from house to house, and finally from person to person. It even crossed over to Germany, though it was not so bad there as with us. During the epidemic, God of His accustomed goodness deigned to grant this grace, that however suddenly men died, almost all awaited death joyfully. Nor was there anyone who died without confessing his sins and receiving the holy viaticum [the Eucharistic bread given to the sick or dying]. . . .

Some said that this pestilence was caused by infection of the air and waters, since there was at this time no famine nor lack of food supplies, but on the contrary great abundance. As a result of this theory of infected water and air as the source of the plague the Jews were suddenly and violently charged with infecting wells and water and corrupting the air. The whole world rose up against them cruelly on this account. In Germany and other parts of the world where Jews lived, they were massacred and slaughtered by Christians, and many thousands were burned everywhere, indiscriminately. The unshaken, if fatuous, constancy of the [Jewish] men and their wives was remarkable. For mothers hurled their children first into the fire that they might not be baptized and then leaped in after them to burn with their husbands and children. It is said that many bad Christians were found who in a like manner put poison into wells. But in truth, such poisonings, granted that they actually were perpetrated, could not have caused so great a plague nor have infected so many people. There were other causes; for example, the will of God and the corrupt humors and evil inherent in air and earth. Perhaps the poisonings, if they actually took place in some localities, reenforced these causes. The plague lasted in France for the greater part of the years 1348 and 1349 and then ceased. Many country villages and many houses in good towns remained empty and deserted. Many houses, including some splendid dwellings, very soon fell into ruins. Even in Paris several houses were thus ruined, though fewer here than elsewhere.

After the cessation of the epidemic, pestilence, or plague, the men and women who survived married each other. There was no sterility among the women, but on the contrary fertility beyond the ordinary. Pregnant women were seen on every side. . . . But woe is me! the world was not changed for the better but for the worse by this renewal of population. For men were more avaricious and grasping than before, even though they had far greater possessions. They were more covetous and disturbed each other more frequently with suits, brawls, disputes, and pleas. Nor by the mortality resulting from this terrible plague inflicted by God was peace between kings and lords established. On the contrary, the enemies of the king of France and of the Church were stronger and wickeder than before and stirred up wars on sea and on land. Greater evils than before [swarmed] everywhere in the world. And this fact was very remarkable. Although there was an abundance of all goods, yet everything was twice as dear, whether it were utensils, victuals, or merchandise, hired helpers or peasants and serfs, except for some hereditary domains which remained abundantly stocked with everything. Charity began to cool, and iniquity with ignorance and sin to abound, for few could be found in the good towns and castles who knew how or were willing to instruct children in the rudiments of grammar.

Jean de Venette vividly describes one of the more bizarre reactions to the terrible plague, the sudden appearance of the Flagellants. Marching like pilgrims across the countryside, the Flagellants were a group of laymen and laywomen who sought divine pardon for their sins by preaching repentance to others and scourging themselves in a quasi-liturgical ceremony in local churches or marketplaces. The movement foreshadowed events in which moral, social, and economic discontent would increasingly manifest itself in the form of religiously justified popular uprisings against civil and clerical authorities.

In the year 1349, while the plague was still active and spreading from town to town, men in Germany, Flanders, Hainaut [east of Flanders], and Lorraine uprose and began a new sect on their own authority. Stripped to the waist, they gathered in large groups and bands and marched in procession through the crossroads and squares of cities and good towns. There they formed circles and beat upon their backs with weighted scourges, rejoicing as they did so in loud voices and singing hymns suitable to their rite and newly composed for it. Thus for thirty-three days they marched through many towns doing their penance and affording a great spectacle to the wondering people. They flogged their shoulders and arms with scourges tipped with iron points so zealously as to draw blood. But they did not come to Paris nor to any part of France, for they were forbidden to do so by the king of France, who did not want them. He acted on the advice of the masters of theology of the University of Paris, who said that this new sect had been formed contrary to the will of God, to the rites of Holy Mother Church, and to the salvation of all their souls. That indeed this was and is true appeared shortly. For Pope Clement VI was fully informed concerning this fatuous new rite by the masters of Paris through emissaries reverently sent to him and, on the grounds that it had been damnably formed, contrary to law, he forbade the Flagellants under threat of anathema [excommunication] to practise in the future the public penance which they had so presumptuously undertaken. His prohibition was just, for the Flagellants, supported by certain fatuous priests and monks, were enunciating doctrines and opinions which were beyond measure evil, erroneous, and fallacious. For example, they said that their blood thus drawn by the scourge and poured out was mingled with the blood of Christ. Their many errors showed how little they knew of the Catholic faith. Wherefore, as they had begun fatuously of themselves and not of God, so in a short time they were reduced to nothing. On being warned, they desisted and humbly received absolution and penance at the hands of their prelates as the pope's representatives. Many honorable women and devout matrons, it must be added, had done this penance with scourges, marching and singing through towns and churches like the men, but after a little like the others they desisted.

Sir John Froissart
THE PEASANT REVOLT OF 1381

In 1381, a rebellion of peasants and poor artisans in England threatened the political power of the ruling class. The rebellion, which was crushed and whose leaders were betrayed and executed, revealed the massive discontent of the lower classes and the specter of social upheaval that hovered over late medieval society. The following account of the rebellion is by Sir John Froissart (c. 1337–c. 1410), a French historian and poet who chronicled the Hundred Years' War between France and England, which wreaked havoc in the countries concerned.

While these conferences [of English nobles] were going forward there happened great commotions among the lower orders in England, by which that country was nearly ruined. In order that this disastrous rebellion may serve as an example to mankind, I will speak of all that was done from the information I had at the time. It is customary in England, as well as in several other countries, for the nobility to have great privileges over the commonality; that is to say, the lower orders are bound by law to plough the lands of the gentry, to harvest their grain, to carry it home to the barn, to thrash and winnow it; they are also bound to harvest and carry home the hay. All these services the prelates and gentlemen exact of their inferiors; and in the counties of Kent, Essex, Sussex, and Bedford, these services are more oppressive than in other parts of the kingdom. In consequence of this the evil[ly] disposed in these districts began to murmur, saying, that in the beginning of the world there were no slaves, and that no one ought to be treated as such, unless he had committed treason against his lord, as Lucifer had done against God; but they had done no such thing, for they were neither angels nor spirits, but men formed after the same likeness as these lords who treated them as beasts. This they would bear no longer; they were determined to be free, and if they laboured or did any work, they would be paid for it. A crazy priest in the county of Kent, called John

Ball, who for his absurd preaching had thrice been confined in prison by the Archbishop of Canterbury, was greatly instrumental in exciting these rebellious ideas. Every Sunday after mass, as the people were coming out of church, this John Ball was accustomed to assemble a crowd around him in the market-place and preach to them. On such occasions he would say, "My good friends, matters cannot go on well in England until all things shall be in common; when there shall be neither vassals nor lords; when the lords shall be no more masters than ourselves. How ill they behave to us! for what reason do they thus hold us in bondage? Are we not all descended from the same parents, Adam and Eve? And what can they show, or what reason can they give, why they should be more masters than ourselves? They are clothed in velvet and rich stuffs, ornamented with ermine and other furs, while we are forced to wear poor clothing. They have wines, spices, and fine bread, while we have only rye and the refuse of the straw; and when we drink, it must be water. They have handsome seats and manors, while we must brave the wind and rain in our labours in the field; and it is by our labour they have wherewith to support their pomp. We are called slaves, and if we do not perform our service we are beaten, and we have no sovereign to whom we can complain or who would be willing to hear us. Let us go to the king and remonstrate with him; he is young, and from him we may obtain a favourable answer, and if not we must ourselves seek to amend our condition." With such language as this did John Ball harangue the people of his village every Sunday after mass. The archbishop, on being informed of it, had him arrested and imprisoned for two or three months by way of punishment; but the moment he was out of prison, he returned to his former course. Many in the city of London envious of the rich and noble, having heard of John Ball's preaching, said among themselves that the country was badly governed, and that the nobility had seized upon all the gold and silver. These wicked Londoners, therefore, began to assemble in parties, and to show signs of rebellion; they also invited all those who held like opinions in the adjoining counties to come to London; telling them that they would find the town open to them and the commonalty of the same way of thinking as themselves, and that they would so press the king, that there should no longer be a slave in England.

By this means the men of Kent, Essex, Sussex, Bedford, and the adjoining counties, in number about 60,000, were brought to London, under command of Wat Tyler, Jack Straw, and John Ball. This Wat Tyler, who was chief of the three, had been a tiler of houses—a bad man and a great enemy to the nobility. . . .

With regard to the common people of London, numbers entertained these rebellious opinions, and on assembling at the bridge asked of the guards, "Why will you refuse admittance to these honest men? they are our friends, and what they are doing is for our good." So urgent were they, that it was found necessary to open the gates, when crowds rushed in and took possession of those shops which seemed best stocked with provisions; indeed, wherever they went, meat and drink were placed before them, and nothing was refused in the hope of appeasing them. Their leaders, John Ball, Jack Straw, and Wat Tyler, then marched through London, attended by more than 20,000 men, to the palace of the Savoy, which is a handsome building belonging to the Duke of Lancaster

[the king's uncle], situated on the banks of the Thames on the road to Westminster: here they immediately killed the porters, pushed into the house, and set it on fire. Not content with this outrage, they went to the house of the Knight-hospitalers of Rhodes, dedicated to St. John of Mount Carmel, which they burnt together with their church and hospital.

After this they paraded the streets, and killed every Fleming [citizen of Flanders] they could find, whether in house, church, or hospital: they broke open several houses of the Lombards [Italian bankers], taking whatever money they could lay their hands upon. They murdered a rich citizen, by name Richard Lyon, to whom Wat Tyler had formerly been servant in France, but having once beaten him, the [scoundrel] had never forgotten it; and when he had carried his men to his house, he ordered his head to be cut off, placed upon a pike, and carried through the streets of London. Thus did these wicked people act, and on this Thursday they did much damage to the city of London. Towards evening they fixed their quarters in a square, called St. Catherine's, before the Tower, declaring that they would not depart until they had obtained from the king every thing they wanted—until the Chancellor [chief financial officer] of England had accounted to them, and shown how the great sums which were raised had been expended. Considering the mischief which the mob had already done, you may easily imagine how miserable, at this time, was the situation of the king and those who were with him. . . .

. . . Now observe how fortunately matters turned out, for had these scoundrels succeeded in their intentions, all the nobility of England would have been destroyed; and after such success as this the people of other nations would have rebelled also, taking example from those of Ghent and Flanders, who at the time were in actual rebellion against their lord; the Parisians indeed the same year acted in a somewhat similar manner; upwards of 20,000 of them armed themselves with leaden maces and caused a rebellion. . . .

John Wycliffe
CHALLENGING PAPAL AUTHORITY

A threat to papal power and to the medieval ideal of a universal Christian community guided by the church came from radical reformers, who questioned the function and authority of the entire church hierarchy. These heretics in the Late Middle Ages were forerunners of the Protestant Reformation.

A principal dissenter was the Englishman John Wycliffe (c. 1320–1384). By stressing a personal relationship between the individual and God and by claiming that the Bible itself, rather than church teachings, is the ultimate Christian authority, Wycliffe challenged the fundamental position of the medieval church: that the avenue to salvation passed through the church alone. He denounced the wealth of the higher clergy and sought a return to the spiritual purity and material poverty of the early church. To Wycliffe, the wealthy, elaborately organized hierarchy of the church was unnecessary and wrong. The splendidly dressed and propertied bishops had no resemblance to the simple people who first followed Christ. Indeed, these worldly bishops, headed by a princely and tyrannical pope, were really anti-Christians, the "fiends of Hell." Wycliffe wanted the state to confiscate church property and the clergy to embrace poverty. By denying that priests changed the bread and wine of communion into the substance of the body and blood of Christ, Wycliffe rejected the special powers of the clergy.

The church deprived the Lollards—an order of poor priests that spread Wycliffe's teachings—of their priestly functions. In the early fifteenth century, some of Wycliffe's followers were burned at the stake.

In the following selection from a pamphlet concerning the pope, Wycliffe contrasts the pope unfavorably with Jesus. The text, originally written in Middle English, was rendered into Modern English by Alfred J. Andrea. The explanatory notes are Andrea's.

Christ was a very poor man from His birth to His death and forswore worldly riches and begging,[1] in accord with the state of primal innocence,[2] but Antichrist, in contrast to this, from the time that he is made pope to the time of his death, covets worldly wealth and tries in many shrewd ways to gain riches. Christ was a most meek man and urged that we learn from Him, but people say that the pope is the proudest man on earth, and he makes lords kiss his feet,[3] whereas Christ washed His apostles' feet. Christ was a most unpretentious man in life, deeds, and words. People say that this pope is not like Christ in this way, for whereas Christ went on foot to cities and little towns alike, they say this pope desires to live in a castle in a grand manner. Whereas Christ came to John the Baptist to be baptized by him, the pope summons people to come to him wherever he might be, yea, as

[1] Apparently, an oblique attack on the mendicant friars, who claimed to follow a life of Apostolic Poverty in imitation of Jesus and his apostles. Wycliffe despised the friars.
[2] The presumed innocence of Adam and Eve before the Fall.

[3] A long-standing tradition.

though Christ Himself, and not the pope, had summoned them to Him. Christ embraced young and poor in token of his humility; people say that the pope desires to embrace worldly prestige and not good people for the sake of God, lest he dishonor himself. Christ was busy preaching the Gospel, and not for worldly prestige or for profit; people say that the pope allows this, but he would gladly make laws to which he gives more prestige and sanction than Christ's law. Christ so loved His flock that He laid down his life for them and suffered sharp pain and death in order to bring them to bliss. People say that the pope so loves the prestige of this world that he grants people absolution that guarantees a straight path to Heaven[4] so that they might perform acts that redound to his honor. And so this foolishiness could be the cause of the death, in body and soul, of many thousands of people. And how does he follow

Christ in this way? Christ was so patient and suffered wrongs so well that He prayed for His enemies and taught His apostles not to take vengeance. People say that the pope of Rome wishes to be avenged in every way, by killing and by damning and by other painful means that he devises. Christ taught people to live well by the example of His own life and by His words, for He did what He taught and taught in a manner that was consonant with His actions. People say that the pope acts contrary to this. His life is not an example of how other people should live, for no one should live like him, inasmuch as he acts in a manner that accords to his high state. In every deed and word, Christ sought the glory of God and suffered many assaults on His manhood for this goal; people say that the pope, to the contrary, seeks his own glory in every way, yea, even if it means the loss of the worship of God. And so he manufactures many groundless gabblings.

If these and similar accusations are true of the pope of Rome, he is the very Antichrist and not Christ's vicar on earth.

---

[4]A reference to the Roman Church's indulgences, which had become increasingly systemized and popular during the twelfth and thirteenth centuries (see page 335).

Peter of les Vaux-de-Cernay
EXTERMINATING THE CATHARS

Catharism (also known as Albegensianism) was the most radical heresy to confront the medieval church. This belief represented a curious mixture of Gnosticism and Manicheanism—Eastern religious movements that had competed with Christianity in the days of the Roman Empire—and of doctrines considered heretical by the early church. Carried to Italy and southern France by Bulgarian missionaries, Catharism gained followers in regions where opposition to the worldliness and wealth of the clergy was already strong.

Cathari tenets differed considerably from those of the church as the first selection from Peter of les Vaux-de Cernay's *Historia Albigensis* (History of the Albigensian Crusade), written between about 1212 and 1218, illustrates. The author, a Cistercian monk, witnessed many of the events described in his narration.

First it should be understood that the heretics maintained the existence of two creators, one of things invisible whom they called the 'benign' God and one of the things visible whom they named the 'malign' God. They attributed the New Testament to the benign God and the Old Testament to the malign God, and rejected the whole of the latter except for certain passages quoted in the New Testament. These they considered acceptable because of their respect for the New Testament. They maintained that the author of the Old Testament was a 'liar'; he said to our first ancestors 'on the day that ye eat of the tree of the knowledge of good and evil, ye shall surely die'; but they did not die after eating the fruit as he had predicted (although, of course, the real truth is that as soon as they had tasted the forbidden fruit they became subject to the misery of death). They also called him 'murderer' because he exterminated the inhabitants of Sodom and Gomorrah by fire and destroyed the world by the waters of the flood; and because he drowned Pharaoh and the Egyptians in the sea. They declared that all the patriarchs of the Old Testament were damned; they asserted that St John the Baptist was one of the chief devils.

Further, in their secret meetings they said that the Christ who was born in the earthly and visible Bethlehem and crucified at Jerusalem was 'evil', and that Mary Magdalene was his concubine—and that she was the woman taken in adultery who is referred to in the Scriptures; the 'good' Christ, they said, neither ate nor drank nor assumed the true flesh and was never in this world, except spiritually in the body of Paul. I have used the term 'the earthly and visible Bethlehem' because the heretics believed there is a different and invisible earth in which—according to some of them—the 'good' Christ was born and crucified. Again, they said that the good God had two wives, Oolla and Ooliba, on whom he begat sons and daughters. There were other heretics who said that there was only one Creator, but that he had two sons, Christ and the Devil; they said moreover that

all created beings had once been good, but that everything had been corrupted by the vials referred to in the Book of Revelations.

All these people, the limbs of the Antichrist, the first-born of Satan, the seed of evildoers, children that are corrupters, speaking lies in hypocrisy, the seducers of simple hearts, had infected almost the whole of the province of Narbonne with the poison of their perfidy. They said that the Roman Church was a den of thieves, and the harlot spoken of in the Book of Revelations. They ridiculed the sacraments of the Church, arguing publicly that the holy water of baptism was no better than river water, that the consecrated host of the holy body of Christ was no different from common bread; instilling into the ears of simple folk the blasphemy that the body of Christ, even if it had been large enough to contain the whole Alps, would by now be wholly consumed and reduced to nothing by those eating of it. They considered that confirmation, extreme unction and confession were trivial and empty ceremonies; they preached that holy matrimony was mere harlotry, and that no one could find salvation in it by begetting sons and daughters. They denied the resurrection of the body, and invented new myths, claiming that our souls are really those angelic spirits who were driven from heaven through their rebellious pride and then left their glorified bodies in the ether; and that these souls after successively inhabiting any seven earthly bodies will then return to their original bodies, as though they had then completed their long penance.

It should be understood that some of the heretics were called 'perfected' heretics or 'good men', others 'believers of the heretics'. The 'perfected' heretics wore a black robe, claimed (falsely) to practice chastity, and renounced meat, eggs and cheese. They wished it to appear that they were not liars although they lied, especially about God, almost unceasingly! They also said that no one should take oaths for any reason. The term 'believers' was applied to those who lived a secular existence and did not try to copy the way of life of the 'perfected', but hoped that by following their faith they would attain salvation; they were separated in the way they lived, but united in their beliefs—or rather unbelief! Those called 'believers' were dedicated to usury, robbery, murder and illicit love, and to all kinds of perjury and perversity; indeed they felt they could sin in safety and without restraint, because they believed they could be saved without restitution of what they had stolen and without confession and penitence, so long as they were able to recite the Lord's prayer and ensure a 'laying-on of hands' by their masters, in the final moments of their lives.

To explain further, they selected from the 'perfected' heretics officials whom they called 'deacons' and 'bishops', and the 'believers' held that no one of them could attain salvation without the laying-on of hands by these clergy just before death; indeed, they considered that however sinful a man might have been, then provided he had undergone this laying-on of hands on his deathbed, and so long as he was able to recite the Lord's prayer, he would gain salvation and (to use their own expression) 'consolation'; to the extent that he would immediately fly up to heaven without making any amends or reparations for wrongs he had committed.

When the Cathari did not submit to peaceful persuasion, Innocent III called on kings and lords to exterminate Catharism with the sword. Lasting from 1208 to 1229 the war against the Cathari in southern France was marked by brutality and fanaticism, as Peter describes in the passage below. Command of the crusading army soon passed to Simon de Montfort, a minor baron with great ambition. De Montfort's army slaughtered suspected heretics throughout the county of Toulouse effectively breaking the power of the nobles who protected the heretics. Innocent III sent legates to the region to arrest and try the Cathari. Under his successor, Dominican and Franciscan inquisitors completed the task of extermination.

Our Count now entered Minerve and went to the place where the heretics were gathered. As a true Catholic he wished them all to win salvation and come to know the way of truth, and he began to urge them to be converted to the Catholic faith. When he could make no progress, he had them taken out of the *castrum*. There were at least a hundred and forty perfected heretics. A huge pyre was made ready, and all were thrown on it—indeed there was no need for our soldiers to throw them on, since they were so hardened in their wickedness that they rushed into the fire of their own accord. Three women only were rescued, whom the noble lady the mother of Bouchard de Marly snatched from the flames and reconciled to the Holy Church. So the heretics were burnt; all the other inhabitants renounced heresy and were reconciled to the Church.

Marsilius of Padua
ATTACK ON THE WORLDLY POWER OF THE CHURCH

The fourteenth century brought a new crisis in church–state relations. King Philip the Fair (1285–1314) tried to raise revenues for the French government by taxing the property and income of the clergy without papal consent, efforts that were resisted by Pope Boniface VIII (1294–1303). When Boniface threatened to excommunicate all who cooperated in such tax collection, the king cut off all papal revenue from France. The struggle continued throughout Boniface's pontificate, ending in an attack in 1303 by French agents on the papal residence in Anagni, Italy, during which the aged pope was physically assaulted. The bitter struggle called forth a series of responses from both sides describing their respective positions on the proper relationship between state and church. Papal theorists, of course, emphasized the superiority of the spiritual power of the church over the temporal power of the state, and insisted that it was the duty of earthly authority to aid the church in the performance of its spiritual duties.

In *The Defender of the Peace*, Marsilius of Padua (c. 1275–1342) made a radical break with traditional medieval political thought. Marsilius argued that Christ never intended that his Apostles or their successors, the bishops, should exercise temporal power. Political life operated according to its own principles and required no guidance from a higher authority; therefore, he said that the state should not be made to conform to standards formulated by the church. For Marsilius, the church was solely a spiritual institution; it possessed no temporal power, and the clergy were not above the laws of the state. Pope John XXII branded him a heretic for publishing this work, and Marsilius was forced to seek the protection of the German prince, Louis of Bavaria. In the following passage, Marsilius outlines the relationship between church and state established by Christ.

. . . I shall first show, that Christ himself came into the world not to dominate men, nor to judge them by [temporal] judgment . . . nor to wield temporal rule, but rather to be subject as regards the status of the present life; and moreover, that he wanted to and did exclude himself, his apostles and disciples, and their successors, the bishops and priests, from all such coercive authority or worldly rule, both by his example and by his words of counsel or command. I shall also show that the leading apostles, as Christ's true imitators, did this same thing and taught their successors to do likewise; and moreover, that both Christ and the apostles wanted to be and were continuously subject in property and in person to the coercive jurisdiction of secular rulers, and that they taught and commanded all others, to whom they preached or wrote the law of truth, to do likewise, under pain of eternal damnation. Then I shall write a chapter on the power or authority of the keys which Christ gave to the apostles and their successors in office, bishops and priests, so that it may be clear what is the nature, quality, and extent of such power, both of the Roman bishop and of the others. For ignorance on this point has hitherto been and still is the source of many questions and damnable controversies among the Christian faithful, as was mentioned in the first chapter of this discourse.

And so in pursuit of these aims we wish to show that Christ, in his purposes or intentions, words, and deeds, wished to exclude and did exclude himself and the apostles from every office of rulership, contentious jurisdiction, government, or coercive judgment in this world. This is first shown clearly beyond any doubt by the passage in the eighteenth chapter of the gospel of John. For when Christ was brought before Pontius Pilate, vicar of the Roman ruler in Judea, and accused of having called himself king of the Jews, Pontius asked him whether he had said this, or whether he did call himself a king, and Christ's reply included these words, among others: "My kingdom is not of this world," that is, I have not come to reign by temporal rule or dominion, in the way in which worldly kings reign. And proof of this was given by Christ himself through an evident sign when he said: "If my kingdom were of this world, my servants would certainly fight, that I should not be delivered to the Jews," as if to argue as follows: If I had come into this world to reign by worldly or coercive rule, I would have ministers for this rule, namely, men to fight and to coerce transgressors, as the other kings have; but I do not have such ministers, as you can clearly see. . . .

. . . It now remains to show that not only did Christ himself refuse rulership or coercive judgment in this world, whereby he furnished an example for his apostles and disciples and their successors to do likewise, but also he taught by words and showed by example that all men, both priests and non-priests, should be subject in property and in person to the coercive judgment of the rulers of this world. By his word and example, then, Christ showed this first with respect to property, by what is written in the twenty-second chapter of Matthew. For when the Jews asked him: "Tell us therefore, what dost thou think? Is it lawful to give tribute to Caesar, or not?" Christ, after looking at the coin and its inscription, replied: "Render therefore to Caesar the things that are Caesar's, and to God the things that are God's." . . . So, then, we ought to be subject to Caesar in all things, so long only as they are not contrary to piety, that is, to divine worship or commandment. Therefore, Christ

wanted us to be subject in property to the secular ruler. . . .

Like Christ and the apostles, then, the Roman bishops and priests and the whole clergy of Rome and the other provinces used to live under the coercive government of those who were the rulers by authority of the human legislator. But later on, certain Roman bishops succumbed to the persuasion and incitation of that ruler of this world, that first parent of arrogance and presumption, that inculcator of all vices, the devil; and they were led, or rather misled, to a path foreign to that of Christ and the apostles. For cupidity and avarice, invading their minds, expelled therefrom that supreme meritorious poverty which Christ had introduced and established in the church. . . . And again, pride and ambition for secular rule, invading their minds, expelled therefrom that supreme humility which Christ had enjoined and commanded the church or whole priesthood to maintain.

This, then, as we have said, is and was the primary source of the present strife and discord between the emperors and the Roman pontiffs, since the controversies over the divine law and over the heresies of certain rulers have died out entirely. For the Roman bishops wrongly wish to possess excessive temporal goods, and refuse to be subject to the laws and edicts of the rulers or the human legislator, thereby opposing the example and teaching of Christ and the apostles. . . .

REVIEW QUESTIONS

1. In the absence of any scientific knowledge about the nature and causes of the bubonic plague, how did the populace react to the mysterious spread of the disease?
2. In the chronicler's opinion, what were some of the long-term moral, social, and economic consequences of the plague?
3. What specific grievances motivated uprisings in England in the late fourteenth century?
4. What political principles were invoked by the leaders of the rebellion of 1381 to justify their demands and actions?
5. Why was John Wycliffe critical of the church? Why did the church regard his teachings as a serious threat to its mission?
6. What church doctrines did the proponents of Catharism repudiate? How did they believe salvation could be achieved? Why did the church call for their extermination?

7. What arguments did Marsilius use to strip the church of its practice of holding or claiming temporal political authority?
8. In Marsilius' opinion, who or what was to blame for the church's claim to exercise temporal political authority?

13 The Medieval World-View

The modern world is linked in many ways to the Middle Ages. European cities, the middle class, the state system, English common law, representative institutions, universities—all had their origins in the Middle Ages. Despite these elements of continuity, the characteristic outlook of medieval people is markedly different from that of people today. Whereas science and secularism shape the modern point of view, religion was the foundation of the Middle Ages. Christian beliefs as formulated by the church made life and death purposeful and intelligible.

Medieval thinkers drew a sharp distinction between a higher, spiritual world and a lower, material world. God, the creator of the universe and the source of moral values, dwelled in the higher celestial world, an abode of perfection. The universe was organized as a hierarchy with God at the summit and hell at the other extremity. Earth, composed of base matter, stood just above hell. By believing in Christ and adhering to God's commandments as taught by the church, people could overcome their sinful nature and ascend to God's world. Sinners, on the other hand, would descend to hell, a fearful place the existence of which medieval people never doubted.

Scholastic philosophy, which sought to demonstrate through reason the truth of Christian doctrines, and the Gothic cathedral, which seemed to soar from the material world to heaven, were two great expressions of the medieval mind. A third was *The Divine Comedy* of Dante Alighieri, the greatest literary figure of the Middle Ages.

Lothario dei Segni (Pope Innocent III)
ON THE MISERY OF THE HUMAN CONDITION

At the center of medieval belief was the image of a perfect God and a wretched and sinful human being. God had given Adam and Eve freedom to choose; rebellious and presumptuous, they had used their freedom to disobey God. In doing so, they made evil an intrinsic part of the human personality. But God, who had not stopped loving human beings, showed them the way out of sin. God became man and died so that human beings might be saved. Men and women were weak, egocentric, and sinful. With God's grace they could overcome their sinful nature and gain salvation; without grace they were utterly helpless. A classic expression of this pessimistic view of human nature was written in the late twelfth century by an Italian canon lawyer, Lotario dei Segni (c. 1160–1216), who was later elected pope in 1198, taking the name Innocent III. His *On the Misery of the Human Condition* was enormously popular and inspired numerous rhetorical writings on the same theme as late as the seventeenth century. Scattered excerpts follow.

• For sure man was formed out of earth, conceived in guilt, born to punishment. What he does is depraved and illicit, is shameful and improper, vain and unprofitable. He will become fuel for the eternal fires, food for worms, a mass of rottenness.

I shall try to make my explanation clearer and my treatment fuller. Man was formed of dust, slime, and ashes; what is even more vile, of the filthiest seed. He was conceived from the itch of the flesh, in the heat of passion and the stench of lust, and worse yet, with the stain of sin. He was born to toil, dread, and trouble; and more wretched still, was born only to die. He commits depraved acts by which he offends God, his neighbor, and himself; shameful acts by which he defiles his name, his person, and his conscience; and vain acts by which he ignores all things important, useful, and necessary. He will become fuel for those fires which are forever hot and burn forever bright; food for the worm which forever nibbles and digests; a mass of rottenness which will forever stink and reek.

• A bird is born to fly; man is born to toil. All his days are full of toil and hardship, and at night his mind has no rest.

• How much anxiety tortures mortals! They suffer all kinds of cares, are burdened with worry, tremble and shrink with fears and terrors, are weighted down with sorrow. Their nervousness makes them depressed, and their depression makes them nervous. Rich or poor, master or slave, married or single, good and bad alike—all suffer worldly torments and are tormented by worldly vexations.

• For sudden sorrow always follows worldly joy: what begins in gaiety ends in grief. Worldly happiness is besprinkled indeed with much bitterness.

• Then, suddenly, when least expected, misfortune strikes, a calamity befalls us, disease attacks; or death, which no one can escape, carries us off.

• Men strive especially for three things: riches, pleasures, and honors. Riches lead to immorality, pleasures to shame, and honors to vanity.

• But suppose a man is lifted up high, suppose he is raised to the very peak. At once his cares grow heavy, his worries mount up, he eats less and cannot sleep. And so nature is corrupted, his spirit weakened, his sleep disturbed, his appetite lost; his strength is diminished, he loses weight. Exhausting himself, he scarcely lives half a lifetime and ends his wretched days with a more wretched death.

• Almost the whole life of mortals is full of mortal sin, so that one can scarcely find anyone who does not go astray, does not return to his own vomit and rot in his own dung. Instead they "are glad when they have done evil and rejoice in most wicked things." "Being filled with all iniquity, malice, fornication, avarice, wickedness, full of envy, murders, contention, deceit, evil, being whisperers, detractors, hateful to God, irreverent, proud, haughty, plotters of evil, disobedient to parents, foolish, dissolute, without affection, without fidelity, without mercy." This world is full of such and worse; it abounds in heretics and schismatics [Christians who reject the authority of the pope], traitors and tyrants, simonists [buyers or sellers of spiritual offices or sacred items] and hypocrites; the ambitious and the covetous, robbers and brigands, violent men, extortionists, usurers, forgers; the impious and sacreligious, the betrayers and liars, the flatterers and deceivers; gossips, tricksters, gluttons, drunkards; adulterers, incestuous men, deviates, and the dirty-minded; the lazy, the careless, the vain, the prodigal, the impetuous, the irascible, the impatient and inconstant; poisoners, fortune tellers, perjurers, cursers; men who are presumptuous and arrogant, unbelieving and desperate; and finally those ensnared in all vices together.

THE VANITY OF THIS WORLD

The following poem, written in Latin by an unknown thirteenth-century author, expresses the medieval rejection of earthly pursuits and preoccupation with the world to come.

Why does the world war for glory that's vain?
All its successes wax only to wane;
Quickly its triumphs are frittered away,
Like vessels the potter casts out of frail clay.

As well trust to letters imprinted in ice
As trust the frail world with its treacherous
    device,
Its prizes a fraud and its values all wrong;
Who would put faith in its promise for
    long?

Rather in hardship's uncertain distress
Trust than in this world's unhappy success;
With dreams and with shadows it leads men
    astray,
A cheat in our work and a cheat at our play.
Where now is Samson's invincible arm,
And where is Jonathan's sweet-natured charm?
Once-famous Solomon, where now is he
Or the fair Absolom, so good to see?[1]

Whither is Caesar the great Emperor fled,
Or Croesus whose show on his table was
    spread?
Cicero's eloquence now is in vain;[2]
Where's Aristotle's magnificent brain?

All those great noblemen, all those past days,
All kings' achievements and all prelates' praise,
All the world's princes in all their array—
In the flash of an eye comes the end of the play.

Short is the season of all earthly fame;
Man's shadow, man's pleasure, they both are the
    same,
And the prizes eternal he gives in exchange
For the pleasure that leads to a land that is
    strange.

Food for the worms, dust and ashes, O why,
Bubble on water, be lifted so high?
Do good unto all men as long as ye may;
Ye know not your life will last after to-day.

This pride of the flesh which so dearly ye prize,
Like the flower of the grass (says the Scripture),
    it dies,

---

[1]In the Old Testament, Samson was the warrior hero of the Israelites; Jonathan was the son of King Saul and the loving friend of David; Solomon was the king of Israel, famous for his wisdom; and Absalom was the most beloved son of David.

---

[2]Croesus was a king of ancient Lydia renowned for his wealth. For Cicero, see page 114.

Or as the dry leaf which the wind whirls away,
Man's life is swept out from the light
  of the day.

Call not your own what one day ye may lose;
The world will take back all it gives you
  to use.

Let your hearts be in heaven, your thoughts in
  the skies;
Happy is he who the world can despise.

Dante Alighieri
THE DIVINE COMEDY

Dante Alighieri was a poet, political philosopher, soldier, and politician. Born
in 1265 in Florence, Italy, he died in exile in 1321. His greatest work, *The
Divine Comedy*, was composed of one hundred cantos (individual poems) and
written not in Latin, the language of learning, but in the Tuscan Italian dialect
of the common people. The poem is an elaborate allegory in which each character and event can be understood on two or more levels—for example, a literal
description of the levels of hell and Dante's (and every Christian's) struggle to overcome a flawed human nature and to ward off worldly sin. Dante, representing all
human beings, is guided through the afterworlds: hell (inferno), purgatory, and
heaven (paradise). The Roman poet Virgil conducts him through hell and purgatory; Beatrice, his long-dead beloved, leads him through heaven to the point
where he sees God in all his glory.

In the descent through the nine concentric circles of hell, Virgil describes the
nature and significance of each region through which they pass. In each section of hell, sinners are punished in proportion to their earthly sins. Over the
entrance gate to hell, Dante reads these words:

THROUGH ME YOU GO INTO THE CITY OF
  GRIEF,
THROUGH ME YOU GO INTO THE PAIN THAT
  IS ETERNAL,
THROUGH ME YOU GO AMONG PEOPLE LOST.

JUSTICE MOVED MY EXALTED CREATOR;
THE DIVINE POWER MADE ME,
THE SUPREME WISDOM, AND THE PRIMAL
  LOVE.

BEFORE ME ALL CREATED THINGS WERE
  ETERNAL,

AND ETERNAL I WILL LAST.
ABANDON EVERY HOPE, YOU WHO ENTER
  HERE.

Dante descends from the first circle to the second circle, where he finds the souls of those
who had been guilty of sins of the flesh.

Now I begin to hear the sad notes of pain,
now I have come to where
loud cries beat upon my ears.

I have reached a place mute of all light
which roars like the sea in a tempest
when beaten by conflicting winds.

The infernal storm which never stops
drives the spirit in its blast;
whirling and beating, it torments them.

When they come in front of the landslide,
they utter laments, moans, and shrieks;
there they curse the Divine Power.

I learned that to such a torment
carnal sinners are condemned
who subject their reason to desire.

And, as starlings are borne by their wings
in the cold season, in a broad and dense flock,
so that blast carries the evil spirits.

Here, there, up, and down, it blows them;
no hope ever comforts them
of rest or even of less pain.

And as cranes go chanting their lays,
making a long line of themselves in the air,
so I saw coming, uttering laments,
shades borne by that strife of winds.

Finally the two poets reach the ninth and
lowest circle, a frozen wasteland reserved
for Satan and traitors.

". . . look ahead,"
my master [Virgil] said, "and try to
discern him."

As, when a thick mist covers the land
or when night darkens our hemisphere,
a windmill, turning, appears from afar,

so now I seemed to see such a structure;
then because of the wind, I drew back
behind my guide, for there was no other
    protection.

Already—and with fear I put it into verse—
I was where the shades are covered in the ice
and show through like bits of straw in glass.

Some were lying, some standing erect,
some on their heads, others on their feet,
still others like a bow bent face to toes.

When we had gone so far ahead
that my master was pleased to show me
the creature (Lucifer)[1] that once had been
    so fair,

he stood from in front of me, and made me
    stop,
saying, "Behold, Dis![2] Here is the place
where you must arm yourself with courage."

How faint and frozen I then became,
do not ask, Reader, for I do not write it down,
since all words would be inadequate.

I did not die and did not stay alive:
think now for yourself, if you have the wit,
how I became, without life or death.

The emperor of the dolorous realm
from mid-breast protruded from the ice,
and I compare better in size

with the giants than they do with his arms.
Consider how big the whole must be,
proportioned as it is to such a part.

If he were once as handsome as he is ugly now,
and still presumed to lift his hand against his
    Maker,
all affliction must indeed come from him.

Oh, how great a marvel appeared to me
when I saw three faces on his head!
The one in front (hatred) was fiery red;

the two others which were joined to it
over the middle of each shoulder
were fused together at the top.

The right one (impotence) seemed between
    white and yellow;

---

[1]Lucifer (light-bringer) was an archangel who led a rebellion against God and was cast into hell for punishment. He was identified with Satan.
[2]Dis was another name for Pluto or Hades, the god of the dead and ruler of the underworld.

the left (ignorance) was in color like those
who come from where the Nile rises.

Under each two great wings spread
of a size fitting to such a bird;
I have never seen such sails on the sea.

They had no feathers, and seemed
like those of a bat, and they flapped,
so that three blasts came from them.

Thence all Cocytus[3] was frozen.
With six eyes he wept, and over his three
   chins
he let tears drip and bloody foam.

In each mouth he chewed a sinner with
   his teeth
in the manner of a hemp brake,[4]
so that he kept three in pain.

To the one in front the biting was nothing
compared to the scratching, for at times,
his back was stripped of skin.

"The soul up there with the greatest
   punishment,"
said my master, "is Judas Iscariot.[5] His head
is inside the mouth, and he kicks with his legs.

Of the other two whose heads are down,
the one hanging from the black face is Brutus;[6]
see how he twists and says nothing.

The other who seems so heavy set is Cassius.[7]
But night is rising again now,
and it is time to leave, for we have seen all."

Dante and Beatrice make the ascent to the
highest heaven, the Empyrean, which is
located beyond Saturn, the last of the seven
planets, beyond the circle of stars that en-
closes the planets, and above the Primum
Mobile—the outermost sphere revolving
around the earth. Here at the summit of the
universe is a realm of pure light that radiates
truth, goodness, and happiness, where God
is found. Dante is permitted to look at God,
but words cannot describe "the glory of Him
who moves us all."

For my sight, growing pure, penetrated
ever deeper into the rays
of the Light [God] which is true in Itself.

From then on my vision was greater
than our speech which fails at such a sight,
just as memory is overcome by the excess.

As one who in a dream sees clearly,
and the feeling impressed remains afterward,
although nothing else comes back to mind,

so am I; for my vision disappears
almost wholly, and yet the sweetness
caused by it is still distilled within my heart.

Thus, in sunlight, the snow melts away;
thus the sayings of the Sibyl [a Roman
   oracle], written
on light leaves, were lost in the wind.

O Supreme Light that risest so high
above mortal concepts, give back to
   my mind
a little of what Thou didst appear,

and make my tongue strong,
so that it may leave to future peoples
at least a spark of Thy glory!

For, by returning to my memory
and by sounding a little in these verses
more of Thy victory will be conceived.

By the keenness of the living ray I endured
I believe I would have been dazed
if my eyes had turned away from it;

and I remember that I was bolder
because of that to sustain the view

---

[3]The Cocytus, a river in western Greece, was alleged to
lead to the underworld.
[4]A hemp brake was a tool used to break up hemp fibers so
that they could be made into rope.
[5]Judas Iscariot was the disciple who betrayed Jesus to the
authorities.
[6]Brutus, a first-century Roman statesman, conspired to
murder Julius Caesar.
[7]Cassius, another Roman statesman, was a co-conspirator
with Brutus.

until my sight *attained* the Infinite Worth
[God].

O abundant grace through which I presumed
to fix my eyes on the Eternal Light
so long that I consumed my vision on it!

In its depths I saw contained, bound with
love
in one volume, what is scattered
on leaves throughout the world—

substances (things) and accidents (qualities)
and their modes
as if fused together in such a way
that what I speak of is a single light.

The universal form (principle) of this unity
I believe I saw, because more abundantly
in saying this I feel that I rejoice.

One moment obscures more for me than
twenty-five centuries
have clouded since the adventure which made
Neptune [the sea god]
wonder at the shadow of the Argo (the first
ship).[8]

Thus my mind with rapt attention
gazed fixedly, motionless and attentive,
continually enflamed by its very gazing.

In that light we become such
that we can never consent
to turn from it for another sight,

inasmuch as the good which is the object
of the will is all in it, and outside of it
whatever is perfect there is defective.

Now my speech, even for what I remember,
will be shorter than that of an infant
who still bathes his tongue at the breast.

Not that more than a single semblance
was in the living light I gazed upon
(for it is always as it was before),

but in my vision which gained strength
as I looked the single appearance,
through a change in me, was transformed.

Within the deep and clear subsistence
of the great light three circles of three colors
and of one dimension (the Trinity) appeared
to me,

and one (the Son) seemed reflected from the
other (the Father)
as Iris by Iris,[9] and the third (the Holy
Spirit)
seemed fire emanating equally from both.

O how poor our speech is and how feeble
for my conception! Compared to what I saw
to say its power is "little" is to say too
much.

O Eternal Light (Father), abiding in Thyself
alone,
Thou (Son) alone understanding Thyself, and
Thou (Holy Spirit)
understood only by Thee, Thou dost love and
smile!

The circle which appeared in Thee
as a reflected light (the Son)
when contemplated a while

seemed depicted with our image within
itself
and of its own (the Circle's) color,
so that my eyes were wholly fixed on it.

Like the geometer who strives
to square the circle and cannot find
by thinking the principle he needs

---

[8]The *Argo*, in Greek legends, was the ship in which the hero Jason and his companions sailed in search of the Golden Fleece. A Greek poet, Apollonius of Rhodes, wrote an epic poem, the *Argonautica*, about it in the mid-third century B.C.

[9]Iris, goddess of the rainbow, was the messenger of the gods.

I was at that new sight. I wanted to see
how the (human) image was conformed
to the (divine) circle and has a place in it,

but my own wings were not enough for
that—
except that my mind was illuminated by
a flash

(of Grace) through which its wish was
realized.

For the great imagination here power failed;
but already my desire and will (in harmony)
were turning like a wheel moved evenly

by the Love which turns the sun and the other
stars.

REVIEW QUESTIONS

1. Compare Innocent III's view of the human condition with that of ancient Greeks such as Homer, Pindar, and Sophocles. What comfort did each offer for the tragic nature of the human condition?
2. Why does the author of "The Vanity of This World" assert that "happy is he who the world can despise"?
3. How did Dante conceive the nature of evil and the moral ordering of specific sins?
4. What was the medieval view of the human condition and its relation to the idea of God? Cite at least two sources from your reading to illustrate your viewpoint.

CHAPTER 9

The Renaissance

THE TRIUMPH OF GALETEA, Raphael, 1513. This fresco from the Palazzo della Farnesina in Rome exemplifies the Renaissance artist's elevation of the human form. The mythological subject is also humanistic in its evocation of the ancient Greek tradition. *(The Triumph of Galatea, 1512–14 (fresco) (see also 108063-4), Raphael (Raffaello Sanzio of Urbino) (1483–1520) / Villa Farnesina, Rome, Italy / Giraudon / The Bridgeman Art Library International)*

From the fifteenth through the seventeenth centuries, medieval attitudes and institutions broke down, and distinctly modern cultural, economic, and political forms emerged. For many historians, the Renaissance, which originated in the city-states of Italy, marks the starting point of the modern era. The Renaissance was characterized by a rebirth of interest in the humanist culture and outlook of ancient Greece and Rome. Although Renaissance individuals did not repudiate Christianity, they valued worldly activities and interests to a much greater degree than did the people of the Middle Ages, whose outlook was dominated by Christian otherworldliness. Renaissance individuals were fascinated by *this* world and by life's possibilities; they aspired to live a rich and creative life on earth and to fulfill themselves through artistic and literary activity.

Individualism was a hallmark of the Renaissance. The urban elite sought to demonstrate their unique talents, to assert their own individuality, and to gain recognition for their accomplishments. The most admired person during the Renaissance was the multitalented individual, the "universal man," who distinguished himself as a writer, artist, linguist, athlete. Disdaining Christian humility, Renaissance individuals took pride in their talents and worldly accomplishments—"I can work miracles," said the great Leonardo da Vinci.

During the High Middle Ages there had been a revival of Greek and Roman learning. Yet there were two important differences between the period called the Twelfth-Century Awakening and the Renaissance. First, many more ancient works were restored to circulation during the Renaissance than during the cultural revival of the Middle Ages. Second, medieval scholastics had tried to fit the ideas of the ancients into a Christian framework; they used Greek philosophy to explain Christian teachings. Renaissance scholars, on the other hand, valued ancient works for their own sake, believing that Greek and Roman authors could teach much about the art of living.

A distinguishing feature of the Renaissance period was the humanist movement, an educational and cultural program based on the study of ancient Greek and Latin literature. By studying the humanities—history, literature, rhetoric, moral and political philosophy—humanists aimed to revive the worldly spirit of the ancient Greeks and Romans, which they believed had been lost in the Middle Ages.

Humanists were thus fascinated by the writings of the ancients. From the works of Thucydides, Plato, Cicero, Seneca, and other ancient authors, humanists sought guidelines for living life well in this world and looked for stylistic models for their own literary efforts. To the humanists, the ancients had written brilliantly, in an incomparable literary style, on friendship, citizenship, love, bravery, statesmanship, beauty, excellence, and every other topic devoted to the enrichment of human life.

Like the humanist movement, Renaissance art also marked a break with medieval culture. The art of the Middle Ages had served a religious function; its purpose was to lift the mind to God. It depicted a spiritual universe in which the supernatural was the supreme reality. The Gothic cathedral, with its flying buttresses, soared toward heaven, rising in ascending tiers; it reflected the medieval conception of a hierarchical universe with God at its apex. Painting also expressed gradations of spiritual values. Traditionally, the left side of a painting portrayed the damned, the right side the saved; dark colors expressed evil, light colors good. Spatial proportion was relative to spirituality—the less spiritually valuable a thing was, the less form it had (or the more deformed it was). Medieval art perfectly expressed the Christian view of the universe and the individual. The Renaissance shattered the dominance of religion over art, shifting attention from heaven to the natural world and to the human being; Renaissance artists often dealt with religious themes, but they placed their subjects in a naturalistic setting. Renaissance art also developed a new concept of visual space—perspective—that was defined from the standpoint of the individual observer. It was a quantitative space in which the artist, employing reason and mathematics, portrayed the essential form of the object as it appeared in three dimensions to the human eye; that is, it depicted the object in perspective.

The Renaissance began in the late fourteenth century in the northern Italian city-states, which had grown prosperous from the revival of trade in the Middle Ages. Italian merchants and bankers had the wealth to acquire libraries and fine works of art and to support art, literature, and scholarship. Surrounded by reminders of ancient Rome—amphitheaters, monuments, and sculpture—the well-to-do took an interest in classical culture and thought. In the late fifteenth and the sixteenth centuries, Renaissance ideas spread to Germany, France, Spain, and England through books available in great numbers due to the invention of the printing press.

1 The Humanists' Fascination with Antiquity

Humanists believed that a refined person must know the literature of Greece and Rome. They strove to imitate the style of the ancients, to speak and write as eloquently as the Greeks and Romans. Toward these ends, they sought to read, print, and restore to circulation every scrap of ancient literature that could still be found.

Petrarch
THE FATHER OF HUMANISM

During his lifetime, Francesco Petrarca, or Petrarch (1304–1374), had an astounding reputation as a poet and scholar. Often called the "father of humanism," he inspired other humanists through his love for classical learning; his criticism of medieval Latin as barbaric in contrast to the style of Cicero, Seneca, and other Romans; and his literary works based on classical models. Petrarch saw his own age as a restoration of classical brilliance after an interval of medieval darkness.

A distinctly modern element in Petrarch's thought is the subjective and individualistic character of his writing. In talking about himself and probing his own feelings, Petrarch demonstrates a self-consciousness characteristic of the modern outlook.

Like many other humanists, Petrarch remained devoted to Christianity: "When it comes to thinking or speaking of religion, that is, of the highest truth, of true happiness and eternal salvation," he declared, "I certainly am not a Ciceronian or a Platonist but a Christian." Petrarch was a forerunner of the Christian humanism best represented by Erasmus (see page 332). Christian humanists combined an intense devotion to Christianity with a great love for classical literature, which they much preferred to the dull and turgid treatises written by scholastic philosophers and theologians. In the following passage, Petrarch criticizes his contemporaries for their ignorance of ancient writers and shows his commitment to classical learning.

. . . O inglorious age! that scorns antiquity, its mother, to whom it owes every noble art—that dares to declare itself not only equal but superior to the glorious past. I say nothing of the vulgar, the dregs of mankind, whose sayings and opinions may raise a laugh but hardly merit serious censure. . . .

. . . But what can be said in defense of men of education who ought not to be ignorant of antiquity and yet are plunged in this same darkness and delusion?

You see that I cannot speak of these matters without the greatest irritation and indignation. There has arisen of late a set of dialecticians [experts in logical argument], who are not only ignorant but demented. Like a black army of ants from some old rotten oak, they swarm forth from their hiding places and devastate the fields of sound learning. They condemn Plato and Aristotle, and laugh at Socrates and Pythagoras.[1] And, good God! under what silly and incompetent leaders these opinions are put forth. . . . What shall we say of men who scorn Marcus Tullius Cicero,[2] the bright sun of eloquence? Of those who scoff at Varro and Seneca,[3] and are scandalized at what they choose

---

[1] The work of Aristotle (384–322 B.C.), a leading Greek philosopher, had an enormous influence among medieval and Renaissance scholars. A student of the philosopher Socrates, Plato (c. 427–347 B.C.) was one of the greatest philosophers of ancient Greece (see Chapter 3). His work grew to be extremely influential in the West during the Renaissance period, as new texts of his writings were discovered and translated into Latin and more Westerners could read the originals in Greek. Pythagoras (c. 582–c. 507 B.C.) was a Greek philosopher whose work influenced both Socrates and Plato.

[2] Cicero (106–43 B.C.) was a Roman statesman and rhetorician. His Latin style was especially admired and emulated during the Renaissance (see page 114).

[3] Varro (116–27 B.C.) was a Roman scholar and historian. Seneca (4 B.C.–A.D. 65) was a Roman statesman, dramatist, and Stoic philosopher whose literary style was greatly admired during the Renaissance (see page 141).

to call the crude, unfinished style of Livy and Sallust [Roman historians]? . . .

Such are the times, my friend, upon which we have fallen; such is the period in which we live and are growing old. Such are the critics of today, as I so often have occasion to lament and complain—men who are innocent of knowledge and virtue, and yet harbour the most exalted opinion of themselves. Not content with losing the words of the ancients, they must attack their genius and their ashes. They rejoice in their ignorance, as if what they did not know were not worth knowing. They give full rein to their license and conceit, and freely introduce among us new authors and outlandish teachings.

Leonardo Bruni
STUDY OF GREEK LITERATURE AND A HUMANIST EDUCATIONAL PROGRAM

Leonardo Bruni (1374–1444) was a Florentine humanist who extolled both intellectual study and active involvement in public affairs, an outlook called civic humanism. In the first reading from his *History of His Own Times in Italy*, Bruni expresses the humanist's love for ancient Greek literature and language.

In a treatise, *De Studiis et Literis* (On Learning and Literature), written around 1405 and addressed to the noble lady Baptista di Montefeltro (1383–1450), daughter of the Count of Urbino, Bruni outlines the basic course of studies that the humanists recommended as the best preparation for a life of wisdom and virtue. In addition to the study of Christian literature, Bruni encourages a wide familiarity with the best minds and stylists of ancient Greek and Latin cultures.

LOVE FOR GREEK LITERATURE

Then first came a knowledge of Greek, which had not been in use among us for seven hundred years. Chrysoloras the Byzantine,[1] a man of noble birth and well versed in Greek letters, brought Greek learning to us. When his country was invaded by the Turks, he came by sea, first to Venice. The report of him soon spread, and he was cordially invited and besought and promised a public stipend, to come to Florence and open his store of riches to the youth. I was then studying Civil Law,[2] but . . . I burned with love of academic studies, and had spent no little pains on dialectic and rhetoric. At the coming of Chrysoloras I was torn in mind, deeming it shameful to desert the law, and yet a crime to lose such a chance of studying Greek literature; and often with youthful impulse I would say to myself: "Thou, when it is permitted thee to gaze on Homer, Plato and Demosthenes,[3] and the other [Greek] poets, philosophers, orators, of whom such glorious things are spread abroad, and speak with them and be instructed in their admirable teaching, wilt thou desert and rob thyself? Wilt thou neglect this opportunity so divinely offered? For seven hundred years, no one in Italy has possessed Greek letters; and yet

[1]Chrysoloras (c. 1355–1415), a Byzantine writer and teacher, introduced the study of Greek literature to the Italians, helping to open a new age of Western humanistic learning.

[2]Civil Law refers to the Roman law as codified by Emperor Justinian in the early sixth century A.D. and studied in medieval law schools (see page 145).

[3]Demosthenes (384–322 B.C.) was an Athenian statesman and orator whose oratorical style was much admired by Renaissance humanists.

we confess that all knowledge is derived from them. How great advantage to your knowledge, enhancement of your fame, increase of your pleasure, will come from an understanding of this tongue? There are doctors of civil law everywhere; and the chance of learning will not fail thee. But if this one and only doctor of Greek letters disappears, no one can be found to teach thee." Overcome at length by these reasons, I gave myself to Chrysoloras, with such zeal to learn, that what through the wakeful day I gathered, I followed after in the night, even when asleep.

ON LEARNING AND LITERATURE

. . . The foundations of all true learning must be laid in the sound and thorough knowledge of Latin: which implies study marked by a broad spirit, accurate scholarship, and careful attention to details. Unless this solid basis be secured it is useless to attempt to rear an enduring edifice. Without it the great monuments of literature are unintelligible, and the art of composition impossible. To attain this essential knowledge we must never relax our careful attention to the grammar of the language, but perpetually confirm and extend our acquaintance with it until it is thoroughly our own. . . . To this end we must be supremely careful in our choice of authors, lest an inartistic and debased style infect our own writing and degrade our taste; which danger is best avoided by bringing a keen, critical sense to bear upon select works, observing the sense of each passage, the structure of the sentence, the force of every word down to the least important particle. In this way our reading reacts directly upon our style. . . .

But we must not forget that true distinction is to be gained by a wide and varied range of such studies as conduce to the profitable enjoyment of life, in which, however, we must observe due proportion in the attention and time we devote to them.

First amongst such studies I place History: a subject which must not on any account be neglected by one who aspires to true cultivation.

For it is our duty to understand the origins of our own history and its development; and the achievements of Peoples and of Kings.

For the careful study of the past enlarges our foresight in contemporary affairs and affords to citizens and to monarchs lessons of incitement or warning in the ordering of public policy. From History, also, we draw our store of examples of moral precepts.

In the monuments of ancient literature which have come down to us History holds a position of great distinction. We specially prize such [Roman] authors as Livy, Sallust and Curtius;[4] and, perhaps even above these, Julius Caesar; the style of whose Commentaries, so elegant and so limpid, entitles them to our warm admiration. . . .

The great Orators of antiquity must by all means be included. Nowhere do we find the virtues more warmly extolled, the vices so fiercely decried. From them we may learn, also, how to express consolation, encouragement, dissuasion or advice. If the principles which orators set forth are portrayed for us by philosophers, it is from the former that we learn how to employ the emotions—such as indignation, or pity— in driving home their application in individual cases. Further, from oratory we derive our store of those elegant or striking turns of expression which are used with so much effect in literary compositions. Lastly, in oratory we find that wealth of vocabulary, that clear easy-flowing style, that verve and force, which are invaluable to us both in writing and in conversation.

I come now to Poetry and the Poets. . . . For we cannot point to any great mind of the past for whom the Poets had not a powerful attraction. Aristotle, in constantly quoting Homer, Hesiod, Pindar, Euripides and other [Greek] poets, proves that he knew their works hardly less intimately than those of the philosophers. Plato, also, frequently appeals to them, and in this way covers them with his approval. If we

---

[4]Q. Curtius Rufus, a Roman historian and rhetorician of the mid-first century A.D., composed a biography of Alexander the Great.

turn to Cicero, we find him not content with quoting Ennius, Accius,[5] and others of the Latins, but rendering poems from the Greek and employing them habitually. . . . Hence my view that familiarity with the great poets of antiquity is essential to any claim to true education. For in their writings we find deep speculations upon Nature, and upon the Causes and Origins of things, which must carry weight with us both from their antiquity and from their authorship. Besides these, many important truths upon matters of daily life are suggested or illustrated. All this is expressed with such grace and dignity as demands our admiration. . . . To sum up what I have endeavoured to set forth. That high standard of education to which I referred at the outset is only to be reached by one who has seen many things and read much. Poet, Orator, Historian, and the rest, all must be studied, each must contribute a share. Our

learning thus becomes full, ready, varied and elegant, available for action or for discourse in all subjects. But to enable us to make effectual use of what we know we must add to our knowledge the power of expression. These two sides of learning, indeed, should not be separated: they afford mutual aid and distinction. Proficiency in literary form, not accompanied by broad acquaintance with facts and truths, is a barren attainment; whilst information, however vast, which lacks all grace of expression, would seem to be put under a bushel or partly thrown away. Indeed, one may fairly ask what advantage it is to possess profound and varied learning if one cannot convey it in language worthy of the subject. Where, however, this double capacity exists—breadth of learning and grace of style— we allow the highest title to distinction and to abiding fame. If we review the great names of ancient [Greek and Roman] literature, Plato, Democritus, Aristotle, Theophrastus, Varro, Cicero, Seneca, Augustine, Jerome, Lactantius, we shall find it hard to say whether we admire more their attainments or their literary power.

---

[5]Ennius (239–169 B.C.) wrote the first great Latin epic poem, which was based on the legends of Rome's founding and its early history. Accius (c. 170–c. 90 B.C.), also a Roman, authored a history of Greek and Latin literature.

Petrus Paulus Vergerius
THE IMPORTANCE OF LIBERAL STUDIES

In *On the Manners of a Gentleman and Liberal Studies,* written in 1392, Petrus Paulus Vergerius (1370–1444), a prominent Paduan scholar, upheld the importance of classical study and made astute observations regarding the educational process. He urged teachers to provide "examples of living men known and respected for their worth" for students to imitate. At an early age, students should learn moral discipline: they should be taught to disdain "arrogance or intolerable self-conceit," "untruthfulness," "idleness of mind," and overindulgence in food, drink, and sleep. They should also be imbued with respect for elders and the ceremonies of the church.

In the following passage from his education treatise, Vergerius discusses the nature and value of a liberal education.

We call those studies *liberal* which are worthy of a free man; those studies by which we attain and practise virtue and wisdom; that

education which calls forth, trains and develops those highest gifts of body and of mind which ennoble men, and which are rightly judged to rank next in dignity to virtue only. For to a vulgar temper gain and pleasure are the one aim of existence, to a lofty nature, moral worth and fame. It is, then, of the highest importance that even from infancy this aim, this effort, should constantly be kept alive in growing minds. For I may affirm with fullest conviction that we shall not have attained wisdom in our later years unless in our earliest we have sincerely entered on its search. Nor may we for a moment admit, with the unthinking crowd, that those who give early promise fail in subsequent fulfilment. This may, partly from physical causes, happen in exceptional cases. But there is no doubt that nature has endowed some children with so keen, so ready an intelligence, that without serious effort they attain to a notable power of reasoning and conversing upon grave and lofty subjects, and by aid of right guidance and sound learning reach in manhood the highest distinction. On the other hand, children of modest powers demand even more attention, that their natural defects may be supplied by art. But all alike must in those early years, . . . whilst the mind is supple, be inured to the toil and effort of learning. Not that education, in the broad sense, is exclusively the concern of youth. Did not Cato[1] think it honourable to learn Greek in later life? Did not Socrates, greatest of philosophers, compel his aged fingers to the lute?

Our youth of to-day, it is to be feared, is backward to learn; studies are accounted irksome. Boys hardly weaned begin to claim their own way, at a time when every art should be employed to bring them under control and attract them to grave studies. The Master {teacher} must judge how far he can rely upon emulation, rewards, encouragement; how far he must have recourse to sterner measures. Too much leniency is objectionable; so also is too great severity, for we must avoid all that terrifies a boy. . . . Not seldom it happens that a finely tempered nature is thwarted by circumstances, such as poverty at home, which compels a promising youth to forsake learning for trade: though, on the other hand, poverty is less dangerous to lofty instincts than great wealth. Or again, parents encourage their sons to follow a career traditional in their family, which may divert them from liberal studies: and the customary pursuits of the city in which we dwell exercise a decided influence on our choice. So that we may say that a perfectly unbiassed decision in these matters is seldom possible, except to certain select natures, who by favour of the gods, as the poets have it, are unconsciously brought to choose the right path in life. . . . For us it is the best that can befall, that either the circumstances of our life, or the guidance and exhortations of those in charge of us, should mould our natures whilst they are still plastic. . . .

{My father}, Jacopo da Carrara, who, though a patron of learning, was not himself versed in Letters, died regretting that opportunity of acquiring a knowledge of higher studies had not been given him in youth; which shews us that, although we may in old age long for it, only in early years can we be sure of attaining that learning which we desire. So that it is no light motive to youthful diligence that we thereby provide ourselves with precious advantages against oncoming age, a spring of interest for a leisured life, a recreation for a busy one. Consider the necessity of the literary art to one immersed in reading and speculation: and its importance to one absorbed in affairs. To be able to speak and write with elegance is no slight advantage in negotiation, whether in public or private concerns. Especially in administration of the State, when intervals of rest and privacy are accorded to a prince, how must he value those means of occupying them wisely which the knowledge of literature affords to him! Think of Domitian[2]:

---

[1]Greek writers such as Plutarch stressed Cato the Elder's anti-Hellenic sentiments, but in *On Old Age* Cicero asserted that Cato learned Greek in his later years as a source of intellectual stimulation.

[2]The Roman emperor Domitian (A.D. 51–96), the son of the emperor Vespasian, succeeded his elder brother Titus as emperor in A.D. 81.

the son of Vespasian though he was, and brother of Titus, he was driven to occupy his leisure by *killing flies!* . . .

Indeed the power which good books have of diverting our thoughts from unworthy or distressing themes is another support to my arguement for the study of letters. Add to this their helpfulness on those occasions when we find ourselves alone, without companions and without preoccupations—what can we do better than gather our books around us? In them we see unfolded before us vast stores of knowledge, for our delight, it may be, or for our inspiration. In them are contained the records of the great achievements of men; the wonders of Nature; the works of Providence in the past, the key to her secrets of the future. And, most important of all, this Knowledge is not liable to decay. With a picture, an inscription, a coin, books share a kind of immortality. In all these memory is, as it were, made permanent; although, in its freedom from accidental risks, Literature surpasses every other form of record.

Literature indeed exhibits not facts alone, but thoughts, and their expression. Provided such thoughts be worthy, and worthily expressed, we feel assured that they will not die: although I do not think that thoughts without style will be likely to attract much notice or secure a sure survival. What greater charm can life offer than this power of making the past, the present, and even the future, our own by means of literature? How bright a household is the family of books! we may cry, with Cicero. In their company is no noise, no greed, no self-will: at a word they speak to you, at a word they are still: to all our requests their response is ever ready and to the point. Books indeed are a higher—a wider, more tenacious—memory, a store-house which is the common property of us all.

I attach great weight to the duty of handing down this priceless treasure to our sons. . . .

We come now to the consideration of the various subjects which may rightly be included under the name of 'Liberal Studies.' Amongst these I accord the first place to History, on grounds both of its attractiveness and of its utility, qualities which appeal equally to the scholar and to the statesman. Next in importance ranks Moral Philosophy, which indeed is, in a peculiar sense, a 'Liberal Art,' in that its purpose is to teach men the secret of true freedom. History, then, gives us the concrete examples of the precepts inculcated by philosophy. The one shews what men should do, the other what men have said and done in the past, and what practical lessons we may draw therefrom for the present day. I would indicate as the third main branch of study, Eloquence, which indeed holds a place of distinction amongst the refined Arts. By philosophy we learn the essential truth of things, which by eloquence we so exhibit in orderly adornment as to bring conviction to differing minds. And history provides the light of experience—a cumulative wisdom fit to supplement the force of reason and the persuasion of eloquence. For we allow that soundness of judgment, wisdom of speech, integrity of conduct are the marks of a truly liberal temper. . . .

The Art of Letters . . . is a study adapted to all times and to all circumstances, to the investigation of fresh knowledge or to the re-casting and application of old. Hence the importance of grammar and of the rules of composition must be recognized at the outset, as the foundation on which the whole study of Literature must rest: and closely associated with these rudiments, the art of Disputation or Logical argument. The function of this is to enable us to discern fallacy from truth in discussion. Logic, indeed, as setting forth the true method of learning, is the guide to the acquisition of knowledge in whatever subject. Rhetoric comes next, and is strictly speaking the formal study by which we attain the art of eloquence; which, as we have just stated, takes the third place amongst the studies specially important in public life. . . .

After Eloquence we place Poetry and the Poetic Art, which though not without their value in daily life and as an aid to oratory, have nevertheless their main concern for the leisure side of existence.

As to Music, the Greeks refused the title of 'Educated' to anyone who could not sing or play. Socrates set an example to the Athenian youth, by himself learning to play in his old age; urging the pursuit of music not as a sensuous indulgence, but as an aid to the inner harmony of the soul. In so far as it is taught as a healthy recreation for the moral and spiritual nature, music is a truly liberal art, and, both as regards its theory and its practice, should find a place in education.

Arithmetic, which treats of the properties of numbers, Geometry, which treats of the properties of dimensions, lines, surfaces, and solid bodies, are weighty studies because they possess a peculiar element of certainty. The science of the Stars, their motions, magnitudes and distances, lifts us into the clear calm of the upper air. There we may contemplate the fixed stars, or the conjunctions of the planets, and predict the eclipses of the sun and the moon. The knowledge of Nature—animate and inanimate—the laws and the properties of things in heaven and in earth, their causes, mutations and effects, especially the explanation of their wonders (as they are popularly supposed) by the unravelling of their causes—this is a most delightful, and at the same time most profitable, study for youth. With these may be joined investigations concerning the weight of bodies, and those relative to the subject which mathematicians call 'Perspective.'

I may here glance for a moment at the three great professional Disciplines: Medicine, Law, Theology. Medicine, which is applied science, has undoubtedly much that makes it attractive to a student. But it cannot be described as a Liberal study. Law, which is based upon moral philosophy, is undoubtedly held in high respect. Regarding Law as a subject of study, such respect is entirely deserved: but Law as practised becomes a mere trade. Theology, on the other hand, treats of themes removed from our senses, and attainable only by pure intelligence.

REVIEW QUESTIONS

1. What do historians mean by the term "Renaissance humanism"?
2. What made Petrarch aware that a renaissance, or rebirth, of classical learning was necessary in his time?
3. Why did Leonardo Bruni abandon his earlier course of studies to pursue the study of Greek literature?
4. What subjects made up the basic course of studies advocated by Bruni?
5. For Vergerius, what is the value of a liberal education?
6. How, according the Vergerius, do history, moral philosophy, and eloquence complement each other?

2 Human Dignity

In his short lifetime, Giovanni Pico della Mirandola (1463–1494) mastered Greek, Latin, Hebrew, and Arabic and aspired to synthesize the Hebrew, Greek, and Christian traditions. His most renowned work, *Oration on the Dignity of Man,* has been called the humanist manifesto.

Pico della Mirandola
ORATION ON THE DIGNITY OF MAN

In the opening section of the *Oration*, Pico declares that unlike other creatures, human beings have not been assigned a fixed place in the universe. Our destiny is not determined by anything outside us. Rather, God has bestowed upon us a unique distinction: the liberty to determine the form and value our lives shall acquire. The notion that people have the power to shape their own lives is a key element in the emergence of the modern outlook.

I have read in the records of the Arabians, reverend Fathers, that Abdala the Saracen,[1] when questioned as to what on this stage of the world, as it were, could be seen most worthy of wonder, replied: "There is nothing to be seen more wonderful than man." In agreement with this opinion is the saying of Hermes Trismegistus: "A great miracle, Asclepius, is man."[2] But when I weighed the reason for these maxims, the many grounds for the excellence of human nature reported by many men failed to satisfy me—that man is the intermediary between creatures, the intimate of the gods, the king of the lower beings, by the acuteness of his senses, by the discernment of his reason, and by the light of his intelligence the interpreter of nature, the interval between fixed eternity and fleeting time, and (as the Persians say) the bond, nay, rather, the marriage song of the world, on David's [biblical king] testimony but little lower than the angels. Admittedly great though these reasons be, they are not the principal grounds, that is, those which may rightfully claim for themselves the privilege of the highest admiration. For why should we not admire more the angels themselves and the blessed choirs of heaven? At last it seems to me I have come to understand why man is the most

fortunate of creatures and consequently worthy of all admiration and what precisely is that rank which is his lot in the universal chain of Being— a rank to be envied not only by brutes but even by the stars and by minds beyond this world. It is a matter past faith and a wondrous one. Why should it not be? For it is on this very account that man is rightly called and judged a great miracle and a wonderful creature indeed. . . .

. . . God the Father, the supreme Architect, had already built this cosmic home we behold, the most sacred temple of His godhead, by the laws of His mysterious wisdom. The region above the heavens He had adorned with Intelligences, the heavenly spheres He had quickened with eternal souls, and the excrementary and filthy parts of the lower world He had filled with a multitude of animals of every kind. But, when the work was finished, the Craftsman kept wishing that there were someone to ponder the plan of so great a work, to love its beauty, and to wonder at its vastness. Therefore, when everything was done (as Moses and Timaeus[3] bear witness), He finally took thought concerning the creation of man. But there was not among His archetypes that from which He could fashion a new offspring, nor was there in His treasurehouses anything which He might bestow on His new son as an inheritance, nor was there in the seats of all the world a place where the latter might sit to contemplate the universe. All was now complete; all things had been assigned to the

---

[1]Abdala the Saracen possibly refers to the eighth-century A.D. writer Abd-Allah Ibn al-Muqaffa.
[2]Ancient writings dealing with magic, alchemy, astrology, and occult philosophy were erroneously attributed to an assumed Egyptian priest, Hermes Trismegistus. Asclepius was a Greek god of healing.

---

[3]Timaeus, a Greek Pythagorean philosopher, was a central character in Plato's famous dialogue *Timaeus*.

highest, the middle, and the lowest orders. But in its final creation it was not the part of the Father's power to fail as though exhausted. It was not the part of His wisdom to waver in a needful matter through poverty of counsel. It was not the part of His kindly love that he who was to praise God's divine generosity in regard to others should be compelled to condemn it in regard to himself.

At last the best of artisans [God] ordained that that creature to whom He had been able to give nothing proper to himself should have joint possession of whatever had been peculiar to each of the different kinds of being. He therefore took man as a creature of indeterminate nature and, assigning him a place in the middle of the world, addressed him thus: "Neither a fixed abode nor a form that is thine alone nor any function peculiar to thyself have we given thee, Adam, to the end that according to thy longing and according to thy judgment thou mayest have and possess what abode, what form, and what functions thou thyself shalt desire. The nature of all other beings is limited and constrained within the bounds of laws prescribed by Us. Thou, constrained by no limits, in accordance with thine own free will, in whose hand We have placed thee, shalt ordain for thyself the limits of thy nature. We have set thee at the world's center that thou mayest from thence more easily observe whatever is in the world. We have made thee neither of heaven nor of earth, neither mortal nor immortal, so that with freedom of choice and with honor, as though the maker and molder of thyself, thou mayest fashion thyself in whatever shape thou shalt prefer. Thou shalt have the power to degenerate into the lower forms of life, which are brutish. Thou shalt have the power, out of thy soul's judgment, to be reborn into the higher forms, which are divine."

O supreme generosity of God the Father, O highest and most marvelous felicity of man! To him it is granted to have whatever he chooses, to be whatever he wills. Beasts as soon as they are born (so says Lucilius)[4] bring with them from their mother's womb all they will ever possess. Spiritual beings [angels], either from the beginning or soon thereafter, become what they are to be for ever and ever. On man when he came into life the Father conferred the seeds of all kinds and the germs of every way of life. Whatever seeds each man cultivates will grow to maturity and bear in him their own fruit. If they be vegetative, he will be like a plant. If sensitive, he will become brutish. If rational, he will grow into a heavenly being. If intellectual, he will be an angel and the son of God. And if, happy in the lot of no created thing, he withdraws into the center of his own unity, his spirit, made one with God, in the solitary darkness of God, who is set above all things, shall surpass them all.

---

[4]Lucilius, a first-century A.D. Roman poet and Stoic philosopher, was a close friend of Seneca, the philosopher-dramatist.

REVIEW QUESTIONS

1. According to Pico della Mirandola, what quality did humans alone possess? What did its possession allow them to do?
2. Compare Pico's view of the individual with that of Saint Augustine and Pope Innocent III.

3 Break with Medieval Political Theory

Turning away from the religious orientation of the Middle Ages, Renaissance thinkers discussed the human condition in secular terms and opened up possibilities for thinking about moral and political problems in new ways. Thus, Niccolò Machiavelli (1469–1527), a Florentine statesman and political theorist, broke with medieval political theory. Medieval political thinkers held that the ruler derived power from God and had a religious obligation to rule in accordance with God's precepts. Machiavelli, though, ascribed no divine origin to kingship, nor did he attribute events to the mysterious will of God; and he explicitly rejected the principle that kings should adhere to Christian moral teachings. For Machiavelli, the state was a purely human creation. Successful kings or princes, he asserted, should be concerned only with preserving and strengthening the state's power and must ignore questions of good and evil, morality and immorality. Machiavelli did not assert that religion was supernatural in origin and rejected the prevailing belief that Christian morality should guide political life. For him, religion's value derived from other factors: a ruler could utilize religion to unite his subjects and to foster obedience to law.

Niccolò Machiavelli
THE PRINCE

In contrast to medieval thinkers, Machiavelli did not seek to construct an ideal Christian community but to discover how politics was *really* conducted. In *The Prince*, written in 1513 and published posthumously in 1532, he studied politics in the cold light of reason, as the following passage illustrates.

It now remains to be seen what are the methods and rules for a prince as regards his subjects and friends. And as I know that many have written of this, I fear that my writing about it may be deemed presumptuous, differing as I do, especially in this matter, from the opinions of others. But my intention being to write something of use to those who understand, it appears to me more proper to go to the real truth of the matter than to its imagination; and many have imagined republics and principalities which have never been seen or known to exist in reality; for how we live is so far removed from how we ought to live, that he who abandons what is done for what ought to be done, will rather learn to bring about his own ruin than his preservation.

> Machiavelli removed ethics from political thinking. A successful ruler, he contended, is indifferent to moral and religious considerations. But will not the prince be punished on the Day of Judgment for violating Christian teachings? In startling contrast to medieval theorists, Machiavelli simply ignored the question. The action of a prince, he said, should be governed solely by necessity.

A man who wishes to make a profession of goodness in everything must necessarily come to grief among so many who are not good. Therefore it is necessary for a prince, who wishes to maintain himself, to learn how not to be good, and to use this knowledge and not use it, according to the necessity of the case.

Leaving on one side, then, those things which concern only an imaginary prince, and speaking of those that are real, I state that all men, and especially princes, who are placed at a greater height, are reputed for certain qualities which bring them either praise or blame. Thus one is considered liberal, another . . . miserly; . . . one a free giver, another rapacious; one cruel, another merciful; one a breaker of his word, another trustworthy; one effeminate and pusillanimous, another fierce and high-spirited; one humane, another haughty; one lascivious, another chaste; one frank, another astute; one hard, another easy; one serious, another frivolous; one religious, another an unbeliever, and so on. I know that every one will admit that it would be highly praiseworthy in a prince to possess all the above-named qualities that are reputed good, but as they cannot all be possessed or observed, human conditions not permitting of it, it is necessary that he should be prudent enough to avoid the scandal of those vices which would lose him the state, and guard himself if possible against those which will not lose it [for] him, but if not able to, he can indulge them with less scruple. And yet he must not mind incurring the scandal of those vices, without which it would be difficult to save the state, for if one considers well, it will be found that some things which seem virtues would, if followed, lead to one's ruin, and some others which appear vices result in one's greater security and wellbeing. . . .

. . . I say that every prince must desire to be considered merciful and not cruel. He must, however, take care not to misuse this mercifulness. Cesare Borgia was considered cruel, but his cruelty had brought order to the Romagna,[1] united it, and reduced it to peace and fealty.

If this is considered well, it will be seen that he was really much more merciful than the Florentine people, who, to avoid the name of cruelty, allowed Pistoia[2] to be destroyed. A prince, therefore, must not mind incurring the charge of cruelty for the purpose of keeping his subjects united and faithful; for, with a very few examples, he will be more merciful than those who, from excess of tenderness, allow disorders to arise, from whence spring bloodshed and rapine; for these as a rule injure the whole community, while the executions carried out by the prince injure only individuals. . . .

Machiavelli's rigorous investigation of politics led him to view human nature from the standpoint of its limitations and imperfections. The astute prince, he said, recognizes that human beings are by nature selfish, cowardly, and dishonest, and regulates his political strategy accordingly.

From this arises the question whether it is better to be loved more than feared, or feared more than loved. The reply is, that one ought to be both feared and loved, but as it is difficult for the two to go together, it is much safer to be feared than loved, if one of the two has to be wanting. For it may be said of men in general that they are ungrateful, voluble, dissemblers, anxious to avoid danger, and covetous of gain; as long as you benefit them, they are entirely yours; they offer you their blood, their goods, their life, and their children, as I have before said, when the necessity is remote; but when it approaches, they revolt. And the prince who has relied solely on their words, without making other preparations, is ruined; for the

---

Alexander VI (1492–1503). With his father's aid he attempted to carve out for himself an independent duchy in north-central Italy, with Romagna as its heart. Through cruelty, violence, and treachery, he succeeded at first in his ambition, but ultimately his principality collapsed. Romagna was eventually incorporated into the Papal State under Pope Julius II (1503–1513).

[2]Pistoia, a small Italian city in Tuscany, came under the control of Florence in the fourteenth century.

---

[1]Cesare Borgia (c. 1476–1507) was the bastard son of Rodrigo Borgia, then a Spanish cardinal, and later Pope

friendship which is gained by purchase and not through grandeur and nobility of spirit is bought but not secured, and at a pinch is not to be expended in your service. And men have less scruple in offending one who makes himself loved than one who makes himself feared; for love is held by a chain of obligation which, men being selfish, is broken whenever it serves their purpose; but fear is maintained by a dread of punishment which never fails.

Still, a prince should make himself feared in such a way that if he does not gain love, he at any rate avoids hatred; for fear and the absence of hatred may well go together, and will be always attained by one who abstains from interfering with the property of his citizens and subjects or with their women. And when he is obliged to take the life of any one, let him do so when there is a proper justification and manifest reason for it; but above all he must abstain from taking the property of others, for men forget more easily the death of their father than the loss of their patrimony. Then also pretexts for seizing property are never wanting, and one who begins to live by rapine will always find some reason for taking the goods of others, whereas causes for taking life are rarer and more fleeting.

But when the prince is with his army and has a large number of soldiers under his control, then it is extremely necessary that he should not mind being thought cruel; for without this reputation he could not keep an army united or disposed to any duty. Among the noteworthy actions of Hannibal[3] is numbered this, that although he had an enormous army, composed of men of all nations and fighting in foreign countries, there never arose any dissension either among them or against the prince, either in good fortune or in bad. This could not be due to anything but his inhuman cruelty, which together with his infinite other virtues, made him always venerated and terrible in the sight of his soldiers, and

without it his other virtues would not have sufficed to produce that effect. Thoughtless writers admire on the one hand his actions, and on the other blame the principal cause of them. . . .

Again in marked contrast to the teachings of Christian (and ancient) moralists, Machiavelli said that the successful prince will use any means to achieve and sustain political power. If the end is desirable, all means are justified.

How laudable it is for a prince to keep good faith and live with integrity, and not with astuteness, every one knows. Still the experience of our times shows those princes to have done great things who have had little regard for good faith, and have been able by astuteness to confuse men's brains, and who have ultimately overcome those who have made loyalty their foundation.

You must know, then, that there are two methods of fighting, the one by law, the other by force: the first method is that of men, the second of beasts; but as the first method is often insufficient, one must have recourse to the second. It is therefore necessary for a prince to know well how to use both the beast and the man. . . .

A prince being thus obliged to know well how to act as a beast must imitate the fox and the lion, for the lion cannot protect himself from traps, and the fox cannot defend himself from wolves. One must therefore be a fox to recognise traps, and a lion to frighten wolves. Those that wish to be only lions do not understand this. Therefore, a prudent ruler ought not to keep faith when by so doing it would be against his interest, and when the reasons which made him bind himself no longer exist. If men were all good, this precept would not be a good one; but as they are bad, and would not observe their faith with you, so you are not bound to keep faith with them. Nor have legitimate grounds ever failed a prince who wished to show [plausible] excuse for the non-fulfilment of his promise. Of this one could furnish an infinite number of modern examples,

---

[3]Hannibal (247–182 B.C.) was a brilliant Carthaginian general whose military victories almost destroyed Roman power. He was finally defeated at the battle of Zama in 202 B.C. by the Roman general Scipio Africanus (see page 108).

and show how many times peace has been broken, and how many promises rendered worthless, by the faithlessness of princes, and those that have been best able to imitate the fox have succeeded best. But it is necessary to be able to disguise this character well, and to be a great feigner and dissembler; and men are so simple and so ready to obey present necessities, that one who deceives will always find those who allow themselves to be deceived. . . .

. . . Thus it is well to seem merciful, faithful, humane, sincere, religious, and also to be so; but you must have the mind so disposed that when it is needful to be otherwise you may be able to change to the opposite qualities. And it must be understood that a prince, and especially a new prince, cannot observe all those things which are considered good in men, being often obliged, in order to maintain the state, to act against faith, against charity, against humanity, and against religion. And, therefore, he must have a mind disposed to adapt itself according to the wind, and as the variations of fortune dictate, and, as I said before, not deviate from what is good, if possible, but be able to do evil if constrained.

A prince must take great care that nothing goes out of his mouth which is not full of the above-named five qualities, and, to see and hear him, he should seem to be all mercy, faith, integrity, humanity, and religion. And nothing is more necessary than to seem to have this last quality, for men in general judge more by the eyes than by the hands, for every one can see, but very few have to feel. Everybody sees what you appear to be, few feel what you are, and those few will not dare to oppose themselves to the many, who have the majesty of the state to defend them; and in the actions of men, and especially of princes, from which there is no appeal, the end justifies the means. Let a prince therefore aim at conquering and maintaining the state, and the means will always be judged honourable and praised by every one, for the vulgar is always taken by appearances and the issue of the event; and the world consists only of the vulgar, and the few who are not vulgar are isolated when the many have a rallying point in the prince. A certain prince of the present time, whom it is well not to name, never does anything but preach peace and good faith, but he is really a great enemy to both, and either of them, had he observed them, would have lost him state or reputation on many occasions.

REVIEW QUESTIONS

1. In what ways was Niccolò Machiavelli's advice to princes a break from the teachings of medieval political and moral philosophers?
2. How does Machiavelli's image of human nature compare with that of Pico della Mirandola, of Pope Gregory VII, and of Innocent III.
3. Would Machiavelli's political advice help or hurt a politician in a modern democratic society?

---

4 The Ideal Gentleman
~~~

By the early sixteenth century, the era of the republics had come to an end in Italy, and the princely courts were the new social and political ideal. At the same time that Machiavelli was defining the new *political* ideal in his *Prince*, Baldassare Castiglione (1478–1529) was describing the new *social* ideal—the Renaissance courtier who served princes—in his *Book of the Courtier* (1528). Born into an illustrious Lombard family near Mantua, Castiglione received a humanist education in Latin and Greek and had a distinguished career serving in the courts of Italian dukes and Charles V in Spain. Castiglione's handbook became one of the most influential books of the day, providing instruction to aristocrats and nonaristocrats alike about how to be the perfect courtier or court lady. By the end of the sixteenth century, it had been translated into every major European language, making Castiglione the arbiter of aristocratic manners throughout Europe.

Like Greco-Roman moralists, Castiglione sought to overcome brutish elements in human nature and to shape a higher type of individual through reason. To structure the self artistically, to live life with verve and style, and to achieve a personal dignity were the humanist values that Castiglione's work spread beyond Italy.

Baldassare Castiglione
THE BOOK OF THE COURTIER

Castiglione chose the court of Urbino as the setting for his *Book of the Courtier*, which he wrote in the form of a conversation among the courtiers and ladies of the court. The participants—such as Guidobaldo, Duke of Urbino; the Duchess, Elisabetta Gonzaga; Count Ludovico da Canossa; and Cardinal Pietro Bembo— were all real people who in Castiglione's day had actual conversations at the court. In the first two books of *The Courtier*, Castiglione describes the ideal courtier as an example of the Renaissance "universal man," a well-rounded person with breadth of interest and versatility of accomplishment. For Castiglione, the courtier is a person of noble birth who is skilled in weaponry, an expert horseman, and adept at all sorts of games. And not only should the courtier be physically gifted; he should be well educated. In the following passages, Count Ludovico declares that he should be learned in the humanities, the new educational curriculum of the Renaissance humanists. Moreover, in the spirit of the "universal man," he should be a musician, and he should display a knowledge of drawing and painting.

"I would have him more than passably learned in letters, at least in those studies which we call the humanities. Let him be conversant not only with the Latin language, but with Greek as well, because of the abundance and variety of things that are so divinely written therein. Let him be versed in the poets, as well as in the orators and historians, and let him be practiced also in writing verse and prose, especially in our own vernacular; for, besides the personal satisfaction he will take in this, in this way he will never want for pleasant entertainment with the ladies, who are usually fond of such things. And if, because of other occupations or lack of study, he does not attain to such a perfection that his writings should merit great praise, let him take care to keep them under cover so that others will not laugh at him, and let him show them only to a friend who can be trusted; because at least they will be of profit to him in that, through such exercise, he will be capable of judging the writing of others. For it very rarely happens that a man who is unpracticed in writing, however learned he may be, can ever wholly understand the toils and industry of writers, or taste the sweetness and excellence of styles, and those intrinsic niceties that are often found in the ancients. . . .

"Gentlemen, you must know that I am not satisfied with our Courtier unless he also be a musician, and unless, besides understanding and being able to read music, he can play various instruments. For, if we rightly consider, no rest from toil and no medicine for ailing spirits can be found more decorous or praiseworthy in time of leisure than this; and especially in courts where, besides the release from vexations which music gives to all, many things are done to please the ladies, whose tender and delicate spirits are readily penetrated with harmony and filled with sweetness. Hence, it is no wonder that in both ancient and modern times they have always been particularly fond of musicians, finding the music a most welcome food for the spirit." . . .

Then the Count said: "Before we enter upon that subject, I would discuss another matter which I consider to be of great importance and which I think must therefore, in no way be neglected by our Courtier: and this is a knowledge of how to draw and an acquaintance with the art of painting itself."

REVIEW QUESTIONS

1. How does Castiglione's ideal gentleman reflect the spirit of Renaissance humanism and art?
2. Compare and contrast Castiglione's ideal courtier with what would be regarded as an ideal type during the Middle Ages.

5 Renaissance Art and Science
—ᴠᴠᴠ—

Renaissance artists were inspired by the art of classical antiquity, which was representational and aspired to show nature as it appeared to the eye. In stressing the importance of depicting the object truly as it is viewed, the Renaissance artist, like his classical predecessors, also emphasized the immeasurable importance of the viewer. Renaissance art gave a renewed and original expression to classical humanism, which celebrated the dignity, worth, and creative capacity of the individual and the beauty of the human form. By defining visual space and the relationship between the object and the observer in mathematical terms, Renaissance art and artistic theory helped pave the way for the development of the modern scientific approach to nature, which later found expression in the astronomy of Copernicus and the physics of Galileo (see Chapter 12).

Leonardo da Vinci
OBSERVATION AND MATHEMATICAL PERSPECTIVE

The works of Leonardo da Vinci (1452–1519)—his drawings, paintings, sculpture, innumerable inventions, and copious writings—exemplify the Renaissance spirit. They announced a new way of looking at nature and the individual. Leonardo examined objects in all their diversity and represented them realistically. For Leonardo, visual art was a means of arriving at nature's truths. Truth was attained when the artist brought both human reason and human creative capacity to bear on the direct experiences of the senses. Leonardo visually delineated the natural world with unprecedented scientific precision and simultaneously asserted his spiritual and intellectual freedom to do so. Through his art, Leonardo helped lay the foundations for modern science.

In his notebooks, Leonardo sketched an infinite variety of objects—inorganic, organic, human—and recorded fragmentary thoughts about them. Everywhere, he demonstrated a concern for the concrete specificity of things, which he depicted in minute detail. In the following excerpts, Leonardo affirms the rigorous and direct observation of nature as a source of truth.

How painting surpasses all human works by reason of the subtle possibilities which it contains:

The eye, which is called the window of the soul, is the chief means whereby the understanding may most fully and abundantly appreciate the infinite works of nature; and the ear is the second, inasmuch as it acquires its importance from the fact that it hears the things which the eye has seen. If you historians, or poets, or mathematicians had never seen things with your eyes you would be ill able to describe them in your writings. And if you, O poet, represent a story by depicting it with your pen, the painter with his brush will so render it as to be more easily satisfying and less tedious to understand. . . .

OF THE ORDER TO BE OBSERVED IN STUDY

I say that one ought first to learn about the limbs and how they are worked, and after having completed this knowledge one ought to study their actions in the different conditions in which men are placed, and thirdly to devise figure compositions, the study for these being taken from natural actions made on occasion as opportunities offered; and one should be on the watch in the streets and squares and fields and there make sketches with rapid strokes to represent features, that is for a head one may make an *o*, and for an arm a straight or curved line, and so in like manner for the legs and trunk, afterwards when back at home working up these notes in a completed form.

My opponent says that in order to gain experience and to learn how to work readily, it is better that the first period of study should be spent in copying various compositions made by different masters either on sheets of paper or on walls, since from these one acquires rapidity in execution and a good method. But to this it may be replied that the ensuing method would be good if it was founded upon works that were excellent in composition and by diligent masters; and since such masters are so rare that few are to be found, it is safer to go direct to the works of nature than to those which have been imitated from her originals with great deterioration and thereby to acquire a bad method, for he who has access to the fountain does not go to the water-pot. . . .

Equally important to Leonardo was the innate ability of the rational mind to use mathematics and to give order, form, and clarity to the individual's experiences of the world. Here he explains the use of mathematical perspective in art.

THE LIFE OF THE PAINTER IN THE COUNTRY

The painter requires such knowledge of mathematics as belongs to painting, and severance from companions who are not in sympathy with his studies, and his brain should have the power of adapting itself to the tenor of the objects which present themselves before it, and he should be freed from all other cares.

And if while considering and examining one subject a second should intervene, as happens when an object occupies the mind, he ought to decide which of these subjects presents greater

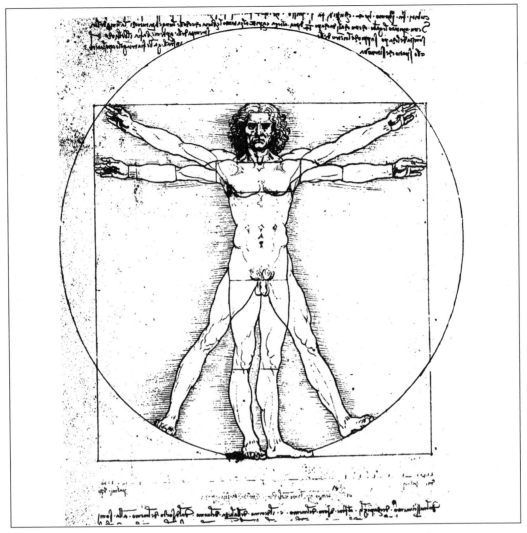

Leonardo da Vinci, *The Proportions of Man,* from his notebooks. See below where Leonardo discusses the proportions that this drawing illustrates. (© *Bettmann/Corbis*)

difficulties in investigation, and follow that until it becomes entirely clear, and afterwards pursue the investigation of the other. And above all he should keep his mind as clear as the surface of a mirror, which becomes changed to as many different colours as are those of the objects within it, and his companions should resemble him in a taste for these studies, and if he fail to find any such he should accustom himself to be alone in his investigations, for in the end he will find no more profitable companionship. . . .

OF THE REQUISITES OF PAINTING

The first requisite of painting is that the bodies which it represents should appear in relief, and that the scenes which surround them with effects of distance should seem to enter into the plane in which the picture is produced by means of the three parts of perspective, namely the diminution in the distinctness of the form of bodies, the diminution in their size, and the diminution in their colour. Of these three divisions of perspective, the first has its origin in the eye, the two others are derived from the atmosphere that is interposed between the eye and the objects which the eye beholds. . . .

WALL OF GLASS

Perspective is nothing else than the seeing of an object behind a sheet of glass, smooth and quite transparent, on the surface of which all the things may be marked that are behind this glass; these things approach the point of the eye in pyramids, and these pyramids are cut by the said glass.

OF THE DIMINUTION OF OBJECTS AT VARIOUS DISTANCES

A second object as far removed from the first as the first is from the eye will appear half the size of the first, although they are of the same size.

A small object near at hand and a large one at a distance, when seen between equal angles will appear the same size. . . .

Perspective is a rational demonstration whereby experience confirms how all things transmit their images to the eye by pyramidal lines. By pyramidal lines I mean those which start from the extremities of the surface of bodies, and by gradually converging from a distance arrive at the same point; the said point being . . . in this particular case located in the eye, which is the universal judge of all objects. . . .

Leonardo was always engaged in a quest for the essential living form of a thing, the relationship of its parts to the whole, the numerical ratios subsisting among the parts, and the laws operative in the ratios. He found such ratios and laws everywhere in both animate and inanimate objects. In the following excerpt he tries to define the ratio of parts to the whole of the male human body. His written observations are accompanied by a marvelous sketch of the body, conceived and framed with realism and mathematical proportion.

If you set your legs so far apart as to take a fourteenth part from your height, and you open and raise your arms until you touch the line of the crown of the head with your middle fingers, you must know that the centre of the circle formed by the extremities of the outstretched limbs will be the navel, and the space between the legs will form an equilateral triangle.

The span of a man's outstretched arms is equal to his height.

From the beginning of the hair to the end of the bottom of the chin is the tenth part of a man's height; from the bottom of the chin to the crown of the head is the eighth of the man's height; from the top of the breast to the crown of the head is the sixth of the man; from the top of the breast to where the hair commences is the seventh part of the whole man; from the nipples to the crown of the head is a fourth part of the man. The maximum width of the shoulders is in itself the fourth part of a man; from the elbow to the tip of the middle finger is the fifth part; from this elbow to the end of the shoulder is the eighth part. The complete hand will be the tenth part. The penis begins at the centre of the man. The foot is the seventh part of the man. From the sole of the foot to just below the knee is the fourth part of the man. From below the knee to where the penis begins is the fourth part of the man.

The parts that find themselves between the chin and the nose and between the places where the hair and the eyebrows start each of itself compares with that of the ear, and is a third of the face.

LEONARDO ON HIS OWN GENIUS

Leonardo possessed extraordinary creative powers that awed his contemporaries. The Renaissance painter and art historian Giorgio Vasari said that Leonardo had "so rare a gift of talent and ability that to whatever subject he turned his attention, no matter how difficult, he presently made himself absolute master of it." In the following application for a position with Ludovico Sforza, Duc of Milan, he lists his many talents.

Most Illustrious Lord: Having now sufficiently considered the specimens of all those who proclaim themselves skilled [designers] of instruments of war, . . . I shall endeavor, without prejudice to anyone else, to explain myself to your Excellency, showing your Lordship my secrets, and then offering them to your best pleasure and [approval] to work with effect at opportune moments on all those things which, in part, shall be briefly noted below.

1. I have a sort of extremely light and strong bridges, adapted to be most easily carried, and with them you may pursue and at any time flee from the enemy; and others, secure and indestructible by fire and battle, easy and convenient to lift and place. Also methods of burning and destroying those of the enemy.

2. I know how, when a place is besieged, to take the water out of the trenches, and make endless variety of bridges and covered ways and ladders, and other machines pertaining to such expeditions.

3. Item. If, by reason of the height of the banks, or the strength of the place and its position, it is impossible, when besieging a place, to avail oneself of the plan of bombardment, I have methods for destroying every rock or other fortress, even if it were founded on a rock. . . .

4. Again, I have kinds of mortars; most convenient and easy to carry; and with these I can fling small stones almost resembling a storm. . . .

5. Item. I have means by secret and [winding] mines and ways, made without noise, to reach a designated [spot], even if it were needed to pass under a trench or a river.

6. Item. I will make covered chariots, safe and unattackable. . . . And behind these, infantry could follow quite unhurt and without any hindrance.

7. Item. In case of need I will make big guns, mortars, and light ordnance of fine and useful forms, out of the common type.

8. Where the operation of bombardment should fail, I would contrive catapults . . . and other machines of marvellous efficacy and not in common use. . . .

9. And when the fight should be at sea I have kinds of many machines most efficient for offense and defense, and vessels which will resist the attack of the largest guns and powder and fumes.

10. In time of peace I believe I can give perfect satisfaction and to the equal of any other in architecture and the composition of buildings public and private; and in guiding water from one place to another.

Item. I can carry out sculpture in marble, bronze, or clay, and also I can do in painting whatever may be done, as well as any other, be he who he may. . . .

And if any one of the above-named things seem to anyone to be impossible, . . . I am most ready to make the experiment . . . in whatever place may please your Excellency.

REVIEW QUESTIONS

1. How did mathematics, an empirical approach, and nature influence the artists of the Renaissance? Why was this a significant development?
2. Which one of Leonardo's claims impressed you the most? Why?

6 The Spread of the Renaissance

The Renaissance spread from Italy to Germany, France, England, and Spain. Exemplifying the Renaissance spirit in France was François Rabelais (c. 1495–c. 1553), a Benedictine monk (until he resigned from the order), a physician, and a humanist scholar. *Gargantua and Pantagruel*, Rabelais's satirical epic, attacked clerical education and monastic orders and expressed an appreciation for secular learning and a confidence in human nature. Like other Renaissance humanists, Rabelais criticized medieval philosophy for its overriding concern with obscure, confused, and irrelevant questions and censured a narrow-minded clergy who deprived people of life's joys. Expressing his aversion to medieval asceticism, he attacked monasticism as life-denying and extolled worldly pleasure as a legitimate need and aim of human nature.

François Rabelais
CELEBRATION OF THE WORLDLY LIFE

The following reading from *Gargantua and Pantagruel* contains a description of life at an imagined monastery, the abbey of Thélème, whose rules differed markedly from those of traditional medieval monasteries. Here Rabelais expressed the Renaissance celebration of the worldly life.

THE RULES ACCORDING TO WHICH THE THÉLÈMITES LIVED

All their life was regulated not by laws, statutes, or rules, but according to their free will and pleasure. They rose from bed when they pleased, and drank, ate, worked, and slept when the fancy seized them. Nobody woke them; nobody compelled them either to eat or to drink, or to do anything else whatever. So it was that Gargantua has established it. In their rules there was only one clause:

DO WHAT YOU WILL

because people who are free, well-born, well-bred, and easy in honest company have a natural spur and instinct which drives them to virtuous deeds and deflects them from vice; and this they called honour. When these same men are depressed and enslaved by vile constraint and subjection, they use this noble quality which once impelled them freely towards virtue, to throw off and break this yoke of slavery. For we always strive after things forbidden and covet what is denied us.

Making use of this liberty, they most laudably rivalled one another in all of them doing what they saw pleased one. If some man or woman said, "Let us drink," they all drank; if he or she said, "Let us play," they all played; if it was "Let us go and amuse ourselves in the fields," everyone went there. If it were for hawking or hunting, the ladies, mounted on fine mares, with their grand palfreys following, each carried on their daintily gloved wrists a sparrow-hawk, a lanneret, or a merlin, the men carrying the other birds.[1]

So nobly were they instructed that there was not a man or woman among them who could not read, write, sing, play musical instruments, speak five or six languages, and compose in them both verse and prose. Never were seen such worthy knights, so valiant, so nimble both on foot and horse; knights more vigorous, more agile, handier with all weapons than they were. Never were seen ladies so good-looking, so dainty, less tiresome, more skilled with the fingers and the needle, and in every free and honest womanly pursuit than they were. . . .

Now every method of teaching has been restored, and the study of languages has been revived: of Greek, without which it is disgraceful for a man to call himself a scholar, and of Hebrew, [other ancient Semitic languages], and Latin. The elegant and accurate art of printing, which is now in use, was invented in my time, by divine inspiration; as, by contrast, artillery was inspired by diabolical suggestion. The whole world is full of learned men, of very erudite tutors, and of most extensive libraries, and it is my opinion that neither in the time of Plato, of Cicero, nor of Papinian[2] were there such facilities for study as one finds today. No one, in future, will risk appearing in public or in any company, who is not well polished in Minerva's [Roman goddess of wisdom] workshop. I find robbers, hangmen, freebooters, and grooms nowadays more learned than the doctors and preachers were in my time.

Why, the very women and girls aspire to the glory and reach out for the celestial manna[3] of sound learning. So much so that at my present age I have been compelled to learn Greek, which I had not despised like Cato,[4] but which I had not the leisure to learn in my youth. Indeed I find great delight in reading the *Morals* of Plutarch, Plato's magnificent *Dialogues*, the *Monuments* of Pausanias, and the *Antiquities* of Athenaeus,[5] while I wait for the hour when it will please God, my Creator, to call me and bid me leave this earth.

Therefore, my son, I beg you to devote your youth to the firm pursuit of your studies and to the attainment of virtue. You are in Paris. There

---

Gargantua writes to his son Pantagruel, studying in Paris; in the letter, he describes a truly liberal education, one befitting a Renaissance humanist.

---

[1]*Palfreys* and *lanneret*, archaic terms, refer respectively to a saddle horse usually ridden by women and to a small male falcon native to the Mediterranean area. A merlin is a small black and white European falcon, now also called a pigeon hawk.

[2]Papinian was a Roman jurist of the late second to early third century A.D. whose legal opinions were considered authoritative in late Roman law.

[3]*Manna* refers to a food miraculously provided by God for the Hebrews during their exodus out of Egypt during Moses' time (Exodus 16:14–36).

[4]Cato the Elder (234–149 B.C.), a Roman statesman, was noted for his conservative morals and hostility to Greek influences in Roman society.

[5]Pausanias was a travel writer famous for his guides to the ancient monuments of Greece, and Athenaeus was a compiler of literary and philosophical writings. Both were Greeks of the second century A.D.

you will find many praiseworthy examples to follow. You have Epistemon for your tutor, and he can give you living instruction by word of mouth. It is my earnest wish that you shall become a perfect master of languages. First of Greek, as Quintilian [Roman educational theorist] advises; secondly, of Latin; and then of Hebrew, on account of the Holy Scriptures; also of Chaldean and Arabic, for the same reason; and I would have you model your Greek style on Plato's and your Latin on that of Cicero. Keep your memory well stocked with every tale from history, and here you will find help in the Cosmographes[6] of the historians. Of the liberal arts, geometry, arithmetic, and music, I gave you some smattering when you were still small, at the age of five or six. Go on and learn the rest, also the rules of astronomy. But leave divinatory astrology and Lully's[7] art alone, I beg of you, for they are frauds and vanities. Of Civil Law I would have you learn the best texts by heart, and relate them to the art of philosophy. And as for the knowledge of Nature's works, I should like you to give careful attention to that too; so that there may be no sea, river, or spring of which you do not know the fish. All the birds of the air, all the trees, shrubs, and bushes of the forest, all the herbs of the field, all the metals deep in the bowels of the earth, the precious stones of the whole East and the South—let none of them be unknown to you.

Then scrupulously peruse the books of the Greek, Arabian, and Latin doctors once more, not omitting the Talmudists and Cabalists,[8] and by frequent dissections gain a perfect knowledge of that other world which is man. At some hours of the day also, begin to examine the Holy Scriptures. First the New Testament and the Epistles of the Apostles in Greek; and then the Old Testament, in Hebrew. In short, let me find you a veritable abyss of knowledge. For, later, when you have grown into a man, you will have to leave this quiet and repose of study, to learn chivalry and warfare, to defend my house, and to help our friends in every emergency against the attacks of evildoers.

---

[6]Cosmographes are books on geography, geology, and astronomy.
[7]Lully alludes to Ramon Lull (c. 1236–1315), a Franciscan friar, a mystic, and a philosopher, who was falsely reputed to have authored various books on magic and alchemy.

---

[8]Talmudists are students of the collection of writings on Jewish civil and religious laws, and Cabalists refers to students of a medieval Jewish occult tradition based on a mystical interpretation of the Hebrew Scriptures.

William Shakespeare
HUMAN NATURE AND THE HUMAN CONDITION

By dealing with classical themes and figures, setting his plays in Renaissance Italy and ancient Greece, and probing the full range of people's motives, actions, and feelings, William Shakespeare (1564–1616), widely regarded as the world's finest playwright, gave expression to the Renaissance spirit. The following passages illustrate Shakespeare's brilliant insights into human nature and the human condition.

THE NOBILITY OF THE HUMAN BEING
Hamlet, Act II, Scene ii. lines 310–313

What a piece of work is a man! How noble in reason! How infinite in faculties! in form and moving how express and admirable! in action how like an angel! in apprehension how like a god! the beauty of the world, the paragon of animals.

THE DARK SIDE OF LIFE
Henry the Eighth, Act III, Scene ii. lines 414–428

Farewell! a long farewell, to all my greatness!
This is the state of man: to-day he puts forth
The tender leaves of hopes; to-morrow blossoms,
And bears his blushing honours thick upon him;
The third day come a frost, a killing frost,
And when he thinks, good easy man, full surely
His greatness is a-ripening, nips his root,
And then he falls, as I do. I have ventur'd,
Like little wanton boys that swim on bladders,
This many summers in a sea of glory,
But far beyond my depth: my high-blown pride
At length broke under me, and now has left me,
Weary and old with service, to the mercy
Of a rude stream, that must for ever hide me.
Vain pomp and glory of this world, I hate ye.

Macbeth, Act V, Scene v. lines 20–29

Tomorrow, and tomorrow, and tomorrow,
Creeps in this petty pace from day to day,
To the last syllable of recorded time;
And all our yesterdays have lighted fools
The way to dusty death. Out, out, brief candle!

Life's but a walking shadow, a poor player
That struts and frets his hour upon the stage,
And then is heard no more. It is a tale
Told by an idiot, full of sound and fury,
Signifying nothing.

Measure for Measure, Act III, Scene i. lines 130–144

Ay, but to die, and go we know not where,
To lie in cold obstruction and to rot,
This sensible warm motion to become
A kneaded clod; and the delighted spirit
To bathe in fiery floods, or to reside
In thrilling region of thick-ribbed ice,
To be imprison'd in the viewless winds,
And blown with restless violence round about
The pendent world; or to be worse than worst
Of those that lawless and incertain thought
Imagine howling: 'tis too horrible!
The weariest and most loathed worldly life
That age, ache, penury and imprisonment
Can lay on nature is a paradise
To what we fear of death.

WAR
The Tragedy of Coriolanus, Act IV, Scene v. lines 219–229

1. Serv[ingman]. Let me have war, say I; it exceeds peace as far as day does night; it's spritely, waking, audible, and full of vent. Peace is a very apoplexy, lethargy; mulled, deaf, sleepy, insensible; a getter of more bastard children than war's a destroyer of men.

2. Serv. 'Tis so: and as war, in some sort, may be said to be a ravisher, so it cannot be denied but peace is a great maker of cuckholds.

1. Serv. Ay, and it makes men hate one another.

3. Serv. Reason: because they then less need one another. The wars for my money.

---

311 faculties: powers
    express: well-modelled
312 apprehension: understanding

---

131 obstruction: stagnation (of the blood)
133 kneaded: i.e., like dough
135 thrilling: piercing with cold
136 viewless: invisible
228 Reason: that is natural

The Life of Henry V, Act IV, Scene i.
lines 125–134

Will[iams]. But if the cause be not good, the
 king himself hath a heavy reckoning to
 make when all those legs and arms and heads
 chopp'd off in a battle shall join together at
 the latter day and cry all 'We died at such
 a place'—some swearing, some crying for
 a surgeon, some upon their wives left poor
 behind them, some upon the debts they
 owe, some upon their children rawly left.
 I am afeard there are few die well that die in a
 battle, for how can they charitably dispose of
 anything when blood is their argument? Now
 if these men do not die well, it will be a black
 matter for the king that led them to it. . . .

THE ROLES WE PLAY
As You Like It, Act II, Scene vii.
lines 143–170

　　All the world's a stage,
And all the men and women merely players.
They have their exits and their entrances,
And one man in his time plays many parts,
His acts being seven ages. At first the infant,
Mewling and puking in the nurse's arms.
Then the whining schoolboy with his satchel
And shining morning face, creeping like snail
Unwillingly to school. And then the lover,
Sighing like furnace, with a woeful ballad
Made to his mistress' eyebrow. Then a soldier,
Full of strange oaths and bearded like the pard,
Jealous in honor, sudden and quick in quarrel,
Seeking the bubble Reputation
E'en in the cannon's mouth. And then the justice,
In fair round belly with good capon lin'd,
With eyes severe and beard of formal cut,

Full of wise saws and modern instances;
And so he plays his part. The sixt age shifts
Into the lean and slipper'd pantaloon,
With spectacles on nose and pouch on side;
His youthful hose well sav'd, a world too wide
For his shrunk shank, and his big manly voice,
Turning again toward childish treble, pipes
And whistles in his sound. Last scene of all,
That ends this strange eventful history,
Is second childishness and mere oblivion—
Sans teeth, sans eyes, sans taste, sans everything.

LOVE AND LOVERS
A Midsummer Night's Dream, Act V,
Scene i. lines 4–11

Lovers and madmen have such seething brains,
Such shaping fantasies, that apprehend
More than cool reason ever comprehends.
The lunatic, the lover, and the poet,
Are of imagination all compact:
One sees more devils than vast hell can hold,
That is the madman; the lover, all as frantic,
Sees Helen's beauty in a brow of Egypt: . . .

Troilus and Cressida, Act III, Scene ii.
lines 144–146

　　But you are wise,
Or else you love not; for to be wise and love
Exceeds man's might. That dwells with gods
 above.

The Two Gentlemen of Verona, Act III,
Scene i. lines 81–105

　DUKE
There is a lady of Verona here,
Whom I affect; but she is nice and coy

---

131 rawly left: poorly provided for
131 die well: i.e., who die a Christian death
132 they . . . anything: settle anything in a spirit of charity
148 Mewling: crying, mewing like a cat
154 pard: leopard
155 Jealous in: suspiciously careful of
157 E'en: Even

160 saws: maxims
　　modern instances: everyday illustrations
161 sixt: sixth
162 pantaloon: old dotard
169 mere: total
170 Sans: without
 11 Helen: Helen of Troy
　　brow of Egypt: gypsy's face

And nought esteems my aged eloquence.
Now therefore, would I have thee to my tutor,—
For long agone I have forgot to court;
Besides, the fashion of the time is chang'd—
How and which way I may bestow myself
To be regarded in her sun-bright eye.

VAL[ENTINE]
Win her with gifts, if she respect not words.
Dumb jewels often in their silent kind
More than quick words do move a woman's
    mind.

DUKE
But she did scorn a present that I sent her.

VAL
A woman sometime scorns what best
    contents her.
Send her another; never give her o'er,
For scorn at first makes after-love the more.
If she do frown, 'tis not in hate of you,
But rather to beget more love in you;
If she do chide, 'tis not to have you gone;
For why the fools are mad if left alone.
Take no repulse, whatever she doth say;
For 'get you gone,' she doth not mean
    'away!'
Flatter and praise, commend, extol their
    graces;
Though ne'er so black, say they have angels'
    faces.

_____

85 forgot: forgotten how
87 bestow: conduct
90 kind: nature
99 For why: because
103 black: dark-complexioned

That man that hath a tongue, I say,
    is no man,
If with his tongue he cannot win a woman.

As You Like It, Act III, Scene ii.
lines 359–364

ROS[ALIND]
But are you so much in love as your rhymes
    speak?

ORL[ANDO]
Neither rhyme nor reason can express
    how much.

ROS
Love is merely a madness and, I tell you,
    deserves as well a dark house and a whip as
    madmen do. And the reason why they are
    not so punish'd and cured is that the lunacy
    is so ordinary that the whippers are in love
    too.*

Much Ado About Nothing, Act II,
Scene iii. lines 60–68

Sigh no more, ladies, sigh no more,
    Men were deceivers ever;
One foot in sea, and one on shore,
    To one thing constant never.
        Then sigh not so,
        But let them go,
    And be you blithe and bonny,
Converting all your sounds of woe
    Into Hey nonny, nonny.

_____

*The whip and the dark room represented the extent of
Elizabethan treatment of the insane.

REVIEW QUESTIONS

1. In what ways did the curriculum recommended by Gargantua reflect the teachings
   of the Renaissance humanists?
2. How does the humanist educational program continue to influence the course of
   studies in modern universities?
3. How did Shakespeare express the Renaissance spirit? Which lines do you consider
   the most insightful? Why?

CHAPTER 10
The Reformation

MARTIN LUTHER AND THE WITTENBERG REFORMERS (c. 1543), by Lucas Cranach, the Younger. With Luther (left) are Frederick of Saxony, Luther's protector, who dominates the painting, and the Swiss reformer Huldreich Zwingli (to the right of Frederick). *(The Toledo Museum of Art; Gift of Edward Drummond Libbey)*

The reformation of the church in the sixteenth century was rooted in demands for spiritual renewal and institutional change. These pressures began as early as the late fourteenth century and came from many sources.

The papacy and orthodox Catholic theology were challenged by English theologian John Wycliffe (c. 1320–1384) and Czech theologian John Huss (c. 1369–1415). Both attacked the bishops' involvement in temporal politics and urged a return to the simple practices of the early apostolic church; and both, claiming that the Bible alone—not the church hierarchy—was the highest authority for Christians, emphasized study of the Holy Scriptures by the laity and sermons in the common language of the people. Wycliffe, though not Huss, also undermined the clergy's authority by denying the priests' power to change the bread and wine into Christ's body and blood during the Mass. Despite severe persecution by church and state, followers of Wycliffe's and Huss's beliefs continued to exist and participated in the sixteenth-century Protestant movement.

Institutional reform from within was attempted through the Conciliar movement, which endeavored to restrict the pope's power through regular meetings of general councils of bishops. The Council of Constance (1414–1418) declared that a general council, not the papacy, was the supreme authority within the church and called for regular assemblies of bishops to consider the church's problems and initiate necessary reforms.

By the mid-fifteenth century, the Conciliar movement had collapsed, and the papacy, unreformed, freely exercised its supremacy. Fearful of losing its autonomy and power, the papacy resisted calling a new council from 1437 until 1512, when the Fifth Lateran Council met in Rome under close papal supervision. The council issued decrees aimed at improving education of the clergy, eliminating many abuses in church administration, and summoning a church council every five years. But the council's decrees were not implemented after the last session ended in 1517, the same year Martin Luther first challenged the papacy, thus starting the Protestant reform movement.

The principal source of the reform spirit was a widespread popular yearning for a more genuine spirituality. It took many forms: the rise of new pious practices; greater interest in mystical experiences and in the study of the Bible; the development of communal ways for lay people to live and work following the apostles' example; and a heightened search for ways within secular society to imitate more perfectly the life of Christ—called the New Devotion movement.

Several secular factors contributed to this heightening of spiritual feeling. The many wars, famines, and plagues of the late fourteenth and the fifteenth centuries had traumatized Europe. The increasing educational level of the urban middle class and skilled laborers and the invention of the printing press allowed the rapid and relatively inexpensive spread of new ideas. Finally, there was the influence of the humanist movement, particularly in northern Europe and Spain. Many humanists dedicated themselves to promoting higher levels of religious education. They stimulated public interest in biblical study by publishing new editions of the Holy Scriptures and the writings of the church fathers, along with new devotional literature. Nearly all the religious reformers of the sixteenth century were deeply influenced by the ideals and methods of the Christian humanist movement.

In Germany, a spirit of discontent with social and economic conditions coincided with the demand for reform of the church and religious life. For several decades before Luther's revolt against the papacy, the economic conditions of the knights, the peasants, and the lower-class urban workers had deteriorated. The knights' grievances included loss of their political power to the centralizing governments of the German princes and increasing restrictions on their customary feudal privileges. Peasants protested that lords had steadily withdrawn certain of their customary rights and had added burdens, increasing the lords' income and control over their estates. The knights and peasants were squeezed into an ever-worsening social and economic niche. In the cities, the lower-class artisans and laborers were similarly oppressed. Those in the urban upper classes, who controlled town governments, enhanced their own economic privileges at the expense of lower-class citizens. The church, which was a major landowner and active in commercial enterprises in the towns, played an important role in these conflicts. All these grievances formed the explosive background to Martin Luther's challenge to the authority of the church and the imperial government.

The success of the reformers, both Protestant and Catholic, depended on support from the ruling political forces in the various kingdoms, principalities, and city-states of Europe. Usually, the rulers' religious preference determined whether the church remained Catholic or became Lutheran, Calvinist, or some combination of all three, as in England. The rulers of large parts of Germany, especially the imperial city-states, and of the Scandinavian kingdoms adopted the Lutheran reform. The Austrian and Spanish Hapsburg emperors and the French kings remained Catholic, although Calvinism had many adherents in France. In Eastern Europe, Protestantism was successful at first, but, under the influence of the Catholic reform movement, Catholicism later recovered its dominance. In Switzerland, allegiance was divided among Catholics and the followers of John Calvin, reformer of the church in Geneva, and of Ulrich Zwingli, reformer of the church in Zurich. Calvinism took root in Scotland, and its influence also grew in England where it inspired the Puritan movement.

These divisions in the Christian church marked a turning point in European history and culture, ending forever the coherent world-view of medieval Christendom. The Reformation split the peoples of Europe into two broad political, intellectual, and spiritual camps: Protestant and Catholic. With the moral, political, and ideological power of the church significantly diminished, post-Reformation society was open to increasing secularization on all fronts. By ending the religious unity of the Middle Ages and weakening the Catholic Church, the Reformation contributed significantly to the rise of modernity.

1   A Catholic Critic of the Church

The greatest scholar and most popular humanist author of the early sixteenth century was the Dutch priest Desiderius Erasmus (1466–1536). Educated under the influence of the New Devotion and well trained in the new humanistic studies, Erasmus dedicated his life to purifying the Latin and Greek texts of the Bible and those of the early fathers of the church. He used his wit and humanistic learning in his preaching to advocate a simpler yet more intense Christian life modeled on Christ. Erasmus castigated those who pandered to the superstitions of people by encouraging magical beliefs about relics, the cults of the saints, indulgences (see the next section), and other abuses of pious practices. He also was hostile to the excessive influence of scholastic philosophers on the church's theology, believing that in their quibbling over obscure philosophical-theological issues, they mocked the Christian faith as revealed in the New Testament. An Augustinian monk who preferred to live outside the monastery, Erasmus severely criticized the lax practices of monks and clergy. He argued, too, that salvation was not based on ascetic and ceremonial acts, but on deeds of love.

Although Erasmus at first welcomed Martin Luther's call for reform, he quickly discerned that Luther was going far beyond what he, Erasmus, felt was wise or necessary. He urged, instead, reform within the church's framework. Although scandalized by a pope leading armies and engaging in international war against other Christians, Erasmus clung loyally to the hierarchical church. He urged peace and civility on all parties, condemned extremist positions, and tried to work for peaceful reconciliation and reform. In 1524, Erasmus wrote a reasoned defense of the role of free will in the process of salvation, taking a Catholic position on this difficult theological problem. Luther was furious with Erasmus for not supporting him, and Erasmus found himself abused by zealots from both camps. To the end, he remained a devout, loyal, but critical Catholic reformer. His preaching, piety, and literary scholarship exemplified the ideals of Christian humanism.

Desiderius Erasmus
IN PRAISE OF FOLLY

Erasmus's most famous work was *In Praise of Folly*, written in 1509, before Luther's first challenge to the church. In the following passages, speaking through the voice of Folly, Erasmus castigates monks, theologians, and other Christians for failing to discern the true purpose of the Christian life: the imitation of Christ. It was said of Erasmus that he laid the egg Luther hatched—a judgment Erasmus did not acknowledge.

As for the theologians, perhaps it would be better to pass them over in silence, "*not stirring up the hornets' nest*" and "not laying a finger on the stinkweed," since this race of men is incredibly arrogant and touchy. For they might rise up en masse and march in ranks against me with six hundred conclusions and force me to recant. And if I should refuse, they would immediately shout "heretic." For this is the thunderbolt they always keep ready at a moment's notice to terrify anyone to whom they are not very favorably inclined. . . .

. . . They are so blessed by their Selflove as to be fully persuaded that they themselves dwell in the third heaven, looking down from high above on all other mortals as if they were earth-creeping vermin almost worthy of their pity. They are so closely hedged in by rows of magistral definitions, conclusions, corollaries, explicit and implicit propositions, they have so many "*holes they can run to*," that Vulcan [Roman god of fire] himself couldn't net them tightly enough to keep them from escaping by means of distinctions, with which they cut all knots as cleanly as the fine-honed edge of "the headsman's axe"— so many new terms have they thought up and such monstrous jargon have they coined. . . .

In all of these there is so much erudition, so much difficulty, that I think the apostles themselves would need to be inspired by a different spirit if they were forced to match wits on such points with this new breed of theologians. Paul could provide a living example of faith, but when he said "Faith is the substance of things to be hoped for and the evidence of things not seen," his definition was not sufficiently magisterial. So too, he lived a life of perfect charity, but he neither distinguished it nor defined it with sufficient dialectical precision in the first epistle to the Corinthians, chapter 13. . . .

. . . But Christ, interrupting their boasts (which would otherwise never come to an end), will say, "Where did this new race of Jews [quibbling theologians] come from? The only law I recognize as truly mine is the only one I hear nothing about. Long ago, not speaking obliquely in parables but quite openly, I promised my Father's inheritance not to hoods [worn by monks], or trifling prayers, or fasts, but rather deeds of faith and charity. Nor do I acknowledge those who too readily acknowledge their own deeds: those who want to appear even holier than I am can go dwell in the heavens of the Abraxasians[1] if they like, or they can order that a new heaven be built for them by the men whose petty traditions they have placed before my precepts." When they hear this and see sailors and teamsters chosen in preference to them, how do you suppose their faces will look as they stare at each other? . . .

Almost as happy as the theologians are those men who are commonly called "religious" and "monks"—though both names are quite incorrect, since a good part of them are very far removed from religion and no one is encountered more frequently everywhere you go. I cannot imagine how anything could be more wretched than these men. . . . For even though everyone despises this breed of men so thoroughly that even a chance meeting with one of them is considered unlucky, still they maintain a splendid opinion of themselves. First of all, they consider it the very height of piety to have so little to do with literature as not even to be able to read. Moreover, when they roar out their psalms in church like braying asses (counting their prayers indeed, but understanding them not at all), then (of all things!) they imagine that the listening saints are soothed and caressed with manifold delight. Among them are some who make a great thing out of their squalor and beggary, who stand at the door bawling out their demands for bread—(indeed there is no inn or coach or ship where they do not make a disturbance), depriving other beggars of no small share of their income. And in this manner these most agreeable fellows, with their filth, ignorance, coarseness, impudence, recreate for us, as they say, an image of the apostles. . . .

Closely related to such men are those who have adopted the very foolish (but nevertheless quite

---

[1] A heretical sect that believed there were 365 "heavens."

agreeable) belief that if they look at a painting or statue of that huge . . . Christopher, they will not die on that day; or, if they address a statue of Barbara with the prescribed words, they will return from battle unharmed, or, if they accost Erasmus on certain days, with certain wax tapers, and in certain little formulas of prayer, they will soon become rich.[2] Moreover, in George they have discovered a new Hercules. . . .[3] They all but worship George's horse, most religiously decked out in breastplates and bosses [ornaments], and from time to time oblige him with some little gift. To swear by his bronze helmet is thought to be an oath fit for a king.

Now what shall I [Folly] say about those who find great comfort in soothing self-delusions about fictitious pardons for their sins, measuring out the times in purgatory down to the droplets of a waterclock, parceling out centuries, years, months, days, hours, as if they were using mathematical tables. Or what about those who rely on certain little magical tokens and prayers thought up by some pious impostor for his own amusement or profit? They promise themselves anything and everything: wealth, honor, pleasure, an abundance of everything, perpetual health, a long life, flourishing old age, and finally a seat next to Christ among the saints, though this last they don't want for quite a while yet—that is, when the pleasures of this life, to which they cling with all their might, have finally slipped through their fingers, then it will be soon enough to enter into the joys of the saints. Imagine here, if you please, some businessman or soldier or judge who thinks that if he throws into the collection basket one coin from all his plunder, the whole cesspool of his

sinful life will be immediately wiped out. He thinks all his acts of perjury, lust, drunkenness, quarreling, murder, deception, dishonesty, betrayal are paid off like a mortgage, and paid off in such a way that he can start off once more on a whole new round of sinful pleasures.

Now who could be more foolish—rather, who could be happier—than those who assure themselves they will have the very ultimate felicity because they have recited daily those seven little verses from the holy psalms? A certain devil—certainly a merry one, but too loose-lipped to be very clever—is believed to have mentioned them to St. Bernard,[4] but the poor devil was cheated by a clever trick. Such absurdities are so foolish that even I am almost ashamed of them, but still they are approved not only by the common people but even by learned teachers of religion. . . .

But why have I embarked on this vast sea of superstitions?

Not if I had a hundred tongues, a hundred
  mouths,
A voice of iron, could I survey all kinds
Of fools, or run through all the forms of folly.[5]

So rife, so teeming with such delusions is the entire life of all Christians everywhere. And yet priests are not unwilling to allow and even foster such delusions because they are not unaware of how many emoluments accumulate from this source. In the midst of all this, if some odious wiseman should stand up and sing out the true state of affairs: "You will not die badly if you live well. You redeem your sins if to the coin you add a hatred of evil deeds, then tears, vigils, prayers, fasts, and if you change your whole way of life. This saint will help you if you imitate his life"—if that wiseman were to growl out such assertions and more like them, look how much happiness he would immediately take away from the minds of mortals, look at the confusion he would throw them into!

---

[2]Christopher refers to Saint Christopher, a popular legendary giant and the patron saint of travelers. Barbara was a widely venerated but legendary early Christian martyr and saint. Erasmus, an Italian bishop and also a saint, was martyred in about A.D. 303.

[3]George, the patron saint of England and of the Crusaders, was believed to have been martyred in about A.D. 300. Saint George's battle with a dragon was a popular legend. Hercules, a Greek hero, performed twelve difficult tasks that won him immortality as a gift of the gods. He was himself worshiped as a god by later Greeks and Romans.

[4]Saint Bernard (1091–1153) was a leading theologian, Cistercian monk, and preacher.

[5]Virgil's *Aeneid* 6.625–627.

REVIEW QUESTIONS

1. What criticisms did Desiderius Erasmus make of the institutional church?
2. What did he see as the solution to the ills afflicting the church?

2   The Lutheran Reformation

The reformation of the Western Christian church in the sixteenth century was precipitated by Martin Luther (1483–1546). A pious German Augustinian monk and theologian, Luther had no intention of founding a new church or over-throwing the political and ecclesiastical order of late medieval Europe. He was educated in the tradition of the New Devotion, and as a theology professor at the university in Wittenberg, Germany, he opposed rationalistic, scholastic theology. Sympathetic at first to the ideas of Christian humanists like Erasmus, Luther too sought a reform of morals and an end to abusive practices within the church. But a visit to the papal court in Rome in 1510 left him profoundly shocked at its worldliness and disillusioned with the papacy's role in the church's governance.

Martin Luther
ON PAPAL POWER, JUSTIFICATION BY FAITH, THE INTERPRETATION OF THE BIBLE, AND THE NATURE OF THE CLERGY

To finance the rebuilding of the church of St. Peter in Rome, the papacy in 1515 of-fered indulgences to those who gave alms for this pious work. An indulgence was a mitigation or remission of the penance imposed by a priest in absolving a penitent who confessed a sin and indicated remorse. Indulgences were granted by papal decrees for those who agreed to perform some act of charity, alms-giving, prayer, pilgrimage, or other pious work. Some preachers of this particular papal indulgence deceived people into believing that a "purchase" of this indulgence would win them, or even the dead, a secure place in heaven.

In 1517, Luther denounced the abuses connected with the preaching of papal indulgences. The quarrel led quickly to other and more profound theological is-sues. His opponents defended the use of indulgences on the basis of papal author-ity, shifting the debate to questions about the nature of papal power within the church. Luther responded with a vigorous attack on the whole system of papal governance. The principal points of his criticism were set out in his *Address to the Christian Nobility of the German Nation Concerning the Reform of the Christian*

Estate, published in August 1520. In the first excerpt that follows, Luther argued that the papacy was blocking any reform of the church and appealed to the nobility of Germany to intervene by summoning a "free council" to reform the church.

A central point of contention between Luther and Catholic critics was his theological teaching on justification (salvation) by faith and on the role of good works in the scheme of salvation. Luther had suffered anguish about his unworthiness before God. Then, during a mystical experience, Luther suddenly perceived that his salvation came not because of his good works but as a free gift from God due to Luther's faith in Jesus Christ.

Thus, while never denying that a Christian was obliged to perform good works, Luther argued that such pious acts were not helpful in achieving salvation. His claim that salvation or justification was attained through faith in Jesus Christ as Lord and Savior, and through that act of faith alone, became the rallying point of the Protestant reformers.

The Catholic position, not authoritatively clarified until the Council of Trent (1545–1563), argued that justification came not only through faith, but through hope and love as well, obeying God's commandments and doing good works. In *The Freedom of a Christian*, published in 1520, Luther outlined his teaching on justification by faith and on the inefficacy of good works; the second excerpt is from this work.

Another dispute between Luther and papal theologians was the question of interpretation of the Bible. In the medieval church, the final authority in any dispute over the meaning of Scriptural texts or church doctrine was ordinarily the pope alone, speaking as supreme head of the church or in concert with the bishops in an ecumenical council. The doctrine of papal infallibility (that the pope could not err in teaching matters of faith and morals) was already well known, but belief in this doctrine had not been formally required. Luther argued that the literal text of Scripture was alone the foundation of Christian truth, not the teaching of popes or councils. Moreover, Luther said that all believers were priests, and the clergy did not hold any power beyond that of the laity; therefore the special privileges of the clergy were unjustified. The third excerpt contains Luther's views on the interpretation of Scripture and the nature of priestly offices.

ON PAPAL POWER

The Romanists [traditional Catholics loyal to the papacy] have very cleverly built three walls around themselves. Hitherto they have protected themselves by these walls in such a way that no one has been able to reform them. As a result, the whole of Christendom has fallen abominably.

In the first place, when pressed by the temporal power they have made decrees and declared that the temporal power had no jurisdiction over them, but that, on the contrary, the spiritual power is above the temporal. In the second place, when the attempt is made to reprove them with the Scriptures, they raise the objection that only the pope may interpret the Scriptures. In the third place, if threatened with a council, their story is that no one may summon a council but the pope.

In this way they have cunningly stolen our three rods from us, that they may go unpunished. They have [settled] themselves within the safe stronghold of these three walls so that they can practice all the knavery and wickedness which we see today. Even when they have been compelled to hold a council they have weakened its power in advance by putting the princes under oath to let them remain as they were. In addition, they have given the pope full authority over all decisions of a council, so that it is all the same whether there are many councils or no councils. They only deceive us with puppet shows and sham fights. They fear terribly for their skin in a really free council! They have so intimidated kings and princes with this technique that they believe it would be an offense against God not to be obedient to the Romanists in all their knavish and ghoulish deceits. . . .

The Romanists have no basis in Scripture for their claim that the pope alone has the right to call or confirm a council. This is just their own ruling, and it is only valid as long as it is not harmful to Christendom or contrary to the laws of God. Now when the pope deserves punishment, this ruling no longer obtains, for not to punish him by authority of a council is harmful to Christendom. . . .

Therefore, when necessity demands it, and the pope is an offense to Christendom, the first man who is able should, as a true member of the whole body, do what he can to bring about a truly free council. No one can do this so well as the temporal authorities, especially since they are also fellow-Christians, fellow-priests, fellow-members of the spiritual estate, fellow-lords over all things. Whenever it is necessary or profitable they ought to exercise the office and work which they have received from God over everyone.

JUSTIFICATION BY FAITH

You may ask, "What then is the Word of God, and how shall it be used, since there are so many words of God?" I answer: The Apostle explains this in Romans 1. The Word is the gospel of God concerning his Son, who was made flesh, suffered, rose from the dead, and was glorified through the Spirit who sanctifies. To preach Christ means to feed the soul, make it righteous, set it free, and save it, provided it believes

the preaching. Faith alone is the saving and efficacious use of the Word of God, according to Rom. 10(:9): "If you confess with your lips that Jesus is Lord and believe in your heart that God raised him from the dead, you will be saved." Furthermore, "Christ is the end of the law, that every one who has faith may be justified" (Rom. 10:4). Again, in Rom. 1(:17), "He who through faith is righteous shall live." The Word of God cannot be received and cherished by any works whatever but only by faith. Therefore it is clear that, as the soul needs only the Word of God for its life and righteousness, so it is justified by faith alone and not any works; for if it could be justified by anything else, it would not need the Word, and consequently it would not need faith.

This faith cannot exist in connection with works—that is to say, if you at the same time claim to be justified by works, whatever their character—for that would be the same as "limping with two different opinions" (I Kings 18:21), as worshiping Baal and kissing one's own hand (Job 31:27–28), which, as Job says, is a very great iniquity. Therefore the moment you begin to have faith you learn that all things in you are altogether blameworthy, sinful, and damnable, as the Apostle says in Rom. 3(:23), "Since all have sinned and fall short of the glory of God," and, "None is righteous, no, not one: . . . all have turned aside, together they have gone wrong" (Rom. 3:10–12). When you have learned this you will know that you need Christ, who suffered and rose again for you so that, if you believe in him, you may through this faith become a new man in so far as your sins are forgiven and you are justified by the merits of another, namely, of Christ alone.

Since, therefore, this faith can rule only in the inner man, as Rom. 10(:10) says, "For man believes with his heart and so is justified," and since faith alone justifies, it is clear that the inner man cannot be justified, freed, or saved by any outer work or action at all, and that these works, whatever their character, have nothing to do with this inner man. On the other hand, only ungodliness and unbelief of heart, and no outer work, make him guilty and a damnable servant of sin. Wherefore it ought to be the first concern of every Christian to lay aside all confidence in works and increasingly to strengthen faith alone and through faith to grow in the knowledge, not of works, but of Christ Jesus, who suffered and rose for him, as Peter teaches in the last chapter of his first Epistle (1 Pet. 5:10). No other work makes a Christian. . . .

Our faith in Christ does not free us from works but from false opinions concerning works, that is, from the foolish presumption that justification is acquired by works. Faith redeems, corrects, and preserves our consciences so that we know that righteousness does not consist in works, although works neither can nor ought to be wanting; just as we cannot be without food and drink and all the works of this mortal body, yet our righteousness is not in them, but in faith; and yet those works of the body are not to be despised or neglected on that account. In this world we are bound by the needs of our bodily life, but we are not righteous because of them. "My kingship is not of this world" (John 18:36), says Christ. He does not, however, say, "My kingship is not here, that is, in this world." And Paul says, "Though we live in the world we are not carrying on a worldly war" (II Cor. 10:3), and in Gal. 2(:20), "The life I now live in the flesh I live by faith in the Son of God." Thus what we do, live, and are in works and ceremonies, we do because of the necessities of this life and of the effort to rule our body. Nevertheless we are righteous, not in these, but in the faith of the Son of God.

THE INTERPRETATION OF THE BIBLE AND THE NATURE OF THE CLERGY

They (the Roman Catholic Popes) want to be the only masters of Scriptures. . . . They assume sole authority for themselves and would persuade us with insolent juggling of words that the Pope, whether he be bad or good, cannot err in matters of faith. . . .

. . . They cannot produce a letter to prove that the interpretation of Scripture . . . belongs to the Pope alone. They themselves have usurped this power . . . and though they allege that this power was conferred on Peter when the keys were given to him, it is plain enough that the keys were not given to Peter alone but to the entire body of Christians (Matt. 16:19; 18:18). . . .

. . . Every baptized Christian is a priest already, not by appointment or ordination from the Pope or any other man, but because Christ Himself has begotten him as a priest . . . in baptism. . . .

The Pope has usurped the term "priest" for his anointed and tonsured hordes [clergy and monks]. By this means they have separated themselves from the ordinary Christians and have called themselves uniquely the "clergy of God," God's heritage and chosen people who must help other Christians by their sacrifice and worship. . . . Therefore the Pope argues that he alone has the right and power to ordain and do what he will. . . .

[But] the preaching office is no more than a public service which happens to be conferred on someone by the entire congregation all the members of which are priests. . . .

. . . The fact that a pope or bishop anoints, makes tonsures, ordains, consecrates [makes holy], and prescribes garb different from those of the laity . . . nevermore makes a Christian and a spiritual man. Accordingly, through baptism all of us are consecrated to the priesthood, as St. Peter says . . . (I Peter 2:9).

To make it still clearer, if a small group of pious Christian laymen were taken captive and settled in a wilderness and had among them no priest consecrated by a bishop, if they were to agree to choose one from their midst, married or unmarried, and were to charge him with the office of baptizing, saying Mass, absolving [forgiving of sins], and preaching, such a man would be as truly a priest as he would if all bishops and popes had consecrated him.

Ulrich von Hutten
RESENTMENT OF ROME

Many Germans were drawn to Luther's message, for it signified a return to the spiritual purity of the first Christians, which had been undermined by a wealthy and corrupt church. Most historians agree that religious considerations—people's yearning for greater holiness and communion with God—were the principal reasons Luther attracted a following. But economic and political factors also drew Germans to him. The urban middle class, in particular, greatly resented the draining of money from German lands in order to provide a luxurious lifestyle for the Roman upper clergy. In a letter written in 1520 to the Elector Frederick of Saxony, Ulrich von Hutten (1488–1523), a distinguished humanist and supporter of Luther, angrily denounced the Roman church for plundering German lands. Hutten's words, excerpted below, also reveal an emerging sense of German national feeling.

We see that there is no gold and almost no silver in our German land. What little may perhaps be left is drawn away daily by the new schemes invented by the council of the most holy members of the Roman curia. What is thus squeezed out of us is put to the most shameful uses. Would you know, dear Germans, what employment I have myself seen that they make at Rome of our money? It does not lie idle! Leo the Tenth gives a part to nephews and relatives (these are so numerous that there is a proverb at Rome, "As thick as Leo's relations"). A portion is consumed by so many most reverend cardinals (of which the holy father created no less than one and thirty in a single day), as well as to support innumerable [auditors, personal secretaries, palace managers, and other high officials] forming the élite of the great head church. These in turn draw after them at untold expense copyists, beadles, messengers, servants, scullions [kitchen help], mule drivers, grooms and an innumerable army of prostitutes and of the most degraded followers. They maintain dogs, horses, monkeys, long-tailed apes and many more such creatures for their pleasure. They construct houses all of marble. They have precious stones, are clothed in purple and fine linen and dine sumptuously, frivolously indulging themselves in every species of luxury. In short, a vast number of the worst of men are supported in Rome in idle indulgence by means of our money. . . . Does not Your Grace perceive how many bold robbers, how many cunning hypocrites commit repeatedly the greatest crimes under the monk's cowl, and how many crafty hawks feign the simplicity of doves, and how many ravening wolves simulate the innocence of lambs? And although there be a few truly pious among them, even they cling to superstition and pervert the law of life which Christ laid down for us.

Now, if all these who devastate Germany and continue to devour everything might once be driven out, and an end made of their unbridled plundering, swindling and deception, with which the Romans have overwhelmed us, we should again have gold and silver in sufficient quantities and should be able to keep it. And then this money, in such supply and value as it may be present, might be put to better uses, for example: to put on foot great armaments and extend the boundaries of the Empire; also that the Turks may be conquered, if this seems desirable; that many who, because of poverty, steal and rob, may honestly earn their living once more, and that those who otherwise must starve may receive from the state contributions to mitigate their need; that scholars may be helped and the study of the arts and sciences, and of good literature advanced; above all that every virtue may receive its reward; want to be relieved at home; indolence banished and deceit killed.

REVIEW QUESTIONS

1. Why did Martin Luther see the papacy as the crucial block to any meaningful reform of the church?
2. How did Luther's teaching undermine the power of the clergy and traditional forms of piety?
3. According to Ulrich von Hutten, why were Germans distressed with the Roman church?

3   The German Peasants' Revolt

After Luther was outlawed as a heretic by the Imperial Diet (parliament) at Worms in 1521, economic and political grievances among the knights, peasants, and lower-class urban workers fostered a series of rebellions. The uprisings were largely local affairs, mostly in southwestern Germany. When the knights revolted against their lords in 1523, they were quickly crushed. A more widespread peasant revolt followed in 1525, accompanied in some places by sympathetic rebellions among the lower-class artisans and laborers of nearby towns. Driven to a frenzy by their grievances and religious enthusiasm, the German peasants seized lords' estates and pillaged churches and monasteries in a rebellion covering a third of the country. Lacking effective training and leaders, however, they were soon crushed by the vengeful lords' armies.

Although Luther was not primarily responsible for the peasants' revolt, his attacks on the abuses of the ruling nobles and the clergy coincided with the growing anger and resentment among knights, peasants, and lower-class townspeople. The peasants had hoped that Luther, who had denounced the lords' cruelty and oppression, would endorse if not lead their revolt. They were completely mistaken. Luther was preoccupied with the individual's relationship with God and with attaining salvation through faith. He did not intend to initiate social revolution and regarded rebellion against the constituted authority of the state as contrary to the Gospel's spirit. To Luther, subjects had the duty to obey state authority, since it was ordained by God.

Anonymous
TO THE ASSEMBLY OF THE COMMON PEASANTRY

In May 1525, at the time of the peasant rebellion, a pamphlet, *To the Assembly of the Common Peasantry*, whose author is unknown, was printed in Nuremberg. The work, excerpted below, clearly states the peasants' grievances.

CHAPTER FOUR

On false and unlimited power,
which one is not obliged to obey.

All the popes, emperors, kings, etc. who puff themselves up in their own estimation above other pious poor Christians, claiming to be a better kind of human—as if their lordship and authority to rule others were innate—do not want to recognize that they are God's stewards and officials. And they do not govern according to his commandment to maintain the common good and brotherly unity among us. God has established and ordained authority for this reason alone, and no other. . . .

Therefore whichever prince or lord invents and sets up his own self-serving burdens and commands, rules falsely, and he dares impudently to deceive God, his own lord. Where are you, you werewolves, with your financial tricks which impose one burden after another on the poor people? This year a labor service is voluntary, next year it becomes compulsory. In most cases this is how your old customary law has grown. In what dementia or camouflage did God, your lord, give you such power that we poor people have to cultivate your lands with labor services? But only in good weather, for on rainy days we poor people see the fruits of our sweat rot in the fields. May God, in his justice, not tolerate the terrible Babylonian captivity in which we poor people are driven to mow the lords' meadows, to make hay, to cultivate the fields, to sow flax in them, to cut it, comb it, heat it, wash it, pound it, and spin it—yes, even to sew their underpants on their arses. We also have to pick peas and harvest carrots and asparagus.

Help us, God! Where has such misery ever been heard of! They tax and tear out the marrow of the poor people's bones, and we have to pay interest on that! Where are they, with their hired murderers and horsemen, the gamblers and whoremasters, who are stuffed fuller than puking dogs? In addition, we poor people have to give them taxes, payments, and interest. And at home [they assume that] the poor should have neither bread, salt nor lard for their wives and small children. Where are they, with their entry fines and heriot dues? Yes, damn their disgraceful fines and robber's dues! Where are the tyrants and raging ones, who appropriate taxes, customs, and user fees, and waste them so shamefully and wantonly, and lose what should go into the common chest or purse to serve the needs of the territory. . . .

God can and will no longer tolerate this great misery and wantonness, which is now found everywhere. May God enlighten his poor lambs through divine grace and with true Christian faith, and protect them against these ravaging wolves. . . .

CHAPTER SEVEN

Whether a community may depose its
authorities or not? . . .

I will speak only briefly about this. All the lords who issue selfish commands stemming from the desires of their hearts and their willful, unjust heads, and who appropriate for themselves— I will remain silent about their plunder—taxes, customs, payments, and what similarly serves the common fund for the protection and maintenance of the common territory, these lords are in truth the real robbers and the declared enemies of their own territory. . . .

CHAPTER EIGHT

*In what form a community may
depose its lords. . . .*

But if the lords always want to be lords and to treat you poor people in the most arbitrary way, contrary to the divine laws which I have discussed above, then follow Solomon and bravely assemble now! Arm yourselves in the spirit of the bold oxen and steers, who gather together staunchly in a ring with their horns outward, not with the intention of rebelling, but only to defend themselves against the ravaging wolves. . . .

After you have assembled, if your opponents still want to have a war, and they pursue this crazy idea of disputing the gospel with lances, halberds, guns, and armor, then it is God's will. Then let happen what cannot happen differently. Their sacrilegious attacks are hated by God. But you trust in God! Be firm in faith! You are not your own but God's

warriors to uphold the gospel and to tear down the Babylonian prison! Each of you should make every effort to deal with the others in all fidelity and love! Do not quarrel among yourselves and be strict with one another! Let each tolerate the others with the greatest discipline and goodness; maintain the fear of God; and do not tolerate any drinkers! In no case allow blasphemers with their damned tongues among you! Then God will surely be your general.

CHAPTER NINE

*Who should be blamed for
being a rebel?*

Some, along with their bloody band, blame you and cry out that you are deviant, treacherous rogues [who have betrayed] your hereditary and natural lords. But do not let yourselves be led astray and do not worry about what they jabber.

Yes, they scream, rant, and curse rebellion so violently, seeking to damn it completely. And in doing this they never think about the cause of the disturbance, which is themselves and their godless nature.

Martin Luther
AGAINST THE THIEVISH, MURDEROUS HORDES OF PEASANTS

A manifesto, The Twelve Articles, was drawn up by the leaders of the peasants of Swabia in southwestern Germany. It blended Lutheran reform ideas with the peasants' demands for relief from their landlords' domination. In a pamphlet published just prior to the peasants' uprising, Martin Luther criticized the Twelve Articles, opposing what he feared was an egalitarian social revolution that threatened the hierarchical order of society and the legitimate property rights of the lords and clergy. He urged peaceful resolution of the crisis, pointing out the just grievances of the peasants.

When in the spring of 1525 the peasants finally took up arms against their manorial lords, they were joined by the lower-class artisans and workers in many towns. In a pamphlet entitled *Against the Thievish, Murderous Hordes of Peasants,* Luther reacted sternly, urging the princes to repress the rebels with every power at their command.

. . . They are starting a rebellion, and are violently robbing and plundering monasteries and castles which are not theirs; by this they have doubly deserved death in body and soul as highwaymen and murderers. Furthermore, anyone who can be proved to be a seditious person is an outlaw before God and the emperor; and whoever is the first to put him to death does right and well. For if a man is in open rebellion, everyone is both his judge and his executioner; just as when a fire starts, the first man who can put it out is the best man to do the job. For rebellion is not just simple murder; it is like a great fire, which attacks and devastates a whole land. Thus rebellion brings with it a land filled with murder and bloodshed; it makes widows and orphans, and turns everything upside down, like the worst disaster. Therefore let everyone who can, smite, slay, and stab, secretly or openly, remembering that nothing can be more poisonous, hurtful, or devilish than a rebel. It is just as when one must kill a mad dog; if you do not strike him, he will strike you, and a whole land with you.

It does not help the peasants when they pretend that according to Genesis 1 and 2 all things were created free and common, and that all of us alike have been baptized. For under the New Testament, Moses does not count; for there stands our Master, Christ, and subjects us, along with our bodies and our property, to the emperor and the law of this world, when he says, "Render to Caesar the things that are Caesar's" (Luke 20:25). Paul, too, speaking in Romans 12 (13:1) to all

baptized Christians, says, "Let every person be subject to the governing authorities." And Peter says, "Be subject to every ordinance of man" (I Pet. 2:13). We are bound to live according to this teaching of Christ, as the Father commands from heaven, saying, "This is my beloved Son, listen to him" (Matt. 17:5).

For baptism does not make men free in body and property, but in soul; and the gospel does not make goods common, except in the case of those who, of their own free will, do what the apostles and disciples did in Acts 4 (:32–37). They did not demand, as do our insane peasants in their raging, that the goods of others—of Pilate and Herod—should be common, but only their own goods. Our peasants, however, want to make the goods of other men common, and keep their own for themselves. Fine Christians they are! I think there is not a devil left in hell; they have all gone into the peasants. Their raving has gone beyond all measure. . . .

. . . I will not oppose a ruler who, even though he does not tolerate the gospel, will smite and punish these peasants without first offering to submit the case to judgment. He is within his rights, since the peasants are not contending any longer for the gospel, but have become faithless, perjured, disobedient, rebellious murderers, robbers, and blasphemers, whom even a heathen ruler has the right and authority to punish. Indeed, it is his duty to punish such scoundrels, for this is why he bears the sword and is "the servant of God to execute his wrath on the wrongdoer," Romans 13(:4).

REVIEW QUESTIONS

1. In referring to the "terrible babylonian captivity," of the peasants, what afflictions did the writer describe?
2. On what grounds did he condemn those responsible for the peasants' misery?
3. What did he propose the peasants should do? How did he justify it?
4. How did Martin Luther use the Scriptures to respond to the peasants' claims?

4 Luther and the Jews

Initially, Luther hoped to attract Jews to his vision of reformed Christianity. In *That Jesus Was Born a Jew* (1523), the young Luther expressed sympathy for Jewish sufferings and denounced persecution as a barrier to conversion. He declared, "I hope that if one deals in a kindly way with the Jews and instructs them carefully from the Holy Scripture, many of them will become genuine Christians. . . . We [Christians] are aliens and in-laws; they are blood relatives, cousins, and brothers of our Lord." When the Jews did not abandon their faith, however, Luther launched a diatribe against them.

Martin Luther
ON THE JEWS AND THEIR LIES

In *On the Jews and Their Lies* (1543), Martin Luther accepted at face value hateful medieval myths about the Jews: that they engaged in sorcery and magic, poisoned the wells of Christians, desecrated the Eucharistic host, and ritually murdered Christian children. In the concluding section, excerpted here, Luther advises civil and clerical authorities to treat the Jews harshly. The authorities did not heed Luther's proposals to raze synagogues and homes—although some anti-Jewish measures were introduced—and for several centuries Lutheran theologians paid little mind to Luther's anti-Judaism. In the late nineteenth century, German nationalists revived Luther's treatise and the Nazis gleefully circulated his words as an authoritative endorsement of their anti-Semitic ideology.[1]

. . . [D]ear Christian, be on your guard against the Jews, who, as you discover here, are consigned by the wrath of God to the devil, who has not only robbed them of a proper understanding of Scripture, but also of ordinary human reason, shame, and sense, and only works mischief with Holy Scriptures through them. Therefore they cannot be trusted and believed in any other matter either, even though a truthful word

may drop from their lips occasionally. For anyone who dares to juggle the awesome word of God so frivolously and shamefully . . . cannot have a good spirit dwelling in him. Therefore, wherever you see a genuine Jew, you may with a good conscience cross yourself and bluntly say: "There goes a devil incarnate." . . .

. . . [D]ear Christian, be advised and do not doubt that next to the devil, you have no more bitter, venomous, and vehement foe than a real Jew who earnestly seeks to be a Jew. . . . Therefore the history books often accuse them of contaminating wells, of kidnaping and piercing children, as for example at Trent, Weissensee, etc. They, of course, deny this. Whether it is true or not, I do know that they do not lack the complete, full, and ready will to do such things either secretly or openly

[1]In 1994 the Church Council of the Evangelical Lutheran Church in America acknowledged "with pain . . . Luther's anti-Judaic diatribes and violent recommendations . . . against Jews. . . . [W]e reject this violent invective, and yet more do we express our deep and abiding sorrow over its tragic effects on subsequent generations. In concert with the Lutheran World Federation, we particularly deplore the appropriation of Luther's words by modern antisemites for the teaching of hatred toward Judaism or toward Jewish people in our day."

where possible. This you can assuredly expect from them, and you must govern yourself accordingly. . . .

. . . [T]heir own vile external life . . . abounds with witchcraft, conjuring signs, figures, . . . idolatry, envy, and conceit. Moreover, they are nothing but thieves and robbers who daily eat no morsel and wear no thread of clothing which they have not stolen and pilfered from us by means of their accursed usury. Thus they live from day to day, together with wife and child, by theft and robbery, as archthieves and robbers, in the most impenitent security. . . .

But for us Christians they stand as a terrifying example of God's wrath. . . . The example of the Jews demonstrates clearly how easily the devil can mislead people, after they once have digressed from the proper understanding of Scripture, into such blindness and darkness that it can be readily grasped and perceived simply by natural reason, yes, even by irrational beasts. And yet they who daily teach and hear God's word do not recognize this darkness but regard it as the true light. O Lord God, have mercy on us! . . .

. . . It serves them right that, rejecting the truth of God, they have to believe instead such abominable, stupid, inane lies, and that instead of the beautiful face of the divine word, they have to look into the devil's black, dark, lying behind, and worship his stench. . . .

. . . [The Jews wish to] lay their hands on the land, the goods, and the government of the whole world. . . . And now a storm breaks over us with curses, defamation, and derision that cannot be expressed with words. They wish that sword and war, distress and every misfortune may overtake us accursed Goyim. They vent their curses on us openly every Saturday in their synagogues and daily in their homes. They teach, urge, and train their children from infancy to remain the bitter, virulent, and wrathful enemies of the Christians. . . .

. . . They have been bloodthirsty bloodhounds and murderers of all Christendom for more than fourteen hundred years in their intentions, and would undoubtedly prefer to be such with their

deeds. Thus they have been accused* of poisoning water and wells, of kidnaping children, of piercing them through with an awl, of hacking them in pieces, and in that way secretly cooling their wrath with the blood of Christians, for all of which they have often been condemned to death by fire. . . .

. . . Furthermore, we do not know to the present day which devil brought them into our country. We surely did not bring them from Jerusalem. . . . For they are a heavy burden, a plague, a pestilence, a sheer misfortune for our country. Proof for this is found in the fact that they have often been expelled forcibly from a country. . . .

What shall we Christians do with this rejected and condemned people, the Jews? Since they live among us, we dare not tolerate their conduct, now that we are aware of their lying and reviling and blaspheming. If we do, we become sharers in their lies, cursing, and blasphemy. . . . I shall give you my sincere advice:

First, to set fire to their synagogues or schools and to bury and cover with dirt whatever will not burn, so that no man will ever again see a stone or cinder of them. This is to be done in honor of our Lord and of Christendom, so that God might see that we are Christians, and do not condone or knowingly tolerate such public lying, cursing, and blaspheming of his Son and of his Christians. . . .

Second, I advise that their houses also be razed and destroyed. For they pursue in them the same aims as in their synagogues. Instead they might be lodged under a roof or in a barn, like the gypsies. This will bring home to them the fact that they are not masters in our country, as they boast, but that they are living in exile and in captivity, as they incessantly wail and lament about us before God.

---

*The element of caution in Luther's phraseology here perhaps indicates some awareness on his part of the unsupported character of such accusations. In 1510, for example, thirty-eight Jews had been executed in Berlin on a charge of desecration of the host. In 1539, however, in the context of a debate on policy toward the Jews at the assembly of Protestant estates at Frankfurt, Philip Melanchthon presented convincing evidence that they had been innocent.

Third, I advise that all their prayer books and Talmudic writings, in which such idolatry, lies, cursing, and blasphemy are taught, be taken from them.

Fourth, I advise that their rabbis be forbidden to teach henceforth on pain of loss of life and limb. . . .

Fifth, I advise that safe-conduct on the highways be abolished completely for the Jews. For they have no business in the countryside, since they are not lords, officials, tradesmen, or the like. Let them stay at home. . . .

Sixth, I advise that usury be prohibited to them, and that all cash and treasure of silver and gold be taken from them and put aside for safekeeping. The reason for such a measure is that, as said above, they have no other means of earning a livelihood than usury, and by it they have stolen and robbed from us all they possess.

In brief, dear princes and lords, those of you who have Jews under your rule—if my counsel does not please you, find better advice, so that you and we all can be rid of the unbearable devilish burden of the Jews, lest we become guilty sharers before God in the lies, the blasphemy, the defamation, and the curses which the mad Jews indulge in so freely and wantonly against the person of our Lord Jesus Christ, his dear mother, all Christians, all authority, and ourselves.

REVIEW QUESTIONS

1. What factors seemed to motivate Martin Luther's attack against the Jews?
2. What steps did Luther advocate to reduce the role of the Jews in German society?

---

5 The Calvinist Reformation

In the first decade of the Lutheran movement, Protestant reform had not spread significantly outside Germany due to suppression by the royal governments in France, Spain, and England. But in 1534 a French clergyman, John Calvin (1509–1564), resigned his church offices and fled to Basel, a Swiss city that had accepted Protestant reforms. There he composed a summary of the new Protestant theology, *The Institutes of the Christian Religion*, which was to be revised four times before his death. Written in the elegant Latin style favored by humanists, the work was translated into French and soon became the principal theological text for French, Swiss, Dutch, Scottish, and English Protestant reformers. Calvin himself settled in Geneva, Switzerland, where his influence dominated the civil and religious life of the townspeople. From Geneva, Calvin carried on an active mission, spreading his reformed faith throughout his native France and elsewhere.

In 1536, the newly Protestant-controlled government of Geneva asked Calvin to draw up a public confession of the reformed faith, a catechism, and rules for liturgical worship. But the Council of Geneva's demand that all citizens be forced to subscribe to the new confession resulted in a change of government at the elections in 1538. Calvin withdrew to Basel. By 1541, the political situation had changed again; Calvin was recalled, and his recommendations for a new government for the church were put into law. He remained the spiritual leader of

Geneva and of many reformed Protestants elsewhere until his death. Calvinism was especially influential in England and Scotland, giving rise to the Puritan movement in seventeenth-century England and the Presbyterian churches in Scotland and Ireland. Both of these religious traditions exercised great influence on the settlers of the English colonies in North America.

John Calvin
THE INSTITUTES OF THE CHRISTIAN RELIGION

One doctrine that assumed greater and greater importance in the four separate revised editions of Calvin's *Institutes* was predestination: the belief that each person's salvation or damnation was already decided before birth. This doctrine raised a question about whether Christ offered salvation for all human beings or only for the elect—a chosen few who were predestined to be saved by God's sovereign will. Some argued that the latter interpretation, one strongly articulated by Saint Augustine, implied that God was a tyrant who created human beings to be damned and that they were not free to acquire salvation by faith. In effect, salvation and damnation were foreordained. To many Christians, this doctrine diminished the justice and mercy of God, made meaningless the idea of freedom of choice in the process of salvation, and stripped good works of any role in gaining salvation. In the following excerpt (from *The Institutes of the Christian Religion*), Calvin offered his definition of predestination and cited Saint Paul as an authority.

The covenant of life is not preached equally to all, and among those to whom it is preached, does not always meet with the same reception. This diversity displays the unsearchable depth of the divine judgment, and is without doubt subordinate to God's purpose of eternal election. But if it is plainly owing to the mere pleasure of God that salvation is spontaneously offered to some, while others have no access to it, great and difficult questions immediately arise, questions which are inexplicable, when just views are not entertained concerning election and predestination. To many this seems a perplexing subject, because they deem it most incongruous that of the great body of mankind some should be predestined to salvation, and others to destruction. . . .

. . . By predestination we mean the eternal decree of God, by which he determined with himself whatever he wished to happen with regard to every man. All are not created on equal terms, but some are preordained to eternal life, others to eternal damnation; and, accordingly, as each has been created for one or other of these ends, we say that he has been predestinated to life or to death. . . .

. . . We say, then, that Scripture clearly proves this much, that God by his eternal and immutable counsel determined once for all those whom it was his pleasure one day to admit to salvation, and those whom, on the other hand, it was his pleasure to doom to destruction. We maintain that this counsel, as regards the elect, is founded on his free mercy, without any respect to human worth, while those whom he dooms to destruction are excluded from access to life by a just and blameless, but at the same time incomprehensible judgment. In regard to the elect, we regard calling as the evidence of election, and justification as another symbol of its manifestation, until it is fully accomplished by the attainment of glory. But as the Lord seals his elect by calling and justification, so by excluding the reprobate either from the knowledge of his name or the sanctification of his Spirit, he by these marks in a manner discloses the judgment which awaits them. . . .

Many controvert all the positions which we have laid down, especially the gratuitous election of believers, which however cannot be overthrown. For they commonly imagine that God distinguishes between men according to the merits which he foresees that each individual is to have, giving the adoption of sons to those whom he foreknows will not be unworthy of his grace, and dooming those to destruction whose dispositions he perceives will be prone to mischief and wickedness. . . .

. . . Assuredly divine grace would not deserve all the praise of election, were not election gratuitous; and it would not be gratuitous, did God in electing any individual pay regard to his future works. Hence, what Christ said to his disciples is found to be universally applicable to all believers, "Ye have not chosen me, but I have chosen you" (John xv. 16). Here he not only excludes past merits, but declares that they had nothing in themselves for which they could be chosen, except in so far as his mercy anticipated. And how are we to understand the words of Paul, "Who hath first given to him, and it shall be recompensed unto him again?"

(Rom. xi. 35). His meaning obviously is, that men are altogether indebted to the preventing goodness of God, there being nothing in them, either past or future, to conciliate his favour.

[T]he Apostle [Paul] goes on to show, that the adoption of Jacob proceeded not on works but on the calling of God. In works he makes no mention of past or future, but distinctly opposes them to the calling of God, intimating, that when place is given to the one the other is overthrown; as if he had said, The only thing to be considered is what pleased God, not what men furnished of themselves. . . .

. . . We learn from the Apostle's words, that the salvation of believers is founded entirely on the decree of divine election, that the privilege is procured not by works but free calling. . . .

. . . Meanwhile, though Christ interpose as a Mediator, yet he claims the right of electing in common with the Father, "I speak not of you all: I know whom I have chosen" (John xiii. 18). If it is asked whence he hath chosen them, he answers in another passage, "Out of the world;" which he excludes from his prayers when he commits his disciples to the Father (John xv. 19). We must indeed hold, when he affirms that he knows whom he has chosen, first, that some individuals of the human race are denoted; and, secondly, that they are not distinguished by the quality of their virtues, but by a heavenly decree. Hence it follows, that since Christ makes himself the author of election, none excel by their own strength or industry.

REVIEW QUESTION

1. Why was the doctrine of predestination so troublesome to many Christian theologians?

---

6 The Catholic Response to Protestantism

The criticisms of Catholic beliefs and practices by Luther, Calvin, and other Protestant reformers generated a host of theological defenses of traditional Catholicism. However, there was a general admission that grave abuses in Catholic clerical morals and discipline had been allowed to go uncorrected.

Almost everyone agreed that a new general council of the church was necessary to clarify and affirm Catholic doctrine and institute reforms in clerical discipline and practices. Despite many promises to summon such a council, the popes delayed. Political conditions never seemed right, and the papacy, remembering the challenge to its power attempted by councils in the fifteenth century, feared that prematurely summoning a council could be a disaster for papal authority.

The council was finally convoked in 1545 at the Alpine city of Trent, on the borders between the German lands and Italy. The papacy was firmly in control and no Protestant theologians participated in the conciliar sessions. The council was suspended several times, the longest hiatus lasting for ten years (1552–1562), and concluded its work in 1563.

The council fathers confessed their responsibility for the evils that had grown up in the church and committed themselves to institutional reforms that would raise the standards of morality and learning among future bishops and other clergy. The most significant pastoral reforms included creating an official catechism outlining the orthodox beliefs of the Roman church, establishing seminaries to direct the education of future clergy, and reforming the bishop's office by increasing his responsibilities for the pastoral life of his diocese.

CANONS AND DECREES OF THE COUNCIL OF TRENT

On doctrinal matters, the council gave an authoritative Catholic response to Protestant teachings on a host of issues. In the following excerpt from the decrees of the Council of Trent (1545–1563), the council condemned the Protestant view that faith alone was necessary for salvation and insisted on the integration of both faith and good works in the process of salvation. This position allowed the council to defend such traditional Catholic practices as monasticism, indulgences, masses for the dead, almsgiving, pilgrimages, veneration of saints, and other pious works.

THE NECESSITY OF PREPARATION FOR JUSTIFICATION [SALVATION] IN ADULTS, AND WHENCE IT PROCEEDS

It is furthermore declared that in adults the beginning of that justification must proceed from the predisposing grace of God through Jesus Christ, that is, from His vocation, whereby, without any merits on their part, they are called; that they who by sin had been cut off from God, may be disposed through His quickening and helping grace to convert themselves to their own justification by freely assenting to and cooperating with that grace; so that, while God touches the heart of man through the illumination of the Holy Ghost, man himself neither does absolutely nothing while receiving that inspiration, since he can also reject it, nor yet is he able by his own free will and without the grace of God to move himself to justice in His sight. Hence, when it is said in the sacred writings: *Turn ye to me, and I will turn to you* [Zach. 1:3], we are reminded of our liberty; and when we reply: *Convert us, O Lord, to thee, and we shall be converted* [Lam. 5:21], we confess that we need the grace of God. . . .

HOW THE GRATUITOUS JUSTIFICATION OF THE SINNER BY FAITH IS TO BE UNDERSTOOD

But when the Apostle [Paul] says that man is justified by faith and freely, these words are to be understood in that sense in which the uninterrupted unanimity of the Catholic Church has held and expressed them, namely, that we are therefore said to be justified by faith, because faith is the beginning of human salvation, the foundation and root of all justification, *without which it is impossible to please God* [Heb. 11:6] and to come to the fellowship of His sons; and we are therefore said to be justified gratuitously [unearned, as a freely given gift], because none of those things that precede justification, whether faith or works, merit the grace of justification. For, *if by grace, it is not now by works, otherwise*, as the Apostle says, *grace is no more grace* [Rom. 11:6]. . . .

IN WHAT THE JUSTIFICATION OF THE SINNER CONSISTS, AND WHAT ARE ITS CAUSES

. . . For though no one can be just except he to whom the merits of the passion of our Lord Jesus Christ are communicated, yet this takes place in that justification of the sinner, when by the merit of the most holy passion, *the charity of God is poured forth by the Holy Ghost in the hearts* [Rom. 5:5] of those who are justified and inheres in them; whence man through Jesus Christ, [with] whom he is [now one], receives in that justification, together with the remission of sins, all these infused at the same time, namely, faith, hope and charity. For faith, unless hope and charity be added to it, neither unites man perfectly with Christ nor makes him a living member of His body. For which reason it is most truly said that *faith without works is dead* [James 2:17, 20] and of no profit, and *in Christ Jesus neither circumcision availeth anything nor uncircumcision, but faith that worketh by charity* [Gal. 5:6, 6:15]. This faith, conformably to Apostolic tradition, catechumens [candidates for baptism] ask of the Church before the sacrament of baptism, when they ask for the faith that gives eternal life, which without hope and charity faith cannot give. Whence also they hear immediately the word of Christ: *If thou wilt enter into life, keep the commandments* [Matt. 19:17]. . . .

The council also condemned individual interpretation of the Bible and set up controls over the publication and sale of unauthorized religious books. It approved the cult of the saints and the use of images, practices condemned by Calvin and the Anabaptists.

Furthermore, to check unbridled spirits, it [the council] decrees that no one relying on his own judgment shall, in matters of faith and morals pertaining to the edification of Christian doctrine, distorting the Holy Scriptures in accordance with his own conceptions, presume to interpret them contrary to that sense which holy mother Church, to whom it belongs to judge of their true sense and interpretation, has held and holds, or even contrary to the unanimous teaching of the [church] Fathers, even though such interpretations should never at any time be published. Those who act contrary to this shall be made known by the ordinaries [bishops] and punished in accordance with the penalties prescribed by the law.

And wishing, as is proper, to impose a restraint in this matter on printers also, who, now without restraint, thinking what pleases them is permitted them, print without the permission of ecclesiastical superiors the books of the Holy Scriptures and the notes and commentaries thereon of all persons indiscriminately, often with the name of the press omitted, often also under a fictitious press-name, and what is worse, without the name of the author, and also indiscreetly have for sale such books printed elsewhere, (this council) decrees and ordains that in the future the Holy Scriptures, especially the old Vulgate [Latin] Edition, be printed in the most correct manner possible, and that it shall not be lawful for anyone to print or to have printed any books whatsoever dealing with sacred doctrinal matters without the name of the author, or in the future to sell them, or even to have them in possession, unless they have first been examined and approved by the ordinary [the local bishop], under penalty of anathema [condemnation and excommunication] and fine. . . .

ON THE INVOCATION, VENERATION, AND RELICS OF SAINTS, AND ON SACRED IMAGES

The holy council commands all bishops and others who hold the office of teaching and have charge of the *cura animarum* [care of souls], that in accordance with the usage of the Catholic and Apostolic Church, received from the primitive times of the Christian religion, and with the unanimous teaching of the holy Fathers and the decrees of sacred councils, they above all instruct the faithful diligently in matters relating to intercession and invocation of the saints, the veneration of relics, and the legitimate use of images, teaching them that the saints who reign together with Christ offer up their prayers to God for men, that it is good and beneficial suppliantly to invoke them and to have recourse to their prayers, assistance and support in order to obtain favors from God through His Son, Jesus Christ our Lord, who alone is our redeemer and savior. . . . Also, that the holy bodies of the holy martyrs and of others living with Christ, which were the living members of Christ and the temple of the Holy Ghost, to be awakened by Him to eternal life and to be glorified, are to be venerated by the faithful, through which many benefits are bestowed by God on men. . . . Moreover, that the images of Christ, of the Virgin Mother of God, and of the other saints are to be placed and retained especially in the churches, and that due honor and veneration is to be given them. . . .

The Council of Trent condemned the Protestant view that clergy were no different than lay people and reaffirmed the Catholic belief that the clergy are specially ordained intermediaries between God and human beings and are responsible for the administration of the church's sacraments. Whereas Luther admitted only three sacraments—baptism, the Eucharist, and penance or confession—and Calvin only two—baptism and the Eucharist—the Council of Trent decreed that there were seven sacraments in the Catholic Church, including ordination of the clergy.

CANONS ON THE SACRAMENTS IN GENERAL

Canon 1. If anyone says that the sacraments of the New Law were not all instituted by our Lord Jesus Christ, or that there are more or less than seven, namely, baptism, confirmation, Eucharist, penance, extreme unction, order and matrimony, or that any one of these seven is not truly and intrinsically a sacrament, let him be anathema [cursed]. . . .

Can. 10. If anyone says that all Christians have the power to administer the word and all the sacraments, let him be anathema. . . .

CANONS ON THE SACRAMENT OF ORDER

Canon 1. If anyone says that there is not in the New Testament a visible and external priesthood, or that there is no power of consecrating and offering the true body and blood of the Lord and of forgiving . . . sins, but only the office and bare ministry of preaching the Gospel; or that those who do not preach are not priests at all, let him be anathema. . . .

Can. 4. If anyone says that by sacred ordination the Holy [Spirit] is not imparted and that therefore the bishops say in vain: *Receive ye the Holy [Spirit]*, or that by it a character is not imprinted, or that he who has once been a priest can again become a layman, let him be anathema.

Can. 5. If anyone says that the holy unction which the Church uses in ordination is not only not required but is detestable and pernicious, as also are the other ceremonies of order, let him be anathema.

Can. 6. If anyone says that in the Catholic Church there is not instituted a hierarchy by divine ordinance, which consists of bishops, priests and ministers, let him be anathema.

Can. 7. If anyone says that bishops are not superior to priests, or that they have not the power to confirm and ordain, or that the power which they have is common to them and to priests, or that orders conferred by them without the consent or call of the people or of the secular power are invalid, or that those who have been neither rightly ordained nor sent by ecclesiastical and canonical authority, but come from elsewhere, are lawful ministers of the word and of the sacraments, let him be anathema.

REVIEW QUESTIONS

1. What was the Catholic doctrine on justification by faith defined by the Council of Trent, and how did it differ from the views of Luther and Calvin?
2. How did the Council of Trent approach the problem of authoritative interpretation of the Scriptures and of church doctrines?

7 Religious Persecution

The passions aroused by the Reformation culminated in vicious religious persecution. Regarding Protestants as dangerous heretics who had affronted God and threatened his church, Catholic clergy and rulers tried to eliminate them, often by fire and sword. Protestants also engaged in persecution, principally against the Anabaptists, a Protestant sect that deviated from the teachings of the main Protestant reformers.

Chronicle of King Francis I
BURNING OF PROTESTANTS IN PARIS

One day in the autumn of 1534 Protestants in several French cities plastered walls and doors with anti-church tracts. Fearing that Protestant heresy would prove calamitous to his realm and undermine his authority, Francis I (1515–1547) in 1535, after an elaborate ceremony, had Protestants publicly burned in Paris as a warning to Protestant dissenters. Following is a contemporary account of the spectacle.

The most Christian king [*Francis I*], our sovereign lord, knowing that certain damnable heresies and blasphemies swarmed in his kingdom and desiring with the aid of God to extirpate the same decreed that a sacred procession should be held in this city of Paris on the twenty-first day [*actually the twenty-ninth*] of January 1535. The streets were adorned with gorgeous tapestries and the crowds held in order by archers in uniform. First came the crosses and banners of the Diocese of Paris followed by citizens and merchants carrying torches, then the four monastic orders with relics, next priests and canons of the parochial churches with relics, and the monks of Saint Martin with the head of that saint. Another carried the head of Saint Philip, one of the most precious relics in Paris. The body of Madame Saincte Geneviève was borne by six citizens in their shirts. Then followed the Canons of Notre Dame, the Rector of the University, and the Swiss Guard with their band of violins, trumpets, and cornets. Among the relics were the true cross of Christ and the crown of thorns and the lance that pierced his side. Then came a great number of the archbishops and bishops with the blood of our Saviour, the rod of Moses, and the head of John the Baptist. Next the cardinals. The precious body of our Lord was carried by the archdeacons on a velvet cushion of violet adorned with *fluers de lys*. Following the Holy Sacrament came the King alone with bare head carrying a lighted taper. After him marched Monseigneur the Cardinal of Lorraine, then all the princes and knights and members of the *Parlement*, etc. The Holy Sacrament was taken to the church of Notre Dame and there deposited with great reverence by the Bishop of Paris. Then the King and his children, the Queen and her attendants and many notables had dinner with the Bishop of Paris. After dinner the King made a speech against the execrable and damnable opinions dispersed throughout his kingdom. While the King, the Queen, and their court were with the Bishop of Paris, into their presence were brought six of the said heretics and in front of the church of Notre Dame they were burned alive. A number of other heretics went to the stake during the days following so that all over Paris one saw gibbets [gallows] by which the people were filled with terror.

THE PERSECUTION OF ANABAPTISTS: THE EXAMINATION OF ELIZABETH DIRKS

The break with the Roman church and the rapid growth of a reformed church party in Germany under Luther's leadership was soon complicated by the appearance of other anti-Roman Protestants who differed with both the papacy and Luther on questions of theology and church discipline. In the Swiss city of Zurich, enthusiastic reformers like Ulrich Zwingli (1484–1531) and Conrad Grebel (c. 1500–1526) overthrew the local Catholic authorities but failed to agree fully with Luther or with each other on several theological matters. Grebel and his supporters, called Anabaptists, held that admission to membership in the church must be a voluntary act by adults, and condemned the practice of baptizing infants. When Zwingli insisted that no reforms in ecclesiastical practices should be undertaken without permission of the public authorities, the Zurich Anabaptists refused to comply, declaring the complete freedom of the church from state control. Condemned by Zwingli and forced into exile, the Zurich Anabaptists soon spread their ideas throughout the German-speaking lands.

Although the majority of Anabaptists renounced the use of force to impose any religious practice, the Anabaptist reformers in Münster, a city in northwestern Germany, did not. After winning control of the city council, they expelled all citizens who refused to become Anabaptists. Under the influence of "prophets," some Münster Anabaptists adopted practicing polygamy, communal ownership of property, and violence in anticipation of the imminent end of the world. In 1535, the forces of neighboring German princes captured Münster, slaughtering the Anabaptists.

The excesses of the Münster sect caused both Protestant and Catholic authorities to persecute more peaceful and orthodox Anabaptists wherever they were discovered. The movement remained small, fervent, but oppressed and was confined to an underground existence. Modern Christian churches that acknowledge the sixteenth-century Anabaptists as their spiritual forebears are the Mennonites and Amish, the Plymouth (Pilgrim) Separatists, and the English and American Baptists.

In January 1549, Elizabeth Dirks was arrested in Holland, at that time under Catholic control. A former nun, she had come to doubt whether monastic life was truly Christian and fled the convent. Following is a verbatim account of her trial before Catholic examiners. Condemned to death, Elizabeth Dirks was drowned in a sack.

EXAMINERS: We understand that you are a teacher and have led many astray. We want to know who your friends are.

ELIZABETH: I am commanded to love the Lord my God and honor my parents. Therefore I will not tell you who my parents are. That I suffer for Christ is damaging to my friends.

EXAMINERS: We will let that rest for the present, but we want to know whom you have taught.

ELIZABETH: No, my Lords, do not press me on this point. Ask me about my faith and I will answer you gladly.

EXAMINERS: We will make it so tough that you will tell us.

ELIZABETH: I hope through the grace of God to guard my tongue that I shall not be a traitor and deliver my brother to death.

EXAMINERS: What persons were with you when you were baptized?

ELIZABETH: Christ said, "Ask those who were present." (John 18:21).

EXAMINERS: Now we see that you are a teacher because you make yourself equal to Christ.

ELIZABETH: No indeed. Far be it from me, for I count myself no better than the [lowest] from the house of the Lord.

EXAMINERS: What do you mean by the house of the Lord? Don't you consider our church to be the house of the Lord?

ELIZABETH: I do not, my Lords. For it is written, "You are the temple of the living God" (2 Cor. 6:16). As God said, "I will dwell with you" (Lev. 26:11).

EXAMINERS: What do you think of our Mass?

ELIZABETH: My Lords, I have no faith in your Mass but only in that which is in the Word of God.

EXAMINERS: What do you believe about the Holy Sacrament?

ELIZABETH: I have never in my life read in Scripture about a Holy Sacrament, but only of the Supper of the Lord.

EXAMINERS: Shut your mouth. The devil speaks through it.

ELIZABETH: Yes, my Lords, this is a little matter, for the servant is not greater than his Lord (Matt. 10:24).

EXAMINERS: You speak with a haughty tongue.

ELIZABETH: No, my Lords, I speak with a free tongue.

EXAMINERS: What did the Lord say when he gave the supper to his disciples?

ELIZABETH: What did he give them, flesh or bread?

EXAMINERS: He gave them bread.

ELIZABETH: Did not the Lord continue to sit there? How then could they eat his flesh?

EXAMINERS: What do you believe about the baptism of children, seeing that you have had yourself baptized again?

ELIZABETH: No, my Lords, I have not had myself baptized again. I have been baptized once on my faith, because it is written, "Baptism belongs to believers." [She deduces this from Peter's confession, Matt. 16:15-16.]

EXAMINERS: Are our children then damned because they are baptized?

ELIZABETH: No, my Lords. Far be it from me to judge the children.

EXAMINERS: Do you not think that you are saved by baptism?

ELIZABETH: No, my Lords. All the water in the sea cannot save me. All my salvation is in Christ, who has commanded me to love the Lord, my God, and my neighbor as myself.

EXAMINERS: Do priests have the power to forgive sins?

ELIZABETH: No, my Lords. How should I believe that? I say that Christ is the only priest through whom sins are forgiven.

EXAMINERS: You say that you accept everything in accord with Holy Scripture. Do you not then hold to the word of James?

ELIZABETH: How can I not hold to it?

EXAMINERS: Did he not say, "Go to the elders of the congregation that they should anoint you and pray for you"? (James 5:13).

ELIZABETH: Yes, but would you say, my Lords, that you are such a congregation?

EXAMINERS: The Holy Ghost has made you so holy that you don't need penance or the sacrament.

ELIZABETH: No, my Lords. I freely confess that I have transgressed the ordinances of the pope which the emperor has confirmed with placards. But if you can show me that in any articles I have transgressed against the Lord, my God, I will wail over myself as a miserable sinner.

This was her first hearing.

Then they took her again before the council and brought her to the torture room. Hans, the executioner, was there. The Lords said, "So far we have treated you gently. Since you won't confess we will put you to the torture." The Procurator General said, "Mr. Hans, take hold of her."

Mr. Hans answered, "Oh no, my Lords, she will confess voluntarily." But since she would not, he put screws on her thumbs and on two forefingers till the blood spurted from the nails.

EXAMINERS: Confess and we will ease your pain. We told you to confess and not to call upon the Lord, your God!

But she held steadfastly to the Lord, her God, as above related. Then they eased her pain and she said, "Ask me. I will answer, for I feel no pain any more at all as I did."

EXAMINERS: Then won't you confess?

ELIZABETH: No, my Lords.

Then they put two screws on her legs and she said, "Oh my Lords, do not put me to shame. No man has ever touched my bare body." The Procurator General said, "Miss Elizabeth, we will not treat you dishonorably." Then she fainted and one said, "Maybe she's dead." Reviving she said, "I'm alive. I'm not dead." Then they took off the screws and tried to bend her by blandishments.

ELIZABETH: Why do you try me with candied speech as one does with children?

So they could get from her not a word against her brothers in the faith, nor against any one.

EXAMINERS: Will you recant everything you have said?

ELIZABETH: No, my Lords. I will not, but I will seal it with my blood.

EXAMINERS: We will not torture you any more. Will you now tell us in good faith who baptized you?

ELIZABETH: Oh no, my Lords. I have told you all along that I will not do it.

Then, on March 27, 1549, Elizabeth was condemned to death and drowned in a sack. And thus she offered up her life to God.

Menno Simons
AN ANABAPTIST REJECTION
OF THE USE OF FORCE

Menno Simons (c. 1496–1561), a Dutch priest who converted to Anabaptism in 1536, is considered the founder of the Mennonite church. In the following passages from his collected theological writings, Simons offered a biblical justification for the Anabaptist rejection of using force or state power to impose religious beliefs or practices.

Say, my dear people, where do the holy Scriptures teach that in Christ's kingdom and church we shall proceed with the magistrate, with the sword, and with physical force and tyranny over a man's conscience and faith, things subject to the judgment of God alone? Where have Christ and the apostles acted thus, advised thus, commanded thus? Ah, Christ says merely, Beware of false prophets; and Paul ordains that we shall avoid a heretical person after he has been admonished once or twice. John teaches that we shall not greet nor receive into the house the man who goes onward and does not bring the doctrine of Christ. But they do not write, Away with those heretics, Report them to the authorities, Lock them up, Expel them out of the city and the country, Throw them into the fire, the water, as the Catholics have done for many years, and as is still found to a great extent with you—you who make yourselves believe that you teach the word of God! . . .

Peter was commanded to sheathe his sword. All Christians are commanded to love their enemies: to do good unto those who abuse and persecute them; to give the mantle when the cloak is taken, the other cheek when one is struck. Tell me, how can a Christian defend Scripturally retaliation, rebellion, war, striking, slaying, torturing, stealing, robbing and plundering and burning cities, and conquering countries?

The great Lord who has created you and us, who has placed our hearts within us knows, and He only knows that our hearts and hands

are clear of all sedition and murderous mutiny. By His grace we will ever remain clear. For we truly confess that all rebellion is of the flesh and of the devil.

O beloved reader, our weapons are not swords and spears, but patience, silence, and hope, and the Word of God. With these we must maintain our heavy warfare and fight our battle. Paul says, The weapons of our warfare are not carnal; but mighty through God. With these we intend and desire to storm the kingdom of the devil; and not with sword, spears, cannon, and coats of mail. For He esteemeth iron as straw, and brass as rotten wood. Thus may we with our Prince, Teacher, and Example Christ Jesus, raise the father against the son, and the son against the father, and may we cast down imagination and every high thing that exalteth itself against the knowledge of God, and bring into captivity every thought in obedience to Christ.

True Christians do not know vengeance, no matter how they are mistreated. In patience they possess their souls. Luke 21:18. And they do not break their peace, even if they should be tempted by bondage, torture, poverty, and besides, by the sword and fire. They do not cry, Vengeance, vengeance, as does the world; but with Christ they supplicate and pray: Father, forgive them; for they know not what they do. Luke 23:34; Acts 7:60.

According to the declaration of the prophets they have beaten their swords into plowshares and their spears into pruning hooks. They shall sit every man under his vine and under his fig-tree, Christ; neither shall they learn war any more. Isa[iah] 2:4; Mic[ah] 4:3. . . .

Behold, beloved rulers and judges, if you take to heart these Scriptures and diligently ponder them, then you will observe, first, that your office is not your own but God's, so that you may bend your knees before His majesty; fear His great and adorable name, and rightly and reasonably execute your ordained office. Then you will not so freely with your perishable earthly power invade and transgress against Christ, the Lord of lords in His kingdom, power, and jurisdiction, and with your iron sword adjudicate in that which belongs exclusively to the eternal judgment of the Most High God, such as in faith and matters pertaining to faith. In the same vein Luther and others wrote in the beginning, but after they came to greater and higher estate they forgot it all. . . .

. . . If he is a preacher called by the Spirit of God, then let him show a single letter in all the New Testament that Christ or the apostles have ever called on the magistrates to defend and protect the true church against the attack of the wicked, as, alas, he calls us. No, no. Christ Jesus and His powerful Word and the Holy Spirit are the protectors and defenders of the church, and not, eternally not, the emperor, king, or any worldly potentate! The kingdom of the Spirit must be protected and defended by the sword of the Spirit, and not by the sword of the world. This, in the light of the doctrine and example of Christ and His apostles, is too plain to be defended.

I would say further, if the magistracy rightly understood Christ and His kingdom, they would in my opinion rather choose death than to meddle with their worldly power and sword in spiritual matters which are reserved not to the judgment of man but to the judgment of the great and Almighty God alone. But they are taught by those who have the care of their souls that they may proscribe, imprison, torture, and slay those who are not obedient to their doctrine, as may, alas, be seen in many different cities and countries.

REVIEW QUESTIONS

1. Why was the burning of heretics treated as a public festival?
2. Why were Anabaptists like Elizabeth Dirks considered dangerous to both Catholic and Protestant authorities?
3. What were Simons' reasons for rejecting the use of state power to impose religious belief or practices?
4. What did Simons think of Luther's support of state authority on behalf of the Church?

CHAPTER 11

Early Modern Society and Politics

HERNÁN CORTÉS, Spanish explorer and conqueror of Mexico, meets the Aztec Emperor Montezuma.
(HIP/Art Resource, NY)

The period from the Renaissance through the Scientific Revolution saw the breakdown of distinctively medieval cultural, political, and economic forms. The Renaissance produced a more secular attitude and expressed confidence in human capacities. Shortly afterward, the Protestant Reformation ended the religious unity of medieval Latin Christendom and weakened the political power of the church. At the same time the discovery of new trade routes to East Asia and of new lands across the Atlantic widened the imagination and ambitions of Christian Europeans and precipitated a commercial revolution. This great expansion of economic activity furthered capitalism and initiated a global economy—two developments associated with the modern world.

In the late fifteenth century, many Europeans encountered peoples whose cultures markedly differed from their own. The Portuguese, trying to break the Muslim monopoly over trade between Europe and eastern Asia, explored along the Atlantic coast of Africa, establishing their first links with the peoples and kingdoms of the sub-Saharan regions of modern Guinea, Ghana, Dahomey, and the Congo. Setting up fortified trading posts along the way, they eventually sailed around the Cape of Good Hope at the tip of Africa and reached India in 1498. By 1516, Portuguese merchants had reached the port of Canton in southern China. The Portuguese established fortified trading posts in India and Southeast Asia, some of which (Goa, Timor, Macao) they continued to hold into the late twentieth century.

In India, China, and Japan, the Portuguese found highly advanced civilizations that were able to resist European political and cultural domination fairly effectively. In contrast, the Spaniards, with the discovery of the Caribbean islands by Christopher Columbus in 1492, encountered a local population living in a Stone Age culture. There were no cities, no state structures, no significant architecture or art; technology was primitive, and contacts with other peoples limited. However, after 1518 when the Spaniards landed on the American mainland, they found in Mexico, Yucatán, and Peru advanced civilizations with great cities, well-developed governments, monumental architecture, and extensive commercial networks. The vast regions and diverse peoples of the Americas were gradually linked to Europe's Christian culture and expanding economy during the sixteenth and seventeenth centuries.

Exploration and commercial expansion created the foundations of a global economy in which the European economy was tied to Asian spices, African slaves, and American silver. A wide variety of goods circulated all over the globe. From the West Indies and East Asia, sugar, rice, tea, cacao, and tobacco flowed into Europe. From the Americas, potatoes, corn, sweet potatoes, and manioc (from which tapioca is made) spread to the rest of the world. Europeans paid for Asian silks and spices with American silver.

The increasing demand for goods and a rise in prices produced more opportunities for the accumulation and investment of capital by private individuals, which is the essence of capitalism. State policies designed to increase national wealth and power also stimulated the growth of capitalism. Governments subsidized new industries, chartered joint-stock companies to engage in overseas trade, and struck at internal tariffs and guild regulations that hampered domestic economic growth. Improvements in banking, shipbuilding, mining, and manufacturing further stimulated economic growth.

In the sixteenth and seventeenth centuries the old medieval political order dissolved, and the modern state began to emerge. The modern state has a strong central government that issues laws that apply throughout the land and a permanent army of professional soldiers paid by the state. Trained bureaucrats, responsible to the central government, collect taxes, enforce laws, and administer justice. The modern state has a secular character; promotion of religion is not the state's concern, and churches do not determine state policy. These features of the modern state were generally not prevalent in the Middle Ages, when the nobles, church, and towns possessed powers and privileges that impeded central authority, and kings were expected to rule in accordance with Christian principles. In the sixteenth and seventeenth centuries, monarchs were exercising central authority with ever-greater effectiveness at the expense of nobles and clergy. The secularization of the state became firmly established after the Thirty Years' War (1618–1648); with their states worn out by Catholic–Protestant conflicts, kings came to act less for religious motives than for reasons of national security and power.

Historically, the modern state has been characterized by a devotion to the nation and by feelings of national pride. There is a national language that is used throughout the land, and the people have a sense of sharing a common culture and history, of being distinct from other peoples. There were some signs of growing national feeling during the sixteenth and seventeenth centuries, but this feature of the modern state did not become a major part of European political life until the nineteenth century. During the early modern period, loyalty was largely given to a town, to a province, to a noble, or to the person of the king rather than to the nation, the people as a whole.

1   The Age of Exploration and Conquest

In 1498, a Portuguese explorer, Vasco da Gama (c. 1460–1524), sailed a fleet of four ships around Africa into the Indian Ocean and landed at the Indian port of Calicut. His voyage marked the first step in the creation of a Portuguese commercial empire in East Asia. For centuries afterward, Europeans competed by fair means and foul for access to and control of the Asian trade. The Dutch,

English, and French eventually established trading posts and colonies along the same routes pioneered by the Portuguese. Meanwhile, the Spaniards, following the initial discovery of the Caribbean islands by Columbus in 1492, proceeded to explore, conquer, and settle the mainland of Central, South, and North America.

Bernal Díaz del Castillo
THE DISCOVERY AND CONQUEST OF MEXICO

In 1518, Spanish ships explored the mainland coast along the Gulf of Mexico near the Yucatán Peninsula. The following year an expedition under the leadership of Hernando Cortés (1485–1547) landed at the site of modern Veracruz to explore the newly discovered country. There the Spaniards were unexpectedly confronted with ambassadors from Montezuma (c. 1502–1520), the ruler of an extensive Aztec empire; the Aztecs presented Cortés with gifts made of jade, gold, and silver and with rich textiles, and urged that the Spaniards depart—Montezuma feared Cortés was the Aztec god Quetzalcoatl who had come to reclaim his kingdom. Having 555 troops together with 16 horses and some cannons, Cortés refused and announced that he was sent by his king to speak directly with Montezuma. Sinking his ships to prevent his troops from deserting, Cortés marched inland to the Aztec capital, Tenochtitlán, the site of today's Mexico City; the Spaniards found a civilization with a high level of social and political organization and advanced techniques of engineering, architecture, writing, astronomy, painting, and ceramics. Located on islands in the midst of a lake, Tenochtitlán was approached by three stone causeways that converged in a great central square, dominated by a high pyramidal temple. Other magnificent stone temples and palaces, paved marketplaces, canals with boats carrying products needed by the busy inhabitants, and cultivated gardens with aviaries presented impressive urban scenes. Thousands of priests, soldiers, civil servants, artisans, and laborers filled the streets and houses.

The following excerpts are from *The Discovery and Conquest of Mexico*, the personal memoir of Bernal Díaz del Castillo (c. 1492–1581). Díaz accompanied Cortés and wrote an eyewitness account of this first confrontation between Christian and Aztec civilizations. In the following passage Díaz described Montezuma and his courtiers. Although generally favorable in his account of Montezuma, Díaz reported a rumor that the Aztec emperor ate human flesh for dinner. Whether the Aztecs were cannibals is still disputed among scholars.

The Great Montezuma was about forty years old, of good height and well proportioned, slender and spare of flesh, not very swarthy, but of the natural colour and shade of an Indian. He did not wear his hair long, but so as just to cover his ears, his scanty black beard was well shaped and thin. His face was somewhat long, but cheerful, and he had good eyes and showed in his appearance and manner both tenderness and, when necessary, gravity. He was very neat and clean and bathed once every day in the afternoon. He had many women as mistresses, daughters of Chieftains, and he had two great Cacicas [noblewomen] as his legitimate wives. He was free from unnatural offences. The clothes that he wore one day, he did not put on again until four days later. He had over two hundred Chieftains in his guard, in other rooms close to his own, not that all were meant to converse with him, but only one or another, and when they went to speak to him they were obliged to take off their rich mantles [cloaks] and put on others of little worth, but they had to be clean, and they had to enter barefoot with their eyes lowered to the ground, and not to look up in his face. And they made him three obeisances [bows], and said: "Lord, my Lord, my Great Lord," before they came up to him, and then they made their report and with few words he dismissed them, and on taking leave they did not turn their backs, but kept their faces towards him with their eyes to the ground, and they did not turn their backs until they left the room. I noticed another thing, that when other great chiefs came from distant lands about disputes or business, when they reached the apartments of the Great Montezuma, they had to come barefoot and with poor mantles, and they might not enter directly into the Palace, but had to loiter about a little on one side of the Palace door, for to enter hurriedly was considered to be disrespectful. . . .

I have heard it said that they were wont to cook for him the flesh of young boys, but as he had such a variety of dishes, made of so many things, we could not succeed in seeing if they were of human flesh or of other things, for they daily cooked fowls, turkeys, pheasants, native partridges, quail, tame and wild ducks, venison, wild boar, reed birds, pigeons, hares and rabbits, and many sorts of birds and other things which are bred in this country, and they are so numerous that I cannot finish naming them in a hurry; so we had no insight into it; but I know for certain that after our

Captain [Cortés] censured the sacrifice of human beings, and the eating of their flesh, he ordered that such food should not be prepared for him thenceforth. . . .

. . . While Montezuma was at table eating, as I have described, there were waiting on him two other graceful women to bring him tortillas, kneaded with eggs and other sustaining ingredients, and these tortillas were very white, and they were brought on plates covered with clean napkins, and they also brought him another kind of bread, like long balls kneaded with other kinds of sustaining food, and *pan pachol*, for so they call it in this country, which is a sort of wafer. There were also placed on the table three tubes much painted and gilded, which held *liquidambar* [a sort of sweet gum] mixed with certain herbs which they call *tabaco*, and when he had finished eating, after they had danced before him and sung and the table was removed, he inhaled the smoke from one of those tubes, but he took very little of it and with that he fell asleep. . . .

Let us leave this and go on to another great house, where they keep many Idols, and they say that they are their fierce gods, and with them many kinds of carnivorous beasts of prey, tigers and two kinds of lions, and animals something like wolves and foxes, and other smaller carnivorous animals, and all these carnivores they feed with flesh, and the greater number of them breed in the house. They give them as food deer and fowls, dogs and other things which they are used to hunt, and I have heard it said that they feed them on the bodies of the Indians who have been sacrificed. It is in this way; you have already heard me say that when they sacrifice a wretched Indian they saw open the chest with stone knives and hasten to tear out the palpitating heart and blood, and offer it to their Idols, in whose name the sacrifice is made. Then they cut off the thighs, arms and head and eat the former at feasts and banquets, and the head they hang up on some beams, and the body of the man sacrificed is not eaten but given to these fierce animals. They also have in that cursed house many vipers and poisonous snakes which carry on their tails things that sound like bells. These are the worst vipers of all, and they keep them in jars and great pottery vessels with many feathers, and there they lay their eggs and rear their young, and they give them to eat the bodies of the Indians who have been sacrificed, and the flesh of dogs which they are in the habit of breeding.

Let me speak now of the infernal noise when the lions and tigers roared and the jackals and foxes howled and the serpents hissed, it was horrible to listen to and it seemed like a hell. Let us go on and speak of the skilled workmen Montezuma employed in every craft that was practised among them. We will begin with lapidaries [gem cutters] and workers in gold and silver and all the hollow work, which even the great goldsmiths in Spain were forced to admire. . . . Let us go on to the great craftsmen in feather work, and painters and sculptors who were most refined; then to the Indian women who did the weaving and the washing, who made such an immense quantity of fine fabrics with wonderful featherwork designs; the greater part of it was brought daily from some towns of the province on the north coast near Vera Cruz called Cotaxtla.

Díaz records with amazement the great central marketplace with its merchants and myriad products.

. . . When we arrived at the great market place, called Tlaltelolco, we were astounded at the number of people and the quantity of merchandise that it contained, and at the good order and control that was maintained, for we had never seen such a thing before. The chieftains who accompanied us acted as guides. Each kind of merchandise was kept by itself and had its fixed place marked out. Let us begin with the dealers in gold, silver, and precious stones, feathers, mantles, and embroidered goods. Then there were other wares consisting of Indian slaves both men and women; and I say that they bring as many of them to that great market for sale as the Portuguese bring negroes from Guinea; and they brought them along tied to long poles, with collars round their necks so that they could not escape, and others they left free. Next there were other traders who sold great pieces of cloth and cotton, and articles of twisted thread, and there were *cacahuateros* who sold cacao. In this way one could see every sort of merchandise that is to be found in the whole of New Spain [Spain's name for Mexico]. . . .

. . . And we saw the fresh water that comes from Chapultepec [a wooded area near Tenochtitlán] which supplies the city, and we saw the bridges on the three causeways which were built at certain distances apart through which the water of the lake flowed in and out from one side to the other, and we beheld on that great lake a great multitude of canoes, some coming with supplies of food and others returning loaded with cargoes of merchandise; and we saw that from every house of that great city and of all the other cities that were built in the water it was impossible to pass from house to house, except by drawbridges which were made of wood or in canoes; and we saw in those cities Cues [pyramidal temples] and oratories like towers and fortresses and all gleaming white, and it was a wonderful thing to behold; then the houses with flat roofs, and on the causeways other small towers and oratories which were like fortresses.

After having examined and considered all that we had seen we turned to look at the great market place and the crowds of people that were in it, some buying and others selling, so that the murmur and hum of their voices and words that they used could be heard more than a league off. Some of the soldiers among us who had been in many parts of the world, in Constantinople, and all over Italy, and in Rome, said that so large a market place and so full of people, and so well regulated and arranged, they had never beheld before. . . .

When Cortés mocks the Aztec ruler's religious devotion to his gods and proposes setting up the Christian cross and image of the Virgin Mary, Montezuma reproaches him.

. . . Our Captain said to Montezuma through our interpreter, half laughing: "Señor Montezuma, I do not understand how such a great Prince and wise man as you are has not come to the conclusion, in your mind, that these idols of yours are not gods, but evil things that are called devils, and so that you may know it and all your priests may see it clearly, do me the favour to approve of my placing a cross here on the top of this tower, and that in one part of these oratories where your Huichilobos and Tezcatepuca [Aztec gods] stand we may divide off a space where we can set up an image of Our Lady (an image which Montezuma had already seen) and you will see by the fear in which these Idols hold it that they are deceiving you."

Montezuma replied half angrily (and the two priests who were with him showed great annoyance), and said: "Señor Malinche [Aztec name for Cortés], if I had known that you would have said such defamatory things I would not have shown you my gods, we consider them to be very good, for they give us health and rains and good seed times and seasons and as many victories as we desire, and we are obliged to worship them and make sacrifices, and I pray you not to say another word to their dishonour." . . .

The Spaniards decide to build a Christian chapel within the walls of the huge Aztec palace

in which they are quartered, hoping to convert the Aztecs by the example of their own Christian religious devotions. By chance, they discover a secret door to a room filled with treasure.

. . . Now as there was a rumour and we had heard the story that Montezuma kept the treasure of his father Axayaca in that building, it was suspected that it might be in this chamber which had been closed up and cemented only a few days before. Yañes spoke about it to Juan Valásquez de Leon and Francisco de Lugo, and those Captains told the story to Cortés, and the door was secretly opened. When it was opened Cortés and some of his Captains went in first, and they saw such a number of jewels and slabs and plates of gold and chalchihuites [figures of goddesses] and other great riches, that they were quite carried away and did not know what to say about such wealth. The news soon spread among all the other Captains and soldiers, and very secretly we went in to see it. When I saw it I marvelled, and as at that time I was a youth and had never seen such riches as those in my life before, I took it for certain that there could not be another such store of wealth in the whole world. It was decided by all our captains and soldiers, that we should not dream of touching a particle of it, but that the stones should immediately be put back in the doorway and it should be sealed up and cemented just as we found it, and that it should not be spoken about, lest it should reach Montezuma's ears, until times should alter.

REVIEW QUESTIONS

1. What evidence did Bernal Díaz del Castillo offer to show that the Aztecs were a highly civilized people?
2. What moral and religious practices of the Aztecs did the Spaniards find strange and contrary to Christian beliefs?

2 Spanish Oppression of Amerindians

To work the mines and large estates they established in the New World, the Spanish conquistadors reduced the Amerindians to servitude. Outraged by the inhumane treatment of the Amerindians, Spanish missionaries, principally Dominicans, condemned the settlers in fiery sermons and appealed to the Spanish throne to intervene. In a sermon preached on the island of Hispaniola (today the Dominican Republic and Haiti), a Dominican missionary said angrily, "Are these Indians not men? Do they not have rational souls? Are you not obliged to love them as you love yourselves?"

Juan Lopez de Palacios Rubios
JUSTIFYING SPANISH DOMINATION OF AMERINDIANS

The *Requerimiento* (Requirement), drafted in 1513 by Juan Lopez de Palacios Rubios, Spain's chief crown jurist, provided legal and theological justification for Spanish domination of Amerindians. In effect the document, reproduced below, asserted that it was God's will that Amerindians submit to both Catholicism and Spanish rule, that in subduing native people the Spaniards were engaged in a just war. Before launching an attack, the Spaniards read the document aloud to Amerindians who, of course, could not understand Spanish.

On the part of the King, Don Fernando, and of Doña Juana, his daughter, Queen of Castille and León, subduers of the barbarous nations, we their servants notify and make known to you, as best we can, that the Lord our God, Living and Eternal, created the Heaven and the Earth, and one man and one woman, of whom you and we, all the men of the world, were and are descendants, and all those who came after us. But, on account of the multitude which has sprung from this man and woman in the five thousand years since the world was created, it was necessary that some men should go one way and some another, and that they should be divided into many kingdoms and provinces, for in one alone they could not be sustained.

Of all these nations God our Lord gave charge to one man, called St. Peter, that he should be Lord and Superior of all the men in the world, that all should obey him, and that he should be the head of the whole human race, wherever men should live, and under whatever law, sect, or belief they should be; and he gave him the world for his kingdom and jurisdiction.

And he commanded him to place his seat in Rome, as the spot most fitting to rule the world from; but also he permitted him to have his seat in any other part of the world, and to judge and govern all Christians, Moors, Jews, Gentiles, and all other sects. This man was called Pope, as if to say, Admirable Great Father and Governor of men. The men who lived in that time obeyed that St. Peter, and took him for Lord, King, and Superior of the universe; so also they have regarded the others who after him have been elected to the pontificate, and so has it been continued even till now, and will continue till the end of the world.

One of these Pontiffs, who succeeded that St. Peter as Lord of the world, in the dignity and seat which I have before mentioned, made donation of these isles and Tierra-firme to the aforesaid King and Queen and to their successors, our lords, with all that there are in these territories, as is contained in certain writings which passed upon the subject as aforesaid, which you can see if you wish.

So their Highnesses are kings and lords of these islands and land of Tierra-firme by virtue of this donation: and some islands, and indeed almost all those to whom this has been notified, have received and served their Highnesses, as lords and kings, in the way that subjects ought to do, with good will, without any resistance, immediately, without delay, when they were informed of the aforesaid facts. And also they received and obeyed the priests whom their Highnesses sent to preach to them and to teach them our Holy Faith; and all these, of their own free will, without any reward or condition, have become Christians, and are so, and their Highnesses have joyfully and benignantly received them, and also have commanded them to be treated as their subjects and vassals; and you too are held and obliged to do the same. Wherefore, as best we can, we ask and require you that you consider what we have said to you, and that you take the time that shall be necessary to understand and deliberate upon it, and that you acknowledge the Church as the Ruler and Superior of the whole world, and the high priest called Pope, and in his name the King and Queen Doña Juana our lords, in his place, as superiors and lords and kings of these islands

and this Tierra-firme by virtue of the said donation, and that you consent and give place that these religious fathers should declare and preach to you the aforesaid.

If you do so, you will do well, and that which you are obliged to do to their Highnesses, and we in their name shall receive you in all love and charity, and shall leave you, your wives, and your children, and your lands, free without servitude, that you may do with them and with yourselves freely that which you like and think best, and they shall not compel you to turn Christians, unless you yourselves, when informed of the truth, should wish to be converted to our Holy Catholic Faith, as almost all the inhabitants of the rest of the islands have done. And, besides this, their Highnesses award you many privileges and exemptions and will grant you many benefits.

But, if you do not do this, and maliciously make delay in it, I certify to you that, with the help of God, we shall powerfully enter into your country, and shall make war against you in all ways and manners that we can, and shall subject you to the yoke and obedience of the Church and of their Highnesses; we shall take you and your wives and your children, and shall make slaves of them, and as such shall sell and dispose of them as their Highnesses may command; and we shall take away your goods, and shall do you all the mischief and damage that we can, as to vassals who do not obey, and refuse to receive their lord, and resist and contradict him; and we protest that the deaths and losses which shall accrue from this are your fault, and not that of their Highnesses, or ours, nor of these cavaliers who come with us. And that we have said this to you and made this Requisition, we request the notary here present to give us his testimony in writing, and we ask the rest who are present that they should be witnesses of this Requisition.

Bartolomé de Las Casas
THE TEARS OF THE INDIANS

A particularly eloquent defender of the Amerindians was Bartolomé de Las Casas (1474–1566), who spent most of his long life in Spanish America. In *The Tears of the Indians*, also published as *A Short History of the Destruction of the Indies*, Las Casas described in graphic detail the atrocities inflicted on the Amerindians. His account greatly exaggerated the number of Amerindians killed by the Spaniards; disease, for which the Amerindians had no immunity, not Spanish mistreatment, was the principal reason for the decimation of the native population. Las Casas' appeals were instrumental in stimulating reforms by the Spanish throne, but the distance separating Spain from her possessions in the New World often prevented effective enforcement of these reforms. In the following excerpt from *The Tears of the Indians*, Las Casas recounts the brutal behavior of the Spaniards toward the native inhabitants of Hispaniola whom he described as a people "devoid of wickedness and duplicity . . . or desire for vengeance."

On the Island Hispaniola was where the Spaniards first landed, as I have said. Here those Christians perpetrated their first ravages and oppressions against the native peoples. This was the first land in the New World to be destroyed and depopulated by the Christians, and here they began their subjection of the women and children, taking them away from the Indians to use them and ill use them, eating the food they provided with their sweat and toil. The Spaniards did not content themselves with what the Indians gave them of their own free will, according to their ability, which was always too little to satisfy enormous appetites, for a Christian eats and consumes in one day an amount of food that would suffice to feed three houses inhabited by ten Indians for one month. And they committed other acts of force and violence and oppression which made the Indians realize that these men had not come from Heaven. And some of the Indians concealed their foods while others concealed their wives and children and still others fled to the mountains to avoid the terrible transactions of the Christians.

And the Christians attacked them with buffets and beatings, until finally they laid hands on the nobles of the villages. Then they behaved with such temerity and shamelessness that the most powerful ruler of the islands had to see his own wife raped by a Christian officer.

From that time onward the Indians began to seek ways to throw the Christians out of their lands. They took up arms, but their weapons were very weak and of little service in offense and still less in defense. (Because of this, the wars of the Indians against each other are little more than games played by children.) And the Christians, with their horses and swords and pikes began to carry out massacres and strange cruelties against them. They attacked the towns and spared neither the children nor the aged nor pregnant women nor women in childbed, not only stabbing them and dismembering them but cutting them to pieces as if dealing with sheep in the slaughter house. They laid bets as to who, with one stroke of the sword, could split a man in two or could cut off his head or spill out his entrails with a single stroke of the pike. They took infants from their mothers' breasts, snatching them by the legs and pitching them headfirst against the crags or snatched them by the arms and threw them into the rivers, roaring with laughter and saying as the babies fell into the water, "Boil there, you offspring of the devil!" Other infants they put to the sword along with their mothers and anyone else who happened to be nearby. They made some low wide gallows on which the hanged victim's feet almost touched the ground, stringing up their victims in lots of thirteen, in memory of Our Redeemer and His twelve Apostles, then set burning wood at their feet and thus burned them alive. To others they attached straw or wrapped their whole bodies in straw and set them afire. With still others, all those they wanted to capture alive, they cut off their hands and hung them round the victim's neck, saying, "Go now, carry the message," meaning, Take the news to the Indians who have fled to the mountains. They usually dealt with the chieftains and nobles in the following way: they made a grid of rods which they placed on forked sticks, then lashed the victims to the grid and lighted a smoldering fire underneath, so that little by little, as those captives screamed in despair and torment, their souls would leave them.

I once saw this, when there were four or five nobles lashed on grids and burning; I seem even to recall that there were two or three pairs of grids where others were burning, and because they uttered such loud screams that they disturbed the captain's sleep, he ordered them to be strangled. And the constable, who was worse than an executioner, did not want to obey that order (and I know the name of that constable and know his relatives in Seville), but instead put a stick over the victims' tongues, so they could not make a sound, and he stirred up the fire, but not too much, so that they roasted slowly, as he liked. I saw all these things I have described, and countless others.

And because all the people who could do so fled to the mountains to escape these inhuman, ruthless, and ferocious acts, the Spanish captains, enemies of the human race, pursued them with the fierce dogs they kept which attacked the Indians, tearing them to pieces and devouring them. And because on few and far between occasions, the Indians justifiably killed some Christians, the Spaniards made a rule among themselves that for every Christian slain by the Indians, they would slay a hundred Indians.

REVIEW QUESTIONS

1. How did the author of the Requerimiento justify the subjugation of the Amerindians?
2. How do you explain the cruelty of the Spaniards?

3 Toward the Modern Economy: The Example of Holland

The Spanish and Portuguese monopoly of trade was challenged in the late sixteenth century, first by English privateers who preyed on the Spanish fleets crossing the Atlantic and then by the Dutch who were in revolt against their sovereign, the Spanish king Philip II (1556–1598). Earlier, the Dutch had traded with both Spanish and Portuguese ports, but were not allowed to seek markets directly with the Americas or the East Indies. When Philip II, who was also king of Portugal from 1580, excluded the rebellious Dutch from trading in his ports— a policy that was renewed by his son, Philip III (1598–1621)—Dutch merchants decided to break the Portuguese monopoly over trade with the East Indies. In doing so, they launched the first of many commercial wars designed to win control over world trade markets.

To encourage trade with the East Indies, the Dutch government established a private limited stockholding company, the East India Company, and granted it a monopoly over trade and colonization anywhere east of the Cape of Good Hope or beyond the Straits of Magellan at the southern tip of South America. The company was granted the right to build fortresses, to raise armies, to establish laws and courts in territories it captured from the Spanish or the Portuguese, and to enter into diplomatic alliances with other princes. The East India Company was the foundation on which the Dutch built their colonial empire. Other European states established similar corporations to further trade and colonization.

William Carr
THE DUTCH EAST INDIA COMPANY

In 1693, William Carr, the English consul at Amsterdam, wrote a travelers' guide to the leading cities of Holland, Flanders, northern Germany, and Scandinavia. Of these, the largest and wealthiest was Amsterdam in Holland. In less than a century, this once small medieval city had grown to become the most important commercial port in the West and the center of European financial capitalism. In the following selection, Carr describes the commercial trading system of the famous Dutch East India Company, which established trading posts in South Africa, the Persian Gulf area, India, Ceylon, Bangladesh, Indonesia, China, and Japan. Although not mentioned by Carr, the Dutch West India Company conducted similar operations in the Caribbean and North America. The Dutch trading post of New Amsterdam at the mouth of the Hudson River would become the city of New York, the world center of finance capitalism in the twentieth century.

. . . The East India Company of the Netherlands is said to be a commonwealth within a commonwealth, and this is true when you consider the sovereign power and privileges the company has been granted by the States General [the ruling council of the Dutch Republic] and also consider its riches and vast number of subjects, and the many territories and colonies it possesses in the East Indies. The company is said to have 30,000 men in its constant employ and more than 200 capital ships, in addition to its sloops, ketches, and yachts. The company possesses many colonies formerly belonging to Spain, Portugal, and various Indian princes, and as good Christians company members have spread the Gospel of Christ in these lands, printing the Bible, prayer books, and catechisms in Indian languages and maintaining ministers and teachers to instruct those that are converted to the faith. Having said that this company is so extensive—as it were a commonwealth apart—I will demonstrate that it is a commonwealth first by its power, riches, and strength in the East Indies, and second, by its position in Europe. . . . But I will begin at the Cape of Good Hope [Africa] where the company has built a fort where it maintains a garrison to defend its ships when they stop there for fresh water. From there let us view the company on the island of Java, where it has built a fair city called

Batavia and fortified it with bastions like those in Amsterdam. This city is the residence of the company's grand minister of state, called the General of the Indies. He has six privy counsellors (ordinary) and two extraordinary; they oversee the concerns of the company throughout the Indies, including matters of war and peace. . . . The General of the Indies has horse and foot soldiers, officers, and servants—as if he were a sovereign prince—all paid for by the company. . . . So formidable is the company in the East Indies that it looks as though it aims to rule the South Seas. It also has a great trade with China and Japan. . . . With Persia also it has great commerce and is so confident that it wages war with the Persian monarch if he wrongs it in trade. It also has several colonies on the coast of Malabar and Coromandel [west coast of India] and in the country of the Great Mogul. . . . But especially let us examine the company on the rich island of Ceylon [Sri Lanka] where it controls the plains, so the king of the island is forced to live in the mountains while the company possesses the city of Colombo. . . . I will say no more of the company's power in the Indies, but let us examine its position in Europe. To begin with, in Amsterdam the company has two large stately palaces, one being in the old part of the city, and the other in the new; in the old part it keeps its court—where the Resident Committee of the company sits— and sells the company's goods.

REVIEW QUESTION

1. What evidence of the Dutch East India Company's power does Carr provide?

---

4 The Jews of Spain and Portugal: Expulsion, Forced Conversion, Inquisition

For centuries the Jewish community in Spain had distinguished itself in commerce and intellectual pursuits, and Jews had served Spanish kings as ministers and physicians. However, the five-hundred-year struggle, seen as a crusade, to drive the Muslims out of Spain and the vitriolic preachings of clerics, particularly Dominican friars, exacerbated anti-Jewish feelings. In a three-month period in 1391, mobs slew some 50,000 Jews and prompted many others to join the growing number of *conversos* or converts. A century later, in 1492, the Spanish monarchs Ferdinand and Isabella, fearing that converted Jews were being encouraged by their relatives and erstwhile co-religionists to return to Judaism, ordered the expulsion of those Spanish Jews who would not convert to Catholicism. Perhaps as many as 150,000 Jews fled; it is not known how many remained and converted.

Old Christians disdained the *conversos* or New Christians. They accused the converts of secretly practicing Judaism and resented their rise to positions of eminence in business, the professions, government service, and even the church. The hostility to *conversos* also had a racial component, as Old Christians insisted, contrary to Catholic theology, that baptism would not cleanse the bad blood of Jews. Old Christians were obsessed with racial purity, refusing to intermarry

with New Christians, even if the family had been faithful Catholics for generations, and barring their entry into certain military and religious orders. For social
acceptance, one had to prove a lineage that had no Jewish blood.

PROCEEDINGS OF THE SPANISH INQUISITION: THE TORTURE OF ELVIRA DEL CAMPO

For centuries the Spanish Inquisition, established to guard against religious
backsliding by New Christians and run by clergy motivated by church doctrines
that denigrated Jews and Judaism, relentlessly hounded the converts' descendants. The following account taken from the Inquisition's archives typifies the
tribunal's procedures. In 1567, Elvira del Campo, a descendant of converts who
considered herself Catholic and married a Catholic, was reported to the Inquisition by neighbors who observed that she refrained from eating pork (forbidden
to Jews) and put on clean clothes on Saturday (the Jewish Sabbath). The pregnant
Elvira assured the clerical judges that she was a good Christian and that she only
performed these innocent practices in fulfillment of a promise she had made to
her dying mother when she was eleven. Subjected to cruel torture, the pregnant
woman confessed to Judaizing. The court confiscated her property, sentenced
her to three years in prison, and required her to wear the garb of a convicted
heretic. Although released a few months after giving birth, she was reduced to
poverty and shame, and her life was ruined.

She was carried to the torture-chamber and told to tell the truth, when she said that she had nothing to say. She was ordered to be stripped and again admonished, but was silent. When stripped, she said "Señores, I have done all that is said of me and I bear false-witness against myself, for I do not want to see myself in such trouble; please God, I have done nothing." She was told not to bring false testimony against herself but to tell the truth. The tying of the arms was commenced; she said "I have told the truth; what have I to tell?" She was told to tell the truth and replied "I have told the truth and have nothing to tell." One cord was applied to the arms and twisted and she was admonished to tell the truth but said she had nothing to tell. Then she screamed and said "I have done all they say." Told to tell in detail what she had done she replied "I have already told the truth." Then she screamed and said "Tell me what you want for I don't know what to say." She was told to tell what she had done, for she was tortured because she had not done so, and another turn of the cord was ordered. She cried "Loosen me, Señores and tell me what I have to say: I do not know what I have done, O Lord have mercy on me, a sinner!" Another turn was given and she said "Loosen me a little that I may remember what I have to tell; I don't know what I have done; I did not eat pork for it made me sick; I have done everything; loosen me and I will tell the truth." Another turn of the cord was ordered, when she said "Loosen me and I will tell the truth; I don't know what I have to tell—loosen me for the sake of God—tell me what I have to say—I did it, I did it—they hurt me Señor—loosen me, loosen me and I will tell it." She was told to tell it and said "I don't know what I have to tell—Señor I did it—I have nothing to tell—Oh my arms! release me and I will tell it."

She was asked to tell what she did and said "I don't know, I did not eat because I did not wish to." She was asked why she did not wish to and replied "Ay! loosen me, loosen me—take me from here and I will tell when I am taken away—I say that I did not eat it." She was told to speak and said "I did not eat it, I don't know why." Another turn was ordered and she said "Señor I did not eat it because I did not wish to—release me and I will tell it." She was told to tell what she had done contrary to our holy Catholic faith. She said "Take me from here and tell me what I have to say—they hurt me—Oh my arms, my arms!" which she repeated many times and went on "I don't remember—tell me what I have to say—O wretched me!—I will tell all that is wanted, Señores—they are breaking my arms—loosen me a little—I did everything that is said of me." She was told to tell in detail truly what she did. She said "What am I wanted to tell? I did everything—loosen me for I don't remember what I have to tell—don't you see what a weak woman I am?—Oh! Oh! my arms are breaking." More turns were ordered and as they were given she cried "Oh! Oh! loosen me for I don't know what I have to say—Oh my arms!—I don't know what I have to say—if I did I would tell it." The cords were ordered to be tightened when she said "Señores have you no pity on a sinful woman?" She was told, yes, if she would tell the truth. She said, "Señor tell me, tell me it." The cords were tightened again, and she said "I have already said that I did it." She was ordered to tell it in detail, to which she said "I don't know how to tell it señor, I don't know." Then the cords were separated and counted, and there were sixteen turns, and in giving the last turn the cord broke.

She was then ordered to be placed on the potro [a type of ladder with sharp-edged rungs]. She said "Señores, why will you not tell me what I have to say? Señor, put me on the ground—have I not said that I did it all?" She was told to tell it. She said "I don't remember—take me away—I did what the witnesses say." She was told to tell in detail what the witnesses said. She said "Señor, as I have told you, I do not know

for certain. I have said that I did all that the witnesses say. Señores release me, for I do not remember it." She was told to tell it. She said "I do not know it. Oh! Oh! they are tearing me to pieces—I have said that I did it—let me go." She was told to tell it. She said "Señores, it does not help me to say that I did it and I have admitted that what I have done has brought me to this suffering—Señor, you know the truth—Señores, for God's sake have mercy on me. Oh Señor, take these things from my arms—Señor release me, they are killing me." She was tied on the potro with the cords, she was admonished to tell the truth and the garrotes [twisted sticks used to tighten ropes that cut into the flesh] were ordered to be tightened. She said "Señor do you not see how these people are killing me? Señor, I did it—for God's sake let me go." She was told to tell it. She said "Señor, remind me of what I did not know—Señores have mercy upon me—let me go for God's sake—they have no pity on me—I did it—take me from here and I will remember what I cannot here." She was told to tell the truth or the cords would be tightened. She said "Remind me of what I have to say for I don't know it—I said that I did not want to eat it—I know only that I did not want to eat it," and this she repeated many times. She was told to tell why she did not want to eat it. She said, "For the reason that the witnesses say—I don't know how to tell it—miserable that I am that I don't know how to tell it—I say I did it and my God how can I tell it?" Then she said that, as she did not do it, how could she tell it—"They will not listen to me—these people want to kill me—release me and I will tell the truth." She was again admonished to tell the truth. She said, "I did it, I don't know how I did it—I did it for what the witnesses say—let me go—I have lost my senses and I don't know how to tell it—loosen me and I will tell the truth." Then she said "Señor, I did it, I don't know how I have to tell it, but I tell it as the witnesses say—I wish to tell it—take me from here—Señor as the witnesses say, so I say and confess it." She was told to declare it. She said "I don't know how to say it—I have no memory—Lord, you are witness that if I knew how to say anything else I would say it. I know nothing more to say than that I did it and God knows it." She said many times, "Señores, Señores, nothing helps me. You, Lord, hear that I tell the truth and can say no more—they are tearing out my soul—order them to loosen me." Then she said, "I do not say that I did it—I said no more." Then she said, "Señor, I did it to observe that Law." She was asked what Law. She said, "The Law that the witnesses say—I declare it all Señor, and don't remember what Law it was—O, wretched was the mother that bore me." She was asked what was the Law she meant and what was the Law that she said the witnesses say. This was asked repeatedly, but she was silent and at last said that she did not know. She was told to tell the truth or the garrotes would be tightened but she did not answer. Another turn was ordered on the garrotes and she was admonished to say what Law it was. She said "If I knew what to say I would say it. Oh Señor, I don't know what I have to say—Oh! Oh! they are killing me—if they would tell me what—Oh, Señores! Oh, my heart!" Then she asked why they wished her to tell what she could not tell and cried repeatedly "O, miserable me!" Then she said "Lord bear witness that they are killing me without my being able to confess." She was told that if she wished to tell the truth before the water was poured she should do so and discharge her conscience. She said that she could not speak and that she was a sinner. Then [her mouth was held open by an iron prong, her nostrils were plugged, and a funnel was inserted in her throat, through which water slowly trickled] and she said "Take it away, I am strangling and am sick in the stomach." A jar of water was then poured down, after which she was told to tell the truth. She clamored for confession, saying that she was dying. She was told that the torture would be continued till she told the truth and was admonished to tell it, but though she was questioned repeatedly she remained silent. Then the inquisitor, seeing her exhausted by the torture, ordered it to be suspended.

Damião de Gois
THE FORCED CONVERSION OF PORTUGUESE JEWS

Influenced by the recent expulsion of the Spanish Jews, in 1497 King Manuel of Portugal (1495–1521) also demanded the expulsion or conversion of the Jews in his own country. Making the event more harrowing for the unfortunate Jews was the king's order to wrest Jewish children age fourteen or younger from their parents, baptize them, and place them in Christian homes. This wave of persecution was not confined to those who actively practiced the Jewish faith. The recent converts, or New Christians, free of the barriers that had been placed on them as Jews, were rising rapidly in the professions, government service, and business. In 1506, Old Christians, driven by fear and hate and aroused by friars shouting heresy, massacred New Christians. Damião de Gois, a contemporary Christian chronicler, reported that the mob dragged the victims

through the streets with their sons, wives and daughters [and] threw them indiscriminately, dead and alive onto the bonfires, without any mercy. And so great was the cruelty that they even executed children and babies in the cradle, taking them by the legs, cutting them into pieces and smashing them against walls. In these cruelties, they did not forget to sack the houses and steal all the gold, silver and jewels which they found in them, the matter reaching such a frenzy that they dragged [even] from the churches many men, women, boys and girls, tearing them away from . . . the images of our Lord and Our Lady and the other saints, which they had embraced for fear of death, killing and burning without distinction, [and] without fear of God, both women and men.

In the following selection, Damião de Gois describes the events surrounding the forced conversion of Portuguese Jews.

Many of the Jews born in the kingdom [of Portugal] and of those who came from Castile received the water of baptism, and those who did not want to convert then began to arrange matters suitably for their embarkation. At this time the king, for reasons that moved him thus, ordered that on a certain day their sons and daughters, aged fourteen and below, should be taken from them and distributed among the towns and villages of the kingdom, where at his own expense [the king] ordered that they should be brought up and indoctrinated in the faith of our saviour Jesus Christ. This was agreed by the king with his council of state in Estremoz, and from there he went to Evora at the beginning of Lent in the year 1497, where he announced that the appointed day would be Easter Sunday.

Because there was less secrecy among the members of the [royal] council than had been expected, concerning what had been ordered in this matter, on the day on which [this] was to happen, it was necessary for the king to command that the execution of this order should be implemented at once throughout the kingdom, before by means and devices the Jews might have sent their children abroad. This action was the cause, not only of great terror, mixed with many tears, pain and sadness among the Jews, but also of much fright and surprise among the Christians, because no [human] creature ought to suffer or endure having his children forcibly separated from him. And [even] among foreigners [perhaps the native population of Portugal's colonies] virtually the same feeling exists by natural communication [i.e. without Christianity],

principally among the rational ones, because with them Nature communicates the effects of her law more freely than with irrational beasts.

This same law compelled many of the 'old' Christians to be so moved to pity and mercy by the angry cries, weeping and wailing of the fathers and mothers from whom their children were forcibly taken, that they themselves hid [Jewish children] in their houses so that [the Jews] should not see them snatched from their hands. Those [Christians] saved them, knowing that they were thus acting against the law and the pragmatic of their king and lord, and that this same natural law made the Jews themselves use such cruelty that many of them killed their children, by suffocating them and drowning them in wells and rivers, as well as other methods, preferring to see them die in this way rather than be separated from them, without hope that they would ever see them again; and, for the same reason, many of [the parents] killed themselves.

While these actions were being carried out, the king never ceased to concern himself with what was necessary for the salvation of these people's souls, so that, moved by piety, he played a trick on them, by ordering them to be allowed to embark. Of the three ports of the kingdom that were designated for this, he forbade them two and commanded that they should all go to Lisbon to embark, giving them the [quarter of] the Estaos in which to shelter, and more than twenty thousand souls gathered there. Because of these delays, the time that the king had fixed for their departure went by, and thus they all remained as captives. Finding themselves in so wretched a state, many of them placed themselves at the mercy of the king. He returned their children to them and promised them that for twenty years he would inflict no harm upon them and that they would become Christians; [all of] which the king conceded to them, together with many other privileges that he gave them. As for those who did not want to be Christians, he ordered immediate embarkation to be granted to them, thus freeing them from the captivity in which they found themselves; and they all passed over to the lands of the Moors.[1]

Now it appears that we might be regarded as neglectful if we did not state the reason why the king ordered the children of the Jews to be taken from them, but not those of the Moors, because they too left the kingdom because they did not wish to receive the water of baptism and believe what the Catholic Church believes. The reason was that from the seizure of the Jews' children no harm could result for the Christians dispersed throughout the world, in which the Jews, because of their sins, do not have

kingdoms or lordships, cities and towns, but rather, everywhere they live they are pilgrims and taxpayers, without having power or authority to carry out their wishes against the injuries and evils which are done to them. But for *our* sins and punishment, God allows the Moors to occupy the greater part of Asia and Africa and a great part of Europe, where they have empires and kingdoms and great lordships, in which many Christians are under tribute to them, as well as many whom they hold as captives. For all these [reasons], it would be very prejudicial to take the Moors' children away from them, because it is clear that they would not hesitate to avenge those to whom such an injury was done on the Christians living in the lands of other Moors, once they found out about it, and above all on the Portuguese, against whom they would have a particular grievance in this regard. And this was the reason why [the Muslims] were allowed to leave the kingdom with their children and the Jews were not, to all of whom God permitted through his mercy to know the way of truth, so that they might be saved in it.

---

[1]North Africa.

REVIEW QUESTIONS

1. Why did Christians persecute Jews and New Christians with a clear conscience?
2. Why didn't the Portuguese take away the children of Muslims the way they did Jewish children?

---

5 The Atlantic Slave Trade

As the first Portuguese merchants began to penetrate southward along the coast of Western Africa, they found that the local African societies engaged in an extensive trade in slave laborers. African slavers brought their captives, generally prisoners of war and kidnap victims, to coastal slave markets where they were purchased by Europeans. Some slaves were taken back to Europe, but after 1500 the trade shifted largely to the Portuguese colony in Brazil and the Spanish colonies in the West Indies. In addition, Arabs and Portuguese competed in conveying slaves from East Africa to the markets of the Middle East. The widespread use of African slaves marked a new stage in the history of slavery. In the Western world slavery became identified with race; the myth emerged that blacks were slaves by nature.

In the seventeenth century, the Dutch and English entered the West African slave trade, ousting the Portuguese as the principal slave traders to the West Indies and North America. The supply of laborers from Africa was essential to the New World's successful economic development. The Africans proved themselves to be skilled farmers and artisans who could endure the heavy labor of plantation life without the high rate of sickness and death that afflicted the local Native American populations. The Atlantic slave trade continued for more than three hundred years until finally suppressed by European governments in the nineteenth century. During that period, it is estimated that between 9.5 and 12 million African men, women, and children were shipped to the New World as slaves.

Seventeenth-Century Slave Traders
BUYING AND TRANSPORTING AFRICANS

Dealing in slaves was a profitable business that attracted numerous entrepreneurs. Following are two accounts written by slave traders in the seventeenth century.

As the slaves come down to Fida from the inland country, they are put into a booth, or prison, built for that purpose, near the beach, all of them together; and when the Europeans are to receive them, they are brought out into a large plain, where the surgeons examine every part of every one of them, to the smallest member, men and women being all stark naked. Such as are allowed good and sound, are set on the one side, and the others by themselves; which slaves so rejected are there called Mackrons, being above thirty five years of age, or defective in their limbs, eyes or teeth; or grown grey, or that have the venereal disease, or any other imperfection. These being so set aside, each of the others, which have passed as good, is marked on the breast, with a red-hot iron, imprinting the mark of the French, English, or Dutch companies, that so each nation may distinguish their own, and to prevent their being chang'd by the natives for worse, as they are apt enough to do. In this particular, care is taken that the women, as tenderest, be not burnt too hard.

The branded slaves, after this, are returned to their former booth, where the factor [buyer] is to subsist them at his own charge, which amounts to about two-pence a day for each of them, with bread and water, which is all their allowance. There they continue sometimes ten or fifteen days, till the sea is still enough to send them aboard; for very often it continues too boisterous for so long a time, unless in January, February and March, which is commonly the calmest season: and when it is so, the slaves are carried off by parcels, in bar-canoes, and put aboard the ships in the road. Before they enter the canoes, or come out of the booth, their former Black masters strip them of every rag they have, without distinction of men or women; to supply which, in orderly ships, each of them as they come aboard is allowed a piece of canvas, to wrap around their waist, which is very acceptable to those poor wretches. . . . in the aforesaid months of January, February and March, which are the good season, ships are for the most part soon dispatched, if there be a good number of slaves at hand; so that they need not stay above four weeks for their cargo, and sometimes it is done in a fortnight.

The Blacks of Fida are so expeditious at this trade of slaves that they can deliver a thousand every month. . . . If there happens to be no stock of slaves at Fida, the factor must trust the Blacks with his goods, to the value of a hundred and fifty, or two hundred slaves; which goods they carry up into the inland, to buy slaves, at all the markets, for above two hundred leagues up the country, where they are kept like cattle [are kept] in Europe; the slaves sold there being generally prisoners of war, taken from their enemies, like other booty, and perhaps some few sold by their own countrymen, in extreme want, or upon a famine; as also some as a punishment of heinous crimes: tho' many Europeans believe that parents sell their own children, men their wives and relations, which, if it ever happens, is so seldom, that it cannot justly be charged upon a whole nation, as a custom and common practice.

A second slaver describes the loading and transporting of the newly acquired slaves.

When our slaves were come to the seaside, our canoes were ready to carry them off to the long-boat, if the sea permitted, and she convey'd them aboard ship, where the men were all put in irons, two and two shackled together, to prevent their mutiny, or swimming ashore.

The negroes are so wilful and loth to leave their own country, that they have often leap'd out of the canoes, boat and ship, into the sea, and kept under water till they were drowned, to avoid being taken up and saved by our boats, which pursued them; they having a more dreadful apprehension of Barbadoes than we can have of hell, tho' in reality they live much better there than in their own country; but home is home, etc: we have likewise seen [many] of them eaten by the sharks, of which a prodigious

number [swam] about the ships in this place, and I have been told will follow her hence to Barbadoes, for the dead negroes that are thrown over-board in the passage. I am certain in our voyage there we did not [lack] the sight of some every day, but that they were the same I can't affirm.

We had about 12 negroes did wilfully drown themselves, and others starv'd themselves to death; for 'tis their belief that when they die they return home to their own country and friends again.

I have been inform'd that some commanders have cut off the legs and arms of the most wilful, to terrify the rest, for they believe if they lose a member, they cannot return home again: I was advis'd by some of my officers to do the same, but I could not be perswaded to entertain the least thought of it, much less put in practice such barbarity and cruelty to poor creatures, who, excepting their want of christianity and true religion (their misfortune more than fault) are as much the works of God's hands, and no doubt as dear to him as ourselves; nor can I imagine why they should be despis'd for their colour, being what they cannot help, and the effect of the climate it has pleas'd God to appoint them. I can't think there is any intrinsick value in one colour more than another, nor that white is better than black, only we think so because we are so, and are prone to judge favourably in our own case, as well as the blacks, who in odium of the colour, say, the devil is white, and so paint him. . . .

When our slaves are aboard we shackle the men two and two, while we lie in port, and in sight of their own country, for 'tis then they attempt to make their escape, and mutiny; to prevent which we always keep centinels upon the hatchways, and have a chest full of small arms, ready loaden and prim'd, constantly lying at hand upon the quarter-deck, together with some granada shells; and two of our quarter-deck guns, pointing on the deck thence, and two more out of the steerage, the door of which is always kept shut, and well barr'd; they are fed twice a day, at 10 in the morning, and 4 in the evening, which is the time they are aptest to mutiny, being all upon deck; therefore all that time [those] of our men are not employ'd in distributing their victuals to them, and settling them, stand to their arms; and some with lighted matches at the great guns that yaun upon them . . . till they have done and gone down to their kennels between decks. . . .

When we come to sea we let them all out of irons, they never attempting then to rebel, considering that should they kill or master us, they could not tell how to manage the ship, or must trust us, who would carry them where we pleas'd; therefore the only danger is while we are in sight of their own country, which they are loth to part with; but once out of sight out of mind: I never heard that they mutiny'd in any ships of consequence, that had a good number of men, and the least care; but in small tools [vessels] where they had but few men, and those negligent or drunk, then they surpriz'd and butcher'd them, cut the cables, and let the vessel drive ashore, and every one shift for himself. However, we have some 30 or 40 gold coast[1] negroes, which we buy, and are procur'd us there by our factors,

to make guardians and overseers of the Whidaw negroes, and sleep among them to keep them from quarrelling; and in order, as well as to give us notice, if they can discover any caballing or plotting among them, which trust they will discharge with great diligence: they also take care to make the negroes scrape the decks where they lodge every morning very clean, to eschew any distempers that may engender from filth and nastiness; when we constitute a guardian, we give him a cat of nine tails [whip] as a badge of his office, which he is not a little proud of, and will exercise with great authority. We often at sea in the evenings would let the slaves come up into the sun to air themselves, and make them jump and dance for an hour or two to our bag-pipes, harp, and fiddle, by which exercise to preserve them in health; but notwithstanding all our endeavour, 'twas my hard fortune to have great sickness and mortality among them.

Having bought my compliment of 700 slaves, *viz.* 480 men and 220 women, and finish'd all my business at Whidaw, I took my leave of the old king . . . and parted, with many affectionate expressions on both sides, being forced to promise him that I would return again the next year, with several things he desired me to bring him from England. . . .

---

[1]The Gold Coast was a section of coastal western Africa along the Gulf of Guinea, known for its trade in gold.

Malachy Postlethwayt
SLAVERY DEFENDED

While some people attacked African bondage as morally repugnant, its proponents argued that it was a boon to shipping and manufacturing and also benefited Africans by liberating them from oppressive African rulers, who had captured and enslaved them, and placing them in the care of more humane Christian masters, who instructed them in Christian ideals. Malachy Postlethwayt (c. 1707–1767), an English economist, defended slavery in the following excerpt written in 1746.

The most approved judges of the commercial interests of these Kingdoms have ever been of the opinion, that our West-India and African trades are the most nationally beneficial of any we carry on. It is also allowed on all hands, that the trade to Africa is the Branch which renders our American colonies and plantations so advantageous to Great Britain, that traffic only affording our planters a constant supply of negro servants for the culture of their lands in the produce of sugars, tobacco, rice, rum, cotton, pimento, and all other our plantation-produce: so that the extensive employment of our shipping in, to, and from America, the great brood of Seamen consequent thereupon, and the daily bread of the most considerable part of our British manufactures, are owing primarily to the labours of Negroes; who, as they were the first happy instruments of raising our plantations; so their labour only can support and preserve them, and render them still more and more profitable to their mother-kingdom.

The negro-trade, therefore, and the national consequences resulting from it, may be justly esteemed an inexhaustible fund of wealth and naval power to this nation. And by the surplus of negroes above what have served our own plantations, we have drawn likewise no inconsiderable quantities of treasure from the Spaniards, who are settled on the continent of America, . . . for Negroes furnished them from Jamaica. . . .

What renders the negro trade still more estimable and important, is, that near nine-tenths of those negroes are paid for in Africa with British produce and manufactures only; and the remainder with East-India commodities. We send no specie or bullion [coined money] to pay for the products of Africa but, 'tis certain, we bring from thence very large quantities of gold. . . .

And it may be worth consideration that while our plantations depend only on planting by negro servants, they will neither depopulate our own country, become independent of her dominion, or any way interfere with the interests of the British manufacturer, merchant, or landed gentleman: whereas were we under the necessity of supplying our colonies with white-men instead of blacks, they could not fail being in a capacity to interfere with the manufactures of this nation, in time to shake off their dependency thereon, and prove as injurious to the landed, and trading interests as ever they have hitherto been beneficial.

Many are prepossessed against this trade, thinking it a barbarous, inhuman and unlawful traffic for a Christian country to trade in Blacks; to which I would beg leave to observe; that though the odious appellation of slaves is annexed to this trade, it being called by some the slave-trade, yet it does not appear from the best enquiry I have been able to make, that the state of those people is changed for the worse, by being servants to our British planters in America; they are certainly treated with great lenity and humanity: and as the improvement of the planter's estates depends upon due care being taken of their healths and lives, I cannot but think their condition is much bettered to what it was in their own country.

Besides, the negro princes in Africa, 'tis well known, are in perpetual war with each other, and since before they had this method of disposing of their prisoners of war to Christian merchants, they were wont not only to be applied to inhuman sacrifices, but to extreme torture and barbarity, their transportation must certainly be a melioration [improvement] of their condition; provided living in a civilized Christian country, is better than living among savages: Nay, if life be preferable to torment and cruel death, their state cannot, with any color of reason, be presumed to be worsened. . . .

As the present prosperity and splendor of the British colonies have been owing to negro labor, so not only their future advancement, but even their very being depends [on it]. That our colonies are capable of very great improvements, by the proper application of the labour of blacks, has been urged by the most experienced judges of commerce.

The negro princes and chiefs in Africa are generally at war with each other on the continent; and the prisoners of war, instead of being slain, or applied to inhuman sacrifices, are carefully preserved and sold to those Europeans only, who have established interest and power among the natives, by means of forts and settlements; or to such who are admitted to traffic with the natives, by virtue, and under the sanction and protection of such European settlements; which is the case of all the British merchants who trade to Africa at present, at full liberty, under the authority and protection of our Royal African Company's rights and privileges, interest and power among the natives. . . .

John Wesley
SLAVERY ATTACKED

John Wesley (1703–1791) was, with his brother Charles, the founder of the evangelical Methodist movement in England. Inspired by the Great Awakening in the American colonies, he launched a successful revival of Christianity in England in 1739. The rest of his long life was devoted to leadership of the Methodist movement.

Wesley's eyes were opened to the evils of slavery by reading an indictment of the slave trade by a French Quaker, Anthony Benezet. In 1774 he published the tract *Thoughts Upon Slavery*, from which the extracts below are taken. Wesley drew heavily on Benezet's writings for his facts, but in warning participants in the slave trade of divine retribution, he spoke in the cadences of the inspired evangelical preacher.

Wesley became one of the leaders in the movement against slavery and his pioneering work, in which he was supported by the Methodist movement, helped bring about the abolition of slavery in England in 1807.

I would inquire whether [the abuses of slavery] can be defended on the principles of even heathen honesty, whether they can be reconciled (setting the Bible out of question) with any degree of either justice or mercy.

The grand plea is, "They are authorized by law." But can law, human law, change the nature of things? Can it turn darkness into light or evil into good? By no means. Notwithstanding ten thousand laws, right is right, and wrong is wrong still. There must still remain an essential [difference] between justice and injustice, cruelty and mercy. So that I still ask, who can reconcile this treatment of the Negroes first and last, with either mercy or justice? . . . Yea, where is the justice of taking away the lives of innocent, inoffensive men, murdering thousands of them in their own land, by the hands of their own countrymen, many thousands year after year on shipboard, and then casting them like dung into the sea and tens of thousands in that cruel slavery to which they are so unjustly reduced? . . .

But if this manner of procuring and treating Negroes is not consistent either with mercy or justice, yet there is a plea for it which every man of business will acknowledge to be quite sufficient. . . . "D—n justice, it is necessity. . . . It is necessary that we should procure slaves, and when we have procured them, it is necessary to use them with severity, considering their stupidity, stubbornness and wickedness."

I answer you stumble at the threshold. I deny that villainy is ever necessary. It is impossible that it should ever be necessary for any reasonable creature to violate all the laws of justice, mercy, and truth. No circumstances can make it necessary for a man to burst in sunder all the ties of humanity. It can never be necessary for a rational being to sink himself below a brute. A man can be under no necessity of degrading himself into a wolf. The absurdity of the supposition is so glaring that one would wonder anyone can help seeing it. . . .

"But the furnishing us with slaves is necessary for the trade, and wealth, and glory of our nation." Here are several mistakes. For first wealth is not necessary to the glory of any nation, but wisdom, virtue, justice, mercy, generosity, public spirit, love of our country. These are necessary to the real glory of a nation, but abundance of wealth is not.

. . . But, secondly, it is not clear that we should have either less money or trade (only less of that detestable trade of man—stealing), if there was not a Negro in all our islands or in all English America. It is demonstrable, white men inured to it by degrees can work as well as they, and they would do it, were Negroes out of the way, and proper encouragement given them. However, thirdly, I come back to the same point: Better no trade than trade procured by villainy. It is far better to have no wealth than to gain wealth at the expense of virtue. Better is honest poverty than all the riches bought by the tears, and sweat, and blood of our fellow creatures.

"However this be, it is necessary, when we have slaves, to use them with severity." What, to whip them for every petty offence, till they are all in gore blood? To take that opportunity of rubbing pepper and salt into their raw flesh? To drop burning wax upon their skin? To castrate them? To cut off half their foot with an axe? To hang them on gibbets, that they may die by inches with heat, and hunger, and thirst? To pin them down to the ground, and then burn them by degrees from the feet to the head? To roast them alive? When did a Turk or heathen find it necessary to use a fellow-creature thus?

I pray, to what end is this usage necessary? "Why to prevent their running away, and to keep them constantly to their labour, that they may not idle away their time. So miserably stupid is this race of men, yea, so stupid and so wicked." Allowing them to be as stupid as you say, to whom is that stupidity owing? Without question it lies at the door of their inhuman masters who give them no means, no opportunity of improving their understanding. . . . Consequently it is not their fault but yours: you must answer for it before God and man. . . .

And what pains have you taken, what method have you used, to reclaim them from their wickedness? Have you carefully taught them, "That there is a God, a wise, powerful, merciful being, the creator and governor of heaven and earth? That he has appointed a day wherein he will judge the world, will take account of all our thoughts, words and actions? That in that day he will reward every child of man according to his works: that 'Then the righteous shall inherit the kingdom prepared for them from the foundation of the world: and the wicked shall be cast into everlasting fire, prepared for the devil and his angels.'" If you have not done this, if you have taken no pains or thought about the matter, can you wonder at their wickedness? What wonder if they should cut your throat? And if they did, whom could you thank for it but yourself? You first acted the villain in making them slaves (whether you stole them or bought them). You kept them stupid and wicked by cutting them off from all opportunities of improving either in knowledge or virtue. And now you assign their want of wisdom and goodness as the reason for using them worse than brute beasts. . . .

It remains only to make a little application of the preceding observations . . . I therefore add a few words to those who are more immediately concerned, . . . and first to the captains employed in this trade. . . .

Is there a God? You know there is. Is he a just God? Then there must be a state of retribution; a state wherein the just God will reward every man according to his works. Then what reward will he render to you? O think betimes! Before you drop into eternity! Think now: he shall have judgment without mercy, that showed no mercy.

Are you a man? . . . Have you no sympathy? No sense of human woe? No pity for the miserable? . . . When you squeezed the agonizing creatures down in the ship, or when you threw their poor mangled remains into the sea, had you no relenting? Did not one tear drop from your eye, one sigh escape from your breast? Do you feel no relenting now? If you do not, you must go on till the measure of your iniquities is full. Then will the great God deal with *you*, as you have dealt with *them*, and require all their blood at your hands. . . .

Today resolve, God being your helper, to escape for your life. Regard not money! All that a man hath will he give for his life! Whatever you lose, lose not your soul; nothing can countervail that loss. Immediately quit the horrid trade. At all events, be an honest man.

This equally concerns every merchant who is engaged in the slave-trade. It is you that induce the African villain, to sell his countrymen, and in order thereto, to steal, rob, murder men, women and children without number. By enabling the English villain to pay him for so doing, whom you overpay for his execrable labour. It is your money that is the spring of all, that impowers him to go on. . . . And is your conscience quite reconciled to this? Does it never reproach you at all? Has gold entirely blinded your eyes, and stupefied your heart? . . . Have no more part in this detestable business. Be you a man! Not a wolf, a devourer of the human species. Be merciful that you may obtain mercy.

And this equally concerns every gentleman that has an estate in our African plantations.

Yea, all slave-holders of whatever rank and degree, seeing men-buyers are exactly at a level with men-sellers. Indeed you say, "I pay honestly for my goods, and am not concerned to know how they are come by." Nay, but . . . you know they are not honestly come by. . . .

If therefore you have any regard to justice (to say nothing of mercy, nor of the revealed law of God) render unto all their due. Give liberty to whom liberty is due, that is, to every child of man, to every partaker of human nature. Let none serve you but by his own act and deed, by his own voluntary choice. Away with all whips, all chains, all compulsion. Be gentle toward all men. And see that you invariably do unto every one, as you would he should do unto you.

O thou God of love, thou who art loving to every man, and whose mercy is over all thy works: Thou who art the father of the spirits of all flesh, and who art rich in mercy unto all: Thou who hast mingled in one blood all the nations upon earth: have compassion upon these outcasts of men, who are trodden down as dung upon the earth. Arise and help these who have no helper, whose blood is spilt upon the ground like water! Are not these also the work of thine own hands, the purchase of thy Son's blood? Stir them up to cry unto thee in the land of their captivity; and let their complaint come up before thee; let it enter into thine ears! Make even those that lead them away captive to pity them. . . . O burst thou all their chains in sunder; more especially the chains of their sins: Thou, Saviour of all, make them free, that they may be free indeed!

Olaudah Equiano
MEMOIRS OF A FORMER SLAVE

One eighteenth-century African, Olaudah Equiano (c. 1745–1797), an Ibo from what is now Nigeria, wrote about his kidnapping and enslavement in Africa, his subsequent sale to English slave merchants, and his voyage to and first impressions of the West Indian port of Bridgetown, Barbados. Equiano's subsequent life diverged from the pattern of most slaves. He educated himself, engaged in petty trade, purchased his freedom, and traveled to England, Nicaragua, Syria, and New England. In 1786, he was involved in planning the first free black colony, at Freetown, Sierra Leone, in Africa, and he took an active part in the antislavery movement in England. In the following excerpts from his memoir, *The Interesting Narrative of Olaudah Equiano or Gustavus Vasa the African*, published in two volumes in London in 1789, he records his reactions at the age of eleven when he was placed aboard an English slave ship for the voyage to the West Indies.

The first object which saluted my eyes when I arrived on the coast was the sea, and a slaveship, which was then riding at anchor, and waiting for its cargo. These filled me with astonishment, which was soon converted into terror, which I am yet at a loss to describe, nor the then feelings of my mind. When I was carried on board I was immediately handled, and tossed up, to see if I were sound, by some of the crew; and I was now persuaded that I had got into a world of bad spirits, and that they were going to kill me. Their complexions too differing so much from ours, their long hair, and the language they spoke, which was very different from any I had ever heard, united to confirm me in this belief. Indeed, such were the horrors of my views and fears at the moment, that, if ten thousand worlds had been my own, I would have freely parted with them all to have exchanged my condition with that of the meanest slave in my own country. When I looked round the ship too, and saw a large furnace or copper [pot] boiling, and a multitude of black people of every description chained together, every one of their countenances expressing dejection and sorrow, I no longer doubted of my fate; and, quite overpowered with horror and anguish, I fell motionless on the deck and fainted. When I recovered a little, I found some black people about me, who I believed were some of those who brought me on board, and had been receiving their pay; they talked to me in order to cheer me, but all in vain. I asked them if we were not to be eaten by those white men with horrible looks, red faces, and long hair. They told me I was not. . . .

. . . Soon after this, the blacks who brought me on board went off, and left me abandoned to despair. I now saw myself deprived of all chance of returning to my native country, or even the least glimpse of hope of gaining the shore, which I now considered as friendly; and I even wished for my former slavery, in preference to my present situation, which was filled with horror of every kind, still heightened by my ignorance of what I was to undergo. I was not long suffered to indulge my grief; I was soon put down under the decks, and there I received such a salutation in my nostrils as I had never experienced in my life; so that, with the loathsomeness of the stench, and crying together, I became so sick and low that I was not able to eat, nor had I the least desire to taste any thing. I now wished for the last friend, death, to relieve me; but soon, to my grief, two of the white men offered me eatables; and, on my refusing to eat, one of them held me fast by the hands, and laid me across, I think, the windlass, and tied my feet while the other flogged me severely. I had never experienced any thing of this kind before; and, although not being used to the water, I naturally feared that element the first time I saw it; yet, nevertheless, could I have got over the nettings, I would have jumped over the side; but I could not; and, besides, the crew used to watch us very closely who were not chained down to the decks, lest we should leap into the water: and I have seen some of these poor African prisoners most severely cut for attempting to do so, and hourly whipped for not eating. This indeed was often the case with myself. . . .

. . . At last, when the ship we were in had got in all her cargo . . . we were all put under deck. . . . The closeness of the place, and the heat of the climate, added to the number in the ship, which was so crowded that each had scarcely room to turn himself, almost suffocated us. This produced copious perspirations, so that the air soon became unfit for respiration, from a variety of loathsome smells, and brought on a sickness amongst the slaves, of which many died, thus falling victims to the improvident avarice, as I may call it, of their purchasers. This wretched situation was again aggravated by the galling of the chains, now become insupportable; and filth of the necessary tubs, into which the children often fell, and were almost suffocated. The shrieks of the women, and the groans of the dying, rendered the whole a scene of horror almost inconceivable. Happily perhaps for myself I was soon reduced so low here that it was thought necessary to keep me almost always on deck; and from my extreme youth I was not put in fetters. In this situation I expected every hour to share the fate of my companions, some of whom were almost daily brought upon deck at the point of death, which I began to hope would soon put an end to my miseries. Often did I think many of the inhabitants of the deep much more happy than myself; I envied them the freedom they enjoyed, and as often wished I could change my condition for theirs. Every circumstance I met with served only to render my state more painful, and heighten my apprehensions and my opinion of the cruelty of the whites. . . .

. . . In a little time after, amongst the poor chained men, I found some of my own nation, which in a small degree gave ease to my mind. I inquired of them what was to be done with us? They gave me to understand we were to be carried to these white people's country to work for them. I then was a little revived, and thought, if it were no worse than working, my situation was not so desperate: but still I feared I should be put to death, the white people looked and acted, as I thought, in so savage a manner; for I had never seen among any people such instances of brutal cruelty; and this not only shown towards us blacks, but also to some of the whites themselves. One white man in particular I saw, when we were permitted to be on deck, flogged so unmercifully with a large rope near

the foremast, that he died in consequence of it; and they tossed him over the side as they would have done a brute. This made me fear these people the more; and I expected nothing less than to be treated in the same manner. I could not help expressing my fears and apprehensions to some of my countrymen.

The voyage from the African coast to the West Indies covered some 5,500 miles and normally took more than two months. (The mortality rate among the slaves sailing from the Niger Delta in the late eighteenth century averaged 9.7 percent.) Equiano's ship finally reaches Bridgetown, Barbados, where the slaves are to be sold.

. . . The white people got some old slaves from the land to pacify us. They told us we were not to be eaten, but to work, and were soon to go on land where we should see many of our country people. This report eased us much; and sure enough, soon after we landed, there came to us Africans of all languages. We were conducted immediately to the merchant's yard, where we were all pent up together like so many sheep in a fold, without regard to sex or age. As every object was new to me, everything I saw filled me with surprise. What struck me first was, that the houses were built with bricks, in stories, and in every other respect different from those I have seen in Africa: but I was still more astonished on seeing people on horseback. I did not know what this could mean; and indeed I thought these people were full of nothing but magical arts. While I was in this astonishment, one of my fellow prisoners spoke to a countryman of his about the horses, who said they were the same kind they had in their country. . . . We were not many days in the merchant's custody, before we were sold after their usual manner, which is this: on a signal given (as the beat of a drum), the buyers rush at once into the yard where the slaves are confined, and make choice of that parcel they like best. The noise and clamour with which this is attended, and the eagerness visible in the countenances of the buyers, serve not a little to increase the apprehension of the terrified Africans, who may well be supposed to consider them as the ministers of that destruction to which they think themselves devoted. In this manner, without scruple, are relations and friends separated, most of them never to see each other again. I remember in the vessel in which I was brought over, in the men's apartment, there were several brothers who, in the sale, were sold in different lots; and it was very moving on this occasion to see and hear their cries at parting. O, ye nominal Christians! might not an African ask you, learned you this from your God? who says unto you, Do unto all men as you would men should do unto you. Is it not enough that we are torn from our country and friends to toil for your luxury and lust of gain? Must every tender feeling be likewise sacrificed to your avarice? Are the dearest friends and relations, now rendered more dear by their separation from their kindred, still to be parted from each other, and thus preventing from cheering the gloom of slavery with the small comfort of being together, and mingling their sufferings and sorrows? Why are parents to love their children, brothers their sisters, or husbands their wives? Surely this is a new refinement in cruelty, which, while it has no advantage to atone for it, thus aggravates distress, and adds fresh horrors even to the wretchedness of slavery.

REVIEW QUESTIONS

1. When were the African slaves most likely to try to escape? How did the slave traders try to prevent this?
2. How did each of the slave traders regard the captive Africans?
3. What was Malachy Postlethwayt's argument in defense of slavery? What is your response?
4. To whom did Wesley address his arguments against the slave trade?
5. What were the commercial justifications for slavery that Wesley disputed? How did he account for the seeming inferiority of the slaves?
6. Compare the reaction of Olaudah Equiano on first encountering Europeans with that of the Spaniards encountering Aztecs (Section 1).
7. What did Equiano believe to be the worst evil of the slave system?

6 The Witch Craze

In both ancient and medieval times, it was widely believed that certain persons, called sorcerers or witches, had supernatural powers over both nature and human beings and that these powers enabled witches to harm people through magical practices. Those suspected of sorcery were greatly feared and were subject to execution. In the late Middle Ages, Europeans began to view suspected witches as having entered into a pact with the devil. The church began to treat them as devil worshipers, heretics, rebels against the church, and threats to society.

During the sixteenth and seventeenth centuries, both Roman Catholics and Protestants intensified the struggle to destroy alleged witches; thousands were questioned under torture and, if convicted of witchcraft, were put to death, a sentence justified by both the Old Testament and Roman law. Belief in witches was not limited to superstitious peasants and fanatics. Prominent intellectuals, theologians, philosophers, and scientists either supported the prosecution of witches or remained silent. Few doubted the existence of witches, and forced confessions were accepted as proof of sorcery; the idea of witchcraft offered credible explanations for otherwise inexplicable human experiences. Although the number of females accused of witchcraft outnumbered the males, during these times persons of all ages, social classes, education, and occupations could find themselves facing the charge of witchcraft. The regular use of torture during interrogation of suspects probably accounted for most confessions, and the alleged bizarre and sometimes lurid practices of suspects seem to have been the products of mental disorders and popular beliefs in occult powers.

Jakob Sprenger and Heinrich Krämer
THE HAMMER OF WITCHES

Written in 1486 by Jakob Sprenger and Heinrich Krämer, both Dominican inquisitors in Germany, *The Hammer of Witches* became a standard reference work for the beliefs and practices of witches. The work, excerpted below, tells us much about the mindset of early modern Europeans committed to a belief in witches who served the devil.

And this class [of witches] is made up of those who, against every instinct of human or animal nature, are in the habit of eating and devouring the children of their own species. And this is the most powerful class of witches, who practise innumerable other harms also. For they raise hailstorms and hurtful tempests and lightnings; cause sterility in men and animals; offer to devils, or otherwise kill, the children whom they do not devour. But these are only the children who have not been re-born by baptism at the font, for they cannot devour those who have been baptized, nor any without God's permission. They can also, before the eyes of their parents, and when no one is in sight, throw into the water children walking by the water side; they make horses go mad under their riders; they can transport themselves from place to place through the air, either in body or in imagination; they can affect Judges and Magistrates so that they cannot hurt them; they can cause themselves and others to keep silence under torture; they can bring about a great trembling in the hands and horror in the minds of those who would arrest them. . . . [T]hey can at times strike whom they will with lightning, and even kill some men and animals; they can make of no effect the generative desires, and even the power of copulation, cause abortion, kill infants in the mother's womb by a mere exterior touch; they can at times bewitch men and animals with a mere look, without touching them, and cause death; they dedicate their own children to devils; and in short, as has been said, they can cause all the plagues. . . . [I]t is common to all of them to practise carnal copulation with devils. . . .

[T]here are now [such witches], some in the country of Lombardy [in northern Italy], in the domains of the Duke of Austria, where the Inquisitor of Como, as we told in the former Part, caused forty-one witches to be burned in one year; and he was fifty-five years old, and still continues to labour in the Inquisition.

Now the method of profession is twofold. One is a solemn ceremony, like a solemn vow. The other is private, and can be made to the devil at any hour alone. The first method is when witches meet together in conclave on a set day, and the devil appears to them in the assumed body of a man, and urges them to keep faith with him, promising them worldly prosperity and length of life; and they recommend a novice to his acceptance. And the devil asks whether she will abjure the Faith, and forsake the holy Christian religion and the worship of the Anomalous Woman (for so they call the Most Blessed Virgin Mary), and never venerate the Sacraments; and if he finds the novice or disciple willing, then the devil stretches out his hand, and so does the novice, and she swears with upraised hand to keep that covenant. And when this is done, the devil at once adds that this is not enough; and when the disciple asks what more must be done, the devil demands the following oath of homage to himself: that she give herself to him, body and soul, for ever, and do her utmost to bring others of both sexes into his power. He adds, finally, that she is to make certain unguents [ointments] from the bones and limbs of children, especially those who have been baptized; by all which means she will be able to fulfil all her wishes with his help.

We Inquisitors had credible experience of this method in the town of Breisach in the diocese of Basel [in Switzerland] receiving full information from a young girl witch who had been converted, whose aunt also had been burned in the diocese of Strasburg [in Germany]. And she added that she had become a witch by the method in which her aunt had first tried to seduce her. . . .

She said also that the greatest injuries were inflicted by midwives, because they were under an obligation to kill or offer to devils as many children as possible; and that she had been severely beaten by her aunt because she had opened a secret pot and found the heads of a great many children. And much more she told us, having first, as was proper, taken an oath to speak the truth.

And her account of the method of professing the devil's faith undoubtedly agrees with what has been written by that most eminent Doctor, John Nider, who even in our times has written very illuminatingly; and it may be especially remarked that he tells us the following, which he had from an Inquisitor of the diocese of Edua, who held many inquisitions on witches in that diocese, and caused many to be burned.

For he says that this Inquisitor told him that in the Duchy of Lausanne [in Switzerland] certain witches had cooked and eaten their own children, and that the following was the method in which they became initiated into such practices. The witches met together and, by their art, summoned a devil in the form of a man, to whom the novice was compelled to swear to deny the Christian religion, never to adore the Eucharist, and to tread the Cross underfoot whenever she could do so secretly.

Here is another example from the same source. There was lately a general report, brought to the notice of Peter the Judge in Boltingen, that thirteen infants had been devoured in the State of Berne [in Switzerland]; and public justice exacted full vengeance on the murderers. And when Peter asked one of the captive witches in what manner they ate children, she replied: "This is the manner of it. We set our snares chiefly for unbaptized children, and even for those that have been baptized, especially when they have not been protected by the sign of the Cross and prayers" (reader, notice that, at the devil's command, they take the unbaptized chiefly, in order that they may not be baptized), "and with our spells we kill them in their cradles or even when they are sleeping by their parents' side, in such a way that they afterwards are thought to have been overlain or to have died some other natural death. Then we secretly take them from their graves, and cook them in a cauldron, until the whole flesh comes away from the bones to make a soup which may easily be drunk. Of the more solid matter we make an unguent which is of virtue to help us in our arts and pleasures and our transportations; and with the liquid we fill a flask or skin, whoever drinks from which, with the addition of a few other ceremonies, immediately acquires much knowledge and becomes a leader in our sect."

Johannes Junius
A CONFESSION OF WITCHCRAFT EXPLAINED

In 1628 Johannes Junius, lord mayor of Bamberg, a city in Bavaria, Germany, was accused of practicing witchcraft. When Junius denied the charge, he was tortured. He then confessed to having become a witch and was burned at the stake. The reasons for his confession are revealed in a letter he secretly sent to his daughter.

Many hundred thousand good-nights, dearly beloved daughter Veronica. Innocent have I come into prison, innocent have I been tortured, innocent must I die. For whoever comes into the witch prison must become a witch or be tortured until he invents something out of his head and—God pity him—bethinks him of something. I will tell you how it has gone with me. When I was the first time put to the torture, Dr. Braun, Dr. Kötzendörffer, and two strange doctors were there. Then Dr. Braun asks me, "Kinsman, how come you here?" I answer, "Through falsehood, through misfortune." "Hear, you," he says, "you are a witch; will you confess it voluntarily? If not, we'll bring in witnesses and the executioner for you." I said "I am no witch, I have a pure conscience in the matter; if there are a thousand witnesses, I am not anxious, but I'll gladly hear the witnesses." Now the chancellor's son was set before me . . . and afterward Hoppfen Elss. She had seen me dance on Haupts-moor. . . . I answered: "I have never renounced God, and will never do it—God graciously keep me from it. I'll rather bear whatever I must." And then came also—God in highest Heaven have mercy—the executioner, and put the thumbscrews on me, both hands bound together, so that the blood ran out at the nails and everywhere, so that for four weeks I could not use my hands, as you can see from the writing. . . . Thereafter they first stripped me, bound my hands behind me, and drew me

up in the torture. Then I thought heaven and earth were at an end; eight times did they draw me up and let me fall again, so that I suffered terrible agony. . . .*

. . . When at last the executioner led me back into the prison, he said to me: "Sir, I beg you, for God's sake confess something, whether it be true or not. Invent something, for you cannot endure the torture which you will be put to; and, even if you bear it all, yet you will not escape, not even if you were an earl [high nobleman], but one torture will follow after another until you say you are a witch. Not before that," he said, "will they let you go, as you may see by all their trials, for one is just like another." . . .

And so I begged, since I was in wretched plight, to be given one day for thought and a priest. The priest was refused me, but the time for thought was given. Now, my dear child, see in what hazard I stood and still stand. I must say that I am a witch, though I am not,—must now renounce God, though I have never done it before. Day and night I was deeply troubled, but at last there came to me a new idea. I would not

---

*This torture of the strappado, which was that in most common use by the courts, consisted of a rope, attached to the hands of the prisoner (bound behind his back) and carried over a pulley at the ceiling. By this he was drawn up and left hanging. To increase the pain, weights were attached to his feet or he was suddenly jerked up and let drop.

be anxious, but, since I had been given no priest with whom I could take counsel, I would myself think of something and say it. It were surely better that I just say it with mouth and words, even though I had not really done it; and afterwards I would confess it to the priest, and let those answer for it who compel me to do it. . . . And so I made my confession, . . . but it was all a lie.

Now follows, dear child, what I confessed in order to escape that great anguish and bitter torture, which it was impossible for me longer to bear. [He then describes his confession] . . .

Now, dear child, here you have all my confession, for which I must die. And they are sheer lies and made-up things, so help me God. For all this I was forced to say through fear of the torture which was threatened beyond what I had already endured. For they never leave off with the torture till one confesses something be he ever so good, he must

be a witch. Nobody escapes, though he were an earl. . . .

Dear child, keep this letter secret so that people do not find it, else I shall be tortured most piteously and the jailers will be beheaded. So strictly is it forbidden. . . . Dear child, pay this man a dollar. . . . I have taken several days to write this: my hands are both lame. I am in a sad plight. . . .

Good night, for your father Johannes Junius will never see you more. July 24, 1628.

[And on the margin of the letter he adds:]

Dear child, six have confessed against me at once: the Chancellor, his son, Neudecker, Zaner, Hoffmaisters Ursel, and Hoppfen Elss—all false, through compulsion, as they have all told me, and begged my forgiveness in God's name before they were executed. . . . They know nothing but good of me. They were forced to say it, just as I myself was. . . .

Nicholas Malebranche
SEARCH AFTER TRUTH

Greatly influenced by Descartes (see page 423), the French thinker Nicholas Malebranche (1638–1715) supplemented his training in philosophy and theology with the study of mathematics and natural science. His most important work, *Search After Truth*, which appeared in two volumes in 1674 and 1675, treated many technical, philosophical, and theological issues. In this work, from which an excerpt follows, he also analyzed the belief in witchcraft, attributing it to the unchecked power of people's imagination. Malebranche attempted a rational explanation of the witch craze and wanted the courts to dismiss charges of witchcraft. Nevertheless, he still believed that although "true witches are very rare," they do exist.

The strangest effect of the power of imagination is the disorderly fear of the apparition of spirits, of enchantments, of symbols, of the charms of Lycanthropes or Werewolves, and generally of everything which is supposed to depend upon the demon's power.

Nothing is more terrible or more frightening to the mind, or produces deeper vestiges on the brain, than the idea of an invisible power which thinks only about harming us and which is irresistible. Speeches which reveal this idea are always heard with fear and curiosity. Holding on to everything extraordinary, men take bizarre pleasure in recounting these surprising and prodigious stories about the power and malice of Witches, in order to frighten both others and themselves. So it is not astonishing if Witches are so common in some countries, where belief in the Sabbat [a secret meeting of witches where they engage in orgiastic rites] is too deeply rooted; where the most absurd stories about spells are listened to as authentic; and where madmen and seers whose imagination has become disordered. . . . from telling these stories . . . are burned as real Witches.

I well know that some people will take exception to my attributing most witchcraft to the power of imagination, because I know that men want to be made afraid, that they become angry with those who want to demystify them. . . .

Superstitions are not easily destroyed, and they cannot be attacked without finding a large number of defenders. It is easy enough to prove that the inclination to believe blindly all the dreams of Demonographers [those who study demons] is produced and maintained by the same cause which makes superstitious men stubborn. Nevertheless, that will not prevent me from describing in a few words how, I believe, such opinions get established.

A shepherd in his fold after dinner tells his wife and children about the adventures of the Sabbat. As his imagination is moderately inspired by vapours from wine, and since he believes that he has attended that imaginary assembly several times, he does not fail to speak about it in a strong and lively manner. His natural eloquence, together with the disposition of his entire family to hear such a new and terrible subject discussed, should doubtlessly produce strange traces in weak imaginations. It is naturally impossible that a woman and her children not remain completely frightened, full, and convinced of what they have heard said. This is a husband, a father, who is speaking about what he has seen and done; he is loved and respected; why should he not be believed? This Shepherd repeats it on different days. Little by little the mother's and children's imagination receives deeper traces from it. They grow used to it, the fears pass, and the conviction remains. . . .

Several times Witches of good faith have been found, who generally tell everybody that they have gone to the Sabbat, and who are so convinced of it, that although several persons watched them and assured them that they had not left their beds, they could not agree with their testimony. . . . So we should not be astonished if a man who thinks he has been to the Sabbat, and consequently talks about it in a firm voice and with an assured countenance, easily persuades some people who listen to him respectfully about all the circumstances which he describes, and thus transmits in their imagination traces similar to those which deceive him.

When men talk to us, they engrave in our brain traces similar to those which they possess. When they have deep traces, they talk to us in a manner which engraves deep ones in us; for they cannot speak without making us in some way similar to them. Children at their mother's breast only see what their mother sees. Even when they have become worldly-wise, they imagine few things of which their parents are not the cause, since even the wisest men conduct themselves more by the imagination of others, *i.e.*, by opinion and custom, [than] by the rules of reason. Thus in places where Witches are burned, a great number of them are found. Because in places where they are condemned to fire, men truly believe that they commit witchcraft, and this belief is fortified by the speeches which are made about it. If one were to stop punishing them and were to treat them like madmen, then it would be seen in time that there would no longer be any Witches, because those who do it only in imagination (who are surely the greater number) would then abandon their errors.

It is indubitable that real Witches deserve death. . . . But by punishing all [those who believe themselves or are believed by others to be witches] common opinion is strengthened, imaginary Witches are multiplied, and so an infinity of people are lost and damned. It is thus right that many Parlements [French courts] no longer punish Witches. There are many fewer of them in the lands of their jurisdictions; and the envy, hatred, or malice of evil men cannot use this pretext to destroy the innocent. . . .

It is ordinary enough for some people to have fairly lively dreams at night and to be able to remember them exactly when awake, although the subject of their dream is not in itself very terrible. Thus it is not difficult for people to persuade themselves that they have been at the Sabbat, for that merely requires that their brain preserves the traces made there during sleep.

The chief reason which prevents us from taking our dreams for realities is that we cannot link our dreams with the things we have done during our wakefulness. By that we recognize that they were only dreams. But Witches cannot recognize in this way that their imaginary Sabbat is a dream. . . .

I am persuaded that true Witches are very rare, that the Sabbat is only a dream, and that the Parlements who dismiss accusations of witchcraft are the most equitable. However, I do not doubt that Witches, charms, enchantments, etc., could exist, and that the demon sometimes exercises his malice upon men by special permission of a superior power.

REVIEW QUESTIONS

1. According to *The Hammer of Witches*, what anti-Christian practices did witches engage in?
2. According to Johannes Junius, how were apparently innocent people successfully prosecuted for practicing witchcraft? What did the victims of the witch craze and the Inquisition have in common?
3. To what did Malebranche attribute a belief in witchcraft?

7 The Court of Louis XIV

During his seventy-two-year reign, Louis XIV (1643–1715) gave France greater unity and central authority than it had ever known. To prevent the great nobles from challenging royal authority, Louis XIV chose many of his ministers and provincial administrators from the middle class. The great nobles, "princes of the blood," enjoyed considerable social prestige but exercised no real power in the government. The king encouraged these "people of quality" to live at court where they contended with each other for his favor.

As the symbol of France and the greatest ruler of Europe, Louis insisted that the social life at Versailles provide an appropriate setting for his exalted person. During his long reign, France set the style for the whole of Europe. The splendor of Versailles was the talk of Europe, and other monarchs sought to imitate the fashions and manners of the Sun King's court.

Duc de Saint-Simon
AN ASSESSMENT OF LOUIS XIV

Louis de Rouvroi, duc de Saint-Simon (1675–1755), was an astute observer of Louis XIV and his court. The following description of Louis XIV comes from Saint-Simon's extensive *Memoirs*.

Louis XIV was made for a brilliant Court. In the midst of other men, his figure, his courage, his grace, his beauty, his grand mien, even the tone of his voice and the majestic and natural charm of all his person, distinguished him till his death. . . . The superior ability of his early ministers and his early generals soon wearied him. He liked nobody to be in any way superior to him. Thus he chose his ministers, not for their knowledge, but for their ignorance; not for their capacity, but for their want of it. He liked to form them, as he said; liked to teach them even the most trifling things. It was the same with his generals. He took credit to himself for instructing them; wished it to be thought that from his cabinet he commanded and directed all his armies. Naturally fond of trifles, he unceasingly occupied himself with the most petty details of his troops, his household, his mansions. This vanity, this unmeasured and unreasonable love of admiration, was his ruin. His ministers, his generals, his mistresses, his courtiers, soon perceived his weakness. They praised him with emulation and spoiled him. Those whom he liked owed his affection for them, to their untiring flatteries. This is what gave his ministers so much authority, and the opportunities they had for adulating him, of attributing everything to him, and of pretending to learn everything from him. Suppleness, meanness, an admiring, dependent, cringing manner—above all, an air of nothingness—were the sole means of pleasing him.

Though his intellect, as I have said, was beneath mediocrity, it was capable of being formed. He loved glory, was fond of order and regularity; was by disposition prudent, moderate, discreet, master of his movements and his tongue. Will it be believed? He was also by disposition good and just! God had sufficiently gifted him to enable him to be a good King; perhaps even *a tolerably great King*! All the evil came to him from elsewhere. His early education was . . . neglected. He was scarcely taught how to read or write, and remained so ignorant, that the most familiar historical and other facts were utterly unknown to him! He fell, accordingly, and sometimes even in public, into the grossest absurdities.

He was exceedingly jealous of the attention paid him. Not only did he notice the presence of the most distinguished courtiers, but those of inferior degree also. He looked to the right and to the left, not only upon rising but upon going to bed, at his meals, in passing through his apartments, or his gardens of Versailles, where alone the courtiers were allowed to follow him; he saw and noticed everybody; not one escaped him, not even those who hoped to remain unnoticed. He marked well all absentees from the court, found out the reason of their absence, and never lost an opportunity of acting towards them as the occasion might seem to justify. With some of the courtiers (the most distinguished), it was a demerit not to make the court their ordinary abode; with others 'twas a fault to come but rarely; for those who never or scarcely ever came it was certain disgrace. When their names were in any way mentioned, "I do not know them," the King would reply haughtily. Those who presented themselves but seldom were thus characterised: "They are people I never see"; these decrees were irrevocable. He could not bear people who liked Paris [better than Versailles].

Louis XIV took great pains to be well informed of all that passed everywhere; in the public places, in the private houses, in society and familiar intercourse. His spies and tell-tales were infinite. He had them of all species; many who were ignorant that their information reached him; others who knew it; others who wrote to him direct, sending their letters through channels he indicated; and all these letters were seen by him alone, and always before everything else; others who sometimes spoke to him secretly in his cabinet, entering by the back stairs. These unknown means ruined an infinite number of people of all classes, who never could discover the cause; often ruined them very unjustly; for the King, once prejudiced, never altered his opinion, or so rarely, that nothing was more rare. He had, too, another fault, very dangerous for others and often for himself, since it deprived him of good subjects. He had an excellent memory; in this way, that if he saw a man who, twenty years before, perhaps, had in some manner offended him, he did not forget the man, though he might forget the offence. This was enough, however, to exclude the person from all favour. The representations of a minister, of a general, of his confessor even, could not move the King. He would not yield.

The most cruel means by which the King was informed of what was passing—for many years before anybody knew it—was that of opening letters. The promptitude and dexterity with which they were opened passes understanding. He saw extracts from all the letters in which there were passages that the chiefs of the post-office, and then the minister who governed it, thought ought to go before him; entire letters, too, were sent to him, when their contents seemed to justify the sending. Thus the chiefs of the post, nay, the principal clerks were in a position to suppose what they pleased and against whom they pleased. A word of contempt against the King or the government, a joke, a detached phrase, was enough. It is incredible how many people, justly or unjustly, were more or less ruined, always without resource, without trial, and without knowing why. . . .

Never was man so naturally polite, or of a politeness so measured, so graduated, so adapted to person, time, and place. Towards women his politeness was without parallel. Never did he

pass the humblest petticoat without raising his hat; even to chambermaids, that he knew to be such, as often happened at Marly. For ladies he took his hat off completely. . . . He took it off for the princes of the blood, as for the ladies. If he accosted ladies he did not cover himself until he had quitted them. All this was out of doors, for in the house he was never covered. . . .

The King loved air and exercise very much, as long as he could make use of them. He had excelled in dancing, and at tennis and mall [a lawn game]. On horseback he was admirable, even at a late age. He liked to see everything done with grace and address. To acquit yourself well or ill before him was a merit or a fault. . . . He was very fond of shooting, and there was not a better or more graceful shot than he. He had always in his cabinet seven or eight pointer bitches, and was fond of feeding them, to make himself known to them. He was very fond, too, of stag hunting. . . .

He liked splendour, magnificence, and profusion in everything: you pleased him if you shone through the brilliancy of your houses, your clothes, your table, your equipages.

As for the King himself, nobody ever approached his magnificence. His buildings, who could number them? At the same time, who was there who did not deplore the pride, the caprice, the bad taste seen in them? St. Germains, a lovely spot, with a marvellous view, rich forest, terraces, gardens, and water he abandoned for Versailles; the dullest and most ungrateful of all places, without prospect, without wood, without water, without soil; for the ground is all shifting sand or swamp, the air accordingly bad. . . .

Let me now speak of the amours of the King which were even more fatal to the state than his building mania.

Louis XIV in his youth more made for love than any of his subjects—being tired of gathering passing sweets, fixed himself at last upon La Vallière.[1] The progress and the result of his love are well known. . . .

---

[1]Françoise-Louise de La Vallière was Louis XIV's mistress from 1661 to 1667; she held great influence over him and was the mother of four of his children. After being discarded as his mistress she retired to a convent in 1674.

When the King travelled his coach was always full of women; his mistresses, afterwards his bastards, his daughters-in-law, sometimes *Madame*, and other ladies when there was room. In the coach, during his journeys, there were always all sorts of things to eat, as meat, pastry, fruit. A quarter of a league was not passed over before the King asked if somebody would not eat. He never ate anything between meals himself, not even fruit; but he amused himself by seeing others do so, aye, and to bursting. You were obliged to be hungry, merry, and to eat with appetite, otherwise he was displeased and even showed it. And yet after this, if you supped with him at table the same day, you were compelled to eat with as good a countenance as though you had tasted nothing since the previous night. He was as inconsiderate in other and more delicate matters; and ladies, in his long drives and stations, had often occasion to curse him. The Duchesse de Chevreuse once rode all the way from Versailles to Fontainbleau in such extremity, that several times she was well-nigh losing consciousness. . . .

At ten o'clock his supper was served. The captain of the guard announced this to him. A quarter of an hour after the King came to supper, and from the ante-chamber of Madame de Maintenon[2] to the table again, any one spoke to him who wished. This supper was always on a grand scale, the royal household (that is, the sons and daughters of France), at table, and a large number of courtiers and ladies present, sitting or standing. . . .

During all his life, the King failed only once in his attendance at mass. It was with the army, during a forced march; he missed no fast day, unless really indisposed. Some days before Lent, he publicly declared that he should be very much displeased if any one ate meat or gave it to others, under any pretext.

---

[2]Françoise d'Aubigné (Madame de Maintenon) was the widow of a celebrated poet when she became governess to two of the king's children in 1669. He provided her with an estate and later married her secretly.

Liselotte von der Pfalz (Elizabeth Charlotte d'Orleans) A SKETCH OF COURT LIFE

Deprived of power and usefulness, many great nobles lived a frivolous, if not debauched, existence at Versailles. The letters of Elizabeth Charlotte, Duchesse d'Orleans (1652–1722)—her German name was Liselotte von der Pfalz—describe this lifestyle. A native of Germany, the duchesse was married to Louis XIV's only brother and spent fifty years at the king's court. During this period she wrote extensive letters, some of which are reproduced below, to her German relatives.

Versailles, 13 February 1695

Where in the world does one find a husband who loves only his spouse and does not have someone, be it mistresses or boys, on the side? If for this reason wives were to go in for the same behavior one could never be sure, as Godfather so rightly says, that the children of the house are the rightful heirs. Does the young duchess[*] not know that

---

[*]Electress Sophie's daughter-in-law, who was caught in a scandalous adultery with Count Christoph von Koenigsmarck.

a woman's honor consists of having commerce with no one but her husband, and that for a man it is not shameful to have mistresses but shameful indeed to be a cuckold? . . . .

Your Grace would not believe how coarse and unmannerly French men have become in the last twelve or thirteen years. One would be hard put to find two young men of quality who know how to behave properly either in what they say or in what they do. There are two very different causes for this: namely, all the piety at court and the debauchery among men. Because of the first, men and women are not allowed to speak to each other in public, which used to be a way to give young gentlemen polish. And secondly, because they love the boys, they no longer want to please anyone but one another, and the most popular among them is the one who knows best how to be debauched, coarse, and insolent. This habit has become so ingrained that no one knows how to live properly any longer, and they are worse than peasants behind the plough. . . .

It is a great honor to sit next to the King during the sermon, but I would be happy to cede this honor to someone else, for His Majesty will not permit me to sleep. As soon as I go to sleep, the King nudges me with his elbow and wakes me up; thus I can never really go to sleep nor really stay awake. And that gives one a headache.

———

Paris, 14 May 1695

At every gathering here in France people do nothing but play *lansquenet*. This game is all the rage now. . . . The stakes are horrendously high here, and the people act like madmen when they are playing. One bawls, another hits the table with his fist so hard that the whole room shakes, and a third one blasphemes to make one's hair stand on end; in short, they show such despair that one is frightened even to look at them.

———

Saint Cloud, 15 September 1695

The story of Saint Cyr is worse than it is written in the book,[†] and funnier, too. The young maids there fell in love with each other and were caught in committing indecencies together. They say that Madame de Maintenon wept bitter tears about this and had all the relics exposed in order to drive out the demon of lewdness. Also, a preacher was dispatched to preach against lewdness. But he himself said such filthy things that the good and modest girls could not stand it and walked out of the church, while the others, the guilty ones, were so taken by the giggles that they could not hold them in.

———

Versailles, 7 March 1696

I will tell . . . how everything is here, and I will begin with Monsieur. All he has in his head are his young fellows, with whom he wants to gorge and guzzle all night long, and he gives them huge sums of money; nothing is too much or too costly for these boys. Meanwhile, his children and I barely have what we need. Whenever I need shirts or sheets it means no end of begging, yet at the same time he gives 10,000 *talers* to La Carte[‡] so that he can buy his linens in Flanders. And since he knows that I am bound to find out where all the money goes, he is wary of me, afraid that I might speak about it to the King, who might chase the boys away. Whatever I may do or say to show that I do not object to his life, he still does not trust me and makes trouble for me with the King every day; even says that I hate the King. If there is any bad gossip, Monsieur tells the King that I have started it and even adds a few stout lies of his own, and sometimes he himself tells me about the terrible things he has said about me. Thereby he

———

[†]A book that had been sent to Madame by her aunt: among other things, it contained negative accounts of the convent school of Saint-Cyr, which had been founded by Madame de Maintenon.

[‡]One of Monsieur's favorites, a particularly greedy character.

so turns the King against me that I can never be in his good graces. Monsieur also continually stirs up my children against me; since he does not want my son to realize how little is being done for his future, he always indulges him in his debaucheries and encourages them. Then if I suggest to my son that he should try to please the King more and abstain from vice, Monsieur and my son laugh in my face, and in Paris both of them lead an absolutely shameful life. My son's inclinations are good, and he could make something of himself if he were not corrupted by Monsieur. My daughter, thank God, he does not drag into debauchery, and to tell the truth, the girl does not have the slightest propensity for *galanterie* [flirtations and love affairs]. But Monsieur does not let me have control over her, always takes her places where I am not, and surrounds her with such rabble that it is a miracle that she has not been corrupted. Moreover, he is inculcating her with such hatred of the Germans that she can barely stand to be with me because I am German, and that makes me feel that she will end up like my son. . . . It is true that in public Monsieur is polite to me, but in fact he cannot stand me. As soon as he sees that any of my servants, be they male or female, become attached to me, he conceives an utter dislike for them and does them harm whenever he can; those who despise me, on the other hand, have all his favor. Monsieur is doing everything he can to make me hated, not only by the King, but also by Monsieur Le Dauphin, and everyone else too. . . . Indeed, the King is so well aware that Monsieur likes me to be treated with contempt that whenever there is trouble between them, the reconciliation always amounts to extra favors for Monsieur's beloved boys and bad treatment for me. All the silverware that came from the Palatinate Monsieur has melted down and sold, and all the proceeds were given to the boys; every day new ones show up, and all of his jewelry is being sold, pawned, pledged, and given to the young men so that if—God forbid—Monsieur should die today, tomorrow I would be thrown upon the King's mercy and not know where to find my daily bread. Monsieur says quite loudly and does

not conceal from his daughter and from me that since he is getting old now, he feels that there is no time to lose and that he means to spare no expense to have a merry time until his end: he also says that those who will live longer than he will just have to see how they can get along and that he loves himself more than he loves me and his children. And indeed he practices what he preaches. If I were to tell Your Grace all the details, I would have to write a whole book. Everything here [at court] is pure self-interest and deviousness, and that makes life most unpleasant. If one does not want to get involved in intrigues and *galanteries*, one must live by oneself, which is also quite boring. In order to clear my head of these dismal reflections, I go hunting as often as possible, but this will come to an end as soon as my poor horses can no longer walk, for Monsieur has never bought me any new ones and is not likely to do so now. In the past the King used to give them to me, but now times are bad. . . . The young people are so brutal that he has to be afraid of them and does not feel like having anything to do with them: the old ones are full of politics and only seek one's company after they see that one has the King's good graces.

Versailles, 2 February 1698

I firmly believe that the wild life that my son leads, carousing all night long and not going to bed until eight in the morning, will do him in before long. He often looks as if he had been pulled out of the grave: this is sure to kill him, but his father never wants to reprimand him. But since nothing I could say would do any good I will be quiet, although I do want to add that it is truly a shame that my son is being dragged into this profligate life, for if he had been accustomed to better and more honorable ways, he would have become a better person. He is not lacking in wit, nor is he ignorant, and from his youth he had every inclination for that which is good, commendable and befitting his rank; but ever since he has become his own master, a lot of contemptible wretches have attached themselves to him, making him keep company with, begging your leave, the vilest kinds of common whores, and he has changed so much that one does not recognize either his face or his temperament, and since he leads this life he no longer takes pleasure in anything; his pleasure in music, which used to be a passion, is gone too. In short, he has become quite insufferable, and I fear that in the end he will lose his very life over it.

———

Versailles, 16 March 1698

Monsieur is keener than ever on the boys and now takes lackeys out of the antechambers; every last penny he has is squandered in this way, and some day his children will be complete beggars, but he does not care about anything but providing for these pleasures of his. He opposes me in everything and avoids me at all times; he lets himself be ruled completely by these rakes and everything in his and my house is being sold for the benefit of these fellows. It is shameful what goes on here. My son has been completely captivated by Monsieur's favorites; since he loves women, they act as his pimps, sponge off him, gorge and guzzle with him, and drag him so deeply into debauchery that he cannot seem to get out of it; and since he knows that I do not approve of his ways, he avoids me and does not like me at all. Monsieur is glad that my son likes his favorites and not me and therefore puts up with everything from him. My son's wife does not love her husband; just as long as he is away from her, she is content, and in this respect they are well matched; all she cares about is her brothers' and sisters' grandeur. That is how things are here; so Your Grace can imagine what a pleasant life it is for me.

———

Versailles, 8 March 1699

Yesterday at table we talked about the Duchesse de Lesdiguières, who certainly has a strange temperament. All day long she does nothing but drink coffee or tea; she never reads or writes, nor does she do needlework or play cards. When she takes coffee, her chambermaids and herself must be dressed in the Turkish manner; when she takes tea, the servants who bring it must be dressed in the Indian manner. The chambermaids often weep bitter tears that they must change their clothes two or three times a day. If anyone comes to call on the lady, her antechamber is full of pages, lackeys, and noblemen; then one comes to a locked door, and when one knocks, a great big Moor wearing a silver turban and a big sabre comes to open up and lets the lady or gentleman, whoever it may be, enter, but all alone. He leads the caller to a second door, which is also locked, and it is opened by another Moor who bolts it after the people have gone through, just as the first one had done. The same thing happens in the third room. In the fourth one there are two valets who lead the caller to the fifth room, where one finds the Duchess all by herself. All the portraits in her room are of her coach horses, which she had painted. These she has led one by one into the courtyard every morning and watches them from the window wearing spectacles, for she does not see well. In her room she also has a painting of the conclave, done in an unusual manner: the Pope and all the cardinals are depicted as Moors, and she also has a piece of yellow silk embroidered with a whole lot of Moors. In her garden, which is very beautiful, there is a marble column with an epitaph to one of her deceased cats which she had loved very much. If her son wants to see her, he must ask for an audience, and so must his wife: after they have inquired six or seven times whether they might be permitted to see her, she receives them, but with the same ceremonies as if they were strangers.

REVIEW QUESTIONS

1. According to Saint-Simon, what were Louis XIV's likes and dislikes?
2. What were the Duchesse d'Orleans' major complaints about her life at court?

398 Part Three Early Modern Europe

8 Justification of Absolute Monarchy by Divine Right

Effectively blocking royal absolutism in the Middle Ages were the dispersion of power between kings and feudal lords, the vigorous sense of personal freedom and urban autonomy of the townspeople, and the limitations on royal power imposed by the church. However, by the late sixteenth century, monarchs were asserting their authority over competing groups with ever-greater effectiveness. In the seventeenth century, European kings implemented their claim to absolute power as monarchs chosen by and responsible to God alone. This theory, called the divine right of kings, became the dominant political ideology of seventeenth-century Europe.

Bishop Jacques-Benigne Bossuet
POLITICS DRAWN FROM THE VERY WORDS OF HOLY SCRIPTURE

Louis XIV was the symbol of absolutism, a term applied to those early modern states where monarchs exercised power free of constitutional restraints. Theorists of absolutism like Bishop Jacques-Benigne Bossuet (1627–1704) argued that monarchs received their authority directly from God. Following are excerpts from Bossuet's *Politics Drawn from the Very Words of Holy Scripture* (1707).

THIRD BOOK, IN WHICH ONE BEGINS TO EXPLAIN THE NATURE AND THE PROPERTIES OF ROYAL AUTHORITY
Article II, Royal Authority is Sacred

1st Proposition, God establishes kings as his ministers, and reigns through them over the peoples We have already seen that all power comes from God.

"The prince, St. Paul adds, is God's minister to thee for good. But if thou do that which is evil, fear: for he beareth not the sword in vain. For he is God's minister: an avenger to execute wrath upon him that doth evil."

Thus princes act as ministers of God, and his lieutenants on earth. It is through them that he exercises his Empire. . . .

It is in this way that we have seen that the royal throne is not the throne of a man, but the throne of God himself. "God hath chosen Solomon my son, to sit upon the throne of the kingdom of the Lord over Israel." And again: "Solomon sat on the throne of the Lord."

And in order that no one believe that it was peculiar to the Israelites to have kings established by God, here is what Ecclesiasticus says: "Over every nation he set a ruler." . . .

Thus he governs all peoples, and gives them, all of them, their kings; though he governs Israel in a more particular and announced fashion.

2nd Proposition, The person of kings is sacred It appears from all this that the person of kings is sacred, and that to attempt anything against them is a sacrilege. . . . [T]hey are sacred through their charge, as being the representatives of divine majesty, deputized by his providence for the execution of his plans. It is thus that God calls Cyrus his anointed. . . .

One must protect kings as sacred things; and whoever neglects to guard them is worthy of death. . . .

3rd Proposition, One must obey the prince by reason of religion and conscience . . . Even if rulers do not acquit themselves of this duty [punishment of evildoers and praise of the good], one must respect in them their charge and their ministry. "Servants, be subject to your masters with all fear, not only to the good and gentle, but also to the angry and unjust."

There is thus something religious in the respect one gives to the prince. The service of God and respect for kings are inseparable things, and St. Peter places these two duties together: "Fear God, Honor the King."

God, moreover, has put something divine into kings. "I have said: You are Gods, and all of you the sons of the most High." It is God himself whom David makes speak in this way. . . .

4th Proposition, Kings should respect their own power, and use it only for the public good Their power coming from on high, as has been said, they must not believe that they are the owners of it, to use it as they please; rather must they use it with fear and restraint, as something which comes to them from God, and for which God will ask an accounting of them.

FOURTH BOOK, ON THE CHARACTERISTICS OF ROYALTY (CONTINUATION)

First Article, Royal Authority is Absolute

1st Proposition, The prince need account to no one for what he ordains . . . Without this absolute authority, he can neither do good nor suppress evil: his power must be such that no one can hope to escape him; and, in fine, the sole defense of individuals against the public power, must be their innocence. . . .

2nd Proposition, When the prince has decided, there can be no other decision The judgments of sovereigns are attributed to God himself. . . .

[N]o one has the right to judge or to review after him.

One must, then, obey princes as if they were justice itself, without which there is neither order nor justice in affairs.

They are gods, and share in some way in divine independence. "I have said: You are gods, and all of you the sons of the most High."

Only God can judge their judgments and their persons. . . .

It follows from this that he who does not want to obey the prince, is . . . condemned irremissibly to death as an enemy of public peace and of human society. . . .

The prince can correct himself when he knows that he has done badly; but against his authority there can be no remedy except his authority.

3rd Proposition, There is no co-active force against the prince One calls co-active [coercive] force a power to constrain and to execute what is legitimately ordained. To the prince alone belongs legitimate command; to him alone belongs co-active force as well.

It is for that reason also that St. Paul gives the sword to him alone. "If thou do that which is evil, fear; for he beareth not the sword in vain."

In the state only the prince should be armed: otherwise everything is in confusion, and the state falls back into anarchy.

He who creates a sovereign prince puts everything together into his hands, both the sovereign authority to judge and all the power of the state.

REVIEW QUESTION

1. According to Bossuet, why do kings merit absolute obedience, and what duty do they owe to God?

9   A Secular Defense of Absolutism

Thomas Hobbes (1588–1679), a British philosopher and political theorist, witnessed the agonies of the English civil war, including the execution of Charles I in 1649. These developments fortified Hobbes's conviction that absolutism was the most desirable and logical form of government. Only the unlimited power of a sovereign, said Hobbes, could contain human passions that disrupt the social order and threaten civilized life; only absolute rule could provide an environment secure enough for people to pursue their individual interests.

Leviathan (1651), Hobbes's principal work of political thought, broke with medieval political theory. Medieval thinkers assigned each group of people—clergy, lords, serfs, guildsmen—a place in a fixed social order; an individual's social duties were set by ancient traditions believed to have been ordained by God. During early modern times, the great expansion of commerce and capitalism spurred the new individualism already pronounced in Renaissance culture; group ties were shattered by competition and accelerating social mobility. Hobbes gave expression to a society where people confronted each other as competing individuals.

Thomas Hobbes
LEVIATHAN

Hobbes was influenced by the new scientific thought that saw mathematical knowledge as the avenue to truth. Using geometry as a model, Hobbes began with what he believed were self-evident axioms regarding human nature, from which he deduced other truths. He aimed at constructing political philosophy on a scientific foundation and rejected the authority of tradition and religion as inconsistent with a science of politics. Thus, although Hobbes supported absolutism, he dismissed the idea advanced by other theorists of absolutism that the monarch's power derived from God. He also rejected the idea that the state should not be obeyed when it violated God's law. *Leviathan* is a rational and secular political statement. In this modern approach, rather than in Hobbes's justification of absolutism, lies the work's significance.

Hobbes had a pessimistic view of human nature. Believing that people are innately selfish and grasping, he maintained that competition and dissension, rather than cooperation, characterize human relations. Even when reason teaches that cooperation is more advantageous than competition, Hobbes observed that people are reluctant to alter their ways, because passion, not reason, governs their behavior. In the following passages from *Leviathan*, Hobbes describes the causes of human conflicts.

Nature hath made men so equall, in the faculties of body, and mind; as that though there bee found one man sometimes manifestly stronger in body, or of quicker mind than another; yet when all is reckoned together, the difference between man, and man, is not so considerable, as that one man can thereupon claim to himselfe any benefit, to which another may not pretend, as well as he. For as to the strength of body, the weakest has strength enough to kill the strongest, either by secret machination, or by confederacy with others, that are in the same danger with himselfe. . . .

And as to the faculties of the mind . . . men are . . . [more] equall than unequall. . . .

From this equality of ability, ariseth equality of hope in the attaining of our Ends. And therefore if any two men desire the same thing, which neverthelesse they cannot both enjoy, they become enemies; and in the way to their End, . . . endeavour to destroy, or subdue one another. . . . If one plant, sow, build, or possesse a convenient Seat, others may probably be expected to come prepared with forces united, to dispossesse, and deprive him, not only of the fruit of his labour, but also of his life, or liberty. . . .

So that in the nature of man, we find three principall causes of quarrell. First, Competition; Secondly, Diffidence; Thirdly, Glory.

The first, maketh men invade for Gain; the second, for Safety; and the third, for Reputation. The first use Violence, to make themselves Masters of other men's persons, wives, children, and cattell; the second, to defend them; the third, for trifles, as a word, a smile, a different opinion, and any other signe of undervalue, either direct in their Persons, or by reflexion in their Kindred, their Friends, their Nation, their Profession, or their Name.

Hereby it is manifest, that during the time men live without a common Power to keep them all in awe, they are in that condition which is called Warre; and such a warre, as is of every man, against every man. . . .

Hobbes then describes a state of nature—the hypothetical condition of humanity prior to the formation of the state—as a war of all against all. For Hobbes, the state of nature is a logical abstraction, a device employed to make his point. Only a strong ruling entity—the state—will end the perpetual strife and provide security. For Hobbes, the state is merely a useful arrangement that permits individuals to exchange goods and services in a secure environment. The ruling authority in the state, the sovereign, must have supreme power, or society will collapse and the anarchy of the state of nature will return.

Whatsoever therefore is consequent to a time of Warre, where every man is Enemy to every man; the same is consequent to the time, wherein men live without other security, than what their own strength, and their own invention shall furnish them withall. In such condition, there is no place for Industry; because the fruit thereof is uncertain: and consequently no Culture of the Earth; no Navigation, nor use of the commodities that may be imported by Sea; no commodious Building; no Instruments of moving, and removing such things as require much force; no Knowledge of the face of the Earth; no account of Time; no Arts; no Letters; no Society; and which is worst of all, continuall feare, and danger of violent death; And the life of man, solitary, poore, nasty, brutish, and short. . . .

The Passions that encline men to Peace, are Feare of Death; Desire of such things as are necessary to commodious living; and a Hope by their Industry to obtain them. And Reason suggesteth convenient Articles of Peace, upon which men may be drawn to agreement. . . .

And because the condition of Man, (as hath been declared in the precedent Chapter) is a condition of Warre of every one against every one; in which case every one is governed by his own Reason; and there is nothing he can make use of, that may not be a help unto him, in preserving his life against his enemyes; It followeth, that in such a condition, every man has a Right to every thing; even to one another's body. And therefore, as long as this naturall Right of every man to every thing endureth, there can be no security to any man, (how strong or wise soever he be,) of living out the time, which Nature ordinarily alloweth men to live. . . .

. . . If there be no Power erected, or not great enough for our security; every man will and may lawfully rely on his own strength and art, for caution against all other men. . . .

The only way to erect . . . a Common Power, as may be able to defend them from the invasion of [foreigners] and the injuries of one another, and thereby to secure them in such sort, as that by their owne industrie, and by the fruites of the Earth, they may nourish themselves and live contentedly; is, to conferre all their power and strength upon one Man, or upon one Assembly of men, that may reduce all their Wills, by plurality of voices, unto one Will . . . and therein to submit their Wills, every one to his Will, and their Judgements, to his Judgment. This is more than Consent, or Concord; it is a reall Unitie of them all, in one and the same Person, made by Covenant of every man with every man, in such manner, as if every man should say to every man, *I Authorise and give up my Right of Governing my selfe, to this Man, or to this Assembly of men, on this condition, that thou give up thy Right to him, and Authorise all his Actions in like manner.* This done, the Multitude so united in one Person, is called a COMMON-WEALTH. . . . For by this Authorite, given him by every particular man in the Common-wealth, he hath the use of so much Power and Strength . . . conferred on him, that by terror thereof, he is in-abled to forme the wills of them all, to Peace at home, and mutuall [aid] against their enemies abroad. And in him consisteth the Essence of the Common-wealth; which (to define it,) is *One Person, of whose Acts a great Multitude, by mutuall Covenants one with another, have made themselves every one the Author, to the end he may use the strength and means of them all, as he shall think expedient, for their Peace and Common Defence.*

And he that carryeth this Person, is called SOVERAIGNE, and said to have *Soveraigne Power*; and every one besides, his SUBJECT. . . .

. . . They that have already Instituted a Common-wealth, being thereby bound by Covenant . . . cannot lawfully make a new Covenant, amongst themselves, to be obedient to any other, in any thing whatsoever, without his permission. And therefore, they that are subjects to a Monarch, cannot without his leave cast off Monarchy, and return to the confusion of a disunited Multitude; nor transferre their Person from him that beareth it, to another Man, or other Assembly of men: for they . . . are bound, every man to every man, to [acknowledge] . . . that he that already is their Soveraigne, shall do, and judge fit to be done; so that [those who do not obey] break their Covenant made to that man, which is injustice: and they have also every man given the Soveraignty to him that beareth their Person; and therefore if they depose him, they take from him that which is his own, and so again it is injustice. . . . And whereas some men have pretended for their disobedience to their Soveraign, a new Covenant, made, not with men, but with God; this also is unjust: for there is no Covenant with God, but by mediation of some body that representeth God's Person; which none doth but God's Lieutenant, who hath the Soveraignty under God. But this pretence of Covenant with God, is so evident a [lie], even in the pretenders own consciences, that it is not onely an act of an unjust, but also of a vile, and unmanly disposition. . . .

. . . Consequently none of [the sovereign's] Subjects, by any pretence of forfeiture, can be freed from his Subjection.

REVIEW QUESTIONS

1. What was Thomas Hobbes's view of human nature and what conclusions did he draw from it about the best form of government?
2. What has been the political legacy of Hobbes's notion of the state?

10 The Triumph of Constitutional Monarchy in England: The Glorious Revolution

The struggle against absolute monarchy in England during the early seventeenth century reached a climax during the reign of Charles I (1625–1649). Parliament raised its own army as civil war broke out between its supporters and those of the king. Captured by the Scottish Presbyterian rebels in 1646 and turned over to the English parliamentary army in 1647, Charles was held prisoner for two years until the Puritan parliamentary general Oliver Cromwell (1599–1658) decided to put him on trial for treason. The king was found guilty and executed in 1649.

The revolutionary parliamentary regime evolved into a military dictatorship headed by Cromwell. After Cromwell's death, Parliament in 1660 restored the monarchy and invited the late king's heir to end his exile and take the throne. Charles II (1660–1685), by discretion and skillful statesmanship, managed to evade many difficulties caused by the hostility of those who opposed his policies. He attempted to ease religious discrimination by ending the laws that penalized dissenters who rejected the official Church of England. But the religious prejudices of Parliament forced the king to desist, and the laws penalizing both Protestant dissenters and Roman Catholics remained in force. The king's motives for establishing religious toleration were suspect, since he himself was married to a French Catholic and his brother and heir James, Duke of York, was also a staunch Catholic.

When James II (1685–1688) succeeded to the throne, he tried unsuccessfully to get Parliament to repeal the Test Act, a law that forbade anyone to hold a civil or military office or to enter a university unless he was a member in good standing of the Church of England. This law effectively barred both Catholics and Protestant dissenters from serving in the king's government. When Parliament refused to act, James got the legal Court of the King's Bench to approve his decree suspending the Test Act. The court affirmed that the king, due to his sovereign authority, had absolute power to suspend any law at his sole discretion. The prerogatives claimed by the king were seen by many as an attempt to impose absolute monarchy on the English people.

King James further roused enemies by appointing many Catholics to high government posts and by issuing his Declaration of Indulgence for Liberty of Conscience on April 4, 1687. This declaration established complete freedom of worship for all Englishmen, ending all civil penalties and discriminations based on religious dissent. Instead of hailing the declaration as a step forward in solving the religious quarrels within the kingdom, many persons viewed this suspension of the laws as a further act of absolutism because James acted unilaterally without consulting Parliament. This act united the king's enemies and alienated his former supporters.

When the king's wife gave birth to a son, making the heir to the throne another Catholic, almost all factions (except the Catholics) abandoned James II and invited the Dutch Protestant Prince William of Orange and his wife Mary, James II's Protestant daughter, to come to England. James and his Catholic family and friends fled to France. Parliament declared the throne vacant and offered it to William and Mary as joint sovereigns. As a result of the "Glorious Revolution," the English monarchy became clearly limited by the will of Parliament.

THE ENGLISH DECLARATION OF RIGHTS

In depriving James II of the throne, Parliament had destroyed forever in Britain the theory of divine right as an operating principle of government and had firmly established a limited constitutional monarchy. The appointment of William and Mary was accompanied by a declaration of rights (later enacted as the Bill of Rights), which enumerated and declared illegal James II's arbitrary acts. The Declaration of Rights, excerpted below, compelled William and Mary and future monarchs to recognize the right of the people's representatives to dispose of the royal office and to set limits on its powers. These rights were subsequently formulated into laws passed by Parliament. Prior to the American Revolution, colonists protested that British actions in the American colonies violated certain rights guaranteed in the English Bill of Rights. Several of these rights were later included in the Constitution of the United States.

And whereas the said late king James the Second having abdicated the government and the throne being thereby vacant, His Highness the prince of Orange (whom it hath pleased Almighty God to make the glorious instrument of delivering this kingdom from popery and arbitrary power) did (by the advice of the lords spiritual and temporal and divers principal persons of the commons)[1] cause letters to be written to the lords spiritual and temporal, being Protestants; and other letters to the several counties, cities, universities, boroughs and Cinque ports[2] for the choosing of such persons to represent them, as were of right to be sent to parliament, to meet and sit at Westminster upon the two

and twentieth day of January in this year one thousand six hundred eighty and eight,[3] in order to [guarantee] . . . that their religion, laws and liberties might not again be in danger of being subverted; upon which letters elections having been accordingly made.

And thereupon the said lords spiritual and temporal and commons pursuant to their respective letters and elections being now assembled in a full and free representative of this nation, taking into their most serious consideration the best means for attaining the ends aforesaid, do in the first place (as their ancestors in like case have usually done) for the vindicating and asserting their ancient rights and liberties, declare:

That the pretended power of suspending of laws or the execution of laws by regal authority without consent of parliament is illegal.

That the pretended power of dispensing with laws or the execution of laws by regal authority as it hath been assumed and exercised of late is illegal.

That the commission for erecting the late court of commissioners for ecclesiastical causes

---

[1]"The lords spiritual" refers to the bishops of the Church of England who sat in the House of Lords, and "the lords temporal" refers to the nobility entitled to sit in the House of Lords. The commons refers to the elected representatives in the House of Commons.
[2]The Cinque ports along England's southeastern coast (originally five in number) enjoyed special privileges because of their military duties in providing for coastal defense.
[3]The year was in fact 1689 because until 1752, the English used March 25 as the beginning of the new year.

and all other commissions and courts of like nature are illegal and pernicious.

That the levying money for or to the use of the crown by pretence of prerogative without grant of parliament for a longer time or in other manner than the same is or shall be granted is illegal.

That it is the right of the subjects to petition the king and all commitments and prosecutions for such petitioning are illegal.

That the raising or keeping a standing army within the kingdom in time of peace unless it be with consent of parliament is against the law.

That the subjects which are Protestants may have arms for their defence suitable to their conditions and as allowed by law.

That election of members of parliament ought to be free.

That the freedom of speech and debates or proceedings in parliament ought not to be impeached or questioned in any court or place out of parliament.

That excessive bail ought not to be required nor excessive fines imposed nor cruel and unusual punishments inflicted.

That jurors ought to be duly impanelled and returned and jurors which pass upon men in trials for high treason ought to be freeholders.

That all grants and promises of fines and forfeitures of particular persons before conviction are illegal and void.

And that for redress of all grievances and for the amending, strengthening and preserving of the laws parliaments ought to be held frequently.

And they do claim, demand and insist upon all and singular the premises as their undoubted rights and liberties and that no declarations, judgments, doings or proceedings to the prejudice of the people in any of the said premises ought in any wise to be drawn hereafter into consequence or example.

REVIEW QUESTIONS

1. How did the Declaration of Rights limit royal authority? With what result?
2. In what ways did the Glorious Revolution impact upon the American rebellion in the 1770s?

CHAPTER 12

The Scientific Revolution

GALILEO GALILEI'S (1564–1642) support of Copernicanism and rejection of the medieval division
of the universe into higher and lower realms make him a principal shaper of modern science.
(The Granger Collection, New York)

The Scientific Revolution of the sixteenth and seventeenth centuries replaced the medieval view of the universe with a new cosmology and produced a new way of investigating nature. It overthrew the medieval conception of nature as a hierarchical order ascending toward a realm of perfection. Rejecting reliance on authority, the thinkers of the Scientific Revolution affirmed the individual's ability to know the natural world through the method of mathematical reasoning, the direct observation of nature, and carefully controlled experiments.

The medieval view of the universe had blended the theories of Aristotle and Ptolemy, two ancient Greek thinkers, with Christian teachings. In that view, a stationary earth stood in the center of the universe just above hell. Revolving around the earth were seven planets: the moon, Mercury, Venus, the sun, Mars, Jupiter, and Saturn. Because people believed that earth did not move, it was not considered a planet. Each planet was attached to a transparent sphere that turned around the earth. Encompassing the universe was a sphere of fixed stars; beyond the stars lay three heavenly spheres, the outermost of which was the abode of God. An earth-centered universe accorded with the Christian idea that God had created the universe for men and women and that salvation was the aim of life.

Also agreeable to the medieval Christian view was Aristotle's division of the universe into a lower, earthly realm and a higher realm beyond the moon. Two sets of laws operated in the universe, one on earth and the other in the celestial realm. Earthly objects were composed of four elements: earth, water, fire, and air; celestial objects were composed of the divine ether—a substance too pure, too clear, too fine, too spiritual to be found on earth. Celestial objects naturally moved in perfectly circular orbits around the earth; earthly objects, composed mainly of the heavy elements of earth and water, naturally fell downward, whereas objects made of the lighter elements of air and fire naturally flew upward toward the sky.

The destruction of the medieval world picture began with the publication in 1543 of *On the Revolutions of the Heavenly Spheres*, by Nicolaus Copernicus, a Polish mathematician, astronomer, and clergyman. In Copernicus's system, the sun was in the center of the universe, and the earth was another planet that moved around the sun. Most thinkers of the time, committed to the Aristotelian–Ptolemaic system and to the biblical statements that seemed to support it, rejected Copernicus's conclusions.

The work of Galileo Galilei, an Italian mathematician, astronomer, and physicist, was decisive in the shattering of the medieval cosmos and the shaping of the modern scientific outlook. Galileo advanced the modern view that knowledge of nature derives from direct observation and from mathematics. For Galileo, the universe was a "grand book which . . . is written in the language of mathematics, and its characters are triangles, circles, and other geometric figures without which it is humanly impossible to understand a single word of it." Galileo also pioneered experimental physics, advanced the modern idea that nature is uniform throughout the universe, and attacked reliance on scholastic authority rather than on experimentation in resolving scientific controversies.

Johannes Kepler (1571–1630), a contemporary of Galileo, discovered three laws of planetary motion that greatly advanced astronomical knowledge. Kepler showed that the path of a planet was an ellipse, not a circle as Ptolemy (and Copernicus) had believed, and that planets do not move at uniform speed but accelerate as they near the sun. He devised formulas to calculate accurately both a planet's speed at each point in its orbit around the sun and a planet's location at a particular time. Kepler's laws provided further evidence that Copernicus had been right, for they made sense only in a sun-centered universe, but Kepler could not explain why planets stayed in their orbits rather than flying off into space or crashing into the sun. The resolution of that question was left to Sir Isaac Newton.

Newton's great achievement was integrating the findings of Copernicus, Galileo, and Kepler into a single theoretical system. In *Principia Mathematica* (1687), he formulated the mechanical laws of motion and attraction that govern celestial and terrestrial objects.

The creation of a new model of the universe was one great achievement of the Scientific Revolution; another accomplishment was the formulation of the scientific method. The scientific method encompasses two approaches to knowledge, which usually complement each other: the empirical (inductive) and the rational (deductive). Although all sciences use both approaches, the inductive method is generally more applicable in such descriptive sciences as biology, anatomy, and geology, which rely on the accumulation of data. In the inductive approach, general principles are derived from analyzing external experiences—observations and the results of experiments. In the deductive approach, used in mathematics and theoretical physics, truths are derived in successive steps from indubitable axioms. Whereas the inductive method builds its concepts from an analysis of sense experience, the deductive approach constructs its ideas from self-evident principles that are conceived by the mind itself without external experience. The deductive and inductive approaches to knowledge, and their interplay, have been a constantly recurring feature in Western intellectual history since the rationalism of Plato and the empiricism of Aristotle. The success of the scientific method in modern times arose from the skillful synchronization of induction and deduction by such giants as Leonardo da Vinci, Copernicus, Kepler, Galileo, and Newton.

The Scientific Revolution was instrumental in shaping the modern outlook. It destroyed the medieval conception of the universe and established the scientific method as the means for investigating nature and acquiring knowledge, even in areas having little to do with the study of the physical world. By demonstrating the powers of the human mind, the Scientific Revolution gave thinkers great confidence in reason and led eventually to a rejection of traditional beliefs in magic, astrology, and witches. In the eighteenth century, this growing skepticism led thinkers to question miracles and other Christian beliefs that seemed contrary to reason.

1 The Copernican Revolution

In proclaiming that the earth was not stationary but revolved around the sun, Nicolaus Copernicus (1473–1543) revolutionized the science of astronomy. Fearing controversy and scorn, Copernicus long refused to publish his great work, *On the Revolutions of the Heavenly Spheres* (1543). However, persuaded by friends, he finally relented and permitted publication; a copy of his book reached him on his deathbed. As Copernicus anticipated, his ideas aroused the ire of many thinkers.

Both Catholic and Protestant philosophers and theologians, including Martin Luther, attacked Copernicus for contradicting the Bible and Aristotle and Ptolemy, and they raised several specific objections. First, certain passages in the Bible imply a stationary earth and a sun that moves (for example, Psalm 93 says, "Yea, the world is established; it shall never be moved"; and in attacking Copernicus, Luther pointed out that "sacred Scripture tells us that Joshua commanded the sun to stand still, and not the earth"). Second, a body as heavy as the earth cannot move through space at such speed as Copernicus suggested. Third, if the earth spins on its axis, why does a stone dropped from a height land directly below instead of at a point behind where it was dropped? Fourth, if the earth moved, objects would fly off it. And finally, the moon cannot orbit both the earth and the sun at the same time.

Nicolaus Copernicus
ON THE REVOLUTIONS OF THE HEAVENLY SPHERES

On the Revolutions of the Heavenly Spheres was dedicated to Pope Paul III, whom Copernicus asked to protect him from vilification. In the dedication, Copernicus explains his reason for delaying publication of *Revolutions.*

To His Holiness, Pope Paul III, Nicholas Copernicus'
Preface to His Books on the Revolutions

I can readily imagine, Holy Father, that as soon as some people hear that in this volume, which I have written about the revolutions of the spheres of the universe, I ascribe certain motions to the terrestrial globe, they will shout that I must be immediately repudiated together with this belief. For I am not so enamored of my own opinions that I disregard what others may think of them. I am aware that a philosopher's ideas are not subject to the judgement of ordinary persons, because it is his endeavor to seek the truth in all things, to the extent permitted to human reason by God. Yet I hold that completely erroneous views should be shunned. Those who know that the consensus of many centuries has sanctioned the conception that the earth remains at rest in the middle of the heaven as its center would, I reflected, regard it as an insane pronouncement if I made the opposite assertion that the earth moves. Therefore I debated with myself for a long time whether to publish the volume which I wrote to prove the earth's motion or rather to follow the example of the Pythagoreans[1] and certain others, who used to transmit philosophy's secrets only to kinsmen and friends, not in writing but by word of mouth. . . . And they did so, it seems to me, not, as some suppose, because they were in some way jealous about their teachings, which would be spread around; on the contrary, they wanted the very beautiful thoughts attained by great men of deep devotion not to be ridiculed by those who are reluctant to exert themselves vigorously in any literary pursuit unless it is lucrative; or if they are stimulated to the nonacquisitive study of philosophy by the exhortation and example of others, yet because of their dullness of mind they play the same part among philosophers as drones among bees. When I weighed these considerations, the scorn which

I had reason to fear on account of the novelty and unconventionality of my opinion almost induced me to abandon completely the work which I had undertaken.

But while I hesitated for a long time and even resisted, my friends [encouraged me]. . . . Foremost among them was the cardinal of Capua [a city in southern Italy], Nicholas Schönberg, renowned in every field of learning. Next to him was a man who loves me dearly, Tiedemann Giese, bishop of Chelmno [a city in northern Poland], a close student of sacred letters as well as of all good literature. For he repeatedly encouraged me and, sometimes adding reproaches, urgently requested me to publish this volume and finally permit it to appear after being buried among my papers and lying concealed not merely until the ninth year[2] but by now the fourth period of nine years. The same conduct was recommended to me by not a few other very eminent scholars. They exhorted me no longer to refuse, on account of the fear which I felt, to make my work available for the general use of students of astronomy. The crazier my doctrine of the earth's motion now appeared to most people, the argument ran, so much the more admiration and thanks would it gain after they saw the publication of my writings dispel the fog of absurdity by most luminous proofs. Influenced therefore by these persuasive men and by this hope, in the end I allowed my friends to bring out an edition of the volume, as they had long besought me to do. . . .

But you [your Holiness] are rather waiting to hear from me how it occurred to me to venture to conceive any motion of the earth, against the traditional opinion of astronomers and almost against common sense. . . . [Copernicus then describes some of the problems connected with the Ptolemaic system.]

---

[1]Pythagoreans were followers of Pythagoras, a Greek mathematician and philosopher of the sixth century B.C.; they were particularly interested in cosmology.

[2]The Roman poet Horace, who lived in the first century B.C., suggested in *Ars Poetica* that writers should keep a new manuscript in a cupboard "until the ninth year" before publishing it. Only then, he argued, would they have enough objectivity to judge its value. Copernicus is referring to this famous piece of advice.

For a long time, then, I reflected on this confusion in the astronomical traditions concerning the derivation of the motions of the universe's spheres. I began to be annoyed that the movements of the world machine, created for our sake by the best and most systematic Artisan of all [God], were not understood with greater certainty by the philosophers, who otherwise examined so precisely the most insignificant trifles of this world. For this reason I undertook the task of rereading the works of all the philosophers which I could obtain to learn whether anyone had ever proposed other motions of the universe's spheres than those expounded by the teachers of astronomy in the schools. And in fact first I found in Cicero that Hicetas supposed the earth to move. Later I also discovered in Plutarch[3] that certain others were of this opinion. . . .

Therefore, having obtained the opportunity from these sources, I too began to consider the mobility of the earth. . . . I thought that I too would be readily permitted to ascertain whether explanations sounder than those of my predecessors could be found for the revolution of the celestial spheres on the assumption of some motion of the earth.

Having thus assumed the motions which I ascribe to the earth later on in the volume, by long and intense study I finally found that if the motions of the other planets are correlated with the orbiting of the earth, and are computed for the revolution of each planet, not only do their phenomena follow therefrom but also the order and size of all the planets and spheres, and heaven itself is so linked together that in no portion of it can anything be shifted without disrupting the remaining parts and the universe as a whole. Accordingly in the arrangement of the volume too I have adopted the following order. In the first book I set forth the entire distribution of the spheres together with the motions which I attribute to the earth, so that this book contains, as it were, the general structure of the universe. Then in the remaining books I correlate the motions of the other planets and of all the spheres with the movement of the earth so that I may thereby determine to what extent the motions and appearances of the other planets and spheres can be saved if they are correlated with the earth's motions. I have no doubt that acute and learned astronomers will agree with me if, as this discipline especially requires, they are willing to examine and consider, not superficially but thoroughly, what I adduce in this volume in proof of these matters. However, in order that the educated and uneducated alike may see that I do not run away from the judgement of anybody at all, I have preferred dedicating my studies to Your Holiness rather than to anyone else. For even in this very remote corner of the earth where I live you are considered the highest authority by virtue of the loftiness of your office and your love for all literature and astronomy too. Hence by your prestige and judgement you can easily suppress calumnious attacks although, as the proverb has it, there is no remedy for a backbite.

Perhaps there will be babblers who claim to be judges of astronomy although completely ignorant of the subject and, badly distorting some passage of Scripture to their purpose, will dare to find fault with my undertaking and censure it. I disregard them even to the extent of despising their criticism as unfounded. For it is not unknown that Lactantius,[4] otherwise an illustrious writer but hardly an astronomer, speaks quite childishly about the earth's shape, when he mocks those who declared that the earth has the form of a globe. Hence scholars need not be surprised if any such persons will likewise ridicule me. Astronomy is written for astronomers. To them my work too will seem, unless I am mistaken, to make some contribution.

---

[3]Hicetas, a Pythagorean philosopher of the fourth century B.C., taught that the earth rotated on its axis while the other heavenly bodies were at rest. Cicero was a Roman statesman of the first century B.C. Plutarch (A.D. c. 50–c. 120) was a Greek moral philosopher and biographer whose works were especially popular among Renaissance humanists.

---

[4]Renaissance humanists admired Lactantius (c. 240–c. 320), a Latin rhetorician and Christian apologist, for his classical, Ciceronian literary style.

Cardinal Bellarmine
ATTACK ON THE COPERNICAN THEORY

In 1615, Cardinal Bellarmine, who in the name of the Inquisition warned Galileo not to defend the Copernican theory, expressed his displeasure with heliocentrism in a letter to Paolo Antonio Foscarini. Foscarini, head of the Carmelites, an order of mendicant friars in Calabria, and professor of theology, had tried to show that the earth's motion was not incompatible with biblical statements.

Cardinal Bellarmine to Foscarini (12 April 1615)

My Very Reverend Father,

I have read with interest the letter in Italian and the essay in Latin which Your [Reverence] sent me; I thank you for the one and for the other and confess that they are full of intelligence and erudition. You ask for my opinion, and so I shall give it to you, but very briefly, since now you have little time for reading and I for writing.

First, . . . to want to affirm that in reality the sun is at the center of the world and only turns on itself without moving from east to west, and the earth . . . revolves with great speed around the sun . . . is a very dangerous thing, likely not only to irritate all scholastic philosophers and theologians, but also to harm the Holy Faith by rendering Holy Scripture false. For your [Reverence] has well shown many ways of interpreting Holy Scripture, but has not applied them to particular cases; without a doubt you would have encountered very great difficulties if you had wanted to interpret all those passages you yourself cited.

Second, I say that, as you know, the Council [of Trent] prohibits interpreting Scripture against the common consensus of the Holy Fathers; and if Your [Reverence] wants to read not only the Holy Fathers, but also the modern commentaries on Genesis, the Psalms, Ecclesiastes, and Joshua, you will find all agreeing in the literal interpretation that the sun is in heaven and turns around the earth with great speed, and that the earth is very far from heaven and sits motionless at the center of the world. Consider now, with your sense of prudence, whether the Church can tolerate giving Scripture a meaning contrary to the Holy Fathers and to all the Greek and Latin commentators. Nor can one answer that this is not a matter of faith, since if it is not a matter of faith "as regards the topic," it is a matter of faith "as regards the speaker"; and so it would be heretical to say that Abraham did not have two children and Jacob twelve, as well as to say that Christ was not born of a virgin, because both are said by the Holy Spirit through the mouth of the prophets and the apostles.

Third, I say that if there were a true demonstration that the sun is at the center of the world and the earth in the third heaven, and that the sun does not circle the earth but the earth circles the sun, then one would have to proceed with great care in explaining the Scriptures that appear contrary, and say rather that we do not understand them than that what is demonstrated is false. But I will not believe that there is such a demonstration, until it is shown to me. . . . and in case of doubt one must not abandon the Holy Scripture as interpreted by the Holy Fathers. I add that the one who wrote, "The sun also ariseth, and the sun goeth down, and hasteth to his place where he arose," was Solomon [King of ancient Israel], who not only spoke inspired by God, but was a man above all others wise and learned in the human sciences and in the knowledge of created things; he received all this wisdom from God; therefore it is not likely that he was affirming something that was contrary to truth already demonstrated or capable of being demonstrated.

REVIEW QUESTIONS

1. What led Nicolaus Copernicus to investigate the motions of the universe's spheres?
2. Why did he fear to publish this theory about the earth's motion?
3. On what grounds did Cardinal Bellarmine reject the Copernican theory?

---

2 Galileo: Confirming the Copernican System

The brilliant Italian scientist Galileo Galilei (1564–1642) rejected the medieval division of the universe into higher and lower realms and proclaimed the modern idea of nature's uniformity. Learning that a telescope had been invented in Holland, Galileo built one for himself and used it to investigate the heavens. Through his telescope, Galileo saw craters and mountains on the moon; he concluded that celestial bodies were not pure, perfect, and immutable, as had been believed. There was no difference in quality between heavenly and earthly bodies; nature was the same throughout.

With his telescope, Galileo discovered four moons orbiting Jupiter, an observation that overcame a principal objection to the Copernican system. Galileo showed that a celestial body could indeed move around a center other than the earth; that earth was not the common center for all celestial bodies; that a celestial body (earth's moon or Jupiter's moons) could orbit a planet at the same time that the planet revolved around another body (namely, the sun).

Galileo appealed to the Roman Catholic authorities asking them to halt their actions against the theories of Copernicus, but was unsuccessful. His support of Copernicus aroused the ire of both clergy and scholastic philosophers. In 1616, the church placed Copernicus's book on the index of forbidden books, and Galileo was ordered to cease his defense of the Copernican theory. In 1632, Galileo published *Dialogue Concerning the Two Chief World Systems* in which he upheld the Copernican view. Widely distributed and acclaimed, the book antagonized Galileo's enemies, who succeeded in halting further printing. Summoned to Rome, the aging and infirm scientist was put on trial by the Inquisition and ordered to renounce the Copernican theory. Galileo bowed to the Inquisition, which condemned the *Dialogue* and sentenced him to life imprisonment—largely house arrest at his own villa near Florence, where he was treated humanely.

Galileo Galilei
LETTER TO THE GRAND DUCHESS CHRISTINA AND *DIALOGUE CONCERNING THE TWO CHIEF WORLD SYSTEMS— PTOLEMAIC AND COPERNICAN*

The first reading illustrates Galileo's active involvement in a struggle for freedom of inquiry many years before the *Dialogue* was published. In 1615, in a letter addressed to Grand Duchess Christina of Tuscany, Galileo argued that passages from the Bible had no authority in scientific disputes.

The second reading (from the *Dialogue*) reveals Galileo's views on Aristotle. Medieval scholastics regarded Aristotle as the supreme authority on questions concerning nature, an attitude that was perpetuated by early modern scholastics. Galileo insisted that such reliance on authority was a hindrance to scientific investigation, that it is through observation, experiment, and reason that one arrives at physical truth.

BIBLICAL AUTHORITY

Some years ago, as Your Serene Highness well knows, I discovered in the heavens many things that had not been seen before our own age. The novelty of these things, as well as some consequences which followed from them in contradiction to the physical notions commonly held among academic philosophers, stirred up against me no small number of professors—as if I had placed these things in the sky with my own hands in order to upset nature and overturn the sciences. They seemed to forget that the increase of known truths stimulates the investigation, establishment, and growth of the arts; not their diminution or destruction.

Showing a greater fondness for their own opinions than for truth, they sought to deny and disprove the new things which, if they had cared to look for themselves, their own senses would have demonstrated to them. To this end they hurled various charges and published numerous writings filled with vain arguments, and they made the grave mistake of sprinkling these with passages taken from places in the Bible which they had failed to understand properly, and which were ill suited to their purposes. . . .

. . . Men who were well grounded in astronomical and physical science were persuaded as soon as they received my first message. There were others who denied them or remained in doubt only because of their novel and unexpected character, and because they had not yet had the opportunity to see for themselves. These men have by degrees come to be satisfied. But some, besides allegiance to their original error, possess I know not what fanciful interest in remaining hostile not so much toward the things in question as toward their discoverer. No longer being able to deny them, these men now take refuge in obstinate silence, but being more than ever exasperated by that which has pacified and quieted other men, they divert their thoughts to other fancies and seek new ways to damage me. . . .

. . . Possibly because they are disturbed by the known truth of other propositions of mine which differ from those commonly held, and therefore mistrusting their defense so long as they confine themselves to the field of philosophy, these men have resolved to fabricate a shield for their fallacies out of the mantle of pretended religion and the authority of the Bible. These they apply, with little judgment, to the refutation of arguments that they do not understand and have not even listened to.

First they have endeavored to spread the opinion that such propositions in general are contrary to the Bible and are consequently damnable and heretical. . . . Hence they have had no trouble in finding men who would preach the damnability and heresy of the new doctrine from their very pulpits with unwonted confidence, thus doing impious and inconsiderate injury not only to that doctrine and its followers but to all mathematics and mathematicians in general. . . .

. . . They go about invoking the Bible, which they would have minister to their deceitful purposes. Contrary to the sense of the Bible and the intention of the holy [Church] Fathers, if I am not mistaken, they would extend such authorities until even in purely physical matters—where faith is not involved—they would have us altogether abandon reason and the evidence of our senses in favor of some biblical passage, though under the surface meaning of its words this passage may contain a different sense.

I hope to show that I proceed with much greater piety than they do, when I argue not against condemning [Copernicus'] book, but against condemning it in the way they suggest—that is, without understanding it, weighing it, or so much as reading it. For Copernicus never discusses matters of religion or faith, nor does he use arguments that depend in any way upon the authority of sacred writings which he might have interpreted erroneously. He stands always upon physical conclusions pertaining to the celestial motions, and deals with them by astronomical and geometrical demonstrations, founded primarily upon sense experiences and very exact observations. He did not ignore the Bible, but he knew very well that if his doctrine were proved, then it could not

contradict the Scriptures when they were rightly understood. . . .

The reason produced for condemning the opinion that the earth moves and the sun stands still is that in many places in the Bible one may read that the sun moves and the earth stands still. Since the Bible cannot err, it follows as a necessary consequence that anyone takes an erroneous and heretical position who maintains that the sun is inherently motionless and the earth movable.

With regard to this argument, I think in the first place that it is very pious to say and prudent to affirm that the holy Bible can never speak untruth—whenever its true meaning is understood. But I believe nobody will deny that it is often very abstruse, and may say things which are quite different from what its bare words signify. Hence in expounding the Bible if one were always to confine oneself to the unadorned grammatical meaning, one might fall into error. . . .

. . . Now the Bible, merely to condescend to popular capacity, has not hesitated to obscure some very important pronouncements, attributing to God himself some qualities extremely remote from (and even contrary to) His essence. Who, then, would positively declare that this principle has been set aside, and the Bible has confined itself rigorously to the bare and restricted sense of its words, when speaking but casually of the earth, of water, of the sun, or of any other created thing? Especially in view of the fact that these things in no way concern the primary purpose of the sacred writings, which is the service of God and the salvation of souls—matters infinitely beyond the comprehension of the common people.

This being granted, I think that in discussions of physical problems we ought to begin not from the authority of scriptural passages, but from sense-experiences and necessary demonstrations. . . . Nothing physical which sense-experience sets before our eyes, or which necessary demonstrations prove to us, ought to be called in question (much less condemned) upon the testimony of biblical passages which may have some different meaning beneath their words. . . .

. . . I do not feel obliged to believe that that same God who has endowed us with senses, reason, and intellect has intended to forgo their use and by some other means to give us knowledge which we can attain by them. He would not require us to deny sense and reason in physical matters which are set before our eyes and minds by direct experience or necessary demonstrations. . . .

It is obvious that such [anti-Copernican] authors, not having penetrated the true senses of Scripture, would impose upon others an obligation to subscribe to conclusions that are repugnant to manifest reason and sense, if they had any authority to do so. God forbid that this sort of abuse should gain countenance and authority, for then in a short time it would be necessary to proscribe all the contemplative sciences. People who are unable to understand perfectly both the Bible and the sciences far outnumber those who do understand. The former, glancing superficially through the Bible, would arrogate to themselves the authority to decree upon every question of physics on the strength of some word which they have misunderstood, and which was employed by the sacred authors for some different purpose. And the smaller number of understanding men could not dam up the furious torrent of such people, who would gain the majority of followers simply because it is much more pleasant to gain a reputation for wisdom without effort or study than to consume oneself tirelessly in the most laborious disciplines.

Galileo attacked the unquestioning acceptance of Aristotle's teachings in his *Dialogue Concerning the Two Chief World Systems— Ptolemaic and Copernican*. In the *Dialogue*, Simplicio is an Aristotelian and Salviati is a spokesman for Galileo; Sagredo, a third participant, introduces the problem of relying on the authority of Aristotle.

ARISTOTELIAN AUTHORITY

SAGREDO One day I was at the home of a very famous doctor in Venice, where many persons came on account of their studies, and others occasionally came out of curiosity to see some anatomical dissection performed by a man who was truly no less learned than he was a careful and expert anatomist. It happened on this day that he was investigating the source and origin of the nerves, about which there exists a notorious controversy between the Galenist and Peripatetic doctors.[1] The anatomist showed that the great trunk of nerves, leaving the brain and passing through the nape, extended on down the spine and then branched out through the whole body, and that only a single strand as fine as a thread arrived at the heart. Turning to a gentleman whom we knew to be a Peripatetic philosopher, and on whose account he had been exhibiting and demonstrating everything with unusual care, he asked this man whether he was at last satisfied and convinced that the nerves originated in the brain and not in the heart. The philosopher, after considering for awhile, answered: "You have made me see this matter so plainly and palpably that if Aristotle's text were not contrary to it, stating clearly that the nerves originate in the heart, I should be forced to admit it to be true." . . .

SIMPLICIO But if Aristotle is to be abandoned, whom shall we have for a guide in philosophy? Suppose you name some author.

SALVIATI We need guides in forests and in unknown lands, but on plains and in open places only the blind need guides. It is better for such people to stay at home, but anyone with eyes in his head and his wits about him could serve as a guide for them. In saying this, I do not mean that a person should not listen to Aristotle; indeed, I applaud the reading and careful study of

---

[1]Galenist doctors followed the medical theories of Galen (A.D. c. 130–c. 200), a Greek anatomist and physician whose writings had great authority among medieval and early modern physicians. Peripatetic doctors followed Aristotle's teachings.

his works, and I reproach only those who give themselves up as slaves to him in such a way as to subscribe blindly to everything he says and take it as an inviolable decree without looking for any other reasons. This abuse carries with it another profound disorder, that other people do not try harder to comprehend the strength of his demonstrations. And what is more revolting in a public dispute, when someone is dealing with demonstrable conclusions, than to hear him interrupted by a text (often written to some quite different purpose) thrown into his teeth by an opponent? If, indeed, you wish to continue in this method of studying, then put aside the name of philosophers and call yourselves historians, or memory experts; for it is not proper that those who never philosophize should usurp the honorable title of philosopher.

GALILEO CONDEMNED BY THE INQUISITION

The following selection is drawn from the records of the Inquisition, which found Galileo guilty of teaching Copernicanism.

Whereas you, Galileo, son of the late Vincenzo Galilei, Florentine, aged seventy years, were in the year 1615 denounced to this Holy Office for holding as true the false doctrine taught by some that the Sun is the center of the world and immovable and that the Earth moves, and also with a diurnal [daily] motion; for having disciples to whom you taught the same doctrine; for holding correspondence with certain mathematicians of Germany concerning the same; for having printed certain letters, entitled "On the Sunspots," wherein you developed the same doctrine as true; and for replying to the objections from the Holy Scriptures, which from time to time were urged against it, by glossing the said Scriptures according to your own meaning: and whereas there was thereupon produced the copy of a document in the form of a letter, purporting to be written by you to one formerly your disciple, and in this divers propositions are set forth, following the position of Copernicus, which are contrary to the true sense and authority of Holy Scripture:

This Holy Tribunal being therefore of intention to proceed against the disorder and mischief thence resulting, which went on increasing to the prejudice of the Holy Faith, by command of His Holiness and of the Most Eminent Lords Cardinals of this supreme and universal Inquisition, the two propositions of the stability of the Sun and the motion of the Earth were by the theological Qualifiers qualified as follows:

The proposition that the Sun is the center of the world and does not move from its place is absurd and false philosophically and formally heretical, because it is expressly contrary to the Holy Scripture.

The proposition that the Earth is not the center of the world and immovable but that it moves, and also with a diurnal motion, is equally absurd and false philosophically and theologically considered at least erroneous in faith.

But whereas it was desired at that time to deal leniently with you, it was decreed at the Holy Congregation held before His Holiness on the twenty-fifth of February, 1616, that his Eminence the Lord Cardinal Bellarmine should order you to abandon altogether the said false doctrine and, in the event of your refusal, that an injunction should be imposed upon you by the Commissary of the Holy Office to give up the said doctrine and not to teach it to others, not to defend it, nor even discuss it; and failing your acquiescence in this injunction, that you should be imprisoned.

And, in order that a doctrine so pernicious might be wholly rooted out and not insinuate itself further to the grave prejudice of Catholic truth, a decree was issued by the Holy Congregation of the Index prohibiting the books which treat of this doctrine and declaring the doctrine itself to be false and wholly contrary to the sacred and divine Scripture.

And whereas a book appeared here recently, printed last year at Florence, the title of which shows that you were the author, this title being: "Dialogue of Galileo Galilei on the Great World Systems"; and whereas the Holy Congregation was afterward informed that through the publication of the said book the false opinion of the motion of the Earth and the stability of the Sun was daily gaining ground, the said book was taken into careful consideration, and in it there was discovered a patent violation of the aforesaid injunction that had been imposed upon you, for in this book you have defended the said opinion previously condemned and to your face declared to be so, although in the said book you strive by various devices to produce the impression that you leave it undecided, and in express terms as probable: which, however, is a most grievous error, as an opinion can in no wise be probable which has been declared and defined to be contrary to divine Scripture.

Therefore by our order you were cited before this Holy Office, where, being examined upon your oath, you acknowledged the book to be written and published by you. You confessed that you began to write the said book about ten or twelve years ago, after the command had been imposed upon you as above; that you requested license to print it without, however, intimating to those who granted you this license that you had been commanded not to hold, defend, or teach the doctrine in question in any way whatever.

We say, pronounce, sentence, and declare that you, the said Galileo, by reason of the matters adduced in trial, and by you confessed as above, have rendered yourself in the judgment of this Holy Office vehemently suspected of heresy, namely, of having believed and held the doctrine—which is false and contrary to the sacred and divine Scriptures—that the Sun is the center of the world and does not move from east to west and that the Earth moves and is not the center of the world; and that an opinion may be held and defended as probable after it has been declared and defined to be contrary to the Holy Scripture; and that consequently you have incurred all the censures and penalties imposed and promulgated in the sacred canons and other constitutions, general and particular, against such delinquents. From which we are content that you be absolved, provided that, first, with a sincere heart and unfeigned faith, you abjure, curse, and detest before us the aforesaid errors and heresies and every other error and heresy contrary to the Catholic and Apostolic Roman Church in the form to be prescribed by us for you.

And, in order that this your grave and pernicious error and transgression may not remain altogether unpunished and that you may be more cautious in the future and an example to others that they may abstain from similar delinquencies, we ordain that the book of the "Dialogue of Galileo Galilei" be prohibited by public edict. . . .

REVIEW QUESTIONS

1. What was Galileo Galilei's objection to using the Bible as a source of knowledge of physical things? According to him, how did one acquire knowledge of nature?
2. What point was Galileo making in telling the story of the anatomical dissection?
3. What was Galileo's view on the use of Aristotle's works as a basis for scientific endeavors?
4. Why did the Inquisition regard the teaching of Copernicanism as dangerous?

3 Prophet of Modern Science

Sir Francis Bacon (1561–1626), an English statesman and philosopher, vigorously supported the advancement of science and the scientific method. He believed that increased comprehension and mastery of nature would improve living conditions for people and therefore wanted science to encompass systematic research; toward this end, he urged the state to fund scientific institutions. Bacon denounced universities for merely repeating Aristotelian concepts and discussing abstruse problems—Is matter formless? Are all natural substances composed of matter?—that did not increase understanding of nature or contribute to human betterment. The webs spun by these scholastics, he said, were ingenious but valueless. Bacon wanted an educational program that stressed direct contact with nature and fostered new discoveries.

Bacon was among the first to appreciate the new science's value and to explain its method clearly. Like Leonardo da Vinci, Bacon gave supreme value to the direct observation of nature; for this reason he is one of the founders of the empirical tradition in modern philosophy. Bacon upheld the inductive approach—careful investigation of nature, accumulation of data, and experimentation—as the way to truth and useful knowledge. Because he wanted science to serve a practical function, Bacon praised artisans and technicians who improved technology.

Francis Bacon
ATTACK ON AUTHORITY AND ADVOCACY OF EXPERIMENTAL SCIENCE

Bacon was not himself a scientist; he made no discoveries and had no laboratory. Nevertheless, for his advocacy of the scientific method, Bacon is deservedly regarded as a prophet of modern science. In the first passage from *Redargutio Philosophiarum* (The Refutation of Philosophies), written in 1609, a treatise on the "idols of the theater"—fallacious ways of thinking based on given systems of philosophy—Bacon attacks the slavish reliance on Aristotle.

But even though Aristotle were the man he is thought to be I should still warn you against receiving as oracles the thoughts and opinions of one man. What justification can there be for this self-imposed servitude [that] . . . you are content to repeat Aristotle after two thousand [years]? . . . But if you will be guided by me you will deny, not only to this man but to any mortal now living or who shall live hereafter, the right to dictate your opinions. . . . You will never be sorry for trusting your own strength, if you but once make trial of it. You may be inferior to Aristotle on the whole, but not in everything. Finally, and this is the head and front of the whole matter, there is at least one thing in which you are far ahead of him—in precedents, in experience, in the lessons of time. Aristotle, it is said, wrote a book in which he gathered together the laws and institutions of two hundred and fifty-five cities; yet I have no doubt that the customs of Rome are worth more than all of them combined so far as military and political science are concerned. The position is the same in natural philosophy. Are you of a mind to cast aside not only your own endowments but the gifts of time? Assert yourselves before it is too late. Apply yourselves to the study of things themselves. Be not for ever the property of one man.

In these excerpts from *The New Organon* (New System of Logic), in 1620 Bacon criticizes contemporary methods used to inquire into nature. He expresses his ideas in the form of aphorisms—concise statements of principles or general truths.

I. Man, being the servant and interpreter of Nature, can do and understand so much and so much only as he has observed in fact or in thought of the course of nature: beyond this he neither knows anything nor can do anything.

VIII. . . . The sciences we now possess are merely systems for the nice ordering and setting forth of things already invented; not methods of invention or directions for new works.

XII. The logic now in use serves rather to fix and give stability to the errors which have their foundation in commonly received notions than to help the search after truth. So it does more harm than good.

XIX. There are and can be only two ways of searching into and discovering truth. The one

[begins with] the . . . most general axioms, and from these principles, the truth of which it takes for settled and immoveable, proceeds to judgment and to the discovery of middle axioms. And this way is now in fashion. The other derives axioms from the senses and particulars, rising by a gradual and unbroken ascent, so that it arrives at the most general axioms last of all. This is the true way, but as yet untried.

XXIII. There is a great difference between . . . certain empty dogmas, and the true signatures and marks set upon the works of creation as they are found in nature.

XXIV. It cannot be that axioms established by argumentation should avail for the discovery of new works; since the subtlety of nature is greater many times over than the subtlety of argument. But axioms duly and orderly formed from particulars easily discover the way to new particulars, and thus render sciences active.

XXXI. It is idle to expect any great advancement in science from the superinducing [adding] and engrafting of new things upon old. We must begin anew from the very foundations, unless we would revolve for ever in a circle with mean and contemptible progress.

CIX. There is therefore much ground for hoping that there are still laid up in the womb of nature many secrets of excellent use, having no affinity or parallelism with any thing that is now known, but lying entirely out of the beat of the imagination, which have not yet been found out. They too no doubt will some time or other, in the course and revolution of many ages, come to light of themselves, just as the others did; only by the method of which we are now treating they can be speedily and suddenly and simultaneously presented and anticipated.

REVIEW QUESTIONS

1. What intellectual attitude did Francis Bacon believe obstructed new scientific discoveries in his time?
2. What method of scientific inquiry did Bacon advocate?

4 The Circulation of the Blood: Validating the Empirical Method

William Harvey (1578–1657), a British physician, showed that blood circulates in the body because of the pumping action of the heart muscle. Previous belief derived from Galen's theories. Galen (c. 130–c. 200), a Greco-Roman physician, claimed that there were two centers of blood, with the liver being the source of blood in the veins, and the heart being the source of arterial blood. In contrast, Harvey demonstrated that all blood passes through a single central organ, the heart, flowing away from the heart through the arteries and back to it through the veins, and that this constant, rotating circulation is caused by the rhythmic contractions of the heart muscle acting as a pump.

This discovery of the circulation of the blood marked a break with medieval medical ideas (inherited from the ancient world) and signified the emergence of modern physiology. Harvey employed the inductive method championed by Sir Francis Bacon: he drew conclusions after carefully observing and experimenting with living animals.

William Harvey
THE MOTION OF THE HEART AND BLOOD IN ANIMALS

In *The Motion of the Heart and Blood in Animals* (1628), Harvey described the heart as a mechanical pump, a description that corresponded to Newton's view that the universe was a mechanical system. In this reading, Harvey discusses his reasons for writing the book and provides insights into his method.

When I first gave my mind to vivisections [cutting live animals open for experimentation], as a means of discovering the motions and uses of the heart and sought to discover these from actual inspection, and not from the writings of others, I found the task so truly arduous, so full of difficulties, that I was almost tempted to think . . . that the motion of the heart was only to be comprehended by God. For I could neither rightly perceive at first when the systole and when the diastole took place, nor when and where dilatation and contraction occurred,[1] by reason of the rapidity of the motion, which in many animals is accomplished in the twinkling of an eye, coming and going like a flash of lightning; so that the systole presented itself to me now from this point, now from that; the diastole the same; and then everything was reversed, the motions occurring, as it seemed, variously and confusedly together. My mind was therefore greatly unsettled, nor did I know what I should myself conclude, nor what believe from others. . . .

At length, and by using greater and daily diligence, having frequent recourse to vivisections, employing a variety of animals for the purpose, and collating numerous observations, I thought that I had attained to the truth, that I should extricate myself and escape from this labyrinth [a

[1]In dilatation, the heart muscle is relaxed, creating the diastole, or expansion of the heart's chambers, during which they fill with blood. The heart's contraction, or systole, forces the blood out of the chambers in a pumping action.

maze, a confused state], and that I had discovered what I so much desired, both the motion and the use of the heart and arteries; since which time I have not hesitated to expose my views upon these subjects, not only in private to my friends, but also in public, in my anatomical lectures, after the manner of the Academy[2] of old.

These views, as usual, pleased some more, others less; some chid and calumniated me, and laid it to me as a crime that I had dared to depart from the precepts and opinion of all anatomists; others desired further explanations of the novelties, which they said were both worthy of consideration, and might perchance be found of signal use. At length, yielding to the requests of my friends, that all might be made participators in my labours, and partly moved by the envy of others, who, receiving my views with uncandid minds and understanding them indifferently, have essayed to traduce me publicly, I have been moved to commit these things to the press, in order that all may be enabled to form an opinion both of me and my labours. . . .

But lest any one should say that we give them words only, and make mere specious assertions without any foundation, and desire to innovate without sufficient cause, three points present themselves for confirmation, which being stated, I conceive that the truth I contend for will follow necessarily, and appear as a thing obvious to all. First,—the blood is incessantly transmitted by the action of the heart from the vena cava to the arteries in such quantity, that it cannot be supplied from the ingesta,[3] and in such wise that the whole mass must very quickly pass through the organ; Second,—the blood under the influence of the arterial pulse enters and is impelled in a continuous, equable, and incessant stream through every part and member of the body, in much larger quantity than were sufficient for nutrition, or than the whole mass of fluids could supply; Third,—the veins in like manner return this blood incessantly

to the heart from all parts and members of the body. These points proved, I conceive it will be manifest that the blood circulates, revolves, propelled and then returning, from the heart to the extremities, from the extremities to the heart, and thus that it performs a kind of circular motion.

Let us assume either arbitrarily or from experiment, the quantity of blood which the left ventricle[4] of the heart will contain when distended to be, say two ounces, three ounces, one ounce and a half—in the dead body I have found it to hold upwards of two ounces. Let us assume further, how much less the heart will hold in the contracted than in the dilated state; and how much blood it will project into the aorta[5] upon each contraction;—and all the world allows that with the systole something is always projected, a necessary consequence demonstrated in the third chapter, and obvious from the structure of the valves; and let us suppose as approaching the truth that the fourth, or fifth, or sixth, or even but the eighth part of its charge is thrown into the artery at each contraction; this would give either half an ounce, or three drachms, or one drachm [dram: $\frac{1}{8}$ ounce] of blood as propelled by the heart at each pulse into the aorta; which quantity, by reason of the valves at the root of the vessel, can by no means return into the ventricle. Now in the course of half an hour, the heart will have made more than one thousand beats, in some as many as two, three, and even four thousand. Multiplying the number of drachms propelled by the number of pulses, we shall have either one thousand half ounces, or one thousand times three drachms, or a like proportional quantity of blood, according to the amount which we assume as propelled with each stroke of the heart, sent from this organ into the artery; a larger quantity in every case than is contained in the whole body! In the same way, in the sheep or dog, say that but a single scruple [$\frac{1}{3}$ dram, $\frac{1}{24}$ ounce] of blood passes with each

---

[2]*The Academy* refers to the Athens school founded by Plato at which public lectures were given.
[3]The vena cava is the major vein that carries blood returning from the body into the heart. Ingesta refers to solid or liquid nutrients taken into the body.

[4]The heart consists of four chambers: a left and right ventricle (the lower chambers) and a left and right atrium (the upper chambers).
[5]The aorta is the major artery that carries blood out of the heart to the body.

stroke of the heart, in one half hour we should have one thousand scruples, or about three pounds and a half of blood injected into the aorta; but the body of neither animal contains above four pounds of blood, a fact which I have myself ascertained in the case of the sheep.

Upon this supposition, therefore, assumed merely as a ground for reasoning, we see the whole mass of blood passing through the heart,

from the veins to the arteries, and in like manner through the lungs.

But let it be said that this does not take place in half an hour, but in an hour, or even in a day; any way it is still manifest that more blood passes through the heart in consequence of its action, than can either be supplied by the whole of the ingesta, or that can be contained in the veins at the same moment.

REVIEW QUESTIONS

1. What evidence led William Harvey to conclude that blood constantly circulates through the heart?
2. What method did he use to reach his conclusions?
3. Why did some of Harvey's colleagues refuse to believe his conclusions?
4. Why did Harvey publish his book?

---

5 The Autonomy of the Mind

René Descartes (1596–1650), a French mathematician and philosopher, united the new currents of thought initiated during the Renaissance and the Scientific Revolution. Descartes said that the universe was a mechanical system whose inner laws could be discovered through mathematical thinking and formulated in mathematical terms. With Descartes' assertions on the power of thought, human beings became fully aware of their capacity to comprehend the world through their mental powers. For this reason he is regarded as the founder of modern philosophy.

The deductive approach stressed by Descartes presumes that inherent in the mind are mathematical principles, logical relationships, the principle of cause and effect, concepts of size and motion, and so on—ideas that exist independently of human experience with the external world. Descartes, for example, would say that the properties of a right-angle triangle ($a^2 + b^2 = c^2$) are implicit in human consciousness prior to any experience one might have with a triangle. These innate ideas, said Descartes, permit the mind to give order and coherence to the physical world. Descartes held that the mind arrives at truth when it "intuits" or comprehends the logical necessity of its own ideas and expresses these ideas with clarity, certainty, and precision.

René Descartes
DISCOURSE ON METHOD

In the *Discourse on Method* (1637), Descartes proclaimed the mind's autonomy and importance, and its ability and right to comprehend truth. In this work he offered a method whereby one could achieve certainty and thereby produce a comprehensive understanding of nature and human culture. In the following passage from the *Discourse on Method*, he explained the purpose of his inquiry. How he did so is almost as revolutionary as the ideas he wished to express. He spoke in the first person, autobiographically, as an individual employing his own reason, and he addressed himself to other individuals, inviting them to use their reason. He brought to his narrative an unprecedented confidence in the power of his own judgment and a deep disenchantment with the learning of his times.

PART ONE

From my childhood I lived in a world of books, and since I was taught that by their help I could gain a clear and assured knowledge of everything useful in life, I was eager to learn from them. But as soon as I had finished the course of studies which usually admits one to the ranks of the learned, I changed my opinion completely. For I found myself saddled with so many doubts and errors that I seemed to have gained nothing in trying to educate myself unless it was to discover more and more fully how ignorant I was.

Nevertheless I had been in one of the most celebrated schools in Europe, where I thought there should be wise men if wise men existed anywhere on earth. I had learned there everything that others learned, and, not satisfied with merely the knowledge that was taught, I had perused as many books as I could find which contained more unusual and recondite knowledge. . . . And finally, it did not seem to me that our times were less flourishing and fertile than were any of the earlier periods. All this led me to conclude that I could judge others by myself, and to decide that there was no such wisdom in the world as I had previously hoped to find. . . .

I revered our theology, and hoped as much as anyone else to get to heaven, but having learned on great authority that the road was just as open to the most ignorant as to the most learned, and that the truths of revelation which lead thereto are beyond our understanding, I would not have dared to submit them to the weakness of my reasonings. I thought that to succeed in their examination it would be necessary to have some extraordinary assistance from heaven, and to be more than a man.

I will say nothing of philosophy except that it has been studied for many centuries by the most outstanding minds without having produced anything which is not in dispute and consequently doubtful. I did not have enough presumption to hope to succeed better than the others; and when I noticed how many different opinions learned men may hold on the same subject, despite the fact that no more than one of them can ever be right, I resolved to consider almost as false any opinion which was merely plausible. . . .

This is why I gave up my studies entirely as soon as I reached the age when I was no longer under the control of my teachers. I resolved to seek no other knowledge than that which I might find within myself, or perhaps in the great book of nature. I spent a few years of my adolescence traveling, seeing courts and armies, living with people of diverse types and stations of life, acquiring varied experience, testing myself in the episodes which fortune sent me, and, above all, thinking about the things around me so that I could derive some profit from them. For it seemed to me that I might find much more of the truth in the cogitations [reflections] which each man made on things which were important to him, and where he would be the loser if he judged badly, than in the cogitations of a man of letters in his study, concerned with speculations which produce no effect, and which have no consequences to him. . . .

. . . After spending several years in thus studying the book of nature and acquiring experience, I eventually reached the decision to study my own self, and to employ all my abilities to try to choose the right path. This produced much better results in my case, I think, than would have been produced if I had never left my books and my country. . . .

PART TWO

. . . As far as the opinions which I had been receiving since my birth were concerned, I could not do better than to reject them completely for once in my lifetime, and to resume them afterwards, or perhaps accept better ones in their place, when I had determined how they fitted into a rational scheme. And I firmly believed that by this means I would succeed in conducting my life much better than if I built only upon the old foundations and gave credence to the principles which I had acquired in my childhood without ever having examined them to see whether they were true or not. . . .

. . . Never has my intention been more than to try to reform my own ideas, and rebuild them on foundations that would be wholly mine. . . . The decision to abandon all one's preconceived notions is not an example for all to follow. . . .

As for myself, I should no doubt have . . . [never attempted it] if I had had but a single teacher or if I had not known the differences which have always existed among the most learned. I had discovered in college that one cannot imagine anything so strange and unbelievable but that it has been upheld by some philosopher; and in my travels I had found that those who held opinions contrary to ours were neither barbarians nor savages, but that many of them were at least as reasonable as ourselves. I had considered how the same man, with the same capacity for reason, becomes different as a result of being brought up among Frenchmen or Germans than he would be if he had been brought up among Chinese or cannibals; and how, in our fashions, the thing which pleased us ten years ago and perhaps will please us again ten years in the future, now seems extravagant and ridiculous; and I felt that in all these ways we are much more greatly influenced by custom and example than by any certain knowledge. Faced with this divergence of opinion, I could not accept the testimony of the majority, for I thought it worthless as a proof of anything somewhat difficult to discover, since it is much more likely that a single man will have

discovered it than a whole people. Nor, on the other hand, could I select anyone whose opinions seemed to me to be preferable to those of others, and I was thus constrained to embark on the investigation for myself.

Nevertheless, like a man who walks alone in the darkness, I resolved to go so slowly and circumspectly that if I did not get ahead very rapidly I was at least safe from falling. Also, I did not want to reject all the opinions which had slipped irrationally into my consciousness since birth, until I had first spent enough time planning how to accomplish the task which I was then undertaking, and seeking the true method of obtaining knowledge of everything which my mind was capable of understanding. . . .

Descartes' method consists of four principles that place the capacity to arrive at truth entirely within the province of the human mind. One finds a self-evident principle, such as a geometric axiom. From this general principle, other truths are deduced through logical reasoning. This is accomplished by breaking a problem down into its elementary components and then, step by step, moving toward more complex knowledge.

. . . I thought that some other method [besides that of logic, algebra, and geometry] must be found to combine the advantages of these three and to escape their faults. Finally, just as the multitude of laws frequently furnishes an excuse for vice, and a state is much better governed with a few laws which are strictly adhered to, so I thought that instead of the great number of precepts of which logic is composed, I would have enough with the four following ones, provided that I made a firm and unalterable resolution not to violate them even in a single instance.

The first rule was never to accept anything as true unless I recognized it to be evidently such: that is, carefully to avoid precipitation and prejudgment, and to include nothing in my conclusions unless it presented itself so clearly and distinctly to my mind that there was no occasion to doubt it.

The second was to divide each of the difficulties which I encountered into as many parts as possible, and as might be required for an easier solution.

The third was to think in an orderly fashion, beginning with the things which were simplest and easiest to understand, and gradually and by degrees reaching toward more complex knowledge, even treating as though ordered materials which were not necessarily so.

The last was always to make enumerations so complete, and reviews so general, that I would be certain that nothing was omitted. . . .

What pleased me most about this method was that it enabled me to reason in all things, if not perfectly, at least as well as was in my power. In addition, I felt that in practicing it my mind was gradually becoming accustomed to conceive its objects more clearly and distinctly. . . .

Descartes was searching for an incontrovertible truth that could serve as the first principle of philosophy. His arrival at the famous dictum "I think, therefore I am" marks the beginning of modern philosophy.

PART FOUR

. . . As I desired to devote myself wholly to the search for truth, I thought that I should . . .

reject as absolutely false anything of which I could have the least doubt, in order to see whether anything would be left after this procedure which could be called wholly certain. Thus, as our senses deceive us at times, I was ready to suppose that nothing was at all the way our senses represented them to be. As there are men who make mistakes in reasoning even on the simplest topics in geometry, I judged that I was as liable to error as any other, and rejected as false all the reasoning which I had previously accepted as valid demonstration. Finally, as the same precepts which we have when awake may come to us when asleep without their being true, I decided to suppose that nothing that had ever entered my mind was more real than the illusions of my dreams. But I soon noticed that while I thus wished to think everything false, it was necessarily true that I who thought so was something. Since this truth, *I think, therefore I am*, was so firm and assured that all the most extravagant suppositions of the sceptics[1] were unable to shake it, I judged that I could safely accept it as the first principle of the philosophy I was seeking.

---

[1]The skeptics belonged to the ancient Greek philosophic school that held true knowledge to be beyond human grasp and treated all knowledge as uncertain.

REVIEW QUESTIONS

1. Why was René Descartes critical of the learning of his day?
2. What are the implications of Descartes' famous words: "I think, therefore I am"?
3. Compare Descartes' method with the approach advocated by Francis Bacon.

---

6   The Mechanical Universe

By demonstrating that all bodies in the universe—earthly objects as well as moons, planets, and stars—obey the same laws of motion and gravitation, Sir Isaac Newton (1646–1723) completed the destruction of the medieval view of the universe. The idea that the same laws governed the movement of earthly and heavenly bodies was completely foreign to medieval thinkers, who drew a sharp division between a higher celestial world and a lower terrestrial one. In the *Principia Mathematica* (1687), Newton showed that the same forces that hold celestial bodies in their orbits around the sun make apples fall to the ground. For Newton, the universe was like a giant clock, all of whose parts obeyed strict mechanical principles and worked together in perfect precision. To Newton's contemporaries, it seemed as if mystery had been banished from the universe.

Isaac Newton
PRINCIPIA MATHEMATICA

In the first of the following passages from *Principia Mathematica*, Newton stated the principle of universal law and lauded the experimental method as the means of acquiring knowledge.

RULES OF REASONING IN PHILOSOPHY

Rule I.   We are to admit no more causes of natural things than such as are both true and sufficient to explain their appearances.

To this purpose the philosophers say that Nature does nothing in vain, and more is in vain when less will serve; for Nature is pleased with simplicity, and affects not the pomp of superfluous causes.

Rule II.   Therefore to the same natural effects we must, as far as possible, assign the same causes.

As to respiration in a man and in a beast; the descent of stones [meteorites] in *Europe* and in *America*; the light of our culinary fire and of the sun; the reflection of light in the earth, and in the planets.

Rule III.   The qualities of bodies, which . . . are found to belong to all bodies within the reach of our experiments, are to be esteemed the universal qualities of all bodies whatsoever.

For since the qualities of bodies are only known to us by experiments, we are to hold for universal all such as universally agree with experiments. . . . We are certainly not to relinquish the evidence of experiments for the sake of dreams and vain fictions of our own

devising; nor are we to recede from the analogy of Nature, which [is] . . . simple, and always consonant to itself. We no other way know the extension of bodies than by our senses, nor do these reach it in all bodies; but because we perceive extension in all that are sensible, therefore, we ascribe it universally to all others also. That abundance of bodies are hard, we learn by experience; and because the hardness of the whole arises from the hardness of the parts, we, therefore, justly infer the hardness of the undivided particles not only of the bodies we feel but of all others. That all bodies are impenetrable, we gather not from reason, but from sensation. The bodies which we handle we find impenetrable, and thence, conclude impenetrability to be an universal property of all bodies whatsoever. That all bodies are moveable, and endowed with certain powers (which we call . . . {*inertia*}) of persevering in their motion, or in their rest, we only infer from the like properties observed in the bodies which we have seen. The extension, hardness, impenetrability, mobility, . . . of the whole, result from the extension, hardness, impenetrability, mobility, . . . of the parts; and thence we conclude the least particles of all bodies to be also all extended, and hard and impenetrable, and moveable, . . . And this is the foundation of all philosophy. . . .

Lastly, if it universally appears, by experiments and astronomical observations, that all bodies about the earth gravitate towards the earth, and that in proportion to the quantity of matter which they severally contain; that the moon likewise, according to the quantity of its matter, gravitates towards the earth; that, on the other hand, our sea gravitates towards the moon; and all the planets mutually one towards another; and the comets in like manner towards the sun; we must, in consequence of this rule, universally allow that all bodies whatsoever are endowed with a principle of mutual gravitation. . . .

Rule IV.   In experimental philosophy we are to look upon propositions collected by general induction from phenomena as accurately or very nearly true, notwithstanding any contrary hypotheses that may be imagined, till such time as other phenomena occur, by which they may either be made more accurate, or liable to exceptions.

This rule we must follow, that the argument of induction may not be evaded by hypotheses.

Newton describes further his concepts of gravity and scientific methodology.

GRAVITY

Hitherto, we have explained the phenomena of the heavens and of our sea by the power of gravity, but have not yet assigned the cause of this power. This is certain, that it must proceed from a cause that penetrates to the very centres of the sun and planets, without suffering the least diminution of its force; that operates not according to the quantity of the surfaces of the particles upon which it acts (as mechanical causes used to do) but according to the quantity of the solid matter which they contain, and propagates its virtue on all sides to immense distances, decreasing always in the duplicate portion of the distances. . . .

Hitherto I have not been able to discover the cause of those properties of gravity from

the phenomena, and I frame no hypothesis; for whatever is not deduced from the phenomena is to be called an hypothesis; and hypotheses, whether metaphysical or physical, whether of occult qualities or mechanical, have no place in experimental philosophy. In this philosophy particular propositions are inferred from the phenomena, and afterward rendered general by induction. Thus it was the impenetrability, the mobility, and the impulsive forces of bodies, and the laws of motion and of gravitation were discovered. And to us it is enough that gravity does really exist, and acts according to the laws which we have explained, and abundantly serves to account for all the motions of the celestial bodies, and of our sea.

A devout Anglican, Newton believed that God had created this superbly organized universe. The following selection is also from the *Principia*.

GOD AND THE UNIVERSE

This most beautiful system of the sun, planets, and comets could only proceed from the counsel and dominion of an intelligent and powerful Being. And if the fixed stars are the centers of other like systems, these, being formed by the like wise counsel, must be all subject to the dominion of One, especially since the light of the fixed stars is of the same nature with the light of the sun and from every system light passes into all the other systems; and lest the systems of the fixed stars should, by their gravity, fall on each other mutually, he hath placed those systems at immense distances from one another.

This Being governs all things not as the soul of the world, but as Lord over all; and on account of his dominion he is wont to be called "Lord God" . . . or "Universal Ruler." . . . It is the dominion of a spiritual being which constitutes a God. . . . And from his true dominion it follows that the true God is a living, intelligent and powerful Being. . . . he governs all things, and knows all things that are or can be done. . . . He endures for ever, and is every where present; and by existing always and every where, he constitutes duration and space. . . . In him are all things contained and moved; yet neither affects the other: God suffers nothing from the motion of bodies; bodies find no resistance from the omnipresence of God. . . . As a blind man has no idea of colors so we have no idea of the manner by which the all-wise God preserves and understands all things. He is utterly void of all body and bodily figure, and can therefore neither be seen, nor heard, nor touched; nor ought to be worshipped under the representation of any corporeal thing. We have ideas of his attributes, but what the real substance of any thing is we know not. . . . Much less, then, have we any idea of the substance of God. We know him only by his most wise and excellent contrivances of things. . . . [W]e reverence and adore him as his servants; and a god without dominion, providence, and final causes, is nothing else but Fate and Nature. Blind metaphysical necessity, which is certainly the same always and everywhere, could produce no variety of things. All that diversity of natural things which we find suited to different times and places could arise from nothing but the ideas and will of a Being necessarily existing. . . . And thus much concerning God; to discourse of whom from the appearances of things does certainly belong to Natural Philosophy.

REVIEW QUESTIONS

1. What did Isaac Newton mean by universal law? What examples of universal law did he provide?
2. What method for investigating nature did Newton advocate?
3. Summarize Newton's arguments for God's existence.
4. For Newton, what is God's relationship to the universe?

CHAPTER 13

The Enlightenment

RENÉ DESCARTES earned an international reputation for his work in philosophy and mathematics.
Here he is conducting a scientific demonstration at the court of Queen Christina of Sweden, c. 1700.
(The Art Archive/Picture Desk)

The Enlightenment of the eighteenth century culminated the movement toward modernity that started in the Renaissance era. The thinkers of the Enlightenment, called *philosophes*, attacked medieval otherworldliness, dethroned theology from its once-proud position as queen of the sciences, and based their understanding of nature and society on reason alone, unaided by revelation or priestly authority.

From the broad spectrum of Western history, several traditions flowed into the Enlightenment: the rational spirit born in classical Greece, the Stoic emphasis on natural law that applies to all human beings, and the Christian belief that all individuals are equal in God's eyes. A more immediate influence on the Enlightenment was Renaissance humanism, which focused on the individual and worldly human accomplishments and which criticized medieval theology-philosophy for its preoccupation with questions that seemed unrelated to the human condition. In many ways, the Enlightenment grew directly out of the Scientific Revolution. The philosophes praised both Newton's discovery of the mechanical laws that govern the universe and the scientific method that made this discovery possible. They wanted to transfer the scientific method—the reliance on experience and the critical use of the intellect—to the realm of society. They maintained that independent of clerical authority, human beings through reason could grasp the natural laws that govern the social world, just as Newton had uncovered the laws of nature that operate in the physical world. The philosophes said that those institutions and traditions that could not meet the test of reason, because they were based on authority, ignorance, or superstition, had to be reformed or dispensed with.

For medieval philosophers, reason had been subordinate to revelation; the Christian outlook determined the medieval concept of nature, morality, government, law, and life's purpose. During the Renaissance and Scientific Revolution, reason increasingly asserted its autonomy. For example, Machiavelli rejected the principle that politics should be based on Christian teachings; he recognized no higher world as the source of a higher truth. Galileo held that on questions regarding nature, one should trust to observation, experimentation, and mathematical reasoning and should not rely on Scripture. Descartes rejected reliance on past authority and maintained that through thought alone one could attain knowledge that has absolute certainty. Agreeing with Descartes that the mind is self-sufficient, the philosophes rejected the guidance of revelation and its priestly interpreters. They believed that through the use of reason, individuals could comprehend and reform society.

The Enlightenment philosophes articulated basic principles of the modern outlook: confidence in the self-sufficiency of the human mind, belief that individuals possess natural rights that governments should not violate, and the desire to reform society in accordance with rational principles. Their views influenced the reformers of the French Revolution, the Founding Fathers of the United States, and modern liberalism.

1   The Enlightenment Outlook

The critical use of the intellect was the central principle of the Enlightenment. The philosophes rejected beliefs and traditions that seemed to conflict with reason and attacked clerical and political authorities for interfering with the free use of the intellect.

Immanuel Kant
"WHAT IS ENLIGHTENMENT?"

The German philosopher Immanuel Kant (1724–1804) is a giant in the history of modern philosophy. Several twentieth-century philosophic movements have their origins in Kantian thought, and many issues raised by Kant still retain their importance. For example, in *Metaphysical Foundations of Morals* (1785), Kant set forth the categorical imperative that remains a crucial principle in moral philosophy. Kant asserted that when confronted with a moral choice, people should ask themselves: "Canst thou also will that thy maxim should be a universal law?" By this, Kant meant that people should ponder whether they would want the moral principle underlying their action to be elevated to a universal law that would govern others in similar circumstances. If they concluded that it should not, then the maxim should be rejected and the action avoided.

Kant valued the essential ideals of the Enlightenment and viewed the French Revolution, which put these ideals into law, as the triumph of liberty over despotism. In an essay entitled "What Is Enlightenment?" (1784), he contended that the Enlightenment marked a new way of thinking and eloquently affirmed the Enlightenment's confidence in and commitment to reason.

Enlightenment is man's leaving his self-caused immaturity. Immaturity is the incapacity to use one's intelligence without the guidance of another. Such immaturity is self-caused if it is not caused by lack of intelligence, but by lack of determination and courage to use one's intelligence without being guided by another. *Sapere Aude!* [Dare to know!] Have the courage to use your own intelligence! is therefore the motto of the enlightenment.

Through laziness and cowardice a large part of mankind, even after nature has freed them from alien guidance, gladly remain immature. It is because of laziness and cowardice that it is so easy for others to usurp the role of guardians.

It is so comfortable to be a minor! If I have a book which provides meaning for me, a pastor who has conscience for me, a doctor who will judge my diet for me and so on, then I do not need to exert myself. I do not have any need to think; if I can pay, others will take over the tedious job for me. The guardians who have kindly undertaken the supervision will see to it that by far the largest part of mankind, including the entire "beautiful sex," should consider the step into maturity, not only as difficult but as very dangerous.

After having made their domestic animals dumb and having carefully prevented these quiet creatures from daring to take any step beyond the lead-strings to which they have fastened them, these guardians then show them the danger which threatens them, should they attempt to walk alone. Now this danger is not really so very great; for they would presumably learn to walk after some stumbling. However, an example of this kind intimidates and frightens people out of all further attempts.

It is difficult for the isolated individual to work himself out of the immaturity which has become almost natural for him. He has even become fond of it and for the time being is incapable of employing his own intelligence, because he has never been allowed to make the attempt. Statutes and formulas, these mechanical tools of a serviceable use, or rather misuse, of his natural faculties, are the ankle-chains of a continuous immaturity. Whoever threw it off would make an uncertain jump over the smallest trench because he is not accustomed to such free movement. Therefore there are only a few who have pursued a firm path and have succeeded in escaping from immaturity by their own cultivation of the mind.

But it is more nearly possible for a public to enlighten itself: this is even inescapable if only the public is given its freedom. For there will always be some people who think for themselves, even among the self-appointed guardians of the great mass who, after having thrown off the yoke of immaturity themselves, will spread about them the spirit of a reasonable estimate of their own value and of the need for every man to think for himself. . . . [A] public can only arrive at enlightenment slowly. Through revolution, the abandonment of personal despotism may be engendered and the end of profit-seeking and domineering oppression may occur, but never a true reform of the state of mind. Instead, new prejudices, just like the old ones, will serve as the guiding reins of the great, unthinking mass. . . .

All that is required for this enlightenment is *freedom*; and particularly the least harmful of all that may be called freedom, namely, the freedom for man to make *public use* of his reason in all matters. But I hear people clamor on all sides: Don't argue! The officer says: Don't argue, drill! The tax collector: Don't argue, pay! The pastor: Don't argue, believe! . . . Here we have restrictions on freedom everywhere. Which restriction is hampering enlightenment, and which does not, or even promotes it? I answer: The *public use* of a man's reason must be free at all times, and this alone can bring enlightenment among men. . . .

I mean by the public use of one's reason, the use which a scholar makes of it before the entire reading public. . . .

The question may now be put: Do we live at present in an enlightened age? The answer is: No, but in an age of enlightenment. Much still prevents men from being placed in a position. . . to use their own minds securely and well in matters of religion. But we do have very definite indications that this field of endeavor is being opened up for men to work freely and reduce gradually the hindrances preventing a general enlightenment and an escape from self-caused immaturity.

REVIEW QUESTIONS

1. What did Immanuel Kant mean by the terms *enlightenment* and *freedom*?
2. In Kant's view, what factors delayed the progress of human enlightenment?
3. What are the political implications of Kant's views?

2 Political Liberty

John Locke (1632–1704), a British statesman, philosopher, and political theorist, was a principal source of the Enlightenment. Eighteenth-century thinkers were particularly influenced by Locke's advocacy of religious toleration, his reliance on experience as the source of knowledge, and his concern for liberty. In his first *Letter Concerning Toleration* (1689), Locke declared that Christians who persecute others in the name of religion vitiate Christ's teachings. Locke's political philosophy as formulated in the *Two Treatises on Government* (1690) complements his theory of knowledge; both were rational and secular attempts to understand and improve the human condition. The Lockean spirit pervades the American Declaration of Independence, the Constitution, and the Bill of Rights and is the basis of the liberal tradition that aims to protect individual liberty from despotic state authority.

Viewing human beings as brutish and selfish, Thomas Hobbes (see page 400) had prescribed a state with unlimited power; only in this way, he said, could people be protected from each other and civilized life preserved. Locke, regarding people as essentially good and humane, developed a conception of the state differing fundamentally from Hobbes'. Locke held that human beings are born with natural rights of life, liberty, and property; they establish the state to protect these rights. Consequently, neither executive nor legislature, neither king nor assembly has the authority to deprive individuals of their natural rights. Whereas Hobbes justified absolute monarchy, Locke explicitly endorsed constitutional government in which the power to govern derives from the consent of the governed and the state's authority is limited by agreement.

John Locke
SECOND TREATISE ON GOVERNMENT

Locke said that originally, in establishing a government, human beings had never agreed to surrender their natural rights to any state authority. The state's founders intended the new polity to preserve these natural rights and to implement the people's will. Therefore, as the following passage from Locke's *Second Treatise on Government* illustrates, the power exercised by magistrates cannot be absolute or arbitrary.

. . . *Political power* is that power, which every man having in the state of nature, has given up into the hands of the society, and therein to the governors, whom the society hath set over itself, with this express or tacit trust, that it shall be employed for their good, and the preservation of their property: now this *power*, which every man has *in the state of nature*, and which he parts with to the society in all such cases where the society can secure him, is to use such means, for the preserving of his own property, as he thinks good, and nature allows him; and to punish the breach of the law of nature in others, so as (according to the best of his reason) may most conduce to the preservation of himself, and the rest of mankind.

So that the *end and measure of this power*, when in every man's hands in the state of nature, being the preservation of all of his society, that is, all mankind in general, it can have no other *end or measure*, when in the hands of the magistrate, but to preserve the members of that society in their lives, liberties, and possessions; and so cannot be an absolute, arbitrary power over their lives and fortunes, which are as much as possible to be preserved; but a *power to make laws*, and annex such *penalties* to them, as may tend to the preservation of the whole, by cutting off those parts, and those only, which are so corrupt, that they threaten the sound and healthy, without which no severity is lawful. And this *power has its original only from compact*, and agreement, and the mutual consent of those who make up the community. . . .

These are the *bounds*, which the trust, that is put in them by the society, and the law of God and nature, have *set to the legislative* power of every common-wealth, in all forms of government.

First, They are to govern by *promulgated established laws*, not to be varied in particular cases, but to have one rule for rich and poor, for the favourite at court, and the country man at plough.

Secondly, These *laws* also ought to be designed *for* no other end ultimately, but *the good of the people*.

Thirdly, They must *not raise taxes* on the *property of the people, without the consent of the people*, given by themselves, or their deputies. And this properly concerns only such governments, where the *legislative* is always in being, or at least where the people have not reserved any part of the legislative to deputies, to be from time to time chosen by themselves.

Fourthly, The *legislative* neither must *nor can transfer the power of making laws* to any body else, or place it any where, but where the people have. . . .

If government fails to fulfill the end for which it was established—the preservation of the individual's right to life, liberty, and property—the people have a right to dissolve that government.

. . . The *legislative acts against the trust* reposed in them, when they endeavour to invade the property of the subject, and to make themselves, or any part of the community, masters, or arbitrary disposers of the lives, liberties, or fortunes of the people.

The reason why men enter into society, is the preservation of their property; and the end why they chuse and authorize a legislative, is, that there may be laws made, and rules set, as guards and fences to the properties of all the members of the society, to limit the power, and moderate the dominion of every part and member of the society: for since it can never be supposed to be the will of the society, that the legislative should have a power to destroy that which every one designs to secure, by entering into society, and for which the people submitted themselves to legislators of their own making; whenever the *legislators endeavour to take away, and destroy the property of the people*, or to reduce them to slavery under arbitrary power, they put themselves into a state of war with the people, who are thereupon absolved from any farther obedience, and are left to the common refuge, which God hath provided for all men, against force and violence. Whensoever therefore the *legislative* shall transgress this fundamental rule of society; and either by ambition, fear, folly or corruption, *endeavour to grasp* themselves, *or put into the hands of any other, an absolute power* over the lives, liberties, and estates of the people; by this breach of trust they *forfeit the power* the people had put into their hands for quite contrary ends, and it devolves to the people, who have a right to resume their original liberty, and, by the establishment of a new legislative, (such as they shall think fit) provide for their own safety and security, which is the end for which they are in society. What I have said here, concerning the legislative in general, holds true also concerning the supreme executor, who having a double trust put in him, both to have a part in the legislative, and the supreme execution of the law, acts against both, when he goes about to set up his own arbitrary will as the law of the society. He *acts* also *contrary to his trust*, when he either employs the force, treasure, and offices of the society, to corrupt the *representatives*, and gain them to his purposes; or openly pre-engages the *electors,* and prescribes to their choice, such, whom he has, by sollicitations, threats, promises, or otherwise, won to his designs; and employs them to bring in such, who have promised beforehand what to vote, and what to enact. . . .

Locke responds to the charge that his theory will produce "frequent rebellion." Indeed, says Locke, the true rebels are the magistrates who, acting contrary to the trust granted them, violate the people's rights.

. . . Such *revolutions happen* not upon every little mismanagement in public affairs. *Great mistakes* in the ruling part, many wrong and inconvenient laws, and all the *slips* of human frailty, will be *borne by the people* without mutiny or murmur. But if a long train of abuses, prevarications and artifices, all tending the same way, make the design visible to the people, and they cannot but feel what they lie under, and see whither they are going; it is not to be wondered at, that they should then rouze themselves, and endeavour to put the rule into such hands which may secure to them the ends for which government was at first erected. . . .

. . . I answer, that *this doctrine* of a power in the people of providing for their safety a-new, by a new legislative, when their legislators have acted contrary to their trust, by invading their property, is *the best defence against rebellion*, and the probablest means to hinder it: for *rebellion* being an opposition, not to persons, but authority, which is founded only in the constitutions and laws of the government; those, whoever they be, who by force break through, and by force justify their violation of them, are truly and properly *rebels*: for when men, by entering into society and civil government, have excluded force, and introduced laws for the preservation of property, peace, and unity amongst themselves, those who set up force again in opposition to the laws, do [rebel], that is, bring back again the state of war, and are properly rebels: which they who are in power, (by the pretence they have to authority, the temptation of force they have in their hands, and the flattery of those about them) being likeliest to do; the properest way to prevent the evil, is to shew them the danger and injustice of it, who are under the greatest temptation to run into it.

The end of government is the good of mankind; and which is *best for mankind*, that the people should always be exposed to the boundless will of tyranny, or that the rulers should be sometimes liable to be opposed, when they grow exorbitant in the use of their power, and employ it for the destruction, and not the preservation of the properties of their people?

Thomas Jefferson
DECLARATION OF INDEPENDENCE

Written in 1776 by Thomas Jefferson (1743–1826) to justify the American colonists' break with Britain, the Declaration of Independence enumerated principles that were quite familiar to English statesmen and intellectuals. The preamble to the Declaration, excerpted below, articulated clearly Locke's philosophy of natural rights. Locke had viewed life, liberty, and property as the individual's essential natural rights; Jefferson substituted the "pursuit of happiness" for property.

A DECLARATION BY THE REPRESENTATIVES OF THE UNITED STATES OF AMERICA, IN GENERAL CONGRESS ASSEMBLED

When in the Course of human Events, it becomes necessary for one People to dissolve the Political Bands which have connected them with another, and to assume among the Powers of the Earth, the separate and equal Station to which the Laws of Nature and of Nature's God entitle them, a decent Respect to the Opinions of Mankind requires that they should declare the causes which impel them to the Separation.

We hold these Truths to be self-evident, that all Men are created equal, that they are endowed by their Creator with certain unalienable Rights, that among these are Life, Liberty, and the Pursuit of Happiness—That to secure these Rights, Governments are instituted among Men, deriving their just Powers from the Consent of the Governed, That whenever any Form of Government becomes destructive of these Ends, it is the Right of the People to alter or to abolish it, and to institute new Government, laying its Foundation on such Principles, and organizing its Powers in such Form, as to them shall seem most likely to effect their Safety and Happiness. Prudence, indeed, will dictate that Governments long established should not be changed for light and transient Causes; and accordingly all Experience hath shewn, that Mankind are more disposed to suffer, while Evils are sufferable, than to right themselves by abolishing the Forms to which they are accustomed. But when a long Train of Abuses and Usurpations, pursuing invariably the same Object, evinces a Design to reduce them under absolute Despotism, it is their right, it is their duty, to throw off such Government, and to provide new Guards for their future Security. Such has been the patient Sufferance of these Colonies; and such is now the Necessity which constrains them to alter their former Systems of Government. The History of the present King of Great-Britain is a History of repeated Injuries and Usurpations, all having in direct Object the Establishment of an absolute Tyranny over these States. . . .

REVIEW QUESTIONS

1. Compare the views of John Locke with those of Thomas Hobbes regarding the character of human nature, political authority, and the right to rebellion.
2. Compare Locke's theory of natural rights with the principles stated in the American Declaration of Independence.

3 Attack on Religion

Christianity came under severe attack during the eighteenth century. The philosophes rejected Christian doctrines that seemed contrary to reason. Deism, the dominant religious outlook of the philosophes, taught that religion should accord with reason and natural law. To deists, it seemed reasonable to believe in God, for this superbly constructed universe required a creator in the same manner that a watch required a watchmaker. But, said the deists, after God had constructed the universe, he did not interfere in its operations; the universe was governed by mechanical laws. Deists denied that the Bible was God's work, rejected clerical authority, and dismissed miracles—like Jesus walking on water—as incompatible with natural law. To them, Jesus was not divine but an inspired teacher of morality. Many deists still considered themselves Christians; the clergy, however, viewed the deists' religious views with horror.

Voltaire
A PLEA FOR TOLERANCE AND REASON

François Marie Arouet (1694–1778), known to the world as Voltaire, was the recognized leader of the French Enlightenment. Few of the philosophes had a better mind, and none had a sharper wit. A relentless critic of the Old Regime (the social structure in prerevolutionary France), Voltaire attacked superstition, religious fanaticism and persecution, censorship, and other abuses of eighteenth-century French society. Spending more than two years in Great Britain, Voltaire acquired a great admiration for English liberty, toleration, commerce, and science. In *Letters Concerning the English Nation* (1733), he drew unfavorable comparisons between a progressive Britain and a reactionary France.

Voltaire's angriest words were directed against established Christianity, to which he attributed many of the ills of modern society. Voltaire regarded Christianity as "the Christ-worshiping superstition" that someday would be destroyed "by the weapons of reason." He rejected revelation and the church hierarchy and was repulsed by Christian intolerance, but he accepted Christian morality and believed in God as the prime mover who set the universe in motion.

The following passages compiled from Voltaire's works—grouped according to topic—provide insight into the outlook of the philosophes. The excerpts come from sources that include his *Treatise on Tolerance* (1763), *The Philosophical Dictionary* (1764), and *Commentary on the Book of Crime and Punishments* (1766).

TOLERANCE

It does not require any great art or studied elocution to prove that Christians ought to tolerate one another. I will go even further and say that we ought to look upon all men as our brothers. What! call a Turk, a Jew, and a Siamese, my brother? Yes, of course; for are we not all children of the same father, and the creatures of the same God?

———

What is tolerance? . . . We are all full of weakness and errors; let us mutually pardon our follies. This is the last law of nature. . . .

It is clear that every private individual who persecutes a man, his brother, because he is not of the same opinion, is a monster. . . .

Of all religions, the Christian ought doubtless to inspire the most tolerance, although hitherto the Christians have been the most intolerant of all men.

———

. . . Tolerance has never brought civil war; intolerance has covered the earth with carnage. . . .

What! Is each citizen to be permitted to believe and to think that which his reason rightly or wrongly dictates? He should indeed, provided that he does not disturb the public order; for it is not contingent on man to believe or not to believe; but it is contingent on him to respect the usages of his country; and if you say that it is a crime not to believe in the dominant religion, you accuse then yourself the first

Christians, your ancestors, and you justify those whom you accuse of having martyred them.

You reply that there is a great difference, that all religions are the work of men, and that the Apostolic Roman Catholic Church is alone the work of God. But in good faith, ought our religion because it is divine reign through hate, violence, exiles, usurpation of property, prisons, tortures, murders, and thanksgivings to God for these murders? The more the Christian religion is divine, the less it pertains to man to require it; if God made it, God will sustain it without you. You know that intolerance produces only hypocrites or rebels; what distressing alternatives! In short, do you want to sustain through executioners the religion of a God whom executioners have put to death and who taught only gentleness and patience?

———

I shall never cease, my dear sir, to preach tolerance from the housetops, despite the complaints of your priests and the outcries of ours, until persecution is no more. The progress of reason is slow, the roots of prejudice lie deep. Doubtless, I shall never see the fruits of my efforts, but they are seeds which may one day germinate.

DOGMA

. . . Is Jesus the Word? If He be the Word, did He emanate from God in time or before time? If He emanated from God, is He co-eternal and consubstantial with Him, or is He of a similar substance? Is He distinct from Him, or is He not? Is He made or begotten? Can He beget in His turn? Has He paternity? or productive virtue without paternity? Is the Holy Ghost made? or begotten? or produced? or proceeding from the Father? or proceeding from the Son? or proceeding from both? Can He beget? can He produce? is His hypostasis consubstantial with the hypostasis of the Father and the Son? and how is it that, having the same nature—the same essence as the Father and the Son, He cannot do the same things done by these persons who are Himself?

Assuredly, I understand nothing of this; no one has ever understood any of it, and that is why we have slaughtered one another.

The Christians tricked, cavilled, hated, and excommunicated one another, for some of these dogmas inaccessible to human intellect.

FANATICISM

Fanaticism is to superstition what delirium is to fever, what rage is to anger. He who has ecstasies and visions, who takes dreams for realities, and his own imaginations for prophecies is an enthusiast; he who reinforces his madness by murder is a fanatic. . . .

The most detestable example of fanaticism is that exhibited on the night of St. Bartholomew,[1] when the people of Paris rushed from house to house to stab, slaughter, throw out of the window, and tear in pieces their fellow citizens who did not go to mass.

There are some cold-blooded fanatics; such as those judges who sentence men to death for no other crime than that of thinking differently from themselves. . . .

Once fanaticism has infected a brain, the disease is almost incurable. I have seen convulsionaries who, while speaking of the miracles of Saint Paris [a fourth-century Italian bishop], gradually grew heated in spite of themselves. Their eyes became inflamed, their limbs shook, fury disfigured their face, and they would have killed anyone who contradicted them.

There is no other remedy for this epidemic malady than that philosophical spirit which, extending itself from one to another, at length softens the manners of men and prevents the access of the disease. For when the disorder has made any progress, we should, without loss of time, flee from it, and wait till the air has become purified.

———

[1] "St. Bartholomew" refers to the day of August 24, 1572, when the populace of Paris, instigated by King Charles IX at his mother's urging, began a week-long slaughter of Protestants.

PERSECUTION

What is a persecutor? He whose wounded pride and furious fanaticism arouse princes and magistrates against innocent men, whose only crime is that of being of a different opinion. "Impudent man! you have worshipped God; you have preached and practiced virtue; you have served man; you have protected the orphan, have helped the poor; you have changed deserts, in which slaves dragged on a miserable existence, into fertile lands peopled by happy families; but I have discovered that you despise me, and have never read my controversial work. You know that I am a rogue; that I have forged G[od]'s signature, that I have stolen. You might tell these things; I must anticipate you. I will, therefore, go to the confessor [spiritual counselor] of the prime minister, or the magistrate; I will show them, with outstretched neck and twisted mouth, that you hold an erroneous opinion in relation to the cells in which the Septuagint was studied; that you have even spoken disrespectfully ten years ago of Tobit's dog,[2] which you asserted to have been a spaniel, while I proved that it was a greyhound. I will denounce you as the enemy of God and man!" Such is the language of the persecutor; and if precisely these words do not issue from his lips, they are engraven on his heart with the pointed steel of fanaticism steeped in the bitterness of envy. . . .

O God of mercy! If any man can resemble that evil being who is described as ceaselessly employed in the destruction of your works, is it not the persecutor?

SUPERSTITION

In 1749 a woman was burned in the Bishopric of Würzburg [a city in central Germany], convicted of being a witch. This is an extraordinary phenomenon in the age in which we live. Is it possible that people who boast of their reformation and of trampling superstition under foot, who indeed supposed that they had reached the perfection of reason, could nevertheless believe in witchcraft, and this more than a hundred years after the so-called reformation of their reason?

In 1652 a peasant woman named Michelle Chaudron, living in the little territory of Geneva [a major city in Switzerland], met the devil going out of the city. The devil gave her a kiss, received her homage, and imprinted on her upper lip and right breast the mark that he customarily bestows on all whom he recognizes as his favorites. This seal of the devil is a little mark which makes the skin insensitive, as all the demonographical jurists of those times affirm.

The devil ordered Michelle Chaudron to bewitch two girls. She obeyed her master punctually. The girls' parents accused her of witchcraft before the law. The girls were questioned and confronted with the accused. They declared that they felt a continual pricking in certain parts of their bodies and that they were possessed. Doctors were called, or at least, those who passed for doctors at that time. They examined the girls. They looked for the devil's seal on Michelle's body—what the statement of the case called *satanic marks*. Into them they drove a long needle, already a painful torture. Blood flowed out, and Michelle made it known, by her cries, that satanic marks certainly do not make one insensitive. The judges, seeing no definite proof that Michelle Chaudron was a witch, proceeded to torture her, a method that infallibly produces the necessary proofs: this wretched woman, yielding to the violence of torture, at last confessed every thing they desired.

The doctors again looked for the satanic mark. They found a little black spot on one of her thighs. They drove in the needle. The torment of the torture had been so horrible that the poor creature hardly felt the needle; thus the crime was established. But as customs were becoming somewhat mild at that time, she was burned only after being hanged and strangled.

---

[2]The Septuagint, the version of the Hebrew Scriptures used by Saint Paul and other early Christians, was a Greek translation done by Hellenized Jews in Alexandria sometime in the late third or the second century B.C. *Tobit's dog* appears in the Book of Tobit, a Hebrew book contained in the Catholic version of the Bible.

In those days every tribunal of Christian Europe resounded with similar arrests. The [twigs] were lit everywhere for witches, as for heretics. People reproached the Turks most for having neither witches nor demons among them. This absence of demons was considered an infallible proof of the falseness of a religion.

A zealous friend of public welfare, of humanity, of true religion, has stated in one of his writings on behalf of innocence, that Christian tribunals have condemned to death over a hundred thousand accused witches. If to these judicial murders are added the infinitely superior number of massacred heretics, that part of the world will seem to be nothing but a vast scaffold covered with torturers and victims, surrounded by judges, guards and spectators.

Thomas Paine
THE AGE OF REASON

Exemplifying the deist outlook was Thomas Paine (1737–1809), an Englishman who moved to America in 1774. Paine's *Common Sense* (1776) was an eloquent appeal for American independence. Paine is also famous for *The Rights of Man* (1791–1792), in which he defended the French Revolution. In *The Age of Reason* (1794–1796), he denounced Christian mysteries, miracles, and prophecies as superstition and called for a natural religion that accorded with reason and science.

I believe in one God, and no more; and I hope for happiness beyond this life.

I believe in the equality of man; and I believe that religious duties consist in doing justice, loving mercy, and endeavoring to make our fellow-creatures happy.

But, lest it should be supposed that I believe many other things in addition to these, I shall, in the progress of this work, declare the things I do not believe, and my reasons for not believing them.

I do not believe in the creed professed by the Jewish church, by the Roman church, by the Greek church, by the Turkish church, by the Protestant church, nor by any church that I know of. My own mind is my own church. . . .

When Moses told the children of Israel that he received the two tablets of the [Ten] commandments from the hands of God, they were not obliged to believe him, because they had no other authority for it than his telling them so; and I have no other authority for it than some historian telling me so. The commandments carry no internal evidence of divinity with them; they contain some good moral precepts, such as any man qualified to be a lawgiver, or a legislator, could produce himself, without having recourse to supernatural intervention. . . .

When also I am told that a woman called the Virgin Mary, said, or gave out, that she was with child without any cohabitation with a man, and that her betrothed husband, Joseph, said that an angel told him so, I have a right to believe them or not; such a circumstance required a much stronger evidence than their bare word for it; but we have not even this—for neither Joseph nor Mary wrote any such matter themselves; it is only reported by others that *they said so*—it is hearsay upon hearsay, and I do not choose to rest my belief upon such evidence.

It is, however, not difficult to account for the credit that was given to the story of Jesus Christ being the son of God. He was born when the heathen mythology had still some fashion and repute in the world, and that mythology had prepared the people for the belief of such a story. Almost all the extraordinary men that lived under the heathen mythology were reputed to be the sons of some of their gods. It was not a new thing, at that time, to believe a man to have been celestially begotten; the intercourse of gods with women was then a matter of familiar opinion. Their Jupiter [chief Roman god], according to their accounts, had cohabited with hundreds: the story, therefore, had nothing in it either new, wonderful, or obscene; it was conformable to the opinions that then prevailed among the people called Gentiles, or Mythologists, and it was those people only that believed it. The Jews who had kept strictly to the belief of one God, and no more, and who had always rejected the heathen mythology, never credited the story. . . .

Nothing that is here said can apply, even with the most distant disrespect, to the real character of Jesus Christ. He was a virtuous and an amiable man. The morality that he preached and practised was of the most benevolent kind; and though similar systems of morality had been preached by Confucius [Chinese philosopher], and by some of the Greek philosophers, many years before; by the Quakers [members of the Society of Friends] since; and by many good men in all ages, it has not been exceeded by any. . . .

. . . The resurrection and ascension [of Jesus Christ], supposing them to have taken place, admitted of public and ocular demonstration, like that of the ascension of a balloon, or the sun at noon-day, to all Jerusalem at least. A thing which everybody is required to believe, requires that the proof and evidence of it should be equal to all, and universal; and as the public visibility of this last related act was the only evidence that could give sanction to the former part, the whole of it falls to the ground, because that evidence never was given. Instead of this, a small number of persons, not more than eight or nine, are introduced as proxies for the whole world, to say they saw it, and all the rest of the world are called upon to believe it. But it appears that Thomas [one of Jesus' disciples] did not believe the resurrection, and, as they say, would not believe without having ocular and manual demonstration himself. *So neither will I*, and the reason is equally as good for me, and for every other person, as for Thomas.

It is in vain to attempt to palliate or disguise this matter. The story, so far as relates to the supernatural part, has every mark of fraud and imposition stamped upon the face of it. Who were the authors of it is as impossible for us now to know, as it is for us to be assured that the books in which the account is related were written by the persons whose names they bear; the best surviving evidence we now have respecting this affair is the Jews. They are regularly descended from the people who lived in the times this resurrection and ascension is said to have happened, and they say, *it is not true.*

Baron d'Holbach
GOOD SENSE

More extreme than the deists were the atheists, who denied God's existence altogether. The foremost exponent of atheism was Paul-Henri Thiry, Baron d'Holbach (1723–1789), a prominent contributor to the *Encyclopedia*. Holbach hosted many leading intellectuals, including Diderot, Rousseau, and Condorcet (all represented later in this chapter), at his country estate outside of Paris. He regarded the idea of God as a product of ignorance, fear, and superstition and said that terrified by natural phenomena—storms, fire, floods—humanity's primitive ancestors attributed these occurrences to unseen spirits, whom they tried to appease through rituals. In denouncing religion, Holbach was also affirming core Enlightenment ideals—reason and freedom—as the following passage from *Good Sense* (1772) reveals.

In a word, whoever will deign to consult common sense upon religious opinions, and will bestow on this inquiry the attention that is commonly given to any objects we presume interesting, will easily perceive that those opinions have no foundation; that Religion is a mere castle in the air. Theology is but the ignorance of natural causes reduced to a system; a long tissue of fallacies and contradictions. In every country, it presents us with romances void of probability. . . .

Savage and furious nations, perpetually at war, adore, under divers names, some God, conformable to their ideas, that is to say, cruel, carnivorous, selfish, bloodthirsty. We find, in all the religions of the earth, "a God of armies," a "jealous God," an "avenging God," a "destroying God," a "God," who is pleased with carnage, and whom his worshippers consider it as a duty to serve to his taste. Lambs, bulls, children, men, heretics, infidels, kings, whole nations, are sacrificed to him. Do not the zealous servants of this barbarous God think themselves obliged even to offer up themselves as a sacrifice to him? Madmen may every where be seen who, after meditating upon their terrible God, imagine that to please him they must do themselves all possible injury, and inflict on themselves, for this honour, the most exquisite torments. The gloomy ideas more usefully formed of the Deity, far from consoling them under the evils of life, have every where disquieted their minds, and produced follies destructive to their happiness.

How could the human mind make any considerable progress, while tormented with frightful phantoms, and guided by men, interested in perpetuating its ignorance and fears? Man has been forced to vegetate in his primitive stupidity: he has been taught nothing but stories about invisible powers upon whom his happiness was supposed to depend. Occupied solely by his fears, and by unintelligible reveries, he has always been at the mercy of his priests, who have reserved to themselves the right of thinking for him, and directing his actions.

Thus man has remained a child without experience, a slave without courage, fearing to reason, and unable to extricate himself from the labyrinth, in which he has so long been wandering. He believes himself forced to bend under the yoke of his gods, known to him only by the fabulous accounts given by his ministers, who, after binding each unhappy mortal in the chains of his prejudice, remain his masters, or else abandon him defenceless to the absolute power of tyrants, no less terrible than the gods, of whom they are the representatives upon earth.

Oppressed by the double yoke of spiritual and temporal power, it has been impossible for the people to know and pursue their happiness. As Religion, so Politics and Morality became sacred things, which the profane were not permitted to handle. Men have had no other Morality, than what their legislators and priests brought down from the unknown regions of heaven. The human mind, confused by its theological opinions ceased to know its own powers, mistrusted experience, feared truth and disdained reason, in order to follow authority. Man has been a mere machine in the hands of tyrants and priests, who alone have had the right of directing his actions. Always treated as a slave, he has contracted the vices of a slave.

Such are the true causes of the corruption of morals, to which Religion opposes only ideal and ineffectual barriers. Ignorance and servitude are calculated to make men wicked and un-happy. Knowledge, Reason, and Liberty, can alone reform them, and make them happier. But every thing conspires to blind them and to confirm them in their errors. Priests cheat them, tyrants corrupt, the better to enslave them. Tyranny ever was, and ever will be, the true cause of man's depravity, and also of his habitual calamities. Almost always fascinated by religious fiction, poor mortals turn not their eyes to the natural and obvious causes of their misery; but attribute their vices to the imperfection of their natures, and their unhappiness to the anger of the gods. They offer up to heaven vows, sacrifices, and presents, to obtain the end of their sufferings, which in reality, are attributable only to the negligence, ignorance, and perversity of their guides, to the folly of their customs, to the unreasonableness of their laws, and above all, to the general want of knowledge. Let men's minds be filled with true ideas; let their reason be cultivated; let justice govern them; and there will be no need of opposing to the passions, such a feeble barrier, as the fear of the gods. Men will be good, when they are well instructed, well governed, and when they are punished or despised for the evil, and justly rewarded for the good, which they do to their fellow citizens.

To discover the true principles of Morality, men have no need of theology, of revelation, or of gods: They have need only of common sense. They have only to commune with themselves, to reflect upon their own nature, to consult their visible interests, to consider the objects of society, and of the individuals who compose it; and they will easily perceive, that virtue is advantageous, and vice disadvantageous to such beings as themselves. Let us persuade men to be just, beneficent, moderate, sociable; not because such conduct is demanded by the gods, but, because it is pleasure to men. Let us advise them to abstain from vice and crime; not because they will be punished in the other world, but because they will suffer for it in this.—*There are,* says a great man [Montesquieu], *means to prevent crimes, and these means are punishments; there are means to reform manners, and these means are good examples.* . . .

. . . Men are unhappy, only because they are ignorant; they are ignorant, only because every thing conspires to prevent their being enlightened; they are wicked, only because their reason is not sufficiently developed.

REVIEW QUESTIONS

1. What arguments did Voltaire offer in favor of religious toleration?
2. Why did Voltaire ridicule Christian theological disputation?
3. What did Voltaire mean by the term *fanaticism*? What examples did he provide? How was it to be cured?
4. What Christian beliefs did Thomas Paine reject? Why?
5. How did Baron d'Holbach's critique of religion affirm basic Enlightenment ideals?

4 Epistemology

The philosophes sought a naturalistic understanding of the human condition, one that examined human nature and society without reference to God's will. Toward this end, they sought to explain how the mind acquires knowledge; and as reformers, they stressed the importance of education in shaping a better person and a better society.

John Locke
ESSAY CONCERNING HUMAN UNDERSTANDING

In his *Essay Concerning Human Understanding* (1690), a work of immense significance in the history of philosophy, John Locke argued that human beings are not born with innate ideas (the idea of God and principles of good and evil, for example) divinely implanted in their minds. Rather, said Locke, the human mind at birth is a blank slate upon which are imprinted sensations derived from contact with the world. These sensations, combined with the mind's reflections on them, are the source of ideas. In effect, knowledge is derived from experience. In the tradition of Francis Bacon, Locke's epistemology (theory of knowledge) implied that people should not dwell on insoluble questions, particularly sterile theological issues, but should seek practical knowledge that promotes human happiness and enlightens human beings and gives them control over their environment.

Locke's empiricism, which aspired to useful knowledge and stimulated an interest in political and ethical questions that focused on human concerns, helped to mold the utilitarian and reformist spirit of the Enlightenment. If there are no innate ideas, said the philosophes, then human beings are not born with original sin, contrary to what Christians believed. All that individuals are derives from their particular experiences. If people are provided with a proper environment and education, they will become intelligent and productive citizens. "[O]f all the Men we meet with," wrote Locke, "Nine Parts of Ten are what they are, Good or Evil, useful or not, by their Education. 'Tis that which makes the great Difference in Mankind." This was how the reform-minded philosophes interpreted Locke. They preferred to believe that evil stemmed from faulty institutions and poor education, both of which could be remedied, rather than from a defective human nature. Excerpts from *Essay Concerning Human Understanding* follow.

Let us then suppose the mind to be, as we say, white paper, void of all characters, without any ideas:—How comes it to be furnished? Whence comes it by that vast store which the busy and boundless fancy of man has painted on it with an almost endless variety? Whence has it all the *materials* of reason and knowledge? To this I answer, in one word, from EXPERIENCE. In that all our knowledge is founded; and from that it ultimately derives itself. Our observation employed either, about external sensible objects or about the internal operations of our minds perceived and reflected on by ourselves, is that which supplies our understandings with all the *materials* of thinking. These two are the fountains of knowledge, from whence all the ideas we have, or can naturally have, do spring.

First, our Senses, conversant about particular sensible objects, do convey into the mind several distinct perceptions of things, according to those various ways wherein those objects do affect them. And thus we come by those *ideas* we have of *yellow, white, heat, cold, soft, hard, bitter, sweet*, and all those which we call sensible qualities; which when I say the senses convey into the mind, I mean, they from external objects convey into the mind what produces there those perceptions. This great source of most of the ideas we have, depending wholly upon our senses, and derived by them to the understanding, I call SENSATION.

Secondly, the other fountain from which experience furnisheth the understanding with ideas is,—the perception of the operations of our own mind within us, as it is employed about the ideas it has got. . . .

And such are *perception, thinking, doubting, believing, reasoning, knowing, willing*, and all the different actings of our own minds;—which we being conscious of, and observing in ourselves, do from these receive into our understandings as distinct ideas as we do from bodies affecting our senses. This source of ideas every man has wholly in himself; and though it be not sense, as having nothing to do with external objects, yet it is very like it, and might properly enough be called *internal sense*. But as I call the other Sensation, so I call this REFLECTION, the ideas it affords being such only as the mind gets by reflecting on its own operations within itself. By reflection then, in the following part of this discourse, I would be understood to mean, that notice which the mind takes of its own operations, and the manner of them, by reason whereof there come to be ideas of these operations in the understanding. These two, I say, viz. external material things, as the objects of SENSATION, and the operations of our own minds within, as the objects of REFLECTION, are to me the only originals from whence all our ideas take their beginnings. . . .

The understanding seems to me not to have the least glimmering of any ideas which it doth not receive from one of these two. *External objects* furnish the mind with the ideas of sensible qualities, which are all those different perceptions they produce in us; and *the mind* furnishes the understanding with ideas of its own operations.

These, when we have taken a full survey of them, and their several modes, (combinations, and relations,) we shall find to contain all our whole stock of ideas; and that we have nothing in our minds which did not come in one of these two ways. Let any one examine his own thoughts, and thoroughly search into his understanding; and then let him tell me, whether all the original ideas he has there, are any other than of the objects of his senses, or of the operations of his mind, considered as objects of his reflection. And how great a mass of knowledge soever he imagines to be lodged there, he will, upon taking a strict view, see that he has not any idea in his mind but what one of these two have imprinted;—though perhaps, with infinite variety compounded and enlarged by the understanding, as we shall see hereafter.

He that attentively considers the state of a child, at his first coming into the world, will have little reason to think him stored with plenty of ideas, that are to be the matter of his future knowledge. It is *by degrees* he comes to be furnished with them.

Claude Helvétius
ESSAYS ON THE MIND
AND A TREATISE ON MAN

Even more than did Locke, Claude-Adrien Helvétius (1715–1777) emphasized the importance of the environment in shaping the human mind. Disparities in intelligence and talent, said Helvétius, are due entirely to environmental conditions and not to inborn qualities. Since human beings are malleable and perfectible, their moral and intellectual growth depends on proper conditioning.

For this reason he called for political reforms, particularly the implementation of a program of enlightened public education.

In 1758 Helvétius published *Essays on the Mind*, which treated ethics in a purely naturalistic way. Shocked by his separation of morality from God's commands and from fear of divine punishment as well as by his attacks on the clergy, the authorities suppressed the book. His second major work, *A Treatise on Man*, was published posthumously in 1777. Apparently Helvétius wanted to avoid another controversy. The following passages from both works illustrate Helvétius' belief that "education makes us what we are."

ESSAYS ON THE MIND

The general conclusion of this discourse is, that genius is common, and the circumstances, proper to unfold it, very extraordinary. If we may compare what is profane to what is sacred, we may say in this respect, Many are called, but few are chosen.

The inequality observable among men, therefore, depends on the government under which they lie; on the greater or less happiness of the age in which they are born; on the education; on their desire of improvement, and on the importance of the ideas that are the subject of their contemplations.

The man of genius is then only produced by the circumstances in which he is placed.* Thus all the art of education consists in placing young men in such a concurrence of circumstances as are proper to unfold the buds of genius and virtue. [I am led to this conclusion by] the desire of promoting the happiness of mankind. I am convinced that a good education would diffuse light, virtue, and consequently, happiness in society; and that the opinion, that geniuses

and virtue are merely gifts of nature, is a great obstacle to the making any farther progress in the science of education, and in this respect is the great favourer of idleness and negligence. With this view, examining the effects which nature and education may have upon us, I have perceived that education makes us what we are; in consequence of which I have thought that it was the duty of a citizen to make known a truth proper to awaken the attention, with respect to the means of carrying this education to perfection.

A TREATISE ON MAN

Some maintain that, *The understanding is the effect of a certain sort of interior temperament and organization.*

Locke and I say: *The inequality in minds or understandings, is the effect of a known cause, and this cause is the difference of education.* . . .

Among the great number of questions treated of in this work, one of the most important was to determine whether genius, virtue, and talents, to which nations owe their grandeur and felicity, were the effect of the difference of . . . the organs of the five senses [that is, differences due to birth] . . . or if the same genius, the same virtues, and the same talents were the effect of education, over which the laws and the form of government are all powerful.

If I have proved the truth of the latter assertion, it must be allowed that the happiness of nations is in their own hands, and that it entirely depends on the greater or less interest they take in improving the science of education.

---

*The opinion I advance must appear very pleasing to the vanity of the greatest part of mankind, and therefore, ought to meet with a favourable reception. According to my principles, they ought not to attribute the inferiority of their abilities to the humbling cause of a less perfect [endowment], but to the education they have received, as well as to the circumstances in which they have been placed. Every man of moderate abilities, in conformity with my principles, has a right to think, that if he had been more favoured by fortune, if he had been born in a certain age or country, he [would have] himself been like the great men whose genius he is forced to admire.

REVIEW QUESTIONS

1. According to John Locke, knowledge originates in experience and has two sources—the senses and reflection. What does this mean, and what makes this view of knowledge so revolutionary?
2. How does Locke's view of the origin of knowledge compare to that of René Descartes? Which view do you favor, or can you suggest another alternative?
3. What is the relationship between Locke's theory of knowledge and his conceptions of human nature and politics?
4. In what way may Claude Helvétius be regarded as a disciple of John Locke, and how did he expand the significance of Locke's ideas?

---

5 Compendium of Knowledge

A 38-volume *Encyclopedia*, whose 150 or more contributors included leading Enlightenment thinkers, was undertaken in Paris during the 1740s as a monumental effort to bring together all human knowledge and to propagate Enlightenment ideas. The *Encyclopedia*'s numerous articles on science and technology and its limited coverage of theological questions attest to the new interests of eighteenth-century intellectuals. Serving as principal editor, Denis Diderot (1713–1784) steered the project through difficult periods, including the suspension of publication by French authorities. After the first two volumes were published, the authorities denounced the work for containing "maxims that would tend to destroy royal authority, foment a spirit of independence and revolt, . . . and lay the foundations for the corruption of morals and religion." In 1759, Pope Clement XIII condemned the *Encyclopedia* for having "scandalous doctrines {and} inducing scorn for religion." It required careful diplomacy and clever ruses to finish the project and still incorporate ideas considered dangerous by religious and governmental authorities. With the project's completion in 1772, Diderot and Enlightenment opinion triumphed over clerical censors and powerful elements at the French court.

Denis Diderot
ENCYCLOPEDIA

The *Encyclopedia* was a monument to the Enlightenment, as Diderot himself recognized. "This work will surely produce in time a revolution in the minds of man, and I hope that tyrants, oppressors, fanatics, and the intolerant will not gain thereby. We shall have served humanity." Some articles from the *Encyclopedia* follow.

Encyclopedia . . . In truth, the aim of an *encyclopedia* is to collect all the knowledge scattered over the face of the earth, to present its general outlines and structure to the men with whom we live, and to transmit this to those who will come after us, so that the work of past centuries may be useful to the following centuries, that our children, by becoming more educated, may at the same time become more virtuous and happier, and that we may not die without having deserved well of the human race. . . .

. . . We have seen that our *Encyclopedia* could only have been the endeavor of a philosophical century. . . .

I have said that it could only belong to a philosophical age to attempt an *encyclopedia*; and I have said this because such a work constantly demands more intellectual daring than is commonly found in [less courageous periods]. All things must be examined, debated, investigated without exception and without regard for anyone's feelings. . . . We must ride roughshod over all these ancient puerilities, overturn the barriers that reason never erected, give back to the arts and sciences the liberty that is so precious to them. . . . We have for quite some time needed a reasoning age when men would no longer seek the rules in classical authors but in nature. . . .

Fanaticism . . . is blind and passionate zeal born of superstitious opinions, causing people to commit ridiculous, unjust, and cruel actions, not only without any shame or remorse, but even with a kind of joy and comfort. *Fanaticism,* therefore, is only superstition put into practice. . . .

Fanaticism has done much more harm to the world than impiety. What do impious people claim? To free themselves of a yoke, while *fanatics* want to extend their chains over all the earth. Infernal zealomania! . . .

Government . . . The good of the people must be the great purpose of the *government*. The governors are appointed to fulfill it; and the civil constitution that invests them with this power is bound therein by the laws of nature and by the law of reason, which has determined that purpose in any form of *government* as the cause of its welfare. The greatest good of the people is its liberty. Liberty is to the body of the state what health is to each individual; without health man cannot enjoy pleasure; without liberty the state of welfare is excluded from nations. A patriotic governor will therefore see that the right

to defend and to maintain liberty is the most sacred of his duties. . . .

If it happens that those who hold the reins of *government* find some resistance when they use their power for the destruction and not the conservation of things that rightfully belong to the people, they must blame themselves, because the public good and the advantage of society are the purposes of establishing a *government*. Hence it necessarily follows that power cannot be arbitrary and that it must be exercised according to the established laws so that the people may know its duty and be secure within the shelter of laws, and so that governors at the same time should be held within just limits and not be tempted to employ the power they have in hand to do harmful things to the body politic. . . .

History . . . *On the usefullness of history.* The advantage consists of the comparison that a statesman or a citizen can make of foreign laws, morals, and customs with those of his country. This is what stimulates modern nations to surpass one another in the arts, in commerce, and in agriculture. The great mistakes of the past are useful in all areas. We cannot describe too often the crimes and misfortunes caused by absurd quarrels. It is certain that by refreshing our memory of these quarrels, we prevent a repetition of them. . . .

Humanity . . . is a benevolent feeling for all men, which hardly inflames anyone without a great and sensitive soul. This sublime and noble enthusiasm is troubled by the pains of other people and by the necessity to alleviate them. With these sentiments an individual would wish to cover the entire universe in order to abolish slavery, superstition, vice, and misfortune. . . .

Intolerance . . . Any method that would tend to stir up men, to arm nations, and to soak the earth with blood is impious.

It is impious to want to impose laws upon man's conscience: this is a universal rule of conduct. People must be enlightened and not constrained. . . .

What did Christ recommend to his disciples when he sent them among the Gentiles? Was it to kill or to die? Was it to persecute or to suffer? . . .

Which is the true voice of humanity, the persecutor who strikes or the persecuted who moans?

Peace   . . . War is the fruit of man's depravity; it is a convulsive and violent sickness of the body politic. . . .

If reason governed men and had the influence over the heads of nations that it deserves, we would never see them inconsiderately surrender themselves to the fury of war; they would not show that ferocity that characterizes wild beasts. . . .

Political Authority   No man has received from nature the right to command others. Liberty is a gift from heaven, and each individual of the same species has the right to enjoy it as soon as he enjoys the use of reason. . . .

The prince owes to his very subjects the *authority* that he has over them; and this *authority* is limited by the laws of nature and the state. The laws of nature and the state are the conditions under which they have submitted or are supposed to have submitted to its government. . . .

Moreover the government, although hereditary in a family and placed in the hands of one person, is not private property, but public property that consequently can never be taken from the people, to whom it belongs exclusively, fundamentally, and as a freehold. Consequently it is always the people who make the lease or the agreement: they always intervene in the contract that adjudges its exercise. It is not the state that belongs to the prince, it is the prince who belongs to the state: but it does rest with the prince to govern in the state, because the state has chosen him for that purpose: he has bound himself to the people and the administration of affairs, and they in their turn are bound to obey him according to the laws. . . .

The Press   [*press* includes newspapers, magazines, books, and so forth] . . . People ask if freedom of the *press* is advantageous or prejudicial to a state. The answer is not difficult. It is of the greatest importance to conserve this practice in all states founded on liberty. I would even say that the disadvantages of this liberty are so inconsiderable compared to its advantages that this ought to be the common right of the universe, and it is certainly advisable to authorize its practice in all governments. . . .

REVIEW QUESTIONS

1. Why was the publication of the *Encyclopedia* a vital step in the philosophes' hopes for reform?
2. To what extent were John Locke's political ideals reflected in the *Encyclopedia*?
3. Why was freedom of the press of such significance to the enlightened philosophes?

6 Rousseau: Political Reform

To the philosophes, advances in the arts were hallmarks of progress. However, Jean Jacques Rousseau argued that the accumulation of knowledge improved human understanding but corrupted the morals of human beings. In *A Discourse on the Arts and Sciences* (1750) and *A Discourse on the Origin of Inequality* (1755), Rousseau diagnosed the illnesses of modern civilization. He said that human nature, which was originally good, had been corrupted by society. As a result, he stated at the beginning of *The Social Contract* (1762), "Man is born free; and everywhere he is in chains." How can humanity be made moral and free again? In *The Social Contract*, Rousseau suggested one cure: reforming the political system. He argued that in the existing civil society the rich and powerful who controlled the state oppressed the majority. Rousseau admired the small, ancient Greek city-state (polis), where citizens participated actively and directly in public affairs. A small state modeled after the ancient Greek polis, said Rousseau, would be best able to resolve the tensions between individual freedom and the requirements of the collective community.

Jean Jacques Rousseau
THE SOCIAL CONTRACT

In the opening chapters of *The Social Contract*, Rousseau rejected the principle that one person has a natural authority over others. All legitimate authority, he said, stemmed from human traditions, not from nature. Rousseau had only contempt for absolute monarchy and in *The Social Contract* sought to provide a theoretical foundation for political liberty.

[To rulers who argued that they provided security for their subjects, Rousseau responded as follows:]

It will be said that the despot assures his subjects civil tranquillity. Granted; but what do they gain, if the wars his ambition brings down upon them, his insatiable avidity, and the vexatious conduct of his ministers press harder on them than their own dissensions would have done? What do they gain, if the very tranquillity they enjoy is one of their miseries? Tranquillity is found also in dungeons; but is that enough to make them desirable places to live in? The Greeks imprisoned in the cave of the Cyclops lived there very tranquilly, while they were awaiting their turn to be devoured. . . .

Even if each man could alienate himself [relinquish his freedom], he could not alienate his children: they are born men and free; their liberty belongs to them, and no one but they has the right to dispose of it. Before they come to years of discretion, the father can, in their name, lay down conditions for their preservation and well-being, but he cannot give them irrevocably

and without conditions: such a gift is contrary to the ends of nature, and exceeds the rights of paternity. It would therefore be necessary, in order to legitimize an arbitrary government, that in every generation the people should be in a position to accept or reject it; but, were this so, the government would be no longer arbitrary.

To renounce liberty is to renounce being a man, to surrender the rights of humanity and even its duties. For him who renounces everything no indemnity is possible. Such a renunciation is incompatible with man's nature; to remove all liberty from his will is to remove all morality from his acts.

Like Hobbes and Locke, Rousseau refers to an original social contract that terminates the state of nature and establishes the civil state. The clash of particular interests in the state of nature necessitates the creation of civil authority.

I suppose men to have reached the point at which the obstacles in the way of their preservation in the state of nature [are] greater than the resources at the disposal of each individual for his maintenance in that state. That primitive condition can then subsist no longer; and the human race would perish unless it changed its manner of existence. . . .

This sum of forces can arise only where several persons come together: but, as the force and liberty of each man are the chief instruments of his self-preservation, how can he pledge them without harming his own interests, and neglecting the care he owes to himself? This difficulty, in its bearing on my present subject, may be stated in the following terms:

"The problem is to find a form of association which will defend and protect with the whole common force the person and goods of each associate, and in which each, while uniting himself with all, may still obey himself alone, and remain as free as before." This is the fundamental problem of which the *Social Contract* provides the solution.

In entering into the social contract, the individual surrenders his rights to the community as a whole, which governs in accordance with the general will—an underlying principle that expresses what is best for the community. The general will is a plainly visible truth that is easily discerned by reason and common sense purged of self-interest and unworthy motives. For Rousseau, the general will by definition is always right and always works to the community's advantage. True freedom consists of obedience to laws that coincide with the general will. Obedience to the general will transforms an individual motivated by self-interest, appetites, and passions into a higher type of person—a citizen committed to the general good. What happens, however, if a person's private will—that is, expressions of particular, selfish interests—clashes with the general will? As private interests could ruin the body politic, says Rousseau, "whoever refuses to obey the general will shall be compelled to do so by the whole body." Thus Rousseau rejects entirely the Lockean principle that citizens possess rights independently of and against the state. Because Rousseau grants the sovereign (the people

constituted as a corporate body) virtually unlimited authority over the citizenry, some critics view him as a precursor of modern dictatorship.

The clauses of this contract . . . properly understood, may be reduced to one—the total alienation of each associate, together with all his rights, to the whole community; for, in the first place, as each gives himself absolutely, the conditions are the same for all; and, this being so, no one has any interest in making them burdensome to others.

Moreover, the alienation being without reserve, the union is as perfect as it can be, and no associate has anything more to demand: for, if the individuals retained certain rights, as there would be no common superior to decide between them and the public, each, being on one point his own judge, would ask to be so on all; the state of nature would thus continue, and the association would necessarily become inoperative or tyrannical.

Finally, each man, in giving himself to all, gives himself to nobody; and as there is no associate over which he does not acquire the same right as he yields others over himself, he gains an equivalent for everything he loses, and an increase of force for the preservation of what he has.

If then we discard from the social compact what is not of its essence, we shall find that it reduces itself to the following terms:

"Each of us puts his person and all his power in common under the supreme direction of the general will, and, in our corporate capacity, we receive each member as an indivisible part of the whole."

At once, in place of the individual personality of each contracting party, this act of association creates a moral and collective body, composed of as many members as the assembly contains voters, and receiving from this act its unity, its common identity, its life, and its will. . . .

In order then that the social compact may not be an empty formula, it tacitly includes the undertaking, which alone can give force to the rest, that whoever refuses to obey the general will shall be compelled to do so by the whole body. This means nothing less than that he will be forced to be free; for this is the condition which, by giving each citizen to his country, secures him against all personal dependence. In this lies the key to the working of the political machine; this alone legitimizes civil undertakings, which, without it, would be absurd, tyrannical, and liable to the most frightful abuses.

The passage from the state of nature to the civil state produces a very remarkable change in man, by substituting justice for instinct in his conduct, and giving his actions the morality they had formerly lacked. Then only, when the voice of duty takes the place of physical impulses and right of appetite, does man, who so far had considered only himself, find that he is forced to act on different principles, and to consult his reason before listening to his inclinations. Although, in this state, he deprives himself of some advantages which he got from nature, he gains in return others so great, his faculties are so stimulated and developed, his ideas so extended, his feelings so ennobled, and his whole soul so uplifted, that, did not the abuses of this new condition often degrade him below that which he left, he would be bound to bless continually the happy moment which took him from it forever, and, instead of a stupid and unimaginative animal, made him an intelligent being and a man.

Let us draw up the whole account in terms easily commensurable. What man loses by the social contract is his natural liberty and an unlimited right to everything he tries to get and succeeds in getting; what he gains is civil liberty and the proprietorship of all he possesses. If we are to avoid mistake in weighing one against the other, we must clearly distinguish natural liberty, which is bounded only by the strength of the individual, from civil liberty, which is limited by the general will; and possession, which is merely the effect of force or the right of the first occupier, from property, which can be founded only on a positive title.

We might, over and above all this, add, to what man acquires in the civil state, moral liberty, which alone makes him truly master of himself; for the mere impulse of appetite is slavery, while obedience to a law which we prescribe to ourselves is liberty. . . .

The first and most important deduction from the principles we have so far laid down is that the general will alone can direct the State according to the object for which it was instituted, i.e. the common good: for if the clashing of particular interests made the establishment of societies necessary, the agreement of these very interests made it possible. The common element in these different interests is what forms the social tie; and, were there no point of agreement between them all, no society could exist. It is solely on the basis of this common interest that every society should be governed. . . .

It follows from what has gone before that the general will is always right and tends to the public advantage; but it does not follow that the deliberations of the people are always equally correct. Our will is always for our own good, but we do not always see what that is; the people is never corrupted, but it is often deceived, and on such occasions only does it seem to will what is bad.

There is often a great deal of difference between the will of all and the general will; the latter considers only the common interest, while the former takes private interest into account, and is no more than a sum of particular wills: but take away from these same wills the pluses and minuses that cancel one another, and the general will remains as the sum of the differences.

If, when the people, being furnished with adequate information, held its deliberations, the citizens had no communication one with another, the grand total of the small differences would always give the general will, and the decision would always be good. But when factions arise, and partial associations are formed at the expense of the great association, the will of each of these associations becomes general in relation to its members, while it remains particular in relation to the State: it may then be said that there are no longer as many votes as there are men, but only as many as there are associations. The differences become less numerous and give a less general result. Lastly, when one of these associations is so great as to prevail over all the rest, the result is no longer a sum of small differences, but a single difference; in this case there is no longer a general will, and the opinion which prevails is purely particular.

It is therefore essential, if the general will is to be able to express itself, that there should be no partial society [factions] within the State, and that each citizen should think only his own thoughts. . . . But if there are partial societies, it is best to have as many as possible and to prevent them from being unequal. . . . These precautions are the only ones that can guarantee that the general will shall be always enlightened, and that the people shall in no way deceive itself.

REVIEW QUESTIONS

1. What did Jean Jacques Rousseau mean by the "general will"? What function did it serve in his political theory?
2. Why do some thinkers view Rousseau as a champion of democracy, whereas others see him as a spiritual precursor of totalitarianism?

---

7 Humanitarianism

A humanitarian spirit pervaded the philosophes' outlook. Showing a warm concern for humanity, they attacked militarism, slavery, religious persecution, torture, and other violations of human dignity, as can be seen in passages from the *Encyclopedia* and Voltaire's works earlier in this chapter. Through reasoned arguments they sought to make humankind recognize and renounce its own barbarity. In the following selections, other eighteenth-century reformers denounce judicial torture, the abuse of prisoners, and slavery.

Caesare Beccaria
ON CRIMES AND PUNISHMENTS

In *On Crimes and Punishments* (1764), Caesare Beccaria (1738–1794), an Italian economist and criminologist, condemned torture, commonly used to obtain confessions in many European countries, as irrational and inhuman.

The true relations between sovereigns and their subjects, and between nations, have been discovered. Commerce has been reanimated by the common knowledge of philosophical truths diffused by the art of printing, and there has sprung up among nations a tacit rivalry of industriousness that is most humane and truly worthy of rational beings. Such good things we owe to the productive enlightenment of this age. But very few persons have studied and fought against the cruelty of punishments and the irregularities of criminal procedures, a part of legislation that is as fundamental as it is widely neglected in almost all of Europe.

Very few persons have undertaken to demolish the accumulated errors of centuries by rising to general principles, curbing, at least, with the sole force that acknowledged truths possess, the unbounded course of ill-directed power which has continually produced a long and authorized example of the most cold-blooded barbarity. And yet the groans of the weak, sacrificed to cruel ignorance and to opulent indolence; the barbarous torments, multiplied with lavish and useless severity, for crimes either not proved or wholly imaginary; the filth and horrors of a prison, intensified by that cruellest tormentor of the miserable, uncertainty—all these ought to have roused that breed of magistrates who direct the opinions of men. . . .

But what are to be the proper punishments for such crimes?

Is the death-penalty really *useful* and *necessary* for the security and good order of society? Are torture and torments *just*, and do they attain the *end* for which laws are instituted? What is the best way to prevent crimes? Are the same punishments equally effective for all times? What influence have they on customary behavior? These problems deserve to be analyzed with that geometric precision which the mist of sophisms, seductive eloquence, and timorous doubt cannot withstand. If I could boast only of having been the first to present to Italy, with a little more clarity, what other nations have boldly written and are beginning to practice, I would account myself fortunate. But if, by defending the rights of man and of unconquerable truth, I should help to save from the spasm and agonies of death some wretched victim of tyranny or of no less fatal ignorance, the thanks and tears of one innocent mortal in his transports of joy would console me for the contempt of all mankind. . . .

A cruelty consecrated by the practice of most nations is torture of the accused during his trial, either to make him confess the crime or to clear up contradictory statements, or to discover accomplices, or to purge him of infamy in some metaphysical and incomprehensible way, or, finally, to discover other crimes of which he might be guilty but of which he is not accused.

No man can be called *guilty* before a judge has sentenced him, nor can society deprive him of public protection before it has been decided that he has in fact violated the conditions under which such protection was accorded him. What right is it, then, if not simply that of might, which empowers a judge to inflict punishment on a citizen while doubt still remains as to his guilt or innocence? Here is the dilemma, which is nothing new: the fact of the crime is either certain or uncertain; if certain, all that is due is the punishment established by the laws, and tortures are useless because the criminal's confession is useless; if uncertain, then one must not torture the innocent, for such, according to the laws, is a man whose crimes are not yet proved. . . .

. . . The impression of pain may become so great that, filling the entire sensory capacity of the tortured person, it leaves him free only to choose what for the moment is the shortest way of escape from pain. The response of the accused is then as inevitable as the impressions of fire and water. The sensitive innocent man will then confess himself guilty when he believes that, by so doing, he can put an end to his torment. Every difference between guilt and innocence disappears by virtue of the very means one pretends to be using to discover it. (Torture) is an infallible means indeed—for absolving robust scoundrels and for condemning innocent persons who happen to be weak. Such are the fatal defects of this so-called criterion of truth, a criterion fit for a cannibal. . . .

Of two men, equally innocent or equally guilty, the strong and courageous will be acquitted, the weak and timid condemned, by virtue of this rigorous rational argument: "I, the judge, was supposed to find you guilty of such and such a crime; you, the strong, have been able to resist the pain, and I therefore absolve you; you, the weak, have yielded, and I therefore condemn you. I am aware that a confession wrenched forth by torments ought to be of no weight whatsoever, but I'll torment you again if you don't confirm what you have confessed."

A strange consequence that necessarily follows from the use of torture is that the innocent person is placed in a condition worse than that of the guilty, for if both are tortured, the circumstances are all against the former. Either he confesses the crime and is condemned, or he is declared innocent and has suffered a punishment he did not deserve. The guilty man, on the contrary, finds himself in a favorable situation; that is, if, as a consequence of having firmly resisted the torture, he is absolved as innocent, he will have escaped a greater punishment by enduring a lesser one. Thus the innocent cannot but lose, whereas the guilty may gain. . . .

It would be superfluous to [cite] . . . the innumerable examples of innocent persons who have confessed themselves criminals because of the agonies of torture; there is no nation, there is no age that does not have its own to cite.

John Howard
PRISONS IN ENGLAND AND WALES

The efforts of John Howard (1726–1790), a British philanthropist, led Parliament in 1774 to enact prison reform. In 1777 Howard published *State of the Prisons in England and Wales*, excerpts from which follow.

There are prisons, into which whoever looks will, at first sight of the people confined there, be convinced, that there is some great error in the management of them: the sallow meagre countenances declare, without words, that they are very miserable: many who went in healthy, are in a few months changed to emaciated dejected objects. Some are seen pining under diseases, "*sick and in prison;*" expiring on the floors, in loathsome cells, of pestilential fevers, and . . . smallpox: victims, I must not say to the cruelty, but I will say to the inattention, of sheriffs, and gentlemen in the commission of the peace.

The cause of this distress is, that many prisons are scantily supplied, and some almost totally unprovided with the necessaries of life.

There are several Bridewells [prisons for those convicted of lesser crimes such as vagrancy and disorderly conduct] (to begin with them) in which prisoners have no allowance of FOOD at all. In some, the keeper farms what little is allowed them: and where he engages to supply each prisoner with one or two pennyworth of bread a day, I have known this shrunk to half, sometimes less than half the quantity, cut or broken from his own loaf.

It will perhaps be asked, does not their work maintain them? for every one knows that those offenders are committed to *hard labour*. The answer to that question, though true, will hardly be believed. There are very few Bridewells in which any work is done, or can be done. The prisoners have neither tools, nor materials of any kind; but spend their time in sloth, profaneness and debauchery, to a degree which, in some of those houses that I have seen, is extremely shocking. . . .

I have asked some keepers, since the late act for preserving the health of prisoners, why no care is taken of their sick: and have been answered, that the magistrates tell them *the act does not extend to Bridewells.*

In consequence of this, at the quarter sessions you see prisoners, covered (hardly covered) with rags; almost famished; and sick of diseases, which the discharged spread wherever they go, and with which those who are sent to the County-Gaols infect these prisons. . . .

Felons have in some Gaols two pennyworth of bread a day; in some three halfpennyworth; in some a pennyworth; in some a shilling a week. . . . I often weighed the bread in different prisons, and found the penny loaf 7½ to 8½ ounces, the other loaves in proportion. It is probable that when this allowance was fixed by its value, near double the quantity that the money will now purchase, might be bought for it: yet the allowance continues unaltered. . . .

This allowance being so far short of the cravings of nature, and in some prisons lessened by farming to the gaoler, many criminals are half starved: such of them as at their commitment were in health, come out almost famished, scarce able to move, and for weeks incapable of any labour.

Many prisons have NO WATER. This defect is frequent in Bridewells, and Town-Gaols. In the felons courts of some County-Gaols there is no water: in some places where there is water, prisoners are always locked up within doors, and have no more than the keeper or his servants think fit to bring them: in one place they are limited to three pints a day each—a scanty provision for drink and cleanliness! . . .

From hence any one may judge of the probability there is against the health and life of prisoners, crowded in close rooms, cells, and subterraneous dungeons, for fourteen or sixteen hours out of the four and twenty. In some of those caverns the floor is very damp: in others there is sometimes an inch or two of water; and the straw, or bedding is laid on such floors, seldom on barrack bedsteads. . . . Some Gaols have no SEWERS; and in those that have, if they be not properly attended to, they are, even to a visitant, offensive beyond expression: how noxious then to people constantly confined in those prisons!

In many Gaols, and in most Bridewells, there is no allowance of STRAW for prisoners to sleep on; and if by any means they get a little, it is not changed for months together, so that it is almost worn to dust. Some lie upon rags, others upon the bare floors. When I have complained of this to the keepers, their justification has been, "The county allows no straw; the prisoners have none but at my cost."

The evils mentioned hitherto affect the *health* and *life* of prisoners: I have now to complain of what is pernicious to their MORALS; and that is, the confining all sorts of prisoners together: debtors and felons; men and women; the young beginner and the old offender: and with all these, in some counties, such as are guilty of misdemeanors only. . . .

In some Gaols you see (and who can see it without pain?) boys of twelve or fourteen eagerly listening to the stories told by practised and experienced criminals, of their adventures, successes, stratagems, and escapes.

I must here add, that in some few Gaols are confined idiots and lunatics. . . . The insane, where they are not kept separate, disturb and terrify other prisoners. No care is taken of them, although it is probable that by medicines, and proper regimen, some of them might be restored to their senses, and to usefulness in life. . . .

A cruel custom obtains in most of our Gaols, which is that of the prisoners demanding of a new comer GARNISH, FOOTING, or (as it is called in some London Gaols) CHUMMAGE. "Pay or strip," are the fatal words. I say *fatal*, for they are so to some; who having no money, are obliged to give up part of their scanty apparel; and if they have no bedding or straw to sleep on, contract diseases, which I have known to prove mortal.

Loading prisoners with HEAVY IRONS, which make their walking, and even lying down to sleep, difficult and painful, is another custom which I cannot but condemn. In some County-Gaols the *women* do not escape this severity.

Denis Diderot
ENCYCLOPEDIA
"MEN AND THEIR LIBERTY ARE NOT
OBJECTS OF COMMERCE. . . ."

Montesquieu, Voltaire, David Hume, Benjamin Franklin, Thomas Paine, and several other philosophes condemned slavery and the slave trade. In Book 15 of *The Spirit of the Laws* (1748), Montesquieu scornfully refuted all justifications for slavery. Ultimately, he said, slavery, which violates the fundamental principle of justice underlying the universe, derived from base human desires to dominate and exploit other human beings. In 1780, Paine helped draft the act abolishing slavery in Pennsylvania. Five years earlier, he wrote:

> Our Traders in Men . . . must know the wickedness of that SLAVETRADE, if they attend to reasoning, or the dictates of their own hearts, and {those who} shun and stifle all these willfully sacrifice Conscience, and the character of integrity to that Golden Idol. . . . Most shocking of all is the alleging the sacred Scriptures to favour this wicked practice.

The *Encyclopedia* denounced slavery as a violation of the individual's natural rights.

[This trade] is the buying of unfortunate Negroes by Europeans on the coast of Africa to use as slaves in their colonies. This buying of Negroes, to reduce them to slavery, is one business that violates religion, morality, natural laws, and all the rights of human nature.

Negroes, says a modern Englishman full of enlightenment and humanity, have not become slaves by the right of war; neither do they deliver themselves voluntarily into bondage, and consequently their children are not born slaves. Nobody is unaware that they are bought from their own princes, who claim to have the right to dispose of their liberty, and that traders have them transported in the same way as their other goods, either in their colonies or in America, where they are displayed for sale.

If commerce of this kind can be justified by a moral principle, there is no crime, however atrocious it may be, that cannot be made legitimate. Kings, princes, and magistrates are not the proprietors of their subjects: they do not, therefore, have the right to dispose of their liberty and to sell them as slaves.

On the other hand, no man has the right to buy them or to make himself their master. Men and their liberty are not objects of commerce; they can be neither sold nor bought nor paid for at any price. We must conclude from this that a man whose slave has run away should only blame himself, since he had acquired for money illicit goods whose acquisition is prohibited by all the laws of humanity and equity.

There is not, therefore, a single one of these unfortunate people regarded only as slaves who does not have the right to be declared free, since he has never lost his freedom, which he could not lose and which his prince, his father, and any person whatsoever in the world had not the power to dispose of. Consequently the sale that has been completed is invalid in itself. This Negro does not divest himself and can never divest himself of his natural right; he carries it everywhere with him, and he can demand everywhere that he be allowed to enjoy it. It is, therefore, patent inhumanity on the part of judges in free countries where he is transported, not to emancipate him immediately by declaring him free, since he is their fellow man, having a soul like them.

Marquis de Condorcet
THE EVILS OF SLAVERY

Marie Jean Antoine-Nicolas Caritat, Marquis de Condorcet (1743–1794), was a French mathematician and historian of science. He contributed to the *Encyclopedia* and campaigned actively for religious toleration and the abolition of slavery. In 1788, Condorcet helped found The Society of the Friends of Blacks, which attacked slavery. Seven years earlier he had published a pamphlet denouncing slavery as a violation of human rights. Following are excerpts from this pamphlet.

"Dedicatory Epistle to the Negro Slaves"

My Friends,

Although I am not the same color as you, I have always regarded you as my brothers. Nature formed you with the same spirit, the same reason, the same virtues as whites. . . . Your tyrants will reproach me with uttering only commonplaces and having nothing but chimerical [unrealistic] ideas: indeed, nothing is more common than the maxims of humanity and justice; nothing is more chimerical than to propose to men that they base their conduct on them.

Reducing a man to slavery, buying him, selling him, keeping him in servitude: these are truly crimes, and crimes worse than theft. In effect, they take from the slave, not only all forms of property but also the ability to acquire it, the control over his time, his strength, of everything that nature has given him to maintain his life and his needs. To this wrong they add that of taking from the slave the right to dispose of his own person. . . .

It follows from our principles that the inflexible justice to which kings and nations are subject like their citizens requires the destruction of slavery. We have shown that this destruction will harm neither commerce nor the wealth of a nation because it would not result in any decrease in cultivation. We have shown that the master had no right over his slave; that the act of keeping him in servitude is not the enjoyment of a property right but a crime; that in freeing the slave the law does not attack property but rather ceases to tolerate an action which it should have punished with the death penalty. The sovereign therefore owes no compensation to the master of slaves just as he owes none to a thief whom a court judgment has deprived of the possession of a stolen good. The public tolerance of a crime may make punishment impossible but it cannot grant a real right to the profit from the crime.

REVIEW QUESTIONS

1. What were Caesare Beccaria's arguments against the use of torture in judicial proceedings? In your opinion, can torture ever be justified?
2. What ideals of the Enlightenment philosophes are reflected in Beccaria's arguments?
3. List the abuses in British jails that John Howard disclosed.
4. How did Condorcet demonstrate the humanitarianism of the Enlightenment?
5. How did Condorcet show that slaves' rights are destroyed?

8   Literature as Satire: Critiques of European Society

The French philosophes, particularly Voltaire, Diderot, and Montesquieu, often used the medium of literature to decry the ills of their society and advance Enlightenment values. In the process they wrote satires that are still read and admired for their literary merits and insights into human nature and society. The eighteenth century also saw the publication of Jonathan Swift's *Gulliver's Travels* (1726), one of the greatest satirical works written in English.

Voltaire
CANDIDE

In *Candide* (1759), Voltaire's most important work of fiction, he explored the question: Why do the innocent suffer? And because Voltaire delved into this mystery with wit, irony, satire, and wisdom, the work continues to be hailed as a literary masterpiece.

The illegitimate Candide (son of the sister of the baron in whose castle he lives in Westphalia) is tutored by the philosopher Pangloss, a teacher of "metaphysico-theologo-cosmolonigology": that is, a person who speaks nonsense. The naive Pangloss clings steadfastly to the belief that all that happens, even the worst misfortunes, are for the best.

Candide falls in love with Cunegund, the beautiful daughter of the baron of the castle; but the baron forcibly removes Candide from the castle when he discovers their love. Candide subsequently suffers a series of disastrous misfortunes, but he continues to adhere to the belief firmly instilled in him by Pangloss, that everything happens for the best and that this is the best of all possible worlds. Later, he meets an old beggar, who turns out to be his former teacher, Pangloss, who tells Candide that the Bulgarians have destroyed the castle and killed Cunegund and her family. Candide and Pangloss then travel together to Lisbon, where they survive the terrible earthquake, only to have Pangloss hanged (but he escapes death) by the Inquisition. Soon thereafter, Candide is reunited with Cunegund, who, despite having been raped and sold into prostitution, has not been killed. Following further adventures and misfortunes, the lovers are again separated when Cunegund is captured by pirates.

After experiencing more episodes of human wickedness and natural disasters, Candide abandons the philosophy of optimism, declaring "that we must cultivate our gardens." By this Voltaire meant that we can never achieve utopia, but neither should we descend to the level of brutes. Through purposeful and honest work, and the deliberate pursuit of virtue, we can improve, however modestly, the quality of human existence.

The following excerpt from Candide starts with Candide's first misfortune after being driven out of the castle at Westphalia. In addition to ridiculing philosophical optimism, Voltaire expresses his revulsion for militarism.

CHAPTER II
What Befell Candide Among the Bulgarians

Candide, thus driven out of this terrestrial paradise, wandered a long time, without knowing where he went; sometimes he raised his eyes, all bedewed with tears, toward Heaven, and sometimes he cast a melancholy look toward the magnificent castle where dwelt the fairest of young baronesses. He laid himself down to sleep in a furrow, heartbroken and supperless. The snow fell in great flakes, and, in the morning when he awoke, he was almost frozen to death; however, he made shift to crawl to the next town, which was called Waldberghoff-trarbk-dikdorff, without a penny in his pocket, and half dead with hunger and fatigue. He took up his stand at the door of an inn. He had not been long there before two men dressed in blue fixed their eyes steadfastly upon him.

"Faith, comrade," said one of them to the other, "yonder is a well-made young fellow, and of the right size."

Thereupon they went up to Candide, and with the greatest civility and politeness invited him to dine with them.

"Gentlemen," replied Candide, with a most engaging modesty, "you do me much honor, but, upon my word, I have no money."

"Money, sir!" said one of the men in blue to him. "Young persons of your appearance and merit never pay anything. Why, are you not five feet five inches high?"

"Yes, gentlemen, that is really my size," replied he with a low bow.

"Come then, sir, sit down along with us. We will not only pay your reckoning, but will never suffer such a clever young fellow as you to want money. Mankind were born to assist one another."

"You are perfectly right, gentlemen," said Candide; "that is precisely the doctrine of Master Pangloss; and I am convinced that everything is for the best."

His generous companions next entreated him to accept a few crowns, which he readily complied with, at the same time offering them his note for the payment, which they refused, and sat down to table.

"Have you not a great affection for—"

"Oh, yes!" he replied. "I have a great affection for the lovely Miss Cunegund."

"Maybe so," replied one of the men, "but that is not the question! We are asking you whether you have not a great affection for the King of the Bulgarians?"*

"For the King of the Bulgarians?" said Candide. "Not at all. Why, I never saw him in my life."

"Is it possible! Oh, he is a most charming king! Come, we must drink his health."

"With all my heart, gentlemen," Candide said, and he tossed off his glass.

"Bravo!" cried the blues. "You are now the support, the defender, the hero of the Bulgarians; your fortune is made; you are on the high road to glory."

So saying, they put him in irons and carried him away to the regiment. There he was made to wheel about to the right, to the left, to draw his ramrod, to return his ramrod, to present, to fire, to march, and they gave him thirty blows with a cane. The next day he performed his exercise a little better, and they gave him but twenty. The day following he came with ten and was looked upon as a young fellow of surprising genius by all his comrades.

Candide was struck with amazement and could not for the soul of him conceive how he came to be a hero. One fine spring morning, he took it into his head to take a walk, and he marched straight forward, conceiving it to be a privilege of the human species, as well as of the brute creation, to make use of their legs how and when they pleased. He had not gone above two leagues when he was overtaken by four other heroes, six feet high, who bound him neck and heels, and carried him to a dungeon. A court-martial sat upon him, and he was asked which he liked best, either to run the gauntlet six and thirty times through the

———
*I.e., Prussians.

whole regiment, or to have his brains blown out with a dozen musket balls. In vain did he remonstrate to them that the human will is free, and that he chose neither. They obliged him to make a choice, and he determined, in virtue of that divine gift called free will, to run the gauntlet six and thirty times. He had gone through his discipline twice, and the regiment being composed of two thousand men, they composed for him exactly four thousand strokes, which laid bare all his muscles and nerves, from the nape of his neck to his rump. As they were preparing to make him set out a third time, our young hero, unable to support it any longer, begged as a favor they would be so obliging as to shoot him through the head. The favor being granted, a bandage was tied over his eyes, and he was made to kneel down. At that very instant, his Bulgarian Majesty, happening to pass by, inquired into the delinquent's crime, and being a prince of great penetration, he found, from what he heard of Candide, that he was a young meta-physician, entirely ignorant of the world. And, therefore, out of his great clemency, he condescended to pardon him, for which his name will be celebrated in every journal, and in every age. A skillful surgeon made a cure of Candide in three weeks by means of emollient unguents prescribed by Dioscorides. His sores were now skinned over, and he was able to march when the King of the Bulgarians gave battle to the King of the Abares.[†]

CHAPTER III

How Candide Escaped from the Bulgarians, and What Befell Him Afterwards

Never was anything so gallant, so well accoutered, so brilliant, and so finely disposed as the two armies. The trumpets, fifes, oboes, drums, and cannon, made such harmony as never was heard in hell itself. The entertainment began by a discharge of cannon, which, in the twinkling of an eye, laid flat about six thousand men on each side. The musket bullets swept away, out of the best of all possible worlds, nine or ten thousand scoundrels that infested its surface. The bayonet was next the sufficient reason for the deaths of several thousands. The whole might amount to thirty thousand souls. Candide trembled like a philosopher and concealed himself as well as he could during this heroic butchery.

At length, while the two kings were causing *Te Deum*[‡] to be sung in each of their camps, Candide took a resolution to go and reason somewhere else upon causes and effects. After passing over heaps of dead or dying men, the first place he came to was a neighboring village, in the Abarian territories, which had been burned to the ground by the Bulgarians in accordance with international law. Here lay a number of old men covered with wounds, who beheld their wives dying with their throats cut, and hugging their children to their breasts all stained with blood. There several young virgins, whose bellies had been ripped open after they had satisfied the natural necessities of the Bulgarian heroes, breathed their last; while others, half burned in the flames, begged to be dispatched out of the world. The ground about them was covered with the brains, arms, and legs of dead men.

Candide made all the haste he could to another village, which belonged to the Bulgarians, and there he found that the heroic Abares had treated it in the same fashion. From thence continuing to walk over palpitating limbs or through ruined buildings, at length he arrived beyond the theater of war, with a little provision in his pouch, and Miss Cunegund's image in his heart.

[†]I.e., French. The Seven Years' War had begun in 1756.

[‡]A Te Deum ("We praise thee, God") is a special liturgical hymn praising and thanking God for granting some special favor, like a military victory or the end of a war.

Denis Diderot
SUPPLEMENT TO THE VOYAGE
OF BOUGAINVILLE

Enlightenment thinkers often used examples from the non-European world in order to attack European values that seemed contrary to nature and reason. Denis Diderot reviewed Louis Antoine de Bougainville's *Voyage Around the World* (1771) and in the next year wrote *Supplement to the Voyage of Bougainville* (published posthumously in 1796). In this work, Diderot explored some ideas, particularly the sex habits of Tahitians, treated by the French explorer. Diderot also denounced European imperialism and the exploitation of non-Europeans, and questioned traditional Christian sexual standards. In *Supplement*, Diderot constructed a dialogue between a Tahitian (Orou), who possesses the wisdom of a French philosophe, and a chaplain, whose defense of Christian sexual mores reveals Diderot's critique of the Christian view of human nature. Diderot thus used a representative of an alien culture to attack those European customs and beliefs that the philosophes detested. In the opening passage, before Orou's dialogue, a Tahitian elder rebukes Bougainville and his companions for bringing the evils of European civilization to his island.

"We [Tahitians] are free—but see where you [Europeans] have driven into our earth the symbol of our future servitude. You are neither a god nor a devil—by what right, then, do you enslave people? Orou! You who understand the speech of these men, tell every one of us, as you have told me, what they have written on that strip of metal—'This land belongs to us.' This land belongs to you! And why? Because you set foot in it? If some day a Tahitian should land on your shores, and if he should engrave on one of your stones or on the bark of one of your trees: 'This land belongs to the people of Tahiti,' what would you think? You are stronger than we are! And what does that signify? When one of our lads carried off some of the miserable trinkets with which your ship is loaded, what an uproar you made, and what revenge you took! And at that very moment you were plotting, in the depths of your hearts, to steal a whole country! You are not slaves; you would suffer death rather than be enslaved, yet you want to make slaves of us! Do you believe, then, that the Tahitian does not know how to die in defense of his liberty? This Tahitian, whom you want to treat as a chattel, as a dumb animal—this Tahitian is your brother. You are both children of Nature—what right do you have over him that he does not have over you?

"You came; did we attack you? Did we plunder your vessel? Did we seize you and expose you to the arrows of our enemies? Did we force you to work in the fields alongside our beasts of burden? We respected our own image in you. Leave us our own customs, which are wiser and more decent than yours. We have no wish to barter what you call our ignorance for your useless knowledge. We possess already all that is good or necessary for our existence. Do we merit your scorn because we have not been able to create superfluous wants for ourselves? When we are hungry, we have something to eat; when we are cold, we have clothing to put on. You have been in our huts—what is lacking there, in your opinion? You are welcome to drive yourselves as hard as you please in pursuit of what you call the comforts of life, but allow sensible people to stop when they see they have nothing to gain but imaginary benefits from the continuation of their painful labors. If you persuade us to go beyond the bounds of strict necessity, when shall we come to the end of our labor? When shall we have time for enjoyment? We have reduced our daily and yearly labors to the least possible amount, because to us nothing seemed more desirable than leisure. Go and bestir yourselves in your own country; there you may torment yourselves as much as you like; but leave us in peace, and do not fill our heads with a hankering after your false needs and imaginary virtues. Look at these men—see how healthy, straight and strong they are. See these women—how straight, healthy, fresh and lovely they are. Take this bow in your hands—it is my own—and call one, two, three, four of your comrades to help you try to bend it. I can bend it myself. I work the soil, I climb mountains, I make my way through the dense forest, and I can run four leagues [about 12 miles] on the plain in less than an hour. Your young comrades have been hard put to it to keep up with me, and yet I have passed my ninetieth year. . . .

"Woe to this island! Woe to all the Tahitians now living, and to all those yet to be born, woe from the day of your arrival! We used to know but one disease—the one to which all men, all animals and all plants are subject—old age. But you have brought us a new one [venereal disease]: you have infected our blood. We shall perhaps be compelled to exterminate with our own hands some of our young girls, some of our women, some of our children, those who have lain with your women, those who have lain with your men. Our fields will be spattered with the foul blood that has passed from your veins into ours. Or else our children, condemned to die, will nourish and perpetuate the evil disease that you have given their fathers and mothers, transmitting it forever to their descendants." . . .

Before the arrival of Christian Europeans, lovemaking was natural and enjoyable. Europeans introduced an alien element, guilt.

But a while ago, the young Tahitian girl blissfully abandoned herself to the embraces of a Tahitian youth and awaited impatiently the day when her mother, authorized to do so by her having reached the age of puberty, would remove her veil and uncover her breasts. She was proud of her ability to excite men's desires, to attract the amorous looks of strangers, of her own relatives, of her own brothers. In our presence, without shame, in the center of a throng of innocent Tahitians who danced and played the flute, she accepted the caresses of the young man whom her young heart and the secret promptings of her senses had marked out for her. The notion of crime and the fear of disease have come among us only with your coming. Now our enjoyments, formerly so sweet, are attended with guilt and terror. That man in black [a priest], who stands near to you and listens to me, has spoken to our young men, and I know not what he has said to our young girls, but our youths are hesitant and our girls blush. Creep away into the dark forest, if you wish, with the perverse companion of your pleasures, but allow the good, simple Tahitians to reproduce themselves without shame under the open sky and in broad daylight.

In the following conversation between Orou and the chaplain, Christian sexual mores and the concept of God are questioned. Orou addresses the chaplain.

[OROU] "You are young and healthy and you have just had a good supper. He who sleeps alone, sleeps badly; at night a man needs a woman at his side. Here is my wife and here are my daughters. Choose whichever one pleases you most, but if you would like to do me a favor, you will give your preference to my youngest girl, who has not yet had any children."

The mother said: "Poor girl! I don't hold it against her. It's no fault of hers."

The chaplain replied that his religion, his holy orders, his moral standards and his sense of decency all prevented him from accepting Orou's invitation.

Orou answered: "I don't know what this thing is that you call 'religion,' but I can only have a low opinion of it because it forbids you to partake of an innocent pleasure to which Nature, the sovereign mistress of us all, invites everybody. It seems to prevent you from bringing one of your fellow creatures into the world, from doing a favor asked of you by a father, a mother and their children, from repaying the kindness of a host, and from enriching a nation by giving it an additional citizen. I don't know what it is that you call 'holy orders,' but your chief duty is to be a man and to show gratitude. . . . I hope that you will not persist in disappointing us. Look at the distress you have caused to appear on the faces of these four women—they are afraid you have noticed some defect in them that arouses your distaste. But even if that were so, would it not be possible for you to do a good deed and have the pleasure of honoring one of my daughters in the sight of her sisters and friends? Come, be generous!"

THE CHAPLAIN "You don't understand—it's not that. They are all four of them equally beautiful. But there is my religion! My holy orders! . . .

. . . [God] spoke to our ancestors and gave them laws; he prescribed to them the way in which he wishes to be honored; he ordained that certain actions are good and others he forbade them to do as being evil."

OROU "I see. And one of these evil actions which he has forbidden is that of a man who goes to bed with a woman or girl. But in that case, why did he make two sexes?"

THE CHAPLAIN "In order that they might come together—but only when certain conditions are satisfied and only after certain initial ceremonies have been performed. By virtue of these ceremonies one man belongs to one woman and only to her; one woman belongs to one man and only to him."

OROU "For their whole lives?"

THE CHAPLAIN "For their whole lives."

OROU "So that if it should happen that a woman should go to bed with some man who was not her husband, or some man should go to bed with a woman that was not his wife . . . but that could never happen because the workman [God] would know what was going on, and since he doesn't like that sort of thing, he wouldn't let it occur."

THE CHAPLAIN "No. He lets them do as they will, and they sin against the law of God (for that is the name by which we call the great workman) and against the law of the country; they commit a crime."

OROU "I should be sorry to give offense by anything I might say, but if you don't mind, I'll tell you what I think."

THE CHAPLAIN "Go ahead."

OROU "I find these strange precepts contrary to nature, and contrary to reason. . . . Furthermore, your laws seem to me to be contrary to the general order of things. For in truth is there anything so senseless as a precept that forbids us to heed the changing impulses that are inherent in our being, or commands that require a degree of constancy which is not possible, that violate the liberty of both male and female by chaining them perpetually to one another? Is there anything more unreasonable than this perfect fidelity that would restrict us, for the enjoyment of pleasures so capricious, to a single partner—than an oath of immutability taken by two individuals made of flesh and blood under a sky that is not the same for a moment, in a cavern that threatens to collapse upon them, at the foot of a cliff that is crumbling into dust, under a tree that is withering, on a bench of stone that is being worn away? Take my word for it, you have reduced human beings to a worse condition than that of the animals. I don't know what your great workman is, but I am very happy that he never spoke to our forefathers, and I hope that he never speaks to our children, for if he does, he may tell them the same foolishness, and they may be foolish enough to believe it." . . .

OROU "Are monks faithful to their vows of sterility?"

THE CHAPLAIN "NO."

OROU "I was sure of it. Do you also have female monks?"

THE CHAPLAIN "Yes."

OROU "As well behaved as the male monks?"

THE CHAPLAIN "They are kept more strictly in seclusion, they dry up from unhappiness and die of boredom."

OROU "So nature is avenged for the injury done to her! Ugh! What a country! If everything is managed the way you say, you are more barbarous than we are."

Montesquieu
THE PERSIAN LETTERS

Like other philosophes, Charles Louis de Secondat, baron de la Brède et de Montesquieu (1689–1755), was an ardent reformer who used learning, logic, and wit to denounce the abuses of his day. His principal work, *The Spirit of the Laws* (1748), was a contribution to political liberty. To safeguard liberty from despotism, which he regarded as a pernicious form of government that institutionalizes cruelty and violence, Montesquieu advocated the principle of separation of powers—that is, the legislative, executive, and judiciary should not be in the hands of one person or body. Montesquieu's humanitarianism and tolerant spirit is also seen in an earlier work, *The Persian Letters* (1721), published anonymously in Holland. In the guise of letters written by imaginary Persian travelers in Europe, Montesquieu makes a statement: He denounces French absolutism, praises English parliamentary government, and attacks religious persecution, as in this comment on the Spanish Inquisition excerpted below.

LETTER XXIX

Rica to Ibben, at Smyrna

. . . I have heard that in Spain and Portugal there are dervishes who do not understand a joke, and who have a man burned as if he were straw. Whoever falls into the hands of these men is fortunate only if he has always prayed to God with little bits of wood in hand, has worn two bits of cloth attached to two ribbons, and has sometimes been in a province called Galicia!* Otherwise, the poor

devil is really in trouble. Even though he swears like a pagan that he is orthodox, they may not agree, and burn him for a heretic. It is useless for him to submit distinctions, for he will be in ashes before they even consider giving him a hearing.

Other judges presume the innocence of the accused; these always presume him guilty. In doubt they hold to the rule of inclining to severity, evidently because they consider mankind as evil. On the other hand, however, they hold such a high opinion of men that they judge them incapable of lying, for they accept testimony from deadly enemies, notorious women, and people living by some infamous profession. In passing

---

*The references are to a rosary, a scapular, and the pilgrimage shrine of St. James of Campostello in the Spanish province of Galicia.

sentence, the judges pay those condemned a little compliment, telling them that they are sorry
to see them so poorly dressed in their brimstone
shirts,[†] that the judges themselves are gentle
men who abhor bloodletting, and are in despair
at having to condemn them. Then, to console
themselves, they confiscate to their own profit all
the possessions of these poor wretches.

Happy the land inhabited by the children of
the prophets! There these sad spectacles are unknown.[‡] The holy religion brought by the angels
trusts truth alone for its defense, and does not
need these violent means for its preservation.

PARIS, THE 4TH OF THE MOON OF CHALVAL, 1712

[†]Those condemned by the Inquisition appeared for sentenc-
ing dressed in shirts colored to suggest the flames of their
presumed postmortem destination.

[‡]The Persians are the most tolerant of all the [Muslims].

REVIEW QUESTIONS

1. What does *Candide* reveal about Voltaire's general outlook?
2. How did Diderot attempt to use the Tahitians to criticize the sexual morals of
   Europeans?
3. How did Diderot use the concept of the law of nature to undermine Christian sexual
   morality?
4. How does Montesquieu characterize Spanish and Portuguese inquisitors?

9 On the Progress of Humanity

During the French Revolution, the Marquis de Condorcet attracted the enmity of
the dominant Jacobin party and in 1793 was forced to go into hiding. Secluded
in Paris, he wrote *Sketch for a Historical Picture of the Progress of the Human
Mind*. Arrested in 1794, Condorcet died during his first night in prison from
either exhaustion or self-inflicted poison.

Marquis de Condorcet
PROGRESS OF THE HUMAN MIND

Sharing the philosophes' confidence in human goodness and in reason, Condorcet
was optimistic about humanity's future progress. Superstition, prejudice, intolerance, and tyranny—all barriers to progress in the past—would gradually be
eliminated, and humanity would enter a golden age. The following excerpts are
from Condorcet's *Sketch*.

. . . The aim of the work that I have undertaken, and its result will be to show by appeal
to reason and fact that nature has set no term
to the perfection of human faculties; that the
perfectibility of man is truly indefinite; and
that the progress of this perfectibility, from

now onwards independent of any power that might wish to halt it, has no other limit than the duration of the globe upon which nature has cast us. This progress will doubtless vary in speed, but it will never be reversed as long as the earth occupies its present place in the system of the universe, and as long as the general laws of this system produce neither a general cataclysm nor such changes as will deprive the human race of its present faculties and its present resources. . . .

. . . It will be necessary to indicate by what stages what must appear to us today a fantastic hope ought in time to become possible, and even likely; to show why, in spite of the transitory successes of prejudice and the support that it receives from the corruption of governments or peoples, truth alone will obtain a lasting victory; we shall demonstrate how nature has joined together indissolubly the progress of knowledge and that of liberty, virtue and respect for the natural rights of man. . . .

After long periods of error, after being led astray by vague or incomplete theories, publicists have at last discovered the true rights of man and how they can all be deduced from the single truth, that *man is a sentient being, capable of reasoning and of acquiring moral ideas.* . . .

At last man could proclaim aloud his right, which for so long had been ignored, to submit all opinions to his own reason and to use in the search for truth the only instrument for its recognition that he has been given. Every man learnt with a sort of pride that nature had not forever condemned him to base his beliefs on the opinions of others; the superstitions of antiquity and the abasement of reason before the [deception] of supernatural religion [had] disappeared from society as from philosophy.

Thus an understanding of the natural rights of man, the belief that these rights are inalienable and [cannot be forfeited], a strongly expressed desire for liberty of thought and letters, of trade and industry, and for the alleviation of the people's suffering, for the [elimination] of all penal laws against religious dissenters and the abolition of torture and barbarous punishments,

the desire for a milder system of criminal legislation and jurisprudence which should give complete security to the innocent, and for a simpler civil code, more in conformance with reason and nature, indifference in all matters of religion which now were relegated to the status of superstitions and political [deception], a hatred of hypocrisy and fanaticism, a contempt for prejudice, zeal for the propagation of enlightenment: all these principles, gradually filtering down from philosophical works to every class of society whose education went beyond the catechism and the alphabet, became the common faith . . . [of enlightened people]. In some countries these principles formed a public opinion sufficiently widespread for even the mass of the people to show a willingness to be guided by it and to obey it. . . .

Force or persuasion on the part of governments, priestly intolerance, and even national prejudices, had all lost their deadly power to smother the voice of truth, and nothing could now protect the enemies of reason or the oppressors of freedom from a sentence to which the whole of Europe would soon subscribe. . . .

Our hopes for the future condition of the human race can be subsumed under three important heads: the abolition of inequality between nations, the progress of equality within each nation, and the true perfection of mankind. Will all nations one day attain that state of civilization which the most enlightened, the freest and the least burdened by prejudices, such as the French and the Anglo-Americans [by virtue of their revolutions], have attained already? Will the vast gulf that separates these peoples from the slavery of nations under the rule of monarchs, from the barbarism of African tribes, from the ignorance of savages, little by little disappear? . . .

Is the human race to better itself, either by discoveries in the sciences and the arts, and so in the means to individual welfare and general prosperity; or by progress in the principles of conduct or practical morality; or by a true perfection of the intellectual, moral, or physical faculties of man, an improvement which may result from a perfection either of the instruments used to heighten the intensity of these faculties and to direct their use or of the natural constitution of man?

In answering these three questions we shall find in the experience of the past, in the observation of the progress that the sciences and civilization have already made, in the analysis of the progress of the human mind and of the development of its faculties, the strongest reasons for believing that nature has set no limit to the realization of our hopes. . . .

The time will therefore come when the sun will shine only on free men who know no other master but their reason; when tyrants and slaves, priests and their stupid or hypocritical instruments will exist only in works of history and on the stage; and when we shall think of them only to pity their victims and their dupes; to maintain ourselves in a state of vigilance by thinking on their excesses; and to learn how to recognize and so to destroy, by force of reason, the first seeds of tyranny and superstition, should they ever dare to reappear amongst us.

REVIEW QUESTIONS

1. According to Condorcet, what economic, political, and cultural policies were taught by the philosophes?
2. What image of human nature underlies Condorcet's theory of human progress?

Credits

Chapter 1

pp. 4–6: *The Epic of Gilgamesh*, translated by N.K. Sandars (Penguin Classics, 1960, Third edition 1972). Copyright © N.K. Sandars, 1950, 1964, 1972. Reproduced by permission of Penguin Books Ltd.

pp. 11–12: From Adolph Erman, *The Ancient Egyptians*, pp. 279–290, 72, 74, 76–86. Reprinted by permission from Routledge, England.

pp. 13–14: Pritchard, James B. (ed.): *Ancient Near Eastern Texts Relating to the Old Testament—Third Edition with Supplement*. © 1950, 1955, 1969, renewed 1978 by Princeton University Press. Reprinted by permission of Princeton University Press.

pp. 15: From Miriam Lichtheim, *Ancient Egyptian Literature: A Book of Readings*, Volume II, 1976, University of California Press. Reprinted with permission of University of California Press.

p. 16: From Miriam Lichtheim, *Ancient Egyptian Literature: A Book of Readings*, Volume II, 1976, University of California Press. Reprinted with permission of University of California Press.

pp. 18–20: Pritchard, James B. (ed.): *Ancient Near Eastern Texts Relating to the Old Testament—Third Edition with Supplement*. © 1950, 1955, 1969, renewed 1978 by Princeton University Press. Reprinted by permission of Princeton University Press.

Chapter 2

pp. 25–28, 33–43: Reprinted by permission from the National Council of Churches of Christ.

pp. 29–33: Revised Standard Version of the Bible, copyright 1952 [2nd edition, 1971] by the Division of Christian Education of the National Council of the Churches of Christ in the United States of America. Used by permission. All rights reserved.

Source in the public domain are not listed.

Chapter 3

pp. 48–49: From *The Iliad* by Homer, translated by E.V. Rieu. Copyright © the Estate of E.V. Rieu, 1946. Reproduced by permission of Penguin Books Ltd.

pp. 50–52: From *Sappho: Poems and Fragments*, translated by Josephine Balmer, Bloodaxe Books Ltd., 1992. Reprinted with permission of Bloodaxe Books Ltd.

pp. 52–53: From G. S. Kirk, J. E. Raven and M. Scholfield, *The Presocratic Philosophers*. Copyright © 1957, 2nd edition © 1984 by Cambridge University Press. Reprinted with the permission of Cambridge University Press.

pp. 53–54: From *The Presocratic Philosophers* by G. S. Kirk, J. E. Raven and M. Scholfield. Copyright © 1957, 2nd edition © 1984 by Cambridge University Press. Reprinted with the permission of Cambridge University Press.

pp. 54–55: From G. S. Kirk, J. E. Raven and M. Scholfi eld, *The Presocratic Philosophers*. Copyright © 1957, 2nd edition © 1984 by Cambridge University Press. Reprinted with the permission of Cambridge University Press.

pp. 55–56: Reprinted by permission of the publishers and the Trustees of the Loeb Classical Library from *Hippocrates: Volume* II, Loeb Classical Library Volume 148, translated by W.H.S. Jones, Cambridge, Mass.: Harvard University Press, 1923. The Loeb Classical Library® is a registered trademark of the President and Fellows of Harvard College.

pp. 56–57: *History of the Peloponnessian War by Thucydides*, translated by Rex Warner. © 1954. Reproduced by permission of Penguin Books Ltd.

p. 58: Excerpted from *Ancilla to the Pre-Socratic Philosophers* by Kathleen Freeman (Cambridge: Harvard University Press, 1948).

p. 59: From *The Greeks*, Revised Edition, poem translated by H.D.F. Kitto, © 1957. Reproduced by permission of Penguin Books Ltd.

pp. 59–60: Excerpted from *Three Theban Plays: Antigone, Oedipus The King, and Oedipus at Colonus* by Sophocles, edited by Theodore Howard Banks, pp. 13–17, 19–22. Copyright © 1956. By permission of Oxford University Press.

pp. 60–63: *Herodotus, the Histories*, translated by Aubrey de Selincourt, revised by A.R. Burn, Penguin Classics, 1954. © The Estate of Aubrey de Selincourt, 1954, © A.R. Burn, 1972. Reproduced by permission of Penguin Books Ltd.

pp. 63–68: Excerpted from *Three Theban Plays: Antigone, Oedipus The King, and Oedipus at Colonus* by Sophocles, edited by Theodore Howard Banks, pp. 13–17, 19–22. Copyright © 1956. By permission of Oxford University Press.

pp. 68–70: Excerpted from *History of the Peloponnesian War*, by Thucydides, translated by Rex Warner, © 1954. Reproduced by permission of Penguin Books Ltd.

p. 71: From Medea translated by Rex Warner, published by Bodley Head. Reprinted by permission of The Random House Group Ltd.

pp. 72–75: Reprinted by permission from Lysistrata, copyright © 1991 by Ivan R. Dee, Inc., translation copyright © 1991 by Nicholas Rudall. All rights reserved.

pp. 76–81: Excerpted from *History of the Peloponnesian War* trans. by Rex Warner, © 1954. Reproduced by permission of Penguin Books Ltd.

pp. 76–81: Excerpted from *History of the Peloponnesian War* trans. by Rex Warner, © 1954. Reproduced by permission of Penguin Books Ltd.

pp. 86–91: *Republic of Plato* translated by F.M. Cornford (1941), from pp. 178–179, 181, 190–192, 228–231, 282–283, 286, 288–289. By permission of Oxford University Press.

pp. 92–95: From *The Oxford Translation of Aristotle: History of the Animals, Politics & Ethics* edited by W.D. Ross. By permission of Oxford University.

pp. 96–98: Reprinted by permission of the publishers and the Trustees of The Loeb Classical Library from *Plutarch: Moralia-Volume* IV, Loeb Classical Library Volume 305, translated by Frank C.

Babbitt, pp. 328–330, Cambridge, Mass.: Harvard University Press, Copyright © 1936 by the President and Fellows of Harvard College. The Loeb Classical Library® is a registered trademark of the President and Fellows of Harvard College.

pp. 98–99: *Epicurus: The Extant Remains*, translated by Cyril Bailey (1926) from pp. 53, 83, 89, 97, 101, 115, 117, 119. By permission of Oxford University Press.

pp. 101–103: Reprinted by permission of the publishers and the Trustees of the Loeb Classical Library from *Philo: Volume* IV, Loeb Classical Library Volume 261, translated by F.H. Colson and G.H. Whitaker, pp. 495, 497, Cambridge, Mass.: Harvard University Press, Copyright © 1932 by the President and Fellows of Harvard College, and *Philo: Volume* VII, Loeb Classical Library Volume 320, translated by F.H. Colson, pp. 117, 119, 121, 123, Cambridge, Mass.: Harvard University Press, Copyright © 1937 by the President and Fellows of Harvard College. The Loeb Classical Library® is a registered trademark of the President and Fellows of Harvard College.

Chapter 4

pp. 106–107: *The Rise of the Roman Empire* by Polybius, translated by Ian Scott-Kilvert, selected with an introduction by F. W. Walbank (Penguin Classics, 1979) Copyright © Ian Scott-Kilvert, 1979. Reproduced by permission of Penguin Books Ltd.

pp. 108–109: Livy, *The War with Hannibal*, translated by Aubrey de Selincourt. Copyright © 1965 The Estate of Aubrey de Selincourt. Reprinted by permission of Penguin Books Ltd.

pp. 110–111: From *The Roman History of Appian of Alexandria*, translated by Horace White (Macmillan, 1899), Vol. I, pp. 229–232.

pp. 112–113: Translated by Anthony M. Esolen. *On the Nature of Things: De Rerum Natura*, pp. 26–27, 191–193. © 1995 The Johns Hopkins University Press. Reprinted with permission of The Johns Hopkins University Press.

Chapter 5

Chapter 6

Chapter 7

Bernard Lewis. By permission of Oxford University Press, Inc.

pp. 212–213: Excerpt from *Jihad in Classical and Modern Times* edited by Rudolf Peters, pp. 48–49. © 1996 by Markus Wiener Publications.

pp. 213–215: From *Avicenna on Theology* by Arthur J. Arberry, pp. 9–13. © 1951 by John Murray Publishers.

pp. 216–217: *A History of the English Church and People*, by Bede, translated by Leo Sherley-Price, © 1955, revised edition © 1968. Reproduced by permission of Penguin Books Ltd.

pp. 217–218: Einhard, *Life of Charlemagne*, translated by Samuel E. Turner. Copyright ©1960 by University of Michigan Press. Used with permission.

pp. 218–219: Excerpted from J. N. Hillgarth, ed., "Christianity and Paganism, 350–750." From *The Conversion of Western Europe*, pp. 62–63. © 1986 University of Pennsylvania Press. Reprinted with permission of the University of Pennsylvania Press.

pp. 220–221: *Cassiodorus Senator, An Introduction to Divine and Human Readings*, translated by Leslie W. Jones. Copyright 1946, renewed 1974 Columbia University Press. Used with permission.

pp. 222–223: Einhard, *Life of Charlemagne*, translated by Samuel E. Turner. Copyright ©1960 by University of Michigan Press. Used with permission.

pp. 223–224: Einhard, *Life of Charlemagne*, translated by Samuel E. Turner. Copyright ©1960 by University of Michigan Press. Used with permission.

p. 227: Barbara Smythe, *Troubador Poet*. Copyright by Chatto & Windus Ltd. Used with permission.

pp. 228–229: Bishop Adalbero of Laon: "The Tripartite Society" from Jacques le Goff, *Medieval Civilization*, trans. Julia Barrow, 1988, pp. 255–256.

pp. 229–230: *Medieval Civilization* by Jacques le Goff, translated by Julia Barrow. Copyright © 1988 by Blackwell Publishers Ltd. Reproduced with permission of Blackwell Publishing Ltd.

pp. 230–231: Glyn S. Burgess, trans., *The History of the Norman People: Wace's Roman De Rou* by Wace. Copyright © 2004 by Boydell & Brwer Ltd. Reprinted with permission.

Chapter 8

pp. 235–237: Lawrence M. Larson, *The King's Mirror*. Copyright © 1917 by The Scandinavian Foundation. Used with permission.

pp. 240–241: Ephraim Emerton, editor and translator, *The Correspondence of Pope Gregory VII*. Copyright 1932, renewed 1960 Columbia University Press. Used with permission.

pp. 244–245: Babcock, Emily Atwater and A.C. Krey, *A History of Deeds Done Beyond the Sea*. Copyright © 1943 by Columbia University Press. Reprinted with permission.

pp. 247–249: Bernard Gui, "Manual of an Inquisitor," in *Heresies of the High Middle Ages: Selected Sources*, translated by W.L. Wakefield and A.P. Evans. Copyright © by Columbia University Press. Used with permission.

pp. 250–251: From Richard C. Dales, editor, *The Scientific Achievement of the Middle Ages*, pp. 40–45. © 1973 by University of Pennsylvania Press. Reprinted with permission of the University of Pennsylvania Press.

pp. 251–254: Anton Pegis, editor and translator *Summa Contra Gentiles*. Copyright ©1955 by Doubleday, Dell Publishing Group, Inc. Used with permission.

pp. 254–255: From *The Canterbury Tales* by Geoffrey Chaucer, translated by Nevill Coghill, Penguin Classics, 1951, Fourth Revised Edition, 1977. Copyright 1951 by Nevill Coghill, © The Estate of Nevill Coghill, 1958, 1960, 1975.

pp. 255–256: Reprinted from Zeydel, Edwin H. "Student Letters" from *Vagabond Verse: Secular Latin Poems in the Middle Ages*. Copyright © 1966 Wayne State University Press, with the permission of Wayne State University Press.

pp. 256–258: Reprinted from Zeydel, Edwin H. "In The Tavern Let Me Die" from *Vagabond Verse: Secular Latin Poems in the Middle Ages*. Copyright

© 1966 Wayne State University Press, with the permission of Wayne State University Press.

pp. 258–259: August C. Krey, editor, *The First Crusade*. Copyright © 1921 by Princeton University Press. Reprinted by permission of Princeton University Press.

pp. 263–265: From *The Teachings of Maimonides*, ed. A. Cohen, 1968, pp. 289–293.

pp. 266–268: From *Songs of the Troubadors* by Anthony Bonner. Copyright © 1972. Reprinted by permission of the author.

pp. 270–272: From *The Book of the City of Ladies*, by Christine de Pizan. Translated by Earl Jeffrey Richards. Copyright © 1982 by Persea Books, Inc. Reprinted by Permission of Persea Books, Inc., New York.

pp. 273–275: From *A Medieval Home Companion: Housekeeping in the Fourteenth Century*, translated and edited by Tania Bayard. © Tania Bayard 1991. Reprinted by permission of Tania Bayard.

pp. 277–278: From Peter Damian *Book of Gomorrah: An Eleventh-Century Treatise Against Clerical Homosexual Practices*, trans. Peter J. Payer, pp. 63–65, 72–73. Copyright © 1982 by Wilfrid Laurier University Press. Reprinted with permission.

pp. 279–280: Excerpted from *The Statesman's Book of John Salisbury*, translated by John Dickenson, © 1963 by Russell & Russell, pp. 335–336.

pp. 280–281: From J.C. Holt (ed.), *Magna Carte*. Copyright © 1976. Reprinted by permission of Cambridge University Press.

pp. 282–284: R.A. Newhall, editor, *The Chronicle of Jean de Venette*, translated by Jean Birdsall. Used with permission.

pp. 285–286: John Froissart, *The Chronicles of England, France and Spain*, translated by Thomas Johnes.

pp. 288–290: Reprinted with permission from Brewer & Boydell Ltd.

pp. 290–292: *Marsilius of Padua* by Alan Gewirth, translator. Copyright 1956 by Columbia University Press. Reproduced with permission of Columbia University Press.

pp. 293–295: Adapted from *On the misery of the Human Condition: Pope Innocent* III, 1st Edition, by R. Donald Howard and Margaret Mary Dietz (trans.). ©1969 by Pearson Education, Inc.

Chapter 9

pp. 311–312: Excerpt from Pico della Mirandola "Oration on the Dignity of Man" translated by Elizabeth L. Forbes. From *The Renaissance Philosophy of Man*, edited by Ernst Cassirer, Paul Oskar Kristeller and John H. Randall, Jr., pp. 223–225. Copyright © 1948 by the University of Chicago Press. Reprinted by permission.

pp. 313–316: Excerpted from *The Prince*, by Niccolo Machiavelli, translated by Luigi, revised by E.R.P. Vincent, © 1935, pp. 92–93, 97, 98–99, 101–103.

pp. 317–318: From *The Book of the Courtier* by Baldesar Castiglione, Illus. edited by Edgar Mayhew, translated by Charles Singleton, copyright © 1959 by Charles S. Singleton and Edgar de N. Mayhew. Used by permission of Doubleday, a division of Random House, Inc.

pp. 318–321: Jonathan Cape for permission to quote from *The Notebooks of Leonardo da Vinci*, edited and translated by Edward MacCurdy.

pp. 323–325: *The Histories of Gargantua and Pantagruel*, translated by J.M. Cohen. Copyright © 1995 J.M. Cohen. Reproduced by permission of Penguin Books Ltd.

pp. 325–328: From *The Yale Shakespeare*, ed. Wilbur L. Cross and Tucker Brooke, 1993.

Chapter 10

pp. 332–334: Excerpted from *In Praise of Folly*, translated by Clarence H. Miller, pp. 63, 87–88, 90, 98–99, 100–101. Copyright © 1979. Reprinted by permission from Yale University Press.

pp. 335–338: Excerpted from *Luther's Works*, Vol. 44, James Atkinson, ed. pp. 310–314. Copyright © 1966 by Augsburg Fortress Publishers. Used by permission.

pp. 341–342: From Michael G. Baylor (editor), *The Radical Reformation*, pp. 107–110, 118, 122–124. Copyright © 1991. Reprinted with the permission of Cambridge University Press.

pp. 342–343: Excerpted from *Luther's Works,* Vol. 46, edited by Robert C. Schultz, pp. 316. Copyright © 1967 by Augsburg Fortress Publishers. Used by permission.

pp. 344–346: Excerpted from *Luther's Works*, Vol. 46, edited by Robert C. Schultz, pp. 231, 217, 242, 253, 256, 264–65, 268–70, 273. Copyright © 1967 by Augsburg Fortress Publishers. Used by permission.

pp. 349–352: From H.J. Schroeder, tr., *Canons and Decrees of the Council of Trent.* Copyright ©1979 by TAN Books and Publications, Inc.

pp. 353–355: From Roland H. Bainton, *Women of the Reformation in Germany and Italy*, pp. 145–149. Copyright © 1971 by Augsburg Fortress Publishers. Used by permission.

pp. 356–357: Excerpts from pp. 537, 550, 555, and 779 in *The Complete Works of Menno Simons*, 1956, edited by John C. Wanger and translated by Leonard Verduin.

Chapter 11

pp. 367–368: Excerpted from *The Devastation of the Indies a Brief Account,* translated by Herma Briffault, pp. 32–34.

pp. 373–375: Edwards, J.H., ed. and trans., *The Jews in Western Europe* 1400–1600. Copyright © 1994 by J.H. Edwards. Reprinted with permission.

pp. 376–378: From *Documents Illustrative of the History of the Slave Trade to America*, Vol. I edited by Elizabeth Donnan. Copyright © 1935, published by Carnegie Institution. Reprinted by permission of Carnegie Institution of Washington.

pp. 382–385: Reprinted by permission of Waveland Press, Inc. from Philip D. Curtin, *Africa Remembered: Narratives by West Africans from the Era of the Slave Trade* (Long Grove, IL; Waveland Press, Inc., 1967 [reissued 1997]). All rights reserved.

pp. 386–387: From *Witchcraft in Europe, 1100–1700*: A Documentary History edited by Alan C. Kors and Edward Peters. Copyright 1972 by the University of Pennsylvania Press. Reprinted by permission of the publisher.

pp. 389–391: In Nicolas Malebranche, Recherche de la Vérité, Oeuvres Complites, published under the direction of Audré Robinet, Volume I, pages 370 to 376, *Vrin*, Paris, 1962. Reprinted by permission.

pp. 392–394: From *Memoirs of the Duc De Saint-Simon* edited by W.H. Lewis. Copyright © 1964.

pp. 394–397: Von der Pfalz, Liselotte. A *Woman's Life in the Court of the Sun King: Letters of Liselotte Von Der Pfalz*, Elisabeth Charlotte, Duchesse d'Orleans, 1652–1722, pp. 87–88, 90–92, 106–107, 111–112. © 1984 The Johns Hopkins University Press. Reprinted with permission of The Johns Hopkins University Press.

pp. 398–399: Bishop Jaques-Benigne Bossuet, *Politics Drawn from the Very Words of Holy Scripture*, trans. & ed., by Patrick Riley, pp. 57–61, 81–83 © 1990. Reprinted by permission of Cambridge University Press.

Chapter 12

pp. 409–411: Copernicus, Nicolaus, *On the Revolutions*, translated by Edward Rosen, edited by Jerry Dbrzycki. Reprinted by permission of Macmillan Ltd.

pp. 412–413: Maurice A. Finocchiaro, editor, *The Galileo Affair: A Documentary History*. Copyright © 1989 The Regents of the University of California. Reprinted by permission of the University of California Press.

pp. 414–417: From Galileo Galilei, translated by Stillman Drake, *Dialogue Concerning the Two Chief World Systems*. 1962, University of California Press. Reprinted with permission of University of California Press.

pp. 417–418: Galileo Before the Inquisition from Giorgio de Santillana, *The Crime of Galileo*, pp. 306–308, 310. Copyright © 1955 by the University of Chicago Press. Reprinted by permission.

pp. 419–420: Benjamin Farrington, ed. and trans., *The Philosophy of Francis Bacon*, pp. 114–115. Copyright © 1970 by Liverpool University Press. Reprinted with permission.

Chapter 13

pp. 432–433: From *The Philosophy of Kant* by Immanuel Kant, translated by Carl Friedrich, copyright 1949 by Random House, Inc. Used by permission of Random House, Inc.

pp. 438–441: Excerpted from *Candide and Other Writings by Voltaire*, edited by Haskell M. Block, Copyright © 1956 and renewed 1984 by Random House, Inc.

pp. 445–446: *Some Thoughts Concerning Education* by John Locke (1989): Extracts from *Essay Concerning Human Understanding* by John Locke (pp. 83, 103, 105, 111, 112, 113–114, 115–116, 134, 142). By permission of Oxford University Press.

pp. 448–450: Denis Diderot, *The Encyclopedia Selections*, edited and translated by Stephen J. Gendzier. Copyright © 1967 by Harper. Used with permission.

pp. 451–454: From Jean Jacques Rousseau, *The Social Contract in the Social Contract and Discources*, trans. G.D.H. Cole, pp. 8–9, 13–15, 18–19, 23, and 26–28. Reprinted by permission of J.M. Dent & Sons and Everyman's Library.

pp. 454–456: *On Crimes and Punishments* by Beccaria, translated by H. Paolucci, © 1963. Reprinted by permission of Prentice-Hall, Inc., Upper Saddle River, New Jersey.

p. 458: Denis Diderot, *The Encyclopedia Selections*, edited and translated by Stephen J. Gendzier. Copyright © 1967 by Harper. Used with permission.

p. 459: From *Sketch for a Historical Picture of the Progress of the Human Mind* by Antonie-Nicolas de Condorcet, translated by June Barraclough. Copyright © Weidenfeld & Nicolson, an imprint of The Orion Publishing Group.

pp. 460–462: Excerpted from *Candide and Zadig*, translated by Tobias George Smollett, edited by Luenter G. Crocker, Pocket Books, pp. 6–15, 20–21.

pp. 463–466: Denis Diderot, *The Encyclopedia Selections*, edited and translated by Stephen J. Gendzier. Copyright © 1967 by Harper. Used with permission.

pp. 466–467: From Montesquieu *The Persian Letters*, pp. 53–54, 88–89, 92–93, 165–66 © 1964.

pp. 467–469: From *Sketch for a Historical Picture of the Progress of the Human Mind* by Antonie-Nicolas de Condorcet, translated by June Barraclough. Copyright © Weidenfeld & Nicolson, an imprint of The Orion Publishing Group.